Retailing

8TH EDITION

8TH EDITION

Retailing

Patrick M. Dunne

Texas Tech University

Robert F. Lusch

University of Arizona

James R. Carver

Auburn University

SOUTH-WESTERN
CENGAGE Learning·

Australia · Brazil · Japan · Korea · Mexico · Singapore · Spain · United Kingdom · United States

© Purestock/Thinkstock

© Juanmonino/iStockphoto

© scanrail/iStockphoto

© Losevsky Pavel/Shutterstock

© Moxie Productions/Getty Images

SOUTH-WESTERN
CENGAGE Learning

Retailing, Eighth Edition
Patrick M. Dunne; Robert F. Lusch;
James R. Carver

Senior Vice President, LRS/Acquisitions &
Solutions Planning: Jack W. Calhoun

Editorial Director, Business & Economics:
Erin Joyner

Editor-in-Chief: Joe Sabatino

Acquisitions Editor: Mike Roche

Developmental Editor: Elizabeth Lowry

Editorial Assistant: Megan Fischer

Marketing Communications Manager:
Linda Yip

Media Editor: John Rich

Manufacturing Planner: Ron Montgomery

Rights Acquisition Director:
Audrey Pettengill

Rights Acquisition Specialist, Text and
Image: Deanna Ettinger

Art and Cover Direction, Production
Management, and Composition:
PreMediaGlobal

Cover Images:
© Moxie Productions/Getty Images;
© Juanmonino/iStockphoto; © scanrail/
iStockphoto; © Losevsky Pavel/
Shutterstock; © Purestock/Thinkstock

Exam*View*® is a registered trademark of eInstruction Corp. Windows is a registered trademark of the Microsoft Corporation used herein under license. Macintosh and Power Macintosh are registered trademarks of Apple Computer, Inc. used herein under license.

© 2014 Cengage Learning. All Rights Reserved.

Library of Congress Control Number: 2012948792

ISBN-13: 978-1-133-95380-7

ISBN-10: 1-133-95380-8

South-Western
5191 Natorp Boulevard
Mason, OH 45040
USA

Cengage Learning is a leading provider of customized learning solutions with office locations around the globe, including Singapore, the United Kingdom, Australia, Mexico, Brazil, and Japan. Locate your local office at: **www.cengage.com/global**.

Cengage Learning products are represented in Canada by
Nelson Education, Ltd.

For your course and learning solutions, visit **www.cengage.com**

Purchase any of our products at your local college store or at our preferred online store **www.cengagebrain.com**.

Printed in Canada
1 2 3 4 5 6 7 16 15 14 13 12

Dedication

To:

Virginia, for everything you have done for our family.

Robert Lusch

To:

Bob and Virginia Lusch, for carrying much of the load on this edition as I continue to work to recover and heal from all my surgeries on my leg; y'all are fantastic writers and friends.

James Carver

FOREWORD

The retail industry has faced many challenges, but one thing is certain: The industry is resilient and will come out on top. Retailers are innovative and dynamic, and the retail landscape is competitive. The many changes in the world of retailing also offer exciting times for retailers and consumers alike.

This eighth edition of *Retailing* gives the reader an insight into all aspects of retailing in a well thought out and methodical approach that is sensitive not only to the industry's current environment but also to its future changes. Professors Dunne, Lusch, and Carver have conducted the highest level of research to stay current with the industry. This enables the reader to engage in a well-rounded dialog about the retail industry. To gain the best possible understanding about the industry, this latest edition covers all major disciplines for retailing including m-commerce, e-commerce, human resources, operations, marketing, merchandising, multichannel retailing, finance, supply-chain management, and more. The conversational writing style presented in the book makes even the most critical issues easy to understand.

The National Retail Federation co-brands this eighth edition of *Retailing* by Dunne, Lusch, and Carver to encourage people who may be considering careers in retailing and others who may be beginning their journey into understanding retailing.

As the world's largest retail trade association and the voice of retail worldwide, NRF's global membership includes retailers of all sizes, formats and channels of distribution as well as chain restaurants and industry partners from the United States and more than 45 countries abroad. In the U.S., NRF represents an industry that includes more than 3.6 million establishments and which directly and indirectly accounts for 42 million jobs—one in four U.S. jobs. The total U.S. GDP impact of retail is $2.5 trillion annually, and retail is a daily barometer of the health of the nation's economy.

It is our hope that your study of the retail industry reveals diverse challenges and opportunities for a fulfilling career that can last a lifetime.

Daniel Butler
Vice President Retail Operations
National Retail Federation

PREFACE

This edition continues to focus on the exciting and dynamic changes in retailing and its competitive environment, which is increasingly becoming global. In fact, this book has a stronger focus on global aspects of retailing and places more emphasis on the important world of fashion retailing. Because in difficult economic times strong financial performance is increasingly difficult to achieve, we, in this edition, emphasize in greater detail the key profit drivers in retailing. The writing style continues to be conversational, a style praised by students using our previous editions.

This edition of *Retailing*, like retailing itself, has undergone major revisions from previous editions. Due to the rapid change in the retail landscape, especially around the Internet and service(s), we have a new Chapter 14, which concludes the book. This chapter is very forward looking and is titled "Reframing Retail Strategy." It vividly discusses how any retailer can be more service- and customer-centric, more focused on co-creating value with customers, suppliers, and other stakeholders. To accomplish this, the retailers need to reframe many parts of their business models and create more opportunities for customer engagement.

Most of the book's story boxes ("Service Retailing," "Retailing: The Inside Story," and "What's New?") are new or updated. Many of the end-of-chapter cases are new and reflect the rapid changes occurring in retailing. More national retailers such as Macy's, Buffalo Wild Wings, Zumiez, and Genuine Auto Parts are featured in these cases. We also now have integrative cases for each of the five parts of the book. This was something instructors requested and which students will benefit from by helping them improve the ability to integrate important retailing concepts and principles. These integrative cases are on such well-known retailers as Target, Walmart, Nordstrom, and Lowe's. Because more students are considering launching their own retail enterprise, we have also included mini-cases and short exercises called "Starting Your Own Entrepreneurial Retail Business," at the end of each chapter.

Given the growth of the Internet and e-tailing, we increase our coverage of this topic. We also discuss how the emergence of m-commerce, or retailing accomplished via the mobile phone, has become so critical to success in retailing. It is amazing how consumers and channel partners, in addition to retailers, are using the Internet and e-commerce and m-commerce in innovative ways. Hence, we offer an in-depth coverage of the topics that readers have come to expect. Consequently, we believe that students and instructors will like this edition even more than they did the highly successful first seven editions.

With retail supporting one in four jobs in the United States or 42 million jobs (www .retailmeansjobs.com), we strongly believe that retailing offers one of the best career opportunities for today's students. Thus, *Retailing* was written to convey that message, not by using boring descriptions of retailers and the various routine tasks they perform, but by making the subject matter come alive by focusing on the excitement that retailing offers its participants in an easy-to-read conversational style filled with pictures and exhibits. This text demonstrates to the student that retailing as a career choice can be fun, exciting, challenging, and rewarding. Thus, excitement arises from selecting a merchandise assortment at market, determining how to present the merchandise in the store, developing a promotional program for the new assortment, and planning next season's sales in an ever-changing economic environment. And the reward comes from doing this better than the competition. While other texts may make retailing a series of independent processes, this edition, like the first seven editions of *Retailing*, highlights the excitement, richness, and importance of retailing as a career choice. *Retailing* provides the student with an understanding of the interrelationship of the various activities that retailers face daily. To do this, we attempt to show how retailers must use both creativity and analytical skills in order to solve problems and pursue opportunities in today's fast-paced environment.

In keeping with our goal of maintaining student interest, *Retailing* focuses on the material that someone entering the retailing field would need to know. We were more interested in telling the student what should happen, and what is happening, than in explaining the academic "whys" of these actions. Thus, when knowledge of a particular theory was needed, we generally ignored the reasoning behind the theory for a simple explanation and an example or two of the use of the theory. In presenting these examples, we drew from a rich array of literature sources, as well as from our combined 90 years of work in retailing.

Students and teachers have responded favorably to the "personality" of *Retailing* because the numerous contemporary and relevant examples, both in the text itself and in each chapter's various story boxes, provide realistic insights into retailing. One student wrote to say "thanks" for writing a book that was "so interesting and not too long." A faculty member noted she was "so pleased with the writing style because it was easier to understand, and the examples used were very appropriate and helped to present the material in a meaningful and easy-to-grasp manner for students." Still another liked *Retailing* because the writing style was "conversational," lending itself to very easy reading, so that she felt confident that her students would read the chapters. "The content coverage was excellent. Terms were explained in easy-to-understand language. And although most of the topics of an advanced retailing text were presented, the extent and presentation of the material was very appropriate to an introductory course." Another reviewer was especially pleased that we were able to incorporate so many current examples.

Text Organization

Retailing, which features an attractive, full-color format throughout the entire text, is divided into five parts that are, in turn, divided into 14 chapters, which can easily be covered over the course of the term. Part 1 serves as an introduction to the study of retailing and provides an overview into what is involved in retail planning. Part 2 examines the environmental factors that influence retailing today: the behavior of customers, competitors, channels, as well as our legal and ethical behavior. Part 3 examines the role that location plays in a retailer's success. Part 4 deals with the operations of a retail store. This section begins with a chapter on managing the retailer's finances. Special attention in this section is given to merchandise buying and handling, pricing, promotion and advertising, personal selling, and store layout and design. The book concludes with Part 5, which focuses on the future of retailing and specifically how to reframe a retail enterprise for higher customer centricity and financial performance.

Chapter Organization

Each chapter begins with an "Overview" that highlights the key topic areas to be discussed. In addition, a set of "Learning Objectives" provides a description of what the student should learn after reading the chapter. To further aid student learning, the text material is integrated with the learning objectives listed at the beginning of the chapters and the summaries at the end. In addition, the text features key terms in bold typeface, with the definition in the margin to make it easier for students to check their understanding of these key terms. If they need a fuller explanation of any term, then the discussion is right there—next to the definition.

The body of the text has photos, exhibits, tables, and graphs that present the information and relationships in a visually appealing manner. Each chapter has three retailing box features that cover the inside story of a particular retailing event or decision ("Retailing: The Inside Story"), retailers that provide services ("Service Retailing"), and what are new trends and technologies in retailing ("What's New?"); and all cases are connected to issues presented in the chapter. Incidentally, many of the boxes feature global aspects of retailing. All of the boxes are lengthier real-world examples than can be incorporated in the regular flow of text material. Some of these box features are humorous, while others present a unique way to solve problems retailers faced in their everyday operations.

Every chapter ends with a student study guide. The first feature of this section of the text is the "Summary" of the learning objectives followed by "Terms to Remember." These are followed by the traditional "Review and Discussion Questions," which are also tied into the learning objectives of the chapter. These questions are meant to test recall and understanding of the chapter material and provide students with an opportunity to integrate and apply the text material. Another feature is the "Sample Test Questions" with multiple-choice questions that cover each chapter's learning objectives. The answers to these questions are at the end of the book.

The second half of the study guide is designed as an "application of what's been learned" section, which opens with the "Writing and Speaking Exercise." This exercise attempts to aid the instructor in improving the students' oral and written communication skills as well as their teamwork skills. Here the student or group of students is asked to make a one-page written report or oral presentation to the class incorporating the knowledge gained by reading the chapter. Some instructors may prefer to view these as "mini-cases."

The "Retail Project" section has the student visiting either a library or a website or finding an answer to a current retail question. Next there is the "Planning Your Own Entrepreneurial Retail Business" section, which can also be viewed as another "mini-case." These mini-cases thrust the student into the role of a budding retail entrepreneur. Many of these cases reinforce the importance of understanding the key profit drivers in retailing.

The next feature of each chapter's study guide is the "Case" section. Most cases are drawn from actual retail situations and firms many students will recognize. The authors believe that the ability to understand the need for better management in retailing requires an explanation of retailing through the use of case studies. These cases cover the entire spectrum of retail operations and involve department stores, specialty shops, direct retailing, hardware stores, grocery stores, apparel shops, discount stores, and restaurants.

Supplementary Material

The Instructor's Resource CD-ROM (IRCD) includes an overview of the chapter, several detailed teaching tips for presenting the material, a detailed outline, the answers to questions for review and discussion, suggestions for handling the writing and speaking exercises, retail projects, cases, and planning your own entrepreneurial retail business. The IRCD also includes the following:

- The test bank contains more than 2,000 questions. These questions are true-false and multiple choice. The test bank is available in Word as well as ExamView—Computerized Testing Software. This software is provided free to instructors who adopt the text.
- PowerPoint slides include the chapter overview, key terms and definitions, charts, tables, and other visual aids by learning objectives.
- The Instructor's Manual includes an overview, learning objectives, an outline, answers to the end-of-chapter material, and a "teaching in action" section.
  A DVD supplement offers a professionally written and produced video case package that provides intriguing, relevant, and current real-world insight into the modern marketplace. Each video is supported with application questions located on the website of Penn State University, Erie.

CourseMate

Cengage Learning's Marketing CourseMate provides instructors with all of the reporting tools needed to track student engagement, while students can access interactive study tools in a dynamic, online learning environment.

CourseMate features include:

- **Engagement Tracker**, a Web-based reporting and tracking tool, allows you to monitor your students' use of course material and assess their engagement and preparation.
- An **Interactive eBook** provides students with an interactive, online-only version of the printed textbook.
- **Interactive Teaching & Learning Tools** including quizzes, flashcards, videos, and more—all online with CourseMate.
- It's **Affordable**—about half the cost of a traditional printed textbook.

In addition, CourseMate contains "The House," which is a spreadsheet analysis of the financial performance of a clothing store in a small college town. As students read and work with the material in "The House", instructors can answer the problems and, if necessary print out their answers. The software used is Microsoft Office, which integrates word processing (Word) and spreadsheet analysis (Excel). Instructors will be able to work the problems as they are.

Acknowledgements

Many people contributed to the development of this text over eight editions and 25 years. For their helpful suggestions as reviewers of the various editions of this text, we are especially grateful to the following individuals:

Avery Abernethy,
Auburn University

Phyllis Ashinger,
Wayne State University

Charles S Areni,
University of Sydney

Chad W. Autry,
Texas Christian University

Steve Barnett,
Stetson University

Barbara Bart,
Savannah State College

Holly E. Bastow-Stoop,
North Dakota State University

Pelin Bicen,
Penn State University, Erie

Jeffrey G. Blodgett,
University of Illinois at Springfield

Jerry E. Boles,
Western Kentucky University

Elten D. Briggs,
University of Texas at Arlington

Doreen Burdalski,
Albright College

Melinda Burke,
University of Arizona

David Burns,
Xavier University

Doze Yolaine Butler,
Southern University

Louis D. Canale,
Genesee Community College

Jason M. Carpenter,
University of South Carolina

John Clark,
California State University–Sacramento

Victor Cook,
Tulane University

Christy A. Crutsinger,
University of North Texas

Ron Daigle,
Sam Houston State University

John A. Dawson,
University of Stirling

Carol A. Decker,
Tennessee Wesleyan College

Dennis Degeneffe,
University of Minnesota

Farrell Doss,
Radford University

Janice Driggers,
Orlando College

Mary Ann Eastlick,
University of Arizona

Joanne Eckstein,
Macomb Community College

Jonathan Elimimian,
Johnson C. Smith University

Sevo Eroglu,
Georgia State University

Kenneth R. Evans,
University of Oklahoma

Ann E. Fairhurst,
University of Tennessee–Knoxville

Lori Feldman,
Purdue University, Calumet

John Fernie,
Heriot-Watt University

Robert C. Ferrentino,
Lansing Community College

Susan Fiorito,
Florida State University

Alan B. Flaschner,
Touro University International

Judy Zaccagnini Flynn,
Framingham State College

Sandra Forsythe,
Auburn University

Sally L. Fortenbery,
Texas Christian University

D. Elizabeth Goins,
University of Illinois at Springfield

Linda K. Good,
Michigan State University

Donald H. Granbois,
Indiana University

Blaine S. Greenfield,
Bucks County Community College

Sejin Ha,
Purdue University

Carol Hall,
University of South Carolina

Jared Hansen,
University of North Carolina at Charlotte

Norman E. Hansen,
Northeastern University

Allan W Hanson,
St. Edwards University

Jack Hartog,
Hanze University

Shelley S. Harp,
Texas Tech University

Joseph C. Hecht,
Montclair State University

Patricia Huddleston,
Michigan State University

Charles A. Ingene,
University of Mississippi

Marian H. Jernigan,
Texas Woman's University

Julie Johnson-Hillery,
Northern Illinois University

Laura Jolly,
University of Georgia

Mary Joyce,
Bryant College

Maria Kalamas,
Kennesaw State University

Jikyeong Kang,
University of Manchester

William Keep,
Quinnipiac College

Astrid Keel,
Auburn University

J. Patrick Kelly,
Wayne State University

Karen W. Ketch,
University of Kentucky

Jiyoung Kim,
The Ohio State University

Tammy Lamb Kinley,
University of North Texas

Gail H. Kirby,
Santa Clara University

Dee K. Knight,
University of North Texas

Jim Kress,
Central Oregon Community College

Grace Kunz,
Iowa State University

Frederick Langrehr,
Valparaiso University

Marilyn Lavin,
University of Wisconsin–Whitewater

Marilyn Lebahn,
Northwest Technical College

Dong Lee,
Fairmont State College

Melody L. Lehew,
Kansas State University

Deborah Hawkins Lester,
Kennesaw State University

Michael A. Levin,
Otterbein College

Bruce Klemz,
Winona State University

Michael Levin,
Otterbein College

Michael W. Little,
Virginia Commonwealth University

John W. Lloyd,
Monroe Community College

Dolly D. Loyd,
University of Southern Mississippi

Paul MacKay,
East Central College

Elizabeth L. Mariotz,
Philadelphia University

Shawna L. Mahaffey,
Delta College

Louise Majorey,
Cazenovia College

Raymond Marquardt,
Arizona State University

Michael McGinnis,
University of Southern Alabama

Paul McGurr,
Fort Lewis College

Ron McNeil,
Iowa State University

Bob Miller,
University of Central Michigan

Nancy J. Miller,
Iowa State University

Diane Minger,
Cedar Valley College

Linda Minikowske,
North Dakota State University

Marguerite Moore,
University of South Carolina

Michelle A. Morganosky,
University of Illinois – Urbana

Mark Mulder,
Grand Rapids Junior College

David W. Murphy,
Madisonville Community College

Pamela S. Norum,
University of Missouri

Elaine M. Notarantonio,
Bryant College

Katherine A. Olson,
Northern Virginia Community College

Jan P. Owens,
Carthage College

Shiretta Ownbey,
Oklahoma State University

Charles R. Patton,
University of Texas at Brownsville

V. Ann Paulins,
Ohio University

John Porter,
West Virginia University

Dawn Pysarchik,
Michigan State University

Abe Qastin,
Lakeland College

Denise Reimer,
Iowa Lakes Community College at Emmetsburg

Glenn Richey,
University of Alabama

Lynne Ricker,
University of Calgary

Jacqueline Robeck,
University of Wisconsin–Stout

Robert A. Robicheaux,
University of Alabama at Birmingham

Rod Runyan,
University of Wisconsin–Stevens Point

Nancy K. Ryan,
Averett University

Ben Sackmary,
State University College at Buffalo

Kare Sandivek,
Buskerud University College

Robin Schallie,
Fox Valley Technical College

Duane Schecter,
Muskegon Community College

Jean Shaneyfelt,
Edison Community College

Soyeon Shim,
University of Arizona

Ian Sinapuelas,
San Francisco State University

Donna Smith,
Ryerson University

Leigh Sparks,
University of Stirling

Cynthia L. J. Spencer,
University of Hawaii

Samuel A. Spralls III,
University of Central Michigan

Robert Stassen,
University of Arkansas

Brenda Sternquist,
Michigan State University

Leslie D. Stoel,
The Ohio State University

Pauline M. Sullivan,
Texas State University–San Marcos

Patrick Swarthout,
Central Lakes College

Harriet P. Swedlund,
South Dakota State University

William R. Swinyard,
Brigham Young University

Paul Thistlewaite,
Western Illinois University

Jane Boyd Thomas,
Winthrop University

Jeff W. Totten,
McNeese State University

James A. Veregge,
Cerritos Community College

Irena Vida,
University of Tennessee

Mary Margaret Weber,
Emporia State University

Scarlett C. Wesley,
University of Kentucky

Deborah Whitten,
University of Houston–Downtown

Mike Wittmann,
University of Southern Mississippi

Allen Young,
Bessemer State Tech College

Deborah D. Young,
Texas Woman's University

We would be remiss if we failed to thank all those in the retailing industry for their input in the text. We particularly want to thank Sue Busch Nehring, Best Buy; Ellen Spiess, Savers, Inc.; Doral Chenoweth and Marvin J. Rothenberg, both retired consultants; Mike Kehoe, Bain & Company, Inc; Susan Pistilli, International Council of Shopping Centers; Kevin Coupe, morningnewsbeat.com; Jim Duddleston and Zack Adcock, Whitewave Food; Wally Switzer, 4 R's of Retailing, Inc.; Jim Maurer, Pierce's Northside Market; William R. Davidson and Katherine Clarke, Kantar Retail; Jim Lukens, D. W. Green; Teddy Tenenbaum, Mr. Handyman of Los Angeles; Mickey Reali, Orville's; Chris Gorley, Starbucks; and Wayne Copeland, Jr., entrepreneur extraordinary. We also want to acknowledge our gratitude for permission to use boxes or cases from Claes Fornell, University of Michigan; Stephen Bell, ShangBy Inc.; Steve Seabury, Pitney Bowes MapInfo; Jay Townley, The Gluskin Townley Group; James Moore, Moore's Bicycle Shop, Inc.; Professor Lislie D. Stoel, Ohio State University; Charles W. Mayers, Anne Alenskis, Idaho Power Company; Carol J. Greenhut, Schonfeld & Associates, Inc.; Bill Kirk, Weather Trends International; Jared Hansen, University of North Carolina at Charlotte; Marijayne Manley, Leeton School District; Mark Fallon, Jeffrey R. Anderson Real Estate; Simon Hay, Dunnhumby; Alison M. Chestovich, breast cancer survivor; Stephen Lusch, PhD Student at University of Arizona; Mark Lusch, MBA Student at University of Wisconsin; Dee Lincoln, Stuart Morris, itravel2000.com.; Jan Owens, Carthage College; and Lynne Ricker, University of Calgary.

A special thanks to the following individuals for their significant contributions to this eighth edition. These individuals offered timely suggestions to early drafts of many of these chapters. For their insight and encouragement, we are especially grateful. Thanks again to Dan Butler, National Retailing Federation; Paul Adams, Paul Adams and Associates, Ray Serpkenci, Retailing Research & Strategy Group Toronto; and Katherine R. Clarke, Kantar Retail.

We offer thanks and gratitude to Virginia Lusch who began gathering many industry examples in 2010 for the new edition and also provided guidance on writing style, photos, and contemporary retail and shopping examples.

To the team at Cengage, we can only say we're glad you let us be a part of the team. These individuals include: Mike Roche, former vice president/editor-in-chief and current senior project fixer-upper; Elizabeth Lowry who served a third shift as our development editor; Robin LeFevre, marketing manager; Jerusha Govindakrishnan, production manager; and Corey Geissler, photo editor.

Robert F. Lusch   Tucson, Arizona
James R. Carver   Auburn, Alabama

ABOUT THE AUTHORS

Patrick M. Dunne

Patrick M. Dunne, who recently retired from the Rawls School of Business at Texas Tech University, received his PhD in marketing from Michigan State University and his BS from Xavier University.

In more than 40 years of university teaching, Dr. Dunne has taught a wide variety of marketing and distribution courses at both the undergraduate and graduate levels. His research has been published in many of the leading marketing and retailing journals. In addition, he has authored more than 20 books, many with Dr. Lusch. These books have been printed in seven languages. Dr. Dunne has also been honored with several university teaching awards.

Dr. Dunne has also taught at Michigan State University, Drake University, and the University of Oklahoma. In addition, he served as vice president of both the Publications and Association Developmental Divisions of the American Marketing Association. Professor Dunne also was an active consultant to a variety of retailers ranging from supermarkets to shopping malls.

Robert F. Lusch

Robert F. Lusch received his PhD in business administration from the University of Wisconsin and his MBA and BS from the University of Arizona. He holds the Jim and Pamela Muzzy Chair in Entrepreneurship at the Eller School of Management, University of Arizona.

His expertise is in the area of retailing, entrepreneurship, marketing strategy, and distribution systems. Professor Lusch has served as the editor of the *Journal of Marketing*. He is the author of more than 150 academic and professional publications, including 18 books. The Academy of Marketing Science awarded him its Distinguished Marketing Educator Award, the American Marketing Association awarded him the IOSIG Lifetime Achievement Award, and the American Marketing Association has twice presented him the Harold Maynard Award.

Professor Lusch has served as president of the Southwestern Marketing Association, vice president of Education, and vice president–finance of the American Marketing Association, chairperson of the American Marketing Association, and trustee of the American Marketing Association. He has also actively consulted with many retail organizations and was instrumental in the development and guidance of three enterprises that became Inc. 500 firms.

James R. Carver

James Carver, an assistant professor at the Lowder College of Business, Auburn University, received his PhD in marketing from the University of Arizona and his MBA and BBA from Texas Tech University.

In his career, Dr. Carver has taught a wide variety of marketing and supply-chain management courses at both the undergraduate and graduate level. His research has been published in top-ranked retailing and marketing management journals. In addition to co-authoring the seventh and eighth editions of *Retailing*, he assisted the two lead authors in the fifth and sixth editions.

Dr. Carver's research interests include retailer pricing policies, supply-chain management, consumers' use of price apps and m-commerce, and the role of chief marketing officers within the retail firm.

BRIEF CONTENTS

CONTENTS

PART 2   The Retail Environment   85

Chapter 3

Chapter 4

Chapter 5

PART 4   Managing Retail Operations   309

Chapter 8

PART 5   Retailing's Future   591

Chapter 14

Part 1

Introduction to Retailing

© Purestock/Thinkstock

© Juanmonino/iStockphoto

© scanrail/iStockphoto

© Losevsky Pavel/Shutterstock

© Moxie Productions/Getty Images

1

Perspectives on Retailing

Overview

In this chapter, we acquaint you with the nature and scope of retailing. We present retailing as a major economic and social force in all countries around the world and as a significant area for career opportunities. Finally, we introduce the approach to be used throughout this text as you study and learn about the strategy and operating details that lead to successful retail enterprises.

Learning Objectives

After reading this chapter, you should be able to:

1 Explain what retailing is and why it is undergoing so much change today.

2 Describe the five methods used to categorize retailers.

3 Understand what is involved in a retail career and be able to list the prerequisites necessary for success in retailing.

4 Explain the different methods for the study and practice of retailing.

What Is Retailing, and Why Is It Undergoing So Much Change Today?

LO 1

Explain what retailing is and why is it undergoing so much change today.

It is easy to take for granted the impact retailing has on our economy and lifestyle. The full importance of this statement was recently pointed out to one of the authors when his niece, after working in New York City and Atlanta, made a career move to a town of 15,000 in the upper Midwest. While the town had a regular Walmart (not a Supercenter), she was now 41 miles from a Target and Walmart Supercenter and almost three hours from many of the retailers she had previously loved to shop like Macy's, Nordstrom, REI, Best Buy, and The Limited. While she now spent less time in stores, she was frustrated by the lack of fashionable clothing and eclectic merchandise that larger cities like Atlanta could offer. Most of all she missed one of her favorite pastimes—having lunch and window shopping with her girlfriends. To overcome the limited selection of her new town, she began shopping online more, but she still missed the in-store shopping experience. In the end, her overall retail merchandise spending declined, but she used these savings to travel more.

This situation illustrates the impact retailing has on the lifestyles of individual consumers, and by extension, the economic prosperity of any nation. History has shown that the nations that have benefited from the greatest economic and social progress have been those with a strong retail sector.[1] If you travel to China or Eastern Europe and talk with the people who have lived there for decades, you will hear their excitement about the

2

phenomenal increase in the quality and diversity of retailers they have recently witnessed. After all, it is retailing that is responsible for matching the individual demands of the consumer with vast quantities of supplies produced by a huge range of manufacturers and service providers.

Retailing's contribution to a nation's economic growth can be further highlighted with two examples. First, in 2006, the Nobel Peace Prize was given to Muhammad Yunus, a Bangladesh economist who received his Ph.D. in economics from Vanderbilt University, and the Grameen Bank, a microretail bank he founded decades earlier. The prize committee recognized the importance of financing the business aspirations of "millions of small people" with loans as little as $20 to help some of the world's most impoverished people start businesses so that they could work to bring about their own development by establishing small retail outlets that helped build the retailing sector of the economy. Today, Grameen Bank is so successful that it has over 2,000 branch offices.

The second example can be found by looking at the impact of the world's largest retailer, Walmart, on the U.S. economy. One business writer suggested tongue in cheek that Walmart, which was founded in Arkansas less than 50 years ago, deserved the Nobel Peace Prize. Since the award is given to an individual and not an organization and since Sam Walton is deceased, the company will never be considered for such an award. Nonetheless, consider the retailer's many contributions to society, which include the following.[2]

- Walmart provides employment to more than 2.1 million people. The best defense against poverty is a job.
- The company pays over $4 billion each year in dividends that help fund the retirement of millions of people.
- Walmart sells food, clothing, and other necessities at prices that are 15 to 25 percent below what conventional supermarkets charge. This helps millions of low-income families as well as other families stretch their dollars. In fact, the major tagline that you see displayed in Walmart's advertisements as well as on their trucks is "Save money. Live better."
- Walmart's low prices also help to push down the inflation rate and keep interest rates low. This is particularly beneficial for millions of families when making payments on their homes, household appliances, or autos. (In fact, one study concluded that Walmart has raised consumer discretionary income by almost 1 percent per year because of its low prices.[3]) Even Warren Buffett, the famous investor, noted that the retailer has "contributed more to the financial well-being of the American public than any other institution I can think of." His own back-of-the-envelope calculation of this contribution: $10 billion a year.[4]
- Walmart is willing to locate stores in small markets, often as small as 5,000 people, and thus provide shopping alternatives for many people in these markets. In total, it has over 8,500 stores to serve customers.
- Walmart has developed an emergency-relief standard to get supplies to areas devastated by hurricanes, fires, and tornados that has resulted in better coordination between private companies and the Federal Emergency Management Agency (FEMA).[5]
- Walmart distributes more than $600 million in cash and in-kind merchandise annually to 100,000 charitable organizations around the world.
- The company enhances the business of other nearby stores because the retailer increases the geographic area from which to attract customers.
- Walmart has been pursuing environmental sustainability from windmills to recycling to other energy-saving measures.[6]
- Walmart sells more organic produce than most of its competitors.

Still, not everyone likes and admires Walmart. For example, in *Fortune* magazine's annual poll of chief executive officers (CEOs), Walmart has gone from being the world's most admired company (in both 2003 and 2004) to 4th in 2005, 12th in 2006, 19th in 2007, and off the Top 20 list entirely in 2008.[7] However, most retail analysts attribute this drop-off to growing criticism of its nonunion policy by two labor union–funded groups (Walmart Watch and Wake-Up Walmart),[8] the settlement of 63 lawsuits about shortchanging employees on overtime wages,[9] and a slumping stock price since 2000. Further, many retail analysts believed that Walmart's attempt to go more upscale and try to match Target and JCPenney in terms of fashionable merchandise may have resulted in its core customer being abandoned.

However, the northwest Arkansas retailer has since returned to its core retail strategies and worked closely with activists to improve its labor, health care, and environmental practices.[10] In fact, during the spring of 2011, a promotional campaign, "It's Back," was launched to inform its traditional core customer that it was bringing back core merchandise that had been removed in an attempt to be a bit more upscale. As a result of these proactive strategic realignments and the resulting increase in popularity with consumers and investors, the company was ranked 11th in 2009[11], 9th in 2010, and 11th in 2011. In 2012, the ranking dropped to 24th; however, perhaps the more relevant ranking is how Walmart is only a few spots behind Nordstrom at 21 and ahead of Target, Kohl's, and Macy's.[12]

Another criticism of Walmart is the popular belief that Walmart has a significant negative effect on the mom-and-pop business sector. Academic research, however, has found that such beliefs are statistically unfounded. The research concluded that "after examining a plethora of different measures of small business activity and growth … it can be firmly concluded that [Walmart] has had no significant impact on the overall size and growth of U.S. small business activity."[13] Thus, while Walmart may cause some poorly managed mom-and-pop businesses in outlying towns to fail, those failures actually pave the way for the entry of other new small businesses that increase overall consumer satisfaction and productivity.

Yet aside from these two examples illustrating how retailing contributes to a nation's economic growth and stability, what about those countries without an efficient and effective retailing system? History has clearly shown that nations that have failed to develop a productive and customer-centric retailing system will ultimately have to devise one in order to improve their populations' well-being. One reason Eastern European countries experienced such low rates of economic growth when they were under Communist control was their lack of a vibrant retail structure. Consumers were forced to shop in stores that offered outdated merchandise and were barely the size of a large living room. Interestingly, when American and Western European retailers opened for business in these countries, they became instant successes. The joy and excitement these new forms of retailing provided the citizens was amazing and illustrated the value people of all cultures place on a retailing system that is responsive to their needs and wants. Even Albania, a nation of 3 million and one of Europe's most depressed countries due to its long-standing communist rule, had its first modern mall open in 2009. This 150-store center, which includes a hypermarket, is located between Tirana and Durres. The mall has generated great excitement as consumers, especially young people, can now save time and do all their shopping at one place.[14] Therefore, the rest of this text will be dedicated to showing how a retail system works and how it can always be improved.

Retailing, as we use the term in this text, consists of the final activities and steps needed to either place a product in the hands of the consumer or to provide a service to the consumer. In fact, retailing is actually the last step in a supply chain that may

retailing
Consists of the final activities and steps needed to place merchandise made elsewhere into the hands of the consumer or to provide services to the consumer.

stretch from Europe or Asia to your hometown. Therefore, any firm that sells a product or provides a service to the final consumer is performing the act of retailing. Regardless of whether the firm sells to the consumer in a store, through the mail, over the telephone, through the Internet, door-to-door, with a push cart on the street, or through a vending machine, the firm is involved in retailing. And it doesn't matter what is being sold—Chipotle fresh Mexican food, Wells-Fargo branch banks, Firestone tire outlets, Holiday Inn Express motels, Lens Crafters eyeglass stores, Thread-less t-shirts sold mostly online, e-Bay or Amazon selling a wide assortment of goods, local pawn shops or house cleaning service firms or the local zoo or art museum—all are a form of retailing.

The Nature of Change in Retailing

Many observers of the business scene believe that retailing is the most "staid and stable" sector of business. While this observation may have been true in the past, quite the contrary is occurring today. Retailing includes every living individual as a customer and accounts for 20 percent of the worldwide labor force, and consumer spending represents nearly a third of America's total economy. As the largest single industry in most nations, retailing, or spending by consumers, is necessary for businesses to "grow and hire again." Therefore, anything that affects whether or how consumers choose to spend money affects the retailing industry.

Consider that when households are financially stressed due to job loss or other factors, it shows up in their retail purchases. Instead of $3 lattes every day, purchasing a new car, or even installing new windows in the home, many families will only have a latte on the weekend or eliminate them all together while simultaneously cutting electricity usage in the home and postponing durable purchases like windows so as to have more money to spend on food and other necessities. Retailers must be vigilant in identifying and understanding any factors that might affect families' spending priorities if they are to remain successful. Take Subway's $5 foot-long sub; during the 2008–2009 economic recession, Subway recognized that people were eating out less for fast food and borrowed an idea from one its franchisees in Florida. The retailer believed the $5 price would be an eye catcher, as families pondered whether to eat out on any given evening, and the strategy seems to have paid off as it credits a 17 percent rise in sales during 2008 to the $5 sub.[15]

The opposite occurs when households begin to experience improvements in their financial condition. In 2010, as the U.S. economy began to rebound, many retailers experienced healthy gains in sales; yet, the expected gains were from a less-anticipated source. During that year, men planned to spend 3 percent more than they had in 2009, whereas women planned to spend 1 percent less![16] Therefore, it wasn't surprising when the December 2010 and 2011 holiday season concluded and sales of iPads, Kindle Fires, and other tablet computing devices, priced from $200 to $700, were very strong.

Today, retailing is undergoing many exciting changes, only a few of which will be covered in this chapter. Every retailer must consider how a change in any facet of the external environment could impact its current and future retail plans, as well as the entire retail sector within which it competes. To that end, every chapter will include several boxes intended to illustrate how successful retailers are trying to stay ahead of the changing environment. For example, each chapter of this text has a "Retailing: The Inside Story" box explaining the rationale or method behind one retailer's attempt to make itself more competitive in the face of changing environmental conditions. Recognizing that technological change is also an area that will continue to alter future retail

Retailing in China is undergoing rapid change as household incomes rise and Chinese consumers have more discretionary income.

activity, each chapter includes a "What's New?" box, which focuses exclusively on how technology, particularly the Internet, affects retailing.

E-Tailing

Interestingly, embedded in the word *retail* is one of the most important trends in the retail industry, and that is e-tailing—just remove the "r" from retailing and you have e-tailing.

The great unknown for retail managers is what the ultimate role of the Internet will be. Contrary to the fears of many retailers a decade ago, the Internet hasn't destroyed **bricks-and-mortar retailers** (or retailers that operate out of a physical and geographic based building or store). The most recent statistics find that the Internet accounts for approximately 4.2 percent of total retail sales.[17] However, if the sales of categories not commonly bought online—automobiles, fuel, and food services—are excluded, sales over the Internet account for about 10 percent of all retail sales.[18]

It's truly astounding how in about two decades time the Internet has come to represent approximately $36 billion of total U.S. retail spending.[19] But focusing solely on online sales diminishes or overlooks where the Internet's truly making an impact on retailing: consumer expectations and behavior. Today, customers, especially the younger ones, are accustomed not only to the speed and convenience of purchasing online but also to the control it gives them. E-tailing, after all, enables consumers to shop when they like and from where they like. In addition, it provides access to vast amounts of information, ranging from a product's attributes to who has the lowest price. No real-world store can match that.

The fastest growing form of e-tailing or e-commerce is beginning to be known as m-tailing or m-commerce.[20] This is where shoppers use their smartphones to purchase

bricks-and-mortar retailers
Retailers that operate out of a physical building.

WHAT'S NEW ?

Do You Have a Room for Rent? How About Just a Bathroom?

As we are in the early stages of exposing you to the study and performance of retailing and retail management, it is perhaps easiest to illustrate how the Internet and technology continue to push forward and blur the boundaries of retailing by asking a simple question. *What would you do, or what would you buy, if you could cut your rent in half this month?*

Would you go buy a new pair of heels? How about on a trip?

It's quite possible that a question like the one just posed, or some derivation thereof, is the reason hundreds of thousands of individuals chose to rent out their spare bedrooms, their apartment, or home for a night or weekend over 4 million times during 2011 with the assistance of Air Bed & Breakfast (www.airbnb.com). It's also quite possible that many of these renters or "hosts" neglected to realize that in renting out their home, they're performing the act of retailing; it might be beneficial at this time to review our definition of retailing. Yet while many of these hosts may overlook the power of retailing to affect their lives, the founders of AirBnb.com surely didn't.

In 2007, two roommates, Joe Gebbia and Brian Chesky, recognized that a prominent design conference was coming to their hometown of San Francisco only to have all the nearby hotel rooms already sold out. Looking around their apartment, Joe and Brian decided to offer up their place to a few conference attendees believing that they could provide a better San Francisco experience than any local hotel. Not only would Joe and Brian not charge their guests $5 or more for a Coca-Cola or Snickers bar, but guests would stay with hosts who could provide a more genuine or authentic experience. A "true" San Francisco experience they believed required dining at local favorite restaurants, shopping in less touristy areas, frequenting nightly attractions unknown to outsiders. A Hilton or Holiday Inn, they felt, couldn't provide such experiences; only a "local," interested in doing so, could.

With an idea of how to enhance one's travelling experience on one hand and a couple of air mattresses on the other, Joe and Brian began AirBnB.com. AirBnB.com, they believed, would become a destination for travelers seeking authenticity and community while simultaneously providing hosts with income. They appear to have been right, at least for those Generation X and Y consumers that see tourist spots as "campy." In five years, the company based on providing new retail outlets to travelers has expanded from an operation in two guys' living room to a $1.3 billion enterprise.

The real question the authors still have after all AirBnB.com's success is: Will renting out one's bathroom also be a huge success? Those at Community-Loo (www.Cloo-app.com) surely think so, and they've already developed a mobile app for those seeking to rent time in someone's personal bathroom rather than enter a public facility.

Just think, you could enter the wild world of retail by renting out your bathroom later today!

Sources: AirBnB.com Company Website (2012) "Airbnb Began by Solving a Problem," [online] Available at: www.airbnb.com/home/story [Accessed: January 28, 2012]; Alpert, Lukas (2011) "CLOO App Helps People Who Need to Use a Bathroom Find Strangers Willing to Open Up Their Homes," [online] Available at: www.articles.nydailynews.com [Accessed: January 28, 2012]; Greenfield, Rebecca (2012) "Airbnb Got Over Its Reputation for Meth and Property Damage," [online] Available at: www.theatlanticwire.com [Accessed: January 28, 2012]; Heussner, Ki Mae (2011) "Case Study: Inside AirBnB's Growth," [online] Available at: www.adweek.com [Accessed: January 28, 2012]; Levy, Ari and Douglas MacMillan (2011) "Airbnb Venture Funding Said to Value Travel-Rental Startup at $1.3 Billion," [online] Available at: www.bloomberg.com [Accessed: January 29, 2012]; "For Turning Spare Rooms Into the World's Hottest Hotel Chain," *Fast Company* (March 2012): 106–108, 148.

not only traditional merchandise and services, but also virtual service providers, which are commonly referred to as *apps*. Apps are digital services that can be downloaded to one's phone or tablet. Services provided range from those designed to enable the playing of an electronic game, to viewing a magazine such as *Time* or *Newsweek*, locating a restaurant, or even getting medical advice. eBay is witnessing its mobile app downloaded between a half million and a million times a week.

M-tailing, which is only a small fraction of e-tailing—less than 2 percent—is projected by the authors to be over 25 percent of e-tailing by 2020. The trend toward m-tailing is particularly good for retailers that sell mobile phones such as Radio Shack, Verizon, AT&T, and Sprint. Best Buy is capitalizing on this trend by opening mobile stores that are considerably smaller than their larger format stores that offer more product breadth.

With the growth of Web 2.0, the Internet has become much more interactive and social in nature. This has important implications for retailers. For instance, in 2007, Macy's did not spend any money on digital advertising and social media; in 2010, it spent $120 million.[21] Also, many retailers have been surprised that the extent to which they can control their communications through their sponsorship of advertising is dwindling. For instance, with some Internet websites, such as Groupon and Meetup, individuals can band together for group buying; the group is then able to negotiate with a retailer or manufacturer for a large transaction size represented by dozens or even hundreds of potential customers. Also, many e-tailers offer personalized help online. For instance, K-Swiss allows visitors to its website to chat with a customer service representative seven days a week, 24 hours a day. Some forward thinking and innovative retail CEO's are even using Twitter to become part of the dialogue and conversation with customers, suppliers, and other stakeholders. This includes Tony Hsieh, who is the CEO of Zappos, a highly successful e-tailer that sells shoes. If you are planning to interview for a job in retailing, you should see if their CEO or other senior management are tweeting and begin to follow them and learn more about the retail enterprise and its culture.

To combat e-tailing, bricks-and-mortar retailers must give their customers more control over the shopping experience, even if it means bringing web-style technology into the store in an attempt to replicate the best things about online shopping, but in a more personal way. Retailers should not fight this trend because the customer is already bringing the web into the store. For instance, young shoppers with smartphones send photos of a potential purchase to their friends and then friends text message back, which allows the young shopper to get input on the potential purchase. These savvy shoppers also use their phones to scan Universal Product Code (UPC) bars to immediately see if the price is competitive with other retailers in the area or online. Consequently, the retailer needs to get on and grow with the web technology trend. In-store kiosks, for example, are particularly useful to show the final product before a special, customized order is placed. They allow a shopper to see the finished product before purchasing and provide an online experience in the store. Other retailers have set up their own websites, while others have begun to use nontraditional methods to reach out to the consumer.

However, the most important thing for bricks-and-mortar retailers to grasp is the shift in power between retailers and consumers. Traditionally, the retailers' control over pricing information provided them with the upper hand in most transactions. Today, the information dissemination capabilities of the Internet have made consumers better informed. This has increased their power when transacting and negotiating with retailers. The web has provided consumers with detailed pricing information about products ranging from bikes to office supplies to digital televisions, thus enabling them to negotiate better deals. Some bricks-and-mortar retailers may have to discontinue some product categories as consumers engage in an activity called **channel surfing**. Channel surfing occurs when the customer gets needed information (such as proper size or how to assemble a product) in the stores and then orders it online for a lower price and to avoid paying state sales tax.

Retailers must keep experimenting with various strategies, both in-store and online, because the next generation of technology will change the consumers' expectation of what they demand from their retailers. That is why stores like JCPenney, Target Corp.,

channel surfing
when the customer gets needed product information within a store and then chooses to order the product online for a lower price or to avoid paying state sales tax.

Best Buy, and Amazon.com, Inc. are pushing new mobile programs. They hope these efforts make it easier for customers to shop online with their smartphones. Even if the prices touted digitally are basically the same as those offered in the store, retailers say customers can get news of sales earlier than with other methods, such as commercials or circulars. After all, failure to keep up with the Internet will spell failure for the retailer.

Price Competition

Some people claim that America's fixation with low prices began after World War II when fair-trade laws, which allowed the manufacturer to set a price that no retailer was allowed to sell below, were abolished, paving the way for America's first discounter, E. J. Korvette. Actually, this revolution more than likely began with the birth of Walmart in Rogers, Arkansas, in 1962. At the time, there were 41 publicly held discount stores and another two dozen privately owned chains already in business.[22] What Sam Walton did that forever changed the face of retailing was to realize, before everybody else, that most of any product's cost gets added after the item is produced. As a result, Walton began enlisting suppliers to help him reduce these costs and increase the efficiency of the product's movement from production to placement on store shelves. Also, Walton, who had never operated a computer in his life, made a major commitment to computerizing Walmart as a means to reduce these expenses. As a result of the introduction of the computer to retail management, Walmart's selling, general, and administrative costs as a percentage of sales reached a low of only 16 percent by the early 1990s. Since that time they have risen to 19 percent, and this has been due to global expansion efforts, higher corporate overhead, and a variety of other factors. Importantly, both in the 1990s and today, all of its competitors' operating expenses are 3 percent to 5 percent higher, which continues to put Walmart at a relative competitive advantage. Simply put, Walmart became the world's largest retailer by relentlessly cutting unnecessary costs, improving operating efficiency, and demanding that its suppliers do the same. A popular measure of *operating efficiency* is operating costs as a percentage of sales. This cost and efficiency focus continues, and recently Walmart has suggested that its suppliers focus on their core competency, which is manufacturing products, and that Walmart provide the transportation service from manufacturing plants to Walmart distribution centers in situations when the retailer can do it more efficiently.[23] Those who claim that Walmart is obsessed with its bottom line (profits) miss the point: Walmart is obsessed with its top line (sales), which it grows by focusing on the consumer's bottom line.

Costco, ranked in 2012 by *Fortune* magazine as the 20th most respected business in the world,[24] is another retailer that seeks to boost store traffic by getting shoppers to come in for a "super, low price" on key products. Consider gasoline. The chain uses gas as a *loss leader* (selling a product near, at or below its cost) to generate traffic and increase its inside-of-the store sales. The success of this strategy is shown by the fact that during the 2008–2009 recession, almost a third of the U.S. population used an alternative gasoline retailer, such as warehouse clubs and supercenters, to get gas. This was up 50 percent from three years earlier.[25] In addition, Costco's 29 million member households need a membership card, which costs $50 to $100 a year and goes straight to the firm's bottom line (net profit on an income statement).[26]

In Exhibit 1.1, you will see how discount or low-price retailing allows retailers to improve their operating efficiency and thus enables them to continue to lower prices. This occurs because when operating a store, many costs are fixed, such as rent and occupancy. Thus, as sales rise, the rent and occupancy costs as a percentage of sales decline. Follow the simple math in Exhibit 1.1 to make sure you understand this relationship.

Exhibit 1.1
How Lower Prices Can Improve Operating Efficiency

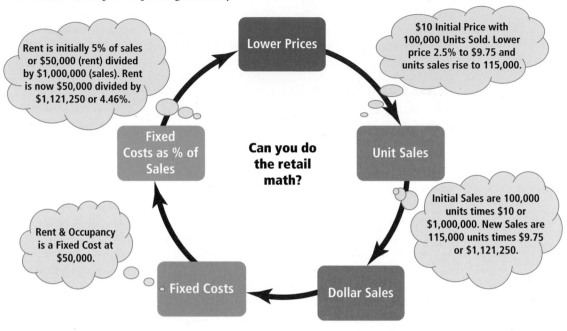

Rent is initially 5% of sales or $50,000 (rent) divided by $1,000,000 (sales). Rent is now $50,000 divided by $1,121,250 or 4.46%.

$10 Initial Price with 100,000 Units Sold. Lower price 2.5% to $9.75 and units sales rise to 115,000.

Lower Prices

Fixed Costs as % of Sales

Can you do the retail math?

Unit Sales

Rent & Occupancy is a Fixed Cost at $50,000.

Fixed Costs

Dollar Sales

Initial Sales are 100,000 units times $10 or $1,000,000. New Sales are 115,000 units times $9.75 or $1,121,250.

Demographic Shifts

Other significant changes in retailing over the past decade have resulted from changing demographic factors such as (1) the fluctuating birthrate, (2) the growing importance of the 70 million Generation Y consumers (those born between 1978 and 1994), (3) the move of Generation X (those born between 1965 and 1977) into middle age, (4) the beginning movement of the baby boomer generation (those born between 1946 and 1964) into retirement, and (5) the increasing number of women relative to men attending and graduating from college and concurrent rise in unemployment among

Consumers are attracted to Costco due to its low gasoline prices. Costco benefits by creating more store traffic that results in higher sales and profit.

men relative to women. Many retailers simply failed to realize how these factors, which had profound effects on our society, could also impact retailing. For example, a decade ago many people realized the advent of the three-generation household, where not only the kids return after college but also the grandparents move in instead of entering an assisted living quarters. Some experts believe that "ParentCare Centers" will soon replace today's KinderCare Centers. In addition, consider how America's recent immigrants have made once-exotic foods like sushi and burritos everyday options. Also, with more women in the workforce, there has been a trend toward quick meals of all sorts that can now be found in supermarkets, convenience stores, even vending machines. Even supermarkets, which were long thought to be the only retailer capable of catering to all market segments, must be aware of the effect of these demographic changes on their business.

Successful retailers must become more service oriented, offering better value in price and quality as well as more convenient store hours; more informative and helpful advertising to include more effective and useful in-store signage; and better attuned to their customers' needs. For instance, the household of today, with both parents or partners working, places more value on one-stop shopping and thus supermarkets that can offer not only food ingredients but also prepared meals, fresh flowers, a pharmacy, a retail banking outlet, cooking classes, party catering service, and perhaps a café within the store are able to offer better value.

same-store sales
Compares an individual store's sales to its sales for the same month in the previous year.

Further, with population growth slowing and with the increasing trend towards e-tailing and m-tailing, traditional retailers will no longer be able to sustain their long-term profit projections simply by building new stores to gain additional sales as they did in the past. Profit growth must come by either increasing same-store sales at the expense of the competition's market share or by reducing expenses without reducing services to the point of losing customers. **Same-store sales** is a retailing term that compares an individual

© Katerina Havelkova/Shutterstock

How rue21 Thrives in a Slow-Improving Economy

Even though the American economy is rebounding from one of its darkest periods outside the Great Depression of the 1930s, many middle-ground fashion retailers like Macy's, JCPenney, and Gap continue to struggle as their target market, the "middle class," rebuilds from a time when the Dow Jones stock index had fallen over 40 percent to below 7,500 for the first time in 16 years, unemployment had surpassed 10 percent, and one in seven Americans found themselves living below the poverty line. True, total sales for the retail fashion industry are up since 2010, but much of this growth has come from high-end chains like Saks and Nordstrom as approximately 50 percent of total sales

have come from the upper 10 percent of American shoppers (normally they account for more than 30 percent). But, one value-oriented fashion retailer has stood out from the rest and outperformed many of its competitors since before the latest recession, rue21.

Since 2006, this specialty clothing retailer from western Pennsylvania named for the French word for *street* (i.e., *rue*) and the age everyone looks forward to being (i.e., 21) has more than doubled its store count to 700 stores in 43 states, experienced a 181 percent gain in total sales revenues, and increased its profits by more than 223 percent. But these successes are not simply the result of cleverly figuring out what will be the new "hot" clothing trends each season; instead, they stem from rue21's unique strategy of "going to market."

(continued)

Unlike many fashion retailers, rue21 is not bound by location type; strip malls, outlet centers, and malls are all a part of its store portfolio. rue21 also prefers to operate small retail outlets, often 5,000 square feet or less, in rural and secondary markets with populations smaller than 250,000, but its growth has come from a more recent focus on markets with fewer than 50,000 people and average household incomes of less than $55,000. The logic behind this small-town strategy is two-fold. First, in small towns, rue21 is likely to be the only specialty fashion retailer in town, which limits competition and creates immediate excitement and fanfare in their teen audience. Second, new store investments are approximately $160,000, including build-out costs, and they begin selling merchandise within six weeks of signing the lease due to the large amount of retail selling space often available in such areas, as well as cheap rents.

rue21 also chooses to source their products from a network of third-party vendors, utilizing more than 450 domestic suppliers and imports (most of whom source overseas). In so doing, they minimize their reliance on any one vendor, enhance their flexibility to deal with sourcing issues, and lessen the potential for inflation in any one country or area of the world to significantly impact the cost of their merchandise. Further, they contract a small portion of their merchandise to be made privately within the United States so as to maximize speed to market on key fashion items.

Lastly, rue21 sees itself as unique from many of its competitors in that it offers value in all aspects of fashion. It not only attempts to sell most of its merchandise, all of which is exclusive to rue21, for less than $35, but also seeks to provide a one-stop shopping experience where customers can create an entire look without traveling from store to store. In 2006, rue21 introduced its "rue21 etc!" store concept, to highlight five new categories of merchandise—footwear, fragrance/beauty, jewelry, intimate apparel/sleepwear, and accessories. Using a "shop-in-store" layout, customers can now create an entire outfit from their head to their toes, all without leaving the store.

By operating in less-congested markets, sourcing product from multiple vendors, selling only private label goods, and incorporating all the accessories necessary to "complete" an outfit, rue21 has propelled itself forward in the fashion industry during a time when many others are struggling to remain profitable.

Sources: Eckholm, Erik. "Recession Raises U.S. Poverty Rate to a 15-Year High," *New York Times*, September 17, 2010: A1; Healy, Jack. "Dow Industrials Plunge to a 6-Year Low," *New York Times*, February 20, 2009: B8; Holmes, Elizabeth. "Rue21 Builds Business in Smaller Towns," *The Wall Street Journal*, May 27, 2010: B8; Van Riper, T. (2011) "The Fastest-Growing Retailers," [online] Available at: www.forbes.com [Accessed: Feb. 8, 2012]; and the company's 2011 annual report.

rue21, a fashion oriented retailer with low prices, has a very hands-on CEO.

market share
Is the retailer's total sales divided by total market sales.

store's sales to its sales for the same month in the previous year, while **market share** refers to a retailer's sales as a percentage of total market sales for the merchandise line or service category under consideration.

As a result, today's retail firms must be run by professionals who are able to look at the changing demographics and see opportunities, exert enormous buying power over manufacturers, and anticipate future changes before they impact the market rather than just react to these changes after they occur.

Store Size

Over the last few decades, the emphasis for many retailers was to increase store size because of the old axiom that said: "The more merchandise customers see, the more they will buy." This idea can best be seen by looking at the country's two largest drug-store chains: Walgreens and CVS. Drug stores, in addition to selling over-the-counter remedies and prescriptions at the back of the store, now have clinics that millions of Americans can use instead of going to emergency rooms for common ailments.[27] In addition, they use the front end of these stores to sell general merchandise. In fact, the majority of their sales come from many different unrelated nondrug items, such as food products, apparel goods, photo supplies, greeting cards, seasonal items such as school supplies, gardening supplies, and Christmas decorations. This phenomenon is referred to as **scrambled merchandising**.

scrambled merchandising
Exists when a retailer handles many different and unrelated items.

Scrambled merchandising is the result of the pressure being placed on many retailers to increase profits by carrying additional, unrelated merchandise or services (with higher profit margins) so as to increase store traffic. As a result, nearly half of the consumers entering a drugstore are not there to have a prescription filled (low-margin business) but to purchase substantially higher margin items from the front end of the store. Another example of scrambled merchandising is the convenience store that sells low-margin gasoline but makes its money selling higher-margin bread, milk, beer, cigarettes, magazines, lottery tickets, and fast food.

Yet scrambled merchandising need not simply pertain to tangible merchandise, it also applies to services, such as ATMs, phone cards, gift cards to a local restaurant (e.g., Red Lobster or the Olive Garden), and car wash services. For example, many drugstores have recently added medical clinics, and supermarkets have added banking and dry cleaning services inside their stores. Today, the practice of scrambling products and services has become so common that one supermarket in England has even introduced a dental clinic,[28] and Xpress in Opelika, Alabama, offers car wash and detailing services to customers while they get a haircut or perm.

But not all retailers are seeking to get bigger or scramble their merchandise to the extent of Xpress. Over the last few years many retailers have found that reducing their store size is a pathway to improved profitability.[29] For instance, Anchor Blue, an apparel store that caters to teenagers, has found that reducing the size of its stores by about 50 percent, to approximately 2,500 square feet, led to an increase in both foot traffic and sales. rue21, as pointed out in this chapter's "Retailing: The Inside Story," is another apparel retailer that prefers to operate out of small retail outlets so as to appear more like a specialty fashion retailer rather than a discount apparel chain. But smaller stores can be advantageous for all types of retailers, not simply those in the fashion and apparel industry. First, many consumers actually prefer to shop in smaller stores due to the convenience of being able to get "in and out" faster, as well as the more personalized customer service that seems to accompany these shopping venues. For example, an Ace or True Value hardware store is often less than 8,000 square feet compared to the over 100,000 square feet of a big box retailer such as Lowe's or Home Depot. Although

RediClinics are small health clinics located in grocery stores, often near the pharmacy.

both of these big box retailers pride themselves on customer service, they cannot match the feeling of intimacy an 8,000-square-foot store provides. Also, for some products, such as power tools and paints, a customer can benefit immensely from a knowledge-able retail clerk who can also offer a bit of customer education. Larger stores, on the other hand, run the risk of some shoppers becoming so overwhelmed by the product selection and lack of available sales clerks that they choose to exit the store without purchasing anything.

A second advantage of small stores is that the retailer needs a smaller geographic area from which to draw its customers and, thus, can locate stores more conveniently near where people live or work. In fact, many Ace and True Value hardware retailers, by locating their stores between the big box stores and local neighborhoods have a more convenient location for customers. Finally, with a smaller store, the retailer can more easily find a location than if it had a larger store that requires more parking and, therefore, more overall land.

Two retail formats that have recently seen not only a significant decrease in average store size but also a decrease in number of stores are department stores and category killers. Department stores are closing their downtown locations, which often were their largest stores, because the downtown areas of many cities have become "ghost towns." Also, what initially made the department stores successful—having a large selection of different merchandise categories under one roof—was superseded by the shopping mall.

In an attempt to stop the loss of customers to the more convenient shopping centers anchored by stores like Best Buy, PetSmart, Home Depot, and Target, Sears Holdings, which is a combination of the Sears and Kmart chains, chose to convert some old Kmart stores into a new retail format called Sears Grand. The thought was these stores, which were near the smaller shopping centers, could lure customers back by making their successful product lines like Kenmore washers, Craftsman tools, and Diehard car batteries more convenient. The project flopped despite the fact that Sears later renamed the stores Essentials, but not because Kmart shoppers rejected Sears products. It failed because the experiment seemed to consist only of tossing Kenmore stoves and Craftsman hammers into an old Kmart store, rather than creating a vibrant new shopping experience.[30] In addition, several other department store chains have either gone out of business or merged with another chain negating the need for the merged chain to continue to operate two stores at a given location—be it downtown or in the small mall.

category killer
Is a retailer that carries such a large amount of merchandise in a single category at such good prices that it makes it impossible for customers to walk out without purchasing what they need, thus "killing" the competition.

The term **category killer** derives from its marketing strategy: Carry a large amount of merchandise in a single category at such low prices that it makes it impossible for customers to walk out without purchasing what they need, thus "killing" the competition.

Toys "R" Us, which began operations in 1948 and became publicly traded in 1978, was the first category killer.[31] Sadly, the company also has the unfortunate distinction of being the largest category killer to fail. In 2005, the entire company, in an attempt to avoid bankruptcy, was sold to a group of investors as it and other independent toy retailers suffered from the highly competitive toy merchandising efforts of Walmart and Target. These two discounters introduced brutally low prices year-round on a limited selection of toys, but expanded their toy section to three or four times its normal size during the all-important holiday shopping season, when busy parents were already in the discount stores. Today, however, the future looks a little brighter for Toys "R" Us, who in 2008, after closing almost 100 stores the previous two years, began replacing its older stores with larger superstores combined with Babies "R" Us outlets.[32]

Other well-known category killers include Best Buy, Home Depot, Hobby Lobby, Office Depot, Total Wine & More, PetSmart, and Bed Bath & Beyond. In addition, category killers have diverted business away from traditional wholesale supply houses. For example, Home Depot appeals to the professional contractor and Office Depot to the business owner who traditionally purchased supplies from hardware wholesalers and office-supply and office-equipment wholesalers. However, in recent years, several other "killers"—Borders, Circuit City, FAO Schwarz, and CompUSA—have fallen on bad times.

Experience and Niche Retailing

It is easy to start to believe that what large and highly successful global retailers, such as Walmart and Carrefour, practice in terms of retailing will engulf the globe, and there will be no alternative formats and choice. Undoubtedly, Walmart and Carrefour will continue to build hypermarkets or superstores with nearly 100,000 stock-keeping units (SKUs) in over 140,000 square feet of space. Nonetheless, as these mass merchandisers continue their global expansion and as markets become more overstored, the global trend and opportunity is to create exciting and engaging shopping experiences coupled with more customized offerings.

In fact, a careful study around the world clearly demonstrates that there is a revival of uniqueness and novelty, in many cases, centered on creating unique, and not mass-produced, merchandising and shopping experiences. Consider, for example, the Museum of Contemporary Art in Los Angeles, which recently created a merchandising event especially for Japanese artist Takashi Murakami by offering Louis Vuitton handbags as well as other luxury merchandise. The Louis Vuitton handbags featured designs by Murakami. Shoe companies are moving toward more mass customization, and this not only includes Nike but also Steve Madden, who offers customized heels designed by customers. Schedoni, an Italian leather crafter, has teamed up with PUMA to produce a line of custom footwear. Recently, Burberry has gotten on the mass customization trend by launching Burberry Bespoke, which is an online customization service that enables customers to co-create a trench coat. Imagine designing a trench coat that pulls from 12 million different combinations of fabric, buttons, length, faux fur collars, etc.

VivoCity is a destination shopping center in Singapore that offers an exciting and engaging shopping experience.

By being involved in co-creating their trench coat, these consumers can express their unique personality via their clothing.[33] Oh yes, we forgot to mention the prices range from $1,800 to $8,800.

Another trend is also occurring in the renovation of shopping malls to transform them into more exciting experience platforms. Consider Tokyo Midtown, which is part of a multi-use development that has been upgraded to appeal to upscale shoppers. Even more extreme is when a shopping center can be built from the ground up. For instance, VivoCity in Singapore not only has 300 retailers under one roof but also an outdoor amphitheater, a 300-meter harbor front promenade, and a 20,000-square-foot open plaza. While shopping in VivoCity, one finds constant surprise and nonstandardized offerings. For instance, Eu Yan Sang is a major health-care brand in Asia, and it has created a Chinese medicine clinic that includes a yoga studio, spa, and health food café. In the store, it sells traditional Chinese medicine products to complement the services offered by the Chinese medicine clinic.

In São Paulo, Brazil, where Carrefour entered the retail market over 30 years ago and Walmart in the last decade, there still remains creative merchants who cater to niche markets and provide highly differentiated offerings. For instance, an independently owned and operated nonchain bookstore in São Paulo has an in-house movie theater (which helps to build store traffic) and a large children's section in which an over 30-foot-tall dragon captures the attention and builds the imagination of children. Another local merchant in São Paulo is a family-owned grocery store that has been operating for over 75 years and is able to position itself to avoid direct mass market and merchandising competition with Carrefour and Walmart by serving a local niche market of high-income households. From the photo here you can guess that having a wine selection with prices as high as 6,600 real (about US$3,000) means that their target market is the wealthy and well-to-do citizens of São Paulo.

Robert Lusch

This wine shop in a grocery store in Sao Paolo, Brazil, carries wines that sell for up to the equivalent of $3,000 U.S. dollars.

Responding to Change

Success in retailing depends on a retail manager's ability to properly interpret what societal changes are occurring and what these changes mean to the store's customers and then build a strategy to respond to these changes. Therein lies the excitement and challenge of retailing as a career.

Of course, the future can never be predicted with certainty. This text attempts to provide you with the tools to meet these upcoming challenges and be a success in retailing. The answer to what the future will bring lies in the disquieting fact that retailers do not operate in a static, closed environment; they operate in a continuously changing and competitive one. Retailing21.com is a website that you will find especially useful in keeping abreast of the forces and environments influencing change in retailing. The changes occurring in retailing are discussed in greater detail in Chapters 3 through 6. For now, we will concentrate on the following environmental elements: the behavior of consumers, the behavior of competition, and the behavior of supply-chain members (the manufacturers and wholesalers that the retailer buys from), the legal system, the state of technology, and the socioeconomic nature of society. Exhibit 1.2 depicts these elements.

A final comment about responding to the changing face of retailing: Remember, business entrepreneurs are not obliged to conform to old norms and social standards. They are free to forge new retail approaches that capitalize on emerging market opportunities. In retailing, this is all the more evident when we consider fashion trends; what in the past would have lasted for years now may last only a few months.

Exhibit 1.2
External Environmental
Forces Influencing the
Retail Firm

LO 2

Categorizing Retailers

Describe the five
methods used to
categorize retailers.

Categorizing retailers can help the reader understand competition, retail strategy, and the changes that occur in retailing. There is no single acceptable method of classifying retail competitors, although many classification schemes have been proposed. The five most popular schemes used today are described in Exhibit 1.3.

NAICS code

The U.S. Bureau of the Census, for purposes of conducting the Census of Retail Trade, classifies all retailers using three-digit North American Industry Classification System (NAICS) codes. The website for locating these codes is www.census.gov/epcd. Some examples of these NAICS codes are shown in Exhibit 1.4.

Exhibit 1.3
Categorizing Retailers

NAICS code	Number of Outlets	Margin/Turnover	Location	Size
3-digit NAICS code	Single unit	Low margin/low turns	Traditional	By sales volume
4-digit NAICS code	2–10 units	Low margin/high turns	Central shopping districts	
5-digit NAICS code	11+ units	High margin/low turns	Shopping centers	By number of employees
		High margin/high turns	Free-standing nontraditional	

Exhibit 1.4
Using NAICS Codes

Code	Type of Business	Number of Establishments (thousands)	Percentage of Total	Sales (billions)	Percentage of Total	Number of Employees (thousands)	Percentage of Total
44-45	Retail Trade	1,123	100%	$3,688	100%	15,339	100%
441	Motor Vehicle & Parts Dealers	129	11%	886	24%	1,948	13%
442	Furniture & Home Furnishings Stores	66	6%	112	3%	576	4%
443	Electronics & Appliance Stores	50	4%	102	3%	469	3%
444	Building Material & Garden Equipment and Supplies Dealers	87	8%	327	9%	1,263	8%
445	Food & Beverage Stores	153	14%	515	14%	2,938	19%
446	Health & Personal Care Stores	85	8%	209	6%	1,037	7%
447	Gasoline Stations	117	10%	374	10%	909	6%
448	Clothing & Clothing Accessories Stores	151	13%	202	5%	1,556	10%
451	Sporting Goods, Hobby, Book, & Music Stores	61	5%	82	2%	631	4%
452	General Merchandise Retailers	46	4%	525	14%	2,671	17%
453	Miscellaneous Store Retailers	128	11%	108	3%	820	5%
454	Nonstore Retailers	50	4%	247	7%	521	3%

As a rule, these three-digit NAICS codes are too broad to be of much use to the retail analyst. Four-digit NAICS codes provide much more information on the structure of retail competition and are easier to work with. For example, NAICS 454 is nonstore retailing, which consists of approximately 50,000 retailers. Within this is NAICS 4541, which consists of 16,000 electronic shopping and mail-order houses, such as L.L. Bean (www.LLBean.com), Harry and David (www.harryanddavid.com), and I love blue sea (www.ilovebluesea.com), and NAICS 4543, which consists of 28,000 direct-selling establishments such as Mary Kay Cosmetics and Tom James menswear, and so on.[34]

In almost all instances, the NAICS code reflects the type of merchandise the retailer sells. A major portion of a retailer's competition comes from other retailers in its NAICS category. General merchandise stores (NAICS 452) are the exception to this rule. General merchandise stores, due to the variety of general merchandise carried, compete with retailers in most other NAICS categories. For example, Macy's and other department stores compete for clothing sales with specialty apparel stores, such as Gap, Abercrombie and Fitch, J. Crew, Anne Taylor, and The Limited; mail-order retailers, such as L.L. Bean; or off-priced stores, such as T.J. Maxx or Ross Dress for Less. In fact, most retailers must compete to a considerable extent with general merchandise stores because these larger stores usually handle many of the same types of merchandise that smaller, more limited retailers sell. In a very broad sense, all retailers compete with each other since they all compete for the same limited consumer dollars.

A second cautionary note about using this Census Bureau data is that comparisons between years may not be accurate. In a note on its website, the Census Bureau cautions that sales made to a customer in a foreign country through a U.S. website are included in the bureau's estimates. Thus, when the dollar is weak, many foreign customers may purchase from an American e-tailer given the advantageous exchange rates and vice versa when the dollar is strong, Americans may purchase on overseas websites.

Another shortcoming of using the NAICS codes is that they do not reflect all retail activity. The Census Bureau's definition equates retailing only with the sale of "tangible" goods or merchandise. However, by our definition, selling of services to the final consumer is also retailing. This suggests that retailing is also conducted by businesses such as barber and beauty shops, health clubs, dry cleaners, banks, insurance agencies, funeral homes, movie theaters, amusement parks, maid services, medical and dental clinics, tutoring centers, and so on. For instance, NAICS 772, which is not classified under retail trade, consists of almost 490,000 eating and drinking establishments, and many of these are some of the most rapidly growing retailers through their expansion efforts. Remember, any time the consumer spends money, whether on tangibles (merchandise) or intangibles (services), retailing has occurred.

Number of Outlets

Another method of classifying retailers is by the number of outlets each firm operates. Generally, retailers with several units are a stronger competitive threat because they can spread many fixed costs, such as advertising and top management salaries, over a larger number of stores and can achieve economies in purchasing. However, single-unit retailers, such as your neighborhood IGA grocery store or ACE hardware store, do have several advantages. They are generally owner- and family-operated and tend to have harder-working, more motivated employees. Also, they can focus all their efforts on one trade area and tailor their merchandise to that area while gaining buying efficiencies by being a member of the IGA or ACE wholesale buying organization. In the past, such stores were usually able to spot emerging customer desires sooner and respond to them faster than the larger multi-unit operations.

Any retail organization that operates more than one unit is technically a chain, but this is really not a very practical definition. Therefore, this text will only consider a retail operation to be a chain if it has 10 or more stores. Various trade associations estimate that chain stores account for 43 percent of all retail sales (including 99 percent of all department store sales and 66 percent of all grocery store sales). Though chain operations account for 60 percent of nondurable goods sales, they account for only about 23 percent of durable goods sales. After all, most auto dealerships, barbers and beauticians, bicycle stores, jewelry stores, furniture stores, and florists are still independent or have less than 10 units.[35]

Restaurants are one of the most rapid growth areas for retail chains. Twenty-five years ago it was still popular for each community to have plenty of family-owned and -operated restaurants. However, just like the local family-owned retailer of the 1950s and prior periods has largely disappeared, the same is becoming true of family-owned and -operated restaurants. However, for the college graduate this may be a positive trend since these chain restaurants need store managers as well as regional and national managers. Thus,

Peter Etchells/Alamy Limited

Restaurants with proven and successful formats can expand and grow rapidly. Consequently, they offer many employment opportunities as they open new locations.

employment opportunities you may not have considered exist at enterprises such as The Cheesecake Factory, Chipotle, In-and-Out Burger, Pei-Wei, Olive Garden, and Panera Bread as well as many others. Of course, you could also be a restaurant entrepreneur and launch your own retail chain as Andrew Cherng, a graduate of Kansas State University, did over thirty years ago when he noted a void in fast casual Asian food. Andrew is the founder of the Panda Restaurant Group, a privately owned chain that now operates restaurants mostly under the Panda Express brand.[36] Panda Express caters to the rapidly rising interest in Asian food in North America and now has over 1,500 restaurants in the U.S. and Puerto Rico. Another retail entrepreneur is Steve Ells, whose Chipotle chain now has more than 1,000 stores that provide quick, but freshly-prepared, Mexican food.[37]

Yet not all chain operations enjoy the same advantages. Small chains are local and may enjoy some economies in buying and in having the merchandise tailored to their market needs. Large chains are generally regional or national and can take full advantage of the economies of scale that centralized buying, accounting, training, advertising, and information systems and a **standard stock list** can achieve. A standard stock list requires that all stores in a retail chain stock the same merchandise. Other national chains such as JCPenney, recognizing the variations of regional tastes, use the **optional stock list** approach,

standard stock list
Is a merchandising method in which all stores in a retail chain stock the same merchandise.

optional stock list
Is a merchandising method in which each store in a retail chain is given the flexibility to adjust its merchandise mix to local tastes and demands.

which gives each store the flexibility to adjust its merchandise mix to local tastes and demands. After all, as one JCPenney executive told the authors, stores in the Rio Grande Valley of Texas sell primarily smalls and mediums in men's shirts, while in Minnesota the chain sells a preponderance of larger sizes. Perhaps this is why Macy's, in 2008, implemented an initiative called My Macy's,[38] where local market managers oversee about a dozen stores each and help to tailor merchandise assortments to local tastes and needs; such as more swimsuits near water parks.

Both types of stock lists provide scale advantages in other retailing activities. For example, promotional savings occur when more than one store operates in an area and can share advertising, even while tailoring specific merchandise to specific stores.

Finally, chain stores have long been aware of the benefits of taking a leadership role in the marketing supply chain. When a chain store retailer is able to achieve critical mass in purchases, it can get other supply-chain members—wholesalers, brokers, and manufacturers—to engage in activities they might not otherwise engage in, and it is then referred to as the **channel advisor** or **channel captain**. For example, the chain store retailer might get other supply-chain members to include direct-to-store deliveries, increased promotional allowances, extended payment terms, or special package sizes, all of which help the retailer operate more efficiently.

In recent years, chains (as will be discussed in greater detail in Chapter 4) have relied on their high level of consumer recognition to engage in **private-label branding**. Private-label branding may be *store branding*, when a retailer develops its own brand name and contracts with a manufacturer to produce the product with the retailer's brand, or *designer lines*, where a known designer develops a line exclusively for the retailer. Thus, instead of competing with another retailer selling the same brand, here the retailer is the only one selling the product. Today, the whole concept of private labels has taken on a new dimension as retailers have nationally promoted these items. These private labels are advertised as brands in a variety of media and are heavily promoted in stores.

In the past, private labels were inexpensive knockoffs of popular items. Today, though, some of the best retailers have significantly increased the quality and style of their private merchandise to promote it front and center. Retailers target these private labels, which have their own distinct personality, to specific markets and advertise them in their own promotional pieces. Consider, for example, the American Living brand, JCPenney's comprehensive lifestyle brand created by a division of Polo Ralph Lauren. It includes a full range of apparel for women, men, and children, along with footwear, accessories, home furnishings, and textiles offering an updated classic style with impeccable quality at a smart price. Just as many consumers believe Arizona Jeans to be a national brand, Penney's hopes to do the same with its American Living brand. In addition, Walmart recently expanded its private-label line of food and household cleaners to take advantage of recession-pinched consumers' increasing desire to buy cheaper store brands rather than more expensive brand-name products.[39]

Another reason why private labels are so popular with retailers is that by designing and manufacturing their own labels, retailers can cut out the designer and the middleman. Doing so can translate into profit margins that can be at least 20 percent better than a manufacturer's name-brand label and in addition they don't need to compete with other retailer's price cutting on the same brand.

The major shortcoming of using the number-of-outlets scheme for classifying retailers is that it addresses only traditional bricks-and-mortar retailers. This scheme thus ignores many nontraditional retailers such as catalog-only sellers and e-tailers. How many outlets does Amazon.com have? One could argue that each new online computer or smartphone is a potential retail outlet for the e-tailing giant.

---

channel advisor or channel captain
Is the institution (manufacturer, wholesaler, broker, or retailer) in the marketing channel that is able to plan for and get other channel institutions to engage in activities they might not otherwise engage in. Large store retailers are often able to perform the role of channel captain.

private-label branding
May be store branding, when a retailer develops its own brand name and contracts with a manufacturer to produce the product with the retailer's brand, or designer lines, where a known designer develops a line exclusively for the retailer.

ZUMA Press/Newscom

Target Stores has developed Archer Farms as a private-label brand.

Margins versus Turnover

gross-margin percentage
A measure of profitability derived by dividing gross margin by net sales.

gross margin
Is the difference between net sales and cost of goods sold.

operating expenses
Are those expenses that a retailer incurs in running the business other than the cost of the merchandise.

inventory turnover
Refers to the number of times per year, on average, that a retailer sells its inventory.

high-performance retailers
Are those retailers that produce financial results substantially superior to the industry average.

Retailers can also be classified with regard to their gross-margin percentage and rate of inventory turnover. The **gross-margin percentage** shows how much **gross margin** (net sales minus the cost of goods sold) the retailer makes as a percentage of sales; this is also referred to as the *gross-margin return on sales*. A 40-percent gross margin indicates that on each dollar of sales the retailer generates 40 cents in gross-margin dollars. This gross margin will be used to pay the retailer's **operating expenses** (the expenses the retailer incurs in running the business other than the cost of the merchandise—e.g., rent, wages, utilities, depreciation, and insurance) and generate a profit. **Inventory turnover** refers to the number of times per year, on average, that a retailer sells its inventory. Thus, an inventory turnover of 12 times indicates that, on average, the retailer turns over or sells its average inventory once a month. Likewise, an average inventory of $40,000 (retail) and annual sales of $240,000 means the retailer has turned over its inventory six times in one year ($240,000 divided by $40,000), or every two months.

High-performance retailers, those who produce financial results substantially superior to the industry average, have long recognized the relationship between gross-margin percentage, inventory turnover, and profit. One can classify retailers into four basic types by using the concepts of margin and turnover: (1) low margin, low turnover; (2) high margin, low turnover; (3) low margin, high turnover; and (4) high margin, high turnover.

Typically, the **low-margin, low-turnover retailer** will not be able to generate sufficient profits to remain competitive and survive. Thus, there are no good examples of successful retailers using this approach. In fact, as any seasoned retailer knows if you have both low margins and low turnover you better figure out a way to increase one or both or go out of business!

High-margin, low-turnover retailers (bricks and mortar) are quite common in the United States. Furniture stores, high-end women's specialty stores and furriers, jewelry stores,

low-margin/low-turnover retailer
Is one that operates on a low gross margin percentage and a low rate of inventory turnover.

high-margin/low-turnover retailer
Is one that operates on a high gross margin percentage and a low rate of inventory turnover.

low-margin/high-turnover retailer
Is one that operates on a low gross margin percentage and a high rate of inventory turnover.

high-margin/high-turnover retailer
Is one that operates on a high gross margin percentage and a high rate of inventory turnover.

gift shops, funeral homes, and most of the mom-and-pop stores located in small towns across the country are generally good examples of high-margin, low-turnover operations. Another example includes Pawn Shops that take merchandise as collateral for small loans. The Pawn Shop dealers are astute and also take a risk, so often the value of the merchandise held as collateral is considerably higher than loaned against it. Predictably, many borrowers do not return to pay their loan and reclaim their merchandise and thus the Pawn Shop operator has an item to sell which will yield a high margin but may take quite awhile to sell.

On the other hand, the **low-margin, high-turnover retailer** only really developed after World War II with the advent of the discount store. Sam Walton ran a Ben Franklin five-and-dime store and was among the first to see that selling one item a week for 99 cents with a 50-cent margin wasn't as good as selling six of those items a week at 69 cents and making 20 cents on each. Bernie Marcus and Arthur Blank revolutionized the hardware business by starting Home Depot with its low-margin, high-turnover strategy and replacing smaller hardware stores using a high–low approach. Today, most mass merchandiser retailers, and especially the big box stores and category killers, use a low-margin, high-turnover strategy. Amazon.com is probably the best known example of a low-margin, high-turnover e-tailer.

Finally, some retailers find it possible to operate as **high-margin, high-turnover retailers**. As you might expect, this strategy can be very profitable. Probably the most popular examples are convenience food stores such as 7-Eleven, Circle K, and Quick Mart; and the concessions and sports apparel businesses at major athletic events. Another common example is flea markets where unfortunately much of the merchandise is either stolen or counterfeit brands.

Although there is a lack of examples of high-margin, high-turnover retailers on the Internet, it is actually fairly common on various home shopping networks. Of course, you may not think that is the case because the prices on these shopping channels appear so low; but take a moment and look at the shipping and handling charges which is the big margin booster for this form of retailing. You should also note the next time you watch a home shopping network that often there is a clock displayed that shows how many units are being sold per time period (usually minute). The operators of these shopping networks will not invite a vendor back to display their merchandise unless sales and, therefore, turnover is high.

As noted previously, the low-margin, low-turnover retailer is the least able of the four to withstand a competitive attack because this retailer is usually unprofitable or barely profitable; when competition increases, profits are driven even lower. On the other hand, the high-margin, high-turnover retailer is in an excellent position to withstand and counter competitive threats because profit margins enable it to finance competitive price wars.

While the margin and turnover scheme provides an encompassing classification, it fails to capture the complete array of retailers operating in today's marketplace. For example, service retailers and even some e-tailers such as Priceline.com carry no inventory. Thus, while this scheme provides a good way of analyzing retail competition, it neglects an important type of retailing: service retailers. Keep in mind, however, that with a bit of imagination the concept may still apply. Often in a service-retailing business such as a restaurant or barber or beauty shop, what the retailer needs to turn is not inventory but people. If you have worked in a restaurant, then you probably know the concept called "turning the tables," which is the practice of getting customers in and serving them quickly and efficiently and getting them out so the table can be used to serve other guests. In a fine-dining establishment, a dinner can take three hours and thus the turnover of tables or customers is low, but the gross margin on the food and beverages is quite high. On the other hand, in a cafeteria the visitors go through the serving line and are seated and depart in 30 minutes. Margins are lower, but turnover of tables or customers is higher. Think of how this concept could apply to a beauty shop.

Location

Retailers have long been classified according to their location within a metropolitan area, be it the central business district, a regional shopping center, or a neighborhood shopping center or as a freestanding unit. These traditional locations will be discussed in greater detail in Chapter 7. However, the last 10–15 years saw a major change in the locations that retailers selected. Retailers are now aware that opportunities to improve financial performance can result not only from improving the sales per square foot of traditional sites but also from operating in new and nontraditional retail areas.

In the past, rather than expand into untested territories, many retailers simply renovated their existing stores. Not today. Now retailers are reaching out for alternative retail sites. North American retailers today are testing all types of nontraditional locations to expand their businesses. For example, McDonald's and Taco Bell have locations in travel stop plazas along interstate highways, airports, university student unions, and even in some Walmart stores. Loblaw, a Canadian grocer, has a women's health club in its store near Toronto; E*Trade, the online brokerage firm, is expanding its non-Internet presence with financial service centers in Target stores. Even the bricks-and-mortar banks now realize that their locations are now less of a vehicle for transactions and much more a vehicle for selling financial products: mutual funds, mortgages, trusts, and investment services. As a result, they are putting in pharmacies, little post offices, and even Starbucks in their buildings as a means of increasing traffic.[40]

Also, given the high income levels of many airline travelers and the increasing amount of layover time between flights and the absence of food on many flights, many retailers have opened stores in airports, an idea that originated with and has long been used by European and Asian retailers. Airport retailers have been able to succeed by offering fast service, convenience, pleasant and clean environments, product variety and quality, entertainment, and competitive prices. For example, one of New York City's

Airports are increasingly the location of a wide variety of retail formats from restaurants to luxury merchandise and even health spas and hotels.

toniest retail venues today—where shoppers can browse in boutiques featuring merchandise from DKNY, adventure sports outfitter ExOfficio, Japanese housewares retailer Muji, Ron Jon Surf Shop, H. Stern Jewelers, and Danish designer Sand—isn't on Fifth or Madison avenues. It's The Shops at John F. Kennedy International Airport. In addition, a wide selection of food is available from full service restaurant chains such as Chili's, TGI Fridays as well as fast food options such as Burger King, Wendy's and Pizza Hut.

You can also find a spa and pharmacy with an on-site nurse if you need them. Travelers can also find Brooks Brothers and Ermenegildo Zegna in Atlanta's airport and Coach and Body Shop in San Francisco's. So popular have these stores become with passengers that retail rents now account for over 50 percent of airport revenues.[41] In addition, every major airport has one or more hotels operating on the airport premise such as Hilton Hotels or Marriott Hotels, and all of these have meeting and conference centers for the business traveler.

Probably, the most significant of the new nontraditional shopping locations today is the combination of culture with entertainment and shopping, something that was unheard of a decade ago. Today, such locations, such as Bass Pro hunting and fishing superstores, have proven that the edges are blurring between shopping and entertainment for the masses.

Retailers do not want to miss out on urban or inner-city neighborhoods, which frequently have large minority populations. By 2015, it is projected that the spending power of Latinos and African Americans will reach $1.4 trillion and $1.1 trillion, respectively. Dollar Tree, Dollar General, Jewel-Osco, and Pathmark are leaders in opening stores in urban locations. Walkable urban grocers are popping up in cities around the United States. For example, Fresh & Easy Market, a division of British-owned Tesco, is expanding in northern California with 10,000- to 12,000-square-foot urban and suburban stores, and Local D'Lish, at 2,000 square feet, in Minneapolis, Minnesota, provides a walkable alternative for residents of the North Loop. An even smaller urban grocer is Mayberry Foodstuffs in downtown Cincinnati, Ohio, which is only 500 square feet.[42]

Before ending our discussion of location, it is important to point out that this is an area of retailing that may undergo significant changes in the next decade. The Internet suggests that future locations may be as close as a consumer's tablet computer, smartphone, or the electronic dashboard of their automobile. Also, consider that many retail offerings may be digital in nature. For instance, of the tens of thousands of apps you can access via your smartphone or other digital device, many of them target retail customers. In fact, some of the most successful retail entrepreneurs of this decade will be young entrepreneurs (sometimes less than 14 years old) writing and becoming wealthy with clever apps that offer value to shoppers and customers.

Size

Many retail trade associations classify retailers by sales volume or number of employees. The reason for classifying by size is that the operating performance of retailers tends to vary according to size; that is, larger firms generally have lower operating costs per sales dollar than smaller firms. For example, based on the recently available information from various trade associations, the authors concluded that operating expenses were 39 percent for firms with sales between $5 million and $45 million and 35 percent for larger operations. These retail trade associations provide confidential information to their members showing similar breakdowns on gross margins, net profits, net markups, sales per square foot of selling space, and so forth. Retailers will find this information meaningful when comparing their results against others of a similar size within their product category.

While store size has been useful in the past, it is unclear whether the changes brought about by technology will make this classification obsolete. For example, imagine a fully automated retailer where, as a consumer places an order online, an automated stock-picking warehouse packages the selected merchandise and forwards it to the shipping area to be sent by UPS or Federal Express to the customer. If Netflix can make video rental stores such as Blockbuster obsolete, can the traditional store-based retailer be eliminated?

A Retailing Career

LO 3

What is involved in a retail career and what are the prerequisites necessary for success in retailing?

Retail is the largest industry in the nation. That means there are many different kinds of retail entities that fuel the nation's economy. Someone once said that "managing a retail store is an easy job. All you have to do is get consumers to visit your store (traffic) and then get these consumers to buy something (convert the traffic into customers) while operating at a lower cost than your competition (financial management)." Assuming that this simplistic statement is correct and forgetting what is involved in each of these tasks, what type of person is needed to manage a retail store?

an economist	Yes _____	No _____
a fashion expert	Yes _____	No _____
a buyer	Yes _____	No _____
a marketer	Yes _____	No _____
a financial analyst	Yes _____	No _____
a personnel manager	Yes _____	No _____
a logistics manager	Yes _____	No _____
an information systems analyst	Yes _____	No _____
an accountant	Yes _____	No _____

In reality, the answer is "yes" to all of these roles. A retail store manager needs to be knowledgeable in all these areas. As we have pointed out, few industries offer a more fast-paced, ever-changing environment where results are quickly seen on the bottom line than retailing. Few job opportunities will train you to become an expert not in just one field but in all business disciplines. Retailing offers you the economist's job of forecasting future sales, the fashion expert's job of predicting consumer behavior and how it will affect future fashion trends, the buyer's job of sourcing and negotiating terms for merchandise that will sell and the marketing manager's job of determining how to promote, price, and display your merchandise. Further, it offers the financial analyst's job of seeking ways to reduce various expenses; the personnel manager's job of hiring the right people, training them to perform their duties in an efficient manner, and developing their work schedules; the logistics manager's job of arranging delivery of a "hot item"; the information systems analyst's job of analyzing sales and other data to determine opportunities for improved management practices; and the accountant's job of arriving at a profitable bottom line.

In summary, a retailer is like a master chef. Anyone can buy the ingredients, but only a master chef can make a masterpiece meal and only the master restaurateur can create the atmosphere and level of service that creates a memorable dining experience. Over the course of a career in retailing, you will have to deal with many issues. Among them are:

1. what product(s) or service(s) to offer
2. what group of customers to serve

3. where to locate the store
4. how to hire, train, and motivate your employees
5. how to use your advertising to promote merchandise and also build the store image
6. what price level to use and when to lower price
7. what levels of customer service (store hours, credit, staffing, parking, etc.) to offer your customers
8. how to lay out and design the store
9. how to control store-operating expenses and police employees and customers to cut down on shoplifting and employee theft of merchandise
10. how to leverage the Internet and social media to support your mission

Exhibit 1.5 illustrates the career paths available to the college graduate at a typical retailer. Note that there are two major paths: store management and buyer. (For a more detailed discussion of the various careers available today in retailing, including jobs in accounting, finance, advertising, information technology, logistics, and store design, see the excellent discussion of retailing careers at www.macyscollege.com/college/careers/careerpaths. In addition, CareerBuliders.com provides information on all aspects of the job search. This site offers tips on resume writing, distributing the resume, interviewing, and even career assessment.)

If you elect the **store-management** path, you will have many decisions to make that affect the store's profitability. Selecting, training, evaluation, and all other aspects of personnel management are your responsibility. This path is very people-skill oriented as you will be responsible for in-store promotions, displays, customer service, building maintenance, and store security. In addition, there is a need to coordinate your efforts with buyers and department managers in order to meet customers' needs, thus maximizing store sales. This career path does require frequent moves as you increase your

store management
The retailing career path that involves responsibility for selecting, training, and evaluating personnel, as well as in-store promotions, displays, customer service, building maintenance, and security.

Exhibit 1.5
Retailing's Two Career Paths

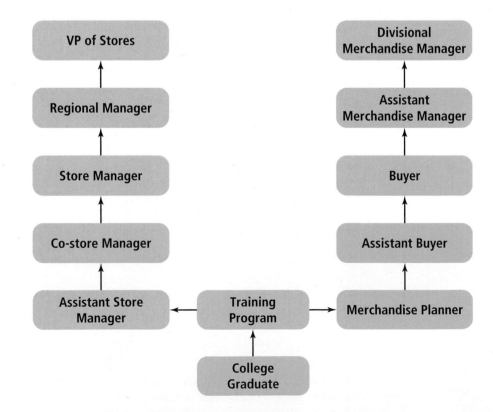

responsibilities. In addition, this path involves working weekends and evenings; however, more retailers are finding ways to enable managers on this career path to spend time with family and have balance in their lives. The career is, however, demanding but many of our former students who have chosen this career path say they loved being a store manager. Every day is different from the previous one, but most of all, they loved teaching, mentoring, and coaching the young people who are in their first job. What the ex-students disliked most about being a manager was dealing with "poor work ethic" and unreliable employees and internal theft from employees and external theft from shoplifters.

Still, this path offers a very rewarding pay package as you advance to store manager and beyond. Several of the ex-students, in their late 20s and their 30s, were making substantial six-figure incomes.

buying
The retailing career path whereby one uses quantitative tools to develop appropriate buying plans for the store's merchandise lines.

If your inclination is toward **buying**, you can follow that career path. After spending some time as an assistant buyer, you will be promoted to buyer, which is the equivalent of the CEO of a small business unit. Buyers will use quantitative tools such as the merchandise budget and *open to buy* in their work. For now, think of open-to-buy as the amount of funds you have to spend on merchandise (we will more succinctly define it in Chapter 9; it is sort of similar to the balance in your checking account, but as an assistant buyer or head buyer it can be in the millions and sometimes hundreds of millions of dollars. Buyers, who usually work out of the retailer's main office but do spend a great amount of time traveling, have to develop appropriate buying plans for their merchandise lines. Also, buyers are not only responsible for selecting the merchandise but also must select the vendors and negotiate terms with them. In fact, as a buyer you could also serve on a team with the retailer's product development staff as it works with a supplier to design a private-label offering for your store. Finally, buyers must coordinate with store managers to ensure that they are meeting the customers' needs. The former students who have chosen this path say that the high they get after a successful buying trip to market cannot be matched. At the same time, there is no low like the one you get when you realize you've bought a product your customers don't want. And in retailing there is no way of hiding this from the senior buyer or general merchandise manager who incidentally is also being evaluated on your performance.

If you consider that there are at least 10,000 possible combinations of products and at least 10 possible combinations of the other seven issues, then there are more than 10 billion different possible retailing formats. No wonder no other occupation offers the immediate opportunities and challenges that retailing does. Yet many students do not consider retailing when exploring career opportunities or they do not consider all they can do in a retailing career. One of the greatest opportunities for people entering a retailing career is in online retailing, or e-tailing. One particular e-tailing field that is attracting many job seekers is the retailing of online information, which is providing unheralded opportunities to those seeking new challenges.

Common Questions about a Retailing Career

As a student considering your future career, you may have certain questions about what opportunities a career in retailing may offer. To help you understand both the positive and negative sides of retailing, we will examine a few of the most frequently asked questions.

Salary

Are salaries in retailing competitive? Generally, starting salaries in executive-training programs will be around $45,000 to $58,000 per year, depending on the geographic area. That, however, is only the short-term perspective. In the long run, the retail manager or buyer is directly rewarded on individual performance. Entry-level retail managers or buyers who do exceptionally well can double or triple their incomes in three to five years, and often within seven to ten years can have incomes twice those of classmates who chose other career fields. As mentioned earlier, it is not uncommon for a college graduate with five to eight years of experience to earn a six-figure income. In fact, Macy's Chairman and CEO Terry Lundgren, was president of Federated Department Stores at age 35 and president of Neiman-Marcus a few years later.

Keep in mind another option is for you to become a retail entrepreneur either out of college or afterwards. If that is the case, the concept of a guaranteed salary disappears. Most retail entrepreneurs take a small compensation package that allows them to barely meet their household obligations. As a retail entrepreneur, you will want to build the profitability of your enterprise which will, if you do well, ultimately create a very high level of economic wealth. However, keep in mind that most or all of the profits in a rapidly growing retail enterprise need to be retained to finance the growth.

Career Progression

Can one advance rapidly in retailing? Yes. Obviously, this answer depends on both the retail organization and the individual. A person capable of handling increasing amounts of responsibility can move up quickly. There is no standard career progression chart; http://retailindustry.about.com/od/retailjobscareers/Retail_Jobs_Career_ Advancement.htm shows career opportunities available with many of the country's leading retailers by geographic area as well as other fine companies seeking college graduates. Keep in mind that franchising (discussed in Chapter 5) is also a potential career option at some point in your retailing career and is often a good substitute for being a retail entrepreneur and not nearly as risky. Even when he sold his retail chain (Mervyns) to Dayton-Hudson over 25 years ago, Mervyn Morris decided he wanted to become a Cadillac dealer and thus became the operator of a franchise business.

Geographic Mobility

Does a retailing career allow one to live in the area of the country where one desires? Yes and no. Retailing exists in all geographic areas of the United States with sufficient population density. In the largest 300 cities in the United States, there will be sufficient employment and advancement opportunities in retailing. In order to progress rapidly, a person must often be willing and able to make several moves, even if the changes may not be attractive in terms of an individual's lifestyle. Rapidly growing chain stores usually find it necessary to transfer individuals, especially those in the store-management career path, in order to open stores in new geographic areas. Fortunately, these transfers are generally coupled with promotions and salary adjustments. Finally, a person may stay in one geographic area if he or she desires; however, this may cost that person some opportunities for advancement and salary increases.

Societal Perspective

Professional merchants are considered respected and desirable members of their communities, state, and nation. Leading retail executives are well-rounded individuals with a high social consciousness. Many of them serve on the boards of nonprofit organizations, as regents or trustees of universities, as active members of the local chambers of commerce, on school boards, and in other service-related activities. Retailers serve society not only outside their retailing career but also within it as well. For example, civic events such as holiday parades are often sponsored by local merchants. In addition, many retail firms support local groups and charities with cash, food, and other goods and services as a means to "reinvest" some of their profits in the communities they serve.

Despite the many positive things retailers and other businesses do for society, there are many negative examples. In fact, in a *Time* magazine poll[43] of Americans over the age of 18, only 49% felt that businesses will make socially responsible decisions without the government telling them what to do. Incidentally, they also felt 68% of Americans do not live up to their responsibilities as citizens. Unfortunately, there are also unscrupulous, deceiving merchants that society can do without. This is true in all professions. There are unscrupulous lawyers, bankers, doctors, and police officers who give their professions a negative image at times. On the other hand, there are professional and ethical lawyers, bankers, doctors, and police officers who are good for their professions and for society as a whole. It is not the profession that dictates one's contribution to society but the soundness of one's ethical principles. Early in your career (preferably as a student), you need to develop a firm set of ethical principles to help guide you throughout your managerial career.

Prerequisites for Success

What's required for success as a retail manager? Let's look at several factors that influence a retailer's success.

Hard Work

Most successful retailers, like successful individuals, will respond to the preceding question with a simple "hard work." Beginning retailers have long known that they earn their salary 9 to 5, Monday through Friday, but earn their advancement after 5 o'clock. Still, one can have a balanced and happy life coupled with a retailing career by using good time-management and planning skills. Also, as we suggested earlier, retailers are developing more family-friendly human resource practices.

Analytical Skills

The retail manager must be able to solve problems through numerical analysis of facts and data in order to plan, manage, and control. In each chapter, you will note an exhibit that focuses on retail math (for instance, see Exhibit 1.1 of this chapter). Also, at the end of each chapter there will be an exercise "Planning Your Own Entrepreneurial Retail Business" that will usually include retail math to further enhance your analytical ability.

The retail manager is a problem solver on a day-to-day basis. An understanding of the past and current performance of the store, merchandise lines, and departments is necessary. It is the analysis of these performance data that forms the basis of future actions in the retailing environment. Today's retailer must be able to analyze all the financial data that are available before going to market. For example, Costco has had vendors redesign product packages to fit more items on a pallet—the wooden platforms it uses to ship and display its goods. In one case, the retailer had the manufacturer put cashews into square containers instead of round ones, which enabled the retailer to decrease the number of pallets shipped by 24,000 a year, cutting the number of trucks needed by 600. Likewise, by having other manufacturers reshape everything from laundry detergent buckets to milk jugs, Costco was able to reduce the number of pallets per year by 200,000.[44]

In addition, quantitative and qualitative analysis of customers, competitors, suppliers, and other constituencies often help to identify emerging trends. Combined with current performance results and market knowledge, continual monitoring of these constituencies provides insight into past performance and alerts the retailer to new directions. Many retailers also get information from reading trade journals, such as *Stores*, *Women's Wear Daily*, *Progressive Grocer*, and *Chain Store Age*; discuss current happenings with their buying office; visit markets; and even talk to their competitors as a means to keep up. One successful retailer told the author to not just analyze the merchandise, customers, competitors, and suppliers, but to do the same with its employees. Do they understand the retailer's philosophy, its values, preferred behavior, and code of conduct?

Creativity

The ability to generate and recognize novel ideas and solutions is known as *creativity*. A retail manager cannot operate a store totally by a set of preprogrammed equations and formulas. Because the competitive environment is constantly changing, there is no standard recipe for retailing. Therefore, retail executives need to be idea people as well as analysts. After all, success in retailing is the result of sensitive, perceptive decisions that require imaginative and innovative techniques.

For example, as the American economy continued in its slowdown a few years ago, many retailers were afraid to embrace new ideas. Instead of using their creative power to increase their competitive advantage, these retailers either just continued doing things as they always had done them: cut costs without thinking about the impact on customer satisfaction or copied what their competitors were doing. None of these actions enabled the retailer to actually differentiate itself from the competition. In fact, many students mistakenly assume that price is the only way for retailers to compete and that the arrival of a discount chain always spells disaster for small-town retailers. After all, the small local stores cannot match the discounters' purchasing volume. This is not the case if the retailer is able to use creativity to differentiate itself from the competition. The chapter's "Service Retailing" box illustrates one of the most creative ways a small bike sales and repair retailer took on the big discounters. Moore's Bicycle Shop simply did it by using the discounter as a supply source.

© Smileus/Shutterstock

SERVICE RETAILING

Using Creativity to Take on Walmart

Moore's Bicycle Shop is located in a southern college town of 50,000 and is surrounded by three Walmart Supercenters. A couple of years ago, its owner, James Moore, became frustrated when he noticed customers walking out of his shop without making a purchase when he was unable to offer them a $125 bicycle. His previous source of these "inexpensive" bikes was Mongoose. However, Mongoose had earlier discontinued selling to independent bicycle retailers, such as Moore, in favor of having an exclusive contract with the much larger Walmart.

Recently, Moore began to notice customers bringing in some Walmart bikes for repair. These bikes, which were sold as "clearance specials" consisted of defects or returns Walmart would put on the sidewalk and sold "as is." Unfortunately for the customers, the cost of the work needed to make their bikes safe and functional often exceeded what they originally paid, and the customers often left without getting the necessary repairs.

Using his creativity, Moore wrote to the three Walmart managers, offering to purchase sight unseen all of their returned bicycles on the condition that he get *all* the returns and not just the worst of the batch. He offered a simple rate structure of $10 for kid's bikes and $15 for adult bikes. He also addressed the issue that the practice of selling defective merchandise was not good from a liability standpoint. In addition, he suggested that their customers might feel cheated with their bargains when they learned the "clearance bikes" were not cost-effective to fix. In short, Moore noted that Walmart might be selling potentially dangerous products to disappointed customers.

At first, Walmart offered him 68 bicycles at an average price under $12. A few bikes only needed a flat repaired, most needed a minimal degree of time and parts, while a few were only usable for parts. Moore took the best six bikes and within two hours had them repaired and sold for enough to pay for all 68 used bikes.

Today, Moore prices most of these repaired bikes either at Walmart's regular price or even higher after

(continued)

Mike Moore

Creativity is one of the easiest ways for small retailers to compete with the discounters. Witness the action of Moore's Bicycle Shop in its dealings with Walmart.

explaining that the higher price included the shop's six-month comprehensive warranty and the fact that the bikes had already gone through the critical break-in period (where most adjustments are needed) and had been serviced by "expert" mechanics.

Over the past couple of years, Moore has purchased several hundred more Walmart returns, resulting in a win–win situation for all three parties.

Walmart wins because it no longer has lines of defective merchandise greeting customers at the front door, and the managers are able to clear their storage clutter with one phone call.

The customers win as they are no longer being sold bikes that are unsafe to ride and too costly to repair. More often than not, the victims of these sidewalk "specials" were the customers least able to afford making a buying mistake by purchasing a faulty or unusable product.

Moore won for two reasons. First, he was now able to provide an identical product to the price-conscious shopper at the same price as Walmart. Second, in the future many of his "new" customers would often trade that "inexpensive" bike in for a better-quality bike. The shop also wins because its labor productivity is now maximized as it always has a backlog of Walmart returns to repair during its otherwise slower periods. Consequently, the shop mechanics now work year-round.

However, nothing excites Moore more than the thought that, with a little creativity, he is now able to take a product that costs less than $12 and, after investing about 15 minutes of employee time and $5 in parts, he can sell it for $125.

Source: Based on information supplied by James Moore, Moore's Bicycle Shop, Hattiesburg, Mississippi, and used with his written permission.

Decisiveness

The ability to make rapid decisions and to render judgments, take action, and commit oneself to a course of action until completion is termed *decisiveness*. A retail manager must be an action person. Better decisions could probably be made if more time were taken to make them. However, more time is frequently unavailable because variables such as fashion trends and consumer desires change quickly. Thus, a manager must make decisions quickly, confidently, and correctly in order to be successful even if perfect information is not always available. For example, buyers often make purchase decisions six months to a year before the merchandise arrives at the store.

Flexibility

The ability to adjust to the ever-changing needs of the situation calls for flexibility. The retail manager must have the willingness and enthusiasm to do whatever is necessary (although not necessarily planned) to get the job completed. Because plans must be altered quickly to accommodate changes in trends, styles, and attitudes, successful retail managers must be flexible. For example, changes in e-tailing occur continuously as retailers adjust prices and product offerings to changing consumer tastes and the competitive actions of other retailers.

Initiative

Retail managers are doers. They must have the ability to originate action rather than wait to be told what to do. This ability is called *initiative*. To be a success, the modern retail manager must monitor the numbers of the business (sales volumes, profits, inventory levels, etc.) and seize opportunities for action. Especially, if you decide to be a retail entrepreneur you best have a plentiful amount of initiative.

Leadership

Working in retailing is really working on a team. The ability to inspire the team members to trust and respect your judgment and the ability to delegate, guide, and persuade this team calls for *leadership*. Successfully conducting a retail operation means depending on the team to get the work done; in any large-scale retailing enterprise, one person cannot do it all. A manager succeeds when his or her subordinates do their jobs. In fact, the concept of the team approach is one of the most important hiring criteria for many retailers.

Organization

Another important quality is the ability to establish priorities and plans and follow through to achieve these results. This prerequisite is *organization*. Retail managers are often forced to deal with many issues, functions, and projects at the same time. To achieve goals, the successful retailer must be a good time manager and set priorities when organizing personnel and resources.

Risk Taking

Retail managers should be willing to take calculated risks based on thorough analysis and sound judgment; they should also be willing to accept responsibility for the results. Retail entrepreneurs succeed by taking calculated risks and having the confidence to try something new before someone else does. For example, no one can say that George Zimmer's move from selling men's wear from the trunk of his car to freestanding stores was without risk, or Jeff Bezos's decision to start Amazon.com or Tony Hsieh's decision to start Zappos and sell shoes on the Internet were without risk. The risk taking nature of retailing, however, goes beyond what retail entrepreneurs do. All successful buyers have at one time or another taken the risk of purchasing merchandise that could be labeled as losers. After all, if buyers never made errors, that would mean they were afraid to take "risks" and probably passed up many winners. However, they must have the ability to recognize when they make a mistake.

Stress Tolerance

As the other prerequisites to retailing success suggest, retailing is a fast-paced and demanding career in an ever-changing environment. The retailing leaders of the 21st century must be able to perform consistently under pressure and to thrive on constant change and challenge. The website Retailing21.com will help you prepare for dealing with constant change.

Perseverance

Because of the difficult challenges that a retail career presents, it is important to have *perseverance*. All too often, retailers may become frustrated due to the many things they can't control. For example, a blizzard may occur just before Christmas and wipe out the most important shopping days of the year. Others may become exasperated with fellow employees, the long hours (especially the weekends), or the inability to satisfy some customers. Tony Hsieh with the launch of Zappos and the sale of shoes online had about 25 percent of sales that were drop shipped direct from the shoe manufacturer to the customer.[45] But the problem with this business model was that Zappos could not control customer service and the customer experience that was critical to its long-term success. Thus, he had to slow down and make the tough decision to not drop ship, although these shipments were highly profitable. Tony had to have the perseverance to move to a different business model requiring that 100 percent of the time Zappos had control of the merchandise they sold. Like Tony Hsieh, the person who has the ability to persevere and take all of this in stride will find an increasing number of career-advancement or entrepreneurial opportunities.

Enthusiasm

Successful retailers must have a strong feeling of warmth for their job; otherwise they will convey the wrong image to their customers and department associates. Retailers today are training their sales forces to smile even when talking to customers on the telephone "because it shows through in your voice."[46] Without *enthusiasm*, success in any field will elude you. Herb Kelleher, the co-founder and legendary CEO of Southwest Airlines, recognized the importance of enthusiasm in employees. Flying on an airline is stressful, especially 40 years ago when many people had not actually flown on an airplane. Herb recognized that if the flight attendants were enthusiastic about their jobs, it would show through to the passengers who would then feel less stress.

LO 4

Explain the different methods for the study and practice of retailing.

The Study and Practice of Retailing

As we have seen, two of the prerequisites for success as a retail manager are analytical skills and creativity. These attributes also represent two methods for the study and practice of retailing.

Analytical Method

The analytical retail manager is a finder and investigator of facts. These facts are summarized and synthesized so a manager can make decisions systematically. In doing so, the manager uses models and theories of retail phenomena that enable him or her to structure all dimensions of retailing. An analytical perspective can result in a standardized set of procedures, success formulas, and guidelines.

Consider, for example, a manager operating a Starbucks shop where everything is preprogrammed, including the menu, decor, location, hours of operation, cleanliness standards, customer-service policies, and advertising. This store manager needs only to gather and analyze facts to determine if the pre-established guidelines are being met and to take appropriate corrective action if necessary.

We mentioned earlier in this chapter how Walmart has made use of the sophistication of its computer system when hurricanes, tornados, or other emergencies occur. For example, when a hurricane is approaching a coast, the area's stores are stocked up with bottled water, flashlights, generators, and tarps. The retailer also will have chain saws, mops, and Pop-Tarts (which stay preserved until opened, taste good, and can be eaten by the whole family) in reserve for after the storm. This is the result of analyzing the data from previous storms.

One thing for a small retailer to consider is watching the Russell 2000 Index. This index, which measures the performance of the small-cap segment of the U.S. equity universe, is a great forecasting tool for future business conditions. Thus, even if they don't trade stocks, small retailers should keep their eye on this stock market index. And since most small retailers operate in one or a few cities, they should be aware of the major employers in the area and how they are faring. Although the Russell 2000 Index captures small-cap firms, it is possible that if a large *Fortune* 1000 firm in your local community fails or has a downturn and closes a local manufacturing plant, distribution center, or administrative office, then that will impact what members of the local community can spend at your store.

Creative Method

Conversely, the creative retail manager is an idea person. This retail manager tends to be a conceptualizer and has a very imaginative and fertile mind capable of creating a highly successful retail chain. If we were to ask you, "What grocer or supermarket in North America produces more in sales per square foot than virtually all others?" you

Trader Joe's leads in the USA in terms of sales per square foot as well as in creative merchandising.

might conclude it is Albertsons, Safeway, Kroger, Piggly Wiggly or one of the other large grocery chains. It is actually Trader Joe's, who sells over $1700 per square foot of retail space; often 50 percent to 100 percent higher than leading competitors. You can be sure Trader Joe's has great analytics behind its business model. But, it also is highly creative and has turned grocery shopping into a fulfilling and fun experience. Undoubtedly, some of that experience is finding exotic food items on their shelves, as well as staples. But, part of the experience is your encounter with cheerful employees dressed in Hawaiian shirts where customers are often greeted with high-fives and free cookies.[47]

A Two-Pronged Approach

As shown through the examples of our Starbucks manager and Trader Joe's, retailing can indeed be practiced from both perspectives. The retailer who employs both approaches is most successful in the long run. Aren't stores like Starbucks successful using only the analytical method? No. The Starbucks manager can operate analytically quite success-fully. However, behind the franchisee is a franchisor who is creative as well as analytical. On the creative side was the development of the company name and logo. On the analytical side was the development of standardized layouts, fixtures, equipment, and employee training. It is the combination of the creative with the analytical that has made Starbucks what it is today. For instance, Starbucks recent introduction of Starbuck's branded instant coffee caught many by surprise. How could you have great tasting coffee that was instant; it seemed a contradiction in terms. But with analytical and creative tools and methods Starbuck's demonstrated that the contradiction did not need to exist.

The synthesis of creativity and analysis is necessary in all fields of retailing. One retail expert noted that "many successful merchandisers are fast duplicators rather than originators."[48] To decide who or what to duplicate requires not only creativity but also an analysis of the strategies that retailers are pursuing. This is an exercise in weighing potential returns against risks. Thus, according to this expert, "creativity in retailing is for the sake of increasing the sales and profits of the firm."[49] If creativity is tied to sales and profits, then one cannot avoid analysis; profit and sales statistics require analysis.

Retailers cannot do without either creativity or analytical skills. We will attempt to develop your skills in both of these areas. At the outset, however, you should note that the analytical and creative methods for studying retailing are not that different. Whether you use creativity or analytical skills, they will be directed at solving problems and pursuing opportunities.

A Proposed Orientation

The approach to the study and practice of retailing that is reflected in this book is an outgrowth of the previous discussion. This approach has four major orientations: (1) environmental, (2) management planning, (3) profit, and (4) decision making.

Retailers should have an environmental orientation that will allow them to anticipate and adapt continuously to external forces in the environment. Retailing is not static. With social, legal, technological, economic, and other external forces always in flux, the modern retailer finds it necessary both to assess these changes from an analytical perspective and to respond with creative actions.

Retailers should have a planning orientation that will help them to adapt systemat-ically to a changing environment. A retailer who wants to have the competitive edge must plan today for the future. Exhibit 1.6 illustrates the problems facing a retailer

Exhibit 1.6
The Importance of
Proactive Planning

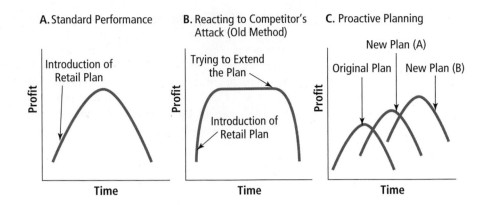

A. Standard Performance

Profit

Introduction of
Retail Plan

Time

B. Reacting to Competitor's
Attack (Old Method)

Profit

Trying to Extend
the Plan

Introduction of
Retail Plan

Time

C. Proactive Planning

Profit

New Plan (A)

Original Plan   New Plan (B)

Time

who is reactive rather than proactive in planning. Exhibit 1.6A shows the standard performance for a retailer's plan: The plan is introduced, sales peak as competitors react to the plan, and finally the plan becomes obsolete. Exhibit 1.6B shows the old method of reacting to a competitor's attack: The retailer tries to extend the sales peak by matching the competitor's plan until another competitor makes both of their plans obsolete. Exhibit 1.6C shows why this text places special emphasis on the development of creative retail strategies. Here the retailer is proactive and already has another plan ready before either the market changes or the competition attacks its original plan.

Retailers also need a profit orientation, since all retail decisions will have an effect on the firm's financial performance. The profit orientation will therefore focus on fundamental management of assets, sales revenues, and expenses. Incidentally, a profit orientation must involve a customer orientation since customers are the source of sales revenue. But a profit orientation also causes the retailer to be supplier oriented since it needs to acquire merchandise from suppliers and find a way where not only it but also the supplier can obtain a fair profit. Finally, a profit orientation focuses on employees since they do all of the work of retailing and thus are responsible for managing assets and expenses. We always advocate taking a long-term perspective on profit and encourage retailers to view customers, suppliers, and employees as their most valuable assets that need to be nurtured, developed, and properly rewarded. Management tools that show how to evaluate the profit impact of retail decisions will be discussed.

Retailers should have a decision-making orientation that will allow them to focus on the need to collect and analyze data for making intelligent retail decisions. To aid in this process, executives need a retail information system to help program their operations for desired results.

The Book Outline

This book is composed of 14 chapters, each with its own study guide and application section. The chapters are intended to reinforce each other. The end-of-chapter materials provide a way to bring the real world into your studies by launching you into the kinds of situations you might face as a retail manager or entrepreneur. Through careful analysis of this material and discussion with fellow students, you will discover retailing concepts that can be vividly retained because of the concrete context. Furthermore, this material will require you to think of yourself as a retail decision maker who must always make decisions with less-than-perfect information.

Introduction to Retailing

This book is divided into five parts. Part 1, "Introduction to Retailing," has two chapters. In Chapter 2, "Retail Strategic Planning and Operations Management," you will be exposed to the basic concepts of strategy, administration, operations planning, and management in retailing, which will be used in the remaining chapters.

The Retailing Environment

Part 2, "The Retailing Environment," will focus on the external factors that the retailer faces in making everyday business decisions. The four chapters examine, in detail, the factors shown in Exhibit 1.2. Chapter 3, "Retail Customers," will look at the behavior of the retail consumer and the socioeconomic environment. Chapter 4, "Evaluating the Competition in Retailing," examines the behavior of competitors as well as the technological advances taking place in the market. Chapter 5, "Managing the Supply Chain," focuses on the behavior of the various members of the supply chain and their effect on the retailer. Chapter 6, "Legal and Ethical Behavior," analyzes the effect of the legal and ethical constraints on today's retailer.

Market Selection and Location Analysis

It has often been said that the three keys to success in retailing are: location, location, and location. In Chapter 7, "Market Selection and Retail Location Analysis," we discuss the various elements to consider in determining the feasibility of targeting a given market segment and entering a given retail market, and then we look at site selection.

Managing Retail Operations

In Part 4, "Managing Retail Operations," we discuss the merchandising operations of a retail firm. This part deals with the day-to-day decisions facing retailers. Chapter 8, "Managing a Retailer's Finances," discusses various financial statements, the key methods of valuing inventory, and the development of merchandise planning budgets by retailers. Chapter 9, "Merchandise Buying and Handling," looks at how a retailer determines what to buy for its market and how these purchases are made. The appendix following Chapter 9 discusses the merchandising of apparel goods. Chapter 10, "Retail Pricing," discusses the importance to the retailer of setting the correct price. In addition to the various markup methods used by retailers, the chapter also looks at markdowns. Chapter 11, "Advertising and Promotion," provides a complete discussion (with the exception of personal selling, which is covered along with services offered by retailers in Chapter 12, "Customer Services and Retail Selling") of how a retailer can and should promote itself. Chapter 13, "Store Layout and Design," discusses the impact of proper layout and design on retail performance.

Retailing's Future

Part 5 of the book provides you our perspective on the future of retailing. In Chapter 14, "Reframing Retailing," we suggest most retail enterprises, and most retail executives need to reframe their mindset away from turning and selling merchandise to what we call a service-dominant logic or mindset. We discuss how retailing is increasingly moving to a collaborative business model. To collaborate with customers, the retailer needs to focus on strategies for customer engagement and offering competitively compelling value propositions.

The text concludes with a glossary of all major terms used in this text, as well as an index of the retailers mentioned.

Summary

This chapter seeks to acquaint the reader with the nature and scope of retailing by discussing its impact on the economy, the types of retailers, and its prerequisites for success.

LO 1

What is retailing and why is it always undergoing so much change?

Retailing consists of the final activities and steps needed to place a product in the hands of the ultimate consumer or to provide a service to the consumer. Retailing is not staid and stable; rather, it is an exciting business sector that effectively combines an individual's skills to make a profit in an ever-changing market environment. That is why some retailers are successful and others, who are either unwilling or unable to adapt to this changing environment, fail.

LO 2

What are the various methods used to categorize retailers?

Retailers can be classified in a variety of ways. Five of the more popular schemes are NAICS code, number of outlets, margins versus turnover, location, and size. None, however, sheds adequate light on competition in retailing.

LO 3

What is involved in a retailing career and what prerequisites are necessary for success in retailing?

In the long run, a retailing career can offer salary comparable to other careers, definite career advancement, and geographic mobility. In addition, a career in retailing incorporates the knowledge and use of all the business activities or disciplines (accounting, marketing, finance, personnel, economics, and even fashion). In retailing, no two days are alike; each offers its own set of opportunities and problems. The prerequisites for success in retailing besides hard work include analytical skills, creativity, decisiveness, flexibility, initiative, leadership, organization, risk taking, stress tolerance, perseverance, and enthusiasm. These are all important, but it is especially vital for the retail manager to develop an attitude of openness to new ideas and a willingness to learn. After all, the market is always changing.

LO 4

What are the different methods for the study and practice of retailing?

To be successful in retailing, an individual must use both analytical and creative methods of operation. The four orientations to the study and practice of retailing proposed in this text are an *environmental orientation*, which allows the retailer to focus on the continuously changing external forces affecting retailing; a *planning orientation*, which helps the retailer to adapt systematically to this changing environment; a *profit orientation*, which enables the retailer to examine the profit implications of any decision; and a *decision-making orientation*, which allows the retailer to focus on the need to collect and analyze data for making intelligent creative retail decisions.

Terms to Remember

retailing
bricks-and-mortar retailers
channel surfing
same-store sales
market share

scrambled merchandising
category killer
standard stock list
optional stock list
channel advisor (channel captain)

private-label branding

gross-margin percentage

gross margin

operating expenses

inventory turnover

high-performance retailers

low-margin, low-turnover retailer

high-margin, low-turnover retailer

low-margin, high-turnover retailer

high-margin, high-turnover retailer

store management

buying

Review and Discussion Questions

LO 1

What is retailing, and why is it always undergoing so much change?

1. Wouldn't a country be better off with fewer retail outlets? After all, with fewer stores, consumers would not waste money making impulsive purchases, and they would save more.
2. Is scrambled merchandising really a good idea? Does it make sense that if you are good in one area of merchandising that you will be good in all areas? Talbots, after all, is excellent in merchandising fashionable women's clothing but failed in selling men's and kids' clothing.
3. What factors are contributing to the recent trend of decreasing store size?
4. Currently, there is a great deal of debate about the future impact of the Internet on retailing. Which of the following items—a vacation package for spring break, a wedding gift for a friend, a pair of jeans for yourself, or an end table for your apartment—would you be least likely to purchase online? Why?
5. Price competition in retailing is pervasive. Explain how lower prices can lead to higher operating efficiency.
6. How can a retailer compete by focusing on shopper or customer experiences?

LO 2

Describe the five methods used to categorize retailers.

7. How can a retailer operate with a high-margin, high-turnover strategy? Won't customers avoid this type of store and shop at a low-margin store?
8. Will retailers with more outlets tend to have lower costs, thus will they always perform better (i.e. bigger is better when it comes to retailing)?
9. Isn't it better for a retail chain to always use a standard stock list? After all, it would confuse a customer if a JCPenney's in Chicago is different from one in Miami.

LO 3

What is involved in a retailing career and what prerequisites are necessary for success in retailing?

10. What concepts or techniques from economics, fashion, accounting, or information systems do you believe would be most useful in retail decision making?
11. What kind of leadership skills does it take to be successful in retailing? Isn't leadership the most important prerequisite for success in retailing?
12. Look at the 11 prerequisites for success as a retail manager. How do you assess yourself on these prerequisites? Which areas are you strong and weak?

LO 4

Explain the different methods for the study and practice of retailing.

13. To be successful in retailing, which skill is most important: being creative or being analytical? Why?
14. Visit a local retailer that you would describe as creative and seek to determine which analytical skills that retailer also possesses.

Sample Test Questions

LO 1   Retailing

    a.   may be defined as any cash purchase for merchandise.
    b.   is the same the world over.
    c.   is the final move in the flow of merchandise from producer to consumer.
    d.   is the sale of an item by the manufacturer to a wholesaler.
    e.   is not necessary to produce economic growth.

LO 2   Which of the following is not one of the ways by which retailers are categorized?

    a.   number of outlets
    b.   size
    c.   margin versus turnover
    d.   location
    e.   gender of the manager

LO 3   Due to increased corporate responsibilities, the manager of a bike shop has asked the assistant manager to take responsibility for screening and hiring new sales associates. The manager is allowing the assistant to make the decisions independently but has scheduled weekly meetings for the two to discuss any issues of concern and to provide any needed insight. The manager is demonstrating which desirable retailing attribute?

    a.   prioritizing
    b.   leadership
    c.   creativity
    d.   laziness
    e.   enthusiasm

LO 4   In attempting to determine whether a branch of a sandwich shop should be opened in a small town outside the original trading area, a retailer gathered information on demographics, competitors' sales, and available real estate in that area. The retailer was employing the _____ method of retail decision making.

    a.   tactical
    b.   strategic
    c.   analytical
    d.   creative
    e.   intuitive

Writing and Speaking Exercise

Nancy, who is your close friend, has just accepted an offer that begins on June 15, from a large U.S. retailer, which is approximately five weeks after she graduates with an undergraduate degree in management. The employment begins with an intensive four weeks of classes and then eight weeks of in-store training where Nancy will be assigned a mentor to provide her guidance and help in skill development. After this program, Nancy will be assigned to work in a store in the region as a sales manager trainee for six to twelve months. After this initial assignment, she will be promoted to be a sales manager of a merchandise department in the store. Nancy is now having second thoughts and has confided in you that she feels it downgrading to have to go back into the classroom to learn and furthermore to then begin her career in sales management. She has also been told that if she is to manage a retail sales force she needs to very early demonstrate that she can herself be a successful retail salesperson.

Prepare a written report for Tony Walker, the Director of College Relations, suggesting how this common concern among new college graduates joining a retail enterprise could be successfully addressed in the recruiting and hiring process.

Retail Project

How would you use the Internet to purchase your next car? Using your smartphone, table computer, or desk computer, select two or three different auto websites. List their web addresses, such as www.autobytel.com, and make a report describing what they have on their websites. Which one do you like best? Why? Can you purchase online from each website? What is the buying process? Can competitors gain anything from looking at these websites? Finally, what is missing from these websites that you feel should be on them?

Planning Your Own Entrepreneurial Retail Business

If you think you might want to be a retail entrepreneur, you can use the "Planning Your Own Entrepreneurial Retail Business" computer exercises at the end of each chapter to assist you in this process. In addition, this text's website (www.cengage.com/marketing/dunne) has an exercise called "The House: Understanding A Retail Enterprise Using Spreadsheet Analysis" that can be used to help you understand the dollars and cents of retailing.

This first exercise is intended to acquaint you with how sensitive your retail business will be to changes in sales volume. Let's assume that you plan that your retail business will generate $650,000 per year in annual sales and that it will operate at a gross-margin percentage of 40 percent. If your fixed operating expenses are $180,000 annually and variable operating costs are 12 percent of sales, then how much profit will you make?

(Hint: sales × gross-margin percentage = gross margin; gross margin − fixed operating expenses − sales × variable operating expenses as % of sales = net profit.) Use a spreadsheet program on your computer to compute your firm's net profits; next, analyze what happens (1) if sales drop 10 percent and (2) if sales rise 10 percent. Why are bottom line results (net profits) so sensitive to changes in sales volume?

CASE

The Changing Role of Funeral Homes

Mike Fallon had looked forward to going home for Christmas. He was about to graduate from a large state university with a degree in accounting and a minor in information technology. Since he wanted to work in a Certified Public Accountant (CPA) firm's tax division, he had even taken a retailing class. After all, he would be dealing with retail customers with his tax work. Still, the last thing he wanted to do at Christmas was discuss school subjects. However, that is just what happened when the family got together for Christmas dinner at his uncle's home.

Mike's mother's youngest brother was a church deacon, and somehow he changed the subject to the fact that so many nonparishioners wanted to use his church for weddings. Most of these requests were declined because of the demand by his current members. Somebody mentioned that with the number of people without church affiliation increasing across the county, she had seen a number of wedding chapels being built in middle- to larger-sized cities. That's when Uncle Bob took you back to your school work, especially that retailing class.

Uncle Bob was the family's funeral director. He and his two sons owned and operated the only locally owned mortuary in a city of 75,000. Over the past decade, he pointed out, his business had been radically changed. No longer do folks want a traditional funeral, complete with casket and burial at the local cemetery. Now, a third of all funerals involved a no-frills cremation and maybe a social "event" instead of a religious service. Since he is planning to remodel, he wants to know what you think about his "scrambled merchandising" idea.

Bob then explains that he is thinking of eliminating the chapel with its stained glass and pews and using the space for a multi-purpose "family center" complete with a catering kitchen in the back where the flower room used to be and adding a 12-foot screen for multimedia memorial presentations. In addition, he wants to partner with a law firm to assist families with estate planning and making wills. Finally, he questions whether he should just remodel the chapel with its current drab entranceway into something brighter and cheerful, complete with an entryway removed from the funeral home. By doing so, he could use the chapel for weddings for the couples who were unable to locate a church.

Questions

1. Do you think couples would mind being married in a chapel located near a funeral home, even if it had a separate entrance and was beautifully decorated?

2. What would happen to those families who want a traditional funeral in a chapel? Would your uncle lose their business?

3. What other creative ideas would you suggest to your uncle?

4. What other data would you suggest that your uncle consider before making any decision?

5. What should your uncle do?

Note: This case was based on "Four Weddings and a Funeral," Business Week, May 14, 2007: 18, and the author's experiences growing up in a family that ran a funeral home.

Retail Strategic Planning and Operations Management

2

Overview

In this chapter, we will explain the importance of planning for the success of retail organizations. To facilitate the discussion, we introduce a retail planning and management model that will serve as a frame of reference for the remainder of the text. This simple model illustrates the importance of strategic planning and operations management. These two activities, if properly conducted, will enable a retail firm to achieve results exceeding those of the competition.

Learning Objectives

After reading this chapter, you should be able to:

1 Explain why strategic planning is so important and be able to describe the components of strategic planning: statement of mission; goals and objectives; an analysis of strengths, weaknesses, opportunities, and threats; and strategy.

2 Describe the retail strategic planning and operations management model, which explains the two tasks that a retailer must perform and how they lead to higher profit.

LO 1

Explain why strategic planning is so important and describe its components.

Components of Strategic Planning

In most endeavors, a well-defined plan of action can mean the difference between success and failure. For example, a driver does not go from Dallas to Kansas City without a well-defined plan of which highways to use. Political candidates and their advisors develop a campaign plan long before the election. Successful college students plan their assignments so that they are not forced to pull an all-nighter just before an assignment is due. Similarly, a clearly defined plan of action is an essential ingredient in all forms of business management.

This is especially true in the highly competitive field of retailing, where consumer demand continues to be relatively soft. Many households have maxed out their use of credit and must cut back on retail expenditures. Unemployment also continues to hover between 9 percent and 10 percent even two years after the economic recovery began in 2010, and the retired are still dealing with significant losses as their returns on certificates of deposit and U.S. Treasury Bonds fell precipitously from 2009 to 2011.[1]

Each of these factors, in addition to countless others, must be planned for in advance if a retailer is going to have a chance at success. Planning is the anticipation and organization of what needs to be done to reach an objective. This sounds simple enough, but as any retail buyer will tell you, it is difficult to know in advance of each upcoming season what styles, quantities, colors, and sizes the customers will want. Superior planning by retailers enables them to offset some of the advantages their competition may have such as a good location.

People not familiar with retailing often wonder how retailers can anticipate what consumers are going to want next season. In reality, success for all retailers, large and small, is generally a matter of good planning and then implementing that plan. For example, years ago the management of Lowe's made the key decision that has defined the retailer ever since. After arguing for months about what direction to take the home-improvement chain, the management decided to become the "customers' first choice for home improvement in each and every market we serve." Lowe's shifted from opening small stores in small markets to building mega-outlets with brighter lights and wider aisles. In addition, the company targeted female customers, which is important because women make 80 percent of home-improvement purchase decisions.[2]

Failure to develop good plans can spell disaster for a retailer. Remember all those easy-to-get "no income, no job, no problem" loans that led to the 2008–2010 housing crisis? Consider also what proved to be a major planning error by Gap Inc. A few years back, the retailer suffered a downturn in sales due in part to having the wrong merchandise mix in its stores and an overlap between its three main divisions—Gap, Old Navy, and Banana Republic. Without a clear definition of what each store should be, customers headed for the low-price: Old Navy. Today, Old Navy is clearly focused on 20-something women, though its customers have included men, teens, and children as well. In addition, the retailer now pushes wardrobe collections, rather than an à la carte approach to fashion, and has introduced business-casual clothing, a departure from Old Navy's past offerings of jeans, T-shirts, socks, and the like. It also uses advertising that is more urbane than its past campy TV spots.[3]

Consider, also, what proved to be a different type of planning error by Barnes & Noble and its website www.barnesandnoble.com. Initially, the chain made the decision not to integrate the website with its stores. Thus, at one of the company's typical bricks-and-mortar stores, there was very little mention of the chain's online alternative. Bricks-and-click integration (using both physical stores and online sales operations) comes at a cost: potentially cannibalizing one's established businesses with the introduction of an e-tailing operation. Barnes & Noble may have had 5 or 6 million customers online, but it had tens of millions walking through its stores. Why promote a website that offered heavy discounts—and at a point in time when no sales tax was charged—to consumers who were willing to pay full price? What Barnes & Noble failed to realize was that if they didn't promote the site, many of its customers would eventually switch to Amazon.

When there is a lot of change and turbulence in the retailer's environment, it may be especially important to be proactive in terms of strategic action. For instance, several retailers have chosen to "jump with both feet" into the digital world and overlook the short-term potential of cannibalizing one's in-store sales. In 2010, JCPenney became the first retailer to place its entire product catalog online within Facebook. Now anything a consumer could buy within a Penney's bricks-and-mortar store or through the company's e-tailing website can be purchased on Facebook. Delta airlines too has chosen to open a "virtual" ticket window on its Facebook page where consumers can purchase, alter, or confirm future travel plans, and 1-800-FLOWERS uses its Facebook shopping site to make the purchase of flowers or gifts more of a social event that can be shared with others.[4] While these retailers may not be sure about the eventual role social media or the Internet may play within their respective industries, each has realized that if they don't plan for the future and take strategic actions today, they risk becoming "forgotten retailers of another era."

strategic planning
Involves adapting the resources of the firm to the opportunities and threats of an ever-changing retail environment.

Strategic planning involves adapting the resources of the firm to the opportunities and threats of an ever-changing retail environment. Through the proper use of strategic planning, retailers hope to achieve and maintain a balance between resources available and opportunities ahead. All retailers want to be among the minority of enterprises able to change the rules of the game being played or, if they can't change the rules, to have a strategy to win the game as it is currently played. That strategy should consist of a specific objective, an area of operation, and the understanding of what makes you better than your competitors. Let's take a closer look at the components of the strategic planning process.

Strategic planning consists of four components:

1. Development of a mission (or purpose) statement for the enterprise;
2. Definition of specific goals and objectives for the enterprise;
3. Identification and analysis of the retailer's strengths, weaknesses, opportunities, and threats—referred to as *SWOT analysis*;
4. Development of strategies that will enable the enterprise to reach its objectives and fulfill its mission.

Mission Statement

The beginning of a retailer's strategic planning process is the formulation of a mission statement. The **mission statement** is a description of the fundamental nature, rationale, and direction of the enterprise. It provides the employees and customers with an understanding of where future growth for the enterprise will come from. Yet not every retailer has a mission statement. In fact, less than 60 percent of all businesses have written mission statements. Consequently, because so many businesses don't know where they want to go and how to get there, they end up as failures. However, the lack of a written statement is not a cause by itself for success or failure if the firm has a clearly understood, even if unwritten, mission and plan of action.

While mission statements vary from retailer to retailer, good ones usually include three elements:

1. How the retailer uses or intends to use its resources;
2. How it expects to relate to the ever-changing environment;
3. The kinds of value it intends to offer in order to serve the needs and wants of the consumer.

A mission statement can be short or long, as long as it provides the retail enterprise with its future. Consider Starbucks' mission statement: "To inspire and nurture the human spirit—one person, one cup, and one neighborhood at a time."[5] You don't have to be a regular latte drinker to understand the coffee retailer's sense of purpose. Or consider REI who does not even use the term "mission" but rather "passion": "REI's passion for the outdoors runs deep. Our core purpose is to inspire, educate and outfit people for a lifetime of outdoor adventure and stewardship." Clearly this passion statement provides clarity for employees, customers, suppliers, and other stakeholders.[6]

James Moore, discussed earlier in Chapter 1, has this mission statement for his bike shop:

Moore's Bicycle Shop is dedicated to bringing the non-cyclists into the sport by matching their recreational needs with the most economical bicycle that will meet or exceed their anticipated cycling demands. While we are capable of serving the professional both in terms of product and services, the entry level cyclists and family cyclists are our focuses. We prefer to downplay the competitive aspect of cycling and promote cycling as an escape from the competitive pressures of life. Our reputation has been built one customer at a time and we realize that it must be maintained in that manner.

Such a statement describes how Moore and another bike shop in town are able to survive. The other shop targets high-end merchandise for sophisticated experienced riders.[7]

As the aforementioned examples point out, a mission statement really answers the question, "What business should the retailer be in?" A critical issue in defining a retail

mission statement
Is a basic description of the fundamental nature, rationale, and direction of the firm.

business is to do so at the most meaningful level of generalization. This is why most mission statements should be general yet still provide direction as well as be motivational.

As a further example of what makes a good mission statement and what doesn't, consider how a poor mission statement can be improved. The Avon Theater, which was located in downstate Illinois near one of the author's hometown, claimed it was "in the movie business and would show only PG 13 movies at the lowest prices in our trading area." Maybe if it had used a better statement such as "We are in the entertainment business and we shall seek to show the movies that customers want at prices that reflect the market's price sensitivity," the theater might still be in business.

As these examples show, just having a mission statement is not enough in today's business climate. The retailer must adhere to its mission and not change with every new fad. During the recent recession, Starbucks' CEO Howard Schultz said that the key to the company's survival was a commitment not to abandon its core values and become a discount-driven brand. After all, "if we are a premium brand, it doesn't mean we can't provide value," Starbucks CEO Howard Schultz remarked.[8] As such, the retailer found ways to compensate for the economic downturn while remaining true to its core values.[9]

However, at times a mission statement must be changed. After trying unsuccessfully to operate on a national scale with an inefficient distribution system, The Great Atlantic & Pacific Tea Co. (A&P) reversed its fortunes by redefining its mission. Once the biggest food retailer in the United States, A&P transformed itself from a fatigued giant into an efficient regional operator. Today, it operates in the Northeast under the A&P, Pathmark, Food Emporium, and Waldbaum's banners.[10]

Statement of Goals and Objectives

The second step in the strategic planning process is to define specific goals and objectives. These goals and objectives should be derived from and give precision and direction to the retailer's mission statement. Goals and objectives should identify the performance results that the retailer intends to bring about through the execution of its major strategies.

Goals and objectives serve two purposes. First, they provide specific direction and guidance to the firm in the formulation of its strategy. Second, they provide a control mechanism by establishing a standard against which the firm can measure and evaluate its performance. If the results are less than expected, then it signals that corrective actions need to be taken.

While goals and objectives can be expressed in many different ways, retailers will usually divide them into two dimensions: (1) market performance, which compares a firm's actions to its competitor's; and (2) financial performance, which analyzes the firm's ability to provide a profit level adequate to continue in business and in many cases grow its business. In addition to the market performance and financial performance objectives, some retailers may also establish (3) societal objectives, which are phrased in terms of helping society fulfill some of its needs; and (4) personal objectives, which relate to helping people employed in retailing to fulfill some of their needs.

Let us examine each type of these goals and objectives in more detail.

Market Performance Objectives

Market performance objectives establish the amount of dominance the retailer seeks in the marketplace. The most popular measures of market performance in retailing are sales volume and **market share** (retailer's total sales divided by total market sales or the proportion of total sales in a particular geographic or product market that the retailer has been able to capture). Usually, when a retailer wants to grow its sales more rapidly than the growth of the overall market or economy, it needs to expand the number of

market share
Is the retailer's total sales divided by total market sales.

Gerardo Mora/Stringer/Getty Images

Disney has redesigned its stores using a neighborhood concept that seeks to enhance shopper experience.

stores it operates. Thus, high sales growth retailing is directly linked to expanding the size of the enterprise's chain of retail stores. Hugo Boss, the German fashion group that is nearly 90 years old, has been seeking its sales growth opportunities by expanding its retail network of company-owned stores across China and the Americas.[11] On the other hand, Urban Outfitters is expanding into Europe with its Anthropologie women's apparel store and hopes to have 100 of each store format within 10 years.[12] Even Disney is getting into using stores to expand sales, but in their case, it is through redesign of existing stores as well as a new design concept[13]—"The best 30 minutes of a child's day." The goal is to create a magical experience for the child and family as they visit the store, facilitated by a layout around different neighborhoods—Princess neighborhood, Cars neighborhood, and a Toy neighborhood.

Research has shown that profitability is clearly and positively related to market share.[14] Three things drive this relationship. A firm gains market share, at least in a stable or growing market, by increasing its' sales faster than competitors, which allows it to gain the operating efficiency that we discussed in Chapter 1 (see Exhibit 1.1). Also, as a retailer gains market share, it has increased recognition among consumers so its advertising expenditures relative to competitors is more efficient. Finally, high–market share retailers have higher store traffic that allows their employees to be more productive. Note, unlike manufacturing, where an employee can work on making something without a customer present, in retailing most employees can only do meaningful work when customers are in the store. Exhibit 2.1 illustrates this relationship.

Thus, market performance objectives are not pursued for their own sake but because they are a key profit path.

Financial Objectives

Retailers can establish many financial objectives, but they can all be conveniently fit into the categories of profitability and productivity.

Exhibit 2.1
The Market Share-Profitability Relationship

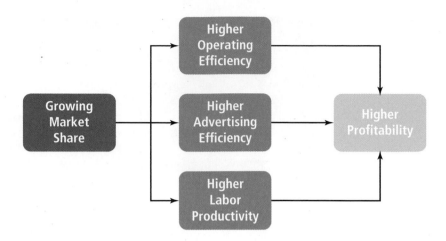

Profitability Objectives

Profit-based objectives deal directly with the monetary return a retailer desires from its business. When retailers speak of "making a profit," the definition of profit is often unclear. The most common way to define profit is the aggregate total of net profit after taxes—that is, *the bottom line of the income statement.* Another common retail method of expressing profit is as a percentage of net sales. However, most retail owners feel the best way to define profit is in terms of *return on investment* (ROI).[15]

This method of reporting profits as a percentage of investments is complicated by the fact that there are two different ways to define the term *investment. Return on assets* (ROA) reflects all the capital used in the business, whether provided by the owners or by creditors. ROI, also referred to as *return on net worth* (RONW), reflects the amount of capital that the owners have invested in the business.

The most frequently encountered profit objectives for a retailer are shown in Exhibit 2.2: the strategic profit model (SPM). The elements of the SPM start at the far left and move right. These five elements include net profit margin, asset turnover, ROA, financial leverage, and RONW.

net profit margin
Is the ratio of net profit (after taxes) to total sales and shows how much profit a retailer makes on each dollar of sales after all expenses and taxes have been met.

1. **Net profit margin** is the ratio of net profit (after taxes) to net sales. It shows how much profit a retailer makes on each dollar of sales after all expenses and taxes have been met. For example, if a retailer is operating on a net profit margin of 2 percent, then it is making two cents on each dollar of sales. In general, retailers operate on considerably lower net profit margins than manufacturers. Whereas a retailer may tend to have a net profit margin of between 2 percent and 5 percent, most manufacturers have net profit margins between 5 percent and 10 percent. The net profit margin ratio is derived exclusively from income or operating statement data and does not include any information or financial data from the retailer's balance sheet. Thus, it does not show how effectively a retailer is using the capital or assets at its disposal.

asset turnover
Is total sales divided by total assets and shows how many dollars of sales a retailer can generate on an annual basis with each dollar invested in assets.

2. **Asset turnover** is computed by taking the retailer's annual net sales and dividing by total assets. This ratio tells the retail analyst and retail management how productively the retailer's assets are being used. Put another way, it shows how many dollars of sales a retailer can generate on an annual basis for each dollar invested in assets. Thus, if a retailer's asset turnover rate is 3.0, it is generating $3 in sales for each $1 in assets annually. The asset turnover ratio incorporates key measures from the income statement (sales) and the balance sheet (assets). As such, it shows how well the retailer is using its capital or assets to generate sales. In general, retailers experience higher rates of asset turnover than do manufacturers. This is because

building and equipping a manufacturing facility such as a steel mill, a microprocessor plant, or an automobile factory is much more capital intensive. For instance, a single modern microprocessor plant (called a fab plant in the industry) costs $5 billion, whereas a big box superstore, including land and equipped with inventory, will cost around $50 million. Thus, one microprocessor fab plant has the investment of 100 big box superstores ($5,000,000,000/$50,000,000 = 100).

return on assets (ROA) Is net profit (after taxes) divided by total assets.

3. **Return on assets (ROA)**, which is annual net profit divided by total assets, depicts the net profit return the retailer achieved on all assets invested regardless of whether the assets were financed by creditors or by the firm's owners. As shown in Exhibit 2.2, ROA is the result of multiplying the net profit margin by asset turnover. For example, a retailer with a net profit margin of 2 percent and an asset turnover of 4.0 would have an ROA of 8 percent (2 percent multiplied by 4 equals 8 percent). See if you can do the retail math in Exhibit 2.3, which is intended to help you better learn the multiplicative relationship between net profit margin and asset turnover and how it yields ROA. In this exhibit, we assume that a retailer wants to achieve a 10 percent ROA, and we show some of the combinations of net profit margin and asset turnover that will yield 10 percent ROA. Your job is to do the math (see the bottom row in the exhibit) for combinations of net profit margin and asset turnover that are not suggested in the exhibit.

financial leverage Is total assets divided by net worth or owners' equity and shows how aggressive the retailer is in its use of debt.

4. **Financial leverage** is total assets divided by net worth or owners' equity. This ratio shows the extent to which a retailer is using debt in its total capital structure. The low end of this ratio is 1.0 times and depicts a situation in which the retailer is using no debt in its capital structure. As the ratio moves beyond 1.0, the retailer is using a heavier mix of debt versus owners' equity. For example, when the ratio is 2.0 times, the retailer has $2 in assets for every dollar in net worth, which is equivalent to a mix of 50-percent debt.

return on net worth (RONW) Is net profit (after taxes) divided by owners' equity.

5. **Return on net worth (RONW)** is net profit divided by net worth or owner's equity. RONW, shown at the far right of the SPM, is usually used to measure performance from the owner's or shareholder's perspective. Note that, as shown in Exhibit 2.2, the ROA multiplied by financial leverage yields RONW. Thus, if a retailer has an ROA of 8 percent and a financial leverage of 2.0, then its RONW would be 16 percent (8 percent times 2.0 equals 16 percent).

Exhibit 2.2
Strategic Profit Model

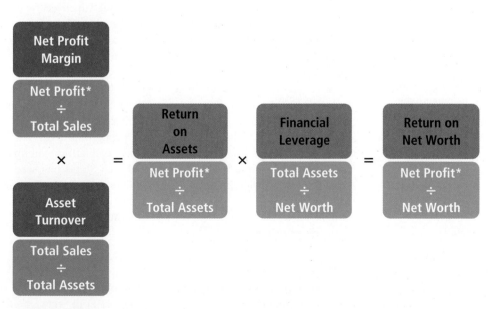

*Net profit after taxes

Exhibit 2.3
Alternative Net Profit Margin and Asset Turnover Goals with 10% Target ROA

Net Profit Margin	×	Asset Turnover	=	Return on Assets
2%		5.0		10.0%
4%		2.5		10.0%
5%		2.0		10.0%
fill in this blank		fill in this blank		10.0%

The important point to remember from this discussion of profitability is that department or specialty stores, which have higher gross margins (net sales minus cost of goods sold) and lower asset turnover rates, compete differently than discounters, which generally have lower gross margins but higher asset turnover. For discounters, this results in less inventory invested per dollar of sales and a need for fewer capital assets such as the fancy fixtures of specialty stores and traditional department stores. Discounters expect to gain a higher asset turnover by reducing their gross margins to drive store traffic and sales, and specialty and department stores expect a lower asset turnover rate with their higher gross margins.

Remember that attempts to increase asset turnover by merely reducing inventory levels can have serious consequences for a retailer. These lower inventory levels may produce higher turnover rates, but they can also lead to **stockouts** (where products are not available for customers when they want them), thus creating a dissatisfied customer who may never return.

Managers are usually evaluated on ROA since financial leverage is beyond their control. In addition to the five elements of the SPM, another measure of profitability is the gross margin percentage, which is gross margin divided by net sales.

All retailers establish some form of profit objective. The specific profit objectives developed will play an important role in evaluating potential strategic opportunities. Incidentally, over the last 25 years the United States has seen relatively low price inflation. But when price inflation rises, retailers as well as other enterprises develop higher profit objectives. Or in the case of individuals, they have higher expectations in terms of annual raises and compensation levels because, with inflation, each dollar is worth less than the prior year.

Productivity Objectives

Productivity objectives state how much output the retailer desires for each unit of resource input. There are three major resources at the retailer's disposal and they are floor space, labor, and merchandise; productivity objectives for each should be established.

stockouts
Are products that are out of stock and therefore unavailable to customers when they want them.

productivity objectives
State the sales objectives that the retailer desires for each unit of resource input: floor space, labor, and inventory investment.

1. *Space productivity*. Space productivity is defined as net sales divided by the total square feet of retail floor space. (In this discussion, whenever we refer to net sales we are talking about annual net sales.) A space productivity objective states how many dollars in sales the retailer wants to generate for each square foot of store space. As we discussed in Chapter 1, declining space productivity was one of the major reasons why some retailers are reducing the size of their stores. We also learned that some retailers like Trader Joe's have over $1,700 in annual sales per square foot of space. However, you should know that most retailers have annual sales per square foot of between $250 and $500.

   Even retailers selling a service, and not a tangible good, have a space utilization problem.

2. *Labor productivity*. Labor productivity is defined as net sales divided by the number of full-time–equivalent employees. A full-time–equivalent employee is one who works 40 hours per week; typically, two part-time workers equal one full-time employee. A labor productivity objective reflects how many dollars in sales the retailer desires to generate for each full-time–equivalent employee. Typically, this is measured on an annual basis but could also reflect weekly or even daily sales per employee such as in retail automobile, furniture store, or jewelry store sales. In the United States, most retailers generate annual sales per full time–equivalent employee of between $150,000 and $250,000. But be aware that norms vary considerably by line of retail trade.

3. *Merchandise productivity*. Merchandise productivity is net sales divided by the average dollar investment in inventory. This measure is also known as the *sales-to-stock ratio*. Specifically, this objective states the annual dollar sales the retailer desires to generate for each dollar invested in inventory. Sometimes the retailer may state this goal for a merchandising season (such as summer) for an apparel store. As we will learn in Chapter 9, merchandise productivity goals are key elements in developing the retailer's merchandising and buying plan.

Productivity objectives are used by a retailer to program its business for high-profit results. For instance, it would be impossible for a supermarket chain to achieve a respectable ROA while experiencing dismal space (sales per square foot), labor (sales per full-time employee), and merchandise productivity (sales per inventory dollars). In short, productivity is a key determinant of profit in retailing.

Societal Objectives

societal objectives
Are those that reflect the retailer's desire to help society fulfill some of its needs.

While generally not as specific or as quantitative as market and financial objectives, **societal objectives** highlight the retailer's concern with broader issues in our society. The five most frequently cited societal objectives are employment objectives, payment of taxes, consumer choice, equity, and being a benefactor.

1. *Employment objectives*. Employment objectives, which were especially significant during the recent recession, relate to the provision of employment opportunities for the members of the retailer's community. In good economic times, they may be even more specific and related to hiring the disabled, social minorities, or students. However, regardless of the economic times, REI is highly committed to being inclusive in hiring people of all backgrounds, thus being a welcoming place of employment for lesbian, gay, bisexual, and transgender people (LGBT).[16] REI has LGBT employees in its stores as well as on the Board of Directors. In addition, its health care coverage for LGBT employees is an industry standard for excellence.

2. *Payment of taxes*. Paying taxes is the retailer's role in helping finance societal needs that the government deems appropriate, from welfare programs to national parks.

In 2011, the total taxes paid by some of the nation's largest retailers were: Walmart: $7.9 billion; Target: $1.5 billion; Macy's: $712 million; Home Depot: $2.1 billion; Best Buy: $709 million; Lowe's: $1.1 billion; The Limited: $377 million.

3. *Consumer choice.* A retailer may have an objective of competing in a way that gives consumers a real alternative. A retailer with such an objective desires to be a leader and innovator in merchandising and thus provide the consumer with choices that previously were not available in the trade area. The best example of this choice is Body Shop. The retailer shuns animal testing of its products, purchases ingredients from environmentally friendly producers in the Amazon rain forest, and keeps packaging and promotional material to a minimum. Still, it does carry such controversial offerings as hemp-based oils and soaps.[17]

4. *Equity.* An equity objective reflects the retailer's desire to treat the consumer and suppliers fairly and not endanger their living conditions. In addition, retailers will not engage in price gouging consumers in instances of merchandise shortages. Consumer complaints will be handled quickly, fairly, and equitably. Further, retailers adopting this objective will inform consumers, to the extent possible, of the strengths and weaknesses of its merchandise. Dollar General, for example, was one of the first retailers to install point-of-sale equipment that protected the privacy of shoppers with visual impairments. These devices allowed those of the retailer's customers who had difficulty reading information on a touch screen to privately and independently enter their confidential information.

5. *Being a benefactor.* The retailer may desire to underwrite certain community activities. For example, many department store retailers make meeting rooms available for civic groups to use for meetings. Other retailers help underwrite various performing arts either with cash donations or by hosting social events that in turn help draw customers to their stores. Local supermarkets often sponsor food drives at Thanksgiving and Christmas to aid the needy. David Green is the entrepreneurial

Hobby Lobby, and its founder, David Green, takes great pride in supporting local communities, particularly Christian colleges and universities.

WHAT'S NEW ?

Location-Based App, Meetup Perks, Enhances Targeting Capabilities

Many location-based apps like Foursquare, Yelp, and Gowalla began as tools to enhance individuals' social-networking experiences. With the help of one's smartphone, users "tag" or "check-in" at different destinations such as places they like to eat, the best place for a massage, or where they are headed at the moment. In so doing, users are able to share their lives and interests with friends and followers while simultaneously learning about new venues to visit in the future through others' check-ins.

The apps were not developed as a marketing tool for driving traffic to one's storefront or to enhance a retailer's conversion rates, but creative retailers have figured out how to do both and the people who developed the apps are loving it. For example, in the summer of 2011 when average gas prices were hovering around $4 a gallon, Murphy USA, a gas station chain with 1,000 locations, offered $2 off a $20 purchase of gas with a Foursquare check-in. The retailer benefited from significant gains in its overall traffic, and Foursquare signed up new users left and right.

The only problem with the existing location-based apps was an inability to effectively target a particular segment of the overall marketplace or build a real relationship with a group of consumers. The apps really were an efficient means of couponing; those that had the app and self-selected to visit and purchase the retailer's products got a discount. The "coupon" was simply directed at everyone, and few retailers sell goods that are attractive to everyone.

As we discuss in this chapter, retailers serve *target markets* because these groups make them the most money for the cheapest cost. Retailers can't afford to target everyone and remain profitable, but the apps didn't allow for segmentation of users. Enter Meetup Perks.

Meetup Perks, was founded on the idea of building relationships between retailers and communities of like-minded consumers through sponsorship. It's a self-service system where retailers can visit the Meetup Perks page, browse all local groups or search by location- or activity-specific criteria (e.g., Ford Mustang enthusiasts in Dallas, Texas), and choose which groups they'd like to sponsor. A sponsorship email detailing a list of "perks" is then sent out to the group's organizer(s) for them to determine whether the group is interested in participating. Perks can be anything of interest to the group but often take the form of discounted or free merchandise, to special tours of "behind-the-scenes" operations, or even free venues to hold group gatherings. Once a sponsorship is accepted, the retailer is charged a nominal fee of $5 per month, per group. If a group originates the request for sponsorship from the retailer; no fee is charged.

With Meetup Perks, retailers can now identify and target specific segments of the local marketplace, market to them in a more efficient manner, and evaluate, after-the-fact, whether the marketing dollars spent were worthwhile. In essence, it offers retailers the ability to build traffic and enhance conversion while being as efficient as possible (i.e., the three general strategies laid out in the chapter, which all retailers must perform in order to have a chance at being successful).

Who knew an idea rooted in the old practice of a local hardware store or diner sponsoring the neighborhood Little League team could be so beneficial for retailers today?

Sources: Davis, Lucia (2011) "Location-Based Apps: What Works, What Doesn't," [online] Available at: www.imediaconnection.com [Accessed: February 3, 2011]; Peters, Meghan (2011) "Meetup Now Lets Businesses Offer Targeted Deals to Group Members," [online] Available at: www.mashable.com [Accessed: February 3, 2011]; Schonfeld, Erick (2011) "Meetup Perks Helps Local Groups Find Local Sponsors," [online] Available at: www.techcrunch.com [Accessed: February 3, 2011]; Wasserman, Todd (2011) "Foursquare Checkins Get Customers Gas Discounts," [online] Available at: www.mashable.com [Accessed: February 2, 2012]; and the personal experiences of one of the authors.

founder of Hobby Lobby who opened his first store in 1972 with a $600 loan. Hobby Lobby now has over 450 stores with annual sales in excess of $2 billion. Unlike many retail chains of this size, Hobby Lobby is privately held and thus Green and his family can decide what to do with the profits they generate. Some of the profits undoubtedly go back into growing Hobby Lobby by building more stores and continuing its expansion throughout the United States. However, David Green is wealthy by any standard, and according to Forbes has a net worth of $2.6 billion. He can pursue any hobby he desires but the one he has selected is traveling the country looking for opportunities to meaningfully give to Christian colleges and universities. Since the late 1990s, Green has donated more than $300 million to these institutions.[18] But retailers need not be as big as Hobby Lobby to act as a benefactor, and as pointed out in this chapter's "What's New?" box, many local retailers are using Meetup.com to find local community groups to sponsor, provide tailored discounts and merchandise to, and become a community-partner with. As these retailers have found out, becoming a benefactor can build a strong sense of community, hopefully later translating into a more loyal customer base.

Personal Objectives

personal objectives
Are those that reflect the retailers' desire to help individuals employed in retailing fulfill some of their needs.

The final set of objectives that retailers may establish is personal. **Personal objectives** can relate to the personal goals of any of the employees, managers, or owners of the retail establishment. Generally, retailers tend to pursue three types of personal objectives: self-gratification, status and respect, and power and authority.

1. *Self-gratification.* Self-gratification focuses on the needs and desires of the owners, managers, or employees of the enterprise and the pursuit of what they truly want out of life. For example, individuals may have opened up a sporting goods store because they enjoy being around athletically oriented people. These individuals may also be avid amateur golfers, and operating a sporting goods store lets them combine work with pleasure. Basically, these individuals are

Starbucks CEO, Howard Schultz, is pushing for retail CEOs to stop giving campaign contributions and instead focus on donating money to retailers' local communities' needs.

experiencing and living the life they really want. You don't have to think of the self-gratification desire or objective as tied only to running a small retail business. Howard Schultz, who is the founder and CEO of Starbucks and the 2011 *Fortune* magazine businessperson of the year, does not want to be a bystander to what is happening in society. In October 2011, he decided that he, along with many others, was fed up with the way government was working, and thus, is on a campaign to encourage CEOs to put a freeze on campaign contributions and to direct their giving to purposes they may find more personally gratifying. One such effort is reflected in a pilot program where a share of profits of two stores in Harlem, New York, will be given to community causes.[19] Note this could also be an illustration of a benefactor objective.

2. *Status and respect.* All people strive for status and respect. In stating this objective, one recognizes that the owners, managers, and employees need status and respect in their community or within their circle of friends. Recognizing this need, the retailer may, for example, give annual awards to outstanding employees.

3. *Power and authority.* Objectives based on power and authority reflect the need of managers and other employees to be in positions of influence. Retailers may establish objectives that give buyers and department managers maximum flexibility to determine their own destiny. They are trusted with the power and authority to allocate scarce resources such as space, dollars, and labor to achieve a profit objective. Many retailers, realizing the importance of keeping customers happy, have empowered their frontline employees with the authority to "make things right" for unhappy customers. Having the power and authority to allocate resources and take care of customers makes employees feel important and gives them a sense of pride when they excel at making things right. Nordstrom is a national retailer with nearly $9 billion in annual sales is legendary for its customer service, which is delivered by empowering employees with the responsibility and authority to make decisions. What is not so well known is that Nordstrom actively pursues a goal of advancing employees from within the enterprise. Thus, it appeals to the power and authority needs of its employees. The program appears to be working, because five of the nine members of the executive committee began at Nordstrom's as retail clerks.[20]

Exhibit 2.4 is a synopsis of the market performance, financial performance, societal, and personal objectives that retailers can establish in the strategic planning process. Clearly revealed in this exhibit is the fact that all retail objectives, of whatever type, must be consistent with and reinforce the retailer's overall mission.

Returning to our earlier discussion, the following are the goals and objectives of another bicycle chain, Bicycle Southwest:

1. Open or acquire one store over the next four years.
2. Remodel one existing store every three years.
3. Increase the operating profit margin in each store by a quarter (0.25) percent for each six-month period.
4. Increase clothing sales in existing stores by 10 percent over the preceding year.
5. Improve the quality of promotion activities, including in-store appearances, publicity, contests, cross-promotions, school promotions, and in-store circulars.
6. Increase awareness and recognition levels of consumers in each new location to equal that of previous existing locations within two years.
7. Improve teamwork among all employees, especially those at similar management levels in order to increase overall labor productivity by 10 percent over the preceding year.

Exhibit 2.4
Retail Objectives

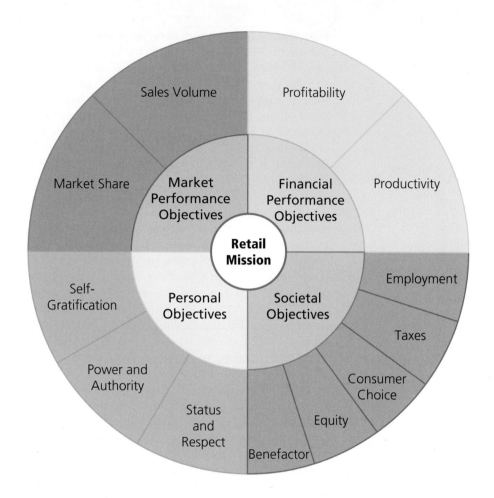

8. Restructure the buying operations so as to coordinate buying activities with other members of the trade association to increase quantity discounts by 20 percent over the next two years.
9. Target 2 percent of each store's profits to the store manager's favorite local charity.
10. Hire at least two ethnic minority applicants chain-wide each year.
11. Maintain payroll costs between 20.5 percent and 22 percent of sales.

Notice how goal 3 did not just say that the retailer wanted to increase operating profits, but stated an amount: It wanted to increase operating profits by a quarter (0.25) percent over each six-month period.

To be effective, goals should identify what the company wants to accomplish, the level that it wants to achieve, and the time period involved. In other words, goals should be measurable and "schedulable," like the chain's first four goals.

As shown here, objectives and goals should be established for each department or performance area in the business. In the Bicycle Southwest example, goals and objectives 1, 2, 5, and 6 are market performance oriented; numbers 3, 4, 6, 7, and 11 are financial performance oriented; numbers 9 and 10 are societal objectives; and number 9 could also be considered a personal objective (self-gratification) for the store managers.

Strategies

strategy
Is a carefully designed plan for achieving the retailer's goals and objectives.

After developing a mission statement and establishing some goals and objectives, a retailer must then develop a strategy. A **strategy** is a carefully designed plan for achieving the retailer's goals and objectives. It is a course of action that when executed will produce the desired levels of performance.[21] Retailers can operate with as few as three strategies:

1. *Get shoppers into your store.* Often referred to as a retailer's *traffic strategy*, many retailers think getting people to visit your website or your store is one of the most difficult tasks in retailing. Sam Walton knew early on how important this task was. There is a funny story of Mr. Sam using a donkey to attract customers to the 1964 grand opening of the second Walmart in Harrison, Arkansas. David Glass, who replaced Mr. Walton as head of the chain, talks about this famous first meeting with Walton and the donkey on the Walmart website (http://walmartstores.com/AboutUs/288.aspx). Today, Walmart knows the importance of getting consumers into its stores. In fact, as this chapter's "Service Retailing" box illustrates, the chain has even become a service retailer in its efforts to attract more consumers to its stores.

2. *Convert these shoppers into customers by having them purchase.* Often referred to as a "retailer's conversion" or "closure" strategy, this means having the right

© Smileus/Shutterstock

SERVICE RETAILING

Is Walmart a Service Retailer?

One of the author's closest friends recently retired and bought a recreational vehicle (RV) to travel around the country. In so doing, he soon discovered that the largest and sometimes most crowded campgrounds for RVs weren't KOA Kampgrounds, Good Sam Club Parks (not related to Walmart), or Passport American Parks. Instead, they were one of the nearly 4,000 Walmart and Sam's Club parking lots.

These locations were more appealing than those other "spaces for rent" campgrounds for several reasons. First, staying a night at Walmart saves about $30, thus allowing these RVers to travel longer and farther on a limited budget. Second, the stores' parking lots are well-lit and many times even have security officers and security cameras. Third, all the Walmarts, but not all the Sam's, stores are open all night, and they have RV supplies, souvenirs, food, tools, and medicine. In addition, many even sell gas and diesel. Fourth, most stores are located just off main interstate routes with easy on- and off-ramps, whereas many of the "for rent" spaces are not as conveniently located. And finally, Walmart does not require reservations, so it is an excellent plan B location if other RV parks in the area are full.

So as to not to offend either competitors, who are probably big customers for the chain, or local townspeople, Walmart doesn't advertise its open invitation to campers, nor do its free parking spaces provide hookups for water, power, or sewage disposal. It also asks campers not to stay more than a couple of nights. After all, visitors sooner or later are going to have to go to a real rentable campsite to get fresh water and drain their tanks. Still, Walmart caters to RVers in not-so-subtle ways. For example, understanding the value of getting customers into its stores, the retailer from northwest Arkansas customizes the Rand McNally road atlas sold at all its stores to include the address of each store and its map coordinates. Campers, after all, are profitable customers. In some cases, a camper may spend more than $300, but the average is between $50 and $100. As a result, stores in heavily traveled areas stock extensive RV and camping supplies, which have high gross margins.

Data from the Recreation Vehicle Industry Association (RVIA) indicate that 8.5 million households in the United States currently own at least one RV, and the RVIA expects that number to grow as baby boomers retire. These people like to travel, like the comforts of their own home, and, best of all, have money to spend. Thus, it seems that Walmart will continue as a service retailer.

Source: Based on information provided by Charles W. Mayers and used with his written permission.

merchandise and services, using the right layout and display, having the right price, and having the right type and quality of employees. The first step, "getting customers into the store," is difficult, but once in the store or on the retailer's website, the visit is often relatively short. In the case of a convenience store such as a 7-Eleven or Texaco StarMart, the visit is often less than 5 minutes, for a grocery store or supermarket, it ranges from 10 to 30 minutes, and for a specialty store or department store it is seldom more than 30 to 60 minutes. However, each year with the exception of food and gasoline retailing and other convenience retailers, the average retailer loses 20 percent to 40 percent of its customers because it didn't take care of them after they entered the store.[22] The customers may claim that there was "no special reason" that no purchase was made. However, the truth is probably that the retailer neglected the customer. This is particularly important to remember since it costs five times as much to get a new customer into a store as it does to make a sale to someone who had already shopped there or to retain a current customer who may be unhappy.

3. *Do this (get shoppers in your store and convert them into customers) at the lowest operating cost possible that is consistent with the level of service that your customers expect.* This is often referred to as a "retailer's cost management" strategy. Remember, as we pointed out in Chapter 1, most of a product's cost gets added after the item is produced and moves from the factory to the retailer's shelf and finally to the consumer. Thus, strategies that reduce operating costs while providing the appropriate level of customer service present significant opportunities for retailers. A great example is a story that Sam Walton loved to tell. He claimed that one of the greatest retail lessons he ever learned, and a major contributor to Walmart's amazing growth rate, came when James Cash Penney visited the Des Moines, Iowa, JCPenney's store where Sam was a trainee. While Mr. Penney was wandering through the store, a customer approached Sam to buy a set of work clothes for her husband.

Mr. Penney watched from a distance while Sam took excellent care of the customer. Sam wrapped the work shirt and pants in a package (using paper off a roll and string to tie it), gave the customer her change, and thanked her for shopping at JCPenney's. Sam was proud of the way he handled the transaction and thought he might even merit praise from Mr. Penney. Sure enough, Mr. Penney came over to Sam and said, "Young man, I want to show you something."

Mr. Penney proceeded to get a set of work clothes, just like the woman had purchased, and wrapped it with paper from the roll that overlapped by less than an inch. Then using half the string Sam used, he tied the package. After handing the newly wrapped package to Sam to examine, he imparted his wisdom: "Young man, you know we don't make money on the merchandise we sell. We make our profit on the paper and string we save."

That lesson was never lost on Sam Walton, and today Walmart's executives still preach it. Little wonder then that one executive was quoted as telling an investor conference that "the misconception is that we're in the retail business. Actually, we're in the distribution business." Furthermore, the executive added, although it is generally believed that Walmart buys and sells at the lowest price, in fact, Walmart sells at the lowest price because it has the lowest distribution costs.[23]

The question is often asked, why would a retailer ever want to get rid of a customer? The answer is simple: If the customer, because of size, location, or other demands, will never be profitable, then that customer must be dropped. Years ago, one of the authors consulted with a mail-order retailer. Ten percent of the retailer's customers would never be profitable since their economic circumstances limited their purchases to less than $50 per year. However, just the cost of sending them four large catalogs per year exceeded $35. After subtracting the cost of the merchandise sold, the retailer was guaranteed to lose money. When management was told to drop these customers, one executive asked "What if they go to our competition?" "You should be so lucky" was the reply. After all, now the rival would have these unprofitable customers, and the client could concentrate only on the profitable customers. Also, if a customer drives other more profitable prospective shoppers away, then the retailer should consider dropping that customer as well. This is also why some malls lament the fact that Friday nights are now prime cruising hours for teenagers. These malls regard the teens as too loud, prone to cussing, and having attitude issues. As a result, they drive away profitable adult shoppers. Thus, despite the fact that teens, especially before they became electronically connected, were once a very profitable segment for a mall, they are now unwanted. These malls now pipe in slow soft music and use overhead lights that accent the teens' pimples.

While the preceding strategies may seem too simple to be operational, they actually do summarize the tasks that every retailer must perform. Many retailers go further and develop strategies that enable them to differentiate themselves from the competition as they accomplish these three tasks.

However, one of the greatest failings in retailing today is that too many retailers have concentrated on just one means of differentiation: price. Dick's Sporting Goods, a *Fortune* 500 enterprise with sales near $5 billion, has been able to avoid the deep price discounting that is prevalent in the industry.[24] Undoubtedly, Dick's faces very tough price competition from discounters such as Target and price-oriented specialty sporting goods retailers such as Big 5 and Modell. The tough competition is evidenced by Herman's going bankrupt and Decathlon, the French retailer, flopping in the United States. Importantly, Dick's Sporting Goods does offer good prices, but it does not build its retail offering around price but rather around a broad merchandise assortment (over 25,000 stock-keeping units or SKUs), excellent customer service, and an exciting shopping experience. These elements are key differentiators for Dick's that lead to its high performance. For instance, many customers will stop by Dick's, especially in bad weather, to practice their golf swing in one of Dick's video golf simulators. Not surprisingly, these visits that were not intended to result in a purchase, often do just that. In part, this is because their two-storey brightly lit stores are the industry standard for visual merchandising and display that seem to pull shoppers into merchandise areas to view, touch, and experience the merchandise. Often, the shopper has trouble walking away without a purchase.

Price promotions usually attract, but rarely hold, customers. As a result of these constant price deals, retailers have taught consumers that if they wait—and, in many cases, this wait is only a matter of days—the desired merchandise will go on sale. While other department stores have weekly sales, Nordstrom only has two major sale events per year.

Unless a retailer has substantially lower operating costs than its competitors, as Walmart does, then aggressively using discounted prices and sales promotions is a very dangerous strategy since the competition can easily copy it, resulting in reduced profits or even losses. Some better forms of differentiation for a retailer are outstanding design of the market offering, the selling process, after-purchase satisfaction, location, and never being out of stock.

1. *Outstanding design of the market offering.* Target follows this strategy with its brilliant and innovative merchandising. It keeps adding apparel by new designers from around the world and also designs it stores with a softer and more engaging

The hottest fashion is no longer solely for those customers with a petite figure. A growing number of retailers have begun to cater to the plus-sized figures of many of their male and female customers.

atmosphere than do other discounters.[25] Retailers have found that a well-designed store can increase sales and profits. As we mentioned earlier, customers usually are in a hurry to shop and spend little time in the store. If a retailer can create speed bumps, which are distractions that shoppers find engaging, then they will purchase more. For instance, in a grocery store, if you can slow the customer down as they travel an aisle and get them to view more merchandise, sales will rise dramatically.[26] Another example of outstanding design is Torrid, a retailer offering cool clothes for plus-sized girls and young women (sizes 12–26), who can now match the style, excitement, and selection available at standard size fashion retailers. Casual Male XL is the men's equivalent of this retailer. However, the best example of a retailer differentiating itself from the competition may be the supermarkets. They have learned to avoid getting into a price war with local supercenters and warehouse clubs. Instead, they focus on less-hectic stores with exotic or difficult-to-match products and greater convenience. In addition, they cut back on drugs and health and beauty products, which are the discounters' strengths, to stress fresh produce, higher-quality meat, and easy-to-prepare foods. Subdued lighting and high-end selections buttress the non-discounter experience.[27]

2. *The selling process.* For example, Nordstrom's, Neiman Marcus and many local jewelers connect with their target customers through their excellent customer service. This also includes speeding up the checkout process. After all, if customers have 30 minutes to spend shopping, they don't want to use five to seven of those minutes just trying to pay the bill.

3. *After-purchase satisfaction.* Some retailers, such as L.L. Bean Inc., achieve this with their "satisfaction guaranteed" programs that enable customers to return any purchase, even after years of use.

4. *Location.* Stores such as Dollar General and Family Dollar excel at this form of differentiation. These stores used to be considered afterthoughts of American retailing, with a marginalized presence in an industry that thrived on larger, more theatrical outlets. Not today. Dollar stores are generating impressive sales increases with a compelling price, value, and convenience model. The growing consumer appeal of these stores is that they are usually located in strip centers en route to a nearby supercenter, capturing shoppers who would rather pick up their toothpaste and motor oil quickly instead of searching a cavernous building offering tires and tomatoes, shirts and soup, and bananas and car batteries. In addition, the small size of their stores gives these retailers advantages in negotiating leases in an industry with a surplus of stores, thus reducing their operating costs.

5. *Never being out of stock.* This means being in stock with regard to the sizes, colors, and styles that the target market expects the retailer to carry. For example, Nordstrom offers a free shirt if it is out of stock on a basic size.

These means of differentiation will not only get more consumers into your store but also result in their buying more once they are there. Note also that in all these examples the retailers are able to develop their own unique niches in the minds of consumers and thus avoid price wars.

So how does a retailer develop a strategy to differentiate itself? This starts with an analysis of the retailer's strengths and weaknesses as well as the threats and opportunities that exist in the environment. This process, which is often referred to as *SWOT* (strengths, weaknesses, opportunities, and threats) *analysis*, involves asking the following questions.

Strengths

What major competitive advantage(s) do we have? (These could be lower prices, unique merchandise, better locations, better store personnel, etc.)

What are we good at? (This might be the ability to anticipate customer demands better than the competition so that the merchandise is there when the customer wants it.)

What do customers perceive as our strong points? (Customers might perceive that we have the best shopping environment or store atmosphere or offer the "best value for the dollar.")

Weaknesses

What major competitive advantage(s) do competitors have over us? (Do they have lower prices, better locations, more effective salespeople, etc.?)

What are competitors better at than we are? (Do they do a better job of selecting merchandise, anticipating demand, or developing their store image through advertising?)

What are our major internal weaknesses? (Do we do a poor job of employee training? Are our stores in need of remodeling? Do we do a poor job at controlling merchandise theft? Do we take too long to respond to changing external environments?)

Opportunities

What favorable environmental trends may benefit our firm? (Is our market size growing? Are family income levels rising in our market? Is merchandise priced correctly for the target market?)

What is the competition doing in our market? (Are new firms entering or are existing firms leaving? Are established firms remodeling their stores? What is the impact on us?)

What areas of business that are closely related to ours are undeveloped? (Is it possible for us to expand into a related field serving the same customers and take advantage of our good name in the marketplace? What services might we combine with the merchandise we sell?)

Threats

What unfortunate environmental trends may hurt our future performance? (Are real estate and sales taxes increasing quicker than the rate of inflation? Has deflation caused consumers to delay purchasing durable goods hoping that next year prices will be significantly lower? As a result, has the consumer become both price and time sensitive? Has this prevented us from raising our prices in order to pass increasing costs on to consumers? How could our competitor's prices, new products, or services hurt us? Could the entrance of new competitors or the loss of suppliers hurt us?)

What technology is on the horizon that may soon have an impact on our firm? (Will some new electronic equipment soon replace our manual way of performing activities? Will we be able to remodel or build new stores that are more energy efficient?)

Exhibit 2.5 could be the SWOT analysis for TrueValue. This family-operated and locally owned hardware store dates back more than 100 years. Although many of these small hardware stores have fallen prey to strong national chain competition from the big box giants such as Home Depot and Lowe's, many continue to survive and prosper in their local communities. This has often been attributed to these independents joining a wholesale cooperative or buying group that helps them achieve efficiencies rivaling those of the national chains. During the 1930s, John Cotter founded Cotter & Company as a retailer-owned wholesale buying cooperative. Cotter & Company was able to pool the purchasing power of many independent retailers to obtain significant buying and distribution economies that allowed the small hardware retailer to compete with the rapidly growing chain stores. In 1997, Cotter & Company merged with ServiStar Coast to Coast, another large retailer-owned wholesale buying cooperative. The combined cooperative was renamed TRU*SERV and had annual sales of more than $6 billion. Today, TRU*SERV supplies more than 6,500 members who operate nearly 10,000 stores. Exhibit 2.5 shows what a SWOT analysis might look like for a successful family-operated TrueValue hardware store.

Now the retailer is ready to develop strategies to accomplish its objectives. Again, notice the close relationship between a retailer's goals and objectives and its strategies. Objectives indicate what the retailer wants to accomplish, and strategies indicate how the retailer will attempt to accomplish those goals with the resources available.

The retailer must develop a retail marketing strategy with strong financial elements. A fully developed marketing strategy should address the following considerations: the specific target market, location, the specific retail mix that the retailer intends to use, and the retailer's value proposition.

target market
The group(s) of customers that a retailer is seeking to serve.

1. The specific **target market** is the group or groups of customers that the retailer is seeking to serve. It is important for retailers to understand that different target markets demand different product offerings. For this reason, successful retailers must determine which customers make them the most money and then segment them carefully, realign their stores, and empower employees to target those favored shoppers with products and services that will encourage them to spend more and come back often.[28] Many women love the legendry Coach brand of leather purses and accessories. However, in 1941 and up until the early 1960s, Coach had an emphasis on men's products. It is now circling back to include men in their target market and has recently opened more than a dozen men's stores.[29] Exhibit 2.6 illustrates an electronics retailer's targeting process. The left side of the box shows five different target markets that Best Buy is trying to reach. The center shows the

Exhibit 2.5
SWOT Analysis for TrueValue

SWOT Analysis Shows How TrueValue Hardware Stores Continue to Succeed

Strengths

What are the major competitive advantages a TrueValue hardware store has over the competition?

TrueValue has a catchy name that combines a key brand (itself) with the name of a local owner—for example, Jim Ruhl's TrueValue Hardware Store. Thus, the store has the integrity of a respected national brand combined with the name of a well-known and respected local operator.

TrueValue's commitment comes from management owning the business. The stores are almost all operated by the people who own the stores. This aligns the interest of the day-to-day managers with the customers. Customer service is generally high because if customers are not served well and do not return, then the financial impact will be immediately felt by the owner–manager.

TrueValue is able to be the only retailer selling a widely recognized, high-quality product such as Stihl. In fact, as a result of a cooperative advertising agreement, TrueValue dealers can run ads saying they carried Stihl products—and that these products weren't available at Lowe's or Home Depot.[30]

Because the stores are locally owned and managed, managers have a very good sense of their trade area and the needs of people in that trade area. Also, since buying is not centralized like it is in a big retail chain, the buying for each store is more in tune with local demand patterns. Many owner–managers know what specific households in the trade area might need and thus order merchandise in anticipation of selling to these households on an individual level. Also, these managers know the names of virtually all of their regular customers and personally greet them when they enter the store. In short, they practice micromarketing.

Most TrueValue stores are in lower-rent facilities that are owned and free of mortgages or debt payments. This allows these retailers to have lower break-even points and to better withstand competitive assaults.

Weaknesses

What are the major competitive advantages that big box retailers have over a TrueValue hardware store?

Home Depot and Lowe's have strong promotional orientations. Often these retailers have local and national television advertising coupled with a heavy use of newspaper inserts. Many times they will run 24–36 newspaper inserts per year, which means these large national chains do a better job of creating customer awareness.

Home Depot and Lowe's offer more than 60,000 items, or SKUs, the lowest level of identification of merchandise, compared to a TrueValue store, which may have fewer than 15,000 items. A big box store will be more than 100,000 square feet; a TrueValue store will generally be less than 12,000 square feet.

Home Depot and Lowe's are much more aggressive in pricing frequently purchased and highly visible items. On high-turnover items such as garden hoses, popular lumber sizes, small tools, and gardening items, they are low-price-point competitors.

What are some of the major internal weaknesses of a typical TrueValue hardware store?

A typical store is not operated by computer-savvy managers. Although some TrueValue operators are capitalizing on information technology, many other owners do not recognize or pursue the potential of a fully computerized inventory management and purchasing system.

Most stores lack depth of management. If the owner is absent from the store for an extended time due to illness, becomes disabled, or dies, there is often not another person in line to take over operations and

(continued)

Exhibit 2.5
(continued)

ownership. Also, since some stores are independently owned, TrueValue stores sometimes present an inconsistent image across the country. Some stores are immaculate and clean and well organized, while other stores may be dusty and cluttered. But there is little that TrueValue can do. After all, it is difficult to enforce standards of operations with independent store owners.

Many stores, because they are operated by the owners, do not have seven days a week, morning to night operating hours. A big box store is open seven days a week and more than 75 hours; a TrueValue store is often open only six days a week and fewer than 60 hours per week.

Opportunities

What favorable environmental trends exist that may benefit a TrueValue Hardware store?

Because dual-income families have less time, people want to shop closer to home. Trips to large malls and shopping areas are declining, and trips to neighborhood shopping centers are on the rise. Also, people are finding that big 100,000-square-foot stores are often too big when a shopper only needs a few items. Most TrueValue stores are small in size and located in small community or strip malls. It is noteworthy that Home Depot has noticed this opportunity and is building a new chain of small stores called Villager Hardware. The number of homeowners planning do-it-yourself home-improvement projects has been increasing yearly for two decades. Although many homeowners enjoy doing these projects, they often need advice during the project. TrueValue retailers, with their focus on customer service and knowledgeable staff, can provide excellent service to this highly profitable customer segment.

The phenomenal growth of the Internet has many more households shopping online for hardware and home-improvement items. This is an opportunity for TrueValue hardware stores because the co-op has built an e-tailing site that allows local customers to purchase an expanded assortment of products from their local TrueValue retailer. Rather than being restricted in items (SKUs) due to space constraints, TrueValue retailers can now offer their customers more than 100,000 SKUs.

Threats

What unfortunate environmental trends exist that may hurt future performance TrueValue retailers?

Many owners are finding that their children do not want to take over the family hardware business. These children are moving to other geographical areas and pursuing other careers. The government reporting requirements on small, single-unit businesses are often as many as for a multi-unit chain store. Consequently, the time required to meet local, county, state, and federal regulations and do all the associated paperwork is becoming increasingly burdensome.

Source: The authors acknowledge the assistance of Professor Leslie D. Stoel, Ohio State University, with this SWOT analysis.

offerings or services that Best Buy will feature in the stores catering to those target markets. The far right lists the customer name that the retailer has assigned each target. According to Best Buy, each of its stores will be aimed at one or two of these customer types.

2. A *location*—whether a traditional store in a geographic space, a person's home in relation to a print catalog or television shopping, or a virtual store in cyberspace—should be consistent with the needs and wants of the desired target market. For instance, Apple Stores because they sell more expensive merchandise, tend to locate in areas of moderate to higher income households.

Exhibit 2.6
Features That Could be Offered by an Electronics Store to Meet Various Customer Types

Customer Type	Feature Offering by Store	Customer "Name"
High Income, High Tech, Home Theater Enthusiast	Storm Zone Home Theater, Tech Troopers	Allen
Multi-tasking, working mom	Personal shopper, on-line order with store pick up, Entertainment zone, Phone zone, lay away, Tech Troopers, Special Offers	Brenda
Small Business Owner	On-line order with store pick up, Tech troopers, Business account option, Business Zone featuring computers and accessories always in stock	Casey
Value Conscious Family	Phone Zone, Tech Troopers, Lay-away, Entertainment Zone, Special Offers	Davis
Early-Adopter Working Single	Phone Zone, Entertainment Zone, Special Offers, Online ordering with store Pickup, Tech Troopers, Auto Audio Zone, Strom Zone Home Theater	Evan

retail mix
Is the combination of merchandise, price, advertising and promotion, location, customer service and selling, and store layout and design.

3. The specific **retail mix** a retailer intends to use to appeal to its target market and thereby meet its financial objectives is the combination of merchandise, price, advertising and promotion, location, customer services and selling, and store layout and design that the retailer uses to satisfy the target market (see Exhibit 2.7). This chapter's "Retailing: The Inside Story" box highlights the plethora of changes JCPenney is making to its retail mix in order to reinvent the department store experience and get shoppers back into its stores.

Exhibit 2.7
Retail Mix

RETAILING — The Inside Story

How JCPenney Plans to Reinvent the Department Store Experience

Many retail analysts believe that the "love affair" Americans had with department stores for apparel and accessories during the 20th century is over, as department stores as a whole represent only 31 percent of the entire market compared to 52 percent in 1992. Yet one chain feels it can rekindle that admiration and is doing everything to prove it: JCPenney.

With the hiring of new CEO Ron Johnson, developer of the Apple Store, Penney is posed to redefine the idea of what a department store should be by 2015. Johnson's plan, which began with much fanfare on February 1, 2012, focuses on overhauling three major areas of the retail operation—promotion, product, and presentation.

During 2011, JCPenney ran 590 unique promotional campaigns at an average cost of $2 million each; yet, the average customer entered only four times. This means over 99 percent of JCPenney's promotions fell flat in getting customers into its stores and cost the retailer over a billion dollars in the process. Johnson is abandoning this promotion-on-top-of-promotion game. Instead, the retailer will have 12 month-long promotions, which coincide with the season or some event going on during a particular month (e.g., February and Valentines). In addition, shoppers will no longer receive an endless supply of mailers in their mailboxes; the retailer will send out a 96-page magazine-like catalog each month detailing new merchandise, in-store services, and fashion advice/tips. JCPenney is also banking on its new spokeswoman's, Ellen DeGeneres, daily television show to assist in driving customers through its doors.

With regard to product changes, JCPenney plans to eliminate hundreds of its private label brands, and the attractive margins associated with such products, and replace them with well-known brands from top designers. Johnson believes that brands are the key; they provide distinctiveness, exclusivity, and pricing power, all of which have been lacking at JCPenney. Some of the newly released lines include those from famed designer Nanette Lepore and Spanish apparel giant Mango to Martha Stewart, who has chosen to align herself with JCPenney even though she faces breach of contract litigation from Macy's. Johnson also plans to routinely roll out new brands each month, as sponsorships from designers are signed on with the retailer.

Finally, JCPenney recognizes all these changes are for not, if it cannot convert consumers into customers once they're in the store, which is why the bulk of the new changes revolve around merchandise presentation and service. Each month, two to three store-within-a-store boutiques will be rolled out in every JCPenney. The boutiques will each focus on a single brand and will employ specialized staff trained to tailor the customer experience to that brand just like one might get when shopping at specialty retailers H&M or Zara. By 2015, every JCPenney will function as 100 individual boutiques; each focused on the sale of a single brand.

JCPenney is also in the process of launching its "Town Square," a take-off on Apple's "Genius Bar". JCPenney's Town Square will take over the 10,000 square feet traditionally reserved for jewelry and cosmetics in the center of the store; however, no selling will take place here. The area will be designed solely to offer support and provide entertainment. Beyond year-round fashion advice and product support, a series of changing services and events tied to each month will be provided, such as cooking demonstrations, "back to school" free haircuts, or free hot dogs and ice cream in July.

Sources: "Apple Stores Chief to Take Helm at J.C. Penney," *The New York Times*, June 15, 2011: B1; "J.C. Penney to Revise Pricing Methods and Limit Promotions," *The New York Times*, January 26, 2012: B1; "J.C. Penney Thinks Different" *The Wall Street Journal*, January 26, 2012: B1; "Penney CEO Says Profit Won't Suffer," *The Wall Street Journal*, January 27, 2012: B6; "Martha, Macy's Debate 'Store'," *Women's Wear Daily*, February 16, 2012: 4; "Too Much Martha," *Bloomberg Businessweek*, February 20–26, 2012: 23–24; "Costs, Weak Sales Hit Penney's," *Women's Wear Daily*, February 27, 2012: 22; "Macy's Answers Stewart Counterclaims," *Women's Weak Daily*, February 29, 2012: 2.

value proposition
Is a clear statement of the tangible and intangible results a customer receives from shopping at and using the retailer's products or services.

4. The retailer's **value proposition** is a clear statement of the tangible and intangible results a customer receives from using the retailer's products or services. It is the difference between the benefits offered by one retailer versus those of the competition. A good value proposition answers the question of "Why should I buy this product or service from this retailer?" Incidentally, if the answer is the "lowest price" then you likely do not have a sustainable value proposition. A sustainable value proposition is one that competitors would find difficult to respond to or copy. Cutting price can be copied both quickly and easily.

Stanley Marcus, founder of Neiman Marcus, underscored the importance of a fully developed marketing strategy when he said: Retailers all too often show a lack of creativity in developing their value proposition. As a result, they usually react to bad economic times and declining sales by cutting back on all expenses and claiming they are going to get back to "basics." No one is really sure what these "basics" are, but shouldn't these retailers have been taking care of the basics all along?

Bad economic conditions are not the time to get aggressive on pricing; they are the time to make sure you have a relevant and easy-to-define value proposition that will transcend good and hard times. After all, if everybody is looking to reduce prices and highlight promotions, then a successful retailer must do something else. It is this something else—the products, the services, the unique take on what a shopper's retail experience should be—that spells out the difference between profit and loss.

The Retail Strategic Planning and Operations Management Model

LO 2

Describe the retail strategic planning and operations management model.

Exhibit 2.8, our strategic planning and operations management model, suggests that a retailer must engage in two types of planning and management tasks: strategic planning and operations management. Each task is undertaken to achieve high-profit results. At this point, take a few moments to study this model.

As explained in Chapter 1, this book has an environmental orientation, a management planning orientation, a profit orientation, and a decision-making orientation. You will note that the environmental orientation is represented by the top and bottom bars in Exhibit 2.8, the management planning orientation by the first five vertical sections (strategic planning and operations management), the profit orientation by the high profit box at the far right, and the decision-making orientation by all the decisions that the retailer must make throughout this model.

Strategic Planning

Strategic planning, as we pointed out at the beginning of the chapter, is concerned with how the retailer responds to the environment in an effort to establish a long-term course of action. In principle, the retailer's strategic planning should best reflect the line(s) of trade in which the retailer will operate, the market(s) it will pursue, and the retail mix it will use. Remember, strategic planning requires a long-term commitment of resources by the retailer. An error in strategic planning can result in a decline in profitability, bankruptcy, or a loss of competitive position. On the other hand, effective strategic planning can help protect the retailer against competitive onslaughts or adverse environmental occurrences.

The initial steps in strategic planning are to define the firm's mission, establish goals and objectives, and perform a SWOT analysis. The next steps are to select the target market and appropriate location(s). It is important to note that most retail managers or executives have very little control over location decisions. A newly appointed manager

Exhibit 2.8
Retail Strategic Planning
and Operations Management Model

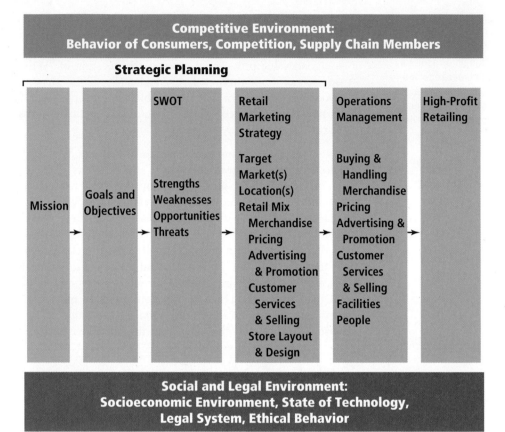

for a chain department store could change promotional strategy, personnel, service levels, credit policies, and even prices but in all likelihood would be constrained by a long-term lease agreement. In fact, only the senior management of most chains is ever involved in location decisions. For the small retailer just starting out, however, or retailers considering expansion, location is an important decision. A full discussion of location and site selection appears in Chapter 7.

After selecting the target market and location, the retailer must develop the firm's retail mix. Retailers can best perform this strategic planning only after assessing the external environment. They should be looking for an opportunity to fulfill the needs of a defined group of consumers (i.e., their target market) in a way that sets them apart from the competition. In other words, retailers should strive to achieve a differential advantage over the competition by providing a compelling value proposition. Retailers will rarely discover a means of gaining a differential advantage by reviewing their own internal operations or by focusing exclusively on the conventional industry structure. Strategic planning opportunities are to be found in the realities of a constantly changing environment. An effective retail strategy can result only from matching environmental forces with a retail marketing program that satisfies the customer better than anybody else. For example, Foot Locker has found success by concentrating on a very narrow segment of the shoe market but offering a very large selection. Williams-Sonoma initially concentrated on the cooking enthusiast or someone who desired to become a better cook and began to offer cooking classes, table-setting demonstrations and food tastings. Thus, it was able to differentiate itself as a luxury retailer rather than being viewed as a shop selling kitchenware.

David Crausby/Alamy

Rather than trying to be a shoe store for all consumers, Foot Locker has succeeded by selling only a few types of shoes, yet offering a wide selection within those shoe categories.

Exhibit 2.8 profiles the major environmental forces that should be assessed. Briefly these are consumer behavior, competitor behavior, supply chain behavior, the socio-economic environment, the technological environment, and the legal and ethical environment.

1. *Consumer behavior.* The behavior of consumers will obviously have a significant impact on the retailer's future. Specifically, the retailer will need to understand the determinants of shopping behavior so it can identify likely changes in that behavior and develop appropriate strategies. When you think about it, the successful retailers are those that didn't wait for their customers to request something. They are the ones who paid attention, used a little imagination, and solved the need before the customers' requests. Amazon.com is an example of a retailer that has automated this process by the use of software that analyzes what customers purchase and compares this to the purchases of other customers and then anticipates other books and products a customer would want to purchase. Some auto dealers keep track of how much you drive and then e-mail or call to remind you that your

auto needs servicing. This is anticipatory marketing, and it is growing considerably in retailing.

2. *Competitor behavior.* How competing retailers behave will have a major impact on the most appropriate strategy. Retailers must develop a competitive strategy that is not easily imitated, which as we mentioned previously happens all too often with price cuts.

3. *Supply chain behavior.* The behavior of members of the retailer's supply chain can have a significant impact on the retailer's future. For example, are certain supply chain members such as manufacturers or wholesalers always seeking to improve their position in the supply chain by establishing their own Internet sites and thus bypassing the retailer? Or are manufacturers who are getting frustrated with retail buyers being too aggressive on negotiating purchase terms experimenting with their own retail stores?

4. *Socioeconomic environment.* The retailer must understand how economic and demographic trends will influence revenues and costs in the future and adapt its strategy according to these changes. Pottery Barn, which incidentally is owned by Williams-Sonoma, was able to see that since Americans were having smaller families and fewer children, they were spending more on the children they had. Thus, they launched Pottery Barn Kids in 1999, which now has nearly 100 stores.

5. *Technological environment.* The technical frontiers of the retail system encompass new and better ways of performing standard retail functions. The retailer must always be aware of opportunities for lowering operating costs. For instance, supermarkets and some big box retailers (i.e., Home Depot) now have self checkout lanes that lower personnel costs. However, the retailer needs to be careful that these cost-cutting technologies do not drive customers away.

6. *Legal and ethical environment.* The retailer should be familiar with local, state, and federal regulations of the retail system. It must also understand evolving legal patterns in order to be able to design future retail strategies that are legally defensible. At the same time, the retailer must operate at the highest level of ethical behavior.

Detailed discussions of these environmental forces will be provided in Chapters 3 through 6. For now, realize that although these forces cannot be controlled by a single retailer, the threats emanating from them are often translated into opportunities by successful retailers. For example, Macy's once was an independent operation that catered to the working classes of New York, but due to increasing competition and the ability to spot future environmental changes, it has now become a major national chain operation with 800 stores and nearly $30 billion in sales. (See the case in this chapter for more on Macy's.)

After reviewing its mission, objectives, and environment and developing its retail marketing strategy, the retailer should be able to develop alternative uses of resources in order to obtain the highest performance level. Next the retailer must determine which strategy will yield the best results. Finally, the retailer will concentrate on operations management.

Operations Management

operations management
Deals with activities directed at maximizing the efficiency of the retailer's use of resources. It is frequently referred to as day-to-day management.

Operations management is concerned with maximizing the efficiency of the retailer's use of resources and with how the retailer converts these resources into sales and profits. In other words, its aim is to maximize the performance of current operations. Speaking of current operations, one of the oldest continually operated retail stores in North America is the over 100-year old Macy's Herald Square store in New York City, which is over 1 million square feet, has 20 million visitors annually, and annual sales of over $850 million. However, the store is substantially out of date, not energy efficient, and does not have a layout that is in tune with today's shopper. Consequently, it is undergoing a $400 million renovation that should be complete by late 2014. When complete, this significant investment of resources should enhance space, inventory, and employee productivity, and therefore profitability.

Most of the retailer's time and energy is devoted to the day-to-day activity of operations management. Our retail strategic planning and operations management model (Exhibit 2.8) shows that operations management involves managing the buying and handling of merchandise, pricing, advertising and promotion, customer services and selling, and facilities. All of these activities require day-to-day attention. For example, the selling floor must be maintained, customers served, merchandise bought and handled, advertisements run, and pricing decisions made each and every day. In other words, operations management is running the store.

Operations management can, however, extend beyond the retail store if the retailer is a chain store retailer and is self-distributing or essentially performs the wholesaling function and buys direct from manufacturers. In this situation, the retailer will operate one or many distribution centers that receives shipments from manufacturers and then sorts the shipments into new shipments of broader assortments for delivery to its stores. Most of the work of transporting and handling merchandise is an operations management function. Incidentally, to give you a sense of the scope of this side of retailing, Walmart operates 120 distribution centers in the United States with each distribution center employing between 500 and 1,000 people.

In Part 4, we will focus on operations management, the real "guts" of retailing. In the first several years of a retailing career, your primary concern will be almost exclusively with the operations management side of retailing. The strategic planning duties will be handled by the senior executives. However, if you enter retailing via a small- or medium-sized firm, you may be making decisions, even strategic ones, immediately. Nevertheless, when a retailer is able to do a good job at operations management—that is, efficiently using the resources available—then the retailer is said to be operations effective.

High-Performance Results

The far right box of the retail strategic planning and operations management model (Exhibit 2.8) suggests that the cumulative effect of well-designed and executed strategic and operations plans will be the achievement of high profit. Mistakes in either of these two areas will severely hamper the retailer's performance and prevent it from being among the leaders in its industry. For example, McDonald's was once hailed as the most successful innovator in the fast food industry. However, by the early to mid-2000s, Mickey D's, by most measures, was doing terribly. It had endured a deluge of negative publicity thanks to movies such as *Super Size Me* and books like *Fast Food Nation* that criticize the quality of its food and blame it for the nation's obesity epidemic. The retailer had just spent more than $5 billion building new stores without increasing operating income. So it decided to focus on existing restaurants by doing a better job of delivering quality, service, cleanliness, and value on a daily basis.[31] It watched the competition, and where Starbucks failed with its meal offering, McDonald's was successful with its premium coffee. Maybe such behavior describes what is meant when retailers say "they are going back to basics." In any case McDonald's is again highly successful.

McDonald's had to reassess its retail strategy, but often, failure to achieve high-performance results is due to poor operations management. You have all probably arrived at the doors of a retailer where the store was to be opened at 9 a.m. but employees are late and the store opens at 9:20 a.m. Or, how many times have you been to a department store and needed to use the restroom only to find it was unsanitary and the ventilation was poor? A common operating problem is the coordination between manufacturers, the retailer's distribution center, and store operations when it comes to holiday sales events. The retailer will need to plan which items to feature in its advertising, and then when shoppers show up at the store, these items need to be stocked and displayed properly. If this does not occur, there is an operations failure and profitability declines.

The need to strive for a high profit is tied to the extremely competitive nature of retailing. It is still relatively easy to start a retail business in comparison to starting a business in other industries. New retail entrepreneurs are continually entering the marketplace. As competition increases and more chains use the same format, profit levels naturally deteriorate. Retailers are therefore well advised to set high but realistic profit objectives so that if their planned profits are not reached, they at least have a chance of achieving average profitability. The retailer that aims only for an average profit often finds itself confronting a rather sobering financial performance. Exhibit 2.9 shows how the SPM results of high-performance retailers compare to the median performance for similar retailers.

As a general rule of thumb, retailers should strive for the following goals when planning their SPM: net profit margin of 2.5 to 3.5 percent, asset turnover of 2.5–3.0 times, and financial leverage of 2.0–3.0 times. Achieving such goals would produce an ROA of 8 percent to 10 percent and an 18 percent to 25 percent RONW. Incidentally, these profit goals are always stated as after payment of corporate income tax. When you set your SPM goals, pay particular attention to the net profit margin, the first financial ratio in the SPM. Note that a rise or decline in the net profit margin has a more than proportionate impact on ROA and RONW. If a retailer has been operating on a net profit margin of 2 percent with an asset turnover of 3.0 and financial leverage of 2.0, then its ROA is 6 percent (2% × 3.0) and its RONW is 12 percent (2% × 3.0 × 2.0). Note what happens if the retailer can develop a strategy and/or improved operations to increase the 2–3 percent. Now, ROA is 9 percent (3% × 3.0) and RONW is 18 percent (3% × 3.0 × 2.0). Therefore, an increase in net profit margin from 2 percent to 3 percent increases RONW from 12 percent to 18 percent. This illustrates why asset turnover and especially inventory turnover and financial leverage are very important in retailing. Successful retailers know that if you can increase your net profit margin only modestly but keep up the job of turning assets (inventory) and leveraging the business then high performance results are often within reach.

Exhibit 2.9
The Strategic Profit Model for Some of the Country's Top Retailers

Company	Net Profit Margin	Asset Turnover	Return on Assets	Financial Leverage	Return on Net Worth
Abercrombie & Fitch	3.1%	1.4×	4.2%	1.6×	6.9%
GAP	5.7%	2.0×	11.2%	2.7×	30.2%
Home Depot	5.5%	1.7×	9.6%	2.3×	21.7%
Staples	3.9%	1.9×	7.3%	1.9×	14.0%
Target	4.7%	1.3×	6.3%	2.9×	18.5%
Walmart Stores	3.5%	2.3×	8.1%	2.7×	2.2%
Kroger	0.7%	3.8×	2.6%	5.9×	15.0%
Macy's	4.8%	1.2×	5.7%	3.7×	21.2%
Nordstrom	6.3%	1.3×	8.0%	4.3×	34.9%
Pier One	11.0%	1.9×	20.5%	1.7×	34.2%
Whole Foods	3.4%	2.4×	8.0%	1.4×	11.5%

Summary

This chapter explains the importance and use of planning in retail management. Toward that end, the chapter introduces a model of retail planning.

LO 1 | **Explain why strategic planning is so important and describe its components.**

Planning and the financial performance of the retailer are intertwined. High-profit performance does not just happen; it is engineered through careful planning. Not all retailers can be leaders, but the ones that are will be those that did the best job of planning and managing. The components of strategic planning include developing a statement of purpose or mission for the enterprise; defining its specific goals and objectives; identifying the retailer's strengths, weaknesses, opportunities, and threats; and developing strategies that will enable the firm to reach its objectives and fulfill its mission. On a generic level, retailers need to have three strategies. First, they need to get shoppers into their store and this is often referred to as the retailers' traffic strategy. Second, they need to convert these shoppers into customers by having them purchase. This is often referred to as the "retailer's conversion" or "closure" strategy. Finally, retailers need to do this (get shoppers in your store and convert them into customers) at the lowest operating cost possible that is consistent with the level of service that the customers expect. This is often referred to as the "retailer's cost management" strategy.

LO 2 | **Describe the retail strategic planning and operations management model.**

Retailers must engage in two types of planning and management tasks: strategic planning and operations management. Strategic planning consists of matching the retailer's mission and goals with available opportunities. The retail marketing strategy that results from this consists of a target market, location(s), retail mix, and value proposition. Operations management consists of planning the efficient use of available resources in order to manage the day-to-day operations of the firm successfully. When retailers succeed at these two levels, they will achieve high-profit results.

Terms to Remember

strategic planning	productivity objectives
mission statement	societal objectives
market share	personal objectives
net profit margin	strategy
asset turnover	target market
return on assets (ROA)	retail mix
financial leverage	value proposition
return on net worth (RONW)	operations management
stockouts	

Review and Discussion Questions

LO 1   **Explain why strategic planning is so important and describe its components**

1. Why is strategic planning so important in retailing today? Should a retailer, even a small retailer, always have a strategy to change the rules of the game as it is currently being played? Why?

2. How do the retail firm's mission statement and its stated goals and objectives relate to the retailer's development of competitive strategy?

3. Many people have either strong favorable or unfavorable opinions of retailers in their community. Suppose you were asked to advise one of the retail businesses near your home, your place of work, or college, what suggestions would you make for it to differentiate itself?

4. Can a mission statement be too narrow in scope? Can it be too broad in scope? Explain your answers.

5. Choose any two supermarkets operating in your community. Compare and contrast their retail mix as they seek to satisfy the needs of their target market given their present location. What changes would you suggest to the management of these retailers as they develop their strategic plans for the coming year?

6. An automobile dealer located near your campus visits your class. During the presentation, the dealer notes that their mission statement is "We will provide the best vehicle sales and service experience for our customers. We will do this in a way that will foster the continuous improvement of our people and our company. We will be a top performing, thoroughly professional, and genuinely caring organization in all that we do." Would you offer any suggestions for changing this mission statement? If so why?

7. Many people are using location-based apps like Foursquare, Yelp, and Gowalla to stay in touch with friends and as described in the chapter's "What New?" box, retailers are now capitalizing on this to increase store traffic or closure. Describe some other ideas not discussed in this chapter that might represent possibilities for retailers to benefit from these apps.

8. Why do you think the strategic profit model is often used in retail planning and management?

9. What is space productivity? Why is it important in retailing?

LO 2   **Describe the retail strategic planning and operations management model**

10. What are the major environmental forces that retailers will face over the next five years? Is any one of these more important than the others?

11. Does strategic planning become more or less important as the uncertainty the retailer faces increases?

12. When doing the strategic planning and operations management tasks described in our model, does the retailer use creative thinking or analytical problem solving?

13. A person once said, "A good manager can overcome a bad plan." Agree or disagree with this statement and explain your reasoning. Use current examples, if possible, in your answer. Would your answer be the same if the person said, "A good plan can overcome a poor manager?"

14. Why is it so important for a retailer to seek high-profit performance? Isn't it enough to be above average?

Sample Test Questions

LO 1 When a retailer sets goals based on a comparison of its actions against its competitors, it is establishing _____ goals.

    a.   competitive analysis
    b.   market performance
    c.   geomarket performance
    d.   societal performance
    e.   financial performance

LO 2 The best way for a retailer to differentiate itself from the competition in the eyes of the consumer is to:

    a.   increase advertising of sale items.
    b.   offer the lowest prices in town.
    c.   always be well stocked with the basic items that customers would expect to find in the store.
    d.   not sell any of the brand names the competition is selling.
    e.   increase its strategic planning effort.

Writing and Speaking Exercise

Dolph Drake, the owner of Bulldog Books, has three bookstores near the campus of a large state university. In the past, he has run his stores very informally. He likes to claim that he is successful because he doesn't think too much and that he makes most of his decisions by the "seat of his pants." Over the past five years profits at each store have increased between 5 percent and 7 percent each year, despite the fact that the average price of textbooks has doubled. Also, Drake has never given much thought to changing his original plans for his bookstores.

While Drake was the first to open off-campus stores and therefore got the prime locations, competitors are beginning to appear near all three of his stores. In fact, just recently an out-of-town competitor gathered the majority of the end-of-semester textbook buy-backs, one of the most profitable activities for a campus bookstore. This out of towner merely set up a drive-through buyback operation at a nearby parking lot so that students could pull up under an awning, hand over their books, and drive off with money within minutes. Even though the competitor left town the next day, Drake expects other book buyers will seek to "hit and run" at the end of the fall semester.

As a result of this recent loss of business, Drake feels that it is time to develop a more structured approach for his business and asks you as part of your summer internship to research the strategic planning process. You are to prepare a memo on the basic steps and tasks that are involved in developing a strategic plan. Be sure to include in your memo a mission statement and a list of objectives that Bulldog Books should seek to achieve.

Retail Project

Go to the library and either look at the most recent annual reports for four or five of the top 25 U.S. retailers listed on the inside cover of this text or locate the 10-Ks of those firms on the Internet. (Note: All publicly held firms need to file their U.S. Security and Exchange Commission 10-Ks, a more complete financial analysis of the firm's performance, electronically. To look up this information, go to www.sec.gov/edgarhp.htm.)

Use the SPM described in Exhibits 2.2 and 2.9 to calculate your own SPM numbers for these retailers.

Finally, after you have calculated these numbers, which retailer do you believe is the best at achieving financial superiority?

Planning Your Own Entrepreneurial Retail Business

In the "Planning Your Own Entrepreneurial Retail Business" exercise in Chapter 1, you learned how to estimate the net profits that your business might earn. You saw what would happen if your sales estimate was off by 10 percent. Now it's time to analyze the dollar investment you need in assets to support your business and how you might finance these assets.

Your investment in assets needs to cover inventory, fixtures, equipment, cash, customer credit (i.e., accounts receivable) and perhaps other assets. These assets could be financed with debt or by investments you or perhaps other investors make in the business.

Compute the strategic profit model ratios under the assumption that your first-year sales are $800,000, net profit is $56,000, total investment in assets is $400,000, and the total debt to finance these assets is $300,000. (Hint: Net worth is equal to total assets less debt.) What would happen to these ratios if net profit rose to $65,000?

CASE

Rethinking Strategy at Macy's

While many business leaders claim to embrace change, Macy's CEO Terry Lundgren may have learned that some parts of the past were valuable keys to customer loyalty.

Throughout its 150-year history, the midrange department store had grown by acquiring small regional department store chains such as Bamberger's in New Jersey (1929), O'Connor Moffat in San Francisco (1945), and John Taylor Dry Goods in Kansas City (1947). These stores were usually renamed Macy's within a few years. Besides economies of scale in advertising and back-office operations, the Macy's management thought that customers would be attracted to the cachet of a New York City icon in their cities and towns. While there was often nostalgia for the traditional local retailer's name, the renamed stores generally prospered.

The purchase-and-rename strategy continued throughout the 1990s as Macy's merged with Federated. Indeed, the merged department store giants were renamed Macy's, Inc., and a strategy was in place to make the Macy's name a national department store brand. However, the recent acquisition of the May Department Store chain by Federated/Macy's meant the demise of some highly regarded regional chains: Filene's, Jordan Marsh, The Broadway, Emporium, Hecht's, Woodward-Lothrop, John Wanamaker, Bullock's, I. Magnin, Abraham & Strauss, Liberty House, Burdine's, Goldsmith's, Lazarus, and Bon Marche.

These acquired chains often had a loyal customer group that relished the unique heritage of the regional brand. The customers of Chicago's Marshall Field's department stores were particularly incensed when they learned in 2006 that Macy's would replace the Field's name. Field's had always positioned itself as an upmarket brand that attracted middle- and upper-income customers, a notch above the typical Macy's positioning. Its enormous flagship on State Street had similar historic associations and ritual destination shopping activity as to Macy's Herald Square location. Macy's may have its Thanksgiving Parade, but Field's had the Walnut Room, Tiffany glass ceilings, and sections of high-end designer goods such as the 28 Shop. Field's had also developed its local identity through its signature Frango mints, as much an embodiment of refined Chicago as the Field's name.

Soon after the announcement of the name change, Field's State Street location saw dozens of customers picketing and protesting. The anniversary of the name change is still marked by demonstration protests from those who had been Fields' most loyal customers. Credit cards were cut up and mailed to Macy's offices. The Macy's outlets that had been Marshall Field's reported slower sales, but the company's strategy would not retreat to the past. While it had continued some signature items such as Frango's mints and Chicago-themed tourist merchandise, Macy's would not try to persuade Fields' former customers to give the store another look. Instead, Macy's would focus on attracting a new group of customers with exclusive merchandise from Martha Stewart, Tommy Hilfiger, and Donald Trump, as well as its Alfani and I.N.C. private label brands. It would further its shop-within-a-shop strategy with Thomas Pink shirts, Levenger leather goods, and an FAO Schwarz toy floor. The updated glitz would come with a wine bar added to the Walnut Room and its Christmas tree decorated by Martha Stewart.

Questions

1. How should Macy's balance the strength in advertising and promotion from having a national branded store with the strength that comes from having a locally branded store? After all, do consumers in Chicago care that much about a Thanksgiving Day parade in New York City?

2. If Macy's continues as a national brand, other than merchandising to local tastes, what can be done to make the store more local?

Note: This case was written by Professor Jan Owens, Carthage College, Kenosha, Wisconsin.

PART 1: INTEGRATIVE CASE
WALMART STORES VERSUS TARGET: A DECADE OF GROWTH

The Current Business of Walmart

Walmart Stores, Inc., with its first discount department store in 1962, currently operates retail stores in various formats around the world and is committed to saving people money so they can live better. We earn the trust of our customers every day by providing a broad assortment of quality merchandise and services at everyday low prices (EDLP), while fostering a culture that rewards and embraces mutual respect, integrity, and diversity. EDLP is our pricing philosophy under which we price items at a low price everyday so our customers trust that our prices will not change under frequent promotional activity.

Currently, our operations comprise three reportable business segments: the Walmart U.S. segment, the Walmart International segment, and the Sam's Club segment.

Walmart U.S.

The Walmart U.S. segment had net sales of $264.2 billion, $260.3 billion, and $259.9 billion for fiscal years 2012, 2011, and 2010, respectively. During the most recent fiscal year, no single supercenter, discount store, neighborhood market, or other small store format location accounted for as much as 1 percent of total company net sales. As a mass merchandiser of consumer products, the Walmart U.S. segment operates retail stores in all 50 states and Puerto Rico, with supercenters in 48 states and Puerto Rico, discount stores in 45 states and Puerto Rico, and neighborhood markets and other small store formats in 18 states and Puerto Rico. Supercenters range in size from 78,000 square feet to 260,000 square feet, with an average size of approximately 182,000 square feet. Our discount stores range in size from 30,000 square feet to 219,000 square feet, with an average size of approximately 106,000 square feet. Neighborhood Markets and other small formats range in size from 3,000 square feet to 64,000 square feet, with an average size of approximately 38,000 square feet. From time to time, Walmart U.S. tests different store formats to meet market demands and needs. Customers can also purchase a broad assortment of merchandise and services online at www.walmart.com. Walmart U.S. does business in the six broad merchandise categories of grocery, entertainment, hardlines, health and wellness, apparel, and home.

Walmart International

The Walmart International segment's net sales for fiscal years 2012, 2011, and 2010 were $125.9 billion, $109.2 billion, and $97.4 billion, respectively. During the most recent fiscal year, no single unit accounted for as much as 1 percent of total company net sales. Our Walmart International segment is composed of our wholly owned subsidiaries operating in Argentina, Brazil, Canada, China, Japan, and the United Kingdom; our majority-owned subsidiaries operating in Chile, Mexico, 12 countries in Africa and 5 countries in Central America; our joint ventures in China and India and our other controlled subsidiaries in China. Walmart International operates units under approximately 70 banners in numerous formats, including discount stores, supermarkets, supercenters, hypermarkets, websites, warehouse clubs, restaurants, and apparel stores. Also, on a limited basis, our Walmart International segment operates banks that provide consumer lending. The merchandising strategy for the Walmart International segment is similar to that of our operations in the United States in terms of the breadth and scope of merchandise offered for sale. While brand name merchandise accounts for a majority of sales, numerous store brands not offered for sale in the U.S. stores and clubs have been developed to serve customers in the different markets in which the Walmart International segment operates. In addition, steps have been taken to develop relationships with local suppliers in each country to ensure reliable sources of quality merchandise.

Sam's Club

The Sam's Club segment had net sales of $53.8 billion, $49.5 billion and $47.8 billion for fiscal years 2012, 2011, and 2010, respectively. During the most recent fiscal year, no single club location accounted for as much as 1 percent of total company net sales. As a membership club warehouse, facility sizes for Sam's Clubs generally range between 71,000 and 190,000 square feet, with an average size of approximately 134,000 square feet. Sam's Club also provides its members with a broad assortment of merchandise and services online at www.samsclub.com. Sam's Club offers brand name merchandise, including hardgoods, some softgoods, and selected private-label items such as "Member's Mark" and three new proprietary brands, "Artisan Fresh," "Daily Chef," and "Simply Right," in five merchandise categories, listed below, within the warehouse club format. The broad merchandise categories for Sam's Club are grocery and consumables, fuel and other, technology office and entertainment, home and apparel, and health and wellness.

Source: Adapted from Item 1 of Walmart 2011 Annual Report.

The Current Business of Target

Target Corporation (the Corporation or Target) was incorporated in Minnesota in 1902. We operate as three reportable segments: U.S. Retail, U.S. Credit Card, and Canadian. Our U.S. Retail Segment includes all of our merchandising operations, including our fully integrated online business. We offer both everyday essentials and fashionable, differentiated merchandise at discounted prices. Our ability to deliver a shopping experience that is preferred by our customers, referred to as "guests," is supported by our strong supply chain and technology infrastructure, a devotion to innovation that is ingrained in our organization and culture and our disciplined approach to managing our current business and investing in future growth. As a component of the U.S. Retail Segment, our online presence is designed to enable guests to purchase products seamlessly either online or by locating them in one of our stores with the aid of online research and location tools. Our online shopping site offers similar merchandise categories to those found in our stores, excluding food items and household essentials. Our U.S. Credit Card Segment offers credit to qualified guests through our branded proprietary credit cards, the Target Visa and the Target Card. Additionally, we offer a branded proprietary Target Debit Card. Collectively, these REDcards® help strengthen the bond with our guests, drive incremental sales, and contribute to our results of operations. Our Canadian Segment was initially reported in the first quarter of 2011 as a result of our purchase of leasehold interests in Canada from Zellers, Inc. (Zellers). This segment includes costs incurred in the United States and Canada related to our planned 2013 Canadian retail market entry.

We operate Target general merchandise stores, the majority of which offer a wide assortment of general merchandise and a more limited food assortment than traditional supermarkets. During the past three years, we completed store remodels that enabled us to offer an expanded food assortment in many of our general merchandise stores. The expanded food assortment includes some perishables and some additional dry, dairy and frozen items. In addition, we operate SuperTarget® stores with general merchandise items and a full line of food items comparable to that of traditional supermarkets. Target.com offers a wide assortment of general merchandise including many items found in our stores and a complementary assortment, such as extended sizes and colors, sold only online. A significant portion of our sales is from national brand merchandise. We also sell many products under our owned and exclusive brands. Owned brands include merchandise sold under private-label brands.

Merchandise is broadly categorized into five groups: household essentials, which includes pharmacy, beauty, personal care, baby care, and cleaning and paper products; hardlines, which includes electronics (including video game hardware and software), music, movies, books, computer software, sporting goods, and toys; apparel and accessories including apparel for women, men, boys, girls, toddlers, infants, and newborns, and also includes intimate apparel, jewelry, accessories, and shoes; food and pet supplies which includes dry grocery, dairy, frozen food, beverages, candy, snacks, deli, bakery, meat, produce, and pet supplies; and home furnishings and décor which includes furniture, lighting, kitchenware, small appliances, home décor, bed and bath, home improvement, automotive, and seasonal merchandise such as patio furniture and holiday décor.

Source: Adapted from Item 1 of Target 2011 Annual Report.

Walmart versus Target: A Decade of Comparative Performance

The decade from year end January 2003 through year end January 2012 witnessed Walmart growth in sales, pre-tax net operating profit, and stores far outstrip Target. These trends are displayed in Exhibits 1–3. During this time frame, Walmart saw its stock price move from $47.80 to $61.36, and Target during this same time frame witnessed its stock move from $28.21 to $50.81 (see Exhibit 4). For the year end January 2012, we can see many other operating performance statistics for these two retailers as displayed in Exhibit 5.

Exhibit 1
Sales Growth at Walmart versus Target

Walmart vs. Target: Sales

	Yr End Jan 2003	Yr End Jan 2004	Yr End Jan 2005	Yr End Jan 2006	Yr End Jan 2007	Yr End Jan 2008	Yr End Jan 2009	Yr End Jan 2010	Yr End Jan 2011	Yr End Jan 2012
◆ Walmart	$229,616	$256,329	$285,222	$312,427	$344,992	$374,526	$401,087	$405,132	$418,952	$443,854
■ Target	$46,781	$40,928	$45,682	$51,271	$57,878	$61,471	$62,884	$63,435	$65,786	$68,466

Exhibit 2
Pre-Tax Operating Profit Growth at Walmart and Target

Walmart vs. Target: Operating Income (Pre-Tax)

	Yr End Jan 2003	Yr End Jan 2004	Yr End Jan 2005	Yr End Jan 2006	Yr End Jan 2007	Yr End Jan 2008	Yr End Jan 2009	Yr End Jan 2010	Yr End Jan 2011	Yr End Jan 2012
◆ Walmart	$12,368	$14,193	$16,105	$17,358	$20,497	$21,996	$20,867	$22,118	$23,538	$24,398
■ Target	$2,960	$2,603	$3,031	$3,860	$4,497	$4,625	$3,356	$3,872	$4,495	$4,456

Exhibit 3
Growth in Store Locations: Walmart versus Target

Walmart vs. Target: Locations

	Yr End Jan 2003	Yr End Jan 2004	Yr End Jan 2005	Yr End Jan 2006	Yr End Jan 2007	Yr End Jan 2008	Yr End Jan 2009	Yr End Jan 2010	Yr End Jan 2011	Yr End Jan 2012
Walmart	4,672	4,906	5,182	6,037	6,809	7,288	7,909	8,459	8,970	10,13
Target	1,475	1,225	1,308	1,397	1,488	1,591	1,682	1,740	1,750	1,763

Exhibit 4
Walmart versus Target: Stock Price

Walmart vs. Target: Stock Price

	Yr End Jan 2003	Yr End Jan 2004	Yr End Jan 2005	Yr End Jan 2006	Yr End Jan 2007	Yr End Jan 2008	Yr End Jan 2009	Yr End Jan 2010	Yr End Jan 2011	Yr End Jan 2012
Walmart	$47.8	$53.8	$52.4	$46.1	$47.6	$50.7	$47.1	$53.4	$56.0	$61.3
Target	$28.2	$37.9	$50.7	$54.7	$61.3	$55.4	$31.2	$51.2	$54.8	$50.8

Exhibit 5

Walmart versus Target Stores: Fiscal Year 2012 Operating Statistics (all data in millions)

	Walmart (year ended 1/31/2012)	Target Stores (year ended 1/31/2012)
Annual Total Sales	$443,854	$68,466
Cost of Merchandise Sold	$335,127	$47,860
Gross Profit	$108,727	$20,606
Selling & General Administrative Expenses	$85,265	$14,106
Net Operating Income (before taxes)	$24,398	$4,456
Total Assets	$193,406	$46,630
Stockholders Equity (net worth)	$71,315	$15,821
Average Inventory Investment	$38,576	$7,757
Provision for Income Taxes	$7,944	$1,527

Questions

1. With the financial data presented in this case, compute the ratios of the strategic profit model for Walmart and Target Stores. Interpret these ratios with special attention to comparing these two major discount retailers.
2. Discuss why Walmart has been growing more rapidly than Target over the last decade. Do you see this trend continuing? Explain your rationale. Note this may require you to do some additional research on these two retailers.
3. Develop a summary of the mission and corporate culture of these two retailers. Note a corporate culture reflects the core values, norms, and behaviors that reflect how it behaves toward employees, customers, and suppliers.

Sources

Target Corporation. "Target Corporation Form 10-K for the Fiscal Year Ended January 28, 2012." *U.S. Securities and Exchange Commission (Home Page).* March 15, 2012. Available at: http://www.sec.gov/Archives/edgar/data/27419/000104746912002714/a2207838z10-k.htm [Accessed April 17, 2012].

Target Corporation. "Target Corporation Form 10-K for the Fiscal Year Ended January 31, 2009." *U.S. Securities and Exchange Commission (Home Page).* March 13, 2009. Available at: http://www.sec.gov/Archives/edgar/data/27419/000104746909002623/a2190597z10-k.htm [Accessed April 17, 2012].

Target Corporation. "Target Corporation Form 10-K for the Fiscal Year Ended January 31, 2004." *U.S. Securities and Exchange Commission (Home Page).* April 5, 2004. Available at: http://www.sec.gov/Archives/edgar/data/27419/000104746904010838/a2130364z10-k.htm#toc_ba1120_1 [Accessed April 17, 2012].

Wal-Mart Stores, Inc. "Walmart Stores, Inc. Form 10-K for the Fiscal Year Ended January 31, 2012." *U.S. Securities and Exchange Commission (Home Page).* March 27, 2012. Available at: http://www.sec.gov/Archives/edgar/data/104169/000119312512134679/d270972d10k.htm [Accessed April 13, 2012].

Wal-Mart Stores, Inc. "Walmart Stores, Inc. Form 10-K for the Fiscal Year Ended January 31, 2009." *U.S. Securities and Exchange Commission (Home Page).* March 27, 2009. Available at: http://www.sec.gov/Archives/edgar/data/104169/000010416909000006/dex13.htm [Accessed April 13, 2012].

Wal-Mart Stores, Inc. "Walmart Stores, Inc. Form 10-K for the Fiscal Year Ended January 31, 2004." *U.S. Securities and Exchange Commission (Home Page).* March 31, 2004. Available at: http://www.sec.gov/Archives/edgar/data/104169/000119312504059900/dex13.htm [Accessed April 13, 2012].

Yahoo Finance. "WMT Historic Prices." *Yahoo Finance.* N.D. Available at: http://finance.yahoo.com/q/hp?s=WMT+Historical+Prices [Accessed April 13, 2012].

Yahoo Finance. "TGT Historic Prices." *Yahoo Finance.* N.D. Available at: http://finance.yahoo.com/q/hp?s=TGT+Historical+Prices [Accessed April 13, 2012].

Note: This case was prepared by Mark Lusch as a basis for class discussion rather than to illustrate either effective or ineffective handling of an administrative situation.

Part 2

The Retail Environment

© Purestock/Thinkstock

© Juanmonino/iStockphoto

© scanrail/iStockphoto

© Losevsky Pavel/Shutterstock

© Moxie Productions/Getty Images

3

Retail Customers

Overview

In this chapter, we examine the effects of the external environment on retailing. We discuss how recent changes in the population and in social and economic trends affect the way consumers behave and the implications of these changes for retailers. We conclude with the development of a consumer shopping and purchasing model that incorporates all of these factors to describe the overall shopping and buying process.

Learning Objectives

After reading this chapter, you should be able to:

1 Explain the importance of population trends on retail planning.

2 List the social trends that retail managers should regularly monitor and describe their impact on retailing.

3 Describe the changing economic trends and their effects on retailing.

4 Discuss the consumer shopping and purchasing model, including the key stages in the shopping and purchasing process.

Introduction

In Chapter 1, we said that retailing consists of the final activities and steps needed to place a product or service in the hands of the consumer. The previous chapters also made the point that to be a high performer, one must be able to differentiate oneself from the competition. In doing so, retail managers must realize that, with the possible exception of supermarkets and gas stations, their stores can't serve all possible consumer types. Some consumers will never shop at a nearby Kohls or Target; others will never shop at a Saks Fifth Avenue, Nordstrom, or Neiman Marcus. Therefore, before developing any plans, the successful retailer must first target a specific segment (or segments) of the overall market and study the environmental factors (competition, the behavior of the other supply-chain members, socioeconomic factors, and legal and ethical factors) that affect that segment. Only after determining what segment(s) to target can the retailer decide on a location, format, retail mix (the combination of merchandise assortment, price, promotion, customer service, and store layout), and value proposition to best serve the selected segment(s).

customer satisfaction
Occurs when the total shopping experience of the customer has been met or exceeded.

The easiest way for retailers to differentiate themselves is to satisfy the customer's needs and wants better than the competition. This customer satisfaction, as we will use the term, is different from customer service. **Customer satisfaction** is determined by whether or not the total shopping experience has met or exceeded the customer's expectation. If it has, then the customer is said to have had a rewarding shopping experience. Customer satisfaction is important because, as was noted in the previous chapter, it costs the average retailer five times as much money to get a new customer into a store as it does to make a sale to someone who has already shopped there before or to retain a current customer who may be unhappy. Not only retailers, but also the nation's economy depends on the customer having a satisfactory shopping experience. Exhibit 3.1 shows the historically strong relationship between changes in the American Customer Satisfaction Index (ACSI) and changes in future consumer spending. The fact that spending and satisfaction generally move together should not be surprising since buyer satisfaction leads to repeat business and increased purchases. After all, a satisfied customer will be encouraged to engage in future spending, while the dissatisfied or unhappy customer will be more hesitant. Little wonder, then, that many economists feel that in the past it was the American consumers' desire to spend that prevented the economy from suffering more severe slowdowns than those that did occur.[1] Perhaps this is why the government is still trying to stimulate consumer spending several years after the 2007–2009 recession.

This chapter's "Retailing: The Inside Story" box discusses the ACSI, and how, as seen at the far right of Exhibit 3.1, retailers have seen the satisfaction levels of their customers rebound from the nearly continuous fall that scores took between the middle of 2009 and the end of 2010—the 18-month period immediately following the official end of the recession in June 2009.[2] The bad news is that the rise in ACSI was minimal and is particularly fragile due to gas prices.

A good portion of the gain in ACSI came during the fourth quarter of 2011, when gas prices fell below $3.25 a gallon nationally; however, by the end of the first quarter of 2012, prices had already precipitously risen past the $3.90 watermark.[3] Hopefully, the United States can get a better grasp on the price of gasoline and energy. Why is this the case? As observed in 2011, when gas prices go up, overall customer satisfaction is likely to go down. This is because the overall price of *shopping in general* increases as gasoline prices rise. The prices of products from eggs and milk, to your designer jeans and computers all must account for the long-term cost associated with getting those products to the retailers' shelves. Additionally, increases in the cost associated with driving one's own car to the store makes shopping trips less enjoyable and necessarily less frequent.

Exhibit 3.1
Personal Consumer Expenditures and Lagged Satisfaction (ACSI)

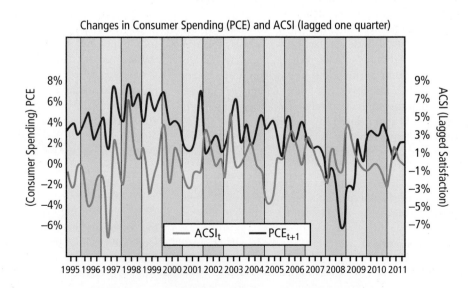

Any fall in ACSI should be concerning and any rise cautiously celebrated. Before the onset of a recession or any downturn in the economy, ACSI begins to go down; conversely, ACSI rises as the economic rebound nears. The interested reader should revisit Exhibit 3.1 and note how in the fall of 2007, prior to the onset of the 2008–2009 recession, ACSI fell and began rebounding early in 2009 prior to the recession's end in June of that year. Why then should one be cautious about celebrating a rise in ACSI? Any rise means consumers' expectations about obtaining gratification from future discretionary spending are increasing. However, to realize a gain in actual consumer spending, it is also necessary that consumers have the means—cash and credit—to spend. As long as there is a lack of spending power, the ability of ACSI alone to predict consumer spending will be limited.

RETAILING — **The Inside Story**

Are Retailers Making the Grade When It Comes to Consumers' Expectations?

Over the last decade, retailers have done a better job at providing a shopping experience that meets or exceeds customers' expectations, but the improvement is minimal. Customer satisfaction with overall retail trade has gone from an ACSI score of 74.8 in 2001 to 76.1 at the end of 2011 (the most recent year for which data had been collected). For those doing the math at home, this corresponds to an increase of approximately 2 percent over a 10-year span. Yet one should not conclude retailers are doing a poor job at meeting their customers' expectations by such marginal rating improvement. The 76.1 ACSI score set a new threshold for service provided by retailers having eclipsed the previous high-water mark of 75.7 set in 1994.

The largest contributing factor for this increase in overall retail trade satisfaction was satisfaction with gasoline stations. In fact, the ACSI score jumped 5.7–74 percent during 2011. The driving force behind this grand improvement was falling gas prices. Although the *national* average retail price for gasoline began 2011 just below $3.07 per gallon and reached a high of approximately $3.96 a gallon, the highest price for gasoline outside the fall of 2008 where it cost approximately $4.12, gas prices fell sharply over the last seven months of the year ending below $3.29. But gasoline prices have since reversed course, which means that consumers are going to be less pleased.

In conjunction with the improvement observed in 2011 ACSI, Q4 retail sales were up approximately 5 percent, and overall retail trade for 2011 rose 8 percent. The good news is that customer satisfaction continues to climb entering 2012, which has a positive effect on consumer demand and economic growth. Consumer spending in Q4 of 2011 was up by 2 percent, which fueled the 2.8 percent Q4 growth in our *gross domestic product* (GDP). It might be beneficial here for the student to reexamine the approximate one-quarter lagged relationship between ACSI and consumer spending illustrated earlier in Exhibit 3.1.

Now let's review what happened in a couple of retail industries and how changes in these industries affected retail's ACSI score.

Supermarkets

The average ACSI score for supermarkets increased 1.3–76 percent despite the continued rise in food prices. In 2011, the cost of food prepared at home rose 6 percent, following a 1.7 percent increase in 2010. Even though this is a price-sensitive market, the negative effect of higher prices on customer satisfaction appears to have been absorbed by a simultaneous enhancement in store aesthetics (e.g., store remodeling and freshening-up), services provision, and merchandise selection; all designed to improve the shopping experience for customers.

As always, Publix Super Markets is king in customer satisfaction among grocers; its score of 84 has held this distinction since ASCI's baseline year of 1994. Conversely, Walmart's grocery business is the lowest of the individual supermarkets measured specifically within the survey. Its score, 69, is down 3 percent from 2010 and significantly below the next

(continued)

highest competitor, Supervalu, at 74, who remained unchanged. In an industry where retailers seek to leverage quality and service for higher prices, Walmart's concentration on price alone appears not to satisfy shoppers; people may shop there because of the everyday low prices, but they're not shopping there because they prefer to. Whole Foods Market on the other hand, who came in second with an ACSI score of 80, continues to inch closer to Publix. Since its inclusion in the survey in 2007, Whole Foods has realized gains in satisfaction each year. In four years, its ACSI rating has grown 10 percent, and its stock price has grown 600 percent! It just goes to show you what satisfied customers will do for your bottom-line.

ACSI Scores for Selected Retailers from 2006 to 2011

	2006	2007	2008	2009	2010	2011
Supermarkets	75	76	76	76	75	76
Publix	83	83	82	86	84	84
Whole Foods		73	75	76	79	80
Kroger	76	75	77	78	78	79
Safeway	74	72	75	72	74	75
Winn-Dixie	76	71	73	74	76	75
Walmart	69	71	68	71	71	69
Department & Discount Stores	74	73	74	75	76	76
Nordstrom		80	80	83	82	84
JCPenny	78	77	78	79	80	82
Kohl's	80	79	80	79	81	81
Dollar General		78	75	79	80	78
Macy's	71	75	74	71	76	77
Sears		72	72	74	75	76
Walmart	72	68	70	71	73	70
Specialty Retailers	75	75	76	77	78	79
Costco	81	81	83	81	82	83
Sam's Club	78	77	79	79	78	81
Staples		77	76	77	81	79
Lowe's	74	75	76	79	77	79
Office Depot		78	75	76	81	79
Barnes & Noble		83	83	84	82	79
Home Depot	70	67	70	72	75	78
Best Buy	76	74	74	74	77	77
Internet Retailers	83	83	82	83	80	81
Amazon	87	88	86	86	87	86
Newegg		87	88	86	84	85
Overstock		80	82	82	83	83
eBay	80	81	78	79	81	81
Netflix		84	85	87	86	74

Note: Blank spaces mean the data collected was not meaningful for that year.

(continued)

Department and Discount Stores

After three consecutive years of growth in overall satisfaction scores, the department and discount stores is the only retail sector tracked to show no change between 2010 and 2011. Pricing pressures remain the greatest challenge to this category of retailer. During 2011, it appeared that this was the only retail sector where price seemed to trump quality in consumers' purchasing decision. As a result, department and discount stores were metaphorically "pinched" as consumers were willing to pay higher prices for greater amounts of service at specialty retailers, thus limiting their ability to compete on service and quality, and category killers, with their quantity buying discounts, were oftentimes able to curtail, or even eliminate, their price competitiveness.

Nordstrom, however, continued to be the exception rather than the rule during 2011. Nordstrom's 84 score again made it the highest ranking department or discount retailer—a distinction the retailer has held every year since ACSI began. Nordstrom's 84 also has the distinction of being the highest score of any traditional, bricks-and-mortar retailer and trails only online, retailing giant Amazon, who scored an 86, and online computer hardware and software retailer Newegg, who scored an 85.

Specialty Retail Stores and Membership Warehouse Clubs

Retailers specializing in particular merchandise lines like category killers Staples, Lowe's, and Best Buy specialty houses for merchandise like fashion or electronics and membership warehouse clubs do the best job of meeting or exceeding customers' expectations when it comes to traditional bricks-and-mortar retailing. The specialty retailing sector's overall ACSI score of 79 is the highest of all traditional retail sectors and only 2 points below the average of the highest retail sector, Internet retailing.

Membership clubs like Costco and Sam's Club lead the way with scores of 83 and 81, respectively. Office supply giants Staples and Office Depot home-improvement giant Lowe's, and last of the big bookstore chains, Barnes & Noble, all tie for third with scores of 79. Interestingly, the biggest gainer in 2011 was OfficeMax, who put a concerted effort into becoming the greatest customer service provider of all office supply retailers. In 2011, the retailer experienced a 5.4 percent increase in its satisfaction scores to 78.

Internet Retail

Like every year since 2000, when Internet retailing was included as a distinct retail category within ACSI, Internet retailers, as a group, received the highest ACSI score, an 81. Online retail giant Amazon led the group with a score of 86, closely followed by Newegg's 85. Both retailers scored higher than any other individually measured retailer included within ACSI.

Yet not all online sellers were as successful at meeting or exceeding the expectations of their customer base like the category average might suggest. Online media retailer, Netflix, scored a dismal 74, placing it third from the bottom; only Walmart (70 and 69 for their department and grocery stores, respectively) and CVS Caremark (73) scored lower. Much of this drop is attributed to the nearly 60 percent price increase during the summer of 2011 and subsequent loss of 800,000 subscribers. It's expected that Netflix will rebound, though, as it continues to transition from their DVD-by-mail to much more of a streaming-media service.

Source: "February 2012 and Historical ACSI Scores," and "Commentary: Customer Satisfaction Slowly Improves as U.S. Economy Continues a Sluggish Recovery by Professor Claes Fornell," ACSI February 21, 2012, Report. Used with the written permission of Professor Claes Fornell; Gasbuddy.com (2012) "Gas Price Historical Price Charts," [online] Available at: http://www.gasbuddy.com/gb_retail_price_chart.aspx? [Accessed: March 3, 2012].

In addition to the merchandise or service offered for sale, another part of the customer's shopping experience is the services provided by the retailer. These **customer services** are the activities performed by the retailer that influence (1) the ease with which a potential customer can shop or learn about the store's offering, (2) the ease with which a transaction can be completed once the customer attempts to make a purchase, and (3) the customer's satisfaction with the product or service after purchase. These three elements correspond to the pre-transaction, transaction, and post-transaction components of customer service.

Common services provided by retailers (in addition to having the product that satisfies the customer's needs and wants) include alterations, fitting rooms, delivery, gift registries, check cashing, credit, extended shopping hours, short checkout lines,

customer services
Consists of all those activities performed by the retailer that influence (1) the ease with which a potential customer can shop or learn about the store's offering, (2) the ease with which a transaction can be completed once the customer attempts to make a purchase, and (3) the customer's satisfaction with the transaction.

gift wrapping, parking, layaway, and merchandise-return privileges, as well as the availability of in-home shopping options such as television, print catalogs, and the Internet. It must be remembered that none of these services is actually the merchandise or service being offered for sale; it merely entices the customers that the retailer is targeting.

If a customer is dissatisfied with either the product offered or the services provided, that customer is less likely to choose that retailer in the future, thus decreasing future sales. (Throughout the remainder of this chapter we will use the term *product* to designate either the physical product or service offered for sale and the term *service* to refer to the services the retailer uses to facilitate that sale. However, in the case of a service retailer, the product offered is, in fact, a service.) Knowing what products to carry, as well as determining which customer services to offer, is a challenging problem for retailers as they seek ways to improve the shopping experience. Imagine listening to a radio with no tuning or volume knob. The receiver picks up many different signals, some in harmony, some in conflict, so that the result is noise coming through the speaker. You're getting something, but you can't understand it. To make sense of the confusing array of available information, retailers use market-segmentation techniques to tune into segments of the population, hoping to hear a series of clear messages that assist them in providing the correct products and services to their customers. Exhibit 2.4 pointed out how an electronics retailer could use a segmentation strategy to meet the needs of the target market served by a particular store. Here the chain customized 20 percent of its merchandise offerings and trained its salespeople to meet the demands of the store's target market. Many nonretailers are surprised to find out that 80 percent of the merchandise in most chain stores is the same nationwide. It is only the remaining 20 percent that is tailored to each store's market.

Understanding different customer segments and their need for convenience might stimulate the retailer to offer additional products through its website, thus providing a critical service component to enhance the customer's experience. As Exhibit 3.2 points out, it is important that the retailer know and understand its customers.

In Exhibit 3.2 we see the three important types of trends—population, social, and economic—that all retailers must monitor because they will affect the way customers undertake the shopping process. As pointed out in Chapter 2, all retailers must perform three basic strategies:

1. Get as many of the targeted consumers into the store as possible,
2. Convert these consumers into customers by having them purchase merchandise, and
3. Perform the first two strategies at the lowest cost possible that is consistent with the level of service customers expect.

Exhibit 3.2
How Current Trends Affect the Way the Consumer Behaves

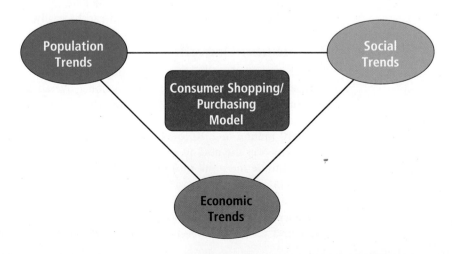

If the retailer doesn't understand its customers, it won't be able to accomplish the first two strategies.

market segmentation
Is the dividing of a heterogeneous consumer population into smaller, more homogeneous groups based on their characteristics.

Market segmentation is the method retailers use to segment, or break down, heterogeneous consumer populations into smaller, more homogeneous groups based on certain characteristics. Market segmentation helps retailers understand who their customers are, how they think, and what they do. It enables the retailer to build a meaningful strategy based on the consumers' needs, desires, perceptions, and shopping behaviors. Only after realizing the various segments to either target or not target can a retailer hope to satisfy consumers' needs better than the competition. For example, in the United States, Walmart has determined that its Supercenters serve three general market segments: *brand aspirationals* (people with low incomes who are obsessed with names such as KitchenAid), *price-sensitive affluents* (wealthier shoppers who love deals), and *value-price shoppers* (who like low prices and cannot afford much more).[4] Failure to spot changes in the marketplace before the competition means the retailer will only be able to react and adapt to what more sensitive retailers have already spotted. Thus, while the high-performance retailer may have spotted an emerging trend and made the necessary changes in its retail mix, the average retailer will only be a follower or "look-alike" retailer. Further, what differential advantage does a "me-too" retailer offer the consumer? Copycat practices have led many retailers into financial difficulties.

As in the case of Walmart Supercenters cited in the previous paragraph, most retailers choose to target only a portion of the overall market. Consider, for example, how the three major membership warehouse club operators go after different customer segments. Sam's club focuses on small businesses, which are said to spend 50 percent more than individual consumers; Costco, despite carrying a third fewer SKUs, has a reputation for bargain prices and surprise designer goods aimed at meeting the needs of its upscale consumers;[5] and BJ's caters to families by offering larger selections. Each of these merchants has excelled at reaching its target customer, although it probably has excluded other available consumer segments.

Now, let's begin our study of the changing consumer to see how an understanding of population, social, and economic trends can help a retailer select a market segment to target.

LO 1

Population Trends[6]

Explain the importance of population trends on retail planning.

population variables
Include population growth trends, age distributions, ethic makeup, and geographic trends.

Retailers often find it useful to group consumers according to **population variables**, such as population growth trends, age distributions, ethnic makeup, and geographic trends. This is useful for two reasons. First, such data is often linked to marketplace needs. Second, the data is readily available and can be easily applied in analyzing markets.

Population Growth

Retailers have long viewed an expanding population base as synonymous with growth in retail markets. Unfortunately, the nation's overall growth rate has declined during each of the past three decades as families have had fewer children. If current average projections are correct, then the U.S. population will increase about 1 percent per year, from 310 million in 2010 to 341 million in 2020. However, it is expected to increase by 42 percent over the next 40 years to 439 million by 2050.[7] The majority of this growth is expected to be the result of immigration.

Implications for Retailers

Any increase in domestic population growth will mean an increased demand for goods and services; however, the growth will be nowhere near the 80-percent increase experienced over the last half-century. Still, even minimal growth in the total population will mean opportunities for retailers. As population growth slows, or perhaps in some areas declines, successful retailers must focus on taking market share away from competitors, managing gross margin by controlling selling price and cost and increasing the productivity of existing stores. Chain store retailers that can operate in hundreds or thousands of different geographic areas also need to pay attention to areas of a city that may be declining in population.

Yet a shrinking number in the overall population of one's shoppers need not mean a retailer should consider closing some existing stores or halt growth plans. For instance, PetSmart continues to expand its retail operations as the number of pet parents and the number of multiple-pet families increase. In fact, growth in this retail sector is likely to continue given that the pet population has outgrown the overall human population.

Another growth opportunity for retailers is international expansion; however, it is likely that this is a limited-time opportunity. Demographers are predicting a major decline in worldwide fertility rates, which will lead to a global population decline—a radical notion in a world brought up on the idea of overpopulation. While it will take some time, global retailers should be prepared for depopulation.

Age Distribution

The age distribution of the U.S. population is changing. In 1980, the median age was 30, but by 2010 it had risen to just over 37.[8] The most significant change today is the bulge of early baby boomers moving into their sixties. This group of 78 million Americans born between 1946 and 1964 accounts for more than 25 percent of the population and spends an estimated $2.3 trillion on consumer goods and services annually.[9] However, many experts claim that, for retail planning purposes, this group is much too large and diverse to share a single lifestyle, life stage, or purchasing proclivity. For example, while the first wave of boomers may have already retired and started collecting full Social Security benefits as of January 1, 2012 (after reaching age 66), many others are 15 or so years away from retirement. Therefore, as these older boomers retire, they may not be spending as they did in the past. This is important because baby boomers accounted for about half of all consumer spending in the United States during the 1990s.[10]

However, as we have suggested before, with any macro trend, there are always micro trends that can go in the opposite direction. Consider, for example, in 2010, denim sales to women over 55 grew 17 percent. As people live longer, they also want to retain their youth and one way to do this is through dress. Consequently, denim brands such as Kut from the Kloth and Not Your Daughter's Jeans have done exceptionally well; after all, the largest women's wear market retailers have to serve is the 55+. Recognizing this trend J. Crew has significantly expanded its denim offering to older women.

Today, many boomers in their late 40s to mid-60s are still spending at levels near their previous pace; however, many have also begun to make a more concerted effort at saving for retirement. This latter group has an increased concern over the long-term viability of Social Security and the likelihood of corporate downsizing, which left many seniors unemployed during the recent recession.

Sadly, the 2008–2009 recession created immediate financial concerns for more than just the pre-retirement boomers. Some boomers and members of the Silent Generation (those born between 1900 and 1945) who had already retired were forced to return to the workforce in order to restore value to their financial holdings. These retirees who just a few years before thought they were "set for life" make up what is now called the *unretired*.[11] *Time* magazine, in a November 1951 cover story,[12] described this generation as hardworking, but docile and detached from the political process. After lives filled with hard work, members of the Silent Generation are now angry: mad at the government, upset with the immigrant problem, and not generally approving of the rise in interracial marriage. In addition, only 45 percent believe the Internet has been a positive development.

As the ramifications from this recent recession continue to unfold, many boomers are now spending less on apparel and clothing, spending more on medicine and recreation, and saving more of their money to pass on to their children in case they don't live to be 100. This chapter's "Service Retailing" box describes the development of a new type of service retailer: consultants, who are combinations of financial planners and attorneys. These individuals are equipped to advise parents and their children on how to manage what will be the largest transfer of wealth in history. Some calculations estimate $41 trillion in wealth—that's $41,000,000,000,000—will be transferred to a younger generation between now and 2052.[13]

As stated previously, seniors should not be viewed as homogeneous. In the past, they were classified as anyone aged 60 and older. However, because people now live longer, more useful categories should be utilized. Octogenarians are people aged 80–89, nonagenarians are 90–99 years, and centenarians are 100 years and above. Today, the United States has more than 70,000 centenarians, a number almost 10 times that of four decades ago. In fact, today one in 50 women and one in 200 men will reach that age.

Another useful way to categorize seniors is in terms of their health (good or poor) and wealth (inadequate or adequate). Doing so creates four types of seniors: good health–adequate wealth, good health–inadequate wealth, poor health–adequate wealth, and poor health–inadequate wealth. Seniors in general have more wealth than several generations ago due to improved Social Security benefits, Medicare, and retirement savings. In addition, seniors are relatively healthier as compared to previous generations. Taking these two factors together, it's not surprising that the population segment with the largest percentage growth over the past five years is the "active" senior who has both the health and the wealth to enjoy himself or herself.

The so-called baby busters or Generation Xers—those born between 1965 and 1977—are another interesting age group. Unlike baby boomers, this age group is a declining percentage of the population. The 47 million Gen Xers are, as a rule, more skeptical, have a more balanced work ethic, and are less impressed by titles, authority, or status than any other group. Xers are especially cynical about things held dear by previous generations, particularly baby boomers. In fact, if the boomers created yuppies (young urban professionals), Gen Xers have given rise to a new kind of elite: yawns (young and wealthy but normal).[14] Some people suggest the behavior of Xers is the result of their growing up during the years leading up to and following the end of the Cold War as well as coming of age during the recession of the early 1990s.

Almost 80 million members of the so-called Generation Y—also called the *Net Generation*, *iGeneration*, *Google generation*, *echo boomers*, and *millennium generation*—are those who were born between 1978 and 1994. This group is emerging as a major buying and consuming force in the economy. In addition to being the last generation of Americans wholly born in the 20th century, this group is racially diverse (more than one in three is not Caucasian) and has been pampered, nurtured, and programmed with a slew of activities since they were preschoolers. Since Yers were the first to grow up with the Internet in its developed form—including music downloads, instant messaging, and camera phones—many of them have never wound a watch, purchased a record, used a typewriter, or had a landline phone in their home or apartment. They think nothing of text messaging rather than calling, downloading music off the Internet, or sharing their accomplishments and lives over Facebook.

SERVICE RETAILING

The Great Money Transfer

Baby boomers, whose parents were raised during the Great Depression, were taught to focus on saving money for that "rainy day." However, it appears that today's middle-aged consumers have something different in mind. They are chasing the trillions of dollars that are expected to transfer among generations as baby boomers and members of the Silent Generation sell their businesses and pass away. These middle-aged consumers expect to inherit money from their parents or take control of the 401(k) money their parents accumulated over lengthy careers.

The authors are friends with several couples who, like many other 50-something boomers, live in fancy homes that are mortgaged to the hilt, drive leased luxury cars, and purchase apparel at Saks and Neiman Marcus. These couples represent the newest behavioral trend among boomers—being a "waiter." In other words, they are "waiting for their inheritance." Sadly, many are not just waiting, but have actually become dependent on what economists say will be the largest amount of money, some $41 trillion, ever set aside for transfer between generations.

However, these boomers may be disappointed given that family assets have dwindled in recent years as savings were depleted not only by fluctuations in the stock market and unpredictable housing values but also by the high costs of nursing homes, long-term care, and prescription drugs—increasingly common expenses since Americans are living longer.

Making matters worse, as these family assets dwindled, the "old school" parents avoided any discussion with their children about their finances or what was in their wills. This has led to many a sibling battle over who gets what and when.

As a result, a new type of service retailer has emerged—a combination financial planner and attorney. These professionals seek to avoid family feuds after a parent's death. To do so, they offer services ranging from extensive will planning to counseling on how retirees can communicate inheritance decisions to their children. This communication is important since baby boomers have a significantly different attitude toward money than their parents. Because of their Great Depression experiences, the parents were savers, whereas baby boomers grew up in the prosperity of the 1950s and 1960s never wanting for the basics. Boomers were the spenders who "shopped till they dropped."

Lifestyle changes also increase the need for these service professionals. The higher divorce rates of recent years and increased number of remarriages have created confusion about the rights of stepchildren and second or third spouses in wills. In addition, wealthy families want someone who not only can help them grow their money but also can guide them through the maze of ever-changing tax laws and other issues that can affect how they hold on to their money until passing it along to the next generation. Today, people don't know how—or don't want to try—to navigate the explosion of investment products or the complexity of tax laws.

Little wonder, then, that these financial planners or lawyers seek to avoid family disputes by placing less emphasis on documenting what a parent wants to say in a will. Instead, these counselors spend their time asking detailed questions about the boomer children, such as financial status, living situations, and relationships with siblings. They encourage parents to include their children in estate-planning meetings so that everyone involved will understand who is getting what and why, all in an attempt to avoid an extended battle after the parents' deaths.

One word of warning: More than half of the respondents in a survey of Americans aged 65 and older stated that they weren't going to divide their assets equally among their children. Instead they plan to give a larger share to the attentive child—the one who provided care, for example.

Sources: Based on "Wealth Management Comes to Financial Services Firms," St. Louis Post-Dispatch, October 7, 2007: D1, D3; "Inherit the Windfall: How to Retire on the Money Your Parent Leave Behind," Wall Street Journal, June 7, 2006: D1; "I Inherited My Money the Hard Way: I Earned It," AARP Bulletin, December 2005: 6; "Not Acting Their Age," U.S. News & World Report, June 4, 2001: 54–60; John C. Carver, "Is It Going to Be 'Share the Wealth,'" Texas A&M University, working paper, 1999; "Going Deeper in Debt," AARP Bulletin, March 2003: 22–24; Roger M. Williams, "The New Breed and the Mega-Bucks," Foundation News and Commentary, September–October 2001: 25; and the authors' observations.

Jupiterimages/Photos.com

As the "active senior" is the fastest growing segment of the senior population, it's not surprising that retailers are looking to highlight recreation and fun for these on-the-move consumers.

In many ways, they are the most "optimistic" generation in this country's history. They tend to have higher disposable incomes than their age group in prior generations, are interested in good health, and tend not to rely on others for their success. Research has also found that Gen Y provides a wealth of potential to employers because of their vigor, enthusiasm, talent, early experience, and high expectations.[15] They want a professional career but place a higher priority on family and home. Three out of four have a working mother, and one out of four is in a single-parent household. Emerging evidence also suggests that Gen Yers' values are more conservative than those of their parents as evident by their tendency to live separately before marriage. However, at the same time, in the 2008 U.S. Presidential election, they voted for Barack Obama over John McCain by 66 percent over 32 percent; whereas adults over 30 voted 50 percent Obama and 49 percent McCain.[16] Exhibit 3.3 illustrates the key differences between these age groups. The Pew Research Center (http:pewresearch.org/pubs/1437/millennials-profile) and Service Management Group (www.smg.com) are excellent sources of information useful to retailers on Generation Y.

Implications for Retailers

The most significant implication of an aging population for retailers, particularly those targeting boomers, is that their customers' big spending years are generally behind

Exhibit 3.3
Boomers, Xers, and Yers

	Baby Boomers	Gen X	Gen Y
Also known as	Boomers	Baby busters	Echo boomers Millennium generation Digital generation
Dates of birth	1946–1964	1965–1977	1978–1994
Number in U.S.	78 million	47 million	80 million
Annual spending	Over $2.3 trillion	Over $800 billion	$1 trillion
Experienced	Birth of rock and roll Space exploration Racial divides Sexual revolution	Growing divorce rate Gang violence Pop culture Information explosion	Age of technology Multilayered information Growth in branding Recycling
Respond to	Authority	Creativity	Learning
Perspective on technology	Fearful	Proficient	Indoctrinated
Attitude	Realistic	Pessimistic	Optimistic

them. However, retailers must resist the temptation to overlook these segments. Despite the fact that boomers still spend an estimated $2.3 trillion on consumer goods and services annually, few retailers fully appreciate today's older boomer consumer. Instead, they continue merchandising and marketing to younger and less affluent Xers and Yers.

Retailers who ignore boomers—thinking they're past their spending prime—are limiting their success. After all, boomers will continue to buy cars, travel, and indulge in expensive "toys" for themselves as well as presents for their kids and grandkids.[17] In fact, Gen X is the fastest growing group of consumers that spend full price for luxury items.[18] This point was driven home to one of the authors by the owner of a successful regional department store. He said "Let Dillard's target the 30- and 40-year-olds. I love having the seniors by myself. I just have to realize that every time a funeral goes by, it was probably one of my customers. Still more and more folks are getting older." Sadly, this chain was taken over by a larger retailer a decade ago and later filed Chapter 11 when the new operator repositioned it to appeal to "hip" 30- to 40-year-olds.

Besides understanding the various needs of each age segment, retailers must also understand what motivates consumers to spend money. Younger adults are by their very nature acquisition oriented. These first-time renters and home buyers need to acquire material objects and usually judge their progress by such possessions; older adults tend to conserve what they have. Therefore, as the population ages, a significant driving force for total economic growth may dry up unless retailers provide consumers with a reason to shop.

This "graying" of America will have enormous consequences for businesses beyond retailing as older consumers tend to be skeptical and less interested in shopping. Retailers must be able to speak the older consumers' language, avoid talking down to or patronizing them, shun "phony friendliness," and understand that, as they age, older consumers need easy-to-navigate store layouts and clearly labeled merchandise.[19]

It is doubtful however that all the baby boomers will behave as their parents did a generation before them. Retailers who make this assumption will be mistaken.

A 50-year-old in 2015 will not act like a 50-year-old in 1995. In fact, they may even keep some of the habits of a 30-year-old in 1995 (which is what they were) tempered with the wisdom of maturity. Many of these so-called Pepsi Generation types will probably enter the "gray market" kicking and screaming. They will demand that retailers embrace their values, such as youthfulness and invincibility, no matter what the product or service: food, insurance, entertainment, or medicine. Therefore, while some firms seek to meet the increased demand for health care services and travel, restaurants (where the over-60 category accounts for more than 30 percent of the breakfast and dinner trade) will have to consider such items as the design of their tables and seats, and financial service firms will have to reconsider their product offerings to this fixed-income category of consumers. This is especially true for women between 50 and 70 who have the time, money, and motivation to take control of their future but are unlikely to be swayed by flashy advertising.

In addition to altering the types of products offered to these aging segments of the population, retailers will also need to shift the types of services provided if they are to gain the consumers' dollar. In general, retailers will have to use bigger print, provide brighter lighting in parking lots, and install fewer displays that block store aisles. Also, they may need more handicap parking spaces in their parking lots or even offer valet parking services. They would also be wise to rethink the way they portray and target senior citizens in their advertising. Today's successful retailers will be those who come up with new and ingenious ways to not just attract this audience but also compel them to walk in the door. For instance, many shopping centers are considering the use of valet parking and lounges with concierge services that make not only shopping easier but also the shopper feel pampered. Once these consumers reach the store, the retailer's job is to convince them that there simply isn't another merchant that can cater to their needs and wishes. On a final note, retailers must also remember that a significant percentage of this group is media and technology savvy; younger consumers are not the only ones buying iPods, iPads, camera phones, and the like.

Although many retailers have some significant planning to do if they are to maintain their boomers' patronage, retailers must also not forget about the Gen Xers and Gen Yers. These two groups are not only different in age but also significantly different in their buying behavior. They will be difficult for retailers to reach without a well-planned and considered effort. In fact, because many of them grew up during the rapid advancements in technology and connectivity (instant messaging, camera phones, the Internet, and iPods), they are more technologically sophisticated than previous generations when it comes to shopping. For instance, when it comes to selecting a restaurant, Yers will commonly text friends or consult reviews on Yelp or Foursquare to validate their selection; rather than, for instance, rely on Zagat or just feel confident in their decision-making.[20] Also, because many have been hard hit by the tough economic times since 2008, and because they are tech savvy, they use their smartphones and tablet computers to help them find bargains or get short-term financing as discussed in this chapter's "What's New" box.[21] Many of the Gen Yers are now in their late 20s and early 30s, graduated from college, and pursuing professional careers. Thus, Brooks Brothers is developing new retail concepts, such as their Flatiron store, to cater to this group with a more casual and hip khaki alternative to the denim worn when they were younger. Predictably, at some point, Brooks Brothers hopes to serve this market as they get even older, with their traditional Brooks Brothers conservative apparel offering.[22] Similarly, Macy's which caters to many of the 76 million baby boomers recognizes that the 70 million Millennials will be the larger group in five years as the baby boomers inevitably face death. Consequently, they have developed distinct merchandising

Even as Brooks Brothers branches out into more modern stores and professional attire, it still maintains its traditional stores and attire which will become increasingly attractive as Gen Yers age.

strategies for the shoppers 13–22 and those 19–30 years of age. Unfortunately, Macy's must confront significant competition for these customer groups because fast-fashion retailers like Zara and H&M are popular with this age group.[23]

The shopping behavior for Gen Yers, for example, is based on different criteria than previous generations. They are concerned with how the product makes them appear and less concerned about the shopping process.[24] Some banks have even lured Gen Yers, not with low interest rates, but with online user friendliness whereby they can drag money from one account to another all on the same screen. Realizing the Yers' interests, many banks are even allowing their customers to set their own rules for transferring funds into savings accounts.[25]

Gen Yers also seem to be turned off by promotions that don't take them seriously. These anti-fashion and anti-establishment consumers still want entertainment or events when they shop; however, the promotions used must be relevant to them, funny, and say, "We understand." Retailers dealing with this market must also remember that 60 percent of 18- to 25-year-olds today rarely carry cash; instead they purchase with debit or credit cards, enticing some observers to call them "Generation P" (for plastic).[26] Finally, probably the biggest difference between the various generations is that 62 percent of web users under age 30 consider the Internet to be the best place to find good deals, while only 32 percent of users aged 65 and older do.[27]

Some retailers have also made a major mistake by overlooking the teenagers and so-called tweeners (those aged 8–14). These younger shoppers spend $40 billion annually and influence another $450 billion in purchases. Retailers of all sorts should target these shoppers in addition to their parents. After all, while their parents might cite price as the primary reason for purchasing a particular item for their children, "child request" was a close second. Teens and tweeners have trained their parents to

Daniel Acker/Bloomberg/Getty Images

While retailers like Abercrombie & Fitch and
A.E. might use sex appeal successfully to target
the high-school and college consumer, such an
approach may not be best for those targeting the
growing tween population, or their parents.

know what to buy for them. While many companies analyze which products appeal to
the older generations, retailers seldom think about marketing specifically to those under
the age of 20. Some retailers are using the Internet to reach out to these young consumers since most of them are more often at their computer than they are at the mall.

One company that has realized the power of the under-20 consumer is Aeropostale.
After originally targeting teenage males, the retailer shifted its strategy to take advantage
of the younger female market. Aeropostale realized that females tend to purchase more
clothes, and female fashion offers higher profit margins. Now instead of going head-
to-head with Abercrombie & Fitch and American Eagle Outfitters for the high-school
and college-age shoppers, the chain carries clothes that are slightly less sexy and revealing to appeal to tweeners and their parents. Aeropostale has also benefited from less
competition for the younger age group.

The recent recession has also introduced another trend for these under-20 shoppers:
buying secondhand. These retailers not only allow the consumer to save money but also
appeal to a growing ecofriendly sentiment among teenagers. Just as their parents discuss
"bargain conquests" at parties, these younger consumers talk of the coolness of getting a
super deal on those vintage jeans. Today's youth are really aware of what is happening to
their economy and to their families.[28]

WHAT'S NEW ?

PawnGo.com Helps Small Retailers Weather Tough Economic Times

It is unlikely that Isaac Newton ever thought about the financial markets when crafting his well-known Third Law of motion (i.e., for every action, there is an equal and opposite reaction), yet this law can easily be observed during any economic downturn, particularly the one the United States is still working to get out from under. Namely, when the financial markets become more volatile, banks hold onto their money more tightly.

Yet it's not uncommon for smaller retail operations to be in need of short-term financing to get themselves through the end of a quarter, fund next week's payroll, or cover the costs associated with a buying error. In such instances, the retailer is not looking to take on any more debt but a short-term solution that has no long-term effect either on its credit rating or debt structuring. Retail banking institutions, however, are often times not equipped to provide such a solution. The cost of the paperwork alone to provide a small loan, say $300 to fix a retailer's only delivery truck, precludes them from making such loans on a regular basis. Add in the "hurdles" of credit ratings, stability of the financial market, and the retailer's existing debt structure, and one can easily see how finding immediate funds for an unsecured, short-term loan is extremely difficult for all but the best of retailers—those less likely to need such assistance in the first place. Where then is the small, mom-and-pop retailer to turn?

One option is a pawn shop. And unless you're a fan of the History Channel's hit series *Pawn Stars*, you're likely thinking, "A pawn shop? Really?" The image that the word *pawn shop* evokes is often some seedy establishment, in some less-than-desirable part of town, full of less-than-desirable people. It's unlikely that you envisioned an institution providing a valuable service to the community similar to that of your local Bank of America.

But pawn shops are a unique and valuable type of lending institution. Loans are collateral-based and short-term in nature making them often times ideal for small retailers looking to get out of a quick jam. Given personal assets are put up as collateral for the loan, applications and credit checks are not used, and loan amounts are not formally reported as part of one's existing debt structure. Further, borrowers need not worry about overextending credit lines or the risk of bankruptcy if they default. Finally, given loans are short-term, principal payments, meaning money paid towards the actual loan amount, are rarely, if ever, collected. Borrowers simply make either a lump-sum payment at the end of the loan period or pay small interest payments on a monthly basis, with the principal due at termination of the loan period.

It's these properties that make pawn shops an ideal source for small retailers who are flush with valuable assets yet limited when it comes to cash on hand. The major factor discouraging more business owners from using such services is the dingy image associated with the pawn industry and personal embarrassment of borrowers needing to "hock" their valuables for cash.

Enter Todd Hill, founder of PawnGo.com, the world's first truly online pawn shop based in Centennial, Colorado (part of the Denver-Aurora metroplex). Having owned and operated pawn shops for over two decades, Mr. Hill was quite familiar with the business model and understood individuals', particularly business owners', desire for pawn services without physically having to carry one's possessions into a store to hock. He believed an online store could enhance the value proposition of a traditional pawn shop by enabling individuals to *discreetly* pawn one's assets for cash without having to feel any public embarrassment.

PawnGo offers small businesses the ability to borrow up to $1 million in less than 24 hours using items they already own as collateral a value proposition few retail banking institutions could provide. The process is simple, quick, and completely private. Prospective borrowers send PawnGo a description and digital photo of any item they wish to pawn. Upon receipt of these materials, an expert appraiser at PawnGo then replies with a loan offer. Once the borrower agrees to the loan amount, the item is sent via free overnight shipping

(continued)

to PawnGo, which deposits the money directly into the borrower's account.

Launched in September of 2011, PawnGo's "Small Business Lending Program" has been a huge success. In less than three months, it had loaned over $3 million in short-term business loans across 46 states. And the privacy component of operating online is a large component of this success. Prior to launching PawnGo, Hill's average loan amount within his bricks-and-mortar stores was approximately $125; online the average loan is $2,400.

An interesting side note to PawnGo's success is that in less than a year of PawnGo's launch, several online pawn shops, like Canada's PawnUp.com, have sprouted up. Soon retailers will be able to use the web to cross-shop pawn brokers for the best loan at the lowest rate possible.

Sources: Larsen, Dave (2011), "Businesses, Homeowners Turn to Pawn Shops for Loans – It's Nothing New, But It's More Prevalent as Bank Credit Lines Tighten," *Dayton Daily News*, August 14, 2011: E1; Brody, Aileen (2011) "PawnGo, the First Online Pawn Shop, Helps Small Businesses Stay Afloat with New Lending Program," *PRWeb Newswire* [online] Available at: www.prweb.com [Accessed: December 8, 2011]; Kornblatt, Lisa (2011) "Online Pawn Shop PawnGo Recognized by Jewelers' Circular Keystone Magazine as one of the '10 Things Rocking the Industry'," *PRWeb Newswire* [online] Available at: www.prweb.com [Accessed: February 10, 2012]; Brody, Aileen (2011) "Pawngo Sets the Standard for Online Pawn Shops With Outstanding Four-Month Numbers," *PRWeb Newswire* [online] Available at: www.prweb.com [Accessed: February 10, 2012].

Ethnic Trends

More than 160 years ago, Ralph Waldo Emerson wrote about America as the utopian product of a culturally and racially mixed "melting pot." Emerson explicitly welcomed the racial intermixing of whites and nonwhites, a highly controversial view during his lifetime. However, it is only in the last half-century that the United States has moved from a predominantly white population to a society rich in racial and ethnic diversity. Today non-Hispanic whites account for only 68 percent of the U.S. population.[29] Further, the ever-growing minority population is comprised of nearly as many Hispanics as blacks, surging numbers of Asians, and a small but growing Native American population. In fact, the U.S. Census Bureau now projects that by 2042 non-Hispanic whites will no longer make up the majority of the population. Instead, they are now expected to fall to 46 percent of the population by 2050, with the Hispanic population rising from 15 percent today to 30 percent by 2050. In addition, African Americans are expected to grow their current 13 percent to 15 percent and Asian Americans from 5 percent to almost 10 percent in 2050. Consequently, the term *minority* is likely to have a very different meaning in the next few decades.

Implications for Retailers[30]

Given the growth projections for the U.S. population overall, retailers must understand Hispanic shoppers and what is projected by 2015 to represent $1.5 trillion in purchasing power.[31] Today, 65 percent of them are under age 35, and they're an average of nine years younger than the overall U.S. population (27.3–36.4 years). However, probably the most important statistic to remember is that between now and 2020, the Hispanic American teen population will grow by 62 percent versus a 10-percent rate for all teens. In fact, by 2020 they will be the largest U.S. teen population, with 88 percent of them born in the United States. The U.S. Census Bureau estimates that by 2050, there will be 132.8 million Hispanics in the United States. JCPenney Company has been on the forefront in media spending directed at Hispanics, but other retailers are following suit, such as Walmart and Macy's. Macy's and other department stores probably need to pay more attention to the fact that Hispanics favor department stores and are quite loyal, when treated well and with respect. Because Hispanics are more likely to shop as a family, the average amount spent per shopping trip can be very attractive.

One of the two of the most common mistakes that retailers make when targeting Hispanics is assuming that their population in the United States is homogeneous.

Most U.S. Hispanics are Mexican, but some are from other Central and South American countries, others are from Spain, and even others are from Caribbean nations such as Cuba, the Dominican Republic, and Puerto Rico. Hispanics in Miami are culturally different from Hispanics in Houston. Also, many Hispanics are moving into the higher income ranks; for instance in 2010, there were over 1.5 million Hispanic families with a household income over $100,000 annually.[32]

The other common mistake made by retailers is that all Hispanics behave the same in the marketplace. Actually, second-generation Hispanic Americans, who have been immersed in American culture, are very different in their shopping behavior than foreign-born Hispanics. First generation Hispanics usually view themselves as completely Hispanic and have minimal contact with or interest in mainstream U.S. culture. However, as their language skills improve, many begin to adopt more mainstream cultural tendencies.

Yet recent consumer data suggests that even as Hispanics become more mainstream, they may maintain shopping tendencies that are unique relative to all shoppers in general. For example, Hispanic shoppers are more likely than the average shopper to know the brands of the products they are going to buy before they go shopping. Yet they are also significantly more likely to take time to browse while shopping, particularly for health and beauty related products, than the average shopper. Further, Hispanic shoppers, as a group, tend to place a higher level of importance on purchasing fresh foods over prepackaged items. One possible reason for this is that Hispanics, relative to all shoppers in general, derive a lot of personal satisfaction from cooking for their families.

Not to be ignored is the fact that African Americans, with a population of 40 million, currently make up 13 percent of the population with a purchasing power of $1.1 trillion. However, while their population is expected to grow to 60 million by 2050, their percentage of the overall population is likely to change by only a few percentage points. Retailers need to recognize the shopping habits of African Americans. For instance, when shopping for groceries, half of African Americans use a shopping list, almost half use coupons, and 61 percent use a frequent shopping card.[33] A recent study by Nielsen reveals among high income shoppers, African Americans spend 300 percent more than their

Relative to the average shopper, Hispanics are more likely to purchase fresh foods, like produce.

The proportion of the U.S. population that is Hispanic and African-American is expected to rise. Retailers will need to adjust their merchandising strategies to appeal to these market segments.

non-African counterparts at high end grocery stores.[34] An excellent source of information useful to retailers in understanding the African American consumer is www.reachingblackconsumers.com.

Conversely, the Asian American population, with 15 million consumers, 5 percent of the total population, and a purchasing power of $670 billion, is expected to double by 2050. You may have noticed that Asian teens and college students are frequent purchasers of fashionable apparel and designer labels. Compared to their white counterparts, they spend 30–40 percent more on apparel. However, if you want to observe an even more dramatic spending pattern on fashion, you need to look to the over 50 million Chinese that travel abroad annually.[35] Many of these are Chinese entrepreneurs that have made enormous fortunes over the last two decades or less; note that it is estimated that there were nearly one million millionaires in China in 2010 and over 270 billionaires. This group of jet setters, in 2010, spent $55 billion on international travel, and signs are this will be growing at 12–14 percent annually for at least the next decade, if not longer.[36] When headed for the United States, the popular destinations are New York City, San Francisco, and Los Angeles where they shop at the high-end fashion stores such as the Louis Vuitton flagship store in Manhattan.

Geographic Trends

The location of consumers in relation to the retailer will often affect how they buy. Retailers should be concerned, not only with the number of people, their ages, and their ethnicity, but also with where they reside. Consumers, especially as they age, will not travel great distances to make retail purchases. All consumers want convenience and will therefore tend to patronize local retail outlets. In fact, your proximity to a retail store is a strong determinant of whether you shop on the Internet for certain merchandise. For instance, if you live a block or two from an office supply store or consumer electronics store, you are less likely to buy office supplies and consumer electronics on the Internet. In this section of overall population trends, we take a closer look at how geographic trends affect retail operations.

Shifting Geographic Centers

Because the U.S. population for the past 200 years has been moving toward the West and the South, growth opportunities in retailing should be greatest in these areas. For example, between 2000 and 2010 the eight fastest-growing states were all in the West and South (Nevada, Arizona, Utah, Idaho, Texas, North Carolina, Georgia, and Florida, respectively).[37] In fact, between now and 2050, the South and West's populations are expected to grow by 44 percent and 45 percent, respectively, whereas the Midwest is expected to only grow 10 percent and the Northeast 7 percent. As will be pointed out later in this chapter, there are marked overall differences in the behavior of consumers based on the region in which they live.

Implications for Retailers

As consumers continue to shift in geographic location, Northeastern and Midwestern retailers are experiencing slower growth, and national retailers are adding stores and distribution centers (warehouses) in the South and West. As this trend continues, retailers must remember, for example, that when people in the North retire to the South, they generally will change the type and style of clothing they purchase year-round (both online and in stores). If the national chains don't plan for this, it could send shock waves up the supply chain all the way back to the textile manufacturers. As a result, it is important that retailers understand the purchasing behavior of consumers in each region of the country.

Yet a common mistake made by retailers is to assume that all consumers in a certain geographic area have the same purchasing habits. While households in the Northeast tend to marry later and spend more on education, food, housing, and apparel as a percentage of consumer expenditures,[38] they don't all spend that way. Midwesterners on average spend more on entertainment, tobacco, smoking supplies, and health care. Those in the South spend relatively more on transportation and make more cash contributions. Finally, those in the West spend more on alcoholic beverages, housing, and entertainment.[39]

Exhibit 3.4 contains another important lesson for retailers. Not only do consumers living in Texas have different consumption patterns than people living in other states but also Texas consumers are quite dissimilar from one another based on their location within the state. (Note the amount of lard used in west Texas, home of two of the authors. It is a common ingredient in many ethnic dishes, including Mexican food.) In fact, these same differences have been found to occur in different parts of the same city. As a result, many of the leading retailers have developed micromarketing merchandising strategies.

Micromarketing involves tailoring merchandise in each store to match the preferences of its neighborhood. It is made possible with the use of the optional stock list approach, discussed in Chapter 1, and computer software programs that match neighborhood demographics with product demand. For example, two of the biggest Sears stores in the area are nearly the same size and do about the same in annual dollar sales; yet the merchandise makeup of the two is quite different. The urban store, which is close to many gourmet bakeries, doesn't carry bread makers, but bread makers are popular items in the more upscale suburban store 15 miles away. The same thing occurs with Macy's in Cincinnati, where the downtown Fountain Place Macy's displays luggage more prominently than other Cincinnati stores because the downtown store attracts more business travelers than other locations, perhaps people attending conventions. Meanwhile, consumers boosted sales of high-end denim at the chain's Kenwood store, a trend that was not as strong with shoppers at other Macy's stores in the region.[40]

micromarketing
Is the tailoring of merchandise in each store to the preferences of its neighborhood.

Exhibit 3.4
Texas Consumers' Percentage of National Average Usage

Product	Dallas/Fort Worth (%)	Houston (%)	San Antonio/ Corpus Christi (%)	West Texas/ New Mexico (%)
Biscuits/Dough	148*	122	103	85
Butter	51	57	39	57
Fresh Eggs	94	112	141	110
Juice/RFG	74	104	76	66
Lard	26	121	**	419
Canned Ham	39	21	22	28
Sausage	134	179	219	73
Baked Beans	82	76	51	60
Cocktail Mixes	118	79	82	112
Pasta	71	80	72	76
Rice/Popcorn Cakes	84	69	58	73
Cosmetics	237	133	329	221
Cold/Sinus Tab/Cough Drops	157	113	125	105
Deodorant	119	118	125	86
Hair Coloring	137	122	238	130
Laxatives	152	116	164	117
Cat Food	88	73	81	67
Diapers	115	135	160	74
Facial Tissue	82	66	64	78
Paper Napkins	71	74	78	68
Motor Oil	112	92	279	114
Shoe Polish & Accessories	147	145	171	147
Tape	163	105	175	149
Hosiery	164	126	156	110

*National average = 100%
**Not measured in this market.

Source: Used with the permission of SymphonyIRI Group

Urban Centers

metropolitan statistical areas (MSA)
Are freestanding urban areas with populations in excess of 50,000.

Most of the U.S. population resides in metropolitan areas with populations greater than 50,000, which the U.S. Census Bureau calls **metropolitan statistical areas** (MSAs). The proportion of the population residing in these cities has increased dramatically, from 64 percent in 1950 to 84 percent today. However, the urban or metropolitan population varies considerably by state. For instance, Massachusetts, Rhode Island, and New Jersey are more than 99 percent metropolitan; whereas Vermont, Montana, and Wyoming are less than 35 percent metropolitan.[41] Further, in the past the migration to MSAs was directed more toward suburban than central city areas, yet some experts feel that a significant increase in gas prices may reverse this trend.

Implications for Retailers

Every shift in consumer population patterns has major implications for retailers, especially when it comes to expenditures made for household products. While these recent shifts have resulted in a slowdown for downtown retail activity, sales increases in free-standing suburban locations have more than offset any decline.

There are also opportunities for retailers in smaller markets. During the past decade, retail activity has grown rapidly in secondary markets, areas with populations less than 50,000. Historically, most chain retailers have ignored these markets. But in addition to their rapid growth, secondary markets are attractive because of the low level of retail competition, lower building costs, cheaper labor, and fewer building and zoning regulations. As MSAs have begun to stabilize, secondary markets have become more attractive.

Mobility

In many countries, people are born, raised, married, widowed, and die in the same city or immediate geographic vicinity. While this was once true in the United States, it certainly is not characteristic of contemporary America. Typically, Americans change residence about a dozen times in a lifetime. This is twice the rate of the British and French and four times as often as the Irish. Two major factors for this heightened mobility is the country's divorce rate and state or regional economic slowdown and hence loss of jobs that varies across the country. Of the 12 percent of the population that moved in 2010, about 75 percent remained in the same county, about 25 percent moved to a new county but stayed in the same state, and approximately 8 percent moved to a new state. (Note the percentages total more than 100 percent due to some Americans having moved more

A large urban city is often composed of many smaller markets or neighborhoods such as this Chinese neighborhood in San Francisco. Retailers operating in these neighborhoods need to adjust their merchandise and services to serve the local markets.

than once that year).[42] Retailers must remember that the farther one moves from a prior residence, the more one needs to establish new retail shopping patterns.

Implications for Retailers

A study regarding mobility has found that in almost half of large families, where the children don't go to college, one child will live within five miles of the parent(s) when the parent(s) reaches age 60, and in more than three-quarters of the cases within 50 miles of the parent(s).[43] Thus, with the recent trend toward higher education (discussed in the next learning objective), which results in more job variations over one's lifetime, retailers can only expect consumer mobility to increase. This presents a problem because retailers serve local markets and tend to cater to well-defined demographic groups. If the population moves, the retailer may find that its target market no longer resides in its immediate area. Likewise, retailers in areas undergoing rapid population growth will want to be prepared to serve these new consumers quickly as many retail-oriented decisions must be made on the spot. After a move, consumers must locate new sources for food, clothing, household goods, and recreation. This presents an advantage for chain stores, since a consumer moving from Des Moines, Iowa, to Baton Rouge, Louisiana, knows what to expect at a Men's Warehouse, T.J. Maxx, Pier One, Old Navy, Brake Max, or Macy's.

LO 2

Social Trends

List the social trends that retail managers should regularly monitor and describe their impact on retailing.

In this section, we continue our examination of demographic factors affecting the modern retailer by looking at several social trends: the increasing level of educational attainment, the state of marriage and divorce, the makeup of the American household, and the changing nature of work. To get the most current data regarding these trends, the reader should visit the home page of the Commerce Department's Census Bureau website (http://census.gov). This site provides easy access to the latest census figures.

Education

The education level of the average American is increasing. In 2010, 87 percent of individuals aged 25 years and older had a high school degree, and 30 percent had a bachelor's or advanced college degree.[44] Gen Xers, who were between ages 33 and 45 in 2010, are the most educated generation ever. (However, as soon as the last members of Gen Y reach age 25, they will become the most educated.) One in three has completed at least four years of college, which is almost as high as the 38 percent of those 25 years and older in 1960 who had a high school degree.[45] Currently, the percentages of men and women receiving *at least* a four-year college degree are equal at 30 percent each;[46] however, figures suggest this trend is rapidly changing given nearly 30 percent more women than men have enrolled in college *each year* since 2000.[47] As a result, it is forecast that by 2020 women—who are increasingly pursuing higher-paying career fields such as business, psychology, biology and life sciences, and engineering—will earn nearly 60 percent of the bachelor's and master's degrees in U.S. colleges and universities.[48]

Implications for Retailers

Educational attainment, which is very closely linked to parents' education, is the single most reliable indicator of a person's income potential, attitudes, and spending habits. Thus, college-educated consumers differ in their buying behavior from other workers of the same age and income levels. They are more alert to price, quality, and advertised claims. However, when retailers use education to segment the marketplace, they often overlook the 33.6 million Americans over age 25 who have some college experience but who failed to earn a degree. In many ways, people with some college best define the term "average" American.[49] They have more money than high school graduates but less than college graduates.[50] They also fall between these groups in their propensity to shop in department stores, spend on apparel, buy new cars, travel, read books, watch TV, and invest in stocks and bonds.

Since education levels for the population, in aggregate, are expected to continue to rise, retailers can expect consumers to become increasingly sophisticated, discriminating, and independent in their search for consumer products. They will also demand a staff capable of intelligently dealing with their needs and wants.

State of Marriage

A relatively new social phenomenon has occurred during the last 40 years. In 1970, less than 10 percent of the U.S. male population between ages 30 and 34 had never married, and slightly more than 6 percent of the same female population had never married. In 2010, these percentages had increased to 37 and 27 percent, respectively.[51] Married couples are one of the slowest-growing household types not only in this country but also worldwide. In 1970, males married at a median age of 23 and females at 21; today, the median age for males is about 28 and 26 for females; however, there are marked regional differences in these numbers.[52] Not only are many people postponing marriage but also some are choosing not to marry at all. In the 45- to 54-year-old age bracket, 15 percent of males and 11 percent of females have never been married.[53] In the United States overall, 28 percent of households are solo households, and this is also a trend in other developed countries. For instance, in Sweden it is 47 percent, Britain 34 percent, Japan 31 percent, and Italy 29 percent.[54]

Implications for Retailers

This trend toward single-person households presents many opportunities for the retailer because of the increased need for a larger number of smaller houses complete with home furnishings. This is especially true for the young adult market. As a result, retailers may need to adjust their store hours to accommodate the needs of this market. In addition, with more men living alone, supermarkets will have to direct promotions toward their needs and habits, particularly since men tend to focus on getting specific items and then getting out of the store as quickly as possible.

Divorce

Since 1960, the U.S. divorce rate has increased by 250 percent. While many have offered potential explanations for this trend, few have given as compelling a justification as Professor Gary Becker of the University of Chicago. Professor Becker was awarded the Nobel Prize for theorizing that families, just like businesses, rationally make decisions that maximize benefits. The theory suggests that in the traditional family, working husbands and stay-at-home wives each performed labor that, when combined, provided the greatest payoff for the time involved. However, as women's wages rose, it became more profitable for them to enter the labor force. As a result, spouses became less dependent on each other and divorce rates increased. An interesting side effect of the soft economy over the last five years is that unemployed spouses became more dependent on the one that had a job, and they were less likely to divorce even if unhappy with their marriage. This trend extended to when both partners were unemployed since there was often little choice but to stay married and try to survive in one household.

As the economy has started to recover and people are moving off unemployment, you can expect a rise in divorces and, as explained earlier, this is generally good for retailers. As an aside, an interesting statistic is that the average divorce occurs approximately 7.2 years after marriage, confirming the conventional wisdom about the proverbial seven-year itch.

Implications for Retailers

When a divorce occurs, many retail purchases are required. A second household, quite similar to that of the never-married individual, is formed almost immediately. These new households need certain items such as furniture and kitchen appliances, televisions and stereos, and even linens. However, they also may be more prone to need or seek more services such as exercise, beauty care, and entertainment that help them to prepare to re-enter the market for another mate. Divorce may also impact the way people shop once they are settled into their new homes. Retailers must make specific adjustments for divorced, working women with children by adjusting store hours, providing more consumer information, and changing the product assortment.[55]

Makeup of American Households

Because households are the basic consumer unit for most products, household growth and consumer demand go hand-in-hand. Yet, because of the differing sizes and habits of various generations, the change in the makeup of households is notoriously hard to predict. The number of households without children increased 18 percent in the 1980s, 11 percent in the 1990s, and 12 percent between 2000 and 2010. In fact, most people are unaware that 55 percent of all households have no children.[56]

Some interesting trends have also occurred over the last two decades. For example, between 1990 and 2010 the number of people living alone ("home aloners") increased by 37 percent to approximately 31.4 million households.[57] This trend, which represents over one-fourth of all households, is the result of an increased desire for privacy, an increase in young adults delaying marriage, an increase in never marrieds, and a large increase in the number of people who live alone after the death of a spouse. Also, the number of unmarried couples ("mingles") has increased by 383 percent from just over 1.3 million in 1980 to just over 6.5 million in 2010.[58] This trend, although it represents only 6 percent of all couple households,[59] is significant to the retailer because it represents a purchasing unit that is hard to understand by conventional household or family norms. The retailer, as well as the social scientist, has little knowledge of how much joint decision making occurs in such a household.

Finally, there are two more interesting facts about the changing American household. The first is called the **boomerang effect**—so called because the parents think the children have left the household for good, but they keep coming back. This was particularly true during the recent recession. The online job site Monster.com reported that nearly half of all 2008 graduates returned home after graduation and that 4 out of 10 from the previous year's class were still living with their parents.[60] Others analysts estimate that, over the next decade, 40 percent of children will return to live with their parents after having previously left. While this projection is extremely sensitive to future economic conditions, several factors will account for the projected 7 million boomerang households: People who marry in their 20s are just as likely to divorce as those who marry as teens, high-school dropouts will not be able to find permanent work, and so on. In addition, when the average college grad owes nearly $20,000 in student loans and has almost $2,900 in credit card debt, living with the folks helps.[61] The second factor to alter the makeup of the American household involves the situation in which parents of the

boomerang effect
The recent trend of children returning to live with their parents after having already moved out.

household's head or spouse move in to live with their children. Often these parents are not healthy enough to live full-time by themselves, but their health is not so bad that they need full-time assistance in a nursing home. When this occurs, it is often referred to as a **sandwich generational family** or **trigenerational family**: all three generations (parents, grandparents, and children) are under the same roof.

sandwich generational family (or) trigenerational family
Occurs when three generations (parents, grandparents, and children) live together in the same house.

Implications for Retailers

Today, the combination of so-called home-aloners, mingles, singles, dinks (dual-income, no-kids households), and empty nesters accounts for nearly 75 percent of all U.S. households. This market is not concerned about back-to-school sales and other family-oriented retail activities. Instead, they're more interested in HDTVs, high social image, and gourmet foods. However, it is important that retailers recognize the differences within this market. Younger women normally spend more on clothing, and men spend more on alcohol, cars, and eating out. As they age, women begin to spend more than men on cars and entertainment while men remain the best customers for eating out. The older segment of the single-household market will require special attention from today's retailers. Between now and 2015, the "wild and crazy single guys" of the 1980s and early 1990s will turn into "tired and pudgy older guys" who no longer live like college students, although some may wish they could. Incidentally, those young people who were part of the boomerang effect we discussed earlier will at some point move out, and retailers will benefit from this trend.[62]

Changing Nature of Work

In the United States and other industrialized economies, work has become less central to one's life. In the past, work was often the way people identified themselves and obtained meaning in their lives. Perhaps because of deterioration in institutional confidence or the overall prosperity of our economy, as Americans we identify less with our employment. At the same time, peoples' hobbies are becoming more work oriented. Many are gardening, investing time and money in learning to cook, developing photography skills, and doing projects around the house. At the same time, we continue to see a rise in self-employed and home-based workers. In 2010 there were nearly 14.9 million incorporated and unincorporated self-employed individuals.[63] However, as a result of the recent recession, these numbers are expected to increase in the coming years. Luckily, the explosive growth of the Internet and cloud computing have allowed many people to set up home-based businesses.

In addition to working from home or running a home business, many consumers are obtaining meaning from consumption. They have literally become durable goods junkies, collecting RVs, boats, workshops, HDTVs, swimming pools, and so on. To pay for these extras, these people often hold several jobs. In 2010, approximately 6.9 million individuals had multiple jobs.[64] Many of these individuals were starting a small business while holding onto their main job; others were earning money to purchase something special, saving for future consumption, or saving for retirement.

Implications for Retailers

Because people are finding less meaning in their work, they are less loyal to their employers. Nineteen percent of all workers have held their job for fewer than 12 months, and the median length of service in a job is 4.4 years.[65] For entry-level personnel in retailing, turnover approaches 75 percent or more per year. Consequently, retailers need to find ways to enrich job experiences and lower turnover. One study found that turnover in the supermarket industry cost $5.8 billion annually. For instance, a cashier who departs costs the retailer $4,212; a department manager, $9,354; and a store manager, $56,844. These costs of employee turnover include paperwork errors, inventory shrinkage, and improper use of equipment. All of these errors occur due to the lack of experience of new employees. These errors lead to lower levels of customer service and satisfaction, which in turn leads to lost sales and profits.[66] One major opportunity for retailers is employing home-based and disabled workers. Home-based workers can handle telephone inquiries and do clerical work or bookkeeping. Likewise, disabled workers may represent a previously untapped pool of talent for the retailer.

Finally, since many individuals are holding multiple jobs, retailers can tap into this pool of individuals for part-time workers. Retailers have done this in the past, primarily at the clerk level. Today, there are opportunities for retailers to employ part-timers in a variety of positions, including accounting, inventory control, merchandising, buying, and store management.

LO 3

Describe the changing economic trends and their effects on retailing.

Economic Trends

In this section, we look at the effects of income growth, the declining rate of personal savings, the increase in the number of working women, and the widespread use of credit on the modern retailer.

Income Growth

In 2010, the median household income was slightly over $60,000, which is a 70 percent increase over the median household income in 1990 (as measured in 2010 dollars).[67] However, not all consumer groups have equally shared in this income increase. When measured in 2010 dollars, the median income of African American and Asian, Pacific-Islander households grew 80 percent and 77 percent, respectively, while Hispanic and Caucasian household incomes grew 70 percent each between 1990 and 2010.[68]

As Exhibit 3.5 points out, incomes are continuing to shift among the various classes of Americans. Today, the American upper classes have a higher share of the nation's aggregate income in comparison to 1980. Further, the top fifth of Americans, those making more than $100,000, accounts for 50.3 percent of the nation's income while the bottom two-fifths, or the 40 percent of Americans who make less than $38,550, account for only 12 percent of the nation's income, down from 14.6 percent in 1980. However, this data is partially misleading because income mobility in the United States is quite

Exhibit 3.5

Share of Aggregate Income Received by Each Fifth and the Top 5% of U.S. Households, 1980–2009

Year	Fifth Lowest	Fifth Second	Fifth Third	Fifth Fourth	Highest Fifth	Top 5%
2009	3.4	8.6	14.6	23.2	50.3	21.7
2000	4.3	9.8	15.4	22.7	47.7	21.1
1990	4.6	10.8	16.6	23.8	44.3	17.4
1980	5.3	11.6	17.5	24.4	41.1	14.6

Source: US Census Bureau, Income, Poverty and Health Insurance Coverage in the United States: 2009, *Current Population Reports*, P60–238, and Historical Tables H1 and H2, September 2010. See also: http://www.census.gov/hhes/www/income.html and http://www.census.gov/hhes/www/income/data/historical/household/index.html. (accessed 9/22/2012)

high. For example, during the 10-year period between 1996 and 2005, over half of all taxpayers moved to a different income quintile (i.e., one-fifth of the population), over half of those in the bottom quintile in 1996 moved up at least one income bracket by 2005, while 75 percent of the top 1 percent of wage earners in 1996 fell at least one income bracket by 2005.[69] Consequently, it is quite possible that those that are rich today will be poorer in the future and vice versa.

Implications for Retailers

The imbalance in income growth across households has created an increased demand for value-oriented retailers such as Costco, Dollar Tree, TJX Companies, and other discounters and manufacturers' outlets. In addition, it explains why many of the upscale retailers (such as Ralph Lauren, Tiffany & Co., Whole Foods Market, Nordstrom, and Neiman Marcus) before the recent recession had not suffered the economic pressures that many of their lower-scale counterparts faced. Retailers of luxury automobiles, lavish foreign vacations, and executive-style houses in gated communities had also done well.

disposable income
Is personal income less personal taxes.

discretionary income
Is disposable income minus the money needed for necessities to sustain life.

Economists tend to view income from two different perspectives: disposable and discretionary. **Disposable income** is simply all personal income minus personal taxes. For most consumers, disposable income is their take-home pay. **Discretionary income** is disposable income minus the money needed for necessities to sustain life, such as minimal housing, transportation, food, and clothing. Retailers who sell necessities, such as supermarkets, like to see incomes rise and taxes decrease. These retailers know that, while consumers won't spend all their increased disposable income on the retailer's merchandise, they will nevertheless increase spending. Retailers who sell luxury goods want to see discretionary income increase. However, the recent economic slowdown has had a negative effect on both types of incomes as the value of the houses and stock market portfolios declined during this slowdown. In addition, many workers lost jobs, and others were forced to take pay cuts. As a result of these factors, the net worth of

Jeff Greenberg/Alamy

As discretionary income rises, men and women can shop for more luxury-type items, like men's ties, that must be overlooked when a household's income is tight.

Americans fell almost 20 percent in 2008. This was the first decline in American household net worth since 2002.[70] For the bottom 80 percent of households the relatively rapid rise in food and gas prices since 2009 have been especially difficult.[71] Consequently, shoppers are becoming more focused on value and quality, and this is especially true in apparel where clothing needs to last longer because the consumer simply needs to first cover the necessities of life such as shelter, transport, and food.[72]

Another, often overlooked, implication for retailers is that many Americans now use the Internet, especially eBay, and Craig's List, as a source to sell unwanted or unneeded merchandise and increase their income. This is especially evident during the first quarter of the year when many Americans use eBay to get rid of that unwanted Christmas scarf or that tie from Aunt Bessie. In fact, a whole new industry has developed to assist consumers who don't use eBay regularly. Drop shops, which will handle the entire selling process for a fee, are listed on eBay's website. Others may "regift" the unwanted merchandise to someone else or donate the item to charity. Also, during the recent recession, many pawn shops experienced a significant increase in business. In the past, pawn shop customers had an average household income of about $29,000. However, this increased to more than $50,000 as middle- and upper-middle-class customers faced ravaged stock portfolios, tightened bank credit, and unexpected layoffs and needed quick cash. In areas dogged by high unemployment and foreclosure rates, the pawn business was especially robust.[73] All of these activities are a variation on garage sales: The seller not only gets rid of stuff he or she doesn't need but also, in many cases, raises spending money.

Personal Savings

A major criticism of the U.S. economic system is that it does not reward personal saving. Expressed as a percentage of disposable income, savings had dwindled from a post–World War II high of 8.8 percent in 1981 to 6.5 percent in 1990, to a dismal 1.4 percent in 2005; however, the trend appears to be changing, as Americans saved 5.9 percent in 2009 and 5.8 percent in 2010.[74] While it appears that the recession of 2008–2009 has altered the savings habits of many Americans, particularly those closer to retirement, many continue to view investing in the stock market as a form of saving despite the risk.

It should also be pointed out that the government's numbers regarding the savings rates fail to address the treatment of capital gains or losses. When the government measures disposable income, it counts wages, interest earned, and dividends; however, it overlooks realized or unrealized capital gains or losses. Consequently, changes in wealth that result from variations in home and equity values are omitted. The government's numbers also count the full cost of purchases made over time—such as cars and appliances. Thus, the government's data tends to undervalue savings because it fails to consider the wealth effect. The *wealth effect* claims that for every $100 of additional wealth generated in an individual's stock market holdings, that individual will spend $4 (4 percent). Such spending lowers the nation's savings rate because, as the stock market rises, spending increases without an increase in wages and salaries. Savings will also be decreased in this example because the government will subtract taxes on the stock market gains from disposable income. While the net wealth of the United States increased by 82 percent between 1992 and 2000, it only increased by 39 percent from 2000 to 2008. Such growth encouraged Americans to spend freely, which in turn furthered the overall economic growth of the country. However, in the last quarter of 2007, net wealth began to fall as stock and housing values slipped. Obviously, these decreases in property values or stock prices will present problems for retailers.[75]

One additional point should also be made. Although the national savings rate in the United States is only a fraction of the rates in Europe, Japan, and China, it must be remembered that each country measures income and savings differently. Thus, comparisons between countries are often unclear.

Implications for Retailers

Retailers have enjoyed continued sales growth over the past decade; however, this growth is not due to significant increases in household income. Instead, retailers have benefited from the spending rather than saving mindset of the consumer. Yet retailers must be prepared for the next decade, when baby boomers and Gen Xers plan for retirement while simultaneously reducing their spending and increasing their savings.

Some economists fear that in another decade retired boomers will begin to remove much of their money from the stock market. If this occurs in great numbers, then the United States could see another declining market that would likely result in a reverse wealth effect. This is because consumers losing money in the stock market tend to save about four cents for every dollar lost (4 percent). Another fear is that because of good health, many boomers may postpone retirement, leading to a surplus in labor supply. As the marketplace becomes saturated with available workers, overall wages fall, which could negatively impact future retail sales.[76]

Women in the Labor Force

Over the past five decades, women have become a dominant factor in the labor force. In 1970, 43 percent of all women over age 16 were in the labor force; today it is just under 59 percent;[77] however, that number climbs to over 72 percent for women with college degrees.[78] This growing trend of women in the labor force is true of all age groups, even women aged 25–34, who might be expected to be raising families. Seventy-five percent of all women aged 25–34 are currently in the labor force;[79] yet this high percentage is not simply due to the postponement of having children. Instead, the percentage of working, married women with preschoolers increased from 30 percent in 1970 to 62 percent in 2010.[80] And these "working moms" aren't just those lucky enough to work for an employer that provides flexible work schedules. Just over one-quarter of all working women with children under the age of six have flexible work schedules.[81] Many likely turn to day-care related retailers or rely on the father to pick up some of the child-rearing responsibilities as just over 30 percent of men with children under the age of six have flexible work schedules—the most of any males in the labor force.[82]

This significant rise in the number of working women has protected many households from inflation and recession. In fact, many economists suggest that the working woman has been the nation's secret weapon against economic hardships. For example, the median household income for married households where both spouses are in the workforce increased over 15 percent (adjusting for inflation) between 1990 and 2010 to almost $86,000.[83] In addition to the working wife, another reason for the huge increase in household income for dual wage-earner families is that, where once a professional man would marry a secretary, nurse, or school teacher (all admirable occupations, but not the highest paying), today many professional men are marrying professional women. As a result, the household income for these couples is increasing faster than the norm. This is not only another cause of the polarization of income shown in Exhibit 3.6, but also creating a new social phenomenon in America—couples too tired for sex.[84]

Implications for Retailers

The rise in the number of working women has many retail implications. First, as the number of dual wage-earner families increases, many of these families have less time for shopping and are more prone to looking for convenience and additional services from retailers. Working men and women are often unable to shop between the hours of 8 a.m. and 6 p.m. Monday through Saturday. Thus, these individuals prefer that retailers hold sales and special events in the evenings or on weekends. Time-pressed shoppers also find that price is sometimes less important than convenience, availability, and service. Bricks-and-mortar retailers—in addition to making the shopping experience pleasant, if not exciting—must develop strategies that accommodate these customers' needs. They must extend store hours (early mornings, evenings, and weekends) and offer conveniences (express checkouts). Bricks-and-mortar retailers should also provide alternatives to in-store shopping, such as catalogs, online shopping, and even delivery if they want to compete for the time-pressed shopper's store loyalty.

Widespread Use of Credit

Retailers, especially department stores and those selling big-ticket items, have long offered their own credit cards to customers. However, today the trend is away from the retailer's store-branded cards and toward third-party cards (Visa, MasterCard, Discover, American Express, etc.). Spurred on in recent years by active promotional campaigns and low interest rates, consumers in 2006 were staggering under an estimated $2.2 trillion in consumer debt.[85] In the United States, more than 70 percent of households have at least one general purpose credit card, and more than 85 percent of households with annual incomes over $50,000 have at least two credit cards.[86]

Credit card firms are seeking for the trend to continue. They offer promotional incentives such as free airline miles, rebates on new auto purchases, and rebates on future purchases. For the retailer, credit card use has increased sales and profits. Consequently, retailers as varied as supermarkets and the family veterinarian are now forced to accept these third-party cards. Other retailers, such as Kroger, Walmart, Nordstrom, and Toys "R" Us, are now co-branding their names with the national card issuers.

Implications for Retailers

Retailers benefit from credit cards. Research shows that customers spend more when they use a credit card than when they must pay in cash. However, since the growth in credit has been outstripping the growth in personal income, it is evident that households will face a liquidity crisis as income growth slows or becomes negative. After all, more than 25 percent of households rarely pay off their credit card balance.[87] Such massive debt loads must be paid off, and that activity will negatively impact future retail sales. Finally, as noted earlier, today's college grad owes nearly $20,000 in student loans and has almost $2,900 in credit card debt. No wonder so many young people postpone getting married, having children, and buying a first house.

LO 4

Consumer Behavior Model

Discuss the consumer shopping and purchasing model.

Now that we have examined the population, social, and economic trends of today, we can develop a model that describes and, to some degree, predicts how these factors come together to affect consumer buying patterns. We call this the *consumer shopping and purchasing model*. Consumers are typically confronted with fundamental decisions when it comes to meeting their needs and wants: What products or brands can potentially fulfill their needs, and where should they purchase these products or brands? Our model is sufficiently general to deal with both of these questions.

Examine the consumer shopping and purchasing model in Exhibit 3.6. This model suggests that consumer behavior is a process with a series of stages or steps. The six

Exhibit 3.6
Consumer Shopping and Purchasing Model

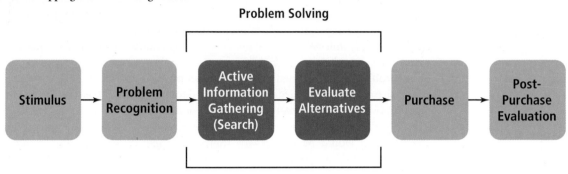

stages in the model are stimulus, problem recognition, search, evaluation of alternatives, purchase, and post-purchase evaluation.

Stimulus

A **stimulus** involves a cue (external to the individual) or drive (internal to the individual). A **cue** is any object or phenomenon in the environment that is capable of eliciting a response. Common examples of retail marketing stimuli are advertisements, point-of-purchase displays, coupons, salespeople, and free samples. All of these examples are cues controlled by the seller or retailer. In addition, there are cues that the retailer does not control. For example, word-of-mouth advertising is common in retailing. Many visits to e-tailing sites are the result of a visitor having a good experience and telling others.

A second type of stimulus is internal to the individual and is referred to as a *drive*. A **drive** is a motivating force that directs behavior. Drives can be physiologically based (hunger and the need to stay warm in the cold) or learned (the desire to spend spring break in Cancun). When drives are strong, they are more likely to prompt purchase behavior. The old adage "never go grocery shopping when you are hungry" illustrates this point.

Individuals can be exposed to both types of stimuli. For instance, one may see an advertisement (cue) for a restaurant at the same time that one is hungry (drive); a person living in Minnesota may be coping with a long, cold winter and browsing the Internet when she sees an advertisement for a vacation on the warm and sunny beaches of Hawaii.

As consumers move through their daily routines in an information economy, they are constantly exposed to hundreds of messages regarding products, services, and where to purchase them. As a result, one of the scarcest resources is human attention. All retailers are competing with virtually all other organizations and individuals for the consumer's attention. Consequently, the individual is always involved in **passive information gathering**, which is the task of receiving and processing information regarding the existence and quality of merchandise, services, stores, shopping convenience, parking, advertising, and any other factor that a consumer might consider in making a decision of where to shop and what to purchase.

Problem Recognition

Stimuli can often lead to problem recognition. **Problem recognition** occurs when the consumer's desired state of affairs departs sufficiently from the consumer's actual state of affairs. When this happens, the consumer is in a state of unrest until he or she finds

stimulus
Refers to a cue that is external to the individual or a drive that is internal to the individual.

cue
Refers to any object or phenomenon in the environment that is capable of eliciting a response.

drive
Refers to a motivating force that directs behavior.

passive information gathering
Is the receiving and processing of information regarding the existence and quality of merchandise, services, stores, shopping, convenience, pricing, advertising, and any other factors that a consumer might consider in making a purchase.

problem recognition
Occurs when the consumer's desired state of affairs departs sufficiently from the actual state of unrest.

a way to resolve this difference. Consider a few examples: (1) While driving across town, you notice that your car's gas tank is almost empty; (2) you hear an advertisement for a new Sony CD player and realize that your 10-year-old stereo needs replacing; (3) you will be graduating from college shortly and do not own any suitable clothes for your new career; and (4) you receive your tax refund and realize you now have money to go to Cancun for spring break.

Not all problems will stimulate the same level of problem-solving activity. The level of one's desire to resolve a particular problem depends on two factors: the magnitude of the gap between the consumer's desired and actual states, and the importance of the problem. Consider the previous example of the gas tank. If your tank were a quarter full, the problem would be less urgent than if the gas gauge were on empty. Next, compare your recognition of the problem about replacing your old CD player with your recognition of the problem of acquiring a new career wardrobe. In all probability, one of these problems is more important to you, and thus you would be more motivated to solve it first.

Problem Solving

The next two stages in the consumer shopping and purchasing model—active information-gathering (or search) and evaluation of alternatives—will determine the degree of problem solving that occurs. Individuals solve problems by searching for information and then evaluating their options or alternatives. The search for information and careful evaluation of alternatives occurs to reduce risk. If consumers do not select the best product, they can incur financial loss (financial risk), personal harm (safety risk), or the decline of respect from family and friends (social risk). Shoppers are finding the Internet and smartphone apps an efficient and effective way to help them solve their purchasing problems. They use the Internet to search for peer ratings on brands, to get advice from friends and the blogsphere, and to find the best price at stores nearby or from e-tailers.

The amount of problem-solving activity consumers engage in varies considerably, depending on their prior experience and the need to reduce financial, personal, and social risk. Consumers learn quickly, and when they locate the product, brands, and retailers that are good at satisfying their needs at a low or acceptable level of risk, then the degree of problem solving decreases. Exhibit 3.7 illustrates the three levels of problem solving. Note that these levels are determined by whether or not the consumer has a strong preference for a specific brand or retail store.

Exhibit 3.7
Degrees of Consumer Problem Solving in Shopping and Purchasing

Brand Preference \ Retailer Preference	Strong	None or Weak
Strong	Habitual Problem Solving	Limited Problem Solving
None or Weak	Limited Problem Solving	Extended Problem Solving

Habitual Problem Solving

habitual problem solving

Occurs when the consumer relies on past experiences and learns to convert the problem into a situation requiring less thought. The consumer has a strong preference for the brand to buy and the retailer from which to purchase it.

With **habitual problem solving**, the consumer relies on past experience and learning to convert the problem into a situation requiring less thought. Here the consumer has a strong preference for the brand to buy and the retailer from which to purchase it. Some consumers are not only habitual users of products but also heavy users. For instance, in fast-food restaurants, only one in five persons is a heavy user; however, they account for 60 percent of fast-food restaurant visits.[88]

By relying on past experience, the consumer has already arrived at an adequate solution to many of their more routine problems. Frequently purchased products of relatively low cost and low risk (e.g., toothpaste, milk, bread, soda pop) tend to belong in this category; however, products of a higher value may also be in this category. For example, when confronted with the need for a new automobile, some people can be loyal to both a particular brand and a specific retailer. Such individuals may be loyal to Ford and may patronize a favorite Ford dealer in their geographic area.

Limited Problem Solving

limited problem solving

Occurs when the consumer has a strong preference for either the brand or the store, but not both.

Limited problem solving occurs when the consumer has a strong preference for either the brand or the store but not both. The consumer may not have a store choice in mind but may have a strong preference for the brand to purchase. In this instance, since the brand has already been determined, the consumer has, in a sense, restricted the problem-solving process to deciding which retailer to patronize among those that carry the brand. Because the consumer may not be aware of all the retailers that carry the item, some searching may be required. To illustrate further, assume the picture tube on your TV fails and you decide to get a new TV. You know that you want a Sony, but since you are new in town, you do not know where to get the best deal. Also, you recognize that your search does not need to be limited to retailers in your community, and the Internet can help you locate the retailer with the lowest price. You prefer a local retailer who can service your set; however, you have decided that this additional convenience is not worthwhile if the local retailer's price is more than 10 percent higher than an out-of-town retailer's price. Although we refer to this category as *limited* problem solving, deciding which brand or store to select may still be an extensive process. Problem solving should therefore be viewed as a continuum.

Extended Problem Solving

extended problem solving

Occurs when the consumer recognizes a problem but has decided on neither the brand nor the store.

Extended problem solving occurs when the consumer recognizes that a problem exists yet does not have a strong preference for either the brand or the store. For example, a woman in her early 20s has recently received a promotion and a 25-percent raise from the bank that employs her. Over the last year, she has postponed purchasing several major durable goods that she wants—a car, living-room furniture, and a Blue Ray DVD player. With the 25 percent raise, she can afford some, but not all, of these items. She has little prior information and experience regarding alternative brands and retailers that sell these products; therefore, she must engage in extensive problem solving to select the products she should buy, determine which brands are appropriate, and learn which retail outlets carry what she wants. Extensive problem solving typically involves infrequently purchased expensive products of high risk. Here, the consumer desires a lot of new information, which implies a need for extensive problem solving.

Problem-Solving Stages

Once consumers recognize that a problem exists and believe a potential product solution exists within the marketplace, they will engage in problem solving. The first

Most major durable goods, like a new car or engagement ring, involve extensive problem solving prior to the consumer selection and purchase.

active information gathering
Occurs when consumers proactively gather information.

set of attributes
Refers to the characteristics of the store and its products and services.

step is **active information gathering**, which is when consumers proactively gather information. Many consumers begin their active information gathering with a search engine such as Google to find out about the desired product or service, its price, and where it is available. Consumers are then confronted with the second stage in problem solving—the evaluation of alternatives. The evaluation of alternatives typically involves three stages:

1. In the first stage, consumers develop a set of attributes on which the purchase decision will be based. The **set of attributes** refers to the characteristics of the store and its products and services. These can include such things as price, product quality, store hours, knowledgeable sales help, convenient parking, after-sale service, and so on. These attributes are often based on general information sources such as preexisting knowledge, advertising, discussions with friends and relatives, and magazines such as *Consumer Reports* as well as the many information sources online.

2. In the second stage, consumers narrow their consideration set to a more manageable number of attributes. Although consumers want to think that they have considered a wide range of options so as not to miss a golden opportunity, they do not want to be confused by myriad options. In this phase, consumers might visit stores or browse online to gather more specific information, such as price ranges, to narrow their list.

3. In the final stage, consumers directly compare the key attributes of the alternatives remaining on their "short list." Here, consumers are very active in their search for specific information and often begin ascertaining actual prices through store visits, browsing the store's website, or preliminary negotiating when appropriate.

One of the most important variables of problem solving is the source of information used by consumers. It is important for retailers to understand what information resources their target market prefers to use and match their communication programs to these resources.

Purchase

Based on information gathered and evaluated in the problem-solving stage, the consumer decides whether to purchase and which product and retailer to choose. However, it is not uncommon for many major purchases such as a new automobile, sofa, or suit that the customer wants to test drive the car, sit on the sofa, or try on the suit. In a sense, this is a form of additional information collection and risk reduction. Interestingly, many auto dealers are seeing a rise in customers who purchase a new automobile without a test drive; something that was unheard of a decade earlier. This trend is being stimulated by more online reviews of products, auto manufacturer websites that give 360-degree views of automobiles to include interiors, and perhaps, more importantly, the disdain many people have for the new car buying experience where aggressive sales tactics are offensive and demeaning. Consequently, many customers just want to get into the transaction and drive away.[89]

Of course, a possible outcome of the problem-solving stage is a decision not to buy or to delay the purchase. A consumer might conclude that an adequate product or service isn't available or that the cost (financial or otherwise) is greater than previously thought. Although a purchase is not made, the information gathered is often mentally recorded and influences future shopping processes.

The purchase stage may include final negotiation, application for credit if necessary, and determination of the terms of purchase (cash, credit card, etc.). Sometimes unexpected, last-minute factors can intervene during the transaction phase and preempt the purchase. For instance, the consumer can become aware of unanticipated costs such as taxes, delivery fees, or other charges and decide not to buy.

The purchase stage is often seen by retailers as an opportunity to use suggestion selling to sell add-on or related purchases such as extended service warranties, batteries for toys, and impulse merchandise. Both online and bricks-and-mortar retailers use this technique. For instance, at Amazon.com once you select books to purchase, the company suggests other titles you might have an interest in buying. If handled properly, consumers view this selling practice as a customer service, as if the retailer were "looking out" for the customer's long-term satisfaction. On the other hand, if handled poorly, the customer can view this as an attempt to gouge them. In extreme cases, the customer may even decide to cancel the initial transaction.

In Exhibit 3.8 we demonstrate the important role of converting shoppers into purchasers or customers. Note that in this exhibit's example, there are 100,000 people that shop the store annually, but that only 75 percent of those are converted into purchasing customers. So, essentially, 25,000 people entered the store to shop and left empty handed.

Post-Purchase Evaluation

The consumer shopping and purchase process does not end with the purchase. Ultimately, consumers are buying solutions to their perceived needs, and successful retailers

Exhibit 3.8
The Economics of
Converting Shoppers
into Customers

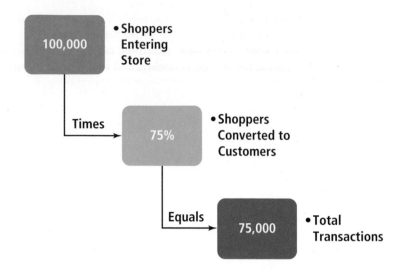

take an active interest in ensuring that their customers feel satisfied over the long term
and that their needs have been resolved. The consumer's use and evaluation of a product
is therefore a critical, although sometimes overlooked, stage in the consumer behavior
process.

One of the most important moments in the use and evaluation stage occurs immediately after the transaction, in the first hours and days in which the consumer uses the
product or service. During this critical time, consumers form lasting impressions regarding the soundness of their purchase decision. These impressions will likely influence all
future purchase decisions. In the event of a problem, consumer dissatisfaction can lead to
post-purchase resentment, where the consumer's dissatisfaction results in resentment
toward the retailer.

If post-purchase resentment is not identified and rectified quickly by the retailer, it
can have a long-term negative effect on the retailer's bottom line. This is because a satisfied customer may tell a few friends, but a dissatisfied customer usually will tell a dozen
or more; however, in cases where an online chat room or Internet complaint site is used,
it may be millions. Just Google any retailer's name followed by the word *sucks* and you
will see the true feelings of many dissatisfied consumers. For instance, in January 5, 2009,
we did a Google Search and found that "Walmart sucks" turned up 1.23 million results,
"Starbucks sucks" turned up 1.18 million results, and "Home Depot sucks" listed 84,900
results. Three years later on January 4, 2012, we conducted the identical Google Search
and found 6.6 million for Walmart, 17.3 million for Starbucks, and 1.6 million for Home
Depot. Predictably this is another indicator of the explosive growth of the Internet.

Fortunately, if the retailer is proactive in its customer-satisfaction program and
responds quickly to budding resentment, it can be overcome. The problem is that many
unhappy consumers do not report their dissatisfaction, so retailers must be diligent in
their monitoring of those "sucks" websites. Retailers also must remember not to get
angry with these posters. In fact, the retailer should be thankful for them because they're
doing the retailer a great favor; they care enough about these retailers to tell them exactly
what went wrong and what needs to be fixed. Other customers may simply head straight
to the competition. By listening to their customers' complaints, establishing proactive
policies such as full-satisfaction guarantees, and boldly communicating these policies to
their target market, retailers are likely to hold on to more of their customers in the event
of a mistake.[90]

**post-purchase
resentment**
Arises after the pur-
chase when the con-
sumer becomes
dissatisfied with the
product, service, or re-
tailer and thus begins to
regret that the purchase
was made.

Beyond this, many retailers have started customer follow-up programs, such as customer-satisfaction reply cards, given out at the time of purchase or mailed to the customer several days later. Electronic cash registers have aided in this process by efficiently gathering the names, addresses, and telephone numbers of customers, recording the merchandise purchased, and automatically mailing the customer satisfaction surveys. It is important that retailers seek to find out why some past customers no longer shop at their stores.

Many large retailers—especially chains where individual stores are not under central control such as franchises and dealerships—have taken this customer-satisfaction process one step further. They have instituted programs that measure customer satisfaction on an ongoing basis and compare customer-service ratings of individual retail locations against pre-established benchmarks or a chain-wide average.

Summary

This chapter focuses on why retailers must continuously monitor those changes in the environment that affect consumer demand. By now it should be clear that the rapid changes occurring in our society require both sensitive management and good retail information systems. Retailers need resourceful managers who not only can provide leadership in handling the challenges of these changes but also can profit from the opportunities they present.

LO 1 Explain the importance of population trends on retail planning.

We began Chapter 3 with a discussion of the major population trends occurring in the United States today and their implications for the future of retailing. These trends include a slowdown in the population growth rate, a change in the age distribution as America gets older, the changing ethnic makeup of America, the geographic shifting of the population to the South and West, the growth of large urban centers, and the increases in consumer mobility.

LO 2 What social trends should be monitored, and what are their impacts on retailing?

Five major social trends and their implications for retailing were discussed. These five trends include the increasing educational levels of consumers, the changing state of marriage (including the expansion of the never-married population), the effect of higher divorce rates, the changing makeup of the American household, and the changes in the nature and importance of an individual's work.

LO 3 How do the changing economic trends affect retailing?

The chapter considers the effects of the imbalance of income growth among various consumer segments, this country's low level of personal savings, the impact of women in the labor force in averting economic crisis, and the impact of the widespread use of credit on retailing.

LO 4 What is involved in the shopping and purchasing model, including the key stages in the buying process?

Shopping and purchasing can be viewed as a six-stage process. A stimulus (stage 1) triggers problem recognition (stage 2); this leads to problem solving. Problem solving consists of two stages: active information gathering or search (stage 3) and evaluation of alternatives (stage 4). The degree of problem solving can vary from habitual, which occurs when the consumer already has a strong preference for both the brand and the retailer from which to purchase it, to extended problem solving, which occurs when the consumer has not decided on the brand or the store. Evaluation of alternatives can lead to purchase (stage 5), and purchase is followed by post-purchase evaluation (stage 6).

Terms to Remember

customer satisfaction	stimulus
customer services	cue
market segmentation	drive
population variables	passive information gathering
micromarketing	problem recognition
metropolitan statistical areas (MSA)	habitual problem solving
boomerang effect	limited problem solving
sandwich generational family or	extended problem solving
trigenerational family	active information gathering
disposable income	set of attributes
discretionary income	post-purchase resentment

Review and Discussion Questions

LO 1

Explain the importance of population trends on retail planning.

1. During the recent recession, some so-called retail experts urged retailers to cut expenses to the bone and not to worry about their customer service levels. Was this a good idea? What is the reasoning behind your answer?

2. Between 2010 and 2050, what type of retailers will be most affected by changes in the ethnic makeup of the population? Will these same retailers be affected by the changing age distribution?

3. It is important for a retailer to understand that as boomers age, they change their shopping behavior. Can you provide one example from current events where a retailer successfully adapted to this changing behavior? Can you provide an example where a retailer hasn't done a good job of adapting to these changes?

LO 2

What social trends should be monitored, and what are their impacts on retailing?

4. What strategies should retailers develop given the higher level of educational attainment today? Explain your reasoning.

5. Should retailers care about trends such as the delay or even postponement of marriage by modern Americans? After all, how does this affect apparel retailing? restaurant retailing? home furnishing retailers?

6. Which recent trend—parents returning to live with their children or children returning to live with their parents—is going to have the most significant impact on retailers? What can retailers do to take advantage of these trends?

LO 3 How do the changing economic trends affect retailing?

7. Why is it more difficult for retailers to manage their businesses when economic turbulence is high?
8. In recent years, the net wealth of the average American has grown at a slower rate, if not declined. Should retailers worry about this? Why?
9. How are retailers affected by the fact that today's college students are graduating with a highest amount of student debt ever? Can you give an example where this will help a retailer? Will this hurt any retailers?

LO 4 What is involved in the consumer behavior model, including the key stages in the buying process?

10. Why is the consumer shopping and purchasing model presented within the text called a *process* model? Explain how understanding this process could affect a retailer's actions.
11. Does a consumer begin the shopping and purchasing process at the need-recognition stage?
12. Why should a retailer care about a customer after a sale has been made?

Sample Test Questions

LO 1 Which of the following statements regarding current U.S. population trends is correct?

a. The baby boomers are now moving into their 30s and 40s.
b. Americans change their residences about a dozen times in their lifetime.
c. Markets with a population of fewer than 50,000 do not present many opportunities for retailers.
d. The U.S. population is expected to increase about 15 percent a year over the next decade.
e. The country's total population is expected to grow at a record rate during the first half of the 21st century.

LO 2 The *boomerang effect* is a relatively new phenomenon that describes:

a. the recent trend for firms to seek bankruptcy protection.
b. the way styles from years ago come back as today's most popular styles.
c. the recent trend of children returning to live with their parents after having already moved out.
d. the use of price as the main means to attract new customers.
e. the recent trend of having most companies report losses for the current quarter.

LO 3 Discretionary income is:

a. all personal income after taxes and retirement savings.
b. all personal income after savings.
c. all personal income minus the money needed for necessities such as food, clothing, housing, and so on.
d. all personal income after taxes minus the money needed for necessities.
e. all personal income after taxes.

LO 4

Post-purchase resentment:

a.   usually only has short-term negative consequences for the retailer.

b.   cannot be fixed.

c.   is easily detected.

d.   is often transferred from the product to the retailer where it was purchased.

e.   is not a problem if the retailer measures customer satisfaction at least every other year.

Writing and Speaking Exercise

When retailers fail to deliver adequate customer service, there isn't much customers can do except shop elsewhere—that is, unless they are willing to go the extra mile. Some retail experts believe that American retailers may not be very creative. However, after years of being in the classroom, the authors know that retailing students certainly are.

A few years ago, a student of one of the authors began collecting information on the executives of any company that failed to meet his service expectations. The list was rather long and covered a wide range of firms. There was the local newspaper for failing to put in all the previous night's sports scores, an airline who left him stuck on the tarmac while on a spring break vacation, a supercenter whose checkout scanner always seemed to overcharge him on "sale" items, the local cable company for just plain lousy service, and so on. Well, anyway, all of these retailers (yes, all of these fit the definition of retailing from Chapter 1) had websites that listed the top executives from president (or head of local operations) to the manager of customer service. For those that listed e-mail addresses, he just copied those. For others, he just compiled his own list of names where a John Jones became johnjones, jjones, or jonesj at the firm's e-mail address. Then he set up a new Yahoo e-mail account. Finally, on Christmas Eve afternoon, he sent all these names e-mails, wishing them a Merry Christmas. What he got back was an inbox full of out-of-office replies, complete with contact information including direct numbers to reach them. In the past when he tried to reach them, he had problems with voicemail routing systems and never could reach these folks. Now, however, he had a list of correct e-mail addresses and direct phone numbers.

Pity anybody who failed to deliver the service he expected (or demanded) the following year.

Prepare a short memo describing what you think the author should have done when he heard about this behavior. Be sure to include in this memo what you think of the student's behavior. Was the student right or wrong in his actions?

Retail Project

By the time you read this chapter, much of the demographic data mentioned in it will be outdated. You can get up-to-date data one of two ways. You can go to the government document section of your local library and use the most current issue of *Statistical Abstract of the United States*. Or you can use your computer to connect with the Census Bureau's website (www.census.gov). A series of easy directions will guide you to the most current available data for any geographic area—from the entire nation to any county or town in any state. Using your mouse you can easily specify what kind of information you want. Also since the census does more than just count people, you can obtain breakdowns on different variables beyond those used in this chapter. For instance, they collect statistics regarding occupations and average pay per occupation (Table S2401), average monthly mortgage by state (Table S0201), education levels by state (Table S0201), and median home value by state (Table GCT2510). (*Note*: The tables provided here correspond to those in the U.S. Bureau of Census, American Fact Finder. Table numbers may change as new editions are published.)

Planning Your Own Entrepreneurial Retail Business

In this chapter, you learned that a major determinant of retail performance is how broadly or narrowly you define your market. In addition, when planning your retail business it will be important that you develop your retail marketing strategy to appeal to this particular market. For example, a women's apparel store could cater to all age groups, professional working women, or teens; it could also target various income groups such as low, moderate, or high income. Further, it could target women of different sizes from petite to full-figured.

For the store you are planning, assume that there are 21,000 households in your community and that these are within a reasonable driving distance. You have determined that if you broadly define your store's market, 64 percent of households in the community would be shoppers at your store and would shop there an average of 3.3 times per year. On the other hand, if you define your market much more selectively by focusing on a well-defined niche, you estimate only 26 percent of households would shop your store; however, they would shop an average of 9.2 times annually.

In this situation, would a broadly or more narrowly defined market create more customer visits to the store? (Hint: Total store visitors, also referred to as *traffic*, is equal to the total number of households in the market multiplied by the proportion that would shop your store, multiplied by their average shopping frequency.) What other factors should you consider when deciding how narrowly or broadly to define your market?

Sonic Drive-Ins: Surviving in Difficult Times

Shawnee, Oklahoma, in 1953 was the stage for the first Sonic Drive-In restaurant to be opened. By 2010 there are 3,500 Sonic Drive-Ins in the United States, operating at year-end 2011 in 43 states. However, Oklahoma and three bordering states (Texas, Kansas, Arkansas) have nearly half of the system-wide drive-ins and Texas itself over one-third). Sonic is primarily a franchise organization with roughly 87 percent of drive-ins operated by franchisees.

Sonic views itself as in the quick-serve restaurant industry where all items are made when ordered and can be highly customized with condiments. Sonic strives to establish a unique dining experience. This experience is built around personalized Carhop service where smiling carhops deliver a customer's order to their car. Customers can eat in their vehicles or also have the option of drive-thru service or patio dining. Sonic Drive-Ins are open all day; usually from 6 or 7 a.m. until 10 p.m. or a bit later. In 2011, 49 percent of sales occurred during lunchtime and dinnertime; 23 percent in the afternoon, 16 percent after dinner and 12 percent in the morning.

The quick-service restaurant industry is highly competitive and can be significantly affected by many factors, including changes in local, regional, and national economic conditions, changes in consumer tastes, consumer concerns about nutritional quality of quick-service food, and increases in the number of, and particular locations of, competing quick-service restaurants. Increases in food and energy costs can also play a significant role.

Unfortunately, after experiencing explosive growth from the late 1980s up until the mid 2000s, performance began to falter. To put this in historical perspective, in 1984 average annual sales per drive-in were $292,000 and in 1990 they were $445,000, and by 2011 were $1,037,000, or a couple percent lower than in 2009. Clearly sales per drive-in had recently plateaued. Another indicator of faltering performance was that total revenues for fiscal year 2007 (fiscal year ends August 31) were $767 million but by 2011 had fallen to $546 million. It should be noted that the total revenues reflect both sales from company-owned drive-ins and franchise fees and leases that franchisees pay to Sonic (the franchisor). The accompanying exhibit provides a variety of financial and operating data on Sonic.

Sonic Corp. Selected Financial (all in 1,000) and Operating Data

	2009	2010	2011
Total Revenues	$706,281	$550,926,000	$545,951
Company Drive-In Sales	$567,436	$414,369	$410,820
Company Drive-In Same Store Sales Change		(8.8%)	1.8%
Advertising Expenditures	$33,000	$22,500	$22,500
Net Income (After Taxes)	$49,442	$21,209	$19,225
Total Assets (Year End)		$737,320	$679,742
Total Stockholders Equity		$22,566	$51,833

Sonic has attempted to make a variety of strategic changes to reverse its declining performance. Since 2005, it has expanded into states in the Northeast, Northwest, and along the U.S. and Canadian border. In 2010 Sonic placed increased emphasis on more high quality food. This included the introduction of real ice cream, footlong quarter pound chili cheese hot dogs, a new line of premium beef hot dogs, bigger and better burgers, and new premium burritos with meat and cheese options. In addition, there was a renewed emphasis on improved customer service and a focus on greater consistency across visits over time and across different locations (both company owned and franchised). As it ended fiscal 2011, the company announced a $30 million common stock repurchase plan effective through August 31, 2012.

Questions

1. What are some of the population, social, and economic trends that may be influencing Sonic's performance?

2. Apply the "consumer shopping and purchasing model" (see Exhibit 3.7) to gain insights into how Sonic can attract more customers.

3. Evaluate whether the strategies that Sonic is pursuing to improve performance are optimal.

4. Analyze Sonic's financial performance over the last couple of years.

Note: This case was prepared as a basis for class discussion rather than to illustrate either effective or ineffective handling of a retail situation. This case is based on the authors' patronage of Sonic Drive-Ins for 30 years, parts of the 1991 Prospectus which was used to take the company public, and 2009–2011 Annual Report to Stockholders.

Evaluating the Competition in Retailing

Overview

The behavior of competitors is an important component of the retail planning and management model. Effective planning and execution in any retail setting cannot be accomplished without the proper analysis of competitors. In this chapter, we begin by reviewing various models of retail competition. The types of competition in retailing are described next. We then discuss the evolution of retail competition. Finally, we examine the retail revolution in nonstore retailing, developing retail formats, global and technological changes, and the use of private labels as a strategic weapon.

Learning Objectives

After reading this chapter you should be able to:

1 Explain the various models of retail competition.

2 Distinguish between various types of retail competition.

3 Describe the four theories used to explain the evolution of retail competition.

4 Describe the changes that could affect retail competition.

LO 1

Explain the various models of retail competition.

Models of Retail Competition

This chapter examines the effects of competition on a retailer's performance. As noted in Chapter 1, retailing was once a growth industry able to increase profits solely on the basis of an increasing population base. Today, though, population growth rates are slowing. As a result, national and regional retailers can grow only by taking sales away from their competition. However, retail competition at the local level is often more complex.

In many regional communities, the area's population and disposable income have grown even as the nation's economic base contracts. For example, for years Tampa, Phoenix, and Las Vegas were like many Sunbelt communities: vibrant local economies that grew as retirees and second-home owners entered the market. Such locals offered retailers the opportunity to grow without having to take sales away from a competitor. Recently, as a result of the housing crises of 2008–2011, this is no longer true. These cities have seen major declines in housing prices and the tripling of unemployment rates. As a result of the wealth effect, explained in Chapter 3, retail sales in these cities have shrunk.

As this example illustrates, a retailer must always be on the offensive, studying the changing competitive environment, especially its local competition, and differentiating itself from that competition. Only by creating a differential advantage that is extremely difficult to copy in both time and money can a retailer hope for continued success.

Prime examples of such differentiation are specialty retailers, like Victoria's Secret or Tiffany's, with their highly specialized selections; Walmart, whose distribution system results in significantly lower operating costs than its competitors; Target, with its more fashionable and contemporary merchandise than other mass merchandise discounters; and the Walt Disney Company and Nordstrom's, which are famous for excellent customer service. Retailers that merely copy the actions of others without a lower cost structure or point of differentiation will experience substandard performance and possibly fail as CompUSA did as they failed to differentiate themselves from Best Buy and other competitors.

The successful retailer will visit retailers of all sizes in its trading area to learn what merchandise and services competitors are and are not offering, which have the most appealing store designs and atmosphere, which offerings receive aggressive pricing emphasis, and which promotional tactics are successful. These tactics are particularly beneficial for smaller retailers. Often, many people believe that local retailers cannot compete with the large discounters, but this isn't true. For example, the small appliance store owner would benefit by understanding that these chains usually carry only a limited selection within a product category and provide little personalized or specialized service. By knowing which kitchen appliances the discounter carries, and how they are priced, the small retailer can match the price on similar units, offer better services, and stock a more complete range of units. Often this more complete range of units allows it to offer items that cannot be found in the national retail appliance chains, and hence the retailer will not have to be as price competitive on these lines.

Other chains have created a niche that has worked well against these discounters. Consider, for example, the tactic used by the dollar stores (Dollar General, Family Dollar, and Dollar Tree). These chains successfully operate small stores within the shadow of the large discounters by providing convenience and low prices on a limited product selection. By enabling their customers to get in and out quickly, these stores are able to compete with the larger chains. Yet the niche served by these dollar stores is risky since they tend to target households earning $30,000 a year or less, a segment that offers little in the way of discretionary spending on high-margin items and requires that the dollar stores make few, if any, errors in their merchandise selection.

Small, locally owned retailers may also use a tactic like the one tried by a variety store in Viroqua, Wisconsin. When Walmart located a store nearby, it gave each of its employees $20 to shop Walmart. Because its employees were local and understood the community, they learned that their store would not be price competitive in health and beauty items or housewares—and that Walmart had few offerings for the agricultural community. Further, the addition of a new private school in town increased the number of residents with more sophisticated tastes than those of the typical Walmart customer. By catering to these underserved customer segments, the variety store has thrived.

A small retailer's competition is not just the large discount stores in the area. Smaller retailers would be wise to check the local drugstore, like CVS, Rite Aid, or Walgreens, that stocks similar items; the Internet for competitive pricing information; and category killers that might offer a deeper selection and a better level of service than the discounter. For example, Best Buy lured female customers away from traditional discounters and small specialty electronics stores by providing merchandise selections tailored to each local market area and training its sales associates not to "talk down" to them, as had often happened in other electronics stores.[1]

It is important to remember that no retailer, however clever, can design a strategy that will completely insulate it from competition. This is true even for the retailer that has done an excellent job in developing and following its mission statement, setting its goals and objectives, and conducting its SWOT analysis; customers will always have shopping choices. The rapid growth of discount department stores, convenience stores, and catalog and Internet retailers attest to this fact. Further, as the cost of entry into retailing is relatively low, as compared with other businesses, and merchandising innovations are often unable to be patented, competition will always remain as other retailers seek to copy a profitable strategy.

Competition in retailing, as in any industry, involves the interplay of supply and demand. One cannot appreciate the nature and scope of competition in retailing by studying only the supply factors—that is, the type and number of competing retailers that exist. One must also examine consumer demand factors as highlighted in Chapter 3. Keeping this in mind, let's examine a formal framework for describing and explaining the competitive environment of retailing.

The Competitive Marketplace

One of the most important tasks to perform prior to examining the competitive environment is deciding how you will compete as a retailer. Competition can be waged on many fronts. A retailer must be clear about what advantages it will emphasize and where its resources will have the greatest impact in attracting and satisfying customers.

This framework helps to identify your primary competitors, as well as threats from secondary competitors. For example, a full-line grocery store competes most directly with similar grocery stores; all of them try to attract the same type of customer in terms of price sensitivity, preferences in merchandise selection, and geographic convenience. A discount grocery store such as Rainbow Foods is also after the grocery store's customer, but it appeals particularly to those who put an emphasis on low prices over a wide selection of specialty items. However, any business that may win the customer's food dollar should also be viewed as a competitor, and in today's hotly competitive supermarket and grocery business this includes: restaurants, farmer's markets, institutional food service (such as at work, in schools, and in hospitals), street vendors, specialty food stores, convenience stores, department stores, home gardens, vending machines, and Internet sellers of food.

Over the past decade, almost a third of a household's food dollar was spent on food consumed outside the home—that is, in restaurants, workplace cafeterias, vending machines, and other venues. The percentage is much higher for certain demographic groups such as higher-income households who can better afford to eat out and young men who prefer not to cook at home. The fact that the same consumer can and will purchase the same product category (food) at different retailers points to the fact that different retailers are more or less competitive to varying degrees given different consumer buying situations and preferences. Customers may choose to shop at traditional grocery stores or supercenters for most groceries, but many will also choose to patronize specialty grocers such as Whole Foods for organically raised meats or Trader Joe's for a particular brand of muesli cereal, shop online for specialty ingredients unavailable within one's area such as Amazon for Il Primo sport peppers to make "Chicago-style" hotdogs, eat in a number of restaurant formats for different reasons throughout the week, and purchase grab-and-go foods from convenience stores.[2]

Retailers compete for target customers on five major fronts or factors:[3]

1. The price for the benefits offered;
2. Service level;
3. Product selection (merchandise line width and depth);
4. Location or access—that is, the overall convenience of shopping the retailer; and
5. Customer experience (the customer's positive feelings and behaviors in the purchase process).

In any competitive environment, retailers must clear a minimum acceptable threshold on each of these criteria in order to attract and retain customers and stay in business. Further, they must distinguish themselves in the marketplace by dominating on one key factor and differentiate themselves on a secondary factor within that primary competitive set. For example, Walmart, Target, Dollar Tree, and Dollar General compete primarily as general merchandise discounters. However, Walmart emphasizes its excellent prices on a wide selection of top name brands, Target highlights its design-forward private-label goods and store atmosphere, and the dollar stores are more convenient than the larger discounters.

Many retailers compete for customers on a local level and must be aware of their direct and secondary competitors in their shopping area. Customers typically will not travel beyond local markets to purchase routine household goods and prefer to shop in the most convenient way possible. When they do travel beyond local markets, however, it is usually because their city or town is too small to support retailers with the selection of merchandise they desire. Some customers will always want to shop out of town, but most cities with populations of more than 50,000 can provide the consumer with sufficient selection in almost all lines of merchandise. In cities with populations less than 50,000, households generally need to travel to another town or city for large purchases such as a new automobile, television, furniture, or for special items of clothing such as a wedding dress or a favored brand name or even for specialty food ingredients such as certain ethnic foods.

Market Structure

Economists use four different economic terms to describe the competitive environment of retailing: *pure competition*, *pure monopoly*, *monopolistic competition*, and *oligopolistic competition*.

pure competition
Occurs when a market has homogeneous products and many buyers and sellers, all having perfect knowledge of the market, and ease of entry for both buyers and sellers.

Pure competition occurs when a market has:

1. Homogeneous (similar) products;
2. Many buyers and sellers, all having perfect knowledge of the market; and
3. Ease of entry for both buyers and sellers—that is, new retailers can start up with little difficulty and new consumers can easily come into the market.

In pure competition, each retailer faces a horizontal demand curve and must sell its products at the going "market" or equilibrium price. To sell at a lower price would be foolish, since you could always get the market price. Of course, you could not sell your merchandise at a higher price because customers know they can buy the item for less.

Pure competition is rare in retailing. Often, neither consumers nor retailers know all the prices in the marketplace without investing extensive time and effort to acquire this knowledge. Further, not all customers value an item similarly. It is seldom also that retailers have homogenous offerings because even if they are selling an identical item, the location of each retailer is unique, and thus, the convenience of traveling to the two stores is different, which results in their offerings not being homogeneous. Even in a very good example of pure competition, such as two vendors located near each other selling bags of peanuts or bottles of water outside a sporting event, customers seldom explore a number of sites before making a choice.

pure monopoly
Occurs when there is only one seller for a product or service.

The second type of economic environment also does not occur very often in real life. In a **pure monopoly**, the seller is the only one selling a particular product and will set its selling price accordingly. However, as the retailer seeks to sell more units, it must lower the selling price. This is because consumers who already have one unit will tend to place a lower value on an additional unit. This is called the *law of diminishing returns* or *declining marginal utility*. For example, a hot fudge sundae would taste great right now, but the second, third, or ninth one, purchased and consumed today, would be less desirable. Similarly, not all customers are equally impressed with a product. The monopolist would have to price more aggressively to entice customers who place a lower value on the item than do its target customers. The customer whose favorite color is hot pink might buy a hot pink blazer at full price, but it is unlikely she will buy another one soon. In addition, the retailer is likely to discount the remaining blazers to customers who are less thrilled with hot pink—that is, hot pink has less "utility" for these customers in the first place.

Even so, situations of near monopoly do exist. The gas station that sells ethanol-free gasoline and/or is many miles from its nearest competitor or the restaurant open late at night on a lonely highway are examples of near monopolies. Similarly, customers can "self-inflict" into a monopoly when a product attribute, such as ethanol-free, or brand name is highly valued, and only one (or a few) retailer controls its sale. Harley-Davidson, like many other luxury-brand sellers, realizes its brand-loyal customers place such a high value on their motorcycles that the company limits areas of distribution and allows its retailers to reap the reward. For a long time, the U.S. Postal Service (USPS) with its thousands of post offices spread across the country believed it had a monopoly on mail and package delivery. But then along came UPS and Federal Express and the rise of the Internet over the last two decades. Consequently, the USPS, in 2010, lost over $5 billion and thus began to aggressively cut employees, close post offices, and consolidate mail sorting and distribution centers.[4] In fact, as a result of the Postal Service's continued oversight of such competitors the government had to step in and provide a $34 billion bailout in April of 2012 to keep the USPS afloat, while simultaneously acknowledging that it would likely lose upwards of $12 billion during the same calendar year due to consumers' increase usage of email and overnight carriers.[5]

Monopolistic competition is a market situation that develops when one of two situations occur:

monopolistic competition
Occurs when the products offered are different, yet viewed as substitutable for each other and the sellers recognize that they compete with sellers of these different products.

1. Retailers sell different (heterogeneous) products in the eyes of consumers that are still substitutes for each other. Here two or more retailers may be selling the same product, for instance Maytag washing machines or Chevrolet autos, but one retailer is able to differentiate itself on another dimension. Thus, consumers perceive the retailers as selling different products, given the total shopping experience.
2. Sellers may be the only ones selling a particular brand but face competition from other retailers selling similar goods and services. For instance, a service station selling Shell gasoline competing with a Quik Trip, Racetrac, or 7-Eleven convenience store selling both gasoline and convenience goods.

The word *monopolistic* means that each seller is trying to control its own segment of the market. However the word *competition* means that substitutes for the product are available. For example, a Pepsi-Cola is a substitute for a Coca-Cola. The degree of the seller's control depends on the extent to which customers view the competitor's product as similar. This is why retailers in monopolistic competition attempt to differentiate themselves with the products or services they offer. Some of the common means of achieving this differentiation are offering better customer service, credit, more convenient parking, larger or more attractive merchandise selection, cleanliness, free setup and delivery, and a more convenient location, as well as the brand or store image created and developed through marketing communications such as advertising or store events.

Oligopolistic competition occurs when a market meets the following conditions:

oligopolistic competition
Occurs when relatively few sellers, or many small firms who follow the lead of a few larger firms, offer essentially homogeneous products and any action by one seller is expected to be noticed and reacted to by the other sellers.

1. Essentially homogeneous products are sold—such as airline travel between two cities on different air carriers.

2. There are relatively few sellers or many small firms who always follow the lead of the few large firms.

3. There is an expectation that any action by one party will be noticed and reacted to by the other parties in the market.

As in pure competition, oligopolies are likely to end up selling at a similar price since everybody knows what others are doing. Nonprice competition is extremely difficult since consumers view the products and services as essentially the same. This is why the major airlines almost always lower their prices on identical travel routes when a low-cost competitor enters one of their markets. As was the case when Southwest Airlines entered the Denver market, American and United both dropped fares to cities served by Southwest.

Retailing is often characterized as monopolistic competition or, in rare cases, oligopolistic competition. The distinction lies in the number of sellers. For an oligopoly to occur, the top four firms need to account for more than 60 percent to 80 percent of the market. Oligopolistic competition rarely occurs on a national level, but consolidation in many industries has left a few large players in some product categories. For example, Home Depot and Lowe's often dominate the home-improvement market, and Macy's and Dillard's have a similar impact on the department store category.

outshopping
Outshopping occurs when a household travels outside their community of residence or uses the Internet to shop in another community.

Oligopolistic competition is more common at a local level, especially in smaller communities, among food stores, specialty stores, and department or discount department stores. However, if prices become too high, merchandise selection too limited, or services too poor, residents of these communities will travel to larger communities to shop. This is known as **outshopping**. However, even when retailing becomes concentrated at the local level, there are several checks on the retailers' market power. One of these checks is nonstore shopping (e.g., the Internet or mailorder). If prices at furniture and other specialty stores become too high, local shoppers may increase their usage of nonstore shopping alternatives. In fact, existing catalog retailers and bricks-and-mortar stores are proving particularly adept at developing multichannel strategies to attract customers from a wider geographic area. L.L. Bean has seen its catalog businesses boom with the addition of an online site, and stores such as Walmart have fine-tuned their Internet offerings. However, the most likely cause for outshopping in the United States today is lawmakers. In New York City, for example, state and city tobacco taxes have risen so many times that the retail cost can exceed $9 a pack—about double the national average. As a result, the Tax Foundation estimates that there is "a 75 percent gap between cigarette sales in the city and cigarette consumption." In other words, three out of four cigarettes smoked by residents of New York City were bought elsewhere.[6]

Interestingly, during the recent energy crisis, the high cost of gasoline limited the growth of outshopping to larger communities. In fact, many rural locations were able to outperform their big city competitors.[7] However, the rising cost of gasoline and transportation costs in general encourages more Internet shopping. Amazon, however, experienced that shoppers will not buy something on the Internet if the shipping and delivery charges are too high a proportion of the purchase price. Why purchase a $8 tank top or belt on-line if the shipping and handling charges are going to be at least as much? Therefore, Amazon.com introduced Amazon.com Prime, which is a membership program that, for $79 annually, offers customers free two-day shipping with no minimum purchase requirement.[8]

The Demand Side of Retailing

As stated previously, most retailers face monopolistic competition, and we assume such a market structure to be the case for the remainder of the text. In a monopolistically competitive market, the retailer will be confronted with a negatively sloping demand curve.

Exhibit 4.1
Demand as a Function of Price

In other words, consumers will demand a higher quantity as price is lowered, assuming the retailer has chosen the merchandise that the customer wants, communicates the value of shopping at his or her store, and makes the product available. Thus, the typical retailer faces a demand function like the one shown in Exhibit 4.1.

One important thing to keep in mind is that the true price (or cost) the customer pays actually includes three components: (1) the price the retailer charges, (2) sales tax on the purchase, and (3) delivery or transportation costs. Consider the purchase of a new automobile. If the car's purchase price is $40,000, for example, it may be prudent to shop outside the city limits, or in another county if sales taxes there are lower. After all, a 1 percent lower sales tax on $40,000 will save $400. Some retailers even run special promotions in which they advertise that they will not charge sales tax on certain purchases, such as school supplies or children's shoes on the weekend before Labor Day. This is the equivalent of a price reduction. The retailers, do indeed, need to pay the sales tax to the city or state tax collectors, but pay it on behalf of the customer. Transportation costs shouldn't be ignored either. A discount appliance store might sell a new Whirlpool or Samsung washer and dryer combination for $50 less than the local appliance store, but they are likely to charge you $75 to $100 to deliver and install the appliances. Some e-tailers will waive shipping charges or give you expedited shipping if your purchase exceeds a certain threshold. Essentially, these are price reductions when you view price from a holistic perspective. And finally, don't forget your transport costs to go shopping! For example, if you travel 250 miles roundtrip to a large metroplex to get a lower price on a new car; you need to keep in mind that you spent money and used your time to make what is most likely a full-day trip. Even on a smaller purchase, deciding to travel 20 miles across town (40 miles roundtrip) to visit friends at a sports bar where your tab and tip is $24 may prove to be more expensive than you thought when you figure out that the 40-mile trip cost you at least $.50 a mile for gasoline and wear and tear on your car or another $20 (40 miles multiplied by $.50).

Such customer behavior implies knowledge of the competitive alternatives. Customers who have greater knowledge of available alternatives and the differences in product features will often patronize a wider range of retailers.[9] Interestingly, this is often exacerbated by retailers themselves. As retailers become more proactive in their marketing efforts (using such tactics as selling over the Internet, aggressive advertising, multiple catalogs, and prospecting for new customers), consumers become increasingly aware of a wider range of alternatives, better prices, better service, and better features. This knowledge leads many customers to migrate from local retailers that do not sufficiently measure up to their growing demands.

Thus, in most cases, higher prices will result in less demand for the retailer because households have limited incomes and many purchase alternatives. This reality should suggest that retailers cannot be profitable by setting prices at the highest possible levels. Retailers will find it necessary to set prices somewhere below the maximum possible price but above zero. Extremely low prices will sell large quantities but not generate sufficient sales revenue to cover costs and generate a profit; retailers are simply unable to meet the maximum customer demand at a profit. At the same time, extremely high prices will result in low quantities sold, and hence, although the price per unit may be high, the sales revenue would not cover both variable and fixed costs. As a result, retailers must routinely monitor competitors' prices in the trade area, as well as understand the impact of catalogs and the Internet. Retailers also need to recognize when a drop in a competitor's prices is temporary and inconsequential to long-term competition (that is, the competitor will be out of business if it prices too low) or when the competitor has set a new permanent pricing standard that requires them to adjust their profit expectations.

Nonprice Decisions

Retailers often believe they must always match or be lower than a competitor's price. This is often not the case. Many customers place a high value on attributes other than price when selecting a place to shop. For instance, some consumers choose to pick up a loaf of bread at a convenience store or bakery, even when it is cheaper at a supercenter or supermarket. These customers are willing to pay a higher price because they place a higher value on their time or have a special preference for certain bakery bread. However, many may be surprised to discover that the special loaf of bread may cost several times the $3.79 price when one considers travel and related costs to the bakery.

© Smileus/Shutterstock

SERVICE ⬦ RETAILING

The "Experience It" Approach

Some retail experts argue that consumers are no longer buying only tangible products and traditional service; instead, they're purchasing an experience. Walt Disney is recognized as the pioneer in this "experience it" approach to retailing. Both Disneyland and Epcot Center were built so that consumers could experience the future. Today, this experience-it approach is found in many retail markets, one being the health spa and resort business.

Canyon Ranch, which was founded in 1979 by Mel Zuckerman in Tucson, Arizona, is considered the pioneer in the high-end health spa and resort business. Canyon Ranch was designed to be more than just a fabulous vacation; it was to be an *experience* that would influence the quality of your life from the moment you arrived to long after you returned home. It was a place to explore your potential for a happier, healthier,

and more fulfilling life. In all promotional material, Canyon Ranch stressed the word *intention* when talking about the experience. Its website stated, "[W]e are more intent than ever on motivating our guests to translate their healthiest thoughts into positive, ongoing action—and we do whatever it takes to make that happen.... Our mission is not selling vacations; it's creating an environment in which you can make a direct, emotional connection between what you know you should do and what you actually do every day."

Thus, this destination spa company was luring guests for body poundings and weight-loss regimens long before the modern spa proliferation was even a gleam in marketers' eyes. With the simple message question "Has there ever been a time when you could have used an escape to Canyon Ranch more?" the resort sought to highlight consumers' need for escape. In fact, this message was very successful during the stressful times of the recent recession.[10]

(continued)

Over the years, Canyon Ranch has expanded and now has a woodlands health resort in the lush Berkshires of Lenox, Massachusetts. It also has SpaClubs in the Venetian Resort on the Las Vegas Strip; Gaylord Palms Resort in Kissimmee, Florida; and on board the Queen Mary II ocean liner. Yet, as in all competitive markets, successful innovators are often copied.

A relatively new resort, Miraval Spa, has entered Canyon Ranch's hometown of Tucson. Ranked as the number-one resort and spa by the prestigious Zagat Survey, Miraval has challenged Canyon Ranch and other competitors in providing the best possible "experience." Miraval positions itself as helping people create a life in balance. To accomplish its mission, it offers a variety of workshops such as "Partners, Pleasure, and Passion: A Couples Retreat"; "Power and Passion: Engaging Feminine Sexual Radiance"; and "Partners and Passion: Taking It to the Next Level." As a result Miraval has a more balanced mix of female and male customers whereas Canyon Ranch is more heavily visited by women. Miraval also has more adventurous sports and offers Native American healing experiences. Well-known holistic and integrative health expert, Dr. Andrew Weil has been recruited as director of integrative health and healing. Predictably, Canyon Ranch is fighting back with its own new and innovative offerings. Yet even these high-end service providers are not exempt from price competition and especially when the economy is faltering.

Winter is the prime season in Tucson because temperatures hover in the 60s and 70s (daily summer temperatures regularly exceed 100 degrees). During this peak winter season, price had always been non-negotiable and extremely high. But this changed in 2006 when Miraval offered a special: a weeklong stay for $4,735 (single occupancy) or $3,780 (double occupancy), which was 15 percent off the regular package price. Even as the economy recovered Miraval used price promotions as an important part of its strategy; for instance, during spring 2012 you could book four nights at the resort and get the fifth free.

Retail service innovators have realized that the spa and resort business is not an exclusively high-end market. In fact, one of the fastest-growing areas of service retailing is stand-alone spas. These provide half-day to full-day treatments with no cost of overnight lodging. Not surprisingly, the cost drops dramatically, with many treatments costing less than $75. Unless you happen to live in a small town of 25,000 or less, you are likely to see numerous "day" spas in your local business directory. However, these spas also have a high failure rate since they are relatively easy to open and may attract individuals with little business and retail training or experience. Undoubtedly, you have witnessed some of these spas failing in your community only after six months of operation.

Another interesting growth area is medical spas. These spas often focus on dermatology, providing such medical treatments as Botox or Restylane, certain chemical peels, and intense-pulsed-light skin treatments. Increasingly, the entrepreneurs are medical doctors who are leaving their traditional medical practices with low insurance reimbursements for cash-paying spa customers. In 2000, there were only a few dozen medical spas in the United States; today, there are more than 1,500, and the number is growing weekly. These spas are successful because they provide a salon-like setting with quick service (sometimes even on a walk-in basis), are conveniently located, and offer attractive prices. The spas are also open weekends and evenings, hours not common in traditional medical offices. Importantly, just as the high-end spas faced price competition as the number of competitors increased, so have medical spas. For example, recently, Lumity MedSpa in west Los Angeles was offering a holiday special of 40 percent off all laser hair removal, and Botox was bargain priced at $9 a unit. Just as the independent day spas mentioned earlier fail at a high rate, the same is true of medical spas. In addition, some of these spa owners have faced litigation related to medical malpractice.

Sources: "Competition Forces Spas to Offer Big Deals," *Wall Street Journal*, February 28, 2006: D1, D7; Joseph B. Pine II and James H. Gilmore, *The Experience Economy* (Boston: Harvard Business School Press), 1999; "Spas in Retail Centers Offer Cosmetic Medical Treatments, *Wall Street Journal*, January 3, 2006: D1; www.miravalresort.com, January 11, 2009, and March 28, 2012; and www.canyonranch.com, January 11, 2009, and March 28, 2012.

This chapter's "Service Retailing" box describes how some spas have used the "experience it" approach to combat price sensitivity. Many American retailers find that their most successful and least price-sensitive product lines are those that either save customers' time or make them feel better or look younger.[11]

Retailers must understand that nonprice elements of the retail mix—merchandise mix, advertising and promotion, customer services and selling, and store layout and

Generally, Hispanic customers are influenced by in-store free samples and demonstrations at a rate of three times that of the average U.S. shopper.

design—can have a significant impact on the quantity of merchandise they sell and the profit levels they achieve. Nonprice variables are directed at enlarging the retailer's demand by offering customers benefits beyond simply the lowest price. For example, some retailers have recently opened more checkout registers to reduce shoppers' time spent in the store. After all, research has found that 42 percent of all New York City shoppers would rather clean their bathrooms and 18 percent would rather visit a dentist than stand in a checkout line.[12]

Similarly, retailers must be aware that certain nonprice variables will be more successful than others given the market segments they choose to target. As discussed in Chapter 3, Hispanics are one of the fastest growing segments in the United States today. Yet as recent consumer data suggests, this segment values certain nonprice variables differently as compared with the rest of U.S. shoppers. As originally pointed out in Chapter 3, Hispanic shoppers are significantly more likely to know the brands of the products they are going to purchase before entering the retail store. However, retail decision makers should not conclude from that finding that in-store marketing will be ineffective on this valuable consumer segment. On the contrary, recent evidence suggests that Hispanic shoppers are two times more likely to report that they were influenced by in-store displays and discounts than the average American shopper.

Just like the rest of American shoppers, Hispanics reported that in-store coupons and price reductions (e.g., temporary sales, BOGOs, etc.) were found to be the most effective of in-store marketing tactics at influencing in-store purchasing behavior. However, nonprice marketing actions were also found to be quite successful at influencing Hispanics' purchase behaviors. In fact, product displays were found to be twice as effective at influencing Hispanic shoppers' purchases than the average American shopper, and free samples or in-store demonstrations were found to be over three times more effective at influencing Hispanic shoppers than all other U.S. shoppers.

Although certain nonprice variables may be more or less advantageous given the retailer's target market, competing on price alone is a no-win situation because price is the easiest variable for competitors to copy. In today's intensely competitive retail marketplace, you can expect exactly that competitive reaction. Therefore, it was not surprising that in late 2011, when overall retail sales were rising as the economy recovered, that long time off-price retailer Filene's Basement (founded in 1909 by William Filene in Boston) filed for bankruptcy[13] (incidentally for the third time). Traditional department stores and discounters as well as many e-tailers were matching prices. After all, if all you have is a low price, then once your competitor matches or beats your price, why should your customers remain loyal, especially when your competitors may have better customer service, more convenient locations, and more merchandise selection.

Consider some of the ways a retailer could use nonprice variables to achieve a protected niche:

store positioning
Is when a retailer identifies a well-defined market segment using demographic or lifestyle variables and appeals to this segment with a clearly differentiated approach.

1. The retailer could position itself as different from the competition by altering its merchandise mix to offer higher-quality goods, greater personal service, special-orders handling, or a better selection of large sizes. (**Store positioning** is the process whereby a retailer distinguishes itself from competitors in specific ways in order to be the preferred provider for certain market segments. It's the act of designing the retailer's merchandise and image so as to occupy a distinct and valued place in the targeted customer's mind.) Such features may increase the maximum price consumers are willing to pay or the distance consumers are willing to travel to shop for these goods, thereby enlarging the retailer's trade area. Neiman Marcus and Nordstrom's have done an excellent job of positioning themselves using this strategy. Exhibit 4.2 details the steps involved in choosing a correct positioning strategy.
2. The retailer can offer private-label merchandise that has unique features or offers better value than do competitors. The strategy of using private-label branding to secure a protected niche is discussed in detail at the end of this chapter.

Exhibit 4.2
How to Implement a Store Positioning Program

1. Assess how shoppers and even competitors view the retailer by asking them to describe the retailer's stores, merchandise, services, and overall image. Determine what's good and bad about the current position. Determine whether the current positioning must be changed to increase sales.
2. Determine what the best position for the retailer is. Next identify how to market the retailer's products, promotions, and image to convey and reinforce this desired position. What are the meaningful differences between the retailer and its competition?
3. Analyze the retailer's current target customers. Are these the correct ones? Who will benefit most from the retailer's new positioning? Does the retailer's target market really value the anticipated change in positioning?
4. Factor in current environmental trends. What trends are on the way that might benefit or harm the retailer's new position?
5. Implement the new positioning strategy but remember that a retailer's business objective drives its market strategy, which drives its positioning strategy. After all, if the business objective is to have fewer customers who spend more per sale by buying higher quality, the strategy must reflect this in the products or services offered. The retailer's positioning strategy will also determine the messages to communicate to its target customer.

Najlah Feanny/Corbis

Neiman Marcus is one retailer known the world over for the top of the line merchandise offerings, great personal service, and luxury image.

3. The retailer could provide other benefits for the customer. For example, as gas prices go up, so does the drawing power of retailers who offer cheap fuel. Because shoppers are more likely to consolidate shopping trips as fuel prices increase, many discounters have followed the lead of warehouse clubs and European grocery stores, sacrificing margins on gasoline to increase sales inside their stores.[14] Other retailers such as Ikea might offer benefits that make it easier to shop such as a kids play center to drop off the kids while the parents shop. Ikea also has in-store restaurants with well-prepared and tasty, but inexpensive, meals.

4. The retailer could master stock keeping with its basic merchandise assortment. For example, Nordstrom strives to always have men's dress shirts in stock and will give the customer a free shirt if the store is ever out of stock in basic sizes. Compare this policy with a competitor who has a similar item in stock only 95 percent of the time. If you go into this store to pick up just five items, the chances are almost one in four that the store will be out of at least one item ($0.95 \times 0.95 \times 0.95 \times 0.95 \times 0.95 = 0.773$).

A variation of nonprice competition is to become a "destination" store for certain products. For example, Hanneford's grocery store in York, Maine, guarantees that it will have hot roasted chickens available and ready for takeout every day between 4 p.m. and 7 p.m. or you get a coupon for a free chicken. (Even so, Hanneford's will always have a chicken ready within 30 minutes during this time period even if it temporarily runs out due to unexpectedly heavy demand.) Another example is Bass Pro Shops, which has become a sportsman's paradise by combining merchandise with in-store demonstrations and experiences, including a trout pond. Its flagship store in Springfield, Missouri, is even located adjacent to the American Fish and Wildlife Museum.

Remember, most retail decision variables, whether price or nonprice, are directed at influencing demand. The profitability of these decisions depends on the marginal cost of the action versus the marginal revenue it generates (see Chapter 10 for a discussion of pricing).

AP Photo/Larry Crowe

Target's Archer Farms private-label brand enables it to attract the value oriented shopper seeking both high quality and a competitive price.

JC Penney logos

JCPenney Arizona private-label clothing is an important part of the JC Penney store positioning strategy.

Competitive Actions

We just discussed how most bricks-and-mortar retailers attract customers from a limited geographic area and that this area expands as prices are lowered. But even at a zero price as we discussed, households can only afford to travel a certain distance to get their goods and services. Therefore, several, if not many, retailers in each line of retail trade are needed to service most cities.

A good measure of competitive activity in a market is the number of retail establishments of a given type per 1,000 households. When the number of stores per 1,000 households gets too large, the market is considered **overstored**. These retailers face a major performance imperative because often their return on investment is below their cost of capital. As a result, they will implement both price and nonprice actions in an attempt to increase both sales and profits. This highly competitive situation reduces the average return on investment and lowers the profitability of all retailers. Some will eventually exit the market. One classic case of a retailer overstoring a trade area is Starbucks. At one time, before closing nearly 600 outlets in 2008, this Seattle-based coffee retailer had multiple stores in the same shopping center and some even across the street from each other.[15]

Exhibit 4.3 demonstrates the economics of overstoring. The scenario begins in a city of 100,000 people that has 20 retail stores selling apparel as a major category. Average monthly apparel purchases are $40 per person or $480 (12 months × $40) annually. Thus, the city has $48 million in annual purchases (demand) for store-purchased apparel. As you will see from the computations in the accompanying exhibit, this results in average sales per store of $2.4 million and average sales per square foot of $480. Consider next what happens when four new retailers enter the market; sales per store decline to $2 million and sales per square foot decline to $400. Predictably, as sales decline and the retailer must cover its fixed costs, the profitability of the stores in the market, on average, declines. Retailing, however, in the United States is highly competitive so you need to actually look at how overstored a market may be in the niche or segment

overstored
Is a condition in a community where the number of stores in relation to households is so large that to engage in retailing is usually unprofitable or marginally profitable.

Exhibit 4.3
Economics of Overstoring

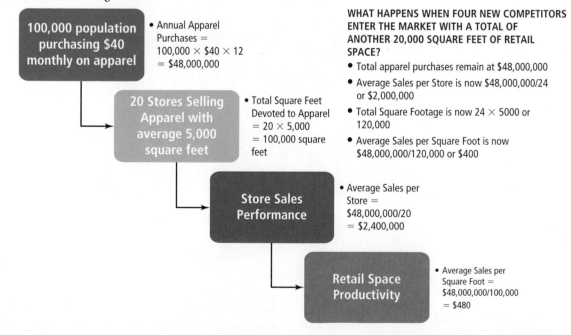

you compete. Take the case of apparel, which consists of the women's, men's, and children's market. Within each of these markets there are niches. For instance, the women's market includes juniors, misses, plus-size, and maternity. The misses market, served by such firms as Talbots, Charming Shoppes, Coldwater Creek as well as JCPenney, Kohl's, Macy's, and Belk who also court the misses' shopper, has faced overstoring for nearly a decade as women cut back on apparel purchases and Gen Yers in their 20s and early 30s turned to e-tailers for many of their apparel purchases. As we learn in Exhibit 4.3 overstoring leads to lower space productivity that leads to deteriorating profitability. Not surprisingly, many of the specialty retailers catering to misses such as Talbots and Charming Shoppes have closed about 10–15 percent of their stores.[16]

A more favorable situation for retailers is when the number of stores per 1,000 households is small in comparison to other markets, and thus the market is said to be **understored**. With too few retailers to adequately service local demand, profits may be high enough to attract new retail competitors, or existing retailers may be enticed to expand. A market is in equilibrium in terms of number of retail establishments if the return on investment is high enough to justify keeping capital invested in retailing, but not so high as to invite more competition. Recognizing that many small towns and cities (under 50,000 population) are understored when it comes to trendy teen apparel, rue21, a teen-apparel retailer located many of its stores in rural markets.[17] For similar reasons, but catering to a broader women's market, Chico's has found good store expansion opportunities in smaller markets.[18]

As just indicated, competition is most intense in overstored markets because many retailers are achieving an inadequate return on investment. It should also be remembered that while e-tailers may not be in close geographic proximity to other e-tailers and retailers,

understored
Is a condition in a community where the number of stores in relation to households is relatively low so that engaging in retailing is an attractive economic endeavor.

Chico's, like a growing number of retailers, is expanding its national footprint by opening stores in smaller towns and cities with populations less than 50,000.

they are easily accessible via a customer's computer or smartphone. From the customer's perspective, this effectively puts e-tailers in very close proximity because they can all be shopped at the same location. Thus, the early exit of many e-tailers was the result of the Internet being overstored given the demand at the time, as well as many e-tailers' inability to control back-office costs.

Suppliers as Partners and Competitors

A retailer's suppliers should be considered both partners and competitors for the customer's dollar. Suppliers, as will be pointed out in Chapter 5, are critical to the retailer's trade, but they are also in competition for gross margins throughout the supply chain. Every extra dollar charged by the supplier is one less for the retailer when retail prices are stagnant. One remedy for the retailer is to develop a loyal group of patrons that encourages the supplier to accommodate the needs of its retail partner. As more manufacturers evaluate their investments and marketing money for retailers and explore their own direct-to-consumer marketing, retailers must determine how they can be most productive for their suppliers yet still maintain profitability.

When they provide a unique product or promotion, suppliers can be a critical competitive advantage to retailers. Many specialty retailers across categories vie to be the first with the latest products or to stock exclusive merchandise. Saks Fifth Avenue prides itself as the first to carry a new perfume in many retail areas. Further, suppliers can cooperate in improved merchandising and operations, such as developing a package design that is easier to read on the shelf or establishing efficient inventory-management systems. For example, OfficeMax has worked with office-supply manufacturers to use more informative labeling and packaging. This has greatly reduced the number of packages that customers rip open in the store to learn if the products are right for them.

Retailers also are recognizing that they can't be successful unless they have the help of their suppliers. For instance, retailers to attract customers need to regularly remodel

British retail chain, Marks and Spencer, is one of many retail chains that is looking to its suppliers to contribute a portion of their annual sales to assist in refurbishing its stores.

or refurbish their stores. Thus, retailers are asking suppliers for financial assistance in keeping their stores fresh and appealing to customers. Mark's and Spencer, a British retail chain dating back to 1884 and operating over 1,000 stores in 40 countries, has recently turned to 60 of its top clothing and home-ware suppliers and asked them to contribute 1.25 percent of their annual sales to help refurbish their U.K. stores.[19]

LO 2

Types of Competition

Distinguish between various types of retail competition.

It is possible to merge the preceding discussion of competition in retailing with the classification schemes used by the Department of Commerce in conducting the Census of Retail Trade.

Intratype and Intertype Competition

intratype competition Occurs when two or more retailers of the same type, as defined by NAICS codes in the Census of Retail Trade, compete directly with each other for the same households.

Intratype competition occurs when two or more retailers of the same type, as defined by North American Industry Classification System (NAICS) codes in the Census of Retail Trade, compete directly with each other for the same household dollars. This is the most common type of retail competition: TGI Friday's competes with Chili's, Avon competes with Mary Kay, Saks Fifth Avenue competes with Neiman Marcus, Family Dollar competes with Dollar General, and Amazon.com competes with bn.com (Barnes & Noble online). It needs to be stressed, however, that independent of the NAICS classification, retailers with the same NAICS do not necessarily compete with each other if one is selling luxury or highly expensive goods and services and the other less expensive. Clearly a TGI Friday competes with Chili's; but neither is competing with Fleming's or Morton's that are both high-priced steak restaurants where the average dinner tab is over $75 per person. Or, consider General Mills that owns Haagen-Dazs ice cream and sells it both through supermarkets and through its franchised ice cream shops in the United States and over 700 shops outside the United States.[20] A potential customer for a $1 soft serve McDonald's ice cream is most likely not the same customer for a $5 single scoop of Haagen-Dazs ice cream. The prior is a convenience good, but the latter is a specialty and luxury good. Incidentally, the Haagen-Dazs store on the Champs Elysees in Paris sells as many as 15,000 scoops of ice cream daily and has $9.5 million in annual sales. However, the fastest growing foreign market for Haagen-Dazs is China, where it already has over 100 stores. There, General Mills recognizes that it is in the luxury and personal indulgence business where its ice cream is merely the means to achieving the experience of feeling special.

Due to the changing nature of retailing, retailers are often forced to alter their strategy as their competition changes. For example, in the early 1990s Sears wanted to compete head on with low-priced discounters such as Walmart and Kmart. Today, after merging with Kmart in 2005, Sears is trying to reposition itself against middle-of-the-road merchants like JCPenney by appealing to women and emphasizing apparel. To generate more up-market store traffic, Sears acquired catalog merchant Lands' End, whose merchandise is now found in most of its stores. Sears has also tried to capitalize on the "nesting" and "cocooning" trend among many consumers by developing the Great Indoors, large freestanding home centers that offer both deeper selections of home furnishings and housewares and the convenience of at-the-door parking. Yet Sears still appears to be trying to find itself: Is it a Kmart or a Sears? After all, its once-dominant household appliance business—with its Kenmore, DieHard, and Craftsman brands—has been chipped away by Best Buy, Home Depot, and Lowe's. Its clothing business has suffered at the hands of JCPenney, Kohl's, and Marshalls, and even its identity as the place for one-stop shopping has been taken over by Walmart.

General Mills' Haagan-Dazs ice cream franchises aren't competitive and successful simply because they sell the newest flavors of ice cream. Unlike McDonald's soft-serve, it sells a luxury experience of personal indulgence.

intertype competition
Occurs when two or more retailers of a different type, as defined by NAICS codes in the Census of Retail Trade, compete directly by attempting to sell the same merchandise lines to the same households.

Every time *different* types of retail outlets (as defined by NAICS codes) sell the same lines of merchandise and compete for the same limited consumer dollars, **intertype competition** occurs. For example, department stores such as Saks, Macy's, or Nordstrom used to be where women shopped for cosmetics, but today, shopping for cosmetics can be at a CVS or Walgreens drugstore that has a limited merchandise assortment of cosmetics, which are competing with Sephora and Ulta Beauty, both operating cosmetics category killer stores, as well as e-tailing options (www.ulta.com and www.sephora.com), which offer a more broad and deep assortment of cosmetics. Actually, the retailing of cosmetics is a good example of the trend by many retailers of using a scrambled merchandising strategy. As discussed in Chapter 1, scrambled merchandising occurs when a retailer carries many different, unrelated product lines, often outside its traditional product mix, as a means of enhancing one-stop shopping convenience for its customers. For instance, when it comes to cosmetics, you not only witness Sephora, Ulta, CVS, Nordstrom, and Saks competing, but also discounters such as Target and grocery stores such as Food Lion.

Other examples of intertype competition and scrambled merchandising include the following:

- Not only have supermarkets (such as Albertsons, Food Lion, Kroger, Safeway, and Whole Foods) taken market share away from fast-food restaurants with their home meal replacements, but also travelers returning from trips are bringing home meal replacements home from the airport. In addition, both discounters and supermarkets with their floral departments, greeting card sections, banks, and pharmacies have changed the competitive landscape for traditional florists, card shops, banks, and drugstores.
- Many auto dealers, needing to create new additional revenue streams due to the recent sluggish economy, are beginning to sell auto insurance. These entrepreneurially driven dealerships have found that the customers like the convenience of having all their needs serviced by one business after a wreck.[21]

- Convenience stores (such as 7-Eleven) sell not only motor oil and related auto care products, but also fast food, lottery tickets, and pain relievers.
- Not only are home improvement retailers, such as Lowe's and Home Depot, and supermarkets, such as Kroger and Safeway, competing against each other, but also they are now engaged in an intertype battle with Walmart, which wants to be the market-share leader in all the lines it carries. Little wonder then that Home Depot has recently been devoting shelf space to home theater systems.

In each of the preceding examples, intertype competition expanded, and gross margins on the respective merchandise lines declined. Declining gross margins translates into lower consumer prices, and with the rise in health care costs, this can help explain how health clinics are the next big trend in intertype competition and scrambled merchandising. You probably first noticed these health clinics in drugstores such as Walgreens, where you could go for flu shots, minor illnesses, or for a checkup. Today, you see supermarkets entering this market. For instance, Little Clinic, a Tennessee-based retailer, partnered with Kroger and Publix because of their loyal customer base, long operating hours, heavy foot traffic, and pharmacies already in place.[22]

Divertive Competition

divertive competition
Occurs when retailers intercept or divert customers from competing retailers.

Another concept that helps to explain the nature of competition in retailing is **divertive competition**. This occurs when retailers intercept or divert customers from competing retailers. For example, a woman in need of a birthday card may plan to purchase one the next time she visits the local shopping mall, which has a well-stocked Hallmark card store. However, while picking up a prescription at the drugstore, she walks by a card stand and decides to purchase the greeting card at the drugstore. In this situation, the drugstore retailer has intercepted this customer from the Hallmark store.

A divertive tactic gaining in popularity today is to operate a gas station on one's property. In doing so, retailers catch customers who have already shopped and do not want to make another stop to get gas. Similarly, consumers who need gas may choose to consolidate shopping trips and shop the retailer's store after purchasing gas. Today, many warehouse clubs, discounters, and supermarkets use this tactic.

pop-up stores
Are temporary stores, which are relatively small in scale, that are set up for a short period of time, usually in conjunction with an event and often in high traffic areas, to explicitly intercept shoppers.

Pop-up stores are temporary stores, relatively small in terms of scale, that are set up for a relatively short period of time often at high shopper traffic points to explicitly intercept shoppers. For instance, eBay over the 2011 winter holiday season, opened up a pop-up store in London with the purpose of getting shoppers to purchase more online. Products were displayed with QR (quick response) codes that, when scanned by a smartphone, took the shopper to the eBay website to purchase the item and have it shipped to their homes.[23] This is a very interesting case of divertive competition because the individual at home shopping online has been a major form of divertive competition; but now online retailers such as eBay are getting more aggressive and setting up pop-up stores to catch shoppers who leave the house and decide to go to their favorite shopping malls.

Another area where divertive competition has been on a rapid escalation over the last few years is attributed to Internet-based innovations such as GROUPON, MeetUp.com, and LivingSocial that enable local retailers to send electronic coupons to households in the retailer's trade area or nearby trade areas. Often these coupons are for items you may have been planning to purchase at your favorite store and in the future but due to the incredible deals that GROUPON, MeetUp.com, and LivingSocial are able to offer, you make the purchase now and with a retailer you had not planned to shop. Another area of rapid growth in divertive competition is flash sale e-tailers. These are member-only websites where merchandise is offered at deep discounts but for a very limited time such as 48 hours or less. Once again, most of the sales that consumers

Richard Levine/Alamy

A growing trend in retailing, the pop-up store, seeks to build clientele by locating near high traffic locations.

make on flash sale websites have not been planned but are opportunistic and thus divert consumer spending away from regularly patronized retailers. Recognizing the rapid growth of flash sales Nordstrom has purchased HauteLook (www.hautelook.com) and Amazon has launched its own flash sale site Myhabit.com; both compete with Gilt Groupe (www.gilt.com) and Rue La La (www.ruelala.com), early innovators in flash sales.[24]

To comprehend the significance of divertive competition, which can be intertype or intratype competition, one needs to recognize that most retailers operate very close to their **breakeven point** (the point where total revenues equal total expenses). For instance, supermarkets, which have extremely low gross margin return on sales, tend to have high breakeven points, ranging from 94 percent to 96 percent of current sales. General merchandise retailers, with a higher gross margin return on sales, face lower breakeven points of 85–92 percent of their current sales. In either case, a modest drop in sales volume could make these retailers unprofitable. As a result, the use of scrambled merchandising and other intercept marketing techniques is growing as retailers seek more of the customer's share of wallet.

breakeven point Is where total revenues equal total expenses and the retailer is making neither a profit nor a loss.

LO 3

Describe the four theories used to explain the evolution of retail competition.

Evolution of Retail Competition

A discussion of the evolution of retailing not only provides a better understanding of the history of retail formats but also enhances our ability to make predictions about their future. Several theories have developed to explain and describe the evolution of competition in retailing. We will review three of them briefly and describe a new concept that helps to explain why a variety of retail formats have the potential to be profitable.

The Wheel of Retailing

The **wheel of retailing theory**, illustrated in Exhibit 4.4, is one of the oldest descriptions of competition in retailing.[25] This theory states that new types of retailers enter the market as low-status, low-margin, and low-price operators. This entry phase allows retailers

Exhibit 4.4
Wheel of Retailing

Moderate to high prices
Elaborate facilities
Increase in services

Trading-Up Phase

Vulnerability Phase

Entry Phase

High prices
Excellent facilities
Excellent service
Declining ROI

Low prices
Limited facilities
Limited service

wheel of retailing theory
Describes how new types of retailers enter the market as low-status, low-margin, low-price operators; however, as they meet with success, these new retailers gradually acquire more sophisticated and elaborate facilities, and thus become vulnerable to new types of low-margin retail competitors who progress through the same pattern.

to compete effectively and take market share away from the more traditional retailers. However, as they meet with success, these new retailers gradually enter a trading-up phase and acquire more sophisticated and elaborate facilities, often becoming less efficient. This creates both a higher investment and a subsequent rise in operating costs. Today, some academics refer to this stage as the "Big Middle," a market space where the largest numbers of potential customers reside.[26] Predictably, these retailers will eventually enter the vulnerability phase and must raise prices and margins to cover rising costs. In doing so, they become vulnerable to new types of low-margin retail competitors who progress through the same pattern. This appears to be the case today with outlet malls. Once bare-bones warehouses for manufacturers' imperfect or excess merchandise, outlet malls quickly evolved into fancy, almost upscale locations where retailers try to outdo each other's accent lighting, private dressing rooms, and generous return policies. As a result, the cost of operating such locations increased and put them in more direct competition with increasingly competitive department stores.

While the wheel of retailing may explain the evolution of some retail forms, it is less clear about the success of some new niche retailers; retailers that successfully compete on nonprice factors, such as luxury retailers or convenience stores, and the role of cost control in improving customer satisfaction as well as competitiveness, as membership warehouse clubs such as Costco, Sam's and B.J.'s have done.

The Retail Accordion

Several observers of the history of retailing have noted that retail institutions tend to evolve from outlets that offer wide merchandise assortments to specialized stores that offer narrow assortments and then return to the wide assortment stores, continuing this pattern again and again. This contraction and expansion of merchandise assortment suggests the term **retail accordion**.[27]

retail accordion
Describes how retail institutions evolve from outlets that offer wide assortments to specialized stores and continue repeatedly through the pattern.

Retail historians have observed that retail trade in the United States was dominated by the general store until 1860. The general store carried a broad assortment of merchandise ranging from wedding dresses to coffins and from farm implements to textiles and food. After 1860, due to the growth of cities and roads, retail trade became more specialized and was concentrated in the central business districts of cities. By 1880–1890, department and specialty stores were the dominant competitive force. Both carried more specialized assortments than the general store. In the 1950s, retailing began to move again to wider merchandise lines. Typical was the supermarket, which added seafood, produce, and dairy products and nonfood items such as kitchen utensils, health and beauty aids, and small household appliances. Today, specialization in merchandise categories has once again become a dominant competitive strategy. Witness, for example, the success of Sports Authority stores, Barnes & Noble bookstores, and Abercrombie & Fitch Co. Or, consider the case of Bill and Erik Young who are Ace Hardware franchisees in North Carolina. Facing competition from Lowe's, they renewed their focus on niche merchandise lines such as Stihl power equipment, Benjamin Moore paint, and high quality pet foods.[28]

However, the accordion theory is vague about the competitive importance of providing wide assortments for various target customer groups. For example, the customer who wants one-stop-shopping convenience has led to success for superstores that Carrefour began to build over 50 years ago and continues to build in Europe and South America and has contributed to the success of other retailers using scrambled merchandising. Simultaneously, many category killers have been successful by specializing in a deep but narrow selection of merchandise lines, and specialty stores like Forever 21 and high-end "hot" designers like Gucci have succeeded by offering a highly edited point of

istock.com

Some analysts suggest that gasoline stations are starting to follow the retail accordion theory as they expand assortments which creates an opportunity for a competitor to narrow assortments back to focusing only on gasoline.

view for their customer segments. Again, a major criticism of this theory is its implication that there is one "right" direction for successful retailing, when many are possible if well executed.

The Retail Life Cycle

retail life cycle
Describes four distinct stages that a retail institution progresses through: introduction, growth, maturity, and decline.

The final framework we will examine is the **retail life cycle**. Some experts argue that retailing institutions pass through an identifiable cycle. This cycle has four distinct stages: It starts with (1) *introduction*, proceeds to (2) *growth* and then (3) *maturity*, and ends with (4) *decline*.

Introduction

This stage begins with an aggressive, bold entrepreneur who is willing and able to develop a different approach to the retailing of certain products. Most often the approach is oriented toward a simpler method of distribution and passing the savings on to the customer. Other times, it could be a different version of an existing product or service centered on a distinctive product assortment, shopping ease, locational convenience, advertising, or promotion. For example, during the recent economic crisis, Americans saw the advent of new forms of rentals. These recent rentals were untraditional in that companies such as Zip Cars rented automobiles by the hour to consumers in large cities or to students on campuses. Other innovative firms offered an alternative to expensive purchases by renting consumers a Coach, Dooney & Bourke, or Dior handbag by the week.[29] Such repacking of traditional products has resulted in many consumers thinking back to the introduction of Starbucks over 25 years ago when consumers questioned the need for a $4 cup of coffee. As might be expected, during this stage, profits are low, despite the increasing sales level, due to amortizing developmental costs and not yet achieving sufficient scale economies.

Growth

During the growth stage, sales and usually profits explode. New retailers enter the market and begin to copy the idea. For example, the rapid growth of e-tailers has encouraged others to enter the market and capture a portion of the growing interest of shopping casually from home. Toward the end of the growth stage, cost pressures arise from the need for a larger staff, more complex internal systems, increased management controls, and other requirements of operating large, multiunit organizations. Consequently, late in this stage, market share reaches its maximum level but profitability begins to decline as retailers cut margins to maintain market share. As growth slows, retailers seek to alter their existing offerings in order to recreate a more profitable and successful niche. This brings up an important point and lesson; even in a slowing and overcrowded market there can be new market opportunity. For instance, consider the growth of population in the United States from India, and the associated interest even among domestics in Indian food. This presented an opportunity for Sushil Malhotra and his son, who launched Café Spice as one of the first Indian fast food retail chains.[30]

Maturity

In maturity, two factors occur that cause market share to stabilize and profits to decline. First, managers have become accustomed to managing a high-growth firm that was simple and small, yet now they must manage a large, complex firm in a nongrowing

RETAILING — The Inside Story

North America's Oldest Retailer

Recently, a television quiz show asked, "What is the oldest retailer in North America?" One contestant answered "A&P" (for the Great Atlantic & Pacific Tea Company), and the other answered "Sears." Both were wrong. A&P was founded in 1859, and Sears, Roebuck and Company started business in 1886. The oldest U.S. retailer is Brooks Brothers, which Henry Sands Brooks opened for business on April 7, 1818, as H. & D. H. Brooks & Co. In 1870, Brooks's four sons inherited the family business and renamed the company "Brooks Brothers." In addition, Lord & Taylor (1826) and Macy's (1858) are both older than A&P. (See the discussion of the current A&P in Chapter 2.)

However, none of these U.S. retailers correctly answers the question. The oldest retailer in North America is Canadian retailer The Hudson's Bay Company, which was chartered by King Charles II on May 2, 1670, to trade fur pelts; it remains one of Canada's major retail players. How "The Bay," as it is known in Canada, has survived the changing retail environment and how it continues to adjust to the retail life cycle is an interesting story.

Throughout its history, The Bay has operated department stores, discount department stores, big-box chains, a smaller regional chain, and an online shopping site. Currently, the company has more than 600 stores in Canada, a country with a population of about 32 million people.

Understanding the changing nature of competition in the marketplace has helped The Bay remain successful over a long period of time. The backbone of the company is its department store chain known as The Bay. The chain has stores from coast to coast in Canada and occupies top-flight downtown, flagship locations in all major cities. It also has a presence in most of the major suburban malls in Canada. Over the years, The Bay has evolved into a mid- to upper-price-point, full-line department store. It focuses on fashion, cosmetics, and soft goods but still carries electronics and appliances. The stores carry many of the same brands as American retailer Macy's as well as a number of brands exclusive to The Bay. Only one other major, national department store remains in Canada: Sears. Others such as Eaton's have disappeared as the department store concept lost popularity and moved into decline.

With department stores in decline, The Bay has been successful by expanding into other retail endeavors. In 1978, The Bay purchased Zellers, a discount department store offering a mass merchandise concept. Using an everyday low-price policy, Zellers has succeeded. The development of a loyalty program for Zellers also helped it weather the storm of Walmart entering Canada in 1994 by buying 122 Woolco stores. Notably, Kmart Canada did not survive. In 1998, Zellers bought all the remaining Kmart stores and converted them to the Zellers format.

Anticipating the growth of the specialty superstore market, The Bay launched Home Outfitters in 1999. This kitchen, bed, and bath specialty superstore is currently the fastest-growing specialty store chain in Canada and has survived the onslaught of many competitors, such as Linens 'n Things, seeking to steal their market share.

In 2000, The Bay launched hbc.com, the company's online store. Hbc.com has been successful for The Bay to date and keeps it moving forward with retail concepts that are in the growth stage.

Throughout this time, The Bay has also hung onto its small value-priced general merchandiser, Fields. Although not very well-known, Fields has continued to be successful. These stores are located only in western Canada and are focused on smaller retail centers, a market somewhat overlooked by larger retailers. Today, many retail analysts are looking forward to watching the evolution of Fields as Walmart expands into smaller centers in Canada.

Jerry Zucker, an American businessman, purchased The Bay in 2006, ending more than 335 years of The Bay as a publicly traded company. In late 2008, NRDC, owner of Lord & Taylor, bought The Hudson's Bay Co. Under this new ownership team, The Bay is looking to continue its successful history as a premier player in Canadian retailing. A portfolio of retail concepts in differing stages of the retail life cycle should ensure continued success.

Source: This box was prepared by D. Lynne Ricker, University of Calgary, and coauthor of this text's Canadian edition.

market. Second, the industry has typically overexpanded, for example, consider the fast food industry and the number of burger outlets or number of pizza restaurants in your local community. Second, competitive assaults increase as firms with new retailing formats or more-efficient methods proliferate in the industry (entrepreneurs starting a new retail life cycle).

Decline

Although decline is inevitable for some formats (few people get their milk delivered to the door anymore) retail managers will try to postpone it by changing the retail mix. These attempts can postpone the decline stage, but a return to earlier, attractive levels of operating performance is unlikely. Sooner or later, a major loss of market share will occur, profits will fall, and the once-promising idea will no longer be needed in the marketplace.

The retail life cycle is accelerating today. New and more competitive concepts move quickly from introduction to maturity since the leading operators have aggressive growth goals and their investors demand a quick return on equity. Once a retail concept is proven successful, a retailer can have a successful public offering of its stock and raise significant funds for a rapid national roll out and expansion. Once a retail concept is proven, it is not unusual for a retailer to open a new store every week or if the stores are smaller, such as in a fast food restaurant concept, one new store every day. For instance, rue21 that we mentioned earlier was a firm that emerged out of a bankruptcy in May 2003 and by 2011 had close to 700 stores and this should reach 1,000 in a few years. This chapter's "Retailing: The Inside Story" box describes how North America's oldest retailer has survived by adjusting to the retail life cycle.

A final word of caution needs to be sounded regarding the retail life cycle. Keep in mind the stage that the retail innovation is country specific. An excellent example would be direct selling channels that are in decline in the United States. This would include firms such as Amway, Avon, Mary Kay, and Tupperware. Over the last couple of decades, direct sellers have done best in fast-growing countries that also lack adequate retail infrastructure. However, even this general rule can be shown to not always fit. For instance, Tupperware saw its worldwide sales rise by 6 percent in 2010, whereas, in France (a country that has been sluggish in growth) they rose 19.2 percent.[31] Of course, we know the French love food and well-prepared meals, but 25- to 45-year-old women were not well trained to cook. Thus, Tupperware has turned its in-home parties into workshops to teach women how to prepare meals. This strategy was coupled with adding more expensive merchandise such as knives and cookware. At many parties, the average sale is over $750.

Resource-Advantage Theory

The final theory to describe the evolution of retail competition is resource-advantage theory.[32] This theory is based on the idea that all firms seek superior financial performance in an ever-changing environment. Retail demand is dynamic because consumer tastes are always changing, and supply is dynamic because, as firm's search for a superior performance, they are forced to change the elements of their retail mix to match changing consumer preferences.

Resource-advantage theory illustrates four important lessons for retailers:[33]

- Superior performance at any point in time is the result of achieving a competitive advantage in the marketplace as a result of some tangible or intangible resource.

- All retailers cannot achieve superior results at the same time.
- The retailer is able to use this resource, such as an innovation regarding location procedures or merchandise selection, to offer greater relative value to the marketplace.
- The retailer is able to use this resource, such as innovation regarding location procedures or merchandise selection, to operate its firms at a lower cost relative to competitors.

Thus, it is important for currently high-performing retailers to maintain their vigilance over the actions of innovative new retailers and lower-performing competitors so as not to be overtaken.

The result is ongoing market turbulence in which new retail forms and offerings continually appear, and consumers continually shift their buying preferences and retail patronage. As retailers compete with each other through different combinations of resources (merchandise selection, pricing, service, communication, positioning, distribution improvements, and relationship building), each of these multifaceted competitive positions can meet the needs of different customer groups. The resulting fragmentation in the marketplace means that many different retail forms are viable, as long as the customer group is sufficiently substantial (i.e., large enough to generate acceptable profit for the retailer) and the retailer is astute in managing its customer relationships and operations. So long as each retailer meets the needs of its target customers better than competitors, while controlling its costs of satisfying those customers, the retailer will prosper.

This is one explanation of why dollar stores such as Dollar General can survive in the same markets with larger discounters that offer better prices, wider assortments, and groceries. Many consumers, lacking personal transportation, rely on Dollar General as a quick, convenient place for sundries and grab-and-go foods. It also explains why Panera Bread can do well despite its higher prices compared with Subway or other fast food retailers such as Burger King. Panera Bread focuses on the consumer's desire for fresh, customizable, convenience that is affordable.[34] Also, they have a relaxed atmosphere where there is no time limit, and thus, it has become a sort of community gathering place and not just a bustling spot to have breakfast, lunch, or a light dinner. Incidentally, at Panera, the average check is nearly $9, whereas at Subway, it is around $7. Also, at Panera average store sales are over twice of Subway. Even more interesting is Five Guys, which only sells hamburgers and French fries and is able to charge higher prices than McDonald's, Burger King, and Wendy's. Five Guys is authentic and real and focuses on the basics of eating in a very plain and simple atmosphere. As some customers have said: "shut up, sit down, and eat."

The fact remains that not all customers are equally knowledgeable about retail alternatives, not all retailers are as astute about understanding their customers, not all customers have similar preferences or access to retail alternatives, and not all retailers have the resources to meet the competition for their traditional customers. Amway, a direct to household selling company, has recently seen retailers, ranging from Walmart to Tractor Supply, make inroads into its suburban and rural base and online merchants tap its traditional "shop-at-home" customers. As a result, Amway is seeking to reposition itself. These marketplace discrepancies allow for less-than-optimal retail environments but also reveal opportunities to the retailer that is willing to study its customers and markets and do a better job in managing its operations. Following these actions, it is then imperative that the retailer communicates its superiority to target customers, thus pushing competition to a new and evolved level. In the "What's New?" box on the next page you will learn how Kohl's is using charitable giving and acts of kindness to get into the hearts and mind of the communities it operates within and thus gives itself a competitive advantage.

WHAT'S NEW ?

Kohl's Cares® for the Kids and Communities in Which They Operate

Business leaders and commentators can occasionally be heard eloquently equating competition with war and battle. The analogy's a bit dramatic, but it underscores the strategic nature of retailing and the multiple "battles" that must be won in order to become, and remain, a high-performance retailer. One battle that Kohl's is fighting, and winning, is a battle for the "hearts and minds" of the people and communities it serves.

And no they're not winning hearts and minds simply by providing that great looking "top" you've been eyeing for the last month at a really great deal.

How then you might ask? Kohl's believes in giving back to the communities it serves not only by providing money and resources, but also by volunteering associates' talent and time. The Wisconsin-based retailer doesn't simply finance community projects; it likes to actually get in there and "get its hands dirty." Through their Kohl's Cares® philanthropic programs the retailer actively supports kids' health and education initiatives, advances environmental solutions, and battles breast cancer on behalf of women's health.

When a minimum of five associates from one Kohl's location volunteer at least three-consecutive hours of their time to any qualifying organization (i.e., a non-profit 501(c)(3) organization), Kohl's provides that non-profit firm with a financial grant to support their cause. In so doing, the charitable organization benefits not only from the money provided, but also the equivalent of 15 hours of free labor—something many non-profits struggle with given their limited amount of funds available to pay wages. Since 2001, Kohl's "Associates in Action" program has resulted in 64,000 volunteer events, more than $35 million in grants, and over 1,200,000 hours of volunteer support for local non-profit organizations geared to help children and/or fight breast cancer.

But the retailer doesn't simply rely upon its associates to identify and support needy charities. No, the retailer wants nonprofits working on behalf of the above initiatives to make themselves known to the manager(s) of

their local Kohl's and inform them of upcoming events. Non-profits can also fill out an "Associates in Action" request sheet online (at http://www.kohlscorporation .com/communityrelations/PDFs/AiARequestNov10.pdf) to ensure any non-profit event is at least considered for support. Likewise, Kohl's provides its own customers with an easy avenue for supporting local children's needs.

Throughout the year, Kohl's sells kid-friendly cause-related merchandise, usually consisting of stuffed animals and matching books (e.g., Bill Martin, Jr. and Eric Carle's "Brown Bear, Brown Bear, What Do You See?" book and corresponding brown bear stuffed-animal), where 100 percent of the net proceeds is donated to support children's health and education initiatives nationwide. Occupying some of the most valuable retail selling space, that area(s) next to the check-out registers commonly reserved for impulse buys like candy, batteries, and the like, Kohl's provides a way for every customer to get involved and help move a child one step closer to getting the opportunity to go to college or get the needed medical attention. And the merchandise program's a huge success: since 2001, it has raised over $180 million for children in need.

Admittedly, Kohl's is a retailer looking to compete, make money, and remain successful just like the thousands of other retailers mentioned within this text and populating your local town. Kohl's just seeks to compete differently than most. The retailer's promise reads "Expect Great Things," and they work extremely hard within each store, and company-wide, to literally make that promise come true every day. Interestingly though, many readers of this story likely never realized that Kohl's term "great things" applies to many areas beyond great merchandise, service, and in-store and online deals the shopper can experience. Kohl's wants every *community* within which it operates to *also* "Expect Great Things."

Sources: Shamion, Vicki and Sam Morris (2012), "Kohl's to Open New Distribution Center to Support E-Commerce Growth," *The New York Times* [online] Available at: http://markets.on.nytimes.com [Accessed: April 8, 2012]; Kohlscorporation.com (2012) "Kohl's Cares" [online] Available at: http://www.kohlscorporation.com/communityrelations/Community01.htm [Accessed: April 8, 2012]; and the authors' communications with several store managers and assistant managers.

LO 4

Describe the changes that could affect retail competition.

Future Changes in Retail Competition

Retailers in today's ever-changing marketplace can expect dynamic changes in competition. Trends shaping the retail landscape include an increase in competition from nonstore retailers, the advent of new retailing formats, heightened global competition, the integration of technology into current operations, and the increasing use of private labels.

Nonstore Retailing

Back in Exhibit 1.3, it was pointed out that nonstore retail sales (NAICS Code 454), including direct sellers, catalog sales, and e-tailing, account for 7 percent of total retail sales. However, most retail analysts predict that, as a result of several key forces at work today, only Internet sales will experience significant growth over the next decade, while the other forms of nonstore retailing, direct selling, and catalog sales will remain steady or decline. Thus, the growth of this form of selling is based on accelerated communication technology and changing consumer lifestyles. Thus, retailers need to continuously monitor developments in nonstore retailing.

E-Tailing

The general belief among retail experts is that electronic, interactive, at-home shopping is definitely the place to be. Every major player in the retail industry, computer industry, telecommunications industry, and the transaction processing industry is committed to this growth. The only prerequisite needed for the Internet's success is having enough consumers with access, whether it is via a personal computer, cell phone, or BlackBerry. Already more than 75 percent of American households are connected either at home or at work, and a rather astonishing fact is that more people now use cell phones and not landline phones as their primary means of phone communication. More important is the fact that today's teens and 20-somethings are the first generation to grow up fully wired and technologically fluent. These consumers, especially college students, use social-networking websites such as MySpace and Facebook as a way to establish their identities; they are also more apt to text message than call a friend.

Most Gen Xers and baby boomers tend to view the Internet as a supplement to their daily lives. They use the Net to gather information, buy items (CDs, books, stocks, gifts, and even fast food), or link up with others who share a passion for their favorite sports team. Yet, for the most part, their social lives remain rooted in the traditional phone call and face-to-face interaction.

Gen Y folks, by contrast, are able to exist in both worlds simultaneously. Increasingly, America's middle- and upper-class youth use social networks as virtual community centers, a place to go and sit for awhile (sometimes hours). While older consumers come and go on the Net for a specific task, Gen Yers are just as likely to socialize online as off. This is partly a function of how much more comfortable young people are on the Web. A recent study on the Internet and American Life by the Pew Foundation revealed 93 percent of those aged 12–17 use the Internet, 95 percent from ages 18–29, 87 percent from ages 31–49, 78 percent from ages 50–64, and 42 percent over 65 years.[35]

As the Internet grows, Americans will make increasing use of it as a shopping method.[36] Many shoppers will opt for its convenience and broad selection. Browsing will be easier and the choices more extensive. (Nevertheless, consumers will still want the social experience of shopping outside the home; after all, with so many stores nearby, shopping at a bricks-and-mortar retailer after doing active information gathering on the computer will become even more convenient.) Exhibit 4.5 reveals some interesting trends on the use of the Internet for shopping. In 1998 the Internet garnered only

Exhibit 4.5
Retail E-Commerce
Market Share: 1998–2017

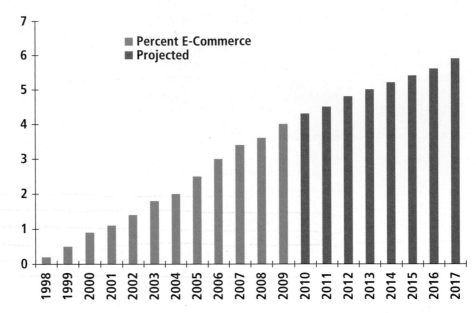

Source: U.S. Census Bureau, "E-Stats, 2009 E-commerce Multi-sector Report," May 2011. For more information: http://www.census.gov/eos/www/ebusiness614.htm http://www.census.gov/econ/estats/ Internet release date 9/30/2011; Data after 2009 is projections by authors.

.2 percent of total retail sales; by 2001 this had grown to 1.1 percent and by 2006 it rose to 3 percent, in 2009 it rose to 4 percent and by 2017 it is projected to be close to 6 percent. If anything the projections may be low.

It is important to remember that the Internet will not increase overall consumer demand. While online sales will definitely cannibalize store and catalog sales, they will not increase the average consumer spending power. Strategies by clicks-and-mortar retailers that integrate a single message and seamless operations will be more powerful than a pure e-tailing strategy. This will be especially true once clicks-and-mortar retailers learn the importance of addressing the total customer experience through any contact point with the customer. A final point to remember is that e-tailers must pay attention to customer service. Most e-tailers do a good job during busy seasons, such as Christmas and Valentine's Day. However, in an effort to reduce operating costs, they reduce their service standards at other times. Customers are demanding such basic services as e-mail confirmation of orders and real-time confirmation of available inventory. Since customer service is a particular vulnerability for traditional retailers, e-tailers should seek their niche here. This is probably even more important as high-income households increasingly use the Internet to purchase expensive and luxury apparel and accessories. These finicky customers want a special type of service and assurance that if something doesn't fit or look right they can easily and quickly return with no hassles.

However, the most significant contribution of the Internet to retailing is that it has enabled everyone to be a retailer, albeit a microretailer, by using eBay. This tremendous impact on individuals of all ages is best seen by the number of training seminars, community colleges, senior centers, and so on, offering classes on how to buy and sell on eBay.

New Retailing Formats

The practice of retailing is continually evolving. New formats are born and old ones die. Innovation in retailing is the result of constant pressure to improve efficiency and effectiveness in a continual effort to better serve the consumer. The pressure to better serve has also resulted in a shortened life cycle for retail formats. However, just as retailers find it extremely difficult to predict what will be the "hot new item" for an upcoming season, especially the December holiday season, they have the same trouble predicting the success of new retail formats.

For example, in the early 1980s, most retail experts agreed that hypermarkets (which are one and one-half times the size of a supercenter) would be retailing's success story of the 1980s. However, despite their overwhelming success in Europe and their limited success in the United States (Meijer's in Michigan and Kroger's Fred Meyer division in the Northwest), these super large stores, which resembled airplane hangars, were instead one of retailing's biggest failures. What happened?

Customers probably felt that any store that had "rest areas" and stockers wearing roller skates was just too big to shop. Also shoppers were unnerved by ceilings and shelves that rose several stories high. In addition, category killers such as Toys "R" Us and Sports Authority offered greater selection, wholesale clubs offered better prices, and supermarkets, discount drug stores, and other discounters offered more convenient locations. Although hypermarkets were a superior competitive offering in Europe, where the traditional alternatives were small, crowded shops with high prices, they did not have a noteworthy competitive advantage in the overstored American retail landscape.

Another retail format that didn't achieve the success predicted was the off-price retailer. **Off-price retailers** were similar to discounters with one important difference. While discounters offer continuity of brands—that is, they carry the same brands day in and day out—off-pricers, which are more opportunistic, carry only brands that they are able to get on special deals from the manufacturer or close-out wholesalers. Thus, the off-price retailers failed because the regular merchants, including discounters, became more competitive on the prices of the brands that the off-pricers were selling. Moreover, the off-price merchandise brands and selection could be wildly unpredictable as manufacturers became better at planning production and inventories.

The three primary examples of off-price retailers are factory outlets, independent carriers, and warehouse clubs. Factory outlets, which are owned and operated by the manufacturer, stock the manufacturers' surplus, discontinued, or irregular products. Independent off-price retailers such as Loehmann's, Stein Mart, TJ Maxx, and websites such as Overstock.com carry an ever-changing assortment of higher-quality merchandise. Warehouse (or wholesale) clubs such as Costco and Sam's were the most successful of the off-pricers. These mature-stage retailers operate out of enormous, low-cost facilities and charge patrons an annual membership fee. They sell a limited selection of brand-name grocery items, appliances, clothing, and miscellaneous items at a deep discount. Warehouse stores, which have low costs because they buy products at huge quantity discounts and use limited labor, usually have low gross margins (gross margin will be explained in detail in Chapter 8) averaging nearly 10–12 percent, which is a third of traditional retailers.

One highly successful retail innovation is the **supercenter**—a cavernous combination of supermarket and discount department store carrying more than 80,000–100,000 SKUs that range from televisions to peanut butter and DVDs. These stores offer the customer one-stop shopping (and as a result are capable of drawing customers from a 50-mile radius in some rural areas) and lower the customer's total cost in terms of time and miles traveled. They are expected to continue being a profitable format for mass merchants.

The supercenter concept has even branched out into the automobile market. Glitzy, computerized auto superstore chains such as AutoNation, Driver's Mart Worldwide, and CarMax Auto Superstores are giving nightmares to the nation's 22,000 traditional car dealers. Since its introduction in the mid-1990s, this new breed of retailer has streamlined an industry in which more than 15 percent of a car's price consists of retailer expenses and has made shopping easier for the customer. These massive, publicly

off-price retailers
Sell products at a discount but do not carry certain brands on a continuous basis. They carry those brands they can buy from manufacturers at closeout or deep one-time discount prices.

supercenter
A cavernous combination of supermarket and discount department store carrying more than 80,000 to 100,000 SKUs that allows for one-stop shopping.

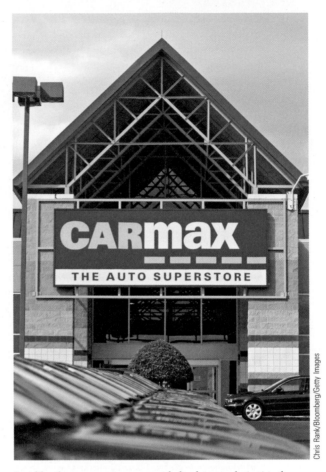

Chris Rank/Bloomberg/Getty Images

Just like the supercenter concept helped to revolutionize the grocery industry, auto-superstores like CarMax have made it easier for customers to buy a new or used automobile.

traded chains sell new and used cars using "cheap" Wall Street money to finance, sell, rent, lease, and repair cars. Just like the supercenters in the grocery industry, these auto superstores are making competition tougher for other auto retailers.

Although the supercenters have achieved their promise while hypermarkets and off-pricers neglected to live up to expectations, three successful formats developed over the last decade are expected to continue: stores that recycle usable merchandise in good condition, such as Gazelle (www.gazelle.com), which buys or recycles used consumer electronics like cell phones, blue ray players, and laptops through an Internet site, liquidators, and rental or trading operations like Swap hand-me-downs (www.swaphandmedowns.com), an online operation that facilitates the trading of children's clothing, toys, and books. These three formats have one thing in common: They offer the consumer value in an untraditional manner.

Recycled Merchandise Retailers

recycled merchandise retailers
Are establishments that sell used and reconditioned products.

Due to their very small numbers just a decade ago, recycled merchandisers have experienced the fastest growth of any retail format over the past five years. As a result of the recent economic slowdown, **recycled merchandise retailers** selling slightly used children's clothes (Once Upon a Child), teen and adult clothing (Plato's Closet), sporting goods (Play It Again Sports), musical instruments (Music-Go-Round), and even building

UNIQLO, one of Japanese retail conglomerate Fast Retailing's branded stores, is making huge profits in the "fast fashion" industry.

materials (Restore www.habitat.org/restores and Elmwood www.elmwoodreclaimedtimber .com), and videogames (Gamestop) have experienced significant growth.[37] In addition, pawn shops, thrift shops, auction houses, consignment shops, flea markets, and even eBay are also considered to be recyclers.

The recycle concept was pioneered by the Salvation Army in London in 1865 to provide merchandise to poor households as well as generate funds to feed and house the poor. Historically, most recyclers were found in the poorer sections of cities, sometimes tucked away in dreary brick buildings with dumpsters on the side. Not anymore. Today these establishments have soft lighting and wide aisles, clothing in neat racks that is coordinated by color and size, plenty of changing rooms, and well-trained and polite salespeople.

As a record number of retailers were seeking bankruptcy protection in 2009, these stores saw a growth rate approaching 20 percent. No longer was conspicuous consumption chic. Today, even the baby boomers who live in big fancy homes in the suburbs and invest in stocks and mutual funds find it fashionable to pull into parking lots with big PAWN SHOP, THRIFT STORE, or SECOND HAND signs while driving their BMWs.[38]

Now that many pre-owned clothes shops are using the same media as traditional retailers to advertise their merchandise, shoppers today may find it difficult to distinguish between recyclers and small specialty shops. Because so much of the merchandise is new, nearly new, or gently used, the tattered appearance of traditional thrift stores is no longer expected. Recyclers have developed to serve specific markets such as pregnant women, people requiring large sizes, and children; or even to offer specific merchandise such as toys, sporting goods, outerwear, or jewelry. Swap hand-me-downs (www .swaphandmedowns.com), is an online operation that facilitates the trading of children's clothing, toys and books. The apparel group accounting for the fewest resale and thrift store sales is men's clothing. It seems that men hang on to their clothes longer than women and children, leaving much less merchandise available for resale.

Liquidators

Between 2008 and 2009, more than 300,000 retail stores, including such well-known retailers as Circuit City, Mervyn's, Linens 'n Things, and Steve & Barry's, closed as a result of bankruptcy. This provided a new retail growth format (albeit another from a very small starting point): liquidators. Often called retailing's undertakers or vultures, firms like Buxbaum Group, Great American Group, and Hilco Organization purchase the entire inventory of the existing retailer and run its "going-out-of-business" sale. They assume responsibility for a retailer's leases, payroll, and other costs and agree either to take a percentage of what they sell or agree in advance to purchase the existing inventory. They are gambling that they will be able to unload the merchandise at prices that will generate a solid profit, which is often the case given they rarely pay more than 30 cents on the dollar for the merchandise. Liquidators do more than $15 billion in sales annually and earn between 3 percent and 7 percent of the sales or they take over the company entirely and take all the risks but make all the profits. Here they will pay a small percent of the cost value of existing inventory.[39]

Some might question why retailers don't do this job themselves, as some manufacturers do with outlet malls. First, the retailers in question usually have problems, or they wouldn't need the liquidator's service in the first place. Second, most liquidators pay cash for the merchandise—a plus for the strapped retailer—and then take all the risks and gain the rewards. In addition, liquidators sometimes augment sales by bringing in new merchandise or by adding leftovers from previous liquidations.[40]

Finally, by having outsiders run the closeouts, management can focus on operating the continuing stores and moving on to (hopefully) more successful merchandising.

Running closeouts requires some very special retailing skills. Liquidators have a talent for pricing merchandise and estimating the expense of everything from ad budgets and payrolls to utility bills. Since most of the employees know they will be out of a job as soon as the liquidation is complete, liquidators have to develop special incentive plans to make it more profitable for store personnel to stay and work rather than quit or walk off with merchandise.

Rentals

The idea of renting and not purchasing an item is not new. Renting has been popular for a limited number of items for decades. Most college students have rented VCR tapes and DVDs. Other consumers have rented furniture on a rent-to-own basis. Similarly, everyone has probably rented a car on a daily or weekly basis. However, the recent slumping economy has generated a renewed interest in this format for an expanded category of products. This chapter will discuss three versions of these new rental formats that are most apt to be used by college students: cars by the hour, fashion items, and textbooks.

Ever needed a car for an hour or so? This is a common problem for college students who live on campus without a car, consumers who live in large cities with extensive mass transit programs and rental spaces that often meet or exceed the car's monthly payment, and retired consumers who live in senior-citizen communities where they have a rather infrequent need for a car. Today, retailers such as Zipcar and Hertz are meeting this need with a retail strategy of renting cars for short periods of time, often by the hour. Zipcar is available on more than 250 university campuses.[41] Such an operation is attractive to customers who make only occasional use of a vehicle.[42] Today, there are more than 700,000 consumers in more than 100 cities and campuses who pay an annual membership fee to use one of the 10,000 vehicles currently involved in this program. Many expect this number to continue growing at an annual rate of 20 percent as consumers recognize the ease and convenience the program offers.

Given the current economic climate, many fashion-conscious consumers now have less cash for that pricey new handbag, designer dress or gown, piece of jewelry, or other accessories. Maybe renting, and not buying, offers the solution. Internet companies such as Rent the Runway (www.renttherunway.com) and Bag Borrow or Steal (www.bagborroworsteal.com) offer designer dresses and handbags for rent for a week, a month, or even longer. In some cases, these online retailers will even apply some of the rental fees toward the purchase of the items.[43]

The final area of rental growth effecting college students is textbooks. Consider the benefits of renting textbooks to the student. The typical college student spends slightly more than $500 a term for textbooks and gets around $200 when selling them back at semester's end, according to federal statistics. In addition, price increases have recently been outstripping inflation. But books cost (typically) only a third that much at the 50 or so schools around the country that rent books. These schools typically charge a "usage fee" of about $7 to $8 per credit hour, meaning a student taking 15 credit hours of classes would only pay either $105 or $120 at the beginning of the semester. After final exams, students simply return the books and they avert those end-of-semester "bookstore won't buy back my book" blues. The major drawbacks for a school trying to adopt such a program are faculty commitment and the huge upfront costs that schools would incur when building the initial inventory of textbooks.[44]

Heightened Global Competition

The rate of change in retailing around the world appears to be directly related to the stage and speed of economic development in the countries concerned, but even the least-developed countries are experiencing dramatic changes. Retailing in other countries exhibits greater diversity in its structure than it does in the United States. In some countries, such as Italy, retailing is composed largely of specialty houses carrying narrow lines. Finnish retailers usually carry a more general line of merchandise. The size of the average retailer is also diverse—from the massive Harrod's in London and Mitsukoshi Ltd. in Japan, both of which serve more than 10,000 customers a day, to the small one- or two-person stalls in developing African and Latin American nations.

New types of retailing have emerged from all areas of the world. These changing formats can be attributed to a variety of economic and social factors that are the same worldwide: a widespread concern for health, a steady increase in the number of working women and two-income families, inflation, consumerism, and so forth. These factors, and their effects on consumer lifestyles, encourage retailers around the world to seek new market segments, make adjustments in their retail mix, alter location patterns, and adopt new multi-segment strategies. In the process, many new retail concepts and formats have emerged and spread.

Still, it is amazing that retailers from larger countries often do not have the same success, compared to that of retailers from smaller countries, when entering a new country. Consider, for example, the fact that at the end of fiscal year 2011 Walmart, in addition to its 3,868 stores in the United States, was operating 88 units in Argentina, 512 in Brazil, 333 in Canada, 622 in Central America, 316 in Chile, 320 in China, 15 in India, 419 in Japan, 2,088 in Mexico, and 541 in the United Kingdom.[45] In 2008 the chain sold its operations in both Germany and South Korea when they failed to meet profit expectations.

In Germany, Walmart found the discount retail market too tough for one to crack as homegrown discount retailers already offered very low prices. Walmart also failed to understand the frugal and demanding ways of German shoppers. For similar reasons, Walmart's biggest global competitor, Paris-based Carrefour, which operates more than

15,000 stores in 29 countries yet is second to Walmart in total sales, never entered the market citing German regulations, restricting store hours, and other retailing basics.[46] Walmart, despite becoming the largest grocery retailer in markets like Brazil, faced similar challenges from Carrefour and others in Britain. Meanwhile, H&M, the Swedish women's apparel chain, and Zara, the vertically integrated women's apparel chain from Spain, both create excitement and sales in most foreign markets they enter. Zara is an especially interesting case study in high-performance retailing. The firm began in a small town in Spain in 1975, and its parent Inditex is the number one apparel retailer in the world with stores in over 75 nations in Africa, America, Asia, Europe, and the Middle East. Zara also owns brands such as Massimo Dutti, Pull and Bear, Oysho, Uterqüe, Stradivarius and Bershka. Not far behind, and aiming to be the world's largest apparel retailer, is Fast Retailing[47] which is a Japanese retail conglomerate that owns retail apparel stores operating under the following names[48]: Uniqlo, GOV Retailing, Cabin Co. Comptoir des Cotonniers, Princesse Tam.Tam Theory and Helmut Lang.

As H&M from Sweden, Inditex from Spain, and Fast Retailing from Japan have experienced explosive global expansion over the last decade, U.S. retailer enterprises such as Kmart, Sears, and JCPenney have all abandoned their foreign-expansion plans. Many successful British merchants such as Conran's Habitat, a housewares chain, and Laura Ashley have not been able to replicate their success in the United States.

Retail experts attribute this failure by large-country retailers to two factors. Some think it is a lack of understanding of the new country's culture. Even Walmart made major mistakes when it entered international markets. In Canada, its cultural faux pas was distributing English-language circulars in French-speaking Quebec. On entering Mexico, the chain built large parking lots at some of its stores only to realize that most of their customers rode the bus and then had to cross these large, empty parking lots carrying bags full of merchandise. Walmart responded by creating a shuttle bus service. This error was especially embarrassing for Walmart since one of the key factors for its overall success was the fact that the company started and stayed in small rural markets until it completely understood its customers and channel partners. It was such a mistake that led Best Buy to buy a 50-percent interest in the United Kingdom's Carphone Warehouse Group. By doing so, the American retailer was able to partner with someone who understood the market environment instead of going alone and stumbling.[49]

The late Michael O'Connor, former president of the Super Market Institute and retail consultant, had another explanation. He felt that the failure of many retailers to succeed in international markets was the result of larger countries having successful economies and retailers becoming accustomed to success. Retailers in smaller countries do not take success for granted and thus tend to take more time and be more careful with key decisions. According to O'Connor, by being a little less sure of themselves, executives from smaller countries sought more counsel and listened to more opinions before developing strategic plans.[50] Along the same lines, smaller country retailers have always had to deal with international issues in order to expand.

One smaller country retailer who has made an impact on international retailing is Ingvar Kamprad, president of Ikea. Ikea was the first to successfully develop a warehouse retailing format that could be followed around the world. The firm's warehouse format, which is based on economies of scale in the areas of marketing, purchasing, and distribution and which utilizes customer participation in the assembly and transportation of the merchandise, generates almost 90 percent of its revenues from global operations—more than any other major worldwide retailer.

Several apparel retailers have also recently entered the American market due to the weak dollar, which reduced the cost of their initial investment, and favorable terms on store leases as landlords looked for new tenants to replace retailers who had gone bankrupt. For example, Sweden's Hennes & Mauritz AB, with nearly 200 U.S. stores, calls the United States its "largest expansion market."[51] Also expanding in the United States are Spain's Zara (owned by Inditex SA) and Mango chains, Germany's luxury sport brand Bogner, Russia's Kira Plastinina, Iceland's Kisan, Japan's Muji, and Britain's Topshop chain and Karen Millen brand.[52]

Opening shop in the United States, of course, isn't a slam dunk. There's no guarantee that the economy—or apparel sales—will recover from the current slump any time soon. What's more, the United States is a low-growth market in which retailers have long had to fight for market share. Nonetheless, the United States remains the world's largest consumer market.

Integration of Technology

One of the most significant trends occurring in retailing is that of technological innovation. Technology is having, and will continue to have, a dramatic influence on retailing. Technological innovations can be grouped under three main areas: supply-chain management, customer management, and customer satisfaction.

The plethora of supply-chain management techniques such as quick response, just-in-time, and efficient consumer response are already being enhanced by new initiatives such as direct store delivery (DSD) and collaborative planning, forecasting, and replenishment (CPFR) systems. DSD systems have the potential to fully automate all retail inventory operations from tracking vendor and item authorization to pricing and order taking. DSD systems provide greater accuracy and increased administrative efficiency, allowing retailers to achieve cost advantages. Advancements in DSD systems will create more efficient operations and stronger partnerships as global competition increases. For example, Giant Food, Inc., eliminated a tremendous amount of paperwork and dramatically increased its administrative efficiency with the implementation of a DSD system.

Many industry experts believe that DSD is the engine that will drive industry profits. However, gross profit numbers alone don't tell the entire story. In fact, gross profit numbers can be somewhat misleading when calculating direct and incremental costs of warehouse-delivered products. Instead, activity-based costing analyses demonstrate that, in categories with mixed distribution, DSD products consistently outperform those just going through the warehouse. Other supply-chain systems—such as CPFR—though still in their infancy, have the potential to move retailers and manufacturers far beyond continuous-replenishment models in terms of reducing excess inventory levels, cutting out of stocks at retail, and efficiently meeting consumer demand. However, technological systems such as DSD and CPFR are but the beginning of the technological revolution occurring within the supply chain. Retailers who continue to use technology in innovative ways within the supply chain will achieve greater efficiency in their operations.

Retailers on the forefront of using technology to understand their consumers will achieve higher levels of effectiveness. For example, retailers might use technology to better target their customers and provide better service to them. Talbot's employs its catalog information to open retail outlets in locations with the greatest opportunity. Talbot's determines new store locations by examining clusters of ZIP codes that have accounted for sales of $150,000 or more annually in the categories of classic women's and children's apparel. Pier One uses similar information to determine where to incorporate direct mail advertising within the first six months of a new store's opening in order to achieve profitability more quickly.

Believe it or not, some of the most sophisticated users of database technology are casinos. In the past, one had to be a high roller to gain any "comps" (free products or services given to customers such as free tickets to shows or a free night's stay). Today, when customers use the casino's gaming facilities (such as gambling at a slot machine), they can insert a card that has been assigned to them that tracks their gaming behavior. Customers then present these cards to the casino to receive individual rewards based on their use of the gaming facilities. Through the use of these cards, a casino not only gains a much better understanding of its customers, enabling it to develop more effective retail strategies, but also rewards gamblers at all levels, thus increasing customer satisfaction.

As technology continues to penetrate the retail marketplace, new advancements in customer service and convenience will be evidenced. For example, what replacements are in store for bar code scanners? One cause of long lines at supermarket checkouts is that each item has to be taken out of a shopper's cart, individually scanned, and then bagged. How might technology change this? Recent testing of radio frequency identifiers (RFIDs) on products might eliminate the item-by-item process completely. The RFID reader generates a low-level radio frequency magnetic field that resonates with the RFID tag's metal coil and capacitor, creating an electrical signal that powers the computer chip, which then transmits its stored data back to the reader. The process works well, but the tags have been expensive—as much as $200 each. However, that cost has recently fallen to less than $1 per tag. Although still too expensive for all but high-priced items, advancements in technology will soon be available, making this system affordable to implement. Imagine bagging your groceries while you shop. Once you have finished, you simply push your cart to the checkout and within a few seconds the cashier scans your entire cart, you pay, and off you go.

These technological advances are but a few of the thousands that will change the nature of retailing. What technological innovations do you see on the horizon for retailers?

Increasing Use of Private Labels

As retailing continues to change, the increased use of private labels has emerged as a key business asset in developing a differential advantage for retailers. Private labels can set the retailer apart from the competition, get customers into their store (or website) and bring them back. Today, retailers are shifting their emphasis on the development of private-label brands into high gear by using a variety of strategies to build the image of their brands, expand brand recognition, and raise their brand images in the marketplace. Walmart, despite its success in America, learned firsthand the importance of private labels when competing internationally. As mentioned earlier in the chapter, Walmart failed in Germany; private-label merchandise played a major factor. In the United States, for example, store-brand goods account for just under a quarter of the unit volume of food sales. This percentage is slightly higher in most European markets (about 30 percent). However, Walmart was unprepared for the fact that its major German competitor, Aldi, generated 95 percent of its sales from private labels. Now the German chain is testing whether the recent economic slowdown will cause Americans to shift to in-store labels.[53] After all, private-label brands often have lower wholesale and marketing costs, resulting in higher levels of profit compared to manufacturers' brands. Retailers must remember, however, that research has shown that most department store shoppers value a product's style more than the product's brand name.[54]

In the past, retailers believed that national brands drew customers into their stores, set the standard, and lent credibility to the retailers. At the same time, retailers felt private-label brands could help retailers differentiate their offerings, reach customers seeking lower prices, and boost margins due to the lower costs of private-label merchandise. However, over the past decade, this thinking has changed. Many retailers are focused on developing strong, proprietary private-label brands as their leading brand and supporting them with major advertising and promotional programs. Private brands, such Target's Archer Farms label, shown in Exhibit 4.4, are now effectively serving as destination draws in their own right while still providing many of the same benefits of traditional private-label programs. Today, it is not uncommon for major retail chains to generate a third or more of their sales from private labels. Saks, a relatively high-end department store, introduced its Saks Fifth Avenue Men's collection, in 2009 and by 2011 had become the largest brand in Saks' men store. Not surprisingly, Saks began in late 2011 to build the Saks Fifth Avenue branded women's merchandise line,[55] hoping for similar results.

The following are some of the private-label branding strategies currently being used by retailers.

1. *Develop a partnership with well-known celebrities, noted experts, and institutional authorities.* Celebrity partnerships—or the use of people as private-label brands— allow retailers to align with an individual whose personal reputation creates immediate brand recognition, image, or credibility. Macy's, for example, has Madonna and Jessica Simpson's junior collections and the Martha Stewart Collection, and Kohl's features the Jennifer Lopez collection (http://www.kohls.com/kohlsStore/ourbrands/jenniferlopez.jsp).

2. *Develop a partnership with traditionally higher-end suppliers to bring an exclusive variation on their highly regarded brand name to market.* Target has a furniture line by Michael Graves and has recently introduced an eco-apparel line by designer Rojan Gregory, which was carried by Barneys, New York, in an attempt to give "new meaning to the phrase 'mass meets class'."[56]

   These partnerships offer both parties a win–win situation. The retailer gets an exclusive private label and the opportunity to expand customer appeal, ratchet up price points, and raise margins. The manufacturer builds volume and gains access to a broad new market spectrum.

3. *Reintroduce products that have strong name recognition but that have fallen from the retail scene.* Old brand names do not die. They get recycled. Retailers can add cachet to their store image by resurrecting former up-market brands that have been discontinued but have not lost their image. Recycled brands can help a retailer achieve differentiation through exclusivity and attract consumers unwilling to risk buying an unknown brand name. By reviving a well-known brand with pedigree, the retailer is able to leverage the brand's equity while still having a proprietary line.

   Walmart, for example, has purchased the rights from Procter & Gamble to its discontinued White Cloud label on diapers and toilet tissues, and Kohl's has recently reintroduced the Hang Ten brand, a label that was popular in the early 1990s.

4. *Brand an entire department or business; not just a product line.* In an approach designed to differentiate its supercenter food offerings from others, Target has taken its private-label branding strategy one step further by branding its entire supermarket section with the Archer Farms name. Not only does the Archer Farm name readily draw an association with the Target brand (the archer's target or bulls-eye) but also it enables Target to separate the two sections of the store. In fact, many consumers believe it to be a different company entirely. This may be a plus for Target, whose customers might not otherwise shop for groceries in a discount store.

   The Archer Farms market-positioning strategy leads the consumer to believe that this is an upscale grocer that places more emphasis on quality and freshness than price. Such a strategy reinforces Target's protected niche image as the "discounter for consumers who don't want to be seen in a discount store." A "fresh from the farm" tagline underscores the market positioning message. Store design features such as green neon perimeter lighting, graphics depicting farm scenes, colorful illustrations of major food categories, and product descriptions and use suggestions all help create a differentiated grocery-shopping environment. The Archer Farms name was also carried into a private-label program featuring approximately 100 SKUs.

Summary

The behavior of competitors is an important component of the strategic retail planning and operations management model. Effective planning and operations management in any retail setting cannot be accomplished without properly analyzing competitors.

LO 1 What are the various models of retail competition?

Competition in retailing, as in any other industry, involves the interplay of supply and demand. Various models of retail competition were described to illustrate certain principles of retail competition. These models suggested that retail competition is typically local but vulnerable to nonstore retailers that provide better selection and convenience; the retail industry is monopolistically competitive and not a pure monopoly, pure competition, or oligopoly. Retailers today are in a struggle to develop strategies that allow them to protect themselves from competitive threats by achieving some type of differential advantage over their competition. As a result of this goal, retailers are developing price and nonprice strategies that look at the supply as well as the demand side of retailing. This opening learning objective concluded by looking at how competitive activity can make a market attractive or unattractive.

LO 2 What are the various types of retail competition?

Competition is most intense in retailing, and various classification schemes were used to describe this intensity. *Intratype* and *intertype competition* describe retailers who compete against each other in the same line of retail trade or in different lines of retail trade, respectively, but still compete for the same customer with similar merchandise lines. *Divertive competition* describes retailers who seek to intercept customers planning to visit another retailer.

LO 3 What are the four theories used to explain the evolution of retail competition?

Retail competition is both revolutionary and evolutionary. Four theories of viewing changing competitive patterns in retailing were discussed. The *wheel of retailing* theory proposes that new types of retailers enter the market as low-margin, low-price, and less-efficient operators. As they succeed, they become more complex, increasing their margins and prices and becoming vulnerable to new types of low-margin competitors, who, in turn, follow the same pattern. The *retail accordion theory* suggests that retail institutions evolve from outlets offering wide assortments to stores with specialized, narrow assortments and then return to wide assortments to repeat the pattern. The *retail life cycle theory* views retail institutions, like the products they distribute, as passing through an identifiable cycle during which the basics of strategy and competition change. Finally, *resource advantage theory* was discussed. This theory is based on the idea that all firms seek superior financial performance in an ever-changing environment. Retail demand is dynamic because consumer tastes are always changing and supply is dynamic because firms searching for a superior performance are forced to change the elements of their retail mix to match changing consumer preferences. Thus, retail evolution is characterized by a variety of viable retail formats, ever-changing opportunities, and customer demands.

LO 4   ## What future changes could affect retail competition?

We concluded this chapter with a discussion of changes that could affect retail competition. Industry analysts contend that nonstore retailing will be a major competitive force in the future. This was followed by a discussion of why two recently introduced formats—hypermarkets and off-pricers—failed while the supercenter format was highly successful. Next we looked at three examples of possible new retailing formats that have recently evolved: recycled merchandise retailers, liquidators, and rentals.

Just as the introduction of new retailing formats in one part of the United States will impact retailers in other parts of the country, so it is for international retailing. Retailing in other countries exhibits even greater diversity in its structure than retailing in the United States. The rate of change in retailing appears to be directly related to the stage and speed of economic development in the countries concerned, but today even the least-developed countries are experiencing dramatic changes in retailing, thereby heightening global retail competition. The global analysis section ended with a discussion of why retailers from smaller countries tend to perform better in international competition.

Other changes in retail formats will result from the significant development of technological advances for use in retailing. The chapter concluded with an in-depth discussion of private-label branding and the various strategies for its use today.

Terms to Remember

pure competition	divertive competition
pure monopoly	pop-up stores
monopolistic competition	breakeven point
oligopolistic competition	wheel of retailing theory
outshopping	retail accordion
store positioning	retail life cycle
overstored	off-price retailers
understored	supercenter
intratype competition	recycled merchandise retailers
intertype competition	

Review and Discussion Questions

LO 1   ## What are the various models of retail competition?

1.   Can a retailer ever operate in a pure monopoly situation? If you believe that this is possible, provide an example and explain what dangers this retailer faces. If you believe this is not possible, explain why not.
2.   Why is it so important for a retailer to develop a protected niche?
3.   Many retailers undoubtedly compete on price. Why is the price the retailer charges for merchandise or services not the same as the total cost the customer pays?
4.   What are the ways a retailer can avoid or minimize competing on price?

LO 2

What are the various types of retail competition?

5. Provide an example of intratype competition that was not mentioned in the text. Provide an example of intertype competition that was not mentioned in the text. Can a retailer face both intratype and intertype competition at the same time? Explain your response.

6. Can divertive competition occur only in intertype competition—that is, where two different types of retailers with a similar product compete with each other?

7. Someone once said that "the supercenter format will kill the grocery retailers." However, this hasn't happened. Can you think of an explanation as to why this hasn't occurred?

LO 3

What four theories are used to explain the evolution of retail competition?

8. Describe the wheel of retailing theory. What are the theory's major strengths and weakness? Does this theory do a good job of explaining what has happened to American retailers today?

9. Describe the retail accordion theory of competition. What are this theory's major strengths and weakness?

10. Would strategies for retailers differ in the four stages of the retail life cycle? What strategies should be emphasized at each of the four stages?

11. If a retail format enters the decline stage of the retail life cycle, does that mean that this format will be gone within the next decade? Or can it linger in the decline stage for years? Can a format ever reposition itself and return to either the growth or maturity stage? Can you think of any current format that could reinvigorate itself?

LO 4

What future changes could affect retail competition?

12. Will the Internet ever completely replace traditional bricks-and-mortar retailing? Provide a rationale for your response.

13. If a new retail format is a hit in one country, it generally will be successful in all countries. Agree or disagree?

14. What do you think about the projected growth of the rental format? Would you rent your textbooks if an outlet was available on your campus? If your best friend was getting married, would you consider renting a gown, handbag, or jewelry to wear for the rehearsal dinner?

15. Several possible explanations were given as to why retailers from smaller countries tend to do better when entering foreign markets than those from larger countries. Do you agree or disagree with these explanations? Explain your reasoning.

16. Is it better for a retailer to develop a new private-label brand or to try to revive a once-prestigious brand that has been discontinued? Explain your reasoning.

Sample Test Questions

LO 1

What type of competitive structure are most retail firms involved in?

a. horizontal competition
b. monopolistic competition
c. vertical competition
d. pure competition
e. oligopolistic competition

LO 2 When Walmart competes with Kroger, Albertsons, and Safeway by adding groceries to its general merchandise products in its new supercenters, what type of competition is this?

    a.   extended niche
    b.   intratype
    c.   scrambled
    d.   intertype
    e.   category killer

LO 3 Walking back to the dorm after class, your roommate complains that she wishes there was a plain old-fashioned hamburger joint, she could go for a simple hamburger, not a fancy triple-decker or one with 17 secret sauces, and not a fast-food restaurant with a playground for 50 kids. Her dilemma describes what theory of retail evolution?

    a.   retail violin
    b.   retail life cycle
    c.   bigger-n-better
    d.   wheel of retailing
    e.   compound growth

LO 4 With regard to international trends in retailing, which of the following statements is true?

    a.   Because of its sheer size, retailing in the United States is more diverse in its structure than any other country.
    b.   Success with a retailing format in one country usually guarantees success in all countries.
    c.   The size of the individual stores does not tend to vary.
    d.   U.S. retailers haven't been as successful in international expansion as some of their competitors from smaller countries.
    e.   No new successful retailing format has been developed outside of the United States in the last half-century.

Writing and Speaking Exercise

Over the past year and half you worked at your church's not-for-profit resale shop. Over this period, while the economic downturn has hurt sales at the nearby shopping center, it has really benefited your shop. In fact, sales have soared as cash-strapped consumers sought out bargains and donors wanted tax deductions. For example, shop prices for blouses and shirts range from $1 to $15 and designer jeans sold for $5 to $25 a pair compared with regular retail prices that were at least triple those amounts. Actually, the shop attracted a wide range of customers ranging from white collar workers who needed work clothes to bargain shoppers who enjoyed the thrill of the hunt. As a matter of fact, the shop's consumers had a wide range in income and age, except for the students at the nearby college.

As you prepared to return to school to graduate, your boss asked you to prepare a report with your ideas on how to attract college students to the shop. As she sees the problem, students only come to the shop in mid- to late-October seeking polyester suits and wide ties to wear to Halloween parties. They fail to realize what good merchandise the shop is actually selling. What can be done to get them to purchase home furnishings from the shop when they decorate their apartments and dorms in the fall and to seek out clothing that is only gently used instead of going to the shopping center? After all, she added, "We have labels like Old Navy, the Gap, Arizona Jeans, and Ann Taylor. It doesn't make any sense to me why students on a limited budget would want to buy anything brand new if the clothes we sell are well taken care of."

Retail Project

You are thinking about buying a Ford Focus after you graduate this semester. Use the Internet to see if you can get a better deal than the traditional auto retailers offer. All you will have to do is make three online connections, all free.

Start by using DealerNet (www.dealernet.com), created by Reynolds & Reynolds, which provides computer services to dealers. You can see a picture of the Ford Focus and find out how it compares with competitors like the Chevrolet Cruze in such key areas as trunk space, fuel economy, and price.

Suppose you decide on the four-door Titanium Model because you really want 17″ sport aluminum wheels and the SYNC voice-activated system. Key over to the prices posted by Edmund Publications (http://www.edmunds.com), a longtime compiler of such information. There you discover what the current sticker price is for the Titanium Model as well as what the dealer pays. You can also explore the Edmunds site to find out what special discounts and financing are available for the car you want. These facts may help you in evaluating the price your local dealer quotes.

When you're ready to order, type in "http://www.autobytel.com." There are several buying services on the Web, but AutoByTel is free. From here you can buy the car using AutoByTel directly or placing your order, and you'll get a call from a nearby dealer. The dealer will charge you a fixed amount over the invoice and deliver the car. Now you've saved enough to buy a copy of this valuable text for all your friends.

Planning Your Own Entrepreneurial Retail Business

As a knowledgeable retail entrepreneur, you recognize how harmful new retail competitors entering the market can be to your business. You opened your bookstore only 18 months ago and already have experienced healthy sales. In the year just ended, sales exceeded $860,000. You have estimated that of the 43,000 households in your market, 39 percent visit your store an average of 4.2 times a year. Due to your excellent merchandising and retail displays, 88 percent of visitors to your store make a purchase (referred to as *closure*) for an average transaction size of $13.89. Unfortunately, last week you learned that Barnes & Noble (a category killer bookstore that also sells music tapes and CDs and serves coffee, refreshments, and pastries) has signed a lease to be part of a new shopping mall in a city of 405,000 located 20 miles north of your store. In this mall there will also be a Lowe's and an Office Depot.

Predictably, you are quite concerned that Barnes & Noble will take customers from your store. It is hard for you to predict the impact of this new competition; at least they are 20 miles away. Nonetheless, you believe that the percentage of households in your market that will shop your store will decline from 39 percent to 35 percent, and average shopping frequency will decline from 4.2 times per year to 4.0 times per year. You believe you can maintain your excellent closure rate and average transaction size. What is the estimated sales impact of gaining Barnes & Noble as a competitor? (Hint: Annual sales can be obtained by multiplying the number of households in the market by the percentage that patronize your store multiplied by their average shopping frequency or number of visits per year. Then multiply this figure by the closure rate and multiple the result by the average transaction size.)

Buffalo Wild Wings: Competing for the Future

Buffalo Wild Wings (BWW) has experienced rapid, and at times explosive growth, since its founding three decades ago. The business, which focuses on Buffalo chicken wings and related fun food, was founded in 1982 with a single location in Columbus, Ohio, near the Ohio State University. Today, the business is an owner, operator, franchisor model; the franchising element began in 1991. Live sporting events are a focus of the customer experience with a typical Buffalo Wild Wing's restaurant having 50 or more televisions for viewing sports. Coordinated marketing and coordinated operational execution has allowed for a consistent brand image across locations; buffalo insignias, yellow and black color scheme, and stylized buffalo images help build this brand image. BWW has been successful in growing restaurant locations with 786 company-owned and franchise locations in 44 states at the end of the third quarter in 2011.

Growth Strategy

BWW needs to determine its strategy for competing for the future in which the restaurant industry is growing increasingly competitive and fragmented. BWW has a stated goal to continue to grow domestically and internationally. In order to grow successfully the focus is on the following strategies.

- Continue to strengthen the Buffalo Wild Wings Brand.
- Deliver a unique guest experience.
- Offer boldly flavored menu items with broad appeal.
- Creating an inviting neighborhood atmosphere.
- Focus on operational excellence.
- Open restaurants in new and existing domestic markets and new countries.
- Increase same-store sales, average unit volumes, and profitability.

The current business concept is thought to be able to support a unit base of 1,400 locations in the United States with a target of 40 percent company owned and 60 percent franchisor owned. The first international play for the company was Canada with the opening of a Toronto location in 2011, with plans to open 50 Canadian locations in the next five years.

Business Operations

A typical Buffalo Wild Wings location is open on a daily basis with operating hours of 11 a.m. until 2 a.m. The hours of operation can vary depending on local regulations and day of the week. In addition, franchisors agree to operate their locations a minimum of 12 hours per day. Dine-in and carryout is facilitated through ordering with traditional table service as well as a counter that takeout orders can be placed at. Purchases of food ingredients and supplies are negotiated on a system-wide basis in order to obtain the best cost possible; additionally all sauces are manufactured by a single company with BWW owning the recipes and seasonings of it's signature sauces to prevent other wing establishments from using the same sauces. Chicken wings are the largest component of the food purchasing costs, and volatility in their prices could have significant impacts on the business. Currently, wings are purchased at market price, although long-term fixed price contracts are a possibility if market conditions warrant the change. BWW restaurants include a full bar, and, in Nevada, gaming; thus the business is subject to the regulations of the appropriate beverage commissions in all states in which it operates and the gaming commission in Nevada.

Financial Performance

A better understanding of the financial performance of BWW can be obtained by examining the data in Exhibits 1–3. Note that net earnings are after-tax net earnings.

Exhibit 1

Revenue & Earnings Growth (in Thousands of Dollars)

	FY 2006	FY 2007	FY 2008	FY 2009	FY 2010
■ Total Revenue	261,910	309,998	397,982	508,253	574,856
■ Net Earnings	16,273	19,654	24,435	30,671	38,400

Exhibit 2

Stock Price & EPS

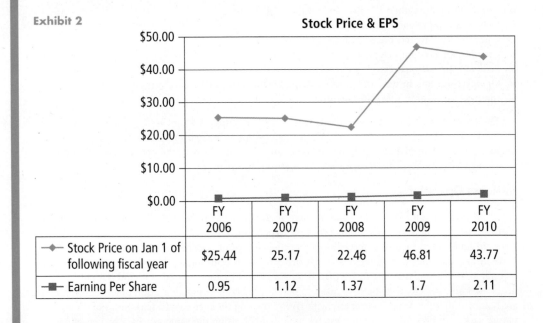

	FY 2006	FY 2007	FY 2008	FY 2009	FY 2010
◆ Stock Price on Jan 1 of following fiscal year	$25.44	25.17	22.46	46.81	43.77
■ Earning Per Share	0.95	1.12	1.37	1.7	2.11

Exhibit 3

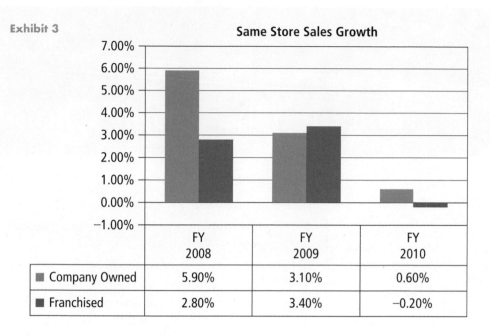

	FY 2008	FY 2009	FY 2010
■ Company Owned	5.90%	3.10%	0.60%
■ Franchised	2.80%	3.40%	−0.20%

Questions

1. If there is a BWW near you, visit the restaurant or if not take a look at them online (www.buffalowildwings.com). Identify what you see as competitors to BWW.

2. What do you see as the competitive advantage of BWW? Be sure to discuss its value proposition.

3. Where would you place BWW and restaurants it competes with in terms of the retail life cycle?

Sources

Buffalo Wild Wings 2010 Annual Report (10k). Available at: http://www.sec.gov/Archives/edgar/data/1062449/000110465911010383/a11-6492_110k.htm;

Buffalo Wild Wings 3Q 2011 Report (10Q). Available at: http://www.sec.gov/Archives/edgar/data/1062449/000110465911060500/a11-25636_110q.htm; and the authors' long-time patronage of BWW.

Note: This case was prepared by Mark Lusch as a basis for class discussion rather than to illustrate either effective or ineffective handling of a retail situation.

5

Managing the Supply Chain

Overview

At the outset of this text, we pointed out that retailing is the final step in the progression of merchandise from producer to consumer. Many other movements occur through time and geographical space, and all of them need to be executed properly for the retailer to achieve optimum performance. Therefore, in this chapter, we will examine the retailer's need to analyze and understand the supply chain in which it operates. After looking at the activities performed within a supply chain, the chapter reviews the various types of supply chains and the benefits each one offers the retailer. The chapter concludes with some practical suggestions to improve supply-chain relationships, especially the use of a category manager.

Learning Objectives

After reading this chapter, you should be able to:

1 Discuss the retailer's role as one of the institutions involved in the supply chain.

2 Describe the types of supply chains by length, width, and control.

3 Explain the terms *dependency*, *power*, and *conflict* and their impact on supply-chain relations.

4 Understand the importance of a collaborative supply-chain relationship.

LO 1

Discuss the retailer's role as one of the institutions involved in the supply chain.

The Supply Chain

Consider the following example. The final movement of a retail item occurred on March 6 at 10:47 a.m. when a customer brought home a garden hose that she had just purchased at a Home Depot in Amarillo, Texas. Thirteen months earlier, a sample of that hose had been in a Hong Kong showroom where a Home Depot buyer ordered 200,000 hoses for the next year's selling season from the showroom's vendor. The buyer then hired a Chinese agent to represent Home Depot after the buyer returned to Atlanta, Georgia. This agent was to make sure that the factories met Home Depot's regulations regarding working conditions and that the hoses and parts met the retailer's quality standards. Over the next nine months, the hoses were assembled in mainland China using nozzles made in Thailand. The hoses were then ocean transported to a warehouse in a free-trade zone in Los Angeles. In late January these hoses were shipped from Los Angeles to the Home Depot distribution center in Texas, for immediate shipment to the Amarillo Home Depot.

In this example, manufacturing occurred in both China and Thailand, a Norwegian owned ship transported the hoses and after clearing customs in Los Angeles they were stored in a warehouse in Los Angeles for several months, and then a U.S. motor carrier was used to deliver them to a U.S. railroad. Within an hour of being received at the distribution center, Home Depot's own trucks were taking the hoses to Amarillo. Thus, before

WHAT'S NEW?

Fast Fashion: It's "Z-Day"

Each year, millions of Americans follow the happenings of February's Fashion Week, hoping to get a glimpse at what will be available in July from designers like Marc Jacobs, Ralph Lauren, and Dolce and Gabbana. However, customers in cities such as Dallas, Atlanta, New York, Miami, and Los Angeles no longer need to wait; in fact, they better not. Fashion has a short shelf life, and at Zara (www.zara.com), it's only a few weeks.

Zara, a clothing company based in La Coruña, Spain, has revolutionized fast turn in fashion. On average, it takes less than two weeks for Zara to spot, design, and ship one of the 300,000 new SKUs it sells in stores each year. Thus, it routinely beats the high-fashion houses to market with nearly identical products that are made with less-expensive fabric and at much lower prices. For example, Zara recently sold a long, pink boucle jacket resembling one of Chanel's current spring and summer offerings for $129 and a pair of black stretch pants similar to a Prada design for $33. The cost of the originals: $7,326 and $350, respectively.

How does Zara do it? Creativity in supply-chain design! First, Zara is part of a corporate-owned, vertical marketing channel, Inditex, which owns and operates retail stores, distribution centers, a design and manufacturing headquarters, and textile-manufacturing facilities.

Second, by controlling all steps in the supply chain, Zara is able to run each step (manufacturing, design, etc.) below full capacity. This is in stark contrast to most competitors who seek large runs to gain economies of scale and the resulting lower costs.

Finally, they produce limited runs of each style; they overlook the possibility of being stocked out on any item. In fact, Zara's business model thrives on these stock outs as they create instant demand.

In addition, Zara has introduced the Z-day concept to its target customers. Z-day, as the Zara faithful know, is the two days a week when new shipments of styles arrive in retail stores. On these days, Zara is packed with 20- and 30-somethings seeking to get their hands on the newest clothes before they're gone. Zara shoppers know that if they find a style they like, they better purchase it immediately or it'll be gone.

Zara's supply chain was designed to create this feeding frenzy. By limiting the number of any one style, customers gain fashion exclusivity while Zara limits the number of discounts taken due to poor-performing lines. In an industry riddled with seasonal discounts, Zara rarely has any because Zara headquarters is in constant communication with its retail stores.

Twice a week (Tuesday and Friday) store managers phone in their orders to market specialists dedicated to each store. During these phone conversations, problems are discussed and new styles are conceived. In addition, customized handheld computers (PDAs) augment these calls and communicate such hard data as orders and sales trends and soft data such as customer reactions, customer requests, and the "buzz" around a new style. Zara's headquarters knows, in real time, what is working and what is not.

By controlling every detail from the dying of fabric and stitching of designs to the delivery and display of fashion within its stores, Zara is able to alter, discontinue, or modify current styles to arrive the following Z-day. To facilitate speed, its headquarters is designed primarily around three halls. Each hall has its own design, planning, manufacturing, and market specialist staff broken down by clothing line: men's, women's, and children's.

The three parallel lines, although expensive, allow information to flow quickly and unencumbered. Using a just-in-time (JIT) model, all aspects of Zara are linked by computer. Designers and market specialists gather data in real time. A small prototype shop is also set up in the corner of each hall to encourage everyone to comment on the new garments as they progress. Once line teams have reviewed the prototypes (often within hours), designers refine them using computer-aided systems and transmit the specs directly to the cutting machines. Bar codes then track the cut pieces of fabric through the various stages of production. Once developed, garments are transferred to a central warehouse where shipments are prepared for every store (usually

(continued)

overnight). Price tags are then placed on the clothes, and necessary items are hung on hangers prior to leaving the warehouse. Clothes shipped to the United States are then loaded on commercial airlines using established schedules, like a bus schedule, and are delivered to each store at the same time every delivery day. Because all clothes have been pre-priced and hung, managers are able to immediately display them the moment they are delivered. Once performed, the entire process starts again the following order day.

Interestingly, it is this last step (hanging) that has really fueled the immediate turnover of fashion.

Customers have realized that clothes are shipped on plastic hangers prior to managers switching them to wooden hangers in the store. As all clothes are immediately displayed on arrival, many customers scan for the telltale sign of a gray, plastic hanger on entering Zara.

Sources: "Zara Thrives by Breaking All the Rules," *Businessweek*, October 20, 2008: 66; "The Mark of Zara," *Businessweek*, May 29, 2000: 98; "Rapid Fire Fulfillment," *Harvard Business Review*, November 2004: 104–110; "Style & Substance: Making Fashion Faster as Knockoffs Beat Originals to Market, Designers Speed the Trip from Sketch to Store," *Wall Street Journal*, February 24, 2004: B1; and "Pace-Setting Zara Seeks More Speed to Fight Its Rising Cheap-Chic Rivals," *Wall Street Journal*, February 20, 2008: B1.

supply chain
Is a set of institutions that move goods from the point of production to the point of consumption.

channel
Used interchangeably with supply chain.

the final retail transaction could take place, several physical movements were needed that involved many firms other than the retailer. As the above example illustrates, retailers cannot properly perform their roles without the assistance of other firms. Retailers are *part* of a supply chain—a valuable component, but not the only one.

In contrast to Home Depot's rather slow-moving supply chain, this chapter's "What's New?" box describes how one Spanish apparel chain, Zara, has revolutionized the fashion world and become the world's second-largest clothing retailer (in sales) by keeping a tight grip on every link in its supply chain.

It is important to understand the retailer's role in the larger supply chain. Retailers have used the term **supply chain** interchangeably with the term **channel**. Traditionally, this consisted of a set of institutions that moves goods from the point of production to

It's important to remember that this Hong Kong seaport, like many others across the globe, represents only one stop in the supply chain or channel that is necessary to move product from a manufacturer on the other side of the world to your local retail store.

Greg Balfour Evans/Alamy

With increased concern by many for the global ecosystem, firms like Tesco are taking an active role in assisting shoppers who seek to recycle.

the point of consumption. However, with increased concern about the physical environment or natural ecosystem, many retailers are beginning to view the supply chain as "dirt to dirt." This broadened view incorporates not only the institutions needed to bring the product to the retailer (the traditional view), but also all the materials that go into manufacturing the good, as well as, the process consumers use to dispose of or recycle the product. Over the last decade, retailers became more aware of the need to expand their view of the supply chain due to harmful ingredients found in products such as lead used in paint for children's toys or foreign substances used in pet food. Some retailers, such as Tesco in the United Kingdom, make it their role to help the customer recycle items such as printer cartridges or old cell phones. In fact, Tesco gives its shoppers extra reward points as part of their frequent shopper program for using Tesco to recycle such items. Other intermediaries such as UPS (transport and logistics) work with manufacturers and retailers to measure their carbon impact, develop eco-responsible packaging, implement carbon neutral shipping, and then impress customers with sustainability information that might influence buying decisions.

Using the more traditional view, the supply chain or channel might include manufacturers, wholesalers, and retailers. For example, the manufacturer could sell directly to an individual for household usage, sell to a retailer for sale to the individual, or sell to a wholesaler for sale to the retailer, who then sells to the individual. Thus, supply chains consist of all the institutions and all the marketing activities (storage, financing, purchasing, transporting, etc.) that are spread over time and geographical space throughout the marketing process. If the retailer is a member of the supply chain that collectively does the best job, that retailer will have an advantage over other retailers.

Why should the retailer view itself as part of a larger channel or supply chain? Why can't it simply seek out the best assortment of goods for its customers, sell the goods, make a profit, go to the bank, and forget about the supply chain? In reality, the world of retailing is not that easy. Profits sufficient for survival and growth would be difficult, if not impossible, to achieve if the retailer ignored the supply chain. This is because both the retailer and the supplier need to make a profit on doing business with each other. Also, if you consider the largest chains such as Target, The Limited, Kroger, or Lowe's, they need many manufacturers or suppliers, both large and small, to help meet their inventory replenishment needs. For instance, Lowe's has over 7,000 suppliers. It is certainly true that a power retailer can put strong demands on suppliers, but suppliers too possess great power; they know they are the only ones that have the production and distribution capacity to deliver 25,000 barbecue grills to dozens of distribution centers and thousands of stores on relatively short notice for a special summer promotion.

We do not mean to suggest that retailers are at the mercy of their manufacturing partners due to their control over the products necessary for retailers' success. Nor do we suggest that retailers sit idly by and neglect altering or improving their supply chain(s). *Innovative retailers are always seeking to find a new method to change the existing supply chain and replace it with a better one.* For example, discounters changed their relationships with vendors when they began to buy directly from manufacturers in large quantities, warehouse the merchandise in efficiently run distribution centers, and ship to their own stores as a means of obtaining lower prices. Prior to this change, discounters purchased smaller quantities from wholesalers only when the merchandise was needed. Today, many local restaurants are buying less from food wholesalers and sourcing more products direct from local producers and farmers. This also helps them to differentiate their offerings by featuring on their menu stories about the locally grown or produced food.

Prior to making changes in the overall channel structure, supply-chain members must understand that all channels are affected by five external forces: (1) consumer behavior, (2) competitor behavior, (3) the socioeconomic environment, (4) the technological environment, and (5) the legal and ethical environment. These external forces cannot be completely controlled by the retailer or any other institution in the supply chain, but they need to be taken into account when retailers make decisions. For example, a change in the inventory tax rate of a state may make it more costly to operate a distribution center in that state and thus result in the distribution center needing to be relocated. Similarly, a rapid rise or fall in fuel prices will result in a shift to using rail and not motor carriers to deliver a product and if fuel prices remain high could alter the optimal number and location of distribution centers.

Consider also how rising fuel prices during 2010 and 2011 affected many other retail decisions beyond simply the choice of transport to use in moving a product to one's distribution centers and ultimately one's store shelves. A rise in fuel prices increases the costs associated with many commodities used to produce other products (e.g., wheat to make flour for your breakfast biscuit sandwich or cotton for the clothes you're wearing). Because farmers now must pay more to fill up and operate the tractors and other heavy machinery necessary to harvest these goods, manufacturers must pay higher prices for the raw materials used to create their products. These associated price increases are often then passed along to the retailer who must either look for cost savings in other areas of their business or pass along the price increase to the final customer in the form of higher prices at market.

It's no wonder then why apparel retailers saw their apparel costs skyrocket, on average over 15 percent, during 2010 and 2011; fuel prices, and natural fabric costs, were higher then than almost any other time in history. Consequently, apparel retailers reacted by offsetting these increases with expense reductions in other areas, increasing long-range booking of purchases of materials or fabrics, shifting to lower cost means of transporting apparel, and narrowing their vendor base so they could have more negotiating power over a smaller vendor base.[1] Incidentally, the supply chain for apparel is global and the inflationary pressures mentioned above had a ripple effect all the way to China, where coupled with rising labor costs in China, many factories cut back

While consumers might not actively monitor the costs of such things like cotton, they do feel the impact at the register when fuel prices and other natural, or raw, materials rise like they did during 2010 and 2011.

production or closed.[2] Supply chains are clearly globally complex and rapidly changing networks of manufacturers, wholesalers, retailers, and consumers.

The retail strategic planning and operations management model (Exhibit 2.8) dramatizes the importance of these external forces in retail decision-making.

Supply-chain or channel structure also depends on the number of tasks or functions each member is willing to perform. Eight marketing functions must be performed by any supply chain or channel: buying, selling, storing, transporting, sorting, financing, information gathering, and risk taking. Most of these functions are self-explanatory; however, the concept of "sorting" requires some explanation. Sorting involves breaking down heterogeneous materials or products into more homogenous groups such as sorting oranges into those that are good for eating versus good for juice or other products. It also involves building up assortments of products that shoppers like to find together in a store—for example, orange juice with muffins, eggs, cereal, or bacon.

A considerable amount of supply chain management for retailers involves storage (inventory), transportation, and sorting, which is mostly performed in the logistics network. The **logistics network** consists of all firms or entities throughout the supply chain that are involved in moving physical inventory from initial source to the retail store. In fact, improving the logistics network represents a considerable opportunity for retailers to improve efficiency, and hence lower costs, and therefore increase profitability. It is not unusual for a retailer that globally sources products for over 10 percent and often as high as 20 percent of its inventory investment, are associated with the time the inventory is in the logistics network and prior to delivery to where the inventory is needed; this is referred to as **logistics inventory**.[3]

Most retailers have had a proliferation of stock-keeping units (SKUs) over the last decade due to rapidly changing consumer trends and competitive pressures, and thus, overall inventory levels are up and inventory turnover is down. Anything that can be done to reduce logistics inventory will, therefore, help to counteract this trend and increase inventory turnover while at the same time lower the costs of holding inventory. Consider the following global supply chain. A retailer sources products from dozens of factories in China, consolidates the production output at Chinese seaports, transports

logistics network
Consists of all the firms throughout the supply chain that are involved in moving physical inventory from its initial source to the retail store.

logistics inventory
Physical inventory that is in the logistics network.

Exhibit 5.1
**Reducing Logistics
Inventory**

Sources of Reduced Inventory	Financial Gain
• Time for factory shipment to seaport drops from 6 days to 4 days • Time it takes to consolidate shipments from five different factories drops from 4 days to 2 days • Import inspection in U.S. port of entry declines from 3 days to 1.5 days	• Retailer has 73 days of supply chain inventory valued at $250 million • 5.5 days of Reduced Logistics Inventory or $5.5/73 = 7.5\%$ inventory reduction • 7.5% times $250 million = $18.75 million reduced inventory • 12% cost of carrying inventory times $18.75 million = $2.25 million in annual savings

the products on ocean carriers across the Pacific, and enters North America through the San Francisco and Los Angeles seaports. Next, the merchandise needs to clear customs and be transported to North American distribution centers and then delivered to retail stores where the inventory sits in a back room and then gets placed on shelves. Note that at all stages, time is consumed and the inventory investment is sitting (stalled) or in transit rather than on the retail shelf where it is available for sale. In Exhibit 5.1 we demonstrate how a retailer who holds $250 million in inventory an average of 73 days is able to reduce this by 5.5 days through logistics inventory reductions and thus generate annual savings of $2.25 million.

As the preceding discussion highlights, subtle changes in one's supply chain can have a dramatic impact on one's bottom line. Therefore, retailers must view their supply chain(s) as extremely fragile and fraught with risk, particularly given so many retailers' supply chains are global.[4] As such, risk taking is an important marketing function that all supply chains, or channels, must consider and manage. Risks within a supply chain can include, but are not limited to, theft, whether on land or on the high seas from pirates; damage due to accidents; and even natural disasters, such as hurricanes and earthquakes. For instance, consider how the 9.0 magnitude earthquake off the coast of Japan in 2011 impacted retailers all around the globe. That earthquake disrupted not only supplies for manufacturing motor vehicles, and by extension the overall inventory of new vehicles, but also the manufacturer of thousands of electronic components used within a variety of industries' products that retailers sell. Hence, many retailers are assessing how much risk global sourcing exposes them to and/or ways to mitigate this risk.

Often the marketing functions are highly integrated. For instance, when sourcing globally, the buying, information gathering, transporting, storage, and risk-taking functions are all intertwined. This can lead to risky and confusing decisions, as in the case of counterfeit merchandise, an especially prominent problem with designer apparel. In fact, in Mexico, it is estimated that six of every ten imported garments are Chinese counterfeits, so Mexico is trying to work out trade agreements with China to reduce this problem.[5] Of course, for every exporter of counterfeit designer apparel from China there is an importer in Mexico that more than likely knows the origin and counterfeit nature of the apparel. However, this is not always the case, for instance, a legitimate shipment of 10,000 units of designer apparel could be mixed during shipment or storage by an illegal merchant who conspires with other intermediaries who then deliver to a unsuspecting retailer counterfeit merchandise. Since goods can flow fairly freely between Canada, Mexico, and the United States as a result of the North American Free Trade Agreement (NAFTA), retailers need to be especially careful when sourcing from intermediaries in Mexico due to the large amount of piracy occurring. Of course, this problem is not systemic only to Mexico. Counterfeiting extends well beyond that of designer apparel to electronic goods, such as Apple computers, and even kitchen appliances. The bottom line is that if you can't track through reliable and valid information your buying, transporting, and storage activities then you are taking on more risk.

Whether the economic system is capitalistic, socialistic, or somewhere in between, every supply chain must perform these eight marketing functions. They cannot be eliminated. They can, however, be shifted or divided in differing ways among the different institutions and the consumer in the supply chain. Increasingly, when firms design supply chains they are considering all of these marketing functions and computing a **total cost of business** versus just looking, for instance, if it is cheaper to manufacture in a lower cost country. Total cost of business is a concept that includes all of the direct and indirect costs of manufacturing, distributing, and marketing a product. Some of these additional costs include the risk of theft of intellectual property, additional travel for managers and executives, additional information on gathering costs and audit controls, and often additional investments tied up in inventory. As a result many manufacturers and retailers are finding that domestic-based sourcing is increasingly competitive from a total business cost perspective.[6]

All forms of retailing were created by rearranging the marketing functions among institutions and consumers. For example, department stores were created specifically to build a larger assortment of goods. They capitalized on the opportunity to perform one or more functions better than the current competition. No longer was it necessary to travel to one store for a shirt and pants, another for shoes, and yet another for cookware; the necessary assortment was available in a single store. Supermarkets too came into existence as a result of shifting the responsibility for the performance of certain marketing functions to the final consumer. Before supermarkets, corner grocers would often select a household's items, deliver those items, and even manage in-store credit accounts that were paid every two weeks when the household received income. With the introduction of the supermarket and the concepts of "self-service" and/or "cash and carry," consumers were now responsible for the information gathering, buying, financing, and transporting functions—consumers had to locate goods within the store, select them from an array of available products, pay for the goods, and transport them home. Some retailers are now even shifting the work of checking out of the store away from retail clerks to the customer via electronic self-service check-out kiosks. Yet as a retailer seeks to have its customers perform more of these eight marketing functions, the consumer must be increasingly compensated in the form of lower prices.

It is important to note that a marketing function does not have to be shifted in its entirety to another institution or to the consumer; instead, it can be divided among several entities. For example, manufacturers that don't want to perform the entire selling function could have the retailer perform part of the job through in-store promotions, local advertising, or promotions on the retailer's website. At the same time, the manufacturer could assume some of the tasks using national advertising and by developing its own website to provide product information such as installation instructions, cleaning directions, and the manufacturer's warranty. A good example of this shared responsibility for the performance of marketing functions can be seen in the sale of new automobiles where the local Ford or Chevrolet dealer will have its own advertising program and website but also Ford and Chevrolet will sponsor notational advertising to build brand image and promote certain models. Each manufacturer will also have its own website where potential customers can learn about different models, design their own car (e.g., www.showroom.ford.com), and/or be directed to their local Ford or Chevrolet dealer.

No member of the channel would want or be able to perform all eight marketing functions entirely. For this reason, the retailer must view itself as an *independent* (in one's ability to make decisions), yet *interdependent* (on other channel members) supply chain member.

total cost of business Is a process where costs beyond simply producing a product are considered and includes all of the direct and indirect costs of manufacturing, distributing, and marketing a product.

Baloncici/Dreamstime LLC

As consumers continue to demand lower prices, retailers are coming up with unique ways to shift more of the eight marketing functions to the consumer as is the case when retailers use self-service check-out kiosks.

primary marketing institutions
Are those channel members that take title to the goods as they move through the marketing channel. They include manufacturers, wholesalers, and retailers.

facilitating marketing institutions
Are those that do not actually take title but assist in the marketing process by specializing in the performance of certain marketing functions.

The institutions involved in performing the eight marketing functions are usually broken into two categories: primary and facilitating. **Primary marketing institutions** are supply-chain members that take title to the goods and services they handle or provide. **Facilitating marketing institutions** are those that do not actually take title to the goods and services they handle or provide, but assist in the marketing process by specializing in the performance of certain functions. A well-known facilitating channel member is UPS, who assists in the movement of products but does not take ownership, or title to, the goods it handles. Exhibit 5.2 classifies the major institutions participating in the supply chain.

Primary Marketing Institutions

There are three types of primary marketing institutions: manufacturers, wholesalers, and retailers.

Because manufacturers produce goods, we don't often think of them as marketing institutions. But manufacturers cannot exist by only producing goods; they must also sell the goods produced. To produce those goods, the nation's 309,000 manufacturers must purchase many raw materials, semi-finished goods, and components. In addition, manufacturers often need the assistance of other institutions in performing the eight marketing functions.

Exhibit 5.2
Institutions Participating in the Supply Chain

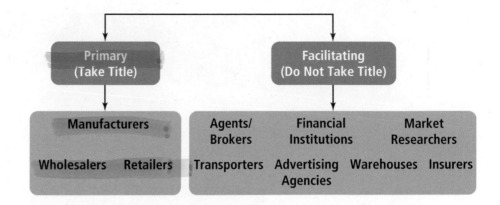

A second type of primary marketing institution is the wholesaler. Wholesalers generally buy merchandise from manufacturers and resell to retailers, other merchants, industrial institutions, and commercial users. An example of a wholesaler is Houston-based Sysco Corporation. Through its subsidiaries, Sysco engages in the distribution and marketing of food and related products primarily to the food-service industry in the United States and Canada. It distributes frozen foods, fully prepared entrees, fruits, vegetables, and desserts, as well as various nonfood items, including disposable napkins, plates, and cups; tableware; cleaning supplies; and restaurant and kitchen equipment to restaurants, hospitals, nursing homes, schools and colleges, hotels and motels. There are 420,000 wholesalers in the United States, each performing some of the eight marketing functions. Just as it is important for retailers to continuously evaluate their own strategies, it is equally important for them to consider the strategies of the wholesalers in their supply chain.

The third type of primary institution is the retailer. Today, there are 1.1 million retail stores or institutions and more than 1.8 million service establishments in the United States. Retailers can perform portions of all eight marketing functions. Remember from Chapter 1 that anyone that sells to the final consumer is a retailer. Zappos, the highly successful e-tailer of shoes, started out primarily collecting orders from customers and then having other companies fill these orders.[7] They used what is called **drop-ship** which is a technique used in supply-chain management in which the retailer does not hold inventory, but instead transmits customer orders and shipment details to either the manufacturer or a wholesaler, who then ships the goods directly to the customer. In the case of drop-ship, the retailer shifts the work and responsibility for storage, transporting, and sorting (three of the eight marketing functions). However, by not performing these marketing functions, it has little control over customer service. This is precisely why the founder of Zappos, Tony Hsieh, halted the practice of drop-ship and became a self-distributing e-tailer by making major investments in inventory, transport, and distribution centers.

It is possible that some firms, such as the membership warehouse clubs (Sam's and Costco), can act as both a wholesaler selling to small businesses and a retailer selling to households. However, for statistical purposes, the Census Bureau considers all membership warehouse clubs to be wholesalers since the majority of their business involves wholesale transactions. Incidentally, Costco has found its business format and appeal to both households and small businesses especially successful in international markets where they have expanded such as Mexico, Japan, Taiwan, Korea, and Australia.[8]

Finally, there are some bold entrepreneurs that are combining manufacturing or production along with distribution and retail functions. Consider, for example, Scott Morrison, who in 2011 launched a new company, called 3x1 (http://3x1.us/) in a 7,300 square foot SoHo space at 15 Mercer Street[9] in New York City. This facility is both a production facility and high-end flagship retail store. Customers can help custom

drop-ship
Is a technique wherein the retailer does not hold inventory, but instead transmits customer orders and shipping details to either the manufacturer or a wholesaler, who then ships the goods directly to the customer.

Bloomberg/Getty Images

Costco, like many other warehouse clubs, is finding that its household appeal is not exclusive to American markets and is beginning to expand into several international markets like Taiwan, Korea, and Australia.

design their jeans by selecting from many fabric and hardware options. Part of the shopping experience is observing the production process from behind a large glass floor to ceiling partition. One more thing, you probably don't need to rush out the next time you are in New York City to buy a pair of 3x1 jeans; unless of course you are prepared to pay $1,200 (minimum).

Facilitating Marketing Institutions

Many institutions facilitate the performance of the marketing functions. Most specialize in one or two functions; yet *none of them takes title to the goods*. Institutions that facilitate the buying and selling functions in the supply chain or channel include agents and brokers, who are independent businesspeople that receive a commission or fee when they are able to bring a buyer and seller together to negotiate a transaction. This chapter's "Service Retailing" box describes a new type of agent broker, a *buyer's* broker, operating within the automobile industry—1Click Auto Brokers. Before moving on, it's important to note that agents or brokers seldom take physical possession of the merchandise they assist in distributing, but some do, like commission merchant, who operates primarily within the agricultural industry. Retailers looking to work with an agent or broker should

SERVICE — RETAILING

Purchasing a New Car Is As Easy As One-Click

Agents and brokers, as discussed within this chapter, typically work on behalf of a supplier or manufacturer, not the end-run consumer, and are often only involved in two of the eight marketing functions—information gathering (i.e., identifying sales prospects) and selling. As such, few would ever think to consider an agent or broker as a retailer, and most often they'd be correct but not always.

Recall how in Chapter 3 we stated that recent college graduates are by their very nature acquisition oriented? Most must immediately find permanent or semi-permanent residences, fill these residences with furniture, and purchase a new, professional, wardrobe. Another common purchase made by these acquisition-hungry individuals is a new automobile; a reward to one's self for finishing four plus years of college and getting a job. And car dealers know this, which is why they gear so many promotions and deals toward recent college graduates. Yet, shopping for a new car is often a miserable experience—shady car salespeople, hidden charges, high-pressure sales tactics, driving all over town to get the best deal only to not, etc. But your *next* car-buying experience, whether leasing or buying, need not be miserable or difficult; a new, and *effortless*, retail channel for purchasing your next automobile exists—1Click Auto Brokers (www.1clickautobrokers.com).

Founded in May 2000, 1Click Auto Brokers is a privately held auto brokerage firm based in Centennial, Colorado. But 1Click Auto Brokers is not a typical agent or broker one commonly finds within the automobile industry; it's a fully licensed and bonded *buyer's* agent, and inclusion of the term "buyer" is important. Most agents/brokers one might come across are nothing more than salespeople who work on behalf of a dealership(s) or manufacturer(s). In so doing, they receive their compensation, often in the form of a commission, from the dealer and/or manufacturer who sells you the vehicle. Thus, it is in *their* best interest for you to pay more for the car as it pads their commission. This is

why so many advertise their brokerage services as "free to the consumer"; the dealer or manufacturer is paying them. [The shrewd reader will realize this is why they're not classified as retailers (see Chapter 1); the service is *not* provided to the consumer but to the manufacturer or dealer.] Others will even "double-dip" by charging both the dealer *and* the customer a fee. 1Click agents are different; they *never* accept *any* form of compensation from a dealer or manufacturer. And this is a critical component of their overall value proposition to the consumer.

How the process works ... Having identified an automobile(s) of interest, one contacts 1Click by phone or email. Agents then proceed to discuss all available "options" on the make/model and have the customer detail *exactly* what one's interested in purchasing. The customer then provides a *fully-refundable* $100 retainer, which is either applied later towards the purchase or refunded to those that "back out" of buying. Agents then scour their network of over 700 dealerships nationwide to find the best priced automobile that meets the customer's "wish list." Automobiles that are found not to be local to the customer are then either delivered to a local dealership or to one's home. On average, the entire purchase process, from start to finish, takes 2–3 days.

It's car buying made simple; the customer gets exactly what they want without any of the hassles. In fact over 98 percent of their customers enjoy the process so much that they refer friends and family and/or plan to use 1Click again for future automobile purchases. And the service is a "steal" when you consider that customers are still able to get all the cash rebates and low interest rates offered by dealers without having to actually enter one.

What's the catch then? It must be real expensive; not true. The fee charged for buying (2 percent) and leasing (2.5 percent) is *based on* the *manufacturer's suggested retail price (MSRP)* of the vehicle, up to $34,000 (that's a maximum of $680 even if you bought an $80,000 car: .02 × $34,000 = $680). Having their fee based on MSRP incentivizes agents at 1Click to get each customer the very best deal. When an agent's fee is tied to

(continued)

the sales price rather than MSRP, the agent is actually incentivized to have the customer pay more as it translates into greater commissions. 1Click brokers only get paid *if* the customer makes a purchase; recall the retainer is refundable. So only those customers who get the very best price will buy, and the fee structure is set so as not to incentivize the agent from working against this goal.

How will you buy your next automobile?

Source: Based on one of the author's own experiences of purchasing automobiles through 1Click and conversations with the head of 1Click Auto Brokers.

carefully scrutinize all possible services offered by each individual agent or broker within their line of trade, as many are increasingly performing more of the eight marketing functions for their business customers in order to remain a relevant option for inclusion within one's future channel arrangement.

Marketing communications agencies, or advertising agencies, also facilitate the selling process by designing effective advertisements and advising management on where and when to place these advertisements.

Institutions that facilitate the transportation function are motor, rail, and air carriers and pipeline and shipping companies. Transporters can have a significant effect on how efficiently goods move through the supply chain. These firms offer differing advantages in terms of delivery, service, and cost. Generally, the quicker the delivery, the more costly it is. However, there is usually a trade-off because faster delivery enables the supply chain to have lower warehousing costs.

public warehouse
Is a facility that stores goods for safekeeping for any owner in return for a fee, usually based on space occupied.

The major facilitating institution involved in storage is the **public warehouse**, which stores goods for safekeeping in return for a fee. Fees are usually based on cubic feet used per time period (month or day). Frequently, retailers take advantage of special promotional buys from manufacturers but have no space for the goods in their stores or storage facilities. As a result, they find it necessary to use public warehouses.

third-party logistics provider (3PL)
Firms that provide service to retailers, and other customers, of outsourced (or 3rd party) logistics services for part, or all, of their storage, transporting, sorting, information gathering, and risk management functions.

One type of facilitating institution that is growing in popularity with retailers is the **third-party logistics provider** (abbreviated **3PL**) which is a firm that provides service to retailers (and other customers) of outsourced (or "third party") logistics services for part, or all, of their storage, transporting, sorting, information and risk management functions in their marketing channel or supply chain. 3PL firms such as Transplace (www.transplace.com) often specialize in integrated operation, warehousing, and transportation services. Pep boys, which operates more than 700 stores in 35 states and Puerto Rico, uses Transplace's Internet-based transportation management system (TMS) to manage its transportation planning and logistics network. This gives Pep Boys a virtual looking glass to view its freight and its movement at anytime and anyplace.[10]

A variety of facilitating institutions also help provide information throughout the supply chain. Increasingly, much of this information is available to customers through the Internet. For instance, Kelley Blue Book (www.kbb.com) for decades was a printed guide available only to bank lending officers and automobile dealers. The Kelley Blue Book provided pricing information on the retail and wholesale price of used automobiles. Today, Kelley Blue Book provides this information to anyone and also provides pricing information on new automobiles and can also help you connect to local auto dealers selling new and used autos.Another example is Lending Tree (www.lendingtree .com) that allows you to find the best deal on a home loan for either a new loan or a refinanced mortgage. The prospective customer is given several loan offers that they can compare using online decision tools to help them make an easier and wiser decision. In both of these cases, Kelley Blue Book and Lending Tree, we witness an information intermediary being the gatekeeper and often key determinant of which local retailers get the business. Consequently, they are an increasing part of a retailer's supply chain.

Other facilitating institutions aid in financing, such as commercial banks, merchant banks, factors, stock and commodity exchanges, and venture-capital firms. These institutions can provide, or help the retailer obtain, funds to finance marketing functions. For example, retailers frequently use factors for short-term loans to fund working-capital requirements (e.g., to finance the increased level of inventory needed for the Christmas selling season) while relying on banks for long-term loans to continue growth and expansion (adding new stores or remodeling). Venture-capital firms are primarily used by retailers starting a new operation or format.

Finally, insurance firms can assume some of the risks in the channel, insuring inventories, buildings, trucks, equipment and fixtures, and other assets for the retailer and other primary marketing institutions. They can also insure against a variety of events such as employee and customer injuries, changes in interest rates, and the impact of terrorist activity. In addition, insurance companies can make it possible for retailers to have what would be otherwise risky promotions. For instance, a retailer may decide to have a promotion that "on any day it rains in the local community that all prices will be cut 35%." In a normal month, perhaps it rains four days, but if after putting in place this promotion the retailer has 17 days of rain in a month, it would be a financial disaster. Buying insurance on this event helps mitigate the risk and make the promotion possible.

Having reviewed the various functions and institutions in the supply chain, we are now ready to examine how the primary marketing institutions are arranged into a supply chain.

LO 2

Describe the types of supply chains by length, width, and control.

Types of Supply Chains

A large part of the supply chain consists of the primary marketing institutions that perform one or more of the eight marketing functions. But how are these functions and institutions arranged into a supply chain? Exhibit 5.3 shows that there are actually three strategy decisions to be made when designing an efficient and competitive supply chain: supply-chain length, width, and control.

Supply-Chain Length

direct supply chain Is the channel that results when a manufacturer sells its goods directly to the final consumer or end user.

As shown in Exhibit 5.4, supply chains can be either direct or indirect; classification is determined by the number of primary institutions involved. A **direct supply chain** or channel occurs when manufacturers sell their goods directly to the final consumer or end user. In these rare cases, the lack of involvement by other middlemen pushes the manufacturer to perform *most* of the marketing functions (e.g., transporting is often

Exhibit 5.3
Strategic Decisions in Supply-Chain Design

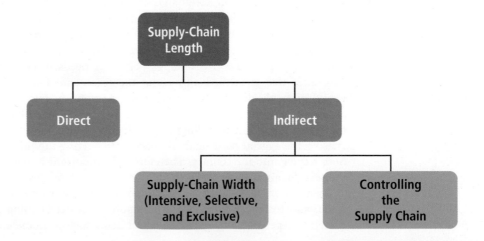

Exhibit 5.4
Direct and Indirect
Supply Chains

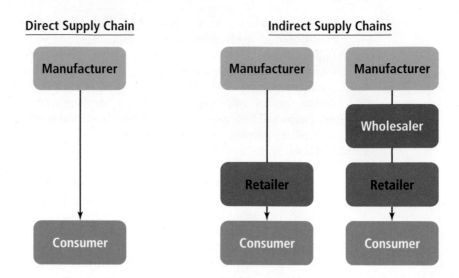

performed by facilitating institutions or even the consumer). An example of such a supply chain is Firestone, which sells some of its tires through company-owned retail outlets to the consumer. The supply chain becomes indirect once *independent* members (wholesalers and retailers) are added between the manufacturer and the consumer. Indirect chains, as shown in Exhibit 5.4, may include just a retailer or both a retailer and a wholesaler. Consider, for example, your neighborhood Avon or Mary Kay representative. This representative is an independent retailer who purchases cosmetic products from Avon or Mary Kay and then sells them to a consumer. This channel is described as being indirect because it goes from manufacturer to retailer to consumer. Similarly, when a local independent grocer purchases some Hunt's ketchup from SuperValu, a large food wholesaler that had already purchased the ketchup from its manufacturer, ConAgra, the channel is also indirect, going from manufacturer to wholesaler to retailer to consumer.

Sometimes the length of a supply chain is hard to determine. For example, when a consumer purchases cosmetics from a manufacturer's website and that manufacturer mails the merchandise directly to the consumer, the chain is said to be a direct manufacturer-to-consumer channel. However, if the consumer makes a purchase from a different manufacturer's website, such as Avon, and an Avon sales representative delivers the merchandise to the consumer from her own inventory, then the channel would actually be indirect—manufacturer to retailer (remember that the Avon lady is an independent businessperson) to consumer.

The desired length is determined by many customer-based factors such as the size of the customer base, geographical dispersion, behavior patterns like purchase frequency and average purchase size, and the particular needs of customers. For example, if the consumer was concerned *only* about the price paid for merchandise, then he or she would probably drive to a farmer's roadside stand to purchase a dozen eggs. However, as we pointed out in Chapter 4, factors other than price influence demand. In this case, the consumer might be willing to pay 20–30 percent more for the convenience of purchasing the eggs at the neighborhood grocer—saving the time and the cost of gas for an hour's drive into the country. Therefore, it is important to remember that, in many cases, indirect channels are actually cheaper in terms of total costs involved.

In addition, the nature of the product—such as its bulk and weight, perishability, value, and technical complexity—is important in determining supply-chain length. For example, expensive, highly technological items such as home entertainment systems will generally use short channels because of the high degree of technical support and liaison needed, which may only be available directly from the manufacturer.

Length can also be affected by the size of the manufacturer, its financial capacity, and its desire for control. In general, larger and better-financed manufacturers have a greater capability to bypass intermediaries and use shorter channels. Manufacturers desiring to exercise a high degree of control over the distribution of their products are also more likely to use a shorter chain (e.g., Zara from this chapter's "What's New?" box).

Retailers, on the other hand, do not always have a lot of control over their channel length. For example, retailers entering Japan will find that their channel's long length is to a great extent predetermined. Japan's channel structure (often referred to as a *multi-tier distribution channel*) was formed in feudal times and is the accepted method of doing business in that country. Sometimes the retailer must learn to operate as efficiently as possible within an inefficient channel.

Supply-Chain Width

intensive distribution
Means that all possible retailers are used in a trade area.

selective distribution
Means that a moderate number of retailers are used in a trade area.

exclusive distribution
Means only one retailer is used to cover a trading area.

Supply-chain width or channel width, shown in Exhibit 5.5, is usually described in terms of intensive distribution, selective distribution, or exclusive distribution. **Intensive distribution** means that all possible retailers are used to reach the target market. **Selective distribution** means that a smaller number of retailers are used, while **exclusive distribution** means only one retailer is used in the trading area.

Although there are many exceptions, as a rule, intensive distribution is associated with the distribution of convenience goods, which are products that are frequently purchased—those for which the consumer is not willing to expend a great deal of effort to purchase. Selective distribution is associated with shopping goods, items for which the consumer will make a price or value comparison before purchasing. Exclusive distribution is identified with specialty goods—usually high-prestige branded products that the consumer expressly seeks out. Thus, soft drinks, milk, and greeting cards (convenience goods) tend to be carried by a very large number of retailers; home appliances and apparel (shopping goods) are handled by relatively fewer retailers; and specialty goods, such as Rolex watches, are featured by only one dealer in a trading area. Some of these specialty goods are so exclusive, Ferrari automobiles (priced generally over $250,000) and Oxxford men's suits (priced generally over $4,000) for example, that many trade areas may not have a retailer handling them.

Exhibit 5.5
Width of Supply-Chain Structure

Exclusive Distribution	Selective Distribution	Intensive Distribution
Only one retailer in trading area sells the product(s)	Moderate number of retailers in each trading area sell the product(s)	All possible retailers in the trading area sell the product(s)

Control of the Supply Chain

The previous discussion was concerned with the length and width of a supply chain. However, a more pressing issue is who should control the supply chain. Many chains consist of independent business firms who, without the proper leadership, may look out solely for themselves, to the detriment of the other members. For this reason, experts agree that *no supply chain will ever operate at a 100-percent efficiency level.* Supply-chain members must have as their goal "to minimize the suboptimization" of the supply chain.

Supply chains follow one of two basic patterns: the conventional marketing channel and the vertical marketing channel. Exhibit 5.6 provides an illustration of these major channel patterns.

Conventional Marketing Channel

conventional marketing channel Is one in which each channel member is loosely aligned with the others and takes a short-term orientation.

A **conventional marketing channel** is one in which each member of the supply chain is loosely aligned with the others and takes a short-term orientation. Predictably, each member's orientation is toward the subsequent institution in the channel. The prevailing attitude is "what is happening today" as opposed to "what will happen in the future." The manufacturer interacts with and focuses efforts on the wholesaler, the wholesaler is primarily concerned with the retailer, and the retailer focuses efforts on the final consumer. In short, all of the members focus on their immediate desire to close the sale or create a transaction. Thus, the conventional marketing channel consists of a series of pairs in which the members of each pair recognize each other but not necessarily the other components of the supply chain.

The conventional marketing channel, which is historically predominant in the United States, is a sloppy and inefficient method of conducting business. It fosters intense negotiations within each pair of institutions in the supply chain. In addition, members are unable to see the possibility of shifting or dividing the marketing functions among all the participants. Obviously, it is an unproductive method for marketing goods and has been on the decline in the United States since the early 1950s.

Exhibit 5.6
Marketing Channel Patterns

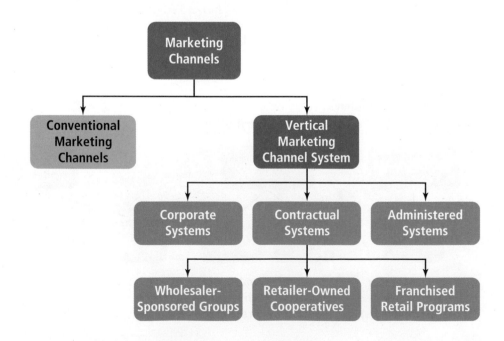

Vertical Marketing Channels

vertical marketing channels
Are capital-intensive networks of several levels that are professionally managed and centrally programmed to realize the technological, managerial, and promotional economies of a long-term relationship orientation.

quick response (QR) systems
Also known as **efficient consumer response (ECR) systems**, are integrated information, production, and logistical systems that obtain real-time information on consumer actions by capturing sales data at point- of-purchase terminals and then transmitting this information back through the entire channel to enable efficient production and distribution scheduling.

corporate vertical marketing channels
Exist where one channel institution owns multiple levels of distribution and typically consists of either a manufacturer that has integrated vertically forward to reach the consumer or a retailer that has integrated vertically backward to create a self-supply network.

Vertical marketing channels are capital-intensive networks of several levels that are professionally managed and rely on centrally programmed systems to realize the technological, managerial, and promotional economies of long-term relationships. The basic premise of working as a system is to operate as close as possible to that elusive 100-percent efficiency level. This is achieved by eliminating the suboptimization that exists in conventional channels, and improving the channel's performance by working together.[11] IKEA leads a vertical marketing channel and recently was able to identify cost savings in using paper shipping pallets versus wood pallets. The pallets, which can hold up to 1,650 pounds, are assembled by IKEA's 1,200 global suppliers and are used only once before being recycled. Because the paper pallets are 90 percent lighter than conventional wood pallets and more compact, IKEA will save $193 million annually.[12]

Formerly adversarial relationships between retailers and their suppliers are now giving way to new vertical channel partnerships that minimize such inefficiencies.[13] Because vertical channel members realize that it is impossible to offer consumers value without being a low-cost, high-efficiency supply chain, they have developed either **quick response (QR) systems** or **efficient consumer response (ECR) systems**. These systems, which are identical despite the differing names adopted by various retail industries, are designed to obtain real-time information on consumers' actions by capturing SKU data at point-of-purchase terminals and then transmitting that information through the entire supply chain. This information is used to develop new or modified products, manage channel-wide inventory levels, and lower total-channel costs. The final section of this chapter discusses category management, which is accomplished when all the members (who would have acted independently in a conventional channel) work as team to apply the ECR concept to an entire category of merchandise.

There are three types of vertical marketing channels: corporate, contractual, and administered. Each has grown significantly over the last half-century.

Corporate Channels

Corporate vertical marketing channels typically consist of either a manufacturer that has integrated vertically forward to reach the consumer or a retailer that has integrated vertically backward to create a self-supply network. The first type includes manufacturers or product design firms such as Apple, Benetton, Dell, Red Wing shoes, Sherwin Williams, Polo Ralph Lauren, and Coach, which have created their own warehousing and retail outlets or Internet selling sites. An example of the second type includes Holiday Inns, which for years was vertically integrated to control a carpet mill, furniture manufacturer, and numerous other suppliers needed to build and operate its motels. To illustrate this point, consider that Holiday Inn had to conduct extensive research to overcome manufacturing problems encountered with the production of cinnamon rolls, the trademark of its Holiday Inn Express units.

In corporate channels, it is not difficult to program the channel for productivity and profit goals since a well-established authority structure already exists. Independent retailers that have aligned themselves in a conventional marketing channel are at a significant disadvantage when competing against a corporate vertical marketing channel.

Contractual Channels

Contractual vertical marketing channels, which include wholesaler-sponsored voluntary groups, retailer-owned cooperatives, and franchised retail programs, are supply chains that use a contract to govern the working relationship between the members. Each of these variations allows for a more coordinated, system-wide perspective than conventional

giacomo giannin/Age Fotostock

Benetton has a corporate vertical marketing channel by creating its own distribution centers and retail outlets.

contractual vertical marketing channels
Use a contract to govern the working relationship between channel members and include wholesaler-sponsored voluntary groups, retailer-owned cooperatives, and franchised retail programs.

wholesaler-sponsored voluntary groups
Involve a wholesaler that brings together a group of independently owned retailers and offers them a coordinated merchandising and buying program that will provide them with economies like those their chain store rivals are able to obtain.

marketing channels. However, they are more difficult to manage than corporate vertical marketing channels because the authority and power structures are not as well defined. Supply-chain members must give up some autonomy to gain economies of scale and greater market impact.

Wholesaler-Sponsored Voluntary Groups

Wholesaler-sponsored voluntary groups are created when a wholesaler brings together a group of independently owned retailers (*independent retailers* is a term embracing anything from a single mom-and-pop store to a small local chain)—grocers, for example—and offers them a coordinated merchandising program (store design and layout, store site and location analysis, inventory management channels, accounting and bookkeeping channels, insurance services, pension plans, trade area studies, advertising and promotion assistance, employee-training programs) as well as a buying program that will provide these smaller retailers with economies similar to those obtained by their chain store rivals. In return, the independent retailers agree to concentrate their purchases with that wholesaler. It is a voluntary relationship; that is, there are no membership or franchise fees. The independent retailer may terminate the relationship whenever it desires, so it is to the wholesaler's advantage to build competitive merchandise assortments and offer services that will keep the voluntary group satisfied.

In the past, local food wholesalers got practically all of their business from independent grocers. Recently, however, as transportation costs have risen, major chains operating over a wide geographic area have also started using local or regional wholesalers. While

Since the mid 1960s wholesaler-sponsored voluntary groups, like NAPA and IGA, have grown in popularity as they assist independent retailers gain economies of scale similar to that of the big-box chains.

welcoming this new business, wholesalers have attempted to keep their independents happy (since they still account for more than 40 percent of their business) by offering them additional services.

Wholesaler-sponsored voluntary groups have been a major force in marketing channels since the mid-1960s. They are now prevalent in many lines of trade. Independent Grocers' Alliance (IGA) and National Auto Parts Association (NAPA) are both examples of wholesaler-sponsored voluntary groups. For instance, NAPA, founded in 1925, now supports over 6,000 NAPA Auto Parts Stores through a strategically located network of over 60 distribution centers. NAPA stores serve both the retail and wholesale customer and have identified its primary customer as the professional installer or the active do-it-yourself auto enthusiast.

Retailer-Owned Cooperatives

retailer-owned cooperatives
Are wholesale institutions, organized and owned by member retailers, that offer scale economies and services to member retailers, which allows them to compete with larger chain buying organizations.

Another common type of contractual vertical marketing channel is **retailer-owned cooperatives**, which are wholesale operations organized and owned by retailers; these are most common in hardware retailing. They include such familiar names as TrueValue (which was highlighted in Exhibit 2.5), Ace, and Handy Hardware, and they offer scale economies and services to member retailers, allowing their members to compete with larger chain-buying organizations.

It should be pointed out that, in theory, wholesale-sponsored groups should be easier to manage since they have only one leader, the wholesaler, versus the many owners of the retailer-owned group. One would assume that in retailer-owned cooperatives, individual members would desire to keep their autonomy and be less dependent on their supplier partner for support and direction. In reality, however, just the opposite has been true. A possible explanation is that retailers belonging to a retailer-owned co-op may make greater *transaction-specific investments*, or investments in assets that are less likely to be applicable to or useful when working with other firms (i.e., assets

Ace Hardware decor specialist Joanne Mendicino points at some new drop bins, part of the new store decor, to Ace retailers Jim and Marylin Berschauer, at a newly remodeled Ace store.

purchased to enhance a relationship between the retailer and the co-op supplier are unlikely to transfer, at least entirely, to any other supplier relationship should the retailer decide to change and increase its buying from a second supplier). Examples of such transaction-specific investments include stock ownership in the co-op, vested supplier-based store identity (e.g., all stores having the same TrueValue banner), and end-of-year rebates on purchases that combine to erect significant exit barriers from the cooperative.[14]

Franchises

franchise
Is a form of licensing by which the owner of a product, service, or business method (the franchisor) obtains distribution through affiliated dealers (franchisees).

The third type of contractual vertical marketing channel is the franchise. A **franchise** is a form of licensing by which the owner of a trademark, service mark, trade name, advertising symbol, or method (the franchisor) obtains distribution through affiliated dealers (franchisees). Each franchisee is authorized by the franchisor to sell its goods or services in either a retail space or a designated geographical area. The franchise governs the method of conducting business between the two parties. Generally, a franchisee sells goods or services supplied by the franchisor or that meet the franchisor's quality standards. This relationship is regulated by Federal Trade Commission laws. In many cases, the franchise operation resembles a large chain store. It operates with standardized logos, uniforms, signage, equipment, storefronts, services, products, and practices—all as outlined in the franchise agreement. The consumer might never know that each location is independently owned.

Franchising is a convenient and economic means of fulfilling an individual's desire for independence with a minimum amount of risk and investment but maximum opportunities for success. This is possible through the utilization of a proven product or service and marketing method. Consider that one of the benefits of franchising is that it permits a franchisee to select a location in a somewhat sophisticated manner based on the various professional forecasting models that use data from earlier units. Another advantage is in the purchasing of key items. Holiday Inn, for example, knows more about how to buy mattresses and furniture than most of its franchisees. However, a franchisee–franchisor relationship requires an ongoing commitment, with each party expected to uphold its end of the contract though active communication, solidarity, and mutual trust. In those cases, where a franchisee–franchisor relationship does not work, it is usually the result of a franchisee misunderstanding the franchising model and the franchisor failing to set expectations or the franchisee not understanding them at the outset. Remember that a franchisee gives up some freedom in business decisions that the owner of a non-franchised business would retain. The most common franchise mistakes result from a franchisee's incorrect perception of himself or herself as a traditional entrepreneur. In order to maintain uniformity of service and to ensure that the operations of each outlet will reflect favorably on the organization as a whole, the franchisor must exercise some degree of control over the operations of franchisees, requiring them to meet stipulated standards of product and service quality and operating procedures. Exhibit 5.7 lists some of the major advantages and disadvantages of franchising for both parties.

There are some 1,200 franchisors in the United States today, and they can be found at any position in the marketing channel (e.g., wholesale operations, broker agencies, and retailers); about 60 percent of them have startup costs of less than $300,000. The franchisor could be a manufacturer such as Chevrolet or Midas Mufflers; a service specialist such as Sylvan Learning, Doctors Express, L.A. Boxing, Stanley Steemer, AAMCO Transmissions, H&R Block, Lawn Doctor, Merry Maids, Mr. Handyman, Supercuts, or Century 21 Real Estate; a retailer such as Gingiss Formalwear or Batteries Plus; or a fast-food retailer such as McDonald's, Dunkin' Donuts, Subway, Domino's Pizza, or KFC. It's important not to simply think of the term, franchising, as synonymous with only fast-food retailing anymore. Consumer service providers such as fitness centers, lawn-care specialists, dance studios, tutoring centers, senior citizen care centers, and pet hotels have not opened the most outlets recently, but they have been the best performing.[15]

Exhibit 5.7
Advantages and Disadvantages of Franchising

ADVANTAGES TO FRANCHISEE	ADVANTAGES TO FRANCHISOR
1. Access to a well-known brand name, trademark, or product	1. Since franchisee is the owner, more motivated managers on site
2. Assistance in location decisions	2. Local identification of the owner
3. Assistance in buying decisions	3. Economics of scale
4. Being part of a successful format	4. Franchisee must make royalty payments regardless of profitability
5. Acquiring rights to well-defined trade area	5. The rapid rollout of a successful concept requires less capital
6. Lower risk of failure	
7. Standardized marketing and operational procedures	
8. By borrowing from the franchisor, the franchisee has access to a lower cost of capital	
DISADVANTAGES TO FRANCHISEE	**DISADVANTAGES TO FRANCHISOR**
1. Higher costs because of fees due to franchisor	1. Loss of some profits
2. Must give up some control of the business	2. Loss of some control
3. Franchisor may not fulfill all promises	3. Franchisee may not fulfill all parts of the agreement
4. Can be terminated or not renewed	

Incidentally, an indicator of the attractiveness of service franchising is the relatively recent entry of Procter & Gamble (P&G)[16] (the consumer packaged goods giant) into the franchising of dry cleaners by using its well-respected Tide brand (see Tide Dry Cleaners at www.tidedrycleaners.com) and into automobile washes through its well-respected Mr. Clean brand (see Mr. Clean Car Wash at www.mrcleancarwash.com).

A more complete list can be found at the International Franchise Association website (www.franchise.org).[17]

Another advantage of being a franchisee was illustrated during the 2008–2010 economic crisis when many financial institutions cut or reduced their loans to the franchisees. Such actions, for example, made it harder for fast-food franchisees to remodel existing locations and buy or open new restaurants.[18] However, while most franchisors normally don't provide financial assistance to existing franchisees, they made an exception during the recent recession. This was because the franchisors were able to get the financing partly because of their historically low default rate on previous loans as well as their current balance sheets. By securing these loans, a franchisor provided capital to be used by the franchisee for expansions, acquisitions, debt consolidation, and refinancing for new and current obligations.[19]

Finally, although only a third of U.S. franchisors are currently operating in foreign countries, another third are looking to expand internationally within the next five years. After all, why compete in overcrowded U.S. markets when many foreign markets are available? Although franchising is seen as an economic-development tool for poor countries, the most widely considered foreign markets are the most prosperous markets of Canada, Japan, Mexico, Germany, the United Kingdom, and, more recently, Southeast Asia—Philippines, Thailand, Taiwan, Singapore, and Indonesia.

Administered Channels

administered vertical marketing channels
Exist when one of the channel members takes the initiative to lead the channel by applying the principles of effective interorganizational management.

The final type of vertical marketing channel is the administered channel. **Administered vertical marketing channels** are similar to conventional marketing channels, yet one of the members takes the initiative to manage (or "administer") the channel by applying the principles of effective interorganizational management, which is the management of relationships between the various organizations in the supply chain. Administered channels, although not new in concept, have grown substantially in recent years. Frequently, administered channels are initiated by manufacturers because channel members have historically relied on manufacturers' administrative expertise to coordinate the retailers' marketing efforts. Suppliers with dominant brands have predictably experienced the least difficulty in securing strong support from retailers and wholesalers. However, many manufacturers with "fringe" items have been able to elicit such cooperation only through the use of liberal distribution policies that take the form of attractive discounts (or discount substitutes), financial assistance, and various types of concessions that protect resellers from one or more of the risks of doing business.[20]

Some of the concessions manufacturers offer retailers are liberal return policies, display materials for in-store use, advertising allowances, extra time for merchandise payment, employee-training programs, assistance with store layout and design, inventory maintenance, computer support, and even free merchandise.

Manufacturers that use their administrative powers to lead channels include Coca-Cola, Sealy (with its Posturepedic line of mattresses), Villager (with its dresses and sportswear lines), Scott (with its lawn-care products), Norwalk (with its upholstered furniture), Keepsake (with diamonds), and Stanley (with hand tools).

Retailers can also dominate the channel relationship. For example, Walmart, as you will learn in this chapter's "Retailing: the Inside Story" box, uses its Retail Link to manage its communication with its vendors. Walmart also was one of the earliest adopters of ECR systems and today administers the relationship with almost all of its suppliers by asking that all money designated for advertising allowances, end-display fees, and so forth be taken off the price of goods instead. By doing this, the giant retailer believes that its supply chains are managed in the most efficient and effective way possible. IKEA is another retailer that administers, or leads, its channel with over 321 stores in 38 countries, 12,000 products and over 1,000 global suppliers. IKEA focuses a lot of its efforts on improving operating efficiency, lowering product costs via good design, and building strong relationships with suppliers and customers.

RETAILING — The Inside Story

Walmart's Not So Secret Weapon: Retail Link

As noted in Chapter 2, Walmart sells at the lowest price because it has the lowest distribution costs. (Remember that operating at the lowest cost is the third of the three tasks that a successful retailer must perform.) A key contributor that enabled Walmart to achieve this goal was the two-way communication system set up between the vendors and Walmart called Retail Link.

Offered at the retailer's expense, Retail Link allows vendors to manage their own lines inside each Walmart store and make informed inventory decisions that are mutually beneficial to the vendor and Walmart. With its constant enhancements, Retail Link is vital to the success of every supplier since it allows it to discover opportunities to grow its business to the benefit of both companies.

Today, Walmart's Retail Link ensures that a supplier has instant access to such vital information as:

- Percentage of stores currently in stock (vendors that fail to meet Walmart's in-stock target are in danger of being replaced),
- The location of any store with low or no stock on hand,
- The sales performance by store for all the vendor's SKUs,
- A list of other items purchased when one of the supplier's SKUs is purchased,
- Sales data for all the vendors' SKUs for the past several years,
- The current number of weeks of inventory on hand at each store based on each store's sell-through rate,
- The effect of promotional activities on sales,
- Sales by time of day and day of week, and
- Current financial projections.

The key to success when developing a system like Retail Link is providing only that information which suppliers deem necessary; too much information is just as bad as too little. To provide such needed information, reports are built from scratch, and suppliers must indicate what level of detail to include in each report. For instance, is the vendor interested in sales units or sales dollars, shipments to the warehouse, or shipments to the stores? What about markdowns, current inventory on hand, or gross margin? In addition, suppliers must also indicate which stores to include. Are they interested in all 3,700 stores or only a particular region, district, or store? Do they want this information for the current year to date, the current or last month only, just yesterday, last year, or the last 10 years? Further, do they want the information reported (aggregated) by the hour, the day, the week, the month, or the year?

As these questions and others demonstrate, there is almost infinite number of available reports—too much information for anyone to handle. Thus, the most important, and sometimes the hardest, thing for a supplier to do is decide what information is necessary for the business decision at hand.

Using such data, the category manager and the supplier might see, for example, that a key SKU's sales may taper off late on Sunday afternoons for several weeks in a row only to pick up on Monday afternoons. Such observations might indicate that the current inventory plan isn't adequate. Perhaps sales dropped off on Sunday due to low stock levels and picked up on Monday after the inventory was replenished.

Retail Link is Walmart's internal information system used by the retailer's buyers and replenishment teams to manage the merchandise. Therefore, whether the Retail Link user is a small, locally owned manufacturer, a global consumer package goods company, or a Walmart employee, each member of the supply chain sees exactly the same screens and reporting options. This consistency allowed Walmart associates to "compare notes" with every manufacturer and ensure that business goals are being met. This usually occurs weekly, if not more often, since most users of Retail Link run several reports every day.

Managing Retailer–Supplier Relations

Explain the terms
dependency, power,
and *conflict* and their
impact on supply-
chain relations.

Retailers that are not part of a contractual channel or corporate channel will probably source their products through a variety of different channels since no single supplier will possess all desired goods. Predictably, these channels will be either conventional or administered. If retailers want to improve their performance in these channels, retailers must strategically manage their relations with wholesalers and manufacturers. And to do so, retailers must understand and apply the three principal concepts of interorganizational management. They are dependency, power, and conflict.

Dependency

As we mentioned earlier, every supply chain needs to perform eight marketing functions, and no one firm can perform all eight on its own and remain profitable. Even direct channels require the use of facilitating members in order to, say, transport a product to the consumer's home after purchase from the manufacturer's website.

None of the respective institutions can isolate itself; each depends on the others to do an effective job in the performance of their responsibilities in order for the channel to be successful. Recall that when Zappos used drop-ship they were dependent on manufacturers and wholesalers for performing the storage (inventory), transportation, and sorting functions.

Consider a channel arrangement where one retailer, A, gets its products from three suppliers, X, Y, and Z. Retailer A is dependent on suppliers X, Y, and Z to make sure that goods are delivered on time and in the right quantities. Conversely, suppliers X, Y, and Z depend on retailer A to put a strong selling effort behind their goods, displaying them properly, and maybe even helping to finance consumer purchases. If retailer A does a poor job in even just one area, then each supplier can be adversely affected; conversely if even one supplier does a poor job, then retailer A is likely to be adversely affected. In every channel arrangement, each member firm, regardless of whether they are primary or facilitating members, depends on the others to do a good job.

This concept was recently driven home to the authors when several giant retailers worked with detergent manufactures to develop a concentrated product that would shrink the package size in half. In return, the retailers would help convince the consumer to pay the same price for a package that was half the size because it provided the same cleaning power. This was a win–win (collaboration) situation for both parties because retailers were able to use less shelf space and manufacturers saved on production costs. However, each party was dependent on the other to achieve these goals.

When each party is dependent on the others, we say that they are *interdependent*. While this interdependency is at the root of the collaboration found in today's supply chains, it is also the major cause of the conflict found in supply chains. To better comprehend this interdependency, an understanding of power is necessary.

Power

power
Is the ability of one channel member to influence the decisions of the other channel members.

We can use the concept of dependency to explain power, but first we must define power. **Power** is the ability of one member to influence the behavior of the other supply-chain members. The more dependent the supplier is on the retailer, the more power the retailer has over the supplier and vice versa. For example, a small manufacturer of grocery products would be very dependent on a large supermarket chain if it wanted to reach the most consumers. In this instance, the supermarket has power over the small manufacturer. Likewise, many suppliers are very dependent on Walmart because it is their biggest customer. For example, today Walmart accounts for 15 percent of P&G's

total revenue, more than the total of many foreign countries.[21] Yet this dependence is not specific to domestic manufacturers. In fact, the *Wall Street Journal* recently ran the following headline across the top of its Marketplace section: "Walmart Sneezes, China Catches Cold" to illustrate the significant dependence so many have on Walmart.[22] Thus, the power one member has over another supply-chain member is a function of how dependent the second member is on the first member to achieve its own goals.

There are five types of power:

reward power
Is based on B's perception that A has the ability to provide rewards for B.

1. **Reward power** is based on the ability of A to provide rewards to B. For instance, a retailer may offer a manufacturer a prominent endcap display in exchange for additional advertising monies and promotional support. Yet liquidity problems due to the 2008–2010 economic slowdown resulted in the use of a different form of reward power: merchandise. Because of the sharp falloff in consumer spending, manufacturers were forced to unload excess inventory to anyone with the means to pay. This resulted in off-price retailers such as like T.J. Maxx, Stein Mart, Ross Stores, and Overstock.com receiving some of the best selections of apparel, accessories, and electronic goods, items they would normally not get, at great prices.[23]

expertise power
Is based on B's perception that A has some special knowledge.

2. **Expertise power** is based on B's perception that A has some special knowledge or superior ability. For example, Midas Muffler (a franchisor) has developed an excellent training program for store managers. As a result, franchisees view Midas as an expert in training effective store managers. Seeking the best managers possible, franchisees give up some of their control in order to gain access to this training program.

referent power
Is based on the identification of B with A.

3. **Referent power** is based on B's desire to be identified or associated with A. Examples of this are auto dealers that want to handle BMWs or Mercedes because of the cars' status, or a manufacturer that wants to have its product sold in Neiman Marcus because of the image that retailer projects.

coercive power
Is based on B's belief that A has the capability to punish or harm B if B doesn't do what A wants.

4. **Coercive power** is based on B's belief that A has the capacity to punish or harm B if B does not do what A wants. For example, franchisors like Burger King have the right to cancel a franchisee's contract if it fails to maintain franchise standards such as restaurant cleanliness, food menu, hours of operation, and employee dress or uniforms.

legitimate power
Is based on A's right to influence B, or B's belief that B should accept A's influence.

5. **Legitimate power** is based on A's right to influence B or on B's belief that B should accept A's influence. The presence of legitimate power is most easily seen in contractual marketing channels. A manufacturer may, for example, threaten to cut off a retailer's supply if the retailer fails to meet certain standards. For example, Deere & Company recently terminated some if its smaller dealerships after years of selling the company's equipment. Deere and Co. stated that many of these smaller dealers simply neglected to run their businesses as needed by the manufacturer; they neglected to develop new revenue streams (customers) while failing to assist the manufacturer in managing inventory costs. Now the company says that dealers must meet established profit and customer-loyalty targets or fear being merged with other dealers.[24]

Also, if the retailer accepts co-op advertising dollars, the manufacturer may control the minimum retail price, since this subject is usually covered in the agreement. Absent such an agreement, the retailer is free to set the selling price. To do otherwise would be a violation of certain federal antitrust laws, which we discuss in the next chapter.

Retailers and suppliers that use reward, expertise, referent, and informational power can foster a healthy working relationship. On the other hand, the use of coercive and legitimate power tends to elicit conflict and harm cooperation in the supply chain. For instance, if an apparel manufacturer wants to have its merchandise displayed more effectively in the retail stores it sells through, it could provide special training and informational programs on merchandising displays and advertisements. This would be much more effective in building strong working relationships than threatening the retailers with pulling the merchandise line if it is not displayed properly (a coercive tactic).

Conflict

Conflict is inevitable in every supply-chain relationship because retailers and suppliers are interdependent. In other words, every channel member is dependent on every other member to perform some specific task. Interdependency has been identified as the root cause of all conflict in marketing channels. There are three major sources of conflict between retailers and their suppliers: perceptual incongruity, goal incompatibility, and domain disagreement.

perceptual incongruity
Occurs when the retailer and supplier have different perceptions of reality.

Perceptual incongruity occurs when the retailer and supplier have different perceptions of reality. A retailer may perceive that the economy isn't coming out of recession, and therefore, may want to continue to keep a low level of inventory investments, while the supplier may believe that the economy is recovering and, therefore, that inventory investments should be maintained or possibly increased. Other areas where the retailer and supplier might perceive things differently include the quality of the supplier's merchandise, the potential demand for the supplier's merchandise, the consumer appeal of the supplier's advertising, and the best shelf position for the supplier's merchandise. Mr. Handyman International is the franchisor of a business model that offers both home repairs as well as repairs for commercial accounts, through local Mr. Handyman franchisees. Mr. Handyman International perceived both the need and opportunity for a national accounts program where they would solicit commercial business, such as a chain of hotels or restaurants, and negotiate the contract to include price, and then assign the account to the various local franchisees.[25] If the local franchisee did not want to serve the account, then the franchisor would subcontract the work. This resulted in a major conflict between the franchisees and Mr. Handyman International because the franchisees perceived that they should be able to set the price and that if subcontractors were used (without their input), then the reputation of their local franchise would be damaged.

goal incompatibility
Occurs when achieving the goals of either the supplier or the retailer would hamper the performance of the other.

A second source of conflict is **goal incompatibility**, a situation in which achievement of either the supplier's or retailer's goals hampers the other in achieving their own goals. In essence, goal incompatibility suggests any two goals are, to some degree, mutually exclusive. For example, Nike and Foot Locker have fought over the retailer's goal of gaining sales with its liberal use of "BOGOs"—industry jargon for "buy one, get one at half-off" sales. Such sales encourage consumers to buy two pairs on a single shopping trip, thereby reducing the chance the consumer would buy the second pair elsewhere.[26] Similarly, some manufacturers don't want their products sold at big-box stores or discounters for fear of cheapening the brand image. That is why Stihl advertises that its power tools "are not sold at Lowe's or Home Depot."

dual distribution
Occurs when a manufacturer sells to independent retailers and also through its own retail outlets.

Another example of incompatibility between retailer and supplier goals is a situation known as **dual distribution**. Dual distribution occurs when a manufacturer sells to independent retailers while simultaneously selling directly to the final consumer through its own retail outlets or through an Internet site. Thus, the manufacturer manages a corporately owned, vertical marketing channel that competes directly with independent retailers that it supplies through a conventional, administered, or contractual marketing channel.

Retailers tend to become upset about dual distribution when the two channels compete at the retail level in the same geographic area. However, as consolidation continues among department stores, some manufacturers, such as Liz Claiborne, have opened stores selling their "power brands"—Juicy Couture, Lucky, Sigrid Olsen, Ellen Tracy,

Kate Spade, and Mexx. This practice has angered traditional retailers that buy from these manufacturers and can have an adverse effect on manufacturer–retailer relationships. In the case of Claiborne, in 2010 JCPenney became the exclusive Liz Claibornee licensee. To avoid any future problems of dual distribution JCPenney, in a bold move in October 2011, bought the brand outright. As a result Liz Claibrone, Inc. changed its name in early 2012 to Fifth & Pacific Companies, Inc.[27] Other manufacturers, such as Oakley and Tommy Bahama, believe that their stores help build brand awareness and thereby sales for the traditional establishments. The fear of upsetting current sales reps caused Tupperware to pull its products out of Target's 1,200 stores. The attempt at dual distribution was meant to reach shoppers too busy to attend sales parties or deal with door-to-door salespeople. However, the easy availability of Tupperware products in the giant retailer's stores had a "detrimental effect" on Tupperware parties.[28]

The problem of goal incompatibility is not necessarily one of profit versus image goals. Even if the retailer and supplier both have a return on investment (ROI) goal, they can still be incompatible, because what is good for the retailer's ROI may not be good for the supplier's ROI. Consider the price element in the transaction between the supplier and the retailer. If the supplier obtains a higher price, then its ROI will be higher but the ROI of the retailer will be lower. Similarly, other key elements in the transaction between the retailer and supplier, such as advertising allowances, cash discounts, order quantity, and freight charges, can result in conflict.

A third source of conflict is **domain disagreements**. *Domain* refers to the decision variables that each member of the marketing channel feels it should be able to control. When the members of the marketing channel agree on who should make which decisions, domain consensus exists. When there is disagreement about who should make decisions, domain disagreement exists.

Consider the situation mentioned earlier where manufacturers were reluctantly forced to sell their upscale wares to off-price retailers. Many of the major department store chains that initially helped the manufacturer *position* those items as high-image brand names in the mind of the consumer felt betrayed.

Another controversial domain disagreement practice in today's retail marketing channels occurs when retailers sell merchandise purchased from the vendor to discounters that the manufacturer does not want selling its products. A **diverter** is an unauthorized member of a channel that buys and sells excess merchandise to and from authorized channel members. For instance, suppose a retailer could buy a name-brand appliance intended to retail for $389 at $185 if it purchases 100 units. However, if the retailer orders 200 units it can purchase the item at $158. What does the retailer do? Some retailers will purchase 200 units even though they need only 100. They in turn sell the 100 extra units at a slight loss, say $155, to a discount store that may retail the item for $219. The net result is the retailer loses $3 a unit on 100 units or $300; however, it bought the remaining 100 units at $27 a unit less, for a savings of $2,700. As a result of this price arbitrage, the retailer is $2,400 ahead on the transaction. However, the manufacturer is likely to be upset because the appliance has been diverted into a retail channel it did not intend and over which it has no direct control. Several manufacturers claim it is because of diverting that Target has been able to offer high-end beauty products from such labels as Kiehl's, Origins, and Bare Essentials in its stores.[29]

Similar to diverting is a practice known as **gray marketing**, whereby genuinely branded merchandise flows through unauthorized channels that *cross national boundaries*. In essence, gray marketing is diverting on an international scale. Gray market channels develop when global conditions are conducive to profits. For example, consider the retailing of prescription drugs. Since Americans pay 67 percent more on average than Canadians for these drugs, the gray market, especially from Canada, has increased

domain disagreements Occur when there is disagreement about which member of the marketing channel should make decisions.

diverter Is an unauthorized member of a channel who buys and sells excess merchandise to and from authorized channel members.

gray marketing Is when branded merchandise flows across national boundaries and through unauthorized channels.

substantially. If you wish to see some of the options for purchasing pharmaceutical drugs from Canada go to (www.canadapharmacy.com).

Diverting and gray marketing can lead to another supply-chain problem: free riding. **Freeriding** occurs when consumers seek product information and usage instructions about products, ranging from computers to home appliances, from a full-service specialty store. Then, armed with the brand's model number, consumers purchase the product from a limited-service discounter or over the Internet. And free-riding is becoming even more common with the proliferation of smart phones; one of the authors had over 50 percent of his students in one class admit that they had purchased a product (e.g., a TV, pair of jeans) from an online discounter using their cell phone while simultaneously getting product information and/or trying on that product within a traditional, retail store.

Yet, not all conflict in a channel is bad. Low levels of conflict will probably not affect any channel member's behavior and may not even be noticed. A moderate level of conflict might even cause the members to improve their efficiency, much the same as happens with some of your classmates when you are working on a team project. However, high levels of conflict will probably be dysfunctional to the channel and lead to inefficiencies and channel restructuring.

freeriding
Is when a consumer seeks product information, usage instructions, and sometimes even warranty work from a full-service store but then, armed with the brand's model number, purchases the product from a limited-service discounter or over the Internet.

LO 4

Collaboration in the Channel

Why is collaborative supply-chain relationship important in supply chains today?

Although all supply chains experience some degree of conflict, the dominant behavior in successful supply chains is collaboration. Collaboration, where both parties seek to solve all problems with a win–win attitude, is necessary and beneficial because of the interdependency of retailers and suppliers. Retailers and suppliers must develop a partnership if they want to deal with each other on a long-term and continuing basis. As a result, many supply-chain members have begun to follow a set of best practices as listed in Exhibit 5.8. This vendor partnership is often a critical factor for the retailer who does not want to confuse the final consumer with constant adjustments in product offerings resulting from constant changes in suppliers.

Exhibit 5.8
Best Practices for a Supply Management

1. All supply-chain members must remember that satisfying the retail consumer is the only way anyone can be successful.
2. Successful partners work together in good times and bad.
3. Never abandon a supply-chain partner at the first sign of trouble.
4. Work together with your partners to offer products at appropriate prices. No one will win if either partner is dishonest or unfair with the other or with the retail customer.
5. Never abuse power in negotiations. Rather, understand your partner's needs prior to negotiations and work to satisfy those needs.
6. Share profits fairly among partners.
7. Limit the number of partners for each merchandise line. By doing so you can signal greater commitment and trust to your partners, thus building stronger relationships.
8. Set high ethical standards in your business transactions.
9. Successful partners plan together to help the supply chain operate efficiently and effectively.
10. Treat your partner as you would wish to be treated.

Facilitating Supply-Chain Collaboration

Collaboration in channel, or supply chain, relations is facilitated by three important types of behavior and attitude. These are mutual trust, two-way communication, and solidarity.

Mutual Trust

mutual trust
Occurs when both the retailer and its supplier have faith that each will be truthful and fair in their dealings with the other.

Mutual trust occurs when the retailer trusts the supplier, and the supplier trusts the retailer. In continuing relations between retailers and suppliers, mutual trust, which is built on past and present performance between members, is critical. This trust allows short-term inequities to exist. If mutual trust is present, both parties will tolerate inequities because they know in the long term they will be fairly treated.[30] For example, a vendor suggests that a retailer purchase a certain product. The retailer does not believe that the product will be successful in its market. However, the vendor insists that many buyers in other markets are purchasing that particular item and even agrees to "make it good" if the product does not sell. In this instance, the buyer will probably buy the merchandise knowing that the supplier can be trusted to make an appropriate adjustment on the invoice amount, such as provide markdown money, or make up this inequity in some other way in the future if the product does not sell.

Without mutual trust, retail supply chains would disintegrate. On the other hand, when trust exists, it is contagious and allows the channel to grow and prosper. This occurs because of reciprocity. If a retailer trusts a supplier to do the right thing and the supplier treats the retailer fairly, then the retailer develops more trust and the process of mutual trust continues to build. In fact, during the past recession, many smaller wholesalers and retailers were able to cut costs by renegotiating contract terms with manufacturers to match deals that the high-volume chains obtained. Here the manufacturers and smaller operators knew that they would need each other, further enhancing the trust between parties and allowing economic recovery to take place.

Two-Way Communication

two-way communication
Occurs when both retailer and supplier communicate openly their ideas, concerns, and plans.

As noted earlier, conflict is inevitable in retail supply chains. Consequently, two-way communication becomes the pathway for resolving disputes and allowing the channel relationship to continue. **Two-way communication** occurs when both parties openly communicate their ideas, concerns, and plans. Because of the interdependency of the retailer and supplier, two-way communication is necessary to coordinate actions. For example, when Jockey decides to run a national promotion on its underwear, it needs to coordinate this promotion with its retail supply chains so that when customers enter stores to shop for the nationally advertised items, they will find them displayed and in stock. Two-way communication is critical to accomplishing this coordination. However, two-way communication does not need to always occur around operational or tactical issues. During industry trade shows, for example, retailers and suppliers have the chance to communicate informally, which can foster good relations.

Sometimes two-way communication can quickly develop into a debate where one party is trying to convince or persuade the other of its view and vice versa. The retailer and supplier can get so involved in trying to win the debate that communication can become heated and failure to reach agreement can arise. For this reason, more and more suppliers and retailers are being taught to engage in dialogue versus merely debate. The concept of dialogue means "learning together" and focuses heavily on learning the other party's perspective and view. Consequently, a dialogical model of communication can be constructive and lead to more win–win situations.[31] Benetton is a good example of a marketing channel where the communication is around dialogue, not only with its extended team of 200 designers but also with customers around the 120 countries where it operates stores. Benetton views this dialogue as a way to better develop its point of view, which has evolved to be around fashion, innovation, and a curiosity for the world.[32]

Communication is not independent of trust. Disputes can be resolved by good two-way communication, and this improves trust. Furthermore, trust facilitates open two-way communication. The process is circular and builds over time. For example, Walmart is not only phasing in energy-efficiency requirements with its suppliers but also pushing gold miners to adopt strict environmental and social standards, verified by independent third parties. With allies Tiffany's and Richline Group, the world's biggest manufacturer of gold jewelry, the retail giant is upsetting miners. However, since mining enough gold to make a typical 18-carat wedding ring leaves behind 20 tons of waste, it appears that two-way communication will demonstrate the benefits of such standards to all parties.[33]

Solidarity

solidarity
Exists when a high value is placed on the relationship between a supplier and retailer.

Solidarity exists when a high value is placed on the relationship between a supplier and a retailer.[34] Solidarity is an attitude and thus is hard to explicitly create. Essentially, as trust and two-way communication increase, a higher degree of solidarity develops. Solidarity results in flexible dealings where adaptations are made as circumstances change. When solidarity exists, each party will come to the rescue of the other in times of trouble. For example, several years ago, Walmart had a problem with shoplifting. It discovered that several P&G products were easy to steal. Because of the relationship that existed between the retailer and supplier, P&G soon altered the packaging of the vulnerable products. Among the changes it made were enlarging and adding an extra layer of plastic to the Crest Whitestrips package and using a clamshell, a flat piece of cardboard covered with plastic, on its Oil of Olay products.[35] Another example of supply-chain partners working together to the benefit of each other recently occurred in the book-publishing industry. Here an industry practice dating from the 1930s allowed retailers to return unsold titles, which amounted to more than a third of all titles shipped, to publishers for full credit and without incurring shipping costs. Later these books were sent back to the same bookstore chains, where they are sold for a substantial discount on the list price. The idea of taking back inventory and then returning it wasn't a good idea for anybody.

Nowhere is this collaboration in today's channels exhibited more clearly than in the shift toward category management.

Category Management

category management (CM)
Is a process of managing all SKUs within a product category and involves the simultaneous management of price, shelf-space, merchandising strategy, promotional efforts, and other elements of the retail mix within the category based on the firm's goals, the changing environment, and consumer behavior.

Category management (CM)[36] involves the simultaneous management of price, shelf-space merchandising strategy, promotional efforts, and other elements of the retail mix within the merchandise category based on the firm's goals, the changing environment, and consumer behavior. The task of category management is accomplished by members of a supply chain working as a team, not acting independently, to apply the ECR concept to an entire category of merchandise such as all breakfast cereals, and not just a particular brand such as Cherios. The manager's goal is to enable the retailer to meet specific business goals such as profitability, sales volume, or inventory levels.

Retailers designate a category manager from among their employees for each category sold. The retailer begins the process by defining specific business goals for each category. The category manager then leverages detailed knowledge of the consumer and consumer trends, detailed point-of-sale (POS) information, and specific analyses provided by each supplier to the category. With this information, the category manager creates specific modulars that may have different facings for different stores as the retailer tailors its offerings to the specific needs of each market. In addition, category managers work with suppliers to plan promotions throughout the year to achieve the designated business goals for the category.

In cases where the solidarity of the channel partners is high, a supplier may serve as the retailer's category manager. In this case, the chosen supplier takes on the designation of *category advisor*. Walmart, for example, uses this strategy wherein the category advisor works closely with the Walmart buyer to ensure that the category achieves peak performance in all stores. Normally, a supplier is chosen to become a category advisor because it is a trend leader in the specific category and can contribute merchandising and market analysis. Often, but not always, this supplier is also the dominant provider within the specific category. As each buyer has responsibility for several related product categories, each category may have a separate category advisor, depending on need. Further, while a supplier may be recognized as a trend leader in one category, a different supplier may be recognized as the trend leader in another.

At one point, category advisers were called *category captains*. While the responsibilities have not changed, retailers have adopted the new terminology (category advisors) to avoid speculation and confusion about who is responsible for making decisions. Also, to ensure fairness, the individual fulfilling the category advisor position is not supposed to have any sales relationships with Walmart. In fact, this person is not supposed to report to anyone with selling responsibility for Walmart. The category advisor receives access to the sales information for all items and suppliers in the designated category. To keep business confidentiality, advisors do not receive access to data on profitability. Also, they are not allowed to share the information with anyone in their company. Given these boundaries, the question arises, why would a vendor want to pay for the category advisor? Most companies would agree that the ability to better understand the retailer's merchandise direction (or thinking and strategy) is enough of a benefit to justify the cost. If you consider, for example, that Walmart purchases $200 million in greeting cards annually from Hallmark, you quickly see the economic logic of investing in a category advisor.

The category captain or category advisor, working closely with the retail buyer, must make sure that the retailer has the best assortment for each store in order to achieve the greatest sales possible. This includes carrying the competition's merchandise. As a result, the supplier's role as the category captain or category advisor has changed greatly in recent years. Whereas in the past the supplier sought to get as many of its items into the retailer's store as possible, today that supplier has to understand how its products help the retailer achieve its objectives, even if this means selecting a competitor's product over its own. For retailers using a single advisor, a yearly review and possible reassignment of the advisor's role to another supplier helps to keep the category advisor's recommendations objective.

To survive strong competition from other retailers, advising suppliers must stay ahead of consumer trends and meet the ever-changing tastes of the consumer. To aid the supplier who serves as a category advisor, the retailer provides the same POS information (except the competition's prices) that it would give its own employee serving as the category manager.

Category managers must be ready to constantly adjust the space given to each item so that the right merchandise is in the right stores, at the right time, and in the right amount. Over the last decade, category management has enabled retailers to do a better job of staying in stock on the best-selling items and avoid being overstocked on merchandise with a lower turnover rate. The category manager must be able to recognize what critical items need to remain in stock at all times to make the assortment complete.

In addition, as will be explained in Chapter 13, the category manager tries to create a shelf layout based on how the consumer shops.

Retailers, however, are far from passive when it comes to accepting a supplier's recommendation. They usually run the supplier's category plan by a second supplier known as the *validator*. Thus, Unilever, for example, could run a reality check for supermarkets using P&G as their category advisor or captain. Even more important, retailers must insist that category advisors adhere to the retailer's strategy with regard to pricing, promotions, and so on.

Category management is now standard practice at nearly every U.S. supermarket, convenience store, mass merchant, and drug chain. Its use is growing because the results of this collaboration benefit both retailer and supplier. Retailers using category management report an increase in sales for both parties, a decrease in markdowns, better in-stock percentages on key items for the retailer, an increase in turnover rates and a decrease in average inventory for both retailers and wholesalers, and an increase in both members' ROI and profit.

However, when all retailers begin to use the same category management approach to optimize each store's layout and maximize the gross margin dollars produced per unit of space, many times stores end up looking just like their competitors. This is why Walmart replaced the "captain" with "advisors" so that they could gain the benefits of different approaches.

Summary

LO 1

What is the retailer's role as a member of the larger supply chain?

In reality, it is the retailer's supply chain, rather than its outlet, that competes against other retailers. If the retailer ignores the supply chain in order to maximize short-run profits, then in the long run the chain will work against the retailer. If the supply chain overlooks the retailer, then profits sufficient for survival and growth will vanish. In learning to work within the supply chain, the retailer needs to recognize the eight marketing functions necessary in all marketing channels: buying, selling, storing, transporting, sorting, financing, information gathering, and risk taking. The retailer can seldom perform all eight functions and therefore must rely on other primary and facilitating institutions in the supply chain. Although marketing functions occur throughout the supply chain, they can be shifted or divided in different ways among the institutions in the marketing supply chain.

LO 2

What are the different types of retail supply chains?

Supply chains can be arranged by length, width, and control. Length is concerned with the number of primary marketing institutions in the chain. The supply chain or channel is said to be direct if it involves only the manufacturer and the consumer. An indirect channel adds either a retailer or a wholesaler or both to the supply chain. The channel's width measures the number of retailers handling the product in a given trading area.

Control looks at the two primary marketing channel patterns—conventional and vertical. A conventional marketing channel is one in which each member of the supply chain is loosely aligned with the others, each member recognizing only those it directly interacts with and ignoring all others. Conventional marketing channels are on the decline in the United States, while vertical marketing channels are becoming dominant. In the vertical marketing channel, all parties to the supply chain recognize each other, and one member programs the supply chain to achieve technological, managerial, and promotional economies. The three types of vertical marketing channels are corporate, contractual, and administered.

LO 3

How do dependency, power, and conflict influence supply-chain relations?

In order to operate efficiently and effectively in any marketing supply chain, the retailer must depend on other channel members for assistance. When a retailer becomes highly dependent on other channel members, it gains power over the retailer. However, other channel members (manufacturers and wholesalers) also depend on the retailer, resulting in interdependency and a sharing of power. Although power and interdependency can lead to conflict, they are more likely to create a high desire for cooperative relationships.

LO 4

Why is collaboration so important in supply chains today?

Because all supply chains experience some degree of conflict, most supply chains today seek to resolve it by using some form of collaboration. Collaboration is necessary and beneficial because of the interdependency of the members and because most retailers and suppliers must nurture a partnership if they want to deal with each other on a long-term basis. This is the only way to perform the marketing functions effectively and efficiently for the benefit of the consumer.

Category management is one of the ways collaboration is used in supply chains today. Category management, where an entire category is managed as a unit, involves the simultaneous management of price, shelf-space merchandising strategy, promotional efforts, and other elements of the retail mix within the category based on the firm's goals, the changing environment, and consumer behavior.

Terms to Remember

supply chain
channel
logistics network
logistics inventory
total cost of business
primary marketing institutions
facilitating marketing institutions
drop-ship
public warehouse
third party logistics provider (3PL)
direct supply chain
intensive distribution
selective distribution
exclusive distribution
conventional marketing channel
vertical marketing channels
quick response (QR) systems or
    efficient consumer response (ECR)
    systems
corporate vertical marketing channels
contractual vertical marketing channels

wholesaler-sponsored voluntary groups
retailer-owned cooperatives
franchise
administered vertical marketing channels
power
reward power
expertise power
referent power
coercive power
legitimate power
perceptual incongruity
goal incompatibility
dual distribution
domain disagreements
diverter
gray marketing
freeriding
mutual trust
two-way communication
solidarity
category management (CM)

Review and Discussion Questions

LO 1

What is the retailer's role as a member of the larger supply chain?

1. Why must a retailer view itself as a member of a larger marketing system? Can't JCPenney, Costco, or Best Buy be successful on its own?

2. Must a retailer be involved in performing all the marketing functions? If it can rely on other members of the channel, what functions can they perform and which members can perform them?

3. Facilitating marketing institutions, since they don't take title to the goods, add no value to a supply chain. Agree or disagree with this statement and explain your reasoning.

LO 2

What are the different types of retail supply chains?

4. For years, Dell was known for selling its computers directly to the consumer. Then it started selling them at Walmart and Best Buy. A classmate contends, "Selling through a middleman is only going to squeeze margins as the retailers demand lower prices. Besides the retailers have to make a profit for themselves." Isn't this clear evidence that a direct supply chain is always the best way to reach a consumer? Agree or disagree and explain your reasoning.

5. Your roommate says he can save money by eliminating the middleman—in this case, the retailer—and purchasing his potato chips at Costco in 8-pound boxes. He says you pay too much by purchasing chips at the nearby 7-Eleven in 4-ounce bags. According to your roommate, the more direct the channel is, the cheaper the item. Who is correct?

6. What is a vertical marketing channel? What is the primary difference between a conventional marketing channel and a vertical marketing channel?

7. You decide you want to open your own retail business. What are the advantages of joining a franchise marketing channel versus opening an independent store?

LO 3

How do dependency, power, and conflict influence supply-chain relations?

8. You are a manufacturer of a popular consumer product that is sold through independent retailers and some department store chains. Today, a large big-box chain approaches you and wants to carry your line. What should you do? How will this affect your relationship with your current retailers?

9. Agree or disagree with the following statement and support your answer. "Retailers should always oppose attempts by the manufacturer to sell its products directly to the consumer from the manufacturer's website."

10. Should it be legal for a manufacturer to prevent a discount retailer from purchasing the manufacturer's name-brand products from a diverter and selling these in the discounter's store?

11. Why are retailers so dependent on other supply-chain members? Couldn't they simply perform all eight marketing functions themselves?

LO 4

Why is collaboration so important in supply chains today?

12. Why is trust so important in a supply chain? Can't the largest and most powerful member of the supply chain simply tell the others what to do?

13. How are communication practices in a supply chain so important and how do these practices relate to trust in the supply chain?
14. With the advent of category management, how has the role of the supplier changed?

Sample Test Questions

LO 1   Facilitating institutions may best be described as specialists that:

    a. take title but not possession of the merchandise.
    b. take title to the merchandise in order to facilitate the transaction.
    c. manage the supply chain so as to increase overall efficiency above 100 percent.
    d. facilitate the transaction by performing all eight marketing functions.
    e. perform certain marketing functions in which they have an expertise for the other supply-chain members.

LO 2   A supply chain in which each member is loosely aligned with the others is a:

    a. highly efficient supply chain.
    b. contractual channel.
    c. supply chain capable of achieving 100-percent efficiency.
    d. supply chain based on the ideals of cooperation and partnership.
    e. conventional marketing channel.

LO 3   The basic root of all conflict in a supply chain is:

    a. each member wants all the power.
    b. each member is dependent on the other members of the supply chain.
    c. each member is fully capable of performing all eight marketing functions.
    d. partnership agreements tend to expire after a year.
    e. everybody wants to work independently of the other members.

LO 4   The key to efficient supply-chain management and the minimization of conflict is:

    a. considering all members as part of the same team and collaborating with each other.
    b. letting the retailer run the supply chain.
    c. never using coercive power.
    d. allowing all members to make at least a 10-percent profit.
    e. allowing the manufacturer to make all the decisions.

Writing and Speaking Exercise

Diva's is a 55-store upscale women's shoe chain targeting businesswomen and college students. Most of its stores are located in regional malls in the Southeast and Southwest. The chain has enjoyed rapid growth over the last decade, and its annual sales volume last year was $180 million with a 6.1 percent net profit margin (before taxes).

    Diva's prices most of its shoes between $39.95 and $119.95. The top-selling shoes are sold using the chain's private label, Avalanche. A primary reason for the success of Diva's has been its vertical marketing channel. The chain has eliminated most suppliers and relies almost entirely on contracting with small manufacturers to make shoes.

Diva's staff designs most of the shoes and has them made to specification by manufacturers in Mexico. As a result Diva is able to operate on a gross margin of 45 percent that is considerably higher than its competitors who do not direct source and use contract manufacturing.

As a result, the chain's shoes are priced approximately 20 percent lower than competitors' shoes of a similar quality. In addition, the chain has a higher markup than stores that buy from manufacturers and wholesalers. Besides these advantages, vertical integration minimizes potential sources of conflict.

This strategy does have its weaknesses, though. Diva's needs a large amount of capital. Money is needed to purchase raw materials and to defray other costs incurred during manufacture. Since Diva needs to supply these raw materials, its total inventory includes raw materials, semi-finished goods, and finished goods and averages $60 million. In addition, since orders are placed approximately nine months to a year in advance of shoe sales, predicting sales is difficult. If orders are placed with manufacturers and business slows down, orders cannot be reduced or canceled. Finally, slow-moving merchandise cannot be returned to vendors. If something does not sell, it has to be marked down in hopes that it will.

Using this strategy, how would the retailer's need for capital affect its return on assets (ROA) during an economic slowdown? (The student might want to refer to the strategic profit model discussed in Chapter 2.) In view of your answer, should the chain change its merchandise mix by adding well-known national brands?

Retail Project

In Chapter 4, we discussed divertive competition and introduced the topic of the break-even point (BEP), or the point where total revenues equal total expenses. Let's see how this topic will help us determine whether to join a franchise or stay independent.

Assume that you own a sandwich shop. In looking over last year's income statement, you see that the annual sales were $250,000 with a gross margin of 50 percent, or $125,000. The fixed operating expenses were $50,000; the variable operating expenses were 20 percent of sales, or $50,000; and your profit was $25,000, or 10 percent of sales.

In discussions with your spouse, you wonder if joining a franchise operation such as Subway or Blimpie would improve your results. Your research has determined that Subway requires a $10,000 licensing fee in addition to an 8-percent royalty on sales and a 2.5-percent advertising fee on sales. Blimpie, while requiring an $18,000 licensing fee, charges only a 6-percent royalty and a 3-percent advertising fee.

Assuming that you wanted to break even, what amount of sales would you have to generate with each channel during the first year, since both your fixed and variable expenses would increase?

Remember, the BEP is where gross margin equals total operating expenses; in equation form, this is:

$$\text{Gross Margin} = \text{Fixed Operating Expenses} + \text{Variable Operating Expenses}$$

Thus, with Subway, your fixed expenses would increase from $50,000 to $60,000, and your variable expenses would increase from 20 percent of sales to 30.5 percent (20% + 8% + 2.5%). Blimpie's would increase fixed expenses by $18,000 and variable expenses by 9 percent. Using the equation, we can calculate the BEP for both.

Subway's BEP:

$$50 \text{ percent (net sales)} = \$60,000 + 30.5 \text{ percent (net sales)}$$
$$\text{Net sales} = \$307,692$$

Blimpie's BEP:

$$50 \text{ percent (net sales)} = \$68,000 + 29 \text{ percent (net sales)}$$
$$\text{Net sales} = \$323,809$$

As a result of the increased franchisee expenses, you would have to increase sales more than 20 percent just to break even. To make the same profit you are already making, you would have to add that profit figure to the equation:

Gross Margin = Fixed Operating Expenses + Variable Operating Expenses + Profit

Subway's BEP with a $25,000 profit:

$$50 \text{ percent (net sales)} = \$60,000 + 30.5 \text{ percent (net sales)} + \$25,000$$
$$\text{Net sales} = \$435,897$$

Blimpie's BEP with a $25,000 profit:

$$50 \text{ percent (net sales)} = \$68,000 + 29 \text{ percent (net sales)} + \$25,000$$
$$\text{Net sales} = \$442,857$$

Thus, to keep the same profit that you currently make, a franchise would have to help you increase sales by more than 75 percent. There is no doubt the image of the franchise will draw additional customers, and its management may even help cut some of your other expenses. However, as these numbers point out, joining a franchise channel is not always a surefire guarantee of success.

Now, by using either a franchise directory in the library (e.g., the International Franchise Association at www.franchise.org) or a franchisor's home page on the Internet, look up two competing franchise channels in the same line of retail trade. After locating the information about these franchises, do the same cost analysis we just did and determine if, based on these figures, joining a franchise is a good investment.

Planning Your Own Entrepreneurial Retail Business

Upon graduation, you decide that you wish to get in on the ground floor of the e-tailing revolution and develop your own online business. You decide that a large opportunity exists in providing private-label apparel to a niche segment of Generation Y consumers. In the process of planning your entrepreneurial business, your preliminary sales forecasts lead you to believe that your first year's sales will be $500,000. You have identified two major manufacturers that can make the merchandise you want to sell online. One manufacturer is in a distant city and is able to promise seven-day delivery on orders of more than $5,000. The second manufacturer is located only 80 miles away and provides next-day delivery on orders of more than $500 placed by 1 p.m. Unfortunately, the nearby manufacturer has slightly higher prices. Consequently, you estimate that by purchasing through this source your gross margin would be 41 percent versus 43 percent by purchasing from the more distant manufacturer. However, because the nearby manufacturer is able to provide more frequent and smaller deliveries, you estimate that your average inventory would be $25,000 versus $30,000 if you used the more distant manufacturer as a supply source. Each manufacturer sells on terms of 2 percent/10 net 30. This means that if the invoice is paid within 10 days, a 2-percent discount can be taken; if not, the net invoice is due within 30 days. Which supply source should you select? (Hint: Compute the gross margin return on inventory investment, which is defined as the gross margin dollars divided by average inventory investment.)

CASE

Build a Belt & Boot (B^3)

Key Nelson was excited about the first six months of operation for Build a Belt & Boot (B^3). After nine months of planning this innovative retail venture, as part of his college major in entrepreneurship and finance at a local university, he was able to raise $100,000 to launch his venture. Luckily he was able to find a vacant store of 7,500 square feet that was easy to divide into two facilities; one his retail showroom and the other the production facility.

B^3 was a relatively simple concept comprised of four key elements: (1) integrate the production and retailing processes, (2) employ state-of-the-art production and information technologies, (3) customize offerings to the customer, and (4) engage the customer in the retail experience. Integrated production and retailing occurred by having a supply chain that provided all of the materials needed to produce boots and belts delivered to the retail store where production would occur. State-of-the-art production included digitally controlled cutting and sewing machines and laser-fitting machines. This was combined with an IT system that built a customer database that was then integrated with production orders. The investment in these technologies did not require any initial outlay of capital since the equipment was obtained on a five-year lease with monthly payments of $4,000. Customized boot offerings for customers occurred through allowing the customer to select from over 600 combinations of hides and tanning materials, four styles of toes for boots, six heel heights, 60 different colors of stitching, and four types of soles. Of course, each boot was custom made to each of the customer's feet since they are often different in size and shape. Similarly, there were over 10,000 combinations of belts that could be made and this did not consider length, something always customized. Engagement of the customer not only occurred through involving them in the design of their boots, but also during the two-week production, the customer could sign onto a website to check the status of their boots and be alerted of times when they could view a webcam and could see their boots being fabricated. When customers registered on the website, they were told the names of the team members that would be making their boots (usually three individuals) and send e-mails to the team if they had questions. Incidentally, all team members signed the boots on the inside of the left boot.

Sally Rider, who operated a local accounting firm, and who Key used to prepare monthly financial statements, recently briefed Key on the first six months of operation. The firm had achieved sales much more quickly than anticipated; projections for the first six months were $150,000 but came in at an astounding $441,000. Sales the first two months were very slow and were $8,000 and $13,000, but once early customers took delivery of their boots (always promised in two weeks) and began to wear them and show their friends, store traffic and sales skyrocketed. Assisting in the sales growth was very favorable PR; one story in the local newspaper in the Sunday business section and one local television newscast where a camera crew visited the B^3 and filmed a customer being fitted and then taking delivery two weeks later.

As Sally reviewed the financials, she paid particular attention to the growing investment in inventory. Key initially started his venture with nearly half of his $100,000 investment in inventory. Since he had not established his creditworthiness, he had to pay for all raw materials immediately and without any credit terms from vendors. Since then, he has established trade credit and is usually able to purchase with 30 days of credit before payment is required. Key can get a 2 percent discount if he can pay within 10 days of invoice. But right now, he doesn't have the free cash flow to pay upfront and take advantage of the cash discount. As Key saw orders skyrocket beginning around the ninth week of business, he aggressively began to expand his purchases of hides and materials for soles and heels. In fact, from an initial inventory investment of $44,000 his inventory investment is now $212,000. However, with sales running between $64,000 and $80,000 per month he feels that he must have on hand the materials needed to build boots and get them delivered in two weeks.

Currently, Key is purchasing all of his materials from wholesalers since he can usually get delivery within three days of order (if he uses UPS or Federal Express and pays the extra charges). Key asked Sally if she could do some projections on the economic viability of sourcing hides direct from tanneries. This would result in a 25 percent cost savings but require an order lead-time of between 15 and 45 days. For some of the exotic skins such as alligator, python, and zebra, it is not possible to source direct. However, Key estimates that for 80 percent of his hides (cattle, horse, and mule), he can source direct from tanneries. Each of these hides can usually be used to make four to eight boots. The hides cost an average of $120 if sourced from a wholesaler but $90 if sourced direct.

There was one final thing that Key asked Sally to consider. He had initially planned to open the second store in 18 months after his initial store, but now feels he should open the second store in 90 days and has identified an ideal site in a city 75 miles north of the current location. Also, due to the heavy publicity the retail concept is generating, he is fearful it will be copied quickly. Thus, he is thinking that after getting two locations firmly established, he should franchise the concept. With that in mind, he believes he can open 20 stores the third year, 50 stores in the fourth year, and 100 in the fifth year. The initial pro-forma income statement for a franchise store projects annual sales of $900,000 with a net profit (before taxes and franchise royalties) of $165,000. Since the franchisees could lease equipment and also their building, the only upfront costs would be a $125,000 franchise fee to pay for store fixtures and a two-week training program that Key would conduct at one of the two founding stores. Also, a continuing franchise fee based on a percent retails sales would be charged.

Questions

1. At this stage of development should B^3 be sourcing hides through wholesalers or direct from tanneries?

2. What can Key do to put in controls on inventory investments to make sure he is not over invested in inventory?

3. In order to grow his retail enterprise should Key use franchise marketing channel? What are the advantages and disadvantages?

4. What do you think would be a reasonable continuing franchise fee to charge the franchisees?

6

Legal and Ethical Behavior

Overview

In this chapter, we discuss how the legal and ethical environment influences retailers' decision-making. The discussion covers the legal aspects of decisions made on pricing, promotion (including the use of credit), products or merchandise, and marketing supply chains. The chapter concludes with a discussion of the major ethical decisions facing the retailer today.

Learning Objectives

After reading this chapter, you should be able to:

1 Explain how legislation constrains a retailer's pricing policies.

2 Differentiate between legal and illegal promotional activities.

3 Explain the retailer's responsibilities regarding the products sold.

4 Discuss the impact of government regulation on a retailer's behavior with other supply-chain members.

5 Describe how various state and local laws, in addition to federal regulations, must be considered in developing retail policies.

6 Explain how a retailer's code of ethics will influence its behavior.

In addition to studying the changing consumer (Chapter 3), competition (Chapter 4), and supply-chain environment (Chapter 5), retailers must also monitor the legal environment. Many large retailers operate in several states, where local laws and regulations often differ from state to state. As a result, most large retailers maintain legal departments and lobbyists to keep abreast of, interpret, and even influence government regulations. The same can be said for retailers who operate in more than one country. Such activities, though, are usually beyond the resources of small businesses. Yet governments and the business media do a reasonably good job of keeping all retailers informed of pending and new legislations. In addition, retailer associations such as the National Retail Federation (NRF) operate in every state in the United States, as well as most major countries, and work to keep retailers informed of proposed changes in state laws while seeking to protect retailers' interests in terms of federal policy and legislation. Matthew R. Shay, President and CEO of the National Retail Federation, is very proactive in looking out for retailers' interests and this goes even as far as writing the President of the United States to advise him on preparing for his annual State of the

Union address and the importance of the retail sector to the nation's economy.[1] You may want to visit www.nrf.com and look at all the areas of government relations that NRF is active in advocating. Also, interested readers might want to visit the Federal Trade Commission's (FTC's) website (www.ftc.gov) to review some basic primers on various activities related to the United States that will be discussed in this chapter.

We will now explore the final set of external constraints that affect retail decision-making: the legal and ethical environment. These forces are shown in Exhibit 6.1. After reviewing Exhibit 6.1, consider how retailers were affected with the passage of each of the following new regulations:

- The U.S. Food and Drug Administration (FDA), seeking to cut down on underage smoking, required a photo ID from any person appearing to be younger than 18 years and wanting to buy cigarettes or smokeless tobacco.
- Passage of various state and local laws that prevent smoking in public places, especially restaurants and bars.

Exhibit 6.1
Ethical and Legal
Constraints Influencing
Retailers

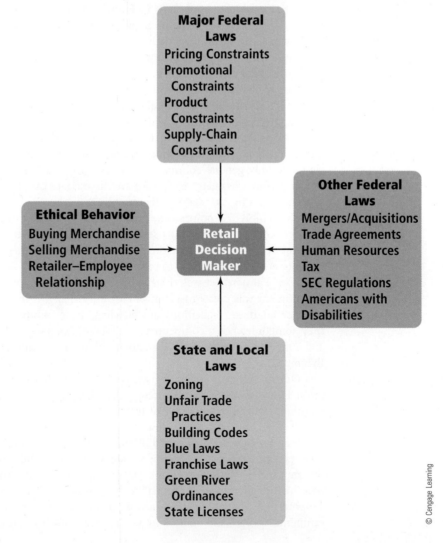

Major Federal Laws
Pricing Constraints
Promotional Constraints
Product Constraints
Supply-Chain Constraints

Ethical Behavior
Buying Merchandise
Selling Merchandise
Retailer–Employee Relationship

Retail Decision Maker

Other Federal Laws
Mergers/Acquisitions
Trade Agreements
Human Resources
Tax
SEC Regulations
Americans with Disabilities

State and Local Laws
Zoning
Unfair Trade Practices
Building Codes
Blue Laws
Franchise Laws
Green River Ordinances
State Licenses

© Cengage Learning

- Regulations in most states concerning the sale of over-the-counter cold medicines containing pseudoephedrine, an ingredient used in the illegal manufacture of methamphetamine, or crystal meth.
- Cities that have "sign ordinances" regulating retailers' use of billboards and even the signage on retailers' buildings.

Some cities have gone so far as to ban the sale of certain products. For instance, in 2011 the West Hollywood City Council voted 3-1 to ban fur apparel sales.[2] The law takes effect on September 21, 2013, allowing retailers sufficient time to clear their shelves. As a frame of reference, this is some of the priciest retail space in the United States and includes the shopping along Sunset Boulevard and Melrose Avenue.

All these laws affect retailers' ability to serve the needs and wants of their target market. In addition, ethical issues influence retailers' decisions.

To avoid costly blunders, the retailer needs to understand the potential legal and ethical constraints that exist within not only each country but also each city and state in which it operates. In fact, while domestic laws can cause headaches for many retail decision-makers, the differences in the laws across countries can drive global retailers crazy. For example, regulations in France require that products be sold to all retailers—big and small alike—for the same price, thus making it tough for discounters to get any kind of pricing advantage without relying heavily on offering private-label products. However, they also present some interesting opportunities for the retailer who is alert enough to take advantage of the situation.

Due to the myriad of country-specific laws, this chapter will deal primarily with various federal constraints that can affect a retailer's decision-making process when it comes to pricing, promotion, products, and supply-chain relationships in the United States. However, due to their sheer number, we will not be able to discuss all of the other federal laws that impact retailers. Also, since state and local laws are quite varied and often more complex, we make only general comments on a few of them. For the most part, we leave it up to you and your classmates to discuss and investigate the impact of state and local laws on retail activities in your state or community.

As Exhibit 6.2 points out, most federal laws affecting retailing seek to "promote competition." These fall into several categories. First, the Sherman Antitrust Act, the Clayton Act, the FTC Act, the Celler-Kefauver Antimerger Act, and the Hart-Scott-Rodino Act were passed to ensure a "competitive" business climate. Second, the Robinson-Patman Act was designed to regulate pricing practices. Third, the Wheeler-Lea Amendment was created to control false advertising. Although some people may question whether all these regulations are bleeding the economy dry, many others believe that they sometimes boost competitiveness. Other laws have been passed to protect consumers and innocent third parties. A sampling of these consumer protection laws is shown in Exhibit 6.3.

One area that is still in legislative flux is whether states can tax e-tailers or Internet sales. However, over the last few years, there has been mounting pressure for taxing e-tailing.[3] During the writing of this book, over 20 states, with California[4] being one of the most recent, had passed laws to tax Internet sales. On November 11, 2011, several senators introduced a Senate bill that would allow states to force e-tailers to collect sales tax and remit to the appropriate state where the customer resides. The bill had the support of Walmart, Home Depot, Best Buy, and surprisingly Amazon.com[5] who had historically argued against such legislation. The NFR has also been a strong supporter of this legislation because most retail jobs are local, and local and state governments forego $25 billion in tax revenue due to the current legislation that only

Exhibit 6.2
Primary U.S. Laws That Affect Retailing

Legislation	Impact on Retailing
Sherman Act, 1890	Bans (1) "monopolies or attempts to monopolize" and (2) "contracts, combinations, or conspiracies in restraint of trade" in interstate and foreign commerce.
Clayton Act, 1914	Adds to the Sherman Act by prohibiting specific practices (e.g., certain types of price discrimination, tying clauses) "whereas the effect … may be to substantially lessen competition or tend to create a monopoly in any line of commerce."
Federal Trade Commission Act, 1914	Establishes the Federal Trade Commission, a body of specialists with broad powers to investigate and to issue cease-and-desist orders to enforce Section 5, which declares that "unfair methods of competition in commerce are unlawful."
Robinson-Patman Act, 1936	Amends the Clayton Act, adds the phrase "to injure, destroy, or prevent competition." Defines price discrimination as unlawful (subject to certain defenses) and provides the FTC with the right to establish limits on quantity discounts, to forbid brokerage allowances except to independent brokers, and to ban promotional allowances or the furnishing of services or facilities except when made available to all "on proportionately equal terms."
Wheeler-Lea Amendment to the FTC Act, 1938	Prohibits unfair and deceptive acts and practices regardless of whether competition is injured.
Lanham Act, 1946	Establishes protection for trademarks.
Celler-Kefauver Antimerger Act, 1950	Amends Section 7 of the Clayton Act by broadening the power to prevent corporate acquisitions where the acquisition may have a substantially adverse effect on competition.
Hart-Scott-Rodino Act, 1976	Requires large companies to notify the government of their intent to merge.

© Cengage Learning

Exhibit 6.3
Examples of Laws Designed to Protect Consumers

Legislative Action	Examples of Laws Designed to Protect Consumers
Mail Fraud Act, 1872	Makes it a federal crime to defraud consumers through use of the mail.
Pure Food & Drug Act, 1906	Regulates interstate commerce in misbranded and adulterated foods, drinks, and drugs.
Flammable Fabrics Act, 1953	Prohibits interstate shipments of flammable apparel or material.
Automobile Information Disclosure Act, 1958	Requires auto manufacturers to post suggested retail prices on new cars.
Fair Packaging and Labeling Act, 1966	Regulates packaging and labeling; establishes uniform sizes.
Child Safety Act, 1966	Prevents the marketing and selling of harmful toys and dangerous products.
Truth in Lending Act, 1968	Requires lenders to state the true costs of a credit transaction; established a National Commission on Consumer Finance.
Fair Credit Report Act, 1970	Regulates the reporting and use of credit information; limits consumer liability for stolen credit cards to $50.
Consumer Product Safety Act, 1972	Created the Consumer Product Safety Commission.
Magnuson-Moss Warranty/ FTC Improvement Act, 1975	Empowers the FTC to determine rules concerning consumer warranties and provides for consumer access to means of redress, such as the "class action" suit; expands FTC regulatory powers over unfair or deceptive acts or practices.
Equal Credit Opportunity Act, 1975	Prohibits discrimination in credit transactions because of gender, marital status, race, national origin, religion, age, or receipt of public assistance.
Consumer Product Safety Improvement Act of 2008	Significantly enhances the ability of the Consumer Product Safety Commission (CPSC) to monitor, track and recall unsafe products with special attention to products such as toys for children.
Credit Card Act of 2009	Prohibits arbitrary rate increases and use of misleading credit terms and establishes more protection to consumers' use of gift cards.

© Cengage Learning

allows e-tailers to collect taxes if they operate a bricks-and-mortar store in the state where the customer resides.

Note that all aspects of retailing—price, promotion, product, and supply chains—are regulated. We will begin our discussion by looking at pricing regulations.

Pricing Constraints

How does legislation constrain a retailer's pricing policies?

Retailers consider a number of factors when establishing prices for the many items they sell including market demand, internal (firm-specific) cost pressures, likely reactions from competitors, etc. Pricing laws also influence retailers in determining what price they should pay for a product. In making these decisions, retailers have considerable, but not total, flexibility. The major constraining factors are summarized in Exhibit 6.4.

horizontal price fixing
Occurs when a group of competing retailers (or other channel members operating at a given level of distribution) establishes a fixed price at which to sell certain brands of products.

Horizontal Price Fixing

Horizontal price fixing occurs when a group of competing retailers establishes a fixed price at which to sell certain products. For example, all retail grocers in a particular trade area may agree to sell eggnog at $2.49 a quart during the Christmas season. Regardless of its actual or potential impact on competition or the consumer, this price fixing by the retailers would violate Section 1 of the Sherman Antitrust Act, which states that "every contract, combination in the form of trust or otherwise, or conspiracy, in restraint of trade or commerce among the several states, or with foreign nations is declared to be illegal."[6] It is also illegal for retailers to reach agreements with one another regarding the use of double (or triple) coupons, rebates, or other means of reducing price competition in the marketplace.

Occasionally, retailers have argued that the Sherman Act does not apply to them, since they operate locally and not "among the several states," the definition of interstate commerce. However, because the merchandise that retailers purchase typically originates in another state, the courts view retailers as involved in interstate commerce even if all their customers are local. In fact, even if a product is sourced locally the courts will

Exhibit 6.4
Pricing Constraints

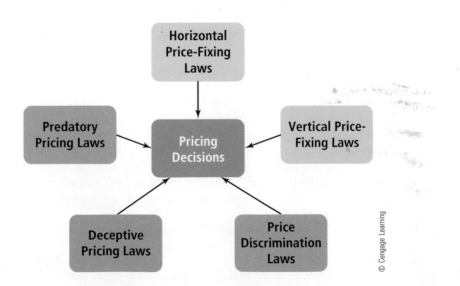

© Cengage Learning

argue that the retailer has other supplies that are interstate, such as the purchase of insurance or a banking relationship. Consequently, virtually all retailers today in the United States are involved in interstate commerce. Also, most states have laws similar to the Sherman Act, prohibiting such restraints of trade as horizontal price fixing on a strictly local level.

Vertical Price Fixing

vertical price fixing
Occurs when a retailer collaborates with the manufacturer or wholesaler to resell an item at an agreed upon price.

Vertical price fixing occurs when a retailer collaborates with the manufacturer or wholesaler to resell an item at an agreed-upon price. This is also often referred to as *resale price maintenance* or fair trade. Until recently, these agreements were considered illegal and were viewed as a violation of Section 1 of the Sherman Act. However, a 2007 Supreme Court ruling involving handbag sales at a Dallas mom-and-pop store upended that original 1911 precedent, and it potentially could alter the face of U.S. discount retailing. The Court ruled that a "rule of reason" standard should apply to such agreements, weighing their anticompetitive effects against their benefits. The justices felt that allowing manufacturers to require minimum retail prices could lead retailers to offer better customer service such as honoring warranties. Manufacturers also argued that if a small retailer is protected against discount competition, then the retailer has more of an incentive to invest in a highly trained sales force. Without such protection, the store owner would face a free-rider problem, which was discussed in the previous chapter, whereby consumers learn about a great new product at a local store, then go home and buy it over the Internet.

Proponents acknowledge that the lack of resale price maintenance increases intrabrand competition (competition among retailers selling the same brand). However, since the repeal gives retailers incentives to compete on a nonprice basis, these advocates expect that interbrand competition (competition among retailers selling different brands) will increase. After all, they claim that this is what antitrust laws were set up to do.

Thus, if consumers are slaves to fashion, this ruling may deprive them of some discount channels for buying the hottest brands. But the ruling should make it easier for an upstart brand to challenge entrenched competitors.[7]

It's important to note that the Supreme Court doesn't give a blanket blessing to resale price maintenance. Manufacturers must prove that its use has a procompetition motive and isn't, for example, designed to prop up a certain group of stores or to hinder others such as discounters or Internet retailers.

Price Discrimination

price discrimination
Occurs when two retailers buy an identical amount of "like grade and quality" merchandise from the same supplier but pay different prices.

Laws can also influence the price that the retailer has to pay for the merchandise it wants to sell. **Price discrimination** occurs when two retailers buy identical amounts of "like grade and quality" merchandise from the same supplier but pay different prices. However, these laws do not mean that the retailer cannot sell identical products— for example, a new car—to two different customers at different prices. These laws are meant to protect *competition* by making sure that the retailers are treated fairly by suppliers. Thus, the laws are intended to protect competitors from unfair practices by each other. In Exhibit 6.5 we see how a 5 percent lower price that one retailer obtains from a supplier enhances its performance versus other retailers the supplier serves.

Not all forms of price discrimination are illegal, however. Federal legislation addressed the legality of price discrimination in the Clayton Act, which made *certain forms* of price discrimination illegal. The Clayton Act was amended and strengthened by the passage of the Robinson-Patman Act. The latter act had two primary objectives: (1) to prevent

Exhibit 6.5
Price Discrimination
Illustrated

© Cengage Learning

suppliers from attempting to gain an unfair advantage over their competitors by discrimination among buyers either in price or in providing allowances or services and (2) to prevent buyers from using their economic power to gain discriminatory prices from suppliers so as to gain an advantage over their own competitors.

For price discrimination to be considered illegal, it must meet two conditions. First, the transaction must occur in interstate commerce. Trade between states, which is the definition of interstate commerce, covers virtually all retailers as we explained previously. Second, while competition does not actually have to be lessened, the *potential* for a substantial lessening of competition must exist. In addition, the act provides that any buyer who knowingly receives the benefit of discrimination is just as guilty as the supplier granting the discrimination.

Considerable attention has been given to the phrase "commodities of like grade and quality." What does this phrase mean? To begin with, commodities are goods and not services. This implies that discriminatory pricing practices in the sale of advertising space or the leasing of real estate are not prohibited by the act. For example, shopping center and mall developers frequently charge varying rates for equivalent square footage, depending on the tenant, the type of merchandise to be sold, and its ability to draw customers to the center.

"Like grade and quality" has been interpreted by the courts to mean identical physical and chemical properties. This implies that different prices cannot be justified merely because the labels on the product are different. Therefore, private labeling of merchandise does not make it different from identical goods carrying the seller's brand. However, if the seller can demonstrate that an actual physical difference in grade and quality exists, then a differential in price can be justified.

The preceding discussion may have led you to believe that the illegality of price discrimination is clear-cut and that retailers no longer have to fear being discriminated against by their suppliers. This is not always the situation. Buyers and sellers use a variety of defenses that enable some types of price discrimination to legally occur. These defenses include cost justification, changing market conditions, and meeting competition in good faith.

Cost Justification Defense

Such a defense would attempt to show that a differential in price could be accounted for on the basis of differences in cost to the seller in the manufacture, sale, or delivery arising from differences in the method or quantities involved. The burden of such a defense is with the seller.

Changing Market Conditions Defense

This defense would attempt to justify the price differential based on the danger of imminent deterioration of perishable goods or on the obsolescence of seasonal goods. This may be common with items such as produce or model changeover in home appliances such as televisions, refrigerators, and laundry equipment or in mobile phones or tablet computers.

Meeting Competition in Good Faith Defense

The seller can attempt to show that its lower price to a purchaser was made in good faith in order to meet an equally low price of a competitor, provided that this "matched price" did actually exist and was lawful itself.

Therefore, it is legally possible that one retailer—a large warehouse club purchasing 10,000 cases, for example—might have a lower cost per case than a smaller retailer purchasing only 15 cases. However, the retailer that knowingly receives a discriminatory price from a seller (assuming the goods are of like grade and quality) should be relatively certain that the seller is granting a defensible discrimination based on any of the three preceding criteria. Although the Robinson-Patman Act is mainly concerned with illegal activities of the sellers, if a buyer knowingly misrepresents to the seller a price that another seller is willing to offer and the seller meets that "factious" offer, then the buyer and not the seller is liable.

Sellers are prohibited not only from discrimination in price but also from providing unequal services and payments to different retailers. These services and payments frequently include advertising allowances, displays, and banners to promote the goods, in-store demonstrations, distribution of samples or premiums, and credit terms. The Robinson-Patman Act deals specifically with these practices, and it states that such services and payments or consideration must be made available on proportionately equal terms to all competing customers.

Finally, it is important to point out that most of the United States' trading partners do not have laws, such as the Robinson-Patman Act, that ban price discrimination, as well as many of the other regulations to be discussed in this chapter. As a result, many U.S. retailers have been shocked by what they perceived as an "unfair" playing field when they entered foreign markets.

Deceptive Pricing

deceptive pricing
Occurs when a misleading price is used to lure customers into the store and then hidden charges are added; or the item advertised may be unavailable.

Retailers should avoid using a misleading price to lure customers into the store. Advertising an item at an artificially low price and then adding hidden charges is **deceptive pricing**, which is an unfair method of competition. The Wheeler-Lea Amendment of the FTC Act made illegal all "unfair or deceptive acts in commerce." Not only is the retailer's customer being unfairly treated when the retailer uses deceptive pricing, but also the retailer's competitors are being potentially harmed because some of their customers may deceitfully be diverted to that retailer. In addition, FTC Guide 233.1 prohibits the advertisement of an inflated former price to emphasize a price reduction (a clearance or sale). The FTC is also concerned with the comparisons between a retailer's price and supposedly that of a competitor when the comparison price is higher than the competitor's actual price. Another concern of the FTC and state regulators: the misuse of rebates in promoting a price because retailers and manufacturers both know that rebates give the perception of saving money. However, in reality, most of these rebates are never claimed due to simple "consumer inertia" in a system where shoppers treat rebates as a discount in the store but seldom find the motivation to mail in the original cash-register receipt, the Universal Product Code (UPC) from a 12-pack of soda, and a correctly filled out claim form to collect a $1.00 rebate on the 12-pack.

Seeking to avoid any charges of deceptive pricing, some retailers have asked manufacturers not to use the word *free* on special packs of merchandise. These retailers have felt the word *free* to be often misleading after they received customer complaints that merchandise marked "free" really should be free of charge, not just a bigger size at the same price. Recently, these retailers have expanded this policy to also apply to shrink wrapping two products together as in a "two-for-the-price-of-one" package.[8]

Predatory Pricing

predatory pricing
Exists when a retail chain charges different prices in different geographic areas to eliminate competition in selected geographic areas.

Predatory pricing exists when a retailer charges different prices in selected geographic areas in order to eliminate competition in those areas. This is a violation of the Robinson-Patman Act, which also forbids the sale of goods at lower prices in one area for the purpose of destroying competition or eliminating a competitor, or the sale of goods at unreasonably low prices for such purpose. Generally, predatory pricing charges are difficult to prove in federal court.

LO 2

What is the difference between legal and illegal promotional activities for a retailer?

Promotion Constraints

The ability of the retailer to make any promotion decision is constrained by two major pieces of federal legislation: the FTC Act and the Wheeler-Lea Amendment of the FTC Act. The retailer should be familiar with three promotional areas that are potentially under the domain of the FTC Act and the Wheeler-Lea Amendment: deceitful diversion of patronage, deceptive advertising, and deceptive sales practices. Exhibit 6.6 depicts these three areas of constraint.

Deceitful Diversion of Patronage

If a retailer publishes or verbalizes falsehoods about a competitor in an attempt to divert patrons from that competitor, then the retailer is engaging in an unfair trade practice. The competitor would be afforded protection under the FTC Act but also could receive protection by showing that the defamatory statements were libel or slander. In either case, the competitor would have to demonstrate that actual damage had occurred.

palming off
Occurs when a retailer represents that merchandise is made by a firm other than the true manufacturer.

Another form of deceitful diversion of patronage that occurs in retailing is **palming off**. Palming off occurs when a retailer represents merchandise as being made by a firm other than the true manufacturer. Incidentally, these items are often also referred to as knockoffs. For example, an exclusive women's apparel retailer purchases a group

Exhibit 6.6
Promotional Constraints

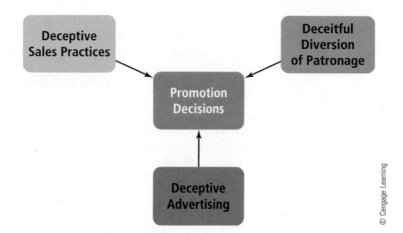

of stylish dresses at a bargain price and replaces its labels with those of a top designer. This is deception as to source of origin, and litigation can be brought under the FTC Act and the Wheeler-Lea Amendment. Also, if the designer's dress label were a registered trademark, then protection would also be afforded under the major piece of federal trademark legislation, the Lanham Act (1946). Canada, European countries, and many others have similar legislation. In 2011 three Canadian companies were ordered to pay damages to Louis Vuitton and Burberry for selling knockoffs of their handbags. All three of the firms were heavily involved in large-scale manufacturing, importing, and retailing of fake handbags.[9] In the United States, a $37.4 million judgment was awarded by a New Jersey judge against Concept Designs Unlimited (CDU) Inc. a jeweler selling counterfeit Cartier and Van Cleef & Arpels baubles.[10] CDU manufactured the counterfeits in its facility in New York's Diamond District on 47th street. Usually counterfeits are sold at a substantial retail discount. What was interesting in this case was the price points were identical to the original pieces (around $30,000). This coupled with forged certificates of authenticity help to deceive the consumer into believing they were purchasing originals.

Although it is difficult to quantify an actual number, the World Customs Organization believes counterfeiting accounts for 5–7 percent of global merchandise trade, equivalent to lost sales of as much as $600–650 billion a year,[11] which is consistent with estimates by the U.S. Immigration and Customs Enforcement.[12] As a result, companies are deploying detectives around the globe in search of counterfeits, pressuring foreign governments to crack down, and trying everything from electronic tagging to redesigned products and aggressive pricing to thwart the counterfeiters.[13] However, hundreds of different products, ranging from counterfeit avian flu vaccines to fake bottles of Hennessy cognac have been copied overseas and shipped to the United States for retail sale, sometimes even by the authorized manufacturer of the product. As a result, many plaintiff attorneys are suing not only the foreign manufacturers, but also the retailers and even their landlords, who may have unknowingly sold the product.[14] The top categories for counterfeit products are video games and other electronic software, apparel, watches, and golf clubs. Recall we mentioned at the outset of the chapter that West Hollywood had banned fur apparel sales by retailers. In late 2011, the continuing controversy over selling animal hides as apparel took an interesting twist when the Humane Society of the United States filed a legal petition with the FTC charging 11 retailers for alleged false advertising and mislabeling of fur-trimmed apparel. The retailers were advertising the items as made with "faux" fur, even though the items contained real animal fur. So, it appears as though if you claim a real product is a fake or a fake product is the "real" thing, it is in both cases deceiving the consumer.[15]

Not all the blame for such actions should be placed on retailers though. After all, a great deal of the merchandise sold in the United States is produced in foreign countries. In many of these foreign countries trademark law is relatively new and the concept of such protection is not always clear to the workers. When informed of questionable merchandise being sold in their stores, most retailers will discontinue all future purchases and work out some type of agreement with the injured party to sell any remaining stock. After all, the retailers know their reputation is on the line. Of course, the counterfeiters keep finding ways to deceive retailer buyers. For instance, many counterfeits come from South Korea and China, but the counterfeiters set up businesses in the United States or Europe and ship goods to these locations. Then, when a retailer places an order from a U.S. or European based distributor, they are led to believe the merchandise is authentic.

Today, however, knockoff artists don't need to operate in parking lots, flea markets, or other retail buildings. They have the Internet. Its anonymity and reach make it perfect for selling knockoffs. In fact, some industry analysts see the Internet as "ground zero," so to speak, in the war on counterfeits since it is estimated that 80 percent of counterfeits are sold online.[16] However, the question facing the courts today is "if landlords can be held responsible for the actions of their tenants, can eBay be held to the same standard?" Well, in a recent French court decision, Hermès International scored a victory against eBay for selling counterfeit luxury goods. The judge found that eBay, plus the individual seller, had "committed acts of counterfeit" and "prejudice" against it by failing to monitor the authenticity of goods being sold on its website.[17] However, at the same time as the French decision, a federal judge in New York ruled that eBay Inc. fulfilled its legal obligation and took adequate precautions to block the sale of counterfeit Tiffany and Co. jewelry on its site, delivering the first significant victory to the e-commerce company in its running battle with luxury goods companies over fake merchandise.[18]

Not only are product trademarks an issue but also the trademark of a retailer's name may be. The U.S. Supreme Court ruled recently that Victoria's Secret was not damaged by an Elizabethtown, Kentucky, store named "Victor's Little Secret." According to the court, the use of the name neither confused any consumers or potential consumers, nor was it likely to do so, since the Kentucky store sold adult-themed items in addition to lingerie. While the court unanimously agreed that Victoria's Secret had a valid interest in protecting its name, it resupported the notion that trademark law requires evidence that the competitor actually caused harm to a retailer by using a sound-alike or knockoff name.[19]

Therefore, when choosing a store name, the retailer must make sure that no one else has trademarked the name that it wants. Even names that just resemble trademarks might infringe on the rights of others as this chapter's "Retailing: The Inside Story" box points out. After all, trademarks are names and marks that identify the source of a product as a particular company. So, for instance, if your name is Kroger, you don't want to open up a store called "Kroger's" or even "Kroger's Store" because you'd be infringing on the trademark of the well-known supermarket chain.

Another potential problem area for retailers concerns patents. Most retail buyers assume that the wholesaler or manufacturer dealing with them has a valid patent on the merchandise being offered. As a rule, if the patent is ever questioned, a retail buyer should discontinue the product. After all, it is easier and involves less court time to replace the questionable item with a substitute.

RETAILING — The Inside Story

A Name Is Just a Name, Until It Isn't

What is a name really? Without careful thought, the passive reader might be inclined to agree with Shakespeare's Juliet when she says unto Romeo, "What's in a name? That which we call a rose, by any other name would smell as sweet," (*Romeo and Juliet*, II, ii, 1–2). Juliet suggests that a name is just a name; it's meaningless, and it's the person (Romeo in this example) that is meaningful. Perhaps she's right when it comes to people, but retailers will argue the opposite every time.

In the context of retailing, a name is much more than just a name; it's an idea, a promise, a value proposition. It's a symbol of the expectation a customer has when considering to shop a particular store. Retailers spend billions of dollars annually creating and maintaining their names, and they don't like when others have even a similar name, much less the same name. It muddies the brand and confuses the consumer, or at least that's what Target Corp. (USA) has argued for over a decade in the Canadian court system.

The target (pun intended) of Target Corp.'s lawsuits is Isaac Benitah and his company, Fairweather Ltd., which owns several stores across Canada called Target Apparel, and has a logo similar to that of Target Corp. Benitah acquired the name from a failing retailer, Dylex Ltd., in 2001, first using it as a label for clothing it manufactured and later in 2005 as the name of its own retail clothing chain. Since 2001, the two have gone back and forth at each other in the courts arguing that each owns the right to the name *Target* in Canada, and the other should pay damages.

At the heart of Target Corp.'s argument is the belief that Canadian consumers, familiar with the American "Target" moniker, will mistakenly infer that a Target Apparel store is affiliated with the Minneapolis, Minnesota, based retailer, enter and, based upon their experiences, believe Target Corp. has chosen to lower its standards in Canada. Yet as late as June 2011, the Canadian courts had denied Target's request for a preliminary injunction against Benitah and have allowed his company to maintain current operations. While the judge did agree that consumers could be confused by the similar name, he didn't believe that Target would suffer irreparable damage if the Target Apparel stores continued to operate until a full trial could be held in late November 2012.

Target Corp. doesn't plan to open its first store in Canada until 2013, but it desperately wants into Canada. Canadians are extremely familiar with the American retailer's value proposition (10 percent have shopped at Target stores in America in the last year, and 70 percent are cognizant of the brand), and it already owns the leases of 220 Zellers stores it purchased from Hudson Bay in 2011. It simply has to own the name *Target* within Canada's borders prior to entry. And many retail experts are saying it could cost the American chain a check with eight to nine digits to do so.

Future readers of this box will be able to look back at the court's ruling on the case beginning November 2012, as well as any settlements thereafter, to understand just how valuable a name like *Target* is in the world of retailing. It appears Juliet, and by extension Shakespeare, simply couldn't comprehend the value some place on a name.

Sources: Zimmerman, Ann and Stuart Weinberg. "Corporate News: Target Goes to Canadian Court—In a Battle with Apparel Chain, the Retailer Seeks Exclusive Rights to Its Name," *The Wall Street Journal*, May 2, 2011: B3; Zimmerman, Ann, "Corporate News: Canadian Judge Rebuffs Target in Bid for Name," *The Wall Street Journal*, June 27, 2011: B3.

---

deceptive advertising Occurs when a retailer makes false or misleading advertising claims about the physical makeup of a product, the benefits to be gained by its use, or the appropriate uses for the product.

Deceptive Advertising

Deceptive advertising occurs when a retailer or other member of the marketing channel makes false or misleading advertising claims about the physical makeup of a product, the benefits to be gained by its use, or the appropriate uses for a product. Deceptive advertising is illegal. However, it is often difficult to distinguish between what is false or misleading and what is simply "puffery" or "laudatory language," which retailers can legally use. Puffery occurs when a retailer or its spokesperson states what is considered to be an opinion or a judgment about a product, not a statement of fact. An example is a salesperson saying,

"This is an excellent buy, and you cannot afford to pass it up." Probably most important for the retailer to recognize is that the FTC's concern is not the intent of the advertiser but whether the consumer was misled by the advertising. When the FTC challenges any claim contained in advertising or promotional material, several requirements must be met before the commission can find actionable deception: (1) the FTC must prove that the challenged claim is contained in the advertisement, (2) the claim must be deceptive, and (3) the deceptive claim must be material.[20] There is disagreement over whether the above statement was a change in, rather than a summary of, FTC policy toward deception. However, it appears that, for example, an advertisement for "Danish pastry" would not be considered deceptive because only a few misguided souls believe … that all 'Danish pastry' is made in Denmark." However, in 2011 Reebok International agreed with the FTC that they would pay $25 million to consumers because the FTC found their advertising of toning shoes as deceptive because it was claimed they would strengthen leg and buttock muscles and provide extra tone.[21] The FTC viewed these claims as more than puffery. Incidentally, this decision of a high-profile firm and brand put similar brands and firms on notice not exaggerate claims that their products strengthen and tone muscles.

bait-and-switch advertising Advertising or promoting a product at an unrealistically low price to serve as "bait" and then trying to "switch" the customer to a higher-priced product.

Bait-and-switch advertising is another type of deceptive advertising. Bait-and-switch advertising is promoting a product at an unrealistically low price to serve as "bait" and then trying to "switch" the customer to a higher-priced product. However, the scope of the FTC's ban on bait-and-switch is much broader than the typical bait-and-switch scenario, and this strictness could, at least theoretically, pose problems for many retailers. For example, federal regulations outlaw all acts or practices by an advertiser that would discourage the purchase of the advertised merchandise as part of a bait scheme to sell other merchandise. Among those forbidden acts or practices are:

1. refusing "to show, demonstrate, or sell the product offered":
2. disparaging, by word or deed, the advertised product or the "guarantee, credit terms, availability of service, repairs or parts, or in any other respect, in connection with it";
3. failing to have sufficient quantities of the advertised product to meet "reasonable anticipated demands" at all outlets listed in the advertisement, unless the advertisement clearly discloses that supply is limited or available only at certain locations;
4. "refusal to take orders for the advertised merchandise to be delivered within a reasonable period of time"; and
5. "use of a sales plan or method of compensation for salesmen…designed to prevent or discourage them from selling the advertised product."[22]

Deceptive Sales Practices

There are basically two illegal deceptive sales practices: (1) failing to be honest or omitting key facts in either an advertisement or a sales presentation and (2) using deceptive credit contracts.

Deceptive activities essentially deal with misrepresenting the ability of a product or service to solve the consumer's problem or meet their need. If you stay up late at night, you might see the infomercials from J.K. Harris & Co., a tax-consulting firm that advertises about being able to help you negotiate your unpaid Internal Revenue Service (IRS) tax obligations. After paying fees to J.K. Harris & Co., many consumers find that the firm has substantially overstated its ability to reduce taxpayers' IRS debts. Recently, this service retailer agreed to pay $800,000 in refunds to some of its customers (well, in law they call them "clients) in Texas[23]. Deceptive sales practices involve not only the failure to tell the customer vital facts during the sales presentation, but also repackaging a used product and reselling it as new. All retailers expect customer returns. Rather than ship the product back to the manufacturer, most retailers resell these items as "open."

However, to avoid frustrating or deceiving purchasers of these "open items" because parts are missing or there are different processes that come into play for warranties and service plans, retailers must have procedures in place to ensure that open-item products are labeled as such, which includes a list of missing or damaged parts or documentation of what has been repaired.[24]

With regard to deceptive credit, federal laws attempt to "assure a meaningful disclosure of credit terms so that the consumer will be able to compare more readily the various credit terms available to him and avoid the un-informed use of credit."[25] These laws were the result of unscrupulous practices on the part of retailers attempting to hide the true cost of merchandise in unrealistically (and sometimes illegal) high credit terms. For example, the retailer might sell a car at a very low price but then tack on a high (and often hidden) finance charge. Many states have laws limiting these hidden charges. Incidentally, if you are in the market for a new car, be wary of the yo-yoing practice of some unscrupulous car dealers. Yo-yoing, also known as spot delivery, occurs when the dealer gets you into a new (or used) car at an attractive interest rate saying they just need to get your credit approved. Nonetheless, they let you drive the car you thought you just purchased home. After a couple of weeks they call and tell you to come back to the dealership to discuss your contract and then they tell you they couldn't get you approved. At this point they inform you they need to charge you a higher interest rate or get you into a lower priced car. If you refuse, you forfeit your down payment and/or the car you traded. All of this is documented in the pages of fine print on the back of the contract you signed and of course failed to take an hour to read (with the help of a magnifying glass).[26]

During the last 25 years the use and marketing of credit cards grew explosively to the point that even teenagers were being signed up by banks for credit cards. Many of the practices were seen as negative for consumers, which fueled national sentiment for a credit card consumer bill of rights and culminated in President Obama signing

Customers should (but usually don't) thoroughly read the fine print on credit agreements before they sign them. Retailers should print font size that is easily readable.

Kristoffer Tripplaar/Alamy

President Obama signed the Credit Card Act in May of 2009 providing some protection for credit card and gift card holders.

the Credit Card Act on May 22, 2009. Some of the more prominent provisions dealt with providing cardholders protection against arbitrary rate increases, not penalizing cardholders who pay on time, protecting cardholders from misleading terms, and the protection of vulnerable consumers from fee-heavy subprime credit cards.

While the Credit Card Act (2009) dramatically enhanced credit protection for many consumers, it also affected retailers' use of gift cards, which also grew in popularity over the last two decades. Importantly, retailers were prohibited from establishing expiration dates less than five years after the card is purchased. Retailers could no longer charge inactivity or service fees unless the card has not been used for at least 12 months. If fees are to be charged after this 12-month period, the details of such fees must be clearly established and placed on the card and retailers cannot assess more than one fee per month.

LO 3

What responsibilities does a retailer have regarding the products sold?

Product Constraints

A retailer's major goal is to sell merchandise. In order to accomplish this goal, the retailer must assure customers that the products they purchase will not be harmful to their well-being and will meet expected performance criteria. Three areas of the law have a major effect on the products a retailer handles: product safety, product liability, and warranties. They are highlighted in Exhibit 6.7.

Product Safety

Retailers are in a difficult position when it comes to product safety. Most retailers do not produce the goods they sell but purchase them from wholesalers or manufacturers. Retailers have little to say about product quality or safety. Their only weapon is choosing

Exhibit 6.7
Product Constraints

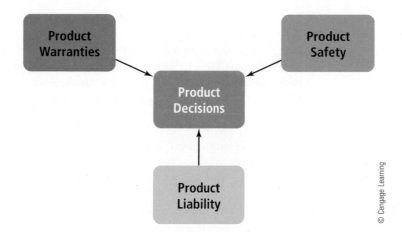

reputable suppliers so as not to carry merchandise they consider unsafe. However, even reputable suppliers can inadvertently sell products that are unsafe. For instance, Chanel Inc. in 2011 had to recall some pure silk garments that did not meet federal flammability standards. So a store such as Neiman Marcus may even be at risk when buying from a well-established source such as Chanel Inc.

According to the Consumer Product Safety Act, retailers have always had specific responsibilities to monitor the safety of consumer products.[27] Today, as a result of the Consumer Product Safety Improvements Act (2008), retailers face even stronger requirements.[28] This new law was the aftermath of a public outcry over imports of tainted toothpaste and pet food, as well as the infamous importation of lead-laden toys from Asia, especially China in 2007; which became known as the Year of the Recall when the Consumer Product Safety Commission (CPSC) made 473 product recalls, and this did not include actions taken by the U.S. FDA regarding food product recalls. The new regulation applies to all members of the supply chain (retailers, as well as manufacturers, other intermediaries, and importers) and sets new limits for plastic-softening chemicals called *phthalates* in children's products, as well as toughening standards for lead content. However, in many instances, retailers, such as CVS, Toys "R" Us, Walmart, had already stopped selling baby bottles containing the chemical bisphenol-A because animal studies had linked small doses of the chemical to cancer and other health issues.[29]

Product Liability

product liability laws Deal with the seller's responsibility to market safe products. These laws invoke the foreseeability doctrine, which states that a seller of a product must attempt to foresee how a product may be misused and warn the consumer against the hazards of misuse.

Product liability laws invoke the "foreseeability" doctrine, which states that a seller of a product must attempt to foresee how a product may be misused and warn the consumer against the hazards of misuse. The courts have interpreted this doctrine to suggest that retailers must be careful in how they sell their products. This is of particular importance to restaurant, nightclub, and bar owners who fail to consider the consequences of serving a consumer who appears intoxicated. In addition to the federal laws covering product liability, all states have their own regulations.

Warranties

Retailers are also responsible for product safety and performance under conventional warranty doctrines. Under the current warranty law, the fact that the ultimate consumer may bring suit against the manufacturer in no way relieves the retailer from its responsibility for the fitness and merchantability of the goods. The disheartening fact that confronts the retailer is that the buyer in many states has been permitted to sue both the retailer and the manufacturer in the same legal suit.

expressed warranties
Are either written or verbalized agreements about the performance of a product and can cover all attributes of the merchandise or only one attribute.

implied warranty of merchantability Is made by every retailer when the retailer sells goods and implies that the merchandise sold is fit for the ordinary purpose for which such goods are typically used.

implied warranty of fitness Is a warranty that implies that the merchandise is fit for a particular purpose and arises when the customer relies on the retailer to assist or make the selection of goods to serve a particular purpose.

Retailers can offer expressed or implied warranties. **Expressed warranties** are the result of the interaction between the retailer and the customer. They may be either written into the contract or verbalized. They can cover all characteristics or attributes of the merchandise or only one attribute. An important point for the retailer (and its salespeople) to recognize is that an expressed warranty can be created without the use of the words *warranty* or *guarantee*. For example, a car salesperson might tell a buyer, "Everybody we've sold this type of car to has gone at least 60,000 miles with no problems whatsoever, and I see no reason why you cannot expect the same. I would not be surprised if you are able to drive 100,000 miles without any mechanical problems." This statement could create an expressed warranty. The court would, however, be concerned with whether this was just sales talk (puffery) or a statement of fact or opinion by the salesperson.

Implied warranties are not expressly made by the retailer but are based on custom, norms, or reasonable expectations. There are two types of implied warranties (which overlap a bit): (1) an implied warranty of merchantability and (2) an implied warranty of fitness for a particular purpose.

Every retailer selling goods makes an **implied warranty of merchantability**. By offering the goods for sale, the retailer implies that they are fit for the ordinary purpose for which such goods are typically used. The notion of implied warranty applies to both new and used merchandise. For example, imagine that a sporting-goods retailer located close to a major lake resort sells used inner tubes for swimming. A customer purchases one; the tube bursts while the person is floating on it; and the person subsequently drowns. This retailer may be held liable. Because of the potential legal liability that accompanies an implied warranty, many retailers, especially many online operators, will expressly disclaim, at the time of sale, any or all implied warranties and seek to mark a product "as is."[30] This is not always legally possible; some retailers will not be able to avoid implied warranties of merchantability.

The **implied warranty of fitness** for a particular purpose arises when the customer relies on the retailer to assist or make the selection of goods to serve a particular

Ariel Skelley/Jupiter Images

When shopping for high priced goods, such as cars, large appliances and power tools, warranties can be a deciding factor.

purpose. Consider a customer who is about to make a cross-country moving trip and plans to tow a 4-foot-by-4-foot two-wheel trailer behind her SUV. She needs a pair of tires for the rear of the SUV and thus goes to a local tire retailer and asks the salesperson for a pair of tires that will allow her to tow the loaded trailer safely. The customer in this regard is ignorant and is relying on the expertise of the retailer. If the retailer sells the customer a pair of tires not suited for the job, then the retailer is liable for breach of an implied warranty of fitness for a particular purpose. This is true even if the retailer did not have in stock a pair of tires to safely perform the job but instead sold the customer the best tire available.

Consumer product warranties frequently have been confusing, misleading, and frustrating to consumers. As a consequence, the Magnuson-Moss Warranty Act was passed. Although nothing in federal law requires a retailer to warrant a product under this act, anyone who sells a product for more than $15 and gives a written warranty (only written warranties are covered by federal laws, while many types of warranties are subject to state laws) to the consumer is required to provide the consumer with all the details of the warranty.[31]

<table>
<tr><td>**LO 4**</td></tr>
</table>

Supply-Chain Constraints

How does government regulation influence a retailer's behavior with other supply-chain members?

Retailers are restricted in the relationships and agreements they may develop with supply-chain or channel partners. These restrictions can be conveniently categorized into four areas as shown in Exhibit 6.8.

Territorial Restrictions

territorial restrictions Are attempts by the supplier, usually a manufacturer, to limit the geographic area in which a retailer may resell its merchandise.

As related to retail trade, **territorial restrictions** can be defined as attempts by a supplier, usually a manufacturer, to limit the geographic area in which a retailer may resell its merchandise. The courts have viewed territorial restrictions as potential contracts in restraint of trade and in violation of the Sherman Antitrust Act. Thus, even though the retailer and manufacturer may both favor territorial restrictions, the courts will often frown on such arrangements because of the lessening of competition between retailers selling the brand in question. The law does not, however, prevent manufacturers and retailers from establishing territorial limits as long as they do not exclude all other retailers or restrict the sale of the manufacturer's products. Franchise agreements have long

Exhibit 6.8
Supply-Chain Constraints

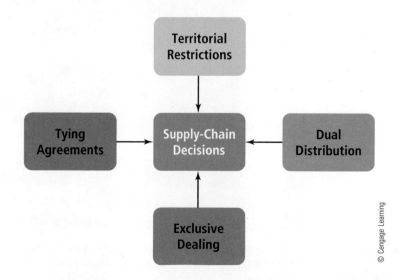

© Cengage Learning

had territorial restrictions that provide a protected zone for the franchisee. Because of these zones, the franchisee is able to develop primary demand for the product without fear of cannibalization by another entry in the protected zone. In cases where the franchisor has permitted another franchisee to invade the "exclusive territory" of another franchisee as outlined in a contract, the original franchisee could sue the parent chain under a breach-of-contract claim. However, a federal appeals court ruling found that when a franchise contract expressly spells out that a franchisee does not have an exclusive territory, the franchisor has the power to place other outlets nearby.[32] It is legal for a franchisor to also restrict a franchisee from opening another outlet without the permission of the franchisor. This can also be the case where a franchisee decides it wants to open a temporary store such as at a sporting event or a local carnival or festival. This practice is almost always expressly prohibited in the franchise contract. Thus, a local McDonald's franchisee cannot open a temporary outlet even if it would capture extra business for the franchisor.

Dual Distribution

dual distribution
Occurs when a manufacturer sells to independent retailers and also through its own retail outlets.

As discussed in the previous chapter, a manufacturer that sells to independent retailers and also through its own retail outlets is engaged in **dual distribution**. Thus, the manufacturer manages a corporately owned vertical marketing system that competes with independent retailers, which it also supplies through a conventional, administered, or contractual marketing channel. Retailers tend to become upset about dual distribution when the two supply chains compete at the retail level in the same geographic area. For example, Ralph Lauren operates wholly owned retail stores and, in addition, uses major independent retailers as outlets. Such supply-chain strategy can have an adverse effect on manufacturer–retailer relationships. Independent retailers will argue that dual distribution is an unfair method of competition and thus is in violation of the Sherman Act. As indicated in Chapter 5, the Internet has created new opportunities for dual

Ralph Lauren engages in dual distribution by operating wholly owned retail stores and selling through a conventional marketing channel to independent retailers.

distribution, which has increased the levels of channel conflict. Dual distribution also takes place when manufacturers sell similar products under different brand names for distribution through different channels as with private labels.

The courts have not viewed dual-distribution arrangements as antitrust violations. In fact, they have reasoned that dual distribution can actually foster competition. For example, the manufacturer may not be able to find a retailer to represent it in all trade areas, or the manufacturer may find it necessary to operate its own retail outlet to establish market share and remain competitive with other manufacturers. The courts will apply a rule-of-reason criterion. Thus, the independent retailer suing a manufacturer for dual distribution will have to convince the court that it was competed against unfairly and damaged. The retailer's best bet would be to show that the manufacturer-controlled outlets were favored or subsidized (for instance, with excessive advertising allowances or lower prices) to an extent that was detrimental to the independent retailer.

Exclusive Dealing

Retailers and their suppliers occasionally enter into exclusive dealing arrangements. In a **one-way exclusive-dealing arrangement**, the supplier agrees to give the retailer the exclusive right to sell the supplier's product in a particular trade area. The retailer, however, does not agree to do anything in particular for the supplier, hence the term *one-way*. For example, a weak manufacturer often has to offer one-way exclusive-dealing arrangements to get shelf space at the retail level. Truly one-way arrangements are legal.

A **two-way exclusive-dealing agreement** occurs when the supplier offers the retailer the exclusive distribution of a merchandise line or product if the retailer agrees to do something for the manufacturer in return. For example, the retailer might agree not to handle certain competing brands. Two-way agreements violate the Clayton Act if they substantially lessen competition or tend to create a monopoly. Specifically, the courts have generally viewed exclusive dealing as illegal when it excludes competitive products from a large share of the market and when it represents a large share of the total sales volume for a particular product type.

Tying Agreements

When a seller with a strong product or service forces a buyer (the retailer) to purchase a weak product or service as a condition for buying the strong one, a **tying agreement** exists. For example, a large national manufacturer with several very highly demanded lines of merchandise may try to force the retailer to handle its entire merchandise assortment as a condition for being able to handle the more popular merchandise lines. This is called a *full-line policy*. Alternatively, a strong manufacturer may be introducing a new product and, in order to get shelf space or display space at the retail level, may require retailers to handle some of the new products before they can purchase better-established merchandise lines.

Tying arrangements have been found to be in violation of the Clayton, Sherman, and FTC Acts. Tying is not viewed as a violation per se, but it is generally viewed as illegal if a substantial share of commerce is affected. The most serious problems involving tying arrangements are those associated with franchising. Quite often, franchise agreements contain provisions requiring the franchisee to purchase all raw materials and supplies from the franchisor. The courts generally consider tying provisions of a franchise agreement legal as long as there is sufficient proof that these arrangements are necessary to maintain quality control. Otherwise, they are viewed as unwarranted restraints of competition.[33] For instance, franchisees of Wendy's, McDonald's, Taco Bell, and so on

---

one-way exclusive-dealing arrangement Occurs when the supplier agrees to give the retailer the exclusive right to sell the supplier's product in a particular trade area.

two-way exclusive-dealing agreement Occurs when the supplier offers the retailer the exclusive distribution of a merchandise line or product in a particular trade area if in return the retailer will agree to do something for the manufacturer, such as heavily promote the supplier's products or not handle competing brands.

tying agreement Exists when a seller with a strong product or service requires a buyer (the retailer) to purchase a weak product or service as a condition for buying the strong product or service.

cannot be forced to purchase paper goods or food ingredients from the franchisor unless the products are of a quality that the franchisee could not obtain otherwise.

LO 5

Other Federal, State, and Local Laws

What is the impact of various state and local laws, in addition to other federal regulations, in developing retail policies?

Several other federal laws also affect retailers, but a detailed discussion of their impact is beyond the scope of this text. However, some limited comments follow. One such set of these laws, which is shown in Exhibit 6.1, is extremely important today because it deals with mergers and acquisitions. As retailers seek to consolidate their operations by selling off unprofitable stores, expand into new markets, or acquire the outlets of other retailers, they must consider the impact on the competitive environment.[34]

Various U.S. trade agreements regulating the amount of importing and exporting American firms can conduct with firms in various countries sometimes limit, if not totally forbid, a retailer's ability to purchase merchandise from certain foreign countries. At one extreme, the United States currently bans all merchandise from Cuba, while at the other extreme our North American Free Trade Agreement membership attempts to reduce all barriers to trade with Mexico and Canada. Such regulations present problems for American retailers operating globally. Consider, for example, Walmart's dilemma. As a U.S. company, the firm can't sell textiles made in Cuba. However, since Canada has no such restrictions against Cuban merchandise, the retailer is not allowed to exclude Cuban-made products due solely to their country of origin. This makes for an interesting problem as to which country's laws are to be followed.

Retailers must also be aware of laws that deal with minimum wages and hiring practices since labor is a retailer's largest operating expense. Chapter 13, "Store Layout and Design," will consider how the Americans with Disabilities Act affects the layout and design of the retailer's store. Finally, Chapter 7, "Market Selection and Retail Location Analysis," will discuss the issue of eminent domain powers used by cities for economic development purposes. Tax laws and Securities and Exchange Commission rules and regulations that deal with the legal form of ownership (sole proprietorship, partnership, or corporation) and shareholder-disclosure requirements are not covered in this text.

In addition to federal laws, many states and municipalities have passed legislation regulating retail activities. Exhibit 6.9 illustrates how state and local laws affect the retailer. Zoning laws, for example, prohibit retailers from operating in certain locations and

Exhibit 6.9
State and Local Regulations Affecting Retailers

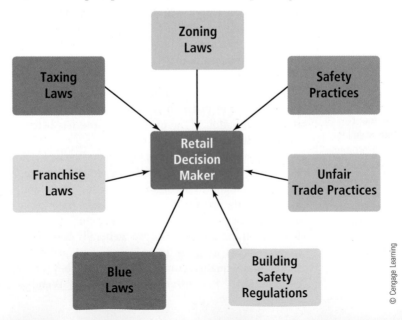

© Cengage Learning

require building and sign specifications to be met. Many retailers have found these codes to be highly restrictive, especially since some existing firms have been able to influence this type of legislation, thereby protecting their already established local businesses. For example, several states ban the sale of caskets over the Internet. Their laws dictate that coffins can be provided to the public only by licensed funeral directors. And a Louisiana statute prohibits flower selling without a license. These "shut-out" competitors claim these laws are a deliberate attempt by legislators to protect the entrenched businesses that fear competition.[35] In addition, while most states don't allow picketing on a retailer's or a shopping center's property, some states are now allowing such behavior claiming that owners of public retail sales areas have no right to prevent demonstrators from calling for the boycott of a retailer or mall.[36]

Safety practices have become a new rallying point for state and local governing bodies. Today, laws in San Francisco and Boston ban the sale of cigarettes by pharmacies. Over a dozen states ban the shipping of wine directly to a consumer's home by a winery, whether it is located in or out of state.[37] Numerous cities have followed Ireland's lead and have either banned outright the use of plastic shopping bags or imposed a fee on their use. Some states, among them New York and California, have begun banning fast-food places by restricting the use of certain ingredients, regulating menu information, and now dictating whether restaurants are healthy enough to open in their communities. Proponents say these actions are crucial in the fight against obesity, diabetes, and other diseases and health conditions. In fact, by early 2009, 27 states had already imposed small tariffs of 7–8 percent on vending machine snacks such as candy, soda, and baked goods to combat obesity.[38] Foes say the rules go too far, violating important freedoms.[39] Finally, some cites are opposed to Domino's new ad slogan: "You Got 30 Minutes." While it has been two decades since Domino's last promised to deliver a pizza to someone's door within 30 minutes or it was free, that pledge is still stuck in many customers' heads. These cities fear that the use of this slogan will lead to a rash of accidents as the pizza delivery drivers may drive too fast or run stop lights.[40]

With regard to unfair trade practices, most states have established their own set of laws that prevent one retailer from gaining an unfair advantage over another retailer. As a general rule, *unfair trade practices* laws regulate retailers' competitive behavior (usually relating to pricing, advertising, merchandise stocked, and employment practices). For example, because shoppers are more likely to consolidate their trips when gas prices are high, some retailers that sell general merchandise along with gasoline may seek to sell gas below cost. Thirteen states have laws against such pricing strategies. The specific content of these laws varies, but usually they prohibit the retailer from seeking unfair advantages from vendors or selling merchandise below cost (or at cost plus some fixed percentage markup—6 percent is typical) with the intent of using profits from another geographic area or from cash reserves to destroy or hurt competition. A number of states have also introduced laws preventing both zero-down car leases and zero-percent financing programs because they claim such programs mislead consumers. Also, the franchise laws in many states assume that, unless otherwise spelled out in the franchise agreement, there is an implied agreement not to locate another outlet near a current location without the current franchisee's permission. These state laws are often in conflict with federal regulations. As a result, in many instances, state laws regulating retailers have either been declared unconstitutional or amended to meet federal guidelines.

Many localities have strong building codes that regulate construction materials, fire safety, architectural style, height and size of building, number of entrances, and even elevator usage. Some local ordinances are attempts to aid retailers, such as the attempt by traffic engineers in some cities to reduce downtown traffic to less than 20 miles per hour so that consumers can observe local businesses and their display promotions. Other

WHAT'S NEW ?

Nothing Is More Certain than Death and Taxes

Mark Twain once wrote that only two things are certain in life: death and taxes. After years in which consumers did not have to pay taxes on Internet purchases, developments in 2008 dictate that Mark Twain's view of the world is right once again.

Prior to the recent developments, retailers relied on the 1992 *Quill Corp. v. North Dakota* ruling from the Supreme Court that stated that forcing retailers to learn the ins and outs of every local sales tax was too burdensome. Thus, merchants cannot be required to collect sales tax from a customer in another state unless they have a "physical presence" in the customer's state, usually defined as a store, office, or warehouse. After all, with more than 7,600 state and local sales tax jurisdictions, each with varying rates, lists of taxable items, and definitions of items, the court reasoned that a retailer otherwise couldn't be expected to know how much tax to charge.

As a result of this ruling, state laws in the 45 states that have sales taxes used the "physical presence" clause to collect the tax from e-tailers. (The only states without sales taxes are Alaska, Delaware, Montana, New Hampshire, and Oregon.) This tax was collected on all non–tax exempt merchandise sold to customers whether through stores, Internet sites, or catalogs.

Therefore, many online retailers structured their Internet operations to avoid having facilities or property in most states.

However, this all changed when New York became the first (and so far only) state to require online retailers to collect sales tax even when they have no physical presence in the state, such as a store, a warehouse, or even a sales rep. The state's two main targets were Amazon and rival Overstock.com. Both claimed the law was unconstitutional and filed suit against the state.

The key to this change in the collection status was that New York amended its law to say that having a New York–based affiliate or associate—such as bloggers or other websites that link to an e-tailer and that are paid a percentage of the sale—is tantamount to having a presence in the state. As a result, Amazon collected the tax while awaiting a court decision. However, Overstock took a different route, choosing instead to drop its 3,400 New York affiliates.

Most legal experts don't expect a final decision on this case until 2012. However, several states are already preparing similar legislation. As one legal scholar noted to the author, it is going to take Roto-Rooter to clean up this mess.

Sources: This box is based on information supplied to the authors by the National Retail Federation, "Attention, Online Shoppers: Taxes Ahead," *Businessweek*, June 16, 2008: 89; and "States Push for Taxation on Internet Sales," *St. Louis Post-Dispatch*, January 13, 2009: C1.

states enforce *blue laws* that restrict the sale of certain products such as automobiles on Sundays. Many states have passed strong regulations on topics not covered by federal regulations governing the relationship between franchisors and franchisees in order to protect the individual businesspeople of their states. These laws require a full disclosure of all the pertinent facts involved in owning a local franchise. Many experts believe that these state franchise laws protect the current antiquated and inefficient automobile dealerships, which were discussed in Chapter 5, from newer, more efficient forms of competition because the dealers provide 20 percent of state sales tax revenues and are usually the largest advertisers in the local media. Given such a concentration of political clout, most state governments will make it difficult for discounters and Internet sellers to enter the new-car business or for Detroit to control the pricing and promotion of its own products. However, Internet businesses that serve as automotive brokers are emerging as discussed in the previous chapter's "Service Retailing" box. These businesses bring together purchasers and franchised dealers who will sell cars to purchasers at prices negotiated by the Internet brokers. This chapter's "What's New?" box illustrates that many state and local governments, which must operate with balanced budgets, now view Internet purchases as a cash cow.

Sometimes states pass laws that don't fit into any of the categories listed in Exhibit 6.8 but which may present problems for retailers. One such issue is what to do with the unused portion of gift cards. Customers often leave a little money on the plastic cards and sometimes lose them altogether. Roughly 10 percent of all cards are unredeemed, allowing many stores and restaurants to keep the spare change, which adds up to an estimated $5 billion a year or more. While most retailers continue to carry the value of the unredeemed cards as a liability on their books, Home Depot and Best Buy recently increased their profits by recording unredeemed but expired cards as income. Since introducing their cards, Best Buy and Home Depot have realized $43 million and $29 million worth of income from such cards repeatedly.[41]

With budgets to balance and with so much unclaimed money at stake, many states are seeking these funds for their treasuries. Since all states have laws that allow them to take custody of funds abandoned by its residents and hold them until the rightful owner claims them, it is not surprising that every state regards unredeemed gift cards as unclaimed property. Retailers disagree with these laws, arguing that when the state *escheats* an unused gift card, the retailer is deprived of the profit it expected to earn when the card was redeemed for merchandise. They further point out that the retailer actually loses money on the gift card because it has to cover the expense of issuing and accounting for the card but then must turn the value of the card over to the state. Today, about half the states claim the full value of gift cards or some portion (such as 60 percent). Some retailers have tried to avoid turning the unredeemed money over to states by imposing conditions on gift cards such as expiration dates or monthly service fees that whittle away the value of the gift cards. That way, the cards have no value by the time the state would lay claim to their unredeemed value. However, expiration dates that diminish the value of gift cards are unpopular with consumers. A dozen states now regulate the imposition of an expiration date or service fees. For the most current summary of the various state regulations regarding gift cards, visit www.consumersunion.org and use their search engine to find information on "gift cards."

In addition, state court systems sometimes make rulings that affect retailers operating across the country. For example, various cities have passed laws governing retailing such as Green River Ordinances (named after the town in Wyoming that first passed them) that restrict door-to-door selling. Other communities restrict the excessive use of garage sales, lottery promotions, or sale of obscene materials and dangerous products. In addition, states and cities might require licenses to operate certain retail businesses such as liquor stores and massage parlors.

For further information about these various laws, a retailer should consult the local Better Business Bureau, the NRF, state and local retail trade associations, or state and local regulatory agencies.

<table>
<tr><td>**LO 6**</td><td></td></tr>
</table>

Ethics in Retailing

How does a retailer's code of ethics influence its behavior?

ethics
Is a set of rules for human moral behavior.

Ethics is a set of rules for moral human behavior. These rules or standards of moral responsibility often take the form of dos and don'ts. Some retailers have an **explicit code of ethics**, which is a written policy that states what constitutes ethical and unethical behavior. However, most often an implicit code of ethics exists. An **implicit code of ethics** is an unwritten but well understood set of rules or standards of moral responsibility. This implicit code is learned as employees become socialized into the organization and the corporate culture of the retailer.

explicit code of ethics
Consists of a written policy that states what is ethical and unethical behavior.

implicit code of ethics
Is an unwritten but well understood set of rules or standards of moral responsibility.

Regardless of whether the code of ethics is explicit or implicit, it is an important guideline for making retail decisions. We will shortly review some retail decision areas where ethical considerations are common. However, before doing so, it should be pointed out that legal behavior and ethical behavior are not necessarily the same. Unethical actions may be legal. Laws, after all, represent a formalization of behavioral standards through the political process into rules or laws. Therefore, a retailer needs to behave legally since laws represent a formalized set of ethical rules. In addition, retailers need to look beyond laws and engage in practices that are also ethical. One problem, though, is that reasonable people may disagree as to what is right and wrong behavior. For this reason, retailers should develop explicit codes of ethical behavior for their employees to provide a formal indication of what is right and wrong.

Let's look at three retail decision areas that involve ethical considerations:

1. Buying merchandise,
2. Selling merchandise, and
3. Retailer–employee relationships.

In each of these situations, the retailer faces an ethical dilemma, and what is legal may not necessarily represent the best ethical guideline.

Ethical Behavior in Buying Merchandise

When buying merchandise, the retailer can face at least four ethical dilemmas. These relate to product quality, sourcing, slotting fees, and bribery.

Product Quality

Should a retailer inspect merchandise for product quality or leave that to the customer? Although the law does not require such inspections, most retail buyers want to ensure that their merchandise meets the expectations of the store's customers. As a result, some retailers have developed laboratory testing programs to verify that the quality of their private-label products, as well as the manufacturers' own brands, adhere to stricter ethical and environmental standards that go beyond existing government regulations.

Sourcing

Should a retailer inspect the working conditions at all plants producing products sold by the retailer? What about foreign merchandise sources using child labor or that fail to pay fair levels of wages? The only way U.S. retailers can be sure that they are not buying illegal merchandise is to inspect all suppliers down to the smallest subcontractors. However, some retailers are also having troubles with American suppliers. A program of careful vigilance to overcome such activities can be expensive, and it is doubtful whether American consumers would be willing to bear the cost. Seeking to overcome such complaints, many retailers have begun using private investigators to check out vendors to make sure they are not buying from unsavory characters. Many other major American retailers have agreed to allow independent observers, including human-rights officials, to monitor working conditions in their foreign factories. Consumers can check the websites of the U.S. Department of Labor (www.dol.gov) or CorpWatch (www.corpwatch.org), a private group dedicated to holding corporations responsible, to see if a particular retailer has issues in this area.

Sustainability

Should a retailer be concerned with the natural resources that are used by its suppliers in manufacturing and distribution? Should they actively encourage or even require suppliers to engage in sustainable business practices? P&G, with such well known brands as Crest, Pantene, Tide, Pringles, and dozens of other highly recognized brands, has not only been encouraged by retailers such as Walmart but also its customers. In fact, P&G is asking its suppliers such questions as how many gigajoules of energy and fuel are used per unit of output and how many metric tons of direct and indirect Kyoto greenhouse gases are emitted[42]? Patagonia (www.patagonia.com) has launched the "Our Common Waters" initiative (visit website and click under environmentalism) to help save one of our most valuable natural resources: fresh water. It just so happens that it takes 703 liters of water (four average bathtubs) to produce a single cotton shirt and the water consumption to produce a pair of jeans is considerably higher.[43] One step Patagonia has taken is to produce jeans from organic cotton fields in India that only rely on rainwater. They also have become members of the Sustainable Apparel Coalition that develops uniform methods to measure the environmental effects of producing and bringing apparel to market. Incidentally, some of the other members of this coalition include Gap Inc., Levi Strauss & Co., Adidas AG, Nike Inc., and Walmart Stores Inc.[44]

Slotting Fees

slotting fees (slotting allowances) Are fees paid by a vendor for space or a slot on a retailer's shelves, as well as having its UPC number given a slot in the retailer's computer system.

Should retailers demand money from a manufacturer for agreeing to add a new product to their inventory? **Slotting fees** (also called **slotting allowances**) are fees paid by a vendor for space, or a slot, on a retailer's shelves, as well as for having a slot in the retailer's computer system for its UPC number. After all, if an item's UPC code is not in the system, then individual stores cannot stock it. Retailers claim that such fees help defray the extra expenses of adding warehouse space, replacing existing items in the store, and placing the new items in the inventory-control system and provide a form of insurance by guaranteeing at least some profit from carrying the new item. It is estimated that these fees now account for more than 16 percent of new product introduction costs. In the only major academic study to date on the subject, the authors found support for the rationale that slotting allowances enhance market efficiency by optimally allocating scarce retail shelf space to the most successful products. They also concluded that the fees do not thwart competition but helped balance the risk of new product failure between manufacturers and retailers, helped manufacturers signal private information about potential success of new products, and served to widen retail distribution for manufacturers by mitigating retail competition.[45] However, most manufacturers still claim that such fees were only an attempt by retailers to make money buying goods rather than selling goods that meet their customers' needs. Thus, smaller food manufacturers complain that slotting fees limit competition and translate into higher prices for consumers. The competition to get a product into a store is fierce given that a typical grocery store has room for only about 40,000 items and more than 100,000 grocery items are available for consideration. Still the question remains, are slotting fees really necessary?

Bribery

Should a retailer or its employees be allowed to accept a bribe? Bribery occurs when a retail buyer is offered an inducement (which the Internal Revenue Service considers to have a value greater than $25) for purchasing a vendor's products. Such inducements, it should be noted, are legal in many foreign countries. The reader may want to visit the document and publication section at the Transparency International website (www .transparency.org) to see in which countries bribes are still considered part of normal business behavior. However, in the United States, the Foreign Corrupt Practices Act bans bribes as anticompetitive. It is, after all, hard to develop a healthy relationship between a retailer and supplier when bribes are expected.

Many believe that Walmart not only failed to abide by the Foreign Corrupt Practices Act but also acted unethically when it was alleged in a *New York Times* investigation to have paid $24 million bribes to local officials in Mexico to help smooth the way for new store construction.[46]

To many long-time Walmart loyalists, including the authors, this was a shocking and disappointing allegation. After all, Walmart, renowned to outsiders for its elbows-out business tactics, is known internally for its bare-knuckled, no-expense-spared investigations of employees who break its ironclad ethics rules. Walmart's employees are not allowed to accept any gifts (including samples) from vendors, not even a cup of coffee or a soft drink when visiting a supplier's showroom. Today, many of the nation's top retailers require not only all their managers and buyers but also their vendors to sign an integrity pledge. Despite such actions, lapses do occur. Home Depot recently fired four merchandise-purchasing employees for allegedly receiving kickbacks to ensure certain flooring products were stocked by the retailer and put in prominent positions.[47]

Since retail buyers are often compensated based on their buying performance, a modern version of bribery occurs when retailers shakedown vendors for markdown money. **Markdown money** is the funds that retailers arbitrarily deduct from vendors' payments when the merchandise doesn't sell briskly enough. This topic will be covered in greater detail in Chapter 10.

markdown money
Markdown money is what retailers charge to suppliers when merchandise does not sell at what the vendor intended.

Ethical Behavior in Selling Merchandise

Ethics can also influence the selling process with regard to the products sold and the various selling practices that salespeople use.

Products Sold

Should a retailer sell any product as long as it is not illegal? For example, should a convenience store operator located near a school carry cigarette paper for those few customers who prefer to roll their own and risk selling the paper to students who might use it for smoking marijuana? Other people have questioned Walmart's decision not to sell adult-themed sex magazines. Long before actions by some states and communities, many drug store and general merchandise chains banned the sale of pseudoephedrine, an ingredient found in most popular over-the-counter cold medicines, and lithium batteries because both pseudoephedrine and lithium are used in the production of crystal meth (methamphetamine). Other retailers have chosen not to sell "unrated" movie DVDs, the ones with raunchy humor and explicit sex scenes, despite the fact that they tend to outsell the original versions.[48]

Sometimes not carrying products can add to a retailer's profit. For example, Trader Joe's, the California-based specialty food retailer, performed a sales analysis on all its cigarettes by company and brand and found that only Marlboro merited the space allocated. Therefore, rather than carry just that one brand, the retailer dropped all cigarettes.[49] Today, the topic of what products should be sold has reached the Internet's service providers. This chapter's "Service Retailing" box highlights the issue of what happens to all that information that Internet search engines gather about their users.

SERVICE — RETAILING

Privacy and Search Engines

A popular urban legend revolves around the college student who used an Internet search engine to have someone write a term paper for him. After all, the student reasoned, if American companies can go online to outsource their work, why can't students outsource their homework? However, in this case, the term-paper writer, who charged only $100, was the student's professor.

Search engines have become so popular for this type of activity that today it is as easy to buy four pages, complete with bibliography, about the "Ethical Aspects of Walmart's Operation" as it is to download a song.[50] To combat this problem, companies such as Turnitin.com and iThenticate.com help professors in their attempts to stop such plagiarism.

A simpler solution to this problem might be to allow professors to check with the search engines to find out who used their services. Sound far-fetched? After all, wouldn't this be an invasion of privacy and thus illegal? Many people thought so until recently.

However, Internet firms such as Locatecell.com now offer complete searches of phone calls from cell phones. Imagine having someone look up your phone records. Worse yet is the question, how private are the records of your online use of search engines such as Yahoo or Google? Google, for example, uses a cookie that expires in two years but renews itself when a Google service is used. Can someone get them?

Yahoo, for example, was once suspected of supplying information to China's government that led to the jailing of a journalist. His crime was sending an internal Communist Party memo to foreign-based websites. Yahoo said it was only complying with China's laws.

In an even more important case, the United States government asked Google to turn over data on customers' web searches for certain types of porn. Of course, Google resisted. The Justice Department wanted the California-based company to turn over 1 million random web Internet protocol (IP) addresses and records of all Google searches from any one-week period. The issue at hand was to see whether online pornography sites were accessible by minors. Google resisted on privacy grounds and said it would "vigorously" oppose any subpoena for web search information.

The government responded by saying it only requested "anonymous data" (the computer's IP address) and that Google's rivals, including Time Warner's AOL, Microsoft's MSN, and Yahoo, had already complied. By the way, the court ruled in Google's favor, recognizing the privacy implications of turning over search terms. However, the refusal by Google—whose guiding philosophy is "Don't be evil"—overlooked an important issue: "Why was a search engine keeping so much information at all?"

Thus, the question remains: Do today's college students want their kids to know in 20 years what Internet sites they searched while they were in school?

Selling Practices

Can a salesperson, while not saying anything false, be allowed to conceal certain facts from a customer? Also, should selling the "wrong" product for the customer's needs be permitted? Many retailers have ethical standards against such practices. However, as long as salespeople are paid on commission, we can expect such behavior to occur. Some highly successful retailers such as Home Depot and Best Buy have sought to overcome this dilemma by never putting their employees at odds with their own code of ethics. Bernie Marcus, the founder of Home Depot, has been quoted as saying, "The day I'm laid out dead with an apple in my mouth is the day we'll pay commissions. If you pay commissions, you imply that the small customer is not worth anything."[51] When Best Buy switched its compensation plan from commissions to salary in 1989, manufacturers such as Toshiba and Hitachi that depended on salespeople to push premium-price items were opposed. However, customers liked the no-pressure atmosphere and sales soon outpaced all rivals.[52] It should be pointed out, however, that paying commissions could be difficult in self-service operations like Home Depot and Best Buy. A rather difficult situation involved the recent switch from analog TV to digital TV. The law required that retailers not sell televisions lacking a digital tuner within two years of the 2009 switch. However, did the retailers have an obligation to inform those customers about the upcoming changeover who may have wanted to purchase an analog set in late 2006 for a Christmas gift?

Ethical Behavior in the Retailer–Employee Relationship

Ethical standards can also influence the retailer–employee relationship in three ways: misuse of company assets, job switching, and employee theft.

Misuse of Company Assets

Most people would agree that the stealing of merchandise is illegal, but what about other types of stealing? What about an employee who surfs the web or trades stock on company time? Also, what about taking an extra break or using the retailer's phone for a personal long-distance call? All of these, while not subject to criminal prosecution, are forms of employee theft and should be considered when an employee develops his or her code of ethics.

Advancements in computer technology and the growth of the Internet have recently challenged one of the most treasured of American rights—the right to privacy. Most retailers have an asset that would have been unheard of a generation ago. In a situation similar to that described above regarding Google, retailers today have databases that contain heretofore private information about nearly every American that most consumers do not even know exists. These databases are constructed in a number of ways, including computer cookies as well as purchased information from state governments (for example, driver's license bureaus or voting records). As a result, current laws provide for consumers to opt out of such databases.

Many e-tailers, for example, know not only what purchases you made from them but also what sections of their website you visited. The majority of e-tailers disclose their privacy policies on their websites. Exhibit 6.10 shows the NRF's Principles on Customer Data Privacy. In general, most of the major retailers in this country adhere to the NRF's principles. However, the shakeout in e-tailing during the early part of this decade showed just how consumers' rights to privacy could be violated by retailers who had no intention of doing so.

Job Switching

Do employees have the right to work for whomever they want? Of course, but employees have a responsibility to their previous employers. These firms provided them with training and access to confidential information such as vendor costs, customer lists, and future plans. When an employee leaves one retailer for another, the employee should respect the previous employer's right to retain the confidentiality of this information.

At the same time, the retailer should not seek to replace an employee, usually a manager or executive with a lower-paid, younger person just because the employee reaches the so-called 20-40-80 plateau (20 years or more with the firm, 40 years or older, and making more than $80,000 a year).

Exhibit 6.10
National Retail Federation's Principles on Customer Data Privacy

GENERAL RULE

National Retail Federation Principles on Customer Data Privacy

The privacy of information collected by a retailer about its customers during the course of transactions with those customers should be maintained with the degree of confidentiality that the retailer reasonably anticipates would be expected of it by the typical shopper purchasing that type of merchandise from the retailer. Departures from this standard should be disclosed to customers at or before each time of occurrence, unless previously consented to by the customer or otherwise expressly permitted by law.

PRACTICE PRINCIPLES

Each retailer should adopt a customer privacy policy explaining its practices with respect to the information it collects about its customers.

Policies could either be corporate-wide or divisional depending upon the manner in which the company believes customers view its retail operations.

A retailer should make reasonable efforts to inform its customers of the existence of its customer privacy policies, and make the substance of such policies available, on a regular basis.

At a minimum, a customer privacy policy should allow a customer to elect whether he or she wishes to prevent the marketing of his or her name to other unaffiliated corporations, or to "opt out" of future promotional solicitations from the company(s) to which the policy applies, or both.

Retail companies should develop procedures to reasonably ensure that customer information is not accessible to, or used by, its employees or others in contravention of its policies and customer elections, and that access to personally identifiable data for non-promotional purposes is limited to those individuals with a customer servicing need to know.

Employee Theft

Even as the misuse of company assets is actually a type of theft, outright stealing by employees is an even more serious issue. After all, just as employers have a responsibility to be fair to their employees, so employees have a responsibility to be honest and fair with their employers. However, at a time when retailers attribute almost half of their missing inventory to employee theft, many workers admit to stealing from their employers. Employee theft or *shrinkage* is most prevalent in food stores, restaurants, bars (the subject of restaurant and bar theft is discussed in greater detail in Exhibit 9.7), department stores, and discount stores. Considering that these types of stores are usually larger in size, sales volume, and number of employees, the lack of close supervision might contribute to this problem. Some retailers are trying to address this problem by offering cash bonuses just before Christmas if the store not only makes its profit goal but also keeps shrinkage under a predetermined limit.

This discussion is not meant to be an all-inclusive list of the ethical dilemmas facing retailing today. It does, however, provide the reader with a big picture of the role of ethics in retailing.

Summary

We began this chapter by describing the multi-faceted legal environment that confronts retailers in the United States. We identified constraints on retailers' activities in six broad categories: (1) pricing, (2) promotion, (3) products, (4) supply-chain relations, (5) other federal laws, and (6) state and local regulations. Within each of these broad constraints, we summarized some specific activities that are regulated.

LO 1 ## Does legislation constrain a retailer's pricing policies?

With regard to pricing—the issue that most frequently confronts retailers—the retailer should first be familiar with two methods of price fixing: with other retailers (horizontal) and with supply-chain members (vertical). In addition, the retailer must consider all the ramifications of price discrimination when purchasing merchandise. In setting retail prices, two other areas of concern are deceptive pricing and predatory pricing.

LO 2 ## Is there a difference between legal and illegal promotional activities for a retailer?

The retailer should focus on three areas that constitute illegal promotional activities: (1) deceitful diversion of patronage, which includes selling counterfeit or fake products; (2) deceptive advertising, including making false claims about a product and using bait-and-switch tactics; and (3) deceptive sales practices, which include not being completely honest in discussions about merchandise and the use of deceptive credit contracts.

LO 3 ## What responsibilities does a retailer have regarding the products sold?

With regard to product constraints, the retailer should be aware of legislation dealing with product safety, product liability, and both expressed and implied warranty requirements as they relate to retailing.

LO 4 ## How does government regulation influence a retailer's behavior with other supply-chain members?

Since all retailers are members of some type of supply chain, it is important to understand supply-chain relationships in terms of the legality of territorial restrictions, dual distribution, exclusive dealing, and tying agreements.

LO 5 ## What is the impact of various state and local laws, in addition to federal regulations, in developing retail policies?

The retailer must be aware of state and local laws, which include regulations on zoning, safety, unfair trade practices, building safety, blue laws, franchises, and taxes.

LO 6 ## How does a retailer's code of ethics influence its behavior?

Laws and regulations do not cover every situation a retailer might face in the day-to-day operations of a business. In such cases, codes of ethics for both retailer and employee behavior will provide guidance. A code of ethics is particularly important in buying merchandise, selling merchandise, and managing the retailer–employee relationship.

Terms to Remember

horizontal price fixing	implied warranty of fitness
vertical price fixing	territorial restrictions
price discrimination	dual distribution
deceptive pricing	one-way exclusive-dealing arrangement
predatory pricing	two-way exclusive-dealing agreement
palming off	tying agreement
deceptive advertising	ethics
bait-and-switch advertising	explicit code of ethics
product liability laws	implicit code of ethics
expressed warranties	slotting fees (slotting allowances)
implied warranty of merchantability	markdown money

Review and Discussion Questions

LO 1

How does legislation constrain a retailer's pricing policies?

1. A busy corner intersection in Houston has gasoline stations on all four corners. These dealers always seem to have identical prices for their gasoline or, at least, they are within one cent of each other. Is this evidence of horizontal price fixing? Why or why not?

2. Does vertical price fixing (resale price maintenance) help or hurt the small independent retailer? What about consumers? Why?

3. Deceptive pricing harms not only the consumer but also competition. Agree or disagree and explain your reasoning.

LO 2

What is the difference between legal and illegal promotional activities for a retailer?

4. If a student goes to a flea market and buys what he knows to be a fake Polo shirt for $18, is this an example of "deceitful diversion of patronage"? Is anyone hurt by this transaction? Who? Explain your reasoning.

5. Should all types of "puffery" be removed from ads? Explain your reasoning.

6. Do you believe that fake merchandise is sold on eBay? If so, what can eBay do about it, within reason?

7. A New York judge recently ruled that a retailer with the first name of John committed trademark infringement when he renamed one of his existing stores "Trader John's" and redesigned it to look like a nearby Trader Joe's. Was the judge right in his ruling? Why?

LO 3

What responsibilities does a retailer have regarding the products sold?

8. Should a McDonald's franchisee be held liable for selling a Happy Meal to an already overweight child? Why?

9. Should a retailer be held liable for statements made by its sales staff, even if the staff was instructed not to make such statements? Explain your reasoning.

LO 4

How does government regulation influence a retailer's behavior with other supply-chain members?

10. Could a decision by a manufacturer to engage in dual distribution be harmful to the consumer and members of the supply chain? Explain your reasoning.
11. How could two-way exclusive dealing arrangements be harmful to consumers and competition?
12. Discuss the concept of exclusive dealing. Are exclusive dealing arrangements in the retailer's best interest? Are they in the consumer's best interest?

LO 5

What is the impact of various state and local laws, in addition to other federal regulations, in developing retail policies?

13. Should a retailer be allowed to sell products below cost in attempt to increase store traffic? Why?
14. In a free-market system such as the one we have in the United States, should cities be allowed to use zoning laws to prevent big-box discounters from entering their markets?
15. Should online retailers be required to collect the sales tax on all their sales for the individual states?

LO 6

How does a retailer's code of ethics influence its behavior?

16. Retailers should abide by the philosophy that "as long as it is legal, it is ethical." Agree or disagree and explain your reasoning.
17. Because of religious or personal beliefs, a convenience owner may not want to stock a particular product—say, cigarettes or beer—that is normally sold by its category of store. Can government force the retailer to carry a full line of merchandise if that retailer is the only store in a community?
18. Many retailers face the problem of small amounts of unredeemed money that remain on a gift card. Does this "breakage" belong to the retailer as part of its profit, does it belong in the state's treasury, or should it go into the state's unclaimed money fund to the consumer? Explain your reasoning.

Sample Test Questions

LO 1

Ben Cooper's Chevrolet charges two different customers (one a man, the other a woman) two different prices for identical automobiles. This is in all probability a violation of the

    a.   Clayton Act.
    b.   your state's Unfair Trade Practices Act.
    c.   Robinson-Patman Act.
    d.   Sherman Act.
    e.   This is not illegal since it involved a sale to a final consumer, not just sales between supply-chain or channel members.

LO 2

An example of deceitful diversion of patronage would be

    a.   spreading rumors about a competitor, even if the rumors do not hurt the competitor's business.
    b.   telling the truth about a competitor that will hurt the competitor's business.

   c.   advertising a product at a very low price and then adding hidden charges.

   d.   putting extra large signs in your store's front window offering lower prices than your competitor next door.

   e.   illegally using another company's trademark or brand name, which results in the loss of sales for the other company.

LO 3 When a customer relies on the retailer to assist the customer or to select the right goods to serve a particular purpose, the retailer is establishing:

   a.   an implied warranty of fitness.
   b.   an implied warranty of merchantability.
   c.   a price discrimination defense.
   d.   an expressed warranty of fitness.
   e.   an expressed warranty of merchantability.

LO 4 D-A Pet Products Company has an extremely popular line of cat food. The company has recently started insisting that retailers who carry its cat food must also carry its rather overpriced cat litter. Due to its price, the litter is not a big seller, and it takes away shelf space from more profitable products. Requiring stores that stock the cat food to also stock the litter is an example of:

   a.   a consent agreement.
   b.   a tying contract.
   c.   unfair advertising.
   d.   monopolistic competition.
   e.   power marketing.

LO 5 The most stringent laws governing franchises are typically enacted at the _____ level.

   a.   federal
   b.   state
   c.   county
   d.   local
   e.   international

LO 6 Which of the following is not an ethical dilemma that a retailer faces when buying merchandise?

   a.   whether the buyer believes he or she can sell the merchandise
   b.   the source of the merchandise
   c.   the issue of product quality
   d.   whether to demand a slotting fee
   e.   whether to ask for a bribe

Writing and Speaking Exercise

As assistant manager for an online flooring retailer, you have been approached by your manager to develop a competition-based pricing policy. Your manager indicates that, since your market is national and pricing of carpets and hardwoods varies by both product and delivery costs, he would like you to develop a pricing strategy based on what online competitors are charging. Your manager believes that your firm could effectively compete on selection and service if only it could establish a pricing policy that would match or beat competitors, thus eliminating their competitive advantage. In other words, he wants you to gather competitive intelligence from your competitors' websites in order to develop a pricing policy that would, in effect, make your flooring cheaper by 2–3 percent or, at worst, the exact same price (when delivery charges are included) as your competitors. You wonder if this is legal and ethical.

Prepare a response to the manager outlining your position on the potential legal and ethical implications of the strategy.

Retail Project

Having enjoyed the entertainment, as well as the refreshments, at your local drinking establishment during your academic career, you decide to open a bar of your own after graduation. However, based on the material presented in this chapter, you realize that there are quite a few regulations governing these types of retail facilities. Investigate the laws regarding operating a bar and grill. Be sure to consider all local and state regulations about the location of such establishments. Also determine what, if any, laws about security and liability are involved.

In addition, determine the ethical issues involved. For example, do you want to locate near a high school or a rehabilitation center? Do you want to hire people who are less than drinking age to work in the food section?

Planning Your Own Entrepreneurial Retail Business

You are the general manager and partner for a local Ford dealership with a net worth of $1,800,000. At your regular Friday morning meeting with the sales force, you congratulate your staff on being ahead of its sales quota for the year.

Things could not be better, you think to yourself, as you leave the meeting and return to your office. You are going to exceed your $8.5 million sales goal for the year. Your cost of merchandise sold is expected to average 88 percent of sales, and your fixed operating costs are being held to $30,000 a month. With variable costs averaging 5 percent of sales, you are expecting to produce almost a quarter of a million dollars in profit before taxes this year.

Just when things look so great, your partner calls to ask if you read the article in the morning newspaper about last night's city council meeting. It seems that in order to reduce local property taxes and thus keep voters happy, a council member has suggested that the city increase its sales tax by 1 percent. This tax would cover everything sold in the city, including automobiles.

While you hate to see any type of sales tax increase since it raises the price of your automobiles, this one in particular could present your dealership with a major problem. Just last year, several dealers representing most major domestic and foreign car manufacturers moved to a nearby suburban location, creating a sort of "car mall" where shoppers could easily move from one dealership to another and compare the various offerings. One of those car mall dealers was the city's other Ford dealer. This dealer's customers would not have to pay this additional sales tax since the suburb's government planned to keep local sales taxes at the current level and instead reap the benefits of an increase in retail sales as consumers flocked to suburban merchants to get lower prices.

What should you do? Should you absorb the additional tax to keep your prices competitive? What would this do to your profits? Or should you lobby city hall to persuade the council to see the errors of this tax increase?

The Changing Face of Tobacco Retailers

Over the last half-century, Americans have become accustomed to the idea of being able to buy cigarettes at a variety of retail outlets ranging from vending machines in bars to restaurants, airports, supermarkets, convenience stores, gas stations, and discount stores. However, federal legislation may soon change the way tobacco is sold in the United States.

Walmart was one of the first major retailers to address the tobacco issue. In 1990, Sam Walton admitted in a letter to a consultant that he was "still in a quandry [sic] on our direction for this very important issue."[53] The next year, the retailer announced the banning of smoking on all Walmart property, including the stores, as well as the removal of any cigarette vending machines. At the time, Walton was not aware of any vending machines, but as a precaution, he issued the "ban" order. Later, when Walmart expanded into Canada by purchasing 127 Woolco stores, Walton met with the pharmacists from the newly acquired stores. At their request, Walmart dropped the sale of tobacco in its Canadian stores. Members of the chain's executive committee decided to continue with the sale of cigarettes after Mr. Walton's death.

At the same time, various state and local agencies began to enforce age restrictions on the sale of cigarettes and other products such as firearms, spray paint (which was used for painting gang slogans), and even glue. Walmart even introduced a program into its scanners that froze the cash register when the stock-keeping unit (SKU) for one of these products was recorded until the clerk ascertained the age of the purchaser. As a result of the increased enforcement, some retailers, especially supermarkets and drug stores, began to drop tobacco. How would this affect the sale of these legal products, which account for more than $60 billion in sales per year?

If such a change were to occur, what retailers would benefit? Some experts think that if cigarettes are dropped by the mass sellers, one of the best prepared retailers is John Roscoe's family-owned Cigarettes Cheaper chain. This is a 400-store operation already doing $500 million in sales each year.

Cigarettes Cheaper, which sells only cigarettes in 1,200-square-foot outlets located primarily in strip malls, is second only to Walmart in total cigarette sales; it is a spin-off of Roscoe's Customer Company convenience store chain. The name Customer Company was a reflection of Roscoe's appreciation for his consumers. As a result, he offered the lowest possible prices on everything in the store. His tobacco stores follow the same philosophy by charging 20 percent less than nearby competitors for the average pack or carton of cigarettes.

The chain is able to charge such prices by taking advantage of every manufacturer discount available and realizing that its customers are not apt to buy just a pack or even a carton but will more likely purchase 10–12 cartons at a time. But low prices are not the only attraction. Roscoe's store (and similar operations) has a broader range of brands and packaging than other retailers, a regular diet of promotions, and a welcoming attitude toward smokers that is not always the case elsewhere.

These facts about Roscoe's operation are most impressive:

- No member of John Roscoe's family smokes, nor do any of them encourage anyone else to smoke.
- The stores put in a great deal of effort into controlling underage customers. All stores have a large sign stating "No Minors Allowed Inside," and a manager could lose his or her job for violating this rule.

Many retail experts think this might be the way all cigarettes are sold in the future. What do you think?

Roscoe says his stores are just there to serve the market. Do you agree with his right to do this? Do you agree with his decision to do this?

Note: This case is based on information supplied by William Davidson and the late Robert Kahn, the two individuals to whom the third edition of this textbook was dedicated.

identifies. If you wish you could do this analysis of performance for 2009–2011.

Nordstrom, Inc. "Nordstrom, Inc. Form 10-K for the Fiscal Year Ended January 28, 2012." *U.S. Securities and Exchange Commission (Home Page)*. March 16, 2012. Available at: http://www.sec.gov/Archives/edgar/data/72333/000119312512119641/d264543d10k.htm [Accessed April 13, 2012].

Note: This case was prepared by Mark Lusch. It was developed as a basis for class discussion rather than to illustrate either effective or ineffective handling of an administrative situation.

Part 3

Market Selection and Location Analysis

7 *Market Selection and Retail Location Analysis*

Market Selection and Retail Location Analysis

Overview

In this chapter, we will review how retailers select and reach their target markets through their choice of location. The two broad options for reaching a target market are store-based and nonstore-based locations. The chapter primarily focuses on the decision process for selecting store-based locations. We describe the various demand and supply factors that must be evaluated for each geographic market area under consideration. We conclude with a discussion of alternative locations that retailers consider as they select a specific site.

Learning Objectives

After reading this chapter, you should be able to:

1 Explain the criteria used in selecting a target market.

2 Identify the different options, both store-based and nonstore-based, for effectively reaching a target market and identify the advantages and disadvantages of business districts, shopping centers, and freestanding units as sites for retail location.

3 Define geographic information systems (GIS) and discuss their potential uses in a retail enterprise.

4 Describe the various factors to consider when identifying the most attractive geographic market for a new store.

5 Discuss the various attributes to consider when evaluating retail sites within a retail market.

6 Explain how to select the best geographic site for a store.

LO 1

Explain the criteria used in selecting a target market.

Selecting a Target Market

Many retail experts say (1) selecting a target market and (2) evaluating alternative ways to reach this target market are the two most critical determinants of success in retailing. Traditionally, for retailers desiring to reach a given target market, this has meant selecting the best location for a store. In fact, according to an oft-repeated story, a famous retailer once said that the three major decisions in retailing are location, location, and location. There is truth in that statement because, while the other elements of the retail mix are also important, customers must be able to conveniently reach your store if those elements are to affect shopping behavior. The easier it is to reach a store, the more traffic a store will have, which will lead to higher sales and profit.

Today, however, as retailers are finding alternative ways to reach customers, the term, location, must be thought of as more than just a store's *physical* location. For example, Dell sells computers and peripherals at Best Buy and Costco, through the mail, over the Internet, and by phone; the University of Phoenix offers an MBA online via a computer in the student's home or place of business, as well as at its own campuses located in major U.S. cities; eBay has established virtual fashion outlet stores in the U.K., (www.ebay.co.uk/) Germany, and recently in the United States (www.ebay.com/fashion/outlet);[1] and Tupperware continues to sell most of its kitchenware via in-home parties.

As noted in Chapter 1, the Internet is becoming a major force in retailing. The most recent statistics reveal that the Internet accounts for approximately 4.2 percent of total retail sales;[2] however, that percentage rises dramatically, to approximately 10 percent, if the sales of categories not commonly bought online, like automobiles, fuel, and foodservices, are excluded.[3] And this growing trend is likely to continue given over 71 percent of American households in 2010 had the capability of making an Internet purchase at home rather than having to rely on using a computer at work.[4]

The equivalent of a store on the Internet is a retailer's website on the World Wide Web (usually denoted by www). When stopping at an e-tailer's website, visitors first view the firm's **home page**, which is essentially the e-tailer's storefront. From the home page, a person can be linked to other pages that provide more detailed information about merchandise, credit, warranties, terms of trade, and even job information and application forms. The total collection of all the pages of information on the retailer's website is known as its **virtual store**. Whereas a traditional store is located in geographic space, a virtual store is located in cyberspace. No longer are retailers downplaying the significance of the Web as many did only five years ago. Almost universally, retailers today are struggling to meet their sales goals and thus incremental sales of a few percent or sometimes over 10 percent gained through a virtual store can make a difference between a low- and a high-performance retailer. For instance, Neiman Marcus Last Call with its own Web presence (www.lastcall.com) decided to be part of eBay's Fashion Outlet in order to achieve additional sales opportunities.

Today, it is possible for a shopper in North America to not only view merchandise but also barter on price in real time with a merchant halfway across the world. This is illustrated in the "Retailing: The Inside Story" box that follows.

The cyberspace counterpart to a convenient location is the **ease of access** a consumer has to the site. Ease of access refers to the consumer's ability to easily and quickly find a website in cyberspace. To gain access to a site, a consumer can use a retailer's name (for example, http://www.target.com) or a search engine such as Google or Yahoo. Exhibit 7.1 illustrates how the importance of easy access increases as the number of websites increases. For this reason, retailers use website optimization services to help move their stores up the list whenever a potential customer searches for a particular merchandise category the retailer handles. This is similar to a practice in the not-too-distant past in which many small local retailers would place advertisements in the telephone yellow pages (which were organized alphabetically) and refer to their business as ABC Automotive Repair, or ABC Landscaping, and so on to gain the advantage of being listed first.

Regardless of whether a retailer is planning a traditional store in geographic space, a virtual store in cyberspace, or both, the first step is to develop a cost-effective way to reach the household or individual consumer that the retailer has identified as its target market. It is important to realize that failure to clearly identify one's target market will result in a significant waste of marketing expenditures.

Market Segmentation

In Chapter 3, market segmentation was defined as the method retailers use to segment, or break down, heterogeneous consumer populations into smaller, more homogeneous groups based upon certain characteristics deemed attractive by the retailer. Since any single retailer cannot serve all potential customers, it is important that it segment the

home page
Is the introductory or first material viewers see when they access a retailer's Internet site. It is the equivalent of a retailer's storefront in the physical world.

virtual store
Is the total collection of all the pages of information on the retailer's Internet site.

ease of access
Refers to the consumer's ability to easily and quickly find a retailer's Web site in cyberspace.

RETAILING — The Inside Story

The Thrill of the Hunt

Every consumer loves hunting for and then finding bargains. Consequently, many are keenly aware that prices for products vary widely, depending on shopping location (e.g., store, city, or even country). One such category where this is particularly true is jewelry. As most jewelry buyers will tell you, the available selection of pearls and other semiprecious stones is often greatest where production takes place.

Since China produces 95 percent of the world's freshwater pearls, the prices for pearl products in China are often 40 percent to 80 percent below those charged in the United States. Unfortunately, for most of us, the closest we will ever get to China is watching the Travel Channel. Enter Stephen Bell, an entrepreneur.

In 2006, while walking though a Shanghai shopping district with his teenage son, Bell came up with the creative idea of selling jewelry online. Jewelry is not only small and easy to ship but also the most popular item purchased by China's tourists. He realized that if the district had Wi-Fi, he could use it to allow consumers in cities ranging from Des Moines to Lexington to experience the joys of shopping in China, and even haggling over price, from their home.

Recognizing American shoppers' desire for deals and the increased fascination with China as the result of the upcoming 2008 Olympics, Bell soon started ShangBy.com, an Internet retailer based in Shanghai and Texas featuring Chinese jewelry. To avoid legal issues, he insisted that the company stay away from cheap Chinese knockoffs; only nonbrand items would be listed on his site. After all, what American consumer could pass on a Tahitian pearl pendant, even if it was nonbrand, that retailed for $2,000 at the local jewelry store but was available in China for only $400?

Operating under the slogan "Shop the World," ShangBy lets consumers travel halfway across the globe to make a virtual shopping trip to China for pearls and other jewelry without ever leaving their homes, making the process extremely simple. For example, a consumer in Tucson can log on to the website and let ShangBy's tour guide cruise the jewelry shops of Shanghai with a video crew, broadcasting live on the Internet. The Tucson "ShangBuyer" can even call a toll-free number and ask the guide and the video crew to zoom in on particular items while haggling over the price with store owners. After each ShangBy show, all the items purchased, as well as anything else the ShangBuyer examined, are listed on the retailer's website for other shoppers to purchase at that same price. This is accomplished by having a ShangBy employee return to the store to buy and ship the item to the customer.

ShangBy.com has become such a whirlwind success that even American talk-show hosts are getting in on the act. On a recent Rachael Ray show, taped live, Shangby.com allowed her and her viewers to visit various vendors in Shanghai where the prices of jewelry were well below those found down the street from her New York City studios. During the show's taping, Rachael purchased two strings of pearls (normally around $300 in the United States) for $62.50 each and had them sent express mail using FedEx.

Today, ShangBy.com is a growing and profitable business that offers as many as three live shopping tours and shows a day during the Christmas season and one or two tours and shows per week during slower shopping periods. According to company management, the most popular time to take a "live" virtual trip around the world to do some pearl shopping is from 9 p.m. to 11 p.m. Eastern Standard Time (8–10 p.m. Central, 6–8 p.m. Pacific). Just think how nice it is for the East Coast shopper to shop China's jewelry markets while sipping a glass of wine and being comfortably attired in robe and slippers.

Source: Based on information supplied by Stephen Bell, founder and CEO of ShangBy, and used with his written permission.

target market
Is the group of customers that the retailer is seeking to serve.

market and select a target market. A **target market** is that segment of the market that the retailer decides to pursue through its marketing efforts. Retailers in the same line of retail trade often pursue different target markets. For example, Ann Taylor appeals to a more upscale female, The Limited appeals to the moderate-income female, and Ross Dress for Less targets the budget-conscious shopper. Other women's clothiers have

Exhibit 7.1
Ease of Access

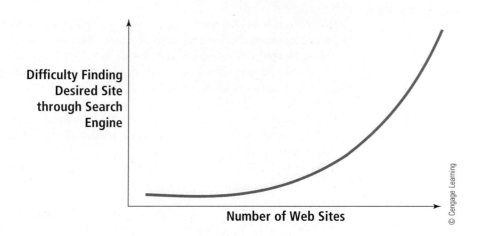

segmented customers based on characteristics such as age, size, education, ethnic group, and geographic location. For example, Charming Shoppes, Inc., with its three distinct brands—Lane Bryant (young, 25–35), Fashion Bug (young, 20–49), and Catherines (baby boomers, 40–65)—has the ability to serve every plus-size woman in the country. The Gap, Inc. has five distinct brands that cater to different market segments and these include The Gap, Old Navy, Banana Republic, Athleta (which you probably have not heard of yet due to its small number of outlets), and the online footwear retailer Piperlime (http://piperlime.gap.com).

The topics of target-market selection and location analysis are combined here because a retailer must identify its target market before it decides how to best reach that market. Reaching the target market can be achieved through a store-based location in which the consumer travels to the store, or through a nonstore retailing format in which products and services are offered to the consumer at a more convenient or accessible location. These are related topics because individuals of different characteristics are not randomly spread over geographic space. In fact, it has been repeatedly demonstrated that people of similar backgrounds live near each other and have similar media habits, consumption habits, activities, interests, and opinions. Because of this, retailers such as Pier One, AutoZone, and Red Lobster know where to geographically locate their stores, and merchants such as Williams-Sonoma (which has a very successful mail-order catalog for high-quality kitchenware) know which ZIP codes, geographic areas, and specific households should receive their catalogs.

Identifying a Target Market

To reach a target market successfully, the market segment should be measurable, substantial, and accessible. First, the retailer should seek a *measurable* market segment. This requires the retailer to rely on objective measures for which there is data available (e.g., age, gender, income, education, ethnic group, and religion). Subjective measures, like personality, are too problematic. For example, how would a retailer reasonably or cost-effectively measure the number of compulsive shoppers with red as their favorite color in the United States? Therefore, retailers most often rely on objective demographic data, which the U.S. Census Bureau (www.census.gov) provides to businesses at no cost or for a small fee. A number of data integration firms such as National Planning Data Corporation can get this publicly available data into a more usable format for the retailer's intended purpose. Buxton Company of Fort Worth, Texas (http://buxtonco .com), is a leading data integrator that provides analytical models to help retailers better locate stores to match up with their desired target market. For instance, Red

Wing Brands of America, Inc. is over a century old and is known for high quality footwear, especially for industrial workers. Buxton analyzed its existing over 400-plus stores, located coast-to-coast and found that 75 percent of its current customers drive 24 minutes to shop at a Red Wing Shoes store; thus clearly, the stores are a destination and a specialty brand. Buxton helped Red Wing develop a plan to open an additional 125 stores over five years, mostly in the Northeast, Mid-Atlantic, Southeast, and South.[5] Interestingly, Red Wing also has a multiple channel strategy and serves the business customer with a shoe truck that visits industrial sites where workers can fulfill their shoe needs at work.

A second criterion is *accessibility,* or the degree to which the retailer can target its promotional or distribution efforts to a particular market segment. Do individuals in the target market watch certain television programs, listen to particular radio programs or podcasts, follow certain people on Twitter, frequently visit the same websites (i.e., cluster in cyberspace), or cluster together in neighborhoods? Increasingly, individuals are becoming members of web-based communities or what are referred to as *tribes.* For instance, if you go to www.tribe.net you will see many of the tribes that are being formed and quickly note how relevant they are for many lines of retail trade.

As we will see in this chapter, the location decision is largely determined by identifying the most effective way to reach a target market. Think about your web browsing activity; it probably matches fairly well with your attitudes, interests and opinions (AIOs), and your demographics. Then, notice the advertisements that flash or pop up on these websites. They are intended, although not always successful, to catch the eye of a person in a particular target market.

Finally, successful target marketing requires that the segment be *substantial,* or large enough to be profitable for the retailer. Consider, for example, Joe Albertson's actions before he opened the first Albertson's grocery store in 1939. He drove through neighborhoods looking for diapers on clotheslines and tricycles in driveways. He knew that these were the signs of families with many mouths to feed and neighborhoods that promised profitability for his grocery stores.[6] Size of the target market is critical to being able to attract enough customers to the store for it to be successful. Recall that in Chapter 2, we emphasized that one of the key strategies every retailer needs to perform in order to simply have a chance at success is getting shoppers into its store (i.e., a traffic strategy). Well, if there are not many potential customers that fit one's target market within a reasonable driving distance of the store, then whatever a retailer does, it will fail at this first strategy.

To illustrate this point, assume you operate a store that caters to pregnant women. Pregnant women are a very small percentage of the overall population in general, and the number is even more limiting when you consider any particular geographic area. Couple this with the fact that most pregnant women do not purchase maternity wardrobes until the second trimester of their pregnancies (around month four). You need to carefully select your retail location if you are going to be successful over the long run; you have to make sure you operate in a market where enough women are getting pregnant on a routine basis if you're to remain profitable. What you don't want to do is to place a store in a large retirement community. Destination Maternity is a maternity superstore or category killer (as discussed in Chapter 1) that appeals to a broad group of women of various ages, socioeconomic levels, and ethnic groups. But, also, since Destination Maternity has an average store size of 25,000 square feet it needs to locate in fairly large metro areas of usually over 300,000 population. On the other hand, Pea in the Pod, a division of Destination Maternity Corp., caters to the affluent pregnant[7] and operates stores of approximately 2,500 square feet. Therefore, Pea in the Pod will locate in specialty shopping malls, often with a fashion flair, in the more expensive

Destination Maternity stores are generally 25,000 square feet in size, so in order to be profitable, they need to locate in fairly large metro areas where there is a substantial population of women of child-bearing age.

neighborhoods of major cities such as Phoenix, Dallas, Chicago, St. Louis, Atlanta, Miami, Boston, Los Angeles, or in leased departments of retailers like Macy's Babies "R" Us and Boscov's.

Clearly, a retailer can develop a store to appeal to any market segment regardless of size, such as a store for fans of the Green Bay Packers. However, the retailer would have to ask whether enough Packer fans live within its trade area to make the store profitable. While there are surely enough Packer fans in Wisconsin to support such a retailer, a nonstore location such as a website on the Internet would be a more effective way to market to Packers fans worldwide.

Reaching Your Target Market

LO 2

Identify the different options, both store-based and nonstore-based, for effectively reaching the retailer's target market and identify the advantages and disadvantages of business districts, shopping centers, and freestanding units as sites for retail location.

As noted above, once a retailer identifies its target market, it must determine the most effective way to reach this market. Exhibit 7.2 illustrates the two basic retail formats that can be used to reach one's target market: store-based and nonstore-based retailing. **Store-based retailers** operate from a fixed store location and require customers to travel to the store to view and purchase merchandise and/or services. Essentially, the retailer requires that the consumer perform part of the transportation function, which was one of the eight marketing functions discussed in Chapter 5.

Nonstore-based retailers reach customers at home, at work, or at places other than a store where they might be open to purchasing. As mentioned earlier, many retailers now reach customers on the Internet. Or, more accurately, the customer chooses to access the retailer on the Internet.

Location of Store-Based Retailers

As shown in Exhibit 7.2, there are four basic types of store-based retail locations: business districts, shopping centers and malls, freestanding units, and nontraditional locations.

Exhibit 7.2
Retail Formats for Accessing Your Target Market

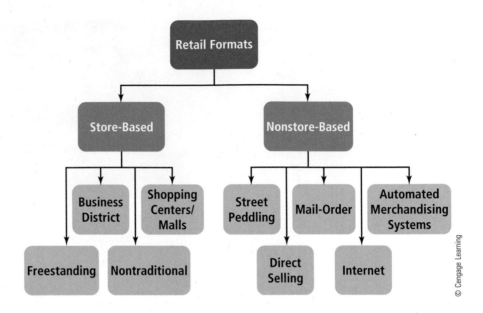

© Cengage Learning

store-based retailers
Operate from a fixed store location that requires customers to travel to the store to view and select merchandise or services.

nonstore-based retailers
Intercept customers at home, at work, or at a place other than a store where they might be susceptible to purchasing.

central business district (CBD)
Usually consists of an unplanned shopping area around the geographic point at which all public transportation systems converge; it is usually in the center of the city and often where the city originated historically.

No one type of location is inherently better than the others. Many retailers such as McDonald's, Panda Express, Pizza Hut, and Taco Bell have been successful in all four location types. Each type of location has its own characteristics relating to the composition of competing stores, parking facilities, affinities with nonretail businesses (e.g., office buildings, hospitals, universities), and other factors.

Business Districts

Historically, many retailers were located in a **central business district (CBD)**, usually an unplanned shopping area around the geographic point where all public transportation systems converge. Many traditional department stores are located in the CBD along with a good selection of specialty shops such as jewelers, cosmetics and beauty aid stores, women's and men's wear and shoe stores, and home furnishings. Uniqlo, the well-respected Japanese retailer of men's and women's wear, targets a lot of its U.S. growth in central business districts, including a new flagship store on Fifth Avenue that opened in late 2011.[8] Also in 2011, REI opened a store in Manhattan's Puck Building, a Romanesque Revival style building which dates back to 1885.[9]

The makeup or mix of retailers in a CBD, however, is generally not the result of any advanced planning and instead largely depends on history, retail trends, and luck. When you notice, for example, along Fifth Avenue and Park in New York City, Bergdorf Goodman, Tiffany's, and other high-priced specialty retailers, it is due to only these retailers being able to afford the high rents, which often exceed $100 per square foot annually. Thus, the invisible hand of the market creates what appears to be a well-planned shopping district. Recall when we stated that households of similar characteristics tend to flock together in neighborhoods; well, so too do retailers. When only retailers that cater to the relatively rich can afford the rents along Fifth Avenue and Park in NYC, there doesn't need to be any master planning to prevent Dollar General from locating next door!

Yet for those of us who do not work or live "downtown," shopping in a CBD can be time consuming and expensive. This is why many CBD merchants often offer free parking or shop and ride coupons that are good on public transit. In addition, some communities have tried to reinvigorate their city centers by enhancing the shopping experience or using other nonshopping attractions such as river walks, art fairs, music festivals, and entertainment and sports districts to get shoppers to overlook the costs associated with frequenting their historic CBDs. For instance, one recent major urban redevelopment is the $15 billion, 26-acre Hudson Yards that is being built in midtown Manhattan in NYC. When completed, the project will have six million square feet of office space, 12 acres of parks, 5,000 apartments, a cultural center, a hotel, and a major retail shopping center. The development is planned at 750,000 square feet of retail space and due to the high cost of real estate it is necessary to build the shopping center on five or six levels.[10] At the same time, across the United States in San Francisco, one can witness a blighted San Francisco neighborhood that is adjacent to fashion-oriented Union Square being redeveloped as more value-based retail.[11] It will be interesting to follow over the next 5–10 years how these redevelopment projects perform. Many similar efforts in the past have not worked well.

In addition, several U.S. cities have seen a resurgence of "antichain" sentiment, which makes it difficult for some retailers to expand.[12] These rules, which are particularly restrictive toward chain retailers that operate big-box stores (often over 100,000 square feet), are, in reality, attempts by local merchants to keep the Walmarts and Home Depots out of their localities.[13] For example, as of February 2011, 431 cities were listed on the www.sprawl-busters.com website as victories. This meant that they had some sort of antichain or big-box regulations in place.[14] The supporters of these laws believe that the introduction of big-box stores will destroy their quaint, close-knit downtown business districts that feature coffee shops, boutiques, clothing stores, and maybe even small locally owned department stores. This action, however, is not limited to the United States. When one of the authors was visiting New Zealand, the editorial page and letters to the editor section were devoted to the issue of stopping a Mitre 10 Mega Store in Dunedin.[15]

Such antichain action may actually have a negative impact on neighborhoods and independent retailers in the long run. Areas that vigorously fight against chains stand to lose the reinvestment ability that only a large corporation can provide.[16] To combat these regulations, chains across the country are mustering up community support, especially in times of economic slowdown, as well as producing custom storefront designs and interior schemes that blend with the aesthetics of the other merchants. Walmart, for example, recently tried to overcome these laws when it took advantage of the recent economic problems to expand in the Chicago market. It stressed the promise of new jobs and added sales-tax dollars.[17]

The CBD has several strengths and weaknesses. Among its strengths are easy access to public transportation; wide product assortment; variety in store images, prices, and services; and proximity to commercial activities. Some weaknesses to consider are inadequate (and usually expensive) parking, older stores, high rents and taxes, traffic and delivery congestion, a potentially high crime rate, and the often-decaying conditions of many inner cities. However, despite these disadvantages, JCPenney recently joined Target, Best Buy, Home Depot, Walmart, Burlington Coat Factory, REI, Staples, and The Container Store by deviating from their historical suburban location policies and adapting their formulas to the most urban of urban environments—New York City.[18] Despite the high costs and other disadvantages of such locations, the chain felt that the high traffic and more than double its national average in sales per square foot of space made these locations economically viable.

Often, the weaknesses of CBDs have resulted in a retail situation known as inner-city retailing. This occurs when only the poorest citizens are left in an urban area. Despite the fact that such areas annually contribute 2 percent to 3 percent of all retail spending, product and service offerings in these areas have decreased while prices have held steady or even increased. Although many consumers are aware that basketball great Magic Johnson has found success in opening movie theaters in Harlem as well as in the inner cities of Los Angeles, Cleveland, and Houston, they may not be knowledgeable about the success of other retailers in these urban areas. Retailers such as Dollar General, Vons, Stop & Shop, Supermarkets General, Jewel-Osco, Kroger, First National Supermarkets, A&P, American Stores, Pathmark, Whole Foods, and even service retailers such as Sterling Optical, Sprint, and Verizon have used good merchandise selection and heavy public relations to find success in previously underserved inner-city areas. One of the key reasons for their success in these markets is that they have tailored their inventories to the special needs and tastes of inner-city residents. In addition, these retailers have leveraged an underutilized workforce with high retention in an overall tight labor market.

In larger cities, secondary and neighborhood business districts have also developed. A **secondary business district (SBD)** is a shopping area that is smaller than the CBD, revolves around at least one department or general merchandise store, and is located at a major street intersection. In fact, Carrefour, the highly French hypermarket, selected its name because it communicates the cross-roads where it typically located its huge stores. A **neighborhood business district (NBD)** is a shopping area that evolves to satisfy the convenience-oriented shopping needs of a neighborhood. The NBD generally contains several small stores, with the major retailer being either a supermarket, a bank, or a variety store, and is located on a major artery of a residential area. An increasing number of national retail chains are finding the neighborhood business district an attractive location for new stores. These chains include retailers such as Ann Taylor, Auto Zone, the Body Shop, Starbucks, Crate & Barrel, Williams Sonoma, Ritz Camera, Radio Shack, and Pottery Barn.

If you recall from Chapter 2, retailing is in a constant state of change because external environments are in flux. One example of this involves the increased frustration and costs that households experience from long commutes to work that often involve wasted time in traffic, which is leading people to reconsider where and how they live.[19] For those that work in the CBD, they are increasingly looking at the first inner-ring of suburbs that developed around the CBD; often these developed during the 1940s and 1950s. These areas have become especially attractive to aging baby boomers who are shunning retirement and remaining in the work force, or who are retiring and want to be closer to the CBD where many cultural and sporting events are held. Not surprisingly, therefore, there is a retail revival and small office revival in these inner-ring suburbs around SBDs and NBDs.

The single factor that distinguishes these business districts from a shopping center or mall is that they are usually unplanned. Like CBDs, the store mixture of SBDs and NBDs evolves partly by planning, partly by luck, and partly by accident but mostly by the invisible hand of the market for retail space. No one plans, for example, that there will be two department stores, four jewelry stores, a day spa, two camera shops, three shoe shops, twelve apparel shops, four restaurants, and one theater in an SBD.

Shopping Centers and Malls

America has had a love affair with shopping centers. These "temples of consumption" experienced their first major growth wave just after World War II. A **shopping center**, which actually traces its history back to Kansas City almost a hundred years ago, is a centrally owned or managed shopping district that is planned, has balanced tenancy (the stores complement each other in merchandise offerings), and is surrounded by parking facilities. A shopping center has one or more **anchor stores** (dominant large-scale stores that are expected to draw customers to the center) and a variety of smaller stores. In the past, these anchors were department stores. However, the recent consolidation of department store companies, largely around Macy's becoming a national retailer by acquisition of regional department store chains, has reduced the number of stores, either chain or independent, that are available to serve as magnets to draw consumers to the center. Today, as a result, many centers are now anchored by a

Margin glossary

secondary business district (SBD)
Is a shopping area that is smaller than the CBD and that revolves around at least one department or variety store at a major street intersection.

neighborhood business district (NBD)
Is a shopping area that evolves to satisfy the convenience-oriented shopping needs of a neighborhood, generally contains several small stores (with the major retailer being a supermarket or a variety store), and is located on a major artery of a residential area.

shopping center (or mall)
Is a centrally owned or managed shopping district that is planned, has balanced tenancy (the stores complement each other in merchandise offerings), and is surrounded by parking facilities.

anchor stores
Are the stores in a shopping center that are the most dominant and are expected to draw customers to the shopping center.

single department store, along with a Cheesecake Factory or Olive Garden; Bed, Bath and Beyond; Michael's; Dick's Sporting Goods; PetSmart; Office Depot; Old Navy; Cost Cutters; or even the occasional Home Depot or a multi-screened movie theater.

To ensure that these smaller stores complement each other, the shopping center often specifies the proportion of total space that can be occupied by each type of retailer. Similarly, the center's management places limits on the merchandise lines that each retailer may carry. In addition, a unified, cooperative advertising and promotional strategy is followed by all the retailers in the center. Because of the many advantages shopping centers and malls can offer the retailer, they are a fixture of American life and account for usually over 50 percent of the retail sales in a community (this excludes new and used automobile sales). Remember that cities tax retail sales, and this is why, when a new major shopping center locates just outside of the city limits, the city council becomes quite concerned. A million square foot shopping center can generate $250 million in annual sales and if the city sales tax is 2 percent then it loses $5 million in annual tax revenue.

Some of the advantages a shopping center or mall provides over a CBD location are:

1. heavy traffic resulting from the wide range of product offerings,
2. cooperative planning and sharing of common costs,
3. access to highways and available parking,
4. lower crime rates, and
5. a clean and neat environment.

Despite these favorable reasons for locating in a shopping center, the retailer operating in a mall does face several disadvantages, such as:

1. inflexible store hours (the retailer must stay open during mall hours and cannot be open at other times),
2. high rents,
3. restrictions as to what merchandise or services the retailer may sell,
4. inflexible operations and required membership in the center's merchant organization,
5. potentially too much competition or the fact that much of the traffic is not interested in a particular product offering, and
6. an anchor tenant's dominance of the smaller stores.

Shopping-center image, preferences, and personality all attract various subsets of consumers, giving retailers located at the center a competitive advantage over other retailers. Therefore, it is extremely important that a retailer considering a shopping-center location be aware of the makeup, image, preferences, and personality of the center under question. For example, the open-air Rookwood Center in Cincinnati developed a whole new trade area for retailers. Prior to its development in the economically depressed area of Norwood, retailers had to locate either in downtown Cincinnati or in the more distant suburbs.

As Exhibit 7.3 shows, according to the International Council of Shopping Centers, there are eight different types of shopping centers and malls, each with a distinctive function. Last on this list is the Outlet Center, which is often populated by manufacturers' factory outlets. Retailers also often locate their outlet stores, which are used to dispose of excess or out of season inventory, in Outlet Centers because they are often located away from cities in rural or hinterland areas. They also can be the outlet for retailers who move to these Outlet Centers, inventory that does not sell in their regular stores or is overstocked in distribution centers where prices are drastically slashed. To overcome some of the problem of the stores in these centers competing with traditional retail channels, they are often located away from cities in rural or hinterland areas.

Exhibit 7.3
ISCS Shopping Center Definitions

Type	Concept	Sq. ft. (Inc. Anchors)	Acreage	Typical Anchor(s) Number	Typical Anchor(s) Type	Anchor Ratio*	Primary Trade Area**
Neighborhood Center	Convenience	30,000–150,000	3–15	1 or more	Supermarket	30–50%	3 miles
Community Center	General Merchandise; Convenience	100,000–350,000	10–40	2 or more	Discount dept. store; super-market; drug; home improvement; large specialty/discount apparel	40–60%	3–6 miles
Regional Center	General Merchandise; Fashion (Mall, typically enclosed)	400,000–800,000	40–100	2 or more	Full-line dept. store; jr. dept. store; mass merchant; disc. dept. store; fashion apparel	50–70%	5–15 miles
Superregional Center	Similar to Regional Center but has more variety and assortment	800,000+	60–120	3 or more	Full-line dept. store; jr. dept. store; mass merchant; fashion apparel	50–70%	5–25 miles
Fashion/Specialty Center	Higher end, fashion oriented	80,000–250,000	5–25	N/A	Fashion	N/A	5–15 miles
Power Center	Category-dominant anchors; few small tenants	250,000–600,000	25–80	3 or more	Category killer; home improvement; disc. dept. store; warehouse club; off-price	75–90%	5–10 miles
Theme/Festival Center	Leisure; tourist-oriented; retail and service	80,000–250,000	5–20	N/A	Restaurants; entertainment	N/A	N/A
Outlet Center	Manufacturers' outlet stores	50,000–400,000	10–50	N/A	Manufacturers' outlet stores	N/A	25–75 miles

*The share of a center's total square footage that is attributable to its anchors
**The area from which 60–80% of the center's sales originate

Bicester Village, near London, England, is a designer outlet with 130 luxury fashion and homeware outlet boutiques that attracts shoppers from all over the world.

Outlet Centers were popular in the United States from the 1980s to 1990s, but have now declined in popularity. As a result, many have closed because retailing is so highly price competitive among existing retailers in the United States that the Outlet Centers have less of price advantage than they did historically. This, however, is not the case in China, which is witnessing the rapid growth of Outlet Centers,[20] especially those focused on luxury fashion apparel. Value Retail is a firm that operates nine luxury outlets (they call them villages) in Europe and is opening similar centers in China. The first is a 600,000 square foot Outlet Center in Suzhou, 50 miles west of Shanghai. The project is called "Suzhou Village" and is modeled after Bicester Village, 65 miles northwest of London, which actually attracts a large number of Chinese Tourists. Suzhou Village, when fully built out, should have 300 stores between 1,000 and 5,000 square feet.[21]

Shopping centers and malls now account for one-half of all retail sales, excluding automotive, in the United States. However, as was recently demonstrated, this love affair can cause a problem for the malls. After all, since personal consumption amounts to some 70 percent of the American economy, if Americans don't spend, then the economy is in trouble. Fiscal health isn't possible until money is again rushing into the cash registers of every shopping center or mall retailer. However, during the 2008–2009 recession, shopping centers and malls struggled with slowing consumer spending and store closings by retailers. By 2012, well after the recovery began in 2010, there was still evidence of a decade of overbuilding as many retail store fronts were still vacant.

In short, it may take a decade for America to overcome the current surplus of retail space. In the United States, retail selling space is now nearly 47 square feet for every person; consider that in the U.K. it is 23, Canada 13, India 2, and Mexico 1.5.[22] To put this in perspective, you should know that the amount of inventory investment per square foot of retail space is often $50 and beyond. Thus, if you multiply 47 square feet of retail space for every person by $50, you get $2,350 in inventory waiting for each person, and this does not count what is sitting in the distribution centers of retailers and e-tailers.

This is essentially a pantry that all of us have, but for which we do not need to pay the storage cost or invest in the inventory. Due to this oversupply of space, retailers may get lower rents for the next couple of years, but they too will face another economic problem. Once Americans start earning again, and thus spending again, they are also likely to save more and thus not overshop and overconsume. After all, they each have this additional pantry of merchandise available when they need it!

The preceding analysis suggests that the oversupply of retail space will not disappear anytime soon. In fact, 2011 could be called "The Year of Store Closings" with the following retail chains closing a significant number of stores: Blockbusters, Borders, Gap, Foot Locker, Talbot's, Rite Aid, Destination Maternity, Abercrombie & Fitch, Lowes, Big Lots, Sonic Drive-Ins, and Denny's. These are only the statistics for a small number of more visible retailers.

Nevertheless, despite their problems, the country's thousands of shopping centers and malls are still a part of our lifestyle. Some seniors engage in their daily exercise there, families find malls a good source of low-cost entertainment, and teens use them as social outlets. In many cases, the loyalties of shoppers toward a specific center or mall have over time become equal to or greater than their loyalties to a particular retailer.

Freestanding Location

freestanding retailer
Generally locates along major traffic arteries and does not have any adjacent retailers to share traffic.

Another location option is to be freestanding. A **freestanding retailer** generally locates along major traffic arteries without any adjacent retailers selling competing products to share traffic. Freestanding retailing offers several advantages:

1. lack of direct competition,
2. generally lower rents,
3. freedom in operations and hours,
4. facilities that can be adapted to individual needs, and
5. inexpensive parking.

However, freestanding retailing does have some limitations including:

1. lack of drawing power from complementary stores,
2. difficulties in attracting customers for the initial visit,
3. higher advertising and promotional costs,
4. operating costs that cannot be shared with others,
5. stores that may have to be built rather than rented, and
6. zoning laws that may restrict some activities.

The difficulties of drawing and then holding customers to an isolated or freestanding store is the reason that only large, well-known retailers such as the category killers discussed in Chapter 1, should attempt it. Small retailers may be unable to develop a loyal customer base since customers are often unwilling to travel to a freestanding store that does not have a wide assortment of products and a local or national reputation. Discounters and wholesale clubs, with their large selections, are most often thought of when discussing this location strategy. When these large national chains acquire land for a freestanding store, they are seeking to acquire land in areas in which they expect the community will grow in the future. As a result, they often acquire more than they need and then "out-parcel" (i.e., sell or lease) the remaining land to smaller retailers. Note, for instance, that a Walmart super store or a Lowe's may have on its perimeter an Olive Garden or Denny's, a Hampton Inn or Holiday Inn Express, or a Sprint or Verizon store. Some astute local retailers and small regional chains have found it quite attractive to buy or lease this excess land and build stores, even at a premium price, because of the traffic a large discounter like Walmart generates.

Nontraditional Locations

Increasingly, retailers are identifying nontraditional locations that offer greater convenience. Recognizing, for example, that a significant number of travelers spend several hours in airports and could use this time to purchase merchandise they might otherwise purchase in their local communities, today many airport concourses now look like real regional malls, complete with national brands, casual dining, service kiosks, and entertainment and infotainment venues. After all, the increased security measures of the TSA mean that people are arriving earlier for their flights, leaving them with more time to shop. Also, cutbacks in the food services offered on many flights have caused more people to seek sustenance in the airport.[23]

College campuses are also experiencing an influx of nontraditional locations. Not only are the number of food courts in student unions and cosmetic counters in campus bookstores increasing, but also they are now allowing temporary "pop-up" stores on major walking paths throughout campuses. For example, Victoria's Secret's Pink, a young women's clothing brand of Limited Brands Inc., opens these campus pop-up stores for a day or two, selling merchandise, handing out promotional items, and collecting used clothing for charity. Ford Motor Company also did this on some campuses when it introduced the Ford Fiesta in 2010, which was squarely targeted at the youth market. In addition, cell-phone retailers such as AT&T, Sprint, and Verizon and credit-card providers such as MasterCard and Visa are often seen on campus malls selling to students. Truck and travel stops along interstate highways are also incorporating food courts. Some franchises such as Taco Bell, Arby's, Burger King, and Dunkin' Donuts are putting small food-service units in convenience stores, university libraries, and classroom buildings. Embassy Suites, a Hilton Hotels chain, saw an opportunity to offer guests additional entertainment, dining, and shopping amenities and built new units next to shopping centers. Hospitals are not only building emergency-care clinics near where people live in the suburbs, but also larger hospitals like the Mayo Clinic in Rochester, Minnesota, whose clientele come from all around the globe, often for weeks, if not months, are opening malls complete with restaurants and retailers selling fashion apparel, technology, and books within their basements to service the needs of their long-term patients and family members. Lawyers and financial planners are also opening storefront offices wherever there is high pedestrian traffic, and dry cleaners and copying services, as well as Yoga studios, are locating in major office buildings. Today, some Wells Fargo banks have mini-marketplaces featuring Starbucks coffee bars, dry cleaners, delis, and postal centers. Other banks have opened branch offices in retirement centers. Incidentally, Starbucks is doing more than serving coffee in banks but using its traditional 7000 outlets in the United States to encourage micro-lending, a form of lending very small amounts of money to small businesses and entrepreneurs. During late 2011, Starbucks announced a $5 million contribution to partner with the Opportunity Finance Network to launch "Create Jobs for USA." More importantly, Starbucks will use their stores to encourage customers to purchase $5 wristbands with the message "Indivisible" written in red, white, and blue with the proceeds going to further fund the Opportunity Finance Network.[24] The bottom line is that even cause-related organizations are seeking ways to use nontraditional locations to raise money.

Some service retailers are an exception, however, since their products are delivered to consumers at home. For example, plumbers, heating and air conditioning service providers, house painters, maid services, carpet cleaners, and lawn-care firms may not be concerned with their location. Enterprise Rent-A-Car will even deliver your rental car or truck to you. Incidentally, Home Depot recognized that many customers do not have a motor vehicle of sufficient size to transport their purchases, so the company will rent customers a suitable truck by the hour.

Nonstore-Based Retailers

There is a great diversity and variety of nonstore-based retailers. Perhaps the oldest form is the street peddler who sells merchandise from a pushcart or temporary stall set up on a street. Street peddling is still common in some parts of the world such as Mexico, Turkey, Pakistan, India, and many parts of Africa and South America. But it

© Rashevskyi Viacheslav/Shutterstock

WHAT'S NEW ?

GBTV Expands the Boundaries of Consumer News and Entertainment

Love him or hate him; it seems almost everyone has an opinion of Glenn Beck—nationally syndicated radio host, 6-time *New York Times* best-selling author, former television host, founder of Mercury Radio Arts and now, *GBTV*. What few can *honestly* criticize though is his ability to connect with his customer audience and generate headlines.

But it's perhaps the list above, and so many peoples' need to classify things into lists, that makes it difficult to understand how or why Mr. Beck has chosen to begin *GBTV*, a subscription-based Internet TV network, which began on September 12, 2011 after he left Fox News and his wildly successful 5-o'clock show. Many people see Mr. Beck as a conservative-leaning radio and television host—in essence a personality. He doesn't. In a recent interview with *The Wall Street Journal*, Mr. Beck said, "I'm a content provider."

Mr. Beck, like many successful businessmen and retail giants, realizes his true value proposition, the content, not the location or venue used to deliver that product or service. He's overcome the tendency for *marketing myopia*, where too much attention is paid to the specific product or service that the benefits and experiences are overlooked, and locked in on a growing trend, entertainment via mobile or computing device. In fact, in the same interview, Mr. Beck stated, "When the audience of 65 and over dies off, then TV is in trouble if they haven't found a new way to connect with the next vibrant and mobile generation." The 18 to 35 consumer is increasingly looking to "cut the cord" with cable and satellite television, with their annual contracts and lofty prices associated with channel tiers, opting instead for online content delivered when they want it and at a "reasonable" price (if not free).

Perhaps this is why Mr. Beck and GBTV turned to the experts in live-streaming technology, Major League Baseball, to ensure the best online experience for the audience regardless of *their* location. Based on the NexDef platform, a downloadable software developed by MLB, GBTV makes the most of one's Internet speed for the best streaming possible; no more "pause-and-load" experiences. If one is watching on their cell phones with one-bar or at home through a Roku device, the consumer gets the best experience possible.

The eventual goal of GBTV—to become a 24/7 network that provides original content that is based solely online; GBTV's location—live anywhere there's an Internet connection. As of the summer of 2012, the video network airs four hours of Mr. Beck's radio show alongside six more hours of shows—Liberty Treehouse, a history and news program for children, to the Glenn Beck program and Real News, to a reality program called "Independence USA," where a family explores living life "off the grid." And the cost for this on-demand news and entertainment, well that's somewhat "have it your way" too; you can pay $4.95 for access to Mr. Beck's daily show and 30-day archive or $9.95 for access to everything above plus original documentaries and other original content including an animated comedy series from Icebox, the production company founded by the writers of "The Simpsons" and "King of the Hill".

It appears Mr. Beck, who sometimes likes to poke fun at his weight, is trying to steal a page from Burger King and make television entertainment available "your way." Future readers of this box will know if he succeeds.

Sources: Stewart, Christopher S. "Glenn Beck Rallies Troops For Revolution Against TV," *The Wall Street Journal Online*, March 15, 2012; Klimas, Liz. "What Makes GBTV Fundamentally Different? How About Cutting-Edge Technology," *The Blaze Online*, September 12, 2011; Stelter, Brian. "Online, Beck will Impose a Fee Model," *The New York Times*, June 7, 2011: B1; Stelter, Brian. "Beck Uses Last Show on Fox to Allude to his New Venture," *The New York Times*, July 1, 2011: B3; Schuker, Lauren. "Glenn Beck to Charge for Online Network," *The Wall Street Journal Online*, June 7, 2011; and based one of the author's own experiences as a GBTV subscriber.

is also seen in the North America in such places as New York City, Montreal, Miami, Washington D.C., and San Francisco, where street-corner vendors sell T-shirts, watches, books, magazines, tobacco, candy, hot dogs, and other products. Peddlers also operate in many other U.S. cities, oftentimes using family members to operate kiosks and carts in heavily traveled areas such as malls and the parking lots at sporting events.

Chapter 4, "Evaluating the Competition in Retailing," discussed several popular forms of nonstore retailing, which are depicted in Exhibit 7.2 (direct sellers, catalog sales, and e-tailing). Yet, because retailing in the United States will continue to be predominantly store-based for the foreseeable future, we focus our attention on location analysis for these retailers. However, it should be noted that an increasing number of retailers are using multiple retail formats to reach their target markets. For example, JCPenney not only continues to build and remodel traditional stores but also has extensive mail and online operations where different catalogs are developed to target specific customer segments. In fact, most experts predict that over the next few years virtually every traditional store-based retailer will have developed multiple retail formats to reach its target markets. Interestingly, as you can read in the "What's New?" box, even entertainment and television is being delivered through new formats and channels that actually eliminate the television! With the growth of mobile computing, the ways in which people shop and how they are entertained are rapidly changing.

Geographic Information Systems

LO 3

Define geographic information systems (GIS) and discuss their potential uses in a retail enterprise.

geographic information system (GIS)
Is a computerized system that combines physical geography with cultural geography.

culture
Is the buffer that people have created between themselves and the raw physical environment and includes the characteristics of the population, man-made objects, and mobile physical structures.

Growing in popularity over the last decade has been the use of **Geographic Information Systems (GIS)**, which is a computerized system that combines physical geography with cultural geography. Physical geography is the latitude (north–south) and longitude (east–west) of a specific point in physical space and its related physical characteristics (water, land, temperature, annual rainfall, etc.). Cultural geography consists of the things that people have put in place in that space. To understand this, one needs to appreciate that **culture** is the buffer that humankind has created between itself and the raw physical environment. It includes characteristics of the population such as age, gender, and income, as well as human-made objects placed in that space like fixed physical structures (factories, stores, apartment building, schools, churches, houses, highways, railroads, airports, etc.) and mobile physical structures (e.g., cars and trucks). In reality, culture includes anything that humans can put onto a physical space, which then becomes an attribute of the physical space. For example, Scottsdale, Arizona, has become known for its very high density of golf courses, but these golf courses were put there by people, not by nature. Other areas are known as high-crime areas, but nature did not put crime there, people did.

Recent advancements in GIS have allowed the retail analyst to also describe the lifestyle (activities, interests, opinions) of the residents of geographic areas. This can be quite helpful in selecting locations for stores that are highly lifestyle sensitive such as Pittsburgh-based Dick's Sporting Goods, Inc. Dick's is a category killer in the sporting goods market and operates more than 400 stores in 40 states. In fact, executives speaking at a research conference held by the International Council of Shopping Centers noted that with the increased user-friendliness of GIS mapping technology, they have become more research-driven in locating stores. They no longer have to rely on information supplied by real estate brokers that may not be relevant to their business such as "the supermarket across the street is doing $30 million in sales annually."[25] With the large number of store closings that many retail chains experienced between 2009 and 2011, GIS was

Exhibit 7.4
GIS Components

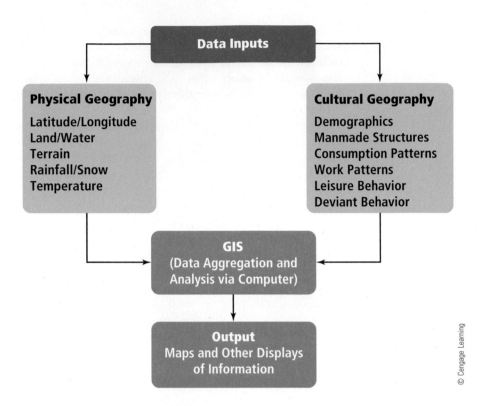

helpful in understanding why some stores disproportionately lost sales during the downturn yet others maintained, if not grew, sales.[26]

Exhibit 7.4 shows the key components of geographic information systems.

Thematic Maps

Historically, it was not unusual for a retailer to push pins into a map of a city where it was located. Each pin represented where a customer lived. An even more sophisticated retailer might have colored the map to represent different areas of the city in terms of income levels or ethnic composition. This was an early form of thematic mapping. **Thematic maps** are area maps that use visual techniques such as colors, shading, lines, and so on to display cultural characteristics of the physical space. Thematic maps can be very useful management tools for retailers. They can help the retailer visualize a tremendous amount of information in an easy-to-understand format. Today, thematic maps are an important feature of geographic information systems and are fully computerized, making them easy for retailers to develop. Google Earth displays satellite images of varying resolution of Earth's surface, allowing users to visually see things like cities, houses, buildings, or vacant lots. The degree of resolution available is based somewhat on the points of interest and popularity of the site being considered. Today, retailers, especially the smaller ones, are beginning to use Yahoo or Google maps as an inexpensive means of selecting or reviewing possible retail expansion ideas. Google Earth even has the capability to show buildings and structures, such as major highways and bridges, and the service recently added a feature that allows users to monitor traffic speeds at loops located every 200 yards in real time. Finally with the use of other search engines, the retailer can enter the address of neighbors and determine the type of business being operated and various other information factors about them—a far cry from the way Sam Walton selected his early sites a half-century ago. Sam would select a town or city and then

thematic maps
Use visual techniques such as colors, shading, and lines to display cultural characteristics of the physical space.

fly over it in his private plane during the rush hour to determine traffic patterns and scout out possible locations.

Uses of GIS

As a management technology, GIS has a variety of important uses in retailing. Some of the more popular uses are identified as follows.

1. *Market Selection.* A retailer with a set of criteria in mind, such as the demographics of its target market and the level of over- or understoring in a market, can have the GIS identify and rank the most attractive cities, counties, or other geographic areas to consider for expansion.

2. *Site Analysis.* If a retailer has a particular community in mind, a GIS can identify the best possible site or evaluate alternative sites for their expected profitability.

3. *Trade Area Definition.* If the retailer develops a database of where its customers reside, a GIS can automatically develop a trade area map and update this daily, weekly, monthly, or annually.

4. *New Store Cannibalization.* A GIS can help the retailer evaluate how the addition of another store in a community might cannibalize sales from any of its existing stores.

5. *Advertising Management.* A GIS can help the retailer allocate its advertising budget to different stores based on the market potential in their respective trade areas. Similarly, a GIS can help the retailer develop a more effective direct-mail campaign to prospective customers.

6. *Merchandise Management.* A GIS can help the retailer develop an optimal mix of merchandise based on the characteristics of households and individuals within its trade area.

7. *Evaluation of Store Managers.* A GIS can provide an important human resource function. It can help assess how well a store manager is performing based on one's trade area characteristics. Consider that two stores of the same size could be performing quite differently because of the demographics and competitive conditions in the two trade areas. Thus, it would be inappropriate to either reward or punish a manager for things over which the manager has no control.

Although most large retailers are using a combination of mapping and demographics during the site-selection process, many small- to medium-sized retailers are not using GIS technology to its full potential. This may be due to a lack of technical expertise in using complicated software; if a program isn't easy to use, many firms won't use it. Visualization of these maps is improving, but it isn't possible to make a perfect model of the world. A mall, for example, has to have anchors that draw traffic for the other stores. As soon as an anchor leaves, the economics of the GIS model are changed. This is happening with more frequency today as the consolidation of department store chains and mall saturation has caused malls to seek a new type of anchor. Not only are Home Depots and Best Buys now anchoring some regional malls, as discussed earlier in this chapter, but so are Bass Pro Shops and Dick's Sporting Goods. Some centers house for-profit universities such as the University of Phoenix, churches, and nonprofit art cooperatives where artists sell their art. Other centers are trying different approaches to filling the voids left created by these departing stores. Some are trying to recruit mid-priced restaurants and theater chains to draw evening visitors and encourage shoppers to convert a quick stop into a day-long excursion. Others are avoiding the addition of new stores and instead adding entertainment or amusement operations such as Legoland Discovery Centres (LDCs). These LDCs are smaller versions of the famous Legoland theme parks, measuring roughly 40,000 square feet and containing a smaller selection of the offerings at the larger parks. They feature rides, 4-D movies (special effects constitute the fourth dimension), miniature replicas of their host cities built from Legos, children's play area, and a boutique.[27]

Market Identification

LO 4

Describe the various factors to consider when identifying the most attractive geographic market for a new store.

trading area
The geographic area from which a retailer, group of retailers, or community draws its customers.

The location decision for store-based retailers involves three sequential steps. First, the retailer must identify the most attractive market or **trading area**—the geographic area from which a retailer, group of retailers, or community draws its customers—in which to operate. For some like Aldi, Carrefour, Home Depot, Walmart, and IKEA, this includes geographic expansion into foreign countries.

One such location is China. Over the last decade, most American and European retailers have identified China as an attractive market for expansion. Sweden's IKEA is one retailer that has found China to be a very attractive market. By late 2011, it had nine stores in China with an additional five under construction. IKEA's China expansion has been a resounding success; for example, their 463,000 square foot store in Beijing has 20,000 visitors on an average day, but this can spike to 30,000.[28] Many retailers, such as IKEA, contend that China is the most lucrative market for the early to mid-21st century because it has the world's largest population.

Retailing in a foreign country though, particularly one whose culture is substantially different from where the retailer initially or primarily operates represents a major challenge in terms of learning cultural norms, institutions, and political processes. For that reason, some retailers choose to license their store concept to a domestic partner in a foreign country. Saks Fifth Avenue has pursued this method of international market entry with licensed stores in Mexico City; Kazakhstan; Riyadh and Jeddah, Saudi Arabia; Dubai; and Manama, Bahrain.[29]

On the other hand, many retailers such as Kohl's and Kroger, as well as most smaller merchants, concentrate on the United States, and when considering new locations, evaluate only the attractiveness of domestic markets. Further, some retailers chose to concentrate on a small region of the United States, possibly a single state or even city. Golfsmith is a retail chain that focuses on golf and tennis merchandise and service offerings. They are relatively small, with around 80 stores, and thus their growth plans are in the United States. Golfsmith, however, is able to enter different sizes and types of geographic markets because they have three store models; one around 18,000 square feet, another at 25,000 square feet, and a larger 35,000 square feet store. Golfsmith has found a GIS solution helpful in determining which of these three formats fit best in any given market.[30]

The second step in the retail location process is to evaluate the density of demand and supply within each market and identify the most attractive sites available within each market. Essentially, this means identifying sites most consistent with the retailer's target market while simultaneously accounting for those markets that may be under- or overstored.

The third step involves selecting the best site (or sites) available. This stage involves estimating the revenue and expenses of a new store at various locations and then identifying the most profitable ones. These three steps are illustrated in Exhibit 7.5.

Exhibit 7.5
Selecting a Retail Location

Identify the most attractive markets in which to operate → Identify the most attractive sites that are available within each market → Select the best site(s) available

© Cengage Learning

Retail Location Theories

The most attractive retail markets are not necessarily the largest. A variety of other factors need to be considered in identifying attractive markets (e.g., the level of competition, zoning laws, average wages, and real estate costs). But to start, three methods are especially useful for identifying the best markets.

Retail Gravity Theory

retail gravity theory
Suggests that there are underlying consistencies in shopping behavior that yield to mathematical analysis and prediction based on the notion or concept of gravity.

Reilly's law of retail gravitation
Based on Newtonian gravitational principles, explains how large urbanized areas attract customers from smaller rural communities.

point of indifference
Is the breaking point between two cities where customers are indifferent to shopping in either city.

Retail gravity theory suggests that there are underlying consistencies in shopping behavior that allow for mathematical analysis and prediction based on the notion or concept of gravity. **Reilly's law of retail gravitation,**[31] named after its developer, William Reilly, dealt with how large urbanized areas attracted customers from smaller communities. In effect, it stated that two cities attract trade from an intermediate location approximately in direct proportion to the population of the two cities and in inverse proportion to the square of the distance from these two cities to the intermediate place. In other words, people will tend to shop in the larger city if travel distance is equal or even somewhat farther because they believe that the larger city has a better product selection and will be worth the extra travel.

Two decades later, Reilly's original law was revised in order to determine the boundaries of a city's trading area or to establish a point of indifference between two cities.[32] This **point of indifference** is the breaking point at which customers would be indifferent to shopping at either city. The new formulation of Reilly's law can be expressed algebraically as:

$$\mathbf{D}_{ab} = \frac{d}{1 + \sqrt{\frac{P_b}{P_a}}}$$

where $\mathbf{D}_{ab}$ is the breaking point from A, measured in miles along the road to B;
d is the distance between A and B along the major highway;
P_a is the population of A; and
P_b is the population of B.

For example, if Levelland and Norwood are 65 miles apart and Levelland's population is 100,000 and Norwood's is 200,000, then the breaking point of indifference between Levelland and Norwood would be 26.9 miles from Levelland and 38.1 miles from Norwood. This means that if you lived 25 miles from Levelland and 40 miles from Norwood, you probably would choose to shop in Levelland since it is within your zone of indifference for Levelland and is beyond your zone of indifference for Norwood. (Readers may want to calculate this for themselves, using Norwood as A and Levelland as B.)

Exhibit 7.6 shows how Reilly's law can be used to determine a community's trading area. As shown in Exhibit 7.6, A has a population of 240,000. City B, with a population of 14,000, is 18 miles north of A, and its breaking point is 14.5 miles north of city A (point X on Exhibit 7.6). City C, with a population of 21,000, is 14 miles southwest of A, and its breaking point is 10.8 miles southwest of A (point Z). Finally, D, with a population of 30,000, is 5 miles southeast of A, and its breaking point is 3.7 miles southeast of city A (point Y on the diagram).

Retail gravity theory rests on two assumptions: (1) the two competing cities are equally accessible from the major road, and (2) population is a good indicator of the differences in the goods and services available in different cities. Consumers are attracted to the larger population center not because of the city's size, but because of the larger number of stores and wider product assortment available, thereby making the increased travel

Exhibit 7.6
Trading Area for City A

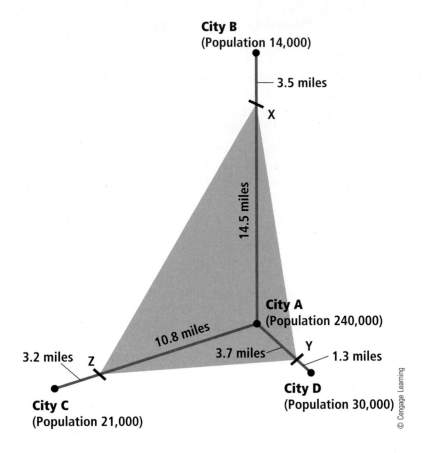

City B
(Population 14,000)

3.5 miles

X

14.5 miles

City A
(Population 240,000)

Y

1.3 miles

10.8 miles

3.7 miles

3.2 miles Z

City C
(Population 21,000)

City D
(Population 30,000)

© Cengage Learning

time worthwhile. This is why in large cities around the world such as New York, Paris, London, Istanbul, Mexico City, São Paulo, Shanghai, and Tokyo, you can find virtually any merchandise or service that is known to humankind.

However, in its simplicity, retail gravity theory does have several limitations. First, city population does not always reflect the available shopping facilities. For example, two neighboring cities, each with a population of 20,000 and similar demographics, would not be reflected equally if one of the cities had a shopping center with Target as the anchor store and the other did not. Second, distance is measured in miles, not the time involved for the consumer to travel that distance or the consumer's perception of that distance or time involved. Given our current highway system, this limitation is extremely important. Traveling 20 miles on an interstate highway to a mall located at an exit may be easier than the stop-and-start travel involved in going 6 miles through downtown traffic. Therefore, some retailers will substitute travel time for mileage. Finally, while the theory works reasonably well in rural areas, where distance is a major decision factor, it is not flawless.

Research on outshopping by residents of rural areas—that is, leaving your community to shop elsewhere—suggests that factors other than those considered by retail gravity theory are also important. For example, Paramus, New Jersey, is probably the nation's outshopping capital as it generates roughly $5 billion a year in retail sales, an amount about equal to the gross domestic product of Cambodia, Nicaragua, or the sultanate of Brunei. Paramus has four major malls and dozens of smaller shopping centers packed into 10 square miles. Take a look at The Outlets at Bergen Town Center (http://www .bergentowncenter.com). What makes this town of 27,000 residents such a magnet of outshoppers? Well, it is just a few minutes away from New York City and has a lower sales tax than New York City (7 percent compared with 8.375 percent). In addition, New Jersey has no tax on clothing and shoes while New York only exempts clothing and shoe taxes on purchases of less than $110.[33]

Some other factors that retail gravity theory fails to consider include perceived differences between local and other trading centers, variety-seeking behavior, and other services provided such as medical services or entertainment facilities. One such city that draws consumers from cities and states several hours away is Auburn, Alabama, where one of the authors currently lives. Auburn is home to Auburn University and its nationally recognized veterinary school. Many times a week, individuals from all over the southeast drive several hours to come to a town, with a population less than 54,000, in order to have their beloved family pet(s) seen. In fact, on one occasion, this author met a family who had driven from North Carolina just to have their dog seen by a university oncologist. The family planned to stay in Auburn for at least two additional days simply to shop and "make their trip worthwhile." Also, gravity theory is less useful in metropolitan areas where consumers typically have a number of shopping choices available within the maximum distance they are willing to travel.

Saturation Theory

Another method for identifying attractive potential markets is based on retail saturation, which examines how the demand for goods and services in a potential trading area is being served by current retail establishments in comparison with other potential markets. Such analysis produces three possible outcomes:

1. **Retail store saturation** is a condition under which existing store facilities are utilized efficiently and meet existing customer needs. Retail saturation exists when a market has just enough store facilities for a given type of store to serve the population of the market satisfactorily and yield a fair profit to the owners.
2. When a market has too few stores to satisfactorily meet the needs of the customer, it is **understored**. In this setting, average store profitability is quite high.
3. When a market has too many stores to yield a fair return on investment, it is **overstored**. Overstored markets are quite costly in terms of lost profit opportunities or, in many cases, losses due to the intense competition.

Saturation theory, therefore, implies a balance between the number of existing retail store facilities (supply) and their use (demand). As indicated in Chapter 4, one typically measures saturation, overstoring, and understoring in terms of the number of stores per thousand households. The consensus among retail location experts is that the United States is currently highly saturated or overstored with retail establishments, and thus retailers are taking a second look at some long-ignored markets such as older downtown areas and also nontraditional locations.

A possible indicator of understored versus overstored markets is the **index of retail saturation (IRS)**.[34] The IRS is the ratio of demand for a product or service divided by available supply and can be measured as follows:

$$IRS = (H \times RE)/RF$$

where IRS is the index of retail saturation for an area, H is the number of households in the area, RE is the annual retail expenditures for a particular line of trade per household in the area, and RF is the square footage of retail facilities of a particular line of trade in the area (including square footage of the proposed store). If you multiply the two terms in the numerator together (households and retail expenditures per household), you obtain dollar sales. Recalling that the denominator is square footage of retail space, it is

---

retail store saturation
Is a condition where there are just enough store facilities for a given type of store to efficiently and satisfactorily serve the population and yield a fair profit to the owners.

understored
Is a condition in a community where the number of stores in relation to households is relatively low so that engaging in retailing is an attractive economic endeavor.

overstored
Is a condition in a community where the number of stores in relation to households is so large that to engage in retailing is usually unprofitable or marginally profitable.

index of retail saturation (IRS)
Is the ratio of demand for a product (households in the geographic area multiplied by annual retail expenditures for a particular line of trade per household) divided by available supply (the square footage of retail facilities of a particular line of trade in the geographic area).

easy to see that the IRS is essentially the sales per square foot of retail space in the marketplace for a particular line of retail trade.

When the IRS takes on a high value in comparison with the line of trade in other cities, it indicates that the market is understored and thus a potentially attractive opportunity. When the IRS takes on a low value, it indicates an overstored market, which precludes the potential for significant profits. Many retailers monitor their sales per square foot for a store because it recognizes that if this ratio is too high, customers may not be well served and competition may be invited into the market. The retailer can then use GIS to identify where to locate additional stores that will minimize cannibalizing the existing store base, yet block competing retailers from entering the understored market.

Until recently, retail scholars believed that it took at least two competitors to saturate a trade area. However, Starbucks has managed to achieve that status all by itself. This achievement was hinted at in 2007 when the *Wall Street Journal* ran a story titled "Why Did Starbucks Cross the Road?" with the subtitle "To Get to the Customers on the Other Side."[35] The story included an interview with a Starbuck's executive lamenting the fact that the chain only had outlets on three of the four corners at Mission and Fourth in San Francisco. He went on to explain that Starbuck's growth had to come from new stores, and as a result the company planned to open more than 10,000 new stores within four years, which would have increased the chain's total to more than 23,000. After all, "if you're over there, you are not likely to cross the street." And Starbuck's growth came from selling that incremental cup of latte, macchiato, or Frappuccino.[36] Little wonder that a year later, when the nation's economy tanked in 2008, the coffee king's first action was to announce closings of 600 to 700 of its 11,000 U.S. locations.

As an example of how the index of retail saturation is used, consider an individual planning to open a jewelry store in either city A or B. This individual has the following information. Households of both cities spend $120 annually per household at jewelry stores. The total number of households in both cities is also the same— 40,000. City A, however, has 20,000 square feet of retail jewelry facilities and city B has 16,000 square feet, and your proposed store will have a square footage of 1,500 square feet. Given this information and using our formula for IRS, we can find the IRS for each city:

$$\text{IRS (city A)} = (40{,}000 \times 120)/(20{,}000 + 1{,}500) = \$223.26$$
$$\text{IRS (city B)} = (40{,}000 \times 120)/(16{,}000 + 1{,}500) = \$274.29$$

Thus, based solely on these two factors of demand (number of households and average expenditure for products by each household) and one factor of supply (the square footage of retail space serving this demand), the individual would choose to locate in B, since its value of $274.29 is higher than A's $223.26.

As nonstore-based retailing continues to grow, retailers need to recognize that the index of retail saturation may become less useful. This is because it incorporates only store-based retailing in the supply component of the index. Consider the following e-tailers: Overstock.com (www.overstock.com), Blue Nile (www.bluenile.com/jewelry), ShangBy (www.ShangBy.com), which you read about in the "What's New?" Box a few pages earlier, or one of the jewelry sales channels on cable TV, like JTV (www.jtv.com), where households in the two preceding communities could purchase jewelry.

Other Demand and Supply Factors

In addition to using retail gravity theory and the index of retail saturation, which are useful in evaluating various potential markets, the successful retailer will also look at some other demand and supply factors for each market.

Market Demand Potential

In analyzing the market potential, retailers identify certain criteria that are specific to the product line or services they are selling. The criteria chosen by one retailer might not be of use to a retailer selling a different product line. The major components of market demand potential are as follows:

1. *Population Characteristics.* Population characteristics are the criteria most often used to segment markets. Although total population figures and their growth rates are of primary importance to a retailer in examining potential markets, the successful retailer can obtain a more detailed profile of a market by examining school enrollment, education, age, sex, occupation, race, and nationality. Retailers should seek to match a market's population characteristics to the population characteristics of people who desire their goods and services.

2. *Buyer Behavior Characteristics.* Another useful criterion for analyzing potential markets is the behavioral characteristics of buyers in the market. Such characteristics include store loyalty, consumer lifestyles, store patronage motives, geographic and climatic conditions, and product benefits sought. This data, however, is not as easily obtainable as population data.

3. *Household Income.* The average household income and the distribution of household incomes can significantly influence demand for retail facilities. Further insight into the demand for retail facilities is provided by Engel's laws, which imply that spending increases for all categories of products as a result of an income increase but that the percentage of spending in some categories increases more than for others. Thus, as average household income rises, the community will exhibit a greater demand for luxury goods and a more sophisticated demand for necessity goods.

4. *Household Age Profile.* The age composition of households can be an important determinant of demand for retail facilities. In communities where households tend to be young, the preferences for stores may be different from communities where the average household is relatively old. For example, consumers aged 55 and older spend almost four times as much at drugstores as do 30-year-olds.

5. *Household Composition.* If we hold income and age constant and change the composition of the household, we will be able to identify another determinant of the demand for retail facilities. After all, households with children have different spending habits than childless households with similar incomes, as alluded to in Chapter 3.

6. *Community Life Cycle.* Communities tend to exhibit growth patterns over time. Growth patterns of communities may be of four major types: rapid growth, continuous growth, relatively stable growth, and finally decline. The retailer should try to identify the communities that are in a rapid or continuous growth pattern since they will represent the best long-run opportunities.

7. *Population Density.* The population density of a community equals the number of persons per square mile. Research suggests that the higher the population density, the larger the average store should be in terms of square feet, and thus the fewer the number of stores that will be needed to serve a population of a given size.

8. *Mobility.* The easier it is for people to travel, the more mobile they will be.[37] When people are mobile, they are willing to travel greater distances to shop. Therefore, there will be fewer but larger stores in the community. In other words, in a community where mobility is high, there will be a need for fewer retailers than in a community where mobility is low.

The most attractive market areas are those in which the preceding criteria are configured in such a way that they represent maximum market potential for a particular

Exhibit 7.7
Identifying Communities with High Demand Potential for a Fast-Food Drive-In Restaurant

Demographic Characteristic	Desired Target Market	Community A	Community B
Population per square mile	over 400	375	423
Median family income	over $31,000	$28,024	$32,418
% population 14–54	over 60%	48%	63%
% white collar	over 50%	38%	54%
% people living in 1–3 person units	over 70%	61%	72%
% workforce traveling 0–14 minutes to work	over 75%	49%	74%
Average annual household expenditure on eating out	over $600	$521	$619

retailer. This will vary by the type of retailer and the product lines it handles. In assessing different market areas, a retailer should first establish the market demand potential criteria that characterize the target market it would like to attract. Exhibit 7.7 illustrates this concept with a fast-food drive-in chain that sells hamburgers, hot dogs, and drinks. This fast-food chain, with more than 3,000 units from coast to coast, is a 1950s-style drive-in where people usually order burgers and drinks in their autos with carhops providing service.

Exhibit 7.7 shows that the chain has determined that there are seven demographic factors that have a positive impact on fast-food restaurant sales. One of these factors may need explanation. Through research, the chain has determined that its restaurants do better when at least 75 percent of the workforce travels to work in less than 14 minutes. When people have to travel longer to work, they get tired and frustrated about being in their cars and thus are not likely to be interested in eating in their autos at a drive-in restaurant. You might examine the other six demographic factors and develop an explanation for why they would be related to the success of a fast-food drive-in restaurant. The information in Exhibit 7.7 shows the desired target market and data on the seven demographic factors for two possible communities. From analyzing this data, you should conclude that community B is the most attractive market to enter from a demand potential basis.

Market Supply Factors

In deciding to enter a new market, the successful retailer will also spend time analyzing the competition. The retailer should consider square feet per store and square feet per employee, store growth, and the quality of competition.

1. *Square Feet per Store.* It is helpful to obtain data on the (average) square feet per store in the communities that are being analyzed. This data will indicate whether the community tends to have large- or small-scale retailing. In addition, this is important in terms of assessing the extent to which the retailer's standard type of store would blend with the existing structure of retail trade in the community. Generally in high population density communities stores are smaller due to the higher cost of real estate.

2. *Square Feet per Employee.* A measure that combines two major supply factors in retailing, store space and labor, is square feet of space per employee. A high number for this statistic in a community indicates that each employee is able to handle more space; this could be due to either a high level of retail technology in the community or more self-service retailing. Since retail technology is fairly constant across

communities, any difference in square feet per employee is most often due to the level of service being provided. In communities currently characterized by retailers as offering a high level of service, there may be a significant opportunity for new retailers that are oriented toward self-service (and vice versa). It should also be kept in mind that service levels vary considerably by country due to cultural issues.

3. *Growth in Stores*. The retailer should look at the rate of growth in the number of stores for the last one to five years. When growth is rapid, the community is likely to have better-located stores with more contemporary atmospheres. More recently located stores will coincide better with the existing demographics of the community. Their atmosphere will also better suit the tastes of the marketplace, and they will tend to incorporate the latest in retail technology. All of these factors hint that the strength of retail competition will be greater when the community has recently experienced rapid growth in the number of stores. Retailers, as well as entrepreneurs, can obtain the information needed for computing the square feet per store, square feet per employee, and growth in stores from the Urban Land Institute's *Dollars and Cents of Shopping Centers*, the National Mall Monitor's *Retail Tenant Directory*, and Lebhar-Friedman's *Chain Store Guide*.

4. *Quality of Competition*. The three preceding supply factors reflect the quantity of competition. Retailers also need to look at the strength or quality of competition. They should attempt to identify the major retail chains and local retailers in each market and evaluate the strength of each. Answers to questions such as the following would be insightful: What is their market share or profitability? How promotional- and price-oriented are they? Are they customer-oriented? Are they community-oriented and do they financially sponsor many civic and community activities? Do they tend to react to new market entrants by cutting price, increasing advertising, or improving customer service? A retailer should think twice before competing with Walmart on price, Saks Fifth Avenue on fashion, Kohl's on community involvement, and Nordstrom's on service or shoe selection.

Quite often when a discounter enters a small community and adds 80,000 to 100,000 square feet of retail space, existing small-town retailers feel they cannot compete and must close down. This is undoubtedly true for the already poor-performing retailers; however, despite the discounter's enormous buying advantages, small-town retailers can compete with the out-of-towners by providing better customer service, having unique product assortments or brands not handled by discounters, adjusting prices on products carried by the discounters, knowing their customers on a personal basis, and remaining open Sundays and evenings. Customers will appreciate the increased standard of living that the discounter's prices make possible, and as a result, the trading area will increase. The apparel retailer, for example, should cut down on basic stock items like socks and underwear but increase its inventory of specialty or novelty items. The sales lost on basic items will be overcome with these newer items and the larger trading area the discounter provides. Another hidden benefit of having a discounter such as Target enter a community is that the discounter's $50 million in retail sales results in households in the community saving from 5 percent to 10 percent or more on its sales. This translates into potentially an additional $5 million in purchasing power left over for the local community's retailers. How they spend their savings will be largely be determined by what the astute small retailer has to offer that does not replicate the discounter's.

Unfortunately, sometimes there are cases when a small community can no longer support retail establishments. This is especially true when a shopping magnet such as a discounter or supercenter arrives in a nearby town. The magnet store may actually benefit other retailers in its town, provided the retailers make the adjustments discussed above. However, the retailers in the nearby smaller communities are the ones most likely to suffer.

LO 5

Site Analysis

Discuss the various attributes to consider when evaluating retail sites within a retail market.

site analysis
Is an evaluation of the density of demand and supply within each market with the goal of identifying the best retail site(s).

Once a retailer has identified the best potential market, the next step is to perform a more detailed analysis of the market. Only after careful analysis of the market can the retailer choose the best site (or sites) available. **Site analysis** consists of an evaluation of the density of demand and supply within each market. It should be augmented by an identification of the most attractive sites that are currently available within each market. The third and final step, site selection, is the selection of the best possible site. One of the lessons from the 2008–2009 recession, and the large store closings through 2011, is that the quality of the retail site is more important than ever.[38] When the economy was going strong, a lot of retailers and their site evaluation teams got lax and opened stores on sites that were not all that good, but it was assumed that demand would grow and make the store eventually successful. Of course, when demand faltered in 2008–2009, the opposite occurred. If you were to open a store today, you would need to be wary of very low priced sites and vacant stores, although you may be drawn by the slashed prices. In fact, as there is a flight to quality sites, the best deals are often the sites that have maintained their value or increased. Why? It is the old principle that the three most important things in retail real estate are location, location, location! Paying higher rent may actually be more profitable. This is illustrated in Exhibit 7.8.

Site analysis begins by evaluating the density of demand and supply in various areas within the chosen market. To do so, retailers commonly use census tract data, ZIP-code areas, or some other meaningful geographic factor to identify the most attractive sites, given the retailer's requirements, that are available for new stores. One of the advantages of using census tract data is that it's readily available from the Census Bureau.

Census tracts are relatively small statistical subdivisions that vary in population from about 2,500 to 8,000, yet are designed to include fairly homogeneous populations. They are most often found in cities and counties of metropolitan areas—that is, the more densely populated areas of the nation. On an even smaller scale, the retailer can use Yahoo or Google, as described earlier in the GIS section of this chapter, to study the site.

Size of Trading Areas

Earlier we discussed the general trading area of a community. Our attention will now shift to how to determine and evaluate the trading area of specific sites within markets. In other words, we will attempt to estimate the geographic area from which a store located at a particular site will be able to attract customers.

Exhibit 7.8
Can High Rents Lead to High Profits?

Low Rent Option ($200,000)	High Rent Option ($400,000)
■ Annual Customers = 100,000	■ Annual Customers = 100,000
■ Average Transaction Size = $50	■ Average Transaction Size = $60
■ Gross Margin = 40%	■ Gross Margin = 40%
■ Gross Profit = (100,000*$50)*40% or $2 million	■ Gross Profit = (100,000*$60)*40% or $2.4 million
■ Gross Profit less Rent ($2 million less $200,000) = $1,800,000	■ Gross Profit less Rent ($2.4 million less $400,000) = $2,000,000

Exhibit 7.9
Customer Spotting Map for a Supermarket

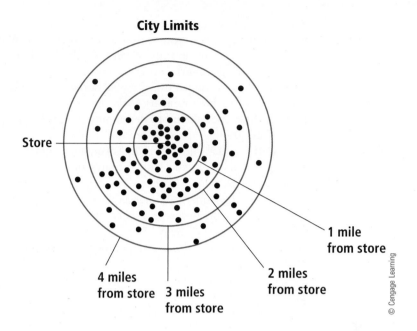

City Limits

Store

1 mile from store

2 miles from store

3 miles from store

4 miles from store

© Cengage Learning

At the same time that Reilly was developing retail gravity theory to determine the trading area for communities, William Applebaum designed a technique specifically for determining and evaluating trading areas for an individual store. Applebaum's technique was based on customer spottings. For each $100 in weekly store sales, a customer was randomly selected or spotted for an interview. Incidentally, Applebaum developed this technique more than 50 years ago, and thus we now recommend that for each $500 (versus the original $100) in weekly sales, a customer is randomly selected for spotting. These spottings usually did not require much time since the interviewer requested only demographic information, shopping habits, and some pertinent consumer attitudes toward the store and its competitors. After the home addresses of the shoppers were plotted on a map, the analyst could make some inferences about trading area size and the competition.[39] Exhibit 7.9 is an example of a map generated using customer spottings.

Thus, it is relatively easy to define the trading area of an existing store. All that is necessary is to interview current customers of the store to determine where they reside. For a new store, however, the task is not so easy. There is a fair amount of conventional wisdom that has withstood the test of time about the factors that are related to trading area size, which can be summarized as follows:

1. Stores that sell products the consumer wants to purchase in the most convenient manner will have a smaller trading area than so-called specialty stores.
2. As consumer mobility increases, the size of the store's trading area increases.
3. As the size of the store increases, its trading area increases because it can stock a broader and deeper assortment of merchandise, which will then attract customers from greater distances.
4. As the distance between competing stores increases, their trading areas will increase.
5. Natural and human-made obstacles such as rivers, mountains, railroads, and freeways can abruptly limit the boundaries of a trading area.

Description of Trading Area

Retailers can access, at relatively low cost, information concerning the trading area for various retail locations and the buyer behavior of the trading area. If you use your search engine to locate the websites of any of the firms providing geographical information services, you will see how readily available this information is to the typical retailer. For example, consider the work of Pitney Bowes MapInfo (www .pbbusinessinsight.com).

Pitney Bowes MapInfo is a global software company that integrates software, data, and services to help retailers make more insightful location decisions. As a market-research firm specializing in developing psychographic, demographic, or lifestyle analyses of geographic areas, it produces solutions that are available in 20 languages in 65 countries. MapInfo's PSYTE Advantage segmentation system, which breaks down all neighborhoods in the United States into 72 different clusters, is based on the old adage that birds of a feather flock together. In other words, even though the total makeup of the American marketplace is very complex and diverse, neighborhoods tend to be just the opposite: People tend to feel most comfortable living in areas with others who are like them. Think for a moment of the place where you are living now as a student and of your parent's home, and you will most likely see the truth of this adage.

Consumers may live in homogeneous neighborhoods for many possible reasons. The most obvious is income level, since people must be able to afford the homes. However, income is probably not the only answer, since many neighborhoods have similar income levels. Factors such as age, occupation, family status, race, culture, religion, population density, urbanization, and housing types can all distinguish between very different types of neighborhoods that have similar incomes. Therefore, these other factors are usually more important for the retailer to consider than income alone.

In distinguishing between neighborhood types, PSYTE Advantage and similar products use two basic criteria. First, each type of neighborhood must be different enough from all the others to make it a distinct marketing segment. Second, there must be enough people living in each type of neighborhood to make it a worthwhile segment to retailers. (Note the similarity in their criteria to those guidelines we presented earlier regarding target markets.)

Utilizing a variety of databases, including U.S. census data and proprietary computer software, Pitney Bowes MapInfo found 72 neighborhood types in the United States. These types are distinguished from each other in many ways. Some are based primarily on income, some are family-oriented, some are race-oriented, some are urban, some suburban, and some rural. Most combine two or more distinguishing demographic characteristics. The reason Pitney Bowes MapInfo settled on 72, and not some other number of clusters, was that in "solution after solution this number afforded the maximum amount of discrimination with the fewest number of clusters."[40] Exhibit 7.10 identifies these 72 neighborhood types or clusters.

The neighborhood names attempt to capture the essence of the neighborhood and provide an easy way of remembering distinctions. Also associated with the neighborhoods are demographics, lifestyles, retail opportunities, and financial and media habits. Still, in some cases the information about a cluster may be confusing. Consider, for example, cluster 68, which is "College Towns." This segment's behavior cannot be based solely on household income because nearly 40 percent of the cluster's population lives in group quarters such as college dorms. This neighborhood type, which is typical of neighborhoods surrounding college campuses across the country, can be characterized by the fact that more than one-third of its population is between ages 18 and 24. Without considering the fact that mom and dad are supporting the kids, the makeup of cars owned and amount of travel would seem contradictory to the cluster's income level.

Exhibit 7.10
PSYTE US ADVANTAGE Cluster Demographics

Cluster	Cluster Name	Population	Households	Mean Hhld Income	Average Hhld Size	Owner Occupied Dwellings	Renter Occupied Dwellings	Median Yr Structure Built	Median Home Value	Family Hhlds	Married Couple Family Hhlds	Bachelors Degree	Managerial and Professional Occ
1	Tuxedo Trails	2,346,218	798,935	$206,840	2.92	93.0%	7.0%	1970	$604,704	84.6%	77.4%	34.6%	62.1%
2	Executive Domain	6,811,130	2,301,069	$155,901	2.91	94.1%	5.9%	1974	$359,016	85.8%	78.9%	35.4%	61.4%
3	Nouveau Manors	2,605,221	860,385	$108,265	3.05	91.3%	8.7%	1993	$220,505	84.9%	77.0%	36.4%	55.3%
4	Parchment Hill	1,240,796	681,790	$181,190	1.97	41.6%	58.4%	1953	$932,092	36.7%	31.6%	37.4%	70.1%
5	Professional Duos	2,583,257	2,583,257	$115,481	2.59	82.0%	18.0%	1954	$378,810	71.2%	59.5%	28.5%	56.5%
6	Balancing Acts	4,780,580	1,562,464	$102,681	3.06	93.4%	6.6%	1981	$205,768	86.5%	77.6%	27.7%	47.3%
7	Equestrian Heights	3,477,347	1,285,906	$100,504	2.69	92.0%	8.0%	1969	$201,777	80.7%	71.9%	27.2%	50.4%
8	Suburban Establishment	2,417,513	1,016,377	$115,613	2.39	67.0%	33.0%	1959	$363,990	59.6%	51.4%	27.9%	57.3%
9	Suburban Wave	6,038,879	2,127,283	$85,833	2.82	85.6%	14.4%	1985	$176,466	79.4%	68.5%	26.3%	44.9%
10	Exurban Tide	5,215,523	1,823,588	$81,251	2.85	90.2%	9.8%	1975	$163,254	81.7%	71.0%	18.1%	37.2%
11	Only in America	7,451,644	2,770,832	$86,247	2.72	72.1%	27.9%	1956	$237,965	71.0%	57.1%	21.3%	43.1%
12	Rural Renaissance	3,391,449	1,186,953	$81,207	2.84	89.7%	10.3%	1973	$166,355	81.5%	71.3%	18.4%	36.7%
13	Sierra Snuggle	7,412,402	2,520,107	$80,178	2.96	82.1%	17.9%	1982	$182,630	79.1%	65.1%	21.2%	39.3%
14	Empty Nest West	2,795,297	1,093,111	$83,877	2.55	83.9%	16.1%	1973	$217,796	74.8%	64.5%	22.4%	44.6%
15	Western Sprawl	1,942,651	661,896	$76,811	3.04	71.8%	28.2%	1976	$244,826	72.0%	57.7%	22.6%	41.6%
16	Frontier Towns	2,638,276	786,164	$71,234	3.35	82.6%	17.4%	1977	$167,145	83.9%	66.9%	13.6%	30.7%
17	Up-Country Environs	2,148,895	815,417	$78,153	2.59	84.9%	15.1%	1976	$156,293	77.3%	66.7%	19.4%	40.5%
18	The Professoriat	1,836,804	818,867	$80,872	2.23	59.3%	40.7%	1959	$234,204	55.0%	44.2%	29.0%	58.2%
19	East Meets East	6,542,899	1,946,981	$68,347	3.41	63.7%	36.3%	1965	$197,506	78.3%	56.7%	14.6%	29.5%
20	Empty Nest East	3,837,941	1,463,478	$67,225	2.61	88.5%	11.5%	1964	$125,850	77.0%	65.8%	14.8%	33.4%
21	Towns in Transition	3,100,265	1,260,106	$68,090	2.45	69.1%	30.9%	1968	$149,311	66.1%	52.3%	21.9%	40.1%
22	Kids, Dogs, Vans	6,538,444	2,296,919	$63,585	2.84	80.5%	19.5%	1981	$125,414	78.7%	63.4%	14.7%	31.0%
23	Life s a Peach	5,549,405	2,377,528	$66,999	2.31	51.8%	48.2%	1980	$163,045	59.0%	44.3%	25.9%	42.6%

(continued)

Exhibit 7.10
(continued)

288

Cluster	Cluster Name	Population	Households	Mean Hhld Income	Average Hhld Size	Owner Occupied Dwellings	Renter Occupied Dwellings	Median Yr Structure Built	Median Home Value	Family Hhlds	Married Couple Family Hhlds	Bachelors Degree	Managerial and Professional Occ
24	Urban Villagers	3,569,556	1,946,619	$80,047	1.84	32.1%	67.9%	1951	$334,249	32.1%	24.0%	33.8%	59.4%
25	Cruisin' Couples	3,852,000	1,703,188	$73,553	2.23	78.8%	21.2%	1965	$162,361	64.6%	54.7%	21.2%	44.3%
26	Suburban Melange	3,480,114	1,441,204	$67,547	2.39	49.9%	50.1%	1970	$230,955	57.9%	41.9%	22.7%	40.4%
27	Retirement Horizons	2,541,929	1,077,550	$69,424	2.32	76.1%	23.9%	1963	$143,127	65.7%	53.9%	20.7%	41.5%
28	Quiet Streets	3,832,188	1,397,819	$63,713	2.73	86.4%	13.6%	1964	$117,827	78.4%	68.0%	11.6%	28.6%
29	Family Acres	3,728,309	1,375,025	$62,731	2.70	85.6%	14.4%	1970	$126,122	77.6%	66.0%	11.9%	29.4%
30	Moo's and Modems	4,859,978	1,786,334	$62,483	2.71	86.0%	14.0%	1975	$117,908	79.2%	67.8%	12.3%	29.9%
31	Home to Mama	6,279,909	2,445,660	$60,359	2.56	82.0%	18.0%	1956	$121,654	70.3%	54.5%	12.7%	29.7%
32	Echo Boomtown	1,871,787	951,361	$63,970	1.96	22.5%	77.5%	1973	$197,990	40.0%	28.0%	31.3%	51.1%
33	Live to Work	2,926,580	1,142,731	$60,377	2.49	53.0%	47.0%	1962	$152,576	60.0%	43.7%	17.5%	35.1%
34	Changing Places	6,695,306	3,178,347	$60,699	2.09	54.9%	45.1%	1960	$151,786	51.8%	38.9%	23.3%	42.8%
35	Cultural Exchange	1,201,709	375,759	$59,157	3.22	62.4%	37.6%	1965	$190,666	78.6%	56.4%	10.9%	24.4%
36	Active Seniors	5,168,842	2,587,011	$63,542	1.99	83.3%	16.7%	1978	$176,354	61.8%	54.2%	15.7%	34.6%
37	Outback USA	6,460,640	2,254,249	$52,661	2.88	78.4%	21.6%	1975	$101,617	76.7%	59.1%	8.2%	22.6%
38	New Neighbors	4,163,111	1,620,324	$51,471	2.56	62.5%	37.5%	1954	$108,856	62.9%	43.2%	12.0%	26.6%
39	Duty Calls	2,639,047	912,924	$53,807	2.89	73.7%	26.3%	1952	$89,032	72.7%	37.3%	9.6%	26.6%
40	The Neighborhood	3,591,669	1,284,191	$55,668	2.90	33.2%	66.8%	1947	$209,608	65.3%	43.0%	14.6%	30.6%
41	Old Metro, New Hands	1,641,679	533,845	$52,392	3.05	49.6%	50.4%	1947	$134,006	71.3%	46.6%	8.7%	21.0%
42	Country Roads	3,986,319	1,663,802	$51,168	2.37	68.9%	31.1%	1955	$95,546	64.3%	49.2%	12.1%	27.3%
43	Family Farm Belt	6,302,256	2,457,564	$51,583	2.55	83.8%	16.2%	1962	$83,540	74.7%	63.6%	9.2%	27.0%
44	Middleburgh	3,926,238	1,560,768	$50,364	2.47	66.4%	33.6%	1965	$95,967	67.8%	50.8%	12.4%	27.7%
45	Opportunity Knocks	3,232,502	1,298,000	$49,330	2.45	58.5%	41.5%	1970	$123,940	62.7%	46.1%	14.4%	29.6%
46	Service Corps	3,276,230	1,112,352	$49,188	2.96	63.1%	36.9%	1959	$84,693	73.8%	38.7%	10.0%	24.6%
47	Here to Stay	4,898,779	2,074,688	$53,947	2.32	81.1%	18.9%	1975	$131,886	69.4%	58.6%	12.5%	30.0%

48	Farm and Factory	2,841,983	$48,095	2.63	81.9%	18.1%	1971	$85,424	75.5%	61.3%	6.5%	21.2%
49	Singles Place	4,640,273	$51,147	2.13	27.2%	72.8%	1965	$153,907	44.9%	28.6%	22.2%	37.3%
50	Rust Belt Blues	2,353,937	$48,185	2.31	76.4%	23.6%	1954	$85,702	64.8%	49.5%	10.3%	27.0%
51	Irrigation Nation	1,960,960	$47,797	2.65	81.5%	18.5%	1975	$82,136	76.1%	61.7%	7.3%	22.7%
52	Military Towns	1,092,769	$48,026	3.46	3.9%	96.1%	1968	$70,418	94.5%	86.0%	15.1%	31.2%
53	Southern Country	5,836,530	$47,622	2.64	83.0%	17.0%	1978	$79,069	76.6%	62.1%	6.9%	22.4%
54	Home Town Harbor	4,154,531	$47,999	2.42	51.1%	48.9%	1963	$98,356	60.6%	41.3%	11.8%	26.8%
55	Plow and Plateau	4,466,139	$47,983	2.59	77.5%	22.5%	1961	$79,426	71.6%	60.1%	10.4%	29.4%
56	Agrarian Edge	5,707,990	$43,732	2.92	63.1%	36.9%	1969	$91,238	73.4%	51.7%	7.3%	21.3%
57	Backwoods Blues	2,851,388	$42,905	2.58	80.9%	19.1%	1969	$71,758	73.8%	58.4%	5.7%	20.5%
58	Latino Quarter	6,443,375	$45,167	3.99	35.5%	64.5%	1959	$147,683	79.0%	50.5%	6.0%	15.3%
59	Exurban Refuge	4,342,508	$45,029	2.30	70.8%	29.2%	1958	$73,007	64.2%	50.2%	9.8%	26.9%
60	Hispanic Hopes	2,524,486	$42,487	3.35	30.7%	69.3%	1953	$95,416	71.8%	40.2%	6.6%	15.1%
61	Amer-Indian Corners	4,595,317	$39,787	2.82	52.5%	47.5%	1957	$71,058	66.5%	38.5%	6.4%	18.4%
62	Hip Nation	3,048,802	$34,138	2.81	10.7%	89.3%	1953	$100,281	63.9%	25.7%	6.7%	20.8%
63	Help Wanted	4,917,158	$39,512	2.59	24.0%	76.0%	1969	$111,058	54.6%	32.0%	11.6%	23.2%
64	Extraction Action	4,946,371	$39,943	2.50	81.1%	18.9%	1970	$59,469	72.8%	57.8%	5.4%	21.3%
65	Village Americana	7,930,361	$37,783	2.38	58.6%	41.4%	1955	$65,155	61.7%	40.8%	6.7%	19.8%
66	Border Zone	3,479,233	$36,447	3.59	64.7%	35.3%	1964	$57,157	82.3%	57.3%	3.4%	14.4%
67	Senior Circles	3,505,446	$35,979	2.01	37.5%	62.5%	1958	$83,381	45.4%	29.5%	9.9%	25.0%
68	College Towns	3,756,878	$40,723	2.23	21.9%	78.1%	1961	$117,974	31.8%	21.4%	24.2%	36.4%
69	Black Memoirs	6,853,884	$35,309	2.69	63.8%	36.2%	1964	$54,609	69.0%	36.8%	5.6%	18.5%
70	Workin' on the Dream	5,820,914	$31,613	2.70	29.1%	70.9%	1957	$67,125	63.9%	24.3%	6.5%	19.1%
71	Project Renewal	2,769,233	$42,486	2.37	49.6%	50.4%	1962	$80,948	55.7%	38.5%	5.5%	24.7%
72	Urban Stress	1,905,734	$33,125	3.03	40.6%	59.4%	1947	$58,781	66.4%	22.2%	4.2%	17.7%

Source: PSYTE is a trademark of Pitney Bowes Software Inc. This exhibit is used with the written permission of Pitney Bowes Software Inc., 4200 Parliament Place, Suite 600, Lanham, MD 20706 (http:// www.pbbusinessinsight.com).

Demand Density

The extent to which potential demand for the retailer's goods and services is concentrated in certain census tracts, ZIP-code areas, or parts of the community is called **demand density**. To determine the extent of demand density, retailers need to identify what they believe to be the major variables influencing their potential demand. One such method of identifying these variables is to examine the types of customers who already shop in the retailer's present stores. The variables identified should be standard demographic variables such as age, income, and education since this data will be readily available. Let's construct an example.

A retailer is evaluating the possibility of locating in a community that has geographic boundaries as shown in Exhibit 7.11. It comprises 23 census tracts. The community is bordered on the west by a mountain range, on the north and south by major highways, and on the east by railroad tracks. The retailer has decided that three variables are especially important in determining the potential demand: median household income above $40,000, households per square mile in excess of 1,200, and average growth in population of at least 3 percent per year over the last three years. In Exhibit 7.11, a thematic map shows the extent to which these three conditions are met for each of the 23 census tracts in the community undergoing evaluation. Thus, you can easily visualize the density of potential demand in each tract. Note that only three tracts (6, 10, and 17) meet all three conditions.

demand density

Is the extent to which the potential demand for the retailer's goods and services is concentrated in certain census tracts, ZIP code areas, or parts of the community.

Exhibit 7.11
Demand Density Map

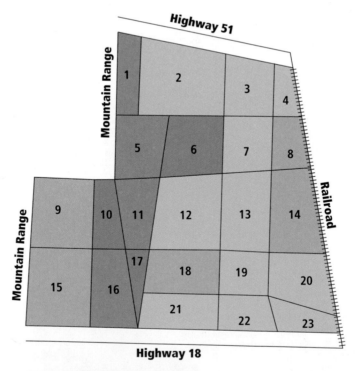

Three-Variable Demand Density Map
Variable 1 = Median income over $40,000
Variable 2 = Greater than 1,200 households per square mile
Variable 3 = Average growth in population over last 3 years
             in excess of 3 percent per year
Number of Variables Met

 0   1   2   3

© Cengage Learning

Supply Density

While the demand-density map allows you to identify the area within a community that represents the highest potential demand, the location of existing retail establishments should also be mapped. For example, for nearly three decades, ZIP code 07652 in Paramus, New Jersey, which was discussed earlier in this chapter, has had the largest dollar volume in retail sales of any ZIP code in the United States because it benefits from drawing shoppers from nearby high-taxed New York City. In addition, Paramus is located in Bergen County, which has a population of more than a million and is ranked among the top 20 American counties in terms of household income. Not surprisingly, Paramus has few vacancies and also commands some of the highest rents for retail space in the country. This information about the lack of available space as well as the number of retailers already serving the market is most important because it allows the retailer to examine the density of supply—that is, the extent to which retailers are concentrated in different areas of the market under question.

Exhibit 7.12 shows the density of stores in the community we saw in Exhibit 7.11. Exhibit 7.11 reveals that two census tracts (10 and 17) out of the three most attractive ones have a lack of stores. Also, in the census tracts with fairly attractive demand density (two of the three conditions met), there are currently no retail outlets (see tracts 1 and 5).

Site Availability

Just because demand outstrips supply in certain geographic locations does not immediately imply that stores should be located in those locations. Sites must be available. (*Note:* The

Exhibit 7.12
Store Density and Site Availability Map

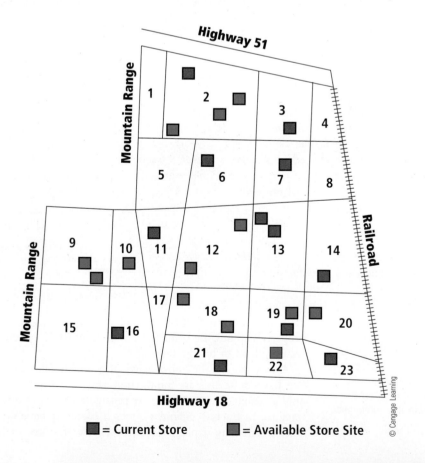

= Current Store   = Available Store Site

© Smileus/Shutterstock

SERVICE — RETAILING

Get Me to that Church!

Banks, medical offices, day spas, nail salons, and real estate offices are among a group of service retailers that has returned to malls and shopping centers as the traditional anchors have either merged with other anchors or gone out of business. This was because the more affordable (i.e., lower) rents and higher traffic counts made these locations attractive. An early example of this trend was the strategy of placing big-box retailers and grocery stores within malls. Today, however, some retailers have found a new and more exciting place for locating outlets: your old neighborhood church.

In past recessions, many times when a retailer closed shop, the landlord was willing to rent to anybody running a legal operation. However, today some retailers are seeking to be creative by differentiating themselves and not just becoming "me-too" types renting unused shopping center space because the price was cheap. These successful retailers realize the importance not only of their location but also of the building's structure in attracting customers.

Some real estate experts trace this creative location trend back to what happened to the old St. Mary's Church in Dublin. This former Church of Ireland structure was built in the early 1700s and is an early example of a gallery-style church. After closing some 50 years ago, it first became an oversized retail outlet. However, it has recently been converted to a most unique establishment—a combination of pubs and restaurants—and is simply called "the Church." Now this restored former church, situated in the heart of Dublin's shopping district, is a major tourist stop as well as a place for locals to gather. (For more information on this internationally known service retailer, see www.thechurch.ie.)

Recently, on the campus of the University of Cincinnati, a similar trend toward taking advantage of an empty church's structure has taken place. Here a local Cincinnati developer, Mark Fallon, purchased the Third Protestant Memorial Church building and transformed this former place of worship into a place of unabashed retail activity. In additional to having roughly 15,000 square feet on two levels, the church had a much coveted parking lot on a college campus. As a result, the vacant church, which had seen its parishioners move to the suburbs, became the logical destination for one of the country's hip and modish retailers Urban Outfitters.

Urban, which is considered to be the brand of choice for well-educated, urban-minded young adults because of its fashion with a retro flair, embraced the opportunity to retrofit the church. After all, the structure was originally built in 1929, and it clearly stood out among the typical campus eclectic mixes of bookstores, coffee shops, and fast-food empires. Today the location is the catalyst for a complete redevelopment of the area. It has attracted more than $100 million in both student and general population housing, as well as more than 100,000 square feet of retail and restaurants. In addition, it has also resulted in new garages holding more than 1,400 parking—spaces. All of this is attributable to the creative reuse of a church that today stands as the anchor location of the retail corridor at a major university.

Currently, other real estate developers are using this Urban Outfitters store as a model to determine if other urban neighborhoods can be moved from areas of potential blight to an exciting retailing infrastructure with the potential for reinvigorating an area.

Source: This box was prepared with written permission of Mark Fallon, Vice President of Real Estate, Jeffrey R. Anderson Real Estate, Inc., Cincinnati.

---

eminent domain law
Is the inherent power of the government to seize private property without the owner's consent in order to benefit the community.

case at the end of this chapter goes into great detail on how some developers have made use of **eminent domain law**—the inherent power of the government to seize private property without the owner's consent in order to benefit the community—as a means of securing land to build retail outlets.)

A map should be constructed of available sites in each community being analyzed. We have done this in conjunction with the supply-density map in Exhibit 7.12. The only available site in the top six census tracts (in terms of demand density) is in census tract 10. In tracts 1, 5, and 17, which currently have no retail outlets, no sites are available, which may explain the current lack of stores in these areas. Perhaps these tracts

Exhibit 7.13
Checklist for Site Evaluations

Local Demographics
Population and/or household base
Population growth potential
Lifestyles of consumers
Income potential
Age makeup
Educational makeup
Population of nearby special markets, that is, daytime
 workers, students, and tourists, if applicable
Occupation mix

Traffic Flow and Accessibility
Number and type of vehicles passing location
Access of vehicles to location
Number and type of pedestrians passing location
Availability of mass transit, if applicable
Accessibility of major highway artery
Quality of access streets
Level of street congestion
Presence of physical barriers that affect trade area shape

Retail Competition
Number and types of stores in area
Analysis of key players in general area
Competitiveness of other merchants
Number and location of direct competitors in area
Possibility of joint promotions with local merchants

Site Characteristics
Number of parking spaces available
Distance of parking areas
Ease of access for delivery
Visibility of site from street
History of the site
Compatibility of neighboring stores
Size and shape of lot
Condition of existing building
Ease of entrance and exit for traffic
Ease of access for handicapped customers
Restrictions on sign usage
Building safety code restrictions
Type of zoning

Cost Factors
Terms of lease/rent agreement
Basic rent payments
Length of lease
Local taxes
Operations and maintenance costs
Restrictive clauses in lease
Membership in local merchants association required
Voluntary regulations by local merchants

© Cengage Learning

are zoned totally for residential use. Or maybe, while there aren't any traditional retail locations available, there are some available to a creative thinker. As described in this chapter's "Service Retailing" box, many service retailers are not only returning to shopping centers but also moving into some vacant but very unconventional locations.

Although Exhibit 7.12 seems to show only one good potential site, several more may exist. Census tract 9 borders the high-density tract 10, in which there are no present stores and in which only one site is available for a new store. Tract 9, however, has two available sites. Furthermore, tract 12 has an available site that is close to the borders of tracts 11 and 17, which are both attractive but, lack available sites. This same kind of analysis can be done with our high-fashion chain in looking over the Los Angeles market. Some retailers have developed a checklist of all the items they want to consider during the site analysis stage. One such list is shown in Exhibit 7.13.

LO 6

Site Selection

Explain how to select
the best geographic
site for a store.

After completing the analysis of each segment in the desired market and identifying the best available sites within each market, retailers are now ready to make the final decision regarding location: selecting the best site (or sites) available. Small to medium-sized retailers without an in-house real estate department are well advised to use the assistance of a real estate professional at this stage. Even if the retailer or its staff has done all the analysis to this point, the assistance of a real estate professional is important. In fact, more and more large retailers set up separate corporations just to handle their real estate transactions.

100-percent location
Is when there is no better use for a site than the retail store that is being planned for that site.

In principle, all retailers should attempt to find a **100-percent location** for their stores. A 100-percent location is one where there is no better use for the site than the retail store that is being planned. Retailers should remember that what may be a 100-percent site for one store may not be a 100-percent site for another; the best location for a supermarket may not be the best location for a discount department store.

How is the 100-percent location or site identified? Unfortunately, there is no best answer to this basic question. There is, however, general agreement on the types of things that the retailer should consider in evaluating sites: the nature of the site, traffic characteristics, type of neighbors, and the terms of purchase or lease.

Nature of Site

Is the site currently a vacant store, a vacant parcel of land, or the site of a planned shopping center? Many of the available retail sites will be vacant stores. This is because 10 percent to 15 percent of stores go out of business each year. This does not mean that because a men's apparel store failed in a particular location that a bookstore is doomed to do likewise. However, sometimes a piece of property becomes known as "jinxed" or "snakebit" because of the high number of business failures that have occurred there. Every town usually has one or more such areas. Restaurants, which are among the toughest businesses to get off the ground, seem to try these locations the most. Even a shopping center can appear to be under an unlucky star. For example, Cincinnati Mills has had six owners in its 20-year history and ended 2008 with a vacancy rate of 44 percent.[41] Therefore, when the retail site that appears to be best suited to the retailer's needs is a vacant parcel of land, the retailer needs to investigate why it is vacant. Why have others passed up the site? Was it previously not for sale or was it priced too high? Or is there some other reason?

Finally, the site may be part of a planned shopping center. In this case, the retailer can usually be assured that it will have the proper mix of neighbors, adequate parking facilities, and good traffic. Sometimes, of course, the center has not been properly planned, and the retailer needs to be aware of these special cases. It is difficult to succeed in a shopping center in which a high percentage of space is not rented.

Traffic Characteristics

The traffic that passes a site, whether it is vehicular or pedestrian, can be an important determinant of the potential sales at that site. However, other factors than traffic flow must be considered. The retailer must determine whether the population and traffic are of the type desired. For example, a retailer of fine furs and leather coats may be considering two alternative sites—one in the central business district and the other in a group of specialty stores in a small shopping center in a very exclusive residential area. The CBD site may generate more total traffic, but the alternative site may generate more of the right type of traffic. Also, because of its convenient location near exclusive neighborhoods, shoppers may visit the store more often and this could lead to higher sales.

The retailer should evaluate two traffic-related aspects of the site. The first is the availability of sufficient parking, either at the site or nearby. One of the advantages of shopping centers and malls is the availability of adequate parking space. If the site is not a shopping center, then the retailer will need to determine if the parking space will be adequate. It is difficult to give a precise guideline for the space that will be needed.

Generally, it is a function of four factors: size of the store, frequency of customer visits, length of customer visits, and availability of public transportation. As a rule of thumb, shopping centers estimate that there should be five spaces for every 1,000 square feet of selling space in medium-sized centers and 10 spaces per 1,000 square feet in large centers. In some cases, where retailers, especially high-end fashion retailers or expensive restaurants, do not have convenient parking, they offer valet parking service.

A second traffic-related aspect the retailer should consider is the direction of traffic relative to the shopping area. Many shoppers prefer not to have to make left-hand turns from a busy roadway into a shopping area. A third consideration is the ease with which consumers can reach the store site. Are the roadways in good shape? Are there traffic barriers—rivers with a limited number of bridges, interstate highways with limited crossings, one-way streets, or a high level of street usage resulting in congestion that limits exits to the site? Remember, customers normally avoid heavily congested shopping areas and shop elsewhere in order to minimize driving time and other difficulties.

Type of Neighbors

What neighboring establishments surround the site? There can be good and bad neighbors. What constitutes a good or bad neighbor depends on the type of store being considered at the site. Suppose that you plan to open a children's apparel store and are considering two alternative sites. One site already has a toy store and a gift shop; the other site has a bowling alley and an adult book store. Obviously, in this case, you know who the good and bad neighbors are.

However, determining the good and bad neighbors may not always be that easy, especially for an entrepreneur. A good neighboring business will be one that is compatible with the retailer's line of trade. When two or more businesses are compatible, they can actually help generate additional business for each other. For example, a paint store, hardware store, and auto parts store located next to one another may increase total traffic and thus benefit them all. One of the authors knew a jewelry store with multiple locations that always tried to locate next to an expensive women's apparel store and ideally a furrier. This was because most furriers provided summer storage of furs, which resulted in at least two major visits per year to the furrier as customers picked up furs for the winter and returned them in the summer. Both times were ideal for the neighboring jewelry merchant to intercept customers. In fact, he often had joint promotions with the furrier.

store compatibility
Exists when two similar retail businesses locate next to or nearby each other and they realize a sales volume greater than what they would have achieved if they were located apart from each other.

Research has found that retailers experience a benefit from **store compatibility**. In other words, when two compatible or very similar businesses (e.g., two shoe stores) locate near each other, they will show an increase in sales volume greater than what they would have achieved if they were located separately.[42] For example, when Lowe's opened a store near a Home Depot in Lewisville, Texas, the Home Depot store went from a category B to a category A store. This meant that the addition of a nearby competitor increased Home Depot's sales by 20 percent. Another example is PetSmart, which doesn't mind locating near a PETCO outlet. PetSmart likes to "shove their stores down the competition's throat"—that is, have its stores so close to the competition that customers can easily compare prices and service. However, when PETCO has PetSmart beat on convenience, PetSmart will back away.[43] A final case is Big Lots, a close-out specialist, which likes being near Walmart. In fact, the large discounter is not only a competitor for Big Lots but also its biggest landlord. Today, Big Lots operates 40 stores on sites where Walmart shut down to open a larger unit nearby. An executive for the smaller chain told a real estate conference that many of our customers "like to comparison shop, and if the competition is across the parking lot rather than across town, we feel like we'll win."[44]

retail clusters
Are groups of stores closely located that share similar characteristics such as product category, store format, or customer demographics.

Retail clusters are groups of stores closely located that share similar characteristics such as product category, store format, or customer demographics. Contrary to what some may think, clustering is not another description for Starbuck's saturation location strategy. Rather, the term dates back to the 1950s, when the choicest location for a gas station was believed to be an intersection that already had three other stations. It is seen today with shoe stores in malls, auto dealerships, furniture stores, and restaurants. The major benefit of clustering is two-fold for customers. First, once potential customers identify a need for a line of merchandise or service, they don't need to decide on the specific store to visit but just need to decide to travel to the retail cluster. Consider how often a family does this when it decides to go out to dinner and heads in the direction of restaurant row (cluster) and then, when in transit or on arrival at the cluster, selects a specific restaurant for dining. Second, retail clustering allows customers to walk from store to store, comparing prices, products, and service. However, grouping stores doesn't always benefit competitors. Consider membership retailers such as wholesale clubs and fitness centers. After all, if consumers have already paid to use one of the retailers, it is doubtful that they would pay to shop at the other. In such cases, one of three things would happen:

1. The retailers would fight it out to the death, and both would lose.
2. The trade area could expand to become big enough so that both could succeed.
3. One retailer would be forced to completely differentiate itself from the other, and even then they might not both survive.

Terms of Purchase or Lease

Another consideration for the retailer at this point is the lease terms. The retailer should review the length of the lease (it could be too long or too short), the exclusivity clause (whether or not the retailer will be the only one allowed to sell a certain line of merchandise), the guaranteed traffic rate (a reduction in rent should be offered if the shopping center fails to achieve a targeted traffic level), and an anchor clause (which would also allow for a rent reduction if the anchor store in a developing center does not open on time or when the retailer opens). Lease arrangements generally call for either a fixed payment in which the rental charge is usually based on a fixed amount per month or a variable payment in which rent is a specified percentage of sales with a guaranteed minimum rent. It is important for the retailer to choose the one that is best under the circumstances—perhaps a combination of the two methods.

When the retailer decides to locate in a shopping center, it usually has no other choice than to lease. However, in the case of a freestanding location, an outright purchase is often possible. When purchasing a freestanding location, the retailer needs to carefully examine any zoning regulations that might prevent the use of the property as the retailer intends. It should also make sure that there are no liens on the property or hazardous wastes that the retailer may need to clean up. For instance, some vacant parcels of land may have hidden fuel tanks from a prior occupant such as a gasoline station. These tanks may have leaked fuel and created a hazard that the retailer is responsible for remediating. Or, a retailer that purchases a piece of property that has an old building that it plans to remodel, should be aware of any asbestos that may need removing or changes that may have to be made to the building to bring it up to safety standards.

Expected Profitability

The final step in site-selection analysis is construction of a pro forma (expected) return-on-asset model for each possible site. The return-on-asset model comprises three crucial variables: net profit margin, asset turnover, and return on assets.

For purposes of evaluating sites, the potential return on equity is not relevant. This is because the financial leverage ratio (total assets divided by equity) is a top-management decision; it represents how much debt the retail enterprise is willing to assume. Most likely, the question of how to finance new store growth has already been answered or at least contemplated. The retailer should already have determined that it has or can obtain the capital to finance a new store. It is therefore reasonable and appropriate to evaluate sites on their potential return on assets and not return on equity.

If the retailer is to evaluate sites on their potential return on assets, then it will need at least three estimates: total sales, total assets, and net profit. Each of these is likely to vary, depending on the site. Sales estimates will be different for alternative sites because each will have unique trade area characteristics, such as the number and nature of households and the level of competition. Estimated total assets could vary because the alternative sites will likely have different prices; the cost of construction could also vary. Finally, estimated profits could vary not only due to varying sales for the different sites but also because of different operating costs. For example, some sites may be in areas where labor expenses, taxes, or insurance rates are higher.

Summary

Selecting a target market and determining which retail format will most effectively reach this market are two of the most important decisions a retailer will make. The retailer can reach potential customers through both store-based retail locations and nonstore retail formats. Geographical information systems can help the retailer gain knowledge of its potential customers and where they reside and how they behave. This can help the retailer better determine how to reach its target market.

Most of the chapter discussed how to select a location for a store-based retailer. The choice of retail location involves three decisions: (1) market identification, or identifying the most attractive markets; (2) site analysis, or evaluating the demand and supply within each market; and (3) site selection, or selecting the best site (or sites) available.

LO 1 | ### Explain the criteria used in selecting a target market.

We began this chapter by stating that an effective target market must be one that is measurable, accessible, and substantial. *Measurability* concerns whether or not objective data exists on the attributes of the target market. *Accessibility* deals with the extent to which marketing efforts can be uniquely targeted at a particular segment of the market. *Substantiality* relates to whether the target market is large enough to be economically worth pursuing.

LO 2 | ### Identify the different options, both store-based and nonstore-based, for effectively reaching the retailer's target market and identify the advantages and disadvantages of business districts, shopping centers, and freestanding units as sites for retail location.

We next reviewed the four store-based location alternatives available to the retailer: the business district, the shopping center or mall, the freestanding unit, and the nontraditional store location. The central business district is generally an unplanned shopping area around the geographic point where a city originated and grew up. With the growth of the cities, we have witnessed an expansion of two newer types of business districts: the secondary business district and the neighborhood business district.

A shopping center or mall is a centrally owned or managed shopping district that is planned, has balanced tenancy, and is surrounded by parking facilities. It has one or more anchor stores and a variety of smaller stores. Because of the many advantages shopping centers can offer the retailer, they are a fixture of America and account for 55 percent of all retail sales in the United States.

A freestanding retailer generally locates along major traffic arteries. There are usually no adjacent retailers selling competing products with which the retailer will have to share traffic.

The retailer also has five nonstore-based options: street peddling, mail order, automatic merchandising machines, direct selling, and the Internet.

LO 3 Define geographic information systems (GIS) and discuss their potential uses in a retail enterprise.

Higher-quality market selection and retail location decisions can be made with the use of geographic information systems, which are computerized systems combining physical geography with cultural geography. The GIS technology can be used not only for market selection, site analysis, and trade area definition but also to evaluate new store cannibalization, advertising management, merchandise management, and store-manager performance. With the advent of Yahoo! and Google, this technique is available to even the smallest of retailers.

LO 4 What are the various factors that should be considered in identifying the most attractive retail market?

We began our analysis of market selection by looking at a trio of theories that can aid in the location decision. *Retail gravitation theory* assumes that as the population of a community rises relative to nearby communities, it will have relatively more merchandise assortments and availability, which serves as a drawing power for the community to draw customers into its retail shopping district. The *index of retail saturation* reflects the total demand for the product under question and whether the area is overstored or understored, which is the availability of current retailers to service or supply current demand. We concluded our discussion on market identification by looking into other factors that could influence a community's supply (square feet per store, square feet per employee, growth in stores, and quality of competition) or demand (market population, buyer behavior, household income, age, and composition, community life cycle, density, and mobility) for goods and services.

LO 5 What attributes should be considered in evaluating retail sites within a retail market?

After reviewing the three location theories, we discussed the second of our three steps in the location process: *site analysis*, which is an evaluation of the density of demand and supply within each possible market. This process begins by determining the size, description, and density of demand and supply of various areas within the chosen market and then identifying the most attractive sites, given the retailer's requirements that are available for new stores within each market.

LO 6 How is the best geographic site selected?

Finally, the retailer should conduct a site-selection analysis of the top-ranking sites in each market. The goal is to select the best site or sites. Retail-site analysts suggest that the following factors should be considered at this stage: nature of the site, traffic characteristics, type of neighbors, terms of lease or purchase, and finally the expected profitability or return on assets.

Terms to Remember

home page	trading area
virtual store	retail gravity theory
ease of access	Reilly's law of retail gravitation
target market	point of indifference
store-based retailers	retail store saturation
nonstore-based retailers	understored
central business district (CBD)	overstored
secondary business district (SBD)	index of retail saturation (IRS)
neighborhood business district (NBD)	site analysis
shopping center (or mall)	demand density
anchor stores	eminent domain law
freestanding retailer	100-percent location
geographic information system (GIS)	store compatibility
culture	retail clusters
thematic maps	

Review and Discussion Questions

LO 1 **What criteria are used in selecting a target market?**

1. Why should retailers be concerned about selecting the right target market? How are target market selection and location related?
2. What three criteria should be met to successfully target a market?

LO 2 **Identify the different options, both store-based and nonstore-based, for effectively reaching the retailer's target market, and identify the advantages and disadvantages of business districts, shopping centers, and freestanding units as sites for retail location.**

3. What types of retailers would be best suited for locating in a lifestyle center?
4. Why are some shopping centers and malls now using big-box stores such as Home Depot, Bass Pro Shops and Kaplan's as anchors? Aren't anchor stores supposed to be department stores?
5. What lines of retail trade do you believe will be most affected by the growth of retailing on the Internet?
6. Why isn't Walmart a good choice to be an anchor at a mall?

LO 3 **Define geographic information systems (GIS) and discuss their potential uses in a retail enterprise.**

7. How have improvements in the user-friendliness of GIS mapping technology caused retailers to become more research-driven in locating stores?
8. How is it possible for small retailers to use GIS? Isn't it expensive to use GIS?
9. Why do GISs include both physical and cultural geography? Provide some examples of physical and cultural data that should be included in a GIS.

LO 4 **What factors should be considered in identifying the most attractive retail market?**

10. Someone once said "build a better mousetrap and the world will beat a path to your door." If this is true, why is it important for a retailer to select the correct site within a trading area? Explain your answer.

11. What is the index of retail saturation? How is it used in making a location decision?

12. With the growth of Internet retailing, will the IRS increase or decrease in importance? Why?

13. According to Reilly's law of retail gravitation, cities attract trade from an intermediate place based on what two factors? How are these factors used in making a location decision?

14. Compute the index of retail saturation for the following three markets. The data for restaurants is:

Market	A	B	C
Annual retail expenditures per household	$739	$845	$903
Square feet of retail space	610,000	494,000	801,000
Number of households	126,000	109,000	163,000

Based on this data, which market is most attractive? What additional data would you find helpful in determining the attractiveness of the three markets?

LO 5 — What attributes should be considered in evaluating retail sites within a retail market?

15. Identify the factors you would consider most important in locating a fast-food restaurant. Compare these factors with the factors you would use in selecting a site for a supermarket.

16. Explain the concepts of demand density and supply density. Why are they important to retail decision making?

LO 6 — How is the best geographic site selected?

17. Why is it so hard to find that 100-percent retail location?

18. Why do some stores cluster around each other? Doesn't being so close to their competition hurt their profitability?

Sample Test Questions

LO 1 — Which of the following is not a criterion used to successfully reach a target market?

a. The market segment should be measurable.
b. Promotional efforts can be directed at the market segment.
c. The market segment should create high sales.
d. The market segment should be profitable.
e. Distribution efforts can be directed at the market segment.

LO 2 — Freestanding retailers offer the following advantages:

a. lack of direct competition
b. high drawing power from nearby complementary stores
c. higher traffic than shopping malls
d. lower advertising costs
e. stores must be leased

LO 3 Geographic information systems can be used for the following purposes:

a. site analysis
b. trade area definition
c. advertising management
d. merchandise management
e. all of the above

LO 4 The three sequential stages involved in selecting a location for a store-based retailer are:

a. identify the most understored markets, identify the most attractive sites that are available within each market, select the best site(s).
b. identify the most attractive markets, identify the most attractive sites that area available within each market, select the best site(s).
c. identify the most attractive markets, identify the vacant parcels of real estate within each market, select the best site(s).
d. identify the most understored markets, identify the vacant parcels of real estate within each market, negotiate terms for the best site.
e. identify the most attractive markets, identify the most attractive sites that are available within each market, negotiate for the lowest priced site.

LO 5 Site analysis consists of:

a. analysis of density of demand.
b. consideration of the type of neighbors.
c. analyzing sources of financing for the site (i.e., debt or equity financing).
d. determining the expected profitability from operating a store at the site.
e. considering the ease with which consumers can reach the site.

LO 6 Which of the following is not an important consideration in selecting the best site for a new retail store?

a. nature of the site
b. traffic characteristics of the site
c. alternative investments available to the retailer
d. potential profitability of the site
e. type of neighbors

Writing and Speaking Exercise

You have a summer job with a small florist shop, Forget-Me-Knot, in Troy, Illinois, a growing area a half-hour east of St. Louis, Missouri. Until recently, Forget-Me-Knot and a smaller flower shop located a mile away in the center of town were able to easily satisfy the demand for flowers and floral arrangements in the area. Kathy Kistenmacher, the owner, believes there is room for another store because of the increasing number of people moving from St. Louis to the small suburban town. In fact, between 2000 and 2010, the city's population increased from 11,000 to 15,500. Kistenmacher sells more than just flowers, which gives her a competitive advantage over other flower shops. She also sells novelty items such as figurines, candles, potpourri, and houseplants. These other items make up 25 percent of Kathy's gross sales.

The shop has been very busy, and sales are growing rapidly. The store is often very crowded between 4:30 p.m. and 6:30 p.m. Therefore, Kistenmacher is contemplating either expanding her current business or opening another store at a new location before someone else sees the opportunity. She does not have the financial capability to do both. The expansion would be less expensive, but another store might attract more customers. Current customer information is given in Exhibit 1.

Exhibit 1

1. Current sales: $452,000
2. Sales growth rate (annually since 2000): 15 percent annually
3. Percentage of customers living within 3 miles: 43 percent
4. Percentage of customers living within 3 to 6 miles: 30 percent
5. Percentage of customers living more than 6 miles: 27 percent
6. Average income of those living within 3 miles: $32,000
7. Average income of those living within 3 to 6 miles: $61,000

© Cengage Learning

Forget-Me-Knot is currently located at the edge of town 2 miles from the interstate to St. Louis on the main traffic artery from the interstate. Kistenmacher is considering two possible locations: One is in the middle of town, a half-mile from her current location and only two blocks from her competitor; the other location is next to the Interstate.

The in-town possibility is centrally located, and Kathy feels that this location would attract many people who shop at the renovated downtown shopping area. The highway location, on the other hand, is conveniently located in a small shopping complex. This location would appeal to commuters returning to the town proper from St. Louis. It would also be accessible to other commuters who live in the new subdivisions across the interstate.

Kathy feels that she has to make a change, but she cannot decide which location to choose, or whether she should renovate and expand the existing store. She can choose only one alternative.

Since you have taken a retailing class, Kathy asks for your advice. Therefore, based on the available information, write a memo telling Kathy if she should open another store or just expand her current location. Explain how you determined this strategy. If you recommend an additional store, tell her why you chose that location.

Retail Project

Small as well as large retailers can benefit immensely from knowing the trade area of their store. Identify a small local retailer such as a florist, pet store, apparel store, gift store, or restaurant. Contact the store owner or manager and tell him or her that you are a student studying retailing and would like to volunteer to construct a map of the retailer's trade area. To do this, you need to obtain the addresses of all the patrons over a one-week period and plot these on a map. Review the customer-spotting map for a supermarket in Exhibit 7.8 on page 288. Develop a method to collect the needed data and construct the map of the trade area. What percentage of customers are within 1 mile of the store? within 3 miles? within 5 miles?

Planning Your Own Entrepreneurial Retail Business

The retail store you are planning has an estimated circular trade radius of 4 miles. Within this 4-mile radius there is an average of 1,145 households per square mile. In a normal year, you expect that 47 percent of these households would visit your store (referred to as *penetration*) an average of 4.3 times (referred to as *frequency*). Based on those figures, what would you expect to be the traffic (i.e., number of visitors to your store per year)? (*Hint:* Traffic can be viewed as the square miles of the trade area multiplied by the household density multiplied by penetration, which is in turn multiplied by frequency.)

Once you answer this question, do some *sensitivity analysis*, which is an assessment of how sensitive store traffic is to changes in your assumptions about penetration and frequency. What happens if penetration drops to 45 percent or rises to 50 percent? What happens if frequency drops to 4.0 times annually or rises to 4.5 times annually? In this analysis, change only one thing at a time and hold all other assumptions constant.

Nordstrom Market Selection

Background

Founded in 1901 as a retail shoe business in Seattle, Nordstrom later incorporated in the state of Washington in 1946. Today, Nordstrom is one of the nation's leading fashion specialty retailers, with stores located in 30 states as of March 16, 2012. The west and east coasts of the United States are the areas in which Nordstrom has the largest presence.

As of March 16, 2012, Nordstrom included 116 'Nordstrom' branded full-line stores, an online store at www.nordstrom.com, and 105 off-price 'Nordstrom Rack' stores. Other retail channels include their online private sale subsidiary 'HauteLook' acquired in February 2011, two 'Jeffrey' boutiques, one philanthropic 'treasure&bond' store and one clearance store that operates under the name 'Last Chance.' HauteLook is a LosAngeles based e-tailer that offers flash sales on designer fashion merchandise may be a key to Nordstrom's future growth. HauteLook (www.hautelook.com) offers merchandise at 50-75% off regular price.

Growth Through Market Expansion

In the U.S. market it has been difficult for retailers to grow since household income adjusted for inflation is often flat if not negative. And even though Nordstrom appears to upper middle class households they have also been hit hard by the economy. Thus Nordstrom has grown via expansion into other states outside its home in Seattle, Washington. This actually is somewhat of a continuation of its store growth strategy going back twenty-five years but store growth and market expansion is more important than ever.

Between 2008 and 2011 continued its geographic expansion as shown in exhibits 1 and 2. Nordstrom generally opened between a dozen and 20 stores annually with the major focus on opening of Nordstrom Rack Stores. Over the last five years Nordstrom Rack stores have almost doubled. At the same time the firm experienced inconsistent financial and operating performance as shown in exhibit 3. In fact 2011 operating profits were lower than in 2007; a rather sobering experience for the senior management team. Some analysts are surprised why with this inconsistent operating performance the firm continues to increase its dividend to shareholders.

Exhibit 1
Nordstrom Store Growth (2008–2011)

State Store Opened In	2008	2009	2010	2011
Arizona			1	1
California	1	4	4	4
Colorado			1	1
Delaware				1
Florida	2	1	4	1
Georgia			1	
Hawaii	1			
Illinois	1	1	1	
Indiana	1			1
Kansas				1
Maryland				1
Massachusetts	2	1	2	1
Michigan	1			
Minnesota		1		
Missouri			1	1
New Jersey		2		1
New York	1		1	1
North Carolina			1	1
Ohio	1	2		
Oregon				1
Pennsylvania	1			
Tennessee				1
Texas	1	2	1	3
Utah		1		
Virginia			2	
Washington D.C.				1

Exhibit 2
Nordstrom Store Openings (2008–2011)

Exhibit 3

Nordstrom Financial and Operating Performance (fiscal year ended January 2007–2011)

	2007	2008	2009	2010	2011
Annual Sales	$8,828	$8,272	$8,258	$9,310	$10,497
Gross Profit	$3,302	$2,855	$2,930	$3,413	$3,905
Net Profit (After Taxes)	$715	$401	$441	$613	$683
Same store sales growth/decline	3.90%	−9.00%	−4.20%	8.10%	7.20%
Sales per square foot of retail space	$435	$388	$368	$397	$431
Inventory Turnover	5.16	5.20	5.41	5.56	5.56
# of Stores					
Nordstrom	101	109	112	115	117
Nordstrom Rack (and others)	55	60	72	89	108
Earnings per Share (Fully Diluted)	$2.88	$1.83	$2.01	$2.75	$3.14
Dividends per Share	0.54	0.64	0.64	0.76	0.92
# of New Stores		13	15	20	22

Note: Sales, Gross Profit, Net Profit in millions ($)

Questions

1. Why do you believe Nordstrom is opening more Nordstrom Rack Stores than its traditional Nordstrom stores?

2. Analyze Nordstrom's financial and operating performance and store growth and draw conclusions on the effectiveness of the market expansion strategy.

3. Register for the HauteLook website and evaluate if you think Nordstrom should put more of its emphasis on growth sales via e-tailing and less on its brick and mortar stores. Do the same for Nordstroms online store (www.nordstrom.com).

4. Should Nordstrom expand to markets outside the United States? If so, what markets do you think would be most attractive?

Source

SEC 10-K and Annual Report to Shareholders for Nordstrom, fiscal years 2007–2011. Three decades of authors experience as a Nordstrom shopper and observer of its retail competitive strategy.

Note: This case was prepared as a basis for class discussion rather than to illustrate either effective or ineffective handling of an administrative or strategic decision.

PART 3: INTEGRATIVE CASE
ZUMIEZ: WHERE TO EXPAND NEXT?

Zumiez, a publicly traded retailer, is a specialty retailer focusing on those in the teen to early 20s market who are seeking the action sports or "rider" lifestyle. These sports include snowboarding, skateboarding, surfing, BMX, and motocross. The merchandise mix reflects brands, which support and are symbols of this lifestyle. Zumiez has been successful in creating a store format that gives the store an independent specialty shop feel, despite the fact that it is a large chain. The company was founded in 1978, and by 2011, had grown to over 400 stores with a presence in 37 states.

In order to set itself apart from competition in the market, Zumiez focuses on a handful of competitive strengths to create its unique place in the market.

- *Attractive Lifestyle Retailing Concept*: The Zumiez brand not only appeals to action sports participants, but also those who aspire to associate with the lifestyle.
- *Differentiated Merchandising Strategy*: A wide variety of soft goods and hard goods across brands are carried in a Zumiez store. In fact, the highest selling brand (including private labels) in a given year typically represents roughly 7 percent of total sales. The depth of the merchandise assortment means that Zumiez typically carries products that cannot be found at other stores in the mall. Action sports gear and apparel is a trend style driven business and Zumiez's attempts to react to trends as quickly as possible to have a fresh assortment available in store. Finally, product assortment may vary by geographic region, based upon local preferences.
- *Deep-rooted Culture*: Customer service is a very important aspect of Zumiez's culture, and the company strives to promote management from within to maintain a consistent culture from top to bottom in the organization.
- *Distinctive Store Experience*: A typical Zumiez store is set up to encourage a longer shopping experience or simply "hanging out." Features such as couches encourage customers to interact with each other and store employees, creating a familiar environment that encourages frequent visits.
- *Disciplined Operating Philosophy*: A combination of measuring results, comprehensive training, and incentives to drive performance.
- *High Impact, Integrated Marketing Approach*: Zumiez focuses on reaching customers in their environment to fully immerse the company in the action sports lifestyle, to build the brand reputation, and to gather feedback from action sports participants. Activities such as local sporting and music event promotions, social media, and the Zumiez Couch Tour help build this relationship with customers. An annual free event which began in 2000, the Zumiez Couch Tour, features professional skateboarding exhibitions, live music, participative activities, and giveaways for festival goers. In 2011, the tour visited 12 cities, featured demos by 11 professional skate teams, and was headlined by the popular band Forever the Sickest Kids. Zumiez utilizes Facebook, YouTube, Twitter, and a Zumiez Couch Tour Ipad/Iphone app to provide interaction spaces for event goers, fans, and Zumiez customers.

Zumiez has been growing rapidly over the past five years, opening 233 new stores from 2006 to 2011. In 2011, Zumiez expanded into the Canadian market with the opening of stores in Toronto and Vancouver areas for a total of five Canadian locations. In addition to store expansion, Zumiez has an opportunity to grow its e-commerce sales. Currently e-commerce represents a small portion of Zumiez's business, especially for a target age range that is more likely to shop online than some others. E-commerce represented 1.7 percent, 2.5 percent, and 4.7 percent of Zumiez's sales in fiscal years 2008, 2009, and 2010, respectively.

Questions

1. Should Zumiez continue to expand in the United States and Canada or now try to enter other foreign countries? What foreign countries might represent viable markets?
2. Would Zumiez be better off focusing its growth strategy around enhancing its e-tailing venture?
3. Identify an area in the state or country you live in where you would see the potential for opening a Zumiez store. Explain your rationale.

Sources

Zumiez 2010 Annual Report (10k) Available at: http://www.sec.gov/Archives/edgar/data/1318008/000119312511067226/d10k.htm

Zumiez Couch Tour 2011, Available at: www.zumiezcouchtour.com/ [Accessed January 13, 2012].

Zumiez 2011 3Q Report (8Q) Interactive Data. Available at: http://www.sec.gov/cgi-bin/viewer?action=view&cik=1318008&accession_number=0001193125-11-328190&xbrl_type=v#

The author's multiple visits to Zumiez outlets over several years.

Note: This case was prepared by Mark Lusch as a basis for class discussion rather than to illustrate either effective or ineffective handling of an administrative situation.

Part 4

Managing Retail Operations

© Purestock/Thinkstock

© Juanmonino/iStockphoto

© scanrail/iStockphoto

© Losevsky Pavel/Shutterstock

© Moxie Productions/Getty Images

8

Managing a Retailer's Finances

Overview

In this chapter, we begin by looking at how a merchandise budget is prepared and how it is used when making plans for an upcoming merchandise season. Next we describe the basic differences among an income statement, a balance sheet, and a statement of cash flow, as well as discuss how a retailer uses these accounting statements in controlling its merchandising activities. Finally, we discuss the accounting inventory systems and pricing methods available to value inventory.

Learning Objectives

After reading this chapter, you should be able to:

1 Describe the importance of a merchandise budget and know how to prepare a six-month merchandise plan.

2 Explain the differences among and the uses of these three accounting statements: income statement, balance sheet, and statement of cash flow.

3 Explain how the retailer is able to value inventory.

LO 1

Describe the importance of a merchandise budget and how to prepare a six-month merchandise plan.

The Merchandise Budget

In Chapter 7, we described the role location plays in a retailer's success. Location is important and was discussed prior to the other elements of the retail mix because, for most new retailers, it is the first decision made. Also, once the location decision is made, it is difficult and costly to change.

Another important element of the retail mix is merchandising, which includes not only the merchandise to offer but its pricing. Some experts suggest that all other elements of the retail mix revolve around merchandising, especially when considering chain store operators. After all, most of the merchandise in a JCPenney's store in Grand Rapids, Michigan, is the same as that in Tulsa, Oklahoma; slight variations are most often due to climate. The same may be said about a Carrefour store in Buenos Aires, Argentina, and one in Paris, France. Only after these merchandising decisions are made can retailers concern themselves with the other retail mix elements: promotion, store layout and design, and customer service. However, before we can explain how to make these merchandising decisions, we must first discuss the retailer's means of controlling these activities.

Many people believe that the terms *retailing* and *merchandising* are synonymous; they are not. Retailing includes all the business activities necessary to sell goods and services to the final consumer. **Merchandising** is only one of these activities and is concerned with the planning and control involved in the buying and selling of goods and services to help the retailer realize its objectives. Success in merchandising is the result of total

merchandising
Is the planning and control of the buying and selling of goods and services to help the retailer realize its objectives.

financial planning and control. This chapter is divided into three sections: the merchandise budget, retail accounting statements, and inventory valuation.

Successful retailers must have good financial planning and control of their merchandise. The retailer invests money in merchandise for profitable resale to others. A poor choice of merchandise will result in low profits or maybe even a loss. Therefore, to be successful in retailing, the retailer must have a plan of what is to be accomplished. In retailing, this plan of operation is called the *merchandise budget*. A **merchandise budget** is a plan of projected sales for an upcoming season, when and how much merchandise is to be purchased, and what markups and reductions are likely to occur. The merchandise budget forces the retailer to develop a formal outline of all merchandising activities for the upcoming selling season.

In developing the merchandise budget, the retailer must answer five major merchandising questions:

merchandise budget
Is a plan of projected sales for an upcoming season, when and how much merchandise is to be purchased, and what markups and reductions will likely occur.

1. What are the anticipated sales for the department, division, or store?
2. How much stock on hand is needed to achieve this sales plan, given the level of inventory turnover expected?
3. What reductions, if any, from the original retail price are likely to be needed in order to dispose of all merchandise brought into the store?
4. What additional purchases must be made during the season?
5. What **gross margin** (the difference between sales and cost of goods sold) is the department, division, or store likely to contribute to the overall profitability of the company, given this merchandising plan?

gross margin
Is the difference between net sales and cost of goods sold.

When preparing the merchandise budget, a retailer must employ the following four rules. First, a merchandise budget should always be prepared in advance of the selling season. This is because buyers for particular departments often prepare their budgets for later approval by a divisional merchandising manager or general merchandising manager. As a result, most retail firms selling apparel or hard-line goods begin the process of developing a merchandise budget three to four months in advance of the budget period. Yet this is not always the case with some specialty retailers. For example, fine restaurants can easily order special selections like fresh fish on a daily basis. However, most retailers have only two seasons a year: (1) spring–summer, usually February through July; and (2) fall–winter, August through January. (Some small retailers may use a three-month budget where the four seasons begin in February, May, August, and November.) The buyer for a particular department will usually begin to prepare merchandise budgets in early March and September for the upcoming seasons.

Second, since the budget is a plan that management expects to follow during the upcoming merchandise season, the language must be easy to understand. The merchandise budget illustration contained in this chapter has only 11 items; however, the number of items contained in a budget may vary by company due to differences in the particular merchandise and market characteristics. Remember, unless the budget is understood by all decision makers, it serves no useful purpose.

Third, because the economy is consistently changing, the merchandise budget must be planned for a relatively short period of time. Six months is the norm for most retailers, although some retailers choose to use a three-month, or even shorter, plan. Forecasting future sales is difficult enough without complicating the process by projecting too far into the future. The firm's senior management should be concerned with long-term trends; buyers should focus more on short-term decisions that may influence the merchandise budget.

Fourth, the budget should be flexible enough to permit changes. All merchandise budgets are plans or estimates of predicted future events. As competition and consumers'

double_p/iStockphoto.com

Most retailers can plan their merchandise budgets three to four months in advance, but as the merchandise becomes more specialized and demand is unpredictable, it is more difficult, but just as important, to budget wisely.

tastes are not always predictable, particularly in regard to fashion preferences nor is weather accurately predictable, any forecast is subject to error and will need revision.

Keeping in mind this discussion of merchandising decisions and rules, review the blank six-month merchandising budget for the housewares department of a major department store shown in Exhibit 8.1. Do not be alarmed if Exhibit 8.1 is not clear to you at this point. As the chapter continues, we will describe why the budget is set up in this form. In addition, we will explain all the analytical tools necessary to calculate the numbers required when developing a six-month merchandise budget or plan.

Exhibit 8.1 may appear more confusing than it really is because each element is broken into four parts: last year, plan for the upcoming season, revised plan, and actual. This is merely a means of providing the decision maker with complete information. "Last year" refers to last year's sales for the period; "Plan" (plan for the upcoming season) is what the original plan projected; "Revised" shows the results of any revisions made due to changes in market conditions after the original plan was accepted; and "Actual" corresponds to the final, or realized, results.

Exhibit 8.2 presents the same material in a simpler form. Here we will only attempt to show you how and why a retailer develops a six-month merchandising plan. Exhibit 8.3

Exhibit 8.1
Sample Six-Month
Merchandise Budget

			SIX-MONTH MERCHANDISE BUDGET Housewares Department					
		February	March	April	May	June	July	Total
BOM Stock	Last Year							
	Plan							
	Revised							
	Actual							
Sales	Last Year							
	Plan							
	Revised							
	Actual							
Reductions	Last Year							
	Plan							
	Revised							
	Actual							
EOM STOCK	Last Year							
	Plan							
	Revised							
	Actual							
RETAIL PURCHASES	Last Year							
	Plan							
	Revised							
	Actual							
PURCHASES @ COST	Last Year							
	Plan							
	Revised							
	Actual							
INITIAL MARKUP	Last Year							
	Plan							
	Revised							
	Actual							
GROSS MARGIN DOLLARS	Last Year							
	Plan							
	Revised							
	Actual							
BOM STOCK/SALES RATIO	Last Year							
	Plan							
	Revised							
	Actual							
SALES PERCENTAGE	Last Year							
	Plan							
	Revised							
	Actual							
RETAIL REDUCTION PERCENTAGE	Last Year							
	Plan							
	Revised							
	Actual							

STOCKTURN: Last Year_____ Plan_____ Actual_____
ON ORDER – BEGINNING OF SEASON_____ Plan_____ Actual_____
EOM INVENTORY FOR LAST MONTH_____ Plan_____ Actual_____
REDUCTION PERCENTAGE_____ Plan_____ Actual_____
MARKUP PERCENTAGE_____ Plan_____ Actual_____

© Cengage Learning

is a summary of how all the numbers in the merchandise budget are determined. Exhibit 8.2 shows the spring–summer season, February through July, for the Two-Seasons Department Store, Department 353, with projected sales of $500,000, planned retail reductions of $50,000 (10 percent of sales), planned initial markup of 45 percent, and a planned gross margin on purchases of $208,750.

Exhibit 8.2

Two-Seasons Department Store, Department 353, Six-Month Merchandise Budget

	February	March	April	May	June	July	Total
1. Planned BOM Stock	$225,000	$300,000	$300,000	$250,000	$375,000	$300,000	--
2. Planned Sales	75,000	75,000	100,000	50,000	125,000	75,000	$500,000
3. Planned Retail Reductions	7,500	7,500	5,000	7,500	6,250	16,250	50,000
4. Planned EOM Stock	300,000	300,000	250,000	375,000	300,000	250,000	--
5. Planned Purchases at Retail	157,500	82,500	55,000	182,500	56,250	41,250	575,000
6. Planned Purchases at Cost	86,625	45,375	30,250	100,375	30,937.50	22,687.50	316,250
7. Planned Initial Markup	70,875	37,125	24,750	82,125	25,312.50	18,562.50	258,750
8. Planned Gross Margin	63,375	29,625	19,750	74,625	19,062.50	2,312.50	208,750
9. Planned BOM Stock-to-Sales Ratio	3	4	3	5	3	4	--
10. Planned Sales Percentage	15%	15%	20%	10%	25%	15%	100%
11. Planned Retail Reduction Percentage	10%	10%	5%	15%	5%	21.67%	10%

Planned Total Sales for the Period	$500,000
Planned Total Retail Reduction Percentage for the Period	10%
Planned Initial Markup Percentage	45%
Planned BOM Stock for August	$250,000

© Cengage Learning

Exhibit 8.3

Formulas for the Six-Month Budget

Determining Planned Sales for the Month

(Planned Sales Percentage for the Month) × (Planned Total Sales) = Planned Sales for the Month)

Determining Planned BOM Stock for the Month

(Planned Sales for the Month) × (Planned BOM Stock-to-Sales Ratio for the Month) = (Planned BOM Stock for the Month)

Determining Planned Retail Reductions for the Month

(Planned Sales for the Month) × (Planned Retail Reduction Percentage for the Month) = (Planned Retail Reductions for the Month)

Determining Planned EOM Stock for the Month

(Planned BOM Stock for the Next Month) = (Planned EOM Stock for the Current Month)

Determining Planned Purchases at Retail for the Month

(Planned Sales for the Month) + (Planned Retail Reductions for the Month) + (Planned EOM Stock for the Month) − (Planned BOM Stock for the Month) = (Planned Purchases at Retail for the Month)

Determining Planned Purchases at Cost for the Month

(Planned Purchases at Retail for the Month) × (100% − Planned Initial Markup Percentage) = (Planned Purchases at Cost for the Month)

Determining Planned Initial Markup for the Month

(Planned Purchases at Retail for the Month) × (Planned Initial Markup Percentage) = (Planned Initial Markup for the Month)
    or
(Planned Purchases at Retail for the Month) − (Planned Purchases at Cost for the Month) = (Planned Initial Markup for the Month)

Determining Planned Gross Margin for the Month

(Planned Initial Markup for the Month) − (Planned Retail Reductions for the Month) = (Planned Gross Margin for the Month)

© Cengage Learning

Determining Planned Sales

The initial step in developing a six-month merchandise budget is to estimate planned sales for the entire season as well as for each month. The buyer begins by examining the previous year's recorded sales. Adjustments are then made when planning sales for the upcoming merchandise budget. When comparing this year's sales to last year's sales, retailers do not always compare exact dates (i.e., comparing February 13, 2013, sales to February 13, 2012). This is because dates fall on different days of the week each year. For instance, as shown in Exhibit 8.4, February 13, 2012, is a Monday, normally a slow day in terms of retail sales, whereas the same date is a Wednesday in 2013. Therefore, retailers use a retail reporting calendar (see Exhibit 8.4), which divides the year into two seasons, each with six months. Thus, February 3, 2014, the first Monday of the 2014 spring season (and the first Monday of February for a retailer using the calendar), would be compared to February 4, 2013, which is the first Monday of the 2013 spring season. In the year 2012, the first Monday of the spring season was January 30.[1]

By using this calendar, retailers are better prepared to make direct comparisons to prior years. Yet many retailers such as those in fashion or apparel experience problems

Exhibit 8.4
Retail Reporting Calendar

SPRING 2013

FEB

S	M	T	W	T	F	S
3	4	5	6	7	8	9
10	11	12	13	14	15	16
17	18	19	20	21	22	23
24	25	26	27	28	1	2

MARCH

S	M	T	W	T	F	S
3	4	5	6	7	8	9
10	11	12	13	14	15	16
17	18	19	20	21	22	23
24	25	26	27	28	29	30
31	1	2	3	4	5	6

APRIL

S	M	T	W	T	F	S
7	8	9	10	11	12	13
14	15	16	17	18	19	20
21	22	23	24	25	26	27
28	29	30	1	2	3	4

MAY

S	M	T	W	T	F	S
5	6	7	8	9	10	11
12	13	14	15	16	17	18
19	20	21	22	23	24	25
26	27	28	29	30	31	1

JUNE

S	M	T	W	T	F	S
2	3	4	5	6	7	8
9	10	11	12	13	14	15
16	17	18	19	20	21	22
23	24	25	26	27	28	29
30	1	2	3	4	5	6

JULY

S	M	T	W	T	F	S
7	8	9	10	11	12	13
14	15	16	17	18	19	20
21	22	23	24	25	26	27
28	29	30	31	1	2	3

FALL 2013

AUG

S	M	T	W	T	F	S
4	5	6	7	8	9	10
11	12	13	14	15	16	17
18	19	20	21	22	23	24
25	26	27	28	29	30	31

SEPT

S	M	T	W	T	F	S
1	2	3	4	5	6	7
8	9	10	11	12	13	14
15	16	17	18	19	20	21
22	23	24	25	26	27	28
29	30	1	2	3	4	5

OCT

S	M	T	W	T	F	S
6	7	8	9	10	11	12
13	14	15	16	17	18	19
20	21	22	23	24	25	26
27	28	29	30	31	1	2

NOV

S	M	T	W	T	F	S
3	4	5	6	7	8	9
10	11	12	13	14	15	16
17	18	19	20	21	22	23
24	25	26	27	28	29	30

DEC

S	M	T	W	T	F	S
1	2	3	4	5	6	7
8	9	10	11	12	13	14
15	16	17	18	19	20	21
22	23	24	25	26	27	28
29	30	31	1	2	3	4

JAN

S	M	T	W	T	F	S
5	6	7	8	9	10	11
12	13	14	15	16	17	18
19	20	21	22	23	24	25
26	27	28	29	30	31	1

SPRING 2014

FEB

S	M	T	W	T	F	S
2	3	4	5	6	7	8
9	10	11	12	13	14	15
16	17	18	19	20	21	22
23	24	25	26	27	28	1

MARCH

S	M	T	W	T	F	S
2	3	4	5	6	7	8
9	10	11	12	13	14	15
16	17	18	19	20	21	22
23	24	25	26	27	28	29
30	31	1	2	3	4	5

APRIL

S	M	T	W	T	F	S
6	7	8	9	10	11	12
13	14	15	16	17	18	19
20	21	22	23	24	25	26
27	28	29	30	1	2	3

MAY

S	M	T	W	T	F	S
4	5	6	7	8	9	10
11	12	13	14	15	16	17
18	19	20	21	22	23	24
25	26	27	28	29	30	31

JUNE

S	M	T	W	T	F	S
1	2	3	4	5	6	7
8	9	10	11	12	13	14
15	16	17	18	19	20	21
22	23	24	25	26	27	28
29	30	1	2	3	4	5

JULY

S	M	T	W	T	F	S
6	7	8	9	10	11	12
13	14	15	16	17	18	19
20	21	22	23	24	25	26
27	28	29	30	31	1	2

FALL 2014

AUG

S	M	T	W	T	F	S
3	4	5	6	7	8	9
10	11	12	13	14	15	16
17	18	19	20	21	22	23
24	25	26	27	28	29	30

SEPT

S	M	T	W	T	F	S
31	1	2	3	4	5	6
7	8	9	10	11	12	13
14	15	16	17	18	19	20
21	22	23	24	25	26	27
28	29	30	1	2	3	4

OCT

S	M	T	W	T	F	S
5	6	7	8	9	10	11
12	13	14	15	16	17	18
19	20	21	22	23	24	25
26	27	28	29	30	31	1

NOV

S	M	T	W	T	F	S
2	3	4	5	6	7	8
9	10	11	12	13	14	15
16	17	18	19	20	21	22
23	24	25	26	27	28	29

DEC

S	M	T	W	T	F	S
30	1	2	3	4	5	6
7	8	9	10	11	12	13
14	15	16	17	18	19	20
21	22	23	24	25	26	27
28	29	30	31	1	2	3

JAN

S	M	T	W	T	F	S
4	5	6	7	8	9	10
11	12	13	14	15	16	17
18	19	20	21	22	23	24
25	26	27	28	29	30	31

SPRING 2015

FEB

S	M	T	W	T	F	S
1	2	3	4	5	6	7
8	9	10	11	12	13	14
15	16	17	18	19	20	21
22	23	24	25	26	27	28

MARCH

S	M	T	W	T	F	S
1	2	3	4	5	6	7
8	9	10	11	12	13	14
15	16	17	18	19	20	21
22	23	24	25	26	27	28
29	30	31	1	2	3	4

APRIL

S	M	T	W	T	F	S
5	6	7	8	9	10	11
12	13	14	15	16	17	18
19	20	21	22	23	24	25
26	27	28	29	30	1	2

MAY

S	M	T	W	T	F	S
3	4	5	6	7	8	9
10	11	12	13	14	15	16
17	18	19	20	21	22	23
24	25	26	27	28	29	30

JUNE

S	M	T	W	T	F	S
31	1	2	3	4	5	6
7	8	9	10	11	12	13
14	15	16	17	18	19	20
21	22	23	24	25	26	27
28	29	30	1	2	3	4

JULY

S	M	T	W	T	F	S
5	6	7	8	9	10	11
12	13	14	15	16	17	18
19	20	21	22	23	24	25
26	27	28	29	30	31	1

FALL 2015

AUG

S	M	T	W	T	F	S
2	3	4	5	6	7	8
9	10	11	12	13	14	15
16	17	18	19	20	21	22
23	24	25	26	27	28	29

SEPT

S	M	T	W	T	F	S
30	31	1	2	3	4	5
6	7	8	9	10	11	12
13	14	15	16	17	18	19
20	21	22	23	24	25	26
27	28	29	30	1	2	3

OCT

S	M	T	W	T	F	S
4	5	6	7	8	9	10
11	12	13	14	15	16	17
18	19	20	21	22	23	24
25	26	27	28	29	30	31

NOV

S	M	T	W	T	F	S
1	2	3	4	5	6	7
8	9	10	11	12	13	14
15	16	17	18	19	20	21
22	23	24	25	26	27	28

DEC

S	M	T	W	T	F	S
29	30	1	2	3	4	5
6	7	8	9	10	11	12
13	14	15	16	17	18	19
20	21	22	23	24	25	26
27	28	29	30	31	1	2

JAN

S	M	T	W	T	F	S
3	4	5	6	7	8	9
10	11	12	13	14	15	16
17	18	19	20	21	22	23
24	25	26	27	28	29	30

once a season when attempting these comparisons. Complications arise due to the movement of Easter (March 31 in 2013, April 20 in 2014, and April 15 in 2015) and Thanksgiving. For example, Easter is the 20th day of April in the 2014 reporting calendar, and the 15th day of April in 2015, but is on the last reporting day of the 2013 March calendar. As a result, March's sales will receive all the benefit of the 2013 Easter season, only half of the 2015, and will be somewhat better in April 2014 since Easter is on the 20th that year. In addition, Easter sales in 2014 should see an improvement from the warmer weather of later April, as many consumers in northern climates don't want to put a coat over a new Easter outfit.

Retail planning is also complicated by the number of "shopping days" between Thanksgiving and Christmas. During the fall season, the period between Thanksgiving and Christmas can vary in length by as much as a week. Since Thanksgiving is the fourth Thursday of November, it can fall between November 22 and 28. As a result, the number of days in the Christmas shopping season will vary from year to year. For example, the number of days between Thanksgiving and Christmas varies from 26 days in 2013 to 30 days in 2016.

The day of the week that a holiday falls on can also impact retailers. Consider Valentine's Day. When Valentine's falls on a Wednesday, many retailers are adversely affected, particularly restaurants. After all, it means an abbreviated romantic evening because most people have to get up early for work the next day. However, for others, like florists, a middle-of-the-week Valentine's is a plus. Midweek days (Tuesday, Wednesday, and Thursday) routinely translate into more flowers, particularly those pricey long-stemmed roses. After all, many of the recipients won't be taking a three- or four-day weekend and therefore will be getting the flowers at work where fellow workers will see them.

Still even the use of a retail reporting calendar cannot overcome many of the uncontrollable and unexpected variables retailers encounter when forecasting sales. Retailers are just now learning how to deal with the greatest uncontrollable variable they must face—the weather. As the chapter's "Service Retailing" box describes, the consequences of weather can have a major impact on a retailer's planned sales projections. During 2011, the Mississippi River experienced disastrous flooding, which had severe negative economic impact on Louisiana, Mississippi, Tennessee, and Missouri, and this impacted nearly a half million businesses and millions of people. Due to this, many individuals lost jobs, and consequently, retail sales were hurt, which resulted in more job loss. Such happenings tend to support the statement one retailer told an author years ago: "Retail sales forecasts are made so that astrologists look good with their projections."

Sometimes weather can produce unexpected consequences for retailers. For example, several years ago when Texas experienced an unusual number of days with 100°-plus heat, the tanning salons were surprisingly busy for a summer season. The simple explanation was that the outdoor heat was simply too intense for many normal "swimming pool tanners." The result was record business for the air-conditioned tanning salons. At the same time, however, business at local putt-putt courses was off nearly 50 percent. Similarly, in another part of the country, drier weather during winter resulted in the closure of many car washes that normally were busy clearing ice and snow remains off cars. After all, winter was their busiest time of the year.

In each of these situations, retailers were caught off guard by uncharacteristic changes in consumer buying behavior caused by the weather. Today, in view of the above-mentioned weather effects, even the smallest retailer should review the weather bureau's long-range forecast before making buying plans. For years, the late Robert Kahn, a respected retail consultant and long-time member of Walmart's board of directors, tried to convince Sam Walton that the effective use of weather forecasts presented the giant

© Smileus/Shutterstock

SERVICE — RETAILING

How Weather Forecasts Can Improve Retail Performance

Consider the case of auto-service retailers and car battery sales. As anyone who has lived above the Mason-Dixon line knows, finding your car battery dead on a cold morning is one of life's most unpleasant surprises. While all consumers know that frigid weather is the number-one cause of dead batteries, many car owners tend to postpone replacing their battery and are often unprepared when a battery problem occurs.

How can retailers use this information when forecasting sales? To start, it is imperative that they know the most conducive weather for a product's sales—in this case, car batteries—before developing a merchandising budget or planning promotional events.

Figure 1, for example, shows the deviation from average automotive battery sales in Minneapolis,

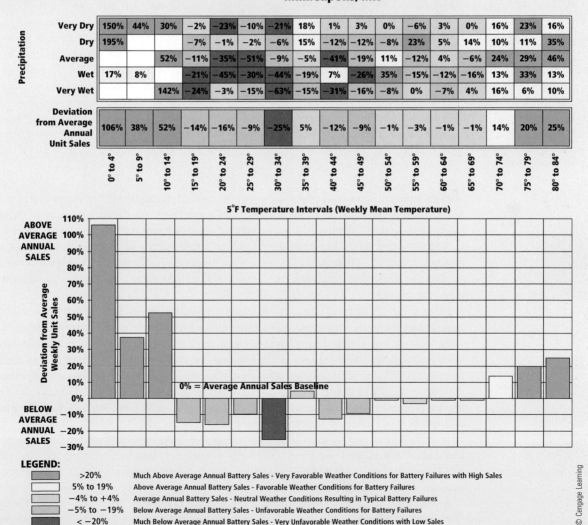

AUTOMOTIVE BATTERY SALES VS WEATHER
Minneapolis, MN

Precipitation	0° to 4°	5° to 9°	10° to 14°	15° to 19°	20° to 24°	25° to 29°	30° to 34°	35° to 39°	40° to 44°	45° to 49°	50° to 54°	55° to 59°	60° to 64°	65° to 69°	70° to 74°	75° to 79°	80° to 84°
Very Dry	150%	44%	30%	−2%	−23%	−10%	−21%	18%	1%	3%	0%	−6%	3%	0%	16%	23%	16%
Dry	195%			−7%	−1%	−2%	−6%	15%	−12%	−12%	−8%	23%	5%	14%	10%	11%	35%
Average			52%	−11%	−35%	−51%	−9%	−5%	−41%	−19%	11%	−12%	4%	−6%	24%	29%	46%
Wet	17%	8%		−21%	−45%	−30%	−44%	−19%	7%	−26%	35%	−15%	−12%	−16%	13%	33%	13%
Very Wet			142%	−24%	−3%	−15%	−63%	−15%	−31%	−16%	−8%	0%	−7%	4%	16%	6%	10%
Deviation from Average Annual Unit Sales	106%	38%	52%	−14%	−16%	−9%	−25%	5%	−12%	−9%	−1%	−3%	−1%	−1%	14%	20%	25%

5°F Temperature Intervals (Weekly Mean Temperature)

ABOVE AVERAGE ANNUAL SALES

Deviation from Average Weekly Unit Sales

0% = Average Annual Sales Baseline

BELOW AVERAGE ANNUAL SALES

LEGEND:

	>20%	Much Above Average Annual Battery Sales - Very Favorable Weather Conditions for Battery Failures with High Sales
	5% to 19%	Above Average Annual Battery Sales - Favorable Weather Conditions for Battery Failures
	−4% to +4%	Average Annual Battery Sales - Neutral Weather Conditions Resulting in Typical Battery Failures
	−5% to −19%	Below Average Annual Battery Sales - Unfavorable Weather Conditions for Battery Failures
	< −20%	Much Below Average Annual Battery Sales - Very Unfavorable Weather Conditions with Low Sales
	Blank	No Sales in the Data Set Occurred in This Precipitation & Temperature Interval

© Cengage Learning

(continued)

Minnesota, in 5° intervals across five precipitation categories. Temperatures are defined as a weekly mean temperature. Therefore, when it is really cold, with weekly mean temperatures below 14° (implying high temperatures in the middle 20s and low temperatures in the middle single digits), there is a 52-percent increase in battery sales due to weather-driven failures. (Notice that there is a 66-percent swing in sales with just a 5° drop from 19° to 14°.)

Consider the problems a retailer might face if it planned a battery promotion for a particular winter week in Minneapolis only to see temperatures rise unexpectedly to a balmy weekly mean of 32° (high temperatures in the 40s) that week. There probably wouldn't be an increase in battery sales, and the advertising dollars would be wasted!

Figure 1 illustrates the importance of using weather forecasts when projecting sales. Historically, when the Minneapolis area has a weekly mean of 32° along with very wet conditions (200 percent above average rain or snowfall), battery sales will fall 63 percent below average sales. Conversely, if colder weather is predicted—say, 0° to 4°—sales should increase by 106 percent over average. The product–weather matrix also illustrates that temperatures between 15° and 49° generally result in fewer battery failures and resulting lower sales.

Between 50° and 69°, battery sales are near average, with little impact due to weather. However, when temperatures are 70° or higher, failures increase 14 percent to 25 percent above average, and extremely hot weather—above 80° with average precipitation—results in peak summer sales of nearly 50 percent above average. (High temperatures would be in the middle 90s in Minneapolis.) By using a reliable weather forecast to determine the most likely really cold and really hot weeks, Minneapolis retailers are better prepared to strategically plan battery inventory levels and craft-effective retailing promotional plans. Conversely, battery retailers located in Southern cities, which do not get cold enough in the winter months to result in failures, should make forecasts based on hot summer weather.

The product–weather matrix can be done for any category by assessing weekly unit sales against past weather conditions for several years to identify the optimal combination of temperature and precipitation for sales of a particular product. Sales can then be grouped by temperature and precipitation intervals and expressed as a unit value or deviation from average annual sales.

Source: The information used in this box was based on Bill Kirk, "Better Business in Any Weather," *ICSC's Research Review*, Vol. 12, no. 2 (2005): 28–34, and used with the written permission of Bill Kirk, CEO and cofounder of Weather Trends International (www.wxtrends.com).

retailer with an opportunity to gain a competitive advantage over its competitors.[2] As a result, most large retailers have now elected to use the sophisticated services of private forecasters such as Weather Trends International (www.wxtrends.com) that have historical data tied to product category sales and tailored to all the locations where the retailer is located. These specific weather projections aid the retailer's sales forecasting so that its gross margins aren't damaged, out of stocks are reduced, and inventory turns are boosted.

Of course, not all sales forecasts are based on weather predictions; many other factors, such as the economy, must also come into consideration. One retailer known for considering a wide variety of factors when estimating future sales is San Francisco–based Williams-Sonoma. Best known for its catalog for cooks, Williams-Sonoma's secret for forecasting sales rests highly on its automated mailing lists. Its database of 5 million customers tracks as many as 150 different pieces of information per customer. With a few keystrokes, the retailer can tell you what you've bought from each of its five annual catalogs (an estimated 60 percent of customers have bought from more than one), what time of the year you tend to buy, how often you buy, what category of merchandise you lean toward, and so forth. Through a complex cross-referencing of the data, Williams-Sonoma's two fulltime statisticians are able to project, within 5 percent (on average), each catalog's sales.

Forecasting is most important for service retailers because their services are perishable. Services present unique forecasting problems for retailers because, unlike physical products, they cannot be produced or manufactured, boxed, stored, and shelved.

AP Photo/David Zalubowsk

When perishability is a problem, forecasting is difficult at best, especially when sales get impacted by things like the weather.

In fact, services theoretically perish the moment they are produced. This perishability is not a problem when demand is steady. However, when demand fluctuates, service retailers have problems. As a result, service retailers often try to balance their demand and supply by continually altering their retail mix in an attempt to better manage sales.

Many restaurant chains now seek to balance their supply and demand with the aid of a computer program that tracks the sales of every menu item on an hourly basis and sets cooking schedules based on the program. After consulting the printout, the restaurant's manager can determine how many baked potatoes to cook and when to put them in the oven so as to meet the expected demand. While it's not completely accurate, the computer bats close to 90 percent, according to one Texas steak-house manager. The same program can also be used to order merchandise and schedule hourly employees. The computer program alone saves the Texas retailer more than 25 hours a week in hand calculations.

One of the high-technology developments that allow retailers to forecast sales more accurately is the **prediction market**. A prediction market is a market where a synthetic financial security reflects if a future event will or will not occur and individuals then buy and sell this security. For instance, the financial instrument could represent such events as: (a) December retail sales for the company will grow by greater than 4 percent compared to last year, (b) the Father's Day promotion of chain saws will result in sales exceeding 2500 units, (c) the stores in our Western Region will have the highest same-store-sales growth during calendar year 2014. When retailers use prediction markets, they give employees artificial currency to buy and sell these securities with special prizes for those traders that create the most artificial currency. Prediction markets are especially useful in large retail organizations where it is difficult for employees to directly share their insights and knowledge with the CEO or President. You can learn how Best Buy is using prediction markets in the following YouTube video (http://www.youtube.com/watch?v=keVL0PkCpaQ), and also learn more about these markets in general at the following link (http://www.youtube.com/watch?v=YtocVDXZbHQ). Incidentally, Consensus Point (http://www.consensuspoint.com) is a market research firm that has

prediction market
A market where a synthetic financial security reflects if a future event will or will not occur and individuals then trade (buy and sell) this security.

developed prediction market software. It has found that events such as the success of a new product introduction or forthcoming promotion that are six to eight weeks in the future can be predicted very well by customers, supply chain partners, or employees.

Now let's return to the example in Exhibit 8.2. After reviewing the data available, the buyer for Department 353 forecasts that $500,000 was a reasonable total sales figure for the future season. Both June, with a projected 25 percent of the total season's sales, and April, with 20 percent, are expected to be the busiest months. May, with only 10 percent, is expected to be the slowest month. The remaining months will have equal sales. Since April, May, and June account for 55 percent of total sales, then February, March, and July's total must be 45 percent or 15 percent per month since they are equal. The buyer is able to determine planned monthly sales by multiplying the planned monthly sales percentage by planned total sales. Since we know February's planned monthly sales are 15 percent of the total planned sales of $500,000, February's planned sales must be $75,000 (15% × $500,000 = $75,000).

It is important to use recent trends when forecasting sales. All too often retailers in nongrowth markets merely use last season's figures for the current season's budget. This method overlooks two major influences on projected sales volume: inflation and competition. If inflation is 10 percent and no other changes have occurred in the retail environment, then the retailer planning on selling the same physical volume as the previous year should expect a 10-percent increase in this season's dollar sales. Of course, recently, prices have not increased much; for instance, in 2010 a Hermes Kelly Bag in Calfskin was priced at $7300 and in 2012 the same bag was $7,500, or a modest 2.7 percent increase over two years. But nonetheless, if a fashion retailer sold 100 of these purses annually the sales in 2012 would be $750,000 versus $730,000 in 2010. Similarly, if the exit of a competitor across town is expected to increase the number of customer transactions by 5 percent, this increase should be reflected in the budget. Suppose that last year's sales were $100,000, inflation is 10 percent, and the retailer expects its market share to increase by 8 percent while the total market remains stable. What should the projected sales be? A simple equation used in retail planning is

$$\text{total sales} = \text{average sale} \times \text{total transactions}$$

In the preceding example, average sales would increase by the 10 percent level of inflation to 1.10 times last year's sales, and total transactions would increase by the 8 percent gain in market share to 1.08 times last year's total transactions, for an increase in total sales of 1.188 times (or 1.10 × 1.08). This increase will then result in a total sales increase of $18,800 or budgeted total sales of $118,800.

Determining Planned BOM and EOM Inventories

Once the buyer has estimated seasonal and monthly sales for the upcoming season, plans can be made for inventory requirements. In order to achieve projected sales figures, the retailer will generally carry stock or inventory in excess of planned sales for the period, be it a week, month, or season. The extra stock or inventory provides a merchandise assortment deep and broad enough to meet customer needs. A common method of estimating the amount of stock to be carried is the **stock-to-sales ratio**. This ratio depicts the amount of stock to be on hand at the beginning of each month to support the forecasted sales for that month. For example, a ratio of 5:1 would suggest that the retailer have $5 in inventory (at retail price) for every $1 in forecasted sales. Planned average beginning-of-the-month (BOM) stock-to-sales ratios are often either (1) based on industry averages which are available from retail trade associations like the National Retail Federation in the United States (www.nrf.com) and the Australian Retailers Association (www.ara.com.au) or (2) calculated directly from a retailer's planned turnover goals.

stock-to-sales ratio
Depicts the amount of stock to have at the beginning of each month to support the forecasted sales for that month.

To calculate a retailer's stock-to-sales ratio based on its desired turnover rate, suppose a retailer wants a target turnover rate of 4.0. By dividing the annual turnover rate into 12 (the number of months in a year), the average BOM stock-to-sales ratio for the year can be computed. In this case, 12 divided by 4.0 equals 3.0. Thus, the average stock-to-sales ratio for this retailer's upcoming season would be 3.

Generally, stock-to-sales ratios will fluctuate month to month because sales tend to fluctuate monthly. Nevertheless, it is important to always review these ratios because, if they are set too high or too low, too little or too much inventory will be on hand to meet the sales target. Remember, it is just as bad to have too much inventory on hand as it is to have too little. Stocking too much inventory could result in inventory-holding costs that offset much if not consume all of the gross margins to be made on the sale of merchandise.

Returning to our earlier example, based on available data, the buyer for Department 353 in Exhibit 8.2 used a planned stock-to-sales ratio of 3.0 for February, April, and June; a ratio of 4.0 for March and July; and a ratio of 5.0 for May. The buyer was able to determine that $300,000 worth of merchandise was needed beginning March 1 due to a planned stock-to-sales ratio of 4.0 and planned sales of $75,000 (line 1). Two things should be noted. First, stock-to-sales ratios always express inventory levels at retail, not cost. Second, the BOM inventory for one month is equal to the end-of-the month (EOM) inventory for the previous month. This relationship can be easily seen by comparing the BOM figures (line 1) for one month with the EOM figures for the previous month (line 4).

Determining Planned Retail Reductions

All merchandise brought into the store for sale to consumers is not actually sold at the planned initial markup price. Therefore, when preparing the merchandise budget, the buyer should make allowances for reductions in the dollar level of inventory that results from nonsale events. Generally, these planned retail reductions fall into three types: markdowns, employee discounts, and stock shortages. These reductions must be planned because, as the dollar value of the inventory level is reduced, the BOM stock that is planned to support next month's forecasted sales will be inadequate unless adjustments are made this month. A buyer must remember that reductions are part of the cost of doing business.

A small number of retailers do not include planned reductions in their merchandise budgets. They simply treat them as part of the normal operation of the store and feel they should be controlled without being a separate line item in the budget. This gives management an understated, conservative planned-purchase figure, thereby having the effect of holding back some purchase reserve until the physical inventory reveals the exact amount of reductions. We have chosen to include planned reductions in this text for two reasons: (1) to reflect the additional purchases needed for sufficient inventory to begin the next month and (2) to point out that taking a reduction is not a bad thing. All too often, inexperienced retailers believe that taking a reduction is an admission of error, and therefore they fail to mark down merchandise until it is too late in the season. A buyer must remember that reductions are part of the cost of doing business. Methods available to the retail buyer for minimizing retail reductions caused by retailer mistakes are discussed in Chapter 10.

It should be noted that the reductions in our six-month budget are listed as a percentage of planned sales. The buyer in our example has estimated monthly retail reduction percentages as shown on line 11. To determine planned retail reductions for March (line 3), planned monthly sales are multiplied by the planned monthly retail reduction percentage to yield the planned monthly retail reduction of $7,500 ($75,000 × 10% = $7,500).

Reductions are one of the major items in the merchandise budget subject to constant change. One reason is that the planned reductions may prove inadequate in light of actual conditions encountered by the retailer. If retailers delay too long in taking reductions, especially those resulting from unexpected weather, they may be forced to take even larger price cuts later as the merchandise style depreciates even more in value. Alternatively, consider what happens when the department manager does such an effective merchandising job that not all the reduction money is needed for the period. The solution to both these dilemmas is found in the rules for developing a budget; namely, keeping it flexible so it can be intelligently administered.

Determining Planned Purchases at Retail and Cost

We are now ready to determine whether additional purchases must be made during the merchandising season. The retailer will need inventory for (1) planned sales, (2) planned retail reductions, and (3) planned EOM inventory. Planned BOM inventory represents purchases that have already been made. In the six-month merchandise budget shown in Exhibit 8.2, the March planned purchases at retail for Department 353 are $82,500 (line 5). This figure was derived by (1) adding planned sales, planned retail reductions, and planned EOM inventory and (2) subtracting planned BOM inventory:

$$\$75,000 + \$7,500 + \$300,000 - \$300,000 = \$82,500$$

Once planned purchases at retail are determined, planned purchases at cost can be easily calculated. The retail price always represents a combination of cost plus markup. If the markup percentage is given, then the portion of retail attributed to cost, or the cost complement, can be derived by subtracting the markup percentage from the retail percentage of 100 percent. Given that the markup percentage is 45 percent of retail for Department 353, the cost complement percentage must be 55 percent (100% − 45% = 55%). Planned purchases at cost for March (line 6) must be 55 percent of planned purchases at retail or $45,375 ($82,500 × 55% = $45,375). Planned initial markup for March (line 7) must be 45 percent of planned purchases, or $37,125 ($82,500 × 45% = $37,125).

Determining the Buyer's Planned Gross Margin

The buyer is accountable for the purchases made, the expected selling price of these purchases, the cost of these purchases, and the reductions that are involved in selling merchandise the buyer has previously purchased. Therefore, the last step in developing the merchandise budget is determining the buyer's planned gross margin for the period. As already discussed, in making plans the buyer recognizes that the initial selling price for all the products will probably not be realized and that some reductions will occur. Referring to Exhibit 8.2, the buyer's planned gross margin for February (line 8) is determined by taking planned initial markup (line 7) and subtracting planned reductions (line 3) ($70,875 − $7,500 = $63,375).

LO 2

Explain the differences among and the uses of these three accounting statements: income statement, balance sheet, and statement of cash flow.

Retail Accounting Statements

Successful retailing also requires sound accounting practices. The number and types of accounting records needed depend on management's objectives. Large retailers generally require more detailed information, usually based on merchandise lines or departments. Smaller retailers may be able to make firsthand observations of sales and inventory levels and make decisions before financial data are available. For example, a retailer in a developing country owning and operating a 100-square-foot store can easily use observation to obtain a general idea of the store's inventory. Still, the small retailer should consult the accounting records to confirm personal observations.

Properly prepared financial records provide measurements of profitability and retail performance. In addition, they show all transactions occurring within a given time period. However, these financial records must provide the manager not only with a look at the past but also a preview of the future so as to allow the manager to plan. Financial records not only indicate if a retailer has achieved good results but also demonstrate what growth potential and problem areas lay ahead. Some examples are:

1. Is one merchandise line outperforming or underperforming the rest of the store?
2. Is the inventory level adequate for the current sales level?
3. Is the firm's debt level too high (does the firm owe too much money)?
4. Are reductions, including markdowns, too high a percentage of sales?
5. Is the gross margin adequate for the firm's profit objectives?
6. Is the payroll expense out of line in relation to sales volume?

These are just a few of the questions that the financial data must answer for the retailer. The authors know of one company where merchandise line "X" was generating an annual profit of $800,000, and merchandise line "Y" was losing money at the rate of $600,000 a year. Management was totally unaware of the situation, just happy to be making $200,000! They were astounded when a little accounting work revealed the true situation.

Let's look at the three financial statements most commonly used by retailers: the income statement, the balance sheet, and the statement of cash flow.

Income Statement

income statement
Is a financial statement that provides a summary of the sales and expenses for a given time period, usually a month, quarter, season, or year.

The most important financial statement a retailer prepares is the income statement (also referred to as the *profit and loss statement*). The **income statement** provides a summary of the sales and expenses for a given time period, usually monthly, quarterly, seasonally,

Small retail firms should examine their financial statements and use that information just like large retailers that are traded on the New York Stock Exchange.

Dreamstime.com/Americanspirit

or annually. Comparison of current results with prior results allows the retailer to notice trends or changes in sales, expenses, and profits. However, given the large number of recent accounting scandals, the mere fact that a company reports increased earnings each year and the income statement looks great should not lead one to believe that everything is fine.

Income statements can be broken down by departments, divisions, branches, and so on, enabling the retailer to evaluate each subunit's operating performance for the period. The most common breakdown is the individual store, and hence if you are a chain store manager, expect to be evaluated on how your store's income statement looks; probably on a monthly or at least quarterly basis. Probably the regional manager is going to pay close attention to your gross margin and also payroll expenses. Exhibit 8.5a shows the basic format for an income statement, and Exhibit 8.5b shows the income statement for TMD Furniture.

Gross sales are the retailer's total sales, including sales for cash or for credit. **Returns and allowances** are reductions from gross sales. Here the retailer makes a financial adjustment for customers who became dissatisfied with their purchases and returned the merchandise to the retailer. Since these reductions represent cancellations of previously recorded sales, the gross sales figure must be reduced to reflect these changes.

Net sales, gross sales less returns and allowances, represents the amount of merchandise the retailer actually sold during the given time period. Sometimes it is difficult to determine what figure to report for net sales. For instance if a retail automobile dealer offers a rebate of $1000 on used automobiles, is the $1000 a reduction in net sales or treated as a promotional expense? If treated as a promotional expense then a car that sells for $12,000 plus a $1000 rebate would reflect net sales of $13,000; whereas if the rebate is treated as a reduction of net sales the net sales would be $12,000. If this auto dealer had 10 such sales during its special "rebate" sales event then the net sales could be either $130,000 or $120,000! Yes, accounting methods and procedures do make a difference.

Cost of goods sold is the cost of merchandise that has been sold during the period. While this concept is easy to understand, the exact calculation of the cost of goods sold is somewhat complex. For example, like their own customers, retailers may obtain some return privileges or receive some allowances from vendors, such as a cash discount for prompt payment (which will be discussed in Chapter 9). Also, there is the issue of determining how inventory levels will be carried on the company's books. This will be fully discussed in the next section of this chapter.

Gross margin is the difference between net sales and cost of goods sold or the amount available to cover operating expenses and produce a profit.

gross sales
Are the retailer's total sales including sales for cash or for credit.

returns and allowances
Are refunds of the purchase price or downward adjustments in selling prices due to customers returning purchases, or adjustments made in the selling price due to customer dissatisfaction with product or service performance.

net sales
Are gross sales less returns and allowances.

cost of goods sold
Is the cost of merchandise that has been sold during the period.

gross margin
Is the difference between net sales and cost of goods sold.

Exhibit 8.5a
Retailers' Basic Income Statement Format

Gross Sales		$_____
—Returns and Allowances	$_____	
Net Sales		$_____
—Cost of Goods Sold	$_____	
Gross Margin		$_____
—Operating Expenses	$_____	
Operating Profit		$_____
±Other Income or Expenses	$_____	
Net Profit Before Taxes		$_____

© Cengage Learning

Exhibit 8.5b
Sample Income Statement

TMD Furniture, Inc.
Six-Month Income Statement
July 31

			Percentage
Gross Sales		$393,671.79	
Less: Returns and Allowances		16,300.00	
Net Sales			
Less: Cost of Goods Sold		$377,371.79	100%
Beginning Inventory	$ 98,466.29		
Purchases	218,595.69		
Goods Available for Sales	$317,061.98		
Ending Inventory	103,806.23	213,255.75	56.5%
Gross Margin		$164,116.04	43.5%
Less: Operating Expenses			
Salaries & Wages:			
Managers	$18,480.50		
Selling	17,755.65		
Office	7,580.17		
Warehouse & Delivery	6,685.99	50,502.31	
Advertising		$ 15,236.67	
Administration and Warehouse Charge		800.00	
Credit, Collections, and Bad Debts		1,973.96	
Contributions		312.50	
Delivery		1,434.93	
Depreciation		5,398.56	
Dues		23.50	
Employee Benefits		566.26	
Utilities		3,738.74	
Insurance		3,041.75	
Legal and Auditing		1,000.00	
Merchandise Service & Repair		1,439.16	
Miscellaneous		602.00	
Rent		9,080.00	
Repairs & Maintenance		1,576.99	
Sales Allowances		180.50	
Supplies, Postage		1,135.40	
Taxes:			
City, County, & State	$ 2,000.00		
Payroll	3,902.90	5,902.90	
Telephone		1,520.09	
Travel		404.92	
Warehouse Handling Charges		12,216.86	118,088.00	31.3%
Operating Profit		$ 46,028.04	12.2%
Other Income:			
Carrying Charges		$ 3,377.48	
Profit on Sale of Parking Lot		740.47	4,117.95	1.1%
Net Profit Before Taxes		$ 50,145.99	13.3%

operating expenses
Are those expenses that a retailer incurs in running the business other than the cost of the merchandise.

Operating expenses are those expenses that a retailer incurs while running the business other than the cost of the merchandise sold (e.g., rent, wages, utilities, depreciation, advertising, and insurance).

Retailers must consider not only Generally Accepted Accounting Principles (GAAP) regulations when presenting their income statement, but also Internal Revenue Service (IRS) rulings. The IRS provided a tax break for retailers by ruling that they may estimate inventory shrinkage (the loss of merchandise through theft, loss, and damage).[3] This enables retailers to reduce ending inventory and thus taxable earnings. Prior to this change, which resulted from court cases involving Kroger and Target, the IRS did not permit retailers to estimate shrinkage from the last physical inventory to the end of the retailer's tax year, usually the end of January. Since it is not feasible for most retail chains to physically count their entire inventory in a single day in late January, most chains check inventory on a rotating basis throughout the year and can now estimate their losses without being challenged by the IRS.

operating profit
Is gross margin less operating expenses.

other income or expenses
Includes income or expense items that the firm incurs which are not in the course of its normal retail operations.

Operating profit is gross margin less operating expenses.

Other income or expenses includes income or expense items that the firm incurs outside the course of its normal retail operations. For example, a retailer might have purchased some land to use for expansion and, after careful deliberation, postponed the expansion plans. Now suppose the retailer rents that land. Since renting land is not in the normal course of business for a retailer, the rent received would be considered other income. Likewise, many convenience stores place income from selling money orders under other income, and supermarkets report the rent received from banks and pharmacies operating in their buildings as other income.

It is also on this line of the income statement that most grocery chains report the revenue from their nonselling activities such as slotting fees, promotional allowances, and free goods, because this revenue is considered to be earned by buying merchandise rather than selling it.

net profit
Is operating profit plus or minus other income or expenses.

Net profit is operating profit plus or minus other income or expenses. Net profit is the figure on which the retailer pays taxes and thus is usually referred to as net profit before taxes.

Many retailers actually divide the income statement into two sections: the *top half*, those items above the gross margin total, and the *bottom half*, those items below the gross margin total. Sales and cost of goods sold are essentially controllable by the buying functions of the retail organization. In more and more retailing operations today, the buying organization is separate from the store management team, which is primarily concerned with the operating expenses that are shown below gross margin. As a result, store managers often look at gross margin from the bottom up and use this formula:

$$\text{gross margin} = \text{operating expenses} + \text{profit}$$

Sometimes retailers use the terms *top line* (sales), *gross* (gross margin), *line above the bottom* (other income), and *bottom line* (profit) when referring to the key elements of their income statement.

Finally, it is important to point out that, just as they do in the reporting of revenues, GAAP allows for variations in how retailers report certain expenses. Preopening expenses, for example, can be expensed as they occur, during the month the store opens, or capitalized and written off over several years. Advertising can be written off when the ad runs or when payment is made. Store fixtures can be depreciated over five years, 40 years, or some increment in between. Thus, when comparing the financial statements of different retailers, it is important to know how each retailer treated these and other expenses.

asset
Is anything of value that is owned by the retail firm.

current assets
Are assets that can be easily converted into cash within a relatively short period of time (usually a year or less).

accounts and/or notes receivable
Are amounts that customers owe the retailer for goods and services.

prepaid expenses
Are those items for which the retailer has already paid, but the service has not been completed.

retail inventories
Comprise merchandise that the retailer has in the store or in storage and is available for sale.

Balance Sheet

The second accounting statement used in financial reporting is the balance sheet. A balance sheet shows the financial condition of a retailer's business at a particular point in time, as opposed to the income statement, which reports on the activities over a period of time. The balance sheet identifies and quantifies all the firm's assets and liabilities. The difference between assets and liabilities is the owner's equity or net worth. Comparing a current balance sheet with one from a previous time period enables a retail analyst to observe changes in the firm's financial condition.

A typical balance sheet format is illustrated in Exhibit 8.6. As Exhibit 8.6a shows, the basic equation for a balance sheet is

$$\text{assets} = \text{liabilities} + \text{net worth}$$

Hence, both sides always must be in balance. Exhibit 8.6b shows the balance sheet for TMD Furniture.

An **asset** is anything of value that is owned by the retail firm. Assets are broken down into two categories: current and noncurrent.

Current assets include cash and all other items that the retailer can easily convert into cash within a relatively short period of time (generally, a year). Besides cash, current assets include accounts receivable, notes receivable, prepaid expenses, and inventory. **Accounts receivable** and **notes receivable** are amounts that customers owe the retailer for goods and services. Frequently, the retailer will reduce the total receivables by a fixed percentage (based on past experience) to take into account those customers who may be unwilling or unable to pay. **Prepaid expenses** are items such as trash collection or insurance for which the retailer has already paid but the service has not been completed. **Retail inventories** make up merchandise that the retailer has in the store or in storage and is available for sale.

Exhibit 8.6a
Retailers' Basic Balance Sheet Format

Current Assets			Current Liabilities		
Cash	$___		Accounts Payable	$___	
Accounts Receivable	$___		Payroll Payable	$___	
Inventory	$___		Current Notes Payable	$___	
Prepaid Expenses	$___		Taxes Payable	$___	
Total Current Assets		$___	Total Current Liabilities		$___
Noncurrent Assets			Long-term Liabilities		
Building (less depreciation)	$___		Long-term Notes		
Fixtures and Equipment			Payable	$___	
(less depreciation)	$___		Mortgage Payable	$___	
Total Noncurrent Assets		$___			
Goodwill		$___	Total Long-term Liabilities		$___
			Net Worth		
			Capital Surplus	$___	
			Retained Earnings	$___	
			Total Net Worth		$___
			Total Liabilities and		
Total Assets		$___	**Net Worth**		$___

Exhibit 8.6b
Sample Balance Sheet

TMD Furniture, Inc.
Balance Sheet
July 31

Current Assets		Current Liabilities	
Cash	$ 11,589	Accounts Payable	$57,500
Accounts Receivable	71,517	Payroll Payable	1,451
Inventory	103,806	Current Notes Payable	14,000
		Taxes Payable	1,918
Total Current Assets	$186,912	Total Current Liabilities	$ 74,869
Noncurrent Assets		Long-term Liabilities	
Building (less depreciation)	$ 61,414	Long-term Notes Payable	$52,750
Fixtures and Equipment		Mortgage Payable	38,500
(less depreciation)	11,505		
Total Noncurrent Assets	72,919	Total Long-term Liabilities	$ 91,250
Goodwill	100	Net Worth	93,812
		Total Liabilities and	
Total Assets	$259,931	**Net Worth**	$259,931

Nordstrom has created a high degree of brand equity for the Nordstrom name by focusing on high levels of personalized customer service. Nonetheless, accounting standards in the United States do not allow the brand equity to be recorded on Nordstrom's balance sheet.

noncurrent assets
Are those assets that cannot be converted to cash in a short period of time (usually 12 months) in the normal course of business.

goodwill
Is an intangible asset, usually based on customer loyalty, that a retailer pays for when buying an existing business.

total assets
Equal current assets plus noncurrent assets plus goodwill.

liability
Is any legitimate financial claim against the retailer's assets.

current liabilities
Are short-term debts that are payable within a year.

accounts payable
Are amounts owed to vendors for goods and services.

long-term liabilities
Are debts that are due in a year or longer.

total liabilities
Equal current liabilities plus long-term liabilities.

net worth (owner's equity)
Is total assets less total liabilities.

Noncurrent assets are those assets that cannot be converted into cash in a short period of time (usually, 12 months) in the normal course of business. These noncurrent or long-term assets include buildings, parking lots, the land under the building and parking lot, fixtures (e.g., display racks), and equipment (e.g., air-conditioning systems). These items, except land, are carried on the books at cost less accumulated depreciation. Depreciation is necessary because most noncurrent assets have a limited useful life; the difference between the asset and depreciation is intended to provide a more realistic picture of the retailer's assets and prevent an overstatement or understatement of these assets' value. However, as every retailer has learned, the value of real estate can fluctuate greatly over time.

Some retailers also include goodwill as an asset. **Goodwill** is an intangible asset, usually based on customer loyalty, that reflects the portion of the book value of a business entity not directly attributable to its assets and liabilities. Goodwill normally occurs only when a retailer purchases an existing business and the dollar value assigned to goodwill is minimal.

Total assets equals current assets plus noncurrent assets plus goodwill.

The other part of the balance sheet reflects the retailer's liabilities and net worth. A **liability** is any legitimate financial claim against the retailer's assets. Liabilities are classified as either current or long-term.

Current liabilities are short-term debts that are payable within a year. Included here are accounts payable, notes payable (which are due within the year), payroll payable, and taxes payable. **Accounts payable** are amounts owed to vendors for goods and services. Payroll payable is money due to employees on past labor. Taxes due the government (federal, state, or local) are also considered a current liability. Some retailers also include interest due within the year on long-term notes or mortgages as a current liability.

Long-term liabilities include notes payable and mortgages not due within the year. **Total liabilities** equals current liabilities plus long-term liabilities.

Net worth, also called **owner's equity**, is the difference between the firm's total assets and total liabilities and represents the owner's equity in the business. The figure reflects the owner's original investment plus any profits reinvested in the business less any losses incurred in the business and any funds that the owner has taken out of the business.

In actuality, the balance sheet does not reflect all the retailer's assets and liabilities. Specifically, such items as store personnel can be an asset or a liability to the business. These items might not appear on the balance sheet but are extremely important to the success of a high-performance retailer. Other items that could be either assets or liabilities, although not in the strict accounting sense, are goodwill, customer loyalty, and even vendor relationships. Each of these items can contribute to the success or failure of a retailer.

Statement of Cash Flow

A third financial statement that retailers can use to help in understanding their business is the statement of cash flow. A statement of cash flow lists in detail the source and type of all revenue (cash inflows) and the use and type of all expenditures (cash outflows) for a given time period. When cash inflows exceed cash outflows, the retailer is said to have a *positive* cash flow; when cash outflows exceed cash inflows, the retailer is said to be experiencing a *negative* cash flow. Thus, the purpose of the statement of cash flow is to enable the retailer to project the cash needs of the firm. Based on projections, plans may be made to either seek additional financing if a negative flow is projected, or to make other investments if a positive flow is anticipated. Likewise, a retailer with a positive cash flow for

WHAT'S NEW ?

Walmart's Buyback of Its Stock

Sam and Bud Walton founded Walmart in 1962 when they opened their initial store in Rogers, Arkansas. In 1972 shares were listed on the New York Stock Exchange. It took 17 years to reach $1 billion in sales in 1979, six years later it ended 1985 with $8.4 billion in sales and a decade later it had $93.6 billion in sales, and in the year ending January 31, 2012, sales were $445 billion. During the first 30 years it was normal for Walmart to grow at double-digit rates and often over 25 percent per year. When a retailer is growing this quickly it doubles sales approximately every three years. But as a result of that aggressive growth the retailer needs to use all of its profit and often, additional debt to finance its growth.

From 2007 to 2011, Walmart faced a very different situation. By 2007 it had reached daily sales of over $1 billion or $375 billion for the year. However, over the next four years sales had only grown by 18.5 percent to $445 billion. Predictably, that is not terrible since many retailers faltered during this period and faced sales decline. Nonetheless, the longer-term problem is that it is very difficult to grow at a high rate when you are already the world's largest retailer. Consider for instance that in 2011 JCPenney had a bit over $17 billion in annual sales and Walmart grew its total sales by nearly $25 billion. It would be totally unreasonable to expect Walmart to grow at the 25 percent plus historical growth rate during its heyday because that would translate to annual sales gains of over $100 billion or nearly the total sales of six retail chains the size of JCPenney! After-all, Walmart already serves 200 million customers a week from its 9,000 plus stores.

Thus, since 2007, Walmart has been using the large excess cash it is generating to purchase back shares of its common stock. See the exhibit below for more details. In support of this strategy consider the stock price trend over the last decade (see exhibit below). On December 31, 2002, the stock closed at $50.51 and a decade later on December 30, 2011, it closed at $59.76; however, profits had more than doubled

from $6.7 billion to $15.7 billion and sales had grown from $218 billion to $445 billion. It is thus not surprising that Walmart has been purchasing back shares of its common stock, that it sees as one of its best investments to increase shareholder value. Note that when a retailer purchases its stock there are fewer shares outstanding and thus making it possible to increase the dividend per share. Incidentally dividend growth has also been very strong since 2002 as show in the exhibit below.

There is no shortage of rumors about what this practice may lead to for the future of Walmart. Some speculate that the company may go private and perhaps return into the hands of the founding family that owned 38 percent of the stock in March 2003 but controlled 48 percent as of March 2011 and may soon control 50 percent of the outstanding stock. This means that Walmart could go private even if other shareholders dissent because the Walton family, through entities they control that hold the shares, could vote to go private. And if they vote to go private and control over 50 percent of the common shares they could avoid having to pay a premium to buy back shares on the open market.

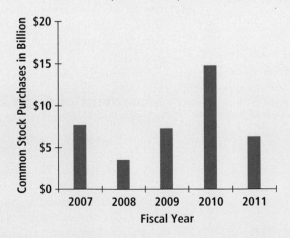

WALMART STORES STOCK PURCHASES
(2007–2011)

(continued)

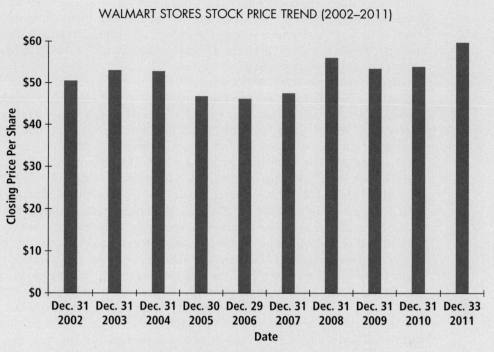

WALMART STORES STOCK PRICE TREND (2002–2011)

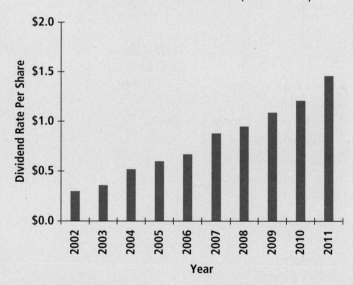

WALMART STORES DIVIDEND RATE (2002–2011)

Sources: Walmart Stores, Inc. SEC Form 10-K for fiscal year ended January 2002 through 2012. "Walmart Unveils Mega Stock Repurchase Program," (June 6, 2011). http://www.edividendstocks.com/2011/06/walmart-unveils-mega-stock-repurchase-program/ (accessed on April 9, 2012). "Walmart Plans $15 Billion Buyback That May Boost Walton Family's Control," (June 3, 2011). http://www.bloomberg.com/news/2011-06-03/walmart-approves-15-billion-buyback-program-as-profit-growth-accelerates.html (accessed on April 9, 2012). Also based on author's long-term investment and tracking of Walmart Stores, Inc. performance and strategy.

the period might be able to take advantage of "good deals" from vendors. In the "What's New?" box you will learn how the retailer uses its positive cash flow to take advantage of what it sees as a good deal, "buying back shares of its stock."

A statement of cash flow is not the same as an income statement. In a statement of cash flow, the retailer is concerned only with the movement of cash into or out of the firm. An income statement reflects the profitability of the retailer after all revenue and expenses are considered. Often expenses will be incurred in one time period but not paid until the following time period. Thus, the retailer's income statement and statement of cash flow are seldom identical. Consider the example of TMD Furniture for the month of August as shown in Exhibit 8.7a.

August is a slow month for furniture sales because many customers are taking vacations; as a result, TMD is expecting sales of only $40,000 for the month. Of that amount, $15,450 will be for cash, and TMD expects to collect $24,998 on its account receivables. Along with a tax-refund check due from the state for $97, TMD has projected a cash inflow of $40,545 for August. However, because August is the month that several notes and accounts payable are due, TMD Furniture is expecting to have to pay out $48,372 during August. This will result in a negative cash flow for the month of $7,827. TMD has prepared for this by having cash on hand (as reported on the July 31 balance sheet) of $11,589. In reality, many retailers forget about cash and realize the difference between cash flow and profit only after the coffers are empty. In the case of TMD Furniture, paying off the notes and accounts payable had no effect on the income statement. Likewise, the statement of cash flow considered only that part of purchases that were paid for with cash, not those purchased on credit. These credit purchasers had no direct effect on the cash flow. Exhibit 8.7b lists the typical retailer's cash inflow and outflow items. It should be noted that retailers who decide to use major credit cards, instead of handling their own credit operations, are able to convert sales much more quickly into cash because they do not need to wait for customers to pay for their purchases—some other party such as a bank assumes this financing function.

Exhibit 8.7a
Sample Statement of Cash Flow

TMD Furniture, Inc.
Cash Flow Statement
August 31

Cash Sales	$15,450	
Collection of Accounts Receivable	24,998	
Refund on State Taxes	97	
Total Cash Inflow		$40,545
Cash Outflow		
Rent	$ 1,513	
Purchases at Cash	5,750	
Salaries	8,483	
Utilities	1,450	
Advertising	2,300	
County Taxes	173	
Supplies	921	
Telephone	150	
Paying Off Accounts Payable	20,632	
Paying Off Notes Payable	7,000	
Total Cash Outflow		$48,372
Total Cash Flow		($ 7,827)

© Cengage Learning

Exhibit 8.7b
Typical Cash Inflows and Outflows Categories

Cash Inflows	Cash Outflows
Cash sales	Paying for merchandise
Collecting accounts receivable	Rent expenses
Collecting notes receivable	Utilities expenses
Collecting other debts	Wages and salary expenses
Sale of fixed assets	Advertising expense
Sale of stock	Insurance premiums
	Taxes
	Interest expenses
	Supplies and other expenses
	Purchase of other assets
	Paying off accounts payable
	Paying off notes payable
	Buying back company stocks
	Paying dividends

© Cengage Learning

The economic downturn experienced between 2008 and 2009 resulted in an increasing number of retailers becoming aware of the critical nature of cash flow. In fact, the number-one cause of retailing bankruptcies in recent years has been cash flow problems. A retailer can be growing quickly and be profitable, yet fail due to inadequate cash flow. However, as we stated in Chapter 2, the soft economy has helped some retailers such as Dollar General who opened 600 stores in 2010 and 625 stores in 2011; Dollar Tree that opened 235 stores in 2010 and 300 in 2011; and Family Dollar that opened 200 stores in 2010 and 300 in 2011. Another retail sector that has grown recently is automotive parts; witness that AutoZone opened nearly 200 stores in 2010 and 2011, as well as O'Reilly Automotive that opened over 150 stores in both years.[4] Importantly, this aggressive rate of store openings results in significant capital expenditures that are not possible without the retailer being able to generate significant cash flow.

However, many retailers have a lack of a sufficient cash flow this scenario is not limited to those large troubled chains you hear about on television. Many a small entrepreneur has come up with a brilliant idea for a retail operation only to fall short. In fact, more than a quarter of all retail operations fail during the first two years due to a lack of positive cash flow. The entrepreneur's problems usually start by overestimating revenues and underestimating costs, resulting in a negative cash flow. By not ensuring they have enough cash on hand to withstand a rocky two-year start-up period, many retailers are assuring themselves of failure. In fact, according to one of the author's mentors, the first thing to look at when examining a retailer's financial records is its accounts payable, particularly government payroll taxes. It seems that when retail firms get into a cash bind, they tend to postpone payments to the government so that they can pay their suppliers and employees. After all, they believe that they can always pay their taxes later. Unfortunately, the government does not always agree with such thinking.[5] As a result, some of these unsuccessful retailers often resort to questionable tactics to improve their financial statements.

Dressing up Financial Statements

Accounting rules give companies wide discretion in calculating their earnings. By accruing, or allotting, revenues and expenses to specific periods, retailers aim to allocate income to the quarter or year in which it was effectively earned. This *accrual accounting* method is supposed to provide a more accurate picture of what's happening to the business at a given time, and often it does. However, retailers, especially small retailers, have learned that lenders judge the worth and creditability of a business by its financial statements. Thus, today, many retailers are using aggressive accounting methods to make their statements look as good as possible. Listed below are several methods retailers have used to window dress their books.

> *LIFO liquidation.* Retailers using the standard LIFO (last-in, first-out) inventory accounting know that profits look better when the older and less costly goods are sold at inflated prices during periods of inflation. Therefore, earnings can be improved by reducing the basic stock level, the minimum amount of an item to be carried at all times. (Basic stock will be discussed in greater detail in Chapter 9.) This will therefore result in some less-expensive older inventory being sold. However, the retailer's future earnings could be hurt when it replaces the inventory at higher prices.

current ratio
Current assets divided by current liabilities.

> *Improving the current ratio.* Since a retailer's **current ratio** (current assets divided by current liabilities) is probably the easiest and most common way for lenders to analyze a balance sheet, some retailers try to improve their ratios even by paying off small portions of their current debt prior to vendor review. For example, suppose a retailer has $20,000 in cash, $30,000 in other current assets, and $30,000 in current liabilities; its current ratio is equal to 1.67:1. Yet lenders prefer to see the current ratio closer to 2:1. In this case, the retailer can use $10,000 of its cash to reduce debt and improve its ratio significantly to 2:1.

> *Massage cash.* Another simple method for retailers to pump up their cash is to sell some of their receivables to a third party.

> *Convert short-term loans to long-term loans.* A few years ago, some retailers took advantage of another method of improving their financial statements when long-term interest rates declined quickly and closely approached short-term rates. (In normal times, long-term rates are one to two percentage points higher than short-term rates.) With so many willing lenders offering extremely low long-term interest rates, these retailers were able to refinance a portion of their short-term debt for long-term debt.

> *Extend the payment time.* Another method troubled retailers have used to improve the appearance of their balance sheet is to have vendors agree to a slower repayment schedule, enabling the retailer to build up its cash balance.

Connecting the Retail Accounting Statements

Although we have discussed the retailer's income statement, balance sheet, and cash flow statement separately, they are tightly intertwined. As illustrated in Exhibit 8.8, this is because wisely investing in assets leads to enhancing operating performance, which leads to enhanced cash flows. More specifically, a retailer should invest in facilities and equipment and information technology that enable it to lower operating expenses, or cost of goods sold, or increase sales, thereby enhancing gross margins and net profit

Exhibit 8.8
Connecting the Retail Accounting Statements

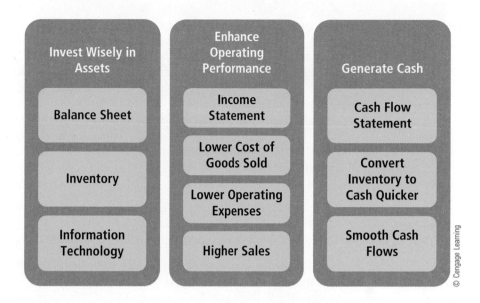

© Cengage Learning

margins, which should result in enhanced cash flow as the retailer is able to more quickly convert inventory into cash and smooth its cash flows. Importantly, by smoothing cash flow (having less volatility in cash flow) the retailer enterprise is viewed by bankers and investors as less risky and this has a long-term effect on lowering its borrowing costs, which further enhances cash flow. As a retailer has enhanced cash flow, it is able to make additional investment in assets and the process repeats. Of course, the opposite happens if bad asset investments are made, operating performance deteriorates as well as cash flow. Stated alternatively, retailers can either get in a death spiral of lower and lower productivity and cash flow or a positive cascading effect of higher productivity and higher cash flow and generally move toward better and better high performance retailing, as discussed in Chapter 2.

Inventory Valuation

LO 3

Explain how the retailer is able to value inventory.

Due to the many different merchandise lines often carried by retailers, inventory valuation is quite complex. A retailer must make two major decisions with regard to valuing inventory: (1) the accounting inventory system to implement and (2) the inventory-pricing method to use.

Accounting Inventory System

Two accounting inventory systems are available for the retailer: (1) the cost method and (2) the retail method. We will describe both methods on the basis of the frequency with which inventory information is received, difficulties encountered in completing a physical inventory and maintaining records, and the extent to which stock shortages can be calculated.

The Cost Method

cost method
Is an inventory valuation technique that provides a book valuation of inventory based solely on the retailer's cost of merchandise including freight.

The **cost method** of inventory valuation provides a book valuation of inventory based solely on the retailer's cost, including freight. It looks only at the cost of each item as it was recorded in the accounting records when purchased. When a physical inventory is taken, all items are counted, the cost of each item is taken from the records or the price tags, and the total inventory value at cost is calculated.

One of the easiest methods of coding the cost of merchandise on the price tag is to use the first 10 letters of the alphabet to represent the price. Here A = 1, B = 2, C = 3, D = 4, E = 5, F = 6, G = 7, H = 8, I = 9, J = 0. A product with the code HEAD has a cost of $85.14. The cost method is useful for those retailers who sell big-ticket items and allow price negotiations by customers. Sales personnel know from the code how much room there is for negotiation while still covering the cost of the merchandise plus operating expenses.

The cost method of inventory valuation does have several limitations:

1. It is difficult to do daily inventories (or even monthly inventories).
2. It is difficult to cost out each sale.
3. It is difficult to allocate freight charges to each item's cost of goods sold.

The cost method is generally used by those retailers with big-ticket items and a limited number of sales per day (e.g., an expensive jewelry store or an antique furniture store), where there are few lines or limited inventory requirements, infrequent price changes, and low turnover rates.

The Retail Method

The retail method of inventory values merchandise at current retail prices. It overcomes the disadvantages of the cost method by keeping detailed records of inventory based on the retail value of the merchandise. However, the fact that the inventory is valued in retail dollars does make it a little more difficult for the retailer to determine the cost of goods sold when computing the gross margin for a time period.

There are three basic steps in computing an ending inventory value using the retail method: calculation of the cost complement, calculation of reductions from retail value, and conversion of the adjusted retail book inventory to cost.

Step 1. Calculation of the Cost Complement   Inventories, both beginning and ending, and purchases are recorded at both cost and retail levels when using the retail method. Exhibit 8.9 shows an inventory statement for Whitener's Sporting Goods for the fall season.

In Exhibit 8.9, the beginning inventory is shown at both cost and retail. Net purchases, which are the total purchases less merchandise returned to vendors, allowances, and discounts from vendors, are also valued at cost and retail. Additional markups are the total increases in the retail price of merchandise already in stock that were caused by inflation or heavy demand and are shown at retail. Freight-in is the cost to the retailer for transportation of merchandise from the vendor and is shown in the cost column.

Exhibit 8.9
Inventory Available

	Cost	Retail
Beginning Inventory	$199,000	$401,000
Net Purchases	70,000	154,000
Additional Markups		5,000
Freight-In	1,000	
Total Inventory Available for Sale	$270,000	$560,000

© Cengage Learning

Using the information from Exhibit 8.9, the retailer can calculate the average relationship of cost to retail price for all merchandise available for sale during the fall season. This calculation is called the *cost complement*:

$$\text{cost complement} = \text{total cost valuation/total retail valuation}$$
$$= \$270,000/\$560,000 = 0.482$$

Since the cost complement is 0.482, or 48.2 percent, 48.2 cents of every retail sales dollar is composed of merchandise cost.

Step 2. Calculation of Reductions from Retail Value
During the course of day-to-day business activities, the retailer must take reductions from inventory. In addition to sales, which lower the retail inventory level, retail reductions can lower retail inventory levels. These reductions include markdowns (sales, reduced prices on end-of-season, discontinued, or damaged merchandise), discounts (employee, senior citizen, student, religious, etc.), and stock shortages (employee and customer theft, breakage). Markdowns and employee discounts can be recorded throughout an accounting period, but a physical inventory is required to calculate stock shortages.

In Exhibit 8.9, it was shown that Whitener's had inventory available for sale at retail of $560,000 for the upcoming fall season. This must be reduced by actual fall season sales of $145,000, markdowns of $12,000, and discounts of $2,000. This results in an ending book value of inventory with a retail level of $401,000. This is shown in Exhibit 8.10.

Once the ending book value of inventory at retail is determined, a comparison can be made to the physical inventory to compute actual stock shortages; if the book value is greater than the physical count, then a stock shortage has occurred. If the book value is lower than the physical count, then a stock overage has occurred. Shortages are due to thefts, breakages, overshipments not billed to customers, and bookkeeping errors (the most common cause). These errors result from a failure to properly record markdowns, returns, discounts, and breakages. Many retailers have greatly reduced their original shortage estimate by reviewing the season's bookkeeping entries. A stock overage, an excess of physical inventory over book inventory, is also usually the result of bookkeeping errors, either miscounting during the physical inventory or improper book entries. Exhibit 8.11 shows the results of Whitener's physical inventory and the resulting adjustment.

Because a physical inventory must be taken in order to determine shortages (overages), and retailers take a physical count only once or twice a year, shortages (overages) are often estimated in merchandise budgets as shown in Exhibits 8.1 and 8.2. As a rule of thumb, retailers may estimate monthly shortages between 0.5 and 3 percent.

Exhibit 8.10
Whitener's Sporting Goods Ending Book Value

	Cost	Retail
Inventory Available for Sale at Retail		$560,000
Less Reductions:		
Sales	$145,000	
Markdowns	12,000	
Discounts	2,000	
Total Reductions		159,000
Ending Book Value of Inventory at Retail		$401,000

© Cengage Learning

Exhibit 8.11
Whitener's Sporting
Goods, Stock Shortage

	Cost	Retail
Ending Book Value of Inventory at Retail		$401,000
Physical Inventory (at Retail)		398,000
Stock Shortages		3,000
Adjusting Ending Book Value of Inventory at Retail		$398,000

Step 3. Conversion of the Adjusted Retail Book Inventory to Cost The final step to be performed in using the retail method is to convert to cost the adjusted retail book inventory figure in order to determine the closing inventory at cost. The procedure here is to multiply the adjusted retail book inventory ($398,000 in the case of Whitener's) by the cost complement (0.482 in the Whitener's example):

$$\text{closing inventory (at cost)} = \text{adjusted retail} \times \text{cost complement book inventory}$$
$$= \$398,000 \times 0.482 = \$191,836$$

Although this equation does not yield the actual closing inventory at cost, it does provide a close approximation of the cost figure. Remember that the cost complement

In order to know Ending Book Value of Inventory, a physical inventory must be taken and kept up to date.

Exhibit 8.12
Whitener's Sporting
Goods Income Statement

	Cost	Retail
Sales		$145,000
Less: Cost of Goods Sold:		
Beginning Inventory (at Cost)	$200,000	
Purchases (at Cost)	70,000	
Goods Available for Sale	$270,000	
Ending Inventory (at Cost)	191,836	
Cost of Goods Sold		78,164
Gross Margin		$ 66,836
Less: Operating Expenses		
Salaries	$ 30,000	
Utilities	1,000	
Rent	19,000	
Depreciation (Fixtures + Equipment)	2,200	
Total Operating Expenses		52,200
Net Profit Before Taxes		$ 14,636

© Cengage Learning

is an average. Now that ending inventory at cost has been determined, the retailer can determine gross margin as well as net profit before taxes, if operating expenses are known. We will discuss expenses in more detail later. In the Whitener's example, let's use $30,000 for salaries, $1,000 for utilities, $19,000 for rent, and $2,200 for depreciation. These figures are shown in Exhibit 8.12.

The retail method has several advantages over the cost method of inventory valuation:

1. Accounting statements can be drawn up at any time. Inventories need not be taken for preparation of these statements.
2. Physical inventories using retail prices are less subject to error and can be completed in a shorter amount of time.
3. The retail method provides an automatic, conservative valuation of ending inventory as well as inventory levels throughout the season. This is especially useful in cases where the retailer is forced to submit insurance claims for damaged or lost merchandise.

A major complaint against the retail method is that it is a "method of averages." This refers to the fact that closing inventory is valued at the average relationship between cost and retail (the cost complement) and that large retailers offer many different classifications and lines with different relationships. This disadvantage can be overcome by computing cost complements for individual lines or departments.

Another limitation is the heavy burden placed on bookkeeping activities. The true ending book inventory value can be correctly calculated only if there are no errors when recording beginning inventory, purchases, freight-in, markups, markdowns, discounts, returns, transfers between stores, and sales. As noted earlier, many of the retailers' original shortages have later been determined to be bookkeeping errors. Most retailers today use the retail method of inventory valuation, which was created in the early 1900s.

FIFO
Stands for first in, first out and values inventory based on the assumption that the oldest merchandise is sold before the more recently purchased merchandise.

Inventory-Valuation Systems

The two methods of valuing inventory are FIFO and LIFO. The **FIFO** (first in, first out) method assumes that the oldest merchandise is sold before the more recently purchased merchandise. However, merchandise on the shelf will reflect the most current replacement price. During inflationary periods, this method allows "inventory profits" (caused by selling the less expensive earlier inventory rather than the more expensive newer inventory) to be included as income.

LIFO

Stands for last in, first out and values inventory based on the assumption that the most recently purchased merchandise is sold first and the oldest merchandise is sold last.

The **LIFO** (last in, first out) method is designed to cushion the impact of inflationary pressures by matching current costs against current revenues. Costs of goods sold are based on the costs of the most recently purchased inventory, while the older inventory is regarded as the unsold inventory. During inflationary periods, the LIFO method results in the application of a higher unit cost to the merchandise sold and a lower unit cost to inventory still unsold. In times of rapid inflation, most retailers use the LIFO method, resulting in lower profits on the income statement but also lower income taxes. Most retailers also prefer to use LIFO for planning purposes since it accurately reflects replacement costs. The IRS permits a retailer to change its method of accounting only once.

Let's study an example of the effect of the LIFO and FIFO methods of inventory valuation on a firm's financial performance. Suppose you began the year with a total inventory of 15 home-theater packages, which you purchased on the last day of the preceding year for $500 each. Thus, if these home-theater packages were the only merchandise you had in stock, your beginning inventory was $7,500 (15 × $500). Suppose also that during the year you sold 12 packages for $900 each for total sales of $10,800; that in June you purchased eight new home-theater packages (same make and model as your old ones) at $525; and that in November you bought four more at $550. Thus, your purchases would equal $4,200 in June and $2,200 in November for a total of $6,400, and you would still have 15 home-theater packages in stock at year end. Under the LIFO inventory approach, your ending inventory would be the same as it was at the beginning of the year ($7,500) since we would assume that the 12 packages sold were the 12 purchased during the year. However, using the FIFO approach, we would assume that we sold 12 of the original $500 packages and had three left. These three home-theater packages, along with June's and November's purchases, result in an ending inventory of $7,900 [(3 × $500) + (8 × $525) + (4 × $350)]. Now let's see how these approaches can affect our gross margins.

	LIFO	FIFO
Net sales	$10,800	$10,800
Less: Cost of goods sold		
Beginning inventory	$7,500	$7,500
Purchases	6,400	6,400
Goods available	$13,900	$13,900
Ending inventory	7,500	7,900
Cost of goods sold	6,400	6,000
Gross margin	$4,400	$4,800

The issue of which inventory valuation method (LIFO or FIFO) to use is one of the key issues facing retailers and accountants around the world as they seek to find a common method of reporting financial transactions. For example, under International Accounting Standards, the use of LIFO is disallowed. Therefore, if an American retailer wants to comply with international standards, it must use the FIFO method. As the Retailing: The Inside Story that follows illustrates, U.S. retailers, such as Walgreens, can end up paying more taxes as a result of this International Accounting Standard.

RETAILING — The Inside Story

International Accounting Rules, Inventory Valuation, and the LIFO Reserve

The International Accounting Standards Board, formerly the International Accounting Standards Committee (IASC), has been working to achieve uniformity in accounting principles since 1973. Today the organization has representatives from approximately 100 countries and has issued 41 international accounting standards. One particular departure between the Generally Accepted Accounting Principles (GAAP) used in the United States and the International Financial Reporting Standards (IFRS) is the valuation of inventory.

Under GAAP, a corporation has the choice between LIFO, FIFO, and the weighted average cost method. However, under IFRS only FIFO and the weighted average cost method are permissible. According to the American Institute of Certified Public Accountants, 36 percent of U.S. companies currently use LIFO, including large retailers such as Walgreen, Macy's, and PetSmart . In addition, GAAP requires companies who choose to use LIFO to disclose what is known as the "LIFO Reserve," which is an account that represents the difference between the inventory valued using LIFO and what it would be valued at using FIFO. Therefore, by looking at the LIFO reserve, we can get an idea as to what a company would have to report under IFRS. Let's look at an example:

Inventory Purchases for 2012

Date	Quantity Purchased	Price per Unit	Total Price
1/15/2012	200	$7	$1400
3/10/2012	350	$8	$2800
4/3/2012	50	$9	$450
7/21/2012	400	$9	$3600
9/13/2012	475	$10	$4750
11/18/2012	325	$12	$3900
Total	1800		$16,900

The company in the example purchased a total of 1,800 units of inventory during 2012 for a total purchase price of $16,900. Now let's assume the company sells 1,200 of the 1800 units during 2012, this leaves 600 units of inventory at the end of 2012 that must be valued for financial reporting purposes. This is where the aforementioned valuation methods are used. Remember, a total of 600 units need to be accounted for; however, the choice between LIFO and FIFO will result in different valuations of these 600 units because different assumptions are made in regard to the flow of inventory.

Valuation of Inventory for 2012

LIFO	FIFO
$200 \times \$7 = \$1,400$	$325 \times \$12 = \$3900$
$350 \times \$8 = \$2,800$	$275 \times \$10 = \$2,750$
$50 \times \$9 = \$450$	
600 units = $4,650	600 units = $6,650

On the 2012 balance sheet, the inventory account if the company reports using LIFO will be $4,650, while the inventory account if the company uses FIFO will be $6,650. The relation of FIFO reporting higher ending inventory values than LIFO will hold as long as price continues to rise. Therefore, the value of the 600 units of inventory reported under LIFO does not clearly portray the cost to replace those units of inventory. It is for this reason that GAAP requires a LIFO reserve to be reported. Under this example, a company reporting using LIFO would also report a LIFO reserve of $2,000 ($6,650–$4,650). This allows financial statement users to determine what inventory would be valued at using the FIFO method, which is also informative for financial statement users who are trying to determine the impact of a switch to IFRS from GAAP on a company's financial statements.

However, the true cost to a switch from GAAP to IFRS for retail companies who use LIFO is related to taxes. The Internal Revenue Code (IRC) requires conformity between the inventory method used for financial reporting and the inventory method used for tax purposes. As LIFO creates higher values of cost of goods sold and lower values of ending inventory in times of rising prices, LIFO also results in lower taxable income. If a taxpayer changes his or her inventory reporting method from LIFO to FIFO for tax purposes,

(continued)

he or she is required to recognize the LIFO reserve as taxable income and pay the tax due on that reserve over the next four years. For a company with a very large LIFO reserve this could result in a significant additional cash outflow for income taxes. Let's look at Walgreen's financial statements to get a better picture:

USD in millions	Aug 31, 2011	Aug 31, 2010	Aug 31, 2009
Inventories at LIFO (as reported)	$8,044	$7,378	$6,789
Add: LIFO reserve, ending balance	$1,587	$1,379	$1,239
Inventories at FIFO (adjusted)	$9,631	$8,757	$8,028

Source: from Walgreen Co. 2009, 2010, 2011 Annual Reports and 10Ks.

So for the year ended August 31, 2011, Walgreen reported inventory on their balance sheet of $8,044 million. However, if Walgreen reported using FIFO their inventory balance would have been $9,631. In addition, the cumulative account of LIFO reserve is increasing in each of the three years, which is a signal that inventory prices are increasing for Walgreen. If Walgreen switched their inventory reporting method to FIFO, they would be required to also switch to FIFO for tax purposes and recognize an additional $1.587 billion of taxable income. Assuming this is taxed at the U.S. statutory tax rate of 35 percent, Walgreen would owe additional taxes of $555.45 million, which can be paid over a four year period. To put the magnitude of this additional tax payment in context, Walgreen's total assets on August 31, 2011, were $27,454 million; therefore, this additional tax payment represents 2 percent of total assets.

Currently, standards issued by the IASB are not mandatory unless a particular country adopts them. This explains the wide variation in reporting requirements. The European Union and Australia mandated the use of international standards for consolidated reporting beginning in 2005. That mandate has gone a long way toward standardizing worldwide practices.

Still, while U.S. retailers may complain about differences between GAAP and IASB rulings as well as IRS regulations, it could be worse. The *Wall Street Journal* reported that a Chinese premier reminded Chinese taxpayers that "tax evasion can result in death by execution."

Source: This box was contributed by Stephen J. Lusch, a PhD accounting student at the University of Arizona.

Summary

LO 1 **Why is a merchandise budget so important in retail planning, and how is a merchandise budget prepared?**

The purpose of this chapter was to introduce you to the major financial statements and their importance in retail planning. We began our discussion with the six-month merchandise budget. This statement projects sales, when and how much new merchandise should be ordered, what markup is to be taken, what reductions are to be planned, and the target or planned gross margin for the season. The establishment of such a budget has several advantages for the retailer:

1. The six-month budget controls the amount of inventory and forces management to control markups and reductions.
2. The budget helps to determine how much merchandise should be purchased so that inventory requirements can be met.
3. The budget can be compared with actual or final results to determine the performance of the firm.

We concluded our discussion of the six-month merchandise budget by showing how each of the figures is determined. We illustrated how to estimate sales, inventory levels, reductions, purchases, and gross margin.

LO 2

What are the differences among and the uses of these three accounting statements: income statement, balance sheet, and statement of cash flow?

The second section of this chapter explained how the retailer uses three important accounting statements: the income statement, the balance sheet, and the statement of cash flow. The income statement gives the retailer a summary of the income and expenses incurred over a given time period. A balance sheet shows the financial condition of the retailer at a particular point in time. The statement of cash flow lists in detail the sources and types of all revenue and expenditures for a given time period. The accounting statements are connected because wise investments in assets that are reflected on the balance sheet should enhance the income statement through lower operating costs, lower cost of goods sold, or higher sales.

LO 3

How does a retailer value its inventory?

The final section of this chapter described two decisions a retailer must make with regards to inventory record keeping: which accounting system (cost or retail) to use and whether to use the LIFO or FIFO valuation method.

The cost system is the simplest, but the retail system is the most widely used because of these advantages:

1. Accounting statements can be drawn up at any time.
2. Physical inventories using retail prices are less subject to error and can be completed in a shorter amount of time.
3. The retail method provides an automatic, conservative valuation of ending inventory as well as inventory levels throughout the season.

The FIFO method assumes that the oldest merchandise is sold before the more recently purchased merchandise, so merchandise on the shelf more accurately reflects the replacement cost. During inflationary periods this method allows "inventory profits" to be included as income. The LIFO method is designed to cushion the impact of inflationary pressures by matching current costs against current revenues. Cost of goods sold is based on the costs of the most recently purchased inventory, while the older inventory is regarded as the unsold inventory. In times of rapid inflation most retailers use the LIFO method, resulting in not only lower profits on the income statement, but also lower income taxes. Most retailers also prefer to use LIFO for planning purposes, since it accurately reflects replacement costs.

Terms to Remember

merchandising	operating expenses
merchandise budget	operating profit
gross margin	other income or expenses
prediction market	net profit
stock-to-sales ratio	asset
income statement	current assets
gross sales	accounts and/or notes receivable
returns and allowances	prepaid expenses
net sales	retail inventories
cost of goods sold	noncurrent assets
gross margin	goodwill

total assets	net worth (owner's equity)
liability	current ratio
current liabilities	cost method
accounts payable	FIFO
long-term liabilities	LIFO
total liabilities	

Review and Discussion Questions

LO 1   **Why is a merchandise budget so important in retail planning, and how is a merchandise budget prepared?**

1. Name a couple of local retailers that can be impacted by unexpected changes in weather patterns. How does weather affect their sales, and what can they do to prevent such fluctuations?
2. It costs money to carry inventory, yet retailers must carry an amount of inventory in excess of planned sales for an upcoming period. Why?
3. Why isn't it a bad thing to take a reduction? After all, aren't reductions an admission of making a mistake?
4. Why should a retailer be allowed to change its merchandise budget after the start of a season? If changes can be made, what would cause such changes?
5. A retailer who last year had sales of $900,000 plans for an inflation rate of 2 percent and a 3-percent increase in market share. What should planned sales for this year be?
6. A retailer believes that since a major competitor has just left the local market, the number of transactions for this year's upcoming season will increase by 4 percent; but because of a slowing rate of inflation, the value of the average sale will increase by only 1 percent. If sales last year were $1,500,000, what will they be this year?

LO 2   **What are the differences among and the uses of these three accounting statements—income statement, balance sheet, and statement of cash flow?**

7. In what ways are the balance sheet and the income statement different? How do retailers use these two financial statements?
8. What accounting statement reports on the retailer's financial performance over a period of time, and which statement reports a retailer's financial condition at a given point in time?
9. What is the difference between a statement of cash flow and an income statement?
10. How would the following activities affect a retailer's balance sheet and income statement for the current year?
    a. The retailer overestimates the amount of year-ending inventory that is obsolete, thus reducing inventory.
    b. The retailer overestimates the breakage on a current rebate program.
    c. The value of your inventory shrinks by a higher than expected amount. You had planned for $46,500 shrinkage, but your July count was $68,200 lower.
    d. The retailer switches from LIFO to FIFO.
11. You are working as a loan officer at a local bank. Earlier today, a former high-school classmate came in to see you about a loan for the family's retail business. After looking over the store's financial statements, you notice that the store is posting a strong net income growth. However, these statements also reveal that the

store has had a negative cash flow for the last two years and that account receivables have almost doubled over the same time span. Should this concern you?

12. The Alamo Hardware Store is trying to determine its net profit before taxes. Use the following data to find Alamo's net profit.

Rent	$36,000	Salaries	$94,000
Purchases	$400,000	Sales	$586,000
Ending inventory	$163,000	Utilities	$45,000
Beginning inventory	$148,000	Other income	$5,300

13. A sporting goods store with sales for the year of $400,000 and other income of $32,000 has operating expenses of $123,000. Its cost of goods sold is $207,000. What are its gross margin, operating profit, and net profit in dollars?

14. Explain how a retailer's accounting statements are connected and illustrate with a apparel store, hardware store, or grocery store.

LO 3

How does a retailer value its inventory?

15. List the advantages and disadvantages the retail method of inventory valuation has over the cost method.

16. Define FIFO and LIFO and the reasons for using one or the other.

17. Because of the Christmas season, most retailers tend to end their fiscal year at the end of January. Does this make it difficult to determine the value of inventory when preparing financial statements?

Sample Test Questions

LO 1

Which one of the following factors is not found on a six-month merchandise budget?

a. planned gross margin
b. current liabilities
c. planned sales percentage
d. planned BOM stock
e. planned purchases at retail

LO 2

The _____ provides the retailer with a picture of the organization's profit and loss situation.

a. expense report
b. index of inventory valuation
c. statement of cash flow
d. income statement
e. statement of gross margin

LO 3

The total cost valuation of a retailer's inventory is $120,000, while the total retail valuation of sales was $200,000. Approximately how much of every retail sales dollar is made up of merchandise cost?

a. 12 cents
b. 40 cents
c. 60 cents
d. $1.20
e. $1.50

Writing and Speaking Exercise

During the economic slowdown of 2008 the U.S. consumer price index was a mere .1 percent but by 2011 the CPI was 3 percent and is expected to remain around that level through 2012. However, some economic forecasters can't seem to agree on the future trend. One group predicts that the inflation rate will double over the next couple of years to 6 percent. The other group seems to believe that there won't be any inflation or maybe even a slight amount of deflation. The cost of goods sold at your family-owned menswear shop mirrors the country's inflation rate, so based on the two forecasts you expect your costs to either remain constant or to increase by 6 percent. Your father asks you to prepare a memo detailing how either of these two forecasts will impact the profitability of the business if it continues to use a FIFO method of valuing inventory.

Retail Project

Go to the library and look at the most recent annual reports of some retailers. (If you are using the Internet, go to the retailer's home page or to http://finance.yahoo.com and then enter the retailer's stock symbol and then click "profile.") Using the financial data from these reports, compare the net cash flow to the net income for each of the retailers you chose and explain the reason for the differences.

Planning Your Own Entrepreneurial Retail Business

You are unsure what level of sales to forecast for your new drugstore, which you plan to open on New Year's Day. Consequently, you have decided to make some assumptions. You believe that it is reasonable to assume that your trade area will encompass about 35 square miles. The city planning department has told you that within this area the population density is 1,157 people per square mile. You conservatively estimate that 40 percent of these individuals will visit your store an average of four times annually and that 85 percent will purchase something on a typical visit. You expect them to purchase an average of $26 per visit. Information from industry sources suggests that drugstores do more business in the fall and winter. In fact, you expect sales during each of the months of November, December, January, and February to be 10 percent of your annual volume. The remaining eight months will share equally the 60 percent of remaining sales. You believe that for your business to be profitable, you need to have a beginning-of-month inventory-to-sales ratio of 3.0 for October through November and 2.5 for the remaining months. You want to plan your beginning-of-month inventory for each of the next 12 months. You also want to begin the first month of your second year of business with $300,000 in inventory at retail prices. Please compute the beginning of the month inventory for each of the next 12 months.

Dolly's Place

After years of teaching retailing and marketing at the University of Southern Mississippi, Dolly Loyd decided to retire and return to her first love—running an apparel store on the Gulf Coast. Because she used to run such a department for a major retail chain before teaching, she kept up with the current trends in the industry. Dolly gained the support of an ex–high-school classmate who, after making millions with an Internet startup, financed her new endeavor.

Today Dolly is beginning to make plans for the upcoming fall season. Dolly anticipates planned sales of $400,000 for the fall season based on a planned initial markup of 48 percent. Within the season, planned monthly sales are projected to be as follows: 15 percent in August and September, 10 percent in October, 20 percent in November, 30 percent in December, and 10 percent in January. To ensure a profitable season, trade association records were consulted. The records indicated the following: (1) The stock-to-sales ratios need to be 3.5 for August, 3.0 for September, 4.0 for October, 3.0 for November, 2.5 for December, and 5.5 for January; (2) reductions can be planned at 10 percent for the first four months, 20 percent for December, and 40 percent for January; and (3) with Valentine's Day approaching, an inventory of $220,000 will be necessary to begin the spring season. Complete a six-month merchandise budget for Dolly.

Dolly's Place **Six-Month Merchandise Budget** **Spring/Summer** **Fall/Winter**				Date: May 23 Season: Fall			
	Aug	**Sept**	**Oct**	**Nov**	**Dec**	**Jan**	**Seasonal Total**
1. Planned BOM Stock							
2. Planned Sales							
3. Planned Retail Reductions							
4. Planned EOM Stock							
5. Planned Purchases @ Retail							
6. Planned Purchases @ Cost							
7. Planned Initial Markup							
8. Planned Gross Margin							
9. Planned BOM Stock/Sales Ratio	3.5 ×	3.0 ×	4.0 ×	3.0 ×	2.5 ×	5.5 ×	—
10. Planned Sales Percentage	15%	15%	10%	20%	30%	10%	100%
11. Planned Retail Reduction	10%	10%	10%	10%	20%	40%	16%

Planned total sales for the period	$400,000
Planned total retail reduction percentage for the period	16%
Planned initial markup percentage for the period	48%
Planned BOM stock for February	$220,000

Note: The reduction percentage for Dolly's is 16 percent, which is the amount of total reductions ($64,000) divided by total sales ($400,000). Because the sales in each month are different, you cannot add up the reduction percentage for each month and divide the sum by the number of months in the budget.

9

Merchandise Buying and Handling

Overview

In this chapter, we explain the planning that retailers must do regarding their merchandise selection. We also analyze how a retailer controls the merchandise to be inventoried. The selection of and negotiations with vendors are also discussed, as well as the security measures used when handling the merchandise in order to prevent theft.

Learning Objectives

After reading this chapter, you should be able to:

1 Describe the major steps in the merchandise buying and handling process.

2 Explain the differences between the four methods of dollar-merchandise planning used to determine the proper inventory stock levels needed to begin a merchandise selling period.

3 Explain how retailers use dollar-merchandise control and describe how open-to-buy is used in the retail buying process.

4 Describe how a retailer determines the makeup of its inventory, including what cross-referencing in the merchandise item file means and how a category-item line review works.

5 Describe how a retailer selects proper merchandise sources.

6 Describe what is involved in the vendor–buyer negotiation process and what vendor contract terms can be negotiated.

7 Discuss the various methods of handling the merchandise once it is received in the store so as to control shrinkage, including vendor collusion, and theft.

Major Steps in Merchandise Buying and Handling

Describe the major steps in the merchandise buying and handling process.

Retailing involves many important activities, but retailers that experience strong performance are excellent merchants. According to an old retailing adage, "Goods well bought are half sold." Another common adage is "Retail is detail." One of the authors' adage is "Goods not properly transported, handled, and merchandised will be stolen; either by employees, vendors, or customers." In this chapter, we will look at the details of merchandise management—the merchandise buying and handling process and its effect on a store's performance.

merchandise management
Is the analysis, planning, acquisition, handling, and control of the merchandise investments of a retail operation.

Merchandise management is the analysis, planning, acquisition, handling, and control of the merchandise investments in a retail operation. *Analysis* is used in the definition because retailers must be able to correctly identify their customers before they can determine the needs and wants of their consumers. They also have to analyze how the individual items they purchase from suppliers will result in meeting forecasted sales, profits, and markdowns so as to develop their merchandise budgets (discussed in Chapter 8). *Planning* is included because retailers must often purchase their merchandise 6–12 months in advance of the selling season. This requires retailers to predict what the economy, employment, weather, and other trends (e.g., movies, music, clothing styles, and colors) will be in the future. After all, these factors will impact future sales. The term *acquisition* is used because, with the exception of service retailers, merchandise needs to be bought from others, either distributors or manufacturers. Besides, all retailers, even those selling only services, must acquire the equipment and fixtures needed to complete a transaction. Proper *handling* ensures that the merchandise is where it is needed and in the proper shape to be sold and not stolen. Finally, *control* of the large dollar investment in inventory is important to ensure an adequate financial return on the retailer's merchandise investment.

Whatever career path you decide to take in retailing, you cannot avoid at least some contact with the firm's merchandising activities. This is because merchandising is the day-to-day business of all retailers.

There are many steps involved in merchandising, and it can be confusing trying to see how they all fit together. It can also be confusing trying to connect merchandise management to financial performance (discussed previously in Chapter 8) or pricing and promotions (discussed next in Chapters 10 and 11). However, after reading this chapter, it will be easy to see.

The people involved in each step of the merchandise buying process shown in Exhibit 9.1 will often change, depending on the size of the retailer and who makes the various decisions. For example, the product development team at Target makes most of the product design choices while the buying team focuses on purchasing. In contrast, most of the product design choices are made by the buyers at Walmart, while the product-development team serves as trend consultants by providing buyers with event and holiday style guides. Several fashion-forward firms have been placing more responsibility (i.e., power) in the hands of buyers and decreasing the role of fashion designers.[1] For smaller firms, several of the steps in the buying process may be done by executives rather than buyers. Of course, it is possible for a new entrepreneurial retail venture that

Exhibit 9.1
Major Steps in the Merchandise Management Process

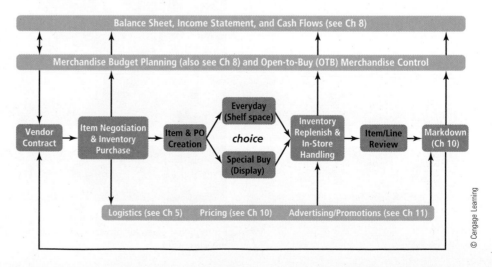

© Cengage Learning

one person may make all decisions in the merchandise management process. In some retail firms, the buying process is decentralized—department managers in each store place most of the merchandise orders. Conversely, others, like JCPenney and Macy's, have moved from a more decentralized to a more centralized buying process where corporate buyers in the company's headquarters perform most of the purchasing. To minimize confusion, the rest of this section will assume that the retailer uses a buyer to do all the activities.

As shown in Exhibit 9.1, the process normally starts with dollar-merchandise planning (which is discussed in the next section). Next, the buyer uses an open to buy figure to plan the merchandise assortment for the upcoming selling season. The buyer must then determine the source of the different product inventories. Some of the merchandise might be purchased from suppliers that the retailer has done business with in the past; some might be purchased from new suppliers. Regardless of who the retailer purchases from, the buyer must negotiate a vendor contract. Indeed, many retailers try to update the vendor contracts each year.

After agreeing to the terms of the vendor contract, the buyer negotiates and purchases merchandise. In doing so, the buyer must consider how the merchandise will be priced, promoted, shipped, and so on (the green box at the bottom of Exhibit 9.1). The buyer must also account for how both the initial and replenishment purchases will affect the retailer's merchandise budget and open-to-buy (OTB) calculations; both affect the retailer's financial reports.

An important, but often overlooked, step in the buying of merchandise is adding items to the retailer's computer system. Doing so allows the merchandise to be tracked and purchase orders (POs) created. If a buyer forgets to do so or links it incorrectly, customer service and sales problems are bound to occur, and the buyer is likely to be reprimanded or fired.

A good merchandise manager will discuss his or her promotional plans for incoming merchandise with the sales team.

Buyers must also determine whether each product purchased will be a basic stock item or a special buy. This is important because basic items are included in the retailer's *planogram*. A planogram, discussed in greater detail in Chapter 13, is a schematic that illustrates how and where a retailer's merchandise should be displayed on the shelf in order to increase customer purchases. It is often maintained with the input of vendors.

Finally, all merchandise should be reviewed on a continual basis to see if any pricing, promotion, or logistical changes are necessary. At the end of each season, a formal planogram review should be made in which all basic stock items are reviewed. Items that don't make the cut for the next season need to be marked down, which impacts the merchandise budget and so on. Buyers must also normally review their vendor contracts as they start looking at new items for purchase.

<table>
<tr><td>

LO 2

Explain the differences between the four methods of dollar-merchandise planning used to determine the proper inventory stock levels needed to begin a merchandise selling period.

</td><td>

Dollar-Merchandise Planning

As inventory is sold, new stock must to be purchased, displayed, and sold once again. This is why merchandising, while only a subfunction of retailing, is the heartbeat of every retailer. Those that do a superior job at managing their inventory investments will be highly successful. If a retailer's inventory continues to build up, then the retailer either has too much money tied up in inventory or is not making the sales it was expecting; both situations are problematic. Although the largest of retail chains such as REI, Kohl's, Banana Republic, and certainly Walmart and Target have sophisticated demand forecasting software and information systems, many of the smaller regional chains were slow to adopt this technology. An interesting example is Harrods, which was incidentally previously owned by Mohamed Al Fayed, an Egyptian tycoon, whose son Dodi Fayed was killed along with Princess Diana in a 1997 Paris car crash. In 2010, Mohamed Al Fayed sold Harrods for $2.37 billion to Qatar Holding, who became the fifth owner of the retailer. The new owner quickly discovered that Harrods was using a very antiquated inventory management system, based on an outdated Microsoft Excel software program. Surprisingly, the retailer could not do sophisticated assortment planning because they could not go down to the micro level of styles, colors, and sizes.[2] Today, Harrods has a state of the art inventory management system. Other examples of being a technology laggard are more understandable such as Bob's Stores, a 34-store chain in the Northeast which only recently adopted an information system that allows them to analyze past performance and consumer demand patterns to more accurately forecast sales. In Bob's case, they were able to cut inventory at distribution centers by 16 percent and in-store inventory by 9 percent while maintaining sales levels and gross margins.[3]

</td></tr>
</table>

Retailers need to be careful to not cut back too much on stock levels because the retailer who is frequently out of stock will quickly lose customers. This is why the business-trade press and retailers take such an interest in inventory levels as different seasons approach. For example, Christmas, which traditionally accounts for 25 percent to 30 percent of annual sales,[4] can be ruined by the lack of inventory to support sales. On the other hand, if the inventory is not sold, the costs involved in carrying excess inventory can force the retailer into taking extra markdowns in addition to having to pay interest on the inventory investment.

<table>
<tr><td>

gross margin return on inventory (GMROI) Is gross margin divided by average inventory at cost; alternatively, it is the gross margin percent multiplied by net sales.

</td><td>

Because inventory is the largest investment retailers make, often over 40 percent of a retailer's total assets, high-performance retailers use a model called **gross margin return on inventory** (GMROI) when analyzing the performance of their inventory. GMROI incorporates how quickly inventory sells and profit into a single measure. It can be computed as follows:

$$\text{(gross margin/net sales)} \times \text{(net sales/average inventory at cost)}$$
$$= \text{(gross margin/average inventory at cost)}$$

</td></tr>
</table>

Here the gross-margin percentage (gross margin/net sales) is multiplied by net sales/dollars invested in inventory to get the retailer's gross-margin dollars generated for each dollar invested in inventory. Net sales are typically computed on an annual basis. (Note, however, that sales/dollars invested in inventory is not the same as inventory turnover. Inventory turnover measures sales/inventory at retail. In the GMROI equation, we use inventory at cost to reflect the investment in carrying merchandise.) Thus, if a particular item has a gross margin of 45 percent and annual sales per dollar of inventory investment of 4.0, its GMROI would be $1.80 ($.45 × 4). Note that this could also be equated to 180 percent GMROI. In other words, for each dollar invested in inventory, on average the retailer obtains $1.80 in gross margin annually. Gross-margin dollars are used to first pay the store's operating expenses (both fixed and variable), with the remainder equaling the retailer's before-tax profit.

You might be wondering what are some of the GMROI performance statistics for retailers you recognize and we mention often in our examples throughout this book. We list these statistics for a dozen retailers, including Abercrombie & Fitch, Best Buy, Gap, Home Depot, Kroger, Pier 1, Tiffany & Company, and Target. You might notice the lowest GMROI performance comes from Tiffany & Company, which has a very low sales to inventory ratio of 1.8; however, it has a very strong gross margin of 63.2 percent, which together yield a relatively unattractive GMROI of 111 percent. Consider on the other hand, Abercrombie & Fitch, with a similar gross margin of 66.2 percent but also a very strong sales-to-inventory ratio of 7.3 that together generate a GMROI of 482.8 percent. In most lines of retailing GMROI performance of over 200 percent is expected.

Before continuing the discussion of merchandise management, you may want to review a couple of earlier chapters. Because all retailing activities are aimed at serving the customer's needs and wants at a profit, you may want to revisit Chapter 3 on the customer. Likewise, because merchandise management is concerned with the acquisition of inventory from other supply-chain members, you may also want to review Chapter 5 on the behavior of the different supply-chain members. Remember the discussion of cash flow in Chapter 8, and consider that if suppliers provide a retailer with credit and thus delay the outlay of cash, then the retailer's cash flow situation is improved. Also, consider that a key driver of GMROI is the sales to inventory ratio and as this improves, the retailer will also improve its cash flow. Why? Because cash comes into the retailer as soon as it sells merchandise; unless it sells on store credit and not many retailers do that anymore, but prefer credit or debit cards where they get their funds immediately.

Exhibit 9.2
GMROI for 12 National Retailers (2011)

Retailer	Gross Margin	Sales/Inventory	GMROI
Abercrombie & Fitch	66.2%	7.3×	482.8%
Best Buy	26.7%	8.8×	236.2%
Bed Bath & Beyond	41.4%	4.6×	189.7%
Gap	40.3%	9.0×	363.2%
Home Depot	34.5%	6.8×	235.0%
Kroger	20.9%	17.7×	369.2%
Limited Brands	43.1%	10.4×	447.8%
Pier One	42.4%	4.8×	202.2%
Target	34.5%	7.9×	272.3%
Tiffany & Company	63.2%	1.8×	111.0%
TJX	29.4%	7.9×	231.4%
Walmart Stores	26.5%	10.9×	289.7%

As pointed out in Chapter 8, successful merchandise management revolves around planning and control. It takes time to buy merchandise, have it delivered, record the delivery in the company records, and properly display the merchandise; therefore, it is essential to plan. Buyers need to decide today what their stock requirements will be weeks, months, or even seasons in advance. When the retailer operates a chain of stores, it also needs to decide how to allocate its inventory to various stores. In fact, one of the early jobs that retailers assign to recent college graduates is to allocate inventory to stores and this is always done with sophisticated inventory management information systems.

As planning occurs, it is only logical that the retailer exercise control over the merchandise (dollars and units) that it plans to purchase. A good control system is vital. If the retailer carries too much inventory, then the costs of carrying that inventory might outweigh the gross margin to be made on the sale, especially if the retailer is forced to reduce the selling price. At times, a retailer could actually improve GMROI by decreasing the retail price if the sale excites customers to the point that they buy more of the product—at a level where the sales-to-inventory ratio increase is more than enough to offset the gross-margin reduction from the reduced sales price. This is illustrated in Exhibit 9.3 where we see that although a retailer cuts price and thus lowers its gross margin from 50 percent to 42.9 percent, that its sales to inventory ratio rises from 4.0 to 4.9, and thus GMROI moves from 200 percent to 210 percent.

After concluding our discussion on the dollar amount of inventory needed for stock requirements, the remainder of this chapter will look at the other merchandising decisions facing the retailer: calculating the dollar amount available to be spent, managing one's inventory, choosing and evaluating merchandise sources, handling vendor negotiations, handling the merchandise in the store, and evaluating merchandise performance.

Working with upper management, buyers are responsible for the dollar planning of merchandise requirements. In the previous chapter, we described the various factors that must be considered in making the sales forecast, the first step in determining inventory needs. Once planned sales for the period in question have been projected, buyers are then able to use any one of four different methods for planning dollars invested in merchandise: (1) basic stock, (2) percentage variation, (3) weeks' supply, and (4) the stock-to-sales-ratio method.

While our discussion in this chapter will focus on retailers who sell tangible goods, the same basic principles may be applied to service retailers, with one exception. Whereas tangible products are first produced, then sold, and finally consumed, services are first sold but then produced and consumed simultaneously. Thus, service retailers, be they beauty parlors or hospitals, are prevented from stockpiling their inventories, whether it is a hair highlighting process or a heart bypass operation, in anticipation of

Exhibit 9.3
Lower Prices May Lead to Higher GMROI

	Initial Situation	Price Cut Scenario
Unit Price	$40	$35
Unit Cost	$20	$20
Unit Gross Margin	$20	$15
Unit Sales	1000	1400
Unit Inventory	500	500
Inventory Investment	$10,000	$10,000
Gross Margin	$20,000	$21,000
GMROI (Gross Margin/ Inventory Investment)	$20,000/$10,000 = 200%	$21,000/$10,000 = 210%

© Cengage Learning

SERVICE — RETAILING

This Hotel Has Gone to the Dogs (and Cats)

It used to be a bad sign when it was said that a hotel "went to the dogs." Not anymore. PetSmart has identified a large group of pet owners that the company refers to as "pet parents," not "pet owners." Pet parents are passionately committed to their pets, and pets are seen as family members by these individuals.

In seeking to address the needs of this group, the retailer focused on providing these customers with a one-stop shopping destination that offered everything needed by these family members in an easy-to-shop, full-service specialty environment. In doing so, PetSmart recognized a unique market segment not being met by the competition—pet boarding. Enter PetSmart's PetsHotel, a boarding and day-care facility for dogs and cats that caters to their every need—even if this includes frequent tender loving care. By mid-2012 PetsHotel had been so successful that PetSmart operated hotels in 35 states and in Ontario, Canada and is an important component of PetSmart growth plan over the next decade.

PetSmart recognized that precisely because there are few competitive barriers to entering the pet care and boarding market that quality and reliability of care is a major problem when it comes to selecting a place to board your family pet. Because of this PetSmart, an already trustworthy retailer, along with PetsHotel, offer a compelling value proposition. First, their employees (pet caregivers) are hand-picked for their love of pets. Second, these caregivers are safety-certified and trained in all aspects of personalized pet care. Third, a Veterinarian is always on call.

Each hotel provides three daily meals prepared just the way their four-legged guests like, free DVDs, and a daily dose of lactose-free ice cream. In addition, PetsHotel offers its guests many amenities not offered by a traditional kennel, such as 24-hour supervision, an on-site veterinarian, air-conditioned rooms and suites, daily specialty treats, play time, and the ability to call and talk with your pet through the bone booth. On holidays, the hotel serves a special meal designed especially for pets. On Thanksgiving, for example, dogs feast on turkey and stuffing, followed by a cranberry apple crumb dessert. Felines indulge in turkey and giblets, followed by kitty milk and cookies. Each dinner is served on special turkey-shaped plates. Of course, dogs (in the Atrium area) and cats (in the Kitty Cottages) are kept in separate areas with separate ventilation systems so they don't smell each other.

However, just as all service retailers must use forecasting tools to adjust their retailing mix and make preparations, especially regarding personnel, to satisfy their customers' wants, this is especially difficult for PetsHotel's management. While regular hotels might experience some fluctuations in demand based on a multitude of factors, they can always count on an occupancy level of between 40 percent and 100 percent. Thus, they will always need someone at the front desk and to work in maintenance and to make repairs overnight. Not so with PetsHotel. Many days, especially during the school year, family travel is limited, and no guests require their services. However, during holidays and summer months, occupancy is likely to reach capacity many days. Even the slightest change in weather can affect occupancy rates as pet parents may decide to leave the four-legged "child" outside while they go on a two-day business trip. Thus, it is very important for service retailers, especially those offering a new type of service, to manage their merchandise mix and personnel needs. However, with careful planning, success is quite possible.

Source: Based on the textbook authors' experiences as pet parents and information found at http://PetsHotel.PetSmart.com, Accessed on: April 7, 2012.

future demand. Given the limited ability to stockpile inventories, service retailers must pay special attention to forecasting demand. This is because even though they do not inventory merchandise, they do inventory or have available personnel to provide services. Thus, a barber shop needs to determine how many barbers to schedule, and a bank needs to decide how many bank tellers to schedule. In a sense, traditional retailers also face this challenge because they need to schedule cashiers or retail clerks in relation to customer traffic flow to provide customer service. In addition, as shown in the "Service Retailing" box on PetsHotel, these service retailers must adjust their retailing mix and make preparations, especially regarding personnel, to satisfy their customers' wants and needs.

Basic Stock Method

basic stock method (BSM)

Is a technique for planning dollar inventory investments and allows for a base stock level plus a variable amount of inventory that will increase or decrease at the beginning of each sales period in the same dollar amount as the period's expected sales.

The **basic stock method (BSM)** is used when retailers believe that it is necessary to have a stable level of inventory available at all times. It requires that the retailer always have a base level of inventory investment regardless of the predicted sales volume. In addition to the base stock level, there will be a variable amount of inventory that will increase or decrease at the beginning of each sales period (one month in the case of our merchandise budget) in the same dollar amount as the period's sales are expected to increase or decrease. The BSM can be calculated as follows:

Average monthly sales for the season	= Total planned sales for the season/ Number of months in the season
Average stock for the season	= Total planned sales for the season/ Estimated inventory-turnover rate for the season
Basic stock	= Average stock for the season − Average monthly sales for the season
Beginning-of-month (BOM) stock at retail	= Basic stock + Planned monthly sales

To illustrate the use of the basic stock method, let's look at the planned sales for Department 353 of the Two-Seasons Department Store shown in Exhibit 8.2. Assume that the inventory-turnover rate for the six months, or the number of times the average inventory is sold for the season is 2.0.

Average monthly sales for the season	= Total planned sales for the season/ Number of months
	= \$500,000/6 = \$83,333
Average stock for the season	= Total planned sales for the season/ Inventory turnover
	= \$500,000/2 = \$250,000
Basic stock	= Average stock − Average monthly sales
	= \$250,000 − \$83,333 = \$166,667
BOM @ retail (Feb.)	= Basic stock + Planned monthly sales
	= \$166,667 + \$75,000 = \$241,667
BOM @ retail (Mar.)	= \$166,667 + \$75,000 = \$241,667
BOM @ retail (Apr.)	= \$166,667 + \$100,000 = \$266,667
BOM @ retail (May)	= \$166,667 + \$50,000 = \$216,667
BOM @ retail (Jun.)	= \$166,667 + \$125,000 = \$291,667
BOM @ retail (Jul.)	= \$166,667 + \$75,000 = \$241,667

In the middle of these two would be a retailer such as Sports Authority, selling a complete range of sporting apparel and equipment. One of the key decisions that restaurants such as McDonald's faces is how much variety to have on their menu. McDonald's is known for burgers and fries but added the Filet-O-Fish in 1962, Southwest Salad in 2007, and Mac Snack Wraps in 2010 and have had many other expansions of their menu variety. Incidentally, this variety did not come from a creative merchandise manager, but from Chef Daniel Courdreaut, who after being trained at the Culinary Institute of America and running the elaborate and gracious kitchen at the Four Seasons Resort and Club outside Dallas, joined McDonalds as Director of Culinary Innovation and Menu Management.[5]

Breadth

breadth (or assortment)
The number of merchandise brands that are found in a merchandise line.

Breadth, also called **assortment**, refers to the number of brands that are found in a single merchandise line. For example, a supermarket will have a wide breadth or assortment in the number of different brands of mustard it carries: six or seven national or regional brands, a private brand, and a generic brand. The 7-Eleven convenience stores, however, will offer very little breadth in generally carrying only one or two brands in any merchandise line. The breadth might change with time. For example, many clothing retailers now have as much as three times the selection in the misses department over the petites department (as customer sizes[6] and manufacturer product styles have changed). Or a high-end specialty menswear retailer or department store may have multiple brands of men's suits catering to different tastes. For the man looking for a classic look, they might handle Ralph Lauren Purple Label (http://www.ralphlauren.com); for the fashion forward and probably younger male, they may feature Rick Owens (http://www.rickowens.eu), and finally for the customer that wants a bit more fashion beyond classic but not heavily fashion forward, they may handle Giorgio Armani (http://www.armani.com).

Fashion buyers attend fashion shows of various designers in order to build an assortment that will appeal to the retailer's target customers.

Breadth is particularly a problem for retailers selling private-label brands. Retailers seek a proper balance between their own private labels and the national brands they carry. This is because private-label brands, as noted in Chapter 4, offer the retailer lower costs and higher gross margins, and this is primarily why in 2011 over 30 percent of the 14,400 new food and beverage items introduced in the United States were private label brands; most often introduced by Safeway, Kroger and Supervalu which account for 40 percent of U.S. retail supermarket sales.[7]

battle of the brands
Occurs when retailers have their own products competing with the manufacturer's products for shelf space and control over display location.

Retailers also need national brands to draw customers into its store. Yet sometimes a powerful manufacturer may try to tie some of its merchandise lines together. In other words, if the retailer wishes to carry one product, the manufacturer stipulates that the retailer must also carry its entire product line. When retailers are faced with such a dilemma, a **battle of the brands** can occur in which the retailer, in determining the breath of its product assortment, has its own brands competing with the manufacturer's brands for shelf space and control over display location. One consequence of such a battle of the brands is that many retailers now stock one or both of the top brands in a product line or category as well as their own private brand. Other retailers are handling this battle of the brands by working with designers to develop exclusive lines.[8] For instance you can find Miley Cyrus's line of apparel only at Walmart, for Jennifer Lopez's line, or the American Idol Collection, you must go to Kohl's and for Demi

To overcome the "battle of the brands," some retailers, are working with designers to develop exclusive lines, like Kohl's did with their Jennifer Lopez collection.

Lovato's apparel you need to shop at Target. As a result of this battle of the brands, there is one negative consequence, many so-called third-tier brands, often by regional manufacturers, have been left off store shelves.

Depth

Merchandise **depth** refers to the average number of stockkeeping units (SKUs) within each brand of the merchandise line. In the preceding example, the supermarket manager must decide which sizes and types of French's mustard to carry. The convenience store will probably carry only the regular nine-ounce jar of French's. In apparel retailing, depth can be a constant challenge because customers have such different color and style preferences. For instance, with women's apparel, it is not just an issue of how many fancy dresses to stock, but how many with full-length sleeves or at quarter length, and you always need to be careful with skirts to have different lengths to appeal to different women. In addition, fashion is about novelty, and this requires even more selection. Even experienced retailers, such as J.Crew, can occasionally have a merchandising season where they simply didn't get their merchandise assortment correct.[9] Depth is an acute problem today because all too often retailers are restricted in the number of SKUs they can carry by specific constraining factors.

Constraining Factors

Research indicates that the merchandise mix, in addition to satisfying customer wants, can actually shape those wants and impact whether and what customers purchase.[10] Exhibit 9.4 details the four constraining factors that may restrict the retailer's design of the optimal merchandise mix. Remember, just as the trading areas for each store in a chain are different, the optimal mix will be different for every store. Merchandise mix decisions are a blend of financial plans that consider the retailer's dollar and turnover constraints, the store's space constraints, and the constraints caused by the actions of competitors.

Dollar-Merchandise Constraints

There seldom will be enough investment dollars to emphasize variety, breadth, and depth simultaneously. If the decision is made to emphasize variety, it would be unrealistic to expect the retailer to also have a lot of breadth and depth. For instance, assume for the moment that you are the owner or manager of a local gift store. You have $70,000 to invest in merchandise. If you decide that you want a lot of variety in gifts (jewelry, crystal, candles, games, cards, figurines, ashtrays, clocks, and radios), then you obviously cannot have much depth in any single item such as crystal glassware.

Some retailers try to overcome this dollar constraint by shifting the expense of carrying inventory back on the vendor. When a retailer buys a product on **consignment**, the vendor retains the ownership of the goods, usually establishes the selling price, and is paid only when the goods are sold. (This is different from the use of the word *consignment* to describe customers taking products to stores like Play It Again Sports to resell merchandise to other customers with the store taking a percentage of the profit). **Pay from scan** is a more recent term that some retailers are beginning to use when describing consignment. Pay from scan (or consignment) helps reduce risk for seasonal products such as greeting cards, books, magazines, or dated food products (e.g., chips or soda). The manufacturer usually sends a field representative to the retail store to pull the remaining product off the shelf when the sell-by date passes. One of the benefits of pay from scan is that a retailer can have a lot of holiday greeting cards or promotional displays and not worry about having to (1) put them in storage somewhere for a year or

(2) spend precious markdown dollars on them. However, consignment doesn't come free. Manufacturers usually pass along a higher initial cost to the retailer to cover the returns. Still, retailers don't have to worry about magazines or potato chips expiring every month. It's a trade-off that retailers must make product by product or category by category: higher initial margin or less risk.

extra dating (EX)
Allows the retailer extra or interest-free days before the period of payment begins.

Another approach the retailer might try to get is **extra dating**, where the vendor allows the retailer some extra time before paying for the goods. For example, the Christmas season is a prime time for toys to be sold. However, the toy manufacturers need to fill their supply chain and get the toys in the retailers' warehouses and stores by mid- to late October. Most of these toys will be sold the last week of November and in December. Thus, a toy manufacturer, who may usually provide 30 days of interest-free financing on purchases, may give an extra 30 days (60 days in total) for the retailer to pay.

Space Constraints

The retailer must also deal with space constraints. If depth or breadth is wanted, then space is needed. If variety is to be stressed, then it is also important to have enough *empty* space to separate the distinct merchandise lines. For example, consider a single counter containing cosmetics, candy, fishing tackle, women's stockings, and toys. This would obviously be an unsightly and unwise arrangement. As more variety is added, empty space becomes necessary to allow the consumer to clearly distinguish between distinct product lines. In the case of some upscale department stores, such as Saks Fifth Avenue, much of the space is used to carve out highly focused and artistically designed shops for key vendors and designers, such as Eileen Fisher, Elie Tahari, Ralph Lauren, Prada, Gucci, Hugo Boss, Burberrry, and Red Valentino.

Most retailers have operation guides that tell how much space should be between each fixture, rack, display, and so forth. They also have to decide how tall they want their fixtures to be. A retailer could have taller shelf sections (gondolas) that hold more products; however, at some point, it would start to feel like a warehouse. Conversely, the retailer could use shorter shelves that customers find more visually appealing, but this tactic provides less space for products. For example, Walmart is taking out many of its risers in its stores to be more visually appealing. While this impacts store atmospherics, it also reduces how much inventory the total store can hold. It either has to give up products (go narrower in breadth or depth), go leaner on inventory (risking out of stocks) and have more trucks on the road, or have more trailers behind the store (in which there is usually more theft, product and package damage, and outside temperature changes that can freeze or melt some products), where permitted.

Retailers, especially in the grocery business, have been able to turn this space constraint into an advantage by charging manufacturers slotting fees, discussed in both Chapters 6 and 8, to carry their products.

Merchandise-Turnover Constraints

As the depth of the merchandise is increased, the retailer will be stocking more and more variations of the product to serve smaller and smaller segments. Consequently, inventory turnover will deteriorate as the retailer attempts to decrease the chances of being out of stock. One does not have to minimize variety, breadth, and depth to maximize turnover, but one must know how various merchandise mixes will affect inventory turnover. One tactic some retailers are using is to offer to order the out-of-stock item or the item not regularly carried by the retailer. Often this is done via the retailer's Internet site. This reinforces the point made in Chapter 7 that more and more retailers are using multiple channels to reach customers. Retailers that operate multiple stores in a community also are often able to check the inventory on hand at their other stores in the area and either direct the customer to that store or have the merchandise delivered to the customer's home.

Market Constraints

Market constraints also affect decisions on variety, breadth, and depth. The three dimensions have a profound effect on how the consumer perceives the store and consequently on the customers that the store will attract. The consumer perceives a specialty store as one with limited variety and breadth of merchandise lines but considerable depth within the lines handled. An individual searching for depth in a limited set of merchandise lines such as formal menswear will thus be attracted to a menswear retailer specializing in formal wear. On the other hand, the consumer perceives a general merchandise retailer such as Target as a store with lots of variety and breadth in terms of merchandise lines but with a more constrained depth. Therefore, someone who needs to make several purchases across several merchandise lines and is willing to sacrifice depth of assortment would be more attracted to the general merchandise retailer. Often, when there is an innovation in a product you sell, then as a retailer in this market you must add this new product. For example, about eight years ago we witnessed the emergence of barefoot, lightweight, or what some refer to as the minimalist shoe; Barefoot Footwear with its Vibram FiveFingers shoe is the most popular but the Minimus line by New Balance, which uses the tagline "like barefoot only better," is growing quickly. Today, you can't claim to be an athletic shoe store without handling multiple brands in the new minimalist line of shoes. In brief, the market often dictates parts of your merchandise mix.

The constraining factors make it almost impossible for a retailer to emphasize all three dimensions. However, retailers can take some comfort in the fact that greater product selection does not necessarily mean that the consumer will get more enjoyment from the shopping experience. Research has found that retailers can cut SKUs without lowering consumer perceptions of selection. In fact, Proctor & Gamble (P&G) claims that in the laundry category 40 percent of SKUs could be eliminated and 95 percent of consumer needs would still be met.[11] Some consumers may even be more satisfied with the smaller selection.[12] This is important for retailers using the category management system

ZUMA Wire Service/Alamy

Sometimes the market can dictate part of the merchandise mix because customers expect new product categories to be carried in their favorite stores. The minimalist line of athletic shoes is one example of how the market dictated the merchandise be added.

to remember. After all, category management, in its effort to increase profits, typically reduces the number of SKUs as it seeks to increase inventory turnover. Nevertheless, if you are going to lose customers, you should seek to lose the less-profitable ones by properly mixing your merchandise in terms of variety, breadth, and depth within the dollar, space, turnover, and market constraints.

Managing the Inventory

After deciding the relative emphasis to be placed on the three dimensions of the merchandise mix, you need to decide when to order and reorder the desired merchandise lines and items. Ideally, as shown in Exhibit 9.5, a retailer selling a basic stock item, one that should always to be in stock, would receive the reordered merchandise just as it is needed. However, a retailer selling a seasonal item, as shown in Exhibit 9.6, would want to be completely sold out at the planned out-of-stock date.

Both Exhibits 9.5 and 9.6 recognize the fact that it annually costs the retailer between 15 percent and 20 percent to carry inventory. Some of these costs are direct, such as product spoilage, shrinkage, interest on the money borrowed to pay for the inventory or insurance and warehousing expenses, and other costs may be indirect, such as what the retailer could have made elsewhere when it uses its own money to pay for the inventory.

The retailer tries to achieve the optimization of its inventory dollars by closely monitoring its inventory. One of the great difficulties many retailers face is that inventory figures, including "perpetual inventory" (real-time updating) are often wrong as much as 40 percent of the time.[13] Thus, retailers need to do a physical audit of their actual inventory, which involves counting every single item on the shelves, and this can take from a half to a full-day. Some retailers even use firms that specialize in counting inventory. More retailers are moving to wireless handheld auditing terminals and some are now in the form of an electronic tablet computer that records and wirelessly transmits inventory data to the retailer's information systems department and computer files and records are instantly updated.[14]

One way to fix (or decrease) the problem is to use radio frequency identification (RFID) barcode data. An RFID tag consists of a tiny digital signal processor embedded in a product, package, or box. It allows retailers to account for merchandise without the use of hand counts, which often leads to missed items in the stockroom, on risers, on the wrong shelves, or in customer carts. They also allow for faster reorders (as the merchandise is being sold). Macy's has been one of the early adopters of RFID. They credit this technology with being able to accurately maintain inventory at 97 percent

Exhibit 9.5
Inventory Management for a Retailer Selling a Basic Stock Item

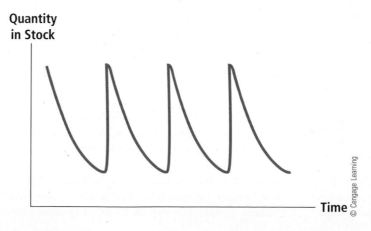

Exhibit 9.6
Inventory Management for a Retailer Selling a Seasonal Item

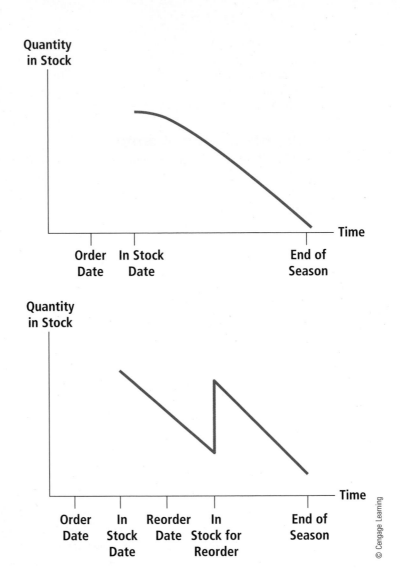

or higher; that is having the right merchandise at the right store at the right time.[15] However, even with Macy's, the focus has been on regularly stocked and replenished basic items versus fashion merchandise that changes rapidly. In this chapter's What's New: RFID Friend or Foe, you will learn that RFID although an exciting technology faces many hurdles.

Another problem can arise when retailers use the wrong baseline in making their forecast. It is well known that sales are heavily driven by the price; however, one of the key determinants of price is what the retailer pays for merchandise both at the factory and the cost of transport. Thus, to manage inventories properly, the retailer also has to forecast the factors that will drive production and distribution costs. In apparel and food, the prices retailers pay for merchandise rose rapidly in 2011, and thus, retailers found ways to work with producers to lower costs.[16] Have you noticed for some packaged foods how the container size is shrinking, and how with apparel, the buttons are not quite as classy as historically, or your pockets are not quite as deep. As we learned, many retailers are using a lot of private labels, and if the retailer directs the producer to use cheaper buttons on a blouse and it saves 20 cents and the retailer sells a million blouses a year, then that is $200,000 in annual savings.

comp shopping
When an employee of one retailer goes into another retailer and checks prices on a select few items to see how competitive they are on a local basis.

WHAT'S NEW ?

RFID: Friend or Foe?

Every major retailer's chief information officer believes that the widespread adoption of RFID tags is a sure thing and will ultimately enable him or her to track every single product from point of manufacture to checkout. Already the biggest names in global retailing— Carrefour, Home Depot, Marks & Spencer, Metro AG, Tesco and Walmart—have lined up behind RFID's promise of absolute inventory control, its consequent cost reductions, and profit-margin improvements.

However, before realizing these advantages, RFID tagging will require a high initial investment in technology and training costs. RFID tagging will produce reams of information ranging from when and where the merchandise was produced to its current location in the supply chain in addition to the customer profile of the purchaser of that merchandise. Without a proper information system, the data provided will create mountains of paperwork for retailers to handle. This data will have to be stored, transmitted in real time, and shared with store management, warehouse management, inventory management, and the retailer's financial systems.

As an innovative retail technology, RFID is infinitely more powerful than barcodes, although it still has a few drawbacks. For one, while RFID offers a great advantage to retailers that sell high-ticket merchandise or that wish to tag at the case, carton, or pallet level, there is a major technical obstacle to widespread adoption that still needs to be overcome: The radio waves used by the tags to communicate are absorbed by liquids and distorted by metal, making RFID useless for tracking, say, cans of soda or jugs of milk.

A second obstacle is that some consumer privacy groups have expressed concerns that products could even be tracked to customers' homes. Therefore, before being accepted by consumers, retailers will have to convince consumers that RFID tags are not a threat to personal privacy. Retailers must overcome the issues raised by consumer associations such as Consumer Against Supermarket Privacy Invasion and Numbering, which is strongly opposed to the adoption of RFID technology by retailers.

There are still other challenges that no one has yet brought up. Some of these challenges have to do with competition and information. For example, a third obstacle is that *anyone* with a RFID handheld scanner would know what is in a retailer's store. For the magnitude of this obstacle to become clear, you have to understand the current situation of what retailers can do. Currently, most retailers do what is called **comp shopping**: An employee of one retailer goes into another retailer and checks prices on a select few items to see how competitive they are on a local basis—for example, does the retailer need to drop prices to match a competitor's sale?. Most retailers do it, and most retailers turn a blind eye to others doing it on a limited basis.

With RFID, however, any associate could walk into another retailer's store and instantly have a complete tally of every UPC being carried by the competing retailer with on-hand quantities. Taking this competitive information threat a step further, if the person made a scan a couple times a day for several days, *they would have an idea of the sales volume of the retailer* for every item. Now consider that Walmart stopped letting Information Resources, Inc. (IRI), and Nielsen collect data from its store scanners a few years ago because it thought its competitors were gaining more value than Walmart was through the industry scanner data reports. Likewise, there is a lot of debate about what percent of any particular retailer's sales is coming from different brands or from branded products versus private-label products. Thus, when RFID catches on, a manufacturer's sales representative could just walk into a retailer's store a few times with the RFID handheld scanner if he or she were interested in how much one of their competitors was selling at retail. Local governments could do the same if they wanted to project taxes for certain items, or the Federal Trade Commission could do it if it was interested in investigating market concentration among manufacturers or retailers.

Of course, retailers could try to ban people from bringing RFID scanners into the stores. Two things would probably happen. One, people would disguise them—they'd look like a blackberry or cell phone or be hidden in a purse. Second, they could simply stand

(continued)

on a public sidewalk along the street a block from the retailer and scan the trucks coming to the retailer—which would give an even more accurate feed of the exact sales movement over time of the retailer at the individual store level. (Perhaps ACNielsen or IRI will start hiring people to do this since they can no longer gather data from Walmart's Retail Link database.) If it had a strong interest, a manufacturer or government could simply mount an RFID tracker to a building or sign that it owns on the truck's route close to the store. It could do this for *any* or *every* retailer. Even small businesses or people selling on E-bay who ship items in unmarked boxes would be shipping products in what could be called "invisible packaging" because anyone with an RFID scanner could learn what's inside it.

Third, and building on the second point, hijackers (e.g., organized crime, pirates, etc.) would have the ability to know what is in every passing truck, cargo container, or mail package. While there is a decent rule of law in the United States, manufacturers and retailers often go to great lengths to disguise or not call attention to their shipments of expensive electronics versus, say, pillows. Now every thug could know which truck to hold up on the road (and even which box to take off the truck) or which container to break open on a cargo ship at sea. Thus, while RFID can be a great friend to a retailer trying to improve its perpetual inventory system, it could turn out to also be a terrible foe.

Source: Used with permission of Professor Jared Hansen, University of North Carolina at Charlotte.

Using the Item File to Manage Inventory

Once a retail buyer has finished negotiating the purchase of an item, the buyer has to oversee the creation of the item in the retailer's computer system. Creating an item in a retailer's computer system may sound easy, but it involves several steps. For example, the buyer or assistants have to determine which subcategories and categories of merchandise the item will be assigned to. When inventory of the item is purchased from the supplier or sales are made to customers, the item's performance will be linked to that category on both the OTB and merchandise planner workbooks that the company keeps.

The buyer also has to decide how many items to create in the system. For example, if a buyer purchases a striped T-shirt that comes in five sizes and four colors, there are as many as 20 items that could be created and cross-referenced in the system. Does the buyer want to track sales by size and color or just by the shirt style? Tracking at a very detailed level can lead to less average inventory needed to be in stock in order to meet customer demand. It can also lead to "analysis paralysis." If the buyer has 20 items for the shirt and one or two of them are not correctly cross-referenced, then some of the items may get missed if the buyer creates a PO or sends a markdown, which can be costly at the stores.

Further, the buyer has to decide if there are any existing items that the new item should be linked to. Continuing with the shirt example, if the widths of the stripe or patterns change throughout the season as they often do, the retailer has to decide how to track the new shirts in its inventory system. Will they use the same item numbers? If not, will the new item numbers be cross listed with the narrower striped shirts' item numbers? Another way of thinking about it is, do all of the shirts get marked down at the same percentages off at the same time? If they are to be managed separately, then they need to be created as separate items. Further, was a similar shirt sold last year that the item should be cross-referenced to so that the merchandise analyst can compare year-to-year performance? Maybe the prior year it was bought from a different supplier, so it needs to be created as a new item in the system (to reflect the different supplier and costs) but linked to the other item for comparison. It might sound easy to do this for one shirt, but the process has to be done for every item that's going to the stores. Some retailers may decide the information gained from this type of item-level tracking isn't worth the costs of doing so, and they simply place stickers with prices on the item. Most of the larger, national retailers use very advanced tracking software so they can reorder products for each store in a way that the stores stay in stock, but not overstocked. Some large-scale retailers have a corporate purchasing order department solely to create and manage items and purchase orders in the retailer's computer system.

The other decision facing the buyer is, will the item be displayed everyday on permanent store fixtures (described in Chapter 13) or will the item be a "special buy"— a display item featured on a stack base in the aisle, at the front of the store, or on end-caps (displays at the end of aisles)? While both methods require inventory management, adding it to the shelf means another item has to be deleted and marked down to free up space for the new item. Making a shelf-space drawing (normally called a *planogram* or *modular*) takes several weeks of measuring product dimensions, uploading them, and adding the UPCs to the shelf-space software (i.e., programs like sas (www.sas.com) or Spaceman (www.acnielsen.com.au/ssl/files/SPACEGLB.PDF)). Stores have to reset the shelves (which takes valuable store employee time and wages). To not overwhelm the store employees or customers, most retailers have an annual shelf-space review calendar. When possible, each department is assigned a different week or time of the year to physically reset the shelves in the stores.

Basic stock items then need to be replenished, which means setting up a forecast usually based on the history of a similar item. Buyers need to be careful in deciding which existing items to use for the new item's history. For example, say a retailer decided to carry a new line of fashion-print bedsheets. If the retailer used an existing white bedsheet item for the sales pattern, then it might be in trouble toward the end of the year. White sales at many retailers have a sales bump toward the end of October that fashion sheets wouldn't have. Why? Because some customers buy the white sheets to use in homemade Halloween costumes. Using the white sheets as a history would result in an overstock of the fashion sheets in early November.

Sometimes special buys might also be replenished to avoid sending too much inventory at one time. Replenishment (buying and selling inventory) affects the merchandise budget and, in turn, the retailer's financial statements. Replenishment can be difficult because so many things can affect it—from weather to transportation problems (like dock strikes or backlogs in port inspections) to manufacturing problems. Manufacturing problems aren't just related to assembly lines. Competitors are always trying to find ways to gain an edge over the competition, and they increasingly seem to be using the court system to impact competition.

Conflicts in Stock Planning

Stock planning is an exercise in compromise and conflict. The conflict is multidimensional because not everything can be stocked. Some of the more common conflicts are described below.

1. Maintain a strong in-stock position on genuinely new items while trying to avoid the 90 percent of new products that fail in the introductory stage. The retailer wants to carry the new products that will satisfy customers. If the consumer is sold a poor product, it hurts the retailer as much as, if not more than, the manufacturer. The problem becomes one of screening out poor products before they reach the customer. Any screening device, however, has error; the retailer might end up stocking some losers and turning down winners. Thus, a basic conflict arises, but even the best of buyers will make some mistakes and be forced to use markdowns to unload slow-selling merchandise.

2. Maintain an adequate stock of the basic popular items while having sufficient inventory dollars to capitalize on unforeseen opportunities. Many times, if the

retailer fills out the model stock with recommended quantities, there is little if any money left over for the super buy that is just around the corner. But if the retailer holds out that money and cuts back on basic stock, then customers may be lost and that super buy may never surface. For this reason, it is important that retailers realize that they should never be out of stock on staples and best-selling products.

3. Maintain high inventory-turnover goals while maintaining high gross-margin goals. This is perhaps the most glaring conflict. Usually, items that turn over more rapidly have thinner gross margins. Therefore, developing an inventory plan that will accomplish both objectives is surely challenging.

4. Maintain adequate selection for customers while not confusing them. If customers are confronted with too many similar items, they will not be able to make up their minds and may leave the store empty-handed and frustrated. On the other hand, if the selection is inadequate, the customer will again leave empty-handed. Thus, a delicate balance needs to be struck between too little and too much selection.

5. Maintain space productivity and utilization while not congesting the store. Take advantage of buys that will utilize the available space but avoid buys that cause the merchandise to spill over into the aisles. Unfortunately, some of the best buys come along when space is already occupied. For instance, in the retail toy market, buyers need to anticipate during late spring and summer, what the hot Christmas toys will be, and thus, often they have their shelves filled and ready for the holiday season shopper. But, it seems like every year there is a big surprise on what becomes the hot selling toy.

Reviewing Inventory Performance

At the end of the selling season, the buyer reviews all of the merchandise performance in what many retailers call a *line review*. The process takes a few weeks. The buyer meets with all of the suppliers one–on–one (usually in one-hour meetings) where they use the supplier performance card and reports showing how each item supplied by the supplier did over the selling season (as compared to the category average and total). They might try to renegotiate the vendor contract or simply jump right into item negotiations, including which items are going to be discontinued and marked down (and who will fund the markdown), which items will stay, and which new items might be added to either the planogram or as seasonal displays. Hundreds of reports are run by the buyer. Some buyers will run an **80-20 report**, showing how much sales do the top 20 percent of the items generate for the retailer. Often 20 percent of the items will do 80 percent of a retailer's business. This also means that 80 percent of the items may only generate 20 percent of the retailer's sales. Other buyers will also run a **sell through report**. Sell through is the percentage of the stock of a particular item or group of items from a particular vendor that sold during the merchandise season. Sell through is computed as: units sold/(units on hand at end of season plus units sold). For instance, if a retailer sold 30 units and had 20 units on hand at the end of the season, then the sell through is 60 percent or (30/(30 + 20)). Various merchandise lines face different expectations in terms of sell through. For instance in apparel a sell through of 60 percent may be required to eliminate the item from being dropped, whereas in a luxury jeweler a sell through of 40 percent on watches over $5,000 may be acceptable. Both the 80-20 report and the sell through report are used to help decide which items to drop.

Deciding which items to drop however is a tricky decision and the merchandise analyst needs to be careful to ignore the overall market basket of related items a retailer

80-20 report
Shows how much sales the top 20% of merchandise items generate in terms of sales. Usually the top 20% generate at least 80% of sales.

sell through report
Lists the percentage of the stock or merchandise item or group of items from a each vendor sold during the prior merchandise season.

may sell. Often a given item may not be a top performer, but maybe it's one of the factors that draw people to the store. For instance a jewelry store may stock an assortment of Cartier watches that generally range in price from $7,500 to $90,000. A current popular model for men is the Calibre De Cartier (see the YouTube: http://www.youtube.com/watch?v=84PtPrKr8K4), which in gold retails for $23,000 and $7,100 in stainless steel and both items may have a fairly good sell through. The retailer may also stock the Cartier Ballon Bleu Tourbillon men's watch, which has a retail price of $104,000 and only sell one every couple of years; an obviously poor sell through. Nonetheless, this $104,000 masterpiece of time keeping makes the $23,000 Calibre De Cartier look like a bargain. Consequently, dropping the Cartier Ballon Bleu Tourbillon may be foolish because most of the salespeople in the store will tell you that it helps to generate considerable interest in the more modestly priced watches in the $7,500 to $30,000 price range.

Line reviews involve taking a lot of data and trying to summarize it in a digestible manner. They also involve understanding trends and fashion. Thus, to be successful, buyers need to have both creative and quantitative analysis capabilities. If they don't, they often are paired with assistants who can complement their strengths.

As should be readily evident at this point, inventory management is no easy task. Equally challenging is the selection of vendors from whom to purchase merchandise.

LO 5

Describe how a retailer selects proper merchandise sources.

Selection of Merchandising Sources

After deciding on the type and amount of inventory to be purchased, the next step is to determine where the retailer is to obtain its merchandise. All too often people have misconceptions about how retailers choose and negotiate with vendors. In reality, with proper planning and control, it can be a very rewarding experience, especially

Retail buyers and manufacturers meet at trade shows such as the international CES (Consumer Electronics Show) pictured here.

Private Label Merchandising is High-Risk

As you learned in prior chapters, there is a trend toward retailers developing more of their own private brands that allow them to have a more distinctive merchandise assortment. However, this is not as simple as it sounds because, if the retailer truly wants distinctive merchandise, it needs to invest in product design and arrange for production of the item(s), distribution and warehousing, and often many international trade details, because most manufacturing will be done in a foreign country. Predictably all of this takes time and money, and a lot of bottlenecks can occur, and of course this is accompanied by more business risk.

To put this in perspective, here are the details of how the development, distribution, and sale of a private label fashion apparel item would occur over an approximate 18-month period.

January	The retailer holds a series of planning meetings for fashion items for the following spring (approximately 14 months forward)
February	Decision is made to move forward to design a new junior wear women's collection for the following spring
March-April	Design work on the new private label apparel line
May	Samples made and redesigns worked on as needed
June	Branding and marketing campaign work commences
July	Evaluate potential off-shore cut-and-sew operations
July-August	Retailer buys materials and supplies (fabric, zippers, buttons, etc.). Note that most cut and sew operations require the retailer to purchase and ship to them all materials
September	Offshore cut-and-sew factory selected and contract finalized
October	Materials and supplies shipped to offshore factory. Branding and marketing campaign completed
December	Production is completed and items shipped to retailer's distribution center in North America
January	Merchandise is allocated to stores
February	Merchandise arrives in stores
March	Merchandise is available in stores and advertised
June	First markdowns on merchandise
July	Last markdowns on merchandise
August	Unsold merchandise liquidated

Keep in mind that the above timelines are only a general guideline, and some highly experienced retailers that regularly design their own private labels (such as the Limited Brands and Zara) can speed this process up considerably. Also here are some general guidelines on costs as the items moved through the process described above. The retailer will spend money on design, and this could be very low or, if they contract to a major design firm, it could run into hundreds of thousands of dollars. The cost of producing samples is done on a custom basis, so it will cost several times what a normal garment costs to produce. Let's next consider that for the assortment and volume the retailer projects it needs for the spring season, it must purchase $600,000 in fabric, fasteners, and so forth, and ship this to the cut-and-sew factory. The cut-and-sew operation then performs labor tasks, and the price the retailer then pays is usually .8 times the material cost. Thus $600,000 translates into $480,000 ($8 \times $600,000) for the apparel cut-and-sew labor and overhead. The cost of the material ($600,000) and the labor and overhead cost ($480,000) are summed ($1,080,000) and multiplied by 2.5 to get the retail price or $2.7 million ($1,080,000 \times 2.5). If the retailer is lucky, it will sell 60 percent at full retail or $1,620,000 (.6 \times $2.7 million) and the remaining $1,080,000 ($2.7 million less $1,620,000) at 40 percent of retail or $432,000 (.4 \times $1,080,000). Below we can see the profit from this complex and risky venture. In this example, we project a $200,000 advertising budget and $80,000 for various transportation costs to ship materials to factories, ship finished goods to the North American distribution center, and then to ship from the distribution center to the retailer's stores.

(continued)

Sales at Full Retail	$1,620,000
Sales at Discount	$ 432,000
Total Sales	$2,052,000
Less:	
Cost of Design and Samples	$100,000
Cost of Materials	$600,000
Labor Costs	$480,000
Transport Costs	$80,000
Advertising	$200,000
Total Costs	$1,460,000
Profit	$ 592,000

Of course it is possible that the spring fashion is a flop and the retailer has to sell most of the merchandise at a substantial discount or even liquate it for ten cents on the dollar. Predictably this would generate a very large loss; as we mentioned, private brand design and sourcing is a high-risk business.

© Cengage Learning

when customers react positively to merchandise selection. However, no matter how rewarding a buying experience is, it will also be grueling. Retail buyers must not only determine what merchandise lines to carry but also select the best possible vendor to supply them with these items while simultaneously negotiating the best deal possible with that vendor.

Unless the retailer owns a manufacturing or wholesale operation or both, the retailer must consider many criteria when selecting a merchandise source. In fact, even if the retailer designs its own merchandise and outsources manufacturing and distribution to other organizations, it still has to do a lot of selection among the competing organizations that can perform these outsourced activities. To help you understand the considerable time and effort involved in designing and sourcing private label merchandise, we have prepared the Retailing: The Inside Story. After you read this story, you may have second thoughts on if private label branding is as attractive as you may have initially envisioned.

The criteria used to evaluate merchandise sources depend on the retailer's type of store and merchandise sold. Generally, the following criteria, which may vary across merchandise lines, should always be considered: selling history, consumers' perception of the manufacturer's or wholesaler's reputation and brand, reliability of delivery, trade terms, projected markup, quality of merchandise, after-sales service (such as helping manage the retailer's replenishment system or perform annual shelf-space reviews), transportation time, distribution-center processing time, inventory carrying cost, country of origin, fashionability, and net cost.

The retail buyer also has to consider the size of the vendor. Is the vendor large enough to provide product to all of the retailer's stores in a timely and reliable manner? If so, is it big enough to replenish the items so they stay in stock without having too much inventory on hand? Is the vendor big enough to staff any support functions for the retailer? Pepsi and Coke can both send field employees into retail stores to restock and rotate soda products. A unique, local mom-and-pop beverage manufacturer probably couldn't do that. Further, if the retailer decided to drop the item to pursue a different strategy, is the vendor big enough that dropping the item won't hurt the vendor? If Target dropped handling one item from Unilever or General Mills, it would not do major damage to these firms. However, if a larger-scale retailer started doing business with a small, entrepreneurial manufacturer who had a single blockbuster product, what would happen if the retailer needed to discontinue it? Would the vendor go out of business? Would the retailer be accused by the manufacturer, the media, or customers of *putting* the vendor out of business?

Country of origin is also becoming a more important issue every day as governments use trade agreements to limit the amount of merchandise that can be imported from various countries. In addition, consumers are becoming aware of sweatshops and the use of child labor in certain countries, and they are rebelling against the buying of products manufactured in these areas. While laws regulating country of origin have long applied to apparel, one of the many initiatives found in the Farm Security and Rural Investment Act of 2002 requires country-of-origin labeling for beef, lamb, pork, fish, perishable agricultural commodities, and peanuts. This is increasingly important for buyers to consider given there were recently several situations in which dozens of manufacturers in China used melamine, a plastic derivative, in baby formula, chocolate, and pet food to make the products look like they had more protein in them. Many toys were also recalled over the last few years because several China-based manufacturers used lead paint beyond the level permitted by law. (The lead-based paint is shinier and requires less primer.) The public outrage over the children and pets that became sick or died has resulted in a renewed and stronger call for labeling where products are made and testing what is in them.

Although consumers say they want to know where their food comes from and what is in it, most are unaware of the costs associated with tracking and testing these products, the amount of record keeping needed, and the loss of sales resulting from the higher prices. The Grocery Manufacturers of America claim such laws are unworkable and will do little to maintain the safety and purity of the U.S. food supply. Is the cost worth it? Are you willing to pay the extra nickel or dime on every product to know where your food, clothing, and electronic purchases were made? And how do such laws apply to retailers in the resale markets? For example, as we discussed in Chapter 6, the U.S. federal government, in 2008, passed stronger consumer protection legislation in which all products for children younger than 12 (regardless of when they were made) have to be tested for lead and certain other chemicals.[17] This means thrift stores, consignment shops, and online auctions and resellers (like eBay or Amazon) are going to encounter a lot of difficulty or need to shut down a big part of their business. However, some local manufacturers have used the situation to help their locally produced products. For example, they'll have "Made in the USA" stickers on them when selling in the United States.

Taking the assortment reduction a step further, several retailers are rediscovering smaller stores.[18] For example, Tesco has recently started putting in very small "Fresh & Easy" stores in the United States with its initial stores in California, Nevada, and Arizona. Fresh & Easy thinks of itself as a lean, green, savings machine with a focus on healthy and nutritious food and meals at affordable prices. It also does some of its own manufacturing and processing to further control quality, an effort supported by the firm's own food technology and engineering specialists. Walmart has also moved to smaller stores through its new Walmart Express stores (about 10,000 to 15,000 square feet), which are half the size of the existing, small Neighborhood Market stores. These smaller stores have considerably less selling space than a 208,000-square-foot Supercenter store. (In addition, these stores don't have any reference to Walmart in them as the giant retailer tries to position these units as a friendly neighborhood grocer.) With a lot less space, these retailers have to decide which few items from their long list of available items they will sell.

Like everything else, tailoring merchandise assortments to each individual store involves a trade-off that the retailer must consider. By creating a "store of the community," the retailer may successfully meet most local needs, but this tailoring of merchandise may increase the frustrations of tourists or other outshoppers. For example, when customers

Fresh & Easy, a division of Tesco, does some of its own
manufacturing and processing to control quality.

visit a McDonald's, Kohl's, or Target store in any part of the country, often they expect to
have the same products across the chain. Further, at some point, the scale advantage (of
buying for hundreds or thousands of stores) could disappear as each store assortment is
customized. Part of the lower costs that large-scale retailers enjoy is due to their large purchases of each item.

   In selecting sources, retailers cannot ignore the advertising or merchandise display
support offered. Essentially, this reduces the retailer's costs and thus makes it more competitive. Of course, manufacturers offer advertising and merchandise display support
because it helps to sell their merchandise. Because the retailer will be advertising the supplier's products, they often need to check to see whether the same merchandise will
be made available to a nearby competitor; in such cases, it may be advantageous for the
retailer to use a private label. Another reason to use a private label is that some manufacturers will not sell a product to certain retailers. For example, some discounters that
try to offer lower prices by carrying only the "hottest" toys claim that some vendors will
not sell them the hot toys for fear of losing business to smaller chains and independents
that sell toys year-round and not just at Christmas.

   One of a retailer's greatest assets when dealing with a vendor is the retailer's
past experiences with that vendor. Whether you are a small retailer doing all the

Exhibit 9.7
Vendor-Profitability Analysis

Vendor Name	Purchases Cost	Purchases Retail	Discount and Anticipation (%)	Freight (%)	Markup % Landed Loaded	Markdown $	Markdown %	Gross Margin Percentage	Vendor No.
Anderson Sports	62,481	129,861	7.1	1.4	50.7	20,211	15.6	46.2	273359
Jack Frost, Inc.	26,921	53,962	8.0	1.3	49.4	3,233	6.0	50.5	818922
Sue's Fashions	25,572	51,930	8.1	1.8	49.9	6,667	12.8	47.1	206284
Jana Kantor Asso.	14,022	29,434	8.0	0.8	52.0	481	1.6	55.1	050187
Pierce Mills	12,761	25,438	9.5	1.7	49.8	7,858	30.9	33.1	132886
Ray, Inc.	2,196	4,416	8.0	1.8	49.4	754	17.1	43.8	148296
Dusty's Place	2,071	4,332	8.0	1.3	51.6			55.4	662411
Lady Carole	1,050	2,100	8.0	2.1	48.9			52.9	676841
Jill Petites	740	1,584	10.4	0.5	54.2	640	40.5	29.2	472977
Andrea's	198	410	8.0	0.8	51.1			55.0	527218

Cost: your cost
Retail: your original selling price
Discount and anticipation %: discount received for early payments
Freight %: your shipping expenses
Markup % Landed Loaded: [Retail selling price − (Cost + Freight)]/Retail selling price
Markdown: Amount original selling price is reduced
Gross Margin %: [Actual selling price − (Cost + Freight − Discount and Anticipation)]/Actual selling price

© Cengage Learning

vendor profitability analysis statement
Is a tool used to evaluate vendors and shows all purchases made the prior year, the discount granted, the transportation charges paid, the original markup, markdowns, and finally the season-ending gross margin on that vendor's merchandise.

buying yourself or a new buyer for a large chain, you should always approach vendors with two important pieces of information: the vendor-profitability analysis statement and the confidential vendor analysis. The **vendor-profitability analysis statement** (see Exhibit 9.7) provides a record of all the purchases you made last year, the discount granted you by the vendor, transportation charges paid, the original markup, markdowns, and the season-ending gross margin on that vendor's merchandise.

The **confidential vendor analysis** (see Exhibit 9.8) lists the same information as the profitability analysis statement but also provides a three-year financial summary as well as the names, titles, and negotiating points of the entire vendor's sales staff. This last piece of information is based on notes taken by the buyer during and after the previous seasons' buying trips.

confidential vendor analysis
Is identical to the vendor profitability analysis but also provides a three-year financial summary as well as the names, titles, and negotiating points of all the vendor's sales staff.

Based on the information obtained in the previous two reports, some retailers classify vendors into different categories (called class A, B, C, D, or E vendors) using both performance and brand-positioning information and the retailer's opinion on the vendor's other attributes. Regarding performance and positioning, if the supplier can produce very profitable items but doesn't have a brand the retailer needs, then the supplier could make private-label products for the retailer. If the supplier has an important brand but not the best prices, then it can still fill an important niche. When the supplier doesn't carry a needed national product *and* it doesn't have the best prices, the supplier is not very valuable unless it can provide information, trends, or something else that the retailer needs.

Exhibit 9.8
Confidential Vendor Analysis

Trip Dates __Fall Market__   City __Dallas__   Buyer's Name __Cooper__   Dept. Name __Women's Wear__   Dept. No. __491__

Vendor/Address Phone No./Floor No.		Volume History 200X	200X	200X	Markup History 200X	200X	200X	Markdown History 200X	200X	200X	Vendor Executives & Titles	Remarks
West Texas Blouse	Spring	590.5	719.4	330.8	47.5	47.7	46.7	2.4	5.3	4.4	Larry Wilcox (VP)	Cash Discount
	Fall	1002.8	706.7		47.3	47.5		3.4	7.8		Julie Davin	Prone to co-op
	Year	1593.3	1426.1		47.4			3.1			Ted Rombach	ads
	Objectives:											
	Results As of 5/22:											
Flatland Fashions	Spring	224.5	230.2	210.8	47.7	50.0	47.2	6.5	8.5	3.8	Joe Hall (P)	
	Fall	175.8	230.5		47.3	47.6		17.0	9.0		Richard Reel	Will deal on
	Year	400.3	460.7		47.5	48.8		11.1	8.7			transportation
	Objectives:											
	Results As of 5/22:											
Southern	Spring	-0-	42.3	50.7		48.4	45.4	-0-	9.1	4.2	Jackie Poteet (SM)	
	Fall	37.0	69.2		47.1	42.3		7.7	7.8		Boonie Hanley	"Quantity"
	Year	37.0	112.5		47.1	44.7		7.7	8.2		Carol Little	
	Objectives:											
	Results As of 5/22:											
Gallo	Spring	21.7	195.0	55.6	46.9	50.0	48.3	1.3	0.2	1.2	Ruth Wilson (P)	
	Fall	-0-	13.9		-0-	46.7		-0-	2.0		John Murphy	Easier of the
	Year	21.7	33.4		46.9	48.6		1.3	0.9			two
	Objectives:											
	Results As of 5/22:											

LO 6

Vendor Negotiations

Describe what is involved in the vendor-buyer negotiation process and what vendor contract terms can be negotiated.

Even buyers who choose not go to market and instead have their vendors come to them evaluate their vendors. For years, many grocers felt that firms like Procter & Gamble treated retailers poorly. These grocers needed the many products that P&G manufactured, but they did not appreciate P&G's "We win, you lose" attitude, which forced retailers to purchase the complete line of P&G products in order to earn merchandising money. Over the last half-decade, however, P&G has developed a program in which it helps all its customers formalize their merchandising plans for the coming months and no longer requires grocers to purchase slow-moving products. This new attitude of "Let's both win" has seen many supermarket managers reclassify P&G as more of a collaboration relationship. With some retailers, P&G is even working together to design new products and advertising copy, building a co-creation relationship. P&G has obviously determined that it can only be as successful as its retailers let it be.

After selecting the vendors, the retailer still must make decisions on the specific merchandise to be bought. Some products, such as the basic items for a particular department, are easy to purchase; others, especially new items, require more careful planning and consideration. Retailers should concern themselves with several key questions prior to selecting a product for purchase:

1. Where does this product fit into the strategic position that I have staked out for my department?
2. Will I have an exclusive with this product, or will I be in competition with nearby retailers?
3. What is the estimated demand for this product in my target market?
4. What is my anticipated gross margin for this product?
5. Will I be able to obtain reliable, speedy stock replacement?
6. Can this product stand on its own or is it merely a "me-too" item?
7. What is my expected turnover rate with this product?
8. Does this product complement the rest of my inventory?

negotiation
Is the process of finding mutually satisfying solutions when the retail buyer and vendor have conflicting objectives.

The climax of a successful buying plan is active **negotiation**, which involves finding mutually satisfying solutions for parties with conflicting objectives. The effectiveness of this buyer–vendor relationship depends on the negotiation skills of both parties and the economic power of the firms involved.

The retail buyer must negotiate price, delivery dates, discounts, promotional allowances, shipping terms, and return privileges. All of these factors are significant because they affect both firms' profitability and cash flow. Often the negotiation may also include a guarantee sell-through rate that if not met, the vendor agrees to take back or compensate the retailer for unsold items.

In recent years, both manufacturers and retailers have become increasingly aware of the cost of carrying excess inventory. Likewise, both parties have become more concerned with the time value of money and the resulting effect on each firm's cash flow. Since both parties involved in the negotiation process are aware of these costs and are trying to shift them to the other party, most negotiations produce some conflict. Often, vendors encourage retailers to have high inventory levels for upcoming seasons, such as having winter, spring, or summer apparel or ample inventory of a new flat screen television. However, when sales do not materialize at the level anticipated, retailers aggressively cut price and often reopen negotiations with vendors and ask for additional markdown money.[19] Also as we mentioned previously it is possible that they had a sell-through clause in their purchase agreement. This can be especially effective when the retailer is handling competing merchandise lines. Even without mentioning anything, the vendor knows that if they don't provide you a guaranteed sell-through or with additional markdown money and a competitor does, that next season more of the business will go to their competitor. Negotiations can be that subtle or implicit.

Despite the perceived need and impulse to negotiate aggressively, a successful negotiation is usually accomplished when both parties realize that the other should serve as its partner during the upcoming merchandising season. Both the buyer and the vendor are seeking to satisfy the retailer's customers better than the competition. Therefore, buyers and vendors must resolve their conflicts and differences of opinion, remembering that negotiation is a two-way street and that a long-term profitable relationship is the goal. After all, the vendor wants to develop a long-term relationship with the retailer as much as the retailer does with its customers.

What can be negotiated? There are many aspects to the terms of a sale (prices, credit, freight, delivery dates, method of shipment and shipping costs, exclusivity, sell-through rate or guaranteed sales, markdown money, promotional allowances, return privileges, and discounts), and life is simplest when there are no surprises. Therefore, the smart buyer leaves nothing to chance and discusses everything with the vendor prior to signing the purchase orders. The buyer and seller must together work out future plans using the buyer's merchandise budget and planned turnover. Therefore, the buyer and seller should seek to make negotiations a win–win situation or collaboration in which neither side feels like a loser. The essence of negotiation is to trade what is cheap to you but valuable to the other party for what is valuable to you but cheap to the other party.

The smart buyer puts all the upcoming areas of negotiations and previous agreements in letter form and distributes it before going to market. This helps to eliminate any misunderstandings afterward. Price, of course, is probably the first factor to be negotiated, but it is always smart to begin negotiating on factors where agreement can be reached most easily. Negotiations that tend to focus too much on the "difficult" terms early tend to become more problematic and leave each party feeling as though it's in a battle rather than a partnership. Consequently, the new buyer would be smart to remember the old adage "First you get along, then you go along" when entering into negotiations.

As price is often the hot topic on many buyer's minds, they should attempt to purchase the desired merchandise at the lowest possible net cost yet not expect unreasonable discounts or price concessions. Also, keep in mind the advice offered in Chapter 6 to stay within the law and not negotiate a price that would be discriminatory and give you unfair advantage over your competitors. Buyers must be familiar with the prices and discounts allowed by each vendor. This is why past records are so important. However, the buyer must remember that his or her bargaining power is a result of his or her planned purchases from the vendor. As a result, a large retailer may be able to purchase goods from a vendor at lower prices than a small mom-and-pop retailer. Five different types of discounts can be negotiated: trade, quantity, promotional, seasonal, and cash.

Trade Discount

trade discount
Is also referred to as a **functional discount** and is a form of compensation that the buyer may receive for performing certain wholesaling or retailing services for the manufacturer.

A **trade discount**, sometimes referred to as a **functional discount**, is a form of compensation that the buyer may receive for performing certain wholesaling or retailing services for the manufacturer. Because this discount is given for the performance of some service, the size of the discount will vary with the type of service performed. Thus, variations in trade discounts are legally justifiable on the basis of the different costs associated with doing business with various buyers.

Trade discounts are often expressed in a chain, or series, such as "list less 40-20-10." Each figure in the chain of discounts represents a percentage reduction from the list price of an item. Assume that the list price of an item is $1,000 and that the chain of discounts is 40-20-10. The buyer who receives all these discounts would actually pay $432 for this item. The computations would look like this:

List price	$1,000
Less 40%	−400
	600
Less 20%	−120
	480
Less 10%	−48
Purchase price	$432

To see how the various chains of discount permit a vendor to compensate the members of the supply chain for their marketing activities, let's look at the preceding example. Assume that the manufacturer sells through a supply chain that includes manufacturer's agents, service wholesalers, and small retailers. The purchase price of $432 is accorded to the manufacturer's agent, who negotiates a sale between the manufacturer and the service wholesaler. The manufacturers' agent then charges the service wholesaler $480 for the item, thus realizing $48 for rendering a number of marketing activities. The service wholesaler, in turn, charges a retailer $600 for the item, thus making $120. The retailer then sells the item at the suggested list price of $1,000, thus making $400 in gross margin to cover expenses and a profit.

Trade discounts are legal where they correctly reflect the costs of the intermediaries' services. Sometimes, large retailers want to buy directly from the manufacturer and pay only $432 instead of $600. This action would enable the large retailer to undercut the competition and is illegal, unless one of the three defenses of the Robinson-Patman Act explained in Chapter 6 can be applied.

Quantity Discount

quantity discount
Is a price reduction offered as an inducement to purchase large quantities of merchandise.

noncumulative quantity discount
Is a discount based on a single purchase.

cumulative quantity discount
Is a discount based on the total amount purchased over a period of time.

free merchandise
Is a discount whereby merchandise is offered in lieu of price concessions.

A **quantity discount** is a price reduction offered as an inducement to purchase large quantities of merchandise. Three types of quantity discounts are available:

1. A **noncumulative-quantity discount** is a discount based on a single purchase.
2. A **cumulative-quantity discount** is based on total amount purchased over a period of time.
3. **Free merchandise** is a discount whereby merchandise is offered in lieu of price concessions.

Noncumulative-quantity discounts can be legally justified by the manufacturer if costs are reduced because of the quantity involved or if the manufacturer is meeting a competitor's price in good faith. Cumulative discounts are more difficult to justify since many small orders may be involved, thereby reducing the manufacturer's savings.

For an example of how a quantity discount works, consider the following schedule:

Order Quantity	Discount from List Price (%)
1 to 999	0
1,000 to 9,999	5
10,000 to 24,999	8
25,000 to 49,999	10

If a retailer that had already purchased 500 units wanted another 800 units, it would have to pay list price if the vendor uses a noncumulative policy. However, the retailer would receive a 5-percent discount on all purchases if the vendor uses a cumulative pricing policy.

Quantity discounts might not always be in the seller's best interest and should always be viewed by the buyer as an invitation for further negotiations. Consider the following price schedule published by a computer manufacturer:[20]

Quantity	Unit Price ($)
1–19	795
20–49	749
50–149	699
150–249	659

Let's say that you, a buyer for a retail chain, want 19 of these computers, and your cost is $15,105 (19 × $795). But 20 would cost only $14,980 (20 × $749). What do you do? You actually have four choices:

1. Tell the manufacturer to ship 20 computers for $14,980 and you keep the extra one.
2. Tell the manufacturer to ship you 19 computers at $14,980 and have it keep the other one.
3. Order 20 but tell the manufacturer to ship you only 19 and to credit you for the other computer at $749.
4. Negotiate a purchase price.

Whenever quantity discounts are offered, buyers should always check to see if the total purchase price may be lower if they order more.

Many times, retailers can make a quick profit from utilizing quantity discounts by selling the extra merchandise to a diverter to sell in a gray market. The diverter, who is not an authorized member of the marketing supply chain but still functions as an intermediary, will be able to purchase these goods cheaper from the retailer than it can from the manufacturer and will then sell this excess merchandise to other retailers. Also, such discounts allow the manufacturer to have its products sold in discount stores without offending all of its authorized retailers. However, many authorized retailers are upset when diverters provide discounters with such merchandise. Some department stores have dropped cosmetic lines when discounters, most of whose cosmetics are diverted, started to carry the lines.

Consider the previous retailer who needed only 19 computers and purchased 20. Here the retailer sold the extra computer to a diverter for $600. As a result, the retailer was better off by $725 (the $125 difference in price between ordering 20 versus 19 units plus the $600 from the diverter) than it would have been had it bought only 19 computers at $795 each. The diverter could now profit by selling the computer to another retailer for something more than $600.

Today, diverters are important members of the retailer's supply chain, especially in the grocery and computer fields. However, despite the problems discussed in Chapter 5 that some manufacturers have with diverters, not all manufacturers or retailers feel the same way about them. In fact, some manufacturers develop their pricing policies to enable diverters to function economically. By doing this, they can increase sales by reaching markets they can't enter under normal operating conditions.

Promotional Discount

promotional discount Is a discount provided for the retailer performing an advertising or promotional service for the manufacturer.

A third type of discount is a **promotional discount**, which is given when the retailer performs an advertising or promotional service for the manufacturer. For example, a vendor might offer a retailer 50 extra jeans if (1) the retailer purchases 1,250 jeans during the season and (2) runs two newspaper advertisements featuring the jeans during the season. One of the main reasons manufacturers offer such discounts is that the rates newspapers charge local retailers are often lower than the rates charged to national manufacturers. These discounts are legal as long as they are available to all competing retailers on an equal basis.

Seasonal Discount

seasonal discount
Is a discount provided to retailers if they purchase and take delivery of merchandise in the off season.

Retailers can earn a **seasonal discount** if they purchase and take delivery of the merchandise in the off-season (e.g., buying swimwear in October). However, this does not mean that all seasonal discounts result in the purchase of merchandise out of season. Retailers in resort areas often take advantage of these discounts since swimwear is never out of season for them. As long as the same terms are available to all competing retailers, seasonal discounts are legal.

Cash Discount

cash discount
Is a discount offered to the retailer for the prompt payment of bills.

The final discount available to the buyer is a **cash discount** for prompt payment of bills. Cash discounts are usually stated as 2/10, net 30, which means that a 2-percent discount is given if payment is received within 10 days of the invoice date and the net amount is due within 30 days.

end-of-month (EOM) dating
Allows the retailer to take a cash discount and the full payment period to begin on the first day of the following month instead of on the invoice date.

Although the cash discount is a common method for encouraging early payment, it can also be used as a negotiating tool by delaying the payment due date. This future-dating negotiation may take many forms. The following are several of the most common:

1. **End-of-month (EOM) dating** allows for a cash discount and the full payment period to begin on the first day of the following month instead of on the invoice date. End-of-month invoices dated after the 25th of the month are considered dated on the first of the following month.

middle-of-month (MOM) dating
Allows the retailer to take a cash discount and the full payment period to begin on the middle of the month.

2. **Middle-of-month (MOM) dating** is similar to EOM except the middle of the month is used as the starting date.

3. **Receipt of goods (ROG) dating** allows the starting date to be the date goods are received by the retailer.

receipt of goods (ROG) dating
Allows the retailer to take a cash discount and the full payment period to begin when the goods are received by the retailer.

4. **Extra (Ex) dating** merely allows the retailer extra or free days before the period of payment begins.

5. A final discount form to be considered, but which is not widely used today, is anticipation. **Anticipation** allows a retailer to pay the invoice in advance of the expiration of the cash discount period and earn an extra discount. However, anticipation is usually figured at an annual rate of 7.0 percent, which is below the current cost of money.

anticipation
Allows the retailer to pay the invoice in advance of the end of the cash discount period and earn an extra discount.

Many vendors have eliminated the cash discount because retailers, especially department stores, have been taking 60 to 120 days to pay and still deduct the cash discount. In fact, many vendors require new accounts to pay up front until credit is established.

Delivery Terms

free on board (FOB) factory
Is a method of charging for transportation where the buyer assumes title to the goods at the factory and pays all transportation costs from the vendor's factory.

Delivery terms are another factor to be considered in negotiations. They are important because they specify where title to the merchandise passes to the retailer, whether the vendor or buyer will pay the freight charges, and who is obligated to file damage claims. Retailers will often be quoted a different cost or price from a vendor if the *free on board* (FOB) is the vendor's factory versus the retailer's factory versus the retailer's stores. Both the location of title transfer and who pays transportation can be negotiated together or separately. The three most common shipping terms are:

1. **Free on board factory**. The buyer assumes title at the factory and pays all transportation costs from the vendor's factory.

free on board (FOB) shipping point
Is a method of charging for transportation in which the vendor pays for transportation to a local shipping point where the buyer assumes title and then pays all further transportation costs.

free on board (FOB) destination
Is a method of charging for transportation in which the vendor pays for all transportation costs and the buyer takes title on delivery.

2. **Free on board shipping point**. The vendor pays the transportation to a local shipping point, but the buyer assumes title at this point and pays all further transportation costs.
3. **Free on board destination**. The vendor pays all transportation costs, and the buyer takes title on delivery.

For consignment (pay-from-scan) merchandise, the FOB is at the retailer's cash register. Consignment is not usually discussed as an FOB point because there is no specified time of transfer (it could be purchased by a customer one day after arriving in the store or several months after sitting on the self). The other FOB points usually have explicit dates or windows of time printed on each purchase order. While delivery terms (including consignment) may not appear to be a big deal at times, the author saw 10-percent to 20-percent differences on vendors' price quotes to a major mass merchandise retailer across products in home furnishing, apparel, and household products. Most retailers don't take advantage of price differences in logistics because the buyers normally don't get rewarded for it on their annual performance evaluation (e.g., a buyer would be better off with a vendor warehouse FOB that has a higher gross margin but lower net margin than selecting a store FOB with a lower gross margin but a higher net margin).

Packaging

While not a discount, packaging is becoming a hot negotiation point, especially with many retailers asking for more PDQs (cardboard display boxes that often have to be painted by manufacturers to match store marketing guides) and for more sustainable (i.e., environmentally friendly) packaging materials. Whether the product is shrink wrapped or in a clam shell, a blister pack, or a solid paperboard box, each packaging display method changes the cost and is usually negotiated as part of the price.

LO 7

Discuss the various methods of handling the merchandise once it is received in the store so as to control shrinkage, including vendor collusion, and theft.

In-Store Merchandise Handling

The retailer must have some means of handling incoming merchandise. For some types of retailers (e.g., a grocery store), this need will be significant and frequent; for others (e.g., a jeweler), it will be relatively minor and infrequent. Frequent and large deliveries entail considerable planning of merchandise receiving and handling space. For instance, consider that a full-line grocery store must have receiving docks to which 40- to 60-foot semitrailers can be backed up. Similarly, space may be needed for a small forklift to drive between the truck and the merchandise receiving area to unload the merchandise. Subsequently, the merchandise will need to be moved from the receiving area, where it will be counted and marked, to a storage area, either on the selling floor or in a separate location.

The point at which incoming merchandise is received can be a high-theft location. The retail manager needs to design the receiving and handling area to minimize this problem. Some thefts involve the retail employees themselves; others involve outsiders. In 2010, the National Retail Security Survey found that the average shrinkage rate for the nation's largest retailers was 1.5 percent of their annual sales, up from 1.44 in 2009. In 2007, the shrinkage percentage was the lowest number in the 17-year history of the survey. The survey that year claimed that the decrease in shrinkage was due to retailer investment in deterrence technology. The increases in the years since indicate that thieves are finding ways to work around the loss prevention efforts, meaning that retailers need to always be upgrading their systems. (**Shrinkage**, which is calculated "at

shrinkage
Represents merchandise that cannot be accounted for due to theft, loss, or damage.

retail," is the loss of merchandise due to theft, loss, damage, or bookkeeping errors.) Therefore, several types of shrinkage caused by theft will be mentioned in the following discussion. Most discussions of shrinkage attribute theft to one of four culprits—vendors, employees, customers and organized crime. Incidentally, shrinkage is such a major problem that the National Retail Federation (NRF) holds the annual three-day "NRF Loss Prevention Conference and Expo" usually during June of each year. The event is attended by thousands of loss and theft prevention retail and supply chain specialists and executives.

vendor collusion
Occurs when an employee of one of the retailer's vendors steals merchandise as it is delivered to the retailer.

Vendor collusion includes the types of losses that occur when merchandise is delivered. Typical losses involve the delivery of less merchandise than is charged for, removal of good merchandise disguised as old or stale merchandise, and the theft of other merchandise from the stockroom or off the selling floor while making delivery. This type of loss often involves both the delivery person and the retail employee who signs for the delivery with the two splitting the profit.

employee theft
Occurs when employees of the retailer steal merchandise where they work.

Employee theft occurs when employees steal merchandise where they work. Although no one knows for sure how much is stolen annually from retailers (since all shrinkage statistics are based only on apprehensions), as many as 30 percent of American workers admit to stealing from their employers, even if they take only small items like a pen or pencil. The National Retail Federation estimates that 43.7 percent of total loses in 2010 was due to employee theft.[21] Although some of the stolen goods come from the selling floor, a larger percentage is taken from the stockroom to the employee lounge and lockers, where it is kept until the employees leave with it at quitting time. Employee theft, which amounts to more than $800 per apprehension, is most prevalent in food stores, department stores, and discount stores. Considering that these types of stores are usually larger in size, sales volume, and number of employees, the lack of close supervision probably contributes to this problem. Exhibit 9.9 shows 50 ways that an employee can steal from a bar.

customer theft
Is also known as shoplifting and occurs when customers or individuals disguised as customers steal merchandise from the retailer's store.

Customer theft is also a problem. In fact, more than a dozen shoppers are caught for every case of employee theft, although the average amount of merchandise recovered is less than $50. Stealing merchandise from the stockroom and receiving area may be easier than taking it from the selling floor for several reasons. First, much of the stockroom merchandise is not ticketed, so it is easier to get it through electronic antishoplifting devices. Second, once the thief enters the stock area, there is very little antitheft security. Most security guards watch the exits and fitting rooms (and even grandmothers stuffing clothing into a stroller do get caught—as witnessed by one of the authors). Third, there is usually an exit in the immediate area of the stockroom through which the thief can carry out the stolen goods. Some retailers have wired these exits to set off an alarm when opened without a key, helping to reduce thefts somewhat. Another innovative retailer, after determining that employees were hiding merchandise in the compressed and discarded boxes that were left out as trash, started using a special spiked baler that punched holes in boxes to damage any stolen merchandise.

organized crime theft
Is when professional thieves steal merchandise when it is in transit to the store, or in the store.

Organized crime theft is when professional thieves steal merchandise and this can occur either when it is in transit to the store, or in the store. This type of theft has been on the rise because of the cut back on retail staffing levels but also because it is easier to traffic in stolen merchandise through e-commerce channels. In a National Retail Federation survey, it was found that 95 percent of retailers mentioned being a victim of organized retail crime in the year ended May 31, 2011.[22] This translates into an industry-wide net loss of $30 billion.[23] In response, many retailers have formed their own special organized-crime-prevention units.

Exhibit 9.9
Fifty Tricks for Bartenders

IT IS A DUMB BARTENDER WHO CAN'T BUY OUT THE BOSS IN 6 MONTHS.

1. The "Phantom Register" trick: Set up an extra register in bar for use only during busy times. The income from this register is not totaled on master tape and funds are skimmed by the bartender.
2. Serve and collect while register is being read between shift changes.
3. Claim a phony walkout and keep money received from customer.
4. Pick up customer's cash when he or she isn't paying attention.
5. Fake a robbery of the night deposit on way to bank. It is difficult for owners to prove this fake occurred.
6. Add phantom drinks to a customer's "running tab."
7. The "Phantom Bottle" ploy: Bring your own bottle of liquor onto shift and pocket cash from its sale.
8. The "Short Pour" trick: Just pour less than shot to cover "giveaway" liquor costs.
9. Don't ring up any sale and keep the cash.
10. The "Short-ring" trick: Under-ring the correct price of item and pocket the difference.
11. The "Free-Giveaway" trick: Give drinks to friends in anticipation of larger tips.
12. Mislead the owner regarding the number of draft beers that can be poured from a keg.
13. Undercharge for drinks with the anticipation of a larger tip.
14. Reuse register drink receipts.
15. Trade drinks to the cook for meals.
16. Add water to liquor bottle to maintain inventory.
17. Substitute lower-priced liquor when asked for call brands.
18. Collude with the delivery person, sell "stolen" products that he or she provides, and split the profit.
19. Ask for kickbacks from liquor distributor.
20. Dispense and register one shot on computerized dispenser system, while short-shotting the liquor into two glasses.
21. Short-change a customer when he or she is a "little under the weather" and claim it was an "honest" mistake if caught.
22. Claim a returned drink: Extra drink produced and can be sold by bartender.
23. Count missing bottles as "to go sale" when bar is selling both liquor to go and by the drink.
24. The "Owner Is a Jerk" ploy: You, the bartender, are the only person in charge of liquor pickup, check-in, and stocking.
25. Maids sell complimentary cocktail or wine coupons from hotel room to bar personnel, which you can place in register for cash.
26. Add two different customer drinks together and charge both customers, claiming misunderstanding in who was purchasing the round.
27. Ring food items on liquor key to cover high liquor cost percent.
28. Sell "after-shift drinks" to customers, not having them consumed by other employees.
29. Pour not enough liquor into blended fruit drinks to cover other shortages.
30. Have customer sign credit card voucher in advance and then overcharge the ticket.
31. Claim opening bank was short.
32. Total out register in midshift. Start new tape. You keep both new tapes and cash.
33. Incorrect "overring" or "void" of register.
34. Make sales during tape changes.
35. Mistotal the amount on the credit card or change the amount after customer leaves.
36. Take money from the game machines or jukeboxes.
37. Accumulate the guest checks to ring up after customer leaves so as to change the amount or leave out items.
38. Run credit card through twice.
39. Sell empty kegs and returnable bottles to an off-premise retailer.
40. Place the tip jars next to cash register—easy to place cash in tip jar and ring "no sale" for register activity.
41. Falsify cumulative register readings and "losing" tape.
42. Add extra hours to your time card and split it with the shift manager.
43. Help the shift manager claim a fictitious employee on payroll.
44. Take home food or liquor or fake a burglary.
45. Take funds from vending machines.
46. Ring up sales at happy hour prices, but charge regular bar prices to the customer when he or she is keeping receipts.
47. Servers charge for happy hour hors d'oeuvres and bar snacks.
48. Hold back bank deposits for a couple days and invest or borrow money or just don't deposit money (or lesser amount) and keep difference.
49. Handwrite bar tabs and ring up lesser amounts on the register.
50. Wrap booze into garbage can for later retrieval.

© Cengage Learning

Source: Copyrighted 1996 by Patrick Dunne and Chuck Mayers. All rights reserved. May not reproduce without the written permission of Patrick Dunne or Chuck Mayers.

Although organized crime is spreading throughout the United States and world, it is often concentrated in large cities where there is a lot of retail activity and transport. In the United States, the top five cities where criminal gangs that steal merchandise from retailers are: Los Angeles, Miami, New York, Chicago, and Houston. Recently, a major retail theft gang was uncovered in Los Angeles that was highly sophisticated and included a supply chain where stolen merchandised was sourced from other cities in the United States. The warehouse used in this organized crime operation was found by the Los Angeles Police and the FBI and had $30 million of stolen Levi's jeans.[24] Obviously, the thieves were sent to stores with a very specific shopping list!

The retailer must be aware that there are numerous opportunities for receiving, handling, and storage thefts. Therefore, steps should be taken to reduce these crimes. The retailer cannot watch the employees every minute to see whether or not they are honest, but some surveillance is helpful. However, the retailer must consider the employees' and customers' rights to privacy versus the retailer's right to security. Legislation is currently being considered by several states that would, if approved, allow the use of electronic monitoring by video and audio systems only when advance notice is given. In effect, workers and shoppers must be informed when they are being monitored. They also have to decide which theft is worth prosecuting. Walmart just revised its rules to allow prosecution of 16-year-olds (it was 18 or older before) and call police regardless of the child's age or theft amount if the store cannot reach the child's parent within 30 minutes or the parent doesn't show within 60 minutes after contact.[25] For example, a man in Florida was charged with shoplifting (valued at $2) and trespassing when an off-duty sheriff's deputy confronted him over 10 raspberry jellybeans he had sampled in the candy area.[26] The man said he just wanted to try them to see if he wanted to buy them. This customer had been shopping at the grocery for 30 years, and assuming he has another 20 or so years of shopping, the store probably lost his customer lifetime value over the $2 shoplifting and trespassing charge. Further, it probably got a lot of other people mad who read about it in the local papers. Retailers obviously have a right and a need to protect their investments. Sometimes, though, they need to think about the reasonableness of it—and the total impact on future sales.

The amount of storage space the retailer needs is related to the physical dimensions of the merchandise and the safety stock level needed to maintain the desired rate of stock turnover. For example, furniture is bulky and requires considerable storage space; grocery items turn over frequently, so more merchandise is usually needed than can be displayed on the shelves. This excess inventory causes retailers to stack boxes and cartons on the floor of the stockroom. In most cases, however, this scenario is inefficient and costly given that the retailer is probably paying employees anywhere from $5 to $15 per hour to keep the storeroom in order. Thus, in most cases, some type of mechanized equipment will be used to increase productivity. For instance, rather than simply hand carry incoming merchandise, employees might use one of the numerous types of carts especially made for this purpose. Also, instead of stacking the cartons and boxes directly on the floor of the stockroom where they must remain packed and risk being damaged, the merchandise can be unpacked, checked, inventoried, ticketed, and then placed on shelves or in bins until needed. By doing this, one can increase the amount of merchandise stored per square foot by decreasing the amount of packing material. A tidy, well-ordered stock area is less tempting to dishonest employees.

Although much theft results from in-store merchandise handling, retailers must also be aware of how theft in transit may influence their ability to have the appropriate amount of merchandise on hand. Therefore, retailers must not only plan to have the appropriate amount of merchandise on hand for customers but also ensure that the merchandise purchased for the store shelves actually arrives. Whether a retailer outsources its logistics or employs its own transportation force, ensuring that the merchandise makes it from the warehouse to the retail floor is critical for success.

So what can happen to merchandise in transit? Hijacking. A significant amount of shipment hijacking does occur in the United States, but the global playing field can be truly fraught with peril. Consider, for instance, the case of a truck carrying a load of consumer electronics bound for Paraguay. Deep in the heart of the Brazilian jungle, the driver sees that the road ahead is blocked. As he comes to a stop, the driver realizes that his truck is about to be hijacked. Luckily, he has brought an off-duty Brazilian police officer with him to help protect the shipment. The police officer exits the cab of the truck, and the driver immediately senses the feeling of familiarity between his security officer and one of the bandits. It seems that the bandit is also a police officer. After a brief discussion, the truck is allowed to move on with its shipment. This may sound like fiction but it is a true story. And even though the shipment was consumer electronics, other high-value products such as apparel, perfume, cigarettes, and alcohol are also subject to hijacking. Whether on land, sea, or air, hijacking is a relatively common occurrence in the retail supply chain.

The probability of theft in transit varies considerably from region to region. Although relatively few shipments are hijacked in Canada, the United States, and Western Europe, regions such as Eastern Europe, Latin America, Russia, and Southeast Asia are the most dangerous. Deteriorating economic conditions in these regions have increased organized-crime activity, resulting in increased theft of cargo. For many people in these regions, hijacking one shipment of consumer electronics can generate more cash than the average person in the area makes in a lifetime.

Although statistics related to the theft of cargo is difficult to obtain because few companies want to publicize their security problems, losses due to hijacking and the resulting disruption to retail operations are a major concern. However, losses due to hijacking are avoidable to a degree. Here are some tips that retailers and their supply-chain partners can employ to minimize the threat of hijacking.

1. Eliminate the retailer's name from the side of containers carrying the cargo. For a consumer electronics company such as Best Buy, putting its name on the truck signals to all that a shipment of consumer electronics is inside. It's tantamount to saying, "Steal me."
2. Install electronic monitoring devices on all shipment vehicles. Whether shipping via land, sea, or air, being able to track the container in which the merchandise is shipped can help determine its location when hijacked.
3. Carefully screen all internal transportation personnel as well as third-party logistics personnel in each global market. Given the nature of their jobs, these personnel are under loose supervision, and higher security standards are therefore critical.
4. Hire security personnel for each shipment. It is much easier for a single person to collude with others than for multiple people to conspire.

As retailers continue to expand globally, the risks involved in international hijacking will continue to grow. As mentioned earlier, RFID also poses a problem here because anyone with an RFID scanner could sit on the side of a road or go through a shipping dock and immediately know exactly what is inside any truck or container. However, by implementing a few security measures, retailers can minimize disruption to their supply of merchandise, thus increasing the level of satisfaction to customers by minimizing out of stocks.

Summary

Merchandise management is the analysis, planning, acquisition, and control of inventory investments and assortments in a retail enterprise. An understanding of the principles of merchandise management is essential to good retail management. A major part of merchandise management is planning. The retailer needs to plan (1) how many dollars to invest in inventory at different times of the season and (2) what to purchase with these dollars.

LO 1

What are the major steps in the merchandise buying and handling process?

The major steps include dollar-merchandise planning, dollar-merchandise control, inventory planning, selection of merchandise source, vendor negotiations, item creation and location (shelf or special display), replenishment and in-store handling, merchandise-line review, and markdowns.

LO 2

What is the difference between the four methods of dollar-merchandise planning used to determine the proper inventory stock levels needed to begin a merchandise selling period?

In the section on dollar-merchandise planning, we discussed how four types of inventory methods are used in retailing today: the basic stock (which is used when retailers believe that it is necessary to have a given level of inventory available at all times plus a variable amount of inventory that is tied to forecasted sales for the period), percentage variation (which assumes that the percentage fluctuations in monthly stock from average stock should be half as great as the percentage fluctuations in monthly sales from average sales), weeks' supply (where the beginning inventory level should be set equal to a pre-determined number of weeks' supply), and stock-to-sales (where the retailer wants to maintain a specified ratio of inventory to planned sales).

LO 3

How does a retailer use dollar-merchandise control and open-to-buy in the retail buying process?

Once the buyer has planned the dollar merchandise to have on hand at the beginning of each month (or season), it is essential that the buyer does not make commitments for merchandise that would exceed the dollar plan. In short, the dollars planned for merchandise need to be controlled by a technique called *open-to-buy*. OTB represents the dollar amount that a buyer can currently spend on merchandise without exceeding the planned dollar stocks discussed previously.

The OTB figure should not be set in stone because it can be exceeded. Consumer needs are the dominant consideration. If sales exceed planned sales, then additional quantities should be ordered above those scheduled for purchase according to the merchandise budget. Usually this is done by decreasing future quantity for a different merchandise line that is not performing as well.

LO 4

How does a retailer determine the makeup of its inventory?

The dollar-merchandise plan is only the starting point in determining a merchandise line, which consists of a group of products that are closely related because they are intended for the same end use, are sold to the same customer group, or fall within a similar price range. Once the retailer has decided how many dollars can be invested in inventory, the dollar plan needs to be converted into inventory. However, there seldom will be enough dollars to emphasize all three inventory dimensions: variety, breadth, and depth. Therefore, retailers must select a merchandise mix that appeals to the greatest number of profitable market segments.

LO 5 ## How do retailers select proper merchandise sources?

In addition to deciding what and how much to purchase, successful merchandise management must also consider vendor selection and negotiations. In this section, we reviewed the major factors (selling history, consumers' perception of the manufacturer's reputation, reliability of delivery, trade terms, projected markup, quality of merchandise, after-sale service, transportation time, distribution-center processing time, inventory carrying cost, country of origin, fashionability, and net landed cost) that are important in the selection of a vendor and how a buyer prepares for a buying trip.

LO 6 ## What is involved in the vendor–buyer negotiation process and what terms of the contract can be negotiated?

The climax of a successful buying plan is the active negotiation, which involves finding mutually satisfying solutions for parties with conflicting objectives, with those vendors that the retailer has identified as suitable supply sources. The effectiveness of this buyer–vendor relationship depends on the negotiation skills of both parties and the economic power of the firms involved. The retail buyer must negotiate price, delivery dates, discounts (trade, quantity, promotional, seasonal, and cash), delivery term, and return privileges. All of these factors are significant because they affect both the firm's profitability and cash flow.

LO 7 ## What are the various methods of handling the merchandise once it is received in the store to control shrinkage, including vendor collusion, and theft?

The chapter has a discussion on in-store merchandise receiving, handling, and storage as a means to control losses by theft. Not only can theft occur from employees and customers but also vendor collusion and organized crime is a major source of loss.

Terms to Remember

merchandise management
gross margin return on inventory
   (GMROI)
basic stock method (BSM)
percentage variation method (PVM)
weeks' supply method (WSM)
stock-to-sales method (SSM)
merchandise line
category management
variety
breadth (or assortment)
battle of the brands
depth
consignment (pay from scan)
extra dating (EX)
comp shopping
80-20 report
sell-through report
vendor-profitability analysis statement
confidential vendor analysis
negotiation

trade discount (functional discount)
quantity discount
noncumulative-quantity discount
cumulative quantity discount
free merchandise
promotional discount
seasonal discount
cash discount
end-of-month (EOM) dating
middle-of-month (MOM) dating
receipt of goods (ROG) dating
anticipation
free on board (FOB) factory
free on board (FOB) shipping point
free on board (FOB) destination
shrinkage
vendor collusion
employee theft
customer theft
organized crime theft

Review and Discussion Questions

LO 1

What are the major steps of the merchandise buying and handling process?

1. How often do most retailers renegotiate vendor contracts?
2. What must happen after a buyer agrees to purchase a product before a purchase order can be created?
3. How do replenishment orders affect the merchandise dollar planner and open-to-buy calculation?
4. Study Exhibit 9.3 and compute what happens to GMROI if the retailer is able to generate 1500 unit sales when it drops its price from $40 to $35.

LO 2

What are the differences between the four methods of dollar-merchandise planning used to determine the proper inventory stock levels needed to begin a merchandise selling period?

5. If your annual inventory-turnover rate is four times, which inventory stock level method would you use and why?
6. The Corner Hardware Store is attempting to develop a merchandise budget for the next 12 months. To assist in this process, the following data have been developed. The target inventory turnover is 4.8, and forecast sales are:

Month	Forecast Sales
1	$27,000
2	26,000
3	20,000
4	34,000
5	41,000
6	40,000
7	28,000
8	27,000
9	38,000
10	39,000
11	26,000
12	28,000

Develop a monthly merchandise budget using the basic stock and percentage variation methods.

LO 3

How do retailer's use dollar-merchandise control? Describe how open-to-buy is used in the retail buying process.

7. What problems can occur to buyers open-to-buy if they misjudge planned sales?
8. What does the term *open-to-buy* mean? How can it be used to control merchandise investments?
9. A buyer is going to market and needs to compute the open-to-buy. The relevant data are as follows: planned stock at end of March, $319,999 (at retail prices); planned March sales, $149,999; current stock on hand (March 1), $274,000; merchandise on order for delivery, $17,000; planned reductions, $11,000. What is the buyer's open-to-buy?

LO 4 **How does a retailer use unit stock planning and model stock plans in determining the makeup of a merchandise mix?**

10. What are the major constraints in designing the optimal merchandise mix?
11. How can merchandise lines have too much breadth yet not enough depth?
12. To the extent that the merchandise mix can actually shape customers' wants and impact whether and what customers purchase, what level of ethical responsibility does the retailer have toward the customer?
13. Manufacturers of so-called third-tier brands argue that they are being squeezed out of many stores by the major brands. Do you agree with that statement? Why?
14. What does *item cross-reference* mean?
15. If a shirt came in five sizes, four colors, and three styles, how many item numbers should be created to best manage the inventory?
16. Who is involved in a merchandise-line review?
17. Compute the sell-through for the following items.

ITEM	UNITS SOLD	UNITS ON HAND (END OF SEASON)	SELL-THROUGH PERCENTAGE
A	3	6	
B	7	9	
C	4	12	
D	12	4	
E	6	6	
F	9	5	
G	13	3	
H	2	10	

18. How long does a merchandise-line review normally take?

LO 5 **How does a retailer select proper merchandise sources?**

19. What do you think is the most important criterion in selecting a vendor? Why?
20. Why should a new buyer look over the previous buyer's confidential vendor analysis before going to market?

LO 6 **What is involved in the vendor–buyer negotiation process, and what terms of the contract can be negotiated?**

21. If a vendor ships you $1,000 worth of merchandise on April 27 with terms of 3/20, net 30 EOM, how much should you pay the vendor on June 8?
22. A retailer purchases goods that have a list price of $7,500. The manufacturer allows a trade discount of 40-25-10 and a cash discount of 2/10, net 30. If the retailer takes both discounts, how much is paid to the vendor?
23. How can cumulative-quantity discounts be considered to be anticompetitive?
24. How can manufacturers stop retailers from diverting their brand-name goods to discounters?

LO 7 **What methods are available to the retailer for controlling loss through shrinkage, vendor collusion, and theft?**

25. What is the worst type of shrinkage—employee theft or customer theft? What is your reasoning?

26. Should a retailer's right to security take precedence over an employee's and a customer's right to privacy when the retailer sets up an electronic monitoring system in its stores to curb losses from theft?

27. Where should retailers draw the line when it comes to prosecuting shoplifting? Should customers who eat grapes "to test them" be prosecuted?

Sample Test Questions

LO 1   Which of the following impact dollar-merchandise planners?

a. product purchases
b. markdowns
c. both of the above
d. none of the above

LO 2   Determine the buyer's BOM for August using the percentage variation method based on the following information: planned sales for August = $170,000; average monthly sales = $142,000; average stock for the season = $425,000.

a. $466,900
b. $390,000
c. $254,400
d. $425,000
e. $453,800

LO 3   The open-to-buy concept provides information about how much the buyer can order at:

a. the beginning of a merchandising period.
b. the middle of a merchandising period.
c. the end of a merchandising period.
d. anytime during the merchandising period.
e. anytime a vendor fails to ship merchandise on time

LO 4   Which of the following factors is not a constraint on the retailer's optimal merchandise mix?

a. space
b. merchandise turnover
c. legal issues
d. dollar merchandise
e. market

LO 5   A vendor-profitability analysis statement:

a. is a vendor's financial statement that is made available to all retailers.
b. is a retailer's analysis of the profitability of the different vendors and their lines from the prior year.
c. is a schedule maintained by the retailer that shows each vendor's initial data for new lines, shipment of orders, and gross margins.
d. is a retailer's financial statement used by the vendor for determining credit limits.
e. contains a list of who provided the retailer with discounts during the prior three years.

LO 6 A cumulative-quantity discount is based on:

a. a single purchase.
b. the total amount of merchandise purchased over a period of time.
c. the total amount of merchandise purchased since you began dealing with a vendor.
d. the amount of free merchandise a vendor is offering.
e. buyer purchases of more than 50,000 units.

LO 7 Which two parties are usually involved in losses due to vendor collusion?

a. delivery people and customers
b. retail employee signing for the delivery and delivery person
c. vendor sales representative and retail employee signing for the delivery
d. customers and vendor sales representative
e. vendor sales representative and retailer's accountant

Writing and Speaking Exercise

As the newly hired intern in the shoe department for a mid-sized apparel chain operating in six Northeastern states, you have been invited to attend your first buyer's meeting. Teresa, the new junior and misses buyer stood up during a weekly merchandise meeting at the retailer's corporate office to show off the newest trend in fashion junior clothing: sweatpants and shorts with words like "hottie," "angel," and "devil" printed in bold letters across the seat of the pants. At the time, a few other retail chains were just beginning to sell similar pants and shorts with writing across the seat of the pants. She showed the crowd of other retail buyers and operational heads several examples of the product. She highlighted the high margin and strong chance of market success. When she asked if there were any questions, another buyer raised his hand. He asked, "I wonder if we should be selling this to teenage girls? Do we have a moral responsibility to not sell a product like this that could increase promiscuity or simply decrease girls' self-worth or self-esteem?" An executive vice president of merchandise then stood up and responded, "Retailers don't have a moral responsibility. That's the media's role. We just sell the product."

Just then your boss asked you, "What do you think Theresa should do?" Explain your reasoning.

Retail Project

There is a trend away drinking of hard liquor and toward wines and therefore more grocery stores are handling a larger assortment of wines in their beer, liquor, and wine departments. Of course there is only so much space and grocers also face market, inventory turnover, and dollar merchandise constraints. As retailers expand more SKUs into the wine category they need to look for ways to spot consumer trends and then translate these into merchandising opportunities. One possibility is to listen to the advice of Robert Parker who is the editor and publisher of *The Wine Advocate*. Robert Parker as "The Independent Consumer's Guide to Fine Wines" (www.eRobertParker.com). To learn more about Robert Parker see Wikipedia (http://en.wikipedia.org/wiki/The_Wine_Advocate). Of course there are other sources such as *The Wine Spectator* (http://www.winespectator.com). See what you can learn about wine from these sources and other blogs and twitter dealing with wine. What useful information is available and how can it be used in the merchandise buying process? Do you think the information is trustworthy?

Planning Your Own Entrepreneurial Retail Business

Anne Cummins is in the process of developing the merchandise budget for a beachwear shop she is opening in Maui, Hawaii, next year. She has decided to use the basic stock method of merchandise budgeting. Planned sales for the first half of next year are $240,000, and this is divided as follows: February = 9 percent, March = 10 percent, April = 15 percent, May = 21 percent, June = 22 percent, and July = 23 percent. Planned total retail reductions are 9 percent for February and March, 4 percent for April and May, and 12 percent for June and July. The planned initial markup percentage is 48 percent. Alexia desires the rate of inventory turnover for the season to be two times. Also, she wants to begin the second half of the year with $100,000 in inventory at retail prices.

Develop a six-month merchandise budget for Anne.

CASE

The Poe Ranch Gift Shop

Charles Poe grew up on the 12,000-acre Poe Ranch in Montana that his great grandfather established with an initial 1,000 acres in 1929. Growing up on the ranch, Charles acquired a lot of practical skills through hard work and a lot of what he thought of as needless tasks. When he was 14 he could not figure out why his father (David) had him work for a year as a clerk in the small family business office that handled all of the payments the ranch made to various suppliers and vendors and also the payroll of 14 ranch employees. Of course, although he found the work boring, it was a good break from the hard physical labor he was used to doing on the ranch.

When Charles was twenty and attending college, his mother (Heather) decided it would be good for the family to turn part of the ranch into a tourist destination. Increasingly people were looking for unusual vacations that also connected them to nature and perhaps a way of life they had only read about or seen in the movies. Several of the ranches in Montana and Wyoming had built small lodges for guests and offered 3–7 day vacations where the guests worked on the ranch and experienced many facets of ranch life. Heather and David decided to capitalize on this trend and in 2009 and constructed the 9,000-square-foot Poe Ranch Lodge with eight bedrooms and a large dining hall that allowed them to accommodate from 8 to 30 guests at the ranch. The lodge was open for guests from May 1 through September 15. After the first season (2010), which had a total of 378 guests and generated gross revenue of $412,000, Heather began to talk to David about the possibility of opening a small gift shop. She had found that many of the visitors wanted to purchase something during their visits as a gift for someone or for themselves, but that was not an option. What captured Heather's imagination at the same time was a small house, dating back to 1942, that was one of the early buildings on the ranch. This structure was not being used and was falling into disrepair, and she felt it was important to preserve it before it was too late. Luckily, it was only 600 feet up a dirt road from the new Lodge. During the 2010 Christmas holiday, David and Heather decided to remodel this simple rustic structure and establish the Poe Ranch Gift Shop. The gift shop would open in May 2012, which gave them 18 months to remodel, plan, and acquire inventory.

During the summer of 2011, Charles was home for the summer after completing his junior year studying business at Colorado State University. Heather asked Charles to help her plan the business. Together Heather and Charles were able to look at past guest records and found that 25 percent of the visitors were from Western and Northern Europe, 12 percent from Asia, 48 percent from the United States and primarily from the East Coast, and the remaining 15 percent from various other countries. Also, even though they did not have information on age, Heather, who had gotten to know the guests quite well during their short stays at the ranch, estimated that 70 percent were between 40 and 60 years and very seldom were children included among the visitors. Charles had recommended that for the U.S. visitors, they look at their zip codes and/or home addresses (which they often had on file). Using U.S. census data and Google Earth, he was able to determine that the U.S. visitors were high-income households (probably mostly with incomes over $200,000 per year). Heather generally felt that the foreign visitors were also high-income households.

Heather and David had earlier projected that the ranch lodge would most likely peak at 630 guests per year and reach this level by 2012. Heather, with assistance from Charles, estimated 75 percent of the guests would purchase something at the Poe Ranch Gift Shop and that the average purchase would be $200. In addition, they would ask all shoppers and guests to register for their e-tailing version of the Poe Ranch Gift Shop. Although trying to project e-tailing sales is very difficult, they nonetheless projected that sales would be $12,000 in year one and then double to $24,000 the second year and to $36,000 the third year. The e-tailing business would also be used to discount the merchandise that did not sell at the ranch store. The merchandising philosophy for the store was to not discount any merchandise at the gift shop but to sell it at full retail price that would allow a 60 percent gross margin. On the other hand, the e-tailing venue had a planned gross margin of 30 percent. Heather felt strongly that part of the vacation experience included the desire to take home something special to remember the vacation. Of course, on the 12,000-acre ranch, the gift shop was the only shopping venue and the nearest town was 38 miles away and it had poor shopping options, especially for gift items.

The overall budget for opening of the Poe Ranch Gift Shop was $125,000. This included $66,000 for remodeling, $20,000 for shelving and fixtures, $3,000 for website development and the remainder for inventory and other working capital needs. David also felt they should add $15,000 for contingencies, so they finally decided on a total project cost of $140,000.

As they were ready to finalize the project, Charles brought up the idea one evening over dinner that perhaps the Poe Ranch Gift Shop should be an extension of The Poe Ranch Lodge. When he mentioned this, both Heather and David were a bit confused at what was meant. Charles went on to explain that the inventory investment of approximately $30,000 may not be enough for an optimal merchandise mix and also that some of his financial modeling suggested the venture may not be able to break-even. He then mentioned that perhaps the furniture, bedding, art, and room accessories at the Poe Ranch Lodge could be for-sale. Enthusiastically, he argued these items were already marvelously merchandised in each of the eight bedrooms in the Lodge. In the case of the art, if a guest wanted to purchase an item, it could be taken with them or they could have it shipped. However, in the case of furniture, bedding, and room accessories the guest would be shipped a new identical item. Heather got really excited about this idea. She already had planned to offer tableware at the Poe Ranch Gift Shop since she had a small local potter who she had used to make plates, bowls, and cups for the Poe Ranch. As she got more excited about almost everything being for-sale at the Poe Ranch Lodge, David suggested that both Charles and Heather were getting a bit too creative and moving away from what Heather had initially planned.

Questions

1. What type of merchandise should the Poe Ranch Gift Shop offer? Explain your rationale.

2. What should be the initial inventory investment? Explain how you arrived at this amount.

3. Evaluate the idea that Charles developed of using the Poe Ranch Lodge as an extension of the Poe Ranch Gift Shop.

Note: This case has been prepared for educational purposes and does not represent the appropriate or inappropriate handling of retailing situations. All places and names have been disguised.

10

Retail Pricing

Overview

In this chapter, we examine the retailer's need to make pricing decisions. We begin with a discussion of the impact of a firm's objectives on its pricing policies and strategies. After reviewing several strategies, we look at why initial markups and maintained markups are seldom the same. We also discuss how a retailer establishes an initial markup. We conclude this chapter with a discussion of why and how a retailer takes markdowns during the normal course of business.

Learning Objectives

After reading this chapter, you should be able to:

1 Discuss the factors a retailer should consider when establishing pricing objectives and policies.

2 Describe the differences between the various pricing strategies available to the retailer.

3 Describe how retailers calculate the various markups.

4 Discuss why markdown management is so important in retailing and describe some of the errors that cause markdowns.

LO 1

Discuss the factors a retailer should consider when establishing pricing objectives and policies.

Pricing Objectives and Policies

Although most retailers have grown savvy about cutting costs, few have figured out how much money they have passed up by using outdated pricing strategies and tactics. After all, pricing is an important contributor to profitability. The price of an item multiplied by the quantity sold is equal to the retailer's sales revenue, and Chapter 8 illustrated the correlation between sales revenue and profit. Nevertheless, retailers today tend to routinely overprice some products and underprice others.

When making pricing decisions, retailers must remember that they are never going to be right every time. However, such decisions are a great deal less difficult and more likely to be correct if the retailers have been performing their other activities correctly. Pricing, as we pointed out in our retail strategic planning and operations management model (Exhibit 2.8), is an interactive decision made in conjunction with the firm's mission statement, goals and objectives, strategy, operational management (i.e., merchandise planning, promotional mix, building and fixtures, and level of service), and administrative management.

Today, when one retailer cuts prices, everyone seems to follow. This seems to be especially true during high shopper traffic periods such as the Christmas holiday and the back-to-school period in August and September. The rationale behind this trend is that many retailers carry identical nationally branded merchandise and the customers now have the capacity with their smartphones and Internet to find if the exact item is available in a nearby store or via an e-tail channel for a lower delivered price. With adjusted-for-inflation household incomes often lower than what they were one or two decades ago, this type of price or deal shopping behavior is not likely to decline. This is yet another reason why retailers, as discussed in prior chapters, have been moving more and more to developing store brands, where the merchandise offering cannot be precisely copied.

For retailers selling services, pricing is even more difficult. This is because services are intangible, not easily stored, and cannot be returned to the vendor for credit. For instance, Six Flags Amusement Parks, which operate in many areas of the United States, have the same fixed costs of being open regardless of whether it is a rainy day with lower attendance or a bright and sunny day but not too hot. The amusement park manager cannot resell excess capacity on slow attendance days.

yield management
Is where the retailer focuses on optimizing the total sales revenue, or yield, from its capacity to provide services.

Many retailers selling services such as airlines, hotels, and golf courses use yield-management techniques when making pricing decisions. **Yield management** is where the retailer focuses on optimizing the total sales revenue or yield from its capacity to provide services. Thus, you may find that a hotel room has a normal price of $195 but that a few weeks prior the hotel room if not yet booked would be priced at $139 and then a few days before at $124. We are sure you have noticed the same for other services,

Imagebrokers/Photoshot

Hotel chains, such as Marriott, use yield management techniques when pricing unsold rooms. By lowering prices at selected times, overall revenue increases.

but often it may be closer to the use of the service such as in an airline, and an unsold seat may go for a higher price especially if only a few are available.

Interactive Pricing Decisions

As shown in Exhibit 10.1, pricing decisions should be interactive. Specifically, the decision to price an item at a certain level should be related to the retailer's decisions on lines of merchandise carried, location, promotion, credit and check cashing, customer services, desired store image, and the legal constraints discussed in Chapter 6.

Remember that just as each retailer is different, each retailer's pricing decision must also be different.[1] After all, price is the easiest element of the retail mix for a competitor to copy. Consider for a moment the price of gas. When a gas station lowers its price, all the other stations in the immediate area soon match or beat that price. Or, when Burger King cuts prices on burgers, it is common to see Wendy's and McDonalds follow. This is why a long-term, competitive differential advantage based on price is difficult, if not impossible to obtain.[2] In fact, if you are going to compete on price, you better be the lowest cost operator and continue to maintain that edge which, as we learned about in Chapter 4 when we discussed the wheel of retailing, is highly unlikely.

Merchandise

Retailers should not set prices without carefully analyzing the attributes of the merchandise being priced. Does the merchandise have attributes that differentiate it from comparable merchandise at competing retailers? What is the value of these attributes to the consumer? Consider, for example, Wright's Market in Opelika, Alabama, a small town near Auburn University. Jimmy Wright has made a success of a small grocery business (his store is only 22,000 square feet) by offering the highest quality meat available. Using the slogan "We have the best meat at the best price," more than 50 percent of his $160,000 weekly sales come from the meat department. Or consider Whole Foods and Trader Joe's with more organic and natural food that in turn allow these grocery retailers to charge higher prices and have higher gross margins than

Exhibit 10.1
Interaction Between a Retailer's Pricing Objectives and Other Decisions

© Cengage Learning

The one situation where price interacts only with merchandise for sale and not with the other retail decision areas is in the case of liquidators.

mass-market conventional supermarkets. Note that Kroger, a conventional supermarket, operates on a low gross margin of 21 percent, whereas Whole Foods has a healthy 38 percent gross margin.

Merchandise selection presents the retailer with another decision: the range of prices to be made available to the consumer. Remember, the retailer's controllable element of price can be either the cost of goods sold or the gross margin that is added to the cost. The retailer, in deciding to buy an item to sell at a specific price, may either purchase lower-cost merchandise and have a high gross margin to offset the higher expenses needed to sell at that price or purchase more expensive goods and reduce the gross margin and expenses in order to sell at a given price.

The one situation in which price interacts only with merchandise for sale and not with the other retail decision areas is in the case of liquidators. Liquidators purchase the entire inventory of a "dead" retailer only to run a *going-out-of-business* (GOB) sale. They generally assume responsibility for everything and agree to take a percentage of what they sell. In some cases, they may agree in advance to purchase the existing inventory and gamble that they will be able to unload all merchandise at prices sufficient to generate a solid profit. All this is done within a given time period, usually eight weeks. Thus, GOB sales are unique in that there is a beginning and an end. They must hit their sales goals each week and be gone in eight weeks. Consequently, they don't concern themselves with long-term commitments, offering additional services, or even offending customers.[3]

Location

The location of a retail store, as discussed in Chapter 7, has a significant effect on the prices that can be charged. The closer the store is to competitors with comparable merchandise and customer service, the less pricing flexibility the retailer has. The distance between the store and the customer is also important. From the 1950s through most of the 20th century, Las Vegas had almost a monopoly on gambling. But as more and more states introduced lotteries and American Indian Nations opened gaming casinos, Las Vegas found it had to be more competitive, not only on price but also on promoting its distinctive advantages.

Generally, if the retailer wants to attract customers from a greater distance, it must either increase its promotional efforts or lower prices on its merchandise. This is because of the increased travel costs (in both time and dollars) consumers incur when they are located farther from the store. Travel costs cut into the amount the customer is able or willing to pay for the merchandise or services, thus forcing the retailer to lower prices to attract more distant customers. To help counteract the cost of travel, some large regional shopping malls will offer discount coupon books to shoppers who have an out-of-state driver's license. In addition to regional shopping malls, factory outlet malls increasingly face problems in attracting customers since these malls are usually 30–60 miles outside major population areas, which translates to a 60–120-mile roundtrip shopping excursion. With gasoline costs often running 30 cents a mile, this can translate into $36 (.30 × 120), and thus buying a pair of jeans and shirt for $85 actually costs you $116 ($36 plus $85). This is why for many consumers it is cheaper to purchase the merchandise at a nearby retailer. However, catalog and online retailers break down location barriers by providing a national and worldwide presence. Pricing for these retailers is balanced between charging higher prices for providing greater convenience to customers and lower prices for products with higher volume and lower operating expenses.

Just as a situation when you are located far away from the customer you need to have a more attractive price, the opposite is true if you are nearby. This should be evident if you notice the price you pay for beverages and food in vending machines on your campus, or what you pay for refreshments at a football, basketball, baseball, or other sporting event or concert. Or, consider the price you might pay to rent an automobile in a downtown area of a big city versus in the outlying suburbs.

Promotion

Chapter 11 illustrates how promotion can increase demand for a retailer's merchandise. However, this does not mean that pricing and promotion decisions are independent. Rather, retailers that promote heavily while remaining very price-competitive may experience increases in demand greater than either a high-promotion or lower-price strategy would produce independently. Imagine, for example, a retailer establishing low prices but not promoting them in the marketplace. How would consumers know of the price cuts? Alternatively, imagine heavy promotion but no cut in prices. Obviously, each would generate demand, but the interactive and cumulative effects of both are likely to be much greater. Costco, who is a leader in the warehouse membership market business, initially did not promote or advertise but relied on its low prices to attract its membership base. However, today, it regularly mails promotional pieces along with additional price-off coupons to its members.

Credit and Check Cashing

For a given merchandise price level, retailers that offer to finance your purchase will charge higher prices. You probably notice those attractive furniture or household appliance advertisements that promise you what appears to be a very attractive price with nothing down and 36 months interest free to pay, with the first payment not due in 90 days. Think about it a moment; although the financing appears free, it costs the retailer money, and there is always a risk to the retailer that the customer will not pay

Costco uses coupons and promotional advertisements sent through the mail as well as posters and hand-outs at the stores to keep their customers informed about current specials.

and not return the merchandise. In brief, the retailer has necessarily built these additional costs and risk into the product's selling price. A retailer that offers to accept a bank card as payment or check-cashing services will often experience greater demand than those that offer neither. Some retailers will offer both a cash price and a credit card price; for instance, for gasoline retailers this can mean charging cash customers 3–5 cents a gallon less for fuel. In the case of large purchases of durable goods such as $30,000 to $60,000 automobiles, the auto retailer may limit the use of credit cards to $5,000 of the purchase price. After all, the banks charge the retailers 2–3 percent on credit cards and thus a $50,000 credit card payment would net the retailer only $49,000 if the fee were 2 percent.

In addition, retailers who provide both financial services may be able to charge slightly higher prices than those who do not while generating the same level of demand. This has become increasingly true for check-cashing services over the past decade as a large number of consumers don't have bank accounts.

Customer Services

Retailers that offer many customer services (e.g., delivery, gift wrapping, alterations, more pleasant surroundings, sales assistance) tend to have higher prices. A decision to offer many customer services will automatically increase operating expenses and thus prompt management to increase retail prices to cover these additional expenses. However, such a policy may also result in higher profits. Consider the case of women's dresses. Customer service used to be common in department stores that took 50-percent to 60-percent initial markups, but pricing pressure by discounters has forced most department stores to respond by cutting markups and service. Women purchasing dresses began to feel neglected in department stores, especially when they had to start paying for alterations. Specialty stores have picked up on this; as a result, they offer the consumer greater assistance in selecting and trying on a dress, something unheard of in the low-price stores. At the extreme high end of customer service, some specialty women and menswear retailers will bring trunks of merchandise to the homes of wealthy patrons for them to try on and select for purchase.

Providing customer services and exceptional customer service can actually help protect a retailer from price competition. Stated alternatively, if you operate a store that doesn't provide customer services or exceptional customer service, then a competing retailer that offers a lower price becomes very attractive. In fact, many consumers are willing to pay more for extra service. This is why the more expensive health clubs or hairstylist, higher priced furniture and housewares retailers, and gift shops are more profitable. Consequently, it is important to remember that customer service decisions interact strongly with pricing decisions.

It is also important to note that service standards vary greatly by country. For example, Japan has extremely high service standards in retail operations. In Japan, gift wrapping is customary, and retailers commonly accept merchandise for return even after the product has been well used. Alternatively, many countries throughout the world do not accept returns regardless of reason. In these retail operations, once the product is sold, it is no longer the retailer's concern. This is truly a situation of *caveat emptor*—let the buyer beware. Given differences in expected service levels, retailers must adapt pricing levels accordingly. Nonetheless, the competitive environment may breakup old practices. For instance, it was unheard of in the United States for a new car dealer to allow you to take a new car purchase home and return it within a few days or even weeks if you were not happy, but this is now occurring in more and more cases. A variation on this occurred during summer 2011 when Kia offered new car buyers a guaranteed trade-in price should they trade for a new Kia in three to four years.

Store Image

One of the cues a customer uses in determining a retailer's image is the retailer's prices. If not offset by a poor location with poor service and merchandise selection, prices aid the customer in developing an image of the store, either consciously or unconsciously. If an exclusive, high-fashion store, such as Saks Fifth Avenue or Bergdorf-Goodman,

Ermenegildo Zegna, based in Milan, Italy, projects an image of affluence. Drastic price cuts would negatively affect that image.

started to discount its merchandise heavily, it simply would not be the same store in the eyes of its customers. Zegna is an excellent example since it sells off-the-rack suits for men starting at about $1,000 and bespoke garments at near $10,000. Zegna's parent company, Ermenegildo Zegna is based in Milan, Italy, and sources 2 million meters of sumptuous wool, cashmere, and mohair fabric each year from its mountainside factory in the village of Trivero. Zegna now has over 60 stores in China, where customers can easily find cheaper "made in China" garments; but the Chinese customer of a Zegna boutique is on a journey to total affluence, and the store image of Zegna and its Italian suits plays well to that ambition. In this situation, cutting price would destroy that desired image.[4]

Legal Constraints

Pricing decisions must be made only after examining the impact of the legal environment. This is especially true for the retailer seeking to operate in more than one state or country, as laws often vary between states and countries. As pointed out in Chapter 6, a retailer may not set a price in collusion with a competitor, may not offer different prices to different retail customers, may not sell below cost, and may not claim or imply in any advertisements that a price has been reduced unless it really has.

The other environmental factors we discussed in Part 2 (consumer behavior, competitor behavior, channel relationships, the socioeconomic environment, and the technological environment) should also be considered when the retailer is developing its overall pricing and market strategy. Still, pricing decisions are easy to make in the United States when compared with some other countries' retail environments. For instance, laws in France require that products be sold to all retailers—big and small alike—for the same price, thus making it tough for discounters to get any kind of pricing advantage.

In the United States, there are laws against vertical monopolies and other restraints on trade to ensure fair competition. American consumers can buy from a full-price retailer or a discounter. American discounters depend on bulk-purchase discounts from manufacturers, rapid inventory turnover, inexpensive real estate, and price-conscious shoppers who are willing to perform some marketing-channel functions themselves.

Pricing Objectives

A retailer's pricing objectives should be in agreement with its mission statement and merchandising policies. Some objectives may be profit-oriented, some may be sales-oriented, and some may seek to leave things just as they are. However, by beginning with the proper pricing objectives, the retail manager can establish pricing policies that will complement the retailer's other decisions and help attract the desired target customers.

Profit-Oriented Objectives

Many retailers establish the objective of either achieving a certain rate of return or maximizing profits.

Target Return

target-return objective
Is a pricing objective that states a specific level of profit, such as percentage of sales or return on capital invested, as an objective.

A **target-return objective** sets a specific level of profit as an objective. This amount is often stated as a percentage of sales or of the retailer's capital investment. A target return for a supermarket might be 2-percent net profit on sales or pricing to yield an 8-percent return on assets; in both cases the returns are after tax. Target-return pricing is popular in retailing because of its alignment of the strategic profit model discussed in Chapter 2, which is very popular in retail financial planning.

Profit Maximization

profit maximization
Is a pricing objective that seeks to obtain as much profit as possible.

skimming
Is a pricing objective in which price is initially set high on merchandise to skim the cream of demand before selling at more competitive prices.

penetration
Is a pricing objective in which price is set at a low level in order to penetrate the market and establish a loyal customer base.

The objective of **profit maximization** seeks to obtain as much profit as possible. Some people claim that this pricing policy "charges all the traffic will bear." Retailers know that if they follow such a policy, they are inviting competitors to enter the market. Thus, in general, a retailer should seek to set prices, not to get as much as possible from each customer, but at a level conducive to build customer loyalty and withstand the competition. However, in some cases, a retailer may have a temporary monopoly and want to take advantage of it. The first fast-food outlets in a university's student center, knowing that others would follow shortly, often charged high prices, only to lower them when competition finally entered the market. This is known as **skimming** or trying to sell at the highest price possible before settling on a more competitive level.[5] Other retailers may take the opposite approach and use **penetration**, which seeks to establish a loyal customer base by entering the market with a low price. For example, many locally owned retailers such as coffee shops often charge low prices, hoping to make stopping at their store a habit for their customers before a large chain operator such as Starbucks enters their trade area.

Auction pricing is one way that the retailer can be assured of getting the maximum price and hence profit; but, of course, auctions always have some time limit on them and thus the retailer never knows if they should have extended the time period; or perhaps put a minimum reserve price on the item. Auction pricing is common in e-tailing and became popularized by eBay. However, you can also find auction pricing in many antique and art galleries and the sale of classic automobiles and even luxury houses as found at Sotheby's (www.sothebys.com). Barrett-Jackson Auto Auction (www.barrett-jackson.com) held in Scottsdale annually has become so popular that it is now televised. At this highly anticipated auction, you can see live on television competing buyers bid up the price of some autos to over $1 million. You wonder if when there is this fierce bidding between two buyers and they are on television around the world if they are not also buying a bit of stardom for a few thousand dollars extra!

Sotheby's uses auctions to get the maximum prices it can on antiques, artwork and luxury properties.

Sales-Oriented Objectives

Sales-oriented objectives seek some level of unit sales, dollar sales, or market share but do not mention profit. Two of the objectives most commonly used in retailing are growth in market share and growth in dollar sales. Although both of these objectives are used by many retailers today, especially smaller retailers, the achievement of either does not necessarily mean that profits will also increase. After all, if a retailer lowers prices, gross margin will go down and sales may improve, but the retailer will not necessarily make more money. Nonetheless, for publicly traded retailers, one of the metrics watched by financial analysts is the change in same-store sales month by month from the prior year. This is usually reported a couple days after the end of each month, and the financial analysts and CNBC, Bloomberg, and Fox Business make a big deal out of, for instance, Target's same-store sales compared to 12 months ago are rising more quickly than at Walmart or vice versa or a similar comparison between Lowe's and Home Depot. What this implies is that one retailer is gaining market share over the other and that profit gains will follow.

Status Quo Objectives

Retailers who are happy with their market share and level of profits sometimes adopt status quo objectives or "don't rock the boat" pricing policies. You may have noted that dollar or 99 cent stores are beginning to pop up, especially in areas of economic downturn. To maintain the legitimacy of their image, they work hard to source items around the world that they can sell for 99 cents. Buyers should, however, be wary because many of these items would normally be priced lower; but because of the smaller package size, lower quality, or just the alluring sound of 99 cents, they sound like incredible bargains.

Many supermarkets gave up on the extra profits and increases in market share that "double coupons" might have brought because they were afraid of what competitive actions would result. It should be noted that pricing actions such as double couponing are not always effective and profitable. Many times, especially when other retailers match the promotion, coupons are used only by the retailer's regular customers, which simply reduces the retailer's profit.

Also, some retailers prefer to compete on grounds other than price. Convenience stores, for example, seldom match the prices of nearby supermarkets. Still, retailers such as McDonald's and Burger King, who want the consumer to focus on factors such as quality of food, service, and locational convenience instead of price, are sometimes forced to drop prices by promoting "value meals" in the face of mounting competition just to maintain status quo market share.

Pricing Policies

Pricing policies are rules of action, or guidelines, that ensure uniformity of pricing decisions within a retail operation. A large retailer has many buyers who are involved in pricing decisions. By establishing the store's overall pricing policies, top merchandising executives provide these buyers with a framework for adopting specific pricing strategies for the entire organization.

A retail store's pricing policies should reflect the expectations of its target market. Very few retailers can appeal to all segments of the market. Low- and middle-income consumers are usually attracted to low-priced, discount stores. The middle-class market often shops at moderately priced general merchandise chains. Affluent consumers are frequently drawn to high-priced specialty stores that provide extra services. Only supermarkets are able to cross the various income lines, and even then there is some basis for segmentation. Successful retailers carefully position themselves in a market and then

Off 5th, a division of Saks, Inc., caters to a target customer looking for below market pricing.

direct their specific pricing strategies toward satisfying their target market. Many times the proper pricing policies influence consumers to patronize one store over another. Recognizing this reality, Saks, Inc. has been careful to focus most price cutting at its Off 5th outlet stores and its e-tailing business which tend to cater to a different market segment. Incidentally, Saks views the outlet and e-tailing business as its major avenue for growth over the next decade.[6]

In establishing a pricing policy, retailers must decide whether they should price below, at, or above market levels.

Pricing Below the Market

Because of the economic recession during 2008–2009 and the slow and inconsistent recovery, a large segment of any trade area now buys primarily on the basis of price, and this includes customers looking for luxury merchandise at a below-market price. For instance, Gilt (www.gilt.com), an e-tailer that sells luxury fashion and designer apparel at deep discounts as high as 80 percent was launched by two Harvard MBA graduates in 2007 and has over 1.4 million members.[7] A **below-market pricing policy** is also attractive to many retailers such as discounters and warehouse clubs. Such a policy doesn't mean that the retailer sells every item in its store at a price lower than can be found elsewhere in its trading area. Rather, the retailer is more intent on how its prices are perceived versus those of the competition. Consequently, a retailer may strive to have the lowest total cost for all items purchased in a typical market basket.

Below-market retailers must buy wisely, which may include closeouts and seconds, stock fast-selling merchandise, curtail customer services, and operate from modest facilities. For instance, Ryanair (www.ryanair.com), which connects many European cities, flies out of outlying smaller airports that are lower cost. Ryanair also squeezes as many passengers onto their airplanes as possible and runs a very high occupancy level, which all allow it to keep costs very low to support its below-market pricing. Some retailers that use below-market pricing choose to stock private-label brands extensively and enhance

below-market pricing policy
Is a policy that regularly discounts merchandise from the established market price in order to build store traffic and generate high sales and gross margin dollars per square foot of selling space.

WHAT'S NEW ?

Retailers Get Dynamic with Their Pricing

"Fewer things frustrate tourists in Egypt more than skin-dependent pricing. Have Irish freckles? Expect to pay double in a Cairo taxi. An Italian tan? The price of that basalt model of the Sphinx just shot up 200 percent. Have glowing blue eyes? Some restaurants suddenly have no menus, and prices are delivered orally. I've been overcharged by more merchants in this country than I can tally in Excel," says Justin Martin of *Christian Science Monitor.*

While overcharging people based on their physical characteristics in the United States is illegal, and rightfully so, if you consider for a moment how prices have been established over the course of human history, you'll realize that most prices charged over time are not "fixed" so that all customers simply pay the same price; such is the result only of modern, large-scale retailing. Instead, most prices over the course of human history have been the result of negotiation between the buyer and the seller (i.e., variable pricing). And retailers, particularly those with online channels, are beginning to question whether the fixed-price approach is best.

No; online retailers are not considering basing their prices on the color of your skin or whether your hair is wavy or straight, but they are beginning to charge different prices to different individuals based upon particular circumstances. And the technique is called dynamic pricing. *Dynamic pricing*—or adjusting prices in real-time, or near real-time, to meet the characteristics and needs of individual shoppers and purchasing situations—isn't new to retailing or business in general. Travel-related industries such as hotels, rental cars, and airline tickets, as well as markets for energy and online mortgages have long relied on software programs to enhance their bottom-lines.

Yet a majority of online retailers are only now, following the Great Recession of 2008–2009, taking a serious look at the technology and software widely available from such leading firms as SAP's Revenue Management and Price Optimization Solutions to ProfitLogic's Spotlight Solutions. What the recent recession and years following have underscored for these retailers is that profits aren't guaranteed, and every additional penny collected could be the difference between success and failure. Thus, if some people are willing to pay more than others for a given product or service, retailers would be wise to charge those individuals more. The only hurdle is identifying those individuals.

In its most basic form, companies customize their offers and prices based on the specific characteristics and behaviors of customers gleaned from information within the cookies kept on their computer browsers or from the purchase history when logged into a site. Consider the following example. Yesterday you were on your computer customizing a new BMW and looking at rings at Tiffany and Co.'s website after purchasing first-class tickets to Rome and ordering new Bose Noise Canceling headphones for the trip. Now you go online to purchase a new sofa. Odds are you're going to pay more for that sofa than someone who has been surfing discount retailer websites and shopping with online coupons. And why not; the retailer knows you can obviously afford it.

It is impossible to know exactly which retailers change a price on a customer depending on their browser or cookies or which retailers change prices for customers after they have clicked to put a product in their shopping cart on a previous shopping occasion only to later walk way. But such retailers do exist and their number is rising. Retailers simply know most shoppers will question the practice, if not despise them for doing so. Therefore, retailers rarely admit to using such tactics publically unless caught red-handed. Yet many retailers offer disclaimers implying they are aware of price discrepancies. One higher-end furniture retailer, for example, answers the FAQ question, "Why is the price of an item in my saved shopping cart different from when I selected it?" on its site. The answer, "Prices are subject to change—including temporary reductions as well as permanent increases. The prices of items in your cart represent the current price for which you will be charged."

Sources: Martin, Justin, "Dynamic Pricing: Internet Retailers Are Treating Us Like Foreign Tourists in Egypt," *Christian Science Monitor,* January 7, 2011; Lowrey, Annie, "How Online Retailers Stay a Step Ahead of Comparison Shoppers," *The Washington Post Online,* December 12, 2010; Rishe, Patrick, "Dynamic Pricing: The Future of Ticket Pricing in Sports," *Forbes Online,* January 6, 2012; Smith, Ethan, "Ticketmaster to Tie Prices to Demand," *The Wall Street Journal Online,* April 18, 2011; "ProfitLogic Acquires Spotlite Solutions in Price Optimization Market," *Internet Retailer,* Available at: http://www.internetretailer.com/2003/09/10/profitlogic-acquires-spotlight-solutions-in-price-optimization-m [Accessed June 3, 2012]; Heun, Christopher, "Dynamic Pricing Boosts Bottom Line," *Information Week,* Available at: http://www.informationweek.com/news/6507202 [Accessed June 3, 2012].

their low-price image by promoting the price differences between their private brands and comparable national brands. That some retailers are successful with such a policy is evident by the fact that many local retailers, especially restaurants, now use warehouse clubs and supercenters as their suppliers.

Besides being known as a "tough, obnoxious, and insane" competitor, the retailer who uses this policy benefits by discouraging some competitors from entering a given trading area so as to avoid head-to-head battles.[8] However, for retailers to consistently price below the market and be profitable, they must concentrate on generating gross-margin dollars per square foot of space, not the gross-margin percentage. After all, profitability is not directly related to the gross-margin percentage of the product sold but the amount of gross margin per unit sold times the number of units sold. Consequently, below-market retailers must always try to increase the sales per square foot of store space since they have already reduced their markups.

A growing number of retailers today are becoming increasingly concerned that the growth of the Internet will forever change the way retailers set prices. As discussed within this chapter's "What's New?" box, the capabilities now exist for online retailers to leverage the information stored within the cookies of customers' online browsers in order to change products' prices in near real-time so as to charge as high a price as a customer's likely willing to pay.

Pricing at Market Levels

price zone
Is a range of prices for a particular merchandise line that appeals to customers in a certain market segment.

Most merchants want to be competitive with one another. Retailers' use of comparison shoppers—that is, having employees visit competitors' retail outlets in order to compare prices—stems from this basic premise. Competitive pricing involves a **price zone**, a range of prices for a particular merchandise line that appeals to customers in a certain demographic group, such as Target selling women's tops in three price zones: under $14, $15 to $24, and $25 to $49. However, it is important to remember that zones may vary across groups. Dillard's does not necessarily need to match the prices of Target, yet Dillard's should maintain prices similar to those of Macy's, particularly when they compete in the same mall. Alternatively, Target should be competitively priced with Walmart and Kohl's. Pricing at market levels is extremely important for e-tailers given the ease with which consumers can compare prices across different Internet retailers. Pricing at the market is also used by universities where they annually look at the other universities and colleges they compete with and then try to set their tuition for the next year to be in-line with the market price at similar schools.

The size of a retail store affects its ability to compete on price. Small retailers usually pay more for their merchandise and have higher operating expenses as a proportion of sales than larger retailers. Although many small retailers have joined voluntary wholesale cooperative chains as discussed in Chapter 5 to reduce their expenses through quantity discounts, they continue to experience a cost disadvantage. For these reasons, small retailers such as mom-and-pop grocery stores, hardware stores, and convenience stores often stress convenience and service rather than price in their retailing mix. However, even in these cases, it is important that one's prices not be too far out of line.

Sometimes, as this chapter's "Service Retailing" box illustrates, circumstances force retailers to price at the market but at a price so low that it generates a very low profit. This is what is happening today with new car dealers as a result of the recent recession.

Pricing above the Market

above-market pricing policy
Is a policy where retailers establish high prices because nonprice factors are more important to their target market than price.

Some retailers, either by design or circumstance, follow an **above-market pricing policy**. Certain market sectors are receptive to high prices because nonprice factors are more

© Smileus/Shutterstock

SERVICE RETAILING

For Auto Dealers, Profit Isn't Always in the Showroom

A half-century ago, many Americans were "shade tree mechanics," performing many minor repairs and services on their own cars. Even a decade ago, many continued to use a neighborhood mechanic to work on their cars. Not anymore. Today's automobile has more than 100 microprocessors (computers on a chip), all to ensure that the car runs smoothly. This is great as long as the microprocessors work; however, when they fail, today's car must be hooked to more monitors than you'd typically see in an operating room. These repairs are expensive, too. Consider, for example, when the computer chip that drives an electronic fan blade fails—it can cost upward of $500 to replace. Similarly, a computer-assisted six-speed transmission could run into the thousands of dollars in repair costs. As a result, dealers now know that servicing has become the most profitable part of their business; the other two sources of profit are new and used vehicle sales.

New vehicle sales aren't as profitable as they used to be because price competition is near perfect. After all, anyone can now go online and access the dealer's cost. In addition, the customer can not only negotiate with local dealers but also shop over the Internet with dealers hundreds, if not thousands, of miles away. For example, one of the authors had a close friend who was able to purchase a 2009 Chevrolet Corvette, listed at $58,000, for $47,750 from a dealer on the East Coast, some 2,000 miles away. Even with the delivery charge to his home, the price was still thousands less than the best offer from his local Chevrolet dealer. Perhaps this is why, after paying the salesperson's commission, a typical dealer's profit on a new vehicle sale is only a small amount. Used car sales, on the other hand, offer a better opportunity for profit. After all, every used vehicle is different in terms of condition, even if it is the same model year, which makes price negotiation more difficult. Therefore, gross margins on the sales of used vehicles are more profitable than those on new vehicles—often between 15 percent and 20 percent.

However, the real profit opportunity for dealers isn't selling cars, but servicing them. After all, the sale of parts and services has gross profit margins of more than 50 percent. Thus, successful new car dealers today realize that their profits depend not only on selling new units but also on developing repeat business from their customers. This is especially true today given that Americans are now keeping their cars for an average of 8–11 years.

There are several strategies to gain this repeat business. First, the dealer can convince new car purchasers that it is less risky to prepay for costly auto repairs by purchasing an extended warranty, which is a form of insurance. This allows the dealer to actually make money on the expected service problems, regardless of where the repairs are performed. The extended warranty on a $40,000 automobile can cost anywhere from $1,500 to $3,000, depending on the length and components covered. Incidentally, the dealer and the insurance carrier usually split the revenue, thereby adding an extra $750 to $1,500 profit to the sale. Some dealers have even found they can increase the sale of such packages by adding it to the monthly payment so that the monthly fee on a 60-month finance contract is only $30 to $60 more (or roughly a dollar or two a day). Of course, the person selling the warranty is careful to mention that a single component could cost that amount if it failed.

Another option that a number of dealers are now pursuing is providing lifetime oil, lube, and tire-rotation services every 5,000 miles for free. You might ask, "How can someone make money giving away a product and service for free?" In this case, the approximate $15 cost for the labor, oil, and filter is an opportunity for service mechanics to check whether alignment issues are present, test the shocks or struts for excessive wear, examine the brakes, and determine whether the tires need replacing. In addition, the service technician can identify items in need of repair that are under warranty and bill these costs to the auto manufacturer. Further, the oil and lube service provides the service representative an opportunity to sell fuel filters, fan belts, and transmission or radiator flushes.

(continued)

All in all, the sale of warranties or the provision of free oil and lube services represents a great profit opportunity for dealers. These services not only entice the owner to repeatedly visit the dealer throughout the life of the automobile but also lure him or her into the showroom to look at new vehicles because these types of services can usually be done in 60 minutes. Yes, people still buy autos on impulse and do fall in love with new models. By providing such services, the dealer is performing retailing's first task—get customers into your store several times a year. Besides, this activity is often cheaper than advertising. After all, the cost of a full-page advertisement in the local newspaper of a large city on the weekend or a few 60-second spots during a local television show could cost $5,000 to $10,000. If this ad brought in 200 potential customers, it would cost the dealer about $50 per showroom visitor generated (significantly more than the cost of an oil change).

important to them than price. Some retailers such as Nordstrom offer such outstanding service that they have minimal price competition. Nordstrom also sells more of their merchandise at full-price because they limit sales to two per year, and rather than cut price at their regular stores if merchandise doesn't sell, they ship it to their outlet stores (http://shop.nordstrom.com/C/nordstrom-rack). Other retailers, such as small neighborhood drugstores and hardware stores, are forced to price above the market because of their high cost structure and low sales volume. Often you will hear criticism that the residents in poor areas of a city and especially downtown areas pay more for consumer purchases such as food, apparel, appliances, and hardware. This is accurate but it is not because these retailers are making more profit but because they have a variety of higher costs that include occupancy, high employee turnover, higher theft, higher insurance costs, and higher store repair and maintenance costs. Unfortunately, these costs need to be passed on to the customer and thus prices are set higher.

Occasionally, retailers may use high prices to drive certain customer groups away from their places of business. This sounds counter-intuitive; however, consider a cocktail lounge or bar that sets prices on beer at $9 and mixed drinks at $12 versus the normal prices of $5 for beer and $7 for cocktails. The cocktail lounge or bar is almost guaranteeing that patrons that are well to do financially visit the establishment and others go down the street to the lower price alternative. For the financially better-off patrons, this could be an advantage as they may seek to socialize with others of financial means. Some other factors that permit retailers to price above market levels include the following.

- Merchandise Offerings. Some consumers will pay higher-than-average prices for specialty items, an exclusive line, or unusual merchandise. Prestige retailers such as Tiffany, Gucci, and Neiman Marcus carry high-priced specialty items.
- Services Provided. Many communities have service-oriented merchants with a loyal group of customers who are willing to pay higher prices to obtain an array of services ranging from wardrobe counseling to delivery. Nordstrom's clerks, for example, have a habit of doing such special things as dropping off purchases at a customer's home, sending thank-you notes to customers, and even ironing a newly purchased shirt so the customer can wear it that day.
- Convenient Locations. The convenient location of gift shops and business service centers in hotels, airline terminals, and even downtown office buildings allows them to charge higher prices. A supermarket could provide a home meal delivery service that offers the ultimate in convenient location and charge a higher price.
- Extended Hours of Operation. By remaining open while other stores are closed, some merchants are able to charge higher-than-average prices. Service plazas on interstate highways justify their higher prices by never closing. Or, a gasoline station open late at night can charge a higher price.

LO 2

Specific Pricing Strategies

Describe the differences between the various pricing strategies available to the retailer.

Various pricing strategies are adopted by the traditional bricks-and-mortar retailers in an effort to achieve certain pricing objectives. The pricing strategies should be in accord with the other components of the store's retail mix: location, promotion, display, service level, and merchandise assortment.

Customary Pricing

customary pricing
Is a policy in which the retailer sets prices for goods and services and seeks to maintain those prices over an extended period of time.

Customary pricing occurs when a retailer sets prices for goods and services and seeks to maintain those prices over an extended period of time. Movies and vending-machine products are common examples of items that use customary pricing. Here, retailers, such as movie theaters with their $8 ticket prices, seek to establish prices that customers can take for granted over long periods of time. Or some fast food restaurants may seek to maintain a $5 value meal price or budget motels seeking to maintain a $39 single occupancy rate.

Variable Pricing

variable pricing
Is a policy that recognizes that differences in demand and cost necessitate that the retailer change prices in a fairly predictable manner.

Variable pricing is used when differences in demand and cost force the retailer to change prices in a fairly predictable manner. Flowers, for example, tend to be priced higher when demand is greatest around Mother's Day and Valentine's Day. It is a common practice for most resorts to increase their rates on premium rooms in June, a busy wedding time, or for destination resorts in Hawaii, Florida, Arizona, and Southern California to have higher rates during the winter season. If you go to the theatre you will often witness variable pricing where the best seats in the house, for instance, for a Broadway hit, will go as high as $400 ($800 for a pair of tickets) on a prime weekend of high demand versus seats in the back row of the second balcony which may go for less than $100. At the local level, in every city or town with a movie theatre, lower prices for weekday mid-afternoon showings will be offered. Fresh fruits tend to sell for less during their growing seasons when the retailer's costs are down. In addition, many restaurants offer the same meal at lunch as for dinner but with a discounted lunch price (often 10–30 percent lower) to increase demand.

Flexible Pricing

flexible pricing
Is a policy that encourages offering the same products and quantities to different customers at different prices.

Flexible pricing means offering the same products and quantities to different customers at different prices. Retailers generally use flexible pricing in situations calling for personal selling. The advantage of using flexible pricing is that the salesperson can make price adjustments based on the customer's interest, a competitor's price, a past relationship with the customer, or the customer's bargaining ability. Most jewelry stores and automobile dealerships and many furniture stores use this pricing policy, although not all customers like it.[9]

Many types of retailers use flexible pricing by varying their prices and giving discounts to special consumer groups such as loyalty club members, senior citizens, military personnel, and the clergy. Interestingly enough, some analysts predict that since a baby now reaches age 60 every 8 seconds, senior-citizen discounts can be expected to disappear over the next decade. Today, some employee groups, credit unions, and housing or neighborhood groups have negotiated price discounts with selected retailers. In fact, the recent downturn in the economy has increased the importance of flexible price as more shoppers are engaging in old-fashioned haggling. This has forced retailers eager to make sales to become flexible. While most major chains don't want to go on record saying they will engage in price negotiation, these retailers do say that the increased level of autonomy at the store level seems to be good for creating the impression that these are neighborhood stores, not just uncaring national chains.

However, Americans are nowhere near what some Chinese consumers do to negotiate lower flexible prices. In China, to the dismay of many retailers, some of the country's 1.3 billion consumers have started shopping in teams to haggle for bigger discounts. This team purchasing practice begins in Internet chat rooms (such as 51tuangou.com—the Chinese word *tuangou* means "I want to team buy"), where they hatch plans to buy appliances, furnishings, food, and even cars in bulk. Next, they show up en masse at stores to demand discounts.[10]

Flexible pricing, although popular because it seeks to match levels of supply and demand, does have its disadvantages. Costs can dramatically increase, and revenues decrease, as customers begin to bargain for everything. Similarly, customers may get mad at the retailer and take their business elsewhere when they find that they paid more than a friend did for the same product. This is why the one-price policy is so popular in the United States.

One-Price Policy

one-price policy
Is a policy that establishes that the retailer will charge all customers the same price for an item.

Under a **one-price policy**, the retailer charges all customers the same price for an item. A one-price policy may be used in conjunction with customary or variable pricing. For example, all people buying a Big Mac at the same McDonald's will pay an identical price. Roland Hussey Macy, the founder of Macy's Department Store, is often credited with the one-price policy, but recently the authors found evidence that a Sacramento retailer, Weinstock & Lubin, was using this policy in 1875, nearly four decades before Macy's.[11] This policy allowed for efficiency and fairness in handling customer transactions in a large store, where the selling activity is delegated to salespersons that have varying degrees of loyalty to the retailer. If salespersons are permitted to bargain over price, then customers who are shrewd and assertive could conceivably negotiate terms that are unprofitable to the retailer.

A one-price policy, therefore, speeds up transactions and reduces the need for highly skilled salespeople. Most catalog operators adopt a one-price policy since they are forced to retain their prices until the expiration date of the catalog, which can be six months from its issuance. Many manufacturers encourage retailers to follow a one-price policy to maintain the image of their products. They do so by advertising the suggested retail price on the packaging and using personal selling techniques to persuade retailers to maintain that price. However, such a pricing policy will work only if the vast majority of retailers voluntarily agree to stick to the plan. Otherwise, a flexible price retailer will know the price it has to beat. This has been part of the challenge that some retail auto dealers have confronted when they went to a one-price policy on new automobiles. They pursued this strategy with the intent to avoid the aggressive negotiations between customers and a retail salesperson that often takes a half-day or more. Also, the one-price strategy would allow the salesperson to focus on serving customers by providing useful information to assist them in selecting the best car for their needs. However, this strategy largely backfired because when a Chevrolet or Toyota dealer put a reasonable but non-negotiable price on their cars, of say $24,300, then the Chevrolet or Toyota dealer across town knew that a deal could probably be reached with most customers for a one to two hundred dollars less.

Price Lining

To simplify pricing procedures and help consumers make merchandise comparisons, some retailers establish a specified number of price lines or price points for each merchandise category. Once the price lines are determined, these retailers purchase goods

price lining
Is a pricing policy that is established to help customers make merchandise comparisons and involves establishing a specified number of price points for each merchandise classification.

trading up
Occurs when a retailer uses price lining and a salesperson moves a customer from a lower-priced line to a higher one.

trading down
Occurs when a retailer uses price lining, and a customer initially exposed to higher-priced lines expresses the desire to purchase a lower-priced line.

that fit into each line. This is called **price lining**. For example, in men's slacks, the price lines could be limited to $29.95, $49.95, and $69.95. The monetary difference between the price lines should be large enough to reflect a value difference to consumers. This makes it easier for the salesperson to either trade up or trade down a customer. **Trading up** occurs when a salesperson moves a customer from a lower-priced line to a higher one. **Trading down**, which gained in popularity during the recent slowdown, occurs when a customer is initially exposed to higher-priced lines but expresses the desire to purchase a lower-priced line.

Retailers select price lines that have the strongest consumer demand. By limiting the number of price lines, a retailer achieves broader assortments, which leads to increased sales and fewer markdowns. For example, a retailer who stocks 150 units of an item and has six price lines would likely have an assortment of only 25 units in each line. On the other hand, if the 150 units were divided among only three price lines, there would likely be 50 units in each line.

When retailers are limited to certain price lines, they become specialists in those lines. This permits them to concentrate all their merchandising and promotional efforts on those lines, thus defining the store image more clearly. In addition, they direct their purchases to vendors who handle those lines. The vendors, in turn, provide favored treatment to their large-volume retailing customers. Other advantages of price lining include buying more efficiently, simplifying inventory control, and accelerating inventory turnover. From the shopper's perspective, it is easy to shop when price lining is used because differences are perceived among the various price points. Saks Fifth Avenue has recently remerchandised the fourth floor of its flagship store in NYC to have a merchandise assortment and price line that is more affordable than high fashion designer apparel that the store is best known. This new floor, called the Wear floor, will have jackets priced $500 to $700; trousers, $150 to $300; tops, $175 to $300; knitwear, $150 to $400.[12]

An analysis of a store's best-selling price lines is essential prior to making any decision to alter them. Generally, middle-priced lines should account for the majority of one's sales. When the bulk of sales occur at the extremes of the price lines, the retailer should take corrective actions. These include altering the assortments in the current price lines, changing the price lines, redirecting the salespersons' efforts, developing more effective promotions, or adjusting the total marketing mix to a new target market.

Odd Pricing

odd pricing
Is the practice of setting retail prices that end in the digits 5, 8, 9—such as $29.95, $49.98, or $9.99.

The practice of setting retail prices that end in the digits 5, 8, or 9—such as $29.95, $49.98, or $9.99—is called **odd pricing**. A quick look at retail advertisements in the newspaper or on the Internet will reveal that many retailers use an odd-pricing policy. Retailers feel that this policy produces significantly higher sales, and recent evidence suggests they might be correct[13] as pointed out in this chapter's "Retailing: The Inside Story" box.

While recent evidence suggests retailers may benefit from the way consumers perceive—or, more accurately, misperceive—odd prices, a more plausible explanation for its initial adoption back in the early part of the 20th century was the lack of a sales tax. In those days, merchandise was priced in even dollars, thus making it easy for salespersons to pocket the occasional $1, $5, or $10 bills or gold piece since they did not have to make change for the customer. When Marshall Field caught on to this, he devised the first odd-numbered pricing system to stop the practice. Field ruled that, "We'll charge 99 cents instead of even dollars. This will force the clerks to ring up the sales, open the cash register, put the money in and give the customer a receipt and change."

Because odd prices are associated with low prices, they are typically used by retailers who sell either at prices below the market or at the market. Retailers selling above the

How Is the Price $13.99 Really Perceived? As Essentially $14, or Is It Just $13?

Recent surveys find that the practice of odd pricing by retailers is increasing with as many as 30 percent of all items being priced with odd ending digits. The question is why? Is a price, say $13.99, really different than $14.00, just 1 cent higher? The casual reader of this box may say no. Some may even assume that they "always round up" such prices, as one of the author's family members commonly tells him—not believing that odd-pricing "really works."

Yet whether you remain a skeptic about the power of odd pricing or not, the evidence suggests that it works; and it works well. But if you're skeptical, it's okay. It's the large number of skeptics that have made the use and impact of odd pricing (also referred to as "99-ending" or "just below" pricing) one of the most studied pricing issues in retailing over the past several decades.

So what are the findings? Well, odd-pricing seems to have two general effects on consumer behavior. First it impacts consumer price comparisons when two products' prices are compared during a single shopping occasion. For instance, if you were to pick up two substitute products, one priced at $ 4.00 and the other $2.99, research indicates you would likely perceive the $2.99 product as substantially cheaper than the $1.01 difference. This effect would not occur if the second product had been priced at $3.00. The reason is because people truncate, or fixate, primarily on the digits left of the decimal and neglect the "cents" portion of a price, or what is termed a *left-digit effect*. In essence, the second price is perceived as essentially $2.00, not one-cent less than $3.00. This would create a scenario where in the above example a shopper would perceive the second product as about half the first product's price, which is not the case. As a result, you might choose to buy more than you would have had you perceived the second price correctly. Interestingly, the same effect occurs if a retailer lowers the price of a product by putting it on sale. If the

price of a product *was* $4.00 and advertises a lowered price of $2.99, consumers will perceive the discount as greater (again about half the original cost) than it really is.

Second, odd pricing has been found to impact consumers' ability to remember prices. For example, recent research tested whether students could be shown a product's price, say $4.99, one day and notice whether the price increased, decreased, or stayed the same during a following class meeting two days later. When the price was 00-ending, like $5.00, students recognized more often if the price changed. When the price was 99-ending, they could not correctly state whether a price had changed or in what direction.

And you might be thinking two days is a long time to remember a price. When was the last time you shopped for groceries at the same store within a two-day period? Odds are that's not a common occurrence for you. But let's assume you're right that two days is a long time; what would you think the odds are students could recall a price correctly after 10 minutes?

Research has shown that 99-ending prices are less likely to be accurately recalled than 00-ending prices, even when one is asked to recall a price they saw *less than 5 minutes before*. Pair these findings with those above and you begin to see why odd-pricing can significantly affect retailers' bottom-lines; most consumers won't notice if the retailer increases its prices or even if it changes its prices after 5 minutes!

Sources: Manning and Sprott, "Price Endings, Left-Digit Effects, and Choice," *Journal of Consumer Research*, 36 (August 2009): 328–335; John C. Carver, "Left Behind: The Potential Downside of Odd-Ending Pricing," Texas A&M University, Working Paper, 2002; Schindler, "The 99 Price Ending as a Signal of a Low-Price Appeal," *Journal of Retailing*, 82(1), 2006: 71–77; Schindler and Kirby, "Patterns of Rightmost Digits Used in Advertising Prices: Implications for Nine-Ending Effects," *Journal of Consumer Research*, 24 (September 1997): 192–201; Thomas and Morwitz, "Penny Wise and Pound Foolish: The Left-Digit Effect in Price Cognition," *Journal of Consumer Research*, 32 (June 2005): 54–65.

market, such as Neiman Marcus and Nordstrom, usually end their prices with even numbers, which have come to denote quality. These retailers would likely sell an item for $90.00 rather than $89.99. Prestige-conscious retailers are not seeking bargain hunters as customers.

Multiple-Unit Pricing

multiple-unit pricing
Occurs when the price of each unit in a multiple-unit package is less than the price of each unit if it were sold individually.

With **multiple-unit pricing**, the price of each unit in a multiple-unit package is less than the price of each unit if it were sold individually. Grocery retailers use multiple-unit pricing extensively in their sales of cigarettes, light bulbs, candy bars, and beverages. Apparel retailers often sell multiple units of underwear, hosiery, and tops. Multiple-unit pricing is also common in restaurants that offer the second meal at a 50 percent or more discount. You also see this practice with other service retailers such as dry cleaners that will offer dry cleaning of three sweaters or slacks for $9.95 where the regular unit price may be $4 to $5. Some car washes, to encourage repeat business, will sell booklets of wash tickets, for instance, five washes for $36, whereas the regular price maybe $9 or $10 per car wash.

Retailers use multiple-unit pricing to encourage additional sales and to increase profits. The gross margin that is sacrificed in a multiple-unit sale is more than offset by the savings that occur from reduced selling and handling expenses. Generally, multiple-unit pricing can be effectively employed for items that are either consumed rapidly or used together.

Bundle Pricing

Bundling generally involves selling distinct multiple items offered together at a special price. For instance, Red Lobster will occasionally offer a four-course meal for a bundled price of $15 (soup, salad, entrée, and desert). Joseph A. Banks is another retailer often using bundled pricing where it offers, for instance, a sports coat, two pairs of slacks, three shirts, and two ties for an attractive bundled price. Here the perceived savings in cost or time for the bundle justifies the purchase. At the same time, bundling can increase the retailer's revenue since the customer may actually purchase more items than originally planned. For example, while airlines have been actively unbundling their prices, many travel agencies are now bundling their vacation packages. Here they package airfare, hotel, transfers, and meals together as a means of reducing price comparisons and increasing the number of options sold.

Today, a small number of retailers are testing nontraditional forms of bundling to encourage customers to patronize their establishments by providing nonrelated services gratis or for a small fee. For example, some movie theaters have found that the main obstacle encountered by parents when coming to the movies is finding child care. As a result, some theaters now offer either "Monday Night Is Baby's Night" for very young babies or child-care centers for children aged 2–8. This latter bundling program seems to be going over well with parents who previously could only consider attending PG movies.

Grocery stores and physical fitness centers are also testing the addition of child-care facilities. Such action shows that retailers are becoming more oriented toward their customers' needs, especially when child and adult activities significantly diverge. Some parents, especially single parents, believe that certain errands and tasks, such as trips to the grocery store, can be sharing activities; however, these parents are also aware that most of the time their youngsters get bored sitting in a shopping cart.

The economic conditions of recent years have also caused some retailers, especially those selling services, to drop the idea of bundling their merchandise and instead unbundle them. These retailers hope that by unbundling their offerings they'll increase revenues without offending their customers. For example, apartments near universities now charge for parking spaces rather than provide them for free. However, this strategy can backfire as when some high-end retailers slash prices on apparel but then add charges for alternations, which used to be included in their retail price. Even though the final price for the customer is still attractive, this practice tends to offend long-time and loyal customers who think they have earned a special sale price with no extra charges added. One of the authors was recently charged an extra fee by his eye-doctor. The fee was in addition to the eye examination and was $30 for writing a prescription.

Leader Pricing

leader pricing
Is when a high-demand item is priced low and is heavily advertised in order to attract customers into the store.

When **leader pricing** is used, a high-demand item is priced low and advertised heavily in an effort to build store traffic. The items selected for leader pricing should be widely known and purchased frequently. In addition, information should be available that will permit consumers to make price comparisons. National brands of convenience goods such as Crest toothpaste, Mitchum antiperspirant, Maxwell House coffee, Budweiser, and Coca-Cola are often designated as leader items.

Leader pricing is usually part of a promotional program designed to increase store traffic. A successful program will produce additional sales for all areas of a store. In many instances, the price of the leader item is reduced only for a specific promotion. Some retailers, such as supermarkets, however, regularly feature leader items. Today, many convenience stores use gasoline as a leader. These retailers reduce their gas prices by a few pennies to get customers into their store. Once in the store, customers are exposed to fast-food sandwiches, groceries, fresh produce, beverages, and even fresh flowers. In such stores, the inside merchandise contributes more than 70 percent to the store's gross-margin dollars and subsidizes its gasoline business. For those customers who just want gas, these stores have pay-at-the-pump facilities.

A retailer using leader pricing should carefully evaluate its usefulness. If consumers are limiting their purchases to only those leader items, then the policy is ineffective. Because leader items may be sold at or near a retailer's cost, higher-markup items must also be sold to generate a profit for the retailer. However, recent research has found that in the supermarket industry "cherry pickers," shoppers who buy only items on sale, aren't as numerous or as profit-draining as the industry once feared.[14]

loss leader
Is an extreme form of leader pricing where an item is sold below a retailer's cost.

An item that is sold below a retailer's cost is known as a **loss leader**. For example, every St. Patrick's Day, many supermarkets sell corned beef at a loss and a week before Thanksgiving Day sell turkeys at a loss (but limit often to one per customer) in hopes of attracting consumers to their stores and making a profit on the rest of their purchases. For instance, a Thanksgiving Feast for eight that is home prepared translates into a grocery bill of $200 or more.

high–low pricing
Involves the use of high every day prices and low leader "specials" on items typically featured in weekly ads.

The pricing actions of discounters using below-market pricing have forced manufacturers to change their pricing strategies, thus endangering another group of retailers—those using leader pricing. Retailers using everyday low prices want vendors to offer them constant prices throughout the year by phasing out virtually all deep discounts and offering them the same low price every day. For example, instead of selling retailers a case of peanut butter for $20 one week and offering it on sale the next week for $15, they want it priced at $18 every week. This would limit the ability of leader pricers such as supermarkets to continue their use of high–low pricing. **High–low pricing** involves the use of high everyday prices and low leader specials on featured items for their weekly advertisements.

Bait-and-Switch Pricing

bait-and-switch pricing
Advertising or promoting a product at an unrealistically low price to serve as "bait" and then trying to "switch" the customer to a higher-priced product.

The practice of advertising a low-priced model of a shopping good such as a television or a computer merely to lure shoppers into a store is called **bait-and-switch pricing**. Once the shoppers are in the store, a salesperson tries to persuade them to purchase a higher-priced model. This pricing strategy is almost always tied to a sales force compensation plan that is heavily based on commissions, and in fact, when bait-and-switch pricing is used, the salespeople get no commission on the deeply discounted item that has been used to lure customers to the store. That is why when you visit stores with a bait-and-switch pricing strategy, the salespeople, if they learn that all you want is the deeply discounted item, seem to find ways to move away from you such as "I will be right back, I need to help another customer." Bait-and-switch pricing, which was discussed in Chapter 6, is considered by the Federal Trade Commission to be an illegal practice when the low-priced model used as bait is unavailable to shoppers. Some in the industry describe the *bait* merchandise as being "nailed to the floor."

Private-Label Brand Pricing

A private-label brand can often be purchased by a retailer at a cheaper price, have a higher markup percentage, and still be priced lower than a comparable national brand. Private labels also permit the retailer a large degree of pricing freedom because consumers find it difficult to make exact comparisons between the private and national brands. Many retailers, like Marks & Spencer, Sears, and Walmart, price their private brands below the market.

Other retailers seeking to differentiate themselves from competitors are now using an above-market pricing approach for their private labels. Department stores that have been battered on price by discounters and specialty stores are now using private labels to improve their own image. Target has had some success with its Archer Farms private brand, especially with its cereals, which come in a distinctive canister. In some cases, the Archer Farms brand product actually sells for a higher per ounce price than the national brands for a comparative product and size.[15]

LO 3

Describe how retailers calculate the various markups.

Using Markups

A retail buyer should be able to calculate rapidly whether a proposed purchase will provide an adequate markup or gross margin. The markup can be expressed in dollars or as a percentage of either the selling price or the cost of the good. There are times, however, when a retail buyer needs to compute the markdown, which is a reduction in the selling price of the goods. Markdowns are made in order to move certain merchandise, especially when the color or size assortments are no longer complete.

Calculating Markup

To calculate the selling price (or *retail price*), the retailer should begin with the following basic markup equation:

$$SP = C + M$$

markup
Is the selling price of the merchandise less its cost, which is equivalent to gross margin.

where C is the dollar cost of merchandise per unit, M is the dollar markup per unit, and SP is the selling price per unit.

Thus, if the retailer has a cost per unit of $16 on a shirt and a dollar markup of $14, then the selling price per unit is $30. In other words, **markup** is simply the difference between the cost of the merchandise and the selling price, which is the same as gross margin.

This markup is intended to cover all of the operating expenses (wages, rent, utilities, promotion, credit, etc.) incurred in the sale of the product and still provide the retailer with a profit. Occasionally, a retailer will sell a product without a markup high enough to cover the cost of the merchandise in order to generate traffic or build sales volume. For instance, many e-tailers originally expected high turnover to allow them to be profitable. However, low margins coupled with low traffic caused many to close before volume could make up for their low margins. This chapter, however, will only be concerned with using markup to produce a profit on the sale of each item.

Markup Methods

Markup may be expressed as either a dollar amount or as a percentage of either the selling price or cost. It is most useful when expressed as a percentage of the selling price because it can then be used in comparison with other financial data such as last year's sales results, reductions in selling price, and even the firm's competition. The equation for expressing markup as percentage of selling price is

$$\text{Percentage of markup on selling price} = (SP - C)/SP = M/SP$$

Although some businesses, usually manufacturers or small retailers, express markup as a percentage of cost, this method is not widely used in retailing because most of the financial data the retailer uses are expressed as a percentage of selling price. Nevertheless, when expressing markup as a percentage of cost, the equation is

$$\text{Percentage of markup on cost} = (SP - C)/C = M/C$$

Several problems occur when we attempt to equate markup as a percentage of selling price with markup as a percentage of cost. Since the two methods use different bases, we really are not comparing similar data. However, there is an equation to find markup on selling price when we know markup on cost:

$$\text{Percentage of markup on selling price} = \text{Percentage of markup on cost}/$$
$$(100\% + \text{Percentage of markup on cost})$$

Likewise, when we know markup on selling price, we can easily find markup on cost:

$$\text{Percentage of markup on cost} = \text{Percentage of markup on selling price}/$$
$$(100\% - \text{Percentage of markup on selling price})$$

The preceding equations convert percentage markup on cost to percentage markup on selling price and vice versa. Exhibit 10.2 shows a conversion table for markup on cost and markup on selling price. Let's go back to our original example of the shirt and see how easy it is to determine markup on selling price when we know the markup on cost and vice versa.

The retailer purchased the shirt for $16 and later sold it for $30. The difference between the selling price and the cost is $14. This $14 as a percentage of selling price (markup on selling price) is 46.7 percent ($14/$30). This same $14, however, represents 87.5 percent ($14/$16) of the cost (markup). In this example, if all we knew was that the shirt had an 87.5-percent markup on cost, we could determine that this was the same as a 46.7-percent markup on selling price:

$$\text{Percentage of markup on selling price} = \text{Percentage of markup on cost}/$$
$$(100\% + \text{Percentage of markup on cost}) = 87.5\%/(100\% + 87.5\%) = 46.7\%$$

Exhibit 10.2
Markup Conversion
Table

Markup Percentage on Selling Price	Markup Percentage on Cost	Markup Percentage on Selling Price	Markup Percentage on Cost
4.8	5.0	32.0	47.1
5.0	5.3	33.3	50.0
8.0	8.7	34.0	51.5
10.0	11.1	35.0	53.9
15.0	17.7	36.0	56.3
16.7	20.0	37.0	58.8
20.0	25.0	40.0	66.7
25.0	33.3	41.0	70.0
26.0	35.0	42.8	75.0
27.3	37.5	44.4	80.0
28.0	39.0	47.5	90.0
28.5	40.0	50.0	100.0
30.0	42.9	66.7	200.0

© Cengage Learning

Likewise, if we knew we had a 46.7-percent markup on selling, we could easily determine markup on cost:

Percentage of markup on cost = Percentage of markup on selling price
(100% − Percentage of markup on selling price) = 46.7%/(100% − 46.7%) = 87.5%

Exhibit 10.3 gives you the total picture of the relationships between markup on cost and markup on selling price. In Exhibit 10.3, you can see that dollar markup does not change as the percentage changes on cost or selling price. Dollar markup is presented as a percentage of cost or selling price.

Exhibit 10.4 reviews the basic markup equations.

Using Markup Formulas When Purchasing Merchandise

Although quite simple in concept, the basic markup formulas will enable you to determine more than the percentage of markup on a particular item. Let us work with the markup on selling price formula to illustrate how an interesting and common question might be answered. If you know that a particular type of item could be sold for $8 per unit and that you need a 40-percent markup on selling price to meet your profit

Exhibit 10.3
Relationship of Markups
Expressed on Selling
Price and Cost

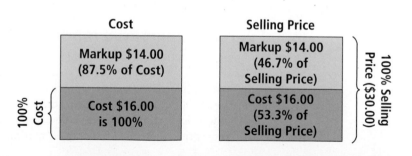

© Cengage Learning

Exhibit 10.4
Basic Markup Formulas

$$\% \text{ Markup on Selling Price} = \frac{\text{Selling Price} - \text{Cost}}{\text{Selling Price}} = \frac{\text{Markup}}{\text{Selling Price}}$$

$$\% \text{ Markup on Cost} = \frac{\text{Selling Price} - \text{Cost}}{\text{Cost}} = \frac{\text{Markup}}{\text{Cost}}$$

Finding % Markup on Cost When % Markup on Selling Price Is Known:

$$\% \text{ Markup on Cost} = \frac{\% \text{ Markup on Selling Price}}{100\% - \% \text{ Markup on Selling}}$$

Finding % Markup on Selling Price When % Markup on Cost Is Known:

$$\% \text{ Markup on Selling Price} = \frac{\% \text{ Markup on Cost}}{100\% + \% \text{ Markup on Cost}}$$

Finding Selling Price When Cost and % Markup on Cost Are Known:

$$\text{Selling Price} = \text{Cost} + \% \text{ Markup on Cost(Cost)}$$

Finding Selling Price When Cost and % Markup on Selling Price Are Known:

$$\text{Selling Price} = \frac{\text{Cost}}{(1 - \% \text{ Markup on Selling Price})}$$

objective, then how much would you be willing to pay for the item? Using our equation for markup on selling price, we have

$$\text{Percentage of markup on selling price} = (SP - C)/SP$$
$$40\% = (8 - C)/8$$
$$C = 4.80$$

Therefore, you would be willing to pay $4.80 for the item. If the item cannot be found at $4.80 or less, then it is probably not worth stocking.

Likewise, if a retailer purchases an item for $12 and wants a 40-percent markup on selling price, how would the retailer determine the selling price? Returning to our original equation ($SP = C + M$), we know that $SP = C + .40\%$ since markup is 40 percent of selling price. If markup is 40 percent of selling price, then cost must be 60 percent since cost and markup are the complements of each other and must total 100 percent. Thus, if

$$60\% \, SP = 12$$

then divide both sides by 60 percent:

$$SP = 20$$

Initial versus Maintained Markup

Up to this point, we have assumed that retailers have been able to sell the product at the price initially set when the product arrived at the store. We have assumed that the initial markup (the markup placed on the merchandise when the store receives it) is equal to the maintained markup or achieved markup (the actual selling price less the cost). Since in many cases the actual selling price for some of the firm's merchandise is lower than the original selling price, the firm's maintained markup is usually lower than the initial markup. Thus, maintained markup differs from initial markup by the amount of reductions:

$$\text{Initial markup} = (\text{original retail price} - \text{cost})/\text{original retail price}$$
$$\text{Maintained markup} = (\text{actual retail price} - \text{cost})/\text{actual retail price}$$

Five reasons can account for the difference between initial and maintained markups. First is the need to balance demand with supply. Since most markup formulas are cost-oriented, rather than demand-oriented, adjustments in selling prices will occur. This is especially true when consumer demand changes, and the only way for retailers to reduce their inventory and make their merchandise salable is by taking a markdown or reduction in selling price. A second reason is stock shortages. Shortages can occur from theft by employees or customers and by mismarking the price when merchandise is received or sold. In either case, the selling price received for the goods will be less than the price carried in the inventory records. In fact, clerical error probably accounts for more stock shortages than theft. Third, there are employee and customer discounts. Employees are usually given some discount privileges after they have worked for the firm for a specified period of time. Also, certain customer groups (e.g., religious and senior-citizen groups) may be given special discount privileges.

The fourth reason is the cost of alterations. Some fashion-apparel items require alterations before the product is acceptable to the customer. While men's clothing is often altered free of charge, there is usually a small charge for altering women's wear. Nevertheless, this charge usually does not cover all alteration costs, so alterations are actually a part of the cost of the merchandise.

A fifth and final reason that initial markup may be different from maintained markup is cash discounts, which are offered to retailers by manufacturers or suppliers to encourage prompt payment of bills. Any cash discounts taken reduce the cost of merchandise and therefore make the maintained markup higher than the initial markup. This is just the opposite of the first four factors.

Some large retailers ignore cash discounts in calculating initial markup because the buyer may have little control over whether or not the discount is taken. The reason for this is that achieving discounts through prompt payment is thought to be the result of financial operations rather than merchandising decisions, and therefore the buyer should not be penalized if the discounts are not taken.

Planning Initial Markups

As the previous discussion illustrates, retailers do not casually arrive at an initial markup percentage. The initial markup percentage must be a carefully planned process. Markups must be large enough to cover all of the operating expenses and still provide a reasonable profit to the firm. In addition, markups must provide for markdowns, shortages, employee discounts, and alteration expenses (all of these together are referred to as *total reductions*), which reduce net revenue. Likewise, cash discounts taken, which increase net revenue, must be included.

Initial Markup Equation

To determine the initial markup, use the following formula:

Initial markup percentage = (operating expenses + net profit + markdowns
+ stock shortages + employee and customer discounts
+ alterations costs − cash discounts)/(net sales
+ markdowns + stock shortages
+ employee and customer discounts)

We can simplify this equation if we remember that markdowns, stock shortages, and employee and customer discounts are all retail reductions from stock levels. Likewise, gross margin is the sum of operating expenses and net profit. This produces a simpler formula:

Initial markup percentage = (gross margin + alterations costs − cash discounts + reductions)/(net sales + reductions)

Because some retailers record cash discounts as other income and not as a cost reduction in determining initial markup, the formula can be simplified one more time:

Initial markup percentage = (gross margin + alterations costs + reductions)/(net sales + reductions)

Regardless of which of the three formulas is used, the retailer must always remember the effect of each of the following items when planning initial markup: operating expenses, net profits, markdowns, stock shortages, employee and customer discounts, alterations costs, cash discounts taken, and net sales.

At this point, a numerical example might be helpful. Assume that a retailer plans to achieve net sales of $1 million and expects operating expenses to be $270,000. The net profit goal is $60,000. Planned reductions include $80,000 for markdowns, $20,000 for merchandise shortages, and $10,000 for employee and customer discounts. Alteration costs are expected to be $20,000, and cash discounts from suppliers are expected to be $10,000. What is the initial markup percentage that should be planned? What is the cost of merchandise to be sold?

The initial markup percentage can be obtained by using the original equation:

Initial markup percentage = (270,000 + 60,000 + 80,000 + 20,000 + 10,000 + 20,000 − 10,000)/(1,000,000 + 80,000 + 20,000 + 10,000) = 40.54%

The cost of merchandise sold can also be found. We know that the gross margin is operating expenses plus net profit ($330,000). This gross profit is equivalent to net sales less cost of merchandise sold, where cost of merchandise sold includes alteration costs and where cash discounts are subtracted. Thus, in the problem at hand, we know that $1 million less cost of merchandise sold (including alterations costs and subtracting cash discounts) is equal to $670,000. Since the alterations costs are planned at $20,000 and cash discounts at $10,000, the cost of merchandise is equal to $660,000 ($670,000 − $20,000 + $10,000).

We can verify our result by returning to the basic initial markup formula: asking price minus cost divided by asking price. The asking price is the planned net sales of $1 million plus planned reductions of $110,000 ($80,000 for markdowns, $20,000 for shortages, and $10,000 for employee and customer discounts). The cost is the cost of merchandise before the alteration costs and prior to cash discounts, or $660,000. Using the basic initial markup formula, we obtain ($1,110,000 − $660,000)/$1,110,000, or 40.54 percent. This is the same result we achieved earlier.

The preceding computations resulted in a markup percentage on retail selling price for merchandise lines storewide. Obviously, not all lines or items within lines should be priced by mechanically applying this markup percentage, since the actions of competitors will affect the prices for each merchandise line. Thus, the retailer will want to price the mix of merchandise lines in such a fashion that a storewide markup percentage is obtained. To achieve this, some lines may be priced with considerably higher markups and others with substantially lower markups than the storewide average that was planned using the initial markup planning equation. It will be helpful to explore some of the common reasons for varying the markup percentage on different lines or items within lines.

Markup Determinants

In planning initial markups, it is useful to know some of the general rules of markup determination. These are summarized as follows:

1. As goods are sold through more retail outlets, the markup percentage decreases. On the other hand, selling through few retail outlets means a greater markup percentage. For instance, the markup on apparel is lower when a manufacturer uses intensive retail distribution versus exclusive distribution.
2. The higher the handling and storage costs of the goods, the higher the markup should be. For example, grocery retailers need to markup produce and fruits more than dry groceries.
3. The greater the risk of a price reduction due to the seasonality of the goods, the greater the magnitude of the markup percentage early in the season. For instance, swimsuits are marked up high early in the season and drop substantially as the swimming season ends.
4. The higher the demand inelasticity of price for the goods, the greater the markup percentage. For instance, the demand for soda and other refreshments is relatively inelastic during major sporting events and thus the markups are substantial.

Although these rules are common to all retail lines, other rules are unique to each line of trade and are learned only through experience in the respective lines—for example, how much to mark up produce in a supermarket during different seasons.

LO 4

Markdown Management

Discuss why markdown management is so important in retailing and describe some of the errors that cause markdowns.

markdown
Is any reduction in the price of an item from its initially established price.

Although retailers would prefer to have their initial markup (the one placed on the merchandise when the store receives it) equal to the maintained markup (the actual selling price less the cost), this seldom happens. **Markdowns**, which are reductions in the price of an item taken in order to stimulate sales, result in a firm receiving a lower price for its merchandise than originally asked. The markdown percentage is the amount of the reduction divided by the original selling price:

$$\text{Markdown percentage} = \text{Amount of reduction/original selling price}$$

Thus, maintained markup (sometimes referred to as *gross margin* or just plain *gross*) is the key to profitability because it is the difference between the actual selling price and the cost of that merchandise.

For effective retail price management, markdowns should be planned. This is true in principle because pricing is not a science with high degrees of precision but an art form with considerable room for error. If retailers knew everything they needed to know about demand and supply factors, they could use the science of economics to establish a price that would maximize profits and ensure the sale of all the merchandise. Unfortunately, retailers do not possess perfect information about supply and demand factors. As a result, the entire merchandising process is subject to error, which makes pricing difficult. Four basic errors can occur: (1) buying errors, (2) pricing errors, (3) merchandising errors, and (4) promotion errors.

Buying Errors

Errors in buying occur on the supply side of the pricing question. They result when the retailer buys the wrong merchandise or buys the right merchandise in too large a quantity. The merchandise purchased could have been in the wrong styles, sizes, colors, patterns, or price range. Too large a quantity could have been purchased because demand was overestimated or a recession was not foreseen. Whatever the cause of the buying error, the net result is a need to cut the price to move the merchandise. Often the resulting prices are below the actual cost of the merchandise to the retailer. Thus, buying errors can be quite costly. As a consequence, you might expect that the retail manager would wish to minimize buying errors. However, this is not the case. The retailer could minimize buying errors by being extremely conservative. It would buy only what it knew the customer wanted and what it could be certain of selling. Buying errors would be minimized, but at the expense of lost profit opportunities on some riskier types of purchase decisions. Recall that when we reviewed the determinants of markups we mentioned that the greater the risk of potential price reductions, the higher the markup percentage. This is simply another way of recognizing that taking a gamble on some purchases that may be buying errors can be profitable if initial markups are high. You may want to review the most common buying errors discussed in Chapter 9.

Chapter 3 explained that the demographics for baby boomers are different from those of Gen X or Gen Y consumers. These groups are not only different in age, but also in their buying behavior. However, many retailers employ buyers who are from the baby boomer generation. When boomers are buying for Gen X and Gen Y customers, it can be difficult for them to prevent buying errors unless they make an intentional effort to avoid such mistakes.

Pricing Errors

Errors in pricing merchandise can be another cause of markdowns. Errors occur when the price of the item is too high to move the product at the speed and in the quantity desired. The goods may have been bought in the right styles, at the right time, and in the right quantities, but the price on the item may simply be too high. This would create purchase resistance on the part of the typical customer.

An overly high price is often relative to the pricing behavior of competitors. Perhaps, in principle, the price would have been acceptable, but if competitors price the same item substantially lower, then the original retailer's price becomes too high.

Merchandising Errors

Although many new retailers believe that carrying over seasonal or fashion merchandise into the next merchandising season is the most common merchandise error, it really isn't. Failure by the buyer to inform the sales staff of how the new merchandise relates to the current stock, ties in with the store's image, and satisfies the needs of the store's target market is the most common merchandising error. Another mistake is the failure to keep the department manager and sales force informed about the new merchandise lines. Too many times, the new merchandise is left in the storeroom or the salespeople are not informed of the key features of the new item, and thus the customer will never be able to become excited about the new merchandise. Another merchandising error is improper handling of the merchandise by the sales staff or ineffective visual presentation of the merchandise. Mishandling errors include failure to stock the new merchandise behind old merchandise whenever possible or simply misplacing the merchandise. All too often a slow seller is a "lost" bundle of merchandise.

Promotion Errors

Finally, even when the right goods are purchased in the right quantities and are priced correctly, the merchandise often fails to move as planned. In this situation, the cause is most often a promotion error. The consumer has not been properly informed or prompted to purchase the merchandise. The advertising, personal selling, sales-promotion activities, or in-store displays were too weak or sporadic to elicit a strong response from potential customers.

Markdown Policy

Retailers will find it advantageous to develop a markdown timing policy. In almost all situations, retailers will find it necessary to take markdowns; the crucial decisions become when and how much of a markdown to take. In principle, there are two extremes to a markdown timing policy: early and late.

Early Markdown Policy

Most retailers who concentrate on high inventory turnover pursue an early markdown policy. Markdowns taken early speed the movement of merchandise and also generally enable the retailer to take less of a markdown per unit to dispose of the goods. One of the author's first bosses taught him early in his retailing career that "the first markdown is the cheapest to take. Therefore, once you take it, do not look back." In other words, when you as a buyer make a merchandising error, take your loss early and do not look back because taking that early markdown will allow the dollars obtained from selling the merchandise to be used to help finance more salable goods. At the same time, the customer seems to benefit, since markdowns are offered quickly on goods that some consumers still think of as fashionable, and the store has the appearance of having fresh merchandise. For example, the top 20 percent of women's apparel shoppers usually visit their favorite store three to four times a month. Thus, it is important for the retailer to always have the appearance of presenting fresh merchandise. Therefore, many fashion retailers use the following set of rules when taking early markdowns.

- After the third week, mark it down 25 percent from the original price.
- After the seventh week, mark it down 50 percent from the original price.
- After the 11th week, mark it down 75 percent from the original price.
- After the 16th week, sell it to an outlet store, give it to charity, or place it on an online auction.[16]

Another advantage of the early markdown policy is that it allows the retailer to replenish lower-priced lines from the higher ones that have been marked down. For instance, many women's wear retailers will regularly take slow-moving dresses from higher-priced lines and move them down to the moderate- or lower-priced lines.

Late Markdown Policy

Allowing goods to have a long trial period before a markdown is taken is called a *late-markdown* policy. This policy avoids disrupting the sale of regular merchandise by too frequently marking goods down. As a consequence, customers will learn to look forward to a semiannual or annual clearance in which all or most merchandise is marked down. Thus, the bargain hunters or low-end customers will be attracted only at infrequent intervals.

Regardless of which timing policy a retailer follows, it must plan for these reductions. Markdowns are not always the result of buyer errors. They may simply be selling merchandise that is late in the season and before larger markdowns must be taken. Remember, when preparing a merchandise budget, the retailer must estimate reductions for that time period.

Amount of Markdown

An issue related to the timing of markdowns is their magnitude. If the retailer waits to use a markdown at the last moment, then the markdown should probably be large enough to move the remaining merchandise. As was mentioned earlier in this chapter's

"Retailing: The Inside Story" box, the average American now considers 40-percent off the original price of an item to be a bargain. Thus, a late markdown should be at least this much. However, such a large amount is not necessary with an early markdown. An early markdown only needs to be large enough to provide a sales stimulant. Once sales are stimulated, the retailer can watch merchandise movement; when it slows, the retailer can provide another stimulant by again marking it down. Which strategy is more profitable depends on the situation. One rule of thumb for early markdowns is that prices should be marked down at least 20 percent in order for the consumer to notice. Recently, because they have lost their impact with the consumer, large chains have begun to move away from chain-wide sales late in the selling season. They are now focusing on using early markdowns region by region based on supply and demand considerations.[17] Remember, however, that while some general rules regarding markdown percentage were presented, the actual markdown percentage should vary with the type of merchandise, time of season, and competition.

Often retailers are able to have their suppliers supplement their markdown losses with *markdown money* or some other type of price reductions.[18] Here's how it works: Let's say Acme Clothing Company delivers 100 sweaters to Judy's Dress Shop at the wholesale price of $40 each. Judy in turn plans to take her customary markup of 50 percent on the selling price in order to sell each sweater for $80, thus producing a gross margin of $4,000.

However, after three months, Judy still has 50 of the sweaters in stock, which she puts on sale for $50 each in order to move the merchandise. After selling the remaining sweaters, Judy's gross margin is only $2,500: $(50 \times \$80) + (50 \times \$50) - (100 \times \$40)$.

The following month, Judy goes to market and visits the Acme showroom. Judy wants Acme to pay her the $1,500 she lost in taking the markdowns on their sweaters. Judy threatens Acme with a loss of future orders if it does not cover her losses. Does this sound fair to you?

Actually, this type of scenario happens quite frequently when buyers go to market. Buyers maintain that manufacturers should share in the responsibility when the merchandise does not sell as promised. Buyers claim that if the supplier cannot deliver the gross margin desired, then there is no reason to reorder from that supplier again. From the retailers' standpoint, when the manufacturer contributes markdown money, the manufacturers are really asking for a second chance to prove the salability of their lines. This markdown money could be in the form of cash payments or discounts on future purchases.

Now let's look at how the maintained markup percentage is determined. A retailer purchases the shirt used in an earlier example for $16 with the intent of selling it for $25 (an initial markup of 36 percent). However, the shirt did not sell at that price, and the retailer reduced it to $20 in order to sell it. This would result in a maintained markup of 20 percent:

$$\text{Maintained markup} = (\text{actual selling price} - \text{cost})/\text{actual selling price}$$
$$= \$4/\$20 = 20\%$$

The following formula can also be used to determine the maintained markup percentage:

$$\text{Maintained markup percentage} = \text{initial markup percentage} - [(\text{reduction percentage})(100\% - \text{initial markup percentage})]$$

where

$$\text{Reduction percentage} = \text{amount of reductions}/\text{net sales}$$

In the preceding example,

$$\text{Maintained markup percentage} = 36\% - [(\$5/\$20) \times (100\% - 36\%)]$$
$$= 36\% - 16\% = 20\%$$

Summary

LO 1 **What factors should a retailer consider when establishing pricing objectives and policies?**

Pricing decisions are among the most frequent a retailer must make. They cannot be made independently because they interact with the merchandise, location, promotion, credit and check cashing, customer service, and store-image decisions the retailer has already made as well as with federal and state legal constraints.

The pricing objectives the retailer ultimately sets must also agree with the retailer's mission statement and merchandise policies. These objectives can be profit oriented, sales oriented, or seek to maintain the status quo.

After establishing its pricing objectives, the retailer must next determine the pricing policies to achieve these goals. These policies must reflect the expectations of the target market.

LO 2 **What are the various pricing strategies available to the retailer?**

Among the strategies discussed were customary pricing, variable pricing, flexible pricing, one-price policies, price lining, odd pricing, multiple-unit pricing, bundle pricing, leader pricing, bait-and-switch pricing, and private-label brand pricing.

LO 3 **How does a retailer calculate the various markups?**

The basic markup equation states that, per unit, the retail selling price is equal to the dollar cost plus the dollar markup. Markups can be expressed as either a percentage of selling price or a percentage of cost to the retailer. Since the initial selling price that the retailer puts on a newly purchased item may not be attractive enough to sell all the inventory of that item, the price may need to be reduced. When we talk of actual selling prices versus initial selling prices, we mean the difference between an initial and a maintained markup.

Initial markups should be planned. Next, the initial storewide markup percentage can be determined by using operating expenses, net profit, alterations costs, cash discounts, markdowns, stock shortages, employee and customer discounts, and sales. The retailer must recognize that not all items can be priced by mechanically applying this markup percentage. Some lines will need to be priced to yield a considerably higher markup and others a substantially lower markup. The initial markup is seldom equal to the maintained markup because of three kinds of reductions: markdowns, shortages, and employee and customer discounts.

LO 4 **Why is markdown management so important in retailing?**

Because the retailer does not possess perfect information about supply and demand, markdowns are inevitable. Markdowns are usually due to errors in buying, pricing, merchandising, or promotion. Because markdowns are inevitable, the retailer needs to establish a markdown policy. Early markdowns speed the movement of merchandise and also allow the retailer to take less of a markdown per unit to dispose of the merchandise. Late markdowns avoid disrupting the sale of regular merchandise by too-frequent markdowns. The best policy from a profit perspective depends on the particular situation.

Student Study Guide

Terms to Remember

yield management	price lining
target-return objective	trading up
profit maximization	trading down
skimming	odd pricing
penetration	multiple-unit pricing
below-market pricing policy	leader pricing
price zone	loss leader
above-market pricing policy	high–low pricing
customary pricing	bait-and-switch pricing
variable pricing	markup
flexible pricing	markdown
one-price policy	

Review and Discussion Questions

LO 1

What factors should a retailer consider when establishing pricing objectives and policies?

1. How does a store's location affect the price it can charge?
2. Is pricing really an interactive decision? Provide an example of how pricing should interact with the services offered by the retailer.
3. Why are retailers of services most likely to use yield management?
4. When should a retailer use the penetration pricing objective?
5. If a retailer wants to use an above-market pricing policy, how should that retailer's retailing mix be different from the competition?

LO 2

What are the various pricing strategies available to the retailer?

6. What is the difference between variable and flexible pricing? Does the demand for the item being sold affect either of these strategies?
7. Despite the lack of supportive research, odd-numbered pricing is still used in retailing today. Shouldn't gas stations drop those .9 cents from their posted prices and round them to the nearest penny?
8. Would you prefer to buy a car from a dealer using a flexible or a one-price policy? Why?
9. What type of retailer is most likely to use leader pricing?

LO 3

How does a retailer calculate the various markups?

10. Compute the markup on selling price for an item that retails for $49.95 and costs $31.20.
11. Complete the following:

	Dress Shirt	Sport Shirt	Belt
Selling price ($)	40.00	49.99	15.00
Cost ($)	23.00	25.35	6.50
Markup in dollars ($)			
Markup percentage on cost (%)			
Markup percentage on selling price (%)			

12. A buyer tells you that she realized a markup of $50 on an interview suit for a college senior. You know that her markup is 25 percent of retail. What did the suit cost her?

13. If the markup on cost is 76 percent, what is the markup on selling price?

14. Which is more important to a retailer—initial or maintained markup?

15. Can an initial markup ever be equal to the maintained markup? Explain.

16. Intimate Apparel wants to produce a 9-percent operating profit this year on sales of $1,200,000. Based on past experiences, the owner made the following estimates:

Net alteration expenses	$1,100	Employee discount	$5,400
Markdowns	61,000	Operating expenses	275,000
Stock shortages	12,200	Cash discounts earned	4,100

Given these estimates, what average initial markup should be asked for the upcoming year?

LO 4 Why is markdown management so important in retailing?

17. Why should a retailer plan on taking markdowns during a merchandising season?

18. Somebody once said, "Buyers only need to take a markdown when they make mistakes. Therefore, good buyers should never have to take markdowns." Do you agree with that statement? Explain your answer.

19. Which markdown policy would be best for sporting goods? Explain your reasoning. Would your answer be the same for a specialty apparel store?

20. The buyer for the women's sweater department has purchased wool sweaters for $35.69. She uses an odd pricing policy and wants to sell them at a 49-percent markup on selling price. At what price should each sweater be sold?

21. The buyer for men's shirts has a price point of $45 and requires a markup of 45 percent. What would be the highest price he should pay for a shirt to sell at this price point?

22. A buyer submits the following plans to his general merchandise manager: planned sales = $135,000; planned initial markup = 40 percent; planned reductions = $41,000. Based on these projections, what is the planned maintained markup percentage?

Sample Test Questions

LO 1   What word best describes the relationship between a retailer's pricing decisions and the merchandise, location, promotion, credit and check cashing, services, image, and legal decisions that retailers must make?

    a. independent
    b. separate
    c. interactive
    d. competitive
    e. multifaceted

LO 2 If a retailer is offering the same products and quantities to different customers at different prices, the retailer has what kind of pricing policy?

a. two-price
b. customary
c. flexible
d. leader
e. variable

LO 3 If a retailer buys a product for $25 and sells it for $45, what is the markup percentage if the markup is based on the selling price?

a. 44.4 percent
b. 80 percent
c. 75 percent
d. 100 percent
e. 55.5 percent

LO 4 An item was marked down to $19.99 from its original retail price of $29.99. What is the reduction percentage for this item?

a. 33.3 percent
b. 25 percent
c. 50 percent
d. 41.3 percent
e. 66.7 percent

Writing and Speaking Exercise

Jack Woodward is home for the summer from college and working in a major league baseball park as a marketing intern. He is in an office with two other interns and the general manager has asked them to prepare a presentation on ticket pricing. Your intern-team has decided to recommend a profit maximization strategy for ticket pricing and to implement that with auction-pricing. Some of the strongest evidence you have to support this proposal is the secondary market price for single tickets versus their face value. For the baseball team you are interning for, the face value of a ticket is $26; however, the secondary market price is often between $38 and $62. You have also obtained some evidence that in 2011 the average major league baseball ticket price was substantially below the secondary market for many teams. For instance, the average face value of tickets for the Toronto Blue Jays was $24.35, and the secondary market price was $72.62, for the Boston Red Sox the face value was $53.38, but the secondary market was at $92.23, and for the Oakland Athletics the face value was $21.52 versus $51.82 in the secondary market. Prepare a presentation and limit it to eight PowerPoint slides.

Retail Project

On your next trip to a mall, visit all the anchor stores and leading apparel stores. Look around at displays and notice if they are having sales. Now, based on the amount of merchandise on sale and the amount of reductions, determine if each store is using an early or late markdown policy. Explain your reasoning for each store and especially explain the reasoning for differences between the stores. (Note: You can also do this project for different websites.)

Planning Your Own Entrepreneurial Retail Business

The online retail operation you recently opened is doing well, but you are uncertain of your pricing strategy. Currently, the typical customer purchases four items at an average price of $11.96 and for an average transaction size of $47.84. The cost of goods is 60 percent of sales, which yields a gross margin of 40 percent. You are considering lowering prices by 10 percent across the board so you can better compete with other music e-tailers. If you lower prices by 10 percent, you believe that the average number of items purchased per customer would rise by 25 percent. Assuming your assumptions are correct, should you lower prices by 10 percent across the board? If not, do you have an alternative pricing strategy to propose?

CASE

America's Car-Mart

Business Description

America's Car-Mart (CRMT stock ticker; incorporated in Texas, principal offices in Bentonville, Arkansas) is a pre-owned automobile seller that focuses its business on the mid- to low price used or pre-owned motor vehicle market. Car-Mart's business integrates automotive sales and financing in the same business and offers financing to the vast majority of its customers. Many of its customers would not be able to receive traditional financing elsewhere due to limited financial resources or past credit problems. Car-Mart has a focus on treating customers in a manner that encourages them to be repeat customers of the company; it wants its customers to be successful in purchasing, financing, and paying off a vehicle. America's Car-Mart has been in business for 30 years, going public in 1999. The company had 106 dealerships at the end of fiscal year 2011, across eight states.

Retail Dealership and Customer Growth

Growth in retail dealerships and customers is key to the success of Car-Mart's business. As mentioned previously there are currently 106 dealerships in eight states (Arkansas, Oklahoma, Texas, Missouri, Kentucky, Alabama, Tennessee, and Indiana). 70 percent of Car-Mart's dealerships are in towns of fewer than 50,000 residents. Growing that dealership base is part of Car-Mart's current strategy as well as operating existing dealerships in a way that encourages repeat business and a drive to increased same-store sales. Car-Mart has been successful in growing same-store sales, its active customer file, and units sold. Car-Mart terms its retail dealer growth strategy as "controlled organic growth"; meaning that it will focus on improving the performance of existing dealerships and will open additional dealerships as long as justified by the current dealer base performance and growth.

Dealer Operations

Car-Mart operates in a decentralized management structure with individual dealers carrying out the majority of tasks and dealer-level decision-making with the corporate office taking on the role of setting financial controls, standards for down-payments and contract terms, as well as the operation of the proprietary customer credit scoring. The corporate office also employs corporate buying agents who are assigned to dealerships to buy automobile inventory on their behalf, although it is important to point out that the decisions on inventory buying lie at the dealer level. Dealers are responsible for buying inventory, pricing, selling, credit worthiness decisions, and collection of the contracts they write. Many customers actually make payments by visiting the dealership. A typical dealer carries an inventory of between 25 and 100 cars and turns its inventory 9–10 times per year. Dealers sell cars "as is" but also offer a few limited warranty options, in which the service is contracted because Car-Mart dealers have little or no facilities on site to handle vehicle service.

Financing

Car-Mart provides financing to almost all of their customers who purchase automobiles. The company writes installment sales contracts with average down payments of 7 percent and an average term of 27 months and a weighted average interest rate of 14.4 percent. Car-Mart structures payments to coincide with the days that customers are paid by their employers. Car-Mart works hard to keep delinquency percentages low on its outstanding contracts and uses repossession of vehicles as a last resort in managing collections. Car-Mart does not rely on securitizations as a financing source, and thus has been relatively unaffected by the current constrictions in the credit market. In the fiscal year 2011, Car-Mart has a provision for credit losses of 20.8 percent of sales; and that is considered a realistic loan loss reserve in this market segment.

Financial Performance

Fiscal year 2011 was a strong year of financial performance for America's Car-Mart. Record profit of $28.22 million was reported on $379.25 million of revenues. 34,424 vehicles were sold in fiscal year 2011 at an average price of $9,367 (a 2.5 percent increase from fiscal year 2010). The active customer file was 50,229. The following exhibits show growth for Car-Mart from the fiscal year ending April 30, 2009, to the fiscal year ending April 30, 2011.

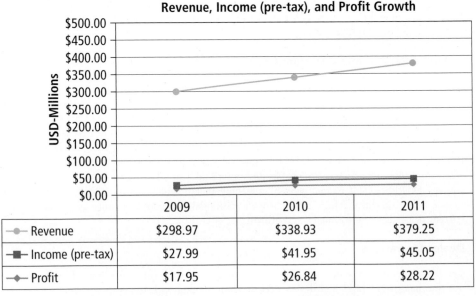

Revenue, Income (pre-tax), and Profit Growth

	2009	2010	2011
Revenue	$298.97	$338.93	$379.25
Income (pre-tax)	$27.99	$41.95	$45.05
Profit	$17.95	$26.84	$28.22

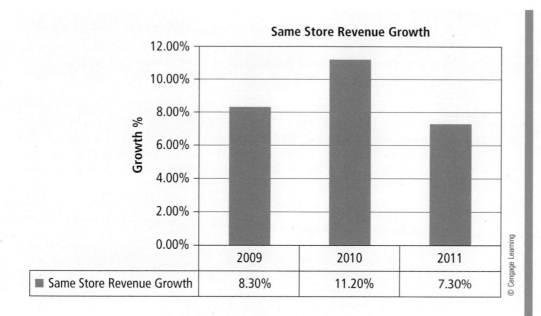

Same Store Revenue Growth

	2009	2010	2011
■ Same Store Revenue Growth	8.30%	11.20%	7.30%

© Cengage Learning

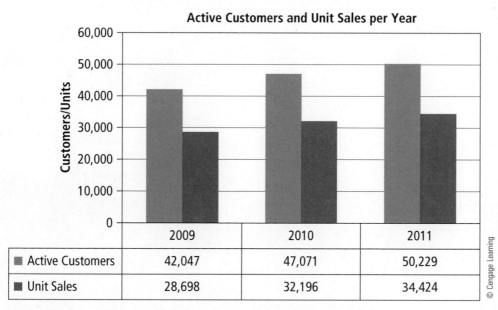

Active Customers and Unit Sales per Year

	2009	2010	2011
■ Active Customers	42,047	47,071	50,229
■ Unit Sales	28,698	32,196	34,424

© Cengage Learning

*Active accounts are defined as those accounts that are not paid off or charged off.

Questions

1. How can Car-Mart justify an interest rate of nearly 15 percent on average when in 2011 most used car automobile finance at banks or credit units was 6–7 percent or less?

2. Car-Mart has a gross margin of 40 percent whereas most used cars that are sold at a new car dealership (often obtained as new car trade-ins) have a gross margin of around

20–25 percent. Is the higher gross-margin and thus higher price by Car-Mart a good strategy?

3. Do you have any suggestions for pricing strategies that Car-Mart could use to enhance its performance?

Source

This case was prepared primarily from data and information in Annual Reports to Stockholders and SEC 10K filings between 2009 and 2011. The case was prepared by Mark Lusch as a basis for class discussion rather than to illustrate either effective or ineffective handling of an administrative situation. Case used with permission of Mark Lusch.

Advertising and Promotion

Overview

Promotion is a major stimulant of demand in retailing. In this chapter, we focus on the role of advertising, sales promotion, social media, and publicity in the operation of a retail business. Retail selling, another important element of promotion, will be discussed in Chapter 12. Our discussion here is directed at describing how retailers should manage their firms' promotional resources.

Learning Objectives

After reading this chapter, you should be able to:

1 Name the five basic components of the retailer's promotional mix and discuss their relationship with other decisions.

2 Describe the differences between a retailer's long-term and short-term promotional objectives.

3 List the seven steps involved in developing a retailer's advertising campaign.

4 Explain how retailers manage their sales promotion and publicity.

LO 1

The Retail Promotion Mix

Name the five basic components of the retailer's promotional mix and discuss their relationship with other decisions.

promotion
Is a means that retailers use to bring traffic into their stores, and it includes advertising, sales promotion, publicity, and personal selling.

Retailers use **promotion** to generate sales by making their targeted customers aware of current offerings. This does not mean that sales cannot occur without using promotion. Some sales will always take place, even if the retailer spends no money on promotion. For example, households close to a retailer may shop there strictly for convenience, a passerby might occasionally visit the store for an impulse purchase, or friends may use Twitter and Facebook to share with others information on their purchases or anticipated purchases, and this can help to promote a product and/or retailer. This is an example of what has become known in the last few years as social media (or "social" for short)—one of the fastest growing media influencing customer and shopper behavior. Most retailers, however, use a combination of location, price levels, displays, merchandise assortments, customer service, and promotion, including social, as a means to generate store traffic and sales.

Retailers make trade-offs between the different elements of the retailing mix. Some retailers like Buckle, which handles medium- to higher-priced casual apparel, footwear, and accessories for fashion-conscious young men and women and has almost 400 mall locations in 41 states, prefer to use prime, high-traffic mall locations. By paying a higher rent for the mall location, the retailer can participate in mall-sponsored promotions rather than develop its own to generate customer interest. As a result, the Nebraska-based chain spends only 1 percent of its sales on promotions.

The Waffle House is another retailer that spends only a small percentage of its sales on sales promotion. The Waffle House instead chooses to use its location, often in high traffic areas or close to tourist destinations (like hotels and motels) and along highways to spur its sales. Additionally, most of its "formal" promotion is geared towards word-of-mouth advertising, which it facilitates through its "First Mile" campaign. The First Mile refers to the one-mile trade radius that surrounds any one location. Store managers are then expected to visit every business within that one mile, spend time with the employees, and hand out coupons for discounted meals. In so doing, the Waffle House hopes that the next time an individual enters, for example, a hotel and asks where to get a quick bite to eat when the kitchen is closed, the hotel's employees immediately refer the traveler to the local Waffle House.

Thus, while direct promotional expenditures (e.g., the coupons given out by Waffle House employees) are not always a prerequisite for generating sales, they are a means of achieving sales above those that could be obtained merely by offering a lower price range, having a better location, or providing outstanding service. Many of today's successful retailers use promotion to not only bring traffic into their stores but also move the traffic to the various selling areas of the store and entice the traffic into purchasing merchandise. Remember that in e-tailing traffic is also a driver of sales. And with e-tailing, it is very easy to track not only what customers have in their online cart, but also what pages of the website they are viewing, how long they view a page or an item on the page, and how frequently they return to the website. All of this information can be used to offer the online customer special deals or recommend merchandise to them.[1] But as you will read toward the end of the chapter in the "Retailing: The Inside Story," box, traditional brick-and-mortar retailers continue to struggle with tracking and measuring the impact of any promotion beyond the simplest of online coupons and discounts codes.

Yet even with the difficulties associated with tracking the impact of an online promotion, say a banner advertisement or Twitter feed, on a bricks-and-mortar retail store, technology is still affecting the way in which traditional stores operate and compete. "Smart" shopping carts can now track not only the shopper's movements throughout a store, but also the contents of one's shopping cart, and smartphones and tablet computers have become a platform for promoting to and assisting the shopper. In fact, as this chapter's "What's New?" box points out, big-box retailers, cell phone carriers, banks, and even credit card issuers have all begun to develop different software platforms that transform a consumer's smartphone into a "smart wallet" that is capable of not only making retail transactions easier and faster to complete but also enhancing *all* retailers' ability to promote, individually, to consumers. But as the box also points out, enhancing the tracking and personalization of digital promotions may not be the only reason for all the interest in smart-wallet technology; it also presents an opportunity for some to generate additional revenue dollars in the future if their platform becomes the "standard" upon which all future smart wallets are based.

Types of Promotion

Promotion has five basic components: advertising, sales promotion, social media, publicity, and personal selling. Collectively, these components make up the retailer's promotional mix. Each component is defined as follows and will be discussed from a managerial perspective.

1. **Advertising** is paid, nonpersonal communication through various media by organizations or individuals who are in some way identified in the advertising message and who hope to inform [or] persuade members of a particular audience; advertising

---

advertising
Is paid, nonpersonal communication through various media by business firms, nonprofit organizations, and individuals who are in some way identified in the advertising message and who hope to inform or persuade members of a particular audience; includes communication of products, services, institutions, and ideas.

© Rashevskyi Viacheslav/Shutterstock

WHAT'S NEW ?

The "Digital Wallet"—Just a Tool for Enhancing Retailers' Promotional Efforts, or a Battleground for Additional Revenues?

The term *digital wallet* is increasingly becoming synonymous with a smartphone that stores a person's credit and financial credentials in order to carry out financial transactions (i.e., the purchase of a good or service) without the need for cash or other physical forms of payment (e.g., credit cards). To pay for merchandise using a digital wallet, the consumer simply waves his or her smartphone in front of a small reader at the checkout counter, and the transaction is complete.

The digital wallet represents a significant step forward in the evolution of NFC, or "near-field communication," which is a set of *contactless*-systems standards based on radio frequency identifier (RFID) technology (initially introduced in Chapter 4), but such *contactless-payment* solutions aren't new. As early as 1997, Exxon-Mobil Corp. was using its "Speedpass" key-fob, which allowed drivers to pay for gas at the pump simply by waving a fob, electronically tied to one's credit card, across a small, circular "reader." The digital wallet, however, is a leap forward because of what it's tied to, or embedded within—a mobile communication device, namely the smartphone. Consumers, particularly those of younger generations, *live* on their mobile phones; they email, text, socially network, twitter, and talk about every single aspect of their lives via their mobile devices. And it's estimated that as early as 2014, over 70 percent of all U.S. consumers will have smartphones; 52 percent of which will be NFC-capable.

But what makes the co-mingling of NFC technology and smartphones so important, particularly for retailing? To answer this question, consider the following example of how a digital wallet might impact a consumer's future purchasing behavior.

A man gets a reminder on his phone that his anniversary is the following week. The phone knows, given all his purchases are stored within the phone's software, that he has yet to buy his wife a gift, at least not one considered "romantic." The phone then sends him a 20-percent-off coupon to an upscale, women's clothing store and directs him to a floral shop around the corner from his office that currently has roses on sale, then emails him a list of "fancy" restaurants with open reservations for the night of their anniversary.

Where do you think this man is likely to shop for his wife's gift? What are the odds that if he decides to purchase flowers, he's going to go to the florist around the corner? Do you think he will choose a restaurant from the list he was just emailed or do his own "leg-work" to find another restaurant that is fancy and available?

No one can positively predict the answers to the questions above, but each of us can see that the co-mingling of NFC and smartphone technology can dramatically enhance the effectiveness of promotional messages. This is because the purchasing history stored within one's digital wallet will help to better target promotions to the most appropriate of individuals at the most appropriate of times.

Digital wallets do afford consumers with a faster, less-cumbersome way to pay for merchandise, but that's not why Google, in conjunction with MasterCard, Citigroup, Sprint Nextel, and VeriFone Systems Inc., was the first to begin rolling out its digital wallet platform, "Google Wallet," in mid-2011. Google sought *to boost its advertising business* by making mobile payments easier. Google and its partners see the ability to sell advertisements and other services to local retailers as a significant growth frontier for Internet companies.

If consumers use their smartphones to pay for all their purchases, Google can not only track, and centrally store, purchasing behavior across consumers, retailers, and credit cards, but also use this information to assist retailers to better target particular consumers with personalized promotions at appropriate times. At its core, Google Wallet can simply be viewed as a tool designed to build a valuable database that can then be used to extract revenues from retailers seeking to enhance their promotional spending. As we discuss in this chapter and the next, successful retailers don't institute promotions or provide services unless they're likely to provide a *positive cash flow* (readers may want to return to Chapter 8 for a

(*continued*)

discussion on this topic). In this instance, the provision of a digital wallet to the consumer is a means to increasing advertising revenue, and Google is not the only firm to see the potential for increased revenues.

The nation's largest cell phone operator, Verizon, has partnered with rival cell phone carriers, AT&T, Inc. and T-Mobile USA to produce their own software platform, "Isis." Isis is undergoing market trials in 2012 but is designed to provide not only similar payment and promotional services to that of Google Wallet, but also "side benefits" like the ability to unlock a deadbolt to one's home (by waiving the phone in front of the lock), or adjusting the seating and mirror positions within one's car (just to name a few). The Isis team believes that in order to combat Google Wallet's "first-mover" advantage and build a sizable pool of consumer and retailer adopters, it must provide additional services.

Walmart and Target have also joined the mobile-payment race, but these long-time competitors are not competing with their own versions of software. Instead, Walmart, Target, and roughly two-dozen other retailers including Alon Brands Inc., which operates more than 300 7-Eleven stores and Fina gasoline stations, are developing their own digital wallet platform. The retailers believe they are in the best position to know what additional services the consumer wants or needs. However, they also cite that their own research suggests that by 2016 the market for mobile payments will exceed $600 billion annually.

Future readers of this box are likely to know who wins and loses in this battle to define the digital wallet ecosystem, but one thing is clear today—while the digital wallet does afford future consumers with the ability to pay for merchandise without carrying a wallet full of credit cards and cash, the driver of this technology race is control over a valuable database of consumer purchasing history and the ability to market that information to retailers looking to enhance their future promotional campaigns.

Sources: Efrati, Amir and Robin Sidel, "Google Sets Role in Mobile Payment," *Wall Street Journal*, March 28, 2011: B1; Gottfried, Miriam, "The New Basics: Their Hands, Your Wallet: Mobile Banking Is Getting More Convenient, but It May Cost You Your Privacy," *Wall Street Journal*, July 9, 2011: B8; Efrati, Amir and Anton Troianovski, "War Over the Digital Wallet: Google, Verizon Wireless Spar in Race to Build Mobile-Payment Services," *Wall Street Journal*, December 7, 2011: B1; Bensinger, Greg, "Pushing Mobile Payments: Amid Slow Consumer Adoption, Companies Tout the Technology's 'Side Benefits'," *Wall Street Journal*, January 13, 2012: B7; Sidel, Robin, "Retailer Join Payment Chase: Walmart and Target Join Project Aiming to Make Plastic Obsolete," *Wall Street Journal*, March 2, 2012: C1.

sales promotion
Involves the use of media and nonmedia marketing pressure applied for a predetermined, limited period of time to stimulate trial, increase consumer demand, or improve product availability.

social media
Term given to a host of electronic information technologies that enable and stimulate social interaction between humans.

publicity
Is non-paid-for communications of information about the company or product, generally in some media form.

includes communication of products, services, institutions, and ideas. Retailers most commonly use the following advertising media: Internet, newspapers, radio, television, billboards, and printed circulars.

2. **Sales promotions** involve the use of media and nonmedia marketing efforts for a predetermined, limited period of time to stimulate trial and customer purchasing. The most popular sales promotion tools in retailing are premiums, frequent-buyer programs, coupons, window and in-store displays and signage, contests and sweepstakes, product demonstrations, and sampling.

3. **Social media** include a host of electronic information technologies that enable and stimulate social interaction among humans. Most social media are facilitated by the Internet and include forums, weblogs, social blogs, microblogging, podcasts, social bookmarking, sharing of video, pictures, and information such as product or retailer ratings.

4. **Publicity** is nonpaid-for communication of information about the company or product, generally in some media form. Popular examples are Macy's Thanksgiving Day parade and local retail support of various civic and educational groups. Note that when Macy's puts on the annual parade, the retailer is paying for all the facilities, floats, etc. that it must have in order to put on the event; it is not paying for the media coverage (or communication) of the event. Increasingly, publicity is coming via social media versus the traditional print and television broadcast media.

5. **Personal selling** involves personal interaction with the consumer with the purpose to create a sale or transaction. Note that the interaction does not need to be direct

By using electronic billboards, retailers can tailor their messages and change them quickly.

personal selling
Involves a face-to-face interaction with the consumer with the goal of selling the consumer merchandise or services.

primary trading area
Is the geographic area where the retailer can serve customers in terms of convenience and accessibility better than the competition.

secondary trading area
Is the geographic area where the retailer can still be competitive despite a competitor having some locational advantage.

face-to-face but can be done via electronic channels such as Skype or video conferencing. Personal selling is often used during the sale of shopping goods and is designed to assist the customer in gathering product information while simultaneously convincing the customer to purchase the retailer's particular products or services.

All five components of the retailer's promotional mix need to be managed from a total systems perspective. In other words, they need to be effectively blended together to achieve the retailer's promotional objectives and reinforce each other. If the advertising conveys quality and status, so too must the sales personnel, publicity, and sales promotion; otherwise, the consumer will receive conflicting or inconsistent messages about the retailer, which will result in confusion and loss of patronage. The biggest challenge facing retailers is that social media cannot be as well managed as the other elements and thus requires some special skills and programs that will be briefly covered.

The management of promotional efforts in retailing must also fit into the retailer's overall strategy. Promotion decisions relate to and must be integrated with other management decisions such as location, merchandise, credit, cash flow, building and fixtures, price, and customer service. For example:

1. There is a maximum distance consumers will travel to visit a retail store. Thus, a retailer's *location* will help determine the target for promotions. A retailer should direct its promotional dollars first toward households in its **primary trading area**, the area where the retailer can serve customers in terms of convenience and accessibility better than the competition, and then to **secondary trading areas**, areas where the retailer is still competitive, even if some competitors have a locational advantage. However, e-tailers who are global in presence must determine specific areas, whether they be countries or communities, in which to focus their promotional efforts. Also, an e-tailer should keep in mind that the products it offers may appeal to a very specific market segment, and individuals who are in this segment may live in a neighborhood where they are the minority, and thus, land-based stores may not stock the

merchandise they need because it is not economical. Consider, for instance, if you are an avid racing cyclist who lives in Fairbanks, Alaska. Since bicycle stores in Fairbanks focus more on off-road bikes you have little selection for the products you need to support your hobby, and thus, you are a very likely candidate for an e-tailer such as Performance Bicycle (www.performancebike.com). Thus, Performance Bicycle may target you with a direct mail piece, although it would not target Fairbanks overall with direct mail advertising. This approach is often referred to as *pin-point marketing*.

2. Retailers need high levels of store traffic to keep their *merchandise* turning over rapidly. Promotion helps build traffic. Of course, the retailer needs to be careful to not build so much traffic with a special promotion that customers end up fighting in line to get into the store or over merchandise bins in the store with drastically reduced merchandise. This also has an equivalent in e-tailing, and that is when the e-tailer has a special promotion and it creates so much traffic that its servers and website can't handle the business and it crashes.

3. A retailer's *credit* customers are more store loyal and purchase in larger quantities. Thus, they are an excellent target for increased promotional efforts. Although the increased use of MasterCard, Visa, and Discover cards has impacted this retail advantage in recent years, many retailers have overcome this problem by developing their own co-branded cards or by using "No interest for 90 days" promotions.

4. A retailer confronted with a temporary *cash-flow* problem can use promotion to increase short-run cash flow. Customers that recognize this reality can also find some incredible deals during off-seasons when business is slow. If you want an incredible deal on a sports car such as a Chevrolet Corvette convertible, find one at a dealer in Northern Iowa in a small farming community in the middle of the long cold winter. Farmers buy their new vehicles after crop harvest and by mid-winter, everyone is hurting for money, especially the auto dealers.

5. A retailer's promotional strategy must be reinforced by its *building and fixtures* decisions. Promotional creativity and style should coincide with building and fixture creativity and style. If the advertisements are exciting and appeal to a particular target market, so should the building and fixtures. One thing to be wary of is liquidators, who may take over a high-end bankrupt furniture store or apparel store. Because the store setting and fixtures present a luxury atmosphere, they often bring in lower quality merchandise from other sources to mix with the inventory of the retailer they are liquidating.

6. Promotion provides customers with more information. That information will help them make better purchase decisions because risk is reduced. Therefore, promotion can actually be viewed as a major component of *customer service*.

The retailer that systematically integrates its promotional programs with other retail decision areas will be better able to achieve high-performance results. One retailer developed a set of basic promotional guidelines that all retailers should follow:

- Try to utilize only promotions that are consistent with and will enhance your store image.
- Review the success or failure of each promotion to help in developing better future promotions.
- Wherever possible, test new promotions before making a major investment by using them on a broader scale.
- Use appeals that are of interest to your target market and that are realistic to obtain. For example, double couponing offers everybody a reward, but a sweepstakes has only one winner.
- Make sure your objectives are measurable.
- Make sure your objectives are obtainable.
- Develop total promotional campaigns, not just advertisements.

- The lower the rent, the higher the promotional expenses generally needed.
- New stores need higher promotional budgets than established stores.
- Stores in out-of-the way locations require higher promotional budgets than stores with heavy traffic.[2]

Today, in a world where we have moved from a one-to-many broadcast model of communication to more social media or many-to-many communication that the retailer has relatively little control over, we would add these additional guidelines.

- Listen to the voice of the customer and market by actively monitoring all social media, and use this to learn about your firm and also your competitors.
- Don't try to convince yourself that what you hear and learn via social media is all wrong and that the customer just doesn't understand you. Remember that in the pre-Internet social media world, when a customer had a bad experience they told 10 friends, but now they tell hundreds of friends and those friends retweet or use other social media so the negative message quickly becomes viral, as other disgruntled customers tweet with their stories.[3]
- When negative news about your enterprise spreads via social media, get on top of it quickly and respond in a positive and proactive manner.

PRIMEZONE/AP Photos

Technology allows retailers to use in-store video displays to increase product understanding, which increases sales and customer satisfaction with the product.

Promotion in the Supply Chain

The retailer is not the only member of the marketing supply chain that uses promotion. Manufacturers also invest in promotion for many of the same reasons retailers do: to move merchandise more rapidly, speed up cash flow, and better retain customer loyalty. However, the promotional activities of the retailer's supply-chain partners may sometimes conflict with the retailer's promotions. There are three major differences in the way retailers and manufacturers use promotion:

1. *Product Image Versus Availability.* The manufacturer's primary goal is to create a positive image for the product itself and differentiate it from competing products. For example, when introducing a new product, a manufacturer will attempt to explain how the product works. Retailers, on the other hand, are primarily interested in announcing to their customers that they have the product available for purchase at a convenient location.

2. *Specific Product Benefits Versus Price.* Manufacturers generally do not care where customers make their purchases as long as they buy their product, which is why they promote the benefits of their products. For instance, Revlon (www.Revlon.com) wants to promote and position its cosmetics as tools to provide women with the inspiration and encouragement to express themselves with more confidence.[4] Retailers, on the other hand, do not care which brand the customer purchases. (Remember, retailers carry products from many different manufacturers.) A retailer just wants the customer to make the purchase in its store rather than from its competitors. Thus, in addition to availability, retailers feature the product's price in their promotion mix.

3. *Focused Image Versus Cluttered Advertisements.* In comparison to manufacturers, most retailers carry a larger variety and breadth of products, while manufacturers produce a greater depth than most retailers carry. Thus, retail advertisements, which are usually geared toward short-term results, tend to be cluttered with many different products as opposed to the manufacturer's advertisement, which focuses on a single-product theme.

Sometimes a lack of promotional harmony between supply-chain members results from other factors. Consider the case of the automobile channel. Assume that the country's rate of real economic growth has been negative for the past year; as a result, the country's auto sales are 20 percent lower than last year. The manufacturer believes that this economy is recovering and therefore does not want to get into a price war by offering major price rebates or other special promotions from the factory. However, the automobile dealers believe that the country is still in the midst of a recession. They feel that the manufacturer's advertising should be increased and that special allowances should be given for increased local advertising. They would also like to see the manufacturer tie in this increased advertising program with cash rebates paid for by the factory. Because the manufacturer and dealer have different beliefs about the economy's future, serious disagreements could occur between them. (The careful reader should realize that this promotional disagreement is due to a perceptual incongruity between the manufacturer and the retailer as originally discussed within Chapter 5.)

A second possible source of problems is when the supply-chain members feel that the chain's promotional campaign is a mistake. Many major supermarket chains, for example, print weekly circulars that allow their suppliers to advertise directly to their customers. In reality, the supermarket makes money on this promotion since together the suppliers are likely to pay more than the actual cost of the circulars. In addition, the suppliers must offer big discounts on the chain's purchases of the advertised items. As a result, many suppliers don't feel this is a good promotional investment. Nevertheless, most suppliers sign up for such a program to avoid angering the retailers that control so much of their business. Such different perceptions show why it is important for retailers to foster a cooperative relationship with their suppliers (discussed in Chapter 5) so that the conflict can be resolved.

LO 2

Describe the differences between a retailer's long-term and short-term promotional objectives.

Promotional Objectives

To efficiently manage the promotional mix, retail managers must first establish their promotional objectives. These promotional objectives should flow from the retailer's overall objectives that were discussed in Chapter 2. They should be the natural out-growth of the retailer's operations management plans. As such, *all promotional objectives should ultimately seek to improve the retailer's financial performance*, since this is what strategic and administrative plans are intended to accomplish.

Exhibit 11.1 shows how promotional objectives should relate to financial performance objectives. As this exhibit shows, promotional objectives can be established to help improve both long- and short-term financial performance.

Long-Term Objectives

institutional advertising
Is a type of advertising in which the retailer attempts to gain long-term benefits by promoting and selling the store itself rather than the merchandise in the store.

Institutional advertising is an attempt by the retailer to gain long-term benefits by selling the store itself rather than the merchandise in it. By doing this, the retailer is creating a positive image for itself in the consumer's mind. Retailers using institutional advertisements generally seek to establish two long-term promotional objectives: creating a positive store image and public service.

Creating a Positive Store Image

The first long-term objective of a promotion is to establish or reinforce a positive store image, relative to its competitors, in its customers' minds. Here the retailer seeks to gain a differential advantage by establishing a favorable impression that is distinct from other retailers. By providing such an image, the retailer hopes to develop an ongoing relationship with the customer. Promotion that fulfills this objective will improve the retailer's long-term financial performance.

Two of the most successful retailers in this area have been Neiman Marcus and Nordstrom. Today, when consumers think of these retailers, they perceive elegantly designed stores, top names in fashion, excellent customer service, and a helpful, knowledge-able sales staff. However, as you might expect, this type of promotion will also assist the retailer in the short run, such as when a consumer is seeking to purchase a gift for

Exhibit 11.1
Possible Promotion Objectives in Retailing

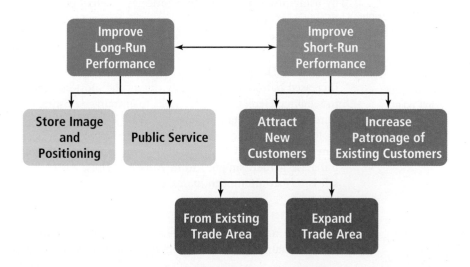

© Cengage Learning

a special friend and the retailer's advertisement suggests that "perfect" gift. A store's promotional efforts have been found to be a key predictor of store choice when gift shopping.

Although we mention two retailers known for a more upscale store image, it needs to be kept in mind that the idea of a positive store image can also be around a more downscale store such as Walmart. In fact several years ago, Stephen Quinn, the new Walmart marketing chief, helped the company brand itself and its image around the simple value proposition of "Save money. Live better." which also became the retailer's statement of corporate purpose or mission. Research revealed an increasing number of people desiring to save money but also recognizing that saving money can allow them to live better, and hence this became the basis of advertising on television and other media to develop Walmart's store image and positioning.[5]

Public-Service Promotion

The second long-term objective is directed at getting the consumer to perceive the retailer as a good citizen within the community. Retailers may sponsor public-service advertisements to honor local athletes, like Wendy's High School Athlete of the Week in Texas, and scholars as well as provide cash and merchandise to local charities. For example, some retailers offer meeting rooms for use by local civic organizations; some supermarkets have begun publishing consumer newsletters with health, cooking, safety, and beauty tips; and still others sponsor programs on public-television stations. Since most new car dealers are family and locally owned, they are often key sponsors of public-service advertisements that support the community. One retailer that stands out in terms of public service is Target, which focuses on education, safe communities, healthy living, and environmental sustainability. Since 1946, Target has given 5 percent of its annual income to communities (see, www.Target.com/HereForGood). An illustration of its commitment to education is a 2011 partnership with The Heart of America Foundation to donate a School Library Makeover including computers, whiteboards, and 2,000 new books to Park Lane Elementary in Aurora, Colorado. Wisely, Target took advantage of this charitable contribution by making it the cover page of an advertising circular in 2011 with the tagline: "Our vision for kids: Giving locally to bring learning to life."[6]

Short-Term Objectives

promotional advertising
Is a type of advertising in which the retailer attempts to increase short-term performance by using product availability or price as a selling point.

Promotional advertising, on the other hand, attempts to bolster short-term performance by using product availability or price as a selling point. The two most common objectives of this type of promotion are increasing patronage from existing customers and attracting new customers.

Increasing Patronage from Existing Customers

Increased patronage is probably one of the most common promotional objectives found in retailing. Here, the retailer seeks to encourage existing customers to make more of their purchases at the retailer's store.

Recently, one of the authors experienced such a promotion after shopping at Amazon.com. Within a few days of making a purchase, he received a $50 coupon to purchase garden supplies from Amazon. Thus, Amazon.com's use of coupons to cross-sell is a clear attempt to increase patronage from its current customers.

Attracting New Customers

Attracting new customers to shop one's store is the second most common short-term promotional objective; however, approaches to achieve such an objective vary, based on where these new customers are located. One approach is to try attracting new customers from within the retailer's primary trading area. For example, there are always some households included within this area that, for a variety of reasons, do not patronize the retailer: They do their shopping at a retailer closer to their place of employment, they do not feel the retailer's store is attractive to their tastes, or they had a poor experience the last time they shopped the retailer's store and vowed never to return.

A second approach to gaining new customers is to focus on expanding one's existing trading area by attracting customers from secondary trading areas. In this case, the retailer might consider using different media to expand the geographic coverage of its promotional efforts.

A third type of new customer is the customer that has just moved into the retailer's trading area. Geographically mobile consumers, for instance, are generally more prone to use national retailers because of the familiarity with their product offerings, service levels, and prices. For example, if you are a pet owner (pet parent) and you move within the United States or Canada, it is likely that you are moving from a city to another city that has one or more of over 1,000 PetSmart stores, and thus, you are likely to rely on this retailer for pet supplies, pet care, and pet lodging as needed. Or, if there is not a local PetSmart store, you may go online to PetSmart.com to get the pet supplies you need. Thus, a local pet store in the city you move to may not have much of a chance to attract you as a new customer. To overcome such issues, local retailers must rely on promotions that inform new customers of their offerings.

Interdependence

The two-way arrow in Exhibit 11.1 suggests that although promotional objectives are often established to improve either long- or short-term financial performance, each is likely to also benefit the other. For example, promotional efforts designed to build long-term financial performance are likely to have both immediate and cumulative effects. Similarly, efforts to promote short-term financial performance are likely to carry over,

Special events, like the London 2012 Olympic and Paralympic Games, are great opportunities for retailers to increase sales and enhance their images through pop-up stores.

affecting the retailer's long-term future. Occasionally, there are special events in a retailer's trade area that can help enhance the retailer's overall image as well as short-term sales. A good example is when a city hosts the Olympics. For instance, the London 2012 Olympic and Paralympic Games had an economic impact of nearly $8 billion. An estimated 880,000 visitors and 5.5 million day-trippers attended the games.[7] Many retailers such as Liberty created pop-up stores to help promote and sell Olympic-themed merchandise resulting in enhanced image for Liberty as well as added sales.

LO 3

List the seven steps involved in developing a retailer's advertising campaign.

Steps in Planning a Retail Advertising Campaign

What is involved in planning a retail advertising campaign? As we discussed in Chapter 2, the elements of a retailer's advertising campaign are just one part of the company's overall strategy. A retailer's advertising campaign is a seven-step process:

1. Selecting advertising objectives,
2. Budgeting for the campaign,
3. Allocating budgeted dollars,
4. Designing the message,
5. Selecting the media to use,
6. Scheduling of advertisements, and
7. Evaluating the results.

Selecting Advertising Objectives

A retailer's advertising objectives should flow from its promotional objectives; however, they should be more specific because advertising itself is a specific element of the promotional mix. Objectives should only be chosen after the retailer considers several factors that are unique to itself: age of the store, its location, merchandise lines being sold, its competition, the size of its trading area, and what support is available from suppliers.

The specific objectives that advertising can accomplish are many and varied, and those chosen depend on the target market the retailer is seeking to reach. Examples of common objectives include the following:

- Make consumers in your trading area aware that you offer the lowest prices;
- Make newcomers to your trading area aware of your existence (e.g., the Welcome Wagon coupons given to new residents of an area);
- Make customers aware of your large stock selection (e.g., Nordstrom's promise of a free shirt if it is out of stock on the basic sizes);
- Inform customers of your product offering (e.g., JCPenney's promotions as the exclusive retailer for Bisou Bisou clothing);
- Increase store traffic at the beginning of an important holiday shopping season;
- Increase traffic during slow sales periods (e.g., many restaurants have special early dinner hour prices where meals between 4 and 5:30 p.m. are discounted);
- Move old merchandise at the end of a selling season (e.g., the after-Christmas clearance sales that all retailers use);
- Strengthen your store's image or reputation (e.g., Neiman Marcus's famous Christmas catalog, which generates news stories around the world when it is mailed to customers);
- Make consumers think of you first when a need for your products occurs, especially if your products are not commonly purchased (e.g., St. Louis service retailer Frederick

Neiman Marcus continues to strengthen its image through its Christmas catalog which is filled with prestigious and unique offerings.

Roofing attempted to differentiate itself from its competitors with the creative but easy-to-remember jingle, "For a hole in your roof or a whole new roof—Frederick Roofing"); and

■ Retain your current customers (e.g., supermarket use of loyalty or frequent-shopper cards).

Although the ultimate goal of every advertising campaign should be to generate additional sales, you should notice that "increase sales" *is not listed as an advertising objective*. This is because elements of the retail mix, beyond advertising, may negatively impact sales. For example, the retailer could select the wrong merchandise for its target customers, charge too high, or too low, a price for its merchandise in comparison to the competition or store's image, or improperly display the merchandise in its store.

Regardless of the objective chosen, it must be (1) aimed at a specific market segment, (2) be measurable, and (3) state the time period necessary in order to realize the desired results. Thus, a good description of a campaign's objective may be "to increase the level of awareness that the retailer has the merchandise customers need, by 30 percent over the next six months among heads of middle-class and upper-middle-class households."

Budgeting for the Campaign

Even though some retailers spend less than 1 percent of sales on advertising, a more common range is 2–4 percent of sales, and for a large department store, this can amount to $40,000 a week or more and thus, careful budgeting is critical. A well-designed retail advertising campaign requires money that could be spent on other areas (e.g., more merchandise or higher wages for employees). The retailer hopes that the dollars spent on advertising will generate sales that will in turn produce added profits, which can then be used to finance the retailer's other activities. In fact, advertising should always be viewed as *an investment* that earns a return just like other investments.

When developing a budget, the retailer should first determine who is going to pay for the campaign; that is, will the retailer be the sole sponsor or will it get coop from manufacturers, distributors, or other retailers?

Retailer-Only Campaigns

If a retailer decides to do the campaign alone, it generally uses one of the following methods to determine the amount of money to be spent on the advertising campaign: the affordable method, the percentage-of-sales method, or the task-and-objective method.

affordable method
Is a technique for budgeting advertising in which all the money a retailer can afford to spend on advertising in a given time period becomes the advertising budget.

The Affordable Method   Many small retailers use the **affordable method** by allocating all the money they can afford for advertising in any given budget period. This method should be employed when the amount spent on advertising will add substantially more profit to the retailer than an alternate use of the funds such as increasing the sales force or adding more fixtures. Too much reliance on this method may lead to an inadequate advertising appropriation or to a budget that is not related to actual needs. A limitation of the affordable method is that the logic of this approach suggests that advertising does not stimulate sales or profits but rather is supported by sales and profits. However, some retailers have little choice but to use this approach. A small retailer cannot go to the bank and borrow $100,000 to spend on advertising. This is unfortunate because the small retailer might benefit more from advertising than from additional inventory or equipment. Thus, we can see that although the affordable method may not be ideal in terms of advertising theory, it is certainly defensible given the financial constraints that confront the small retailer.

percentage-of-sales method
Is a technique for budgeting in which the retailer targets a specific percentage of forecasted sales as the advertising budget.

Percentage-of-Sales Method   The **percentage-of-sales method** of budgeting for advertising is a type of *benchmarking* whereby the retailer uses the industry's best practices as a standard. Here the retailer targets a specific percentage of forecasted sales to be used for advertising based on the assumption that successful similar firms should be used as a guide.[8] Industry data, such as those shown in Exhibit 11.2, are often published by trade associations. These figures are averages, however, and do not reflect the unique circumstances and objectives of a particular retailer. A more suitable guide to the level of advertising expenditures is the retailer's past sales experience *when the level of past expenditures achieved management's objective*. The average percentage of advertising expenditures to sales for the past several years can be applied to the current year.

One weakness of the percentage-of-sales method is that the amount of sales becomes the factor that influences the advertising outlay. In a correct cause-and-effect relationship, the level of advertising should influence the amount of sales. In addition, this technique does not reflect the retailer's advertising goals. Rather than pinching pennies as consumers rein in spending, some retailers plow money into standing out from the crowd, hoping to grab market share and emerge from the economy's slump in better shape than their rivals. One of the author's early retail mentors, Louis Bing, always preached that "he never saw business so bad that he couldn't buy all of it he wanted." By that he meant that when business slowed and all his competitors reduced their advertisement budgets, he would then increase his advertisement expenditures. Without the clutter of competitors' advertisements, consumers became more aware of his advertisements and his sales increased, despite the general sales slowdown affecting the other local merchants. This strategy was built at least partly on the premise that shoppers typically are creatures of habit and that economic slowdowns offer an opportunity to change those habits as households try to economize. Besides, for publicly held companies, Wall Street tends to put less pressure on them to perform when the economy is weak, which

Exhibit 11.2
Advertising as Percentage of Sales by Line of Trade

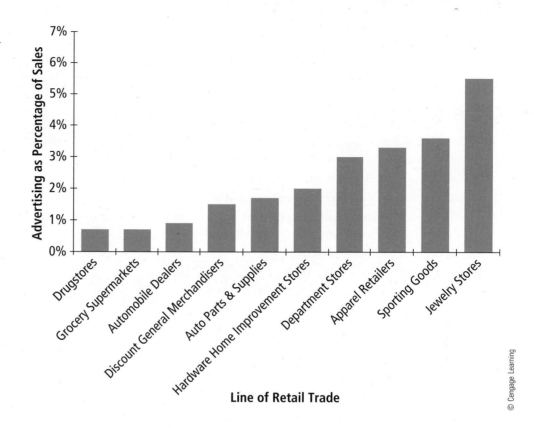

© Cengage Learning

can give these retailers a little room to view advertising as a long-term strategic investment in building a retailer's brand image.

Another weakness of this method is that it gives more money to departments that are already successful and fails to give money to departments that could be successful with a little extra money. Percentage of sales does, however, provide a controlled, generally affordable amount to spend; if spent wisely, it may work out well in practice. Most retailers, especially the smaller ones, do not use advertisement agencies and lack the sophistication required to adequately implement the task-and-objective approach. A percentage-of-sales guideline allows the retailer to follow objectives in an affordable, controlled manner. If the dollars are carefully applied in appropriate amounts over the year in such a way that they relate to expected sales percentages in each month, the percentage-of-sales method can work well.

Task-and-Objective Method   In the preceding budgeting methods, advertising seems to follow sales results. With the **task-and-objective method**, the logic is properly reversed; here retailers can see the relationship between promotions that change attitudes and behavior. Thus, advertising leads to some other measure of financial performance—hopefully, sales. Basically, the retailer prioritizes its advertising objectives and then determines the advertising tasks that need to be performed to achieve those objectives.[9] Associated with each task is an estimate of the cost of performing the task. When all of these costs are totaled, the retailer has its advertising budget. In short, this method begins with the retailer's advertising objectives and then determines the tasks needed to meet those objectives and what it will cost to perform them.

More and more retailers, as well as shopping malls, are moving toward this method as they realize that their shrinking funds can no longer be wasted on promotions that don't

task-and-objective method

Is a technique for budgeting in which the retailer establishes its advertising objectives and then determines the advertising tasks that need to be performed to achieve those objectives.

Exhibit 11.3

Task and Objective Method of Advertising Budget Development

	Objective and Task	Estimated Cost
Objective 1:	Increase traffic during dull periods.	
Task *A:*	15 full-page newspaper advertisements to be spread over these dates: February 2–16; June 8–23; October 4–18	$22,500
Task *B:*	Run 240 30-second radio spots split on two stations and spread over these dates: February 2–16; June 8–23; October 4–18	4,320
Objective 2:	Attract new customers from newcomers to the community.	
Task *A:*	2,000 direct-mail letters greeting new residents to the community	1,000
Task *B:*	2,000 direct-mail letters inviting new arrivals in the community to stop in to visit the store and fill out a credit application	1,000
Task *C:*	Yellow Pages advertising	1,900
Objective 3:	Build store's reputation.	
Task *A:*	Weekly 15-second institutional ads on the 10 p.m. television news every Saturday and Sunday	20,800
Task *B:*	One half-page newspaper ad per month in the home living section of the local newspaper	9,500
Objective 4:	Increase shopper traffic in shopping center.	
Task *A:*	Cooperate with other retailers in the shopping center in sponsoring transit advertising on buses and cabs	3,000
Task *B:*	Participate in "Midnight Madness Sale" with other retailers in the shopping center by taking out 2 full-page newspaper ads—one in mid-March and the other in mid-July	3,000
Objective 5:	Clear out end-of-month, slow-moving merchandise.	
Task *A:*	Run a full-page newspaper ad on the last Thursday of every month	18,000
Task *B:*	Run 3 30-second television spots on the last Thursday of every month	14,000
Total advertising budget		$99,020

pay off. Exhibit 11.3 gives an example of the task-and-objective method. Notice that the retailer has five major advertising objectives and a total of 11 tasks to perform to accomplish these objectives. The total cost of performing these tasks is $99,020. While the task-and-objective method of developing the advertising budget is the best of the three methods from a theoretical and managerial control perspective, not all retailers have adopted it because it is difficult to implement.

Many of the major retailers use a combination of the percentage-of-sales method, which they use to keep pace with competitors, and the task-and-objective method, which reflects the different tasks they must accomplish to reach their objectives. Thus, as shown in Exhibit 11.4, while the percentages for close competitors are similar, they differ somewhat because of circumstances relating to the other elements of their retail mixes. For example, Macy's department stores recently spent 4.9 percent of sales on advertising while some other department stores—Dillard's, Bon-Ton, and JCPenney's—spent 2.3 percent, 4.1 percent, and 6.6 percent, respectively. Target spent 1.9 percent while Walmart spent only .6 percent. Safeway spent 1.3 percent, while A&P spent 1.0 percent, Publix spent .8 percent, and Kroger spent only .7 percent.[10]

A retailer's promotional decisions can't always be determined solely by analytical or scientific methods. On the contrary, promotion offers the opportunity for highly creative thought. In fact, as noted throughout the text, creativity is probably the best way for retailers to differentiate themselves from competitors. This chapter's "Service Retailing" box discusses some of the creative methods used by retailers in one of the most competitive service industries—restaurants.

Co-Op Campaigns

Although most retail advertising is paid for solely by the retailer, sometimes manufacturers and other retailers may pay part or even all of the costs of a retailer's advertising campaign.

vertical cooperative advertising
Occurs when the retailer and other channel members (usually manufacturers) share the advertising budget. Usually the manufacturer subsidizes some of the retailer's advertising that features the manufacturer's brands.

Vertical cooperative advertising allows the retailer and other supply-chain members to share the advertising burden. For example, a manufacturer may pay as much as 40 percent of the cost of a retailer's advertising that focuses on the manufacturer's products to a maximum of 4 percent of annual purchases by the retailer from the manufacturer. If the retailer spent $10,000 on advertising the manufacturer's products, then 40 percent of this amount or $4,000 could be reimbursed, as long as the retailer purchased at least $100,000 during the last year from the manufacturer.

There is a strong temptation among retailers to view vertical co-op advertising money as free. Retailers forget, however, that good advertising, like a good investment, should increase revenues from customers, not just from vendors. In other words, even if the supplier is putting up 50 percent of the expense, the retailer must still pay the other 50 percent. Don't think about it as the supplier paying one-half of your advertising, but the other way around; you are actually paying one-half of the supplier's cost to advertise their product. In addition, since the supplier often exercises considerable control over the content of the advertising and its objectives may be different than the retailer's, the retailer may actually be paying 50 percent of the supplier's cost of advertising rather than vice versa. Also, suppliers know that it is a common media practice to offer local retailers a discount on rates relative to national advertisers. Thus, suppliers often use local retailers to get this discount on their advertisements.

Retailers must prioritize their objectives to determine whether they can get a better return on their money by using vertical co-op dollars or by assuming total sponsorship of advertising a message with high priority. Remember, in earlier chapters, it was pointed out that retailers and their supply-chain partners often have different objectives. As a result, sometimes it can be more profitable for the retailer to pass up a co-op deal on one product line and spend the money on another line that is likely to have a higher sales impact.

To illustrate this line of reasoning, let's consider the following scenario. Assume that a retailer has $10,000 to spend on advertising and is considering the possibility of increasing advertising expenditures for either merchandise line A or line B. With line A, the vendor has offered a co-op deal, which roughly equates to the supplier paying 50 percent of the cost of the advertising. If the retailer selects this option, it would be able to purchase $20,000 of advertising for a $10,000 investment. No co-op deal is being offered by the supplier of line B because it is the retailer's private label, but line B is just now becoming very popular with the retailer's customers, and the retailer believes it could benefit substantially from $10,000 in advertising. What should the retailer do?

The answer to the preceding will depend on two major factors. First, how much will the sales of line A increase as a result of $20,000 in advertising compared with the likely sales increase of line B that would result from a $10,000 increase in advertising? Second, what is the gross-margin percentage for each line? Let's assume these are the facts: Line A has 50-percent gross margin and line B has 60-percent gross margin. Currently, line A has sales of $160,000, and it is expected that a $20,000 advertising program would push sales up to $220,000. At the current time, line B has sales of $36,000, but it is expected that a $10,000 advertising program would increase the sales volume to $120,000.

Exhibit 11.4
Advertising Expenditures
at Leading Retailers as a
Percentage of Sales
(2009–2011)

Retail Sector/Firm	2009	2010	2011
Apparel Retailers			
Men's Warehouse, Inc.	4.3%	4.4%	3.5%
Charming Shoppes, Inc.	3.2%	3.3%	3.1%
Limited Brands, Inc.	5.3%	4.9%	4.6%
Chicos FAS, Inc.	3.8%	4.6%	5.0%
Talbots, Inc.	3.5%	4.7%	5.5%
Burlington Coat Factory	2.0%	1.9%	2.0%
GAP, Inc.	3.6%	3.5%	3.8%
Ross Stores	.7%	.7%	.7%
RUE21 Inc.	.6%	.6%	.7%
TJX Companies, Inc.	1.1%	1.1%	1.2%
Casual Male Retail Group Inc.	4.8%	4.8%	4.9%
Stein Mart, Inc.	4.1%	4.6%	4.9%
Buckle, Inc.	1.0%	1.0%	.8%
Pacific Sunwear Calif, Inc.	1.4%	1.8%	1.8%
Urban Outfitters, Inc.	2.4%	2.6%	2.9%
American Eagle Outfitters, Inc.	2.3%	2.2%	2.3%
Stage Stores, Inc.	4.3%	4.3%	4.3%
Coldwater Creek, Inc.	7.4%	7.4%	7.5%
Automobile Dealers			
AUTONATION, INC.	1.1%	1.0%	.9%
Penske Automotive Group Inc.	.7%	.7%	.6%
America's Car-Mart, Inc.	.9%	1.0%	.9%
Car Max	1.0%	1.0%	1.0%
Auto Parts & Supplies			
Pep Boys	2.8%	2.9%	2.7%
Auto Zone, Inc.	1.2%	1.2%	1.2%
O'Reilly Automotive Inc.	1.5%	1.3%	1.3%
Advance Auto Parts, Inc.	1.2%	1.3%	1.5%
Department Stores			
Dillards, Inc.	2.2%	1.7%	1.4%
Macy's, Inc.	4.6%	4.3%	4.3%
JC Penney Co.	6.7%	6.6%	6.0%
Saks Inc.	1.4%	1.6%	2.0%
Neiman Marcus, Inc.	2.2%	2.1%	2.1%
Nordstrom, Inc.	1.0%	1.2%	1.2%
Belk, Inc.	3.7%	4.1%	4.1%

(continued)

Retail Sector/Firm	2009	2010	2011
Discount General Merchandisers			
Kohl's Corp	5.0%	4.7%	5.1%
Target Corp	1.8%	1.9%	2.0%
Walmart Stores, Inc.	.6%	.6%	.5%
Family Dollar Stores	.1%	.2%	.2%
Dollar General, Corp	.4%	.4%	.3%
Dollar Tree, Inc.	.2%	.2%	.2%
Big Lots, Inc.	2.0%	1.9%	1.9%
Drugstores			
CVS Caremark, Inc.	.3%	.2%	.2%
Rite Aid Corp	1.5%	1.4%	1.4%
Walgreen Co.	.5%	.4%	.4%
Electronics			
Best Buy Co., Inc.	1.5%	1.8%	2.0%
Radioshack Corp	4.5%	4.6%	4.8%
Hardware/Home Improvement			
Home Depot, Inc.	1.4%	1.3%	1.2%
Lowe's Companies, Inc.	1.6%	1.6%	1.6%
Orchard Supply Hardware Stores	3.2%	3.5%	3.3%
Grocery/Supermarket			
Great Atlantic & Pacific Tea Co.	1.1%	1.1%	N/A
Kroger	.7%	.7%	.6%
Publix Supermarkets, Inc.	.7%	.8%	.7%
Safeway, Inc.	1.2%	1.2%	1.1%
Weis Markets, Inc.	.9%	1.0%	.9%
Winn-Dixie Stores, Inc.	1.3%	1.3%	1.2%
Whole Foods Market Inc.	.4%	.4%	.4%
Spartan Stores Inc.	.6%	.6%	.6%
Roundy's Inc.	1.1%	.9%	.8%
Jewelry Stores			
Zale Corp	5.0%	4.7%	4.4%
Tiffany & Co.	5.9%	6.4%	6.4%
Signet Jewelers, LTD	5.1%	5.2%	5.6%
Sporting Goods Stores			
Sport Chalet, Inc.	1.2%	1.2%	1.5%
Hibbett Sports, Inc.	.9%	1.1%	1.1%
Big 5 Sports, Corp	5.1%	5.0%	5.3%
Dicks Sporting Goods, Inc.	3.6%	3.8%	3.6%
Cabelas, Inc.	7.2%	6.7%	6.6%

Source: SEC 10K Corporate Annual Reports and author computations.

SERVICE — RETAILING

Promoting a New Restaurant

For years, restaurant owners have tried to determine the best way to promote a new restaurant. Many restaurant managers have felt the same as John Wanamaker, the merchant prince of Philadelphia department store fame, when he was asked about his advertising budget. He answered that he knew that half of his money was wasted, but he just didn't know which half. Consider the changing trends that have occurred over the last two decades as restaurants have entered the Dallas, Texas, market.

Two decades ago, for example, when Dallas-based sports bar and restaurant chain Dave & Busters first opened, most of its restaurants avoided advertising and relied on word of mouth. That strategy worked out just fine for Dave & Busters. Customers loved the games and good food and spread the word. Doing so, the restaurant used the money that might have been spent on advertising to ensure that every customer had a good experience. In fact, this strategy was so successful that it was widely copied and lost its effectiveness. As a result, Dave & Busters today advertises its new restaurants on local radio supported by direct mail and also conducts a nationwide campaign through drive-time radio and cable television outlets such as ESPN, TNT, TBS, the Comedy Channel, and Fox Sports.

Once word of mouth was no longer effective for promoting a new restaurant, Fox Sports Grill developed a new idea when it entered the restaurant scene in heavily populated North Dallas. (By the way, North Dallas is known as the burial ground for restaurants. Just recently, the famous Smith & Wollensky Steakhouse closed its restaurant in this area.) This sports bar, which features hardwood flooring, set up giant plasma TVs and projection flat screens that offered unobstructed views of all the latest sports action. At the same time, the bar provided sunken private areas complete with smaller televisions for individual viewing. Fox soon became the place to be seen for Dallas area sports figures, as one author can attest. In addition, the restaurant features a menu that includes superior cuisine ranging from pasta to chicken and shrimp to prime rib, as well as all kinds of burgers, sandwiches, and appetizers. All this and at affordable prices.

However, what was truly the creative genius behind the success of this sports bar was the fact that its advertisements featured one simple message: Fox was a sports bar *without smoking*.

(continued)

Another Dallas-based restaurant, Del Frisco's Double Eagle Steakhouse, also realized that word of mouth was no longer effective, so its cofounder, Dee Lincoln, used publicity as an alternative to advertising when she opened a new restaurant in the Denver market. Lincoln paid a then-record $80,000 for a 1,309-pound Maine-Anjou crossbreed steer at Denver's National Western Stock Show. When her winning bid was accepted, an opposing bidder said, "Lady, you must either be really crazy or have too much money." Dee Lincoln got what she wanted—hundreds of thousands of dollars' worth of front-page newspaper coverage, not to mention radio and television publicity, for her high-quality steakhouses.

It was no accident that all the media mentioned the newest restaurant in Denver. However, restaurant owners can't always be as lucky as Ms. Lincoln was to have a publicity-generating event available.

Thus, despite market changes over the last two decades, service retailers, such as restaurants, have come up with creative ideas for promoting their offerings. This is an especially difficult task for restaurants because a dining episode is essentially an experience, and the retailer's promotions must cut through the clutter of all its competitors' advertisements.

Source: Based on conversations with Dee Lincoln and the experience of the authors, all of whom have lived in Texas.

Notice that line B, although its current sales are relatively low, is very responsive to advertising expenditures as compared to the responsiveness of merchandise line A. Here is the numerical analysis:

	Line A		Line B	
	Before	**After**	**Before**	**After**
Sales	$160,000	$220,000	$36,000	$120,000
Cost of goods sold	80,000	110,000	14,400	48,000
Gross margin	80,000	110,000	21,600	72,000
Advertising	0	10,000[a]	0	10,000
Contribution to profit	$80,000	$100,000	$21,600	$62,000

[a]Actually, $20,000 was spent, but the net cost to the retailer was $10,000 since the supplier paid the other $10,000.

As you can see, the numerical analysis suggests that while the increase in line A's contribution to profit would be $20,000 ($100,000 versus $80,000), it would be $40,400 for line B ($62,000 versus $21,600). Therefore, it would be more profitable for the retailer to pass up the co-op deal on line A and spend the $10,000 on advertising line B, its private-label brand.

horizontal cooperative advertising
Occurs when two or more retailers band together to share the cost of advertising usually in the form of a joint promotion of an event or sale that would benefit both parties.

Horizontal cooperative advertising occurs when two or more retailers band together to share the cost of advertising. When used, this approach tends to give small retailers more bargaining power in purchasing advertising than they would otherwise have. Also, if properly conducted, it can create substantially more store traffic for all participants. For example, retailers in shopping malls will often jointly sponsor multiple-page spreads in newspapers promoting special events such as "Santa Land" or "Moonlight Madness" sales, while downtown merchants usually jointly sponsor "Sidewalk Days" or "Downtown Days" sales. The impact of these events on store traffic is evident by the many malls that have recently turned a very slow shopping night (Halloween) into a very successful "Dead Night." By having a store-to-store program that provides a safe place for trick or treating, a mall can pull significantly more people into each retailer's store than each retailer could do individually for the same cost.

Allocating Budgeted Dollars

Regardless of the method by which the retailer determines its budget, the firm will subsequently need to decide how to allocate its advertising dollars. It will probably not be profitable to heavily advertise all merchandise lines or departments. Even if it were, most retail advertising budgets would not be large enough to do so. Thus, in either case, some conscious decision on where to spend advertising dollars is necessary.

Deciding which lines or departments to spend advertising dollars on is not easy. Advertising theory would suggest that the retailer's limited advertising funds be allocated to products or departments that maximize the retailer's overall profitability. In practice, due to uncertainty and inadequate information, such a theoretical rule is difficult to implement. Rather, the retailer must settle for an allocation that is approximately correct. Let us consider the factors that suggest a merchandise line or department is a candidate for a high advertising allocation.

Gross Margin Percentage

Merchandise lines or departments that have a high gross margin percentage are potentially better able than others to benefit or produce a profit from high levels of advertising. If a merchandise line has a gross margin of 20 percent, then to pay for each dollar of advertising at least $5 in merchandise needs to be sold. If the merchandise line has a gross margin of 50 percent, then only $2 in sales have to be created for each dollar of advertising. Here is a little tool to use to figure out how much you have to generate in sales to pay for a dollar of advertising; simply take the gross margin percent and divide that into one; for instance, in the earlier examples if you take 20 percent divided into one (1/.20) you get $5 or if you take 50 percent and divide into one (1/.50) you get $2.

Advertising Elasticity of Demand

The product's advertising elasticity of demand is the percentage of change in sales as a result of a 1 percent change in advertising. For example, an advertising elasticity of demand of 4.0 suggests that as advertising is increased by 1 percent, dollar sales will rise by 4 percent. When demand is more elastic, demand is more expandable, and therefore the product is a better candidate for high advertising expenditure.

In Exhibit 11.5, we illustrate the role that gross margin percent and advertising elasticity play in allocating budget dollars. Make sure you understand the computations in this exhibit (Can you figure out what goes in the blank space?). Incidentally, this exhibit also helps to explain why a luxury jewelry retailer, such as Tiffany's, with an average gross margin of near 65 percent, can spend approximately 6.5 percent of sales on advertising. Tiffany's also caters to the wealthy and has the highest market share among luxury jewelry retailers in the over $50,000 purchase category. Yes, that is for a single piece of jewelry.

Market Share Dominance

Speaking of Tiffany's market share dominance, retailers have found through experience that there is a close association between market share by merchandise category and profit. Also, retailers with large market shares enjoy an unusually large consumer franchise that

Exhibit 11.5
Role of Gross Margin Percent and Advertising Elasticity in Advertising Budget Allocation

Gross Margin Percent	Dollar Sales Needed to Support $1 in Advertising	Advertising Elasticity	Dollar Sales Generated from $1 in Advertising
20%	(1/.2) = $5.00	2.0	$2.00
40%	(1/.4) = $2.50	4.0	$4.00
50%	(1/.5) = $2.00	6.0	$6.00
75%	(1/.75) =	8.0	$8.00

can be protected only with high levels of advertising. Thus, retailers with dominant market share merchandise lines or departments should allocate a disproportionate share of advertising to them. The same also applies to lines or departments that are growing rapidly and have the potential of being dominant in terms of market share.

Sales Displacement and Substitution

Retail promotions, including price reductions, have been shown to increase current period sales substantially. However, in addition to increasing current sales of the advertised brand, retail promotions may also reduce sales of the brand during subsequent nonpromotional periods (i.e., they stockpile goods bought at cheaper prices), referred to as **sales displacement**, and reduce current and future demand for competitive brands, referred to as **substitution effect**. If a promoted brand causes extensive substitution effects, for example, the retailer may be worse off when consumers switch purchases from high-margin unpromoted brands to low-margin promoted brands. Restaurants, for instance, need to be careful that their featured menu items are not priced too attractively and thus may be too disproportionately substituted for higher margin meals the customer may have otherwise purchased. Likewise, sales displacement may have deleterious effects on the retailer's sales if consumers switch from a potentially high-margin time period to low-margin promotional periods.

Backup Resources

A merchandise line or department should not receive a heavy dose of advertising unless it is supported sufficiently by other resources. When a product is to be promoted, retailers must ensure that they not only have enough stock on hand in order to meet increased demand, but they must also ensure they have enough space to display the merchandise and enough staff on hand to handle the increased traffic levels. Additionally, if the advertised merchandise is often sold on store credit, then the retailer should ensure that it has adequate funds on hand to finance the consumer credit.

Critical Mass

The retailer needs sufficient funds to allocate to a department or merchandise line so that the advertising can really make a difference in the line's or department's performance. The question is not whether a line should receive a high proportion of a retailer's advertising budget, but whether that high proportion is sufficiently high enough in absolute dollars to make a difference. If not, the dollars are better spent on another line or department.

Designing the Message

The next step in developing an advertising campaign is to design a creative message and select the media that will enable the retailer to reach its objectives. In reality, these decisions are made simultaneously. Creative messages cannot be developed without knowing which media will be used to carry the message. This text, however, will cover media selection after discussing how retailers design their messages.

Creative decisions are especially important for retailers because their advertising messages generally seek an immediate reaction from the consumer while having a short life span. The development of such messages is one of retailing's major challenges. If you have ever covered the retailer's name in a newspaper advertisement or tuned out the retailer's name in a broadcast advertisement, you know that all too often retailers lack originality in their advertisements. Here are a couple of examples of retailers who have demonstrated creativity when developing a promotional strategy.

T&M Appliance & TV of Clinton, Missouri, population 1,500, used a variation of a Christmas Tree Rental promotion used by IKEA with decorating Halloween pumpkins.

---

sales displacement
Occurs when consumers purchase and stockpile advertised brands during a promotional period and any gains in sales are later offset by sales reductions from average during subsequent nonpromotional periods.

substitution effect
Happens when advertising of a particular branded product during a promotional period reduces the current and future demand for competitive brands.

The five visits here involved picking up a free pumpkin with your parents, turning in the finished pumpkin, coming in to select the best pumpkin, stopping by after the citywide parade to see the store's decorations (including the pumpkins), and returning to select the best costume.

Therefore, in view of this, retail advertisements must accomplish these three goals:

1. Attract and retain attention; that is, they must be able to break through the competitive clutter;
2. Achieve the objective of the advertising strategy; and
3. Avoid errors, especially legal ones.

Accomplishing these goals is, however, an extremely difficult task in today's marketplace, especially given the limited attention span of the time-pressed consumer. After all, newspapers and magazine readership is declining, and more and more consumers use their remote controls to skip or block television commercials. Consumers now spend their time twittering with friends, playing with their PlayStation 3s, and surfing the Internet instead of using mass media for entertainment. Therefore, it is becoming imperative for retailers to find unique ways to break through the competitive clutter and then get and hold the consumer's attention. One retailer in Opelika, Alabama, a city close to Auburn University, told one of the authors that given the overwhelming use of DVRs (digital recording devices) and consumers' tendency to fast-forward through commercials, he (creatively) decided to "hold" his store's logo in the same spot on the television screen throughout the entirety of all his advertisements so as to ensure that consumers are still exposed to his logo even if they're not sure what the actual message is within the advertisement. Some more common approaches that retailers use to gain repeated viewing involve using one of the following styles, or genres, to make the promotion more enjoyable or informative.

Lifestyle:	Shows how the retailer's products fit in with the consumer's lifestyle. (Eddie Bauer magazine advertisements often show their clothing being worn while camping, fishing, and hiking. Toyota's Prius V advertisement "Cargo Space meets Cyberspace", shows how the Prius V fits the driver's lifestyle.)
Fantasy:	Creates a fantasy for the consumer that is built around the retailer's products. (Victoria's Secret, Disney and casinos all use fantasy. Purina uses fantasy in its advertisement for Busy Bone which depicts a dog chewing on the Busy Bone and thinking: "When I chew Busy, it's like… I'm bounding through a world with no fences, running circles around rabbits, showing them who's the boss.")
Humorous:	Builds a campaign around humor that relates to using the retailer's products. (GEICO has several series of advertisements that advertise insurance products through humor. M&M's candy "people", Budweiser's trained dogs and Clydesdale horses, and "Jack" of Jack in the Box fame are other examples.)
Slice of life:	Depicts the consumer in everyday settings using the retailer's products. (Mastercard, "Priceless" ads, Hallmark, Travelocity, Safeway, Macy's, Target, and Holiday Inn all do slice-of-life types of advertising.)
Mood or image:	Builds a mood around using the retailer's products. (Tiffany & Co. and Copenhagen Contemporary Furniture both build a mood of luxury and style in their advertisements. Tully's Coffee has a line of advertisements, which builds a mood around relaxation and hominess.)

Finally, before using the advertisement, the retailer should test it for mistakes. These mistakes could be either accidental or perhaps inserted by an unhappy employee. The authors have seen a promotion for an "early bird special" at a Texas mall sweepstakes in which the customers could drop off their entries between 7 and 10 a.m.; unfortunately, the drawing was to be held at 9:30 a.m. A department store in the Crossroads Mall in Omaha left an author laughing when he saw this sign next to a stairwell: "This store's elevator is in China." In another case, a Sunday circular for a major East Coast retailer offered a special deal on Scrabble games. However, the adjoining picture had two young boys playing the game and one had just spelled the word RAPE. A Philadelphia clothing store's advertisement had this heading: "CLEARANCE SALE! SAVINGS LIKE THESE ONLY COME ONCE A YEAR," and a California florist once advertised a "PRE-GRAND OPENING CLEARANCE."

A few years ago, KFC ran a new product introduction advertising campaign for grilled chicken that *Advertising Age* declared would go down in the "annals of marketing disasters." The ill-fated campaign began when KFC used Oprah Winfrey to offer two free pieces of grilled chicken, two sides, and a biscuit to anyone who downloaded a coupon within a two-day period. Within minutes, it was the number-one topic on Twitter. That night, blogs began reporting "riots" at New York City KFCs. The next day, local news crews across the country interviewed fuming customers getting turned away because some franchisees refused to honor the coupons since the company wouldn't reimburse their costs for the free meal. Consumers complained about rude service, and media complained about a public relations team that seemed asleep at the wheel. On day three, the day after KFC pulled the promotion, National Public Radio was calling KFC "the James Frey of fast food," referring to the author of a memoir praised by Ms. Winfrey that was later exposed as fiction. In the end, KFC made good on the coupons. However, in just a couple of days it strained relationships with KFC's three core constituents—consumers, media, and franchisees—not to mention the fact that it seemed to forget what the "F" in KFC stood for.[11]

Although these errors are serious, they should not present legal problems. Retailers can accidentally violate some advertising laws, even if they are not trying to deceive the consumer. Chapter 6 discussed some of the various federal laws governing retail advertising. All too often, however, the retailer runs into trouble with state or local laws. Some states limit promotions involving games of chance, others regulate the use of advertisements with price comparisons among retail stores, and others restrict the use of certain words in the description of merchandise. For example, the Pennsylvania Human Relations Commission has issued guidelines against the use of the following words in real-estate advertisements because it may tend to discriminate among consumer groups: *bachelor pad, couple, mature, older seniors, adults, traditional, newlyweds, exclusive, children,* and *established neighborhood.*

Internationally, individual countries—or, in some cases, groups of countries such as the European Union—set specific guidelines for advertising content that must be followed. For instance, in the European Union, advertising that is directed at a child or a young person is generally allowed; however, the advertisement must not directly encourage children or young people to buy a product and must not exploit their inexperience and credulity. In addition, the advertisement must not cause them any physical or mental harm. Advertisements cannot exploit the trust children have in parents, teachers, or other persons, and product placement is not allowed in children's programs, and children's programs can be interrupted only if the program runs longer than 30 minutes.[12] In April 2011, the Beijing Administration for Industry and Commerce banned billboards that promoted hedonism or the worship of foreign-made products. In large-part this was a reaction from the growing celebration of conspicuous consumption, wealth, and luxurious lifestyles in China.[13]

In addition, to the aforementioned examples, a smart retailer should prepare a message to be used in case of some type of emergency. For example, a Costco executive was recently quoted as saying as a result of an *E. coli* scare a decade ago that the retailer created a system that matched product purchases with a membership number. Thus, in 2009, when the peanut butter crisis occurred, the retailer was not only able to remove the involved products from its shelves but also immediately contract the 1.8 million members who purchased peanut butter at one of its warehouses.[14]

Media Alternatives

The retailer has many media alternatives from which to select. However, before the retailer selects from the media alternatives, it needs to recognize the behavior of shoppers, and whether or not, and to what degree, they plan their shopping trips. Thirty-six percent of shoppers do not plan their shopping trips until the day they actually go shopping. This is especially the case for purchases of jewelry, clothing, lawn and garden supplies, and toys.[15] Thus, some media choices, such as monthly magazines or weekly magazines, would not be as attractive. At the same time, it makes Internet advertising more attractive.

In the past, retailers generally categorized media as print (which included newspaper, magazines, and direct mail) and broadcast (which lumped radio and television together). Now, however, retailers are beginning to classify media using a managerial perspective that recognizes that newspapers and local television stations that use broadcast programming from the networks are mass-media alternatives aimed at a total market, while cable television, radio, magazines, direct mail, and the Internet can be more easily targeted toward specific markets.

Newspaper Advertising

Historically, the most frequently used advertising medium in retailing was the newspaper, but, newspaper advertising has been declining over the last decade. However, virtually every newspaper now has an Internet version and often this online format is more informative because it often also provides access to other news media such as *USA TODAY* and other regional newspapers. You may have grown up in a household where your parents purchased the local newspaper just to view the advertisements and now, this is being increasingly done online. Incidentally, many fashion conscious consumers purchase the Sunday *New York Times* to view the advertising content where new fashion is featured. Newspaper advertising is popular for retailers because of the following reasons.

1. Most newspapers are local. This is advantageous since most retailers appeal to a local trading area. However, keep in mind that newspapers, with their online version, can attract more than a local audience.
2. A low technical skill level is required to create advertisements for newspapers. This is helpful for small retailers.
3. Newspaper advertisements require only a short interval between the time copy is written and when the advertisement appears. Because some retailers do a poor job of planning and tend to use advertising to respond to crises (poor cash flow, slackening of sales, need to move old merchandise), the short lead time for placing newspaper advertisements is a significant advantage. However, remember that shoppers are also often like retailers in that they often do not plan shopping ahead of time but decide on the day or a few days earlier to make a shopping trip.

However, recently many families, finding they were not reading the local newspaper or finding it redundant with what they could get on the Internet, have discontinued their local newspaper subscriptions or at least cut back their subscriptions to Sundays only.

As a result, many newspapers across the county have either gone out of business or have reduced the number of days published. Another problem for retailers wanting to use this medium is that if the retailer has a specific target market, then much of its advertising money will be wasted using newspapers since their circulation is seldom able to match the retailer's target market. This criticism of newspaper advertising is particularly true for the under-25 segment. This group rarely reads newspapers and gets most of its news from the Internet. Also, retail newspaper advertising presents retailers with the following four disadvantages.

1. The fact that a consumer was exposed to an issue of a newspaper does not mean the consumer read or even saw the retailer's advertisement.
2. The life of any single issue of a newspaper is short—it's read and subsequently discarded.
3. The typical person spends relatively little time with each issue, and the time spent is spread over many items in the newspaper.
4. Newspapers have poor reproduction quality, which leads to advertisements with little visual appeal.

Still, despite these disadvantages, newspapers continue to be an often-used form of advertising for retailers. Many of the large bricks-and-mortar retailers, however, such as Best Buy, Lowe's, Kohl's, and Target, primarily use newspapers to deliver their own centrally produced advertising circulars. In fact, this is a big source of advertising revenue for newspapers.

A recent trend in newspaper advertising is the so-called adzine format. In the past, many consumers simply ignored supermarket advertisements because they were simply lists of items on sale and many of the items didn't pertain to their needs. However, since consumers enjoy reading magazines, grocers have evolved a new style of advertising. These lifestyle adzines, which are often published quarterly, present meal-time ideas

Some retailers, such as Best Buy, Walmart, and Safeway, use newspapers as a means to deliver their own separate advertising circulars.

that incorporate items on sale with recipes, pictures, and informational copy. Still, this concept depends on the newspaper's delivery system to reach all, or a selected group of, consumers, whether they are newspaper subscribers or not.

Local and Cable Television Advertising

Over the past decade, some retailers such as Macy's have shifted from newspapers to television advertising as a means of reaching the elusive full-price shopper. After all, for a brand to be viewed as credible and top of the line, television is a more dynamic medium. Research suggests that, over time, the subtle and gradual effect from TV images on consumer memory is greater than the aural messages received from media such as radio. However, even though television advertising is a great image builder, it is expensive. A well-designed television advertisement may use up the total advertisement budget of a local retailer. Additionally, television advertising is likely to possess coverage well beyond the small- to intermediately sized retailer's trading area, which increases the likely inefficiency of such a media choice.

Another major disadvantage of using television advertising is that competition is high for the viewer's attention, especially with most consumers having access to more than 100 channels, as well as DVDs, not to mention TiVo. Thus, during commercials, the viewer may either use the remote control to surf other channels or, if the program was TiVoed, just skip the advertisements. Another complication for the retailer to consider is that the overall time spent watching television has decreased in recent years as many younger consumers have switched to watching television programming over to the Internet or via a Ruku device, which delivers content on-demand. The phenomenal growth of tablet computers, such as the iPad, have also accelerated this trend.

However, in spite of the preceding drawbacks, television advertising can be a powerful tool for generating higher sales. The American public spends more time relaxing in front of the television than in any other recreational activity. Television has broad coverage; more than 98 percent of homes in the United States have at least one television set. These sets offer the retailer a medium in which both sight and sound can be used to create a significant perceptual and cognitive effect on the consumer. It should be noted that television penetration rates differ across the world, and therefore television's usefulness as a tool to reach consumers differs as well.

Also, the widespread development of cable television has made television attractive to small local retailers without expensively produced commercials. Local cable operators have been selling targeted advertising on cable channels ranging from the Food Network (www.foodnetwork.com) to the Home & Garden Network (www.hgtv.com), Do-It-Yourself Network (www.diynetwork.com) to ESPN (espn.go.com) and Fox Sports (msn.foxsports.com) in hopes of matching a retailer's particular customer profiles.

Radio Advertising

Many retailers prefer to use radio because it can target messages to select groups. Most communities have 5–10 or more radio stations, each of which tends to appeal to a different demographic group. Through the use of proper variations in volume and types of sounds, retailers can use radio to develop distinctive and appealing messages and to introduce a store and its image to current and potential customers. In short, radio offers a lot of flexibility. Also, many radio audiences develop strong affection and trust for their favorite radio announcers. When these announcers endorse a retailer, the audience often listens. In fact, one of the authors recently began using ProFlowers.com (www.proflowers.com) and Goldline International (www.goldline.com) after repeatedly hearing his favorite morning talk-show host mention their products during his shows.

Radio advertising also has its drawbacks. Radio commercials, especially the uncreative ones, are not saved or referred to again like print media advertisements. In fact, some media experts claim that radio's lack of innovation is a major shortcoming. All too often, ad agencies and radio stations lack the creativity to help local retailers. In addition, radio is frequently listened to during work hours and during drive time (to and from work) and therefore tends, over time, to become part of the background environment. Further, since radio is nonvisual, it is impossible to effectively demonstrate or show the merchandise that is being advertised.

One of the big drawbacks to traditional radio, which is laden with advertising commercials that finance the radio station, is satellite radio. Sirius XM (www.siriusxm.com) offers over 140 channels via satellite that can beam music to wherever you are: your automobile, tablet or desktop, television, or smartphone. Importantly, half of the Sirius XM channels are advertising commercial free. Sirius XM currently doesn't have competitors in the satellite radio market, but there are other forms of commercial free radio available where an Internet connection is available. Some other free Internet radio stations, like Pandora (www.pandora.com), Slacker (www.slacker.com), Live 365 (www.live365.com), and Rdio.com (www.rdio.com), allow you to access commercial-free music, for a small monthly fee. So just like consumers being able to avoid advertising on television with TiVo they now can avoid advertising on radio.

Magazine Advertising

Relatively few local retailers advertise in magazines unless the magazine has only a local circulation. Nationally based retailers such as JCPenney, Williams-Sonoma, and Victoria's Secret will allocate some of their advertising budget to magazines, but a majority of these advertisements tend to be institutional in nature.

Magazine advertising can be quite effective. In relation to newspapers, magazines perform well on several dimensions. They have a better reproduction quality and a longer life span per issue, and consumers spend more time with each issue of a magazine than a newspaper. For instance, some subscribers to Motor Trend, Playboy, Architectural Digest, and National Geographic will build collections that span several decades if not more. Many magazines even have the unique characteristic of being shared among family and friends, thus extending the reach of the advertisement. Or, consider that as you wait for a medical or dental appointment or to have your automobile serviced, there are always a host of magazines in the waiting room for you to peruse. Airlines too have realized the value of people seated for a long time as they travel between cities, and often countries, and thus have introduced their own magazines that often have feature stories on hotels, restaurants, and interesting cultural or outdoor aspects of a particular destination. An added benefit is that featured articles in a magazine can put people in the mood for a particular product class. For example, a feature article on home remodeling in *Better Homes and Gardens* can put people in a frame of mind to consider purchasing wallpaper, carpeting, tiling, draperies, paint, and other home-improvement items. The major disadvantage of using magazines is that the long lead time required prevents advertising with price appeals or any urgency in its messages.

Direct Mail

Direct marketing can be a powerful addition to the retailer's promotional strategy. With direct mail, the retailer can precisely target its message to a particular group as long as a good mailing list of the target population is available. Macy's, for example, uses a customer database to select targeted recipients for each of its roughly 300 annual catalog and promotional mailings. In addition, direct mail provides retailers a personal contact with individual consumers who share certain valued characteristics. Thus, while all of Macy's customers receive the Christmas catalog, only those who recently purchased a men's suit will receive a postcard promoting a sale on shirts and ties. Such messages can reach the consumer without being noticed by the competition. Finally, direct-mail results can generally be easily measured, thus providing the retailer with important feedback.

On the negative side, direct-mail advertising is relatively expensive per contact or message delivered. Also, the ability to reach the target market depends totally on the quality of the mailing list: If the list is not kept current, then advertising dollars will be wasted. For example, the University of Phoenix regularly sends the authors a direct-mail advertisement suggesting that they could further their career prospects if they had a bachelor's degree in business. Given that all three authors already have PhDs, is this an instance of wasted advertisement dollars? A related problem is the incidence of unopened or unexamined mail, especially when it is addressed to "Occupant" or is mailed using third-class postage.

Another key challenge for retailers regarding mailing lists is that the typical U.S. household moves every five years and also family composition changes even though the household address may have not changed. Perhaps five years ago you had a 14-year-old and an 18-year-old at home and their purchasing behavior resulted in them having direct mail advertisements or catalogs sent to them. But today these children are 19 and 23 years old and neither lives with you. Or perhaps you decided to purchase stereo components from an out-of-state electronics store and don't intend to purchase electronic components in the foreseeable future, but you still get a monthly catalog which probably costs well over a dollar to print and mail. Thus, the retailer may be spending $20 annually mailing you catalogs. Finally, have you ever received two or three catalogs from the same retailer at your household? This is often because when you purchased you wrote in a slightly different name; perhaps Sally Martha Rider or S.M. Rider or Sally M. Rider but this is picked up as three customers!

Another negative of traditional direct mail is the increasing quantity of electronic direct mail, which is commonly known as *spam*. Although most Americans tolerate direct-mail solicitations, the infestation of unsolicited e-mail irritates nearly everyone. Currently, spammers and consumer groups are trying to settle this issue out of court without infringing on the spammers' right to free speech and their ability to conduct business. However, it appears that only the legal system will be able to settle this issue.

Internet

As we discussed newspapers, radio, television, magazines, and direct mail, we mentioned the disruptive effect of the Internet over the last decade. Clearly the Internet, with its various social networks ranging from MySpace to Facebook and LinkedIn, Twitter to YouTube, is playing an important role as a way for consumers to establish their identities.[16] While TV ratings and newspaper circulation have declined at an accelerating rate in recent years, Internet traffic is continuing to grow rapidly on a national and global basis. By going to www.Alexa.com, you can keep abreast of the Internet websites with the most traffic, by country and category such as art, health, home, kids, science, shopping, etc. For instance, in early 2012, for the U.S. market, the 10 most heavily used sites included:[17] (1) google.com, (2) facebook.com, (3) youtube.com, (4) yahoo.com, (5) amazon.com, (6) wikipedia.org, (7) ebay.com, (8) twitter.com, (9) linkedin.com, and (10) craiglist.org. Undoubtedly, the Internet must be an important promotional medium for retailers who have Facebook pages and Twitter accounts. Through these Internet options, retailers can send messages of sales and special events to specific people who have opted to receive them. This allows the retailers to stay current, and allows the followers to give instant feedback as well.

A key aspect of the Internet is in its ability to provide information on demand to customers. The communication elements of advertising, sales promotion, and public relations are all strategic options a firm can use when communicating with its various publics. For example, retailers may wish to provide online customers with samples of their advertising on their websites as Scottrade (www.scottrade.com) and The Gap (www.gap.com) have done. Another type of sales promotion occurs when retailers such as Edible Arrangements (www.ediblearrangements.com), Hollister (www.hollisterco.com), Famous Footwear (www.famousfootwear.com), Williams-Sonoma (www.williams-sonoma.com), Six Flags (www.sixflags.com), and Amazon offer online coupons on RetailMeNot.Com (www.retailmenot.com).

A retailer can also use its website to share specific information on its good works through press releases and bylined articles. Other uses include advising investors of financial policies and explaining the firm's position on a social issue. Excellent examples of websites used in this manner are Walt Disney Company (www.disney.com) and Target (www.target.com). In essence, the Internet provides a platform for a retailer to employ a relatively low-cost, integrated marketing-communications mix, thus increasing shareholder value by enhancing the retailer's image by providing a variety of highly specialized information. Southwest Airlines' website (www.southwest.com) provides a good example of a fully integrated marketing-communications mix. Southwest offers online ticketing, investor information, and advertising as well as sales promotions and public-relations materials, thus effectively communicating with all of its relevant publics. Also, the Internet can pay off for smart shoppers. Ebates.com and yub.com, for example, offer visitors a cashback refund when they register on the site and then make purchases at dozens of e-tailers.

Equally important for the e-tailer is the fact that various Internet providers offer many tools to improve the effectiveness of their promotions. A search engine such as Yahoo can not only provide the e-tailer with extremely detailed demographic information about the people who click on its advertisements but also predict the probable response rate to the advertisements. It knows what time of day the advertisements are likely to be most effective, and, increasingly, by analyzing "click streams" on its network, a search engine can spot potential buyers at various stages of the consideration process. In other words, by looking at the billions of user clicks that flow through its servers every day, Yahoo is getting better and better at figuring out that a given pattern—say, a user who's looked up scuba diving on Yahoo Sports, checked out romance movies on Yahoo Entertainment, and compared Key West hotel prices on Yahoo Travel—is interested in taking a trip and is just beginning to think about a purchase. Such information is invaluable to a retailer such as Hyatt. Once Yahoo knows when and where a potential customer is in the trip-buying process, it can serve up the appropriate hotel or resort advertisement.

As the previous discussion highlights, Internet promotions appear to offer retailers many advantages over more traditional media, and this is particularly the case for e-tailers. However, as this chapter's "Retailing: The Inside Story" box points out, traditional bricks-and-mortar retailers do face greater difficulties in effectively implementing an online promotional campaign, particularly if they are wanting the same measurement capabilities afforded to e-tailers. At the moment, many service firms are working to better track the effectiveness of promotional spending by bricks-and-mortar retailers; yet, this is still a somewhat infant technology. While the Internet does afford all retailers the ability to communicate with specific consumers on a more personal and targeted basis, the ability to more definitively track consumer actions from the point of exposure to the point of purchase within a physical retail store is much more limited, particularly for those promotions that are not simply digital coupons or discount codes.

A final point worth considering is that although many retailers believe that consumers are visiting their bricks-and-mortar stores to find the products they like and then going home and buying them from an e-tailer, this often not the case. In fact, Forrester research[18] estimates that the volume of sales in bricks-and-mortar stores as a result

RETAILING — The Inside Story

Online and "Social" Promotion May Represent Fruitful Areas for the Future, But It's Complicated to Say the Least

No one can argue that the Internet, and particularly social networking (or "social"), represents fertile opportunities for retailers seeking to increase their traffic and/or conversion rates through promotion. In order for any promotion to have a chance at success, it must have significant coverage (as defined within this chapter), and the Internet, particularly "social," offers great coverage potential.

A report released at the end of 2011 by Nielsen found that social networking and blogs account for one-quarter of all time spent online. Nearly 80 percent of all Internet users visit social networks, with Facebook being not only the most visited of all social sites as of June 2012 (more than three times as many unique monthly visitors, at 800 million, than the next most popular, Twitter with approximately 250 million, and more than 10 times that of MySpace, 70.5 million, and Google+, 65 million), but also the U.S. website Americans spend the most time on per year.

But the coverage (or even reach—also defined within this chapter) afforded by social and other forms of Internet promotion aren't necessarily enough to ensure a retailer's promotional spending is fruitful, particularly for all but the pure-play e-tailer (one whose entire business occurs online). Sure banner ads and click-through media, particularly those that are *pay-per-click* (PPC) wherein the advertiser (i.e., retailer) only pays for an advertisement once it is clicked, offer great efficiency, but traditional brick-and-mortar retailers can't track promotions via click-through rates. Tracking the metaphorical journey of an online promotion to a physical retail store requires significantly more planning and thought.

One result of the Great Recession of 2009 is that consumers are searching for, "clipping," and redeeming more Internet coupons than ever before; 92 percent more coupons are "clipped" than in the years prior to the recession, and of those clipped, significantly more are actually redeemed within stores (a 360 percent increase in redemption since the end of the recession). This is great for all types of retailers as a recent study by Experian

Marketing Services found that online coupons translate into significantly larger transaction sizes than average. The problem is identifying where the consumer was exposed to the coupon or other promotional materials.

Unless a brick-and-mortar retailer varies the types of coupons or promotional offers across every avenue a potential customer might use to come in contact with the retailer's promotion (e.g., using a 10–percent off coupon on Facebook, a buy-one-get-one-free certificate via email, and a "free alterations" package via Twitter), that retailer will be unable to determine which medium is best for generating the desired action (e.g., sales). Alternatively, the retailer could attach different codes or identifiers to each coupon based upon where the coupon is placed online in order to track where the customer came in contact with the promotion, but as we discuss throughout this chapter, promotions are not simply concerned with discounts and coupons. Greater difficulty for all but the pure-play retailers arises when one wants to understand whether the addition of a new series of banner advertisements on Facebook or blog sites boosts one's sales figures.

For example, True Value Hardware Company had been running a $5-off campaign on all purchases over $25 since 2007, and while the campaign led to significantly larger transaction sizes within its stores (an average of $40 without coupons and $46 with coupons), it was unable to understand which coupon placements were best given particular promotional objectives (e.g., which sites were best to use in order to increase traffic within its downtown, urban stores versus its more rural stores) and which were actually failing to generate significant increases in traffic for the money invested. As a result, True Value turned to RevTrax tracking solutions, whose expertise is tracking and measuring the impact of digital media and promotions for brick-and-mortar retailers. Yet, that is unlikely to be enough in the long-run, particularly if True Value seeks to understand the impact of its non-sales-promotion oriented campaigns.

More recent digital solutions, like ClearSaleing's "Barometer," are beginning to be developed in order to fill perceived gaps left by the existing tracking software systems (e.g., their focus primarily on online couponing and discounts). Introduced at the end of

(continued)

2011, Barometer is one of the earliest software-platforms that seeks to "tease-out" the individual effects of any one marketing or promotional activity with the use of simulation software. Using three individual indices as a base for its software (i.e., economic, social, and firm-specific factors), Barometer controls for general market factors that might increase or decrease a firm's sales in the absence of any promotional activity, and once done, factors in the realized difference in sales to determine the effectiveness of any one promotional campaign. Keeping with the home improvement example, assume that a home-improvement retailer opts to begin a new banner advertising campaign. If the housing market is growing at 2 percent and the retailer's sales are growing at 3 percent, it knows that it is outperforming the market, but it's unlikely to know exactly what portion of the gain is due to the banner advertisements. Barometer seeks to isolate these factors by applying advanced statistics and modeling to the data and calculations and segregating the influence of a company's advertising and marketing efforts from the impact of broader industry and market conditions. Only then can it begin to understand the effectiveness of the banner advertisement itself.

As the preceding discussion highlights, online promotion represents a significant opportunity for retailers in the future, given the dramatic increase in online usage within the United States; however, it does have its pitfalls when it comes to effectively measuring how impactful a retailer's promotional spending is on its bottom line. Retailers of the future will be looking for young and inspiring minds to address these problems, and perhaps you, the reader, will be the one to come up with a better solution.

Sources: Giesen, Lauri (2011), "Rate of Redemption: True Value Tracks Effectiveness of Online Offers," *Stores Magazine (Online)*, November (1); Kroll, Karen M. (2012), "Is It the Economy – Or Your Ad?," *Stores Magazine (Online)*, March (1); Experian Marketing Services, (2008), "The Coupon Report: Benchmark Data and Analysis for Email Marketers," [White Paper]; Reda, Susan (2012), "Social Gets Down to Business: Measurement Remains Elusive, But Growing Influence is Undeniable," *Stores Magazine (Online)*, March (1); Stambor, Zak, (2010) "Consumers 'Clipped' 92% More Coupons From the Web Last Year," Internet Retailer *(Online)*, [Accessed: June 19, 2012] from: http://www.internetretailer.com.

of Internet web search is growing rapidly. In brief it appears that the Internet may be stimulating awareness and interest among consumers but they then want to visit a traditional store to touch and view the merchandise in a more realistic setting and then often follow this with a purchase.

Miscellaneous Media

The retailer can also advertise using media other than those previously identified: Yellow Pages, outdoor advertising and especially billboards, transit advertising (on buses, cabs, and subways), electronic information terminals, specialty firms such as Welcome Wagons, and shopping guides (newspaper-like printed material that contain no news). Each of these is usually best used to reinforce other media and should not be relied on exclusively unless the retailer's advertising budget is minimal. Most retailers look on these media vehicles as geared mainly toward specific product advertising by manufacturers. However, that does not mean a retailer cannot make use of them because a new resident is still going to have to purchase food, clothing, and entertainment.

Media Selection

To select the best media, the retailer needs to remember the strengths and weaknesses of each medium and determine its coverage, reach, and frequency.

Coverage refers to the theoretical maximum number of consumers in the retailer's target market that can be reached by a medium—not the number actually reached. For example, if a newspaper is circulated to 35 percent of the 40,000 households in a retailer's trading area, then the theoretical coverage is 14,000 households.

Reach, on the other hand, refers to the actual total number of target customers who come into contact with the advertisement message. Another useful term is **cumulative reach**, which is the reach achieved over a period of time.

coverage
Is the theoretical maximum number of consumers in the retailer's target market that can be reached by a medium and not the number actually reached.

reach
Is the actual total number of target customers who come into contact with an advertising message.

cumulative reach
Is the reach that is achieved over a period of time.

frequency
Is the average number of times each person who is reached is exposed to an advertisement during a given time period.

cost per thousand method (CPM)
Is a technique used to evaluate advertisements in different media based on cost. The cost per thousand is the cost of the advertisement divided by the number of people viewing it, which is then multiplied by 1,000.

cost per thousand— target market (CPM-TM)
Is a technique used to evaluate advertisements in different media based on cost. The cost per thousand per target market is the cost of the advertisement divided by the number of people in the target market viewing it, which is then multiplied by 1,000.

impact
Refers to how strong an impression an advertisement makes and how well it ultimately leads to a purchase.

Frequency is the average number of times each person who is reached is exposed to an advertisement during a given time period.

Different media can be evaluated by combining knowledge of the advertisement cost for a medium and the medium's reach and cumulative reach. The most commonly used methods for doing this are the **cost-per-thousand method (CPM)** and **cost per thousand–target market (CPM-TM)**. The most appropriate way to compute the CPM is to divide the cost for an advertisement or a series of advertisements in a medium by the total number of people viewing the advertisement. For example, if a newspaper advertisement costs $500 and is distributed to 38,200 households, then the CPM is $13.09 [($500/38,200) × 1,000)]. However, the advertisement may reach only 13,860 customers in the retailer's target market; the cost per thousand for the target market is $36.80 [($500/13,860) × 1,000]. As you can see, CPM-TM only measures members of the retailer's target market who are reached by the advertisement.

Comparing CPM and CPM–TM for different media vehicles can also provide information on their effectiveness. For example, let's compare billboard to cable-television advertising. Let's say that the billboard and cable both cost $1,000 a month and each reaches 1 million consumers. Here the CPM for both is $1.00. However, given the focused nature of cable, the retailer may hit 900,000 in its target market, thus having a $1.11 CPM-TM. The billboard, however, reaches only 500,000 of the retailer's targeted customers and as a result has a CPM-TM of $2.00. Comparing CPM-TMs, we can see that cable television (at $1.11) is more effective than the billboard (at $2.00) for the retail outlet. Thus, a medium such as television may cost more based on CPM, but if it has a significantly better CPM-TM, then it may be the better buy.

Lastly, **impact** refers to how strong an impression an advertisement makes and how well it ultimately leads to a purchase. As a result of the increase in media alternatives and the tendency of consumers to spend a stable amount of time on the various media, targeted advertisements have had a sixfold increase over the last decade.

Scheduling of Advertising

When should a retailer time its advertisements to be received by the consumer? What time of day, day of week, week of month, and month of year should the advertisements appear? No uniform answer to these questions is possible for all lines of retail trade. Rather, the following conventional wisdom should be considered.

1. Advertisements should appear on or right before the days when customers are most likely to purchase. If most people shop for groceries Thursday through Saturday, then grocery store advertisements might appear on Wednesday and Thursday.
2. Advertising should be concentrated around the times when people receive their payroll checks. If they get paid at the end of each month, then advertising should be concentrated at that point.
3. If the retailer has limited advertising funds, then it should concentrate its advertising during periods of highest demand. For example, a muffler-repair shop would be well advised to advertise during drive time on Thursday and Friday when the consumer is aware of his or her problem and has Saturday available for the repair work.
4. The retailer should time its advertisements to appear during the time of day or day of week when the best CPM-TM will be obtained. Many small retailers have discovered the advantages of late-night television.
5. The higher the degree of habitual purchasing of a product class, the more the advertising should precede the purchase time.

Many retailers use advertising to react to crises such as an unexpected buildup of inventory due to slow sales. Of course, in these cases the timing of advertisements is not planned in advance and is an ineffective method of scheduling retail advertising. The preceding rules are only suggestions based on conventional wisdom. Depending on the situation, a retailer may use a different scheduling plan to make the best use of its money. For example, earlier in the chapter it was mentioned that one of the author's retailing mentors suggested advertising when others were not and, to avoid getting lost in the crowd, cutting back on advertisements when competitors were advertising.

Evaluating the Results

Will the advertising produce results? It depends on how well the advertisements were designed and how well the advertising decisions were made. A consistent record of good retail-advertising decision making can be made only if the retailer effectively plans its advertising program.

Some retailers try systematically to assess the effectiveness and efficiency of their advertising. **Advertising effectiveness** refers to the extent to which the advertising has produced the desired result (i.e., helped to achieve the advertising objective). **Advertising efficiency** is concerned with whether the advertising result was achieved with the minimum effort (e.g., dollars). This is one area where new technology is being applied to help retailers better evaluate advertising. For instance, some retailers use eye tracking when people view their advertisements to determine which advertisements will work best. One firm that provides this service is EyeTrackShop (www.eyetrackshop.com), which sends e-mails to selected shoppers, perhaps those who recently purchased or did not purchase. During an online survey, the shopper's webcam captures 10–20 photos of eyes per second. The shopper is then exposed to online advertising, and thus the retailer can determine what elements of the advertising are being noticed. Next shoppers are given a survey which measures, like for the retailer's brand, comprehension of the message and purchase intent.[19]

The effectiveness or efficiency of advertising can also be assessed on a subjective basis. Simply ask yourself: Are you satisfied with the results produced? Do you believe you achieved those results at the least cost? Most but not all ineffective advertising is due to one of 10 errors:

1. The retailer bombarded the consumer with so many messages and sales that any single message or sale tended to be discounted. A retailer that has a major sale every week will tend to wear out its appeal.
2. The advertising was not creative or appealing. It may be just more "me too" advertising in which the retailer does not effectively differentiate itself from the competition.
3. The advertisement didn't give customers all the information they needed. The store hours or address may be absent because the retailer assumes that everyone already knows this information. Or information may be lacking on sizes, styles, colors, and other product attributes.
4. Advertising dollars were spread too thinly over too many departments or merchandise lines.
5. There may have been poor internal communications among salesclerks, cashiers, stock clerks, and management. For example, customers may come to see the advertised item, but salesclerks may not know that the item is on sale or where to find it, and cashiers may not know the sale price. Worst yet, for a variety of reasons, the advertised product may not be available when the consumer seeks to purchase it.
6. The advertisement was not directed at the proper target market.
7. The retailer did not consider all media options. A better buy was available, but the retailer did not take the time to find out about it.

advertising effectiveness
Is the extent to which the advertising has produced the result desired.

advertising efficiency
Is concerned with whether the advertising result was achieved with the minimum financial expenditure.

8. The retailer made too many last-minute changes in the advertising copy, increasing both the cost of the advertisement and the chance for error.

9. The retailer took co-op dollars just because they were "free" and therefore presumably a good deal.

10. The retailer used a medium that reached too many people not in the target market. Thus, too much money was spent on advertising to people who were not potential customers.

LO 4

Explain how retailers manage their sales promotion and publicity.

Management of Sales Promotions and Publicity

Retailers also use sales promotions, which provide some type of short-term incentive, and publicity to increase the effectiveness of their promotional efforts. The role of sales promotions and publicity in the retail organization should be consistent with and reinforce the retailer's overall promotional objectives.

Role of Sales Promotion

Sales promotion tools are excellent demand generators. Many can be used on relatively short notice and can help the retailer achieve its overall promotional goals. Furthermore, sales promotions can be significant in helping the retailer differentiate itself from competitors. Retailers have long known that consumers will change their shopping habits and brand preferences to take advantage of sales promotions, especially those that offer something special, different, or exciting. Recognizing the short-term nature of sales promotions, many retailers now use tweeting (www.twitter.com) to get news of their promotions out to shoppers that follow them on Twitter. Perhaps, you are following some retailers on Twitter, but if not, you might do so to learn more about how retailers are using Twitter for promotional purposes.

Retailers must remember that, since all stores are able to shop the same vendors, merchandise alone does not make a store exciting. In-store happenings of sales promotion can generate excitement. Because of their poor record-keeping systems, many retailers fail to recognize that the role of sales promotion is quite large and may represent a larger expenditure than advertising. They know the cost of advertising because most of that is paid to parties outside the firm. However, the cost of sales promotions often includes many in-store expenses that the retailer does not associate with promotion activities. If these costs were properly traced, then many retailers would discover that sales promotions represent a sizable expenditure. Therefore, promotions warrant more attention by retail decision makers than is typically given.

Types of Sales Promotion

As a rule, successful retailers break sales promotions into two categories: those where they are the sole sponsors and those involving a joint effort with other parties. These are shown in Exhibit 11.6.

Sole-Sponsored Sales Promotions

Just like advertising, sales promotions are an expense to the retailer that may or may not be shared with others. With sole-sponsored sales promotions, the retailer has complete control over the promotion but is also completely responsible for its costs. Although there may be some overlap in the sponsorship of these promotions, retailers generally consider the following sales promotions to be sole sponsored.

Exhibit 11.6
Types of Sales Promotion

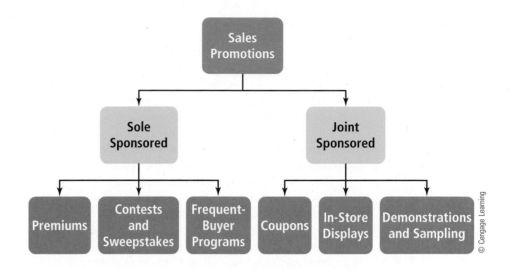

premiums
Are extra items offered to the customer when purchasing promoted products.

contests and sweepstakes
Are sales promotion techniques in which customers have a chance of winning a special prize based on entering a contest in which the entrant competes with others, or a sweepstakes in which all entrants have an equal chance of winning a prize.

loyalty programs
Are a form of sales promotion program in which buyers are rewarded with special rewards, which other shoppers are not offered, for purchasing often from the retailer.

coupons
Are a sales promotion tool in which the shopper is offered a price discount on a specific item if the retailer is presented with the appropriate coupon at time of purchase.

1. **Premiums** are extra items offered to the customer when purchasing a promoted product. Premiums are used to increase consumption among current consumers and persuade nonusers to try the promoted product. Generally, the retailer is solely responsible for such programs, although some exceptions may occur. An example of a successful premium is the free toy McDonald's gives away with the purchase of a Happy Meal.

2. **Contests and sweepstakes**, which face legal restrictions in some states, are designed to create an interest in the retailer's product and encourage both repeat purchases and brand switching. Although such programs usually produce only one grand prize winner, the selection of a prize that will appeal to a large segment of the market and the addition of smaller prizes make such promotions very popular with consumers. Many local restaurants use weekly drawings not only to generate business but also to track their customers.

3. **Loyalty programs**, or frequent-shopper programs, are rapidly growing as retailers realize the importance of combining such promotions with their database systems to solidify their relationships with customers. Some retailers credit loyalty programs for saving their customer base from attack by competitors. Other retailers think the benefits of using these programs are overrated.

Jointly Sponsored Sales Promotions

Jointly sponsored sales promotions offer retailers the advantage of using *other people's money* (OPM). Although in some cases such promotions require the retailer to partially relinquish control, the co-sponsor's monetary offering to the retailer often more than compensates. Retailers generally consider the following promotions to be jointly sponsored.

1. **Coupons** offer the retail customer a discount on the price of a specific item. Roughly 300 billion coupons are distributed annually in the United States, and there are more of them every year, although less than 2 percent of coupons are redeemed. Coupons represent a windfall for retailers worth more than $500 million since they receive, on average, a 10-cent coupon-redemption fee from the manufacturers.

   For manufacturers, a coupon is a form of advertising to entice a consumer to try a product, especially a new product. People may forget their coupon but buy the product anyway because they remember seeing the coupon advertisement. Coupons are also used to maintain a loyal base of customers for older brands such as Kellogg's

Raisin Bran and Wisk, as competitors attempt to get loyalists to switch brands by offering lower prices. However, given the recent downturn in the nation's economy, many retail experts see a shift in the way Americans approach spending money, and the data suggests they're correct. Americans now "clip" almost twice as many online coupons than they did prior to the Great Recession of 2009, and redemption of online coupons, meaning that they were actually *used*, is up over 360 percent.[20]

in-store displays
Are promotional fixtures of displays that seek to generate traffic, highlight individual items, and encourage impulse buying.

endcaps
The display of products placed at the end of an aisle in a store.

register racks
The racks placed near the checkout to encourage impulse buying.

demonstrations and sampling
Are in-store presentations with the intent of reducing the consumer's perceived risk of purchasing a product.

2. **In-store displays** are promotional displays that seek to generate traffic, advertise, and encourage impulse buying. Displays such as **endcaps** (the shelving at the end of an aisle) and **register racks** at checkout stands offer manufacturers a captive audience for their products in the retailer's store. (Remember, the retailer does not care which brand the customer purchases, just as long as the purchase is made in its store.) As a result, the manufacturer is willing to pay for the right to "rent" the space necessary for this display from the retailer.

   Discussions with store managers and vendors indicate that there is a strong correlation between shoppers noticing an in-store promotion and a resulting impulse purchase. However, not all forms of in-store media are equal, nor is the effectiveness the same with different shopper segments. For instance, end-aisle displays and store flyers were the most noticed forms of in-store advertising overall, while shopping cart advertisements and in-store TV advertisements were largely ignored by today's on-the-go shoppers and are viewed by most vendors as a money grab by the retailer.[21] Chapter 13 will provide a greater discussion on in-store displays.

3. **Demonstrations and sampling** are in-store presentations or showings that are intended to reduce the consumer's perceived risk of purchasing a new product. These demonstrations, which accentuate ease, convenience, or product superiority, are paid for by the manufacturer at a price that is usually higher than the retailer's cost for providing that service.

   Joint demonstrations and sampling promotions can be undertaken with entities other than the retailer's suppliers or other retailers. Every spring, retailers, especially

In-store demonstrations are helpful in showing customers how a product can solve problems and fill their needs.

malls, invite landscapers and other lawn-care experts onto their grounds to promote their own merchandise and services because consumers are getting ready to prepare their own lawns for the summer and appreciate the convenience of visiting with all the lawn experts at one location. In addition to bringing merchandise for sale, many lawn professionals also bring samples of their work to place in the mall hallways or parking lot. This is truly a case of using OPM since the retailer and malls bear no expense for this promotion; the lawn-care folks are willing to do it as a form of self-promotion.

Evaluating Sales Promotions

As Exhibit 11.7 indicates, sales promotions are intended to help generate short-term increases in performance. Therefore, they should be evaluated in terms of their sales and profit-generating capability. As with advertising, sales promotions can also be evaluated with sophisticated mathematical models; however, the development and use of such models is usually not cost effective. A simpler approach is to monitor weekly unit volume before the sales promotion and compare it to weekly unit volume during and after the promotion. One area where a retailer can benefit from a more sophisticated method of evaluating sales promotions is when promotions such as coupons are distributed via the Internet on certain websites and/or through social media such as Facebook. There are a variety of companies such as RevTrax (www.revtrax.com), which was discussed in this chapter's "Retailing: The Inside Story" box, that are able to track all of a retailer's digital sales promotions and connect it to store sales. For instance, if a retailer is distributing its coupons through various websites, it can determine if some websites result in a higher redemption. The retailer can also track the average amount spent, as well as from which website the shopper obtained the coupon.[22]

Publicity Management

Publicity was defined at the outset of this chapter as nonpaid-for communications of information about the company or products, generally in some media form; however, this definition is actually misleading because in many instances publicity is a contracted service. An example of this may be the health reports on your local television news program. Sometimes these are, in fact, publicity, but at other times they may be part of the health provider's promotional contract with the station. Even when the retailer does not pay directly for publicity, it can be very expensive to have a good publicity department

Exhibit 11.7
What Sales Promotion Can and Cannot Achieve

Tasks That Sales Promotions Can Accomplish
Get consumers to try a new product
Stimulate the sales of mature products
Neutralize competitive advertising and sales promotions
Encourage repeat usage by current users
Reinforce advertising

Tasks That Sales Promotions Cannot Achieve
Change the basic nonacceptance of an undesired product
Compensate for a poorly trained sales force
Give consumers a compelling reason to continue purchasing a product over the long run
Permanently stop an established product's declining sales trend

that plants commercially significant news in the appropriate places. It may be even more expensive to create news that is worth reporting. Consider Macy's Fourth of July fireworks display in New York, Lowe's and Target's NASCAR sponsorship, McDonald's Ronald McDonald Houses, and Sleepy's "Bedder Days" charitable program to donate mattresses. For instance, Sleepy's, a bedding retailer with over 700 stores, donated more than 50 mattresses to victims of a tornado in Tuscaloosa, Alabama, during April 2011.[23] However, there are few attempts to get publicity that are more expensive, especially if you relate it to the number of stores in the retail chain, than Dee Lincoln's purchase of the crossbreed steer, described earlier in the chapter's "Service Retailing" box. All create favorable publicity, but all are expensive.

Recently, some experts suggested that publicity may be more important to a retailer than advertising. They claim that advertising can only maintain brands that have already been created by publicity. These experts cite examples, such as the Cheese Cake Factory, that have been built with virtually no advertising. Consider the case a few years back when Paris Hilton did an advertisement for Carl's Jr.'s Spicy BBQ Burger. The advertisement generated so much publicity across the country that many called the spicy advertisement nothing more than a naked publicity grab. Yet the media coverage generated was what the restaurant chain wanted. While it is doubtful that publicity is more important than advertising, as these experts claim, these examples do point out the importance of managing your firm's publicity.

Publicity (like other forms of promotion) has its strengths and weaknesses. When publicity is formally managed, it should be integrated with other elements of the promotion mix. In addition, all publicity should reinforce the store's image. Perhaps the major advantages of publicity are that it is objective and credible and appeals to a mass audience. For instance, First Lady Michelle Obama has created considerable publicity for The Gap and H&M when she wears their clothing.

Today, however, the Internet has made it possible for angry consumers to rapidly spread such false stories about any retailers. Unfortunately, only in rare circumstances do retailers ever find out who started the false rumors such as those stating that snakes were found in overcoats, a retailer is selling a cactus filled with a nest of deadly spiders, and another fast-food retailer is slaughtering chickens inhumanely. However, when the originators are located, it can be expensive for them. Recently, for example, Procter & Gamble Co. won a jury award of $19.25 million in a civil lawsuit filed against four former Amway distributors who were accused of spreading false rumors linking the giant manufacturer to Satanism as a means to advance their own business. The distributors were found to have used a voicemail system to tell thousands of customers that part of Procter & Gamble profits went to satanic cults.[24] The most interesting thing about all these falsehoods is that the events related in the stories never actually happened to the people sending you the e-mail, but rather to some "friend of a friend."

For retailers to be able to handle these falsehoods, they must first be aware of them, so it is important for retailers to maintain a systematic program of monitoring the online rumor mill. For many retailers, simply checking general websites such as urbanlegends.com or urbanlegands.about.com may be effective. Remember back in Chapter 3 we pointed out the enormous number of websites with a retailer's name followed by the word *sucks*? These sites begin with the originator's complaints and soon generate both additional complaints and questionable events that, whether true or not, contribute to a negative public perception of the retailer. In other cases, individuals have created websites that work on misspellings of the retailer's name; examples include Untied Airlines: the Most Unfriendly Skies (untied.com) which is aimed at United Airlines and (unitedpackagesmashers.com) which targets United Parcel Service. Others use a play on the retailer's name such as againstthewal.com, which focuses on Walmart.

As a result, successful retailers who want to prevent such behavior have adopted a four-pronged plan:

1. Buy the URLs for their name followed by "sucks.com" or preceded by "ihate." In another example of creative planning, Neiman Marcus owns the "needlessmarkup" website, which takes customers to the regular Neiman Marcus home page.
2. Locate the website's creator and determine why he or she is angry. If possible, apologize and then fix the problem before it irritates others.
3. Tell your side of the story on your own website, as Starbucks has done.
4. When all else fails, take the hate-site creators to court. Many will back away from a costly court battle. The courts will find in favor of the retailer if libel or slander can be proven. There are a couple of legal precedents to keep in mind though. First, the Sixth Circuit Court of Appeals has held that a domain name holder's use of another's trademark in a "fan" site did not run afoul of Section 1114 of the Lanham Act because of the presence of both a prominent disclaimer on the site disavowing any affiliation with the mark owner and a link to the plaintiff's official website. Second, the domain holder's use of the trademarks in conjunction with the word *sucks* in the domain names of non-commercial complaint sites did not violate Section 1114 of the Lanham Act because there was no likelihood of consumer confusion arising from that type of use, and because such speech is protected by the First Amendment of the U.S. Constitution.

Summary

LO 1 **What are the five basic components of the retailer's promotion mix, and how are they related to other retailer decisions?**

A retailer's promotion mix comprises advertising, sales promotions, social media, publicity, and personal selling. All five components need to be managed from a total systems perspective and must be integrated not only with each other but also with the retailer's other managerial decision areas such as location, merchandise, credit, cash flow, building and fixtures, price, and customer service. In addition, the retailer must realize that its promotional activities may be in conflict with the way other supply-chain members use promotion.

LO 2 **What are the differences between a retailer's long-term and short-term promotional objectives?**

A retailer's promotional objectives should be established to help improve both long- and short-term financial performance. Long-term or institutional advertising is an attempt by the retailer to gain long-term benefits by selling the store itself rather than the merchandise in it. Retailers seeking long-term benefits generally have two long-term promotion objectives: creating a positive store image and promoting public service.

Short-term or promotional advertising attempts to bolster short-term performance by using product availability or price as a selling point. The two most common promotional objectives are (1) increasing the patronage of existing customers and (2) attracting new customers.

LO 3 **What seven steps are involved in developing a retail advertising campaign?**

Developing a retail-advertising campaign is a seven-step process: (1) selecting advertising objectives, (2) budgeting for the campaign, (3) allocating budget dollars, (4) designing the message, (5) selecting the media to use, (6) scheduling the advertisements, and (7) evaluating the results.

Student Study Guide

The advertising objectives should flow from the retailer's promotion objectives and should consider several factors that are unique to retailing such as the store's age and location, the merchandise sold, the competition, the size of the market, and the level of supplier support. The specific objectives that advertising can accomplish are many and varied, and the ones chosen depend on these factors.

When developing a budget, retailers must decide whether they can get a better return on their money with co-op dollars or by total sponsorship of advertising. In budgeting advertising funds, retailers tend to use the affordable method, the percentage-of-sales method, or the task-and-objective method. While most retail advertising is paid for solely by the retailer, sometimes manufacturers and other retailers may pay part or all of the costs for the retailer's advertising campaign. For example, vertical cooperative advertising allows the retailer and other supply-chain members to share the advertising burden while horizontal cooperative advertising enables two or more retailers to band together to share the cost of advertising.

In allocating budget dollars, the retailer needs to consider the difference in gross margin percent and advertising elasticity of different merchandise lines or departments and favor those with higher gross margins and high advertising elasticity. Also, it should consider that market share and profitability are positively associated, and thus, in some cases, advertising can be a strategic investment to grow market share. It needs to carefully consider the effect of the advertising on displacing sales that may occur over the next few weeks or months and also may substitute for higher markup merchandise the retailer may normally purchase. Additionally, the retailer needs to make sure it has sufficient backup resources for items it advertises; such as adequate inventory, floor space, and credit availability. Finally, if the retailer can't devote a critical mass of advertising budget to a merchandise line or department, it may be best not to make the advertising investment.

Retailers must develop a creative retail advertisement that accomplishes three goals: attracts and retains attention, achieves its objective, and avoids errors. Some of the common approaches that retailers use to gain repeated viewing include showing how the retailer's products fit in with the consumer's lifestyle, creating a fantasy for the consumer that is built around the retailer's products, designing the campaign around humor that relates to the uses of the retailer's products, depicting the consumer in everyday settings using the retailer's products, and building a mood around using the retailer's products. Before publishing any advertisement, the retailer should test it with both consumer groups and legal experts for errors.

Once the budget is established, it should be allocated in such a way that it maximizes the retailer's overall profitability. In determining allocations, retailers can choose from a variety of media alternatives, primarily newspapers, television, radio, magazines, direct mail, and the Internet. Each medium has its own advantages and disadvantages. To choose among the media, the retailer should know their strengths and weaknesses, coverage and reach, and the cost of an advertisement.

After the retailer selects a medium, it must decide when the advertisement should appear. While there is no single "right" time to run an advertisement, conventional wisdom suggests that the advertisements should (1) appear on or slightly precede the days when customers are most likely to purchase, (2) be concentrated around the times when people receive their payroll checks, (3) be concentrated during periods of highest demand, (4) be timed to appear during the time of day or day of week when the best CPM (or CPM-TM) will be obtained, and (5) precede the purchase time, especially for habitual purchased products.

Advertising results can be assessed in terms of efficiency and effectiveness. Effectiveness is the extent to which advertising has produced the result desired. Efficiency is concerned with whether the result was achieved with minimum cost.

LO 4 ## How do retailers manage their sales promotion and publicity?

Retailers use sales promotions, which provide some type of short-term incentive, and publicity to increase the effectiveness of their promotional efforts. The role of sales promotions and publicity in the retail organization should be consistent with and reinforce the retailer's overall promotion objectives.

Sales-promotion tools are excellent demand generators. Many can be used on relatively short notice and can help the retailer achieve its overall promotion goals. Retailers usually break sales promotions into two categories: those where they are the sole sponsors (premiums, contests and sweepstakes, and loyalty programs) and those involving a joint effort with other parties (coupons, displays, and demonstrations and sampling).

Although retailers may not pay for publicity directly, the indirect cost can be quite significant. Most retailers do not have formal publicity departments or directors, but some of the larger and more progressive retailers do. The major advantages of publicity are that it is objective, credible, and appeals to a mass audience. The major disadvantage is that publicity is difficult to control and schedule.

Terms to Remember

promotion	reach
advertising	cumulative reach
sales promotions	frequency
social media	cost per thousand method (CPM)
publicity	cost per thousand–target market
personal selling	(CPM-TM)
primary trading area	impact
secondary trading area	advertising effectiveness
institutional advertising	advertising efficiency
promotional advertising	premiums
affordable method	contests and sweepstakes
percentage-of-sales method	loyalty programs
task-and-objective method	coupons
vertical cooperative advertising	in-store displays
horizontal cooperative advertising	endcaps
sales displacement	register racks
substitution effect	demonstrations and sampling
coverage	

Review and Discussion Questions

LO 1 ## What are the four basic components of the retailer's promotion mix and how are they related to other retailer decisions?

1. What features should a retailer promote in its advertisements for national branded products? Are these the same features that should be promoted by the retailer for its private-label products?

2. Why are the desired promotional outcomes for other members of a retailer's supply chain different from the retailer's promotional goals? Isn't the marketing supply chain supposed to be a partnership?

LO 2 | **What are the differences between a retailer's long-term and short-term promotional objectives?**

3. Explain how a long-term promotional objective can affect the firm over the short run.
4. What do you think is the most important short-term objective for a retailer: increase patronage from existing customers or attract new customers? Explain the reasoning behind your answer.

LO 3 | **What seven steps are involved in developing a retail advertising campaign?**

5. Why don't retailers list "increasing sales" as their number-one advertising objective?
6. Describe the three methods available to the retailer for determining the amount to spend on advertising. Which one is the best one to use? Which one is most commonly used by small retailers?
7. Some retailers decline a vendor's offer of cooperative advertising; is this smart? After all, aren't they passing up "free" money?
8. An old proverb claims, "Doing advertising without planning is like running a giant manure spreader; your advertising department throws words out the back faster than you can shovel money in the front." Do you agree or disagree with this statement? Explain your reasoning.
9. How does the gross margin percent and advertising elasticity for a merchandise line influence how much a retailer should budget for advertising?
10. From the creative standpoint, it is said that a retail advertisement should accomplish three goals. What are these goals, and is one of these more important than the others?
11. How should a small-town retailer use the Internet?

LO 4 | **How do retailers manage their sales promotion and publicity?**

12. What is sales promotion? How is it different from advertising?
13. What is publicity? Isn't this always free to the retailer? How does publicity fit into a retailer's promotional efforts?
14. What can retail managers do to prevent bad publicity about their stores from circulating on the Internet?

Sample Test Questions

LO 1 | Which of the following areas should not be taken into consideration by a retailer when formulating a promotional strategy?

    a. the retailer's credit customers
    b. the price level of the merchandise
    c. merchandise inventory levels
    d. the retailer's building and fixtures
    e. the retailer's net worth

LO 2 | The two objectives of institutional advertising include:

    a. creating a positive store image and public-service promotion.
    b. increasing patronage from existing customers and attraction of new customers.
    c. publicity and sales promotion.
    d. advertising a sale and generating store traffic.
    e. using other people's money and using co-op money.

LO 3 Which of the following should not be part of The Campus Shoppe's advertising campaign's objectives. "The Campus Shoppe desires to increase awareness

    a. of its two locations

    b. among incoming freshmen

    c. to 40 percent

    d. over the next three months."

    e. All the above belong in the retailer's advertising objectives.

LO 4 Consumer premiums are considered to be a form of:

    a. joint-sponsored sales promotion

    b. publicity that utilizes OPM

    c. advertising

    d. personal selling

    e. sole-sponsored sales promotion

Writing and Speaking Exercise

Most airline, hotel and motel, and even car-rental companies offer special discounts to large groups traveling together or going to the same location for a conference, meeting, or convention. These special discounts are made available by assigning a special code for the group members to use when making reservations. For example, in August 2012, if an individual had gone to the shopping-center meeting in Las Vegas, American Airline's special 25-percent to 30-percent discount code was Star #SZ9Z1K1, and the Delta code was File #ZX232. An individual attending the apparel market in Dallas during the same time period would be given different airline codes but be offered a similar discount. In addition, if some apparel buyers had desired to rent a car, they could have used code 79242, Group G3, at Hertz for an extra discount. These travel companies, however, don't want members of the general public to be able to use their codes to reduce travel costs.

Over the summer, you interned at a travel agency that obtained access to these codes and used them to generate a substantial sales increase by publishing an e-mail newsletter featuring an extensive list of locations and dates when these discounts were available. The customers could only take advantage of these discounts by purchasing their tickets and hotel and car reservations through your travel agency. Several airlines objected to this action, but since the recession had reduced their traffic, they let the travel agency continue to use the discounts. Besides, it was because of this additional business that the agency was able to hire you for the summer.

One night you were telling your mother about this situation, and she asked if you were happy about it happening. How would you answer her?

Retail Project

If you don't subscribe to GROUPON, register on their website (www.groupon.com). Study all of the coupons being offered by retailers in your area and evaluate if you believe these coupons are creating any sales displacement or substitution. Write up a short report (no more than two pages) on this topic for two local retailers and their use of GROUPON.

Planning Your Own Entrepreneurial Retail Business

Your Uncle Nick has agreed to sell you his supermarket where you have worked for seven years since graduating from college. Uncle Nick is 72 years old and is ready to step down from day-to-day management.

After operating the Crest Supermarket on your own for six months, you begin to analyze how you can increase store traffic and, consequently, annual sales and profitability. During a recent trip to the Food Marketing Institute convention, you ran across several successful grocers. Some of them competed largely on price, while others competed more on promotion and advertising.

You decide to pursue a heavy promotion-oriented strategy. Consequently, you budget to increase advertising by $20,000 monthly or $240,000 annually and to also have a weekly contest where you give away $100 in groceries to 25 families. This will cost you $130,000 (52 × $100 × 25) annually.

Currently, Crest Supermarket serves a trade area with a 2-mile radius and a household density of 171 per square mile. Seventy percent of these households shop at Crest an average of 45 times per year. Of those that visit Crest, 98 percent make a purchase that averages $24.45. Crest operates on a 25-percent gross margin.

You estimate that with your new promotion program, the radius of Crest's trade area will increase to 2.5 miles. Assuming that all other relevant factors remain constant (171 households per square mile, 70 percent of households shop Crest, 98-percent closure rate, $24.45 average transaction size, 25-percent gross margin percent), is the planned promotion program and investment of an additional $370,000 (annually) a profitable strategy?

(Hint: Assume the trade area is circular and thus its size in square miles can be computed as pi (3.142) times the radius of the circle squared. The total square miles of the trade area can be multiplied by the number of households per square mile to obtain total households in the trade area. This in turn can be multiplied by the percentage that shop at Crest, which in turn can be multiplied by the average number of trips annually to Crest, which will yield total traffic. This traffic statistic can be multiplied by the percent of visitors that make a purchase, which will yield total transactions. You should be able to figure out on your own the rest of the computations that are needed to determine if the promotional strategy is profitable.

© Sarunyu_foto/Shutterstock

CASE

The Bandanna

The following letter was sent to a mall recently.

Alison Stiles
5319 Walnut Hill Drive
Indianapolis, Indiana 46202
aestiles@hotmail.com
October 4, 2011

To Whom It May Concern:

Last weekend, I drove four hours from my home in Indianapolis, Indiana, to visit my boyfriend, a grad student at Washington University, St. Louis. It wouldn't have been a noteworthy trip, except that the last time I came to St. Louis I ended up at Barnes-Jewish Hospital for a week with a dangerous infection—I have breast cancer and am undergoing chemotherapy, so my immune system is not what it once was. After that scare I decided to wait until my immune system was up before making the trip again. I had my final infusion last month, the drugs ran their course, and so at long last I packed my weekend bag. My bag probably has a somewhat different style than most women with breast cancer—mine is usually filled with low-rise jeans and baby-tees. Did I mention that I'm 29? I'm 29.

Like most other women with breast cancer, my hair called it quits when the chemotherapy started. So, I'm a hip bald chick. I'll admit that around friends and family I'm pretty comfortable showing scalp, but in public I try to cover up—fewer stares that way. But, I've found that most traditional headscarves and hats cramp my style. I prefer a simple bandanna. Classic.

On the Saturday of my grand return to St. Louis, my boyfriend and I hit the town. We did some shopping, visited the Landing, saw the Arch, and then were going to cap off a great day with a trip to Riverside. I was having a perfect day—the kind of day when I can forget, for a few hours or so, that I am 29 and have cancer. That day, I was just a normal, healthy 29-year-old visiting her boyfriend.

We had been wandering around Riverside Mall for about a half an hour or so when I was approached by a security guard. At first I didn't realize he was speaking to me—my boyfriend and I had been waiting for the show at the Fudgery to begin, not bothering anyone, not creating anything resembling a disturbance. Why would he be speaking to me? Once he got my attention, he told me that I would have to take off my bandanna.

And then—whomp!—I remembered. I have cancer. Reality. I took a step towards him and, trying not to draw attention, lifted the bandanna just enough that he could see the few wisps of hair left on my scalp. I then had to say the words I have come to hate: "I have cancer."

I thought that would be enough; that he might apologize and leave me be. But he didn't. He told me that my condition didn't matter—there were no bandannas allowed. Never mind that I have never been asked to remove my chosen headwear before; not anywhere in Indianapolis, not anywhere in Chicago; not anywhere in Louisville. If I wanted to continue wearing it I would have to put on a medical bracelet. He very kindly offered to have a bracelet provided to me for my bandanna-wearing purposes.

So, now I was 29, had cancer, and was being tagged. Don't get me wrong; I can guess why bandannas are prohibited mall attire. I would imagine it would have something to do with gangs and gang violence. Now, St. Louis may have a problem with gang violence of which I am unaware. But I am aware that those of us in the "Breast Cancer Gang" are less inclined to violence than your average gang member. We're a rather peaceful bunch, really. Something about the unending fatigue, the humiliation of losing much of your dignity (not to mention your hair), and the regular vomiting just drives the urge to hurt others right out of you.

Which is why, when I felt the tears in my eyes at the thought of having to put on a stupid medical bracelet to walk through a stupid mall instead of taking out the months of humiliation, loss of dignity, frustration, fear, and plain old anger out on the guard who was just trying to enforce a policy that he didn't institute but was paid to enforce, I left your mall. But I also promised myself that I would never, ever return—and that I would send out this letter voicing how the experience made me feel. An overreaction? Maybe. But, the way I see it, I've already had to put up with quite a lot. Arbitrary and ineffective mall rules cross the line. And, I hate to say it, but in my mind St. Louis is no longer the city I thought I knew. I grew up in St. Louis, but now instead of thinking of the old neighborhood and the Arch and the Botanical Gardens and the Cardinals, I'll think of cancer and gangs and insensitivity, all thanks to the policies of a place which calls itself "the number one attraction in St. Louis."

Ironically, October is "Breast Cancer Awareness Month." And believe me, I am aware. I hope that others become aware, too, and that the proud women who follow me in treatment and survival wear whatever they damn well please on their bald heads and go wherever they damn like. I hope Riverside and any other public place which has any policy against any type of headwear rethinks that policy, or at least makes an exception for women who are engaged full-time with a battle for their lives and have other things to worry about. And, I hope that someday, no woman will have to say at any age, to a mall security guard or anyone else, "I have cancer."

Sincerely,
Alison Stiles

cc: Riverside Mall
Mayor Francis G. Slay
KSDK-TV, St. Louis
Fox 2, St. Louis
St. Louis Post Dispatch
Susan G. Komen Foundation
Young Survival Coalition
American Cancer Society

The mall responded with the following e-mail letter.

From: "Stacy Barnes" <stacybarnes@stlus.com>
To: <aestiles@hotmail.com>
Subject: response letter
Date: Tuesday, 14 Oct 2011 16:37:42 -0500

Dear Ms. Stiles,

Thank you for expressing your thoughts and concerns regarding our code of conduct. We appreciate your comments and regret any hard feelings.

It is important that you know that our primary goal at Riverside Mall is to offer a safe and comfortable shopping environment for all of our visitors. We are committed to treating our shoppers in a fair, consistent, and sensitive manner and are upset that you felt that you were treated unfairly.

Our policy was put in place five years ago to ensure the safety of our more than 6 million shoppers annually, and this is the first time that a reaction of this type has occurred. The policy is quite specific in its language so that it addresses only those types of apparel that are worn to support gang activity. Unfortunately, your head covering fell into that category. The dress code does have an exception for those with medical conditions, such as yourself.

In an effort to accommodate every person and every kind of situation with sensitivity, when those with medical conditions such as cancer are stopped for non-compliance with the dress code, they are asked to wear a small wristband to enable them to continue to shop without being stopped again by the public safety officers. The intention is not to single out any individual, but to avoid any further interruption to your visit.

We regularly review the policies and the code to make sure they are up to date and are appropriate for the current environment.

We thank you again for your comments and we assure you that we will review our policies in the near future with your situation in mind.

Sincerely,

Stacy
Stacy L. Barnes
Marketing Director
Riverside Mall
314-555-5555 ext. 7032
314-555-5556 fax

Questions

1. If you were the marketing director for a retailer and received such a letter, would you have replied the same way as Ms. Barnes?

2. Does a retailer's imposition of hard and fast rules cause bad public relations? (After all, a breast cancer victim wearing a bandanna could hardly be mistaken for a gang member. The lack of hair, missing eyelashes, and a general pale complexion should have been a clue.)

3. Since the press was copied on Ms. Stiles' letter, should the mall copy them on its reply?

Note: While the names of the individuals, date and the mall have been changed, everything else is as it occurred.

Customer Services and Retail Selling

12

Overview

In this chapter, we demonstrate how customer services, including retail selling, generate additional demand for the retailer's merchandise and services. We also examine the determination of an optimal customer-service level. We conclude the chapter by looking at the unique managerial problems that retailers must address.

Learning Objectives

After reading this chapter, you should be able to:

1 Explain why customer service is so important in retailing.

2 Describe the various customer services that a retailer can offer.

3 Explain how a retailer should determine which services to offer.

4 Describe the various management problems involved in retail selling, salesperson selection, training, compensation, and evaluation.

5 Describe the retail selling process.

6 Understand the importance of a customer service audit.

LO 1

Explain why customer service is so important in retailing.

Customer Service

The old rules about customer loyalty are obsolete. Today's customers are tired of making a series of wishes (see the shopper's wish list in Exhibit 12.1) before embarking on their planned purchases. Customers instead define loyalty on their terms, not those of the retailer. Little wonder, then, that the average retailer is expected to lose half of its customers every five years. Further, even those customers who continue to shop with a particular retailer are not always loyal. Many routinely cross shop several retailers offering the same, or similar merchandise, in hopes of finding a better customer service experience than that which they are currently receiving. Without exception, it is a fact of life that all retailers must give consideration to the service level and services they offer their customers.

high-quality service
Is the type of service that meets or exceeds customers' expectations.

Delivering **high-quality service** means delivering service that meets or exceeds customers' expectations. Note that this definition mentions no absolute level of quality service. Instead, only service that meets and exceeds the expectations of customers is considered high quality. For example, suppose a consumer has lunch at a restaurant where he or she expects to have slow service but is instead served in 10 minutes. The next day at lunch, the same consumer eats at another restaurant where he or she expects to have fast

Exhibit 12.1

A Shopper's Wish

Please …

- Let me find a parking place near the store.
- Do not let me pay too much.
- Have the sales staff pretend that they care.
- Do not make me have to return anything.
- Get me in and out as fast as possible.
- Do not make me wait in line to make my purchase.
- Let this experience be somewhat enjoyable.
- Do not make me have to deal with other obnoxious shoppers.

service and again is served in 10 minutes. Even assuming that other factors such as cleanliness, friendliness, and food quality are equal, this consumer might report the service quality to be better in the first restaurant, because the 10-minute service was faster than expected, and report lower service quality in the second restaurant, because the 10-minute service was slower than expected. On an absolute basis, the service was the same in each case—good food in 10 minutes—but the customer's evaluation was different due to different expectations.

It's important for the the student not to infer from the previous discussion that high-quality service is necessarily time-sensitive (i.e., that providing a service faster will always be a good thing). In fact, there are many instances wherein quicker service provision may ruin the customer's experience entirely. Instead, customer service is *context dependent*.

When you visit a fine-dining restaurant like Smith and Wollensky steakhouse, what are you expecting? How much personal service is appropriate when your dinner bill is likely to hit $200–300? Do you expect to have your food delivered to your table immediately as if it were already prepared, or do you anticipate waiting a little bit in order to get the food cooked exactly like you wish? How long are you likely to spend relaxing and conversing at the table with your guests following the meal?

As the preceding questions highlight, 10-minute service may be perceived as a highly unsatisfactory "rush job" when dining at a fine-dining establishment because it prevents you from visiting with friends, enjoying your meal, and relishing the experience. What the customer is paying for when they seek out fine-dining restaurants is an experience, and slow-paced dining is a positive value proposition in such a context.

Another illustration of this concept occurs when customers have a problem with a purchase. When problems are handled swiftly and politely (above their expectations), customers will end up being more loyal to the retailer than those who never encountered a problem. The bottom line then in retailing is: *always strive to meet or exceed customer service expectations*.

Remember back in the previous chapter when we quoted one of the author's mentors as saying that when business slowed and all his competitors reduced their ad budgets, he would then increase his ad expenditures? After all, without the clutter of competitors' ads, consumers became more aware of his ads and his sales increased, despite the general sales slowdown affecting the other local merchants. The same thing can be said about customer service. In 2008, as the economy plunged into the Great Recession, many retailers felt forced to trim costs, often cutting services so deeply that they drove away customers. However, as this chapter's "Retailing: The Inside Story" box points out, successful retailers, like the Waffle House, Nordstrom, and Amazon.com, who are often cited as providing high levels of customer service, safeguarded their competitive positions within their respective industries by maintaining their pre-recession service levels.[1]

Service is context dependent. When eating at a fast-food restaurant, 10-minute service may be desired; however, at a fine-dining establishment it would be seen as unsatisfactory by customers.

relationship retailing
Comprises all the activities designed to attract, retain, and enhance long-term relationships with customers.

One way in which retailers provide the high-quality service expected and reduce customer defections is through relationship retailing programs.[2] **Relationship retailing** includes all the activities designed to attract, retain, and enhance customer relationships. Retailing is no longer driven by the expansion of large, homogeneous, big-box chains offering only low prices. Profitable retailers of the future will be those who concentrate on building long-term relationships with customers by promising, and consistently delivering, high-quality products backed by high-quality service, shopping aids to ease the purchase process, and honest pricing to build and maintain a reputation for absolute trustworthiness. After all, loyal customers are less prone to shop other retailers selling the same

RETAILING — The Inside Story

"Waffling" on the Yield Management Trend

Pun intended, the Waffle House has "waffled" when it comes to the growing trend among restaurants to adopt yield management techniques designed to minimize the amount of servers and staff on duty during "nonpeak" times. And Waffle House management sees this action, or perhaps more appropriately stated, in-action, as one of the keys to their success and exemplary service record.

The dictionary defines the act of "waffling" as acting evasively toward, or avoiding, something or someone, and that's exactly what the Waffle House has done when it comes to the, sometimes die-hard, adherence that so many other restaurant chains have to the yield management principles of scheduling restaurant staff only when peak patronage is expected. As the United States and the global economy struggle to rebound from the Great Recession of 2008–2009, restaurants and other retailers are increasingly incentivized to identify any area(s) representing that proverbial "fat" to be trimmed from the budget. One area on many restaurants' radar is the number of employees "on the clock" during slower periods of the day and week. Many are the restaurants that schedule a bare-bones staff during all but the peak dinner and lunch rushes or "cut" wait-staff immediately upon realization that customer levels during a particular shift are not in line with what was expected. It's quite likely that many of the readers of this box have been "cut" at least once during a shift.

From a cost-management perspective, such techniques of closely monitoring one's sales and service staff makes sense; retailers need not waste money on employees standing around assisting no one. Yet a service-oriented perspective, like that of the Waffle House, suggests such actions can leave the firm vulnerable to inadequate and improper service provision.

As we've discussed repeatedly throughout the text thus far, every retailer is essentially selling a *service*, not a product; the same is true at the Waffle House. Sure when you go to a Waffle House, you're expecting excellent eggs, cooked just like you like, alongside hash browns, bacon, toast, and a waffle, but there are many breakfast retailers out there; you likely select the Waffle House due to their speed (ideally less than 20 minutes), courteousness, convenience, and quality. And Waffle House management realizes that a bare-bones staff impedes the restaurant's ability to offer that quality meal *with speed*.

Yes, the Waffle House keeps diligent records of sales per day, week, and month. And yes, they use this information to plan their seasonal staffing needs. For instance, can you guess the busiest day of the year for a Waffle House? Christmas day. Assuredly, your local Waffle House will have a full staff on hand every Christmas morning. But what it won't do is "cut" servers the next day afternoon when customer numbers appear low; they'll maintain their staff levels to ensure that every customer who walks into the restaurant will be greeted, seated, served, and checked-out *on time* (approximately 20 minutes or less). The retailer has strict standards for all such actions, and they're unwilling to become vulnerable to lapses in service quality simply due to the added cost associated with keeping an employee "on the clock" when demand varies from expected.

For a firm who has little a budget for formal promotions and does not advertise on television, word-of-mouth is crucial. Have a bad experience, and you'll likely tell everyone you know. The Waffle House's major tool for driving traffic to their restaurants is word-of-mouth advertising; they bank on *your* communication of a great experience. And the facilitator of that great experience is a fully staffed restaurant waiting to take your order and get you in-and-out in less than half an hour with a full stomach and a smile on your face.

Source: Based on personal discussions a few of the authors have had with Waffle House managers while eating breakfast (of course).

merchandise mix and are less price conscious.[3] In addition, a U.S. Department of Commerce's Office of Consumer Affairs study found that it costs a retailer five times more money to attract a new customer as it does to convince a former customer to return.[4]

As a result of the preceding trends, today's retailers are not trying to maximize the profit on each transaction but are instead seeking to build a mutually beneficial relationship with their customers. Consider what retailers can learn from the hotel industry about relationship retailing. High-end hotels like the Ritz-Carlton are dedicated to not only meeting customers' needs, but also *anticipating* them prior to travelers' arrivals. Each day, hotel staff, from those at the front desk to those in housekeeping and even maintenance, discreetly observe and record even the smallest of guest preferences. Then every morning, management and staff review the files of all new arrivals who have previously stayed at a Ritz-Carlton and prepare a list of suggested "extra touches" for each guest, from knowing whether one needs a nonallergenic pillow, to how one likes the blinds positioned, and what type of coffee one's most likely to drink. In fact, if management can get a hold of a picture of a guest's pet, it will make a copy, frame it, and have it displayed in the guest's room prior to arrival.[5] Or consider Harrah's, the well-known casino gaming retailer from Las Vegas. Harrah's has one of the most sophisticated relationship retailing programs in existence. It not only knows a lot about each of its frequent patrons (gamblers), but if you are new to Harrah's, it also can predict fairly accurately your behavior. For instance, Harrah's has found that women gamble more frequently than men, and women who are older will gamble more than any other demographic group.[6]

Harrah's Casino does an outstanding job with it relationship retailing programs by providing special incentives and personal services to its frequent patrons.

customer relationship retailing
An integrated information system which uses relevant information about the customer to predict future behavior and customer manage relationships.

Most often, supporting relationship retailing is an information technology infrastructure that the industry refers to as **customer relationship management (CRM).** CRM is composed of an integrated information system in which the fundamental unit of data collection is the customer; supplemented by other relevant information about the customer, including purchasing behavior, demographics, customer complaints, and often more. However, keep in mind that if you are a small entrepreneurial retailer, you probably don't need to initially invest in an expensive CRM system. We know of one enterprising young pizza restaurant entrepreneur who catered to the community around a major college campus. Note that this was 40 years ago, long before desktop computers, but nonetheless, this entrepreneur had a small file box with a card for each customer, organized by city blocks, apartment buildings, and dormitories. For each customer, there were notes such as days of the week and time of day he or she ordered pizza. This entrepreneur had a growing home delivery service. When he would get a phone call for a pizza, say at 5:30 p.m. on Wednesday night from Charlie at 830 Adams Street, he would quickly look at his file of city blocks and call other frequent customers on Adams Street who had a tendency to order pizza on Wednesday night and mention to them "we are delivering a pizza in your neighborhood and wanted to call to see if you wanted us to also prepare one for you." This retailer not only increased his business, he also better controlled his home delivery costs. Today, small retailers could set up a similar system on their computers with relative ease.

In using CRM systems, there is an important lesson for retailers to remember: *Keep your firm's mission in mind* when evaluating and adopting a CRM program. For instance, if you are a retailer who emphasizes everyday low prices (EDLP), then you want your CRM program to help you have merchandise in-stock at all times.[7] If you are not a price-oriented retailer and focus more on nonprice value propositions, then your CRM program may have a different purpose. Crabtree & Evelyn, the skin-care and home accessories chain, learned the importance of never forgetting the firm's

Crabtree & Evelyn's CRM program has evolved from a "one-size-fits-all" program into one that specifically targets and rewards different loyalty customers.

mission after its early CRM and loyalty program treated all regular customers the same and offered them special price discounts and rewards the first week of each month, regardless of when or how often they shopped the store. Today, Crabtree & Evelyn's CRM program has matured, and now it is able to more finely cluster or segment and specifically target customers by focusing on an element of surprise with more indulgence-based, special experiences such as a free short massage.[8]

The new operating maxim for all the retailers should be: "Proper management of relationships will produce a satisfied customer who will become a repeat customer. And repeat customers produce long-term profits." Leo Shapiro, a well-known retail consultant, claimed that the "dollars that walk out of a store every day to be spent at a competitor's store represent the most immediate, major source of potential sales and profit growth."[9] Robert Kahn, another retail consultant discussed earlier in the text, often argued that just reducing the amount of customer defections by as little as 10 percent can often double a retailer's profits. However, in what was probably the most powerful statement about the importance of customer relationships, one executive of a leading discount mass merchandiser told the authors that the loss in future revenues to the chain from losing just one customer would exceed $200,000.[10] One sad note about customer service is that while modern retailing is spreading around the world, creating new retail stores may prove to be far easier than establishing good sales skills. Surliness, odd policies, and slow service appear to be common complaints in underdeveloped markets, especially from expatriates who are used to more customer-friendly policies.[11] Also, retailers that expand too quickly often find that they are not able to keep up with the need for more assistant managers and store managers as stores open. In fact, this was one of the reasons Starbucks, several years ago, intentionally slowed growth of store openings; it allowed them to focus more on customer service and training the entire management and worker team to focus on the customer. Chapter 14 places a lot of emphasis on customer-centric retailing and how to build long-term relationships with customers.

Profitable retailers can develop these relationships with their customers by offering two general types of benefits: financial and social.

1. *Financial benefits* increase the customer's economic rewards. Examples are the frequent-purchaser discounts or product upgrades already offered by some supermarkets, airlines, and hotels.
2. *Social benefits* increase the retailer's interaction with the customer. Chapter 13 will discuss how shopping can be a pleasant experience for the customer. Retailers must not forget that their stores must offer benefits other than economic but offer only those that customers desire. Thus, for some stores, such as a high-end women's apparel store, customers may want an exciting and pampered shopping experience. Whereas, for a retail banking transaction, many customers may want an experience where all of the little details simply work well, such as the line being short, forms easy to fill out, and tellers polite and knowledgeable. Or, as one analyst put it, some shoppers may want your store to simply bore them to death by getting all of the little distractions removed that characterize bad service and then deliver boring but accurate and high-quality customer service.

Exhibit 12.2 highlights the three basic tasks or activities that every retailer must perform in order to simply have a chance at success. These tasks were first mentioned in Chapter 3: get consumers from your trading area into your store, convert these consumers into loyal customers, and do so in the most efficient manner possible. Chapter 7 described how retailers determine their trading area. The earlier chapters of Part 4, Chapters 8 through 11, discussed the first task: how retailers budget for and select their merchandise and then price and promote this merchandise. In addition, Chapter 8 covered the third task by describing the basic method for controlling inventory cost. The next two chapters

Exhibit 12.2
Three Basic Tasks
of Retailing

1 Get Consumers into Your Store

2 Convert Them into Customers

3 Operate As Efficiently as Possible

© Cengage Learning

will focus upon the second and most important task: converting the consumer from your trading area who has decided to try your store into a loyal (and thus profitable) customer.

As you examine Exhibit 12.2, we want you to also recognize that better customer service has a positive effect on each of the three basic tasks of retailing. When a retailer establishes its reputation around great customer service, that retailer will actually expand its trade area, which will lead to higher customer traffic. Also, great customer service will result in better addressing customers' needs, which increases a retailer's closure rate, as well as the average transaction size. Finally, as a retailer focuses more on the customer and on exceeding the customer's needs, retailing errors (e.g., wrong merchandise, poor quality merchandise, merchandise stocked on the wrong shelf, etc.) decrease, which in turn decreases the costs associated with correcting an error, which naturally increases the retailer's overall efficiency. Exhibit 12.3 illustrates this process.

Yet due to the overstoring of the North American market and the rapid growth of e-tailing, the second task (converting consumers into customers) has become even more difficult. Retailers today are so standardized in either their physical layout or website design, with each one carrying the same merchandise styles and colors, that customers often cannot tell them apart. More importantly, many current retailers have either a nonexistent sales force or an indifferent and undertrained sales force. As a result, there is a complete breakdown of what is essential for a retailer to succeed: providing exciting merchandise backed up by outstanding service and personal selling that generates loyal customers. In recent years, intense competition from discounters has caused many retailers to lower customer-service levels as a means of staying price competitive. These

Exhibit 12.3
Influence of Customer
Service on Profitability

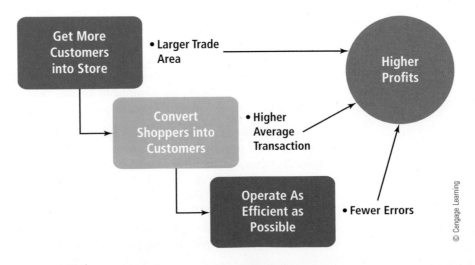

Get More Customers into Store

• Larger Trade Area

Convert Shoppers into Customers

• Higher Average Transaction

Operate As Efficient as Possible

• Fewer Errors

Higher Profits

© Cengage Learning

retailers felt that reduced service levels would lower their operating costs, thus allowing increased price competitiveness. For most customers, it is no wonder that shopping trips do not always meet their expectations and result in an unsatisfying experience.[12]

Retailers must differentiate themselves by meeting the needs of their customers better than the competition. Thus, successful retailers have again come to realize that customer service is a key source of competitive strength and advantage. Instead of frustrating the customer by not having the necessary merchandise on hand or the proper selling support on the sales floor, today's profitable retailers realize that customer service is a major demand generator. However, it is important that retailers also remember that when they encourage high customer expectations, the slightest disappointment in service can be a catastrophe. Even Nordstrom, the retailer most famous for its outstanding service, cannot please all its customers all the time. One blog quoted an unhappy customer as saying, "I ordered a jacket two weeks ago when it just went on sale. I called in and they said that there is one left in my size so I ordered it. The shipping came super fast, like in three days, however when I got my package it says it was a pair of men's pants. I was so confused as I did not order anything else from there but the jacket. I opened my package and it was a SKIRT!!!"[13] In this case, the Nordstrom salesperson probably made a mistake, causing the retailer to fail to live up to the very high expectations that it had trained its customers to expect. However, the retailer corrected the mistake, and most other bloggers praised the Seattle-based retailer not only for its great service but also for going the extra mile in solving their problems.

Customer service consists of all those activities performed by the retailer that influence (1) the ease with which a potential customer can shop or learn about the retailer's offering, (2) the ease with which a transaction can be completed once the customer attempts to make a purchase, and (3) the customer's satisfaction with the transaction. These three elements are the *pretransaction*, *transaction*, and *posttransaction* components of customer service. Some common services provided by retailers include alterations, fitting rooms, delivery, gift registries, check cashing, in-home shopping, extended shopping hours, gift wrapping, charge accounts, parking, layaway, and merchandise-return privileges. It must be remembered that none of these services are altruistic offerings; they are all designed to entice the customers with whom the retailer is seeking to develop a relationship. After all, successful retailers don't try to satisfy customers just because customers deserve it. Rather, they do it because "firms that actually achieve high customer satisfaction also enjoy superior economic returns."[14]

Retailers should design their customer-service program around the pretransaction, transaction, and posttransaction elements of the sale in order to obtain a differential advantage. After all, in today's world of mass distribution, most retailers have access to the same merchandise, so retailers can seldom differentiate themselves from others solely on the basis of merchandise stocked. The same can be said regarding location and store-design advantages. Retailers can, however, obtain a high degree of differentiation through their customer-service programs.

A retail shopping experience is more than negotiating your way through the retailer's store, website, or catalog; finding the merchandise you want; interacting (or not interacting) with the staff; and paying for the merchandise. It also involves your actions before and after the transaction. Therefore, serving the customer before, during, and after the transaction can help to create new customers and strengthen the loyalty of current customers. If customer service before the transaction is poor, then the probability of a transaction occurring will decline. If customer service is poor at the transaction stage, then the customer may back out of the transaction. And if customer service is poor after the transaction, then the probability of a repeat purchase at the same store will decline. The customer who visits a retailer and finds the service level below expectations

customer service
Consists of all those activities performed by the retailer that influence (1) the ease with which a potential customer can shop or learn about the store's offering, (2) the ease with which a transaction can be completed once the customer attempts to make a purchase, and (3) the customer's satisfaction with the transaction.

transient customer
Is an individual who is dissatisfied with the level of customer service offered at a store or stores and is seeking an alternative store with the level of customer service that he or she thinks is appropriate.

or the product out of stock will become a **transient customer**. This transient, or temporary, customer will seek to find a different retailer with the level of customer service he or she feels is appropriate. At any given moment, for all lines of retail trade there are a significant number of transient customers. And, increasingly these transient customers are using their smartphones or tablet computers to find new places to shop, and, of course, Internet banner ads try to dislodge them from their traditional shopping patters, and e-mails from Groupon and directly from retailers attempt to capture these transient customers. The performance mandate, therefore, is for retailers to develop a superior customer-service program that will have a significant advantage in not allowing customers to exit and become transients other retailers can capture and/or to convert transients it can attract to its store or website into loyal customers. Thus, customer service can play a significant role in building a retailer's sales volume and profitability.

Customer service cannot happen all by itself but must be integrated into all aspects of retailing. That is why the profitable retailers of the future will know that the demand for their merchandise is not simply price elastic, as economists would have us believe. It is also *service elastic*, which means that an increase of 1 percent in service levels provided will result in more than a 1 percent increase in sales.

Merchandise Management

Chapter 9 discussed the importance of merchandise management since one of the best ways a retailer can serve its customers is by having what they want in inventory. There are few things more disturbing to a customer than making a trip to a store for a specific item only to discover that the item is out of stock. This is why Nordstrom offers its customers a free dress shirt if it is ever out of stock on any of the basic sizes. This retailer wants its customers to be confident of locating any style, color, or size. Basically, the better the store is at allocating inventory in proportion to customer demand patterns, the better the customer will be served.

Building and Fixture Management

Retailers' decisions regarding building and fixtures can also have a significant effect on how well the customer is served. For example, consider how the following noncomprehensive list of building and fixture dimensions might influence customer service: heating and cooling levels; availability of parking space; ease of finding merchandise; layout and arrangement of fixtures; well-functioning elevators and/or escalators, placement and cleanliness of restrooms and lounge areas; location of the check-cashing desk, complaint desk, and returns desks; level of lighting; places to sit and rest; clean and well-lighted restrooms; and width and length of aisles.

Promotion Management

Promotion provides customers with information that can help them make purchase decisions. Therefore, retailers should be concerned with whether the promotion programs they develop, including those online, assist the consumer. The following questions can help the retailer assess whether its promotion is serving the customer:

1. Is the advertising informative and helpful?
2. Does the advertising provide all the information the customer needs?
3. Are the salespeople easy to find or identify based on a uniform, name badge, or other identifier?

4. Are the salespeople helpful and informative?
5. Are the salespeople friendly and courteous?
6. Are the salespeople easy to find when needed?
7. Are sufficient quantities available on sales-promotion items?
8. Do salespeople know about the ad, what's being promoted, and why?

This list is not comprehensive. It is intended only to show that customer-service issues need to be considered when designing promotional programs.

Price Management

Price management will also influence how well the customer is served. Are prices clearly marked and visible? Is pricing fair, honest, and straightforward? Some supermarkets have experimented with charging a different price for shoppers late at night where usually the demand is more inelastic; however, most shoppers, if they found out about this practice, would be outraged and not patronize the store in the future. Are customers told the true price of credit? These questions suggest that the pricing decision should not be isolated from the retailer's customer-service program.

Credit Management

The management of credit, in-house or co-branded with a bank or large financial institution, should also be integrated into the customer-service program. After all, credit, along with the retailer's layaway plans, is a significant aid in both encouraging loyalty and helping consumers purchase merchandise. However, this facet of the retailer's business must be monitored closely. Target in 2007, for example, was one of the nation's top credit-card issuers. The Minneapolis-based retailer developed various promotional campaigns whereby users of the Target-branded financial products were given compelling reasons to shop at Target more often, as well as to spend more on each visit.[15] In addition, Target's financial products contributed more than 20 percent to the retailer's 2007 profits.[16] However, at the end of Target's 2007 fiscal year, the company had $8.62 billion in loans outstanding on Visa cards, which could be used anywhere, and its private-label cards, which are for purchases at Target only. This amount was 29 percent greater than the total ($6.71 billion) at the end of 2006.[17] Thus, as the economy slowed during 2008 and the credit crisis grew, Target found out that it had offered too much credit to struggling borrowers who would soon be unable to pay off their debt. As a result, in early 2009 Target posted a 22-percent drop in yearly earnings as the discount chain struggled with a lower growth in sales and a major increase in bad-debt expenses.[18] By year end 2011, Target had decreased the gross card receivables to $6,314 million.[19] This decrease was due, in part, to the fact that Target "no longer issues new Target Visa accounts, and it undertook risk management and underwriting initiatives that reduced available credit lines for higher-risk cardholders during 2009 and 2010."[20]

A Recap

Integration between the elements of the retail mix is important when retailers develop their customer-service programs. Much of what has already been discussed in this book relates, either directly or indirectly, to one of the three broad categories of customer service: pretransaction, transaction, and posttransaction. Successful retailers view customer service as a way to gain an advantage over the competition. As a result, even discounters are beginning to empower all their employees, not just management, to do whatever is reasonable to take care of the customer.

LO 2

Describe the various
customer services
that a retailer
can offer.

Common Customer Services

Much of the discussion in previous chapters on location, merchandise, pricing, and promotion had implications for serving the customer. However, many of the more popular types of customer service have not been mentioned or have received sparse coverage. Let us review some of them.

Pretransaction Services

**pretransaction
services**
Are services provided
to the customer prior to
entering the store.

The most common **pretransaction services**, which are provided to the customer prior to entering the store, are convenient hours, ease of parking, and information aids. Each service makes it easier for the potential customer to shop or to learn of the retailer's offering.

Convenient Hours

The more convenient the retailer's operating hours are to the customer, the easier it is for the customer to visit the retailer. Convenient operating hours are the most basic service that a retailer should provide to its customers. Retailers must ascertain what their customers want and weigh the cost of providing those wants against the additional revenues that would be generated. If a retailer's target customers want longer hours because of their work schedules, then the retailer should do so, provided it is profitable. Some retail entrepreneurs are now serving their time-deprived customers with round-the-clock food service, auto-repair, and medical services. Some merchant groups have even started banding together to offer a concierge service at the local commuter train station that—for a fee paid by the merchants—will return video rentals, handle dry cleaning, pick up prescriptions, and do other shopping chores for the commuter.

A retailer's operating hours also depend on the competition. If a competitor is willing to stay open until 9 p.m. six nights per week to serve customers, it would probably not be wise to close every night at 6 p.m. unless a lease provision requires it. Several years ago, many bricks-and-mortar retailers transformed themselves into bricks-and-click retailers to compete with retailers who offer the most convenient hours: 24/7/365. However, in reaction to the economic downturn, many retailers, especially supermarkets, are now shutting down during the midnight to 6 a.m. shift. These decisions are only being made on a case-by-case basis after management determines the real value of these hours to their customers. In addition to reducing labor costs, most retailers closing during the early morning period often see a reduction in insurance fees. This is due to the fact that store robberies peak during that period.

The retailer must also remember that local and national laws, which were described in Chapter 6, may restrict the retailer's ability to set its hours of operations. For example, some states employ blue laws to restrict certain types of retailers from operating on Sundays. In Oklahoma and Texas, for example, new-car dealers must be closed one day each weekend.

Parking

As we have discussed, traffic is a key driver of store profitability. In fact, as discussed in Chapter 7, that is why stores on streets or intersections with high traffic are more costly in terms of rent or purchase price. However, along with traffic comes the need for easy parking for customers. The amount of parking the retailer needs, in areas where the car is the prime method of transportation for the shopper, will be a function of the average time that customers spend in the store as well as the time of day and time of week where customer traffic is concentrated. For example, if a retailer is open 12 hours a day and it has 600 visitors a day and each spends an hour shopping, then it would need 50 parking spaces (600 divided by 12). However, this assumes that customers are spread evenly throughout the day. This, of course, never occurs. Thus, if the retailer looks at the maximum visitors per hour during the day, and let us say it is 120, then it would need 120 parking spaces; assuming each spends 60 minutes shopping.

Let us now look at one of the counterintuitive results of providing better merchandising and customer service. This could actually result in customers spending more time in the store as they find it enjoyable and the merchandise assortments appealing and exciting. If in the prior example, the average shopper spends 90 minutes in the store and it has 120 new visitors per hour then it would have 180 visitors in 90 minutes (120 times 1.5 hours) and thus it would need 180 parking spaces or an increase of 50 percent. If more parking is not available, then new arriving shoppers will go elsewhere as the happy customers in the store are enjoying their visit and spending more time.

Information Aids

As already mentioned, the retailer's promotional efforts help to inform the customer. Many retailers offer customers other information aids that help them enter into intelligent transactions. Today, for example, with the click of a mouse, consumers can not only search for products or services, but also determine what choices are available in local stores, the location of specific stores, and directions on how to get there. Consumers can also get information about return policies, credit policies, merchandise availability, and even merchandise prices on the websites of most major retailers. There are even websites where consumers experience firsthand a virtual walk through of the store. Other web retailers, such as The Gap, (www.gap.com) and Lands' End (www.landsend.com), let consumers move around images of the latest fashions on the screen to get a feel for how the different outfits will mix and match.

In addition, today's retailers realize that the store, be it a physical store or an online location, is becoming more than merely a vehicle for transactions; it is now a place to encourage purchases even before the customers begin the transaction process. Consider what is currently happening with banks. Deregulation, mergers, and acquisitions, and the proliferation of financial "products"—funds, trusts, and investment services—have, as will be discussed in greater detail in Chapter 13, caused banks to use their physical layouts to generate additional sales. In fact, after the collapse of Washington Mutual, the first thing J. P. Morgan did after taking over the Seattle-based bank was to remodel its 900 branches. Renovations were made so as to free up room for J.P. Morgan to create locations within the building, complete with signage, to pitch credit cards, trust funds, investment services, mortgages, and other products to customers inherited from Washington Mutual.[21] This same concept should be used on the homepage of every retailer's website.

Transaction Services

In the past, retailers believed that transaction services meant employing salespeople who would personally take care of an individual customer. But for the profitable retailers of the future, the term **transaction services** will mean offering the conveniences customers need and then helping them get out of the store as fast as possible with their purchases. The most important transaction services are credit, layaway, gift wrapping and packaging, check cashing, gift cards, personal shopping, merchandise availability, personal selling, and the sales transaction itself. These services help to facilitate transactions once customers have made a purchase decision.

transaction services
Are services provided to customers when they are in the store shopping and transacting business.

Credit

One of the most popular transaction-related services offered by retailers is consumer credit. Offering credit can be of great service to the customer because it enables shopping without the need to carry large sums of money. In addition, it allows the customer to buy now and pay later. Credit can be a benefit to the retailer also: It increases sales by increasing both impulse buying and purchases of expensive items. Of course, in-house credit can decrease profits if the credit policy is too lenient.

One final comment about the use of credit and debit cards: Eighty percent of consumers currently own a debit card, compared to 78 percent who own a credit card and 17 percent who own a prepaid card.[22] As a result, more and more retailers have begun to more aggressively negotiate with banks for the high fees charged to the retailer for using these financial products. In addition, because banks charge a lower fee to the retailer when customers use their PIN numbers rather than signing for the purchase, most retailers now steer their customers toward that form of payment. In addition, on some high-end purchases such as a new automobile, retailers will limit the amount that can be put on a credit or debit card since the fees could end up costing the auto dealer $500 or more.

Layaway

When a layaway service is offered, the customer can place a deposit (usually 20 percent) on an item, and in return the retailer will hold the item for the customer for a specified period of time (usually several months, but for jewelry the layaway could be up to 12 months). The customer will make periodic payments on the item and can take it home when it's paid for in full. In a sense, a layaway sale is similar to an installment credit sale; however, the retailer retains physical possession of the item until the bill is completely paid. Westside International Travel (www.westsideintltravel.com), to address the declining travel market brought on by the declining economy, has introduced a layaway plan for some of its trips, allowing its customers to put down an initial payment and then spread the other payments over 10–12 months, depending upon the trip.

A negative aspect of using layaways is that many items are never picked up by customers. The retailer then has to return a "dated" item to regular inventory, where a markdown, which is usually larger than the first customer's initial payment, is required. Walmart did away with layaway in September 2006 due to its cost in terms of staff time and floor space. However, on September 8, 2011, it announced the return of layaway for the Christmas season. Unfortunately, the program was only for select toys and electronics, and there was a minimum item cost of $50 and a nonrefundable $5 fee. In addition, if the order was cancelled, there was another $10 charge.[23] Incidentally, one indicator of a weak economy is a rise in layaway. When households lose a wage earner or have other economic strain, they start to budget more carefully. Layaway allows these households to acquire items they need but to delay payment and taking physical possession of the merchandise.

Perhaps, you recall the 2011 winter holiday season where what the national press and evening news referred to as "layaway angel" arose out of nowhere and spread throughout the nation. These angels would appear at a store such as Kmart or Sears and pay off thousands of layaway accounts and perhaps leave only a small token outstanding payment of 25 cents. Predictably, the beneficiaries of this wonderful kindness were very happy and at the same time shocked and surprised at the anonymous demonstration of generosity they received.

Gift Wrapping and Packaging

Customers are typically better served if their purchase is properly wrapped or packaged. The service may be as simple as putting the purchase into a paper bag or as complex as packaging crystal glassware in a special shatterproof box to prevent breakage.

The retailer must match its wrapping service to the type of merchandise it carries and its image. A discount grocer or hardware store does quite well by simply putting the merchandise into a paper sack. Specialty clothing stores often have dress and suit boxes that are easy to carry home. Some upscale retailers even put the purchased merchandise in decorated shopping bags or prewrapped gift boxes. This considerably reduces the number of packages that must be gift wrapped. Since it is hard to wrap a new automobile, some dealers will deliver the new car with a gift such as premium candy in a special gift wrapped box.

Many larger department stores and most gift shops offer a gift-wrapping service. Often there is a fee for gift wrapping unless the purchase price exceeds some limit, usually $10 or $25. Many other retailers also offer a courtesy wrap, which consists of a gift box and ribbon, or a store wrap that identifies the place of purchase. This type of wrap is not only a goodwill gesture but also a form of advertising.

Check Cashing

Most retailers offer some form of check-cashing service. The most basic type allows customers to cash a check for the amount of purchase. Most retailers now have online acceptance systems on their registers that make check cashing as easy as using a credit card. Other retailers provide their customers with an identification card that entitles them to pay for merchandise with a personal check. More generous check-cashing retailers allow qualified customers to cash checks for amounts above the purchase price, usually not for more than $20.

Check cashing has been found to be an effective means of attracting certain market segments and is based on the premise that consumers will spend more if they have cash in their pockets. This trend has resulted in some supermarket chains becoming the biggest check-cashing operators in some cities, often times bigger than the banks, especially in urban areas where many customers don't have checking accounts.

Gift Cards

Many consumers continue to view gift cards as the perfect present because they are fun to receive, they make shopping easier, and consumers can use them to take advantage of after-Christmas sales. In fact, according to the National Retail Federation, one in every $6 of future Christmas sales will be used for a gift card.

Gift cards are a year-round service being sold by retailers ranging from Macy's to Starbucks and from Amazon.com to Home Depot. Gift cards for many types of retailers and service providers are often available at "card kiosks" located at supermarkets and drug stores. This way, you don't have to go from store to store to buy gift cards, you can purchase cards, for example, for meals from Red Lobster, movie tickets at Harkins Theatres, a vacation at Disneyland, downloads from iTunes, purchases from Nordstroms, and minutes on a prepaid phone while shopping for your groceries. One key reason for the popularity of today's plastic gift card is that it is a "stored value" card as opposed to an old-fashioned gift certificate. Thus, when a consumer spends $33 from a $100 plastic card, the card automatically updates the balance. This is more efficient and much less time-consuming than making the retailer reissue a new gift certificate for the $67 balance.

The major impact of gift cards on retailers is the postponement of sales since retailers can't count a gift card as a sale at the time of purchase. Instead, they must wait until the gift card is redeemed for merchandise. As a result, most of the more than $25 billion spent on gift cards in November and December will not show up in holiday sales but instead as sales when the gift cards are actually redeemed.[24]

Personal Shopping

Recent changes in family lifestyles have left many Americans, especially when both spouses are working professionals, without enough time to accomplish all they need and want to do. Other shoppers hate browsing in stores more than they hate doing household chores. Successful retailers have sought to aid these consumers by offering personal-shopping services. **Personal shopping** is the activity of assembling an assortment of goods for a customer. This can be as varied a service as picking out clothing, filling a nonstore order (many retailers now offer key customers an 800 phone number or a website address), assembling a supply of groceries and sending them to the customer's home, or selecting a wedding gift. Personal-shopping services are one of the best ways to build a relationship with the customer. A common misconception about personal shoppers is that they cater only to celebrities. However, because most retailers don't charge extra for the service, it is available to everybody.

The newest type of personal shopper is the health advocate. For professionals and other affluent consumers short of time, but with a serious illness, these advocates research new treatments, cut through medical bureaucracy, and frame medical decisions more objectively than stressed-out patients and their family members. Somewhat similar are professionals that assist families in selecting the school and/or college for their children to attend.

Merchandise Availability

Merchandise availability as a service simply relates to whether the customers can easily find the items they are looking for. A customer might be unable to find an item for one of three reasons: (1) The item is out of stock, (2) it is not located where the customer looks for it, or (3) the customer does not know what is really needed. The retailer can minimize out-of-stock conditions by good merchandise management, although some out-of-stock situations are inevitable. The customer's ability to locate a needed item in the store can be increased by having proper in-store signage, displays, helpful and informative employees, and a well-designed layout. The problem of not knowing "what is really needed" is more difficult to overcome. Most major retailers have a bridal registry, both in-store and online, with easy-to-remember phone numbers to help solve one such problem. For example, at Chicago's old Marshall Field's (which has been renamed Macy's, after the merger between Federated and May), the number is 1-800-2-I DO I DO; at JCPenney it is 1-800-JCP-GIFT; and at Target it is 1-800-888-WEDD.

Merchandise availability is an element of customer service that many retailers take for granted, but they shouldn't. When customers do not find items they are looking for in a store—regardless of the cause—they will remember their bad experiences and will probably tell their friends.

Some retailers are also recognizing that today's time-pressured customer is often looking for more one-stop shopping. The most frequently visited retailers are gasoline or fuel stations and grocery stores as well as banks. Some grocers are now selling gasoline but also venturing into banking and financial services. For instance, consider Tesco, a retail powerhouse in Britain with more than 20 million customer visits weekly to its grocery stores. Starting a few years ago, it began to open banks in its supermarkets in England and Scotland that offer insurance, credit cards, savings and checking accounts, and now home mortgages.[25] These branches also have much longer operating hours than the traditional stand-alone bank.

Personal Selling

Another important transactional service that retailers can offer is a strong, customer-oriented retail sales staff. A good job of personal selling, resulting in a need-satisfying experience, or even skilled suggestive selling will greatly enhance customer satisfaction. In fact, one study found that in 73 percent of the cases where the customer had the "best ever shopping experience," there was sales-force involvement. The same study also pointed out the dangers of ineffective sales personnel—81 percent of the time when a customer had the "worst ever shopping experience," there was direct employee involvement.[26] Personal selling will be discussed in detail later in this chapter.

A particularly interesting recent trend is for outlet centers to begin to add more service to complement their historical price-based value proposition. For example, some of the Off Fifth outlet stores (whose parent firm is Saks Fifth Avenue) have allowed consumers to schedule an appointment with a sales associate prior to an upcoming sale and then hold any merchandise selected until the sales begin.[27]

Sales Transaction

The final service to be discussed is the sales transaction itself, or the interaction between the retailer, its employee, and the customer. Some discounters, seeking to invoke a positive, personal touch, made headway with a "greeter" to acknowledge customers when they enter the store. Probably the two most overlooked problems involving transaction services are having clean restrooms and minimizing *dwell time*, which is the amount of time a consumer must spend waiting to complete a purchase.

The majority of all shopping experiences should be recreational and entertaining. This is especially true for retailers selling nonessential products such as books. Therefore, the retailer should never do anything that might drive the consumer away. Leonard Riggio, the feisty CEO of Barnes & Noble, recognized this truth and chose to provide customers Starbucks coffee, comfy chairs, a clubby atmosphere, and, yes, public restrooms.[28] Sam Walton believed that his restrooms should be the best in town so that a woman would never want to leave his stores to rush home for a bathroom visit. In fact, whenever Sam visited a store, he and his wife, Helen, always checked the restrooms.[29]

As noted earlier, all retailers face unique challenges in determining how to deal with customers in their stores. However, as the chapter's "Service Retailing" box illustrates, these decisions are far more complex for those retailers whose interaction with the customer is conducted in the customers' home.

Another issue facing the retailer is how to handle dwell time. As noted earlier, **dwell time** refers to the amount of time a consumer must spend waiting to complete a purchase. This time greatly influences the customer's expectations and evaluations of the retailer. Customers understand that certain waiting periods are required, especially for services that cannot be produced ahead of demand. However, they must perceive that the line or waiting time is shortening. One successful supermarket has determined that more than half the time customers spend in its meat market is spent waiting for their orders. Thus, the supermarket tries to give them meal ideas for their next shopping trip. It not only passes the time but also leads to future sales. You have probably taken your car to the auto dealership or service retailer such as Brake Max or Jiffy Lube for an oil change or other service. To make your wait time more enjoyable, these service retailers often offer television, beverage service, and snacks. Some auto dealers may even invite you into their new auto showroom or invite you to take a test drive of a new automobile.

It may seem like a simple thing, but for any retailer serving hundreds of customers daily, the decision on how to line them up can have a major impact on customer satisfaction. This decision affects all retailers from the U.S. Postal Service to fast-food operations and hotels to banks. Currently, most retailers are moving away from multiple lines and opting for the single, serpentine line. This type of line, which was first made popular at amusement parks, got its name because of its long, snakelike shape. Multiple lines cause customer frustration because other lines inevitably move faster. In recent

dwell time
Refers to the amount of time a consumer must spend waiting to complete a purchase.

SERVICE RETAILING

Etiquette Guidelines for Service Retailers

Many service retailers don't work from their own location but must go to the customer. Some, such as lawn-care specialists, work outside the customer's home but others, such as home-improvement and repair contractors, must enter the customer's home to complete the assigned job. Anytime a service provider enters a private home, there is the possibility of being put in an awkward situation.

Most of the major service franchisors try to avoid these situations by having all franchisees follow a detailed operating-policy manual. This manual covers hiring and training procedures as well as providing operational and financial guidance. One common guideline is to require the franchisee to obtain a police background check on applicants before making the hiring decision. Many service franchisors now insist that all service technicians be bonded, that they wear uniforms with collared shirts and slacks, and that they wear plastic protective shoe coverings when entering a home. Despite these and other similar upgrades in professionalism, not every unfortunate contingency can be anticipated. How does a service retailer prepare its employees for that "once-in-a-million" situation?

One service provider who provides outstanding training in this sensitive area is Ted Tenenbaum, the owner of the Mr. Handyman Franchise in Los Angeles. Mr. Tenenbaum's employees provide all types of home maintenance including electrical, plumbing, drywall repair, painting, and tilling. Like all Mr. Handyman Franchisees across America, Tenenbaum's workers specialize in jobs that are too small for most general contractors. Because his employees spend the bulk of their time inside customers' homes, Tenenbaum's training sessions focus on teaching a "common sense" level of business etiquette that is specific to the nature of the work. Since every situation is different, these guidelines are not written in stone and posted for every employee to memorize. Instead, Tenenbaum attempts to instill the idea that a combination of common sense and basic etiquette will forestall many of the problems that service retailers might encounter. Here is an overview of Ted Tenenbaum's unwritten rules:

Whatever You See, Pretend You Don't See It. Whether it is a pair of racy underwear in the middle of the floor or the homeowner walking around in flimsy clothing, the worker didn't see it.

Don't Stare Too Long at Anything. After all, if you followed the first guideline, you didn't see anything.

Never Get in the Middle of Any Domestic Argument and Agree with Everyone and then Switch the Conversation to Something Else. Feuding parties often like to involve a neutral third party. The third party can never win—so always try to avoid such situations.

Never Be Alone in a Room with a Child. What would happen if a child were to stumble and fall, start crying, and a parent walks in the room to see a service tech with an arm around the child trying to provide comfort? Or what if the child cuts himself on a tool or replacement part?

Be Sure to Compliment at Least One Item or Feature in the Customer's Home. You always want to get on the customer's good side.

Mr. Tenenbaum's final, and probably most important, guideline is

Call Me If You Are Ever Frightened.

With etiquette guidelines such as these, it is little wonder that Hollywood celebrities use his service. But don't ask Ted or his techs about these celebrities. They won't say anything out of school.

Source: Based on information provided by Ted Tenenbaum and used with his written permission.

years, the frustration of waiting to complete the transaction—the dwell time—has become a threat to retailers. According to a study conducted by one major retailer, 44 percent of its customers would rather clean their bathrooms, 20 percent would rather sit in traffic, and 18 percent would rather visit the dentist than stand in a checkout line. Another survey asked more than a thousand women what they found most stressful when shopping. Here 33 percent said the checkout lines.[30] Thus, dwell time is such an important issue that today big chains now monitor checkout times. One retailer explained to an author that it takes an extra minute and three seconds when a customer uses a check instead of a credit card. However, the most frustrating wait for most consumers is the time spent on the phone trying to bypass those annoying voice robots to reach a real, live customer-service agent. One consumer advocate offered four suggestions to the authors as a means to avoid this problem:

1. Mention the name of the company's competitor. Most systems have been set up to recognize these names and to serve you immediately.
2. Call the extension number for new service. If you're a prospective customer, a company will snap to answer your call.
3. Press every number as fast as you can. This makes the system think you're on a rotary phone—or that you're about to disconnect. Either way, you're next in line.
4. Ask for the collections department. In these economic times, the collections department tends to answer calls quickly, and you can jump to the head of the line for your desired department this way.

Posttransaction Services

posttransaction services
Are services provided to customers after they have purchased merchandise or services.

The relationship between the retailer and the consumer has become more complex in today's service-oriented economy. Many products—such as computers, automobiles, travel, and financial services—require an extended relationship between the retailer and the consumer. The longer this period of time can be extended by ensuring the customer's satisfaction with the product, the greater the chances that future sales will result. The most common **posttransaction services**, which are provided after the sale has been made, are complaint handling, merchandise returns, merchandise repair, servicing, delivery, and postsale follow-ups. Posttransaction services are especially important for online retailers since there usually isn't a face-to-face relationship involved; it is all done via the computer.

Complaint Handling

Customer dissatisfaction occurs when the customer's experience with the retailer or product fails to live up to expectations. The proper handling of customer complaints can mean a big difference in retail performance. Dealing with customers is a sensitive issue because it involves employees who make human errors dealing with customers who make human errors. In essence, this doubles the chance of misunderstandings and mistakes between the two parties. Unfortunately, these mistakes and misunderstandings often lead to a poor image of the retailer, no matter whose fault they might be. Therefore, it is essential that retailers try to solve customer complaints effectively. After all, if retailers are able to solve the customer's problem the right way, then the customer will not only continue to shop with the retailer but may also influence others to shop there through the use of word of mouth.[31]

There are several ways of handling and solving customer complaints. Regardless of the method used, retailers should follow the six rules shown in Exhibit 12.4. For a large retailer, the central complaint department is most efficient. Here a staff that is specifically trained for this task handles all customer complaints. This method leaves the sales force free to do its job and allows the customer to deal with someone who has the authority to act on most complaints. Many large retailers have even established an 800 number so that they may properly handle complaints with minimal effort on the part of the customer. Although, as was discussed in the section on dwell time, the long wait to talk to a real live person may only increase the consumer's level of frustration.

Exhibit 12.4

Six Rules to Follow When Handling a Customer's Complaint

1. Acknowledge the importance of the customer. Before the customer even begins to explain his or her problem, acknowledge that the customer is important by telling him or her that you are there to help. Try to ease the customer's frustration.
2. Understand the customer's problem. Ask all the questions needed to completely understand the situation. Determine the responsibilities of each party and what went wrong. Do not assign any fault at this stage.
3. Repeat the problem (as you understand it) to the customer. Without interrupting the customer, paraphrase the problem as you understand it.
4. Think of all possible solutions. Using your creative powers, think of all possible, even wild, solutions that could remedy the problem.
5. Agree on the solution. Determine the solution that is fair to both parties and then have both parties agree to it.
6. Above all, make sure the customer leaves feeling as you would want to feel if you were the customer. If you would not be satisfied with the solution if you were the customer, start over. Remember, it is better to lose a little now than to take a chance on losing a customer for life.

© Cengage Learning

Some retailers have the individual salesperson handle complaints. They believe that a friendly, sympathetic attitude exhibited by the salesperson will have a positive effect on future sales, especially if the complaint is about a product rather than the retailer or sales force. This method does, however, have several disadvantages. First, the individual salesperson often does not have the authority to settle problems and must call in someone else to handle the situation, forcing the customer to restate the problem. A second drawback of this system is the fact that a salesperson who is listening to a past customer complain cannot serve current customers who, incidentally, are overhearing the complaints.

Regardless of the complaint-handling system, the retailer needs to remember three things when handling complaints: The customer deserves courteous treatment, a fair settlement, and prompt action. Remember, even if the sale is lost, the customer need not be lost. The proper handling of complaints has a substantial payback for the smart retailer. Sometimes, however, the customer makes it difficult for even the best retailer to handle a complaint and make the customer happy. Luckily for frontline employees, there are online support groups: www.customerssuck.com and www.retail-sucks.com. Through these websites, employees can share and vent their frustrations regarding unruly and sometimes just plain stupid customers.

Merchandise Returns

A return policy can range from "No returns, no exchanges," to "The customer is always right." The handling of merchandise returns is an important customer service, sometimes making the difference between turning a profit and losing money. As was pointed out earlier, successful retailers are well aware that it costs five times as much money to get a customer into your store as it does to make a sale to someone already there. Therefore, since *customer retention* is so important, why would a retailer ever seek to lose one due to the mishandling of a return? Retailers therefore need to decide if they want to use either of the extreme policies mentioned earlier or a more moderate one. Few services build customer goodwill as quickly as a fair return policy. It is important that the retailer's return policy be consistent with its image. A mistake that some retailers make is to follow the policies (such as "No receipt, no return," having a "30-day limit" on returns, or having a $20 to $30 restocking fee) established by the competition. Since a retailer is trying to differentiate itself from the competition, saying it has a similar return policy as competitors isn't the best strategy. Still, it must be acknowledged that returns are an expense to the retailer.

While no one is sure of an exact figure for fraudulent returns and abuses, most retailers believe the number to be in excess of $20 billion per year. Some common examples of this fraud and abuse are:[32]

1. *Renting, Not Buying.* Some consumers buy merchandise such as a laptop computer to use for a semester with the intention of returning it when done. A customer-service representative of a hardware store told the authors that one of the most commonly returned items is a plunger: "It wouldn't be so bad, but usually they come back in a plastic bag just after they have been used." However, what is probably the most abused return policy is that of an electronic retailer getting back a large screen television set the Monday after the Super Bowl.
2. *Fraudulent Employee Actions.* Typically, employees return merchandise they stole for cash. This may also involve using falsified, stolen, or reused receipts to return the merchandise.
3. *Shoplift Returns:* Items are shoplifted with the intention of returning them for cash.
4. *Price switching:* Lower-priced tags are put on merchandise with the intention of returning them for full retail price—and the original price tag back on the items.

Research has also shown that approximately 75 percent of all shoppers never return purchases and that only 1 percent of consumers are responsible for fraudulent or abusive returns.[33] Even so, it is important that a retailer sets a return policy that considers the effect on both sales and expenses. Thus, retailers must estimate the salvage value of returned merchandise that is probably out of its peak selling season, the probability of losing a customer, and the transaction costs of returning merchandise. There is also an opportunity cost—the foregone interest or return on investment dollars. This money is tied up in merchandise that is in the possession of the customer but will be returned.

One innovative approach to dealing with the 1 percent abusers is a new technology used by retailers that tracks the buying and return activity of shoppers, especially those returns without a receipt. After shoppers reach the retailer's return limit within a given time period,[34] they are informed that they can't make more exchanges at any of the retailer's stores for as long as a year. Such actions allow retailers to offer the other 99 percent of consumers a more lenient and flexible return policy.

Servicing, Repair, and Warranties

Any new product with more than one moving mechanical part is a candidate for future service or repair. In fact, even items without moving parts such as clothing, coffee tables, and paintings are candidates for repair. Retailers who offer merchandise servicing and repair to their customers tend to generate a higher sales volume. And if the work they perform is good, they can also generate repeat business. For example, if the service department of a TV and appliance store has a reputation for doing good work at fair prices, then customers will not only purchase TVs at the store but also tend to purchase radios, stereos, and washing machines.

Repair servicing, especially repairs involving warranties, is perhaps one of the most difficult customer services to manage. While good repair service can stimulate additional sales, many customers will never be satisfied because it is difficult to schedule appointments. In today's urban environment, it is virtually impossible for retailers to schedule a repair call or delivery within even a three-hour time frame. Traffic, parking, and the inability to predict exactly how long each call will take make scheduling uncertain. These factors often make it difficult for today's two-wage-earner families to be home when the retailer's personnel arrive. In addition, buyers can be confused by warranties that involve free replacement parts but not labor or that have prorated values. (The legal issues pertaining to warranties were discussed in Chapter 6.) Although most customers feel inconvenienced having to deal with service warranty work, they will only tell their friends, relatives, and acquaintances of their experiences. However, if they are really unhappy, they will often post their experiences on Facebook or websites such as Hissing Kitty (http://hissingkitty.com) for all to see, like the person who wrote that he would rather pay someone else double than deal with a particular company again.

Delivery

Delivery of merchandise to the customer's home can be a very expensive service, especially because of the high cost of fuel. Retailers such as florists can offer free delivery (which is actually absorbed in slightly higher prices) or they can charge the customer a small fee to help offset the cost. Nonetheless, the extra business derived from providing delivery may be worth the expense if the merchandise and customer characteristics warrant it. For example, when consumers think of delivery, they usually think of Domino's Pizza. When Thomas Monaghan started the company, pizza already enjoyed widespread popularity. He soon realized that success could come by focusing on fast, free delivery— something no one else did.[35] However, with higher gasoline prices, the days of free pizza delivery for Americans may soon end. Despite the risk that extra charges will alienate customers, Pizza Hut, Domino's, and Papa John's have been testing the addition of a delivery fee in an attempt to bolster their bottom line.

Andresr/Shutterstock.com

Delivery of merchandise is often seen as a valuable service component from customers as they become even more time pressed; however, retailers must balance the costs associated with providing delivery with the additional revenues such a service generates.

The final step of the delivery process is installation. As products become more technically advanced, more people are looking for someone who can actually install it for them. Some retailers refer to these consumers, especially senior citizens who did not grow with all the modern technology, as the "do-it-for-me" segment. Best Buy, for example, has taken this delivery and installation process to the next level with its Geek Squad.

Postsale Follow-Up

Retailing's job is not over when the cash register rings. It is only starting. Many retail salespeople spend a great deal of time and energy to get a customer to say yes, but most don't spend enough time trying to keep that purchaser a loyal customer. Earlier in the chapter it was pointed out that it costs a retailer five times as much money to attract a first-time customer as it does to persuade a former customer to return, so it's important that the retailer care for its current customers. This may involve just a follow-up phone call to see how the product is working, to remind a customer about an upcoming sale, or suggest that it might be time to reorder. Southwest Airlines, for example, sends out special deals to its Rapid Rewards (loyalty club) members who haven't flown with the airlines over the past year. Some luxury and specialty retailers, especially in women's wear and jewelry, will follow up with customers to make sure that they are satisfied and also to remind them about new merchandise that may be arriving soon that may interest them. Of course, we also know how well dentists send us a reminder every six months to come in for a cleaning and examination.

One final comment on postsale follow-up: The Internet is rife with sounding boards for disgruntled shoppers, so it is wise to have someone check these blogs on a regular basis. One such blog is http://getsatisfaction.com. This website seeks to bring customers and company employees together into a "community" to make things better for everyone by answering questions, gathering product ideas, gathering marketing data, and building rapport with the others in that chosen "community." It groups issues into four areas: marketing, support, e-commerce, and product. So far, 65,000 "communities," through over 9,600,000 visits to Get Satisfaction's website, worked together to improve more than 21,000 products and services.[36]

| **LO 3** |

Explain how a retailer should determine which services to offer.

Determining Customer-Service Levels

It is not easy to determine the optimal number and level of customer services to offer. Theoretically, however, one could argue that a retailer should add customer services until the additional revenue that is generated by higher service levels is equal to the additional cost of providing those services. In the short run, cutting back on costly customer services can usually increase profits, but such an action may present serious long-run problems as customers may shop elsewhere seeking better services.

Deciding what specific customer services to offer in order to increase sales volume is a difficult question for any retailer. Exhibit 12.5 lists six factors to be considered when determining the customer services to offer: (1) the retailer's characteristics, (2) the services offered by the competition, (3) the type of merchandise handled, (4) the price image of the retailer, (5) the income of the target market, and (6) the cost of providing the service. It is the retailer's job to study these six areas to arrive at the service mix that will increase long-run profits by retaining current customers, enticing new ones, and projecting the right image. Above all else, retailers must remember to be realistic and not expect to satisfy the wants and needs of all customers. No strategy could be less profitable than trying to satisfy everybody. What the retailer is really trying to do is to use its sales staff as the conduit between the vendor's expectations and the customer's expectations, as shown in Exhibit 12.6.

Exhibit 12.5
Factors to Consider
When Determining
Customer Services
to Offer

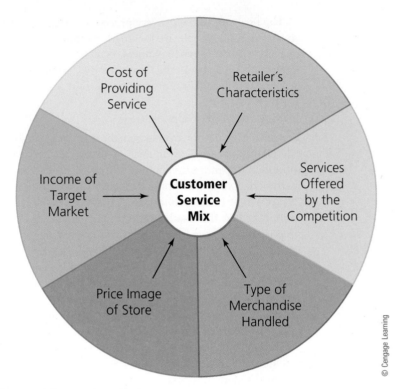

Retailer's Characteristics

Retailer's characteristics include store location, store size, and store type. It is especially important to look at these three characteristics when considering adding a service.

Services offered in the downtown area of a large city would probably be different from those offered by a similar store in a suburban shopping center. For example, a drugstore in the downtown area might offer free delivery of prescriptions to its clientele. This service would be of great benefit to city dwellers without cars and to businesspeople who do not want to wait at the drugstore for a prescription. This same service in a suburban shopping center would not be as important. This druggist might get a better return on investment by offering such services as check cashing, credit, and a drive-through window rather than free delivery of prescriptions.

Exhibit 12.6
How the Retailer's Sales
Force Meets the Expecta-
tions of Both Vendors
and Customers

The size and type of store also determine which services to offer. A major department store would offer a different assortment of services than a supermarket. There would also be a difference between large and small stores of the same type and one among bricks-and-mortar, clicks-and-mortar, and e-tail stores.

Competition

The services offered by competitors will have a significant effect on the level and variety of customer services offered. A retailer must also provide these services or suitable substitutes, or it may offer lower prices.

Suppose there are three clothing stores of the same general type, price range, and quality within a given area. Store A and store B offer free gift wrapping, standard alterations, bank-card credit, and a liberal return policy. Store C, on the other hand, offers only standard alterations and has an exchange-only return policy. Customers who are shopping for gifts will generally prefer stores A and B to store C because they feel confident that whatever they purchase will ultimately be just right. It can even be gift wrapped at the store. If the gift is not suitable, then the receiver can exchange it or get a cash refund. In this situation, store C can do two things to compete: add different services and decrease prices.

Type of Merchandise

The merchandise lines carried can be an indication of the types of services, especially personal selling, to be offered. The principal reason is that certain merchandise lines benefit from knowledgeable sales personnel; for example, would you want a less-than-knowledgeable salesperson to assist you in purchasing an engagement ring for the woman of your dreams? Or worse, would you want your boyfriend buying your engagement ring at a self-service discounter, even if it offers a "diamond guarantee" that it will appraise for double the selling price? In addition, other products benefit from coupling them with complimentary services: bicycles and free assembly, major appliances and delivery, and sewing machines and free sewing lessons.

Price Image

Customers usually expect more services from a retailer with a high-price image than from a discounter. When a customer perceives a retailer as having high prices, he or she also sees the retailer as possessing an air of luxury. Therefore, the services rendered by this retailer should reinforce the image of luxury or status. Some of the typical high-price-image services include personal shopping, a home-design studio, free gift wrapping, free delivery, free alterations, a person that answers the phone versus an automated voice recorder or electronic agent, and sales personnel who are more professional in both appearance and manner.

On the other end of the scale, discounters need not offer luxury services because customers who shop there are seeking low prices, not pampering. A discounter or store with a low-price image might offer such basic services as free parking, layaway, bank-card credit, and convenient store hours.

Target-Market Income

The higher the income of the target market, the higher the price that consumers will pay. The higher the prices consumers will pay, the more services the retailer can profitably provide. Some customers may expect more services than retailers can afford, and retailers must avoid the strong temptation of providing costly services to such consumers. In the long run, the retailer will have to raise prices to pay for the services, and then it will most likely lose customers at the lower income boundary of its target market.

Cost of Services

It is important that retailers know the cost of providing a service so that they can estimate the additional sales needed to pay for the service. For example, a customer service expected to increase costs by $20,000 per year for a store operating on a gross margin of 25 percent would have to stimulate sales by at least $20,000/0.25, or $80,000. However, if a store has a gross margin of 50 percent then it would only need $40,000 in incremental sales to support the $20,000 added cost of service ($20,000/0.50 = $40,000). In this sense, customer services are evaluated in a manner similar to promotional expenditures. The key criterion becomes the financial effect of adding or deleting a customer service. As a result, some national retailers have started charging for their catalogs after decades of providing them free. Research determined that although nearly 20 percent fewer customers received the catalog, those who did felt that they had made an investment ($5). As a result, these customers increased their purchases by 25 percent.

Another way of expressing the cost of having poor service is to examine what the costs would be if a store did not offer good service. After all, retailers should be aware of the loss in revenue from losing a customer. Let's consider what happens to a small 25-store supermarket chain. If this chain alienated only one customer per week per store, the chain would lose almost $100,000 in annual revenue from just the customers lost during one year. (This is based on the assumption that grocery business is repeat business and that the real revenue loss is the $75 that the average customer spends weekly at that chain.) It is important for the retailer to compare the costs of taking care of those unhappy customers to the costs of replacing them. One online broker, for example, has determined that it costs $350 to acquire a new customer and that each customer generates more than $600 in profit.[37] Therefore, always remember that, on average, it costs five times as much money to replace that lost customer as it would have if the old one had been kept. That is why customer service is so important in today's economy.

LO 4

Describe the various management problems involved in retail selling, salesperson selection, training, compensation, and evaluation.

Retail Sales Management

Retail salespeople and the service they provide are a major factor in consumer purchase decisions. For example, if the retail salesperson is rude or unhelpful, customers often walk out of the store empty-handed. The salesperson is a major determinant of a retailer's image. When the salesperson is available, friendly, appropriately dressed, and helpful, customers are often influenced to enter into a transaction with the retailer. The management of the retail sales force plays a crucial role in the success or failure of retail operations.

Types of Retail Selling

In many retail settings, the employees are called *salespersons* or *order takers*. For example, consider the role of salespeople in a typical fast food restaurant such as McDonald's, Burger King, or Wendy's. Most order takers simply ask the customers, "Can I take your order?" Little if anything related to the actual sale occurs. Similarly, in a discount department store such as Target, Kohl's, or Walmart, salespeople may show a customer where a specific product is or, if the product is not on the shelf, may go to the storeroom to attempt to locate the item. However, seldom do they attempt to sell merchandise or demonstrate its use. In fact, one discounter's policy is to provide next to no sales help. Some discounters do not want to get into the business of person-to-person selling. Retailers that employ order takers are appealing to those customers who want value instead of service. Nonetheless, one must recognize that these order takers can influence demand, especially in a negative manner. If you stand at the counter of a McDonald's and no one asks you for your order, you may get frustrated and leave the store without making a purchase.

Retail employees who are most appropriately labeled *salespersons* should be order getters rather than order takers. Order getters are involved in conversations with prospective purchasers for the purpose of making a sale. They will inform, guide, and persuade the customer to culminate a transaction either immediately or in the future. For example, in many restaurants whether or not customers choose to order dessert is related to the relationship they have established with their hosts or hostesses.

The degree of emphasis the retailer places on its employees being order getters depends on the line of retail trade and the retailer's strategy. Retailers that concentrate on the sale of shopping goods (e.g., automobile dealers, furniture retailers, computer retailers, and appliance retailers) want their salespeople to both get and take orders. In lines of retail trade where predominantly convenience goods are sold (gasoline service stations and grocery retailers), the role of the salesperson (or what many call the *retail clerk*) is that of an order taker. In terms of strategic orientation, it is generally true that retailers with high margins and high levels of customer service place more emphasis on order getting. Those with low margins and a low customer-service policy tend to emphasize order taking. Clearly, however, regardless of the line of retail trade and the retailer's strategic thrust, all retail enterprises must carefully evaluate the role of the salesperson in helping to generate demand.

Salesperson Selection

Selecting retail salespeople should involve more than casually accepting anyone who answers an ad or walks into the retailer seeking a job. In fact, the casualness with which many retailers have selected people to fill sales positions is one cause of poor productivity.

Criteria

To select salespeople properly, retailers must decide on their hiring criteria. What is expected from retail salespeople? Are retailers looking for a sales force that has low absenteeism and a willingness to work nights and weekends or the ability to generate a high volume of sales? Are they seeking other qualities or a combination of factors? Unless retailers know what they are looking for in salespeople, they will not acquire a sales force that possesses the proper qualities.

However, good results are dependent not only on the salesperson's characteristics but also on how satisfied the salesperson is with the job and how the sales job was designed. Retail-selling jobs should be designed to have high levels of variety (the opportunity to perform a wide range of activities), autonomy (the degree to which an employee determines the work procedures), task identity (the degree to which an employee is involved in the total sales process), and feedback from supervisors and customers.

Predictors

Once retailers determine the hiring criteria, they must then identify the potential predictors to meet the chosen criteria. The most commonly used predictors in selecting retail salespeople are demographics, personality, knowledge and intelligence, and prior work experience. We will discuss criteria for selecting managerial trainees later in this chapter.

Demographics   Depending on the specific line of retail trade, demographic variables can be important in identifying good retail salespeople. For example, a music store appealing to teens will probably benefit from having retail salespeople who are younger than 30 years of age. A high-fashion women's apparel store appealing to 30- to 50-year-old, career-oriented, and upwardly mobile females would probably not desire inexperienced salespeople just out of high school. Interestingly enough, a famous study by J. D. Power & Associates of more than 33,000 new-car buyers has shown that female salespersons scored higher or at least equal to men in 13 of the 15 categories evaluated. The two items where men scored best were knowledge of models and features and competitive vehicles. Women, however, scored substantially higher in sincerity, honesty, and concern for the buyer's needs.[38] Obviously, there are exceptions to the preceding cases, but the essential point is that demographics play an important role in the retail sales process.

Personality   An applicant's personality can reflect on his or her potential as a retail salesperson. Most retailers prefer salespeople who are friendly, confident, consistent, and understanding of others. These personality traits can be identified either through a personal interview with the applicant or by personality-inventory tests. In most lines of retail trade, the personal interview is sufficient.

Knowledge and Intelligence   Increasingly, many of the products that retailers sell are technically complex. Consider, for example, how fast the technology is evolving with tablet computers, smartphones, and Ruku systems, which are already beginning to make TiVos and DVRs obsolete. In addition, as this chapter's "What's New?" box points out, retail salespeople are increasingly relying upon tablet computers and smartphone apps to assist in delivering customer service.

Technology is radically changing the necessary skills salespeople must have in order to be effective. It's a must that salespeople have basic salesmanship and point-of-sales experience, but that's no longer enough. As a recent Deloitte survey of retail executives listed, "tech-savvy," "brand ambassadorship," and "specialized product knowledge" are the most important skills for retail salespeople; they must not only have knowledge of

© Rashevskyi Viacheslav/Shutterstock

WHAT'S NEW **?**

Enhancing the Service Experience—Tablets and Smartphones

Traditionally, retail salespeople were perceived to have the most information about their products, and consumers relied upon this knowledge in order to make an informed purchase decision, but times have changed. Consumers now have the tools to educate themselves, even within the store, without ever having to turn to a salesperson, and the most popular tools used to educate one's self are smartphones and tablet computers.

A recent study conducted by ComScore in 2012 found that 14 million, of the nearly 100 million smartphone owners in the United States, compared a price or scanned a QR- (Quick Response—black, square-dot modules arranged in a square pattern on a white background) or bar-code inside a retail store; approximately 25 percent

had even done so in a grocery store! Many of today's consumers simply feel they can survive without a retail salesperson; if they have a question, even about frosted flakes, they can quickly look it up online via their smartphones. So it's not surprising why so many consumers are turning to online shopping; online shopping has long afforded lower prices and fast deliveries. And with the advent of smartphone technology and tablet computing, shopping online has also become even more convenient.

But brick-and-mortar retailers, particularly department stores (e.g., Sears), general merchandisers (e.g., Walmart), category killers (e.g., Best Buy), and specialty clothing stores (e.g., Zara), are all beginning to fight back. At the heart of their attempts to regain the lost consumers' dollars spent online is *enhanced service*. But these retailers can't simply expect a more cheerful sales-staff or even personal shopping to overcome the convenience and

(continued)

information capabilities that e-tailing provides. Instead, many are looking to provide more of a "blended" retail environment: one that leverages the best of shopping online with all the advantages of in-store shopping, such as the ability to touch, taste, smell, and try out merchandise in person (i.e., the ability to *experience* the merchandise). In essence, traditional retailers are realizing that to stay competitive they must offer an experience that one cannot get online, and they view technology simply as an avenue for "leveling the playing field" with online retailers like Amazon. And the tools traditional retailers are turning to first in order to blend technology with the in-store environment are tablet computers and smartphones.

Tablet computers, like the iPad and Kindle Fire, and smartphones, like the iPhone, make it possible for sales associates to pull up one's purchase history, help compare options and features, and even check-out customers immediately following product selection. For example, Neiman Marcus's "NM Service" is an iPhone app designed to connect customers with their favorite sales associates. When the customer walks into the store, the app immediately alerts the sales associate. The associate can then quickly review the customer's purchase history and text the customer a message, like "I found the perfect tie and cuff links to go with the suit you bought last week," prior to meeting up with the customer on the sales floor.

But such service isn't limited only to high-end retailers. In 2012, Lowe's distributed over 42,000 iPhones to its workers and developed its "Store Associates App," which includes an estimator to help customers determine how much paint or carpet to buy. Quick-service restaurants, like Buffalo Wild Wings, have also even begun testing mobile app technology, which allows customers to place an order as soon as they sit down. And recent studies have found that restaurants that have developed mobile devices have seen a 25 percent increase in the number of times they can turn a table, thus serving more customers per shift, which is definitely desired by the time-pressed lunch crowd. And even some of the oldest retailers in North America, Sears and Macy's, are increasing their use of quick response (QR) codes throughout their stores near items for which customers would most likely want additional information and are deploying thousands of tablet computers to their sales staff and as displays throughout their stores, so that customers may have access to information on their own in the event a salesperson is not immediately available. And internal studies have found that use of display tablets and additional QR codes have not only assisted customers who do not wish to wait for personal service, but also kept customers focused on the *product rather than the price of the good.*

Sources: Lee, Thomas, "Best Buy's Richfield Store Seeks to Connect on New Scale," *Star Tribune*, June 30: D1; Patel, Kunur, "Retailers Strike Back in Mobile Wars with…People," *Advertising Age*, 83(12), 2012: 18–20; Aquino, Judith, "Tablets and Smartphones Transform the In-Store Customer Experience: Retailers Hope to Give Customers New Incentives to Shop Brick-and-Mortar Stores," *CRM Magazine*, 16 (January 2012): 17–18; Skeldon, Paul (2011), "14m Americans Scanned QR and Bar Codes with Their Mobiles in June 2011," *Internet Retailing – Selling in the Digital Age* [online] Available at http://internetretailing.net [Accessed: May 19, 2012].

current products, but also be familiar with the new products and *technology platforms* that are most likely to be "right around the corner."[39]

Experience   One of the most reliable predictors of success as a salesperson is prior work experience, especially selling experience. If applicants have performed well in prior jobs, then there is a good chance that they will perform well in the future. However, many applicants for retail selling jobs are young and have no prior work experience of any magnitude. These applicants are better assessed on their personal character and apparent ambition, drive, and work ethic. This could be indicated by leadership positions in clubs or student organizations, timely graduation, and the display of ambition during the interview process.

Salesperson Training

After salespeople are selected, they will need some form of training. This is true even if they have selling experience. In their training programs, retailers can explain their own policies. Furthermore, retailers usually want inexperienced salespeople to become familiar with and knowledgeable about their merchandise, warranties, and return policies, the different customer types they may have to deal with, and the selling strategies

Salesperson training teaches new employees about the merchandise, policies and mission of the retailer as well as the general principles of dealing with customers.

appropriate for these different customers. Even order takers need training in greeting a customer, thanking customers, and using a point-of-sale terminal. Best Buy, Coach, Discount Tire, Ethan Allen Furniture, Lexus Auto Dealerships, Nordstrom, University of Phoenix, and Tiffany's do an extremely good job of training new sales employees. Another great source of sales training is at industry trade shows such as the annual home furnishings, toy, hardware, gift, and other trade shows or the annual National Retail Federation conference held in January in New York City. Attendees can take 1-hour to half-day courses on many retail topics that also include retail-selling and merchandising skills. Often these training programs are put on by manufacturers and, thus, have an obvious additional purpose of promoting the manufacturers' merchandise lines, but these programs are also staffed by high caliber and often well-recognized sales trainers.

As illustrated in this chapter's "Service Retailing" box, probably the most important skill the retailer can teach the new sales staff is common customer etiquette and courtesy. Office Depot's employee training manual, for example, says that employees are to offer fanatical customer service by "doing, with truth and compassion, whatever it takes and then some, to win the customer's heart forever." The discount chain insists that its sales staff carry the following "crib sheet" about being customer friendly with them at all times they are on the sales floor.

> *Customer Friendly Means...*
> Smiling
> Greeting the customer
> Being as helpful as you would want somebody to be to you
> Using the customer's name (if possible)
> Saying "Thank You"

The importance of being customer friendly can be shown in studies from the medical field. These studies found that the doctor's competence and prescribed method of treatment played a very small role in determining whether a malpractice suit would be filed. Rather, it was the interpersonal skills that the doctor used with the patient that was the determining factor.[40]

Retailer's Policies

In most situations, the salesperson provides the interface between the customer and retailer. It is thus important for the salesperson to become familiar with the retailer's policies, especially those that may involve the customer directly. Some of these policies relate to merchandise returns and adjustments, shoplifting, credit terms, layaway, delivery, and price negotiation. In addition, the retail salesperson should be knowledgeable about work hours, rest periods, lunch and dinner breaks, commission and quota plans, nonselling duties, and standards of periodic job evaluation. Sales employees should also be informed about the criteria used for promotion and advancement, as well as dismissal and termination, within the retail enterprise.

Merchandise

If the merchandise includes shopping goods, then the retailer will want to familiarize its salespeople with the strengths and weaknesses of the merchandise so they can advise customers on the best items to meet their needs. The retailer may also suggest that the salesperson become knowledgeable of competitors' merchandise offerings and their strengths and weaknesses.

Increasingly, retail salespeople need to be familiar with the warranty terms and serviceability of merchandise the retailer handles. This implies that the salesperson know something about the reputation of each manufacturer the retailer represents.

Customer Types

Many retailers have recognized that an important way to increase customer satisfaction is by having their salespeople identify and respond to certain customer types.[41] Various customer types are described in Exhibit 12.7. By knowing how to handle each of these customers, the salesperson can generate additional sales. Too many times, retailers dwell on handling the technical details of the job rather than the feelings of a customer. One retail salesperson (who should go online at the customerssuck.com website mentioned earlier in the chapter) said this about her training program: "The computer training was real good. I know how to do all this technical stuff, but nobody prepared me for dealing with all these different types of people."

Customer Choice Criteria

The retail salesperson should also learn how to identify the customer's choice criteria and how to respond to them.[42] There are four choice criteria situations: (1) The customer has no active product choice criteria; (2) the customer has product choice criteria but they are inadequate or vague; (3) the customer has product choice criteria but they are in conflict; and (4) the customer has product choice criteria that are explicit and well defined. For each situation, there is an appropriate selling strategy that the salesperson should learn.

No Active Product Choice Criteria   The best sales strategy when the customer does not have a prior criteria set is to educate the customer on the best choice criteria and how to weigh them. For example, a prospective customer enters an automobile dealership to purchase a used automobile but does not know what criteria to use in selecting the best car. The salesperson may present convincing arguments for considering four criteria in the following order of importance: warranty, fuel economy, price, and comfort.

Exhibit 12.7
Various Customer Types

Characteristics	Basic Types		Recommendations
Don't trust any salesperson. Resist communication as they have a dislike of others. Generally uncooperative and will explode at slightest provocation.	**Defensive**		Avoid mistaking their silence for openness to your ideas. Stick to basic facts. Tactfully inject product's advantages and disadvantages.
Intense, impatient personality. Often interrupt salespersons and have a perpetually "strained" expression. Often driven and successful people who want results fast.	**Interrupter**		Don't waste time; move quickly and firmly from one sales point to another. Avoid overkill since they know what they want.
Confident in their ability to make decisions and stay with them. Open to new ideas but want brevity. Highly motivated by self-pride.	**Decisive**		No canned presentations. The key is to assist. Don't argue or point out errors in their judgment.
They worry about making the wrong decision and therefore tend to postpone all decisions. Want salesperson to make decision for them.	**Indecisive**		Avoid becoming frustrated yourself. Determine as early as possible the need and concentrate on that. Avoid presenting customer with too many alternatives. Start with making decisions on minor points.
Friendly, talkative types who are enjoyable to visit with. Many have excess time on their hands (e.g., retirees). They usually resist the close.	**Sociable**		You may have to wait out these customers. Listen for points in conversation where you can interject product's merits. Pressure close is out. Subtle friendly close needed.
Quick to make decision. Impatient, just as likely to walk out as they were to walk in.	**Impulsive**		Close as rapidly as possible. Avoid any useless interaction. Avoid any oversell. Highlight product's merits.

Once the salesperson and customer agree on this list, they can work together at finding the used car that best fits the criteria. Incidentally, as pointed out earlier in this chapter's "What's New?" box, you will soon be witnessing more salespeople with their tablet computers in hand that allow them to pull up inventory at other retail locations, play recorded product demonstrations saved to YouTube or the firm's internal servers, compare models and features, or help the customer order a product online.

Inadequate or Vague Choice Criteria   When the criteria are inadequate or vague, the range of products that will satisfy them is often wide. Perhaps the easiest thing for the salesperson to do is to show that a particular product fits a customer's choice criteria. Because the choice criteria are vague, this would not be difficult, and little actual selling may be involved. However, the customer may have trouble believing that the product the salesperson selected is the best one to meet his or her needs. The customer may therefore choose to shop around at other locations.

If the salesclerk is interested in building repeat business and customer goodwill and has a wide range of products to sell, then a preferable strategy would be to help the customer define his or her problem in order to refine the choice criteria. The customer and salesclerk can work together in defining the criteria of a good product and then select the product that best fits the criteria.

Choice Criteria in Conflict   Prospective customers with choice criteria that are in conflict frequently have trouble making purchase decisions. There are two basic ways in which choice criteria can be in conflict. First, the customer may want a product to possess two or more attributes that are mutually exclusive. For example, a person purchasing a mountain bike may wish it to be of high quality and low price. This person will quickly find that these two attributes do not coexist. The best strategy in this situation is for the salesperson to play down one of the attributes and play up the other. A second way the choice criteria can be in conflict is when a single attribute possesses both positive and negative aspects. Consider a person thinking of purchasing a high-performance automobile. High-performance automobiles have both positive aspects (status, speed, and pleasure fulfillment) and negative aspects (high insurance rates and low mileage per gallon). For this type of conflict, the best selling strategy is to enhance the positive aspects and downplay the negative aspects.

Explicit Choice Criteria   When the customer has a well-defined, explicit choice criteria, the best selling strategy is for the salesperson to illustrate how a specific product fits these criteria. "The salesclerk guides the customer into agreeing that each attribute of his product matches the attributes on the customer's specification. If, at the end of the sales talk, the customer does not agree to the salesclerk's proposition, he appears to be denying what he has previously admitted."[43]

Sales Force Compensation

Compensation is one of the major variables in attracting, retaining, and motivating retail salespeople. Quite simply, the quality of sales personnel or sales managers is directly proportional to the compensation package offered. Naturally, other things besides compensation are important to employees. According to a report by Deloitte & Touche's Human Resource Strategies Group, "more flexible, portable benefits systems with fewer links to age and service" are desired by today's retail associates. In addition, these benefits should be compatible with the employee's lifestyle choices.[44]

Here the term *compensation* includes direct-dollar payments (wages, commissions, and bonuses) and indirect payments (insurance, vacation time, retirement plans). Compensation plans for retail salespeople can have as many as three basic components: a fixed component, a variable component, and a fringe-benefit component. The *fixed component* typically is composed of some base wage per hour, week, month, or year. The *variable component* is often composed of some bonus that is received if performance warrants. Salesclerks may be paid a bonus, usually from 5 percent to 10 percent of sales above some established minimum, and department managers may receive a bonus based on the profit performance of their department. Many of the readers of this text are or have been waiters or servers in a restaurant; the tips you received while working each night were variable components to your overall pay that the retailer did not control. Finally, a *fringe-benefit package* may include such things as health insurance, disability benefits, life insurance, retirement plans, the use of automobiles, and financial counseling.

The best combination of fixed, variable, and fringe-benefit compensation components depends on the person, the job, and the retail organization. There is no set formula. Some top retail sales personnel and managers prefer mostly salary, others thrive on bonuses, and still others would rather have more pension benefits. Therefore, the compensation package needs to be tailored to the individual. We now focus our attention on compensation of the sales force, but the same principles will apply to managers.

Retail sales-force compensation programs can be conveniently broken into three major types: (1) straight salary, (2) salary plus commission, and (3) straight commission. Each method has its advantages and disadvantages.

Straight Salary

In the straight salary program, the salesperson receives a fixed salary per time period (usually per week) regardless of the level of sales generated or orders taken. However, over time, if the salesperson does not help generate sales or take enough orders, he or she will likely be terminated for not performing adequately. Similarly, over time, if the salesperson helps to generate more than a proportionate share of sales or fills more than a proportionate number of orders, then the retailer will be unable to retain the employee without a raise.

Many small retailers use this compensation method because they typically assign tasks such as stock rearranging, merchandise display, and other nonselling duties to their salespeople. Therefore, if the employees were paid on a commission basis, they would spend little time, if any, performing nonselling tasks (as their compensation does not reward them for doing any action beyond selling), and the retail organization would suffer. Many promotional and price-oriented chain stores whose salespeople are merely order takers will use the straight salary method because the salesperson is not much of a factor in generating sales. Also, most clerks and cashiers, as well as other lower-level retail personnel are almost always paid straight salaries.

The salesperson may view this plan as attractive because it offers income security or as unappealing because it gives little incentive for extraordinary effort and performance. Thus, for this method (the easiest plan for the employee to understand) to be effective, it must be combined with a periodic evaluation so that superior salespeople can be identified and singled out for higher salaries.

Salary Plus Commission

Sometimes the salesperson is paid a fixed salary per time period plus a percentage commission on all sales or on all sales over an established quota. Because merchandise lines and items can vary in terms of gross margins, some retailers pay commissions on gross margin dollars generated. Often, the fixed salary is lower than that of the salesperson working on a straight salary plan, but the commission structure gives one the potential to earn more than the person on the straight salary plan. In fact, most salespeople on the salary plus commission program earn more than their counterparts on a straight salary program.

This plan gives the employees a stable base income—and thus incentive to perform nonselling tasks—but it also encourages and rewards superior effort. Therefore, it represents a good compromise between the straight salary and the straight commission programs. In many cases, top management generally receives a salary and a bonus based on overall store or department performance. For example, the Waffle House provides its store managers with a bonus that's equivalent to 10 percent of operating profits.

Straight Commission

The income of some salespeople is limited to a percentage commission on each sale they generate. The commission could be the same percentage on all merchandise or it could vary depending on the profitability of the item.

The straight commission plan provides substantial incentive for retail salespeople to generate sales. However, when the general business climate is poor, retail salespeople may not be able to generate enough volume to meet their fixed-payment obligations (mortgage payment, auto payment, food expenses). Because of that problem, most retailers slightly modify the straight commission plan to allow the salesperson to draw wages against future commissions up to some specified amount per week. A major problem with the straight commission plan is that it may provide the retail salesperson with too much incentive to sell. As a result of the income insecurity features of this plan, the employee may begin to use pressure tactics to close sales, hurting the retailer's image and long-run sales performance. Similarly, the employee may not be willing to perform other duties such as helping customers with returned merchandise or helping to set up displays or restock merchandise when low. After all, compensation is paid to sell, not to handle customer complaints or displays. Generally, sales personnel for high-price merchandise or high-ticket items (such as automobiles, real estates, jewelry, and furniture, as well as those items requiring the sales personnel to prospect or seek out potential customers, i.e., insurance and door-to-door selling) are paid this way.

An Ernst & Young survey reported that 51 percent of the retailers polled used a salary plus commission plan, and 38 percent used straight commission.[45] During the late 1990s, some retailers began to reduce the commission portion of employee-compensation plans and increase the salary portion. This was an attempt to reduce consumer distaste for what was perceived to be "high-pressure selling." However, as retailers have faced a tight labor market and the need to increase productivity in recent years, the trend has begun to reverse.

Supplemental Benefits

In addition to regular wages (salary, commission, or both), retail salespeople also can receive four types of supplementary benefits: employee discounts, insurance and retirement benefits, childcare, and push money. Push money may be new to you so we will explain this type of benefit. Retailers often refer to push money also as *prize money, premium merchandise, spiffs,* or just plain *PM.* The PM, which is paid to the salesperson in addition to base salary and regular commissions, is said to encourage additional selling effort on particular items or merchandise lines.

PMs can be either retailer- or supplier-offered. A retailer may give a PM in order to get salespeople to sell old or slow-moving merchandise. The salesperson who sells the most may win a free trip to Hawaii or some other prize, or everyone who sells an established quantity of merchandise may get a prize or premium. Or the retailer may simply offer an extra $25 bonus for the sale of a specific product—for example, a dining-room table. Suppliers, on the other hand, tend to offer PMs to retail salespeople for selling the top-of-the line or most profitable items in the suppliers' product mix. These supplier-offered PMs are common in the appliance, furniture, jewelry, and restaurant industries. In fact, one of the authors worked his way through high school and college waiting tables in Mexican food restaurants, which are often times rife with PMs from liquor manufacturers. Routinely, the author would show up for an "evening shift" only to find out that there was a $100 prize available to the waiter who sold the most margaritas using, for example, Sauza tequila.

Occasionally, there may be a conflict between the supplier and the retailer over the offering of PMs. This conflict arises because the supplier may be offering the retailer's salespeople an incentive to push an item or merchandise line that may not be the most profitable line for the retailer or the best for the customer, although it may be highly profitable to the supplier. In the aforementioned example, the author routinely would win a nightly PM by pushing Sauza as the base of a margarita even though many of the waiters, including the author, felt other tequilas offered better taste or the same quality at more reasonable prices. Some retailers prefer to keep all PMs for themselves, because they believe they are already paying a fair wage to their salespeople.

Evaluation of Salespeople

Evaluation of salespeople seeks to determine each salesperson's value to the firm. That determination is important as a basis for salary adjustments, promotions, transfers, terminations, and sales reinforcement. The retailer should develop a systematic method for evaluating both individual salespeople and the total sales staff. Rather than subjectively evaluating performance, the manager should develop explicit performance standards.

Performance Standards

Several standards can be developed to measure a salesperson's performance. Some standards apply only to individual efforts, whereas others assess both individual and total sales-force effort.

conversion rate
Is the percentage of shoppers that enter the store that are converted into purchasers.

Conversion Rate   The **conversion rate** is the percentage of all shoppers who make a purchase—that is, who are converted into customers. This is a measure of the sales force's performance, not the individual salesperson's.

A poor conversion rate can be caused by a variety of factors. Perhaps there were not enough clerks on hand when customers needed them. This could have resulted in numerous unassisted searches and long customer waits, causing many customers to exit the store without making a purchase. Or the number of salesclerks could have been adequate to handle the flow of customers, but the salespeople may not have done a good selling job. A poor selling job could have several causes, including giving inadequate product information, disagreeing or arguing too strongly with the customer, demonstrating the product poorly, having an unfriendly attitude, or giving up on the sale too early. However, all of these factors are really related to poor training, which is the underlying reason for poor sales. A low conversion rate might also have been due to factors beyond the salesperson's control, such as inadequate merchandise levels. The important point is that when a substandard conversion rate exists, the retailer should identify the causes and remedy the situation because even a small increase in the conversion rate can have a major impact on retail sales.

Marvin Rothenberg, a retired retail consultant, studied what happened in four chains operating a total of 68 department stores.[46] He found that 131,328,000 sales opportunities a year (i.e., 2.4 million shoppers who averaged 1.9 shopping visits per month and

2.4 departments per trip) produced only 38 million sales transactions. Thus, 93 million departmental shopping visits resulted in "no sale."

In fact, 49 million of the departmental shoppers who made no purchase did not even have contact with a salesperson or a cashier. Another 44 million had contact with a salesperson but did not buy anything. And among these two segments of 93 million shoppers already in the departments, 28 million came into the department with the intent to make a specific purchase! In total, 71 percent of all the departmental shopping visits resulted in shoppers either having no contact with sales personnel or having the wrong kind of contact; as a result, they made no purchase. No wonder that, in another study, Rothenberg found that one-third of customers who entered a store with the expressed intent of making a specific purchase walked out without making any purchase. It is obvious that a small increase in converting these nonpurchasing consumers into customers could increase sales dramatically, even if the shopper is only in the store as a means to combat loneliness.

For example, if these retailers did nothing more than just contact half the 49 million customers who had no sales contact, and if the conversion rate among this group was only half of what it was among those who had sales contact, then the number of sales transactions, currently 38 million, would increase by 15 percent (half of 49 million who had no contact multiplied by half of the conversion rate for those who had contact equals 5.6 million more sales transactions). That's an opportunity to add 15 percent to sales by doing nothing more than what is already being achieved when customers contact a salesperson. Yet for many retailers this is a lost opportunity as they either do not want to or do not know how to train their sales staff in the proper methods of approaching and assisting customers and more generally providing customer service. Worse yet are those retailers who view their sales force as an operating expense and not as an investment. As such they want to cut back on expenses and end up with too few salespeople on duty. Either way, the retailer is missing out on a great opportunity to increase sales.

Some online retailers, realizing the importance of converting as many lookers into buyers as possible, are chatting up customers to get them to stay on their site longer and hopefully buy something. Such strategies are especially beneficial to the small online retailers because it offers a relatively low-cost way to track consumer behavior and concerns and react accordingly. The strategy also allows small online companies, with their limited promotional and research budgets, to copy some of the personalized attention that bricks-and-mortar stores are able to use.

Sales per Hour   Perhaps the most common measure of sales-force performance is sales per hour. Sales per hour is computed by dividing total dollar sales over a particular time frame by total salesperson or sales-force hours. A retailer can compute this simple measure for each salesperson, any group of salespeople, or the entire sales force. It can also be computed for various days, weeks, or months. This simple measure can be quite useful when comparing salespeople like when comparing two automobile salespeople working the identical shift or two waiters in a fine dining restaurant where it can be clearly seen which one does a better job at obtaining more appetizer, drink, and desert orders.

When employing this measure, remember that standards should be specific to the group or person being evaluated for a particular time period. For example, in a department store, the sales per hour of selling effort cannot be expected to be the same for the toy department as for the jewelry department. Nor could one expect the same sales per hour during July and December because of the heavy Christmas demand for toys and jewelry. In some lines of retail trade, particularly those selling high-ticket items such as automobiles, the key performance measure is gross profit generated per salesperson.

Use of Time   Standards can be developed for how salespeople should spend their time. A salesperson's time can be spent in four ways:

1. *Selling time* is any time spent assisting customers with their needs. This could be time spent talking, demonstrating a product, writing sales receipts, or assisting the customer in other potentially revenue-generating ways.
2. *Nonselling time* is any time spent on nonselling tasks such as marking or straightening up the merchandise.
3. *Idle time* is time the salesperson is on the sales floor but is not involved in any productive work.
4. *Absent time* occurs when the salespeople are not on the sales floor. They may be at lunch, in the employee lounge, in another part of the store, or in some inappropriate place.

The retailer may develop standards for each of these ways to spend time. For example, the standard time allocation may suggest that salespeople spend 60 percent of their time selling, 28 percent of their time on nonselling activities, 5 percent idle, and 7 percent absent. Any deviation from these standards should be investigated, and corrective measures should be taken if necessary.

Data Requirements

To establish proper standards of performance, the retailer needs data. What are good standards for the conversion rate? sales per hour? time allocation? Only data will help answer these questions. For bricks-and-mortar retailers, data can come from retail trade associations, consulting firms, or the retailer's own experience.

Once the retailer obtains the data on which to base standards, it must collect additional data continually or at least periodically on actual performance. For example, an increasing number of retailers today survey their customers and use other programs, such as mystery shoppers, to evaluate their salespeople. The results of mystery shopper surveys, along with the employee's actual conversion rate, sales per hour, and time allocation must be compared to their respective standards. If the actual data differ significantly from the standard, then an investigation of the cause is warranted. Both favorable and unfavorable variances should be investigated because a retailer may learn just as much from unusually good performance as from unusually poor performance.

LO 5

The Retail Sales Process

Describe the retail selling process.

Several basic steps occur during the retail selling process. The length of time that a salesperson spends in each one of these steps depends on the product type, the customer, and the selling situation. Exhibit 12.8 details the sales-process model.

Prospecting

prospecting
Is the process of locating or identifying potential customers who have the ability and willingness to purchase your product.

Prospecting is the search process of finding those who have the ability and willingness to purchase your product. Prospecting is particularly important when the store is full of customers. A salesperson should be aware that good prospects generally display more interest in the product than poor prospects that are "just looking." Salespeople should take advantage of the behavioral cues shown in Exhibit 12.8.

Approach

The salesperson may meet hundreds of customers a day, but the customer is only going to meet the salesperson once that day. Therefore, it is extremely important to remember

Exhibit 12.8
The Selling Process in the Retail Environment

Step 1—Prospecting
Decide who can benefit from your product.
a. Find prospects.
b. Qualify prospects (determine whether a prospect has the ability, buying power, and willingness to make a purchase).

Step 2—Approach
The first 15 seconds are the key as they set the mood for the sale.
a. Never say, "May I help you?"
A single "Hello," "Good morning," or "What may I show you?" makes the customer realize that you are glad they are in your store.
b. Determine the customer's needs as early as possible.
Listen—*What you hear* is more important than anything you could possibly tell your customer. Ask a few well-chosen questions—What do I need to know?
1. Product needed or problem to be solved.
2. User of the product (tell me about so-and-so).

Step 3—The Sales Presentation
Get the customer to want to buy your product/service.
a. Pick the right price level.
If uncertain, ask, "Is there a price range you have in mind?" Remember, you can't pick out the *right product* for the uncertain customer if the price is wrong.
b. Pick the right product.
Match user and need with product. Show the customer at least two items.
c. Show the merchandise in an appealing manner.
1. Make the merchandise stand out.
2. Show the item so that its good points will be seen.
3. Let the customer handle the merchandise.
4. Stress the features of the product.
5. Explain the benefits of these features.
6. Appeal to the customer's emotions.
d. Help the customer decide.
1. Handle objections.
2. Replace unneeded items.
3. Watch for unconscious clues.
4. Stress features and benefits of "key" product.

Step 4—Closing the Sale
Reach an agreement.
a. What is going on in the customer's mind?
b. Four effective ways to close:
1. Make the decision for the customer.
2. Assume the decision has already been made.
3. Ask the customer to choose.
4. Turn an objection around.

Step 5—Suggestion Selling
Follow up leads to other sales.

that the first 15 seconds sets the mood for the sale. The salesperson must use this time to begin enhancing the shopping experience of everyone who walks through the front door. Therefore, the sales presentation should never begin with "May I help you?" or any other question to which the customer may respond negatively. A simple "Good morning" (afternoon, evening) or any other greeting acknowledging the customer's presence should do. Nordstrom's trains its sales force to mention an item the customer is wearing as an approach if something better is not evident.

The key to a successful approach is discerning the customer's needs as soon as possible by asking the right questions and listening. What the salesperson hears about the customer's problem or need is more important than anything the salesperson can possibly contribute at this point. The salesperson should ask only a few well-chosen questions to find out more about the need or problem to be solved. The salesperson should also find out if the user of the product is a different individual than the customer. Remember the salesperson should ask only as many questions as needed, and let the customer do the talking. One well-known retail sales trainer was famous for telling her trainees that "you can close more sales with your ears than with your mouth." Listening to the voice of the customer is *key*.

Sales Presentation

Once the initial contact has been established and the salesperson has listened to the customer's problems and needs, the salesperson is in a position to present the merchandise and sales message correctly. How the salesperson presents the product or service depends on the customer and the situation. The key, however, is to get the customer to want to buy your product or service. The salesperson might begin by determining the right price range of products to show the customer. A price too high or too low will generally result in a lost sale. If uncertain, the salesperson should ask the customer about the price range desired.

Next, the salesperson should pick out what he or she believes will be the right product or service to satisfy the customer's needs. The salesperson should be careful not to show the customer too many products so as to avoid confusing him or her.

The salesperson should tell the customer about the merchandise in an appealing way, stressing the features that are the outstanding qualities or characteristics of the product, and have the customer handle the merchandise. The salesperson can then help the customer decide on the product or service that best fulfills the customer's needs. The salesperson should handle any objection that the customer might have, replace the unneeded items, and continue to stress the features and benefits of the product the customer seems most interested in.

Recognizing the importance of the sales presentation and the fact that effective sales presentations require knowledgeable salespeople, it is not unusual for manufacturers to offer sales training for retail salespeople. This is quite a common practice in the retail tire business where independent tire dealers such as Discount Tire and Four Day Tire compete with not only factory-affiliated stores such as Firestone and Goodyear, but also retailers such as Sears and Walmart and Costco that sell competing lines of tires. For instance, Continental Tire offers a program for Discount Tire salespeople in the Texas hill country where they can drive Ford Mustangs equipped with Continental and Goodyear tires (one of Continental's major competitors) on a 1.1 mile asphalt race track so they can compare Continental's tire performance with Goodyear. After a couple of hours of racing, the salespeople are hosted to a Texas-style happy hour and dinner and fishing at a local ranch. Incidentally, Michelin and Goodyear offer similar programs. These programs, often costing $1,000 per retail salesperson, appear to pay off since Continental has found that sales of salespeople at the event experience a 30 percent increase in sales of Continental tires.[47]

Closing the Sale

closing the sale
Is the action the salesperson takes to bring a potential sale to its natural conclusion.

Closing the sale is a natural conclusion to the selling process. However, for most salespeople, closing the sale is the most difficult part of the job. In fact, by some estimates, almost three-quarters of all "lost" sales occur during this stage of the selling process because the salesperson didn't "ask for the sale." The salesperson was either afraid of rejection or, worst, was unaware that the customer was ready to make the purchase. Remember, the salesperson is there to help the customer solve a problem, and so should not be afraid to ask for the sale. The key to closing the sale is to determine what is going on in the customer's mind. Exhibit 12.9 lists some of the things a salesperson should watch for at this stage of the selling process. If the salesperson waits too long or is too impatient in completing this step, then the customer will be gone before the salesperson realizes it. There are four effective ways to close a sale: (1) make the decision for the customer, (2) assume that the decision has been made and ask if the sale will be cash or charge, (3) ask the customer to select the product or service, and (4) turn an objection around by stressing a positive aspect of the product. For example, a salesperson might suggest that, although the initial cost of a product might be high, its longer life span will reduce total cost.

In the discussion of the consumer behavior model in Chapter 3, postpurchase resentment was described. This can occur whether the consumer is buying a car, a blazer, or spring break get-a-way. Usually, the more expensive the purchase, the greater the doubt and the higher the risk of dissatisfaction. Over the years, good salespeople, selling expensive products, have found three easy steps to be effective when dealing with this problem:

1. Always congratulate the customer for making a wise decision. As soon as customers agree to a purchase, assure them that others have been happy with their decision to purchase the same item, and you know they will be equally satisfied.

Exhibit 12.9
Some Closing Signals Salespeople Should Be on the Lookout For

The customer reexamines the product carefully.
The customer tries on the product (i.e., trying on a sport coat or strapping on a wristwatch).
The customer begins to read the warranty or brochure.
The customer makes statements similar to the following:

> I always wanted a compact disc player.
> I never realized that these were so inexpensive.
> I bet my wife would love this.

The customer asks questions like:

> Does this come in any other colors?
> Do you accept Discover cards?
> Can you deliver this tomorrow?
> Do you have a size 7 in this style?
> Do you accept trade-ins?
> Do you have any training sessions available?
> Do you have it in stock?
> What accessories are available?
> Where would I take it to get it serviced?
> Is it really that easy to operate?

2. Always send a thank-you note. Nordstrom's system has shown everyone the value of these notes by the positive customer responses and referrals.

3. Get the customer in possession of the product as quickly as possible. If the products can't be delivered immediately, then send updates on the progress of those orders, even if it is only a phone call or e-mail.

Suggestion Selling

An effective salesperson continues to sell even after the sale has been completed. An additional sale is always possible. The salesperson should find out if the customer has any other needs or if the customer knows of anybody else with needs that can be solved with the salesperson's product line. Many retailers refer to suggestion selling as "filling the basket." A couple of examples would be selling a Valentine's gift to a college student for his girlfriend and then asking if he needs help with a gift for his mother or suggesting an extra ink cartridge to a customer who just purchased a printer (because most cartridges in printers are only half-full).

Many customers appreciate suggestion selling because it often eliminates a second shopping trip. However, it may also decrease a consumer's satisfaction with the retailer as some customers view suggestion selling as an annoyance.

LO 6

The Customer-Service and Sales-Enhancement Audit

Discuss the importance of customer-service audit.

Up to this point, we have discussed the level and type of sales personnel needed in a retail operation; the types of retail selling; the selection, training, compensation, and management of the sales force; the factors to consider when evaluating individual salespeople, and how to sell in a retail store. These are microapproaches to improving the productivity of an individual. How do we get macro answers for the performance of a whole department or a whole store? Remember the example earlier in this chapter of those retailers who had 49 million possible buyers walk out of their stores without any salesperson contact? One solution is an audit of the retailer's customer-services and sales-enhancement programs.

Such an audit, which can easily be performed by the retailer's own staff or by a consultant, provides the direction that enables retailers to capture the unrealized potential of customers who walk out with no salesperson contact. It analyzes current levels of performance by selling area within each store, revealing how customers shop the store, and the extent of the service they receive. It is *not* an attempt to learn what the customers want (e.g., friendly and competent salespeople, low prices, free assembly); instead, it concentrates on the facts of their shopping experience.

The audit is usually performed by having the retailer's staff, or hired researchers, intercept customers as they leave the store and asking about their experience in the store. The number of customers interviewed should reflect the size and shopping patterns of each store. The objectives of the audit are to

- identify the service, salesmanship, and sales-enhancement methods that will produce more sales from the existing shopping traffic;
- target the methods by store and selling area that will produce the most significant improvements; and
- determine the added sales that can be generated by improving the accepted service level, salesmanship, and sales-enhancement programs.

Upon completion, the audit provides management with a detailed analysis of current sales activity by location and by selling area. It identifies how and where additional sales volume is available. It measures, analyzes, and reports on the specific factors.

Basic Service

1. *Customer contact.* In stores that purport to offer service, there can be no sale if the shopper has no contact with a salesperson or a cashier. Increasing the number of shoppers who are approached increases the number of shoppers who are likely to buy.
2. *Salesperson-initiated contact.* Motivated salespeople—those who do not wait for customers to approach them—can prevent walkouts and generate more sales from shoppers who otherwise might have to spend shopping time looking for a salesperson.
3. *Customer acknowledgment.* Greeting customers within a short time frame also prevents walkouts and provides more shopping time. It keeps the shopper in a favorable buying mood.

Salesmanship

4. *Merchandise knowledge.* A salesperson with product knowledge can answer a shopper's questions, enhance the transaction, help to consummate the sales, prevent lost sales, and even add to the purchase.
5. *Needs clarification.* Asking the proper questions enables the salesperson to present and show the proper merchandise.
6. *Active selling.* Actively selling the merchandise and volunteering advice about the use and care of the goods, as well as stating the advantages of ownership, helps to consummate the sale.
7. *Suggestion selling.* Suggesting additional or complementary merchandise may increase the value of the sale. (The audit should also measure the number of times that suggestion selling resulted in an additional purchase.)

Sales Enhancement

8. *Impulse purchasing.* Proper selection of merchandise, packaging, location within a department, presentation, and then servicing the transaction will increase the productivity of shopping traffic.
9. *Walkouts.* Retaining sales that would otherwise be lost is one of the most direct and immediate routes to sales improvement. Offering the desired goods in easy-to-find locations is the most obvious method for reducing walkouts. However, customer contact and salesmanship can be a major deterrent of walkouts among those who come to buy.

These elements of service, salesmanship, and sales enhancement are measured and reported by selling area within each store, enabling management to apply targeted training programs. It is usually not necessary to spend money to train or retrain all personnel in each store for each of the techniques. However, when applied, the method can add significantly to the value of each transaction. For example, for the four chains cited in our earlier example, the incremental sales transactions for the average salesperson after the audit were:

10 percent … when the salesperson initiated the contact with the shopper,

3 percent … when the salesperson acknowledged the customer's presence in a timely manner,

12 percent … when the salesperson was able to answer the customer's questions,

14 percent … when the salesperson asked questions to clarify the shopper's needs,

18 percent … when the salesperson actively "sold" the merchandise, and

48 percent … when the salesperson suggested additional or complementary merchandise and the suggestion was taken.

No incremental addition to the average salesperson can be calculated for increasing contacts with shoppers, for improving the rate of impulse buying, or for reducing walk-outs. The reason is obvious: When these techniques are applied and are successful, an entirely new transaction is created!

To provide management with an action program, the customer service and sales-enhancement audit includes a series of exception reports that show specifically what improvement is necessary within each selling area at each company store. The dollar value also is listed so that management can know the added volume that is available by applying targeted retraining programs. The report should list the causes of walkouts for each selling area at each location. Management therefore receives an analysis of current performance by selling area at each company location and the specific action necessary to capture unrealized potential. The dollar opportunity is also calculated to highlight the value of each improvement. Exception reports make it easy to implement the program.

Every day, within all types of stores, there are "acres of diamonds in their own backyards." Shoppers are continuing to visit stores in large numbers, many of them will-ing, able, and anxious to be converted into buyers. Management's task is to identify where and how that can be accomplished. That is the function of the audit.

Summary

LO 1   Why is customer service so important in retailing?

This chapter emphasizes that customer service is a key revenue-generating variable for the retailer. To properly manage the customer-service decision area, the retailer needs to build a customer relationship by integrating customer service with merchandise, promo-tion, building and fixtures, price, and credit management. An integrated customer-service program will allow the retailer to expand its retail trade area, increase average transaction size, and improve operating efficiency and thus achieve improved profitability.

LO 2   What are the various customer services that a retailer can offer?

Customer services are classified into pretransaction, transaction, and posttransaction services. Pretransaction services make it easier for a potential customer to shop at a retai-ler's location or learn about the retailer's offering. Common examples are convenient hours and informational aids. Transaction-related services make it easier for the customer to complete a transaction. Popular transaction-related services are consumer credit, gift wrapping and packaging, check cashing, gift cards, personal shopping, merchandise avail-ability, personal selling, and the transaction itself. Posttransaction services influence the customer's satisfaction with the merchandise after the transaction. The most frequently encountered services are handling complaints, merchandise returns, servicing, repairing and warranting, delivery, and postsale follow-up.

LO 3   How should a retailer determine which services to offer?

Conventional wisdom suggests that the retailer should consider six factors when estab-lishing the mix of customer services: retailer's characteristics, competition, type of merchandise, price image, target market income, and cost of the service.

LO 4   What are the various management problems involved in retail selling, salesperson selection, and training, compensation, and evaluation?

This chapter also illustrates the role of managing the retail salesperson. Regardless of whether salesclerks are primarily order getters or order takers, they play an important role in the demand for a retailer's products. However, the role played by the order getter is obviously more important in this regard.

Various criteria to be used in the selection of a selling staff and its training program were discussed. Also, various compensation plans for retail salespeople that often included fixed compensation, variable compensation, and fringe benefits were reviewed. The section ended by reviewing the performance evaluation of retail salespeople.

LO 5   What steps are involved in the retail selling process?

The retail selling process consists of five steps—prospecting, approach, presentation, close, and suggestion selling. The length of time a salesperson spends on each step depends on the product type, customer, and selling situation.

LO 6   What is involved in a customer-service audit?

An audit of the retailer's customer-services and sales-enhancement programs enables retailers to capture the unrealized potential of customers who walk out without being contacted by a salesperson. It analyzes current levels of performance by selling area within each company store, revealing how customers shop the store and the extent of the service they receive. It is *not* an attempt to learn what the customers want but concentrates on the facts of their shopping experience.

Terms to Remember

high-quality service	transaction services
relationship retailing	personal shopping
customer relationship management (CRM)	dwell time
	posttransaction services
customer service	conversion rate
transient customer	prospecting
pretransaction services	closing the sale

Review and Discussion Questions

LO 1   Why is customer service so important in retailing?

1. Your store manager just told you that since profits have been falling over the past year, he has recommended to the owners that they could increase profits by cutting back further on customer services. After all, customers don't really expect service anymore. Agree or disagree with this statement and explain your reasoning.

2. Should the level of service offered by a retailer be directly proportional to the gross margin obtained from the sale of the merchandise? In other words, the more profitable the item, the greater the service level that should be extended. Explain the reasoning behind your answer.

3. Should online customers expect the same type of service that bricks-and-mortar customers get from retailers selling similar merchandise? Explain the reasoning behind your answer.

4. Explain why higher customer service will lead to higher profitability.

LO 2 | **What are the various customer services that a retailer can offer?**

5. A major discounter was recently quoted as saying that he "no longer worries about dwell time. After all, low price is the only factor that drives sales." Do you agree or disagree with this statement? What is your reasoning?

6. Some discounters not only have a "no layaway" policy but also will accept only cash. They don't accept checks or credit and debit cards. Will this hinder these stores in the marketplace? Because of the slowing economy and the high fees banks charge on the cards, as well as bad checks, is the trend moving away from accepting these forms of payment? What would you suggest retailers do? Explain your reasoning.

LO 3 | **How should a retailer determine which services to offer?**

7. How does the type of customer affect the level of customer service a retailer should offer?

8. Shouldn't all retailers seek to exceed their competition's level of customer service? Explain the reasoning behind your answer.

LO 4 | **What are the various management problems involved in retail selling, salesperson selection, training, compensation, and evaluation?**

9. Develop a list of predictor variables you would use to screen applicants for a sales position in (a) a jewelry department in a high-prestige department store, (b) a used-car dealership, (c) a health club, (d) an antique shop, and (e) a home, life, and auto insurance agency.

10. Why is training of retail salespeople generally a wise investment? Can you think of situations in which this training may not be a wise investment? Try to be as specific as possible.

11. Refer to the previous question and suggest how salespeople in these types of retail firms should be compensated.

12. A men's clothing store chain has analyzed the annual sales per salesperson in 10 of its stores nationwide. The sales per salesperson range from a low of $121,000 to a high of $248,000. Develop a list of factors that might help to explain this wide variation.

LO 5 | **What is involved in the retail selling process?**

13. When you are shopping for yourself, do you appreciate it when the salesperson uses suggestion-selling techniques? Does the type of merchandise make a difference in your answer?

14. What should retail salespeople know about customer choice criteria?

15. Why is selling so much more important for retailers of services than it is for retailers selling physical products?

LO 6 | **What is involved in a customer-service audit?**

16. Why is it so important that a retailer's sales personnel be taught that each customer must be contacted by a sales associate each time the customer enters the store? Don't some customers just want to be left alone to look around?

17. How often should a customer-service audit be performed?

Sample Test Questions

LO 1 A transient customer is a consumer who visits a retailer:

    a.   and finds the item desired in a matter of minutes.
    b.   only when his or her regular retailer is closed.
    c.   that does not meet his or her customer-service expectations.
    d.   while on vacation.
    e.   and then visits all the other retailers in the neighborhood.

LO 2 Merchandise availability is an example of:

    a.   cost of sales.
    b.   a pretransaction service.
    c.   an operating cost.
    d.   a posttransaction service.
    e.   a transaction service.

LO 3 Which of the following is not a factor in determining the service level to be offered?

    a.   income of target market
    b.   price image of the retailer
    c.   services offered by the competition
    d.   firm's management structure
    e.   retailer's characteristics

LO 4 Which one of the following factors is not one of the elements that need to be considered when designing a sales job?

    a.   feedback from supervisors
    b.   the number of complaints a salesperson should have to handle
    c.   the amount of variety involved
    d.   the appropriate degree of autonomy
    e.   the level of task identity present

LO 5 What is the first step that a salesperson should take during the sales presentation?

    a.   inform the customer about the merchandise in an appealing manner
    b.   select the right product or service that the salesperson believes will satisfy the customer's needs
    c.   greeting the customer
    d.   help the customer to decide on the product that best fulfills the customer's needs
    e.   determine the right price range of products

LO 6 Which of the following is not an objective of a customer-service audit?

    a.   It is an attempt to learn what are the most important considerations for customers when choosing a store—that is, low prices or ease of the transaction.
    b.   It identifies the service, salesmanship, and sales-enhancement methods that the retailer can use to produce more sales from the existing shopping traffic.
    c.   It targets which methods can be used to produce significant customer-service improvement.
    d.   It helps determine the added sales that can be generated by improving the current level of customer service.
    e.   All of the above are customer-service audit objectives.

Writing and Speaking Exercise

Luther Henderson was a long-term frequent Walmart shopper often spending $325 weekly on groceries and other merchandise for his family of seven. That is, until he lost his part-time job that helped to supplement his regular job as a police officer. Luther, however, knew that in a few months he would be able to find another part-time job. Therefore, he was surprised when he tried to put $794 in holiday gifts on layaway at his local Walmart and discovered that only $144 worth was eligible for layaway because the firm had a policy of not allowing all merchandise to be eligible for layaway. In disgust, he departed without putting any merchandise on layaway and also left $139 in groceries in his shopping cart. That evening, he mentioned his experience to Sally, his wife of 19 years. Sally mentioned that her friend Karen had a similar experience and decided to visit the local Kmart that she had not patronized for over decade. At Kmart, Karen had no problem putting on layaway 15 holiday gifts that totaled over $700. Karen liked the experience so much, and so disliked and was offended by the Walmart layaway policy, that she decided to boycott Walmart. Sally urged Luther to join Karen in her boycott. Luther reminded Sally that his grandfather gave him $100 of Walmart stock when he was born in 1975 and that last year when they prepared income taxes, his $100 of stock had increased to over $200,000. That evening Luther decided, as a long-term Walmart shareholder, he should first write to the senior management about his concern with the layaway policy.

Look up the senior management group at Walmart and decide to whom Luther should write. Compose a letter that you think would be appropriate for Luther to send to Walmart.

Retail Project

As you are approaching graduation, you decide that you need a new suit for interviewing. In considering your shopping alternatives, you decide to compare online clothing stores versus bricks-and-mortar stores.

Determine the difference in the amount of time involved in shopping between the two types of retailers, the time it would take for you to obtain the clothing from each, and prices. Which would you choose to use?

Planning Your Own Entrepreneurial Retail Business

Donnelly's Jewelers, a family business your grandfather started in 1952, had annual sales last year of $900,560. Your parents, who purchased this business from your grandfather in 1981, have asked you to help them develop a strategy to improve sales. Since you plan to open a second Donnelly's Jewelers store on graduation with your family's support, you want to use this opportunity to impress your parents with your business and retail-marketing skills.

In reviewing the records of the store, you were surprised to find that a record had been kept of how many shoppers visited the store on a daily basis. For the most recent year, you computed that there were 15,000 visitors and that 2,803 of these made a purchase. You also have spent the last few weeks observing the salespeople (including your parents) make sales presentations. Your observation is that they do a good job on approaching shoppers and making a sales presentation, but they are quite weak and passive on closing a sale. You also have observed little effort is made to cross-sell merchandise.

Your recommendation is to have a local professor who teaches a course in personal selling conduct a sales-training workshop. This two-day workshop would cost $5,000. After consulting with the professor, you both believe the training should produce an increase in average transaction size of $30 and an increase in the conversion rate of 5 percent.

Based on the preceding information, show the impact on annual sales of the proposed training program.

Jane's Attic

During November 2008, Jane Whitler decided to open a high-end used furniture store. Jane lived in a major metropolitan area in Southwest United States, and part of the growth of the city over the last 35 years was an increasing retired population. Many of the retirees starting to visit the city as snowbirds from the Midwest and Northeast as they neared retirement, then moved to spend their retirement years in the desert Southwest. Many of the first-wave of retirees that moved to this city back in the mid-1970s were now dying. One of the consequences of this aging population was that many estate sales occurred where Jane could purchase fine quality used furniture at very attractive prices. In addition, more and more retirees aged and got tired of the upkeep on the retirement houses they purchased a couple of decades earlier. Increasingly, they were deciding to move into retirement villages, and this triggered sales of their many high-quality home furnishings. By year end 2011, Jane was very pleased with the sales volume of Jane's Attic of nearly $2 million. At the same time, Jane looked back at the last two years and, although sales rose from $650,000 in 2009, she couldn't figure out why she was still losing money. In 2009, she lost $68,000, in 2010 the loss was $31,000, and in 2011 it was down to $20,000. She was determined that 2012 would be profitable. But, she also noticed that sales were beginning to plateau, and thus, she could not expect to easily grow her way out of the problem.

Recognizing that her biggest operating expense was compensation of her 10-person sales force, she decided to consider the possibility of a new sales force compensation plan. The current plan gave each salesperson a $1,500 monthly base salary and an 8 percent commission on sales they generated. Thus, an employee with $200,000 in annual sales would receive 8 percent of $200,000 or $16,000 and also a base of $18,000 or a total of $34,000 annually. On top of this were fringe benefits that averaged 25 percent of compensation. Jane wondered if perhaps she should lower the base salary to perhaps as low as $1,000 monthly and then perhaps increase the commission rate. She asked Ted, her brother, who had spent his entire career in business-to-business sales if she should consider establishing the commission as a percent of gross margin dollars generated on each sale. He felt this was an especially viable option because Jane allowed the salespeople to negotiate the selling price, if the salesperson got her permission. If Jane was not at the store, the salespeople could call her to discuss a price reduction. In fact, recently Jane became concerned that Hector was calling her too often pleading for permission to lower the selling price.

Jane asked John Barnes, her accountant, to prepare some sales statistics that might help her consider different sales compensation plans. The data John prepared is presented in the accompanying exhibit. Jane also wanted to establish some minimum performance goals for her salespeople. John mentioned to her that some of his other retail clients that employed salespeople or order getters versus merely order takers, tried to have each employee generate at least twice and ideally three times their annual compensation and fringe benefits in gross margin dollars. Thus, if a salesperson had total compensation and fringe benefits of $50,000 they needed to generate between $100,000 and $150,000 in gross margin dollars.

Sales Force Performance Data

Salesperson	Average Transaction	Gross Margin Percent	Total Transactions
Joe	$419	48%	378
Hector	$307	40%	412
Sally	$371	46%	329
Amy	$400	43%	401
Jean	$514	47%	395
Mark	$795	44%	412
Jason	$441	48%	470
Irene	$388	42%	401
Wayne	$441	42%	399
Maria	$703	46%	404

Questions

1. Which of Jane's 10 salespeople are the top two performers and which are the bottom two performers?

2. Should Jane lower the base monthly compensation to $1,000 from $1,500? Are there any other changes she should make to the compensation plan?

3. What should be the minimal performance that Jane should expect from her salespeople in order for them to retain their jobs? How soon should Jane decide if a salesperson should be retained or terminated?

Store Layout and Design

13

Overview

In this chapter, we discuss the place where all retailing activities come together—the retail store. The store can be the most meaningful form of communication between the retailer and its customers. Most important, the store is where sales happen—or fail to happen. We will see that, despite its hundreds of elements, the store has two primary roles: creating the proper store image and increasing the productivity of the sales space. We identify the most critical elements in creating a successful retail store and describe the art and science of store planning, merchandise presentation, and design.

Learning Objectives

After reading this chapter, you should be able to:

1. List the elements of a store's environment and define its two primary objectives.

2. Discuss the steps involved in planning the store.

3. Describe how various types of fixtures, merchandise-presentation methods and techniques, and the psychology of merchandise presentation are used to increase the productivity of the sales floor.

4. Describe why store design is so important to a store's success.

5. Explain the role of visual communications in a retail store.

LO 1

List the elements of a store's environment and define its two primary objectives.

Introduction to Store Layout Management

Chapter 11 discussed how customer service and personal selling can be used to develop a relationship with the customer. This chapter examines another tool retailers can use to initiate and continue this relationship—the retail store itself. Retailers must never forget the old axiom that "we all sell discretionary merchandise; therefore, we must package it with theater and excitement." They also must recognize that a retail store is different than an Internet site because for most individuals "shopping is a contact sport." Often consumers want to touch, feel, and experience the merchandise first-hand, and how the store engages and interacts with the shopper is critical to its success. Nonetheless, traditional brick-and-mortar retailers must be careful not to diminish the power that other channels, like the Internet or even catalogs, have or assume that once the consumer is within the retailer's four walls, the retailer need not worry about such potential competitors. As we originally pointed out in the "What's New?" box in Chapter 12, 14 million smartphone users in 2011 used their devices to compare prices with an online retailer while still inside the retailer's store (25% of which were searches comparing prices of grocery items)![1]

Today's finicky customers demand sizzle with their steak. *Setting* and *presentation* are critical factors in serving the customer. To underscore this point, consider the last time you had fajitas or were in a Mexican food restaurant and heard the loud sizzling sound that filled the restaurant as the waiter brought out a skillet full of hot fajitas. The sound you hear is part of the presentation; fajitas need not sizzle at all in order to taste good. In fact, the meat naturally only sizzles for a second or two once the meat is placed on the skillet. As the waiter walks out of the kitchen, a chef or waiter will pour a small amount of liquid, often lime juice or even water, over the meat in order to make it sizzle all the way to the table. The reason for this action: customers perceive the fajitas as more fresh and hot when it sizzles than when it doesn't.

Yet all too often the retailer, realizing the importance of getting customers into a store, develops an excellent promotional campaign only to have the customer become turned off after entering the store. Successful retailers today use their stores as a means to excite their customers so that they will spend more time looking and viewing merchandise, which will subsequently enhance sales. The last thing a retailer needs is for customers to enter the store only to subsequently walk out empty handed.

No other variable in the retailing mix influences the consumer's initial perception of a bricks-and-mortar retailer more than the store itself. Unfortunately, many retailers do not realize how valuable the hundreds of thousands of dollars—and, for larger stores, millions of dollars—invested in a store's design and atmosphere are creating a unique platform that not only assists salespeople in engaging the consumer, but also enhances the overall shopping experience. Successful retailers today are spending a great deal of time and effort making sure the right things happen in their stores so that the right customers enter the stores, shop, and spend money. Simply put, for retailers the store is "where the action is," and this includes such seemingly minor details as the placement and display of merchandise.

Consider, for example, petite sizes are for women who are 5 feet, 4 inches tall or shorter. For years, many department stores located their petite sizes either next to or between the misses and plus sizes. Department stores sold versions of the same products in the misses, women's, and petite departments, often with racks of similar styles in different sizes across the aisle from each. The boundaries between departments were blurred, and department store petite lines were considered frumpy. Thus, the mixing of misses, plus sizes, and petites reduced the possibility of a sale. As a result of this ineffective merchandising, petite departments in some department stores have been eliminated or reduced in size.

There are many consultants available to help the retailer with store design. London-based Shopworks (shopworks.co.uk), for example, uses consumer research, as well as the idea that shopping is all about money and enhancing cash flow, when designing a retailer's selling space. Shopworks designs appealing and engaging stores; more importantly, these store designs enhance space productivity and thus retailer profitability. Unlike some other consulting firms, they also assist in the implementation and execution of their designs. New York–based Envirosell (www.envirosell.com) is another research and consulting firm specializing in studying retail and service environments. Founded by Paco Underhill, one of the first researchers to study how people shop, Envirosell bases its recommendations after videotaping and tracking shoppers in the stores, often for weeks at a time. In fact over a year's time, the firm collects more than 50,000 hours of shopping behavior video. One of the benefits of such research is that Envirosell concluded that consumers now make more decisions about what to buy when they are in the store, not before entering the store.[2]

Although this chapter is concerned with the physical store, the same factors may be used to develop an e-tailer's "virtual store." Just as with a bricks-and-mortar location, the first impression is most important. After all, most consumers spend less than five seconds at a website the first time they visit. Therefore, there is a limited window of opportunity to capture the attention of an online user. Although there is no strict list of dos and don'ts, given that the online "rules" are constantly changing, a few underlying fundamentals have been identified that can drive repeat visits and encourage purchasing:

- *Keep content current.* Online consumers browse frequently, so it is very important to continually update information on the site. Two aspects should be considered: merchandise presentation and merchandise description. In merchandise presentation, the Web offers e-tailers a plethora of presentation options. Not limited by physical restraints, e-tailers can provide consumers with 3-D presentations that allow a 360-degree view of merchandise. In merchandise description, write in "web-ese." Online consumers scan information as opposed to reading it.

- *Make the site easy and enjoyable to use.* Ease of use is a primary concern for online consumers. This means that users with little or no experience either online or with your product category should be able to move easily about the site and find the information they desire. Much like signage in a bricks-and-mortar world, e-tailers must clearly show the way for online consumers.

- *Structure an online community where consumers can interact with one another or contribute to the site's content.* The virtual world allows for new methods of integrating customers into a retailer's business. Offering potential consumers an opportunity to become involved in the site can build a loyal clientele. A breakthrough entrepreneurial e-tailer is Threadless, headquartered in Chicago (www.threadless.com/retail), which involves potential customers by engaging them in regular T-shirt contests. Potential customers design T-shirts, and then the Threadless customer community votes on the designs. Winning designs are then produced for sale either online, as the firm began, and now offline in its retail stores.[3] Uncommon goods (www.uncommongoods.com) is another company that invites its customers to submit designs for products, and also has them vote on potential products for the company to sell through its online and catalog.

Although a store is composed of literally thousands of details, the two primary objectives around which all activities, functions, and goals revolve are store image and space productivity. However, before discussing these two objectives, it is important to identify the elements that compose the store environment (shown in Exhibit 13.1), each of which will be discussed in detail in this chapter.

Exhibit 13.1
Elements That Compose the Store Environment

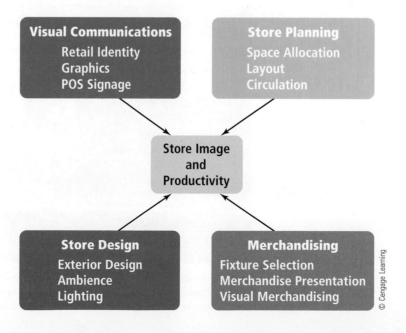

Elements of the Store Environment

The first decision to make in planning a store is how to allocate the retailer's most scarce resource—space. Space is scarce because it is costly, and a retailer has limited capital it can invest in its store. Consider that annual leases can range from $15 per foot to more than $100, and new construction including land and fixtures can exceed $250 per square foot. Even a modest remodel can be expensive.[4] For instance, new flooring can cost $4 per square foot, ceilings $2 per square foot, interior lighting $3 per square foot; heating and cooling $2 per square foot; signage $2 per square foot; display fixtures $9 per square foot; and roofing $3 per square foot. This totals $25 per square foot and thus, a 100,000 big box store would require $2.5 million for a fairly simple remodel. Making productive use of the store space through thoughtful space allocation thus becomes pivotal to enhancing image and space productivity.

The retailer creates a store layout that shows the location of all merchandise departments and the placement of circulation aisles that allow customers to move throughout the store. As discussed above, the merchandise presentation must be exciting so as to catch and hold customers' attention, be easy to understand, and encourage shoppers to browse, evaluate (especially if the decision is being made in the store), and buy. Therefore, the presentation of the merchandise is a critical factor in the selling power of a store and has a significant effect on the store image. Bookstores can display books either with the cover of the book facing out (called a *face-out*) so it is in full view or with only the spine of the book showing where the viewer can see the title and author but not the cover (called *spine-out*). A bookstore with a high percentage of face-outs, for example, can create the image of being a specialty book boutique that carries a limited selection of exclusive titles and is, therefore, a rather pricey place to shop. A bookstore with virtually all spine-outs is often perceived as cramming in a huge selection of titles sold at low prices. Thus, merchandise presentation is a critical factor in determining both store image and productivity.

Most shoppers are accustomed to noticing the layout and design of a store, which is composed of all the elements affecting the human senses of sight, hearing, smell, and touch. An effective store layout and design, including the storefront, creates a comfortable

A bookstore with a high percentage of face-outs creates the image of being a specialty book boutique, while a bookstore with virtually all spine-outs is often perceived as cramming in a huge selection of titles sold at low prices.

environment that enhances the merchandise and entices shoppers to browse and buy. Lighting is an important element that should not be overlooked. Both display and in-store lighting help create the proper image and also draw customers' eyes around the store and onto merchandise, and they ultimately encourage a customer to purchase the product.[5] Likewise, in-store graphics such as art, photography, and signs form an important visual communication link between the store and its customers by providing much-needed information on how to shop in the store. The chapter's "Retailing: The Inside Story" box gives a description of how supermarket managers have perfected the art of store design and layout. Importantly, geographical positioning systems (GPS) are now moving into the store where there are increasingly Wi-Fi networks. This allows retailers to no longer rely on some of the rules of thumb that are discussed in "The Inside Story" but to obtain accurate maps of how their customers navigate through their particular store.[6] Sometimes retailers tend to forget the lessons in the "The Inside Story" box. For example, many managers ignore their own 25-25-50 rule on endcaps. This rule states that 25 percent of all endcaps should be advertised sale merchandise that the customer will seek out and another 25 percent should be unadvertised sale items that will cause the customer to be alert when looking at an endcap. The remaining 50 percent should be regular-priced seasonal or impulse merchandise. Retailers tend to violate this rule when manufacturers offer money for the right to set up their own displays. While the managers will gain a short-term profit by renting out most of their endcap space, they often destroy the long-term profits that a well-defined endcap policy generates.

© Katerina Havelkova/Shutterstock

RETAILING — The Inside Story

Consumer Behavior: Supermarket Style

It's unknown how many supermarket managers took a consumer behavior class in college, but they sure know how to practice the art.

Observe

Not only are most consumers right-handed but also they think "right-headed."

- Since supermarkets make more money on their store's private-label brands, they stock the store brands to the right of the name brands so that the consumer has to reach across the store brand to grab the name brand.
- Since shoppers are more prone to look right, supermarkets display the higher gross-margin merchandise on the right side of an aisle, as gauged from the predominant direction of cart traffic. Also, displays should be set so that they are visible on the right side as shoppers travel the predominant path.
- Since 90 percent of all customers entering a store turn right, that area is the most valuable for the store. Thus, it is no accident that the produce area, a deli, or a bakery is the first section that a customer will reach. That is because they can see, feel, and smell the merchandise. This, in turn, will get their mouths watering and make them hungry. Supermarket managers will tell you that their best customer is a hungry customer.

- When customers enter a store and begin to turn right, they tend to scan the entire store from left to right and then fix their eyes on an object (sign or merchandise) at a 45-degree angle from the point of entry.
- Grocers also use the most recognizable brand to lead off the product category as the consumer is walking toward it. In other words, they use Coca-Cola to lead off soft drinks, Fusion to lead off razors, and Secret to lead off deodorants.

Most consumers think "neatness" counts.

- Merchants sometimes try to make their point-of-purchase displays look like a mess. These so-called dump displays, which are affectionately known

(continued)

by some grocers as "organized chaos," are deliberately arranged in a haphazard fashion so the items inside look cheap and are, therefore, perceived as a great bargain. The same thought process works for merchants leaving out open cartons piled on top of another. Usually the items are not on sale, they merely look "hot" or such a "great deal" that the retailer cannot keep the merchandise in stock.

- For the same reason, handwritten (as long as they are legible) signs create the impression of recently lowered prices (i.e., there has not been time to get the printed signs). Thus, even though they do not always look great, handwritten signs move the merchandise faster than standard printed signs.

Most consumers are likely to focus on a large central display.

- The point-of-purchase displays at the end of each supermarket aisle (known in the trade as *endcaps*) are usually the focus of customers' attention as they wheel their carts through the store. Thus, a smart retailer knows to follow the 25-25-50 rule (i.e., 25% advertised sale merchandise, 25% unadvertised sale items, and 50% should be regular priced seasonal or impulse merchandise).

Consumers are creatures of habit, and when something is out of place they become more sensitive to their environment.

- Every supermarket will make regularly scheduled display changes for staple items such as cake mixes, salad dressings, and cereals. They do not want to move the items to new locations because that may upset time-pressed customers. However, by changing shelf displays of these staples, the grocer draws the attention of the customer, thereby increasing the chances of an impulse sale.

There is a little bit of greed in every one of us.

- Supermarket managers may put a limit on the purchase of a sale item, by advertising "Limit 4 to a Customer." Not only will consumers think that the limit restrictions mean it's a great deal but also they will often buy the limit, even if they don't need that many.
- Another version of the above is the special "10 for $x" where x is a whole dollar amount, such as 10 for $9, or 10 for $6. Many of these promotions are mix and match deals in which the customer can choose among several different items. In many cases, the new "sale" price is slightly higher than the typical sale price. Retailers have found that selling an item on sale at $.79 each usually results in one sale. However, at 10 for $8, or even $9, many consumers will stock up and buy more than one unit.
- Similarly, many customers will get so excited by finding a great price on a staple like peanut butter that they will fail to notice that the item's complementary products—in this case, jelly and bread—may have had their prices increased.

Source: Based on insights provided by Jim Lukens, Paul Adams, Zack Adcock, and Paul Easter.

Objectives of the Store Environment

The two primary objectives of a retail stores environment, which are (1) creating the desired store image and (2) increasing space productivity, amount to an extension of the three basic tasks or strategies, originally presented in Chapter 2 (see pp. 58–60), that all retailers must perform in order to have a chance at success. Again, these tasks include:

- get consumers into your store (*market image*);
- convert these consumers into customers by having them purchase merchandise (*space productivity*); and
- do this in the most efficient manner possible that is consistent with the level of service your customers expect.

As we stated earlier, successful retailers use their stores as a means to excite customers so that they not only enter the store, but also spend time looking and viewing merchandise. This is particularly important when the segment(s) of population a retailer is going after generally tends not to enjoy the act of shopping—that is, men. Yet, as a couple of menswear retailers have realized, men aren't too difficult to attract as long as you have the right store environment. Take for instance, Lost Boys in Washington, D.C., or Kesner in New York's West Village. Upon entering either establishment, or even simply looking through the storefront windows, you might first think either retailer is simply a local bar catering to young professionals. After all, customers can be seen sipping beers and watching television programming on a giant flat-screen television, but you'd be wrong. In both of these stores, the liquor and beer is free of charge; it's simply given to enhance men's experiences of shopping for clothing. Men do not like to shop, and when they do shop, they do so hastily. Like the youngest author, many don't try on clothes within the store; they seemingly view shopping as a time-trial where the faster they can get in and get out the better. Thus, both retailers have tried to create a relaxing shopping atmosphere and put the men at ease with a drink and casual conversation. In so doing, the men appear more relaxed, peruse all the merchandise, and actually end up purchasing more clothing.[7]

Most retailers who have adopted this approach have found that the free liquor is cheaper than investing money in traditional advertising to build store traffic. In fact, a local hair salon in Auburn, Alabama, TRIM, told one of the authors that the addition of two pool tables and a large bar in the center surrounded by flat screen TVs has more than doubled their clientele and weekly visits beyond what their initial advertising and promotional dollars generated. Seldom does traditional media advertising work for men; when it does, they rush into the store and rush out with either nothing or a small purchase. And in the case of TRIM, it definitely doesn't lead to more visits to get one's hair cut, but cocktails and televisions, displaying every possible sporting event, do. Thus, this technique enhances the store image, builds store traffic, and creates additional sales transactions in a cost-efficient way.

Developing a Store Image

The starting point in creating this image, of course, is the merchandise carried in the store, along with the retailer's promotional activities, customer service, cleanliness, and sales force. An example is *Salvation*, a new retail concept from Nike.[8] *Salvation* combines the Nike, Converse, and Hurley brands. The sales force helps the action-sports customer select merchandise and customize it so the shorts or other merchandise become personal art projects. The desire is for the store to help the shopper celebrate the culture of art, design, music, and action-sports. The stores are very clean, simple and have a subtle presentation that avoids screaming out at the customer to purchase. iPads sit on the counter of the store's customization area where shoppers can select from many graphics to customize products, ranging from boardshorts to sneakers.

That the store image serves a critical role in the store selection process is best illustrated by the fact that in the supermarket industry, overall cleanliness is the most important criterion in deciding where to shop. That is why many supermarkets today not only provide moist sanitary wipes for their customers, but also run the shopping carts through a car-wash–type mist where a disinfecting peroxide solution is sprayed onto carts. This is to protect infants and young children from potential contamination due to contact with a shopping cart handle. The other important criteria for selecting a supermarket are low prices, accurate price scanning, pleasant clerks, clearly labeled prices, and well-stocked shelves.

To further illustrate the importance of store image, consider for a moment the words *7-Eleven*. For most people, these words represent more than just two numbers. Together, they form the name of one of the most familiar retailers, the worldwide chain with more than 27,000 convenience stores.

The thoughts and emotions this logo evokes in customers constitute 7-Eleven's store image. Regardless of what its managers would like its store image to be, regardless of what image they have tried to create, the store's actual image exists only in the heads and hearts of consumers. Many factors influence that image.

First, the name itself has a great influence. If the stores were called "8-Twelve," we all might have a different image in our heads. The name was created in 1946 to stress the stores' operating hours, 7 A.M. to 11 P.M. every day, then unheard of in retailing.[9] The rhythm and rhyme of *seven* and *eleven* allow the name to roll easily off the tongue and be memorable, even if the customer does not shoot craps. (In craps, a 7 or an 11 on the shooter's first roll is a winner.) The PMS# 165 orange, PMSA# 485 red, and PMS# 341 green colors of the logo suggest vitality, quality, and well-being. The storefront, historically, a mansard roof that has evolved into a wide flat front, gives a large area for the orange, red, and green stripes and 7-Eleven logo and conveys a heavy, masculine appearance. When you walk in the store, a buzzer warns clerks of entering shoppers, suggesting a concern about safety and theft. The smell of fresh coffee and the sight of sausages and hot dogs rolling around on the hot dogger create a certain atmosphere. By the way, they sell over 100 million hot dogs every year! Even the uniforms worn by the store clerks leave an impression, which joins all other impressions to create 7-Eleven's store image in our minds. The consumer's image of a store, therefore, is a combination of out-of-store factors—location (Chapter 7), advertising and publicity (Chapter 11), and the various services offered (Chapter 12)—plus the dozens of in-store variables perceived by the consumer.

Although advertising and other promotional activities are important in establishing a desired store image, the store itself makes the most significant and lasting impression on our collective consciousness, and it is here that the retailer must focus great energy. Aritzia, a stylish Canadian retailer who has recently entered the United States, is an excellent example of focusing energy. Aritzia focuses on the 18–35 year old female who is not interested in fast-fashion (such as that offered by H&M or Zara) but on sophistication and quality merchandise at affordable prices ($40 to $400). Interiors of the stores help to reinforce its image with natural woods, original art, and funky signage; indie rock soundtracks; and wildlife-inspired window displays. Brian Hill, CEO, states "We try to build stores that are in tune with what's going on with the people, to connect people with the energy of the culture."[10] Earlier we mentioned that retailers spend as much as $250 per square foot in creating their stores; well, Aritzia spends in the vicinity of $300! But the results in terms of space productivity (our next topic) are sensational; $1,500 sales per square foot where the industry norm is less than half.

Increasing Space Productivity

The store's image attracts customers. However, when customers are visiting the store or it's website, the retailer must also convince them to make a purchase. Therefore, a store must increase its space productivity, a goal that is summarized in a simple but powerful truism in retailing: *The more merchandise customers are exposed to that is presented in an orderly manner, the more they tend to buy.* The typical shopper in a department store goes into only two or three shopping areas per trip. By carefully planning the store environment, the retailer can encourage customers to flow through the entire store—or at least through more shopping areas—and see a wider variety of merchandise. As a general rule of thumb, customers need to pass within four feet of the merchandise for it to capture their attention and cause them to slow down. Of course, with poor merchandise display even passing within four feet will not cause the customer to pause and look at the merchandise. The proper use of in-store advertising and displays will let the customer know what's happening in other departments and encourage a visit to those areas.

WHAT'S NEW?

Shopping Carts Go "Smart"

Mention the topic retail store design, and many students begin to think about floor coverings, lighting fixtures, color palettes, and so forth. And perhaps this is due to the growing popularity of television stations like HGTV and the DIY Network with their almost 24/7 line-up of remodeling, interior design, and home renovations. But retail design includes much more; most of which might not be considered "sexy" but that are definitely important to enhancing a retailer's bottom-line.

One item that has a major impact on a retailer's bottom-line, yet many of us take for granted, is the shopping cart. Each of us can probably remember the last time we had one of those carts that seemed hell bent on going any way but straight; how was your shopping experience that day? Exactly. A shopping cart might not be the first thing that comes to mind when you think about designing the retail shopping experience, but the cart alone can have a dramatic effect, particularly if it's a new "Smart" cart.

A smart cart is a term given to a general class of shopping carts that look normal except for an interactive, informational dashboard contained within an 8- to 10-inch color touch screen/scanner combination mounted on the handle-bar near the shopper. Once a shopper swipes a store's loyalty card through the cart's scanner in order to "sign in," shoppers can view customized promotions; access recipes; gain product information like the nutritional value and calories contained; follow a shopping list that is either prepared at home or suggested based upon one's shopping history; and so on. The smart cart truly represents evolution in the history of shopping carts, but it's only a vehicle; one whose form has become somewhat standardized over the last decade.

What continues to change are the software platforms. Since 2003 when IBM demonstrated its smart cart solution at their Industry Solutions Lab in Hawthorne, New York, several firms, including technology-services company Electronic Data Systems Corp. (EDS) and Mercatus Technologies, a Canadian technology firm, have been at the forefront of designing software intended to enhance the customer shopping experience. Some, like Mercatus Technologies, who's been test marketing their Concierge program in Food Lion's "Bloom" supermarkets, even appear poised to begin a large-scale roll out of their software across the United States. But surprisingly, it's the retailers themselves who seem to be slowing down the progress.

A recent survey found that not all retailers are investing in the technology infrastructure needed to make their stores more digitally connected. As of 2012 more than half had no Wi-Fi-enabled stores, and more than one-third had no plans to add Wi-Fi in the future. In order for the carts to operate as intended, retailers must provide, at a minimum, Wi-Fi service. Those wishing to take advantage of the software features that seek to direct customers to particular aisles like "There's a nice white wine in Aisle 6 that would go perfectly with your salmon," need GPS programming too.

Admittedly, recent research conducted by a food-industry body on behalf of EDS found that in a study of 1,000 shoppers, most prefer to get information from labels on the food; perhaps this is why so many retailers are hesitant to invest in technology. But that same study found that a third of shoppers want bar-code scanners fitted to their carts.

Currently, a majority of shoppers may not view static signage, and even more advanced shelf-talkers, as boring or old fashioned, but the information-hungry, 18–25-year-old segment likely does as they increasingly shop with one hand on their smartphone. This segment, and segments like it, wants personalization and instant service, or they want to pay rock-bottom prices. While the smart cart is not solely intended for use in the grocery industry, traditional grocers, with their slim margins, are likely going to need to incorporate smart cart technology soon to enhance the shopper's experience or continue to lose customers to discounters like Walmart who are able to offer everyday low prices.

Sources: Fleenor, D. Gall (2011), "Information, Please," *Stores Magazine (Online)*, November (1); Aquino, Judith (2012), "Tablets and Smartphones Transform the In-Store Customer Experience: Retailers Hope to Give Customers New Incentives to Shop Brick-and-Mortar Stores," *CRM Magazine*, 16 (January), 17–18; Anonymous, "'Smart' Carts Warn Shoppers on Junk Food," *The Wall Street Journal*, October 10, 2007: D5; Vibert-Kennedy, Karen, "Smart Shopping Carts to Roam Grocery Stores of Future," *USA Today (Online)*, October 26, 2003 [Accessed May 19, 2012] from http://www.usatoday.com; Anonymous, "Retailers on Trend with Mobile Technology, *Retail Customer Experience.com*, [Accessed May 19, 2012] from http://www.retailcustomerexperience.com; Anonymous, "Panphonics Unveils New Directional Audio Systems for Retail Stores," *Retail Customer Experience.com*, [Accessed May 21, 2012] from http://www.retailcustomerexperience.com.

Retailers are also finding that incorporating new advances in technology can help stimulate sales.[11] For example, as discussed in this chapter's "What's New?" box, some grocery chains like Food Lion are experimenting with "smart" shopping cart technology to provide consumers with not only more detailed product information like the number of calories within a particular brand of dessert, but also personalized in-store promotions and suggestions about particular aisles that carry complementary products to those already placed within one's shopping cart (e.g., white wine on Aisle 6 to go with a filet of fish purchased from the fish counter). Pacific Sunwear is another retailer that equips its salespeople with iPads that allow them to create outfits for customers and order out of stock items. In 2012, Lowe's too distributed over 42,000 iPhones and developed its own "Store Associates" app, which allows floorwalkers to check inventory, estimate quantities of product to purchase, or make suggestions if an item is out of stock.[12] Many furniture and jewelry stores are also adopting this practice.

Another factor that affects space productivity is amount of merchandise a shopper is generally exposed to on an average shopping trip. A good way to increase sales is to increase the overall amount of merchandise within the store, and thus the amount of merchandise a customer is exposed to; yet, it is important that the retailer not have merchandise pushed into every conceivable nook and cranny of the store so that customers cannot get to it. However, retailers can take the act of trimming one's merchandise for the benefit of wider and cleaner aisles too far. For example, during the recent recession, Walmart, like many other retailers, whittled the number of items it carried (by approximately 9 percent) in order to clear aisles for a cleaner, more appealing look, and to enhance consumers' overall shopping experience. In response customer satisfaction scores soared; yet, despite the increased ratings, the world's largest retailer had one of the longest slides in domestic same-store-sales in company history; customers loved the new store experience, but purchased less (much less). Instead, adding inventory, even within its aisles, increased not only consumers' perceptions of value, but also the amount of merchandise they purchased.[13]

One factor that detracts from space productivity is shrinkage, or the loss of merchandise through theft, loss, and damage, which was discussed in Chapter 9. It is called **shrinkage** because retailers usually do not know what happened to the missing items, only that the inventory level in the store has somehow shrunk. Even stores that move customers through the entire space and effectively use in-store marketing techniques to maximize sales can fall victim to high shrinkage. Remember, when a store sells an item for $1.29, it earns only a small percentage of that sale, perhaps ranging from 15 cents to 60 cents. When that item is stolen, lost, or damaged, however, the store loses the cost of that $1.29 item—for example, 69 cents—and this loss is deducted from the store's overall profit. Shrinkage ranges from 1 percent to 4 percent of retail sales. Although this may seem like a small number, consider that after-tax profit for many retailers is little more than 4 percent, so high shrinkage alone can make the difference between a profit and a loss. Also, because of the high cost of theft, retailers are employing a greater number of security guards and loss-control specialists. This adds to their costs and results in higher prices for legitimate customers. For this reason, all 50 states have passed special laws that they call "civil recovery" that enable retailers to seek more from the shoplifter than the return of the price of the item; these additional charges are often up to three times the cost of the item or more, to help recover the costs of theft protection.[14]

To enhance space productivity, retailers today must incorporate planning, merchandise presentation, and design strategies that minimize shrinkage by avoiding displaying merchandise in hidden areas of the store. They should also seek to reduce the number of times merchandise must be moved, during which time damage and loss can occur.

shrinkage
Represents merchandise that cannot be accounted for due to theft, loss, or damage.

LO 2

Discuss the steps involved in planning the store.

Store Planning

Planning an effective retail store resembles planning an effective piece of writing, and moving through a store as a customer is similar to reading an article or a chapter in a book. The merchandise, like text, is there for you to review, understand, and consume. But just as a book needs more than words to make sense, a store needs more than merchandise to be shopable.

The store's layout and design can be compared to the organization of chapters, sections, and subsections in this book. Grouping the words and thoughts into mental "chunks" makes the book easier to digest and understand. Unless a store specializes in only one product type—for example, candles—it would be impossible to shop if that store were not broken into departments and categories. The books would be mixed in with the shovels, the underwear would be found among the garden plants, and you wouldn't know where to begin.

Signs and graphics are similar to the headings and punctuation, which give cues to understanding the organization of both a book and the merchandise in a store. Without headings and subheadings, this chapter would be a stream of words, very difficult and, worse, boring to read and understand. Similarly, without signs, a store would seem like an endless sea of racks and merchandise, annoying to understand and shop.

Finally, the photos, exhibits, charts, and boxes in this book are the retail equivalent of the visual displays and focal points, where merchandise is pulled off the shelf or racks and displayed in theatrical vignettes. Successful retailers use these settings to break up the store space, illustrate merchandise opportunities in the store, and visually demonstrate how certain merchandise goes together or can work in the consumer's life. Like photos and exhibits in a book, these visual displays elaborate on the text, or the bulk of merchandise on the racks, to make statements.

Most important, a retail store and a piece of writing are very similar in the way they affect the consumer. Many writing coaches teach aspiring writers that each time an uncommon word is used or a punctuation mark is missing, the reader hits a "speed bump" in the writing and must mentally pause to consider what is meant. After hitting three speed bumps, the reader may conclude that the writing is too difficult to understand and quit reading.

The same is true in a retail store. All cues must work subliminally to organize the merchandise and guide shoppers effortlessly through the store. Each time shoppers become a bit confused as to where they are, where they need to go, how much an item costs, or where certain merchandise is, they become frustrated. The first or second instance may not even be consciously noticed, but shoppers may quickly become frustrated and walk out, concluding that the store is too hard to shop. Exhibit 13.2 is a list of warning signs that managers should look for, because each warning sign indicates a speed bump waiting to drive customers away from a store.

Exhibit 13.2
These Warning Signs May Indicate a Space Problem

- Open spaces on the selling floor, even if the product is on hand
- Cluttered and disorganized aisles, hallways, and stockrooms
- Excessive time required to put away new receipts
- Insufficient staging space for large shipments of advertised products
- Sales associates continually required to leave the sales floor to locate additional merchandise
- Poor utilization of vertical space and excessive time required to retrieve products stored on high shelves
- Sales lag expectations for specific locations where space or fixtures are a known issue
- Off-site storage or multiple stockrooms required for a single commodity

Most shoppers cannot consciously identify the elements of a good store, but they certainly know when these elements are missing. We have all experienced the feeling that a store seems to "really have it together"—for example, the Apple Store, Niketown, IKEA, REI, and Bass Pro Shops Outdoor World. These exemplary stores are easy to shop in, fun, and exciting; the merchandise is easy to understand; the associates seem friendly. You conclude that these stores are a great place to shop, and with any luck you are completely oblivious to the thousands of little details that have guided you through the shopping experience.

In retailing, the term **floor plan** indicates where merchandise and customer-service departments are located, how customers circulate through the store, and how much space is dedicated to each department. The floor plan, which is based around the predicted demands of the store's targeted customer, serves as the backbone of the store and is the fundamental structure around which every other element of the store environment takes shape. Successful retailers, such as Walmart with its Retail Link, analyze their sales along with the demographics of the store's trading area when developing a floor plan. These retailers then structure the merchandise to the needs of each store. Thus, it is not uncommon for two Target or Best Buy stores in the same city to be different in both merchandise carried and in its presentation. This is called **microretailing**, and it means that each store's offerings are tailored to the trading area being served. As we mentioned earlier, Wi-Fi combined with GPS is allowing retailers to better understand how to merchandise their stores based on actual store traffic within each store.

In addition, successful retailers place merchandise in key strategic locations. For example, H.E.B. Grocery Company places the jelly next to the peanut butter, facial tissues next to the cold medicines, and chocolate syrup next to the ice cream. (Next time you are in a supermarket, see if it locates such items together.) Other profitable retailers know that toys and movies are kid magnets and thus display snacks right next to them. Another simple rule to follow is to think of the age of the consumer. For example, a retailer should never put a child's toy on the top shelf where kids can't reach it or denture cream on the bottom shelf where seniors can't easily bend down and get it. Therefore, the store's layout and design, including merchandise location, must be carefully planned to meet the retailer's merchandising goals, make the store easy to understand and shop, and allow merchandise to be effectively presented.

Merchandise being arranged alongside other merchandise, or what is often referred to as *adjacencies* in the retail trade, can be especially frustrating for certain customers because they don't fit neatly into predetermined merchandise categories. Body Central is a Florida-based chain that targets 18–35 year-old women. Recently, it has arranged its merchandise into "club" (evening wear), "casual" (weekend wear), and other customer-relevant groupings of merchandise. The importance of merchandise adjacency can also be observed the next time you visit a supermarket. Notice, for instance, that some products are displayed by keeping all the brands from one manufacturer together (ice cream, frozen pizzas, and salad dressings) while other products are grouped by category (canned corn and peaches, bars of soap, and baking aids such as flour and sugar).[15] You should also note that the concept of adjacencies also applies to the design of shopping centers. For example, a community center that has Whole Foods as an anchor tenant would generally find that shoppers want to stop at a café for breakfast or lunch or at a specialty wine retailer with broader and deeper wine assortments than Whole Foods, and drop their clothing off at a laundry and dry cleaning establishment.

It is interesting to note that some retail innovations have actually broken established retail trade practices when it comes to merchandise adjacencies. One notable example of this is the warehouse club. Costco, for example, uses crazy product positioning as part of its selling formula. The retailer has found that putting toothpaste next to golf clubs

floor plan
Is a schematic that shows where merchandise and customer service departments are located, how customers circulate through the store, and how much space is dedicated to each department.

microretailing
Occurs when a chain store retailer operating over a wide geographic area, usually nationally, tailors its merchandise and services in each store to the needs of the immediate trading area.

and cereals next to computer tables not only increases impulse purchasing but provides customers with a "thrill-of-the-hunt" psychological lift when they find something.[16] Such positioning tends to make customers more alert as to what is available, and retailers know that 30 percent to 50 percent of all brick-and-mortar purchases are impulse buys.[17] Perhaps a more notable example is Ethan Allen, which broke all of the rules in terms of the traditional merchandise adjacencies in furniture retailing. The established practice was to group all couches in one corner, all tables in another corner, all beds in another corner, and so on. Ethan Allen changed all of this by presenting complete rooms of furniture around a theme, which enabled shoppers to visualize how furniture would look in their own homes. Not only did the image of the furniture store improve but also shoppers found themselves purchasing furniture items they had not planned because they could see how various pieces of furniture could be integrated into their homes.

stack-outs
Are pallets of merchandise set out on the floor in front of the main shelves.

Almost as important as merchandise adjacencies is the reduction of **stack-outs**, those pallets of merchandise set on the floor in front of the main shelves. Although stack-outs may improve the short-run sales of the featured product, their negative impact may offset these marginal sales. As Robert Kahn, the late editor of *Retailing Today* and highly regarded retail consultant, pointed out many times in his newsletter, when there is a stack-out and the customer does not have a specific need on that aisle, then the customer will skip that aisle. This phenomenon is known in retailing as the dreaded "butt-brush," which holds that the likelihood of a woman being converted from a browser to a buyer is inversely proportional to the likelihood of her being brushed on her backside while she is examining merchandise.[18] Thus, any item that requires extensive examination by a woman should never be placed in a narrow aisle. Also, since some purchases are impulse, the retailer may actually lose sales when shoppers ignore certain aisles, especially when the product being considered requires some type of examination or inspection. This is especially true of electronic products such as televisions and computers; retailers don't seem to realize that too many merchandise items stuffed onto shelves, display tables, and walls can create congestion and prevent customers from an engaging shopping experience, and thus sales will falter.

Allocating Space

The starting point for developing a floor plan is analyzing how the available store space, usually measured in square footage, should be allocated to various departments. This allocation can be based on mathematical calculation of the returns generated by different types of merchandise. However, before discussing this process, it's important to first recognize that a major current and projected trend in retail over the next decade is a shift to smaller stores. In the United States and many other countries, we have observed for many decades the gradual increase in store size, often to nearly 200,000-square-foot big-box stores. But finally the trend is reversing. For instance, JCPenney is rolling out 50,000- to 60,000-square-foot stores—a stark contrast to its normal 100,000 square foot stores. CityTarget are Target stores for urban areas that are 50,000 to 60,000 square feet and Walmart Express stores are 15,000 square feet.[19]

Additionally, before describing the space allocation process, we must also discuss the various types of space in the store. As you review these, keep in mind that many retailers, as we suggested above, are trying to reduce the size of their stores. Perhaps these cuts won't be as bold as a 50-percent reduction, but almost all will be by 10 percent or more. Thus, a historical 50,000-square-foot supermarket may now need to be planned at 45,000 square feet.[20] All this pressure to reduce store size, due to the cost of construction and related operating costs, puts more pressure on effectively allocating the different types of space a retailer requires for success.

Types of Space Needed

Shoppers are most familiar with the sales floor, but this is not the only element in a retail store with which the planner must contend. There are five basic types of space needs in a store: (1) back room; (2) office and other functional spaces; (3) aisles, service areas, and other nonselling areas of the main sales floor; (4) wall merchandise space; and (5) floor merchandise space. The retailer must balance the quest for greater density of merchandise presentation with the shopability and functionality of the store.

Since space is the retailer's ultimate scarce resource, rarely can the retailer fully achieve all of its desired goals. Rather, most retailers find themselves compromising on one or more dimensions, carefully weighing priorities, strategies, and special constraints. In reviewing each of these space categories, keep in mind that the overall goal is to make the largest possible portion of the space available to hold merchandise and be shopable.

Back Room   To operate virtually any type of retail store, some space is required as back room, which includes the receiving area to process arriving merchandise and the stockroom to store surplus merchandise. The percentage of space dedicated to the back room varies greatly, depending on the type of retailer, but the amount of space is shrinking for all types of retailers. Historically, back room percentages have ranged from nearly 50 percent in some department stores to as little as 10 percent in some small specialty and convenience stores. General merchandise stores have historically dedicated about 15 percent to 20 percent of their store space to the back room. The need to squeeze more sales out of expensive retail space, coupled with new distribution methods allowing smaller, more frequent merchandise deliveries from suppliers (called *quick response inventory* or *efficient consumer response*, depending on the industry involved), has allowed retailers to shrink their back rooms, with department stores cutting back to about 20 percent, and others reducing their back rooms to 5 percent or even less. However, there are always exceptions to general rules and trends. For instance, Saks Fifth Avenue flagship store in New York City has recently expanded its 8th floor shoe department from 22,000 square feet to 32,150 square feet with 15,500 of this space (or nearly 50 percent) going for inventory storage.[21] It is estimated that the shoe category is nearly 10 percent of Saks total annual sales volume and also shoes are a very profitable category for Saks; hence, this expansion of space makes sense.

Some retail formats, such as warehouse clubs, have receiving areas but virtually no back room stock capacity. In these stores, the store fixtures are usually large warehouse racks that carry shopable inventory at reachable heights (up to 84 inches) and large pallets or cartons of excess inventory at higher levels. These racks can be as tall as 15 feet.

By using this strategy, warehouse clubs are taking advantage of not only the width and depth of the store but also the height. In other words, while retailers pay expensive rents for their store space, as measured in *square* footage, the store and the merchandise can be stacked as high as possible at little additional cost, using the *cubic* footage (or volume) of the store. The ability of shoppers to reach does limit the height at which *shopable* merchandise can be stacked, but it does not limit the use of this high space to carry excess inventory. The same inventory carried in the back room would require additional square footage, causing either higher rent or reducing the amount of shopable space. Essentially, the sales floor doubles as the back room. This stocking method visually creates a dramatic low-cost image in the store, which can be advantageous to value-oriented retailers but detrimental to fashion or high-end retailers. This can be observed in how new-car dealers merchandise their inventory in their showrooms and on their car lots. Whereas a Chevrolet, Ford, or Honda dealer may pack its showroom and car lot with hundreds of cars all very close together, a high-end dealer selling Jaguar, Porsche, or Ferrari will have only a sampling of cars in the showroom that are elegantly displayed as almost pieces of art or jewelry, with relatively few models on the car lot.

High-end or high-fashion retailers often make use of vacant space and elegant display rather than tightly packing as much merchandise as possible into an area.

Offices and Other Functional Spaces   Every store must contain a certain amount of office and other functional space. This often includes a break room for associates, a training room, offices for the store manager and assistant managers, a cash office, bathroom facilities for both customers and employees, and perhaps other areas. Though necessary, the location of such functional spaces receives a lower priority than the location of the sales floor and stockroom. Often they are located on mezzanines over the front of the store, over the back stockroom, or in side spaces too small to be stockrooms. Some restaurants create part of their store image around having the food cooking and preparation space an integral part of the customer experience. For example Pei Wei and Paradise Bakery use this practice.

Aisles, Service Areas, and Other Nonselling Areas   Even on the main sales floor, some space must be given up to nonselling functions, the most obvious of which are aisles that move shoppers through the store. The retailer's first step, particularly in larger stores, is to create main aisles through which shoppers will flow on their way through the store and secondary aisles that draw customers back into the merchandise. These aisles must be large enough to accommodate peak crowds, and in bigger stores, they may be as wide as 15 feet. The amount of space dedicated to aisles can be significant. For instance, a 15-foot aisle running around the perimeter of an 80,000 square-foot store (the size of a typical discount store) may consume 12,000 square feet, or 15 percent of the entire space! Retailers also need to pay particular attention to aisle width for disabled persons, and this is especially true in terms of checkout lanes where the width of accessible checkout aisles must be at least 36 inches wide for lengths greater than 24 inches long and at least 32 inches wide for lengths 24 inches or less. Also, depending on the number of checkout aisles a store has, a certain number must be handicapped accessible.[22] In addition, counter height cannot exceed 36 inches. There are many other guidelines for store design for the handicapped or disabled, and some are unique to certain lines of retail such as restaurants and self-service gasoline stations.[23] You can also obtain detailed information on the various legal aspects of the American Disabilities Act at www.ada.gov.

In addition to aisles, space must be given to dressing rooms, layaway areas, service desks, and other customer-service facilities that cannot be merchandised. While the retailer always attempts to minimize the amount of nonselling space, customer service areas are an important part of a store and should not be shortchanged. For example, many retailers skimp on or do not even offer public restrooms. When you consider that shoppers may have been out for several hours shopping, have young children, or older parents along with them, all of which are likely to increase the need for frequent bathroom breaks, it is surprising these retailers are able to retain shoppers in their stores at all. These retailers will argue that restrooms may be a staging ground for shoplifting or that the lost sales from diverting sales space is too costly. What do you think?

Sometimes the nonselling area is dependent on the particular type of retailer. For instance, tire and muffler stores need considerable amounts of nonselling space, given the equipment necessary to work on the customer's vehicle; retail bakeries need space for baking and preparing cakes and pastries; and apparel retailers need dressing rooms where shoppers can try on clothes to see that they fit properly. It is interesting to note, however, that many apparel retailers ignore the important role of dressing rooms in the sale of apparel. Why is this so important? People like to touch clothes that they are considering purchasing. But the best way to touch the clothes is in a private dressing room where the outfit can be touched and worn. In fact, if you are a retail apparel salesperson and you observe a shopper touching a sweater, dress, or slacks, you should ask them if they would like to try on the item(s). Once people try on an apparel item, the probability of purchase rises considerably. Also, to make it convenient for shoppers to try on clothes, be sure to place the dressing rooms in a convenient place.[24]

Wall Merchandise Space   The walls are one of the most important elements of a retail store. They serve as fixtures holding tremendous amounts of merchandise as well as providing a visual backdrop for the merchandise on the floor. For example,

Timberland makes good use of wall space to attractively display all of their shoe styles carried at a particular location.

many shoe stores are narrow at the entrance, sometimes less than 18 feet, but are usually 100 or 200 feet deep. An effective wall display might be to have the entire back wall lined from floor to ceiling with a particular type of shoe, such as athletic shoes, for which the store is known. This actually makes a bold statement that the retailer is in, for example, the athletic shoe business.

Floor Merchandise Space   Finally, we come to the store space with which we as shoppers are most familiar—the floor merchandise space. Here many different types of fixtures are used to display a wide variety of merchandise. Generally speaking, retailers use bulk fixtures on the floor to carry large quantities of merchandise. But increasingly, retailers are realizing that the best approach is not simply to just cram the largest possible amount of merchandise on the floor as possible but to attractively and effectively display the largest amount that customers can understand and shop. In many cases, displaying lesser amounts of merchandise actually increases retailer sales, and thus space productivity. Incidentally, this approach also enables the inventory productivity, as measured by gross margin return on inventory, to be higher.

Space-Allocation Planning

To determine the most productive allocation of space, the retailer must first analyze the profitability and productivity of various categories of merchandise. Our experience, after observing many different types of retailers, is that around 10 to 20 percent of the average retailer's inventory is either obsolete or not wanted by the retailer's target market. Predictably, inventory requires space, and thus, not only does this unnecessary inventory result in a low GMROI, it also lowers a retailer's space productivity.

There are several methods for measuring profitability and productivity. Regardless of the method used, the results must relate some type of output performance measure (e.g., net sales, net profit, or gross margin) to the amount of space used in the store in order to get a productivity figure to help determine the best allocation of the square footage. Two situations may cause a retailer to perform these tasks: revising the space allocation of an existing store and planning a new store.

Improving Space Productivity in Existing Stores   Any retailer that has occupied its store for a decade will always find that it can benefit substantially from a fresh analysis of its existing space allocation. For example, Men's Wearhouse realized that given the growing trend towards casual clothing in the office, the chain could be much more profitable if it began displaying an increased amount of such clothing options in the front of each store.[25] Similarly, Duane Reade, a New York City drugstore chain, realized after evaluating its inventory productivity that much of their merchandise looked eerily like that of Walgreen's and many of its other national competitors and thus decided to allocate more space to its private label brands, many of which also had a strong city appeal, like Christmas in New York.[26]

One easy measure to use is the **space productivity index**, which compares the percentage of the store's total gross margin dollars for a particular merchandise category to its percentage of space utilized. An index rating of 1.0 would be an ideal department size. If the index is greater than 1.0, then the product category is generating a larger percentage of the store's gross margin than the percentage of store space it is using, and the retailer should consider allocating additional space to this category. If the index falls below 1.0, then the product category is underperforming relative to other merchandise, and the retailer might consider reducing its space allocation. The merchandise-productivity analysis shown in Exhibit 13.3 indicates that in this store, softlines (apparel and apparel accessories) categories, with an index of 1.29, are

space productivity index
Is a ratio that compares the percentage of the store's total gross margin that a particular merchandise category generates to its percentage of total store selling space used.

Duane Reade Drugstores tries to differentiate itself from other drugstore chains through private label brands and attractive display.

performing very well and perhaps should be given more space. On the other hand, hardlines (nonapparel products), with an index of 0.86, are underperforming and should be considered for downsizing.

Of course, as with all financial analysis, the space-productivity index is simply a tool to help management make decisions, not a decision-making formula. Even though a certain category may have a low index, senior management may retain its full space because a new buyer has just been hired or because the category is an important image builder. A high-index category might not be given more space if management expects a hot fashion trend to cool off soon and believes the space-productivity index for that category will drop accordingly. Also, the space-productivity indexes can only be computed on merchandise the retailer has a history of selling. For this reason, it does not help to reveal that a hardware store may find it profitable to stock bottled water and soda or that a supermarket may find it profitable to devote space to a branch bank or beauty salon.

Space Allocations for a New Store   When a retailer is creating a new store format, no productivity and profitability data are available on which to base the allocation of space. In these situations, the retailer bases space allocation on industry standards, previous experience with similar formats, or, more frequently, the space required for stocking the number of items specified by the buyers. Kroger, for example, used information obtained from existing stores to revamp its beverage section at new locations. In its newer stores, one side of a 48-foot-long aisle was committed to bottled waters and new energy drinks—some 150 different types. At the same time, Kroger reduced the space normally allocated for traditional colas.

Once a detailed assortment plan has been created, typical stock levels are estimated based on minimum and maximum quantities. The retailer can then determine the amount of shelf space required to carry this merchandise. By determining the space

Exhibit 13.3
Merchandise-Productivity Analysis

Category	Total Sales	Sales as % of Total	Total Sq. Ft.	Sq. Ft. as % of Total	Sales per Sq. Ft.	Total G.M. $	G.M. $ as % of Total	Space Productivity Index
Softlines								
Juniors	259,645	3.9	1,602	2.9	162.08	211,497	4.57	1.58
Dresses	47,829	0.7	608	1.1	78.67	33,426	0.72	0.66
Misses	512,458	7.7	3,702	6.7	138.43	429,403	9.29	1.39
Women	170,819	2.6	1,934	3.5	88.33	148,899	3.22	0.92
Boys	184,485	2.8	2,542	4.6	72.58	144,866	3.13	0.68
Men	751,604	11.3	3,591	6.5	209.30	603,330	13.05	2.01
Infants	204,983	3.1	1,658	3.0	123.63	142,545	3.08	1.03
Toddlers	47,829	0.7	497	0.9	96.24	43,261	0.94	1.04
Girls	191,318	2.9	2,542	4.6	75.27	157,573	3.41	0.74
Lingerie	273,311	4.1	2,431	4.4	112.43	262,548	5.68	1.29
Accessories	245,980	3.7	1,602	2.9	153.55	238,735	5.16	1.78
Jewelry	129,823	1.9	829	1.5	156.60	123,484	2.67	1.78
Total Softlines	3,020,084	45.2	23,537	42.6	128.31	2,539,566	54.92	1.29
Hardlines								
Domestics	498,792	7.5	4,531	8.2	110.08	407,745	8.82	1.08
HBA	464,628	7.0	1,989	3.6	233.60	153,153	3.31	0.92
Housewares	457,795	6.8	3,591	6.5	127.48	254,979	5.51	0.85
Cosmetics	75,160	1.1	608	1.1	123.62	55,913	1.21	1.00
Tobacco	140,187	2.1	221	0.4	634.33	37,349	0.81	2.02
Candy	144,944	2.2	387	0.7	374.53	88,179	1.91	2.72
Sporting Goods	184,485	2.8	2,652	4.8	69.56	129,948	2.81	0.59
Stationery	307,475	4.6	2,763	5.0	111.28	254,150	5.50	1.10
Furniture	75,160	1.1	1,547	2.8	48.58	60,333	1.30	0.47
Home Entertainment	601,284	9.0	2,265	4.1	265.47	255,973	5.54	1.35
Toys	300,642	4.5	2,431	4.4	123.67	143,429	3.10	0.70
Seasonal	145,333	2.2	2,652	4.8	54.80	90,168	1.95	0.41
Hardware/Paint	163,986	2.5	2,100	3.8	78.09	111,274	2.41	0.63
Pet Supplies	13,666	0.2	55	0.1	248.47	13,094	0.28	2.83
Auto Accessories	81,993	1.2	1,271	2.3	64.51	29,227	0.63	0.27
Total Hardlines	3,655,480	54.8	29,061	52.6	125.79	2,084,914	45.08	0.86
Nonselling	—	—	2,652	4.8	—	—	—	—
Total Scores	6,675,564	100.0	55,250	100.0		4,624,480	100.00	1.00

© Cengage Learning

for each item and then for each category and department, the retailer can develop the floor plan for the store. As you can imagine, optimizing a store's space is a grueling process.

Robert Kahn, who was also a member of Walmart's board of directors, once explained to Sam Walton that one of the problems with retailers was that they thought the best way to get higher sales per square foot (which they recognized was an important factor in store profitability, since higher sales would reduce operating expenses as a percentage of sales) was to run more ads and add more merchandise displays. Thus, retailers at the time reduced their aisle space and stacked the merchandise so high that many customers either could not reach the top or were afraid to touch the displays.[27]

Kahn, however, had his own ideas about customer behavior in the store and explained that there was a better formula for higher sales per square foot:

$$\text{Sales per square foot} = f[(\text{number of customers}) \times (\text{length of time they spend in the store})]$$

In Exhibit 13.4, we show how retailers can use this simple equation to understand the profit impact of increased customer traffic and also longer store visits.

According to Kahn's theory, retailers should concentrate on the time customers spend browsing and experiencing the store (this doesn't include the dwell time of waiting in line to check out), not on how much merchandise they are exposed to. Based on this concept, Kahn outlined four things that Walmart should do:

1. Ensure that in every aisle, a customer with a cart can comfortably pass another customer with a cart without having to ask that customer to move.
2. Make the restrooms the best in town so that a customer will never leave the store and rush home to use the bathroom.
3. Put at least one bench in each store, in the alcove at the front door. When Walmart opened the first American hypermarket, Kahn went to the grand opening. Afterward, he kiddingly told Sam to put 10 to 12 benches inside each hypermarket and have a vendor sponsor (pay for) each bench. Sam Walton thought this was a dumb idea because as he told Kahn "if they (the customers) are sitting, they ain't buying."
4. In all large stores, install a coffee stand catty-corner from the snack bar so that customers can recharge themselves in order to spend more time and money shopping.

All these ideas seemed to agree with Sam Walton's concept that a retailer was a failure if, after getting customers to come into the store, the retailer did not do everything possible to satisfy all their needs and did not force them to go elsewhere for merchandise.

Exhibit 13.4
Impact of Customer Traffic and Length of Store Visit

$S = .01C + 9T$

where:

> S = Sales per square foot
> C = number of customer visits annually
> T = length of time (minutes) average shopper spends in the store (excluding dwell time)

Explanation: For each customer that visits the store the retailer gains .01 (one cent) of sales per square foot but for each additional minute in the store by the average customer, sales per square foot rises $9. *In short, time in the store pays the retailer or costs the customer.*

Example: 30,000 customer visits, 30 minutes average time shopping in store

> $S = 30,000(.002) + 9(30)$
> $S = \$60 + \$270$
> $S = \$330$

As an experiment, Walmart built 10 new 85,000-square-foot stores and 10 new 115,000-square-foot versions. The stores had identical amounts of fixtures and merchandise. The larger stores used the extra 30,000 square feet for wider aisles and extra space at the increased number of checkouts (obviously, the time spent in the store was to reflect shopping or browsing time and *not* the dwell time spent waiting to check out) and to project an open, friendlier image. Also, the new restrooms, which were checked every two hours for cleanliness, had tile, not cement, floors; diaper-changing shelves in both the men's and women's restrooms; and easy-to-clean vinyl-covered walls. Eight to ten benches were placed in the main aisles. However, Walmart dropped Kahn's coffee bar idea.

The first indication of the success of the larger store was that its parking lots were always full because shoppers were spending so much more time in the store. Sales figures showed that the larger stores not only had higher sales but were also producing higher sales per square foot of store space than the smaller stores, despite all that "wasted" aisle space. Walmart did not know exactly what the customers were doing in these larger stores, just that they were spending more time and money. As a result, Walmart went with the larger store model and increased the parking spaces from five to six per 1,000 square feet of store space. However, the benches were dropped because, as mentioned earlier, Sam felt that if the customers were sitting, they weren't buying.

Kahn used the experience as the basis in 1998 for his work as an expert witness supporting a suit by two disabled individuals under the Americans with Disabilities Act (ADA). The case involved R. H. Macy Company, which purchased an O'Connor, Moffat & Co. store in San Francisco during the 1940s. Despite three expansions, the store still had inadequately sized aisles. Macy's, along with the California Retailers Association and its own expert witnesses, claimed, "It's pretty basic in retail. Inventory per square foot drives sales per square foot, which drives profit." Kahn used the Walmart experience to show that a "reduction in nonaisle space permitted greater access to merchandise, which in turn leads to an increase in sales. If Macy's was correct, why didn't all retailers eliminate all aisles and stack merchandise to the ceiling to maximize profit?"[28] While this case was settled out of court, five years later a California court ruled that the now-bankrupt Mervyn's department store chain didn't have to expand its aisles to ease shopping for disabled customers because Mervyn's would lose $30 million a year in profits due to remodeling expenses, causing the company to shut down some of its 126 California operations.[29] Despite the rather general guidelines of the ADA, it is important that retailers not lose sight of the fact that 21 percent of the U.S. population has some type of disability. Today, profitable retailers need to understand the relationship between "the store needs and objectives and those of disabled customers."[30] This is especially important with the aging of the population since older customers have more physical disabilities. However, these older disabled individuals still want to eat out, travel, visit museums and other attractions, and shop for themselves and their grandchildren.

planogram
Is a schematic that illustrates how and where a retailer's merchandise should be displayed on the shelf in order to increase customer purchases.

Planograms   After retailers have allocated space for all of their departments, they then decide how and where retail products should be displayed on the store shelves. This is accomplished by using a planogram. A **planogram**, which was first introduced in Chapter 9, is a graphic schematic showing the precise location of every SKU on a shelf or other merchandise display. This schematic points out not only the location of the item but also the desired quantity, including the number of facings and the item's *adjacencies*, or what products it should be displayed alongside. A planogram is designed to allow the retailer to increase space productivity by taking into account inventory turnover, space and inventory investment requirements, and gross margins of the SKUs. Incidentally, one of the first assignments many college graduates have when they go to work for consumer packaged goods companies is to call on retailers and to persuade them to follow the manufacturer's suggested planogram. To create an effective planogram, the developer, which could be the retailer, the manufacturer, or both working together, needs not only to be creative but also to understand the financial aspects of merchandising performance, which was covered in Chapters 8, 9, and 10. The planogram developer should review sales history on a continual basis to see if pricing, promotion, or logistical changes need to be made. At the end of each season, both the retailer and vendor will conduct a formal planogram review to determine the performance of all stock items. Those that don't perform as planned may be discontinued or be marked down. Both decisions will impact the retailer's future merchandise budget. Also, if a product is dropped, space is then available for a new item.

Historically, planograms were developed by manufacturers to help persuade retailers where and how to display their products. Today, however, planogram software is the preferred method for space planning. Two of the most popular software programs are the Apollo space-management program, which is marketed by IRI, and Spaceman, which is marketed by ACNielsen. Both IRI and Nielsen specialize in collecting information on product movement at retail and thus are in an excellent position to be objective and scientific in the development of planograms for retailers.

Circulation

The circulation pattern not only ensures efficient movement of large numbers of shoppers through the store, exposing them to more merchandise, but also determines the character of the store. For instance, upon entering a Bass Pro Shops Outdoor World, the consumer views outdoor scenes through graphic and physical design elements. In addition, the store is usually connected to a lake or other natural feature. These scenes pull customers through the store and allow them to view more merchandise and often test the merchandise.[31] Similarly, Disney Stores are designed to communicate the fun and excitement of the theme parks and famous characters and to entice customers to walk to the back wall. After all, chances are good that when customers get to the back, they will return using a different route. This will expose them to more merchandise and increase the chance of a sale. Four basic types of layout are used today (free flow, grid, loop, and spine), each of which is described in the following discussion. Shoppers have been trained to associate certain circulation patterns with different types of stores, so in reading these descriptions, try to think of how they are used in the various stores you shop and the store image they evoke in your mind.

Free Flow

free-flow layout
Is a type of store layout in which fixtures and merchandise are grouped into free-flowing patterns on the sales floor.

The simplest type of store layout is a **free-flow layout** (Exhibit 13.5) in which fixtures and merchandise are grouped into free-flowing patterns on the sales floor. Customers are encouraged to flow freely through all the fixtures since there are usually no defined traffic patterns in the store. This type of layout works well in small stores, usually less than 5,000 square feet, in which customers wish to browse through all of the merchandise. Generally, the merchandise is of the same type, such as fashion apparel perhaps categorized only into tops and bottoms. If there is a greater variety of merchandise (for instance, men's and women's apparel, bedding, and health and beauty aids), a free-flow layout fails to provide cues as to where one department stops and another starts, confusing the shopper.

Exhibit 13.5
Free-Flow Layout

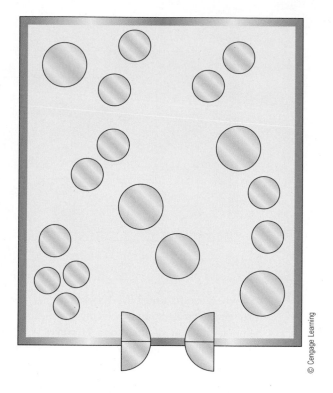

© Cengage Learning

Grid

Another traditional form of store layout is the grid, in which the counters and fixtures are placed in long rows or "runs," usually at right angles, throughout the store. In a grid layout (Exhibit 13.6), customers circulate up and down through the fixtures, and, in fact, the grid layout is often referred to as a *maze*. The most familiar examples of the grid layout are supermarkets and drugstores.

The grid is a both a historically and contemporarily popular shopping layout, best used in retail environments in which the majority of customers wish to shop the entire store. In supermarkets, for instance, many shoppers flow methodically up and down all the fixture runs, looking for everything they might need along the way. However, if the shopper wishes to find only several specific categories, the grid can be confusing and frustrating, because it is difficult to see over the fixtures to other merchandise (especially

Exhibit 13.6
Grid Layout

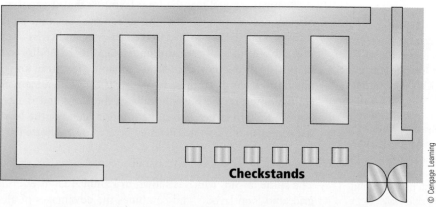

Checkstands

© Cengage Learning

Exhibit 13.7
Loop Layout

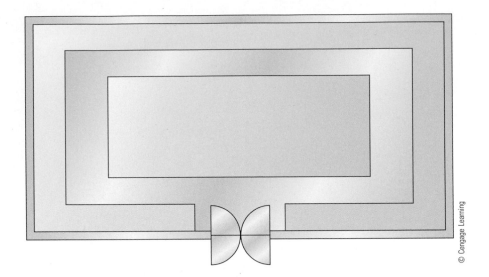

© Cengage Learning

today because fixtures have become higher). For example, supermarkets move customers through the entire store by placing the meats, dairy goods, and other frequently purchased items at the rear of the store. However, retailers should employ this strategy carefully. Forcing customers in a hurry all the way to the back of a large store will frustrate many customers and lead some to go elsewhere for merchandise. For this reason, many supermarkets, such as Albertson's and Kroger, recognizing the high demand for home meal replacements, are placing these freshly prepared take-home meals at the front of the store and often link them to an in-store deli and a place to eat the meal within the supermarket.

Loop

loop layout
Is a type of store layout in which a major customer aisle begins at the entrance, loops through the store—usually in the shape of a circle, square, or rectangle—and then returns the customer to the front of the store.

Over the past two decades, the **loop layout** (sometimes called a *racetrack* layout) has become a popular tool for enhancing the productivity of retail stores. As shown in Exhibit 13.7, a loop provides a major customer aisle that begins at the entrance, loops through the store—usually in the shape of a circle, square, or rectangle—and then returns the customer to the front of the store. While this seems like a simple concept, the loop can be a powerful space-productivity tool. Recently, you may have noticed that Old Navy is updating its store layout by using a loop layout. This type of layout also allows clear sightlines throughout the store so a shopper traveling the loop can see other departments. Old Navy also decided to centralize the fitting rooms so they can be easily reached from any department.

The major benefit of the loop layout is that it exposes shoppers to the greatest possible amount of merchandise. An effective circulation pattern must first guide customers throughout the store to encourage browsing and cross-shopping. Along the way, shoppers must be able to easily see and understand merchandise to the left and right, so ideally the main aisle should never stray more than 60 feet from any merchandise. The way to simultaneously accomplish these two goals is to create a main circulation loop that mirrors the configuration of the outside walls of the store and is never more than 60 feet from the outside wall. In larger stores, the interior island of the loop can itself be too large to easily see across, and internal walls may be created to shorten sightlines to merchandise.

Spine

spine layout
Is a type of store layout in which a single main aisle runs from the front to the back of the store, transporting customers in both directions, and where on either side of this spine, merchandise departments using either a free-flow or grid pattern branch off toward the back side walls.

The **spine layout**, which is shown in Exhibit 13.8, is essentially a variation of the free-flow, grid, and loop layouts and combines the advantages of all three in certain circumstances.

Exhibit 13.8
Spine Layout

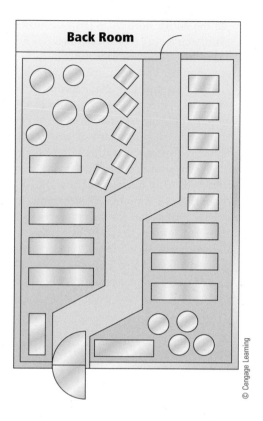

A spine layout is based on a single main aisle running from the front to the back of the store, transporting customers in both directions. On either side of this spine, each merchandise department branches off toward the back or side walls. Within these departments, either a free-flow or grid layout can be used, depending on the type of merchandise and fixtures in use. The spine is heavily used by medium-sized specialty stores, either hardlines or softlines, ranging in size from 2,000 to 10,000 square feet. Often, especially in fashion stores, the spine is subtly set off by a change in floor coloring or surface and is not perceived as an aisle, even though it functions as such.

Shrinkage Prevention

When planning a store's layout and design, the prevention of shrinkage due to theft, damage, and loss must be considered. Some layouts will minimize vulnerability to shoplifters. One of the most important considerations when planning the layout is visibility of the merchandise. Most shoplifting takes place in fitting rooms, blind spots, aisles crowded with extra merchandise, or behind high displays. Fitting rooms, one of the most common scenes of the shoplifting crime, should be placed in visible areas that can be monitored by associates. Historically, display fixtures have been kept no higher than eye level to allow store associates to monitor customers in other aisles. Recently, mass merchandisers have found that increased sales from the greater merchandise intensity of higher fixtures outweigh the increase in shoplifting due to reduced visibility. This depends greatly on merchandise type, however. Expensive items that are easily placed into pockets and handbags, such as compact discs or drill bits in a hardware store, are high-theft items and are usually kept on low fixtures to discourage shoplifting. The manager's office and other security windows can be an excellent deterrent to shoplifting if they are placed in an obvious area above the sales floor level, where managers can easily see the entire store. Also large circular mirrors placed high and reflecting down an aisle allow employees to see customers in aisles—and shoplifters have learned to avoid these aisles. Electronic security systems, including sensor tags and video cameras, have become very popular and are usually in a highly visible location to serve as a deterrent.

Always remember that more than half of shrinkage occurs from employees and not shoppers. Thus, you need to keep in mind that design needs to also consider preventing employees from easy means of theft. For instance, trash cans should be emptied by managers or a rotating team of employees because many employees steal by tossing new merchandise into a trash can and then volunteering to empty the trash, which gets the new merchandise either into the back room or outside the building where it can be easily retrieved. Also, be aware of how fitting rooms can be a place for theft by employees who conspire with shoppers. For example, a friend might try on several outfits, only to leave one or two behind for the employee to retrieve, toss in a corner or in the back room, and then put into the trash or in another location, where it can be easily stolen later on. If the store has a back room, retailers should also be leery if it is always sloppy and disorganized because this becomes a safe haven for tossing merchandise that the employee plans to take home after work. The storeroom should always be organized with everything having a well-defined place.[32]

LO 3 Planning Fixtures and Merchandise Presentation

Describe how various types of fixtures, merchandise-presentation methods and techniques, and the psychology of merchandise presentation are used to increase the productivity of the sales floor.

on-shelf merchandising Is the display of merchandise on counters, racks, shelves, and fixtures throughout the store.

Retailing is theater, and in no area is that more true than in merchandise presentation. Recently, retailers have been increasing their emphasis on presentation as competition has grown and stores try to squeeze more sales out of existing or, as we mentioned earlier, less square footage. Two basic types of merchandise presentation include: visual merchandising and on-shelf merchandising. In thinking of retailing as theater, visual merchandising is analogous to the stage props that set scenes and serve as backdrops.

Merchandise presentation is a complex activity best learned on the retail floor. While this text will not attempt to teach the art and science of merchandise presentation, you should be familiar with a number of basic components of merchandise presentation and their potential impact on store image and sales, including fixture type and selection and certain techniques and methods of on-shelf merchandising.

On-shelf merchandising, which describes the merchandise that is displayed on and in counters, racks, shelves, and fixtures throughout the store, represents the stars on our theater stage. This is the merchandise that the shopper actually touches, tries on, examines, reads, understands, and, we hope, buys. Recall our earlier advice: "Shopping is a contact sport." Shoppers want to see close up, touch, and smell merchandise because shoppers are sensual and shopping is a sensual experience.[33] In fact, it is more important today than ever, that if you operate a land-based versus on-line retail store, that you design the store and on-shelf merchandising to enhance the shoppers' sensual experience. Otherwise, they must just as well purchase the merchandise on-line.

Therefore, on-shelf merchandising must not only present the merchandise attractively but also display the merchandise so it is easy to understand and accessible. Further, it must be reasonably easy to maintain, with customers themselves able to replace merchandise so it is equally appealing to the next shopper. It must not be so overwhelming that the customer is afraid to touch the merchandise. After receiving more than 25,000 complaints a year regarding injuries from falling merchandise, Walmart has sought to reduce the height level of merchandise displays in every store. Despite the efforts of top management, many managers still falsely believe the best way to improve sales (and their year-end bonus) is to cram as much merchandise as possible into the store.

Fixture Types

Store fixtures fall into three basic categories: hardlines, softlines, and wall fixtures.

Hardlines Fixtures

The workhorse fixture in most hardlines departments is known as the *gondola*, so named because it is a long structure consisting of a large base and a vertical spine or wall sticking up as high as eight feet, fitted with sockets or notches into which a variety of shelves, peg hooks, bins, baskets, and other hardware can be inserted. The basic gondola can hold a wide variety of merchandise by means of hardware hung from the vertical spine. Think of your last trip to a discount store or supermarket. The long, heavy-duty fixtures fitted predominantly with shelves are gondolas. In addition to the gondola, a few other types of fixtures are in common use today: tables, large bins, and simple flat-base decks. These fixtures are commonly used in promotional aisles to display advertised or other special-value merchandise.

Softlines Fixtures

The bulky gondola is inappropriate for fashion-oriented softlines merchandise. A large array of fixtures has been developed to accommodate the special needs of softlines, which are often hung on hangers. As shown in Exhibit 13.9, the four-way feature rack and the round rack are the two fixtures most heavily used today. These smaller, specialized fixtures have replaced the straight rack, a long pipe with legs on each end from which rows of apparel were hung, and which for generations was the most prevalent softlines fixture. Although it held a great quantity and was easy to maintain, the straight rack provided few opportunities to differentiate one style or color of garment from another, which merchants have found is the key to selling more. A straight rack is like the hanger rod in your closet, and what you see when you open your closet is nothing

Softlines fixtures, such as open hanging racks, low tables, and visually pleasing bins and cubes, invite customers to experience the merchandise.

Exhibit 13.9
Four-Way Feature Rack and Round Rack

more than sleeves. You know your own clothes, so sleeves are enough to tip you off to what the rest of the garment looks like. When you are shopping, however, the more of the garment you are exposed to and the more varieties of size, silhouette (shape), and color, the more you are apt to buy. So merchants prefer *face-out* presentations over *sleeve-out* presentations. The face-out concept can apply not only to softlines such as apparel but also to hardlines. Often for hardlines the exposure of the full visual of the product can attract the customer to the item. For instance, a new-car dealer can stack its new vehicles in a grid format similar to a normal parking lot; however, all the potential car shopper will then view are hoods and trunks or the back ends of the vehicles. Displaying the autos face-out would create a dramatically different effect and pull the customer to the new vehicles. Of course, face-outs take up more space than sleeve-outs, so it is impractical to face out all or even a high percentage of the total merchandise on the floor.

The round rack is known as a **bulk or capacity fixture** and is intended to hold the bulk of merchandise without looking as heavy as a long straight rack of merchandise. Although it is smaller than the straight rack, it too allows only sleeve-outs unless fitted with special hardware. The four-way rack, on the other hand, is considered a **feature fixture**; even though it holds fewer items, it presents merchandise in a manner that permits the shopper to glimpse at a garment's style and key characteristics (such as color or shape). The ingenious design also allows it to hold a large quantity of merchandise on the hanger arms behind the four face-outs. However, to be easily shopped, all the merchandise on one arm must be the same type of garment with variations only in color and size.

Wall Fixtures

The last type of fixture is designed to be hung on the wall. To make a store's plain wall merchandisable, it is usually covered with a skin that is fitted with vertical columns of notches similar to those on the gondola, into which a variety of hardware can be

bulk or capacity fixture
Is a display fixture that is intended to hold the bulk of merchandise without looking as heavy as a long, straight rack of merchandise.

feature fixture
Is a display that draws special attention to selected features (e.g., color, shape, or style) of merchandise.

inserted. Shelves, peg hooks, bins, baskets, and even hanger bars can be fitted into wall systems. Hanger bars can be hung parallel to the wall, much like a closet bar, so that large quantities of garments can be sleeved-out, or they can protrude perpendicularly from the wall, either straight out (*straight-outs*) or angled down (*waterfalls*), to allow merchandise to be faced out. The primary quality to remember about wall systems is that walls can generally be merchandised much higher than floor fixtures. On the floor, round racks are kept to a maximum of 42 inches so that customers can easily see over them to other merchandise, but on the wall garments can be hung as high as customers can reach, which is generally about 72 inches. This allows walls to be "double hung" with two rows of garments, or even "triple hung" with smaller children's apparel. Therefore, walls not only hold large amounts of merchandise but also serve as a visual backdrop for the department.

Merchandise-Presentation Planning

As we have just discussed, retailers can choose from a large array of fixtures and hardware. This may seem to present an endless variety of ways to merchandise product, but there are essentially six methods:

1. *Shelving.* The majority of merchandise is placed on shelves that are inserted into gondolas or wall systems. Shelving is a flexible, easy-to-maintain merchandise-presentation method.
2. *Hanging.* Apparel on hangers can be hung from softlines fixtures, such as round racks and four-way racks, or from bars installed on gondolas or wall systems.
3. *Pegging.* Small merchandise can be hung from peg hooks, which are small rods inserted into gondolas or wall systems. Used in both softlines and hardlines, pegging gives a neat, orderly appearance but can be labor intensive to display and maintain.
4. *Folding.* Higher-margin or large, unwieldy softlines merchandise can be folded and then stacked onto shelves or placed on tables. This can create a high-fashion image, such as when towels are taken off peg hooks and neatly folded and stacked high up the wall.
5. *Stacking.* Large hardlines merchandise can be stacked on shelves, the base decks of gondolas, or *flats*, which are platforms placed directly on the floor. Stacking is easily maintained and gives an image of high volume and low price.
6. *Dumping.* Large quantities of small merchandise can be dumped in bins or baskets inserted into gondolas or wall systems. This highly effective promotional method can be used in softlines (socks, washcloths) or hardlines (batteries, grocery products, candy), and creates a high-volume, low-cost image.

The method of merchandise presentation can have a dramatic impact on image and space productivity. Different merchandise-presentation methods have been shown to strongly influence buying habits and stimulate consumers to purchase more. There is a certain "psychology of merchandise presentation" that must be carefully considered in developing merchandise-presentation schemes. Only between one-third and one-half of store shoppers make an impulse (unplanned) purchase, and these purchases are made by only 60 percent of the shoppers who actually enter the store with the intent of making a specific purchase. Thus, 40 percent of the shoppers who enter a store to make a purchase are "wasted" because the store failed to use merchandise presentation to generate additional purchases.[34] This is why department store design incorporates a gauntlet of goodies to stimulate impulse buys. For example, cosmetics, usually the store's most profitable department, is always near the main entrance. Typically, the department is leased to cosmetic companies that use their own salespeople to sell the perfume, lipstick, and eye shadow. Other high-impulse items (e.g., jewelry, handbags, and shoes) are usually nearby, while the "demand" products (e.g., furniture) are on upper floors. These stores would be unprofitable if they failed to induce a significant amount of impulse buying.

The following are three key psychological factors to consider when merchandising stores:

1. *Value and fashion image.* One of the most important effects of merchandise presentation is the psychological effect it fosters in the customer's mind of how trendy, exclusive, pricey, or value oriented the merchandise is. For each of the merchandise-presentation methods mentioned previously, we discussed its effect on price image. By changing the merchandise-presentation method, we can change the perception of our towel display from common, high volume, and high value to an exclusive selection of high-fashion merchandise that is typically branded by a well-known designer such as Ralph Lauren, which presumably will be at higher prices. Note that this concept of using merchandise presentation to reinforce a value or fashion image can also be done with service retailers. Consider, for example, how Cost Cutters Family Hair Care displays hair-care products on a high series of shelves in the waiting area that is lighted with fluorescent light fixtures. And then contrast that with how a high-end beauty or barbershop perhaps coupled with a health spa would most likely display the merchandise on glass tables with flowers surrounding the hair-care products and spotlights on the merchandise.

2. *Angles and sight lines.* Research has shown that as customers move through a retail store, they view the store at approximately 45-degree angles from the path of travel, as shown in Exhibit 13.10, rather than perpendicular to their path. Incidentally, this 45-degree angle approximates the extent to which the typical person can turn his or her head. Although this seems logical, most stores are set up at right angles because it is easier and consumes less space. Therefore, merchandise and signage often wind up being at a 90-degree angle to the main aisle. Exhibit 13.10 also shows how four-way feature racks can be more effectively merchandised by being turned to meet the shoppers' sight lines head-on.

3. *Vertical color blocking.* To be most effective, merchandise should be displayed in vertical bands of color wherever possible. As customers move through the store, their eyes naturally view a "swath" approximately two-feet high, parallel to the

Exhibit 13.10
45-Degree Customer Sightline

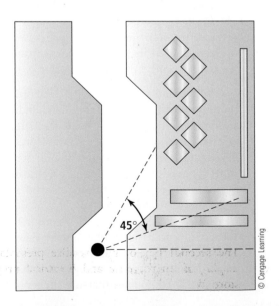

45°

© Cengage Learning

Exhibit 13.11
Vertical Color Blocking

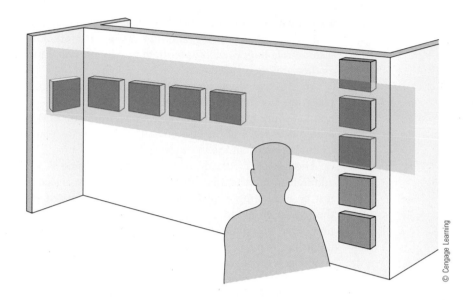

© Cengage Learning

floor, at about eye level. This is shown in Exhibit 13.11. This visual swath of merchandise will be viewed as a rainbow of colors if each merchandise item is displayed vertically by color (e.g., the vertical columns represent different colors, and within these colors could be different sizes). This method of merchandise presentation creates such a strong visual effect that shoppers are exposed to more merchandise, which in turn increases sales. In addition, when shopping for clothing, customers most often think first of color. Thus, they can easily find the column of color on display and locate their size. United Colors of Benetton, with more than 5,500 stores in 120 countries, is perhaps the leader in effectively using vertical color blocking as a signature element of its store designs.

Selecting Fixtures and Merchandise-Presentation Methods

Proper fixtures emphasize the key selling attributes of merchandise while not being overpowering. A good guideline for selecting fixtures—although it is not always possible to follow—is to *match the fixture to the merchandise, not the merchandise to the fixture.* This means you should only use fixtures that are sensitive to the nature of the merchandise. All too often, though, retailers are forced to put merchandise on the wrong fixture.[35]

Consider intimate apparel, for instance. This is a fast-selling, high-margin merchandise category that can enhance a retailer's image in fashion merchandising. Though retailers entering this business might be tempted to place intimate apparel on existing shelves of a gondola, they would be well served to consider special fixtures that enhance the delicate qualities of intimate apparel. A large, metal, bulky gondola will overpower a small, delicate intimate-apparel item, and therefore reduce sales potential. More delicate fixtures made of softer materials will enhance sales. Likewise, it would not be effective to bulk stack fragile merchandise because the weight of items might damage those lower in the stack. It would not make sense to peg hook large, bulky items, because they take up too much room and might be too heavy for the peg hooks.

Visual Merchandising

visual merchandising
Is the artistic display of merchandise and theatrical props used as scene-setting decoration in the store.

The second type of merchandise presentation, **visual merchandising**, is the artistic display of merchandise and theatrical props used as scene-setting decoration in the store. While on-shelf merchandising must be tastefully displayed to encourage shopping, a store with just on-shelf merchandising would be dreary. Many low-price stores contain little visual merchandising, and they do appear more boring than their upscale cousins in fashion retailing, which concentrate heavily on visual merchandising displays, or *visuals*, as they are often called.

An effective visual merchandising display has several key characteristics. Visual displays are not typically associated with a shopable fixture but are located in a focal point, feature area, or other area away from the on-shelf merchandising and perhaps even out of reach of the customer. Their goal is to create a feeling in the store conducive to buying merchandise.

Another characteristic of visual merchandising is its use of props and elements in addition to merchandise. In fact, visuals do not always include merchandise—they may just be interesting displays of items somehow related to the merchandise or to a mood the retailer wishes to create. A prop might be a wooden barrel, a miniature airplane, or a mock tree with autumn leaves. Visuals are like the illustrations and design elements in a book that make it interesting; they tell the customer whether this is an upscale, serious shopping experience; a frivolous, fun shopping experience; or a down and dirty, low-price shopping experience.

To be most effective, however, visuals should incorporate relevant merchandise. In apparel retailing, mannequins or figure forms are used to display merchandise as it might appear on a person rather than hanging limply on a hanger. This helps the shopper visualize how these garments will enhance his or her appearance. Good fashion visuals include more than just one garment to show how tops and bottoms go together and how belts, scarves, and other accessories can be combined to create an overall fashion look. This is called *accessorization*. When successful, visuals help the shopper translate the merchandise presentation from "garments on a rack" to "fashionable clothes that will look good on me." Note this concept can be applied beyond apparel. For instance in furniture retailing, you can display a sofa, dining table, or other key furniture

Alex Segre/Alamy

Good visual merchandising can use mannequins to show how different elements of clothing can be put together to create fully accessorized looks.

pieces with accessories such as lamps, pictures, mirrors, rugs, and pottery. In fact, some furniture stores when they deliver furniture, will also bring along accessories and use this as a second sales opportunity.[36] In another example, consider how some home improvement centers are using accessorization to illustrate how a new outdoor grill or outdoor furniture can be accessorized with related merchandise.

LO 4

Describe why store design is so important to a store's success.

ambience
Is the overall feeling or mood projected by a store through its aesthetic appeal to human senses.

Store Design

Store design is the element most responsible for the first of our two goals in planning the store environment: creating a distinctive and memorable store image. Store design encompasses both the exterior and the interior of the store. On the exterior, we have the storefront, signage, and entrance, all of which are critical to attracting passing shoppers and enticing them to enter. On the inside, store design includes the architectural elements and finishes on all surfaces such as wall coverings, floor coverings, and ceilings. There are literally hundreds of details in a store's design, and all must work together to create the desired store **ambience**, which is the overall feeling or mood projected by a store through its aesthetic appeal to the human senses. For instance, Ulta, a retail specialty beauty store featuring cosmetics, hair and bath products, and beauty services, creates a mini-department store image by offering a wide range of beauty brands across a wide price spectrum to a broad target market by age and income. The stores provide a contemporary shopping environment that is positive and bright which is enhanced with well-lit and clearly signed merchandise displays and friendly, knowledgeable and helpful staff. Of course, Ulta stores also have many wonderful fragrances that further enhance the shopping experience. We mentioned earlier that shoppers are sensual and Ulta plays to this desire by having many open bottles of fragrances and lotions you can sample. Another favorite of many Ulta shoppers is the purse size versions of many popular cosmetics, lotions, and hair sprays that further enhance shoppers trying new products, but also reminding shoppers when they open their purse that their Ulta experience goes beyond the store.

This chapter's "Service Retailing" box provides further illustration of how one restaurant chain, Del Frisco's Double Eagle Steakhouse, designs its individual restaurants based upon the cities within which they are located in order to enhance the overall dining experience of its customers.

Storefront Design

If the retail store can be compared to a book, then the storefront, or store exterior, is like the book cover. It must be noticeable, easily identified by passing motorists or mall shoppers, and memorable. The storefront must clearly identify the name and general nature of the store and give some hint as to the merchandise inside. Generally, the storefront design includes all exterior signage and the architecture of the storefront itself.

In many cases, the storefront includes display windows, which serve as an advertising medium for the store. Store windows must arrest the attention of passing shoppers, enticing them inside the store. Therefore, windows should be maintained with exciting visual displays that are changed frequently, are fun and exciting, and reflect the merchandise and service offering inside. Always remember that in those few seconds that the customer is approaching the store—and especially the last 25 to 50 feet—he or she is already forming an opinion about the store and the merchandise and services in it.

Interior Design

Unless you have ever been responsible for redecorating a house or room, you may be unaware of the dozens of design elements that go into a physical space. We can break

SERVICE ⟩ RETAILING

Del Frisco's Takes Its Designing Cues from Its Cities' Surroundings

What comes to mind when you read the names of the following cities: Dallas, Denver, Boston, New York, and Philadelphia? What architectural features do you see? What "hot spots" do you use as the backdrop of your mental image?

Most likely when you think of Denver, you think of the mountains; hiking in wilderness; trees and nature surrounding you. When you imagine New York, most likely you immediately see Manhattan, Rockefeller Center, a bustling city with sidewalks full of people (even at midnight). In Boston you think of the water, fishing boats coming in from a day of fishing, and in Philadelphia, you likely imagine the birthplace of America or all the old financial and banking institutions with their classic, Greek-style white-marble columns and enormous white-marble steps (like the ones Sylvester Stallone ran up during the Rocky franchise).

But what does this "thought exercise" have to do with dining, particularly fine-(steak) dining? Originally introduced in Chapter 11's "Service Retailing" box, Del Frisco's Double Eagle steak house, which began operations more than 20 years ago in the steakhouse-rich Dallas, Texas, competes by offering not only the best hand-cut steaks, chops, and freshest seafood backed with an extensive, and award-winning, wine and cocktail list, but also via their design. Each restaurant is entirely unique; all pay specific homage to the architectural elements and personalities of each city in which they are located. And in so doing, guests receive a lifestyle-rich experience that goes well beyond simply a choice-cut of meat.

For example, the Dallas location resembles a traditional steakhouse with its stark-white table cloths, richly upholstered wooden chairs, and tufted burgundy leather couches. Dark wood finishes, densely carpeted floors, large mirrors, and heavy draperies used to create semi-private dining are all emblematic of the fine steakhouses found throughout Dallas. The Denver location's design couldn't be more different. This restaurant uses earth-tone paints and wallpaper, more rustic wood, and

natural stone to create an "earthy" or "natural" feel, which is consistent with the personality of Denver.

But perhaps the chain's New York and Philadelphia locations are the best examples of the chain's attempt to merge the cities' personalities with the dining experience. When you think of New York, what do you think of? A city that never sleeps? A city that is modern, hip, and full of life?

When you enter the New York establishment, you see floors that are finished with high-end natural stone and mahogany hardwoods; chairs are tufted with soft, supple fabric, and tables are donned with crisp, white table linens; every finish is precise and rich. But, such elements could be characteristic of any fine-dining eatery, in any part of the world. What makes it an experience is how management has brought the "outside in." Every wall of the main dining room has (three stories high) floor-to-ceiling windows availing patrons of views of 6th Avenue, West 49th Street, and Rockefeller Center. Diners can literally sit, sip a glass of fine red wine, eat their steaks, and see all the action of downtown New York. Diners aren't secluded from the outside world with opaque walls and artwork; no, the city itself becomes part of the scenery and staging of the dining experience. When people go to New York, they want to experience it, and diners experience it while eating some of the finest food in town.

The Philadelphia location too succeeds in bringing the outside-in, but in a different way—via *its location*. As we eluded to in Chapter 7, many retailers are beginning to compete via the use of nontraditional locations, and Del Frisco's is nothing different. The restaurant is situated within the old First Pennsylvania Bank in the center of Philadelphia's financial district. Upon entering, diners are most likely to immediately notice a three-story tall wooden elevator shaft that is now full of the most exquisite wine bottles and runs from the center of the bar on the first floor, past the second floor seating, and on up to the ceiling more than 30 feet above. The restaurant also maintains the original architecture of the bank including several, very large white marble columns that support the original, decoratively-carved coffered ceiling. From these columns are sweeping bolts of red

(continued)

fabric that highlight the crisp red linens that are draped over each tabletop. But the most unique of dining experiences available to Philadelphia's diners is the ability to eat in the restaurant's Vault Room. An actual vault of the old bank, diners pass by a huge, multi-ton circular vault door to enter the dining area. Once in, diners are treated to a large, yet semi-private, dining experience with carpeted floors and walls of stacked wine bottles.

Although you've probably never envisioned yourself eating within a vault, or don't immediately see the uniqueness of doing so, imagine how many people you, or your significant other, would tell if you were to be taken on a date which included eating in a vault! As one of the authors has experienced first-hand, it's nice to have a great steak for dinner, but it does seem to taste a little more special when eating it in a vault (and his date to this day agrees).

Source: Based on two of the authors' personal experiences while dining at different Del Frisco's locations across the country and personal discussions between of the authors and Dee Lincoln, one of the founders of Del Frisco's.

interior design into two types of elements: the finishes applied to surfaces and the architectural shapes. Think of all the elements from the floor to the ceiling. First, we have some type of floor covering placed over a concrete or wood floor. At the least, this finish is stain or paint, but vinyl, carpet, ceramic tile, and marble are more frequently used. Each of these different surfaces creates a different impression on the shopper. An unpainted concrete floor conveys a low-cost, no-frills environment. A color-stained floor can convey a rustic yet sophisticated look and feel. Vinyl floor covering makes another statement; depending on its quality, sheen, color, and design pattern, the image can vary from very

The overall impression of a retailer's store includes how all the aspects of the interior design work together. Everything from the colors used to the display elements, lighting, flooring and space planning is important.

downscale to very upscale. Carpet suggests a homelike atmosphere conducive to selling apparel. Ceramic tile, travertine, and especially porcelain or marble suggest an upscale, exclusive, and probably expensive shopping experience.

Retailers have even more options for covering the walls from paint and wallpaper to hundreds of types of paneling. The ceiling must also receive a design treatment, whether it is finished drywall (a very upscale image because it is an expensive process), a suspended ceiling (very common and economical, though not distinctive), or perhaps even an open ceiling with all the pipes and wires above painted black (which suggests a low-price warehouse approach but also could be successful in sports bars or other casual eating establishments). Then there are thousands of types of moldings that can be applied to the transitions from floor to wall to ceiling, and hundreds of architectural design elements that can be incorporated.

Lighting Design

Another important, though often overlooked, element in a successful store design is lighting. Retailers have come to understand how lighting can greatly enhance store sales. Brighter lighting in a wine store also influences shoppers to examine and handle more merchandise. Department stores, on the other hand, have found that raising lighting levels in fashion departments can actually discourage sales because bright lighting suggests a discount-store image.

Lighting design, however, is not limited to simple light levels. Contemporary lighting design requires an in-depth knowledge of electrical engineering and the effect of light on color and texture. Retailers have learned that different types and levels of lighting can have a significant impact on sales.[37] In addition, the types of light sources available have multiplied quickly. Today, there are literally hundreds of light fixtures and lamps (bulbs) from which to choose. Increasingly, retailers are also recognizing that lighting is a large contributor to energy cost and energy waste, and thus energy-efficient lighting is a very high priority in both new buildings and store remodeling.

Many retailers are actually using too much outdoor lighting today, probably because of the increasing risk of accidents or lawsuits. Lighting is measured in foot-candles. One foot-candle is a unit of illumination equal to one lumen per square foot. Research findings suggest that customers in urban areas feel safest in parking lots lighted to the level of five foot-candles, while those in suburban parking lots prefer three foot-candles. (By comparison, one foot-candle lights most roadways, and full moonlight is 1/100th of one foot-candle.) However, most businesses, especially gas stations, restaurants, and convenience stores, are now lighting at 100 to 150 foot-candle levels. This not only substantially increases costs but also causes "light pollution" for the neighborhood.[38]

Sounds and Smells: Total Sensory Marketing

Effective store design appeals to the human senses of sight, hearing, smell, and touch. Obviously, the majority of design activity in a retail store is focused on affecting sight. For instance, if you have a greeter in your store, it actually has the effect of making shoppers feel welcome and it also slows them down and causes them to more carefully take in a fuller view of the store interior. This single act will result in more sales. Today, supermarkets and other retailers are using a similar tactic with the area between the parking lot and the front door to the store. For this critically important area, they are incorporating "plazas," often with plantings and other attractive amenities, thus allowing their customers to enter the store through an attractively designed area, as opposed to older stores that typically have shopping carts and soda machines at their front doors. Some of the more progressive retailers now have water fountains, plants, and seating areas directly in front of their stores. Others slow down the consumer with a community area near the front of the store, even incorporating small stage areas for local bands to play on the weekends. Thus, rather than a Coke or Pepsi machine parked in the front of the store, they have a BBQ grill with burgers and hot dogs, music, and happy and entertained customers entering the store.

Research has shown that senses other than sight can also be very important, and as a result, many retailers are beginning to engineer the smells and sounds in their stores. Smell is believed to be the most closely linked of all the senses to memory and emotions. Bakeries, coffee shops, popcorn vendors in movie theaters, and specialty shops that sell coffee or tobacco often attract customers through the smells that emanate from their products. Retailers hope that using smells as an in-store marketing tool will put consumers "in the mood."[39] Victoria's Secret has deployed potpourri caches throughout its stores, and in fact now sells them to create the ambience of a lingerie closet. The Walt Disney Company uses the smell of freshly baked cookies on Main Street in the Magic Kingdom to relax customers and provide a feeling of warmth. Regardless of the smell used, it must be consistent with the store's image. For example, a natural foods store should employ natural scents such as potpourri or sandalwood rather than artificial scents that are typical of modern floor cleansers. A large department or grocery store should also create islands within the store with distinct smells. For example, shoppers may find it natural to move from fresh produce, to bakery, to coffee, and then to meats and to seafood. A store should also have neutral zones where shoppers can recover their olfactory senses. Some believe that a strong coffee scent actually serves as a powerful neutralizer. However, the type of aroma to use depends on the merchandise being sold and the target customer. You may want to use a floral aroma for men because it will remind them of their mothers and trigger a happy memory or feeling of security. For teenagers, some retailers have used smells that resemble airplane or automobile exhaust. Shoe stores with the smell of leather, even though many shoes now are not made from leather, will experience higher sales.

Retailers have piped music such as Muzak into their stores for generations, believing that a musical backdrop will create a more relaxing environment and encourage customers to stay longer. Increasingly, music is being seen as a valuable marketing tool because the right music can create an environment that is both soothing and reflective of the merchandise being offered. For example, a jeans retailer might play hip-hop near baggies and classic rock over by the Dockers. Researchers believe that while the tempo of music affects how long shoppers stay in a store, the type of music may be just as influential on how much they purchase. One study found that restaurant patrons spent an average of 10 percent more per meal when classical music was playing and more on after-dinner coffee. The classical music created an air of sophistication, reflected in the more sophisticated (higher-priced) entrées chosen by the diners.[40] Thus, while classical music is soothing and has been shown to encourage customers to linger and select more expensive merchandise,[41] it may be inconsistent with the desired ambience of a trendy fashion store catering to college-age women. Today, some retailers are experimenting with placing advertisements into the background music. Other retailers have found a different use for this canned music. A shopping mall in Australia plays Bing Crosby music to drive out the kids who want to hang out after school. In addition, the mall uses pink fluorescent lights, which supposedly highlight pimples. The New South Wales train service in Australia uses canned music at stops in high-crime areas to keep the undesirable element away.[42]

Retailers also must recognize that different seasons of the year and the holidays or cultural events that surround them can motivate shoppers to purchase and more generally have a memorable shopping experience. As they evolved, humans developed music to celebrate life-cycle events and annual celebrations. Music, thus gave these events and times special meaning. Therefore, retailers need to understand the culture they operate in, as well as the role of music throughout the seasons. Christmas music with a heavy Christian meaning may be appropriate for some situations, but in other cases, Christmas music that is more nondenominational may be a better choice. In even other situations, Arabic, Jewish, or Hindu music may be more appropriate. Also, music could be used to draw attention to "select" merchandise within the store. For example, playing French music to call attention to French wines can result in increased sales.[43]

LO 5

Explain the role of visual communications in a retail store.

Visual Communications

Chapter 14 is devoted to the retail selling process. However, sales associates cannot always be available to assist customers, particularly in this era of increased competitive pressure and reduced gross margins, which have caused many retailers to cut costs by reducing their sales staffs. Even department stores, which staked their reputations on high levels of personal customer service, have had to reduce their service levels and learn to rely on alternative service strategies. How, then, can retailers provide good selling communications and high customer service while controlling labor costs?

The answer is visual communications in the form of in-store signage and graphics. Because these visual communications are inanimate objects that stay permanently in place, they require a one-time-only installation cost and low maintenance and can be relied on to perform their function, the same way, for every shopper. Unlike sales associates, visual communications are never late for work, are never in a bad mood, and never mistreat customers. Of course, neither are they as effective as a good sales associate who provides the personal touch that makes customers feel welcome and comfortable. But when carefully balanced with personal service, visual communications, with their reliability and low cost, can create an effective selling environment and are therefore becoming an important tool in the store designer's toolbox. Recognizing that retail service is sparse, some manufacturers are experimenting with in-store Internet kiosks where customers can go online and have a live chat with a customer-service representative to get their questions answered.

Earlier we likened a retail store to a well-written book. Visual communications are akin to the headlines, subheads, illustrations, and captions that give the reader direction and illustrate the written descriptions. These visual communications must address the questions of the shopper: What is it? Where is it? Why should I buy it? How much does it cost?[44] Without visual communications, a store would resemble a newspaper full of words but no headlines—a jumbled, incomprehensible mess of merchandise. An effective visual communications program includes a range of messages from large and bold directives used sparingly to provide cues to the gross organization of the space to the smaller, more specific, and plentiful messages that describe actual merchandise. A visual communications program includes the following important elements.

Name, Logo, and Retail Identity

The first and most visible element in a comprehensive visual communications program is the retailer's identity, which is composed of the store name, logo, and supporting visual elements. The name and logo are seen not only on the storefront and throughout the interior but also in advertising and all communications with consumers. Therefore, they must be catchy, memorable, and, most of all, reflective of the retailer's merchandising mission. Historically, many retail companies have taken the names of their founders, as is the case with most department stores. That practice has fallen out of vogue, however, as retailing has become a game of crafty store images and catchy retail identities. A founder's name rarely captures the merchandising spirit of a company as well as names such as Bath & Body Works, Office Depot, The Home Depot, and Toys "R" Us. Probably no name captured the essence of its business better than that of a store frequented by Bernie Madoff, the convicted stock swindler. Trillion was the super-high-end men's clothier in Palm Beach. Late-night television hosts joked that it was for people who wouldn't be caught dead at a store called "million" or even "billion."[45] Given the ever-increasing barrage of advertising messages and the waning effectiveness of each message, retailers have found it necessary to choose names that are highly distinctive as well as descriptive of their unique offerings. Today's hottest logos, reflecting "American values," include Nike, Apple, Starbucks, L. L. Bean, Cheesecake Factory, and Old Navy. Sometimes even the names of retailer failures have value. Recently, the sons of Merv Morris, the founder of Mervyns department stores, purchased the department store's name, intellectual property, and online properties with plans to revive the brand. In a similar move, some of the same liquidators that had led other failed stores through their dying days have expressed an interest in buying the brand names Circuit City, Sharper Image, Linens 'n Things, and Bombay. The liquidators say they see themselves as brand-licensing experts who will receive royalties for the products without the need to pay rent or a sales staff. And besides it will be cheaper to open a new operation with a familiar name than developing a new name.[46]

Once a name has been chosen, a logo is developed to visually portray the name in a creative and memorable manner. Again, the key is to keep the logo simple and easy to understand, while making it exciting enough to leave a lasting image in the customers' minds. The logo is often accompanied by taglines that provide more description of the store concept such as Walmart's "Save Money, Live Better." This simple yet compelling tagline communicates that Walmart customers will pay lower prices than if they shopped the competition; as a result, they will be able to use their savings to have a better life.

The logo's most prominent placement is on the outside of the store. This is critical to attracting customers and creating high store traffic. Another reason the store name and logo should be succinct and descriptive is that they often play to motorists passing by at 45 miles per hour.

Institutional Signage

Inside the store, the first level of visual communications is known as *institutional* signage, or signage that describes the merchandising mission, customer-service policies, and other messages on behalf of the retail institution. This signage is usually located at the store entrance to properly greet entering customers, as well as at service points such as the service desk, layaway window, and cash registers. In addition, some retailers place customer-service signage throughout the store to reinforce special policies several times during the shopping trip. This signage might include messages such as "Lowest Price Guaranteed" and "All Major Credit Cards Accepted."

Directional, Departmental, and Category Signage

Directional and departmental signage serves as the highest level of organization in an overall signage program. For instance, when you enter a Lowe's with its more than

25-foot ceilings and large metal warehouse racks organized into a grid shopping pattern and covering several acres of floor space, it would be very difficult to find merchandise without Lowe's use of large and bold signs showing the location of the paint department, plumbing department, electrical department, lumber department, and gardening department. These signs are usually large and placed fairly high, so they can be seen throughout the store. They help guide the shopper through the store and locate specific departments of interest. Not all stores use directional signage. It is not necessary in smaller stores, but in virtually all stores larger than 10,000 square feet, some type of departmental signage is used. Once a shopper locates and moves close to a particular department, category signage is used to call out and locate specific merchandise categories. Category signage is usually smaller since it is intended to be seen from a shorter distance and is located on or close to the fixture itself. For instance, the departmental sign might say "Sporting Goods," be two feet high and six feet wide, and hang from the ceiling. On the other hand, the category signage might be only six inches high and two feet wide, affixed to the top of the gondola, and read "Hunting," "Tennis," or "Fitness."

Point-of-Sale Signage

The next level of signage—even smaller and placed closer to the merchandise—is known as *point-of-sale* (POS) signage. Because POS signage is intended to give details about specific merchandise items, it usually contains more words and is affixed directly to fixtures. POS signage may range in size from 11 by 17 inches to a 3-by-5-inch card with very small type describing an item. Always, however, the most important function of POS signage is to clearly state the price of the merchandise being signed.

POS signage includes a set of sign holders used throughout the store, along with a variety of printed signs that can be inserted into the hardware. Store associates mix and match the signage and hardware as directed by management so that POS signage changes frequently. Special POS signs for sales, clearance, and "As Advertised" are often different colors than the normal price signage to highlight these special values.

Lifestyle Graphics

Visual communications encompass more than just words. Many stores incorporate large graphics panels showing so-called lifestyle images in important departments. These photo images portray either the merchandise, often as it is being used, or simply images of related items or models that convey an image conducive to buying the product. In a high-fashion department, lifestyle photography might show a scene of movie stars arriving at a nightclub in very trendy fashions, suggesting that similar fashions are available in that department. In sporting goods, a lifestyle image might show an isolated lake surrounded by autumn-colored trees, with mist rising off the water and the sun rising in the background.

Retailers must be careful when choosing lifestyle photography; as the saying goes, "Beauty is in the eye of the beholder." One person's lifestyle is not necessarily another's, so lifestyle photography must be kept very general to be attractive to the majority and offensive to none. Increasingly, photo panels and lifestyle imagery, which can be expensive to create, are being provided free of charge to retailers by merchandise vendors, who are looking to gain an advantage for their products on the retail floor.

Summary

LO 1 ## What are the elements of a store's environment?

In this chapter, we focused on the retail store, a key factor influencing the consumer's initial perception of the retailer. It must effectively convey the store image desired by the retailer and provide a shopping environment that is conducive to high sales. The guiding principle in effective store planning, merchandise presentation, and design is that the more merchandise customers are exposed to, the more they tend to buy. This depends largely on planning the name, logo, and visual appearance of the store to convey a desired market-positioning image. Although retailers work diligently to influence their images, true store image is an amalgam of all messages consumers receive from advertising to stories they hear from friends and to the store itself.

LO 2 ## What is involved in store planning?

Store planning refers to developing a plan for the organization of the retail store. First, the retailer must decide how to allocate the available square footage among the various types of selling and nonselling space needed. This is usually accomplished by conducting a statistical analysis of the productivity of various merchandise categories. By comparing the sales or gross margin produced by various categories with the space they use, the retailer can develop a plan for the optimal allocation of available space and a planogram that shows the precise location on a shelf or otherwise of each item. Next the floor plan is created, showing the placement and circulation patterns of all merchandise departments. Finally, thought must be given as to how the floor plan can help reduce shrinkage.

LO 3 ## How are the various types of fixtures, merchandise-presentation methods and techniques, and the psychology of merchandise presentation used to increase the productivity of the sales floor?

Fixture selection and merchandise presentation are critical for exposing customers to the maximum amount of merchandise. There are many types of store fixtures, as well as specific methods of merchandise presentation, that have been shown to maximize merchandise exposure and lead to increased sales. Particularly, there is a psychology of merchandise presentation that utilizes customers' natural shopping behaviors and adapts merchandise presentation to match them. In addition to maximizing sales, fixture selection and merchandise presentation must conform to operational constraints and be easy to maintain.

LO 4 ## Why is store design so important to a store's success?

The most visible elements of the store are the design of its storefront and the interior decor. The storefront or exterior must be eye catching, inviting, and reflective of the merchandise inside. The interior design must be comfortable, put the shopper in the proper buying mood, and provide a backdrop that enhances but does not overpower the merchandise. The store designer must always remember that shoppers are there to look at the merchandise, not the store design.

LO 5 ## What is the role of visual communications in a retail store?

A successful selling environment is based on effective visual communications with the customers. Since shoppers require information even when sales associates are not available, visual communications must be used throughout the store to provide direction, specific information, and prices. A visual communications program begins with the store name and logo and includes a range of interior signage that walks the customer through the buying experience.

Finally, there are literally hundreds of details in a successful retail store, and all must be carefully coordinated to create a cohesive, targeted store image that reflects the retailer's mission.

Terms to Remember

shrinkage	spine layout
floor plan	on-shelf merchandising
microretailing	bulk or capacity fixture
stack-outs	feature fixture
space productivity index	visual merchandising
planogram	ambience
free-flow layout	
loop layout	

Review and Discussion Questions

LO 1 **What are the elements of a store's environment?**

1. Why is it important for retailers to use their stores as a means to excite their customers?
2. What is merchandise presentation, and how does it impact sales?
3. What is the simple but powerful truism in retailing that store planners can follow to increase the space productivity of a store environment? Does this truism also hold true for e-tailers? Why?
4. What is the 25-25-50 rule regarding endcaps? Why shouldn't endcaps be 100-percent sale items?

LO 2 **What is involved in store planning?**

5. Discuss the various types of space in a retail store, describing the role of each.
6. Identify the four main types of store layouts, discussing their differences and impact on customers.
7. What is a planogram? Why must the vendor be involved in helping the retailer develop the planogram?
8. Describe the space-allocation planning process. How is this process different for updating an existing store versus opening a new store?

LO 3 **How are the various types of fixtures, merchandise-presentation methods and techniques, and the psychology of merchandise presentation used to increase the productivity of the sales floor?**

9. Discuss the different uses of bulk or capacity futures and feature fixtures.
10. In what ways should new stores be designed differently from older stores so as to reflect the differences in Gen X and Gen Y customers?
11. If retail space is such a scarce resource, then what is wrong with the mantra of "Stack it high, watch it fly" so as to stock more merchandise in the limited available space?
12. What is the psychology of merchandise presentation, and how is it used? Can it be used by e-tailers?

LO 4 **Why is store design so important to a store's success?**

13. What are the goals of interior and exterior design?

14. Which is more important in achieving retail sales—a store's external or interior appearance?

15. Why is the background music so important to a store's performance?

LO 5 What is the role of visual communications in a retail store?

16. Why are so many people purchasing the brand names of failed retailers? After all, aren't they worthless?

17. Why is the retailer's logo so important? Why isn't the founder's name a good choice for the name of a retail store?

18. Consider the importance of directional, departmental, and category signage and discuss how important each type is in a relatively small food store such as a 3,000–square-foot bakery versus a 60,000 supermarket.

Sample Test Questions

LO 1 The two primary objectives of the store environment are:

  a. effective sales management and creating a distinctive ambience.
  b. creating the store image and increasing space productivity.
  c. creative merchandise presentation and effective store traffic control.
  d. maximizing impulse purchase opportunity and effective shelf space allocation.
  e. maintaining market share and effective merchandise control.

LO 2 The goal of store layout and design in store planning should be to:

  a. maximize customer access to high-profit items.
  b. evenly divide floor space between the five functional areas of a retail store.
  c. make the store easy to understand and shop and allow the merchandise to be effectively presented.
  d. allow for the rapid restocking of valuable shelf space in low-turnover merchandise categories.
  e. maximize the back room stock capacity.

LO 3 The psychology of merchandise presentation refers to the fact that:

  a. different merchandising methods can strongly influence the store's image and its sales.
  b. psychologists should always be hired as merchandisers.
  c. merchandise presentation teaches consumers how to shop effectively.
  d. social factors strongly influence shopping behavior.
  e. shoppers can be classified according to psychological tests.

LO 4 Store design does all but which of the following?

  a. It is responsible for creating a distinctive and memorable store image.
  b. It maximizes sales transactions per customer visit.
  c. It includes the architectural elements and finishes on all surfaces.
  d. It seeks to attract passing shoppers and entice them to enter the store.
  e. It encompasses the store's exterior and interior.

LO 5 Which of the following is not part of a visual communications program?

  a. store name and logo
  b. institutional signage
  c. directional and category signage
  d. lifestyle graphics
  e. television advertising

Writing and Speaking Exercise

Ninety years ago, Paul Jesup, your great grandfather who emigrated from Italy, opened his first grocery store in a small mid-western farming community. That store at 10,000 square feet, was thought of as large, especially compared to the typical corner grocery store of the 1920s. Today, you are president of a chain of 15 supermarkets, with annual sales of $148 million and net profits of $3.1 million that traces its roots back to Paul Jessup. The chain is spread across six mid-western communities between 35,000 and 242,000 in population. One of the communities, with the attraction of a high-quality university, has become the home of many retirees. Recently, Sally Barnes, one of these retirees, began blogging about how both of the supermarkets in the community (the one you operate and one of a national chain) are not well designed for retirees. Within a few weeks she had over 100 community members sharing ideas about how the supermarkets were insensitive to senior citizens.

You had one of your staff summarize the blogging on this topic and also look at other blogs in other communities on this topic. Below is a summary of the major complaints:

1. Some parts of the store are not well lighted, which makes it difficult for those with failing eyesight to see the merchandise as it should be viewed.
2. Too many of the items that senior citizens purchase often, such as adult diapers, over-the-counter medications for pain, and laxatives, are difficult to find due to poor signing. Also, often these items are on lower shelves that are difficult to reach by seniors.
3. Music being played in the store is oriented too much toward young people and not relaxing; some of it they find irritating.
4. The pre-cut and packaged meats are too large in terms of portions.
5. The shopping carts are considerably over-sized for a single or couple only purchasing a few items making them too large to navigate easily, and too deep to easily reach items at the cart bottom.
6. Seniors like to visit the supermarket several times a week in order to get out of their apartment or house, and would like an area of the store where they could gather for conversation and relaxing.

In addition to the preceding list that was common across many of the blogs that were examined, there was one concern that was unique to your supermarket. About three years ago, you decided to slowly replace the senior citizen greeters at the entrance of the store who were doing a good job and appreciated the part-time work, even if it was a minimum wage. As greeters quit, you replaced them with teenagers between ages 16 and 19. In part, you took this action because there was rising unemployment among teenagers, and you felt this was a positive act of community responsibility. Now, the seniors in your community were suggesting that your supermarket go back to only using senior citizen greeters.

As you looked over the concerns of seniors, you noticed many good suggestions, but perhaps some that might be merely cost centers and not revenue generators. You were especially torn by the suggestion of not employing teenagers as greeters. Nonetheless, you decided something had to be done to be responsive to the concerns of seniors. Also, you thought it could be a competitive advantage if your supermarket acted proactively before your competitor. Then, the phone rang and it was Sally Barnes and she asked to meet with you as soon as possible. When you asked the purpose she was rather vague.

Even though you're the president, you are in charge of marketing and communications for your retail chain. You want to be prepared for your meeting with Sally Barnes. Provide an outline detailing of how you want the meeting to go, what topics you want to address right now, and what other steps you might take in the coming months.

Retail Project

Let's look more closely at some of the attributes that often influence choice of patronage at home improvement and hardware stores. Nine frequently cited attributes are:

1. low prices,
2. choice of national versus private labels,
3. ease of parking and loading,
4. fast checkouts,
5. product quality,
6. convenience (including hours, location, ease of entrance and parking, ease of finding items),
7. services (including credit, delivery, return policy, and guarantees),
8. store personnel (including helpfulness, friendliness, and courtesy), and
9. advertised "specials" in stock.

For your assignment, you are to rank these attributes in order of importance to you. After ranking them, take the most important attribute and assign it the value of 10, take the second most important attribute and assign it the value of 9. Continue to do this for your top five attributes, with your fifth attribute getting a value of 6.

Now visit two hardware stores or home improvement centers and assign a value (1 being very poor, 10 being very good) to the stores' performance on your five attributes. Multiply your rank value by their performance value for each attribute and sum the total. Is the store with the highest total points your favorite? If not, why is there a difference?

Planning Your Own Entrepreneurial Retail Business

After graduation from college, you opened a swimwear store called Zig Zag on South Padre Island. The building you located is 400 square feet and had been vacant for 18 months. Because of the limited amount of start-up capital you had to invest in the business, you moved into the building without remodeling either its exterior or its interior.

During the first year, Zig Zag had 13,400 visitors, of whom 3,350 made a purchase. The average transaction size was $38. Zig Zag operates on a gross margin of 55 percent and has annual fixed operating expenses of $30,000. Variable costs were 15 percent of sales. The two primary fixed expenses are rent of $1,100 a month and salaries of $1,200 a month. You keep all profits in the business to reinvest in inventory and other immediate business needs.

Because your first year was profitable, you are now considering remodeling the store. Your landlord will not help with these expenses. To paint the exterior would cost $1,400. For the interior, you are thinking of tiling the floor in a zigzag pattern, which will cost $1,600. In addition, new lighting and some new fixtures would cost $4,000.

You believe these changes will increase traffic by 10 percent and that your closure or conversion rate will increase to 30 percent. Will your proposed changes pay for themselves the first year?

© Sarunyu_foto/Shutterstock

CASE

Peterson's

Peterson's is a women's apparel store that grew out of a bridal store that Liz Peterson's mother started in 1949. When Liz worked at Peterson's while in high school, she was amazed at how hard her mother worked to help would-be brides plan their perfect wedding ensemble. Often the soon-to-be brides and their mothers would make last-minute changes in color themes and fabric, and Liz's mother had to work with her seamstress and fabric suppliers to meet their clients' desires. It was difficult for Liz's mother to charge the real cost for all of these changes, but she felt in the long run that it was good for business. The problem was that the positive word of mouth was too successful. As a result, the community's soon-to-be brides began to expect this level of service with last-minute demands.

Liz returned home in 1967 after graduating with a degree in merchandising from the University of Kentucky to assist her mom in operating the store. Sadly, her mother died in 1973 of an unexpected severe heart attack, and Liz took over the operation of Peterson's. The peak season for weddings is between March and September. After her first peak season in running the store on her own, she decided to close down on October 30 and reopen on March 1 of the following year. When she reopened Peterson's on March 1, 1975, it was at the beginning of the rise of women in professional and managerial roles. She thus designed Peterson's to appeal to the 22- to 40-year-old career-oriented female. The store was a resounding success. In the prior 10 years, the best annual profit was $17,000, but in Liz's first year under this new concept the net profit was $67,000 on sales of $844,000. For a 5,000-square-foot store, this was sensational productivity. In 1977, Liz gave birth to twin daughters, Marcy and Tracy.

Today, Marcy is successfully practicing law, but Tracy returned home in 2007 with the goal of purchasing the store from her mother. Prior to returning, Tracy had worked for a regional department store chain as an assistant buyer in the children's department and then as head buyer for home furnishings. When Marcy joined Peterson's, she got involved in store operations to help her understand that aspect of retailing. At first, Liz made Tracy the assistant store manager; in 2010, she became store manager. Now Liz is semiretired, and Tracy reports to Tony Valesco, who is the general manger of Peterson's and essentially runs the entire operation. Tony has been at the store since 1981 when she began in the stockroom and has not only been a dedicated and loyal employee but also a great merchandiser. Tracy will replace her in 2015 when Tony retires.

Two years ago, Tony decided it was time for Peterson's to undergo a major renovation. Although the store had been remodeled in 1982 and in 1996, it was now time to do a major upgrade. The store needed an entire new heating and cooling system, new flooring and ceilings, exterior renovation, and replacement of the outdated fixtures, some of which dated back to the late-1960s. In addition, the 4,000-square-foot store next door was up for sale, and Tony convinced Liz it would be a good acquisition and would allow Peterson's to nearly double its space and enter into clothing for younger women (juniors) and also for the over-40 age group. Peterson's had been very successful at targeting the career-oriented female, but as these women moved into their 50s and retirement, they found the merchandise selection at Peterson's to be not very relevant to their needs and suited to their fashion tastes. The renovation was expensive and time consuming. Tony felt the entire project could be done in three months and for $1.2 million, but the project extended to six months; when asbestos was discovered in the additional space acquired, the cost escalated to $1.5 million.

Because the store's core customer was now the over-50 woman, Tracy wanted to devote 2,500 square feet of the added space to a juniors and teen department hoping to attract the daughters and granddaughters of her customers and their friends. The floor plan was a loop layout. This layout exposes shoppers to the most amount of merchandise. However, given the dimensions of the store, the rear left and right sections of the store were rather deep; as a result, shoppers and the merchandise often is not in clear view of the associates and management team. In fact, some of the fixtures that Tony selected were a bit too high and easy to hide behind. Tony reasoned she wanted to create a three-dimensional look with a set of fixtures

8 feet high, then 5 feet high, and then 3 feet high. The look was dramatic, but the hidden area behind the 8-feet fixtures appeared to be the source of increased shoplifting by teenage girls patronizing the store.

As part of the process of learning the overall store operations, Tracy was spending a lot of time going over the monthly, quarterly, and annual financial statements. She was surprised that shrinkage had gone from 1.8 percent before the remodel to nearly 3.5 percent. When she mentioned this to Tony as an area of concern, Tony brushed Tracy off with the comment, "I know our shrinkage has almost doubled, but our sales per square foot are up 22 percent and our profits are up 30 percent since the remodel. It is just a cost of doing business, and so let's not worry." Tracy decided to ask two of her student interns from a local university to spend part of their summer analyzing the situation and deciding what could be done to reduce shrinkage. The two students came up with two recommendations. First, redo the store fixtures in the rear corners of the store. This would cost an estimated $47,000. Second, use a new law that had been passed that allowed retailers to prosecute shoplifters for up to three times the cost of merchandise sold. The students argued that if Peterson's prosecutes the few shoppers it catches to the fullest extent possible, then the word would quickly get out to the juniors and teens that theft at Peterson's is not worth the effort. When Tracy sat down at her weekly Monday morning meeting with Tony, she presented these two options. Tony replied, "Tracy, you forgot the option I suggested months ago. Let's just not do anything about this problem. We are making more money, so let's just view the increased theft as a cost of business." When Tracy was having dinner with Liz on Sunday afternoon, she mentioned the problem and asked advice. Liz replied, "Tracy, I think you will find the answer if you think this through carefully. Tony will be retiring in a couple of years, and she has a lot of wisdom, but if you want to challenge her you need to figure out how to proceed. Tony has done a lot for our family, and I want the two of you to work this out and keep me out of the picture. I have confidence in both of you."

Questions

1. Is shoplifting just a cost of doing business? Doesn't Peterson's have an obligation to encourage ethical behavior, especially among teens?

2. How should Tracy settle this issue with Tony? Tracy is beginning to think that perhaps Tony is correct. Perhaps if teenagers were prosecuted, some parents could get angry and stop shopping at Peterson's.

Part 5

Retailing's Future

14 *Reframing Retail Strategy*

14 Reframing Retail Strategy

Overview

In this chapter, we argue that most lines of retailing, most retail enterprises, and most retail executives need to reframe their mindset away from buying and selling merchandise to what we call a service-dominant logic or mindset. To accomplish our objective, we need to examine how retailing has evolved from supplying merchandise to a market of customers, to marketing to customers to get them to purchase more often and in greater magnitude, and is now moving to a collaborative business model of marketing "with" customers. We learn that service is the act of a retailer using its competences or skills and knowledge to benefit the customers, and that a service orientation also views the customer and retailer as co-creators of value. Retailers striving to be service oriented and customer centric must develop strategies for customer engagement. But, they also must recognize that continuous learning is necessary to be able to offer compelling value propositions that make the retailer dynamically competitive. In this regard, the retailer will find that it needs to periodically fundamentally alter its business model by use of form, time, place, and possession reframing strategies.

Learning Objectives

After reading this chapter, you should be able to:

1 Describe the three eras of retailing and what distinguishes them.

2 Define service according to a service-dominant logic and explain the four principles of service-dominant logic.

3 Explain how customer centricity is essential in contemporary retailing.

4 Discuss the central importance and imperative of continuous learning in retailing.

LO 1

Describe the three eras of retailing and what distinguishes them.

Introduction

Retailing is virtually synonymous with merchandising, and merchandising is synonymous with goods or tangible offerings. For hundreds if not thousands of years, merchant traders would travel rural areas in their wagons and carts selling new gadgets, cloth, spices and other things that farmers or rural families could not make for themselves. Town squares were marketplaces where merchandise was displayed periodically (often weekends). The general store, often located at a geographic outpost, was filled to the brim with merchandise and often stocked everything from wedding gowns to funeral caskets.

Despite the abundance of merchandise you now witness in virtually any city around the world, this abundance was not always the situation. In fact, throughout most of human civilization there was a large scarcity of manufactured or processed goods. Several hundred years ago, retail merchants had a difficult time acquiring and building merchandise assortments. Also, during this time, travel was slow before the invention of railroads and motor vehicles, and airplanes. A third major constraint was slow communication. Imagine sending a letter and not receiving a return letter for six months versus the seconds that is possible with the Internet.

Assortment, travel, and communication constraints meant that when consumers visited the village's town square, or the relatively few specialty retail merchants that lined the narrow streets, they saw nothing even remotely similar to what you would find today if you visited retailers within just a couple miles (or perhaps a half dozen blocks) of where you live or work. In fact, because communication technology was so poor, and paper and books were very expensive, most humans could talk, but few could write or read. Thus, as the typical person walked down the village streets, he or she had to be able to identify what a retail merchant was selling. How do you think the retail merchants responded? Quite simply, rather than hanging a sign, they hung out a typical merchandise item; thus, a blacksmith shop hung out iron, and a tailor hung out an item of apparel, and a fruit and vegetable store, a basket of fruit.

By today's standards, this seems very primitive, but we should note that on a relative basis, consumers of this time were quite amazed to see merchandise available for sale that filled many of their needs. This is because when we experience less choice over time, this becomes "normal," so any improvement in choice results in improvement in customer satisfaction and well-being. This is illustrated by a story recently told to one of the authors by a university professor from Leipzig University in Germany. When he was a teenager in 1989, the Berlin Wall that separated East (communist) from West (democracy) Germany fell. It was a heartening moment as hundreds of millions of people around the world watched on television. A week after the fall of the wall, he recalls his mother taking him across the crumbling wall to West Germany. Remember, for several decades, East Germany was cut off from most of the rest of the world, and thus it had access to less merchandise, and travel and communication was restricted. Upon entering a West Germany supermarket, his mother stood in the aisle and cried. Only years later did the son recognize the crying was from the realization of the merchandise assortments and choice that her family had forgone for decades.

Three Eras of Retailing

Over the long history of human civilization, retailing can be characterized as going through three distinct eras. Note that the timing of the three eras is specific to each country and culture. In fact, some parts of the world are still in era one. The three eras can be described as: (1) going to market or "to market" for short, (2) "marketing to" customers, and (3) "marketing with" customers. It is important to understand this short lesson in retailing history because it helps you develop the frame of mind for the direction retailing is headed over the next several decades.

To Market

The "to market" era, for most of the developed world, is generally the time period prior to 1900. In the United States in 1900, less than 30 percent of the population lived in cities; today it is just about the opposite with only 20 percent living in rural areas. The United States in 1900 was still largely rural, and the West and South largely unsettled; for example, Los Angeles had a population of 102,000, Denver 133,000, and Atlanta 90,000. The horseless carriage (automobile) was slightly more than a decade old, and few paved roads existed for travel. Air travel and transport was several decades away. Generally, merchandise and goods moved primarily by railroads and by waterways. During this

John Bergman, N.Y./Miscellaneous Items in High Demand/Library Of Congress

In 1902, Macy's opened its flagship store at Herald & 34th Street in New York City. One way Macy's was able to operate efficiently at that time was to have an apparel factory as part of the store.

era, the major challenge was bringing merchandise to the market. Most retailers could succeed if they could get plentiful and timely supplies of merchandise and keep their stores freshly stocked with new merchandise.

The retail marketplace was synonymous with the city; and the larger the city, the larger the market, the larger the retailer. The largest retailers were the department stores such as Marshall Field in Chicago and Macy's in New York City. Although Macy's dates to the mid-1800s, the flagship New York store at Herald & 34th Street, which incidentally still operates today, was established in 1902. One indication of the transportation and assortment challenges of this period was the fact that at the Herald Macy's store, they had an apparel factory where workers assembled apparel for children, men, and women. It was much more efficient to purchase fabric in bulk and produce garments at the store than to try to obtain a supply of finished garments.

Marketing To

Not long after 1900, as transport and communication systems improved, it became much easier to bring or transport goods to the market. Consequently, there was an increase in retail competition as more and more merchants were able to fill their stores with goods. Some retailers that were successful recognized that they could replicate their stores in different geographic areas of the city and then across cities and across states. The Great Atlantic & Pacific Tea Company (A&P) became the first U.S. based chain store in 1859. However, it was not until the 1920s when rapid growth of chain stores occurred. Some of the popular chain stores of the time were Kroger, Walgreens, Woolworth's, S.S. Kresge, JCPenney, and Sears Roebuck. Incidentally, S.S. Kresge became Kmart and Woolworth became Woolco, a discount department store that closed its U.S. stores in 1982 and in 1994 sold its Canadian stores to Walmart.

Many of the chain stores also became heavily price and promotion oriented, as they developed more efficient stores and used price and promotion to "market to" and sell to customers. After 1900, retail advertising also witnessed rapid growth. Local newspapers were filled with retail advertisements, magazines grew rapidly as did print circulars, outdoor billboards, and radio advertising. This was the golden age of advertising as this persuasive tool was increasingly used to *market to* and persuade customers to shop. World War II brought a slight interruption to the move away from a "to market" to a "marketing to" retailing philosophy due to the shortage of household goods and merchandise. However, after World War II, the growth of retailing and the acceleration of retail competition became even more prominent.

In 1954, Sol Price founded FedMart in San Diego, which was the first discount mass merchandiser. Not long after, Kmart, Woolco, Target, and Walmart were founded; all incidentally in the same year—1962. To be able to compete with the high margin department stores, these retailers had a common mass merchandising formula. First, they located in relatively low-cost facilities in low-rent districts that kept operating costs low. Second, they focused on high turnover of inventory and stimulated this turnover with low prices and sales promotions. They were first to recognize the power of a Gross Margin Return on Inventory (GMROI; see Chapter 9) mindset where the key to success was to earn low margins but turn inventory rapidly. Third, they shifted work to the customer by employing a self-selection, self-service strategy that kept store employees to a minimum, thus lowering operating costs and allowing for low gross margins.

The "earn and turn" mass merchandising formula spread rapidly over several decades as witnessed by retail enterprises such as Home Depot and Lowe's, PetSmart, Office Depot, and Office Max, and membership warehouse clubs such as Costco and Sam's. Along the way retailers not only pursued GMROI-driven strategies but also strategies that boosted Gross Margin Return on Space (GMROS) and Gross Margin Return on Labor (GMROL). Exhibit 14.1 presents the retail resource trinity model. The **retail resource trinity model**

retail resource trinity model
Shows how inventory, space, and labor resources interrelate to yield high resource productivity.

Exhibit 14.1
Retail Resource Trinity Model

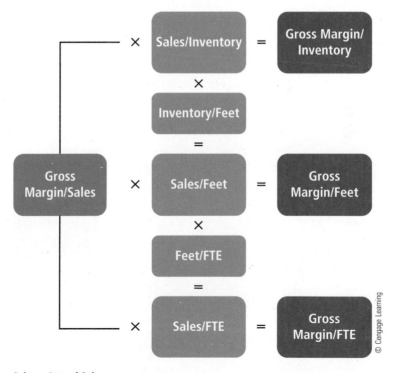

Sales = Annual Sales
Gross Margin = Annual Gross Margin Dollars
Inventory = Average Annual Inventory Investment
Feet = Square Feet of Retail Floor Space
FTE = full time equivalent employees; one employee equals 8 hours per day of work for five days per week or 40 hours of work.

shows how inventory, space, and labor resources interrelate to yield high resource productivity.

What should be noted in the resource trinity model is that the most fixed resource is floor space. A retailer's floor space is hard to change at least in the short to intermediate run. On the other hand, the level of inventory and employees can be changed rather rapidly. Because the mass merchandising formula is very much driven by low gross margins, the retailer must keep its operating costs low. Since 50 percent of the retailer's total operating costs is labor (and fringe benefits), it tries to push more of the work onto the customer via self-service and self-selection, and therefore, it is able to have more square feet of space covered by each employee, and of course, this translates into lower customer service. Retailers also learned that if they could expose shoppers to a lot of merchandise, then they would tend to buy more. This caused retailers' inventory investments per square foot of retail floor space to increase and eventually led many to begin stacking merchandise higher and narrowing aisles.

In summary, during this era, the key drivers became low margins leading to more store traffic, coupled with high merchandising or inventory intensity and high self-service intensity. Unfortunately, this formula for success is easy to replicate and so, on a relative basis over time, becomes less of a competitive advantage. After all, it is a relatively unsophisticated retail strategy that is simply grounded in cutting prices, stuffing the store with more merchandise, and lowering employee or customer service. Because prices are so low, many customers can't resist this value proposition; however, it is not a very exciting retail experience, and as we will see, not one that can sustain itself as a pathway to high performance retailing.

Exhibit 14.2 illustrates how a retailer employing the mass merchandising formula can get trapped in an endless cycle of lower margins, frequent sales promotions, higher traffic, and higher efficiency. Because of the costs of retail space, inventory, and labor, the lure of this trap is tempting. Essentially, resource efficiency wins out over resource effectiveness. And unfortunately, a resource efficiency strategy captures and traps the retailer in an iron cage of efficiency where effective and long-term relations with customers, suppliers, and employees are increasingly difficult, if not impossible, to maintain.

Marketing With

The "marketing with" era of retail marketing can be also thought of the era of active collaboration between retailers and their customers, suppliers and other stakeholders

Exhibit 14.2
The Retail Resource Efficiency Cycle

such as employees. Long-term relationships become a central premise of retail planning. During this era, the retailer begins to view itself as a support system for all of its stakeholders with the customer most central, because only the customer can bring new revenue or cash into the firm. Suppliers and other stakeholders are also important, but usually they are users of cash versus providers of cash.

Triggering or stimulating this era of marketing is a major change in retail management thinking. This change in mindset or thinking is with regard to how the retailer views resources and their management. Historically, business viewed resources as tangible and static things such as natural resources, equipment, fixtures and facilities, or merchandise. These resources actually have a special name, "operand" resources. **Operand resources** are those that humans act upon or do something to in order to create effects. For instance, a block of wood can be shaped and formed to produce a piece of furniture, or fabric can be cut and sewn to create a garment. Operand resources by their static and tangible nature can be exhausted or depleted. Incidentally, they are also the resources that are on the retailer's balance sheet. For instance, at fiscal year end January 31, 2012, Target had $8 billion of inventory, $29 billion of buildings, fixtures, and equipment.

Over the last several decades, it became increasingly recognized that a second type of resource is dynamic and often intangible. **Operant resources** is the label given to these resources because they are those resources that can act on and produce effects. These resources, rather than being depleted, can be expanded and grown. They include such things as employee skills and knowledge, the core competences of an organization or its dynamic capabilities. For instance, Walmart has a core competency in supply chain management that allows it to apply its knowledge to produce supply systems that are highly efficient and the lowest cost in the retail industry. Or, The Limited or Macy's have dynamic merchandising display capabilities that have allowed them to develop the skills and knowledge to create effective merchandise displays that positively correlate to customer purchases, or closure rate. Regardless of whether we are referring to Walmart's supply chain competency or The Limited or Macy's merchandise display capabilities, it should be recognized that neither of these resources is tangible. In fact, because they are not tangible, they are hard for other retailers to precisely copy or replicate.

A retailer's intangible resources are seldom on its balance sheet. In fact, for a publicly held retailer, if you look at its price per share of stock and compare this to the book value of a share of stock (on its balance sheet), you will have one valid indicator of how important these intangible resources are. In Exhibit 14.3 we show the value of intangibles as measured by what is referred to as the **price to book ratio**, where price is the price of a share of stock and book is the book value of a share of stock. The higher price to book ratio, the higher the intangible assets relative to tangible or balance sheet assets. Note, for instance, that JCPenney has a price to book ratio of 1.56, suggesting that for $1 of book value the firm generates $.56 in intangible assets (i.e., take the $1.56 and subtract $1 to get the intangible assets). On the other hand, Whole Foods Market has a 5.08 ratio which suggests that for each dollar of book value it generates $4.08 of intangible assets. Pay particular note that in every situation the value of intangible resources exceeds the value of the largely tangible assets on the retailer's balance sheet!

Another trend that has resulted in a shift to more collaborative relationships with suppliers, employees, and customers is improved and lower cost of telecommunication. During the "marketing to" era, communication was primarily broadcast on the one-to-many model. For instance, a retailer would broadcast a radio or television advertisement or run an advertisement in a newspaper or magazine. With employees and suppliers, much of this one-to-many model of communication was employed because the retailer developed standardized procedures that over time took the form of the

operand resources
Those that humans act upon or do something to in order to create effects. For instance, fabric can be cut and sewn to create a garment. Operand resources by their static and tangible nature can be exhausted or depleted. Incidentally, they are also the resources that are on the retailer's balance sheet.

operant resources
Those resources that can act on and produce effects. These resources, rather than being depleted, can be expanded and grown. They include such things as employee skills and knowledge, the core competences of an organization or its dynamic capabilities.

price to book ratio
The price of a share of stock divided by the book value of a share of stock. The higher the price to book ratio, the higher the intangible assets relative to tangible or balance sheet assets.

Exhibit 14.3
Comparing Tangible vs.
Intangible Resources

Retailer	Price to Book Ratio
Home depot	4.43
TJX	9.73
Kohl's	1.91
Gap	4.66
Lowe's	2.34
Macy's	2.79
Whole foods	5.08
JCPenney	1.56
Target	2.49
Walmart	3.03
McDonalds	6.85
Pier one	4.74

employee handbook or manual or the buyers' handbook or manual. Essentially, these printed documents of rules and procedures were broadcast media that communicated rules and procedures. With the invention and phenomenal growth of the Internet over the last quarter century, coupled with the rapid decline in computation and communication costs, many-to-many communication networks emerged, perhaps best illustrated by social media platforms such as Facebook and Twitter. As you have undoubtedly learned in your use of social media, you, as an individual person, are able to connect to not only your friends, but also to thousands or millions of other people.

Let us return to the importance of how retailers view resources as well as the growth and proliferation of many-to-many networks. In past eras, the retailer often viewed both suppliers and customers and often employees as operand resources. Humans, whether in the role of a supplier, employee, or customer were viewed as objects that you do things to. They were like natural resources—something to be extracted and used.

The typical retailer would heavily negotiate to extract as many concessions as possible from its suppliers. Employees would be tightly controlled and monitored so the retailer could extract as much work from them as possible. Customers were also managed in a way to get them to purchase as much as possible. If retailers could not extract maximum concessions from suppliers, they would switch suppliers. If employees did not put out the highest possible productivity, they would be terminated. Finally, if customers were not highly profitable, retailers would find ways to get rid of them.

Think for a moment about the logic described earlier. If the most valuable things are people and if you view them as static resources to be managed and depleted, then you quickly use up your most valuable resources. Taken to the extreme, before long, you don't have suppliers or employees who want to work with you or for you and customers find more compelling options. Over the long run, this is simply not a very good business model. In fact, entrepreneur and retail history buff, Gary Hoover argues that "those who don't cherish and respect and innovatively serve their customers will not be long for this world."[1] Essentially this boils down to a long-held strategy for retail success, *love your employees and customers*. Topics covered in previous chapters such as buying, pricing, promotion, distribution, and merchandising should never be your central focus.

Customers, or more broadly, people should be your central focus. Everything else is only important to the extent they help the retailer better meet the needs and wants of people and serve them.

Now, couple this with the presence of many-to-many communication networks. All of a sudden, if I am a supplier and I start to get treated in a coercive manner or if I get unfairly terminated, I can and will start to share my experiences with others. In fact, in business-to-business marketing, we witness the emergence of vendor ratings that are shared among network members similar to how you may rate various vendors from whom you buy on e-Bay or Amazon. Employees who are disgruntled begin to share their complaints and frustrations with other employees and the public at large through social media such as blogs. The same behavior occurs among customers and potentially other stakeholders such as community members who attempt to boycott a retailer and use the Internet to organize their grass roots or net roots boycott campaigns. Not to be neglected are the positive effects that can be created when many-to-many networks are used to spread favorable comments about a retailer and its practices.

All of a sudden when retailers start to witness, up close, their suppliers, employees, and customers being proactive in both a negative and positive manner, it becomes very clear that they are not operand resources but operant resources. This is precisely what triggers the management practice of collaborating or *marketing with* suppliers, employees, and customers. In fact, if the retailer does not embrace this orientation then suppliers, employees, and customers may become more of a resistive force versus a resource or partner.

LO 2

A Service-Dominant Mindset

Define service according to a service-dominant logic and explain the four principles of service-dominant logic.

service
The application of knowledge and skills through deeds, processes, and performances for the benefit of another.

Many names or labels could be used to capture the new management mindset that retailers and businesses in general are moving toward. However, it is often referred to as a service-dominant[2] or service-centric mindset. **Service** is defined as the application of knowledge and skills through deeds, processes, and performances for the benefit of another. This definition has the following features:

1. It involves doing something of benefit for the customer, suppliers, and employees.
2. It involves interaction between others because the deeds, processes, and performances that comprise the service are not done in isolation but in interaction with others.
3. It involves the application of knowledge and skills that are operant resources that can provide the retailer with competitive advantage.

Service is not defined as what a good or tangible product is not, but rather service is a transcending concept. Let us explain a bit further.

IHIP Characteristics Misleading

IHIP characteristics
Intangible, heterogeneous, inseparable and perishable.

The traditional–services marketing thought argued that services are distinct from goods and they have less desirable characteristics than goods. These are referred to as the **IHIP characteristics**, or a service is intangible, heterogeneous, inseparable and perishable. Service-Dominant logic takes the perspective that the IHIP characteristics are actually the proper characteristics that all market offerings should strive for regardless of whether they are tangible or not. For instance, with a tangible good, the brand and its meaning are intangible and is what often separates successful from unsuccessful products. Consider, for instance, jewelry in a little blue Tiffany's gift box versus the same or similar jewelry in the box of an unknown jewelry retailer or a department store or Costco. Consider these other tangible goods and how intangible their value actually is: BMW automobile, Harley Davidson motorcycle, Fender guitar, Barbie doll, Heineken beer, Dove soap, Polo jeans, Apple iPad, and Starbuck's coffee. Retailers that recognize that they are selling intangibles, even if their merchandise is tangible, will be able to develop more effective retail marketing strategies. Don't forget to also consider the store itself as an important part of the intangible offering a retailer makes. Finally, remember that if you are only selling tangibles then you are almost guaranteed to become a commodity retailer where the only thing that you can compete on is price, not a very enviable position.

Services are viewed in traditional logic as heterogeneous, since each customer is receiving something different from the service provider. On the other hand, the traditional marketing thought argues that goods are homogenous, because they are produced in a factory where they are standardized and controlled for manufacturing quality, so they all look alike. However, this homogeneity is only from the firm's perspective. It is not so that each customer experiences an identical (homogeneous) physical product, because what the customer experiences is unique, and thus the product is heterogeneous from the customer's perspective. We are sure you have been shopping and looked at or tried on a piece of clothing that you liked and your friend and/or spouse viewed the same piece of clothing quite differently! Therefore, not only are services heterogeneous, so are goods, even if they are standardized and homogeneous from an engineering or manufacturing perspective.

Conventional wisdom also states that with services, the service provider and customer are inseparable. It is believed that since goods are produced in a factory and away from the customer, that separability exists. Inseparability occurs only from the perspective of the producer of the good. Goods, however, are not worth anything, or they have no meaningful value unless they are used. Importantly, in the use of the good, the seller (producer and retailer) and the consumer come together or co-create value. When you drive your BMW, ride your Harley Davidson, wear Polo jeans, or use your Fender guitar or Apple iPad, you are co-creating value with the producer and seller of these tangible goods.

Finally, services are viewed as perishable, and thus they could not be inventoried, whereas goods were viewed as not perishable and thus could be inventoried. This, however, is a very product-centric notion of perishability. Perhaps, education is the best example of the fallacious nature of this argument. Consider the college courses you are enrolled in during this semester. All would agree that education is a service. But is what you are receiving, i.e., an educational experience, something that perishes when you walk out of the classroom or disconnect from your online class each day or when the course ends? Certainly you would hope not. Why would you spend the time studying and learning if you believed that the learning or knowledge gained would disappear when the course ended. This is not an isolated example; consider other services you have used such as a trip to an amusement park, a live concert, a dinner at a nice restaurant with a special person, a surgical procedure, and hospital stay, etc. All of these often bring back vivid memories years and even decades later. So are services perishable? We argue that if the customer experience is your focus, they are not!

Also consider that goods that are not perishable or are not recycled may not be a very good thing for the environment and natural ecosystem, which brings us to the point that goods may not be very good! And this is why we may be witnessing the growth of people sharing goods such as children's clothes, books, automobiles, and as we saw in Chapter 1, people renting spare bedrooms to strangers to substitute for traditional hotel services. Some economic and social analysts have even gone as far as suggesting what is emerging is the sharing economy.[3]

Service Can Take on Three Forms

For service to be perceived as a transcending concept, it needs to be recognized that a service can be provided in three primary forms. Exhibit 14.4 illustrates these ways of providing service.

Probably the way you most often think of service is when it is provided directly to you or in general when one person serves another. We see this all around us and often not in the marketplace, like, when someone prepares a dinner at home for family or guests, serves the dinner, and cleans up the dishes afterwards. In the marketplace, there are many examples of direct service provision such as when a barber or beautician cuts and styles your hair or when a dentist examines your teeth and provides teeth cleaning service or when someone washes your car.

A service can also be provided indirectly through a good. This views all goods as service appliances. Thus, one could purchase a razor and hair clippers to shave and trim their hair or a car wash mitt and soap to clean their car. The person is performing self-service but with the aid of tangible goods or products. You can even view customers as hiring goods to help them do their jobs.[4] Consider this during your next purchase of merchandise; even that stylish new dress or sports coat has a job that it performs for you. Also, note that the large growth of apps is essentially the growth of software as a service—helping the customer do a job (solve a problem). For instance, if you subscribe to the Weather Channel app, it provides you weather service. Keep in mind that because merchandise is a service appliance, that what you are selling is solutions, and not merchandise or goods.[5] Incidentally, the Victorinox Swiss Army Knife has been recently redesigned so it can address problems and solutions that confront today's worker. Consequently, the new knife has more than blades for cutting and snipping, but also a USB thumb drive, laser pointer, wireless Bluetooth remote-control features, and a biometric fingerprint sensor.[6]

Sharon DiMinico is the founder and CEO of Learning Express and provides an excellent example of how a retailer was able to see that the merchandise it offered helps a customer get a job done or, as we suggested, is an appliance that is used to create solutions. Sharon focuses on offering toys that stimulate creativity and learning. She makes sure that her staff of experts can help children and parents or grandparents select the right toys. Importantly, the store atmosphere is designed to encourage kids to try out toys and their skills.[7]

Exhibit 14.4
Service as Transaction

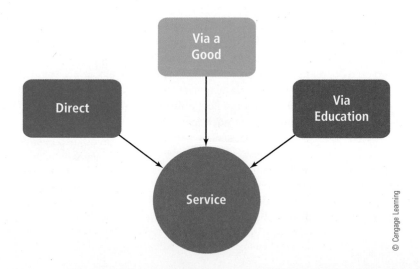

© Cengage Learning

The Augusta Chronicle/ZUMApress.com/Alamy

Sharon DiMinico, founder and CEP of Learning Express focuses on showing how the toys it carries stimulate creativity and learning. Learning Express stores are designed to engage children to stop and try the toys.

Lululemon Athletica sells athletic clothing. But as you will learn in the "What's New" box that follows, the clothing it sells is best thought of as a service appliance that provides the service of self-expression through yoga-influenced athletic clothing. Athletica apparel appeals to the person who wants to make the place a better world by assuming responsibility for a healthy and positive lifestyle.

© Rashevskyi Viacheslav/Shutterstock

WHAT'S NEW ?

Lululemon: Less Is More

Lululemon Athletica is the $1 billion (U.S.) company behind a line of yoga-influenced athletic clothing. Since its founding in Vancouver, Canada, in 2000, it has focused on a "quest to elevate the world from mediocrity to greatness." Astute product development, cost control, and connection to customers are key to its success. Its corporate philosophy calls for each individual to make the world a better place by assuming responsibility for a healthy, positive lifestyle.

Lululemon's strategy includes tight control of merchandise through inventory management, cost control in store management, low-cost consumer research, and cost-effective promotional spending. Limited production runs of 3-, 6-, and 12-month cycles keep merchandise styles and colors fresh and encourage customers to "buy now." "Core" products are stocked throughout the year but are never discounted. Even with typical prices for its yoga pants in the range of $78 to $128, 95 percent of merchandise sells at full price. In contrast, brands such as Lucy, Victoria's Secret PINK, and Athleta price their yoga pants in the $25 to $50 range.

While sales growth has been rapid, a limited number of stores keep overheads low. Each of the approximately 167 stores is carefully planned and justified, as is any expansion. Internet sales are 11 percent and are expected to grow as a percent of overall sales. The merchandise return policy is within 14 days, unworn, and with tags. Markdowns are kept to a minimum.

(continued)

Success is also earned by listening to the customers. However, Lululemon does not depend on extensive database programs or expensive marketing research to understand their needs. It fine-tunes merchandise and captures trends by interviewing yoga instructors, an important and committed group that influences its students. Indeed, Lululemon's use of high-tech fabrics in its apparel was driven by its founder's search for better performance than the typical cotton-based fabrics used in the athletic wear of the time. Further, Lululemon actively seeks customer comments. Sales associates can overhear customers' discussions in the fitting rooms since folding tables are placed nearby. A chalkboard near the fitting room invites customers to leave comments and complaints. The feedback is taken seriously in adjusting designs, fits, and future orders.

Lululemon does little advertising. Instead, it invests in brand ambassadors that espouse the Lululemon philosophy, and are seen as leaders in their communities. These ambassadors are not paid but receive free products and are supported with "friendship, personal development, high performance training, and life-changing adventures." Lululemon cultivates a healthy lifestyle through its website and blog, with educational information about yoga in its many forms, and personal development encouragement in addition to product information (www.lululemon.com). Related blogs of Lululemon fans, such as Lulumum.blogspot.com, have popped up, providing more social marketing opportunities.

These tactics have resulted in sales of $1,800 per square foot—more than three times that of the luxury specialty store, Neiman-Marcus. While quarterly sales rose 30 percent over the last two years, it is difficult to see how that exceptional level can be sustained with a limited number of stores and until stock-outs become less of a problem.

Still, Lululemon has had glitches in its history. Limited production lines may sound good in theory, but there were significant stock-outs during the 2010 Christmas selling season, resulting in lost sales. In 2011, some customers objected to a slogan on the shopping bags that quoted Ayn Rand's *Atlas Shrugged*, a novel that espouses living for self-interest and is against corporate altruism that doesn't directly promote a company's financial performance. This message seemed contradictory to the life-enhancing philosophies that customers had associated with practicing yoga.

Finally, while Lululemon has controlled its store growth, it realized that it needed more stores than one in order to reach a comfortable sales volume to earn a profit. Stores were so busy that its original vision to provide more extensive educational yoga in store had to be dropped. Operationally, it had to compromise and train only store staff to become more expert and deeply involved in yoga to provide expert advice and influence sales. Customers can still access the website for more information about yoga and personal development.

Sources: Written by Professor Jan Owens, Carthage College, Kenosha, Wisconsin, and based on the author's experience with Athleta. Austen, Ian, "Lululemon Athletica Combines Ayn Rand and Yoga," *New York Times*, November 27, 2011; Available at: http://www.nytimes.com/2011/11/28/business/media/combines-ayn-rand-and-yoga.html?_r=1 [Accessed May 30, 2012]; Lululemon corporate website "Lululemon Athletica Invites You to Yoga. Run. Party." Available at: www.lululemon.com/media/index.php?id=217 [Accessed May 30, 2012]; Mattioli, Dana, "Lulu's Secret Sauce," *Wall Street Journal*, March 22, 2012, B1, B2. Available at: http://online.wsj.com/article/SB100014240527023038 12904577295882632723066.html?KEYWORDS=lululemon [Accessed May 31, 2012]; Young, Vicki M, "Lululemon Q4 Profits Rise 34.2%, *Women's Wear Daily*, March 23, 2012. Available at: http://www.wwd.com/markets-news/financial/lululemon-q4-profits-rise-342-5820629 [Accessed May 30, 2012].

Finally, a service can be provided through education. The retailer could, for instance, offer classes in cooking as Williams-Sonoma does, which helps to enable the customer to better use cookware and food ingredients to create a home-cooked meal. Note that often when the retailer provides information or demonstrations of products they are essentially educating the customer on how to use a product and, thus, providing a service. Some apparel stores provide short courses on how to dress, while some department stores do the same for how to apply cosmetics. If you have purchased a new car recently, it is likely you were invited to a lunch or dinner where you were taught how to care for your new vehicle.

The service designation captures very well the "marketing with" era and mode of thinking. When the barber or beautician or the dentist is performing a service, they are doing so in concert with the beneficiary of the service. When a good is a service appliance, it is being used by the beneficiary, which is interaction with the product, so, in a sense, with the creator of the product. Finally, when service is done through education, there is always the need to interact with the learner.

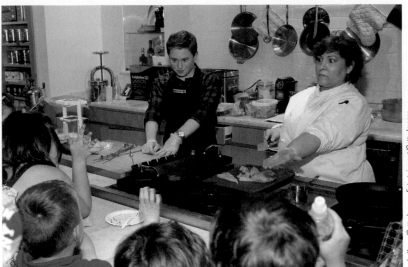

Williams-Sonoma offers workshops for customers of all ages and skill levels. Workshops are offered on topics ranging from knife skills to cupcake baking to preparing complete meals.

Principles of Service-Dominant Logic

Service as a mindset and dominant logic is grounded on four principles. The four principles are: (1) service is the basis of human exchange, (2) people are always co-creators of value, (3) all people are resource integrators, and (4) each person uniquely determines value.

Service as Basis of Exchange

Consider the pre-history of retailing when perhaps we have two individuals or families and one specializes in fishing and the other in growing wheat. Each has developed his or her knowledge and skills to a very high level. Thus, one person has more fish than he or she needs and the other more wheat. They exchange, and each is better off. A common question we ask our students when this story is told is what is being exchanged. Students often think we are tricking them because we essentially told them that fish was being exchanged for wheat and vice versa and that is indeed the common answer. One person is giving up wheat for fish and the other fish for wheat. Unfortunately, from a service-dominant logic perspective this is the wrong answer!

What the standard answer to this question tells us is that we have a tangible goods bias as well as an output bias. We see the result or output of human action but not the processes or performances that led up to this output. That is because these processes and performances are often invisible and always intangible. Using the prior definition of service what we can observe is that the fisher is exchanging his or her sea-based protein-gathering knowledge and skills in return for the farmer's soil-based carbohydrate-growing and -gathering knowledge and skills. Or essentially service is being exchanged for service, and hence service is the fundamental basis of exchange.

Because service is the fundamental basis of exchange it is also the basis of all competition.[8] Ask yourself what differentiates and allowed Walmart to grow from a single store in a small town in Arkansas to be the largest retailer in the world or what allowed Starbucks in two decades to have the largest share of coffee houses in the world? It was not the merchandise or goods that either retailer offered because many other competing retailers offered those goods as well. The service that Walmart offered was in global supply chain and logistics; i.e., getting the merchandise from manufacturer to consumer in the most efficient manner. Starbucks on the other hand offered a third place for people to relax, unwind, read, and enjoy coffee and conversation. The first place in most of our lives is our house or apartment and the second place is our office or place of work. Who would have ever thought that we needed the service of a third place? Stated alternatively, both of these retailers and other high-performing retailers excel at certain business processes that allow them to apply their knowledge and skills to better serve customers. These knowledge and skills are part of the intangible resources we witnessed in Exhibit 14.3. Competing on intangibles always provides the retailer a competitive advantage because intangibles are hard to copy versus tangible resources that can be easily copied or purchased in the marketplace.

Value Co-Creation

A goods-dominant logic leads one to believe that manufacturers or producers of goods create value and then take this value to market and sell it to consumers who in turn consume the value or more succinctly destroy the value that the firm created. This is a rather negative view of humans as consumers—that their primary role is destroying value. A service-dominant mindset views the customer or beneficiary as using what the firm sells to do something valuable or to create value. Thus, each customer or household is similar to a small enterprise that itself is creating resources or things of value.[9]

The food purchased from the supermarket or the dress from the specialty women's wear store is essentially dormant material unless used by the beneficiary to co-create value. It is interesting that we often think of kitchen products as kitchen appliances that imply we use them to create something, but all products are appliances for service provision, and thus, value co-creation is pervasive among customers—not value destruction.

A family co-creates value by taking food ingredients and turning them into a family dinner.

Retailers that recognize that customers are incorporating what they sell into the value co-creation process are able to use this knowledge in their communication. For instance, a supermarket may show a colorful photo mural in its store of a family preparing and eating a meal together and engaged in conversation or a home improvement retailer could have photo murals of various do-it-yourself projects in which families are engaged. Recall our earlier mention that customers hire goods to do a job. Always ask yourself how the goods or merchandise you sell fit into the jobs the customer is doing. Goods are always the means to some end job.

Resource Integration

resource integration Blending three major types of resources: market resources, public resources, and private resources, in order to co-create value to solve problems and pursue opportunities or perform jobs.

A firm-centric or retailer-centric mindset views the customer as purchasing the retailer's value-embedded or laden offering. Although disquieting to retailers, the retailer's sale is probably not the only ingredient the customer will use to co-create value. In fact, it is possible the retailer is a relatively small player or provider in the customer's total value co-creation process. Consider your personal experience and how central any single product or retailer is to the overall value you experience each day, or more broadly, to your personal happiness. Even the smartphones or tablet computers most of us are so occupied with every day or hour of the day are only a small part of our total experience. If you have such an appliance, from Apple or Samsung, but don't have a phone service provider such as AT&T, Sprint, or T-Mobile, then the appliance is not of much value. But then, you also need a network of friends to communicate with, because if you had no friends then the appliance is not of much use; think of friends as resources that are integrated into your use experience. This example helps to illustrate that each of us are always resource integrators.

In Exhibit 14.5 we show that customers actually integrate three major types of resources as they co-create value in their daily lives: market resources, public resources, and private resources. To illustrate the resource integrating nature of customers and their value co-creation, we take something as simple as purchasing seafood, fruits and vegetables, and wine and preparing a home-cooked meal. What you quickly realize is that many resources beyond what the retailer offers are necessary. Incidentally, what the retailer offers are referred to as market resources, since they can be acquired in the retail marketplace. In addition to market resources that the retailer provides, there are public resources and private resources that are integrated into the value co-creation process.

Exhibit 14.5
Customers as Resource Integrators

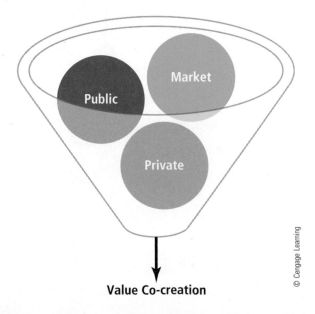

© Cengage Learning

The food ingredients in the earlier illustration are market resources, and they are often available at many competing retailers in a community. However, to travel to the store, the customer drove a car or took public transportation, where, in either case, used some public resources such as roadways and traffic laws and regulations that accommodated the flow of traffic. However, most likely, private resources were also integrated, such as help from another to prepare, serve, or clean up after the meal, or conversation over dinner about the events of the day and plans for the weekend. These private resources are also often called social resources but, in either case, it is important to recognize that they are not purchased in the marketplace. To see that you understand the concept of resource integration and co-creation of value as described previously and portrayed in Exhibit 14.5, see if you can apply it to the course you are taking that uses this book.

A retailer cannot fully understand its customer if it does not go beyond simply trying to understand how customers shop in its store. Retail shopping behavior must be understood within the context of the everyday existence of customers, and how they constantly integrate resources to solve problems and pursue opportunities or, as we suggested earlier, perform jobs. For instance, if a retailer operating a family restaurant understands how its customers normally prepare and eat a meal at home (in modern society), they quickly learn that few families have family members who eat at the same time or within the same place, even if they are all in the same house. Therefore, what eating out together may be about, is not the tangible food offering (which of course needs to be appropriate), but time for family members to share conversation and relax together. Or, mostly integrated are the social relationships among family members. This then, has profound implications for the design of the restaurant and the entire dining experience.

Value as Unique

Retailers, when they sell an item or basket of items, are able to compute the price or economic value of the transaction. In fact, most large retailers and many smaller retailers use information technology and frequent shopper cards to know the precise economic value of each customer, which they often measure as the total sales revenue or profit from a customer over a particular time period such as one to three years.

Economic value, although definitely not to be ignored, is a limited view of value. From the customer's perspective, where the primary value resides is in the use and integration of resources to create uniquely determined customer experiences, and hence, value. Two individuals acquiring the same items will integrate them in a unique manner with other resources and create different experiences or they will co-create value differently. Therefore, in the prior example of the family dining out together, what a mother or father may experience is different than what the 5-year-old is experiencing and that is again different than his 13-year-old sister. Recognizing and capitalizing on the unique experiences of value by each customer is one of the biggest challenges in retailing. However, retailers that can do this well are much more likely to be high performance retailers.

The notion of unique value is especially important when the retail shopper or customer includes not a single individual but a group of individuals, such as a family. Each of these family members, even though they are on the same shopping trip, has unique needs and values things differently. The challenge is how to develop a value proposition that can be attractive to each of the shoppers or customers in the group. For instance, Ikea with its indoor children's play area offers a value proposition that both pleases children as well as their parents who can shop uninterrupted by their children and at the same time the children enjoy the experience of play and not having to be pulled and directed by their parents through the store to look at things they prefer not to see. Or, some specialty women's wear stores will have a sitting area where men who may accompany a female shopper can relax and read magazines or newspapers. Other retailers will cater to the unique value each customer is seeking

By providing a safe play area within its stores, IKEA shows it knows that having happy children leads to having happy parents, which makes the shopping experience better for everyone.

through customization of the offering. An Ace Hardware store (often only 10 percent the size of Home Depot or Lowe's) can provide specialized advice to shoppers to enable them to purchase the proper hardware items for a do-it-yourself project, or to provide a custom installation service for their customers if they prefer others to do it for them.

Customer-Centric Retailing

LO 3

Explain how customer centricity is essential in contemporary retailing.

customer-centric
Putting the customer at the center of the economic and social system within which the retailer operates.

Adopting a service-dominant mindset puts the customer at the center of the economic and social system within which the retailer operates. The **customer-centric** view is so extreme that it suggests that the retailer begins not with its capabilities and skills but with developing a deep understanding of its customers or potential customers and how they are going about their ordinary lives to enhance them. Consider, for instance, your household and what you would envision as the ideal set of retail offerings that were available to you at anytime you wanted them and at the place you wanted them. Of course, this may not be realistic, but the point is to envision the possibility of a 100 percent customer-centric retail offering. Perhaps, as you rise in the morning, you have the freshly cleaned apparel you desire for that day, the ideal breakfast prepared and served before you drive your ideal car to your ideal job, while listening to your favorite tunes and enjoying the perfect second cup of coffee. When you get to work, without any traffic problems, the perfect parking spot awaits, the elevator is waiting and uncrowded, and there is a bouquet of fresh flowers on your desk and throughout the day, everything is provided on demand to your ideal specifications! In a limited, but important sense, Coca-Cola is moving in this on-demand direction. Coca-Cola Freestyle[10] vending machine revolutionizes beverage vending. And remember, selling through a vending machine is a form of retailing, so it may transform beverage retailing. Most vending machines offer a half dozen to perhaps a dozen drink options. With the Freestyle vending machine, the customer has over 100 choices and can invent and mix customized drinks, and they can share these drink ideas with others online. Incidentally, the expertise for this innovative machine came from a collaboration involving Microsoft,

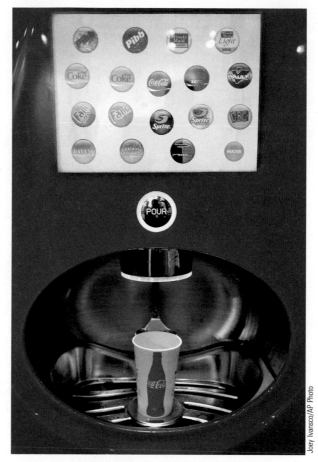

Joey Ivansco/AP Photo

The Coca-Cola Freestyle vending machine takes customer-centricity
to a new level by allowing the customer to custom-mix a soft drink
or choose one of more than 100 programmed options.

Apple, Ferrari, and BMW.[11] Perhaps, the next step is to have your own personal Freestyle vending machine in your home or office. This would be an example of increasing
what is called "density"—the topic discussed next.

Density[12] or the best combination of resources that are mobilized to a time and place
for a particular individual to solve their problem(s) or for them to pursue opportunities
at an optimal value or cost result. Density is actually driven largely by population size
and population density, and this occurs in cities. Living in a city and especially a large
and highly dense city such as New York, Tokyo, Rome, Sao Paolo, etc., creates the concentrated customer demand that enables retailers to offer virtually any offering you can
imagine. And if you have the income (or credit), you can have just about anything you
may desire. Perhaps, that is why for hundreds of years people have been moving to large
cities where in many countries over 75 percent of the population resides.

Density is more and more facilitated via the Internet, which overcomes many
geographic constraints. Probably, the current market offering that comes closest to maximum density is Google or other popular information search engines. They are able to
bring together a large number of information resources at a time and place where needed
for a particular individual seeking specific information. Amazon.com is another example
of an enterprise that tries to provide density by presenting an incredibly large merchandise assortment at the click of a mouse or your touch screen and essentially uses Best

density
The best combination
of resources that are
mobilized to a time and
place for a particular
individual to solve their
problem(s) or for them
to pursue opportunities
at an optimal value or
cost result.

Exhibit 14.6
Customer as an Operant
Resource

© Cengage Learning

Buy and other retailers as Amazon's showroom. But even with Google or Amazon search engines, the information is ranked ordered and not very well integrated. Perhaps, one of the biggest retail opportunities is for retailers to think of themselves as being a customer-consultant[13] and then advise the customer on how to maximize their density. Hence, the retailer becomes the buying agent for the customer, and, in fact, the retailer is probably the best positioned in a marketing system to be the master resource integrator.[14]

Customer centricity also implies the customer is an active participant in the process of creating resources and solutions. They are what we referred to earlier as an operant resource. In Exhibit 14.6 we show the five facets around which customers are operant resources. These are engagement, co-producing, co-creating, relieving, and enabling.

Engagement

engagement
Is about how intensely the customers interface, experience, and connect to various other actors in the economic system to include retailers.

Velcro is a simple product and one that you have probably often used. Velcro allows you to fasten many things together; we not only see it in shoes, apparel, hats, etc., but also use it to hang fabric on walls or to fasten things together so we don't lose them. Velcro is essentially a fastener with the value proposition that it will efficiently and effectively connect things. In retailing, **engagement** is about how the customers interface, experience, and connect to various other actors in the economic system to include retailers. And just like Velcro, the retailer ideally wants to efficiently and effectively engage customers. One of the reasons for the success of Starbucks is that it does an excellent job at engaging customers. On the other hand, many retailers do a very poor job at engagement. Consider, for example, that most providers of cell phone service sign up customers for two-year service plans with high penalties for cancellation, which is a fairly good indicator that their customers don't find their relationship with their provider as engaging.

Keep in mind that engaging the customer is only part of the solution to customer centricity. Employees also need to be engaged with the retail enterprise because engaged employees are satisfied and happy employees and customers notice this quite well. Have you ever met a retail clerk or service worker who was mean, rude, and generally not responsive to your needs? There is a good chance this employee is not engaged and

Exhibit 14.7
Engagement Processes

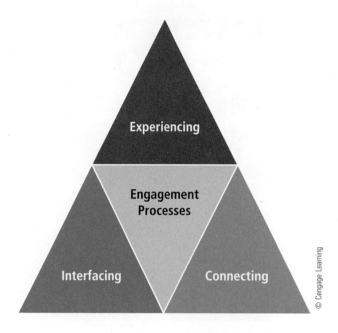

even disenfranchised from the retail enterprise. You can also bet that this employee will share his or her feelings and experiences with friends and acquaintances.

You probably recognize The Walt Disney Company as a global brand with theme parks on several continents and a reputation for outstanding movie making. The Disney Company also is a leader in building brand loyalty that inspires commitment. In fact, on a typical day two out of three guests at a Disney theme park are return visitors. Recognizing the need to create a culture that results in engaged employees and customers, the Disney Company in 1986 launched the Disney Institute (www.disneyinstitute.com) to train executives, managers, and other employees in leadership and customer service. Today, the Disney Institute trains thousands of employees each year for many retailers around the world.

Three processes occur that can help facilitate engagement. These processes are *interfacing*, *experiencing*, and *connecting*, and they are shown in Exhibit 14.7.

Interfacing   An individual interfaces with a retailer every time he or she interacts with the retailer. This interaction can be hard surfaced if it is a tangible interface or soft surfaced if it is an intangible interface. Thus, listening to a television advertisement or reading a newspaper or pop-up advertisement on the Internet is part of soft interfacing. But parking your car in the retailer's parking lot and walking into the store is a form of hard interfacing. And, walking through the store, viewing and selecting merchandise, checking out and paying, etc. are some of the soft and hard interfacing experiences. In Chapter 13, we discussed many good methods and examples of using store design to provide soft and hard interfaces that were synergistic with customer engagement. Again, don't forget employees. If a retail clerk at a supermarket is standing at the checkout register and scanning merchandise, talking with customers, and a host of other chores and is interfacing with equipment, flooring, lighting, etc., then all of these interfaces need to make the employee comfortable and not unnecessarily physically strained.

Experiencing   Experiences are the cognitive and affective responses that result from interfacing. Consider the experience of parking your car and getting upset because the parking spaces are too small for your SUV or that the entry door to the store has a hot handle which creates a burning sensation when you touch it. Consider the feelings you

Joe Burbank/MCT/Landov

Each year, The Disney Institute trains thousands of employees for other organizations in interfacing, experiencing and connecting with customers.

have when you cannot locate the item you want or when you interface with a rude retail salesperson or clerk or when fellow shoppers crowd you out of an aisle.

Thinking carefully about how to use everything the retailer does, when interfacing with the shopper to create a positive experience, can be the source of innovative ideas. For instance, a consignment store in Tokyo enables individuals to recycle their cared for and loved possessions that they no longer need or have space to store. That alone, as you probably know, is not very unique. But what is unique is that each item that is for sale in the consignment shop has a personal story that is written by the owner and attached to the item. This enables the store to help create a store brand that has meaning, social responsibility, and a very strong emotional appeal.[15] Incidentally, using your store and merchandising to tell stories can be a very strong way to create positive customer and shopping experiences.

Most new car dealerships do a very poor job at creating an enjoyable, exciting, and engaging new car shopping experience or a return experience to get your auto serviced. A notable example is Carl Sewell who, for over 25 years, has been designing and operating exciting and customer-centric retail facilities. The recently completed Sewell MINI dealership in North Texas is an excellent example. The showroom is family-friendly and makes the purchasing and servicing of your MINI a memorable and fun experience. Customers have access to Xbox stations, vintage games, iPads, etc. Once again, consider many of the concepts and ideas from Chapter 13 on store layout and design if you want to design an engaging retail experience.

The experiences can thus be positive or negative but they can also be neutral. And often, neutral experiences are what can create an overall great experience as surprising as it sounds! How can this be so; it sounds contradictory. There are many mundane experiences that the shopper simply wants to be bland experiences. They want an adequate parking slot, a not too hot or too cold door handle, and merchandise on the shelf where they expect to find it. However, just because these occur it does not suggest the shopper shouts with joy and has strong positive affective feelings. But overall, when all of these mundane things work, the overall retail experience is wonderful.

Connecting   Only when the interfacing and resulting experiences produce an overall highly positive result, the customer wants to connect or bond with the retailer. Some of this can be instrumental or what can be thought of as economic in nature. That is, the interfacing and experiences result in connecting to the retailer for economic reasons such as the rewards from a frequent shopper program. However, often it goes deeper and results in a form of identification with the retailer. This deeper form of connecting can often relate to shared values that are reflected in interfacing and experiencing with the retailer. For instance, a person may value courtesy and kindness, truthfulness and transparency, and artistic design. When they interface with a retailer that has employees, policies, and a store design that reflect these values, then the Velcro that connects it to the retailer is strong.

Co-Production and Co-Creation

Customers are active participants in creating value as we have discussed. There are two primary ways customers are active participants. First, a retail enterprise can invite or require the customer to do part of the service (work) of retailing. This is actually quite common, especially given the way that mass retail merchandising has evolved over the last century. For instance, in a supermarket, the customers are required to push carts around the store, select merchandise without assistance, and cart their groceries to their automobile or otherwise transport the purchases to their home or place of work. Today, there are even computer checkout counters where customers can scan their own groceries and pay for them electronically without assistance from store personnel. So, **co-production** is the active involvement of the customer in the retailer's core activities. When this occurs, the customer is a co-producer of service.

A second way the customer is an active participant is in the co-creation of value. Although co-production can be optional in that the customer may decide not to do some of the service work or find a retailer to patronize where this is not required, in the case of **co-creation** everyone who purchases a tangible or intangible market offering and uses the offering is viewed as a co-creator of value. This perspective on co-creation gets to the heart of where value is created. With a service-dominant orientation, value is always viewed as being created in the use of things (tangible or intangible). Value in exchange (i.e., price) cannot be ignored but from a customer's perspective the real or true value is in the experience of using things and that is the core of understanding value and its co-creation.

An excellent example of the co-production and co-creation concepts in retailing is Build-a-Bear Workshop.[16] Maxine Clark, the founder, as a seasoned retail executive who had held senior positions at the May Company (now known as Macy's) knew a lot about shoppers and merchandising. She also knew how important it is to engage customers and that today people want customized offerings. This led her to the idea of creating a retail store where individuals could produce a customized stuffed animal, along with apparel for the animal. The customer thus not only obtained a customized animal but also had an engaging experience and often with a young child or grandchild. Of course, once the animal was taken home the child or adult would always remember the experience of creating the animal.

We do not think the preceding example or the example of Ikea customers co-producing the furniture are isolated examples. There is high potential for many retailers to develop a co-production and co-creation strategy. This can often be done with digital and information technology. For instance, at some Barnes & Noble bookstores, there is an online children's self-publishing service.[17] Kids can write and illustrate their own books and then print them in a soft or hardcover format.

co-production

Is the active involvement of the customer in the retailer's core activities. When this occurs, the customer is a co-producer of service.

co-creation

Everyone who purchases a tangible or intangible market offering and uses the offering is viewed as a co-creator of value. With a service-dominant orientation, value is always viewed as being created in the use of things (tangible or intangible).

Andrea Renault/ZUMAPRESS/Newscom

Build-a-Bear Workshop allows customers to co-produce and co-create by designing and making their own custom made stuffed animals.

relieving
The use of other tools, people or other aids to eliminate certain tasks or to make those tasks easier. Examples include wheels and pulleys, automatic washing machines, medications, pre-made food, store signage, ATMs, automatic doors, and knowledge-able retail salespeople and food servers.

enabling
The use of tools, people or other aids that allow people to perform service for themselves or others, and allows someone to do things he or she might have not been able to otherwise.

Relieving and Enabling

Closely related to the concepts of co-production and co-creation are the concepts of **relieving** and **enabling**. Taking a customer-centric view, we can see all individuals as actively involved in service for themselves or for others. That is what we do as spouses, parents, employees, and in our many other roles in life; we simply serve one another and that is what holds society together. In fact, you can argue that humans cannot exist independently, but exist by cooperating and working with others to be of service to each other.

In their daily lives, individuals find it helpful to be "relieved" of doing certain types of service or things. In fact, humans are quite clever as they evolved over millions of years, and especially the last couple of thousand of years, at inventing tools that allow them to be relieved of certain tasks and activities. Simple tools such as the wheel and pulley relieved humans of physical and often mental effort, but modern day appliances such as a robotic floor cleaner, an anti-acid pill, or an automatic washing and/or clothes dryer relieve us of physical and often mental activity, and laundry detergents such as Tide, an iconic Procter & Gamble brand, made washing clothes easier. Finally, remember that not only a knowledgeable retail clerk can be viewed as a reliever but also well-designed store signage and merchandise displays can also be relievers.

Chipotle is a fast food retailer that essentially relieves the customer from the work of determining if the food they are eating is healthy and produced in an environmentally friendly manner. Rather than spending a lot of money on aggressive and often misleading advertising, Chipotle places its efforts on sourcing the finest sustainable food ingredients.[18]

People also invent tools that enable them to perform service for themselves or others. Some of the prior examples such as clothes dryer can be viewed as relieving you of some physical work and effort, but it can also be viewed as enabling you to do things you might have not been able to otherwise. For instance, some clothes dryers are now designed with the technology that allows for dry cleaning and steam cleaning. Individuals on their own may not have the knowledge and skills to perform these tasks and, thus, the clothes dryer becomes an enabler. Or, consider an automobile with an automatic transmission that relieves you of shifting gears and, when coupled with a stereo satellite connected radio, enables you to listen to hundreds of types of music and news formats.

A retailer should consider designing an assortment so as to enhance enabling customers. For instance, in a supermarket if the retailer has a branch bank or café, then the grocery shopper is able to do banking and grab a snack all in one convenient location. When Lowe's or Home Depot offers classes to customers to teach them how to build things or install things in their homes, they are enabling their customers to do things they could not otherwise do. Many enablers can be information technology based. Consider for example, a product such as TurboTax that enables people who are not expert at tax accounting to prepare their own tax returns. A retailer could also have a website where customers could go to learn more about how to use the items they purchased from the retailer. Kroger (http://www.kroger.com), for example, has a website with recipes, meal-planning, party planning, nutrition information, fitness and health information, and much more to enable its customers to use its products in their everyday lives.

Dialogue

A consumer-centric retailer will find itself moving away from (but not fully eliminating) a promotional and advertising program that is one-way and intended to push out a message to customers to simply buy more. The traditional broadcast one-way model of promotion is highly firm centric because it is designed to allow the retailer to primarily sell its merchandise. However, a consumer-centric orientation views advertising and all communications as a service and part of the process of building relationships.[19] It views these tools as providing help and assistance to the customer and shopper. Adopting a dialogical model of communication is therefore more appropriate.[20] Dialogue, as a concept, actually means to learn together, and thus, it is very consistent with a *marketing with* mental model. To learn together, each party needs to be open in their communication with each other. This openness allows them to solve problems and pursue opportunities together.

Rob BonDurant, vice president of marketing and communications for Patagonia, is a strong advocate of using dialogue to advance the retailer's mission. Patagonia's "Common Threads Initiative" uses dialogue to help customers reduce purchases by repairing, reusing, and recycling their belongings. To help stimulate this dialogue, Patagonia ran a full-page advertisement in the *New York Times* on Black Friday 2011. While everyone else was trying to capture the Christmas and holiday shopper with deep discount advertising, Patagonia's message was "Don't Buy This Jacket." The advertisement certainly caught the attention of not only loyal Patagonia customers, but also many others. The R2 Jacket shown in the advertisement was reported as requiring 135 liters of water to create and produced 20 pounds of carbon dioxide or 24 times the weight of the finished product. As the jacket was transported to Reno for redistribution, it left behind an additional two-thirds of its weight in waste. Patagonia wanted to create a dialogue around the culture of consumption and to motivate conversation and dialogue that would improve its business, but in a sustainable manner. Clearly, the evidence from the social media buzz and the public relations impact of the advertising was very positive for Patagonia.[21]

Patagonia is an example of being actively involved with your community. But even without the retailer's active involvement it will increasingly find that its customer community is engaging in dialogue. Often this is through blogs, forums, or other social media. Consider your own social media activity; you are probably a member of Facebook or Twitter or a host of other social media communication channels. Retailers are also establishing social networking for employees to collaborate and tear down departmental silos that all large retailers confront.[22] Also, retailers are starting to establish social networking with suppliers. We therefore recommend the retailer become active in this dialogue.

Value Propositions

In Chapter 2, we defined value propositions. Essentially, value propositions are statements of how the retailer plans to positively affect customers or also employees, suppliers, and other stakeholders. Our focus here is primarily on customers. What a value proposition does is to place the retailer in the role of attempting to see things from the perspective of the customer. From that perspective, it has to understand how the customer views value and how what the retailer offers can positively affect this value. Understanding customer engagement, co-production, co-creation, relieving, and enabling become vital, and using dialogue to learn about these areas even more essential.

Here is what we recommend for developing competitively compelling value propositions. First, we recommend forgetting for a moment the "holy grail" of price or economic value, which virtually all retailers are obsessed with on a daily, if not hourly, basis. Thus, it will be hard to forget about price or sales revenues and all of those things tied to economic value that retailers were taught to focus upon. As you turn your mind away from price and revenues, you focus on the customer's value in use. How do your customers use your offerings to create value? Second, consider the resource integrating nature of your customers. What other resources do they combine or integrate with your offerings and what does this mean for how they create value? Third, go back now to price but to that add the other costs that customers have in the use of your offerings. These can not only be economic costs such as fuel, repair, or operating costs but also psychological or social costs. Finally, consider how the value proposition you develop will not only resonate with your customers but also with employees, suppliers, and other stakeholders. The reason for the latter is because only the customer is the source of cash flowing into the enterprise; however, other entities have a stake in this cash flow. Ideally, the retailer wants a customer value proposition that gets other stakeholders excited about the retailer serving the customer. As we stated earlier, the retailer may also want to develop unique value propositions for these other stakeholders, but they would need to be consistent with the firm's value proposition to customers.

LO 4

Discuss the central importance and imperative of continuous learning in retailing.

Developing a Learning Mindset

Virtually all retailers, like virtually all businesses, in modern society have plans. These plans for a large national or global retailer can include plans for the aggregate enterprise and plans that are mapped out by geography, specific store, merchandise lines, and categories. An important part of these plans are financial goals. These include planned sales, sales growth, gross margins, inventory productivity, labor productivity, and space productivity, as shown in the retail resource trinity model in Exhibit 14.1. Actual results are then compared to the plan. If actual results are equal to or greater than the plan, then all is well, and more ambitious plans and financial goals are set for the next planning horizon (often quarterly or annually). On the other hand, if actual results fall short of planned results, then things are not so well. In fact, in retailing, the failure to meet the plan creates high anxiety and often a feeling of failure among management and employees—not something that is best for the long-term health of the retailer's employees: its most valuable asset.

Actual results can fall short of planned results for a variety of reasons.[23] Some can be environmental, such as adverse weather patterns or economic sluggishness in the trade area the retailer operates. More aggressive competition than anticipated is another potential cause of poor performance, which often translates into stores not being as well managed as the stores of competitors. However, at least in North American retailing, when actual results are less than planned, the fault or blame is laid on management and employees. There is a predominant, and we believe unhealthy, attitude that the "plan" is truth or correct, and failure to achieve the plan is because people did not work hard or smart enough.

At the center of the discussion of what planned versus actual results reflect is our built-in assumptions about learning. When actual results are below plan, it can be viewed as a control problem; get workers and management more in control to work harder to achieve planned results or goals. Or alternatively, it can be viewed as an opportunity to learn how the retailer can improve in the future. Consider your early life and when you learned the most. It probably occurred when you made errors or mistakes, when you fell off your bicycle trying to learn to ride it or when you kept hitting the ball poorly when learning to play golf. In brief, poor performance or failure should be seen as a learning opportunity. Therefore, when a retailer experiences actual results that are below plan it should not be assumed that the problem or cause is management or lazy workers. Rather, the retailer should look deeper or more broadly and try to learn how to take the appropriate corrective action. There are three types of learning[24] and each has profound implications for retail success. These are single-, double-, and triple-loop learning.

Single-Loop Learning

single-loop learning
A single source of feedback about "are we doing things right" to achieve our goals. It is a way of learning in which an action is triggered whenever you drop below your target goal.

Single-loop learning can be compared to a thermostat model of learning and how to correct a situation. With a thermostat there is a programmed-in target temperature and when the temperature falls below the target, an action is taken to turn on the furnace to adjust the temperature. In the case of a retail enterprise, if a target return on assets is 8 percent and if the return is below 8 percent, then it triggers action by the retailer around the two primary determinants of return on assets (as discussed in Chapter 2) or net profit margin and asset turnover. One or both of these would need to be increased to get the return back up to 8 percent. Single-loop learning is also often thought of as "are we doing things right" to achieve our goals.

Double-Loop Learning

double-loop learning
A double source of feedback. Feedback is not only on "are we doing things right" but also on, "are we doing the right things." The later gets at are we targeting the right goals.

Double-loop learning looks at whether the retailer is doing the right things versus merely doing things right. It is thus, a deeper form of learning. In this situation, the retailer may actually be achieving its goals, but the goals may, in fact, reflect not the right things on which it should be focused. For instance, historically, many retailers throughout the world focused on margins—either net or gross. They did not focus on asset and inventory investments and the return these investments generated. But instead, the mindset was how much could be earned per dollar of sales. This sounds logical and appealing. However, retailing is an industry of buying and selling merchandise, so inventory turnover becomes critical to success. Thus, retailers began to focus on GMROI and other models of return on investment or assets.

Of course, there are many goals, as we discussed in Chapter 2, on which a retailer could focus its efforts. Not only are there financial goals, but also market performance such as market share, personal such as self-gratification, and societal such as job creation. In fact, some of these goals may better reflect how effective a retailer is versus merely how economically efficient it is with resources. To repeat, with double-loop learning the retailer asks itself if the goals and measures on which it is focused are the appropriate or "right" goals and measures.

Triple-Loop Learning

triple-loop learning
"What is the right business model" incorporates doing things right, toward the right goals, and being ever cognizant of the opportunity to change your business model.

Perhaps the most sophisticated type of learning is triple loop. As we mentioned, single-loop learning is about doing things right and double loop is about doing the right things. **Triple loop learning** brings forth a deeper and more philosophical question and that is "what is our right business model." A retailer may be doing things right and doing the right things but this can be in the context of its current business model. Duane Reade, a drugstore chain, we have mentioned in earlier chapters and now owned by Walgreen's, is an excellent example of using triple-loop learning by regularly fundamentally challenging the dominant drugstore business model. Its flagship store on Wall Street in New York City has been reconfigured to include a sushi chef, juice bar, nail bar, and hair salon. Management views this store as a "learning store" where it can try out new, sometimes radical ideas and, if successful, roll out throughout the Walgreen's chain.[25] The Inside story on S.S. Kresge is a good historical example of triple-loop learning.

© Katerina Havelkova/Shutterstock

RETAILING — The Inside Story

S.S. Kresge: A Historical Illustration of Triple-Loop Learning

Let us illustrate triple-loop learning with the history of S.S. Kresge, a retailer established in 1897 that grew rapidly during the first half of the 20th century but quickly became a declining old-line variety store chain muddling through the post-World War II era.[26] In 1957, Harry B. Cunningham, the general vice-president of the firm, was assigned to travel the country to study retail trends firsthand. Cunningham traveled for two years and finally confirmed that variety stores—like the earlier five-and-dime stores—had somehow drifted away from their original formula for success: low margins and high inventory turnover. Instead of pricing merchandise to stimulate sales, they were pricing it on the basis of current costs. Variety stores were extremely vulnerable; supermarkets, discount houses, and other new mass merchandisers were beating them at their own game. This set the ideal stage for triple-loop learning. But not many retail executives (or other individuals) have the insights and wisdom

required for triple-loop learning. This is because it means being able to see what the retailer enterprise "is not" versus what "it is" and then developing the insights to transform it into something "it can become".

Let us continue the story of S.S. Kresge and triple-loop learning. In 1959, Cunningham was named president and chief executive officer and ordered another two-year study to focus exclusively on trends in discount retailing in the United States. When the results were in, Cunningham made the decision to transform S.S. Kresge into a discount retailer. He was determined to avoid the merchandising mistakes of the other discounters flooding the market. The result was Kmart, a conveniently located, large-scale, one-stop shopping unit, where customers could buy quality merchandise at discount prices. Cunningham had just engaged in triple-loop learning and discovered that the Kresge business model was flawed and abandoned it. In March 1962, Kresge opened its first Kmart in Garden City, Michigan, and by 1991 Kmart was the second-largest retailer in the United States, with annual sales in excess of $32 billion.

Reframing

reframing
Changing a business model by reconfiguring the resources of time, place and possession around a customer-centric view.

Triple-loop learning brings forth the important role of the title of this chapter "**Reframing** Retailing." In a rapidly changing technological, political, economic, and social world, it is naïve to think that the dominant retail business model of the past will continue to work well. In order to be able to do the triple-loop learning from reframing, the retail enterprise must begin with a customer-centric view for the reasons outlined in this chapter. Obtaining this customer-centric view in order to reframe the retailer's business begins with a consideration of how to create more density for the customer, and this involves analyzing how to reconfigure resources of the current retail business model specifically around changes in form, time, place, and possession.[27] Each of these is now elaborated. Also review the "Service Retailing" box that projects what retailing will look like in a dozen years or 2025.

© Smileus/Shutterstock

SERVICE ▭ RETAILING

Town Center USA: Prototype for 2025[28]

Instead of trying to develop a prototype for a particular type of retail store of the future, we develop a prototype of the shopping center of the future (2025). Since 2025 is only a dozen years away, it is unlikely that this prototype will dominate retailing by 2025. Probably, the development of this prototype is most useful for making explicit the assumptions we make about the future of retailing as you will see the heavy emphasis on services provided by retailers integrated with community services.

Town Center USA is much more than a *shopping center* as we currently use the term. Town Center USA is a community center built to serve a population greater than 100,000. It succeeds because it offers local citizens a community place. This is critical to its success because the community orientation and philosophy has been decaying in America; Town Center USA returns to a community orientation. To bring back a sense of community, people need a place to gather and dialogue, learn, and become enriched. Since people are time constrained, the shopping center is an ideal place of community interaction. Town Center USA will be a new town center, serving community needs for togetherness and individual needs for shopping and materialistic consumption.

Town Center USA will need to begin with the planning of a large physical and digital infrastructure to support community activities. The focal point of the infrastructure will be Main Street USA, a cobble-paved street

that will bisect Town Center USA and serve as the major focal point of the center. Main Street will be used for holiday parades, street festivals, athletic events, organized protests, and street peddlers. It will be a place for civic engagement and social interaction and relaxation. Clusters of benches will be set along Main Street where people can sit and read from their tablet computers or simply old-fashioned hard copy books or wait for the Town Trolley.

Town Trolley USA will be a hybrid–energy powered trolley that will transport individuals throughout Town Center USA. The Town Trolley will be entertaining to ride. Trolley operators will be friendly and conversant with the passengers and dressed in attire that reflects the history of the community. Both outside and inside the trolley, important digital screen advertising for nonprofit organizations and public service messages will be displayed. The Town Trolley will not only go up and down Main Street, but up and down Broadway Street, the other major traffic artery in Town Center USA. As customers near their destination, they will receive customized digital messages on their smartphones or tablet computers from various retailers.

Riverfront USA will flow from a small 10–15 acre man-made lake stocked with ducks and fish. The riverfront will have a tranquil and soothing effect on the visitors to Town Center USA. It will be a place for picnics, festivals, athletic events, and relaxation. River Boat USA will ferry people between restaurants that are positioned along the riverfront. Several of the restaurants

(*continued*)

will have outside eating areas that overlook the river. At the point where the lake flows into the river will be a farmers' market where fresh flowers, vegetables, and other locally produced food items can be purchased. On occasion this open market will be used for the merchandising of arts and crafts or for major-event retailing such as July Fourth, Labor Day, or Memorial Day.

At the intersection of Main and Broadway Streets will be Town Hall USA, which will be used for civic meetings, social clubs, and charitable organizations. Information about all town or community events will be available. The Town Learning Center will also be located at the intersection of Main and Broadway and will rent space to schools, colleges, and universities for a broad variety of educational events. Some of these will be for do-it-yourself instruction, remedial education, and personal enrichment courses. Religious events can also be scheduled in the Town Learning Center. The Town Learning Center will also be mirrored by a web-based center by the same name.

Down the street from the Town Hall will be the Town USA Wellness Center. This will be a facility for wellness and fitness education and training. Community members, on a volunteer basis, will be able to monitor their physical activity and nutrition through smart devices worn on their wrists or embedded under their skin. This information will be uploaded to a personal website that the individual an access 24/7 anyone in the world. This technology will have the ability to sense when an individual is facing degradation in health, and also individual data can be aggregated to get an overall health profile for the community and how it is changing over time.

Town Center USA will have a minimum of 500,000 square feet of retail space that can be configured anywhere from 1,500–square foot shops to 100,000–square foot mass merchandisers. Also pop-up stores will be encouraged and are expected to be a dominant part of the experiential nature of Town Center USA. Due to the rise of e-tailing, Town Center USA will feature eBay and Amazon fulfillment centers that will be joint ventures with some of the largest retailers in the USA. It is also projected that a host of retailers will offer financial, health care, legal, personal care, education, and entertainment as well as other services.

Form Reconfiguration   Form deals with the physical structure of the retail enterprise. This can be around any elements of the enterprise such as the fundamental design of the format of the store or a part of the store such as checkout counters, merchandise fixtures, layout or overall dimensions, or size of the store. For instance, many retail banks in the United States have gone over the last several decades from having large centrally located physical structures to smaller physical structures. Or Walmart has gone through several transitions in terms of the physical footprint of their stores from the 1960s when most of their discount stores were under 40,000 square feet to the 1980s when they were over 70,000 square feet to Walmart supercenters in the 1990s that exceeded 120,000 square feet and now returning to smaller neighborhood markets and convenience stores that are under 20,000 square feet. Or 7-Eleven that went in the 1960s and 1970s from convenience stores of a couple thousand square feet that did not sell gasoline or fast food to stores in the 1980s and beyond to larger stores on larger parcels of land that sold gasoline, fast food, and lottery tickets. In a more dramatic reframing of form, Sears Roebuck went from a mail order retailer in the late 1800s to opening its first retail store in 1925, primarily building physical stores in the 1930s and 1940s.

Time Reconfiguring   A retailer can also reframe its business in terms of the time it performs certain activities and offers service. Grocery stores historically (pre-1940) often displayed fresh meats in a butcher counter and then sliced and wrapped the meat to order based on customer instructions. However, in a radical change in timing of meat slicing, many decided to pre-slice meat and package it in cellophane wrapping and present it in a refrigerated meat display case the customer could select from without assistance. Other retailers changed their time of operating. Up until 1990, many U.S. banks were not open on Saturday and then some innovators began to open until noon on Saturday and then later they remained opened until 5 p.m. Even earlier, most banks opened at 10 a.m. and closed at 3 p.m. and this became known as "bankers' hours" but in the 1970s hours moved to 9 a.m., and by late 1980 closing hours were moved to 5 or 6 p.m. This made obvious sense since most people work Monday through Friday and do not have bankers' hours. Gilt Groupe (www.gilt.com) is only a bit over five years old, but it has been highly successful in reframing the time around sale events. Gilt wanted to create sense of discovery and surprise.[29] With a bricks-and-mortar store it would be extremely difficult to change out the merchandise everyday. But at Gilt everyday when you arrive at their website, it is a new and exciting day with new merchandise and one-day sales also called flash sales. Gilt began by offering women's designer sample sales but now has expanded to menswear, baby and kids, home furnishings, food, and jetsetter vacations. In 2013 sales will exceed $1 billion, a long way from its 2007 sales of $25 million. It seems common sense for Internet retailers to not replicate a bricks-and-mortar store in the quickest or flash of their sales. But often what is common sense is not so obvious and some of the best forms of retail reframing are only common sense after the fact.

Place Reconfiguring   A new logic around the geographic location of a retailer is another way to reframe its business model. For instance, retailers such as Walmart, Coldwater Creek, and Office Depot have developed e-stores and hence are essentially putting the retailer's place of business in the customer's home or office or wherever the customer has access to a computer, electronic tablet, or phone with an Internet connection. Sephora is a leader in developing iPhone and iPad apps that allow the customer to have a Sephora store experience but outside the physical place of the store.[30] Sephora's iPad app (you can download free) brings together Sephora social content, e-commerce, interactive catalogue and how-to videos. You can also get Facebook and Twitter feeds. There is even a virtual mirror where as you look at your iPad you see yourself in a mirror that allows you to follow a how-to video so you can experience how a new look would look on you.

Retailers can also find that by creating stores that are smaller (a type of form restructuring), they can place them in nontraditional locations. Consider, for example, McDonald's and Pizza Hut locating in airports or Federal Express service centers locating in office buildings.

Possession Reconfiguring   Where and how a customer takes physical possession of the merchandise can also be a source of reframing. Often the place of possession is at the retail store, but home delivery is an option and home installation is another way of providing possession. Best Buy with its Magnolia Theatre home entertainment departments takes the home theatre purchase all of the way through delivery and custom installation in the customer's home. Another way of thinking about possession is with regard to the passing of legal title to the merchandise. The tradition in North America and most parts of the world is for the customer to buy a durable good and take ownership of the good. However, if you look at the U.S. sale of new automobiles, an increasing number are leased and thus, the customer is actually purchasing a flow of service such as 12,000 miles a year for three years. Today, there are 500,000 members of Zipcar sharing cars part-time, often for a few hours or day. The same concept of course can be applied to furniture, computers, home appliances, and even clothing. In fact, some of you may have not purchased the book you are reading but rented it for the semester. This is part of a more general trend called collaborative consumption.[31] Capitalizing on this trend, Snapgoods (www.snapgoods.com) assists people in renting and sharing goods via the Internet.

Summary

The logic or mindset for thinking about retail enterprises can be transformative and if a retailer is to survive over the long-run it must at some point be transformative. Should the retailer primarily view itself as supplying merchandise to customers, or marketing and selling merchandise to customers, or as a collaborative partner with the customer? Or, as not selling merchandise to customers but as serving customers in their resource-integrating and resource-creating experiences. This chapter develops the rationale for why the latter is increasingly needed in retailing and the direction in which it is moving. From a service mindset, the retailer and the customer are co-creators of value and the entire retail enterprise must put the customer at the center or simply stated the retailer must be customer centric.

LO 1   What are the three eras of retailing and what distinguishes them?

The three major eras of retailing are: (1) *to market*, (2) *marketing to*, (3) *marketing with*. A "to market" orientation focused on how to get product or merchandise from sources of supply to the retail store and then to the customer. "Marketing to" retailing focuses on how to promote and advertise and otherwise entice customers to purchase merchandise. The third era is "marketing with" which is an orientation that treats the customer as an equal partner and someone to engage in value co-creating activities.

LO 2   What is service according to a service-dominant logic and what are the four principles of service-dominant logic?

Service is defined as the application of knowledge and skills through deeds, processes, and performances for the benefit of another. Service (1) involves doing something of benefit for another actor and this can include not only the customer but also suppliers and employees, (2) involves interaction between actors because the deeds, processes, and performances that comprise the service are not done in isolation but in interaction with actors, and (3) involves the application of knowledge and skills that are operant resources that can provide the retailer with competitive advantage.

The four principles of service-dominant logic are: (1) service is the basis of human exchange, (2) human actors are always a co-creator of value, (3) human actors are resource integrators, and (4) human actors uniquely determine value.

LO 3   What is customer centricity and how is it fostered in retailing?

A customer-centric view of retailing is focused on the retailer developing a deep understanding of its customers or potential customers and how they are going about their ordinary lives to enhance them. Customer centricity views the customer as an active participant in the process of creating resources and solutions. It views the customer as involved in relationships that involve engagement, co-producing, co-creating, and relieving and enabling processes.

LO 4   What is the central importance and imperative of continuous learning in retailing?

Retailers are confronted by continuous, dynamic, and unpredictable change. Thus, the best developed plans and goals are often not achieved. When this occurs, the retailer that has a learning mindset will use this as an opportunity to learn what went wrong and how to take corrective action. There are three types of learning with the most simple being single-loop learning in which the retailer tries to learn how to do the things right. A bit more sophisticated type of learning is double loop where the retailer begins to question if it is doing the right things. Finally, with triple-loop learning the retailer asks the more fundamental question of whether it has the right business model. Triple-loop learning can often lead to reframing of the retailers business model.

Terms to Remember

retail resource trinity model
operand resource
operant resource
price to book value
service
IHIP characteristics
resource integration
customer-centric
density

engagement
co-production
co-creation
relieving
enabling
single-loop learning
double-loop learning
triple-loop learning
reframing

Review and Discussion Questions

LO 1 **What are the three eras of retailing and what distinguishes them?**

1. Should all retailers adopt a collaborative or marketing "with" customer philosophy?
2. Describe and explain the retail resource trinity model. How is it useful for understanding retail resource management?
3. What distinguishes an operand versus operant resource? Should employees and customers be viewed as operand or operant resources? Explain your response.
4. Which retail industries do you believe are further along in term of moving to a collaborative "marketing with" philosophy? Can you identify any particular retailers that are further along?

LO 2 **What is service according to a service-dominant logic and what are the four axioms of service-dominant logic?**

5. How is the concept of service different than the concept of services?
6. How can a tangible good be a service? Explain.
7. Why are the IHIP characteristics of services normatively proper for tangible goods as well as intangible offerings?
8. Develop several examples of co-production in retailing (do not mention those in the text).
9. How can the retailer take better advantage of the fact that all customers are resource integrators?

LO 3 **What is customer centricity and how is it fostered in retailing?**

10. What does customer engagement mean in retailing?
11. Can dialogue with customers fully replace traditional retail advertising? Explain.
12. If value is uniquely defined and experienced by each customer how can a retailer develop an overall value proposition that appeals to all customers?
13. What is relieving? Give examples of how relieving can be a central part of a retailer's strategy.
14. What is enabling? Give examples of how enabling can be a central part of a retailer's strategy.

What is the central importance and imperative of continuous learning in retailing?

15. Define single, double, and triple-loop learning.
16. A retailer has an annual goal of increasing earnings per share by 10 percent and for the last two years it has achieved 8.1 percent and 7.7 percent this year. Explain how a retailer using single, double, and triple-loop learning may respond to these performance results.
17. Reread the Town Center USA feature ("Service Retailing") and identify which features of this shopping center might reflect triple-loop learning for retailers that locate in Town Center USA.
18. Several ways can be used to reframe a retailer's business model. What are they and which do you think is most relevant to retailers today?

Sample Test Questions

LO 1 During the "marketing with" era of retailing the typical retailer:

   a. concentrates its efforts on growing market share
   b. strives to improve gross margins
   c. puts more emphasis on promotion and advertising
   d. views itself as a support system for all its stakeholders
   e. concentrates primarily on working collaboratively with suppliers

LO 2 The service-dominant mindset includes the:

   a. view that goods are distinct from service(s)
   b. view that services are perishable
   c. view that goods can only be tangible and not intangible in any manner
   d. view that all people are resource integrators
   e. view that manufacturers are the primary source of value creation

LO 3 Regarding co-production and co-creation, they:

   a. are what all customers do with all retailers
   b. always occur simultaneously
   c. recognize value-in-use and co-creation go hand-in-hand
   d. position co-creation as optional; however, everyone is a co-producer
   e. are both key drivers of the contemporary retail competitive landscape

LO 4 Single-loop learning as practiced by retailers is:

   a. all that is necessary for high performance success
   b. focused on "doing things right"
   c. focused on "doing the right things"
   d. done primarily by small independent retailers
   e. a deeper form of learning than double-loop learning

Writing and Speaking Exercise

The Village Center is a neighborhood shopping center that was developed and opened in 1948. Henry Prescott recently purchased an Ace Hardware store that is located in the Village Center which is the also the location of Ginger's, a women's apparel store catering to the 50 and over market. Anne, who is Henry's partner, purchased Ginger's three years ago from Ginger Barnes who opened the store in 1979 and operated it for nearly 30 years before she decided to retire at the age of 84. The Village Center has a dozen specialty stores that are mostly locally owned and operated as well as a small grocery store that one of the great grandchildren of the founding family operates. In addition there are several service retailers that include a dry cleaner and laundry, chiropractic center, local café, barber shop, two beauticians, a dentist and a branch of Bank of America. In total there are 20 merchants that are all members of the Village Merchants Association. Although most of the retailers in the center do well, there has been some concern among the merchants that a new shopping center three times the size will be opening in six months only three miles away. This new center will have a 60,000-square foot modern Kroger supermarket, as well as a Home Depot, Best Buy, Old Navy, Dick's Sporting Goods, Pier One, PetSmart, Chipolte, Cheesecake Factory, In-and-Out Burger, and 15 other mostly national retailers as well as an eight-cinema movie theatre.

Prepare a presentation or memo to the Village Merchants Association about how the merchants could collaborate to create a more customer-centric shopping experience.

Retail Project

Carry a camera with you during the week and as you see an example of a retailer that does a good job at interfacing and connecting with customers to create a positive experience take a photo. Print these photos or put them into a PowerPoint presentation and describe how each represents an example of a positive experience. Also provide suggestions for how the retailer could reframe part of its business to improve the experience for shoppers.

Planning Your Own Entrepreneurial Retail Business

You launched your first entrepreneurial venture eight months ago, "The Curiosity Store," which is a toy store that has as its mission "to provide an engaging learning environment where children can develop their inquisitive and curious nature and hence their skills and talents." Sales have been growing each month but you estimate breakeven sales are $40,000 a month, and The Curiosity Store is still 25 percent below that level. You are especially concerned because the last two months sales growth has begun to slow. One of the things you had learned in the retail class you took at the local community college was that customer traffic was a key driver of retail success. At the same time you know that many children and their parents in the trade area you serve shop at Target and Walmart for toys or shop online. Perhaps one possibility for growing sales is to get more customers to shop the store and also do so more frequently. Consequently, you are considering selecting two-dozen toys that will be rented and not sold. The toys have a retail price that ranges from $36 to $78. For toys under $50 the one-week rental fee will be $5 and for toys above $50 the fee will be $7. Incidentally, your cost on the toys is approximately 50 percent of the retail price. When the toys are returned the customer will be offered the toy at the regular retail price less the one-week rental fee and then will receive another 10 percent discount if they purchase the toy. Should you adopt this new strategy?

Genuine Parts Company

Genuine Parts Company (GPC) founded in 1928, "is a service organization engaged in the distribution of automotive replacement parts, industrial replacement parts, office products, and electrical/electronic materials."[32] From annual sales in 1928 of $75,129 with a loss of $2,570, GPC has grown to annual sales of $12.5 billion and a net profit after taxes of $565 million in 2011. Importantly, with the exception of the loss experienced in 1928, its founding year, GPC has operated for 82 years without a loss, something few other businesses have achieved.

The automotive parts group, operating under the NAPA banner is the largest segment of business for GPC. NAPA is the brand for the National Automotive Parts Association and is a wholesaler-sponsored voluntary group (see Chapter 5). NAPA was formed in 1925 to facilitate the nationwide distribution of automotive parts in the United States. GPC is the largest NAPA member, owning approximately 95 percent of NAPA. GPC serves approximately 5,700 NAPA AUTO PARTS stores throughout the United States and approximately 690 wholesalers in Canada. In the United States, 950 of the stores are company-owned and the remainder independently operated. NAPA AUTO PARTS stores have over 435,000 parts available through GPC. Also GPC in conjunction with NAPA offers the store owner-operators a variety of services such as training, cataloging, marketing, and inventory management.

On January 1, 2012, GPC purchased 30 percent of the Exego Group (Exego) for approximately $150 million in cash.[33] Exego distributes after-market automotive parts and accessories. The corporate headquarters for Exego is Melbourne, Australia, and operates over 430 company-owned stores across Australia and New Zealand. GPC has an option to purchase an additional 70 percent of Exego over the next several years.

Regardless of whether GPC is operating in the United States, Canada, Australia, or New Zealand, they face a tough competitive market for automotive replacement parts. Competitors include the original equipment manufacturers, rebuild manufacturers and retail auto dealers, independent repair facilities, warehouse clubs, and specialty auto mass merchants, such as AutoZone and Advantage Auto Parts, and predictably there are many online providers of automotive parts.

Automobiles are becoming more sophisticated in terms of technology and especially electronics. Consequently, fewer people are repairing their own cars. In addition, most people are part of dual-income families, and do not have time to do auto repair for themselves. Thus there is solid growth in automotive repair service. In fact, NAPA Auto Care Centers are quite popular (http://www.napaautocare.com) as are Firestone Complete Auto Care Centers and Brake Max Auto Care centers. Of course, there are also many mom-and-pop auto care and repair centers, but due to the increasing cost of diagnostic equipment and facilities, these are generally in decline as chain retailers enter this business.

Although the financial performance of the automotive segment of GPC is relatively healthy (see the accompanying exhibit), there is some concern that to be competitive in the future, it is necessary to make its stores more contemporary. Although GPC cannot mandate to independent operators how to design and operate their stores, they can certainly provide them advice. And with nearly 1,000 company-operated NAPA stores, it can set the standard for others. As a recent college graduate and new employee at GPC, you have been asked to help work with others to design a store of the future; explicitly one not for next year but for 2020.

Genuine Automotive Parts: Automotive Segment Financial Performance[34] (2007–2011)

	2011	2010	2009	2008	2007
Proportion of Total Company Sales	48.7%	50.0%	52.0%	48.3%	49.0%
Net Sales (thousands)	$6,061,424	$5,608,101	$5,225,389	$5,321,536	$5,311,873
Operating Profit (thousands)	$467,806	$421,109	$387,945	$385,356	$431,180
Assets (thousands)	$2,895,748	$2,854,461	$2,825,693	$2,799,901	$2,785,619

Questions

1. Evaluate the financial performance of the automotive segment of GPC from 2007 to 2011.

2. Apply the concepts from service-dominant logic to developing a new store concept for 2020. Be sure to consider the role of triple-loop learning.

3. How should e-tailing and m-tailing be part of the 2020 store of the future?

PART 5: INTEGRATIVE CASE
LOWE'S AT THE CROSSROADS

Background

Lowe's has a retail heritage that dates back to 1921 when Lucius S. Lowe opened Lowe's North Wilkesboro Hardware in North Wilkesboro, North Carolina. During the 1950s, the company opened many other hardware stores, primarily in small towns in the southeastern United States, and went public in 1961. In 1962 the company operated 21 stores. Lowe's today continues to be publicly held and is the second largest home improvement retailer in the United States, behind Home Depot and ahead of Menards.

Lowe's was very successful not only at merchandising but also at financial management. It was one of the first retailers where senior management embraced the strategic profit model, described in Chapter 2, as a major financial planning and control tool. However, what the retailer did not embrace was the aggressive growth of Home Depot as it expanded at breakneck speed in the 1980s with its big-box format. Lowe's eventually got on the big-box home improvement bandwagon and grew rapidly with this new format during most of the last two decades.

As of February 3, 2012, Lowe's operated 1,745 stores which consisted of 1,712 stores across all 50 United States, 31 stores in Canada and two stores in Mexico. Lowe's also has its sights on Australia for future expansion and in 2009 completed a joint venture agreement with Woolworths Limited, an Australian retailer to jointly develop a chain of home improvement stores for the Australian market. Lowe's is a one-third owner of these joint-venture Australian stores.

Market Served

Lowe's serves customers in several market segments that include homeowners, renters, and commercial business customers. The homeowners and renters can be further divided into those that are more active do-it-yourself (DIY) versus those that is more do-it-for-me (DIFM). Of course, these are not categories *per se* but a continuum. Most of the customers on the commercial side are those who work in construction, repair/remodel, commercial and residential property management, and business maintenance professionals.[1]

Through market research, Lowe's has identified that there is a very active home improvement customer and this active customer visits Lowe's more frequently and spends more. Furthermore, these customers "seek quality tailored experiences, and are on the lookout for new ideas to improve homes,"[2] and also this customer is more discerning and demanding. Lowe's refers to this group of customers as "Creators," and Lowe's has decided to focus on their needs because if they meet the needs of these more discerning customers, they will meet or exceed the needs of other customers.

Lowe's sells and/or reaches customers through multiple channels. Lowe's is primarily a bricks-and-mortar retailer, but it also is an e-tailer with its website www.lowes.com. Lowes.com provides a 24/7 shopping experience and provides information to reduce the complexity of product decisions and to simplify home improvement projects. In addition to these two primary channels, Lowe's has on-site specialists who are available to retail and commercial business customers. These specialists can assist customers with selecting the products and services that are right for their project. Finally, Lowe's can reach customers and vice versa through two call centers: one in Wilkesboro, North Carolina, and another in Albuquerque, New Mexico. These call centers provide direct support to customers who contact Lowe's via phone, e-mail, or letter.

Value Proposition

Lowe's strives to be the first choice among customers for home improvement. The company recognizes that most customers want a full solution to their home improvement projects, and thus Lowe's offers to be a partner through the home improvement process and that includes inspiration, planning, completion, and enjoyment. Lowe's has a goal of executing better than competitors and to create a seamless and simple process for customers. Behind this goal are three principles (possibilities, support, and value) that are described as

> "*Possibilities means providing customers with inspiration and ideas for enhancing and maintaining their homes through innovative solutions. Support means being a trusted partner and resource whenever and wherever customers need us in the home improvement process. Value means offering competitive pries plus helping customers successfully accomplish their home improvement goals.*"[3]

Merchandise Offering

A Lowe's store will stock 40,000 or more items plus many other items available through special order. Lowe's has over 7,000 vendors. The merchandise categories include appliances, lawn and landscape, fashion electrical, lumber, building materials, paint, home fashions, storage and cleaning, rough plumbing, flooring, tools, seasonal living, millwork, hardware, fashion plumbing, nursery, and cabinets and countertops.

Lowe's offers a variety of popular brands across a wide spectrum of merchandise lines. Some of these brands include:

- Levolor (Blinds)
- AquaSource (Fashion bath products)
- Kohler (Fashion bath products)
- Moen (Fashion bath products)
- Delta (Fashion bath products)
- Dekor (Fashion bath products)
- Bel Air (Lighting)
- Sea Gull (Lighting)
- Kichler (Lighting)
- Juno (Lighting)
- Monte Carlo (Ceiling fans and accessories)
- Hunter (Ceiling fans and accessories)
- Bosch (Tools)
- Dewalt (Tools)
- Hitachi (Tools)
- Porter-Cable (Tools)
- Scotts (Lawn and garden)
- BlueHawk (Hardware)
- Schlage (Hardware)
- Kwikset (Hardware)
- Pella (Windows)
- Larson (Doors)
- Perfect Flame, Charbroil, and Masterforce (Grills)
- John Deere (Power equipment)
- Honda (Power equipment)
- Troy-Bilt (Power equipment)
- American Olean (Flooring)
- Emser (Flooring)
- Milliken (Flooring)
- Stainmaster (Flooring)
- Valspar (Paint)
- Olympic (Paint)
- Rust-Oleum (Paint)
- Minwax (Paint)
- Kraftmaid (Cabinets)
- Brainerd (Cabinets and hardware)
- Samsung (Appliances)
- Electrolux (Appliances)
- GE (Appliances)
- KitchenAid (Appliances)
- Maytag (Appliances)
- Whirlpool (Appliances)

Services Offering

Installed sales are an important part of Lowe's offering and in 2011 represented 6 percent of total sales. Installation is offered through independent contractors in areas such as flooring, millwork, and cabinets and countertops. Lowe's also offers extended protection plans and repair services. These plans extend the coverage of the manufacturer's warranty plans. Also Lowe's Authorized Service Repair Network allows a customer to contact Lowe's with an issue and get the problem diagnosed and the solution facilitated. Credit is another important service and consists of a proprietary credit card program for retail customers. This service also offers Lowe's consumer credit card holders with a 5 percent discount on everyday purchases, and with purchases over $299, a customer can choose between a 5 percent discount or no-interest financing. Lowe's also offers proprietary credit programs for commercial business customers. These programs also offer a 5 percent discount to commercial business customers.

Lowe's at a Crossroads

As the data in the following exhibit reveals over the last five years financial performance at Lowe's Companies has been disappointing. Sales are up a mere 4 percent and profits are down 35 percent. As a consequence over the last few years, Lowe's has been on a pathway of strategic renewal that consists of a transformational journey from being a "home improvement *retailer* to a home improvement *company*."[4] Robert Niblock, chairman of the Board, president and chief executive officer, believes that Lowe's needs to deliver better customer experiences, and this will foster long-term sales growth, profitability, and shareholder value. Critical to success is developing deeply engaged customers and employees.

During fall 2011, the firm introduced mylowes (www.mylowes.com), which is representative of how Lowe's wants to simplify the customer experience and make it more engaging. As of late April 2012, the site boasted a registered user base of over 5 million users.[5] The goal is to make managing, maintaining, and improving homes simpler including the ability for customers to create virtual versions of their home, view their purchase history, track previous home improvement decisions such as paint color formulations, access to product manuals, and the ability to set reminders for maintenance such as air filter changes.[6] Customers can also view more than 600 how-to videos at Lowes.com. Lowe's also recognizes it must embrace social media and has developed an internal social business network that allows employees to share information and knowledge with fellow employees.

Another webpage, which Lowe's hosts to enhance the customer experience, is Lowe's Creative Ideas (www.lowescreativeideas.com). This site provides many tips and ideas on home improvement projects for every area of the home and even provides a community for site members to share their home improvement projects with other's seeking ideas and information for home improvement projects. There is also a team of bloggers associated with the site who share their views and stories and encourage site user participation through comments and discussion of each blog post.

In addition to these new web pages, Lowe's has also placed Apple iPhone in the hands of employees, a move to allow employees to better serve customers in the store. Lowe's CIO Mike Brown stated that, "In all of my 27 years at Lowe's, iPhone will go down in history as being the most impactful device we have ever put in our employees' hands."[7] With this technology an employee is able to do things such as help a customer locate a hard to find item, check to see if another Lowe's location has available inventory of an out-of-stock item that a customer wants or even check out the Lowe's competitors' offerings and prices.

Despite these important steps, the transformational journey that Robert Niblock needs to lead is just beginning. In fact, it makes many employees and financial analysts a bit worried as Lowe's attempts to make the biggest transformation since when it transformed itself to a national big-box retail format 25 years ago.

Lowe's Companies' Selected Financial Data (2007–2011) (million of dollars)

Fiscal Year Ended	Net Sales	Net Profit (after tax)	Total Assets	Cost of Goods Sold	Inventory
January 31, 2008	$48,283	$2,809	$30,869	$31,556	$7,611
January 31, 2009	$48,230	$2,195	$32,686	$31,729	$8,209
January 29, 2010	$47,220	$1,783	$33,005	$30,757	$8,249
January 28, 2011	$48,815	$2,010	$33,699	$31,663	$8,321
February 3, 2012	$50,208	$1,839	$33,559	$32,858	$8,355

Source: Lowe's Companies Corporate Annual Reports for respective fiscal years.

Questions

1. What do you think is Lowe's biggest asset (resource) that it needs to draw on for its transformational journey?
2. Develop some ideas for how Lowe's can better deliver on its value proposition and meet its transformational goal.
3. From a household customer perspective how can Lowe's make home improvement projects simpler?
4. What do you see as the major barriers that confront Lowe's in its business transformation?

Note: This case is prepared for classroom instruction and not to illustrate or imply any evaluation of management practices at Lowe's Companies, Inc.

Answers to Sample Test Questions

Chapter 1

1. Answer c is the correct answer. Answer a is wrong because retailing includes credit card purchases. Answer b is wrong because retailing is different in each country. Answer d is wrong because retailing involves selling to the final consumer, not the wholesaler. Answer e is wrong because retailing is a valued sector of the economy, and it does increase economic growth.

2. Answer e is the correct answer as the other four answers were among the five ways of categorizing retailers listed in the chapter. The fifth way, which wasn't listed as a possible answer, was the Census Bureau's NAICS codes. The manager's gender should have no impact on a store's performance; besides, federal sex-discrimination laws would make this an illegal means for categorizing retailers.

3. Answer b is the correct answer. However, we would hope that a retailer possesses the other four possible characteristics as well as being a leader.

4. Answer c is the correct answer as the manager investigated both sources of supply and competition before making her decision.

Chapter 2

1. Answer b is the correct answer since market performance objectives seek to establish the retailer's dominance against the competition. Answers a and c are wrong because they are made-up terms. Answer d is wrong because societal performance is concerned with the broader issues of the world, and answer e is wrong because financial objectives are internally number oriented and dealing with profit or productivity.

2. Answer c is the correct answer. Answers a and b are wrong because price is the poorest way to differentiate yourself. Answer d is wrong because this action would restrict you from selling many of the top brands. Answer e is wrong because the customers really don't see planning, only the results of planning.

Chapter 3

1. Statement b is the correct answer. Americans do move about a dozen times in their lifetime. Answer a is wrong because some baby boomers are already in their 50s. Answer c is wrong because small markets still represent great opportunities for retailers if they satisfy the consumers' wants and needs. Answer d is wrong because the U.S. growth rate is expected to be about 1 percent, and answer e is wrong because the growth rate has been declining in recent years.

2. Item c is the correct answer: The boomerang effect is a relatively new phenomenon that describes something many of today's students will face that previous generations did not have to face—returning home to live with their parents. Statements a, b, and d are at least true statements, but they have nothing to do with the boomerang effect. Item e could be true or not at the time you are reading this, but it also has nothing to do with the question asked.

3. Item d is correct since discretionary income is disposable income (which is all personal income minus personal taxes) minus the money needed for necessities. Statement e is wrong because, as

we just noted, it is the definition of disposable income. The other three possible choices are just made-up definitions.

4. Item d is the correct answer. Answer a is incorrect because such resentment may have a long-term negative impact on the retailer's ability to regain that consumer as a customer. Item b is wrong because if the retailer is proactive with its customer-satisfaction program and responds quickly to the problem, the resentment can be overcome. Statement c is incorrect because most unhappy consumers don't make the retailer aware of their dissatisfaction. Therefore, it is up to the retailer to be vigilant, and monitor customer satisfaction. Item e is not correct either. Retailers must measure customer satisfaction on an ongoing basis and compare customer-service ratings against pre-established benchmarks.

Chapter 4

1. Answer b is correct. Item e is true in rare cases, but the question asked for what structure *most* retailers are involved in. Answer d, while it is a type of market structure, is wrong because retailers don't operate in environments with horizontal demand curves. Items a and c, while sounding good, are made-up terms.

2. Item d is the correct answer because this involves different types of retailers competing with each other with similar products. Answer b is wrong because *intratype* refers to cases in which the same types of retailers compete with each other, and Walmart is a general merchandise store and not a grocer. Item c (scrambled merchandising) can be used to describe what Walmart is doing, but this term does not refer to a type of competition. Answer e refers to a situation in which a retailer dominates a single line of merchandise, not many lines as Walmart is doing with its supercenters. Answer a is wrong because it is a made-up, nonsense term.

3. Answer d is correct. Some might say that the retail accordion theory could be used by saying that the small original hamburger stand expanded to the large McDonald's and Burger King franchises of today and will get smaller as customers rebel. However, this isn't entirely accurate. Nevertheless, we didn't include the accordion theory as a possible answer. Item b is

wrong because it describes a stage of growth that institutions pass through and not why they change formats. The other three possible answers are made-up terms.

4. Item d is the correct answer. Answer a is wrong because retailing is more diverse around the world, and answer b is wrong because success in one country doesn't guarantee success in other countries—witness the hypermarkets in the United States or the fact that Kmart, Sears, and JCPenney have abandoned their foreign expansion plans. Item c is wrong because the size of the average retailer is diverse. Item e is wrong because other countries have also developed successful new retailing formats—witness IKEA.

Chapter 5

1. Answer e is correct since facilitating institutions aid the supply chain by performing tasks that they are more capable of doing than the current supply chain members. Item a is wrong since some facilitating institutions may take possession of the merchandise but none of them take title. Item b is wrong since facilitating institutions do not take title to the goods, and answer c is wrong since they do not manage the supply chain and besides the goal of a supply chain is to minimize suboptimization since they cannot operate at 100-percent efficiency. Answer d is wrong since they cannot do all eight functions without taking title; besides, the text mentions that no one firm would want, or be able, to perform all eight functions.

2. Item e is the correct answer. Answers a and c are wrong since conventional channels, due to their loose alignment, are by their very nature not efficient. Item b is wrong because contractual channels are not loosely aligned since the contract directs each member's duties and responsibilities. Answer d is wrong since there is no feeling of partnership and cooperation in a conventional channel.

3. Answer b is correct. Item a is wrong even though it may be true that each member wants all the power, a supply-chain member is still dependent on the other members. Item c is wrong because no member can perform all eight functions. Answer d is wrong because a partnership should be committed to the life of the supply chain, and answer e is wrong because, if everybody wants to

work independently of each other, there would not be a supply chain in the first place.

4. Answer a is correct because, to be successful, all the channel members must work as a team. Item b is wrong because, in some cases, especially those involving a small retailer and a larger manufacturer, it doesn't make sense to have a retailer direct the channel. Answer e is wrong for the same basic reason; a small manufacturer would never tell Walmart how to act. Answer c is incorrect because at times coercion is necessary to make some members realize that their actions hurt other members. Item d is not the correct answer because it doesn't work to set an arbitrary profit level. Profit should be based on the tasks performed.

Chapter 6

1. Answer e is correct since the major price discrimination law, the Robinson-Patman Act, is meant to protect competition by making sure that retailers are treated fairly by suppliers. The possible other answers pertain to laws covering other situations.

2. Answer e is correct since it involved a deceitful action (using another firm's trademark) that caused damage to the other firm. Item a is wrong because it did not cause damage to the competitor. Item b is wrong because it was not deceitful—the retailer told the truth. Answer c is wrong because it involves deceptive pricing. Answer d is perfectly legal since you did not do anything wrong.

3. Item a is the correct answer since an implied warranty of fitness for a particular purpose arises when the customer relies on the retailer to assist or make the selection of goods to serve a particular purpose. Answer b is wrong because an implied warranty of merchantability means that the retailer implies that the merchandise is fit for the ordinary purpose for which the product is usually purchased. Answer c is wrong because it is a made-up answer. Answers d and e are wrong because no verbal or written guarantee was mentioned in the question.

4. Answer b is correct since the purchase of the cat food was tied to the purchase of the unpopular product—litter. The other answers have nothing to do with the question.

5. Item b is the correct answer. While there are federal laws governing franchise operations, the most stringent laws are usually state laws since the state government wants to protect its citizens and locally owned franchise businesses, as well as voters, from the unfair practices of out-of-state franchisors.

6. Answer a is correct since it is a merchandising decision regarding the success or failure of merchandise. The other four answers pertain to the ethical decisions discussed in the chapter.

Chapter 7

1. Answer c is correct. It is not essential that a market segment create high sales, but it should be profitable. Answers a, b, d, and e are all criteria used to successfully reach a target market and thus are incorrect answers.

2. Item a is the correct answer. Since freestanding retailers are not part of a shopping center or CBD, they do not have direct competition. Answer b is not correct since it is an advantage of retailers in shopping centers. Item c is incorrect since freestanding retailers have more difficulty in attracting customers for the initial visit. Answer d is incorrect because freestanding retailers are not able to share advertising costs with other retailers as in a shopping center. Answer e is incorrect because freestanding stores can be either leased or purchased.

3. Item e is the correct answer. Answers a, b, c, and d are all purposes of geographical information systems, thus any one of these answers is not the single best choice.

4. Answer b is correct. The three steps presented are exactly as discussed in the textbook. Item a is wrong because the first step is incorrect, answer c is wrong because the second step is incorrect, answer d is wrong because all three steps are incorrect, and answer e is wrong because the third step is incorrect.

5. Answer e is correct. Items a and b by themselves are not the best answer because both are needed to do a site analysis. Answers c and d are incorrect because they are irrelevant to site analysis.

6. Item c is correct because alternative investments available to the retailer should not be a consideration in the selection of a site. Answers a, b, d, and e are incorrect because they are all important considerations in selecting the best site.

Chapter 8

1. Answer b is correct since current liabilities are listed on the balance sheet but are not included in the merchandise budget. The other answers are all included in the merchandise budget.
2. Answer d is correct since the income statement is a summary of the sales and expenses for a given time period. Item a is wrong because an expense report, while not mentioned in the chapter, would cover only expenses. Item b is wrong because even though the inventory valuation will affect the retailer's expenses, it also does not include sales. Answer c is wrong because the cash flow statement deals with only the inflow and outflow of cash, and e is wrong because gross margin only considers sales and cost of goods sold and does not include operating expenses.
3. Answer c is correct since the cost ($120,000) divided by sales ($200,000) is 0.6.

Chapter 9

1. Answer c is correct. Both product purchases and markdowns impact dollar-merchandise planners.
2. Item a is the correct answer since $425,000 \times 1/2[1 + (\$170,000/\$142,000)] = \$466,901$. Answer e would be correct if the question is asked for the basic stock method, not the PVM. Item d is the average stock for the season but not the correct answer. The other two answers are made-up numbers.
3. Since the key feature of OTB is that it can be determined at anytime during the merchandise period, item d is the correct answer. The other answers are wrong because they are time-specific.
4. Answer c is correct; the other four answers are the constraints listed in the text.
5. Answer b is correct since it best describes what is involved in a vendor-profitability analysis statement, which was defined in the text as a "record of all purchases you made last year, the discounts granted you by the vendor, transportation charges paid, the original markup, markdowns, and the season-ending gross margin on that vendor's merchandise." Answer a is wrong because it is about the vendor's financial statements, which are seldom provided to retailers. Answer c is wrong because it deals with new lines of merchandise, and answer d is wrong because it deals with the retailer's line of credit granted by the vendor. Answer e is wrong because it covers only one factor (discounts) covered by the vendor-profitability analysis statement.
6. Item b is the correct answer. Answer a is wrong because it describes a noncumulative-quantity discount, and c is wrong because it assumes the discount period starts with the beginning of the year, something that is not always true. Item d is wrong because it describes a different type of discount. Answer e is wrong because it is based on a specific quantity that may be too high or too low given the circumstances of the sale.
7. Answer b is correct since it is the combination of vendor and retail employees that is most often involved in collusion. Answers a and d are wrong because customers are not involved in vendor collusion. Items c and e are wrong because even though the sales representative or accountant may be involved, the people involved with delivery person must also be included.

Chapter 10

1. Answer c is correct since the retailer's pricing objectives must be interactive with all the other decision areas of the firm. Item a is incorrect since pricing cannot be independent of these other decision areas, and b is incorrect since pricing cannot be separate from these other areas. Answer d is wrong because the retailer's pricing objectives should not be in competition with these other areas. Answer e is incorrect since multifaceted has nothing to do with the question.
2. Item c is the correct answer since in this case the retailer offered the same merchandise to different customers at different prices. Answer e is incorrect because variable pricing means that the prices for all customers may change as differences in either demand or costs occur. Nevertheless, all customers will pay the same price unless the retailer also uses a flexible policy. Answer a is wrong because there is no such policy as "two-price." Answer b is incorrect because, with customary pricing, the retailer seeks to maintain the same price for an item over an extended period of time. Item d is incorrect because leader pricing involves taking a popular item and offering it for sale to everybody as a means of drawing these consumers into a store.

3. Answer a is correct since markup on selling price is SP − C/SP [($45 − 25)/$45 = 44.4%]. Answer b is incorrect since the question asked for markup on selling price, and 80 percent is the markup on cost. The other answers are merely made-up numbers.

4. This question was chosen because many students get confused about reduction percentage. Answer c is correct since reduction percentage is the amount of the reduction ($29.99 − $19.99= $10) divided by net sales ($19.99). Answer a is the markdown percentage, which is the amount of the reduction divided by the original selling price ($10/$29.99). The other answers are made-up numbers, although e is the result of dividing the new selling price by the original selling price.

Chapter 11

1. Answer e is the correct answer. Even though the retailer may have a low net worth, this should not be taken into consideration when developing a promotional strategy. After all, the objectives will still be the same. The other four alternatives (credit customers, price level, merchandise, and building and fixtures) are managerial decisions that must be integrated into the retailer's overall plan.

2. The correct answer is a. Institutional, or long-term, advertising tries to create a positive store image and provide public service. Answer b lists the objectives for short-term, or promotional, advertising. Answer c lists the two other types of promotion, and d lists how a retailer might seek to obtain short-term results. Item e lists two other topics covered in this chapter that have nothing to do with the question.

3. Answer e is correct as all four of the alternatives belong as part of an advertisement's objectives.

4. Answer e is correct. Premiums are the extra items offered to customers when they purchased the promoted product. In a limited number of cases, when premiums could be joint-sponsored sales promotions (answer a), such promotions would not be beneficial to the retailer since the consumer could purchase the product from another retailer. The other three answers (b, c, and d) are other forms of promotion.

Chapter 12

1. Answer c is correct since the text explained that a transient customer is an individual who visits a retailer and finds the service level below expectations or the product out of stock. This transient or temporary customer will seek to find a retailer with the level of customer service he or she feels is appropriate. Answer a is wrong because, even though the dictionary defines transient as short-lived or not long-lasting, the term does not refer to length of time spent shopping. The other choices are wrong because they have nothing to do with a transient customer.

2. Answer e is correct since merchandise availability is a transaction service that helps build the relationship with the customer, thus making answers b and d wrong. Answers a and c are wrong because personal shopping is a service, not a cost, despite the fact that there might be some additional cost involved.

3. Item d is wrong because, as shown in Exhibit 12.5, the other alternatives are factors that must be considered when determining the service levels to offer.

4. Answer b is correct since good results are dependent not only on the salesperson's characteristics but also on how satisfied the salesperson is with the job and how the sales job was designed. Retail selling jobs should be designed to have high levels of variety (c), autonomy (d), task identity (e), and feedback from supervisors and customers (a).

5. Item e is the correct answer because once the approach has been completed, the salesperson is in a position to present the merchandise and sales message correctly. The key to the presentation, however, is to get the customer to want to buy your product or service. Therefore, you must have the right price range of products to show the customer. Answer a is wrong because, if the price is too high or too low, the sale will be already lost. Answer b is wrong because you cannot select the right product unless you know the right price. Answer c is wrong because the greeting occurs in the approach stage, and d is wrong because helping the customer decide is the last step of the presentation.

6. Answer a is correct. The audit isn't an attempt to learn what the customers want, rather it concentrates on the facts of their shopping experience. Answers b, c, and d concern that shopping experience.

Chapter 13

1. Answer b is the correct answer since the two primary objectives around which all activities,

functions, and goals in the store revolve are store image and space productivity. Alternatives c and d have two worthwhile activities (merchandise presentation and traffic control; opportunities for impulse buying and shelf management) but by themselves they will not produce high-performance results. Answers a and e are wrong because, while its activities are also good traits, sales management (a) and maintaining market share (e) are not objectives of the store environment.

2. Answer c is correct since the store's layout and design must allow the store to be shopable and the merchandise to be effectively presented. Answer a is wrong because even though the retailer would like all the customers to see every high-profit items, this is not always possible, and nothing was said about presentation of the merchandise. Item b is obviously wrong since it would be foolish to give offices, the back room, wall, and aisles as much space as the selling floor since this is not where sales are generated. Answer d is wrong because why would a retailer care to have rapid replacement in a low-turnover area? Answer e is wrong because retailers today want to minimize the space given to back rooms.

3. Answer a is the correct answer since the method of merchandise presentation has an impact on the store's image and space productivity. Answer b is obviously wrong since it would be foolish to hire a psychologist to do the store's displays. Item c is wrong because, by shopping effectively, the customer might not make any impulse purchases. Answer d is wrong because even though social factors may influence our behavior, this alternative has nothing to do with the question. Answer e is another obviously wrong choice because it would be foolish for this to be done.

4. Answer b is correct since store design is most responsible for developing a store image, which the other four alternatives are concerned with doing. Answer b, however, would not increase the productivity of the store.

5. Answer e is correct since visual communications is concerned with the message within the store, which is covered by the other four possible answers, and not those external to the store.

Chapter 14

1. Answer d is correct. Answers a and b are incorrect because "marketing with" is not directly tied to financial or market performance objectives; answer c is incorrect because with "marketing with" there is less emphasis on promotion and advertising; answer e is incorrect because although working collaboratively with suppliers is part of the "marketing with" philosophy, it is not the primary concentration.

2. Answer d is correct. Answer a, service-dominant logic, does not view goods as distinct from services but that all goods are delivery mechanisms for service. Answer b is incorrect because many services are remembered and especially if the service experience was especially positive or negative. Answer c is incorrect because all goods create intangible impressions and also the brand which is part of the good is intangible. Answer e is incorrect because only the beneficiary can create value as they uniquely experience the market offering.

3. Answer c is correct. Answer a is incorrect because co-production is optional. Answer b is incorrect because co-production and co-creation do not have to occur simultaneously. Answer d is incorrect because co-creation is not optional but co-production is optional. Answer e is incorrect because neither is a key driver of the contemporary retail competitive landscape.

4. Answer b is correct. Answer a is incorrect as there are many factors that lead to high performance success in retailing. Answer c is incorrect because "doing the right things" is referred to as double-loop learning. Answer d is incorrect because single-loop learning is common among both small and large retailers. Answer e is incorrect because double-loop learning is a deeper form of learning.

GLOSSARY

100-percent location   Is when there is no better use for a site than the retail store that is being planned for that site.

80-20 report   Shows how much sales the top 20% of merchandise items generate in terms of sales. Usually the top 20% generate at least 80% of sales.

A

above-market pricing policy   Is a policy where retailers establish high prices because nonprice factors are more important to their target market than price.

accounts and/or notes receivable   Are amounts that customers owe the retailer for goods and services.

accounts payable   Are amounts owed to vendors for goods and services.

active information gathering   Occurs when consumers proactively gather information.

administered vertical marketing channels   Exist when one of the channel members takes the initiative to lead the channel by applying the principles of effective interorganizational management.

advertising   Is paid, nonpersonal communication through various media by business firms, nonprofit organizations, and individuals who are in some way identified in the advertising message and who hope to inform or persuade members of a particular audience; includes communication of products, services, institutions, and ideas.

advertising effectiveness   Is the extent to which the advertising has produced the result desired.

advertising efficiency   Is concerned with whether the advertising result was achieved with the minimum financial expenditure.

affordable method   Is a technique for budgeting advertising in which all the money a retailer can afford to spend on advertising in a given time period becomes the advertising budget.

ambience   Is the overall feeling or mood projected by a store through its aesthetic appeal to human senses.

anchor stores   Are the stores in a shopping center that are the most dominant and are expected to draw customers to the shopping center.

anticipation   Allows the retailer to pay the invoice in advance of the end of the cash discount period and earn an extra discount.

asset   Is anything of value that is owned by the retail firm.

asset turnover   Is total sales divided by total assets and shows how many dollars of sales a retailer can generate on an annual basis with each dollar invested in assets.

B

bait-and-switch advertising   Advertising or promoting a product at an unrealistically low price to serve as "bait" and then trying to "switch" the customer to a higher-priced product.

bait-and-switch pricing   Advertising or promoting a product at an unrealistically low price to serve as "bait" and then trying to "switch" the customer to a higher-priced product.

basic stock method (BSM) Is a technique for planning dollar inventory investments and allows for a base stock level plus a variable amount of inventory that will increase or decrease at the beginning of each sales period in the same dollar amount as the period's expected sales.

battle of the brands Occurs when retailers have their own products competing with the manufacturer's products for shelf space and control over display location.

below-market pricing policy Is a policy that regularly discounts merchandise from the established market price in order to build store traffic and generate high sales and gross margin dollars per square foot of selling space.

boomerang effect The recent trend of children returning to live with their parents after having already moved out.

breakeven point Is where total revenues equal total expenses and the retailer is making neither a profit nor a loss.

bricks-and-mortar retailers Retailers that operate out of a physical building.

bulk or capacity fixture Is a display fixture that is intended to hold the bulk of merchandise without looking as heavy as a long, straight rack of merchandise.

Buying The retailing career path whereby one uses quantitative tools to develop appropriate buying plans for the store's merchandise lines.

C

cash discount Is a discount offered to the retailer for the prompt payment of bills.

category killer Is a retailer that carries such a large amount of merchandise in a single category at such good prices that it makes it impossible for customers to walk out without purchasing what they need, thus "killing" the competition.

category management (CM) Is a process of managing all SKUs within a product category and involves the simultaneous management of price, shelf-space, merchandising strategy, promotional efforts, and other elements of the retail mix within the category based on the firm's goals, the changing environment, and consumer behavior.

central business district (CBD) Usually consists of an unplanned shopping area around the geographic point at which all public transportation systems converge; it is usually in the center of the city and often where the city originated historically.

channel Used interchangeably with supply chain.

channel advisor or channel captain Is the institution (manufacturer, wholesaler, broker, or retailer) in the marketing channel that is able to plan for and get other channel institutions to engage in activities they might not otherwise engage in. Large store retailers are often able to perform the role of channel captain.

channel surfing when the customer gets needed product information within a store and then chooses to order the product online for a lower price or to avoid paying state sales tax.

closing the sale Is the action the salesperson takes to bring a potential sale to its natural conclusion.

co-creation Everyone who purchases a tangible or intangible market offering and uses the offering is viewed as a co-creator of value. With a service-dominant orientation, value is always viewed as being created in the use of things (tangible or intangible).

coercive power Is based on B's belief that A has the capability to punish or harm B if B doesn't do what A wants.

comp shopping When an employee of one retailer goes into another retailer and checks prices on a select few items to see how competitive they are on a local basis.

confidential vendor analysis Is identical to the vendor profitability analysis but also provides a three year financial summary as well as the names, titles, and negotiating points of all the vendor's sales staff.

consignment (pay from scan) Is when the vendor retains the ownership of the goods and usually establishes the selling price; it is paid only when goods are sold.

contests and sweepstakes Are sales promotion techniques in which customers have a chance of winning a special prize based on entering a contest in which the entrant competes with others, or a sweepstakes in which all entrants have an equal chance of winning a prize.

contractual vertical marketing channels Use a contract to govern the working relationship between channel members and include wholesaler-sponsored voluntary groups, retailer-owned cooperatives, and franchised retail programs.

conventional marketing channel Is one in which each channel member is loosely aligned with the others and takes a short-term orientation.

conversion rate Is the percentage of shoppers that enter the store that are converted into purchasers.

co-production Is the active involvement of the customer in the retailer's core activities. When this occurs, the customer is a co-producer of service.

corporate vertical marketing channels   Exist where one channel institution owns multiple levels of distribution and typically consists of either a manufacturer that has integrated vertically forward to reach the consumer or a retailer that has integrated vertically backward to create a self-supply network.

cost method   Is an inventory valuation technique that provides a book valuation of inventory based solely on the retailer's cost of merchandise including freight.

cost of goods sold   Is the cost of merchandise that has been sold during the period.

cost per thousand method (CPM)   Is a technique used to evaluate advertisements in different media based on cost. The cost per thousand is the cost of the advertisement divided by the number of people viewing it, which is then multiplied by 1,000.

cost per thousand—target market (CPM-TM)   Is a technique used to evaluate advertisements in different media based on cost. The cost per thousand per target market is the cost of the advertisement divided by the number of people in the target market viewing it, which is then multiplied by 1,000.

coupons   Are a sales promotion tool in which the shopper is offered a price discount on a specific item if the retailer is presented with the appropriate coupon at time of purchase.

coverage   Is the theoretical maximum number of consumers in the retailer's target market that can be reached by a medium and not the number actually reached.

cue   Refers to any object or phenomenon in the environment that is capable of eliciting a response.

culture   Is the buffer that people have created between themselves and the raw physical environment and includes the characteristics of the population, man-made objects, and mobile physical structures.

cumulative quantity discount   Is a discount based on the total amount purchased over a period of time.

cumulative reach   Is the reach that is achieved over a period of time.

current assets   Are assets that can be easily converted into cash within a relatively short period of time (usually a year or less).

current liabilities   Are short-term debts that are payable within a year.

current ratio   Current assets divided by current liabilities.

customary pricing   Is a policy in which the retailer sets prices for goods and services and seeks to maintain those prices over an extended period of time.

customer relationship retailing   An integrated information system which uses relevant information about the customer to predict future behavior and customer manage relationships.

customer satisfaction   Occurs when the total shopping experience of the customer has been met or exceeded.

customer service   Consists of all those activities performed by the retailer that influence (1) the ease with which a potential customer can shop or learn about the store's offering, (2) the ease with which a transaction can be completed once the customer attempts to make a purchase, and (3) the customer's satisfaction with the transaction.

customer theft   Is also known as shoplifting and occurs when customers or individuals disguised as customers steal merchandise from the retailer's store.

customer-centric   Putting the customer at the center of the economic and social system within which the retailer operates.

D

deceptive advertising   Occurs when a retailer makes false or misleading advertising claims about the physical makeup of a product, the benefits to be gained by its use, or the appropriate uses for the product.

deceptive pricing   Occurs when a misleading price is used to lure customers into the store and then hidden charges are added; or the item advertised may be unavailable.

demand density   Is the extent to which the potential demand for the retailer's goods and services is concentrated in certain census tracts, ZIP code areas, or parts of the community.

demonstrations and sampling   Are in-store presentations with the intent of reducing the consumer's perceived risk of purchasing a product.

density   The best combination of resources that are mobilized to a time and place for a particular individual to solve their problem(s) or for them to pursue opportunities at an optimal value or cost result.

depth   Is the average number of stock-keeping units within each brand of the merchandise line.

direct supply chain   Is the channel that results when a manufacturer sells its goods directly to the final consumer or end user.

discretionary income Is disposable income minus the money needed for necessities to sustain life.

disposable income Is personal income less personal taxes.

diverter Is an unauthorized member of a channel who buys and sells excess merchandise to and from authorized channel members.

divertive competition Occurs when retailers intercept or divert customers from competing retailers.

domain disagreements Occur when there is disagreement about which member of the marketing channel should make decisions.

double-loop learning A double source of feedback. Feedback is not only on "are we doing things right" but also on, "are we doing the right things." The later gets at are we targeting the right goals.

drive Refers to a motivating force that directs behavior.

drop-ship Is a technique wherein the retailer does not hold inventory, but instead transmits customer orders and shipping details to either the manufacturer or a wholesaler, who then ships the goods directly to the customer.

dual distribution Occurs when a manufacturer sells to independent retailers and also through its own retail outlets.

dwell time Refers to the amount of time a consumer must spend waiting to complete a purchase.

E

ease of access Refers to the consumer's ability to easily and quickly find a retailer's Web site in cyberspace.

eminent domain law Is the inherent power of the government to seize private property without the owner's consent in order to benefit the community.

employee theft Occurs when employees of the retailer steal merchandise where they work.

enabling The use of tools, people or other aids that allow people to perform service for themselves or others, and allows someone to do things he or she might have not been able to otherwise.

endcaps The display of products placed at the end of an aisle in a store.

end-of-month (EOM) dating Allows the retailer to take a cash discount and the full payment period to begin on the first day of the following month instead of on the invoice date.

engagement Is about how intensely the customers interface, experience, and connect to various other actors in the economic system to include retailers.

ethics Is a set of rules for human moral behavior.

exclusive distribution Means only one retailer is used to cover a trading area.

expertise power Is based on B's perception that A has some special knowledge.

explicit code of ethics Consists of a written policy that states what is ethical and unethical behavior.

expressed warranties Are either written or verbalized agreements about the performance of a product and can cover all attributes of the merchandise or only one attribute.

extended problem solving Occurs when the consumer recognizes a problem but has decided on neither the brand nor the store.

extra dating (EX) Allows the retailer extra or interest-free days before the period of payment begins.

F

facilitating marketing institutions Are those that do not actually take title but assist in the marketing process by specializing in the performance of certain marketing functions.

feature fixture Is a display that draws special attention to selected features (e.g., color, shape, or style) of merchandise

FIFO Stands for first in, first out and values inventory based on the assumption that the oldest merchandise is sold before the more recently purchased merchandise.

financial leverage Is total assets divided by net worth or owners' equity and shows how aggressive the retailer is in its use of debt.

flexible pricing Is a policy that encourages offering the same products and quantities to different customers at different prices.

floor plan Is a schematic that shows where merchandise and customer service departments are located, how customers circulate through the store, and how much space is dedicated to each department.

franchise Is a form of licensing by which the owner of a product, service, or business method (the franchisor) obtains distribution through affiliated dealers (franchisees).

free merchandise Is a discount whereby merchandise is offered in lieu of price concessions.

free on board (FOB) destination   Is a method of charging for transportation in which the vendor pays for all transportation costs and the buyer takes title on delivery.

free on board (FOB) factory   Is a method of charging for transportation where the buyer assumes title to the goods at the factory and pays all transportation costs from the vendor's factory.

free on board (FOB) shipping point   Is a method of charging for transportation in which the vendor pays for transportation to a local shipping point where the buyer assumes title and then pays all further transportation costs.

free-flow layout   Is a type of store layout in which fixtures and merchandise are grouped into freeflowing patterns on the sales floor.

freeriding   Is when a consumer seeks product information, usage instructions, and sometimes even warranty work from a full-service store but then, armed with the brand's model number, purchases the product from a limited service discounter or over the Internet.

freestanding retailer   Generally locates along major traffic arteries and does not have any adjacent retailers to share traffic.

frequency   Is the average number of times each person who is reached is exposed to an advertisement during a given time period.

G

geographic information system (GIS)   Is a computerized system that combines physical geography with cultural geography.

goal incompatibility   Occurs when achieving the goals of either the supplier or the retailer would hamper the performance of the other.

goodwill   Is an intangible asset, usually based on customer loyalty, that a retailer pays for when buying an existing business.

gray marketing   Is when branded merchandise flows across national boundaries and through unauthorized channels.

gross margin   Is the difference between net sales and cost of goods sold.

gross margin return on inventory (GMROI)   Is gross margin divided by average inventory at cost; alternatively, it is the gross margin percent multiplied by net sales.

gross sales   Are the retailer's total sales including sales for cash or for credit.

gross-margin percentage   A measure of profitability derived by dividing gross margin by net sales.

H

habitual problem solving   Occurs when the consumer relies on past experiences and learns to convert the problem into a situation requiring less thought. The consumer has a strong preference for the brand to buy and the retailer from which to purchase it.

high–low pricing   Involves the use of high every day prices and low leader "specials" on items typically featured in weekly ads.

high-margin/highturnover retailer   Is one that operates on a high gross margin percentage and a high rate of inventory turnover.

high-margin/lowturnover retailer   Is one that operates on a high gross margin percentage and a low rate of inventory turnover.

high-performance retailers   Are those retailers that produce financial results substantially superior to the industry average.

high-quality service   Is the type of service that meets or exceeds customers' expectations.

home page   Is the introductory or first material viewers see when they access a retailer's Internet site. It is the equivalent of a retailer's storefront in the physical world.

horizontal cooperative advertising   Occurs when two or more retailers band together to share the cost of advertising usually in the form of a joint promotion of an event or sale that would benefit both parties.

horizontal price fixing   Occurs when a group of competing retailers (or other channel members operating at a given level of distribution) establishes a fixed price at which to sell certain brands of products.

I

IHIP characteristics   Intangible, heterogeneous, inseparable and perishable.

impact   Refers to how strong an impression an advertisement makes and how well it ultimately leads to a purchase.

implicit code of ethics   Is an unwritten but well understood set of rules or standards of moral responsibility.

implied warranty of fitness   Is a warranty that implies that the merchandise is fit for a particular purpose and arises when the customer relies on the retailer to assist or make the selection of goods to serve a particular purpose.

implied warranty of merchantability   Is made by every retailer when the retailer sells goods and implies that the merchandise sold is fit for the ordinary purpose for which such goods are typically used.

income statement   Is a financial statement that provides a summary of the sales and expenses for a given time period, usually a month, quarter, season, or year.

index of retail saturation (IRS)   Is the ratio of demand for a product (households in the geographic area multiplied by annual retail expenditures for a particular line of trade per household) divided by available supply (the square footage of retail facilities of a particular line of trade in the geographic area).

institutional advertising   Is a type of advertising in which the retailer attempts to gain long-term benefits by promoting and selling the store itself rather than the merchandise in the store.

in-store displays   Are promotional fixtures of displays that seek to generate traffic, highlight individual items, and encourage impulse buying.

intensive distribution   Means that all possible retailers are used in a trade area.

intertype competition   Occurs when two or more retailers of a different type, as defined by NAICS codes in the Census of Retail Trade, compete directly by attempting to sell the same merchandise lines to the same households.

intratype competition   Occurs when two or more retailers of the same type, as defined by NAICS codes in the Census of Retail Trade, compete directly with each other for the same households.

inventory turnover   Refers to the number of times per year, on average, that a retailer sells its inventory.

L

leader pricing   Is when a high-demand item is priced low and is heavily advertised in order to attract customers into the store.

legitimate power   Is based on A's right to influence B, or B's belief that B should accept A's influence.

liability   Is any legitimate financial claim against the retailer's assets.

LIFO   Stands for last in, first out and values inventory based on the assumption that the most recently purchased merchandise is sold first and the oldest merchandise is sold last.

limited problem solving   Occurs when the consumer has a strong preference for either the brand or the store, but not both.

logistics inventory   Physical inventory that is in the logistics network.

logistics network   Consists of all the firms throughout the supply chain that are involved in moving physical inventory from its initial source to the retail store.

long-term liabilities   Are debts that are due in a year or longer.

loop layout   Is a type of store layout in which a major customer aisle begins at the entrance, loops through the store—usually in the shape of a circle, square, or rectangle—and then returns the customer to the front of the store.

loss leader   Is an extreme form of leader pricing where an item is sold below a retailer's cost.

low-margin/highturnover retailer   Is one that operates on a low gross margin percentage and a high rate of inventory turnover.

low-margin/lowturnover retailer   Is one that operates on a low gross margin percentage and a low rate of inventory turnover.

loyalty programs   Are a form of sales promotion program in which buyers are rewarded with special rewards, which other shoppers are not offered, for purchasing often from the retailer.

M

markdown   Is any reduction in the price of an item from its initially established price.

markdown money   Markdown money is what retailers charge to suppliers when merchandise does not sell at what the vendor intended.

market segmentation   Is the dividing of a heterogeneous consumer population into smaller, more homogeneous groups based on their characteristics.

market share   Is the retailer's total sales divided by total market sales.

markup   Is the selling price of the merchandise less its cost, which is equivalent to gross margin.

merchandise budget   Is a plan of projected sales for an upcoming season, when and how much merchandise is to be purchased, and what markups and reductions will likely occur.

merchandise line   Is a group of products that are closely related because they are intended for the same end use (all televisions); are sold to the same customer group (juniormiss clothing); or fall within a given price range (budget women's wear).

merchandise management   Is the analysis, planning, acquisition, handling, and control of the merchandise investments of a retail operation.

merchandising   Is the planning and control of the buying and selling of goods and services to help the retailer realize its objectives.

metropolitan statistical areas (MSA)   Are freestanding urban areas with populations in excess of 50,000.

micromarketing   Is the tailoring of merchandise in each store to the preferences of its neighborhood.

microretailing   Occurs when a chain store retailer operating over a wide geographic area, usually nationally, tailors its merchandise and services in each store to the needs of the immediate trading area.

middle-of-month (MOM) dating   Allows the retailer to take a cash discount and the full payment period to begin on the middle of the month.

mission statement   Is a basic description of the fundamental nature, rationale, and direction of the firm.

monopolistic competition   Occurs when the products offered are different, yet viewed as substitutable for each other and the sellers recognize that they compete with sellers of these different products.

multiple-unit pricing   Occurs when the price of each unit in a multiple-unit package is less than the price of each unit if it were sold individually.

mutual trust   Occurs when both the retailer and its supplier have faith that each will be truthful and fair in their dealings with the other.

N

negotiation   Is the process of finding mutually satisfying solutions when the retail buyer and vendor have conflicting objectives.

neighborhood business district (NBD)   Is a shopping area that evolves to satisfy the convenience-oriented shopping needs of a neighborhood, generally contains several small

stores (with the major retailer being a supermarket or a variety store), and is located on a major artery of a residential area.

net profit   Is operating profit plus or minus other income or expenses.

net profit margin   Is the ratio of net profit (after taxes) to total sales and shows how much profit a retailer makes on each dollar of sales after all expenses and taxes have been met.

net sales   Are gross sales less returns and allowances.

net worth (owner's equity)   Is total assets less total liabilities.

noncumulative quantity discount   Is a discount based on a single purchase.

noncurrent assets   Are those assets that cannot be converted to cash in a short period of time (usually 12 months) in the normal course of business.

nonstore-based retailers   Intercept customers at home, at work, or at a place other than a store where they might be susceptible to purchasing.

O

odd pricing   Is the practice of setting retail prices that end in the digits 5, 8, 9—such as $29.95, $49.98, or $9.99.

off-price retailers   Sell products at a discount but do not carry certain brands on a continuous basis. They carry those brands they can buy from manufacturers at closeout or deep onetime discount prices.

oligopolistic competition   Occurs when relatively few sellers, or many small firms who follow the lead of a few larger firms, offer essentially homogeneous products and any action by one seller is expected to be noticed and reacted to by the other sellers.

one-price policy   Is a policy that establishes that the retailer will charge all customers the same price for an item.

one-way exclusive dealing arrangement   Occurs when the supplier agrees to give the retailer the exclusive right to sell the supplier's product in a particular trade area.

on-shelf merchandising   Is the display of merchandise on counters, racks, shelves, and fixtures throughout the store.

operand resources   Those that humans act upon or do something to in order to create effects. For instance, fabric can be cut and sewn to create a garment. Operand resources by their static and tangible nature can be exhausted or depleted. Incidentally, they are also the resources that are on the retailer's balance sheet.

operant resources Those resources that can act on and produce effects. These resources, rather than being depleted, can be expanded and grown. They include such things as employee skills and knowledge, the core competences of an organization or its dynamic capabilities.

operating expenses Are those expenses that a retailer incurs in running the business other than the cost of the merchandise.

operating profit Is gross margin less operating expenses.

operations management Deals with activities directed at maximizing the efficiency of the retailer's use of resources. It is frequently referred to as day-today management.

optional stock list Is a merchandising method in which each store in a retail chain is given the flexibility to adjust its merchandise mix to local tastes and demands.

organized crime theft Is when professional thieves steal merchandise when it is in transit to the store, or in the store.

other income or expenses Includes income or expense items that the firm incurs which are not in the course of its normal retail operations.

outshopping Outshopping occurs when a household travels outside their community of residence or uses the Internet to shop in another community.

overstored Is a condition in a community where the number of stores in relation to households is so large that to engage in retailing is usually unprofitable or marginally profitable.

P

palming off Occurs when a retailer represents that merchandise is made by a firm other than the true manufacturer.

passive information gathering Is the receiving and processing of information regarding the existence and quality of merchandise, services, stores, shopping, convenience, pricing, advertising, and any other factors that a consumer might consider in making a purchase.

penetration Is a pricing objective in which price is set at a low level in order to penetrate the market and establish a loyal customer base.

percentage variation method (PVM) Is a technique for planning dollar inventory investments that assumes that the percentage fluctuations in monthly stock from average stock

should be half as great as the percentage fluctuations in monthly sales from average sales.

percentage-of-sales method Is a technique for budgeting in which the retailer targets a specific percentage of forecasted sales as the advertising budget.

perceptual incongruity Occurs when the retailer and supplier have different perceptions of reality.

personal objectives Are those that reflect the retailers' desire to help individuals employed in retailing fulfill some of their needs.

personal selling Involves a face-to-face interaction with the consumer with the goal of selling the consumer merchandise or services.

personal shopping Occurs when an individual who is a professional shopper performs the shopping role for another; very upscale department and specialty stores offer personal shoppers to their clients.

planogram Is a schematic that illustrates how and where a retailer's merchandise should be displayed on the shelf in order to increase customer purchases.

point of indifference Is the breaking point between two cities where customers are indifferent to shopping in either city.

population variables Include population growth trends, age distributions, ethic makeup, and geographic trends.

pop-up stores Are temporary stores, which are relatively small in scale, that are set up for a short period of time, usually in conjunction with an event and often in high traffic areas, to explicitly intercept shoppers.

post-purchase resentment Arises after the purchase when the consumer becomes dissatisfied with the product, service, or retailer and thus begins to regret that the purchase was made.

posttransaction services Are services provided to customers after they have purchased merchandise or services.

power Is the ability of one channel member to influence the decisions of the other channel members.

predatory pricing Exists when a retail chain charges different prices in different geographic areas to eliminate competition in selected geographic areas.

prediction market A market where a synthetic financial security reflects if a future event will or will not occur and individuals then trade (buy and sell) this security.

premiums Are extra items offered to the customer when purchasing promoted products.

prepaid expenses   Are those items for which the retailer has already paid, but the service has not been completed.

pretransaction services   Are services provided to the customer prior to entering the store.

price discrimination   Occurs when two retailers buy an identical amount of "like grade and quality" merchandise from the same supplier but pay different prices.

price lining   Is a pricing policy that is established to help customers make merchandise comparisons and involves establishing a specified number of price points for each merchandise classification.

price to book ratio   The price of a share of stock divided by the book value of a share of stock. The higher the price to book ratio, the higher the intangible assets relative to tangible or balance sheet assets.

price zone   Is a range of prices for a particular merchandise line that appeals to customers in a certain market segment.

primary marketing institutions   Are those channel members that take title to the goods as they move through the marketing channel. They include manufacturers, wholesalers, and retailers.

primary trading area   Is the geographic area where the retailer can serve customers in terms of convenience and accessibility better than the competition.

private-label branding   May be store branding, when a retailer develops its own brand name and contracts with a manufacturer to produce the product with the retailer's brand, or designer lines, where a known designer develops a line exclusively for the retailer.

problem recognition   Occurs when the consumer's desired state of affairs departs sufficiently from the actual state of unrest.

product liability laws   Deal with the seller's responsibility to market safe products. These laws invoke the foreseeability doctrine, which states that a seller of a product must attempt to foresee how a product may be misused and warn the consumer against the hazards of misuse.

productivity objectives   State the sales objectives that the retailer desires for each unit of resource input: floor space, labor, and inventory investment.

profit maximization   Is a pricing objective that seeks to obtain as much profit as possible.

promotional advertising   Is a type of advertising in which the retailer attempts to increase short-term performance by using product availability or price as a selling point.

promotional discount   Is a discount provided for the retailer performing an advertising or promotional service for the manufacturer.

prospecting   Is the process of locating or identifying potential customers who have the ability and willingness to purchase your product.

public warehouse   Is a facility that stores goods for safe-keeping for any owner in return for a fee, usually based on space occupied.

publicity   Is non-paid-for communications of information about the company or product, generally in some media form.

pure competition   Occurs when a market has homogeneous products and many buyers and sellers, all having perfect knowledge of the market, and ease of entry for both buyers and sellers.

pure monopoly   Occurs when there is only one seller for a product or service.

Q

quantity discount   Is a price reduction offered as an inducement to purchase large quantities of merchandise.

quick response (QR) systems   Also known as efficient consumer response (ECR) systems, are integrated information, production, and logistical systems that obtain real-time information on consumer actions by capturing sales data at point-of-purchase terminals and then transmitting this information back through the entire channel to enable efficient production and distribution scheduling.

R

reach   Is the actual total number of target customers who come into contact with an advertising message.

receipt of goods (ROG) dating   Allows the retailer to take a cash discount and the full payment period to begin when the goods are received by the retailer.

recycled merchandise retailers   Are establishments that sell used and reconditioned products.

referent power   Is based on the identification of B with A.

reframing   Changing a business model by reconfiguring the resources of time, place and possession around a customer-centric view.

register racks   The racks placed near the checkout to encourage impulse buying.

Reilly's law of retail gravitation   Based on Newtonian gravitational principles, explains how large urbanized areas attract customers from smaller rural communities.

relationship retailing   Comprises all the activities designed to attract, retain, and enhance long-term relationships with customers.

relieving   The use of other tools, people or other aids to eliminate certain tasks or to make those tasks easier. Examples include wheels and pulleys, automatic washing machines, medications, pre-made food, store signage, ATMs, automatic doors, and knowledgeable retail salespeople and food servers.

resource integration   Blending three major types of resources: market resources, public resources, and private resources, in order to co-create value to solve problems and pursue opportunities or perform jobs.

retail accordion   Describes how retail institutions evolve from outlets that offer wide assortments to specialized stores and continue repeatedly through the pattern.

retail clusters   Are groups of stores closely located that share similar characteristics such as product category, store format, or customer demographics.

retail gravity theory   Suggests that there are underlying consistencies in shopping behavior that yield to mathematical analysis and prediction based on the notion or concept of gravity.

retail inventories   Comprise merchandise that the retailer has in the store or in storage and is available for sale.

retail life cycle   Describes four distinct stages that a retail institution progresses through: introduction, growth, maturity, and decline.

retail mix   Is the combination of merchandise, price, advertising and promotion, location, customer service and selling, and store layout and design.

retail resource trinity model   Shows how inventory, space, and labor resources interrelate to yield high resource productivity.

retail store saturation   Is a condition where there are just enough store facilities for a given type of store to efficiently and satisfactorily serve the population and yield a fair profit to the owners.

retailer-owned cooperatives   Are wholesale institutions, organized and owned by member retailers, that offer scale economies and services to member retailers, which allows them to compete with larger chain buying organizations.

retailing   Consists of the final activities and steps needed to place merchandise made elsewhere into the hands of the consumer or to provide services to the consumer.

return on assets (ROA)   Is net profit (after taxes) divided by total assets.

return on net worth (RONW)   Is net profit (after taxes) divided by owners' equity.

returns and allowances   Are refunds of the purchase price or downward adjustments in selling prices due to customers returning purchases, or adjustments made in the selling price due to customer dissatisfaction with product or service performance.

reward power   Is based on B's perception that A has the ability to provide rewards for B.

S

sales displacement   Occurs when consumers purchase and stockpile advertised brands during a promotional period and any gains in sales are later offset by sales reductions from average during subsequent nonpromotional periods.

sales promotion   Involves the use of media and nonmedia marketing pressure applied for a predetermined, limited period of time to stimulate trial, increase consumer demand, or improve product availability.

same-store sales   Compares an individual store's sales to its sales for the same month in the previous year.

sandwich generational family (or) trigenerational family   Occurs when three generations (parents, grandparents, and children) live together in the same house.

scrambled merchandising   Exists when a retailer handles many different and unrelated items.

seasonal discount   Is a discount provided to retailers if they purchase and take delivery of merchandise in the off season.

secondary business district (SBD)   Is a shopping area that is smaller than the CBD and that revolves around at least one department or variety store at a major street intersection.

secondary trading area   Is the geographic area where the retailer can still be competitive despite a competitor having some locational advantage.

selective distribution   Means that a moderate number of retailers are used in a trade area.

sell through report   Lists the percentage of the stock or merchandise item or group of items from a each vendor sold during the prior merchandise season.

service The application of knowledge and skills through deeds, processes, and performances for the benefit of another.

set of attributes Refers to the characteristics of the store and its products and services.

shopping center (or mall) Is a centrally owned or managed shopping district that is planned, has balanced tenancy (the stores complement each other in merchandise offerings), and is surrounded by parking facilities.

shrinkage Represents merchandise that cannot be accounted for due to theft, loss, or damage.

single-loop learning A single source of feedback about "are we doing things right" to achieve our goals. It is a way of learning in which an action is triggered whenever you drop below your target goal.

site analysis Is an evaluation of the density of demand and supply within each market with the goal of identifying the best retail site(s).

skimming Is a pricing objective in which price is initially set high on merchandise to skim the cream of demand before selling at more competitive prices.

slotting fees (slotting allowances) Are fees paid by a vendor for space or a slot on a retailer's shelves, as well as having its UPC number given a slot in the retailer's computer system.

social media Term given to a host of electronic information technologies that enable and stimulate social interaction between humans.

societal objectives Are those that reflect the retailer's desire to help society fulfill some of its needs.

solidarity Exists when a high value is placed on the relationship between a supplier and retailer.

space productivity index Is a ratio that compares the percentage of the store's total gross margin that a particular merchandise category generates to its percentage of total store selling space used.

spine layout Is a type of store layout in which a single main aisle runs from the front to the back of the store, transporting customers in both directions, and where on either side of this spine, merchandise departments using either a freeflow or grid pattern branch off toward the back side walls.

stack-outs Are pallets of merchandise set out on the floor in front of the main shelves.

standard stock list Is a merchandising method in which all stores in a retail chain stock the same merchandise.

stimulus Refers to a cue that is external to the individual or a drive that is internal to the individual.

stockouts Are products that are out of stock and therefore unavailable to customers when they want them.

stock-to-sales method (SSM) Is a technique for planning dollar inventory investments where the amount of inventory planned for the beginning of the month is a ratio (obtained from trade associations or the retailer's historical records) of stock-to-sales.

stock-to-sales ratio Depicts the amount of stock to have at the beginning of each month to support the forecasted sales for that month.

store compatibility Exists when two similar retail businesses locate next to or nearby each other and they realize a sales volume greater than what they would have achieved if they were located apart from each other.

store management The retailing career path that involves responsibility for selecting, training, and evaluating personnel, as well as in-store promotions, displays, customer service, building maintenance, and security.

store positioning Is when a retailer identifies a well-defined market segment using demographic or lifestyle variables and appeals to this segment with a clearly differentiated approach.

store-based retailers Operate from a fixed store location that requires customers to travel to the store to view and select merchandise or services.

strategic planning Involves adapting the resources of the firm to the opportunities and threats of an ever-changing retail environment.

strategy Is a carefully designed plan for achieving the retailer's goals and objectives.

substitution effect Happens when advertising of a particular branded product during a promotional period reduces the current and future demand for competitive brands.

supercenter A cavernous combination of supermarket and discount department store carrying more than 80,000 to 100,000 SKUs that allows for one-stop shopping.

supply chain Is a set of institutions that move goods from the point of production to the point of consumption.

T

target market The group(s) of customers that a retailer is seeking to serve

target return objective Is a pricing objective that states a specific level of profit, such as percentage of sales or return on capital invested, as an objective.

task-and-objective method Is a technique for budgeting in which the retailer establishes its advertising objectives and then determines the advertising tasks that need to be performed to achieve those objectives.

territorial restrictions Are attempts by the supplier, usually a manufacturer, to limit the geographic area in which a retailer may resell its merchandise.

thematic maps Use visual techniques such as colors, shading, and lines to display cultural characteristics of the physical space.

third-party logistics provider (3PL) Firms that provide service to retailers, and other customers, of outsourced (or 3rd party) logistics services for part, or all, of their storage, transporting, sorting, information gathering, and risk management functions.

total assets Equal current assets plus noncurrent assets plus goodwill.

total cost of business Is a process where costs beyond simply producing a product are considered and includes all of the direct and indirect costs of manufacturing, distributing, and marketing a product.

total liabilities Equal current liabilities plus long-term liabilities.

trade discount Is also referred to as a functional discount and is a form of compensation that the buyer may receive for performing certain wholesaling or retailing services for the manufacturer.

trading area The geographic area from which a retailer, group of retailers, or community draws its customers.

trading down Occurs when a retailer uses price lining, and a customer initially exposed to higher priced lines expresses the desire to purchase a lower-priced line.

trading up Occurs when a retailer uses price lining and a salesperson moves a customer from a lower-priced line to a higher one.

transaction services Are services provided to customers when they are in the store shopping and transacting business.

transient customer Is an individual who is dissatisfied with the level of customer service offered at a store or stores and is seeking an alternative store with the level of customer service that he or she thinks is appropriate.

triple-loop learning "what is the right business model" incorporates doing things right, toward the right goals, and being ever cognizant of the opportunity to change your business model.

two-way communication Occurs when both retailer and supplier communicate openly their ideas, concerns, and plans.

two-way exclusive dealing agreement Occurs when the supplier offers the retailer the exclusive distribution of a merchandise line or product in a particular trade area if in return the retailer will agree to do something for the manufacturer, such as heavily promote the supplier's products or not handle competing brands.

tying agreement Exists when a seller with a strong product or service requires a buyer (the retailer) to purchase a weak product or service as a condition for buying the strong product or service.

U

understored Is a condition in a community where the number of stores in relation to households is relatively low so that engaging in retailing is an attractive economic endeavor.

V

value proposition Is a clear statement of the tangible and intangible results a customer receives from shopping at and using the retailer's products or services.

variable pricing Is a policy that recognizes that differences in demand and cost necessitate that the retailer change prices in a fairly predictable manner.

variety Refers to the number of different merchandise lines that the retailer stocks in the store.

vendor collusion Occurs when an employee of one of the retailer's vendors steals merchandise as it is delivered to the retailer.

vendor profitability analysis statement Is a tool used to evaluate vendors and shows all purchases made the prior year, the discount granted, the transportation charges paid, the original markup, markdowns, and finally the season-ending gross margin on that vendor's merchandise.

vertical cooperative advertising Occurs when the retailer and other channel members (usually manufacturers) share the advertising budget. Usually the manufacturer subsidizes some of the retailer's advertising that features the manufacturer's brands.

vertical marketing channels   Are capital-intensive networks of several levels that are professionally managed and centrally programmed to realize the technological, managerial, and promotional economies of a long-term relationship orientation.

vertical price fixing   Occurs when a retailer collaborates with the manufacturer or wholesaler to resell an item at an agreed upon price.

virtual store   Is the total collection of all the pages of information on the retailer's Internet site.

visual merchandising   Is the artistic display of merchandise and theatrical props used as scene-setting decoration in the store.

W

weeks' supply method (WSM)   Is a technique for planning dollar inventory investments that states that the inventory level should be set equal to a predetermined number of weeks' supply, which is directly related to the desired rate of stock turnover.

wheel of retailing theory   Describes how new types of retailers enter the market as low-status, low-margin, lowprice operators; however, as they meet with success, these new retailers gradually acquire more sophisticated and elaborate facilities, and thus become vulnerable to new types of low-margin retail competitors who progress through the same pattern.

wholesaler sponsored voluntary groups   Involve a wholesaler that brings together a group of independently owned retailers and offers them a coordinated merchandising and buying program that will provide them with economies like those their chain store rivals are able to obtain.

Y

yield management   Is where the retailer focuses on optimizing the total sales revenue, or yield, from its capacity to provide services.

ENDNOTES

Chapter 1

1. "Freedom Is Still the Winning Formula," *Wall Street Journal*, January 13, 2009: A17.
2. This list is based in part on information from the MorningNewBeat.com, February 2008.
3. "Walmart Sets Seminar to Assess Economic Impact," *Wall Street Journal*, November 4, 2005: B2.
4. "One Nation Under Walmart," *Fortune*, March 3, 2003: 64–76.
5. "Walmart's Emergency-Relief Team Girds for Hurricane Gustav," *Wall Street Journal*, August 30, 2008: A3.
6. "Walmart Goes Greener," *Shopping Centers Today*, March 2007: 9; "Turning Green into Gold," *Shopping Centers Today*, March 2006: 59–60.
7. "America's Most Admired Companies," *Fortune*, March 17, 2008: 111–116.
8. "The Unending Woes of Lee Scott," *Fortune*, January 22, 2007: 118–122.
9. "Walmart to Settle 63 Lawsuits over Wages," *Wall Street Journal*, December 24, 2008: B1.
10. "Green-Light Specials, Now at Walmart," *New York Times*, January 25, 2009: U1, U5; "Green Gold," *Fortune*, September 15, 2008: 107–112.
11. "The World's Most Admired Companies," *Fortune*, March 16, 2009: 76.
12. "The World's Most Admired Companies," *Fortune*, March 19, 2012: 140.
13. Andrea M. Dean and Russell S. Sobel, "Has Walmart Buried Mom and Pop? *Regulation*, Spring 2008: 38–45.
14. "Retail Relief," *Shopping Centers Today*, September 2008: 133–136.
15. "The Accidental Hero," *Businessweek*, November 16, 2009: 58–61.
16. "Forget Hemlines. Ties May Be the New Indicator," *Bloomberg Businessweek*, December 6-12, 2010: 25.
17. "E-Commerce Sales Rise 14.8% in 2010," [online] www.internetretailer.com, Accessed: January 21, 2012.
18. "US Internet Christmas Sales Are Up 15.4% to $36 Billion & Now Account for 10% of All Retail Sales," [online] www.thedomains.com, Accessed: January 21, 2012.
19. Ibid.
20. "Tech the Talk at NRF," *Women's Wear Daily*, January 19, 2012: 1, 8; "M-commerce on Rise," *Women's Wear Daily*, January 25, 2012: 1, 12; "NRF: Stores Moving Fast on Mobile Landscape," *Women's Wear Daily*, February 15, 2012: 16.
21. "Adapting to a Changing Retail Landscape," *Womens Wear Daily*, April 14, 2011: 8.
22. From a list compiled by the late Robert Kahn.
23. "Why Wal-Mart Wants to Take the Driver's Seat," *Bloomberg Businessweek*, May 31-June 6, 2010: 17–18.
24. "The World's Most Admired Companies," *Fortune*, March 19, 2012: 140.
25. "Fuel Prices Drive Customers to Gas Up at Supercenters, Clubs," *Shopping Centers Today*, August 2008: 9.
26. "Costco's Artful Discounts," *Businessweek*, October 20, 2008: 58–60.

27. "Drugstores, Too, Feel Recession Pain," *New York Times*, January 3, 2009: B3

28. "Root Canal? Try Aisle Five." *Businessweek*, October 13, 2008: 16.

29. "In These Lean Days, Even Stores Shrink," *New York Times*, November 9, 2010.

30. "Saving Sears Doesn't Look Easy Anymore," *New York Times*, January 27, 2008: 1, 8–9.

31. "Toy Story III: The Toys 'R' Us Story." Presentation by Rebecca Caruso at the Establishing a Distinctive Identity in a Changing Global Marketplace Conference at Notre Dame University, September 7, 2001.

32. "Toys 'R' Us Unwraps Plans for Expansion," *Wall Street Journal*, May 22, 2008: B1.

33. "In the Trenches: Will Burberry Customers Pay Big for a DIY Coat?" *Time*, December 5, 2011; 82.

34. U.S. Bureau of Census, *Statistical Abstract of the United States: 2009*, Table 1008.

35. The Census Bureau no longer compiles data on chain store sales as a percentage of total retail sales. This information is based on estimates from various industry experts and older government data.

36. "The Sharin' Huggin' Lovin' Carin' Chinese Food Money Machine," *Bloomberg Businessweek*, November 22-28, 2010: 97–103.

37. "Chipotle's Rise," *Fortune,* October 18, 2010: "Chipotle's Growth Machine," *Fortune*, September 26, 2011: 135–144.

38. "A Leaner Macy's Tries Catering to Local Tastes," *Businessweek*, September 14, 2009: 13.

39. "Walmart Gives Makeover to Its Private-Label Line," *Wall Street Journal*, March 17, 2009: B2.

40. "Branching Out," *Shopping Centers Today*, March 2008: 33–34.

41. "First-Class Shopping, Food for Flyers," *Shopping Centers Today*, December 2008: 9; "On the Fly," *Shopping Centers Today*, November 2008: 59–61; "U.S. Airport Shops Go High-End," *Wall Street Journal*, December 20, 2005: D1, D3; "High-Flying Retail: JFK's The Shops Raises Bar for Airport Retail with Posh Purveyors," *Shopping Centers Today*, May 2005: 213–214.

42. Sam Newberg, "The Rush to Build Walkable Urban Grocery Stores," *Urban Land,* March 22, 2011, [online] urbanland.uli.org/Articles/2011/Mar/NewbergGrocery, Accessed: March 30, 2012.

43. "The Responsibility Revolution," *Time*, September 21, 2009: 38–41.

44. "Costco's Artful Discounts," op. cit.

45. "Etc. Hard Choices," *Bloomberg Businessweek*, May 31-June 6, 2010: 88.

46. "Americans Can't Get No Satisfaction," *Fortune*, December 11, 1995: 194.

47. "Inside Trader Joe's," *Fortune*, September 6, 2010: 86–96.

48. Roger Dickinson, "Creativity in Retailing," *Journal of Retailing*, Winter 1969–1970: 4.

49. Ibid.

Chapter 2

1. "Adapting to a Changing Retail Landscape," *Women's Wear Daily*, April 14, 2011: 8; "Survey: Retailers Cash-Rich, Plan to Spend on IT," *Chain Store Age*, August 2011: 12; "A Winning Game Plan," *Chain Store Age*, March 2011: 26.

2. "Bigger and Bigger," *Fortune*, September 5, 2005: 104–107.

3. "Changing Course," *Shopping Centers Today*, April 2008: 63–64.

4. Chaney, Paul. (2010). "J.C. Penney Moves Entire Product Catalog to Facebook," [online] Available at www.practicalecommerce.com [Accessed: February 3, 2012]; Van Grove, Jennifer. (2010). "Delta Strats Selling Flights on Facebook," [online] Available at www.mashable.com [Accessed: February 3, 2012]; Lee, Jessica. (2010). "1-800-FLOWERS Launches Store Inside Its Facebook Page," [online] Available at www.insidefacebook.com [Accessed: February 3, 2012].

5. Taken from Starbuck's website (www.starbucks.com/mission/default.asp), December 23, 2011.

6. Taken from REI website (http://www.rei.com/stewardship), December 23, 2011.

7. Based on information provided by James Moore.

8. "Starbucks Addresses the Price Issue and Breakfast," *New York Times*, March 3, 2009: B4.

9. "Starbucks Shifts Focus to Value, Cost Cutting," *Wall Street Journal*, December 5, 2008: B1; "At Starbucks, a Tall Order for New Cuts, Store Closures," *Wall Street Journal*, January 29, 2009: B1, B4.

10. "A&P's Supermarket Shuffle," *Shopping Centers Today*, September 2008: 55–57.

11. "Change Agent: After Record Year, Hugo Boss Steps Up Expansion Strategy," *Women's Wear Daily*, March 17, 2011: 1, 7.

12. "Urban Outfitters' Grow-Slow Strategy," *Bloomberg Businessweek*, March 1, 2010: 56.

13. "Growing Disney's Best 30 Minutes," *Chain Store Age*, August/September 2011: 52–53.

14. Sidney Schoeffler, "Nine Basic Findings on Business Strategy," PIMS Letter No. 1. Cambridge, MA: The Strategic Planning Institute, 1977.

15. For a detailed discussion of this material with examples, see "The Profit Wedge: How Five Measure Up," *Chain Store Age*, May 1998: 60–68.

16. "100 Best Companies to Work For," *Fortune*, June 14, 2010: 52.

17. "In Memoriam: Anita Roddick," *Businessweek*, September 24, 2007: 31.

18. "One Family's Hobby," *Fortune*, November 1, 2010: 69–72.

19. "Strong Coffee," *Fortune*, December 12, 2011: 101–114.

20. "100 Best Companies to Work For: No. 53 Nordstrom," *Fortune*, October 18, 2010: 37.

21. For a detailed discussion of how performance objectives link to retail strategies, see: Leonard L. Berry and Robert F. Lusch, "Making Corporate Performance 'Soar'" *Marketing Management*, Fall 1996: 13–24. "Winning Back Lost Customers," *Retail Issues Letter*, March 2001.

22. Jay Fitzsimmons, senior vice president and treasurer of Wal-Mart, quoted in MorningNewsBeat. com, March 24, 2003.

23. "Dick's Sporting Goods Makes Customers, And Its Investors, Happy: Can It Possibly Last?" *Fortune*, May 3, 2010: 165–168.

24. "Staying on Target," *Wall Street Journal*, May 7, 2007: B1, B2.

25. "Zones of Seduction," *Time*, November 7, 2011: 58.

26. "Too Good for Lowe's and Home Depot?" *Wall Street Journal*, July 6, 2006: B1.

27. "At Best Buy, Marketing Goes Micro," *Businessweek*, May 26, 2008: 52–54.

28. "A Modern Classic," *Americanway*, August 1, 2011: 15–16.

29. "How Jim Skinner Flipped McDonald's," *Wall Street Journal*, January 5, 2007: B1, B2.

30. The following sources were used by Dr. Owens in preparing this case: "Macy's Has High Hopes for Company's New Approach," *Cincinnati Enquirer*, February 7, 2009: C1, C3; "Macy's Needs Tailoring to Suit Customers," *St. Louis Post-Dispatch*, July 20, 2008 (http://voipservices. tmcnet.com/news/2008/07/20/3556316.htm); "Federated Plans Corporate Name Change," press release, Cincinnati: Macy's Inc., February 27, 2007 (http://phx.corporate-ir.net/phoenix.zhtml? c=84477&p=irol-newsArticle&ID=967632&highli ght=); Sandra Guy, "Macy's Stores Trying to Go Local," *Chicago Sun-Times*, October 14, 2008; Sandra Jones, "Hard-Core Fans Stay Loyal to Brand," *Chicago Tribune*, September 5, 2006; Sandra Jones, "Macy's: State Street Store 'Doing Badly,'" *Chicago Tribune*, May 19, 2007: p. 1+; David Moin, "Fortifying Flagship: Growth Engines Getting Big Bucks in Tough Times," *Women's Wear Daily*, June 4, 2008; David Moin, "Macy's to Reorganize Divisions," *Women's Wear Daily*, February 6, 2008.

31. "Not Copying Wal-Mart Pays Off for Grocers," *Wall Street Journal*, June 6, 2007: B1, B5.

Chapter 3

1. "Commentary by Professor Claes Fornell," *ACSI Report*, February 21, 2006. Used with the author's permission.

2. If you want to see the most recent data on ACSI data for the nation's leading retailers, go to www. theacsi.org. The index for retailers is updated every February.

3. Gasbuddy.com (2012) "Gas Price Historical Price Charts" [online] Available at http://www.gasbuddy.com/gb_retail_price_chart.aspx [Accessed: March 3, 2012].

4. "It's Not Only about Price at Walmart," *New York Times*, March 2, 2007: C1, C2.

5. "Costco's Artful Discounts," *Businessweek*, October 20, 2008: 58–60.

6. Unless otherwise noted, the statistical data used in this chapter will be the most recently posted information on the Census Bureau's website: http://factfinder.census.gov.

7. U.S. Bureau of Census, *Statistical Abstract of the United States: 2012*, Table 3.

8. U.S. Bureau of Census, *Statistical Abstract of the United States: 2012*, Table 7.

9. "Five Things You Don't Know About Baby Boomers," *Stores*, June 2008.

10. "Boomer Bust: How Will the Economy Rebound without Post-War Babies Financing Their Harleys?" *Wall Street Journal*, October 21, 2008: A13.

11. "The Unretired," *Businessweek*, December 15, 2008: 46–49.

12. "The New Generation Gap," *Time*, November 14, 2011: 36–40.

13. "Wealth Management Comes to Financial Services Firms," *St. Louis Post-Dispatch*, October 7, 2007: D1, D3.

14. "The Rich Are Duller," *Wall Street Journal*, July 13, 2007: W1, W2.

15. HaeJung Kim, Dee K. Knight, and Christy Crutsinger, "Generation Y Employees' Work Experience in the Retail Industry: The Impact on Job Performance, Job Satisfaction and Career Intention." Paper presented at the ACRA 2006 Spring Conference, Springdale, Arkansas, April 7, 2006.

16. Available at http://pewresearch.org/pubs/1437/millennials-profile [Accessed: December 29, 2011].

17. "Five Things . . . ," op. cit.

18. "Gen X a Key Market for Luxury," *Womens Wear Daily*, February 11, 2012: 2.

19. "Older Consumers Don't Believe You," *Advertising Age*, August 14, 1995: 14.

20. "Connecting with the Connected Generation," *Stores*, August 2011 [online] Available at http://www.stores.org/print/book/export/html/6838 [Accessed: August 25, 2011].

21. "U.S. Retailers Face Generational Shift" *Womens Wear Daily*, September 21, 2011: 1, 12.

22. "Brooks Brothers Aims to Attract Younger Shoppers" *Womens Wear Daily Men's Week*, August 18, 2011: MW1, MW4.

23. "Macy's Sets Strategy for Gen-Y Shoppers," *Women's Wear Daily*, March 22, 2012: 1, 6.

24. "Reaching Gen Y on Both Sides of the Cash Register," *Texas A&M's Retailing Issues Letter*, 18(2), 2007.

25. "User-Friendly Finance for Generation Y," *Businessweek*, December 8, 2008: 66.

26. "Generation P: Yearning for a Cashless Society?" *Belleville News Democrat*, May 27, 2007: B5.

27. "Study: Generation Gap with Net Shopping," *Lubbock Avalanche-Journal*, February 15, 2008: B9.

28. "Teens Turn to Thrift as Jobs Vanish and Prices Rise," *Lubbock Avalanche-Journal*, April 20, 2008: D3.

29. Hispanicity, which is independent of race, is the only *ethnic* category, as opposed to *racial* category, which is officially collated by the U.S. Census Bureau. The distinction made by government agencies for those within the population of any official race category, including "white American," is between those with Hispanic ethnic backgrounds and all others of non-Hispanic ethnic backgrounds. In the case of white Americans, these two groups are, respectively, termed *white Hispanics* and *non-Hispanic whites*, the former having at least one ancestor from the people of Spain or Spanish-speaking Latin America, and the latter consisting of an ethnically diverse collection of all others who are classified as white American who are of non-Hispanic ethnic backgrounds.

30. The authors wish to acknowledge the assistance of Retail Forward for providing much of the data in the following section.

31. "Hispanics: A Growing Force," *Womens Wear Daily*, March 23, 2011: 2.

32. U.S. Bureau of Census, *Statistical Abstract of the United States: 2012*, Table 690 and author calculations.

33. Available at http://www.cdph.ca.gov/programs/cpns/Documents/Network-FV-AA-Shopping.pdf [Accessed: December 29, 2011].

34. "African-Americans Wield Considerable Consumer Power," [online] Available at http://www.nielsen.com/us/en/insights/press-room/2011/african-americans-wield-considerable-consumer-power.html [Accessed: September 22, 2011].

35. Lara Farrar, "On Tour in the U.S. With China's New Rich," *Womens Wear Daily*, April 11, 2011: 1, 6, 7.

36. Ibid.

37. U.S. Bureau of Census, *Statistical Abstract of the United States: 2012*, Figure 1.1.

38. U.S. Bureau of Census, *Statistical Abstract of the United States: 2012*, Table 687.

39. Ibid.

40. "Macy's Has High Hopes for Company's New Approach," *Cincinnati Enquirer*, February 7, 2009: C1, C3.

41. U.S. Bureau of Census, *Statistical Abstract of the United States: 2012*, Table 24; and authors' calculations.

42. U.S. Bureau of Census, *Statistical Abstract of the United States: 2012*, Table 30; and authors' calculations.

43. "A Bigger Family Stays Closer to the Nest," *Wall Street Journal*, April 1, 1994: B1.

44. U.S. Bureau of Census, *Statistical Abstract of the United States: 2012*, Table 231.

45. U.S. Bureau of Census, *Statistical Abstract of the United States: 2012*, Table 231; and authors' calculations.

46. Ibid.

47. U.S. Bureau of Census, *Statistical Abstract of the United States: 2012*, Table 226; and authors' calculations.

48. U.S. Bureau of Census, *Statistical Abstract of the United States: 2012*, Table 221; and authors' calculations; "My Daughter, the PhD," *Businessweek*, March 27, 2000: 30.

49. U.S. Bureau of Census, *Statistical Abstract of the United States: 2012*, Table 231; and author calculations.

50. U.S. Bureau of Census, *Statistical Abstract of the United States: 2012*, Table 232.

51. U.S. Bureau of Census, *Statistical Abstract of the United States: 2012*, Table 57.

52. U.S. Bureau of Census, *2010 American Community Survey*, Subject Table B12007.

53. U.S. Bureau of Census, *Statistical Abstract of the United States: 2012*, Table 57.

54. "Living Alone Is the New Norm," *Time*, March 12, 2012: 60–62.

55. For a complete discussion of the consumer's behavior, especially differences between male and female shoppers, see Paco Underhill, *Why We Buy* (New York: Simon & Schuster), 1999.

56. U.S. Bureau of Census, *Statistical Abstract of the United States: 2012*, Table 64.

57. U.S. Bureau of Census, *Statistical Abstract of the United States: 2012*, Table 61; and author calculations.

58. U.S. Bureau of Census, *Statistical Abstract of the United States: 1980*, Table 60; U.S. Bureau of Census, *Statistical Abstract of the United States: 2010*, Table 63; and author calculations.

59. U.S. Bureau of Census, *Statistical Abstract of the United States: 2012*, Table 63; and author calculations.

60. "They're Baaa-aack," *St. Louis Post-Dispatch*, May 3, 2008: 23.

61. "The College Credit-Card Hustle," *Businessweek*," July 28, 2008: 38–42; and "Students Suffocate Under Tens of Thousands in Loans," *USA Today*, February 23, 2006: B1, B2.

62. "When Kids Move Out the Economy Benefits" *Bloomberg Businessweek*, May 16–22, 2011: 9, 10.

63. U.S. Bureau of Census, *Statistical Abstract of the United States: 2012*, Table 605; and author calculations.

64. U.S. Bureau of Census, *Statistical Abstract of the United States: 2012*, Table 610.

65. U.S. Bureau of Census, *Statistical Abstract of the United States: 2012*, Table 612.

66. "Turnover Costs Sack Retailers," *Chain Store Age*, March 2000: 100–102.

67. U.S. Bureau of Census, *Statistical Abstract of the United States: 2012*, Table 697; and author calculations.

68. Ibid.

69. U.S. Treasury Department, *Income Mobility in the U.S. From 1996 to 2005*, November 13, 2007.

70. "Americans See 18% of Wealth Vanish," *Wall Street Journal*, March 13, 2009: A1, A8.

71. "Food, Gas Prices Pinch Shoppers," *WWD*, April 8, 2011: 1, 6.

72. "The Purposeful Shopper: Quality and Value Drive the New Consumer," *WWD*, July 21, 2011: 2.

73. "People Pulling Up to Pawnshops Today Are Driving Cadillacs and BMWs," *Wall Street Journal*, December 30, 2008: A1, A6.

74. U.S. Bureau of Census, *Statistical Abstract of the United States: 2012*, Table 678.

75. "'Wealth Effect' May Be Near Payback Time," *Wall Street Journal*, June 5, 2008: C1.

76. "Age before Beauty. No, Really," *Businessweek*, April 26, 2004: 14.

77. U.S. Bureau of Census, *Statistical Abstract of the United States: 2012*, Table 588.

78. U.S. Bureau of Census, *Statistical Abstract of the United States: 2012*, Table 593.

79. U.S. Bureau of Census, *Statistical Abstract of the United States: 2012*, Table 587.

80. U.S. Bureau of Census, *Statistical Abstract of the United States: 2012*, Table 599.

81. U.S. Bureau of Census, *Statistical Abstract of the United States: 2012*, Table 608.

82. Ibid.

83. U.S. Bureau of Census, *Statistical Abstract of the United States: 2012*, Table 699; and author calculations.

84. "Not Tonight, Honey: The Plight of the Dual-Income, No-Sex Couples," *Wall Street Journal*, April 3, 2003: D1.

85. "Crushed by . . . Savings," *Fortune*, March 6, 2006: 60.

86. U.S. Bureau of Census, *Statistical Abstract of the United States: 2012*, Table 1189.

87. Ibid.

88. "Hamburger Joints Call Them 'Heavy Users'—But Not to Their Face," *Wall Street Journal*, January 12, 2000: A1, A10.

89. "For New-Car Buyers, Taking a Test Drive Now Seems so 1995" *New York Times*, November 21, 2011.

90. "Love the Customers Who Hate You," *Businessweek*, March 3, 2008: 58.

Chapter 4

1. Based on information provided in a speech by Best Buy CEO Brad Anderson at Texas Tech University, November 8, 2005.

2. "Supermarkets," *Shopping Centers Today*, May 2005: 16–35.

3. Fred Crawford and Ryan Mathews, *The Myth of Excellence: Why Great Companies Never Try to Be the Best at Everything* (New York: Crown Business), 2001: 21–39.

4. "Post Office Makeover," *Fortune*, December 12, 2011: 17.

5. "Mail Fraud," *Wall Street Journal Online*, April 26, 2012 [online] Available at http://online.wsj.com.

6. "Cigarette Tax Burnout," *Wall Street Journal*, August 11, 2008: A14.

7. "High Fuel Costs Helping Small-Town Businesses, Pinching Distant Malls," *Lubbock Avalanche-Journal*, July 13, 2008: D4.

8. From Amazon.com Fiscal Year 2004 Annual Report.

9. Anthony J. Capraro, Susan Broniarczyk, and Rajendra K. Srivastava, "Factors Influencing the Likelihood of Customer Defection: The Role of Consumer Knowledge." *Journal of the Academy of Marketing Science*, Spring 2003: 164–175.

10. "Retailers Demanding New Products Carry Category," KPMG Consumer Markets Insiders Focus (www.kpmginsiders.com), May 28, 2003.

11. "Web Can Pay Off for Traditional Retailers," *Wall Street Journal*, December 23, 2006: A7.

12. "Liquidation Ahead For Syms, Filene's" *Women's Wear Daily*, November 3, 2011: 8.

13. "Supermarkets, Warehouse Clubs Gas Up," *Shopping Center Today*, November 2005: 9.

14. "Anxiety Grows Around Starbucks Closings," *Wall Street Journal*, July 9, 2008: B1; "Fewer Starbucks," *Businessweek*, July 14, 2008: 8; "Why Did Starbucks Cross the Road?" *Wall Street Journal*, April 3, 2007: B1, B2.

15. "Once Vibrant Sector Forced to Reinvent," *Women's Wear Daily*, December 21, 2011: 1, 12.

16. "rue21 in Expansion Mode," *Chain Store Age*, June/July 2011: 22.

17. "Chico's in Expansion Mode," *Women's Wear Daily*, February 23, 2012: 8.

18. "Retail in an Age of Austerity," *Women's Wear Daily*, December 30, 2011: 3.

19. "General Mills' Global Sweet Spot," *Fortune*, May 23, 2011: 194–202.

20. "Car Dealer Butch Suntrup Adds Insurance to His Business," *St. Louis Post-Dispatch*, August 13, 2008: C9.

21. "David vs. Goliath" *Fortune*, March 22, 2010: 68.

22. "EBay's Adventures in Brick and Mortar" *Bloomberg Businessweek,* November 28–December 4, 2011.

23. "Vente-Privee Said Set to Unveil U.S. Deal" *Women's Wear Daily*, May 22, 2011: 1, 6.

24. Malcolm P. McNair, "Significant Trends and Developments in the Postwar Period." In A. B. Smith (ed.), *Competitive Distribution in a Free High-Level Economy and Its Implications for the University* (Pittsburgh: University of Pittsburgh Press), 1958.

25. Michael Levy, Dhruv, Robert Peterson, and Bob Connolly, "The Concept of the 'The Big Middle,'" *Journal of Retailing*, 81 (2) (2005): 83–88.

26. Stanley C. Hollander, "Notes on the Retail Accordion," *Journal of Retailing*, Summer 1966: 29–40, 54.

27. "David vs. Goliath," *Fortune*, December 6, 2010: 69.

28. "The Skinny on Handbag-Rental Services," *Wall Street Journal*, July 24, 2008: D2.

29. "Main Street Masala," *Bloomberg Businessweek*, February 6–12, 2012: 70–71.

30. "In France, Vive la Tupperware," *Bloomberg Businessweek*, May 9–15, 2011: 21–23.

31. For a complete discussion of this theory see Shelby D. Hunt, *A General Theory of Competition* (Thousand Oaks, CA: Sage), 2000.

32. Shelby D. Hunt and Robert M. Morgan, "The Resource-Advantage Theory of Competition: Dynamics, Path Dependencies, and Evolutionary Dimensions," *Journal of Marketing*, October 1996: 107–114.

33. "Rising Dough" *Fast Company* (October 2009): 69–71.

34. http://www.pewinternet.org/Infographics/2010/Internet-acess-by-age-group-over-time-Update.aspx [Accessed March 28, 2012]

35. "Click to Buy" *Time*, January 16, 2012: 16.
36. "Used Games Score Big for Gamestop," *Wall Street Journal*, January 21, 2009: B1; and "Thrift Shops on Easy Street," *Businessweek*, October 20, 2008: 60.
37. "People Pulling Up to Pawnshops Today Are Driving Cadillacs and BMWs," *Wall Street Journal*, December 30, 2008: A1, A6.
38. "New Threat to Retailers: Liquidations," *Wall Street Journal*, December 12, 2008: B1, B2; "Selling Out the Bare Walls," *Businessweek*, March 16, 2009; and "With Lots of Liquidation Sales Winding Down, Bargain Hunters Need to Remain Vigilant," *St. Louis Post-Dispatch*, March 7, 2009: A5.
39. "Flush Times for Liquidators," *Wall Street Journal*, January 20, 2009: B1.
40. "Zipcar Rentals Come to Valparaiso," by Amy Lavalley, Available at Posttrib.suntimes.com/news/porter/a0206192/zipcar-rentals-come-to-balparaiso.html? updated Jan. 25, 2012 02:02AM.
41. "Hertz Takes Aim at Zipcar With Car-Sharing Service, *Wall Street Journal*, December 3, 2008: D2.
42. "The Skinny on Handbag-Rental Services," *Wall Street Journal*, July 24, 2008: D2, and company websites.
43. "Students Get a Break by Renting, Rather than Buying, Textbooks," *Kansas City Star*, February 24, 2008: C3.
44. Wal-Mart, *2011 Annual Report*: 6–7.
45. "Carrefour Braces for More Global Weakness," *Wall Street Journal*, January 16, 2009: B1; and "With Profits Elusive, Walmart to Exit Germany," *Wall Street Journal*, July 29, 2006: A1, A6.
46. "Expansion-Minded Uniqlo Aims Big" *Chain Store Age*, December 2011: 22.
47. "Fast Retailing" *Fast Company*, March 2010: 93.
48. "Best Buy Tales a Safe Route," *Wall Street Journal*, May 9, 2008: C3.
49. Michael J. O'Connor, "Global Marketing: A Retail Perspective," *International Trends in Retailing*, December 1998: 19–35.
50. "Apparel Retailers from Overseas Are Hitting the Malls in the U.S." *Wall Street Journal*, July 28, 2008: B1, B2.
51. Ibid.
52. "Aldi Looks to U.S. for Growth" *Wall Street Journal*, January 13, 2009: B1.
53. "Name Brands Are OK, but We Want Style," *Shopping Centers Today*, May 2005: 13.
54. "Saks Boosts Women's Private Label Lines" *Women's Wear Daily*, August 17, 2011: 1, 4.
55. "Target's New Eco-Apparel Line to Debut at Barneys New York." *Wall Street Journal*, May 1, 2008: D6.
56. "In Tough Times, Spas Stress Stress," *New York Times*, February 8, 2009: TR 3.

Chapter 5

1. "Industry Strategizes to Battle Inflation," *Women's Wear Daily*, April 18, 2011: 1–3.
2. "China Industry Being Slammed by Rising Costs," *Women's Wear Daily Style*, March 29, 2011: 1–2; "A Sea Change in the Pearl River Delta," *WWD*, July 12, 2011: 6.
3. "No Room for Logistics Inventory," *Stores*, August 2011; published on http://www.stores.org. [Accessed August 25, 2011].
4. "When Supply Chains Break" *Fortune*, December 26, 2011: 29–32.
5. "Mexico Eyes Antipiracy Deal with China," *Women's Wear Daily*, December 28, 2011: 7.
6. "Time to Head Home for Some Manufacturers," *Bloomberg Businessweek*, February 6–12, 2012: 17.
7. "Etc. Hard Choices," *Bloomberg Businessweek*, May 31–June 6, 2010: 88.
8. "Costco Keeps Formula as It Expands," *Women's Wear Daily*, January 30, 2012: 6.
9. "Morrison, Rothfeld Launch 3x1 Denim," *Women's Wear Daily*, March 10, 2011: 2.
10. "Focus on: Logistics," *Chain Store Age*, June/July 2011: 30.
11. For a more complete discussion of this subject, see the special report "Managing the Trading-Partner Link Is the Key to Success," *Chain Store Age*, June 2003: 1A–12A.
12. "Ikea's Challenge to The Wooden Pallet," *Bloomberg Businessweek*, November 28–December 4, 2011: 64.
13. For a more complete discussion on this subject, the reader should consult Robert Buzzell and Gwen Ortmeyer, "Channel Partnerships Streamline Distribution," *Sloan Management Review*, Spring 1995: 85–96.
14. F. Robert Dwyer and Sejo Oh, "A Transaction Cost Perspective on Vertical Contractual Structure and Interchannel Competitive Strategies," *Journal of Marketing*, April 1988: 21–34.

15. "Service Chains Are Best-Performing Franchisers," *Shopping Centers Today*, April 2008: 11.

16. "P&G Puts Its Big Brands to Work in Franchisees," *Bloomberg Businessweek,* September 6–12, 2010: 20.

17. Another good website to check for current information about franchising is www.entrepreneur.com/franchiseopportunities/index.html

18. "Credit Crunch Squeezes Franchisees," *Wall Street Journal*, September 29, 2008: B1.

19. "On Franchising," *Wall Street Journal*, November 25, 2008: B4.

20. Bert C. McCammon, Jr., "Perspectives for Distribution Programming." In Louis P. Bucklin (ed.), *Vertical Marketing Systems* (Glenview, IL: Scott, Foresman), 1970: 45.

21. "Wal-Mart Era Wanes Amid Big Shifts in Retail," *Wall Street Journal*, October 3, 2007: A1, A17.

22. "Wal-Mart Sneezes, China Catches Cold," *Wall Street Journal*, May 29, 2007: B1.

23. "TJX: Dressed to Kill for the Downturn," *Businessweek*, October 27, 2008: 60.

24. "Why Deere Is Weeding Out Dealers Even as Farms Boom," *Wall Street Journal*, August 14, 2007: A1, A10.

25. "Franchisees Balk at Handyman Plan," *Wall Street Journal*, July 7, 2009: B4.

26. "In a Clash of the Sneaker Titans, Nike Gets Leg Up on Foot Locker," *Wall Street Journal*, May 13, 2003: A1, A10.

27. "Liz Claiborne Reborn As Fifth & Pacific," *Women's Wear Daily*, January 4, 2012: 1.8.

28. "A Deal with Target Put Lid on Revival at Tupperware," *Wall Street Journal*, February 18, 2004: A1, A9.

29. "Target Sneaks into Upscale Beauty Biz," *Shopping Centers Today*, May 2008: 36.

30. Robert Morgan and Shelby Hunt, "The Commitment-Trust Theory of Relationship Marketing," *Journal of Marketing*, July 1994: 20–38.

31. David Ballantyne and Richard J. Varey, "Introducing a Dialogical Orientation to the Service-Dominant Logic of Marketing," in Robert F. Lusch and Stephen L. Vargo (eds.), *The Service-Dominant Logic of Marketing* (Armonk, New York: M.E. Sharpe), 2006: 224–243.

32. "A New Era Begins at Benetton," *Women's Wear Daily* (June 6, 2011): 4.

33. "Green Gold?" *Fortune*, September 15, 2008: 107–112.

34. Jan B. Heide and George John, "Do Norms Matter in Marketing Relationships?" *Journal of Marketing*, April 1992: 32–44; and James C. Anderson and James A. Narus, "A Model of Distributor Firm and Manufacturer Firm Working Partnerships," *Journal of Marketing*, January 1990: 42–58.

35. "P&G's Gillette Edge: The Playbook It Honed at Walmart," *Wall Street Journal*, January 31, 2005: A1, A12.

36. The authors want to acknowledge the contributions of many of their ex-students in this section. These students are now buyers, suppliers, vendors, and category managers. In addition, we want to give special credit to Wally Switzer, president of the 4 R's of Retailing, Inc., and Kevin Blackwell, General Manager of Sales & Marketing-Analytic Solutions, Bristol Technology Inc., for their suggestions in this section.

Chapter 6

1. "Macy's Lundgren, NRF Press Obama on Agenda," *Women's Wear Daily*, January 11, 2012: 12.

2. "W. Hollywood Bans Fur Sales," *Women's Wear Daily,* November 29, 2011: 12.

3. "Pressure Mounting for Taxes on E-tail," *Women's Wear Daily*, June 20, 2011: 1, 7; "More Retailers Back Internet Sales Tax Bill," *Women's Wear Daily*, November 10, 2011: MW7.

4. "California Passes Web Sales Tax," *Women's Wear Daily*, June 30, 2011: 8.

5. "Amazon Backs Web Tax Bill," *Women's Wear Daily,* August 1, 2011: 15.

6. Sherman Act, 26 Stat, 209 (1890) as amended, 15 U.S.C. articles 1–7.

7. "Supreme Court Ruling Won't Hurt Retail Competition," *St. Louis Post-Dispatch*, July 15, 2007: E1, E7.

8. "Free Becomes Fighting Word," *Advertising Age*, January 24, 2005: 14.

9. "$2.5M Awarded in Knockoffs Case," *Women's Wear Daily*, July 1, 2011: 3.

10. "Richemont Gets $37.4M in Fakes Case," *Women's Wear Daily,* September 23, 2011: 2.

11. "Effort to Quantify Sales of Pirated Goods Lead to Fuzzy Numbers," *Wall Street Journal*, October 10, 2007: B1; and "Fighting Fakes," *Forbes*, August 11, 2008: 44–47.

12. "Web Ground Zero in Ongoing War on Counterfeits," *Women's Wear Daily,* April 25, 2011: 4.

13. "Faking Out the Fakers," *Businessweek,* June 4, 2007: 76–80.

14. "Landlords Face Real Fines for Fake Goods," *Shopping Centers Today,* April 2008: 11.

15. "Humane Society Targets Fake Fur Claims," *Women's Wear Daily,* November 23, 2011: 8.

16. "Web Ground Zero in Ongoing War on Counterfeits," *Women's Wear Daily,* April 25, 2011: 1, 4, 5.

17. "eBay Fined over Selling Counterfeits," *Wall Street Journal,* July 1, 2008: B1

18. "eBay Wins in Fight over Tiffany Counterfeits," *Wall Street Journal,* July 15, 2008: B1.

19. "Shop Wins Round in Victoria's Secret Case," *USA Today,* April 5, 2003: 5B.

20. Fred W. Morgan and Allen B. Saviers, "Retailer Responsibility for Deceptive Advertising and Promotional Methods." Paper presented at the Retail Patronage Conference, Lake Placid, NY, May 1993.

21. "Reebok to Pay $25M in Advertising Flap," *Women's Wear Daily,* September 29, 2011: 12.

22. Morgan and Saviers, op. cit.

23. http://lubbockonline.com/filed-online/2011-04-05/jk-harris-tax-consultant-firm-settles-state-consumer-suit#.Tw2ormBvcek [Accessed January 11, 2012].

24. Based on information supplied by Susan Busch, Director, Public Relations–Corporate for Best Buy, January 23, 2006.

25. *N. C. Freed Co., Inc. v. Board of Governors of Federal Reserve System* (CA2 NY) 473 F.2d 1210.

26. "Spot Delivery Puts the Dealer in the Driver's Seat," Ann Zieger, Consumer Affairs.com/automotive, 10/28/2004 [Accessed on January 30, 2012].

27. United States Public Law 92-573, Consumer Product Safety Act (1972).

28. Eileen Flaherty, "Safety First: The Consumer Product Safety Improvement Act of 2008," *Loyola Consumer Law Review* 21 (3) (2008): 372–391.

29. Based on a news report from CNN Money issued July 16, 2008.

30. "How to Right Retailing Wrongs," *Consumer Reports,* May 2006: 5.

31. Magnuson-Moss Warranty Federal Trade Commission Act, Public Law 93-637, 93rd Congress (1975).

32. *Burger King v. Weaver,* United States Court of Appeals, 11th Circuit, 96-5438, 1999.

33. *Eastman Kodak Company v. Image Technical Services* (1992), 112 S. Ct. 2072.

34. For a detailed analysis of the changes taking place in this area of government regulation, the reader should consult: "Antitrust Enforcers Drop the Ideology, Focus on Economics," *Wall Street Journal,* February 27, 1997: A1, A8.

35. "Oklahoma Death Grip," *Wall Street Journal,* March 18, 2005: W15.

36. "Court: No Mall Can Protest the Protests," *Shopping Centers Today,* February 2008: 7.

37. "Wine Lovers See Red over State Laws that Restrict Home Delivery of Bottles," *Wall Street Journal,* September 24, 2008: D1, D7.

38. "Taxing the Rich—Foods, That Is," *Businessweek,* February 23, 2009: 62.

39. "Exiling the Happy Meal," *Wall Street Journal,* July 22, 2008: A14; and "Push for Calories on Menus Gains," *Wall Street Journal,* June 11, 2008: A2.

40. "Will a Twist on an Old Vow Deliver for Domino's Pizza?" *Wall Street Journal,* December 17, 2007: B1, B2.

41. "Best Buy Increases Third-Quarter Net Earnings to $138 Million," a press release issued by Best Buy, December 13, 2005; and "Form 10-Q," a quarterly report issued by Home Depot on June 2, 2005.

42. "Score Two for Sustainability," *Fast Company,* November 2010: 54.

43. "Patagonia Launches Water Initiative," *Women's Wear Daily,* May 31, 2011: 6.

44. "Sustainable Apparel Coalition Created," *Women's Wear Daily,* March 1, 2011: 7.

45. K. Sudhir and Vithala Roa, "Do Slotting Allowances Enhance Efficiency or Hinder Competition," *MSI Reports,* 2005; working paper series, issue 4.

46. "Walmart's Discounted Ethics," *Time,* May 7, 2012: 19.

47. "Home Depot Fires Employees Amid Probe of Kickbacks," *Wall Street Journal,* August 2, 2007: A2.

48. "Uninhibited, Uncut, Unrated DVDs Fly Off Shelves," *Advertising Age,* October 31, 2005: 9.

49. Information supplied by Bob Kahn to the authors.

50. This information was found at www.universitip.com/term-papers/Ethical-Aspects-of-Wal-Mart's-Operation-207218424.html on February 15, 2009.

51. "Companies that Serve You Best," *Fortune*, May 31, 1993: 74–88.

52. "Best Buy's Giant Gamble," *Fortune*, April 3, 2006: 68–75.

53. Letter from Sam Walton to Robert Kahn dated July 6, 1990.

Chapter 7

1. "EBay Set to Launch Outlet Site," *WWD*, August 4, 2011: 6.

2. "E-Commerce Sales Rise 14.8% in 2010," www.internetretailer.com, Accessed: January 21, 2012.

3. "US Internet Christmas Sales Are Up 15.4% to $36 Billion & Now Account for 10% of All Retail Sales," www.thedomains.com, Accessed: January 21, 2012.

4. U.S. Bureau of Census, *Statistical Abstract of the United States 2012*, Table 1155.

5. "Red Wing teams with Buxton to continue its expansion march," *Chain Store Age*, April/May 2011: 71.

6. Albertson's, *Annual Report* (1998): 5.

7. "Maternity's Denim Destination," *Women's Wear Daily*, December 21, 2011: 6.

8. "Uniqlo Has Twin Bill Set for NYC," *Women's Wear Daily*, August 30, 2011: 6.

9. "REI to Open in Manhattan's Puck Building," *Women's Wear Daily*, November 18, 2011: 10.

10. "Retailing by the River: Hudson Yards' Blueprint," *Women's Wear Daily*, May 17, 2011: 8.

11. "San Francisco Neighborhood Set for Revival," *Women's Wear Daily*, April 26, 2011: 3.

12. Antichain legislation actually dates back to the early 1920s; by the middle of the Great Depression, these laws had been passed in 28 states. As noted in Chapter 6, fair trade laws were also antichain.

13. "Anti-Chain Ordinances Choke Some Neighborhoods," *Shopping Centers Today*, May 2008: 32; and "In San Francisco, It's Work to Find Toys," *New York Times*, December 25, 2007: C4.

14. Information taken from www.sprawl-busters.com, March 19, 2009.

15. The opinion page from *The Otago Daily Times*, November 26–27, 2005.

16. "Anti-Chain Ordinances Choke ..." op. cit.

17. "Walmart to Push Into Urban Chicago," *Wall Street Journal*, February 11, 2009: B1.

18. "J.C. Penney Scales Back Plans for New Stores in '09," *Wall Street Journal*, June 26, 2008: B7; "Target to Open Designer-Focused Stores in New York," *New York Times*, September 2, 2008: C3; and conversations with executives from several of these firms during February 2009.

19. "Retail's New Sweet Spot: Inner-Ring Suburbs," *Chain Store Age*, March 2011: 12.

20. "Outlet Malls Proliferate in China," *Women's Wear Daily*, July 7, 2011: 3.

21. "Value Retail to Open Luxe Outlets in China," *Women's Wear Daily*, September 26, 2011: 1.4.

22. "Country by Country Retail Space Comparison," Mish's Global Economic Trend Analysis, http://globaleconomicanalysis.blogspot.com/2011/11/country-by-country-per-capita-retail.html. Accessed on January 20, 2012.

23. "At Kennedy, Shopping and Dining, Followed by a Takeoff," *New York Times*, July 30, 2008: C4.

24. "We are Indivisible," http://www.opportunityfinance.net/createjobsforusa/. Accessed on January 21, 2012.

25. "Big Boxes Dig for Their Own Data," *Shopping Centers Today*, December 2005: 9.

26. "Know Your Business: Technology Helps Retailers Understand Their Customers, Stores and Locations," *Chain Store Age*, April/May 2011; 75–80.

27. "Entertainment Wizard," *Shopping Centers Today*, May 2008: 65–66; and "Malls Race to Stay Relevant in Downturn," *Wall Street Journal*, February 26, 2009: B1, B4.

28. "IKEA Takes on China," *Fortune*, December 12, 2011: 15.

29. "Saks to Open Store in Kazakhstan," *Women's Wear Daily*, July 6, 2011: 2.

30. "Growing Golfsmith: A GIS tool helps one retailer score the right sites," *Chain Store Age*, April/May 2011: 69.

31. William J. Reilly, *Methods for the Study of Retail Relationships* (research monograph no.4) (Austin: Bureau of Business Research, University of Texas, 1929).

32. P. D. Converse, "New Laws of Retail Gravitation," *Journal of Marketing*, January 1949: 379–384.

33. "In This Town, Even a Mall Rat Can Get Rattled," *New York Times*, December 20, 2006: A1, C19.

34. Bernard LaLonde, "The Logistics of Retail Location." In William D. Stevens (ed.), *American Marketing Proceedings* (Chicago: American Marketing Association, 1961): 572.

35. "Why Did Starbucks Cross the Road?" *Wall Street Journal*, April 3, 2007: B1, B2.

36. Ibid.

37. Mobility can be viewed as both a household characteristic and a community characteristic. We chose to treat it as a community characteristic because the design of the community, the availability of public transportation, and the cost of operating an auto in any given area are determinants of mobility and are themselves characteristics of the community.

38. "Developers, Retailers Focus On Quality Sites," *WWD*, June 9, 2011: 1, 6.

39. The essence of Applebaum's work, plus contributions from several of his students, can be found in William Applebaum and others, *Guide to Store Location Research with Emphasis on Supermarkets* (Curt Korhblau, ed., sponsored by the Supermarket Institute) (Reading, MA: Addison-Wesley, 1968).

40. This information is used with the written permission of Pitney Bowes Software Inc., 4200 Parliament Place, Suite 600, Lanham, MD 20706 (www.pbbusinessinsight.com).

41. "Cincinnati Center Never Says Die," *Shopping Centers Today*, April 2009: 5.

42. Richard L. Nelson, *The Selection of Retail Locations* (New York: F.W. Dodge, 1958): 66.

43. "Big-Box Bedfellows," *Shopping Centers Today*, December 2005: 9.

44. Ibid.

Chapter 8

1. The 4-5-4 Calendar, which is widely used by retailers today, was derived in the 1930s to replace the straight comparison of calendar months to report monthly sales. This old method became problematic as Saturdays and Sundays became an increasingly large percentage of sales and the number of weekends in a month varied year to year. However, the layout of the 4-5-4 Calendar (52 weeks × 7 days = 364 days) results in one remaining day each year and, with the occurrence of a leap year, a 53rd week is sometimes added to the end of the calendar for sales reporting purposes only. Many retailers will choose to do this at the end of 2012. However, this text will ignore the 53rd week.

2. Based information contained in a letter from Sam Walton to Robert Kahn, November 30, 1989.

3. IRS Revenue Procedure 97-37.

4. "Focus on: Retail Construction," *Chain Store Age*, December 2011: 32.

5. Based on information supplied by the late Robert Kahn, a retail consultant and editor of *Retailing Today*.

Chapter 9

1. "Fashion Takes a Beating," *Business Today*, March 8, 2009: 20; "Copy Protection for Fall Fashion: Designers' New Formal Looks Are Tougher to Knock Off; A Messy Mutton-Leg Sleeve," *Wall Street Journal*, October 27, 2007: W1, W4.

2. "Harrods graduates from Excel spreadsheets to cloud computing," *Stores*, November 2011.

3. "Bob's Stores reduces on-hand inventory with demand forecasting system," *Chain Store Age*, April/May 2011: 94.

4. For a more detailed discussion of the effect of any retail holiday on retail sales, visit the National Retailing Federation website at www.nrf.com.

5. "McDonald's Has a Chef?" *Time*, February 22, 2010: 88–91.

6. "Dressing Women of a Certain Size," *Wall Street Journal*, August 21, 2008: D1, D8.

7. "Even Better Than The Real Thing," *Bloomberg Businessweek* (November 28-December 4, 2011): 25–26.

8. www.bizjournals.com/milwaukee/news/2012/03/21/kohls-to-add-exclusive-american.html

9. "J. Crew Reports $29.9M Loss," *Women's Wear Daily*, June 10, 2011: 2.

10. Itamar Simonson, "The Effect of Product Assortment on Buyer Preferences," *Journal of Retailing*, Fall 1999: 347–370.

11. "P&G Slams Inefficient Marketing," *Marketing Week*, November 8, 1996: 26–27.

12. Susan Broniarczyk, Wayne Hoyer, and Linda McAlister, "Consumers' Perceptions of Assortment Offered in a Grocery Category: The Impact

of Item Reduction," *Journal of Marketing Research*, May 1998: 166–176; S. Iyengar and M. Lepper, "When Choice Is Demotivating: Can One Desire Too Much of a Good Thing?" *Journal of Personality and Social Psychology*, 6, 2000: 995–1006.

13. Tom Gruen, "Inventory Inaccuracy and Retail Shelf Out-of-Stocks: Understanding the Extent, Impact, and Traditional Measurement," *American Marketing Association Winter Educators Conference*, February 21, 2009; A. Raman, N. DeHoratius, and Z. Ton, "Execution: The Missing Link in Retail Operations," *California Management Review*, 3, 2001: 136–152.

14. "Family Dollar transitions to electronic inventory auditing process," *Chain Store Age*, October 2011: 26, 28.

15. "Macy's Rolling Out RFID," *Women's Wear Daily*, September 29, 2011: 2.

16. "Retailers Getting Prepared To Cope With Soaring Prices," *Women's Wear Daily*, March 11, 2011: 1, 8.

17. "New Lead Test Law Causing Second-Hand Woes," *Times Leader*, January 8, 2009: A1; "Agency Rethinks Its Rules on Testing Products for Lead; Exemptions for Some Items Get a Tentative OK after Thrift Stores and Others Complain," *Los Angeles Times*, January 7, 2009: C3.

18. "Fresh, but Far From Easy," *The Economist*, June 23, 2007: 77–79.

19. "Getting Inventories Right Seen Tougher Than Ever," *Women's Wear Daily*, December 19, 2011: 1, 16.

20. This example is based on "Unauthorized Channels of Distribution: Gray Markets," by Roy Howell, Robert Britney, Paul Kuzdrall, and James Wilcox, *Industrial Marketing Management*, 15, November 1986: 257–263. Used with the permission of the authors.

21. Shrinkage On The Rise, According To Preliminary National Retail Security Survey Findings

22. For Immediate Release Kathy Grannis (202)783-7971 www.nrf.com

23. www.nrf.com/modules.php?name=News&op=viewlive&sp_id=1136 accessed on Feb.7, 2012 2pm.

24. "Organized Retail Crime Grows," *Women's Wear Daily* (June 8, 2011): 2.

25. "Walmart to Crack Down on Young Shoplifters," *Wall Street Journal*, July 11, 2007: B4.

26. "The Price of Sampling, for the Cost of a Few Jelly Beans," MorningNewsBeat.com, October 29, 2007.

Chapter 10

1. For more details on how consumers process price information, see Sangkil Moon, Gary J. Russell, and Sri Devi Duvvuri, "Profiling the Reference Price Consumer," *Journal of Retailing*, 82(1), 2006: 1–11.

2. Roger Dickinson, "Pricing at Retail," *Pricing Strategy & Practice*, 1(1), 1993: 24–35.

3. "Selling Out the Bare Walls," *Businessweek*, March 16, 2009; and "With Lots of Liquidation Sales Winding Down, Bargain Hunters Need to Remain Vigilant," *St. Louis Post-Dispatch*, March 7, 2009: A5.

4. "Luxury Clothier Zegna's Marco Polo Moment," *Bloomberg Businessweek,* June 14-20, 2010: 18.

5. It should be noted some academics consider skimming and even the use of couponing to be a form of price discrimination because it allows different groups of customers to pay different prices depending on what they are willing to pay. Remember, as was pointed out in Chapter 6, price discrimination is not always illegal.

6. "Sadove Sets Tone for Saks Growth Via Outlets, Web," *WWD*, April 27, 2011: 1, 4.

7. "When Cheap Is Exclusive," *The Economist,* September 5, 2009, 73.

8. Dickinson, op. cit.

9. "No-Haggle Pricing Climbs Higher, Finds Fans among Affluent, Educated," *Advertising Age*, August 1, 2005: 23.

10. "Chinese Consumers Overwhelm Retailers with Team Tactics," *Wall Street Journal*, February 28, 2006: A1, A14.

11. Based on material found in the Robert Kahn Collection, University of Oklahoma.

12. "Bridge Work at Saks to Recast Wear," *WWD* July 5, 2011: 4.

13. Robert M. Schindler and Thomas M. Kibarian, "Increased Consumer Sales Response through Use of 99-Ending Prices," *Journal of Retailing*, 72(2), 1996: 187–199.

14. Dinesh K. Gauri, K. Sudhir, and Debabrata Talukdar, "The Temporal and Spatial Dimensions of Price Search: Insights from Matching

Household Survey and Purchase Data," *Journal of Marketing Research*, April 2008: 226–240.

15. Christina Cheddar Berk, "Private-Label Brands Gaining Clout- and Pricing Power," www.cnbc.com/id/46207713, Tuesday, 31, Jan 2012/3:01PM ET [Accessed: February 16, 2012; 3:57PM CT.

16. Charles M. Wood, Bruce L. Alford, Ralph W. Jackson, and Otis W. Gilley, "Can Retailers Get Higher Prices For 'End-of-Life' Inventory Through Online Auctions?" *Journal of Retailing*, 81(3), 2005: 181–190.

17. "Sales May Go Out Like Last Year's Winter Coat," *Advertising Age*, April 25, 2005: 16.

18. "Marked Down," *Fortune*, August 22, 2005: 103–108.

Chapter 11

1. "Cart Culture," *Stores*, August 2011.

2. This list was developed by the late Louis Bing, Bing Furniture Company, Cleveland, Ohio.

3. "Focus on: Innovation," *Chain Store Age*, January 2012: 28–29.

4. "Revlon Saturates 2012 Ads with Color," *Women's Wear Daily*, December 23, 2011: 5.

5. "Walmart's Makeover," *Fortune*, December 26, 2011: 50–55.

6. Target advertising circular authors received in 2011.

7. "Great Expectations for the Olympics," *Women's Wear Daily*, June 11, 2012: 6.

8. Myron Gable, Ann Fairhurst, Roger Dickinson, and Lynn Harris, "Improving Students' Understanding of the Retail Advertising Budgeting Process," *Journal of Marketing Education*, 22(2) (2000): 120–128.

9. Ibid.

10. This information was provided by Schonfeld & Associates, Inc., and is used with the firm's written permission.

11. "Grilled Chicken a Kentucky Fried Fiasco," *Advertising Age*, May 11, 2009: 1.

12. Available at www.responsible-advertising.org/advertisingandchildren.asp [Accessed February 20, 2012; 6:43 p.m].

13. "Out of Luxe: Beijing Bans 'High Class' Billboards," *Women's Wear Daily*, March 23, 2011: 3.

14. "How Do I Keep My Company's Reputation Intact When Our Industry Has Been Tainted by Bad News?" *Fortune*, March 16, 2009: 30.

15. Frank N. Magid Associates, *How America Shops & Spends*, 2011: 4. Available at: www.newspapermedia.com; www.naa.org [Accessed February 5, 2012].

16. "Tips for Using Live Blogging to Promote Events," *Chain Store Age Executive*, November 14, 2011. Available at http://chainstoreage.com [Accessed: July 6, 2012].

17. Available at www.alexa.com [Accessed: February 5, 2012].

18. "Digital World Now Coaxing Shoppers Back to Stores," *Women's Wear Daily*, June 27, 2012: 1, 12.

19. D. Gail Fleenor, "Eye Catching," November 2011 [online] Available at http://www.stores.org [Accessed: July 6, 2012].

20. Stambor, Zak, "Consumers 'Clipped' 92% More Coupons From the Web Last Year," *Internet Retailer* [online] Available at: http://www.internetretailer.com [Accessed: June 19, 2012].

21. Based on information gathered between December 2008 and April 2009.

22. "Rate Redemption" *Stores*, November 2011.

23. "Sleepy's Provides 'Bedder Days'," *Home Furnishings Business*, January 2012: 26.

24. "P&G Wins Rumor Lawsuit," *Cincinnati Enquirer*, March 20, 2007: A7.

Chapter 12

1. "Customer Service in a Shrinking Economy," *Businessweek*, March 2, 2009: 26–40.

2. For a detailed discussion of this topic, see Pratibha Dabholkar, David Shepherd, and Dayle Thorpe, "A Comprehensive Framework for Service Quality: An Investigation of Critical Conceptual and Measurement Issues Through a Longitudinal Study," *Journal of Retailing*, Summer 2000: 139–173.

3. Christian Homburg, Nicole Koschate, and Wayne D. Hoyer, "Do Satisfied Customers Really Pay More? A Study of the Relationship Between Customer Satisfaction and Willingness to Pay," *Journal of Marketing*, April 2005: 84–96.

4. "After All You've Done For Your Customers, Why Are They Still Not Happy?" *Fortune*, December 11, 1995: 178–182.

5. Bush, Michael, "Why You Should Be Putting on the Ritz," *Advertising Age*, June 21, 2010: 1; and Gallo, Carmine, "Employee Motivation the Ritz-Carlton Way," *Businessweek*, February 29, 2008 [Available at: http://www.businessweek.com].

6. "How to Survive in Vegas," *Bloomberg Businessweek*, August 9–15, 2010: 69–75.

7. "Pillars to CRM Success," *Chain Store Age*, April/May 2011: 90.

8. "Loyalty Updated: Crabtree & Evelyn Delivers Targeted Promotions with New CRM Program," *Chain Store Age*, April/May 2011: 88, 90.

9. Leo J. Shapiro, "How to Increase Sales by 20 Percent Without Attracting Any New Customers," *International Trends in Retailing*, December 1998: 37–49.

10. Based on information presented at the Spring American Collegiate Retailing Association Conference, Springdale, AR, April 6–8, 2006.

11. "Customer Service Often Lags Retail in Newer Markets," *Shopping Centers Today*, May 2006: 172.

12. If you want to see the most recent data on ACSI data for the nation's leading retailers, go to www.theacsi.org/index.php. This survey, which is updated quarterly, was discussed in Chapter 3.

13. Quoted from http://forum.purseblog.com/general-discussion/i-hate-nordstrom-242951.html [Accessed April 15, 2009].

14. Eugene W. Anderson, Claes Fornell, and Donald R. Lehmann, "Customer Satisfaction, Market Share, and Profitability: Findings from Sweden," *Journal of Marketing*, 58(3), July 1994: 53–66.

15. *Target's 2007 Annual Report*: 13.

16. Ibid.: 16.

17. Ibid.: 25.

18. *Target's 2008 Annual Report*: 26, 33–34.

19. www.sec.gov//Archives/edgar/data/27419/000104746912002714/a2207838z10-k.htm#dg70701 Item 6. Selected financial data. [Accessed July 3, 2012].

20. Target Annual Report 2011

21. "WaMu's Branches Lose the Smiles," *Wall Street Journal*, April 7, 2009: C1, C3; and "Branching Out," *Shopping Centers Today*, March 2008: 33–34.

22. Source: "The Survey of Consumer Payment Choice," Federal Reserve Bank of Boston, January 2010. Read more at: http://www.creditcards.com/credit-card-news/credit-card-industry-facts-personal-debt-statistics-1276.php#ixzz1nctC279w.

23. "Walmart Layaway Information," Available at www.layawayplans.net/walmart-layaway-information/ [Accessed: February 8, 2012]

24. "Gift Cards Sales to Drop 5 Percent This Holiday, Survey Says," *Shopping Centers Today*, November 2008: 7.

25. "Eggs, Bread, Milk—And a Mortgage," *Bloomberg Businessweek*, March 1, 2010: 20.

26. SIRS presentation at National Retail Federation (NRF) Annual Convention 2000, January 18, 2000.

27. "Outlets Add Service to the Price Proposition," *Women's Wear Daily*, August 1, 2011: 8.

28. "Speaking Volumes," *Dallas Morning News*, April 16, 2000: 1H, 5H.

29. Based on a letter from Sam Walton to Robert Kahn, June 5, 1991.

30. North *American Retail Dears Association Newsletter*, June 22, 2007: 1.

31. James G. Maxham III, Richard G. Netemeyer, "Modeling Customer Perceptions of Complaint Handling Over Time: The Effects of Perceived Justice on Satisfaction and Intent," *Journal of Retailing*, Fall 2002: 239–252.

32. *Second Annual Customer Returns in the Retail Industry*, a study conducted by King Rogers International, September 2004.

33. "Return Fraud and Abuse: How to Protect Profits," *Texas A&M Retailing Issues Letter*, 17(1), 2005.

34. The actual number of returns and the time period involved is confidential and varies by retailer.

35. Domino's press release, September 25, 1998.

36. As of June 2012, Available at http://getsatisfaction.com/corp/ [Accessed: June 3, 2012].

37. "In Search of Easy Money," *Forbes*, January 12, 2009: 36.

38. "Customers Like Buying Cars from Women, Survey Finds," *USA Today*, November 8, 1994: B1.

39. Patel, Kunur, "Retailers Strike Back in Mobile Wars With…People," *Advertising Age*, 83(12), 2012: 18–20.

40. W. Levinson et al., "Physician-Patient Communication. The Relationship with Malpractice Claims Among Primary Care Physicians and Surgeons," *JAMA*, February 19, 1997: 553–559; Gerald B. Hickson et al., "Obstetricians' Prior Malpractice Experience and Patients' Satisfaction with Care,"

JAMA, November 23/30, 1994: 1583–1587; Stephen S. Entman et al., "The Relationship Between Malpractice Claims History and Subsequent Obstetric Care," *JAMA*, November 23/30, 1994: 1588–1591.

41. For a more complete discussion of this subject, see Anne W. Magi, "Share of Wallet in Retailing: The Effects of Customer Satisfaction, Loyalty Cards, and Shopper Characteristics," *Journal of Retailing*, Spring 2003: 97–106; Arun Sharma, D. Michael Levy, "Categorization of Customers by Retail Salespeople," *Journal of Retailing*, Spring 1995: 71–82.

42. Much of the following is based on John O'Shaughnessy, "Selling as an Interpersonal Influence Process," *Journal of Retailing*, Winter 1971–1972: 32–46.

43. Ibid.: 41.

44. "Hot Tamale," *Wall Street Journal*, January 28, 2006: B2.

45. *People in Retail. Ernst & Young Survey*, September 1990: 11.

46. The following information was provided the authors by Marvin J. Rothenberg and is used with his written permission.

47. "To Move More Tires, Try Selling the Salesman," *Bloomberg Businessweek*, July 11–17, 2011: 19–20.

Chapter 13

1. Skeldon, Paul. (2011), "14m Americans Scanned QR and Bar Codes With Their Mobiles in June 2011," *Internet Retailing – Selling in the Digital Age* [Accessed: May 19, 2012] from http://internetretailing.net.

2. "Getting the Most Out of Every Shopper," *Businessweek*, February 9, 2009: 45–46.

3. "Threadless: From Clicks to Bricks," *Business-Week,* November 26, 2007: 84.

4. "Annual Store Construction and Outfitting Survey," *Chain Store Age*, June/July 2011: 34–38.

5. Haim Mano, "The Influence of Pre-Existing Negative Affect on Store Purchase Intentions," *Journal of Retailing*, Summer 1999: 149–172.

6. "WiFi and GPS Move Outdoor Audience Measurement Indoors," *Business Wire*, April 10, 2008.

7. Belly Up to the Bar and Buy Some Jeans," *Wall Street Journal*, April 2, 2009: D1, D6.

8. "Nike Opens Third Salvation Store," *Women's Wear Daily*, July 5, 2011: 2.

9. Alan Liles, *Oh Thank Heaven! The Story of the Southland Corporation* (Dallas: Southland Corporation, 1977).

10. "New Concepts: Five to Watch" *Chain Store Age*, April/May 2011: 16.

11. "Replacing the Extinct Impulse Buyer," *Bloomberg Businessweek*, November 14–20, 2011: 28–29.

12. Patel, Kunur, "Retailers Strike Back in Mobile Wars With…People," *Advertising Age*, 83(12) (2012): 18–20; and Aquino, Judith, "Tablets and Smartphones Transform the In-Store Customer Experience: Retailers Hope to Give Customers New Incentives to Shop Brick-and-Mortar Stores," *CRM Magazine*, 16, January 2012: 17–18

13. Clifford, Stephanie, "Stuff Piled in the Aisle? It's There to Get You to Spend More," *The Ney York Times*, April 8, 2011: A1.

14. "Big Retail Chains Dun Mere Suspects in Theft Demands for Money Can Leave Targets with Little Defense," *Wall Street Journal*, February 20, 2008: A1, A2.

15. This information was provided to the authors by Paul Adams, a supermarket consultant, April 15, 2009.

16. "Costco's Artful Discounts," *Businessweek*, October 20, 2008: 58–60.

17. Angela Hausman, "A Multi-method Investigation of Consumer Motivations in Impulse Buyer Behavior," *Journal of Consumer Behavior*, 17(5), 2000: 403–419.

18. "The Science of Shopping," *The New Yorker*, November 4, 1996: 66–75.

19. "In Major Retail Shift, Stores Begin to Shrink," *Women's Wear Daily*, July 11, 2011: 1, 12.

20. "Smarter Supermarkets: Today's supermarkets are sized, merchandised and operated toward success," *Chain Store Age*, August/September 2011: 74–76.

21. "Saks Pumps Up Shoes," *Women's Wear Daily*, June 18, 2012: 1, 15.

22. "Unhandicapped Access," *Shopping Centers Today*, September 2008: 97–100.

23. William D. Goren, *Understanding the Americans with Disabilities Act*, 2nd ed. (Washington, DC: American Bar Association, 2007).

24. Paco Underhill, ibid., 180–183.

25. "Men's Wearhouse to Roll Out Remodels," *Women's Wear Daily*, March 17, 2011: 6.

26. "Extreme Makeover," *Stores*, March 2011: www.stores.org/print/book/export/html/6321.

27. Based on a November 30, 1989, letter from Sam Walton to Robert Kahn and numerous conversations on the subject with Robert Kahn.

28. Based on conversations with Robert Kahn.

29. "Mervyn's Doesn't Have to Widen Aisles," *Lubbock Avalanche-Journal*, November 6, 2003: D12.

30. Carol Kaufman-Scarborough, "Reasonable Access for Mobility-Disabled Persons Is More than Widening the Door," *Journal of Retailing*, Winter 1999: 479–508.

31. "Store Design Makes Waves for Bass Pro Shops" *Retailing Today*, September 10, 2007: 23.

32. "Inside Job: Tips on Guarding Your Store From Employee Theft," *Home Furnishings Business*, February 2012: 19–23.

33. Paco Underhill, ibid: Chapter 12 "The Sensual Shopper": 171–193.

34. The preceding material was provided for the authors' use by Marvin J. Rothenberg.

35. For a more detailed discussion of this topic, the reader should consult the latest edition of Martin M. Pegler's *Stores of the Year* (New York: Retail Reporting Corporation).

36. "Firing The Imagination," *Home Furnishings Business*, June 2011: 15–19.

37. "Blinded by the Light," *Progressive Grocer*, August 2000: 57–58.

38. Ibid.

39. "Something in the Air," *Shopping Centers Today*, July 2008: 35–37; and "Scents and Sensibility," *Time*, October 16, 2006: 66–67.

40. Adrian C. North and Amber Shilcock, "The Effect of Musical Style on Restaurant Customers' Spending," *Environment and Behavior*, 35(5), 2003: 712–718.

41. Areni and Kim, op. cit.

42. Based on information supplied by Charles Areni, University of Sydney.

43. "Holiday Music Is Inescapable," *Wall Street Journal*, December 13, 2008: W1, W2.

44. Randahl Ramos, "Enhancing Your Customer's Shopping and Learning Experience," *NARDA Independent Retailer*, February 2005: 24.

45. "Shopping Spree Last for Madoff?" *Wall Street Journal*, January 10, 2009: B3.

46. "Brand Names Live After Stores Close," *New York Times*, April 14, 2009: B1, B7.

Chapter 14

1. "The Secret to Long-Term Success: Love People, Love Merchandise," *Chair Store Age*, August/September 2011: 19a.

2. Stephen L. Vargo, Robert F. Lusch. "Evolving Toward a New Dominant Logic for Marketing," *Journal of Marketing*, 68, January 2004: 1–17. Stephen L. Vargo, Robert F. Lusch. "Service-Dominant Logic: Continuing the Evolution," *Journal of the Academy of Marketing Science* 36, Spring 2008: 1–10.

3. "The Sharing Economy," *Fast Company*, May 2011: 88–93, 130, 131.

4. Lance Bettencourt A., Anthony W. Ulwick. "The Customer-Centered Innovation Map," *Harvard Business Review*, May 2008.

5. "Sell Solutions, Not Products," *Stores*, October 2011.

6. "Smart Knife," *Bloomberg Businessweek*, December 19–25, 2011: 85.

7. "Product Mix Gives Edge to Learning Express," *Chain Store Age*, April/May 2011: 22–23.

8. Robert F. Lusch, Stephen L. Vargo, Alan Malter. "Marketing as Service-Exchange: Taking a Leadership Role in Global Marketing Management," *Organizational Dynamics* 35(3), 2006: 264–278. Robert F. Lusch, Stephen L. Vargo, Matthew O'Brien. "Competing Through Service: Insights from Service-Dominant Logic," *Journal of Retailing* 83(1), 2007: 5–18.

9. Stephen L. Vargo, Robert F. Lusch. "It's All B2B...and Beyond: Toward a Systems Perspective of the Market," *Industrial Marketing Management* 40, 2011: 181–187.

10. http://coca-colafreestyle.com/#!/news-updates-buzz/post_panel/push-play-v3-coca-cola-freestyle [Accessed September 30, 2011].

11. "An example of business disruption and brand extension," *Chain Store Age*, August/September 2011: 7a.

12. Richard Normann, *Reframing Business: When the Map Changes the Landscape*. (Chichester: Wiley, 2001): p. 27.

13. Ravi Achrol, Philip Kotler. "Marketing in the Network Economy," *Journal of Marketing* 63(Special Issue), 1999: 146–163.

14. Robert F. Lusch, Stephen L. Vargo, Matthew O'Brien. "Competing Through Service: Insights from Service-Dominant Logic," *Journal of Retailing* 83(1), 2007: 5–18.

15. "Vintage Set to Influence," *Chain Store Age*, August/September 2011: 13a.

16. "Who Built Build-a-Bear?" *Fortune*, March 19, 2012: 49–52.

17. "Getting Engaged: Barnes & Noble Testing HP Touchscreen Solution That Encourages Kids to Be Authors," *Chain Store Age*, April/May 2011: 92–93.

18. "Chipotle: For Exploding All The Rules Of Fast Food," *Fast Company*, March 2012: 125, 126.

19. T. Duncan, S.E. Moriarty. "A Communication-Based Marketing Model for Managing Relationships," *Journal of Marketing* 62(2), 1998: 1–13.

20. David Ballantyne, Richard J. Varey. "Introducing a Dialogical Orientation to the Service-Dominant Logic of Marketing," in Robert F. Lusch and Stephen L. Vargo (eds). *The Service-Dominant Logic of Marketing*. Armonk, New York: M.E. Sharpe (2006): pp. 224–235.

21. "Walking the Talk," *Marketing News*, March 15, 2012: 24–28.

22. "Unique Customer Experience Is Retail's Holy Grail," *Stores*, July 2011.

23. Dipankar Ghosh, Robert F. Lusch, "Outcome Effect, Controllability and Performance Evaluation of Managers; Some Field Evidence from Multi-Outlet Businesses," *Accounting, Organizations and Society*, 25, 2000: 411–425.

24. Normann (2001).

25. "Anything to Get Attention," *Chain Store Age*, August/September 2011: 12a.

26. Robert F. Lusch, Patrick Dunne, Randall Gebhardt. *Retail Marketing* (Cincinnati, Ohio: South-Western Publishing Company, 1993; second edition): 55–57.

27. Robert F. Lusch, Stephen Vargo, Mohan Tanniru (2010), "Service, Value Networks and Learning," *Journal of the Academy of Marketing Science*, 38, February 2010: 19–31.

28. The initial idea for Town Center USA came from conversations with Wayne E. Copeland, Jr. and was featured in Robert Lusch and Patrick Dunne, *Retail Management* (Cincinnati, Ohio: South-Western Publishing Co., 1990): 729–731.

29. "Gilt Groupe," *Fast Company*, March 2010: 77.

30. "Dialing for Dollars in Digital," *Women's Wear Daily*, July 22, 2011: 5

31. "Today's Smart Choice: Don't Own. Share." *Time*, March 28, 2011: 62.

32. Genuine Parts Company, 2011 SEC 10-K Annual Report, Commission File number: 1-5690: 1.

33. Ibid.: 2.

34. Ibid.: F-26

URL INDEX

Company Name	Website
A	
AAMCO Transmission	http://www.aamco.com
Abercrombie & Fitch	http://www.abercrombie.com
Ace Hardware	http://www.acehardware.com
Aeropostale	http://www.aeropostale.com
Air Bed & Breakfast	http://www.airbnb.com
Albertson's	http://www.albertsons.com
Aldi	http://www.aldi.com
Amazon.com	http://www.amazon.com
American Airlines	http://www.aa.com
American Disabilities Act	http://www.ada.gov.com
American Eagle Outfitters	http://www.ae.com
Amway	http://www.amway.com
Ann Taylor	http://www.anntaylor.com
Autobytel.com	http://www.autobytel.com
Australian Retailers Association	http://www.ara.com.au
Avon	http://www.avoncompany.com
B	
Banana Republic	http://www.bananarepublic.com or gap.com
Barnes & Noble	http://www.barnesandnoble.com
Barrett-Jackson Auto Auction	http://www.barrettjackson.com)
Bergen Town Center	http://www.bergentowncenter.com
Blue Nile	http://www.bluenile.com/jewelry
Bass Pro Shops	http://www.basspro.com
Bed Bath & Beyond	http://www.bedbathandbeyond.com
Benetton	http://www.benetton.com
Best Buy	http://www.bestbuy.com
Big Lots	http://www.biglots.com
BJ's	http://www.bjs.com
Black Friday	http://bfads.net/
Bloom	http://www.shopbloom.com/
Borders	http://www.bordersgroupinc.com
Brooks Brothers	http://www.brooksbrothers.com
Buckle	http://www.buckle.com
Buffalo Wild Wings	http://www.buffalowildwings.com
Burger King	http://www.burgerking.com